A Concise History of the American Republic

A CONCISE HISTORY OF THE

An Abbreviated and Revised Edition of

The Growth of the American Republic

NEW YORK OXFORD

AMERICAN REPUBLIC

Second Edition

SAMUEL ELIOT MORISON
HENRY STEELE COMMAGER
WILLIAM E. LEUCHTENBURG

OXFORD UNIVERSITY PRESS 1983

A Concise History of the American Republic is an abbreviated and revised edition of *The Growth of the American Republic.*

Picture Adviser
JUDITH MARA GUTMAN

Library of Congress Cataloging in Publication Data
Morison, Samuel Eliot, 1887–1976
A concise history of the American Republic.
Bibliography: p. Includes index.
1. United States—History.
I. Commager, Henry Steele, 1902– . II.
Leuchtenburg, William Edward, 1922– . III. Title.
E178.M83 1983b 973 82-3621
ISBN 0-19-503179-2 AACR2
ISBN 0-19-503180-6 (pbk.)

Printing (last digit): 9 8 7 6 5 4 3 2 1

Printed in the United States of America

5/84

Preface

A Concise History of the American Republic is a shortened and revised edition of *The Growth of the American Republic,* which first appeared in 1930. Over the next three decades, the two senior authors brought out four more editions. In the fifth edition, which appeared in 1962, Morison was responsible for the period up to the Civil War, and for the chapters on World War II; Commager for the period since 1860, except for the chapters on World War II. In the sixth edition, published in 1969, Leuchtenburg had the main responsibility for revision, and for writing new chapters on the recent period, but Morison and Commager also made revisions.

Leuchtenburg has written *A Concise History of the American Republic,* but the book draws largely upon the work of the two senior authors in *The Growth of the American Republic.* Furthermore, the senior authors made numerous editorial recommendations at different stages in the preparation of the manuscript for the first edition of this book, which was published in 1977. In particular, Leuchtenburg closely followed Morison's suggestions for abridgment for the period up to the American Revolution and Commager's on the most recent period. *A Concise History of the American Republic* aims to reach a wide audience that prefers a more compact historical account, but effort has been made to preserve the essence of *The Growth of the American Republic* and to maintain the stylistic integrity of those volumes. Leuchtenburg has again been responsible for writing this revised edition, which carries the narrative into the second year of the Reagan administration, but Commager has made a number of editorial emendations. In preparing this new edition, we have sorely missed the counsel of Admiral Morison, whose death on 15 May 1976 evoked widespread expressions of sorrow together with a sense of fulfillment for a life so rich in achievement.

Our sincere thanks are extended to authors and publishers who have allowed us to quote passages from prose and poetry, to Esta Sobey for bibliographical assistance and to Delight Ansley, who prepared the index. We are especially happy to have an opportunity to acknowledge our debt to Judith Mara Gutman, whose contribution to illustrating this volume was indispensable, and to Byron S. Hollinshead, Jr., and the proficient staff of the Oxford University Press, especially Nancy Lane, Leona Capeless, and Joyce Berry.

We write for young men and women of all ages. We believe that history embraces the whole of a people's activity: economic and social, literary and spiritual, as well as political and military. We have endeavored therefore to give such stress to these different aspects that our story will be that of a growing and changing civilization in an expanding United States of America.

March 1982

HENRY STEELE COMMAGER
WILLIAM E. LEUCHTENBURG

Contents

Maps

Samuel Eliot Morison

1887–1976

For the whole earth is the sepulchre of famous men, and their story lives on, woven into the stuff of other men's lives.

PERICLES, *The Funeral Speech*

1

The New World

*

?–1615

Indian Culture

One summer day somewhat over 25,000 and less than 40,000 years ago, a Mongolian tribe stood on lofty Cape Dezhnev, the easternmost promontory of Siberia, about 30 miles south of the Arctic Circle. They or their parents had abandoned their old home in what is now the Gobi Desert, because that area was beginning to dry up. They had had a hard trek of at least 3000 miles, living off the country and fighting the natives along the way for several years. Perhaps only the magic of their medicine man, his promise of a new world toward the rising sun, had kept them going. Food was scarce, the latest enemy to resent their intrusion followed hard at their heels, and their skin garments were in tatters; in fact they were a tough-looking lot, even according to Siberian standards of that unrefined era. Looking southeastward over Bering Strait, our hard-pressed wayfarers saw clearly, only 23 miles away, a dome-shaped island over 1700 feet high rising above the sea. They had no experience in navigation, but something had to be done quickly. So, either by fastening together whatever logs and driftwood they could procure, or (more likely) by stealing native kayaks, they ferried themselves over to Big Diomede Island and shook off their pursuers. Big Diomede and its companion Little Diomede, between which runs today the U.S.-U.S.S.R. boundary, are barren, affording little in the way of food. So our harassed pioneers, unconscious that they were men of destiny, resumed their voyage to a high rocky land 25 miles to the eastward on the Seward Peninsula of Alaska, now the westernmost point of continental United States. Our Mongolian pilgrim fathers were the forerunners of the mighty race which Christopher Columbus mistakenly named the Indians.

Indulge your historians this little flight of imagination before they settle down to hard fact! After all, the consensus of scientists is that the American continent was discovered by man in some such way as we have described. *Homo sapiens* is a relative newcomer on our planet, and he must have come from some other continent, because no near relatives, such as the bigger and brighter apes, have been found here. Great animals like the dinosaur had it all their own way in the pre-glacial age, 50,000 years ago and earlier.

This is not to say that all the many million Indians who inhabited North, Central, and South America in 1492 were descended from the passengers on our hypothetical fleet. Biologically it was possible, but other migratory bands from Siberia must have followed the same course to safety and a square meal.

All ancestors of the Indians came from Asia via Siberia, and America received no addition from any other source for at least 25,000 years. Africa was once joined to South America, and there was a bridge for plant and insect life between the Old World and the New; but that was long before humankind appeared on the earth. The 'lost continents' of Atlantis and Mu are myths. The Polynesians, although very skillful in canoe navigation, never reached America, because in the South Pacific the prevailing winds are easterly, and in the North Pacific there is a 2000-mile jump from the Hawaiian Islands to California. An occasional Chinese junk or Japanese fishing boat may have drifted across to the coast of Vancouver Island or Oregon; but the human survivors, if any, were undoubtedly killed and probably eaten.

During the next twenty-five to perhaps thirty-five millennia, these Asiatic immigrants drifted southward, perhaps through a corridor in the ice cap that then covered much of North America, until they had reached the southernmost part of Patagonia. Although they lived in the Western Hemisphere for a period some fifty to seventy times as long as the interval from Columbus's landfall to the present day, we know little of their history save what may be surmised from scattered artifacts and skeletons. In these silent eons, Niagara Falls was created, Crater Lake erupted into birth, and mastodons, enormous ground sloths, and camels roamed the continent. The Indians hunted mammoths with spears tipped with ivory; painted pictures and made beads; and showed their precocity by working copper and planting maize at a surprisingly early point in time.

Somewhere between 500 B.C. and A.D. 500, the pace of Indian life quickened, especially among the Maya of northern Central America, the Inca of Peru, and the Chibcha of Colombia. In Guatemala arose the Maya empire, a civilization so advanced that its calendar was more accurate than the Julian calendar. It abandoned the stone-built cities of Guatemala in favor of Yucatán, where its civilization reached its height around A.D. 1100. About a hundred years later the Toltec, a warrior tribe from the north traditionally led by a remarkable king named Quetzalcoatl, conquered most of the Maya and absorbed their culture, much as the Romans did that of the Greeks. The Toltec empire fell before the onslaught of a new warrior race from the north, the Aztec, a ruthless people who practiced human sacrifice to satisfy the blood lust of their unattractive deities. In South America, the Inca ruled over a great Andean empire; a totalitarian society, it excelled in stone architecture and imperial organization.

The only area north of Mexico where any long historical sequence can be given to Indian life is New Mexico and Arizona. Here a hunting group that had learned the rudiments of agriculture settled down somewhere about the beginning of the Christian era and erected adobe-walled towns with apartment-house dwellings, community courts, and buildings where religious dances and other ceremonies were practiced. These pueblos were so defensible that succeeding waves of Indian conquerors passed them by, and their inhabitants, of the Hopi, Zuñi, and other tribes, were such good farmers and weavers that they seldom lacked food or clothing. First conquered by the Spaniards in the sixteenth century, they managed to throw out their masters in 1680; and although reconquered, they, more than other North American Indians, have been unmolested by Spaniards and Americans, so today they afford the best example of a well-rooted Indian culture.

Using a 'tree-ring' method of dating,[1] one can establish a sequence of basket weaving and pottery for the Pueblos, in different styles, from the first centuries of the Christian era to the present. In the 1300 years that elapsed between A.D. 217 (year of the oldest pueblo roofbeam that can be dated) and

1. Rings of trees make definite patterns, owing to the amount of sunshine and moisture they receive in the growing season. Thus, in the Southwest, where wooden beams were used for the pueblos, the rings on them can be compared with those of a pueblo known to have been destroyed four centuries ago, and these with rings on deeper buried beams, giving us a dating sequence extending about 2100 years.

(Stokes Collection, New York Public Library)

1540, when the Spaniards burst in on them, these Indians became fairly sophisticated. In the oldest culture, that of the basket-makers, the people lived in caves or built round adobe huts, wove baskets in which they stored nubbin-like ears of corn, which they cultivated with a digging-stick, hunted with flint-headed spears, and went completely naked, except for sandals on their feet and fur in the winter. In their second stage, the basket-makers learned to make pottery, as the inhabitants of Mexico had done somewhat earlier, and the women began to adorn themselves with bracelets of shell, seed, and turquoise beads. The bow and arrow, another independent invention of the Indians which had already been adopted in the Old World, replaced the spear. The third Pueblo period, from about A.D. 1050 to 1500, curiously corresponds to the 'glorious thirteenth century' in Europe. It was the golden age of cliff-dwellings, which discouraged enemies, of great masonry-walled communal dwellings built in the open, with terraced set-backs like modern skyscrapers; of big *kivas* like built-in drums where the priests danced. The close-weave basketry and decorated black-on-white pottery of this period are remarkable. After 1300 the area occupied by the Pueblo civilization was seriously reduced; the people were forced together into larger pueblos which had a good water supply, and their arts, ritual, and organization expanded. The Navajo and Apache moved in and absorbed the Pueblo culture, which the Navajo maintain to this day.

This drawing by Jacques Le Moyne, a member of an ill-fated Huguenot expedition to the Floridas in 1564, shows Indian women sowing seeds in coastal Florida. After the men broke and leveled the ground, women planted beans, millet, and maize. This sketch was first published by the gifted engraver Theodor de Bry (1528–98), who, with the aid of the distinguished geographer Richard Hakluyt, initiated the voluminous *Peregrinationum in Indiam Orientalem et Indiam Occidentalem* that gave many Europeans their main impression of the New World. From Theodor de Bry, *America*, part II, 1591. (*Rare Book Division, New York Public Library*)

Of Indian history east of the Rockies even less is known because the Indians there did not stay put, as did those of the pueblos. Whence came the 'mound-builders,' the older Indians of the Ohio and upper Mississippi valley, we do not know. The mound-builders tilled the earth with stone and shell hoes, carved out of stone elaborate tobacco pipes with realistic pictures of birds and fishes, and painted their bodies with red ochre. They were the best metal workers north of Central America before the European discovery, and even used a musical instrument, panpipes of bone and copper.

These disappeared when they disappeared, along with the tunes that a thousand years ago resounded through the oak groves of our Middle West. Above all, these people were famous for the massive earthen mounds, sometimes built in shapes of serpents and birds, in which they buried their dead.

At the time the first white men arrived in North America, the Indians of the Great Plains between the Rocky Mountains and the forested areas bordering on the Mississippi lived mostly by hunting the buffalo, on foot with bow and arrow. Although Europeans regarded all Indians except the Pueblos as nomads (a convenient excuse for denying them title to the land they occupied), only the Plains Indians really were nomadic; and even they did not become so until about A.D. 1550, when they began to break wild mustangs, offspring of European horses brought in by the Spaniards. The horse gave the men mobility in pursuit of the buffalo herds, while women followed with children and baggage on *travois*, shafts attached to big dogs or old horses; or, in winter, on toboggans, another Indian invention.

Semi-sedentary and agricultural, the Algonquin included the Abnaki of Maine and Nova Scotia, all the Indian tribes of southern New England, the Delaware and Powhatan of the Middle States and Virginia, the Sauk and Fox, Kickapoo and Pottawatomi in the Middle West, and Blackfoot in the Plains. The New England settler found the Indians not in the forest primeval but in the fields, tending crops. They cultivated beans, pumpkins, tobacco, and maize, which on many occasions saved English colonists from starvation. The Algonquin was an excellent fisherman with nets and a good hunter. He lived sociably and filthily in long bark-covered communal houses. He invented one of the lightest and most efficient of the world's small boats—the birch-bark canoe; and in regions where no white birch of sufficient girth was available he built dugouts, as did the other coastal Indians. He hunted deer and moose with bow and arrow for meat and skins, and trapped beaver, with which the women made smart jackets. The men went almost naked, even in winter, except for 'shorts' and moccasins of deerskin. They got about easily in winter on snowshoes, an Algonquian invention. These tribes produced some great and even noble characters: Powhatan, Massasoit, King Philip, Tammany, Pontiac, Tecumseh, and Keokuk. The Algonquin were susceptible to Christianity and assimilated European culture somewhat better than most Indians, although some of the chiefs tried to unite their people against the English and perished in the attempt.

The Five Nations (Mohawk, Cayuga, Oneida, Onondaga, and Seneca) of the Iroquois had the reputation of being the toughest fighters in North America; and they had to be, to hold their own against the Algonquin. In 1600, when first seen by Europeans, they occupied the territory from Lake Champlain to the Genesee river, and from the Adirondacks to central Pennsylvania. Hard pressed when the Europeans arrived, the Iroquois survived, and even extended their dominion, partly by Hiawatha's League which prevented war among themselves, and later through alliance with the Dutch and English. Their folkways were similar to those of the Algonquin. Among their famous leaders were Hendrick, Cornplanter, Red Jacket, Brant, and Logan. The Tuscarora, who in 1720 moved north and became the Sixth Nation, and the southern Cherokee were also of Iroquoian stock. The Cherokee produced one of the greatest of American Indians, Sequoya, who invented an alphabet for his people and led them in a great advance in civilization.

In the Southeast the Muskhogean stock, which included the Apalachee, Chickasaw, Choctaw, Creek, Natchez, and Seminole nations, was regarded by Europeans as the elite of North American Indians. They had an elaborate system of castes, from the 'Suns' down to the 'Stinkards,' which were not allowed to intermarry. All Muskhogean tribes were planters of maize, which they accented with the annual 'busk,' or green corn festival; and they were expert potters, weavers, and curers of deerskin for clothing. They learned very quickly from Europeans to plant orchards and keep cattle.

Even the most advanced Indian civilizations never discovered some simple things of immemorial use in Europe. Although they mined, smelted, and worked gold, silver and platinum, tin, lead, and copper, their use of iron was limited to chance finds of meteoric deposits. Indians invented the bark and the dugout canoes, yet only one or two primitive tribes in California learned to build a boat from plank and timber. They never discovered the potter's, or any other kind of wheel; the only beasts of burden in all the Americas (apart from the women) were the dog and the llama. But despite their deficiencies—notably in political organization—the American Indians were a great and noble race.

Indian and European

Since most Indians lived in a state of permanent hostility with their neighbors, and knew nothing of what went on elsewhere, it was possible for Europeans to impinge here and there on the New World without affecting tribes a few hundred miles away. One such impingement, the only one which is positively known to have occurred before Columbus, was that of the Norsemen in the eleventh century A.D. In the ninth century Scandinavians from Norway occupied Iceland, and in the late tenth century a tough Norseman from Iceland named Eric the Red discovered Greenland. On its west coast he founded a colony that flourished for several centuries by raising cattle and exporting walrus ivory and white falcons to Norway. After one Biarni Heriulfson had seen land to the west *c.* 986, Eric's son Leif in 1001 reached a coast where he saw long sand beaches; he spent a winter in northern Newfoundland and returned to Greenland.

Around 1010–15 another Icelander, Thorfinn Karlsefni, with a group of Eric the Red's kindred and neighbors, explored the coast of this 'Vinland the Good,' and attempted to found a colony where Leif had been. They spent two or three winters in northern Newfoundland, but the natives, whom they called 'Skrellings,' proved so hostile that the Norsemen gave up and returned to Greenland. These Norsemen were not Vikings, but ordinary farmers and traders; with weapons little better than those of the American natives, they were unable to cope. The significance of their discovery as the key to a New World never seems to have occurred to the Norsemen, or to anyone else. Biarni Heriulfson may justly be called the European discoverer of America; but he only lifted a corner of the veil, and his people let it drop. Nothing that he or Thorfinn Karlsefni observed was of any interest to a Europe just emerging from the Dark Ages. And there is no trace of Norse influence in the legends or customs of the northern Indians, or in American fauna and flora.

Thus America enjoyed almost five centuries more of complete isolation. Nothing was done to prepare for the next European attack, because the existence of Europe and Asia was unsuspected. No Indian tribe or nation knew much about its own continent a few hundred miles away. Among them there was nothing even approaching a sentiment of racial or continental solidarity, not even a name for race or country. Almost every Indian tribe called itself something equivalent to 'We the People,' and used some insulting title for its near neighbors. Wherever Europeans appeared, for a century or more after 1492, the first thought of the Indians was 'Men from the Sky,' and the second, 'Heaven-sent allies against our enemies.' The white man did not have to divide and conquer; he only had to overcome the tribes piecemeal, and he found plenty of native assistance for the task. Lack of iron and gunpowder, ships and horses, handicapped the Indians, but the earliest Europeans who came had few of these, and the Indians in time learned to use them well enough. Certain tribes, like the Cuna Cuna of Panama and others in Colombia and Brazil, have retained their lands and their cultural integrity to this day because they combined the offensive power of poisoned arrows with lack of anything valuable to Europeans. Primarily, inability to unite was responsible for the European conquest. If, for instance, the Aztec 'emperors' had had a little more time to consolidate their empire, Mexico might have emerged as a native state like Japan. As it was, the three authoritarian Indian empires were the first to fall. For, as a conquistador put it, when you captured *the* Inca or *the* Montezuma, it was as if a keystone fell from an arch. In Mexico, Peru, and Colombia the Spaniards simply took the place of an Indian aristocracy or theocracy, and exploited the natives for their own profit.

There was no consistent pattern of conquest. Certain feeble peoples, such as the Arawak of the

West Indies, were exterminated by being forced to labor. Others, like the Plains Indians, were humbled in the nineteenth century because their food supply was destroyed. Some nations managed for many years to live peaceably side by side with a European colony. But if a tribe wished to keep its virtue, it had to raid or fight; and the lower sort of white men could always be counted on to provoke hostilities, which at best ended in land cession and removal. However, war was far less important in the extermination of the Indian than the ravages of new forms of disease, imported by the white man.

Since Indian societies were diverse, and since their experience with whites differed, the intrusion of the European had a variety of unexpected results. In New England, the Puritans, who regarded the redmen as potential Christians descended from the ten lost tribes of Israel, sought to convert and educate them and to deal with them fairly. In the South, the Indian, adapting himself to the white man's ways, acquired Negro slaves. In the Great Plains, the Spaniards' horses had the unanticipated consequence of the explosive development of the horse-and-bison culture. Yet even where the initial result of the advent of the white man was benign, the ultimate outcome of the pressure of a technologically advanced European civilization on the Indian was almost always extinction or dispersal. Still, the Indians are so far from being exterminated that in the United States and Canada today their numbers are approaching the estimated 1.5 million of 1492.

The Decadence of Europe

At the end of the year 1492 most thinking men in western Europe felt gloomy about the future. Christian civilization appeared to be shrinking in area and dividing into hostile units. For over a century there had been no important advance in natural science, and registration in the universities dwindled as instruction became increasingly lifeless. Many intelligent men were endeavoring to escape the present through studying the pagan past. Islam was expanding at the expense of Christendom. Every crusade to recover the Holy Sepulchre at Jerusalem had failed. The Ottoman Turks, after snuffing out all that remained of the Byzantine Empire, had overrun most of Greece, Albania, and Serbia. In 1492 the papacy touched bottom when Rodrigo Borgia, a corrupt ecclesiastical politician, was elected to the throne of Saint Peter as Alexander VI. If one turned to the governments, the prospect was no brighter. The amiable but lazy Emperor Frederick III, driven from his Austrian lands by the king of Hungary, had retired to dabble in astrology and alchemy. In England the Wars of the Roses were over, but few expected the House of Tudor to last long. Only in the Iberian peninsula, in Portugal and Castile, were there signs of new life; but these kingdoms were too much on the periphery of Europe to alter the general picture of decay. Throughout western Europe the feeling was one of profound disillusion, cynical pessimism, and black despair.

The colophon of the *Nuremberg Chronicle,* dated 12 July 1493, declares that it contains 'the events most worthy of notice from the beginning of the world to the calamity of our time.' That time was painted in the most somber colors, suggesting the end of the world; a few blank pages were left to record events between 1493 and the Day of Judgment. Yet, even as the chroniclers of Nuremberg were correcting their proofs, a Spanish caravel named *Niña* scudded before a winter gale into Lisbon, with news of a discovery that was to give old Europe another chance.

In a few years we find the picture completely changed. Strong monarchs are stamping out privy conspiracy and rebellion; the Church, purged and chastened by the Protestant Reformation, puts her house in order; new ideas flare up throughout Italy, France, Germany, and the northern nations; faith in God revives and the human spirit is renewed. The change is complete and astounding. A new world view has begun, and people no longer sigh after an imaginary golden age in the distant past, but lay plans for a golden age in the near future.

Columbus Discovers America

Christopher Columbus discovered America by accident when looking for Japan and China. Few people cared anything about it, when found; and

Christopher Columbus (1451–1506). No portrait of 'the Admiral of the Ocean Sea' was painted during his lifetime, and various purported likenesses bear no resemblance to him. This sixteenth-century 'giovio' portrait (for a gallery of notable men at Bishop Paolo Giovio's villa at Lake Como) is regarded as the most authentic, although it was not painted until thirty years or more after his death. It depicts the explorer, wearing a sort of monastic robe, in a downcast and reflective mood after his third expedition, which ended with his return to Spain in chains. (*Museo Giovio, Como*)

the Atlantic coast from Hudson's Bay to the Strait of Magellan was explored by navigators seeking a passage to India through or around this unwanted continent. Yet Columbus was the effective discoverer of America for Europe, because he was the first to do anything with it. The 'Enterprise of the Indies,' as he called his plan of sailing west to the Orient, was his very own, suggested by no previous information, produced by no economic forces. He promoted this design for at least eight years before he could persuade any prince to grant him the modest equipment required; and a less persistent or stout-hearted captain would have turned back before reaching land. News of his discovery was immediately spread throughout Europe by the recent invention of printing. Columbus led the first colony to the New World in 1493; he discovered the South American continent in 1498; and he obtained the first definite news of the Pacific Ocean. The history of the Americas stems from his four voyages.

Born at Genoa in 1451, the son of a weaver of woolen cloth, this great mariner went to sea at about the age of twenty, and after making voyages in the Mediterranean, suffered shipwreck in Portugal, settled in Lisbon around the year 1477. Portugal was then the most progressive of the European kingdoms. Under Prince Henry the Navigator, the Portuguese sought a sea route to 'the Indies' (India, China, and the eastern islands), to obtain at their source the spices, drugs, and gems which reached Europe in small quantities over caravan routes, and the gold and silver about which Marco Polo had told tall tales. The most promising route lay to the southward; and by the time Columbus settled in Portugal, the mariners of that nation were opening up new stretches of the West African coast every year. As early as 1460 they had passed the site of Dakar, and had dispelled the Arabian legends of a 'sea of pitchy darkness.' Fifteen years later they had completed the exploration of the Gulf of Guinea, and opened up a trade in gold and ivory, slaves and pepper, that made Lisbon the envy of Europe. For this traffic, which required a round voyage of many thousand miles, the Portuguese developed the caravel, a sailing vessel, which was fast, seaworthy, and weatherly. Ships capable of making the voyage to America and back had existed long before Columbus was born; but the caravel made the voyage far less difficult and dangerous.

Columbus proposed to open a much shorter sea route to 'the Indies' by sailing west, around the world. A poor mathematician, he had satisfied himself by a series of lucky miscalculations that Japan lay only 2400 to 2500 miles west of the Canaries. In 1484 he began his efforts to obtain backing. But the learned men to whom the plan was referred had more accurate notions of the globe than he had. Not that he needed to demonstrate the earth was round. It had been known to be spherical for centuries; a spherical earth was taught in all European universities. Everyone agreed that a westward route to 'the Indies' was theoretically possible, like flying in 1900; but nobody considered it practicable with such means as were then available.

After eight years of agitation, the intuition of Queen Isabella gave Columbus his chance. After all, the man might be right about the size of the earth: it was simply one theory against another. The equipment he asked for was cheap enough; the honors he demanded were not unreasonable, if he succeeded, and the glory and gain for Spain would be incalculable. If he failed, little would be lost. So Ferdinand and Isabella, the joint sovereigns of Spain, undertook to pay the bills and to make Columbus viceroy, governor, and admiral over any lands he might acquire. They gave him a Latin letter of introduction to the Emperor of China, and a passport stating that he was on a legitimate voyage 'to regions of India.'

Columbus sailed from Palos on 3 August 1492, as commander of a fleet of three vessels, *Niña, Pinta,* and *Santa Maria,* each about 70 to 80 feet long. They were manned by about 90 picked Spaniards. His plan was to sail due west from the Canary Islands, because according to the best available maps these lay on the same latitude as Japan; if these islands were missed, the fleet would be sure to hit China. Their course lay along the northern edge of the belt of northeast trade winds which blow steadily in late summer between the Canaries and America. This most important voyage in history was also one of the easiest; they generally enjoyed fair wind, soft air, a serene sky, and an ocean smooth as a river. The three vessels departed the westernmost Canaries on 9 September. Mutiny flared on 10 October but Columbus persuaded his men to go on for three days more. At 10 p.m. on 11 October, Columbus and a few others saw for a short time a dim light ahead. This may have been a brush fire kindled by natives on a high point of an island, whose sand cliffs showed up in the moonlight at 2 a.m. on the 12th. It was the Bahamian island that Columbus named, and we call, San Salvador.

Many other discoveries have been more spectacular than that of this small, low, sandy island that rides out ahead of the American continent, breasting the trade winds. But it was there that the Ocean for the first time 'loosed the chains of things' as Seneca had prophesied, gave up the secret that had baffled Europeans since they began to inquire what lay beyond the western horizon's rim. San Salvador, rising from the sea at the end of a 33-day westward sail, was a clean break with past experience. Every tree, every plant, that the Spaniards saw was strange to them, and the natives were completely unexpected, speaking an unknown tongue and resembling no race of which even the most educated of the explorers had read. Never again may mortal man hope to recapture the wonder, the delight of those October days in 1492 when the New World gracefully yielded her virginity to the conquering Castilians.

Several of the natives, whom Columbus hopefully called Indians, welcomed the 'Men from the Sky,' and several were impressed to act as guides to 'Cipangu' (Japan) and 'Cathay' (China). They piloted Columbus through the Bahamas to northwestern Cuba. There he dispatched his Arabic interpreter inland to meet a cacique whom he took, from the Indians' description, to be the Emperor of China. But the village of thatched huts that they found bore little resemblance to the Cambaluk where Marco Polo had hobnobbed with Kubla Khan. Columbus persisted in his quest, eagerly examining every new plant for evidence that Cuba was the southeastern promontory of China. On *La Isla Española*, 'The Spanish Island,' which we still call Hispaniola, he found golden grains in river sands, rumors of a gold mine upcountry, and an abundance of gold ornaments on the Indians which they readily swapped for brass rings, glass beads, and bits of cloth. When the flagship ran on a coral reef, Columbus built a fort of her timbers, garrisoned it with her crew, and sailed for home on board *Niña*, accompanied by *Pinta*.

Columbus and his men were received as heroes, and everyone assumed that they had discovered islands 'in the Indian Sea,' if not the continent of Asia. The Pope conferred on Spain sovereignty of all lands beyond the meridian 100 leagues (318 nautical miles) west of the Cape Verde Islands. Portugal protested, and by mutual consent the next year the line was moved 270 leagues farther west; this new line of demarcation gave Portugal her title to Brazil. After six months in Spain Columbus sailed in command of a gallant fleet of seventeen vessels which discovered all the Caribbee Islands north and west of Martinique, and Puerto Rico. At Hispaniola, after ascertaining that his garrison had been wiped out, he began building a fortified trading station.

There his troubles began. The first European colony in America was nothing more than a glorified gold hunt. Columbus expected to obtain the precious metal by trade; but the Indians' demand for trading truck was soon exhausted, and the Spaniards began taking gold by force. As elsewhere in America where Europeans came, the newcomers were first welcomed by the Indians as visitors, then resented as intruders, and finally resisted with fruitless desperation. The Spaniards, who had come only for gold, resented their governor's orders to build houses, tend crops, and cut wood; the wine and food supplies from Spain gave out; and before long bands of men in armor were roving the fertile interior, living off the country, and torturing the natives to obtain gold. In the summer of 1494, which Columbus spent exploring the southern coasts of Cuba and Hispaniola and discovering Jamaica, the colonists got completely out of hand; and the Admiral's attempts to impose an iron discipline resulted in malcontents seizing vessels and returning to Spain to complain. So Columbus, leaving his brother Bartholomew in charge, sailed for home in 1496. After a year's lobbying at court, Columbus could only obtain grudging consent to send out convicts as colonists, and to let him make a new voyage in search of the Asiatic continent.

Meantime, a second nation had stumbled on America when searching for Asia, and through the efforts of another Genoese. John Cabot, a compatriot of Columbus but a naturalized citizen of Venice, believed that the Far East could best be reached by sailing westward in the short high latitudes. After making a contract with Henry VII of England similar to that of Columbus with the Spanish sovereigns, he sailed from Bristol in 1497 and reached the New World, probably northern Newfoundland, where he spent less than a month. All we know of Cabot's second voyage in 1498 is that he never returned. The English did practically nothing to follow up Cabot's voyages for three-quarters of a century, and their only influence was to give the English Crown a 'legal' title to North America against the claims of Spain and France.

When on his third voyage Columbus returned to Santo Domingo, the new capital of Hispaniola that had been established in his absence, he found the island in turmoil. Most of the Indians had been brought under subjection, but the chief justice, Francisco Roldán—first of a long line of American rebels—was heading a revolt of ex-criminals and robust individualists against the government of Columbus's brother, in the hope of obtaining a larger share of the women and the gold-diggings. Columbus was forced to appease Roldán. To each man was granted a tract of land with the Indians who lived on it, whose labors he was entitled to exploit as he saw fit. These *encomiendas,* as they were subsequently called, marked the beginning of a system the Spaniards applied throughout their conquests in order to induce settlement and supply the colonists with cheap servile labor.

Several Spaniards who had been officers under Columbus made voyages to South America, and on one of them sailed a Florentine merchant, Amerigo Vespucci. Amerigo's inflated and pre-dated account of a voyage in 1499 made his name familiar to northern Europe. Thus, when a German geographer in 1507 suggested that the new continent be called *America,* after him, the name caught on. A year earlier Columbus, after an unsuccessful fourth voyage to try to find a strait through his 'Other World,' as he called America, had died in obscurity.

No discoverer in the world's history had such marvelous success as Columbus, even though he never found what he first sought; no navigator save Magellan or da Gama may be compared with him for courage, persistence, and skill; no other great benefactor of the human race was so ill rewarded in his lifetime; none other is so justly revered today in the New and Other World of his Discovery.

The Spanish Empire

For about twenty years after the first voyage of Columbus, Hispaniola was the only European colony in America. It was based on cattle and cotton raising, gold mining, and the culture of the sugar cane introduced from the Canaries. In 1512 Hispaniola was exporting annually to Spain not far short of a million dollars in gold. The enslaved Indians died off under forced labor, and were replaced, first by Indians kidnapped from other islands, who suffered the same fate, and then—beginning in 1510—by black slaves, bought from the Portuguese, who procured them in Africa, largely from other blacks. Santo Domingo became the center from which much of the rest of America was explored and colonized.

Juan Ponce de León, the first of the *adelantados* (advancers), explored in 1506 the island of Puerto Rico, which, with Jamaica and Cuba, was conquered and colonized, and then extended his explorations to the mainland. Ponce de León had heard the story of a marvelous spring on an island named Bimini which restored youth and vigor to the old and impotent, and he decided to search for it. In April 1513, after threading his way through the Bahamas and ascertaining that there were neither springs nor streams in the islands, Ponce landed near Daytona Beach and named the land Florida after that fair Easter season (*Pascua Florida*). Hugging the coast to avoid the Gulf stream, he rounded the Florida Keys and sailed up into the Gulf of Mexico, and then discovered Yucatán. But he returned to Puerto Rico without an ounce of gold or a drink of invigorating water. Though St. Augustine was founded by Menéndez de Aviles in 1566 in order to protect the treasure fleets from French and English marauders, Florida during three centuries of Spanish rule remained little more than a military outpost of Mexico and Cuba.

Vespucci 'Discovering' America. In this late sixteenth-century work, Stradanus depicts the New World as an abundantly endowed woman burdening a hammock, while a tapir and a sloth prowl around the trees. In the background cannibals are cooking dinner. Vespucci, in a handsome garment, carries an astrolabe in his left hand; in his right, he holds the Southern Cross. (*The British Museum*)

The Pacific Ocean was discovered by Vasco Núñez de Balboa, a stowaway from Hispaniola who had made himself master of a relatively insignificant Spanish post on the Gulf of Darien. In 1513 Balboa had several hundred Indians hack the way across the difficult isthmus of Darien for him and his 189 hidalgos to the spot where 'silent, upon a peak in Darien,' he first gazed upon the Pacific. The discoverer was soon after put to death by his rival Pedrarias, whose energy was so vast that small sailing vessels and their gear were transported across the divide in sections, and set afloat on *El Mar del Sur,* the great South Sea. Presently the city of Panama was founded, and Spain had a Pacific base.

Across that ocean—how far across nobody had yet guessed—lay the Spice Islands, whence the king of Portugal was deriving far greater wealth than did his Spanish cousins from the gold-washings of Hispaniola, for the epic voyage of Vasco da Gama around the Cape of Good Hope to India had given the Portuguese the long-sought sea route to the Orient. Ferdinand Magellan, a captain who had spent seven years with the Portuguese in the Far East, believed that the Spice Islands—modern Indonesia—could better be reached by sailing westward. Rebuffed by the king of Portugal, he turned to the king of Spain (Charles I, later Emperor Charles V), who gave him a fleet of five ships. They sailed from Seville in August 1519, reached the River Plate in January, and continued south along the coast of Patagonia. While the fleet was wintering, the captains of four ships mutinied; Magellan hanged some of the leaders, and marooned the others. At the Antarctic summer solstice the voyage was renewed, and on 21 October 1520, Magellan discovered the entrance to 'the Strait that shall forever bear his name,' as Camoëns wrote in the *Lusiads*. The fleet, reduced by shipwreck and desertion to three sail, required 38 days to thread the dangerous 334-mile passage that cuts through the tail end of the Andes.

Then came the most terrible part of the voyage. This South Sea was calm enough, once they were off shore—that is why Magellan renamed it the Pacific Ocean—but they were fourteen weeks without sight of land, excepting two small coral atolls where neither water nor food was found. The scurvy-ridden men were reduced to eating sawdust and biscuit which had become mere powder swarming with worms, even to broiling the leather chafing-gear of the yards. Relief was obtained on 6 March 1521, at Guam, and ten days later they reached Leyte Gulf in the Philippines. On the tiny island of Limasawa, off Leyte, there occurred the most dramatic event of the voyage. Magellan's Malay servant Henriquez, whom he had brought home from a previous voyage, was able to make himself understood. West had met East.

After Magellan was slain in a battle and two of the three vessels ran into grief, the *Vittoria*, laden with spices, set forth alone, on 21 December 1521, under Captain Juan Sebastian de Elcano. She crossed the Indian Ocean, rounded the Cape of Good Hope, and on 9 September 1522, this greatest voyage of all time ended at Seville, with only eighteen of the 239 men who set forth three years earlier. Captain de Elcano was ennobled, and Europe for the first time learned the width of the Pacific Ocean and the real relation of the New World to the Orient.

Magellan was already on his way and the entire east coast of South America had been explored before the two most splendid native civilizations in America, Mexico's and Peru's, yielded their secrets. In 1519 the governor of Cuba, wishing to establish a trading post on the Mexican coast, sent an expedition of eleven ships, carrying only 550 Spaniards, under 32-year-old Hernando Cortés. Arriving at a time when the caciques of Mexico were chafing under the cruel sovereignty of the Aztecs, Cortés was welcomed by many as their fabled hero, Quetzalcoatl, and he had the wit to take advantage of it. For all that, the conquest of Mexico was one of the most amazing military and diplomatic feats in the world's history. The march up from Vera Cruz to the great interior plateau, the audacious capture of Montezuma's lake-rimmed capital (1521), and the defeat of a vast army on the plains of Teotihuacan completed the ruin of Aztec power and firmly established Cortés as master of Mexico.

Spanish conquistadors explored the whole southern expanse from South Carolina across to California in search of more valuable treasure and of new empires. Pánfilo de Narváez, who sailed from Spain in 1527, landed somewhere on the Gulf coast of Florida, where he built a fleet from native wood fastened with spikes fashioned from spurs and stirrups, rigged with hair cordage and sails made from the hides of horses which his men had eaten. In these crazy craft Narváez made his way to Texas, where the fleet was wrecked. The survivors, Cabeza de Vaca, two other Spaniards, and a Negro, Esteban, spent six years among the Indians, eventually reaching Mexico with tales of wild 'hunchback cows' that covered the plains as far as the eye could see, and of cities with emerald-studded walls, of which they had heard. These 'Seven Cities of Cibola' were more readily believed in than were the buffalo. In 1539 the viceroy of Mexico sent Fray Marcos, accompanied by Esteban, up into the future New Mexico in search of the fabled 'Seven Cities.' There they discovered the disappointing foundation of this myth, the Zuñi pueblos, and the honest Fray Marcos so reported. Nevertheless the viceroy sent forth the most splendid expedition of all, that of Francisco Vásquez Coronado. One of Coronado's lieutenants discovered the Grand Canyon in 1540; Coronado himself marched eastward across the panhandle of Texas into eastern Kansas, only to return, disappointed, to Mexico. Yet another explorer led on by tales of splendid cities, Hernando de Soto, landed in Florida, marched about the interior of the future Gulf States, and in 1541 came upon the mighty Mississippi.

Owing to their failure to find treasure or a strait, these explorations had no immediate result. Only at the end of the sixteenth century did Juan de Oñate formally take possession 'of all the kingdoms and provinces of New Mexico.' The Pueblos submitted, colonization began, and the next governor founded Santa Fe in 1609. Thus New Mexico, the forty-seventh state to be admitted to the Union, was settled at the same time as the first permanent English colony in North America. Well before then Spain had conquered almost the whole of Latin America. Francisco Pizarro had overthrown the mighty Inca empire of Peru and founded Lima by 1535, and by mid-century the foundations had been laid for every one of the twenty republics of Central and South America, excepting the Argentine.

There has been no other conquest like this in the annals of the human race. In one generation the Spaniards acquired more new territory than Rome did in five centuries. Genghis Khan swept over a greater area, but left only destruction in his wake; the Spaniards organized all that they conquered, brought in the arts and letters of Europe, and converted millions to their faith. Our forebears in Virginia and New England, the pathfinders of the Great West, and the French-Canadian pioneers were stout fellows indeed; but their exploits scarcely compare with those of the conquistadors and friars who hacked their way in armor through solid jungle, across endless plains, and over snowy passes of the Andes to fulfill their dreams of gold and glory, and for whom reality was greater even than the dream.

Hispanic America is rich in paradox. The Spanish, who encountered an Indian population more numerous and more advanced than England and France found, incorporated the Indian into their society, unlike the English and the French, and the intermarriage of whites, Indians, and blacks created a heterogeneous culture less marked by racial prejudice. But it was also a highly stratified social order in which social distinction rested on pigmentation, with a white elite at the top. Guilty of revolting cruelty toward the Indian, Spain also sought persistently to preserve his personal liberty. A medieval society, it nonetheless welcomed modern advances. Mexico City and Lima, the 'City of Kings,' became seats of urban civilization within fifteen years of the conquest; in each a university was founded in 1551; the first printing press in the New World came to Mexico City in 1539. Even today an air of superb magnificence rests on the churches and palaces built by these 'children of the sun' in their provincial capitals hundreds of miles from the sea.

Thus the Spanish empire had more than a century's head start on the English and French; and the stupendous results of that conquest were the envy of every European power. Spanish prestige reached its height in 1580 when Philip II succeeded to the throne of Portugal as well as that of Spain, uniting under his person two vast empires that now stretched their arms around the world, the left arm to the west coast of Mexico, the right arm to Manila. At that moment not another nation had placed a single permanent settler on the shores of the New World.

Yet the end of that monopoly was near. The autumn gales of 1580 blew up the English Channel and into Plymouth harbor Francis Drake in the *Golden Hind,* worm-eaten and weed-clogged after her three years' voyage around the world, laden with the spoil of a Peruvian treasure ship. Only eight years more, and Spain suffered her first major defeat on the ocean that she had mastered; twenty years more, and Virginia was founded.

Enter France and England

Spanish conquest was too swift and successful for the health of Spain. American treasure ruined her manufactures, financed useless military adventures of her kings, and finally led to poverty and stagnation. Yet the immediate success, which alone was visible, stimulated three other nations, France, England, and the Netherlands, to acquire colonial possessions of their own. As early as 1521 French corsairs bagged part of the booty that Cortés was sending home; and this process of muscling into the Spanish empire continued until England and France were firmly established in North America, and the Dutch in the Far East.

Jacques Cartier is the Columbus of French Canada. This hardy seaman of St.-Malo made three voyages to the Gulf of St. Lawrence (1534–41) in search of a passage to the Orient. On the second he discovered the rock of Quebec, in a region which the natives called Canada, and then proceeded upstream, past Montreal (so named by him), to the lowest rapids of the St. Lawrence, the La Chine. From the Indians he collected a cycle of tall tales about an inland kingdom of the Saguenay, where gold and silver were as plentiful as in Peru. Cartier brought back nothing save a shipload of iron pyrites, or fool's gold, and quartz crystals that he believed to be diamonds, but he did discover one of the two leading axes of penetration of the continent. France then fell into a cycle of religious wars, and no progress was made toward an empire in America until the next century.

England approached America gingerly, for it was a small and poor country, hemmed in by enemies and anxious to placate Spain. Yet England was growing stronger year by year. No small share of the treasure from Mexico and Peru went to buy English woolens. Henry VIII's breach with the Church of Rome stimulated English nationalism and made a break with Spain inevitable sooner or later. Under Queen Elizabeth I (1558–1603) it became a religious as well as a patriotic duty to 'singe the king of Spain's beard.' On Francis Drake's memorable voyage to California and around the world (1577–80) he terrorized the coasts of Chile and Peru, and in 1587 Captain Thomas Cavendish bagged the grandest prize of all, a Manila galleon. His ships entered the Thames rigged with damask sails, and each sailor wore a silk suit and a chain of pure gold round his neck.

The great age of Elizabeth and of Shakespeare, in which English genius burned brightly in almost every aspect of life, was reaching its acme.

> This happy breed of men, this little world,
> This precious stone set in the silver sea,

awakened from long lethargy to a feeling of exuberant life, such as few people had known since ancient Greece. That was an age when the scholar, the divine, and the man of action were often one and the same person—for the Elizabethans knew, what many of us have forgotten, that life is empty without religion, that the tree of knowledge is barren unless rooted in love, and that learning purchased at the expense of living is a sorry bargain. Man in those days was not ashamed to own himself an animal, nor so base as to quench the divine spark that made him something better; but above all, he exulted in the fact that he was a man. Chapman spoke for his age when he cried out, 'Be free, all worthy spirits, and stretch yourselves!'

The age of discovery in England was closely integrated with literature and promoted by her governing class. Sir Humphrey Gilbert, Oxonian, educational reformer, and courtier, published a *Discourse of a Discovery for a New Passage to Cataia* (China), and attempted the first English colony. His half-brother Sir Walter Raleigh, courtier, soldier, and historian, founded Virginia and sought El Dorado up the Orinoco. And the Reverend Richard Hakluyt, student of Christ Church, Oxford, compiled his great collection of *Navigations, Voiages, Traffiques and Discoveries of the English Nation* in order to fire his countrymen to worthy deeds overseas. These men wanted an overseas empire that would make England self-sufficient and employ a great merchant marine. It should be in a climate where Englishmen might live, and where they and the natives would provide a new market for English goods. The colonies should produce tar and timber for shipbuilding, gold and silver, dyewoods, wine, spices and olives, and everything else that England was then buying from abroad. The Indians must be converted to Protestant Christianity, in order to stay the progress of the Counter-Reformation, and a passage through to the real Indies was sought.

Yet, with all this energy and gallantry, English colonization in the sixteenth century repeatedly failed. Gilbert took possession of Newfoundland for the Queen in 1583, but was lost on the voyage home. Raleigh then took over his patent to the whole of North America above Florida, named it Virginia, and planted two successive colonies on Roanoke Island. The first gave up after a year; the second, a well-chosen group of 117 men, women,

Sir Walter Raleigh (*c.* 1552–1618), organizer of the Roanoke Island expeditions, failed either to achieve a permanent settlement in Virginia or to find El Dorado up the Orinoco, but quickened interest in colonizing the New World. This portrait by Marcus Gheerhardts the Younger depicts Queen Elizabeth's favorite shortly after he was knighted. (*Colonial Williamsburg*)

and children, had completely disappeared by the time a relief expedition arrived in 1590. The experience of Gilbert and Raleigh proved that 'it is a difficult thing to carry over colonies into remote countries upon private men's purses.' The Crown was too impecunious to finance colonies; and individual enterprise preferred the gay adventure and certain profit of raiding the Spanish Main. So the sixteenth century closed like the fifteenth, without a single Englishman on American soil—unless survivors of Raleigh's lost colony were still wandering through the forests of Carolina.

This should have been discouraging, but the English were past discouragement. For, underlying all their efforts, the earlier failures as well as later successes, was a powerful drive. This *daimon* of the English was the burning desire to found a new England, a new society, in which all the best of the past would be conserved, but where life would have a better quality than anything conceivable in Europe, where men might even create a commonwealth that would be, in a word borrowed from Sir Thomas More's great work of 1516, Utopia.

2

First Foundations

*

1600–1660

Virginia

Two waves of colonizing activity were responsible for founding twelve of the thirteen English colonies which federated as the United States of America, and the French colonies which became the nucleus of the Canadian Commonwealth. The first wave, which began in 1606 and lasted until 1637, planted three groups of English colonies and three French colonies: Virginia and Maryland on the Chesapeake, the Puritan commonwealths of New England, and the British West Indies; French L'Acadie (Nova Scotia), Quebec, and the Antilles; and also the Dutch colony of New Netherland, which became New York.

The death of Elizabeth I and the accession of James I in 1603 brought peace with Spain and Scotland, and released capital and men for fruitful purposes. The lesson that 'private purses are cold comforts to adventurers' had been well learned. Excellent results had already been obtained in foreign trade by joint-stock corporations, which combined the capital of many under the management of a few. The Muscovy Company and the Levant Company had done well in trading with Russia and the Near East; spectacular profits were in store for the East India Company. Each firm received a monopoly of English trade with a specified portion of the world, and full control over whatever trading posts or colonies it might see fit to establish.

In such wise the English colonization of Virginia was effected. Two groups of capitalists were formed, one centering in Bristol and the other in London. Every stockholder could take part in the quarterly meetings (called general courts) and had a vote in choosing the board of directors, known as the treasurer and council. Between these two companies, the English claim to North America was divided. Northern Virginia, renamed New England in 1620, fell to the Bristol group; Southern Virginia, which also included the future Maryland and Carolina, to the Londoners. The Northern Company's one attempt to plant came to grief because of an 'extreme unseasonable and frosty' Maine winter. But the 'Old Dominion' of Virginia was established by the London Company. That corporation was no mere money-making scheme, although the expectation of profit certainly existed; rather was it a national enterprise with hundreds of stockholders great and small.

Three ships under Captain Christopher Newport, *Susan Constant*, *Godspeed*, and *Discovery*, dropped down the Thames at Christmastide 1606, and 'Virginia's Tryalls' (as an early tract was entitled) began at once. The long voyage proved fatal to sixteen of the 120 men on board—no women were taken. The company expected to convert Indians, locate gold, discover the Northwest Passage, and produce 'all the commodities of Europe, Africa and Asia.' But no gold was found, neither the James nor the Chickahominy rivers led to the Pacific, and the only commodities sent home for several years were of the forest, such as oak clapboard. The company proposed to establish a new home for the unemployed who swarmed into English towns, but these 'sturdy beggars' did not care to emigrate as landless wage-slaves. So the first colony consisted largely of decayed gentlemen, released prisoners, and a few honest artisans. For Jamestown Captain Newport had selected a very malarial site which was eventually abandoned. As in Columbus's first colony, the men were upset by the strange food, drenched in flimsy housing, racked by disease, and pestered by mosquitoes and Indians. By the spring of 1608 only 53 Englishmen were left alive; and they were saved only through the bustling activity of Captain John Smith in placating the natives and planting corn.

The Virginia Company sent relief in 1608, and again in 1609—a fleet of nine ships under Sir Thomas Gates. The flagship was wrecked on the Bermudas, providing material for Shakespeare's *Tempest*, and securing for England the lovely islands that are now her oldest colony. When the survivors reached Jamestown, that colony was reduced to the last stage of wretchedness. 'Everie man allmost laments himself of being here,' wrote Governor Dale in 1611. He despaired of making a success with 'sutch disordered persons, so prophane, so riotous . . . besides of sutch diseased and crased bodies.' He hoped the king would send to Virginia, out of the common jails, all men condemned to die; they at least might be glad 'to make this their new Countrie.' One is not astonished at the 'treasonable Intendments' of these workers when one reads of their regime. Twice a day they were marched into the fields by beat of drum or into the forests to cut wood, and twice a day marched back to Jamestown to eat and pray. The only thing that kept the colony alive was the deep faith and gallant spirit of men who believed that they had hold of something which must not be allowed to perish. 'Be not dismayed at all,' says the author of *Newes from Virginia* (1610):

> Let England knowe our willingnesse,
> For that our worke is good;
> *Wee hope to plant a nation,*
> *Where none before hath stood.*

Virginia needed more than faith and gallantry to ensure permanence. She needed a profitable product, a system of landholding that gave immigrants a stake; discipline to be sure, but also liberty. In ten years' time she obtained all these. Between 1615 and 1625 Virginia was transformed from an unsuccessful trading post, ruled by iron discipline and hated by most of the settlers, into a commonwealth that began to open a new and wonderful life to the common man of England.

Tobacco culture, which never entered into the founders' plans, saved Virginia. Smoking was brought to England by Sir John Hawkins in the 1560's. The English complained that the tobacco the Indians cultivated around Roanoke bit the tongue, and so continued to import West Indian leaf through Spain. John Rolfe, husband to Pocahontas, is said to have been responsible for procuring seed from the West Indies around 1613, and the leaves grown from this seed on Virginian soil smoked well. Some 2500 pounds were exported in 1616; 20,000 in 1617; 50,000 in 1618. Here at last was something to attract capital and labor, and make large numbers of Englishmen wish to emigrate.

Private property in land also stimulated growth. As the indentures of hired servants expired, they became tenant farmers on a sharecropping basis; by 1619 tenant farms extended twenty miles along the James. Groups of settlers organized by some man of substance were granted large tracts called 'hundreds,' which formed autonomous communities within the colony. And in 1618 the company devised 'head-rights,' which

L
F
E
K
G
H
I
E
D
B
C
A
T B
20

became the basis of land tenure in all the Southern English colonies. By this system persons who emigrated at their own expense were granted 50 acres free for each member of their party, or for any subsequent immigrant whose passage they paid. Thus private gain was enlisted to build the colony, and the labor supply kept pace with that of arable land.

English law and liberty came as well. In 1618 the company instructed the governor to introduce common law and summon a representative assembly with power to make by-laws, subject to the company's consent in England. Democracy made her American debut on 30 July 1619, when 22 'burgesses,' two from each settled district, elected by vote of all men seventeen and upward, met with the governor's council in the church at Jamestown. From that time forth, government of the people, however limited or thwarted, and the rule of law have been fundamental principles of the English colonies and the United States.

The parent company in England exerted far more power in Virginia than this popular assembly, but the company itself was democratic in spirit. Stockholders in 1619 unseated Sir Thomas Smyth, the London merchant adventurer who had headed it during the most difficult years, and elected Sir Edwin Sandys, an opposition leader in the House of Commons, tolerant in religion and liberal in outlook. Convinced that the colony's exclusive preoccupation with tobacco was unsound, Sandys induced the stockholders to adopt a five-year plan for Virginia. French vines, vintners, and olive trees, lumbermen from the Baltic, ironworkers from England were procured or hired to start new industries, and thousands of poor English men and women were assisted to emigrate. Unfortunately this required more expense than the company could bear, and the colony was ill-prepared to receive an influx of 4000 people in four years. Of those sent from England in the Sandys regime, more than three-fourths perished. Ships were overcrowded, housing facilities inadequate, and the loss of life from typhus, malaria, malnutrition, and overwork was appalling. Plantations were laid out too far apart, defense was neglected, and in 1622 a surprise attack by Indians destroyed the infant ironworks

This depiction of a Pamlico river Indian village in sixteenth-century Virginia derives from a watercolor by John White, a settler on Roanoke Island who subsequently became governor of the doomed colony. It is the earliest printed picture of tobacco fields, marked *E*. In the lower half, as Thomas Hariot explained, *A* indicates a building housing 'the tombes of their kings and princes,' *B* the site of their 'solemne prayers,' *C* where they met with their neighbors to 'make merrie together' after they had feasted with them in a broad plot, *D*. In the structure designated *F* in the upper right, an Indian keeps vigil, 'for there are such nomber of fowles, and beasts, that unles they keepe the better watche, they would devour all their corne. For which cause the watcheman maketh continual cryes and noyse.' From Theodor de Bry, *America*, part I, 1590. (*Rare Book Division, New York Public Library*) at the falls of the James, erased almost every settlement outside Jamestown, massacred more than 300 men, women, and children, and in a night wiped out the gains of three years. This gave the enemies of Sandys a handle against him, convinced the king that the bankrupt, faction-torn colony had been grossly mismanaged, and produced, in 1624, a judicial dissolution of the Virginia Company of London.

Virginia now became a royal province or Crown colony; but she did not lose her large measure of self-government. Assembly and courts of justice were retained, though governor and council were now appointed by the king and subject to royal instructions. Charles I, not unaffected by the large revenue he was obtaining from the duties on tobacco, interfered with the colony less than the company had, and development continued along tobacco plantation lines.

When we think of seventeenth-century Virginia we should first banish from our minds the cavalier myth of gallants and fair ladies living a life of silken ease. We must picture a series of farms and plantations lining the James, the York, and the Rappahannock up to the fall line, and along the south bank of the Potomac. Few houses are more than a mile from tidewater. The average farm, not above 300 or 400 acres, is cultivated by the owner and his family and a few white indentured servants of both sexes. Around a story-and-a-half frame cottage are a vegetable garden and orchard; beyond, corn and tobacco fields, enclosed by zigzag fences of split rails; and beyond that, woodland, where cattle and hogs fend for themselves. In the course of a few years, when the original tobacco fields are exhausted, the woodland will be cleared and put under tillage, while the 'old fields,' after a few diminishing crops of corn, will revert to brush and woodland. Few horses and still fewer wheeled vehicles will be seen outside Jamestown until after 1650, but almost every farmer keeps a yoke of oxen for plowing and a boat on the nearest creek or river. If the owner prospers, he will procure more land from someone who has more head-rights than he cares to take up, or by importing his poor relations as servants.

The few great plantations, established by men who came out with considerable capital, have large houses and more outbuildings, keep a shop for selling English goods to their neighbors, and a wharf and warehouse for handling their tobacco. Every so often the big planter orders the London merchant who handles his tobacco crop to send him out another parcel of indented servants, for each of whom he will obtain 50 acres more land; if no ungranted land is available near the homestead he will 'seat' a second plantation elsewhere, and put his son, or a trusty servant whose time is up, in charge. Virginia was a colony with a sharply defined ruling class, although it took almost a century for a stable aristocracy to develop.

During the first half-century, the manners and customs of Virginia were Puritan. The code of laws adopted by the first Virginia Assembly 'Against Idleness, Gaming, drunkenes and excesse in apparell,' might well have been passed by a New England colony. Yet there were important differences, too, between Virginia and New England. The Church of England was early established in Virginia, and Puritan congregations were outlawed in 1643. And as time flowed on, and great fortunes were built from tobacco, the Puritan tinge faded from the Old Dominion.

Below the independent landowners in Virginia were the English and Irish indented servants, the main source of labor in the Chesapeake colonies throughout this pioneer period. Indented servants were mostly lads and lasses in their late 'teens or early twenties, members of large families in the English towns and countryside, who were looking for a better chance than the overcrowded trades of the old country. Men and women servants alike performed any sort of labor their master required for a period of five years, which might be extended for ill-conduct; at the end of that time they were dismissed with a few tools and clothes; in Maryland each servant was given 50 acres by the Lord Proprietor. The more energetic freedmen would then earn money by wage labor, and set up as farmers themselves. A hard system it was, according to modern lights; yet it enabled thousands of English men and women, and, in the eighteenth century, tens of thousands of Scots, Irish, Germans, and Swiss, to make a fresh start and take an active part in forming the American nation.

A Dutch ship brought the first Africans to

Jamestown as early as 1619. The first blacks appear to have been indented servants; slavery is not mentioned in any statute until after 1660, although it may have developed before that. Slavery did not become a characteristic feature of Virginia until nearly the end of the seventeenth century. It became so then for three reasons: England restricted the emigration of white bond servants; the Royal African Company became more efficient in the slave trade; and a catastrophic fall in the price of tobacco ruined the small farmers, permitting profits only to men who had the capital to purchase cheap and self-propagating labor.

Lord Baltimore's and Other Proprietary Colonies

Maryland, a colony with the same soil, climate, economic and social system as Virginia, owed her separate existence and her special character to the desire of one Englishman to create a feudal domain for his family, and a refuge for members of his faith. Sir George Calvert, first Lord Baltimore, aspired to found his own colony. Ordered out of Virginia because he was a Roman Catholic convert, he asked for and obtained from Charles I a liberal slice of the Old Dominion. Lord Baltimore died while the Maryland charter was going through, but it was confirmed to his son and heir Cecilius, the second Lord Baltimore, who dispatched the first group of colonists in 1634. Cecilius Calvert planned Maryland to be not only a source of profit, but a refuge for Catholics. Yet almost from the start the colony had a Protestant majority. Calvert coped with this situation in a statesmanlike manner by inducing the Maryland Assembly to pass a law of religious toleration in 1649. But civil war broke out in 1654, a class war of Protestant small farmers against the Catholic magnates and lords of manors. The majority won, and the Act of Toleration was repealed; but Lord Baltimore eventually recovered his rights.

In the West Indies, English, French, and Dutch used the proprietary method of colonization with success. The extension of sugar culture around 1650 and the importation of slaves made even the smallest of the islands immensely valuable. Far more money and men were spent on defending and capturing these islands than on the continental colonies that became Canada and the United States, because they were much more profitable.

These West Indian colonies were closely integrated with the English colonies in New England. Slave labor made it more profitable for the planters to concentrate on tropical crops of high profit, and procure elsewhere every other essential, such as salt meat and fish, breadstuffs and ground vegetables, lumber and livestock. These were exactly the commodities that New England produced, yet could find no vent for in England; and New England built the ships to carry these products of her farms, forests, and fisheries to the West Indies. The Chesapeake colonies, and later the Middle Colonies and the Carolinas, also shared this trade and, like New England, imported molasses and distilled it into rum. New England would have long remained a string of poor fishing stations and hardscrabble farms but for commerce with these superb tropical islands set in the sapphire Caribbean.

The Puritan Colonies

New England was founded without reference to the West Indies, and largely as a result of the religious movement known as Puritanism. The Puritans were that party in the Church of England who wished to carry through the Protestant Reformation to its logical conclusion, and establish both a religion and a way of living based on the Bible—as interpreted by themselves. The Church of England, a compromise between Rome and the reform, did not satisfy them. With official Anglican doctrine the Puritans had no quarrel; but they wished to do away with bishops and all clergy above the rank of parish priests, to abolish set prayers, and to reorganize the Church either by a hierarchy of councils (Presbyterianism), or on the basis of a free federation of independent parishes (Congregationalism). They were disgusted with the moral corruption that pervaded English society and wished to establish such patterns of living as would make it possible for people to lead something approaching the New Testament life. Eng-

Cecilius Calvert, second Baron Baltimore, sought to make Maryland a refuge for Catholics, but the settlers turned out to be predominantly Protestant. In this Gerard Soest portrait, he is shown with his young grandson Cecil. (*Enoch Pratt Free Library, Baltimore*)

lish Puritan divines frowned on idleness as a sin, eschewed mysticism and monasticism, and taught that a good businessman served God well, provided he were honest; hence Puritanism appealed to the middle class of tradesmen and rising capitalists whose center was London. It made a wide appeal also in rural regions such as East Anglia and the West Country, where 'the hungry sheep look up and are not fed' (to use Milton's phrase) by the common run of English clergyman, incapable of delivering a proper sermon. And it enlisted the devoted support of many young intellectuals in the universities, especially in Cambridge; hence the stress of the Puritans on education. Puritanism was no class revolt, or economic movement in religious clothing, as sundry writers have claimed, but a dynamic religious revival with a burning desire to do the will of God. Their desires were thwarted by the first two Stuart kings. James I promised to harry the Puritans out of the land if they would not conform, and under Charles I, clergymen who refused to follow the Anglo-Catholic polity of Bishop Laud were persecuted.

The Pilgrim Fathers were a group of Separatists who, unlike the majority of Puritans, despaired of reforming the Church of England and broke away to create a new institution. This small band of humble folk of East Anglia, whose religious meetings were so interfered with that they removed to Leiden in 1609, formed an English Congregational Church in that Dutch city. After ten years' exile in a foreign land where the people were tolerant but the living was hard, and where war threatened, they decided to remove to America. Sir Edwin Sandys procured for them a grant from the Virginia Company, and a group of English merchants financed their migration. The *Mayflower*, after a rough passage, anchored on 11 November 1620 in the harbor of Cape Cod, outside the Virginia jurisdiction. Accordingly, the Pilgrims signed a compact to be governed by the will of the majority until permanent provision should be made for their colony. This Mayflower Compact of 1620 stands, with the Virginia Assembly of 1619, as one of the two foundation stones of American institutions. Nothing similar occurred anywhere else in the world for almost two centuries.

No group of settlers in America was so ill-fitted by experience and equipment to cope with the wilderness as this little band of peasants, town laborers, and shopkeepers; yet none came through their trials so magnificently. For, as Bradford put it, 'they knew they were pilgrims, and looked not much on those things, but lift up their eyes to the heavens, their dearest country.' Their only good luck was to find deserted fields ready for tillage at the harbor already named Plymouth by Captain John Smith, and to be joined by Squanto, a lonely Indian who taught them how to catch fish and plant corn. Half the company died the first winter; but when the *Mayflower* set sail in April not one of the survivors returned in her. Around mid-October 1621, after the gathering of a fair harvest and a big shoot of waterfowl and wild turkey, the Pilgrims held their first Thanksgiving feast, with Chief Massasoit of the Wampanoag and 90 of his subjects, 'whom for three days we entertained and feasted.' For several years thereafter the colony ran neck-and-neck with famine. But the Pilgrims never lost heart, and their stout-hearted idealism made Plymouth Rock a symbol. For, as Governor Bradford concluded his annals of the lean years,

> Thus out of small beginnings greater things have been produced by his hand that made all things of nothing, and gives being to all things that are; and as one small candle may light a thousand; so the light here kindled hath shone unto many, yea, in some sort, to our whole nation.

Only 'small beginnings' were apparent for ten years; at the end of that time the Colony of New Plymouth numbered just 300. In the meantime a dozen straggling fishing and trading posts had been founded along the New England coast from southern Maine to Massachusetts Bay, with or without permission from the Council for New England.

One of these developed into the important Bay Colony. A company, which planted a small settlement at Salem in 1628, was taken over by a group of leading Puritans, including Sir Richard Saltonstall, Thomas Dudley, and John Winthrop, who wished to emigrate. Obtaining from Charles I a royal charter as the Massachusetts Bay Company in 1629, when Anglo-Catholic pressure began to be severely felt, they voted to transfer charter, government, and members to New England. A fleet of seventeen sail bearing 900 to 1000 men and women, the largest colonizing expedition yet sent out from England, crossed in the summer of 1630 to Massachusetts Bay and founded Boston and six or seven nearby towns.

This transfer of the Massachusetts Bay charter had an important bearing on colonial destiny and American institutions. With both charter and company in America, the colony became practically independent of England. The 'freemen,' as stockholders were then called, became voters; the governor, deputy-governor, and assistants whom the freemen annually elected, and who in England had been president and directors of a colonizing company, were now the executives, upper branch of the legislative assembly, and judicial officers of a Puritan commonwealth. A representative system was devised, as it was inconvenient for the freemen to attend the 'general court' or assembly in person, and by 1644 the deputies and assistants had separated into two houses. Neither king nor parliament had any say in the Massachusetts government. The franchise was restricted to church members, which prevented non-Puritan participation in the government; but this did not matter in the long run. What mattered was that this organization made for independence, and that the annual election on a definite date of all officers—governor and upper branch as well as deputies—became so popular in the colonies as to be imitated wherever the king could be induced to grant his consent. This feature survives in the Federal Government, and the corporate precedent has given the American system of government a very different complexion from the parliamentary system that was slowly developing in England.

The Puritan leaders had proposed to set up and maintain what they deemed to be true religion. That included an insistence on sobriety of manners, purity of morals, and an economy that would neither exalt the rich nor degrade the poor. Unlike the Pilgrims of Plymouth, they were not Separatists, but remained nominally within the Church of England. Unlike the Presbyterians, they were Congregationalists, who denied the need for a church superstructure and who stipulated that membership in the church would be restricted to those 'visible saints' who gave unmistakable evidence of their Christian belief. Each Congregational church was formed by a new covenant, and so was each new settlement. It soon appeared that Massachusetts Bay was the sort of colony that English Puritans wanted; for heavy Puritan migration to it continued until the outbreak of civil war in England. By that time New England had some 20,000 people. Most of this emigration, unlike that which was going on at the same time to Virginia, Maryland, and the West Indies, was against the will of the royal government; but nothing could stop it.

The community character of the New England migration dictated the method of land settlement. Neighborhood groups from the old country, often accompanied by an ousted parson, insisted on settling together, obtained a grant of land from the general court, established a village center, laid out lots, and so formed what was called in New England a town. Around each village green were situated the meeting-house (as the Puritans called a church edifice), the parsonage, and the houses of the principal settlers. Each person admitted as an inhabitant received a house lot, a planting lot for his corn, and a strip of river mead or salt meadow for winter forage. The cattle ranged the common woods, attended by the town herdsman. In town meeting, each settlement determined local affairs such as support of the school. Here democracy seeped into New England, unwanted by the founders.

The Puritan leaders were disturbed, too, by the rising spirit of egalitarianism. Men like John Winthrop, a superior statesman of noble character, had no doubt that God had ordained a hierarchy of classes, so that 'in all times some must be rich some poore, some highe and eminent in power and dignitie; others meane and in subieccion.' When a Puritan synod met in 1679, it expressed its concern not only about the rise of bastardy, the attempt to set up a brothel in Boston, and the displaying of naked necks and arms, 'or, which is more abominable, naked Breasts,' but, above all, about the spirit of insubordination of inferiors toward their betters. In particular, the church leaders noted: 'Day-Labourers and Mechanicks are unreasonable in their demands.'

The Puritan clergyman Richard Mather (1596–1669). His grandson Cotton Mather observed: 'His voice was loud and big, and uttered with a deliberate vehemency, it procured unto his ministry an awful and very taking majesty.' This 1670 depiction by John Foster, a recent graduate of Harvard who had been baptized by Richard Mather, is the earliest portrait in a woodcut in America. (*American Antiquarian Society*)

As the population of the towns grew, clashes frequently developed between the first generation, which insisted on respect for rank, and the second generation, determined on winning a share of meadow rights. If demands of the new generation were not met, they would threaten to secede from the town. 'If you persecute us in one city, wee must fly to another,' a Sudbury man warned. When such clashes were unresolved, a few hardy spirits would break away and repeat the process of town-building farther west.

Education was a particular concern of the Puritans. Their movement was directed by university-trained divines, and embraced by middle-class merchants and landowning farmers who had received the excellent education of Elizabethan England. Moreover, it was necessary for godliness that everyone learn to read the Bible. There had come to New England by 1640 about 130 university alumni, who insisted that their children have the same advantages as themselves, or better. Consequently, in the New England colonies, parents were required to teach their children and servants to read, or to send them to a village school. Above these primary schools, about two dozen of the larger New England towns had secondary public grammar schools on the English model, supported by taxation, which boys entered at the age of eight or nine, and where they studied Latin and Greek, and little else, for six years. At the end of that time they were prepared to enter Harvard College, founded by the Massachusetts government in 1636. There, the more ambitious lads studied the same seven arts and three philosophies as at Oxford, using the same Latin manuals of logic and metaphysics, Hebrew and Greek texts. Nor were the fine arts neglected. Seventeenth-century New Englanders had good taste in house design and village layout; artisans fashioned beautiful articles of silver for home and communion table; writers such as Anne Bradstreet produced poetry of great charm. Thus the classical and humanist tradition of the English was carried into the clearings of the New England wilderness.

Three more Puritan colonies, which later formed two states of the Union, sprang up before 1640. Under the lead of the Rev. Thomas Hooker, the first westward migration in the English colonies took place in 1636, to the Connecticut river, where a Bible Commonwealth was organized on the Massachusetts model. New Haven, founded by a London merchant, Theophilus Eaton, and his pastor the Rev. John Davenport, maintained a separate existence from Connecticut until 1662, and spread along both shores of Long Island Sound. Both these colonies were like-minded with the Bay Colony and Plymouth; but Rhode Island, the creation of four separate groups of Puritan heretics, was distinctly otherwise-minded. Anne Hutchinson of Boston, who set up as a prophetess, and the Rev. Roger Williams, who differed with Bay authorities on many matters, were banished, and on Narragansett Bay formed settlements which federated as Rhode Island and Providence Plantations in 1644. Williams denied the authority of civil or ecclesiastical hierarchy over a man's conscience. 'Forced worship,' he asserted, 'stinks in God's nostrils.' Imbued with the spirit of Christian love, he treated Indians as brothers. Under Williams, Rhode Island became a haven for the persecuted, and the ideas of this seventeenth-century Puritan have inspired secular twentieth-century civil libertarians, even though their views of the universe differ greatly from those of this remarkable divine.

One thing these New England colonies had in common until 1680: all were virtually independent, acknowledging allegiance to whatever authority had control in England, but making their own laws, trading where they pleased, defending themselves without help from home, and working out their own institutions.

New Netherland

Between New England and Virginia the indomitable Dutch, with that uncanny instinct for sources of wealth that has always characterized their commercial ventures, planted a colony that in due time became New York. In 1602 Dutch capitalists organized the Netherlands East Indies Company, a corporation in comparison with which the Virginia Company was a petty affair. Inexorably this company pushed the Portuguese out of most of their trading posts in the Far East, where they

New Amsterdam, 1673. This view of the tip of Manhattan Island, Wall Street south to the Battery, is from Brooklyn Heights, which remained the favored perspective for those seeking to depict the city. The engraving, from Carolus Allard, *Orbis Habitablis,* published in Holland, represents the dying gasp of the Dutch empire in North America. The Dutch recaptured the city in 1673 but it was returned to England by treaty the following year. (*Stokes Collection, New York Public Library*)

created a rich empire. The East Indies Company, seeking a shorter way to the Orient than the dangerous Cape route, made several efforts to find a northwest passage. That is what Henry Hudson was looking for in 1609 when he sailed the *Half-Moon* up the noble river that shares his name with the mighty bay where he met his death. The Hudson river proved to be a passage indeed, to the heart of the Iroquois Confederacy and the richest fur-bearing country south of the St. Lawrence. After skippers Block and May had explored the coast from Maine to the Delaware Capes, Dutch fur traders began to frequent the rivers and trade with the natives.

New Netherland began as a trading-post colony in 1624, with the foundation of Fort Orange (Albany) up the Hudson. Fort Amsterdam on the tip of Manhattan Island was permanently established in 1626, Fort Nassau at the site of Gloucester, N.J., in 1623, and Fort Good Hope on the Connecticut river, near Hartford, in 1633. New Netherland was governed much as Virginia had been before 1619, by a governor and council appointed by the company, without representative institutions. As early as 1630 New Amsterdam was a typical sailormen's town, with numerous taverns, smugglers, and illicit traders, as well as a Dutch Reformed Church, and a number of substantial houses. When in 1638 the States General threw open the seaborne trade of New Netherland to all Dutch subjects, New Amsterdam became practically a free port. In 1629 the company made a half-hearted attempt to encourage settlement by issuing the Charter of Privileges to Patroons. Anyone who brought out 50 families of tenants at his own expense could have an extensive tract of land, with full manorial privileges, including holding court. The directors of the company, such as Kiliaen Van Rensselaer, promptly snapped up all the best sites, and these privileges, which were confirmed under the English regime, meant that the most valuable land in the Hudson valley was held in vast estates on a feudal basis. A certain number of Dutchmen and Walloons acquired 'bouweries' (farms) outside the wall on Manhattan, or in the pretty villages of Haerlem, Breucelen on Long Island, or Bergen across the North (as the Dutch called the Hudson) river; a few hundred New England Puritans spilled over into Westchester County and Long Island. Yet New Netherland did not prosper; it was the neglected child of a trading company whose main interests were in the East.

'Diedrich Knickerbocker' (Washington Irving) created a myth of New Netherland that will never die; the jolly community of tipplers and topers, of waterfront taverns, broad-beamed fraus, and well-stocked farms. The actual New Netherland was a frustrated community. The successive governors, of whom Irving drew comic pictures, were, in reality, petty autocrats and grafters who ruled New Amsterdam with a rod of iron, used torture to extract confessions, and mismanaged almost everything. The peg-legged Peter Stuyvesant enlarged New Netherland at the expense of his neighbors. In 1655 he annexed the colony of New Sweden that centered about Fort Christina (Wilmington) on the Delaware. But on the other side, Fort Good Hope on the Connecticut river was squeezed out by English settlers.

When a small English fleet appeared off New Amsterdam one summer's day in 1664 and ordered the Dutch to surrender, Governor Stuyvesant stomped his wooden leg in vain, and New Netherland became New York without a blow or a tear. The population of the city had then reached only 1500, and that of the colony less than 7000; New England outnumbered New Netherland ten to one. But the Dutch stamp was already placed indelibly on New York, and most of the Dutch families, such as the Van Rensselaers, Van Burens, and Roosevelts, prospered under English rule.

Two Decades of Neglect

That 'salutary neglect' by England, which Edmund Burke later asserted to be one of the main reasons for American prosperity, was never more evident than in the twenty years between 1640 and 1660. The civil war and other commotions, lasting from 1641 to 1653, when Oliver Cromwell became Lord Protector of the English Commonwealth, afforded all three groups of colonies a chance to grow with a minimum of interference; and Oliver, too, decided to let well enough alone. When interference was threatened, colonies as far apart as Massachusetts and Barbados stood stiffly on their privileges. The Virginia Assembly, which proclaimed Charles II king after hearing of the execution of Charles I, capitulated without a blow to a parliamentary fleet in 1652, and in return was allowed to elect the governor and council. In Maryland, the only colony where English events touched off a civil war, Lord Baltimore triumphed in the end.

Perhaps the most significant colonial development of the period was the formation of the New England Confederacy in 1643, largely for defense against the Dutch, the French, and the Indians. A board of commissioners representing Plymouth, Massachusetts, Connecticut, and New Haven, the 'United Colonies of New-England,' established a 'firm and perpetual league of friendship and amity, for offense and defense, mutual advice and succor upon all just occasions.' Several boundary controversies between the member colonies and one with the Dutch were settled, provision was made for the return of runaway servants, contributions were taken up for Harvard College, and an English fund for the conversion of the Indians was administered. In several respects the New England Confederacy anticipated the Confederation of 1781; and the league held together long enough to direct military operations during the Indian war of 1675–76.

New France

New France, too, took on substance in this period. Samuel de Champlain, who unfurled the lilies of France on the rock of Quebec in 1608, protected missionaries and attempted, with but a handful of soldiers, to defend the beaver line of his Huron allies to Quebec from Iroquois assaults. But the companies that employed him, up to his death in 1635, were even less interested in settlement than was the Dutch West India Company. Not a furrow was plowed or a seed planted in Canada until 1628. Shortly after, the Company of the Hundred Associates, which then ruled New France, began establishing seigneuries, not unlike the Dutch patroonships, though smaller and more numerous, along both banks of the St. Lawrence. Each seigneur was supposed to bring out a certain number of habitants, or settlers. But the system caught on very slowly. There were two main interests in New France, conversion of the Indians and conversion of beaver into peltry. The French Crown, which wished Canada to be a country of peasant farms like Normandy, abolished the company regime in 1663, and Canada became a Crown colony under the direct government of Louis XIV. But even *Le Grand Monarque* was unable to make his transatlantic empire change character.

Thus, in little more than half a century after the founding of Jamestown, the French, English, and Dutch had a firm foothold on the shores of five American areas—the St. Lawrence, New England, the Hudson, the Delaware, Chesapeake Bay—and the West Indies. They had planted those attitudes, folkways, and institutions which were destined to endure and to spread across the North American continent.

3

The Empire Comes of Age

*

1660–1763

The Acts of Trade and Navigation

Although the English colonies were by this time conscious of themselves, England was not very conscious of them. Every English colony except Virginia had grown up through the uncoordinated efforts of individuals and small groups. The home government as yet had no clear policy about the connection between colonies and mother country.

With the restoration of the monarchy in 1660 came a perceptible drift into something that may be called a colonial policy. Charles II conquered New Netherland, and filled the gap between New England and Maryland with four new English colonies. He extended the southern frontier by founding the Carolinas. Parliament laid down a definite economic policy in the Acts of Trade and Navigation. After James II tried to consolidate all continental settlements into two vice-royalties, Spanish style, a scheme thwarted by his expulsion from England, William and Mary, more tactfully, brought all their American colonies under some measure of control. And England began a protracted struggle with the French and Spanish for North America.

By 1660 the doctrine known as mercantilism, the pursuit of economic power in the interest of national self-sufficiency, was taken for granted by all European states. Even colonists admitted that the profits of an empire should center in the mother country. Spain and Portugal had seen to that since the beginning; but England, what with haphazard colonization and civil tumults, had allowed her overseas subjects to trade with foreign countries in almost everything except tobacco, and even tobacco was often carried abroad in foreign ships. Now, through a series of Acts of Trade and Navigation (1660–72), an effort was made to make the English empire self-sustaining and to confine profits to English subjects.

These acts embodied three principles. All trade between England and her colonies must be conducted by English- or English-colonial-built vessels, owned and manned by English subjects. All European imports into the colonies, save for perishable fruit and wine from the Atlantic Islands, must first be 'laid on the shores of England'—i.e., unloaded, handled, and reloaded—before being sent to the colonies, some of the duties being repaid on re-exportation. And, finally, certain colonial products 'enumerated' in the laws must be exported to England only. In the seventeenth century the enumerated products were tobacco, sugar, cotton, and tropical commodities grown only in the West Indies. Rice and molasses, furs, and naval stores (tar, pitch, turpentine, ships' spars) were added between 1705 and 1722.

Opinions still differ about the effect of this system on the colonies. It certainly did not stop growth in the century after 1660. But the cutting off of direct tobacco exports to the European continent helped to depress the price of tobacco in Virginia. As time went on, more and more colonial products were added to the enumerated list, until, on the eve of the American Revolution, the only important non-enumerated article was salt fish. The enumerated principle was not too severe, as proved by the fact that Americans after independence continued to use England as an entrepôt for rice and tobacco. Nor should it be forgotten that Parliament paid bounties to colonial producers of naval stores and indigo, prohibited the growing of tobacco in England, and laid preferential duties which excluded Cuban and other Spanish-American leaf from the English market. There was no legal bar to the colonists' trading with the French and other foreign West Indies. In fact a large part of the specie circulating in the continental colonies until the Revolution consisted of French and Spanish coins which were procured in the islands in exchange for the products of northern farms, forests, and fisheries. However, skilled artisans were forbidden to leave England for the colonies, and in the last third of the century, English emigration to her colonies dwindled to a mere trickle. A leading English interest was supplying the colonies with slaves, a traffic in which colonial ships and merchants participated to a limited extent.

In the mercantilist perspective the most valuable colonies were those from the Chesapeake south, which produced tropical or semi-tropical raw materials that England wanted, and imported almost every luxury and necessity from home. And the least valuable colonies were those of New England, which were Old England's competitors rather than her complements. In 1698 seven-eighths of England's American trade was with the West Indies, Virginia, Maryland, and the Carolinas. As time went on, and the Northern Colonies acquired wealth through the West Indies trade, this unequal balance was redressed. By 1767, two-thirds of England's colonial exports were to colonies north of Maryland.

Founding of the Carolinas

After 1660 the impulse toward colonial expansion came mainly from three sources: English merchants and shipowners who wanted new areas for trade and exploitation, courtiers and politicians who planned to recoup their shattered fortunes with great colonial estates, and religious dissenters who sought a refuge for members of their faith.

Restoration of the Stuart monarchy set all doubtful English colonial claimants polishing up their old claims and seeking validation from Charles II. The Carolina Proprietors, a group of eight promoters and politicians, obtained from Charles II a proprietary patent to all North America between the parallels of 31° and 36° N (and the next year had this enlarged to embrace all the territory between Daytona, Fla., and the Virginia-North Carolina boundary). This they named Carolina. The two leading spirits among the proprietors were Sir John Colleton, a wealthy Barbadian planter who sought new homes for the surplus white population of Barbados, and Anthony Ashley Cooper, better known by his later title of Earl of Shaftesbury, Chancellor of the Exchequer. Shaftesbury, in collaboration with John Locke, wrote a charter for the colony, the 'Fundamental Constitutions of Carolina' in 120 articles; an extraordinary document which attempted to provide for this pioneer colony a revived feudalism, with five 'estates,' eight supreme courts, a chamberlain and lord high admiral, and native titles of baron, cacique, and landgrave, depending on the amount of land one bought. After several false starts, a small number of colonists from England and several hundred Barbadians founded Charleston in 1670.

Ten years later the proprietors obtained a group of French Huguenots, and in 1683 Scots began arriving; thus South Carolina was racially heterogeneous from the first. By 1700 the population of the colony was about 5000, half of them black slaves; the principal exports were provisions for the West Indies trade, naval stores, and peltry. These early South Carolinians were as expert fur-traders as the French Canadians, sending agents around the southern spurs of the Appalachians into the future Alabama in search of deerskins; and they followed the Spanish example of enslaving Indians. At the turn of the century the cultivation of rice and indigo began on the low coastal plain and along the rivers; and these gradually replaced the more pioneer pursuits. By 1730 South Carolina was a planting colony like Virginia, with different staples, and a centralized instead of a dispersed social and political system. There were no county or local units of government. Every leading planter had a town house near the battery in Charleston where he spent the summer months, when river plantations were unhealthful. The French Huguenots, the most important element in the ruling class, imparted a high-spirited and aristocratic tone to the colony; they quickly adopted the English language and joined the Established Church of England.

In the meantime a wholly different society was developing in the section of the province which became North Carolina. There the original settlers had been adventurers from New England and poor whites from Virginia. The proprietors granted them a separate governor and assembly. Apart from the Swiss-German settlement of New Bern there were few foreigners before 1713, and still fewer colonists of means. The principal products were tobacco and naval stores; and lack of harbors suitable for seagoing vessels meant heavy transportation costs. North Carolina was poor, turbulent, and democratic, with relatively few slaves, and, unlike South Carolina, few plantations. In 1736 the white population was estimated to be one-third greater than that of the southern colony, but the production very much less.

On the whole, the proprietors of Carolina did a good job in planting these two colonies, but they reaped more headaches than profit. All except Lord Granville sold out to the Crown in 1729, when the two halves became the royal provinces of North Carolina and South Carolina.

New York and the Jerseys

The Duke of York's brief and unsuccessful reign as James II should not blind us to the fact that he was an excellent seaman and an able administrator. His brother Charles II appointed him Lord High Admiral at the age of 26. As head of the navy he wished to deprive the Dutch of their base at New Amsterdam, and as an impecunious member of the House of Stuart he needed a profitable colony. With parliamentary approval the king conferred on his brother in 1664 the most extensive English territorial grant of the century: the continent between the Connecticut and Delaware rivers, together with the islands of New England and Maine east of the Kennebec. When Stuyvesant surrendered New Netherland, the Duke of York, aged 30, gained possession of a section of America destined to be the wealthiest area in the world. As Lord Proprietor, he was absolute master of this domain, under the king.

The Duke's rule of New York, as he renamed the Dutch colony, was fairly enlightened. He summoned no assembly, but ordered his governor to treat the Dutch with 'humanity and gentleness,' and made no effort to impose on them the English language or his own religion. But he intended to make money out of the colony, and drew up his own schedule of customs duties, quit-rents, and taxes. That made trouble. There were already too many English in the colony for any proprietor to raise taxes without representation. After two decades of resistance, the Duke's governor summoned a representative assembly in 1683.

Realizing that he had bitten off a little more than he could chew, the Duke began giving away slices of his grant as early as 1664. To his friends Lord John Berkeley and Sir George Carteret he ceded all land between the Hudson and the Delaware as the 'Province of Nova Caesaria or New Jersey.' A few hundred Dutch and English Puritans from New England were already there, and, in order to attract more, Berkeley and Carteret granted freedom of conscience, liberal terms for land, and an assembly. In 1674 Berkeley sold out his half share in New Jersey to two Quakers, who took the southwestern half of the province, while Carteret kept the northeastern part. Carteret's widow in 1680 sold out East New Jersey to a group of proprietors, and the two Quakers let William Penn in on West New Jersey. The net result was a heterogeneous population, little social cohesion, and confused land titles.

Penn's Holy Experiment

The founding of Pennsylvania, more so than any other American commonwealth, is the lengthened shadow of one man and of his faith in God and in human nature.

Out of the religious ferment of Puritan England came the Society of Friends, commonly known as Quakers. They believed that religious authority rested neither in the Bible nor in a priestly hierarchy but in the Inner Light of Jesus Christ in the soul of every man. A mystical faith, Quakerism encouraged not quietistic contemplation but an 'enthusiastic' crusade to persuade their fellow men that they could enter a 'paradise of God' on earth. Since every man had some of God's spirit, all men were brothers and all were equal; they addressed one another as 'thee' and 'thou,' and observed literally the divine command 'thou shalt do no murder,' even under the name of war. Like the early Christians they gathered strength from oppression. Over 3000 Quakers were imprisoned in England during the first two years of the Restoration; yet the sect spread like wildfire. In 1652 the first Quaker missionaries appeared in the English colonies. Severe laws were passed against them in every colony but Rhode Island, and in Boston three were hanged; but finally by passive resistance they wore down the authorities and won a grudging toleration. In England, George Fox and his courageous missionaries converted thousands, especially among the poorer country people and the workingmen of London and Bristol. As Puritanism had been in 1600, and as Methodism would be in 1770, so Quakerism became the dynamic form of English Protestantism from about 1650 to 1700.

With William Penn the Quakers obtained one of the greatest colonies. The founder of Pennsylvania, born in 1644, was the son of Admiral Sir William Penn, conqueror of Jamaica. Young William was converted to Quakerism in 1667, when he listened to the sermon of a Friend on the text 'There is a Faith that overcometh the World.' And for the remaining 51 years of his life, William Penn was steadfast in that faith. The Admiral, who swore great oaths when he heard this news, became reconciled before his death and left his Quaker son a considerable fortune. What the young man wanted was a proprietary colony of his own, where he could experiment with political as well as religious liberty. The Friends no longer needed a refuge; but, like the Puritans of half a century before, they wanted a colony where they could live their ideal of the New Testament life, free from the pressure of bad example and worldly corruption. In 1677 in Germany Penn met members of several sects, some akin to the Quakers in doctrine, who were eager to leave. That tour enlarged his conception of a colony to that of a refuge for the persecuted of every race and sect.

Fortunately, Penn's conversion had never caused him to break with his father's friends, among whom was counted the Duke of York, who owed the Admiral £16,000. The cancellation of that bad debt secured for William and his heirs in 1681 a generous slice of the Duke's grant. The king implemented this grant by a charter creating 'Pennsylvania' a proprietary province on the model of Maryland.

Settlement began without delay. In 1681 Penn published in English, French, German, and Dutch *Some Account of the Province of Pennsylvania.* He urged peasants and artisans to come, and get-rich-quick adventurers to stay away; he gave instructions for the journey, and promised political and religious liberty. Even more persuasive were the easiest terms for land yet offered in North America: a 50-acre head-right free; 200-acre tenant farms at a penny an acre rent; estates of 5000 acres for £100, with a city lot thrown in. In three months Penn disposed of warrants for over 300,000 acres, and in 1682 he came over himself.

Neither the banks of Delaware Bay nor the

lower reaches of the rivers were a wilderness in 1682. About a thousand Swedes, Finns, and Dutch survivors of the colonies of New Sweden and New Netherland were already there. These were given free land grants, and proved useful in providing the first English colonists with food, housing, and labor. Choosing an admirable site for his capital, Penn laid out Philadelphia between the Delaware and the Schuylkill rivers in checkerboard fashion—which had a permanent and pernicious effect on American city planning—and undertook the government himself.

William Penn liked to allude to his province as the 'Holy Experiment,' and he made religious liberty and trust in humanity its cornerstones. Though his tastes were those of the English aristocracy, he believed in the traditional liberties of Englishmen, and intended that they should be respected in his province. Yet Penn was no nineteenth-century democrat. He favored government for the people, by liberally educated gentlemen like himself. And the first *Frame of Government* that he issued for Pennsylvania in 1682 reflected this idea. He appointed himself governor. A small council was elected by taxpayers from landowners 'of best repute for wisdom, virtue and ability,' to initiate bills, and a large elective assembly to accept or reject them—but if the assembly 'turn debaters, you overthrow the charter,' said he. Such a system was unpalatable to discussion-loving Englishmen. It worked fairly well when Penn was in his province, but when he returned to England, his government almost blew up. His too great trust in human nature led him to make unsuitable appointments of land agents who robbed him, and of deputy governors who antagonized or scandalized the people.

Penn returned to Philadelphia in 1699 and issued a Charter of Privileges, which remained the constitution of the colony until 1776. It provided the usual set-up of a governor and council (appointed by the proprietor but confirmed by the king), and an assembly composed of four representatives for each county, elected by a property franchise. The three 'Lower Counties,' as the future state of Delaware was then called, acquired an assembly of their own in 1702, but the Charter of Privileges was their charter too, and the governor of Pennsylvania was their governor.

Pennsylvania began with the most liberal and humane code of laws in the world. Capital punishment, which existed for a dozen different offenses in the other English colonies and for more than twenty in England, was inflicted in Pennsylvania only for murder. But a crime wave at the turn of the century caused the criminal code to be stiffened to such a point that the Privy Council in England rejected half the new laws. Accordingly, by 1717, there was little difference between Pennsylvania and other colonies in the rigor of their laws. However, their severity was mitigated by Quaker compassion. Philadelphia had the most humane prisons in the English colonies.

Pennsylvania prospered as did no other early settlement. Two years after its foundation Philadelphia boasted 357 houses; in 1685 the population of the province was little short of 9000. Germans of the Mennonite sect settled Germantown in 1683; Welsh Quakers founded Radnor and Haverford; a Free Society of Traders, organized by English Quakers, started fisheries and established brick kilns, tanneries, and glass works. Penn could state without boasting in 1684, 'I have led the greatest colony into America that ever any man did upon a private credit, and the most prosperous beginnings that were ever in it are to be found among us.'

William Penn himself fell on evil days at the turn of the century. His business affairs went from bad to worse. He had a protracted boundary controversy with Lord Baltimore—eventually settled in 1763–67 by the Mason-Dixon Line.[1] His eldest son, the second proprietor, turned out a spendthrift and a rake. The quarrels among council and governor and assembly distressed him; 'For the love of God, me, and the poor country,' he once wrote to the leader of the opposition, 'do not be so litigious and brutish!' But he never lost

1. The Mason and Dixon Line lies along latitude 39° 43′ 26.3″ N between the southwestern corner of Pennsylvania and the arc of a circle of twelve miles' radius drawn from New Castle (Delaware) as a center; and along that arc to the Delaware river. It was run by two English surveyors, Mason and Dixon, in 1750. But there have been interstate controversies about parts of it even in the present century.

faith in the Holy Experiment, or in human nature. Pennsylvania was a portent of America to be; the first large community in modern history where different ethnic groups and religions lived under the same government on terms of equality. Pennsylvania interested eighteenth-century philosophers as a successful experiment in the life of reason; Voltaire never tired of holding it up as proof that man could lead the good life without absolute monarchy, feudalism, or religious and ethnic uniformity.

Time of Troubles in Virginia and New England 1675–92

Virginia, ever loyal to the House of Stuart, suffered grievously from its restoration. Charles II appointed Sir William Berkeley governor of Virginia, and in a wave of loyalty the people elected a house of burgesses in 1661 which proved so pliant that Berkeley kept this 'long assembly' going for fifteen years by successive adjournments, and managed to get the whole machinery of government in his hands.

More serious for the Old Dominion were overproduction and low prices for tobacco. The Acts of Trade and the Dutch wars curtailed the foreign market and raised the cost of transportation. In 1662 Governor Berkeley reported the price of tobacco to be so low that it would not pay the cost of freight. 'Forty thousand people are impoverished,' he wrote, 'in order to enrich little more than forty merchants in England.' In 1668 tobacco prices in Virginia reached an all-time low of a farthing a pound, one-quarter of the customs duty on it in England. The assembly for ten years made attempts to curtail production and peg prices; these were thwarted partly by Maryland's refusal to come in, and partly because the English merchants raised prices of goods sent in exchange when they could not make their usual profit. Fifteen years after the Restoration, Virginia, the land of opportunity for poor and industrious Englishmen, had become a place of poverty and discontent. There the first serious rebellion in North American history broke out.

The immediate cause of Bacon's Rebellion was the Indian question. At this time the Indians were restive all along the rear of the English colonies. The Susquehannock, forced south to the Potomac by the Seneca, broke up into small bands and began harrying the Virginia-Maryland frontier in the summer of 1675. Governor Berkeley, hoping to avoid a general Indian war (such as had already broken out in New England), decided on a defensive policy, building a chain of mutually supporting forts around the settled part of Virginia. That infuriated the frontier planters, who believed the Berkeley clique had put the planters' lives in jeopardy in order to profit from the Indian trade. Nathaniel Bacon, an impetuous 28-year-old gentleman fresh from England whose plantation had been attacked, protested: 'These traders at the head of the rivers buy and sell our blood.' As leader of discontented planters, Bacon commanded an unauthorized military force which slaughtered the peaceful Oconeechee tribe, and then advanced on Jamestown. Bacon is said to have exclaimed, 'Damn my blood, I'll kill Governor, Council, Assembly and all!' As this improvised rebel army approached Jamestown, Berkeley decided to dissolve his 'long assembly' and issued writs for a new one, which met shortly and passed some important bills for relief, reform, and defense. What had begun as a sectional quarrel over Indian policy had developed into an assault on political privilege, although in this confused upheaval the poorer farmers had as many grievances against the Bacon faction as against the Berkeley circle.

For a time, Bacon ruled most of Virginia. But Berkeley plucked up courage, called out the loyal militia of the Eastern Shore, and civil war began. Exactly how far Bacon intended to go is not clear, but there is some evidence that he hoped to unite Virginia, North Carolina, and Maryland as a 'free state.' He did set up a government of his own, but cavalier feeling in Virginia was still too strong to support a rebellion against royal authority. After Bacon's premature death (26 October 1676), the rebellion collapsed. Berkeley rounded up the leaders and had twenty-three of them executed for treason. 'That old fool has hanged more men in that naked country than I have done for the murder of my father,' exclaimed Charles II.

Captain Thomas Smith, self-portrait, *circa* 1690. A mariner who arrived in New England in 1650, Captain Smith was a self-taught artist who developed enough proficiency to be commissioned by Harvard in 1680 to paint a portrait. No doubt because he traveled widely, as the naval scene suggests, his work is closer to the more ornate style of Europe than that of his contemporaries in New England, but there is an authentic Puritan emphasis in the skull and the lines beneath it, which bid farewell to a 'World of Evils.' (*Worcester Art Museum*)

New England under the Stuart Restoration not only flourished economically, but preserved its right of self-government. Massachusetts Bay was allowed to continue for a quarter-century longer under her corporate charter, and Connecticut and Rhode Island obtained similar charters from the Crown in 1662 and 1663, with complete self-government. The Connecticut charter included the old New Haven Colony in its boundaries.

Nevertheless, New England, too, had its time of troubles. In 1675–77 broke out the most devastating war in her entire history. King Philip's War it was called, after the Wampanoag chief who began hostilities. The natives were reacting desperately against their diminishing power. Now skilled in the use of firearms, they were able to attack frontier settlements at will, destroy crops, cattle, and houses, and endanger the very existence of white New England. A dozen villages were leveled, and the casualties were distressingly high. But the Puritans had the New England Confederacy, while the Indians were not united; some 2500 converts remained loyal to the whites; and gradually the New England militia, accompanied by loyal Indian scouts, broke up Indian concentrations, destroyed their food supply, and hunted down their bands. With the death of King Philip in August 1676 the rebellion collapsed, and Philip's wife and son were sold into slavery in the West Indies. The power of the natives in southern New England was broken forever; but the Abnaki of Maine and New Hampshire turned to Canada for aid, and kept the English at bay in northern New England for another seventy-five years. Not until 1720 did New England recover the frontier thrown back by this fierce war.

The royal government chose this time to bring the Bay Colony to book for her recalcitrance. Massachusetts offended Charles II by coining the pine-tree shilling, and by purchasing from the Gorges proprietors the Province of Maine, which the king intended to buy for one of his bastards. The province refused to obey the Navigation Acts on the ground 'that the subjects of his majesty here being not represented in Parliament, so we have not looked at ourselves to be impeded in our trade by them.' It declined to allow appeals to English courts, or to grant freedom of worship and the franchise to Anglicans. Consequently, in 1684, the High Court of Chancery declared the old Massachusetts Bay charter to be 'vacated, cancelled and annihilated.' The government was now in the king's hands to do as he saw fit.

James II found the colonial situation disquieting. There were three separate colonies in New England and four in the middle region, each with its own assembly, all of them flouting the Acts of Trade and Navigation as much as they dared. At the same time French Canada seemed menacing again. A great administrator, Count Frontenac, sent explorers like Joliet, Marquette, and La Salle down the Mississippi, and attempted to break the Anglo-Iroquois alliance. Consolidation was the royal solution. Between 1685 and 1688 the New England colonies, New York, and the Jerseys were combined into one viceroyalty called the Dominion of New England. It was ruled by an appointed governor (Sir Edmund Andros) and council, but had no representative institutions. Andros and his council questioned the validity of land titles, which alarmed every farmer in New England, and they taxed without a legislative grant.

When James II was expelled from England in the 'Glorious Revolution' of 1688, which brought in William III and Mary II as joint sovereigns of the British Isles, a succession of popular revolutions overthrew dominion authorities and put the several colonies back where they had been before 1685. The only conspicuous leader in these revolts was Jacob Leisler, a New Yorker of German birth. Leisler, by antagonizing the patroons and other important groups in his colony, and by firing on royal troops sent to take over the government, placed himself in a position where he could be accused of treason. He was judicially murdered in 1691. Elsewhere the Dominion of New England fell apart with scarcely a blow.

By that time King William's War with the French was going full blast, no English frontier farm was safe; and to cap the catalogue of woes in this seventeen-year period of terror and trouble, a witchcraft scare broke out in Massachusetts. To the already vast literature on witchcraft the Reverend Cotton Mather, boy wonder of the New England clergy, contributed a book entitled *Memorable Providences.* In it he described a case of alleged witchcraft in Boston for which a poor old woman was executed, and how he had handled the accusing children to prevent a witch-hunting epidemic. The second edition of this work (1691) got into the hands of a group of young girls in a suburb of Salem. More or less as a prank, they accused a half-Indian, half-Negro family slave of being a witch. Flogged by her master into confessing, to save her skin she accused two respectable goodwives of being her confederates. The 'afflicted' children, finding themselves the objects of attention, persisted in their charges for fear of being found out, and this started a chain reaction. A special court was set up to try the witches. The

LATE
Memorable Providences
Relating to
Witchcrafts and *Poſſeſſions*,
Clearly Manifeſting,
Not only that there are Witches, but that Good Men (as well as others) may poſſibly have their Lives ſhortned by ſuch evil Inſtruments of Satan.

Written by *Cotton Mather* Miniſter of the Goſpel at *Boſton* in *New-England.*

The Second Impression.

Recommended by the Reverend Mr. *Richar. Baxter* in *London*, and by the Miniſters of *Boſton* and *Charleſtown* in *New-England.*

LONDON,
Printed for *Tho. Parkhurſt* at the *Bible* and *Three Crowns* in *Cheapſide* near *Mercers-*Chapel. 1691.

When a copy of this work by the noted Puritan divine Cotton Mather (1663–1728) fell into the hands of some young Massachusetts girls, they made an accusation of witchcraft against a family slave that led to the Salem hysteria of 1692. Before it was over, five men and fourteen women had been hanged and one man pressed to death. (*Library of Congress*)

innocent people whom the girls accused implicated others to escape the gallows, confessing broomstick rides, flying saucers, witches' sabbaths, sexual relations with the devil, and everything which, according to the book, witches were supposed to do. Honest folk who declared the whole thing nonsense were cried out upon for witches. The vicious business continued through the summer of 1692, until nineteen persons, including a Congregational minister and fourteen women, had been found guilty of witchcraft and hanged; and one man pressed to death. About 55 more had pleaded guilty and accused others, 150 of whom were in jail awaiting trial. The frenzy was only halted because the witch-finders were beginning to go after prominent people. On the tardy advice of Increase Mather and other clergymen, the assembly dissolved the special court and released all prisoners.

As a witchcraft scare, the Salem one was small compared with others at the time in Europe; and it had a few redeeming features. The condemned witches were hanged, not burned to death as elsewhere. Almost everyone concerned in the furor later confessed his error (Judge Sewall doing so in open church meeting), and twenty years later the Massachusetts courts annulled the convictions and granted indemnity to the victims. But the record reveals an appalling moral cowardice on the part of ministry and gentry, and credulity and hatred among the people at large. It was one of those times which unfortunately have occurred more frequently in the present century, when evil is given full sway.

Colonial Reorganization

Colonial reorganization took place gradually by a series of typical English compromises. Rhode Island and Connecticut were allowed to keep their corporate charters; New York, and later the Jerseys and Carolinas, became royal provinces; Pennsylvania and Maryland were restored to their proprietors. A part of the Dominion of New England was salvaged by creating the royal province of Massachusetts Bay, including the old Bay colony, the Plymouth colony, and Maine. In all these units, representative institutions were confirmed or granted. By an act of Parliament of 1696, a new system of admiralty courts, requiring no jury trial, was instituted to enforce the Acts of Trade and Navigation. The new system succeeded in suppressing the grosser forms of piracy and smuggling, and stopping direct importations from continental Europe. Submission of all acts of colonial assemblies to the Privy Council for possible disallowance was insisted on, and appeals from colonial courts to the Privy Council were encouraged.

The Crown could balk colonial legislation that it considered undesirable, both by the royal governor's veto which could not be overridden, and by the royal disallowance. About 2½ per cent of all acts passed by colonial assemblies were disallowed by the Privy Council. Most of those thrown out deserved it; for instance, discriminatory legislation against religious minorities, or laws discriminating against ships, products, or subjects of neighboring English colonies. But some good ones, restricting the slave trade, were also nullified. These colonial laws were disallowed after investigation and report by the Board of Trade and Plantations. That body, appointed by the king under an act of 1696, was the nearest thing to a colonial office in the English government; but its powers were only advisory. Most colonial matters were routed through the Board, which meant a certain uniformity in administration, but decisions were made either by the king, the lords of the admiralty, or the war department. This imperial system, as it existed to 1776, would have been cumbrous and inefficient even if competently and honestly administered, as it was not.

The principal officials in the colonies who were expected to enforce English laws and regulations were the royal and proprietary governors. The former were appointed by the king during his good pleasure; the proprietary governors had to be acceptable to the Crown. They had not only an absolute veto over legislation, but the authority to prorogue and dissolve the lower houses in most colonies, and the power to dismiss judges. Nonetheless, most were dependent on the assemblies for their salaries. Executive patronage, which might have been an important lever, was taken away from them both by the English secretary of state, who needed it for his own henchmen, and by the assemblies, which generally elected the colonial treasurer and other minor officials. The royal governors on the whole were honest and able men, and no small number of them were colonists; but they had an unhappy time, for they were expected to enforce the regulations of an overseas government without the power to do so. The assemblies, representing local interests, demanded greater control than the governors' instructions permitted; the governors demanded more power for their royal and proprietary masters than the people were disposed to admit; and distance, as well as the power of the purse, tended to keep the governor's power at a low ebb.

Imperial Wars

William III brought the English colonies into the orbit of world politics. As stadholder of the Netherlands he had organized a league of European states to resist the pretensions of Louis XIV to the hegemony of Europe. Having obtained the English crown, he made that league into the Grand Alliance, which brought the English and French colonies to blows. There then began the

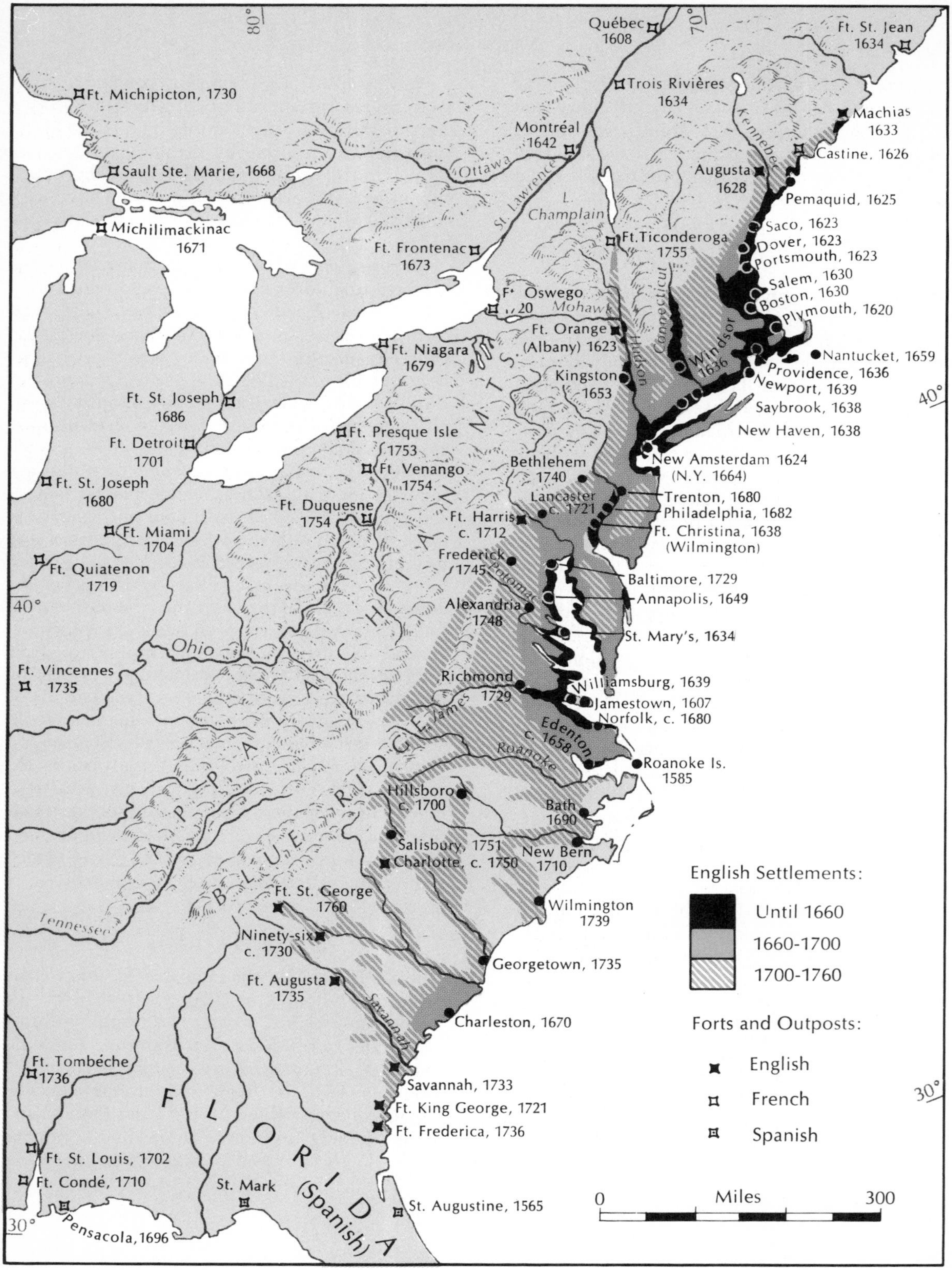
Québec 1608
Ft. St. Jean 1634
Ft. Michipicton, 1730
Trois Rivières 1634
Machias 1633
Montréal 1642
Castine, 1626
Sault Ste. Marie, 1668
Augusta 1628
Pemaquid, 1625
Michilimackinac 1671
L. Champlain
Ft. Ticonderoga 1755
Saco, 1623
Dover, 1623
Portsmouth, 1623
Ft. Frontenac 1673
Salem, 1630
Boston, 1630
Plymouth, 1620
Ft. Oswego 1720
Mohawk
Ft. Orange (Albany) 1623
Nantucket, 1659
Ft. Niagara 1679
Windsor 1636
Providence, 1636
Newport, 1639
Kingston 1653
Saybrook, 1638
New Haven, 1638
Ft. St. Joseph 1686
Ft. Presque Isle 1753
Ft. Detroit 1701
New Amsterdam 1624 (N.Y. 1664)
Bethlehem 1740
Ft. Venango 1754
Ft. St. Joseph 1680
Trenton, 1680
Lancaster c. 1721
Philadelphia, 1682
Ft. Duquesne 1754
Ft. Harris c. 1712
Ft. Christina, 1638 (Wilmington)
Ft. Miami 1704
Frederick 1745
Ft. Quiatenon 1719
Baltimore, 1729
Annapolis, 1649
Alexandria 1748
St. Mary's, 1634
Ohio
Ft. Vincennes 1735
Richmond 1729
Williamsburg, 1639
Jamestown, 1607
Norfolk, c. 1680
Edenton c. 1658
Roanoke Is. 1585
Hillsboro c. 1700
Bath 1690
Salisbury, 1751
New Bern 1710
Charlotte, c. 1750
Ft. St. George 1760
Wilmington 1739
Ninety-six c. 1730
Georgetown, 1735
Ft. Augusta 1735
Charleston, 1670
Ft. Tombéche 1736
Savannah, 1733
Ft. King George, 1721
Ft. Frederica, 1736
Ft. St. Louis, 1702
Ft. Condé, 1710
St. Mark
St. Augustine, 1565
Pensacola, 1696
FLORIDA (Spanish)
APPALACHIAN MTS.
BLUE RIDGE
St. Lawrence
Ottawa
Kennebec
Connecticut
Hudson
Potomac
James
Roanoke
Tennessee
Savannah
English Settlements:
Until 1660
1660-1700
1700-1760
Forts and Outposts:
English
French
Spanish
Miles
0
300
80°
70°
40°
30°

English settlements, 1607–1760
English, French, and Spanish Outposts

first of the international colonial wars,[2] which took up a large part of colonial energy, and which ended with the complete overthrow of French power in North America.

Informal hostilities between England and Spain on the southern border had been going on for years, and a clash between English and French on the northern border was inevitable because of the menace of the Iroquois Confederacy to Canadian trade. Every young Canadian of spirit became an explorer or a coureur de bois, and the more adventurous of these traveling salesmen of the fur business had reached the Dakotas before Englishmen had attained the crest of the Appalachians. The Iroquois Confederacy, whose sphere of influence covered upstate New York, most of Pennsylvania, and the old Northwest, remained faithful to their alliance with the Dutch and the English, who could provide them with cheaper blankets and liquor than did the French. The Iroquois occasionally raided the canoe fur route of the St. Lawrence basin, forcing Canadian fur traders to travel north of and around the Iroquois country in order to reach the upper Mississippi valley, which by 1715 had become a more valuable source of fur than the basin of the Great Lakes.

In the summer of 1682 the Sieur de La Salle, greatest of French explorers, sailed and rowed down the Mississippi, planted the white banner of St. Louis on its banks below New Orleans, and named the region Louisiana. On his next voyage La Salle reached the Gulf coast of Texas, where he was killed by his own men, who were then finished off by the Comanche. These remarkable expeditions so little affected French policy that in 1696 Louis XIV actually issued an edict ordering the Canadian coureurs de bois to take wives, settle down, and cease exploring the wilderness in search of fur! For Louis was entering his pious old age, and the Church objected that these adventurers ruined the work of the missionaries. Governor Frontenac, hand in glove with the fur-trading interests, largely ignored his sovereign's orders.

Louis XIV had no objection to Count Frontenac's using coureurs de bois and friendly Indians to raid the frontiers of New England and New York. So King William's War, as well as that of Queen Anne, took the character of a series of winter attacks on English frontier settlements. Schenectady, New York, was the first place to be destroyed, in February 1690. Other raids followed against the Maine and New Hampshire frontiers, while Canadian privateers from L'Acadie (Nova Scotia) preyed on Yankee fishermen and traders. New England's reply (1690) was to capture Port Royal on the Bay of Fundy, and to send an unsuccessful expedition against Quebec. King William's War ended in Europe with the Treaty of Ryswick (1697), which did not change a single colonial boundary. In New England the war dragged along until 1699. By that time there was hardly a white settler left in the future state of Maine.

During the interval between King William's and Queen Anne's wars, England's rivals in the New World strengthened their positions. In 1696 Spain, which was England's enemy in the next three colonial wars, founded Pensacola. That same year, Father Kino founded the Spanish mission of San Xavier near Tucson, Arizona, and by 1700 the Spanish had reoccupied New Mexico, whence the Pueblo Indians had driven them out in the 1680's. About the same time French Canadians founded three posts—Kaskaskia, Cahokia, and Vincennes—in the Illinois country, partly as a check to Iroquois influence, and partly as connecting links between Canada and Louisiana.

In 1700 came a shifting of European alliances. The king of Spain died without issue, Louis XIV claimed the throne for his grandson, the Grand Alliance supported a rival claimant, and the War

2. The colonial wars may be summarized as follows:

Colonial Name	*European Name*	*Dates*	*Peace Treaty*
I King William's	League of Augsburg	1689–97	Ryswick
II Queen Anne's	Spanish Succession	1702–13	Utrecht
III King George's	Austrian Succession	1745–48	Aachen
IV Old French and Indian	Seven Years War	1754–63	Paris

King George's War began in the Southern Colonies and Caribbean in 1739 as the 'War of Jenkins' Ear' between England and Spain.

The marriage of a Frenchman and an Indian woman, probably an Iroquois. The bridal couple perform a marriage dance, a volume published in London explains, as 'the relations of each party assemble in the hut of the most ancient person among them' where 'they make an entertainment, after the Canadian fashion.' (*Rare Book Division, New York Public Library*)

of the Spanish Succession broke out—Queen Anne's War the colonists called it after their new sovereign. France and Spain now became allies, and the feeble little colonies of Louisiana and Florida became friends. They found a common enemy in the vigorous young English colony of South Carolina, which had developed much the same sort of fur-trading frontier as had the Canadians. By 1700 the Carolinian traders were even obtaining deer and buffalo skins from across the Mississippi. Queen Anne's War on this southern border was a preliminary skirmish in the contest for mastery of the Mississippi. On the northern frontier, Queen Anne's War began with border raids by the French and Indians, including one which wiped out Deerfield, Mass. After two failures, Massachusetts captured Port Royal, this time permanently; it became Annapolis Royal, Nova Scotia.

The Treaty of Utrecht (1713), which ended this war, was a significant event in the territorial history of North America. Great Britain obtained French recognition of her sovereignty over Nova Scotia and Hudson's Bay, where the great fur-trading corporation of that name had been operating since 1670. But the value of Nova Scotia was largely nullified by allowing France to retain Cape Breton Island, where she later constructed Louisbourg, the 'Gibraltar of the New World.' The negotiators at Utrecht paid no attention to the southern frontier. There the Tuscarora Indians in North Carolina rose against the English in 1711. South Carolina came to the aid of her neighbor, defeated the Tuscarora tribe, and carried a large part of it off to be sold as slaves; the remnant withdrew to the Iroquois country and became the sixth nation of that confederacy. Aside from this exception and the brief King George's War, the Treaty of Utrecht marked the beginning of a generation of peace in which the English colonies expanded westward, drew on new sources for their population, diversified their economy, and began to enjoy the fruits of the century of enlightenment.

New Lands, New People

The Treaty of Utrecht opened the last half-century of the old British empire, a period marked by widespread change. Only two new continental colonies, Nova Scotia and Georgia, were founded; but immigrants poured into the other twelve, and the frontier marched westward, creating a new section along the back-country from New Hampshire to South Carolina. Population and trade increased manyfold, and began to strain at the bonds of the Acts of Trade and Navigation. Religion took a new turn with the Great Awakening; new schools and colleges were founded; and in the East an upper class, growing in wealth and in self-confidence, acquired the refinements and the sophistication of eighteenth-century Europeans. Increasingly, the colonists felt that they were Americans as well as Englishmen. In 1713 nobody predicted or suspected that the English colonies would ever seek union, unless in an imperial war, much less free themselves from English rule; in 1763 union and independence were distinct possibilities.

In 1713 the population of the twelve continental colonies was nearly 360,000; in 1760, with Georgia added, it approached 1.6 million, a fourfold increase. Since 1713 the area of settlement had tripled. Whence came this vast increase, proportionally greater than that of any subsequent half-century of our history? Both from large families and from immigration. The two most important contributions were German and Scots-Irish. Discontented Germans came to English America because the German states had no overseas possessions, and no colonies except those of the English would admit foreigners. Many were assisted by the English government; thousands of others were 'redemptioners,' people given free transportation from Europe by shipowners, who recouped themselves by selling their passengers as indented servants. Most Germans entered America at Philadelphia, whence they spread out fanwise into the back-country and became the most prosperous farmers in North America. They brought their own language and culture, established printing presses and newspapers, and at Bethlehem, a musical tradition that eventually flowered into the annual festival devoted to the works of Johann Sebastian Bach.

Equal in importance were the English- (and sometimes Gaelic-) speaking Scots-Irish from Ulster. These were largely descendants of the Scots who had colonized Northern Ireland when the English were first settling Virginia. After 1713 the pressure of the native Catholic Irish and the restrictive legislation of the British Parliament forced them to emigrate in droves. As land was dear in the Eastern colonies, these fighting Celts drifted to the frontier. By 1763 they formed the outer belt of defense against the Indians all the way from Londonderry, New Hampshire, to the upper country of South Carolina. A considerable number of southern Irish, mostly Protestants but including Catholic families like the Carrolls of Maryland, came at the same time; these were mostly men of property who invested in land and remained in the older-settled regions.

A third non-English strain was the French Protestant. In 1685 the revocation of the Edict of Nantes destroyed their religious liberty, and tens of thousands of the most solid and enterprising French subjects fled. Comparatively few Huguenots, as they were called, came to America; but those who did acquired an influence out of proportion to their numbers. They were particularly prominent in South Carolina (Huger,

Ivory-billed woodpecker by Mark Catesby. This engraving of what Catesby called a 'White Bill'd Woodpecker' was first published in 1731–32, twenty years after the English naturalist arrived in America. It is from his seminal work *The Natural History of Carolina, Florida, and the Bahama Islands.* (*Rare Book Division, New York Public Library*)

Petigru), Virginia (Maury), Massachusetts (Revere), and New York (Jay, De Lancey).

About 1726 Germans and Scots-Irish began to pour into the Shenandoah valley. Their motive was to acquire cheap land; for William Penn's heirs, reversing his policy, charged £10 for a hundred acres, as against 10*s* by some of the Virginia speculators. The 'Old Wagon Road' up the valley became a veritable funnel of the frontier. Some settlers sprinkled the Shenandoah valley with log cabins and German names; others turned south, through one of the many gaps in the Blue Ridge, into the piedmont of Virginia and the Carolinas. In North Carolina the defeat of the Tuscarora opened up not only the coastal plain but part of the piedmont, and that colony increased sixteenfold in population between 1713 and 1760. By then it had more people than New York, where Iroquois mastery of the Mohawk valley and the feudal institutions of the Hudson river patroons retarded settlement.

This settlement of the Old West built up new internal tension. South of New York, the older-settled region was English in race and Anglican or Quaker in religion; the West was a mixture of German, Scots-Irish, and English, who were either Presbyterian, Baptist, or German sectarian in religion. People of the eastern belt of settlement controlled the assemblies, which often discriminated against the frontier, building up a West-East antagonism that broke out later in movements like the Paxton Boys, the Regulators, and Shays's Rebellion.

Georgia

The eighteenth century is full of contradictions. This happens in every age when new modes of thought and action, new forms of society and industry, are struggling to emerge from the womb of the past. On the one hand, this was an era of formalism, indifference, and decay in the established churches; on the other, it saw the birth of new religious and philosophical movements, such as Methodism in England, Jansenism in France, the 'natural religion' that stems from Newton, the idealism associated with Berkeley, and the rational philosophy that prepared the way for the French Revolution. In England the age was one of social smugness, brutality, and complacency toward poverty and other evils; yet it was also an age of benevolence, when the first effective protests were made against the slave trade, high infant mortality, and imprisonment for debt. While the colonies as a whole were exploited for the benefit of mercantile classes in England, charitable funds flowed to America from England for the foundation of libraries, schools, and colleges, and for the conversion and education of Indians and Negroes.

The new colony of Georgia was the result of a combination of several charitable individuals and forces for a single well-defined object. James Edward Oglethorpe, a young gentleman of rank and fortune, left Oxford to fight under Eugene of Savoy against the Turks, and then entered Parliament where, 'driven by strong benevolence of soul' (as Alexander Pope wrote of him), he served on a committee to inquire into the state of jails. That state was bad indeed. A debtor once committed to jail could not be released until his debt was paid, and in jail he had no means of discharging it; if released by charity after many years, he was usually incapable of supporting himself. It occurred to Oglethorpe that the way to meet this social evil was to assist poor debtors to emigrate to America under conditions that would enable them to start afresh and lead happy and useful lives. At his instance the Associates of Dr. Bray, an energetic Anglican clergyman who had initiated several benefactions, obtained a proprietary grant, with limited tenure, of the land between the Savannah and the Altamaha rivers, under the name of Georgia. As several of the trustees of Georgia were members of Parliament, they were able to obtain grants of public money to transport and settle the deserving poor. Georgia began as a colony de luxe, the pet project of wealthy and powerful philanthropists.

General Oglethorpe, appointed the first governor, came out with the first shipload of settlers in 1733 and founded Savannah. In the next eight years the trustees sent over 1810 charity colonists, of whom almost half were Germans, Scots, and Swiss, and the rest English. In the same period 1021 persons arrived on their own; 92 of these were Jews. Each settler received 50 acres free, and

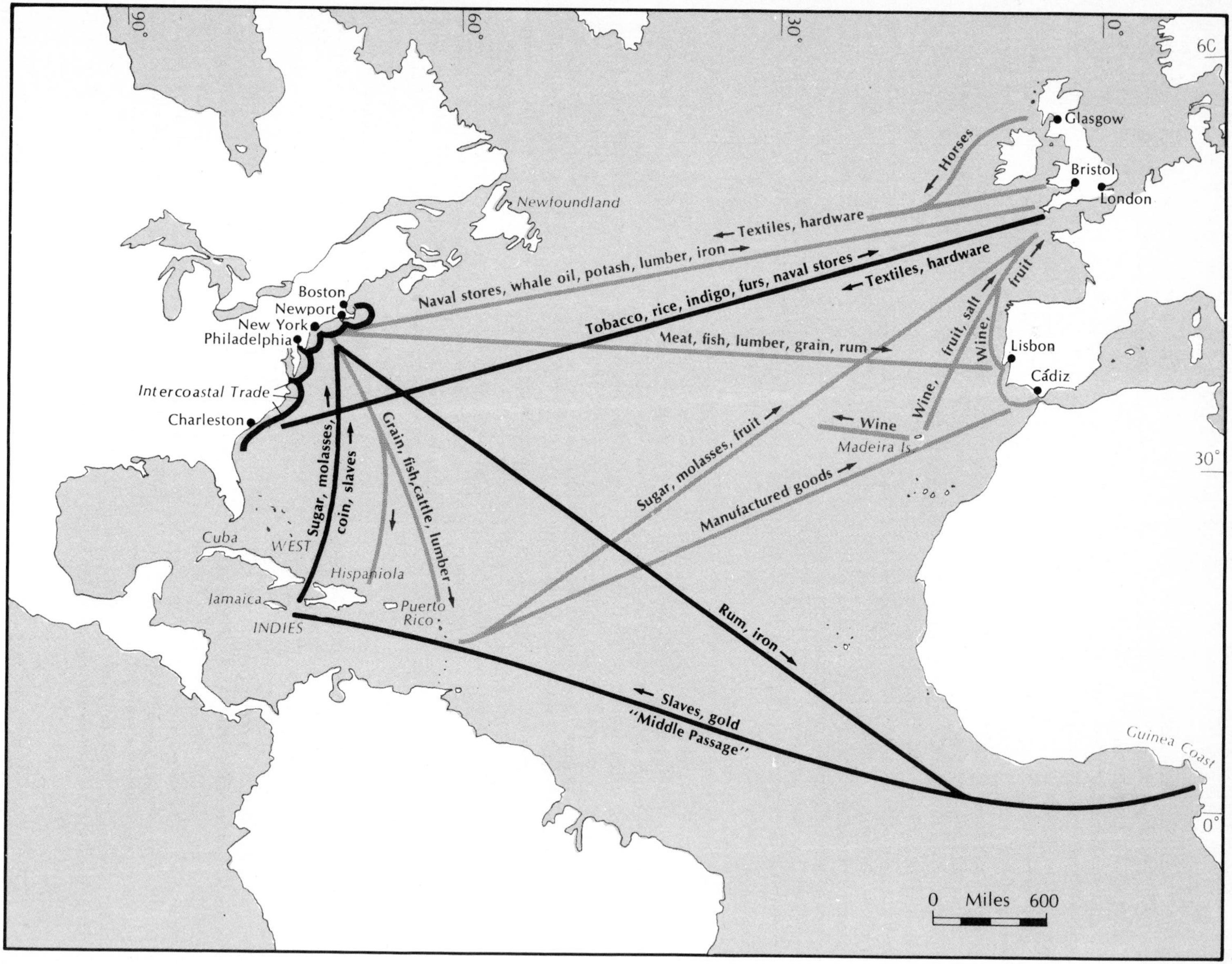
90°
60°
30°
0°
6C
30°
0°
Newfoundland
Glasgow
Bristol
London
Lisbon
Cádiz
Madeira Is.
Boston
Newport
New York
Philadelphia
Intercoastal Trade
Charleston
Cuba
WEST
INDIES
Jamaica
Hispaniola
Puerto Rico
Guinea Coast
Horses
Textiles, hardware
Naval stores, whale oil, potash, lumber, iron
Tobacco, rice, indigo, furs, naval stores
Textiles, hardware
Meat, fish, lumber, grain, rum
Wine, fruit, salt
Wine, fruit
Wine
Sugar, molasses, fruit
Manufactured goods
Sugar, molasses,
coin, slaves
Grain, fish, cattle, lumber
Rum, iron
Slaves, gold
"Middle Passage"
0 Miles 600

Colonial Trade Routes

the trustees forbade the importation of slaves and rum. The charity settlers were not all poor debtors or jailbirds; many were small tradespeople and artisans, for the trustees wished to establish a colony in which many occupations were represented.

Georgia did not prosper under this benevolent despotism. The settlers found it impossible to live off 50 acres; and with no quinine, rum became a necessity in the malarial lowlands. The contrast with South Carolina, where colonists were growing rich through applying slave labor to rice and indigo plantations, attracted the more ambitious to the older colony. The trustees gradually liberalized the conditions of land-owning, removed the slavery and liquor prohibitions, and granted an assembly in 1751; but the colony lost many people through fever and removal—the population was only 1735 whites and 349 blacks in 1752. In that year, when the twenty years' proprietorship lapsed, the trustees were glad to turn Georgia over to the Crown. Gradually the economy of Georgia was assimilated to the rice-plantation pattern of South Carolina, and eventually it received an up-country population by way of the intermountain trough. Yet at the outbreak of the Revolution Georgia was still the weakest and least populous of the Thirteen Colonies. Still, the enterprise did assist several thousand people, whose lives would have been wasted in England, to a new life in the New World.

Industry and Commerce

Despite the tightened controls of the imperial system—perhaps to some extent because of them—the colonial economy prospered as never before during the half-century following the Treaty of Utrecht. The key to this prosperity was a rise in prices for colonial produce. The increased European demand for colonial produce hit first the West Indies; and West Indian prosperity almost automatically affected the continental colonies. The French West Indies were an important source of cheap molasses, which New England and the Middle Colonies made into rum. The British West Indies, annoyed by this competition, induced Parliament in 1733 to pass the Sugar or Molasses Act, charging a prohibitory duty on foreign molasses and sugar entering English colonies. By that time, rum distilleries had become so numerous in towns from Portsmouth to Philadelphia that the French Antilles were necessary as a source of molasses. So the act was simply ignored.

So brisk was the demand for flour in the West Indies that within a few years the export of grain and flour from Chesapeake Bay ports pushed tobacco for first place. Baltimore was founded in 1729, largely because Jones Falls turned mills which ground the wheat of Pennsylvania and up-country Maryland into flour. However, Philadelphia remained the principal place of export for grain and other provisions. Virginia recovered her ancient prosperity with a rise in the price of tobacco and shared in the flour trade as well. And, as in the previous century, the West Indies trade was vital for southern New England, the islands importing more and more salt fish, wood for boxes, barrels, and house construction, work horses, salt meat, and ground vegetables.

The Carolinas shared in the general prosperity. For North Carolina, the export to England of ship timber and pitch and tar was of great importance. In South Carolina fortunes were built out of rice and indigo. In 1731, over 200 vessels cleared from Charleston, carrying 42,000 barrels (about 21 million pounds) of rice, 14,000 barrels of pitch, tar, and turpentine, about 250,000 deer skins, and a large quantity of provisions. Parliament in 1729 allowed rice to be sent directly to all European ports south of Cape Finisterre, and by 1771 South Carolina's rice exports were threefold what they had been in 1731. Indigo, stimulated by a production bounty from Parliament, was introduced about 1740, and quickly produced a crop of 'indigo millionaires.' Both rice and indigo required a large labor force for profitable cultivation, thus accelerating the growth of slavery and the African slave trade.

Although England did not object to the colonists' indulging in crude manufacturing, such as milling grain and distilling molasses into rum, it attempted to suppress competition with leading English industries. Two acts of Parliament were aimed at protecting English staples. On complaint of London's Worshipful Company of Hatters that the colonists were beginning to make up furs into the wide-brimmed beaver hats of the era, instead of importing headgear from England, a law of 1732 limited the number of hatter apprentices and banned exports of hats from one colony to another. In 1750 British iron interests induced Parliament to remove British duties from colonial pig and bar iron, in the hope of encouraging Americans to supplant importations from Sweden to England. The same act forbade the establishment of new slitting mills (which slit bar iron into nail rods) or plating forges using a trip hammer, or steel tool furnaces, in order to protect the export of English ironmongery and steel. But this law was so flagrantly disregarded that Pennsylvania, New Jersey, and Massachusetts even granted bounties for new plants after the law was on the statute books! By 1760 there was a thriving colonial iron industry wherever a combination of surface iron ore, wood for smelting, and water power was found. So, though the acts restraining manufactures were restrictive in motive, they were hardly so in practice.

Far more serious than all Acts of Trade and Navigation as brakes on colonial enterprise were English restrictions on the colonial use of money, and attempts of colonial assemblies to get around them. Nothing that a colonial assembly did in the way of fiat money could legally discharge debts due to English merchants; hence it was the country storekeeper or seaport merchant who suffered from this sort of restriction and sought redress in England. Royal governors were always instructed to veto paper-money laws unless they provided for prompt redemption out of taxes; and when the governor was forced by political pressure to disobey his instructions, the law was disallowed by the Privy Council. Although few colonial assemblies showed sufficient wisdom and restraint to be entrusted with so dangerous a power as the issuance of paper money, the British government did nothing to provide a substitute. By forbidding the colonies to import English coin, or to mint the bullion they acquired from the Spanish West Indies into coin, they made some other form of currency necessary, and inflation inevitable.

Society and Religion

While the Thirteen Colonies were expanding trade and developing a more heterogeneous population, their social and intellectual ties with England were becoming closer. Every royal governor's mansion provided a little court where the latest European fashions were displayed and London coffee-house gossip was repeated. Transatlantic travel, except during winter months, was relatively safe in the small packet ships and 'constant traders' of the day. Merchants in the seaport towns made a point of visiting London every few years, and sent their sons on long voyages as supercargoes; many sons of rich Southern planters attended school in England; or, if they studied at a colonial college, took a medical course at the University of Edinburgh or read law in the Inns of Court. Between 1713 and 1773, thirteen colonial Americans were accorded the highest scientific honor in the English-speaking world, a fellowship in the Royal Society of London.

Professional architects were few. When Harvard College wanted a new building in 1764, Governor Bernard obligingly drew the plans. Local builders, with the aid of books of design from England, erected mansions in the well-proportioned Georgian style and churches modeled on those of Sir Christopher Wren in London. After 1720 paint was used freely to preserve the exterior and adorn the interior of wooden dwelling houses, and white paneled doors surmounted by graceful fanlights replaced the massive nail-studded oak portals that were designed to resist Indian tomahawks. In the South we have the first colonnaded porches, as at Mount Vernon, a balanced layout with detached offices and kitchen, and landscaped grounds. In the back-country and new settlements from Maine to Georgia the log cabin, made either of round logs or of squared timbers well mortised together and chinked with chips and clay, became universal.

Even colonial towns of 2000 or 3000 inhabitants afforded more amenities in the eighteenth century than do American cities today of tenfold times their population. There would always be a market house and merchants' exchange, a tavern where the latest English gazettes were taken in and where clubs of gentlemen or tradesmen met to talk, smoke, drink, and sing; a dancing assembly for the elite; a circulating library; and, in five or six places, a musical society. Philadelphia had a theater as early as 1724, and in 1749 an English company of players began trouping through the colonies south of New England; for in the Puritan colonies only private theatricals were permitted. Fairs gave entertainment to everyone. Williamsburg established semi-annual fairs for livestock, goods, and merchandise, with foot races, horse races, greased pigs to be caught.

The period from 1740 to the French and Indian War was the golden age of the Old Dominion. Peace reigned, high prices ruled for tobacco, immigrants thronged the back-country; and the Virginia of Thackeray and Vachel Lindsay—'Land of the gauntlet and the glove'—came into being. Living in Virginia at that time was like riding on the sparkling crest of a great wave just before it breaks and spreads into dull, shallow pools. In that wholesome rural society with lavish hospitality and a tradition of public spirit was bred the 'Virginia dynasty' which (with some help from elsewhere, one must admit!) would guide the destinies of the young republic yet unborn.

By mid-century, religious dissenters in every colony had made tremendous gains among the common people through the religious revival known as the Great Awakening. This was the first spontaneous movement of the entire English colonial population. The Great Awakening began in three different colonies. The Reverend Theodore Frelinghuysen of the Dutch Reformed Church started a revival in the Raritan valley, New Jersey, in 1719. William Tennent, a Presbyterian Scot, in 1736 established the Log College for revivalists at Neshaminy, Pa. In 1734 Jonathan Edwards, graduate of Yale and minister of Northampton, Mass., began his imprecatory sermons to recall the people to a sense of sin and bring them to that feeling of communion with God which evangelicals call conversion. His description of this revival, *A Faithful Narration of the Surprising Work of God in the Conversion of Many Hundred Souls in Northampton* (Boston, 1737), was promptly reprinted in London and Edinburgh, translated into German and Dutch, and became, as it still is, a classic. John Wesley read it afoot between London and Oxford. 'Surely this is the Lord's doing,' he wrote in his journal; presently he began to obtain the same effects from his own preaching, and in a little while the Methodist Church was born. George Whitefield, an eloquent young minister sent out to Georgia by the trustees, read *A Faithful Narration* in Savannah, and his amazing career as a revivalist dates from that hour.

Whitefield began the second phase of the Great Awakening by preaching at Philadelphia in 1739, and touring New England in 1740. In 73 days he rode 800 miles and preached 130 sermons. His voice could be heard by 20,000 people in the open air. He made violent gestures, danced about the pulpit, roared and ranted, greatly to the delight of the common people who were tired of unemotional sermons from college-bred ministers. He introduced the stage of revivalism with which many parts of America are still familiar—sinners becoming vocally 'saved.' Gilbert Tennent, son of the proprietor of the Log College, and several score of lay exhorters and itinerant preachers followed Whitefield. The 'New Lights,' as their followers called themselves, proved to be the first blossom of that amazing tree that was to bear the Shakers and the Mormons, Holy Rollers and the Millerites, and a score of other sects. Not one colony or county was unaffected by the Great Awakening.

Jonathan Edwards stayed with the movement, although he deplored its excesses; but the backwash of reaction drove him from the pleasant Connecticut valley. He became a missionary to the Indians in Stockbridge, and there, in the solitude of the wilderness, wrote three of his greatest works—*The Nature of True Virtue, Original Sin,* and *Freedom of the Will.* Edwards faced, as few modern men have dared or cared to face, the problem of evil and the problem of free will. The system of Calvinist theology that he and his disciple Stephen Hopkins worked out emphasized the splendid but terrible omnipotence of Almighty

Jonathan Edwards (1703–58), the brilliant Calvinist theologian. This contemporary engraving by Jocelyn shows him in the last year of his life when he agreed to become president of the College of New Jersey at Princeton, only to die within two months as a consequence of a smallpox inoculation. (*Library of Congress*)

God and the miserable impotence of sinful man. And certain passages in his works express more effectively the beauty of holiness and the supreme importance of man's relation to God than any other in American literature.

Although the more extreme religious enthusiasts were anti-intellectual, and even encouraged book-burning, the Great Awakening gave to the colonies three new colleges; for the 'New Lights' soon perceived that without seminaries to educate an evangelical ministry, their movement would be killed by ignorant hot-gospelers. The College of New Jersey at Princeton (1746), the first colonial school of higher learning to be founded since Yale (1701), was the Presbyterian seminary; Dartmouth (1769) was founded by

Eleazar Wheelock, a disciple of Edwards and Whitefield, ostensibly for training Indian preachers; and the Baptists, who hitherto had been without an educated ministry, were driven by competition to build the College of Rhode Island (later Brown University) at Providence in 1764. King's College (Columbia University), founded in New York City in 1754, was Anglican; Queen's College (Rutgers University), founded at New Brunswick, N.J., in 1766, was Dutch Reformed. The Philadelphia Academy (University of Pennsylvania), founded as a secondary school in 1740, was the only colonial college whose impetus and control were wholly non-sectarian.

All these colleges were very small by modern standards; the record colonial graduating class numbered 63. Princeton, Yale, and Harvard offered graduate training in theology; Philadelphia and King's established medical schools in 1765 and 1767. In the two decades before the Revolution, increasing emphasis was given to modern languages and science. But the great majority of undergraduates followed a prescribed course in rhetoric, philosophy, mathematics, and the ancient classics (including a good deal of political theory), which proved an excellent preparation for public life. Most of the important framers of state and federal constitutions were college-trained.

Nevertheless, only one of the three greatest Americans of the age, Jonathan Edwards, was a college graduate. George Washington (born 1732) attained his superb poise, self-discipline, and character that met every test, partly through manly sports, and partly through contact with his gentle neighbors, the Fairfaxes of Belvoir, who employed him as a surveyor in his young manhood. They introduced him to the Stoic philosophy that breathes through Plutarch's *Lives*, Seneca's *Dialogues*, and Addison's *Cato*. Benjamin Franklin, three years younger than Edwards, was the very antithesis of New England's saint. Essentially worldly and practical, he found little time for theology or philosophy, and none for sports. Yet his moral maxims in *Poor Richard's Almanack* provided ethics for the unchurched, and he organized schools and libraries that others might learn. His industry enabled him to accumulate a competence early, after which the application of his inquiring mind to problems made him a leading scientist. His pioneer work on electricity was of the highest significance, and his passion for improvement made him the first inventor of his time. Finding that most of the heat from open fireplaces went up the chimney, he designed the Franklin stove in 1740. Worried by the fires set by lightning, he invented the lightning rod. And during long ocean passages under sail he thought up improvements in the mariner's art, many of which have since been adopted. Franklin loved music, played four different instruments, and invented a fifth, the glass harmonica, for which even Mozart and Beethoven composed music. The most eminent statesmen, scientists, and men of letters in England and France valued his conversation; yet he never ceased to be a good democrat.

Franklin's college was the newspaper office. Colonial journalism began with the colorless *Boston News-Letter* of 1704; within twenty years James Franklin, with teen-aged Ben as printer's devil and anonymous contributor, brought out *The New-England Courant*. 'Mr. Coranto,' as this paper called itself, was a sprightly sheet that attacked Harvard College and the Mather dynasty, even when those clerical autocrats, far ahead of public opinion, were advocating inoculation for smallpox. But when Mr. Coranto attacked the Massachusetts assembly, he got in trouble; and Ben left Boston for Philadelphia. There and in London, Franklin continued his trade of printer; and he was one of the first to sense the use of almanacs to enlighten farm folk who could not afford a newspaper. In 1725 there were only five newspapers in the continental colonies; by 1765 there were twenty-five, two of them in German. All were four-page weekly journals, filled largely with foreign news clipped from London papers, but carrying a certain amount of local items, assembly debates, advertisements of runaway slaves, and 'fine assortments' of English and West Indian goods for sale.

Libel laws in all the colonies were severe, and governments had to be criticized by innuendo rather than directly; yet one of the landmarks in the long struggle for the freedom of the press was the Zenger case. John Peter Zenger, publisher of *The New-York Weekly Journal*, lent his columns

to criticism of the governor, who haled him into court for false and scandalous libel. Andrew Hamilton, an aged Philadelphia lawyer who defended Zenger, offered the unheard of defense that the articles complained of told the truth! Chief Justice De Lancey rejected this contention and insisted on the English common law rule that the greater the truth the greater the libel. Hamilton countered with a ringing appeal to the jury, declaring that the cause of English liberty, not merely the liberty of a poor printer, was at stake, and won a verdict of 'not guilty' in August 1735. Although the Zenger verdict failed either to alter the common law or to provide the basis for a fully developed philosophy of freedom of expression, it encouraged editors to criticize governors. Gouverneur Morris called the Zenger case 'the morning star of that liberty which subsequently revolutionized America.'

It also marked the rise of a lawyer class. In the seventeenth century practitioners were regarded with contempt, and usually deserved it. The increase of commerce brought more litigation and the need for skilled lawyers; and the men of best repute who had defended clients in the courts formed a bar, with rules of entry and of conduct that had the force of law. Prominent lawyers naturally were elected to the assemblies, where they were very clever in tying up the royal governors in legal knots, and making every local dispute a matter of the 'liberties of Englishmen.' So, when weightier matters were at issue in the 1760's, the legal profession as well as the press was prepared.

The Last Colonial Wars, 1739–63

The last colonial war began in 1739 with the 'War of Jenkins' Ear' between England and Spain,[3] which was fought on the Georgia-Florida border and in the Caribbean. There the principal events were raids on Porto Bello and Cartagena by Admiral Vernon, with thousands of volunteers from the continental colonies, nine-tenths of whom succumbed to yellow fever. One survivor was

Benjamin Franklin (1706–90). This engraving, after Mason Chamberlain, shows him with his lightning detector. An avid scientific researcher, the many-sided Franklin set forth the fruits of his work, including the invention of the lightning rod, in *Experiments and Observations on Electricity* (1751–54). (*Metropolitan Museum of Art*)

3. So called because Parliament declared war after being outraged by a smuggler named Jenkins having his ears cropped by a Spanish coast guard.

George Washington's elder brother, who named Mount Vernon after the popular but unlucky admiral.

In 1744 the Anglo-Spanish conflict merged into the War of the Austrian Succession, and France again came to grips with England in North America, where the conflict was called King George's War. Again there was *la petite guerre* along the New York-New England border; and *la grande guerre* but not according to the book. The New Englanders' attack on Acadian Louisbourg, planned by Governor Shirley and led by a Maine merchant, Sir William Pepperell, was one of the maddest schemes in the history of modern warfare, a sort of large-scale 'commando'; but it worked. The Yankee yokels who pitched camp before the 'impregnable' fortress refused to obey any of the rules of war, and so baffled the French governor by their odd antics that he surrendered (1745). By the Treaty of Aachen, which ended this war in 1748, the English restored Louisbourg to France in return for Madras; the disappointment of New England was assuaged by the Crown's paying the entire expenses of the expedition.

This treaty was only a truce in the final conflict for mastery in North America. In Virginia companies were organized with the object of opening a route from the Potomac to the Ohio for Indian trade, and making a profit from Western land. These ventures constituted a threat to communications between Canada, the Illinois country, and Louisiana, which the French could not afford to ignore. In 1749 the governor of Canada sent Céloron de Blainville with several hundred Canadians and Indians in a fleet of bateaux and canoes to take possession of the Ohio valley. This expedition was followed up in 1753 by Marquis Duquesne, who established a chain of log forts on the Allegheny and upper Ohio.

French Canada had a population of only 50,000 or 60,000 farmers and fur-traders in 1750 when the English colonies numbered 1.25 million, and the pretension of France to reserve for herself the unsettled parts of North America was one that the English could hardly be expected to admit. In 1753 Governor Dinwiddie of Virginia commissioned George Washington (aged 22) lieutenant-colonel of Virginia militia, and the next year sent him with 150 men to forestall the French at the forks of the Ohio. But the French had arrived first, and built Fort Duquesne on the site of Pittsburgh. At Great Meadows in western Pennsylvania, the young lieutenant-colonel fired a shot on a French force that began the last and greatest of the colonial wars. The enemy rallied and Washington's troops had to capitulate and go home; for this was only a cold war—not declared for two years more. Both Virginia and New England were eager to call it a hot war and get going. Virginia wished to preserve her ancient charter rights to all the territory west and northwest of her settled area; Massachusetts was still aiming to clear the French out of Canada. But the governments of George II and Louis XV hoped to localize hostilities. So in the fall of 1754 George II sent General Braddock to America with only two regiments, and the powers of commander in chief.

In the meantime eight of the Thirteen Colonies had made an attempt to agree on a plan for common defense. Out of the Albany Congress of June 1754 came the Albany Plan of Union, the work of Benjamin Franklin and Thomas Hutchinson. There was to be a president-general appointed by the Crown, and a 'grand council' appointed by the colonial assemblies, in proportion to their contributions to the common war chest—a typical bit of Ben Franklin foxiness, to ensure that taxes were really paid. The president, with the advice of the grand council, would have sole jurisdiction over Indian relations and the Western territory. The Union would have power to build forts, raise armies, equip fleets, and levy taxes. This plan showed far-sighted statesmanship, in advance of its time, but was a closer union than the Thirteen Colonies were willing to conclude. Whether the British authorities would have accepted it is doubtful; but they never had a chance to express their views. Not one colonial assembly ratified the Plan. Every one refused to give up any part of its exclusive taxing power, even to a representative body. So the ensuing war was carried through under the old system. No British commander had authority to raise troops or money from a colony without the consent of its assembly. As in previous wars, the assemblies of provinces that were not directly menaced, and also some of those that were, like Pennsylvania, refused to make any substantial contribution to the common cause.

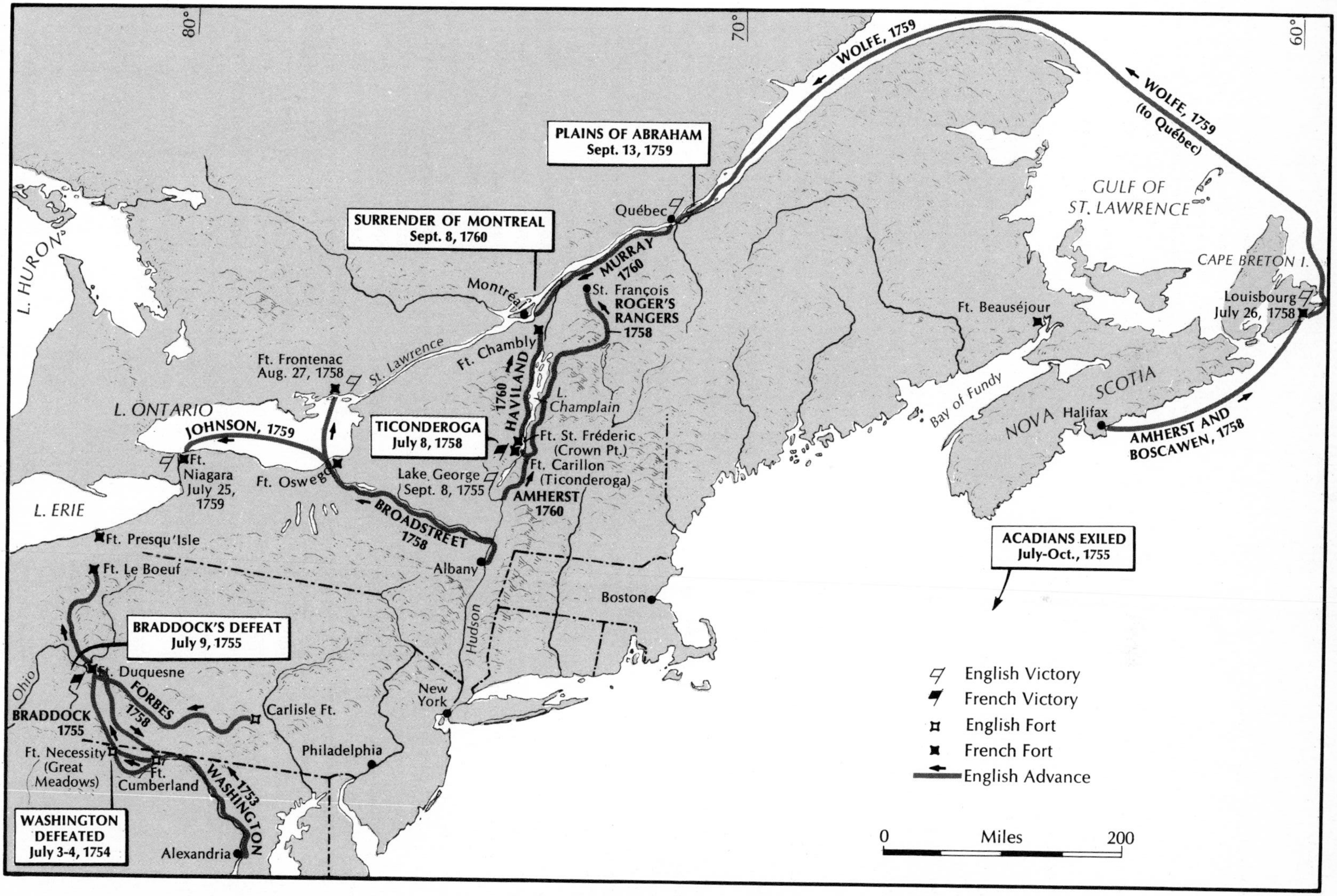

WOLFE, 1759
WOLFE, 1759 (to Québec)
GULF OF ST. LAWRENCE
CAPE BRETON I.
Louisbourg July 26, 1758
AMHERST AND BOSCAWEN, 1758
NOVA SCOTIA
Halifax
Ft. Beauséjour
Bay of Fundy
ACADIANS EXILED July-Oct., 1755
PLAINS OF ABRAHAM Sept. 13, 1759
Québec
SURRENDER OF MONTREAL Sept. 8, 1760
Montreal
MURRAY 1760
St. François
ROGER'S RANGERS 1758
Ft. Chambly
HAVILAND 1760
L. Champlain
Ft. St. Fréderic (Crown Pt.)
Ft. Carillon (Ticonderoga)
AMHERST 1760
TICONDEROGA July 8, 1758
Lake George Sept. 8, 1755
St. Lawrence
Ft. Frontenac Aug. 27, 1758
L. HURON
L. ONTARIO
JOHNSON, 1759
Ft. Niagara July 25, 1759
Ft. Oswego
BROADSTREET 1758
Albany
Hudson
Boston
New York
Philadelphia
L. ERIE
Ft. Presqu'Isle
Ft. Le Boeuf
BRADDOCK'S DEFEAT July 9, 1755
Ft. Duquesne
FORBES 1758
Carlisle Ft.
Ohio
BRADDOCK 1755
Ft. Necessity (Great Meadows)
Ft. Cumberland
WASHINGTON 1753
WASHINGTON DEFEATED July 3-4, 1754
Alexandria
80°
70°
60°
English Victory
French Victory
English Fort
French Fort
English Advance
0
Miles
200

French and Indian War, 1754–1763

Although the Seven Years War (1756–63) was not formally declared for two more years, it was already being hotly waged in America, where it was called the French and Indian War. The haughty Braddock's march against Fort Duquesne ended in total defeat only a few miles from the site of Pittsburgh, lost him his life, brought the Indians of the Northwest over to the French side, and exposed the western settlements of Pennsylvania, Maryland, and Virginia to a series of devastating attacks. The other operations of the English in 1755 were inept, though not disastrous. Governor Shirley failed to take Fort Niagara, the French gateway to the West. William Johnson, a clever Irishman of the Mohawk valley who kept the Six Nations quiet, defeated the French on Lake George and was rewarded with a baronetcy for having gained the only English victory that year. But he was unable to capture Crown Point on Lake Champlain, and the French built Fort Ticonderoga to back up Crown Point.

Before the war was over it had extended to every European power and to all parts of the world. There was naval warfare in the Atlantic, the Mediterranean, the West Indies, and the Indian Ocean; battles on the Asiatic continent between Dupleix and Clive and their East Indian allies, and in the Philippines, where the English captured Manila after hostilities were over in Europe.

The years 1756–57 were disastrous for England. Oswego, the English fort on Lake Ontario, was captured by the French General Montcalm, who then advanced down Lake Champlain to Lake George, and captured Fort William Henry. Admiral Byng lost Minorca in the Mediterranean to the French, and was court-martialed and shot for cowardice, 'pour encourager les autres,' as Voltaire quipped. In India, the British lost Calcutta. On the European continent, Frederick the Great was defeated by the French and Austrians, and an Anglo-Hanoverian army surrendered. At the end of 1757 military experts confidently predicted that France would win hands down and would get all North America.

Yet the whole complexion of the war changed in 1758 when William Pitt, the future Earl of Chatham, became head of the ministry and virtual dictator of the English empire. Pitt had a genius for organization, a knack for grand strategy, and a knowledge of men. While most Englishmen regarded America as a secondary theater, Pitt saw that the principal object for England should be the conquest of Canada and the American West, thus carving out a new field for Anglo-American expansion. Pitt's policy was simple and direct: subsidize Frederick the Great to carry on warfare in Europe; use the navy to command the high seas and contain the French fleet in port; and concentrate the military might of England in America, under young and energetic generals.

James Wolfe, son of a country squire, was a tall, lanky, narrow-shouldered young man with vivid red hair. Ambition, audacity, genius, and a fierce concentration on becoming master of his profession made Wolfe the most Napoleonic soldier in English history. He was only thirty-one in 1758, when Pitt made him first brigadier general under General Jeffrey Amherst, whom Pitt had selected as commander in chief by passing over whole columns of senior officers. These two formed a perfect team with Admiral Boscawen in assaulting Louisbourg, which, though infinitely better fortified than in 1745 and more skillfully defended, was captured in 1758. That same year a force of New Englanders captured Fort Frontenac at the site of Kingston, Ontario; and General Forbes, with George Washington as his right-hand man, seized Fort Duquesne, renaming it Pittsburgh after the great war minister. Clive won the upper hand in India, and Frederick the Great broke out from his encirclement of French, Russian, and Austrian enemies. Then came 1759, England's *annus mirabilis*—the acme of the old empire, when England reached a pinnacle of glory that she had never touched before, and, as Horace Walpole wrote, the very bells of London were worn threadbare pealing out victories. Off the coast of France, Admiral Hawke won the battle of Quiberon Bay, which rendered the French incapable of sending reinforcements to Canada; in the West Indies, a combined naval and military expedition conquered Guadeloupe; in North America, Sir William Johnson captured Fort Niagara, key to the West.

Yet the greatest campaign that year was the one for Canada. Wolfe's army advanced in transports up the St. Lawrence river to Quebec. There Gen-

Quebec in 1758, a year before the climactic battle in which the capital of New France fell to the British. Notice how many of the structures in this Thomas Johnston engraving house Catholic institutions. (*Stokes Collection, New York Public Library*)

eral Amherst with a land force was supposed to co-operate with him. Amherst captured Crown Point and Ticonderoga, but never got within striking distance of Quebec. Thrice in previous wars this failure in co-ordination had meant that the great fortress-city remained French. But Wolfe's forces carried on. After abortive attacks on Quebec from two sides, Wolfe worked out a ruse for placing a force on the plains above the city. And with a single concentrated volley on the Plains of Abraham, Wolfe won Quebec on 13 September 1759—as he learned just before his death on the battlefield.

After the surrender of Quebec in 1759 and Montreal in 1760, French power ceased on the North American continent. War continued only in the West, where after a last flare-up, the conspiracy of Pontiac, the conflict in America flickered to a close. In Europe, Spain came in and the war dragged on. But the new king, George III, dismissed Mr. Pitt, who was becoming altogether too powerful for royalty, and purchased peace by renouncing a number of the conquests. By this Peace of Paris (1763), French Canada and the Spanish Floridas were ceded to Great Britain; while France, in order to compensate Spain for her losses, ceded Louisiana and all French claims to the west of the Mississippi to Spain.

The British empire bestrode the world like a colossus; India gained, all North America to the Mississippi won, and the best of the West Indies; supremacy of the seas confirmed. As the historian Seeley wrote, 'long it continued to be the unique boast of the Englishman,

> That Chatham's language was his mother tongue
> And Wolfe's great name compatriot with his own.'

English, Scots, Irish, and colonists spilled over with expressions of loyalty; and at a meeting in Boston to celebrate the peace, James Otis declaring that the true interests of Britain and her colonies were identical, warned, 'What God in his providence has united, let no man dare attempt to pull asunder!' Yet the war was not paid for, and the price of glory comes high. The French menace was ended forever; but a flock of new problems within the empire clamored for solution.

4

The Revolution Precipitated

*

1763–1776

Liberty and Authority

The American generation that came to maturity between the Peace of Paris and the inauguration of President Washington lived in an era that was revolutionary and destructive for the old British empire, but creative and constructive for the United States. This period from 1763 to 1789 has a singular unity. We must not let the rush of events and the din of arms hide from us its real meaning. Just as the Greek tragedies of the Periclean Age are concerned not merely with the conflicts of gods and heroes, but with the depths of human nature, so we may discern, behind the noisy conflict of the American Revolution, the stirring of a political problem older than recorded history: the balancing of liberty with authority. This ancient question resolves itself into two: the federal problem of distributing power between one central and many regional governments; and the democratic one of how far the masses of mankind shall be entrusted with control. These two problems are the warp and woof of American history through the Civil War; and the circumstances of our own time have simply restated these ancient issues.

By excluding the French from continental North America, the British took over more responsibility than they could handle. Baffling questions of Indian relations, fur trade, land policy, and military and political administration were created. For the next twenty-five years, Great Britain attempted unsuccessfully to solve the great riddle of imperial organization. And the new American government found itself confronted with the same difficulties.

The immense acquisitions of the Seven Years War persuaded British statesmen that their bigger empire required more ships and soldiers. These would cost money; and unless the British taxpayer supplied it all, the colonies, which also benefited, should contribute to the cost. Revenue could be extracted from the colonies only through a stronger central administration, at the expense of colonial self-government. As Governor Hutchinson wrote in a sentence that lost him his job, 'There must be an abridgement of so-called English Liberties in America.' Furthermore, the Acts of Trade were strengthened to an extent that began to impose real hardships on important colonial interests.

During the half-century since 1713 the lower

houses of the colonial assemblies had managed to seize control of the purse and patronage and had taken advantage of the Seven Years War to transform themselves into 'miniature parliaments.' The British government by veto or disallowance was able to prevent things, such as abuse of paper money, that it did not like; but it was unable to get positive things done, such as full co-operation in time of war, or a financial contribution to imperial defense. Despite a panoply of executive powers, the colonial governors were weak. The Board of Trade reported in 1754, with truth, that members of the New York Assembly 'have wrested from Your Majesty's governor, the nomination of all offices of government, the custody and direction of the public military stores, the mustering and direction of troops raised for Your Majesty's service, and in short almost every other part of executive government.' South Carolina even pushed encroachment to the extent that the Anglican churches of the colony were instructed to pray for the assembly instead of the governor!

By 1763 there had been worked out a compromise between imperial authority and colonial self-government. King and Parliament had undisputed control of foreign affairs, war and peace, and overseas trade. Parliament directed colonial trade into channels that it deemed profitable to the empire, colonies included. In almost every other respect the Americans had home rule. They had acquired far more autonomy than Ireland then enjoyed, and infinitely more than the colonies of France, Spain, or any other country had before the next century. So, apart from minor discontents, the Americans were fairly well satisfied with this compromise in 1763. But the government of George III was not. It had devised no method of exacting a uniform contribution from the colonies for defense. And there were still leaks in the enforcement of the Acts of Trade and Navigation. This situation had points of friction, but was not explosive. 'The Abilities of a Child might have governed this Country,' wrote Oliver Wolcott of Connecticut in 1776, 'so strong has been their Attachment to Britain.' But the Americans were a high-spirited people who claimed all the rights for which Englishmen had fought since Magna Carta, and would settle for nothing less.

Make no mistake; the American Revolution was not fought to *obtain* freedom, but to *preserve* the freedom that the colonies already had. Independence was no conscious goal, but a last resort, reluctantly adopted, to preserve 'life, liberty, and the pursuit of happiness.'

The West

The West created the most pressing problem of imperial reorganization. This problem had many strands: the international and military question, the Indians, the fur trade, the dilemma of territorial administration and land policy, and the political issue, particularly with reference to French Canadians.

The international question was whether the West would be won by France, Spain, or Great Britain, or partitioned among them. This was only partially solved by the Seven Years War. To the south and west of the new British possessions lay the rich Spanish empire. Spain was still a power to be reckoned with, still the largest empire in the New World, embracing most of South America and all Central America, together with California, Texas, and everything west of the Mississippi. In spite of her acquisition of a new bulwark in the shape of Louisiana, she was eager to recover the two Floridas which had gone to England, and the east bank of the Mississippi as well. Although the Peace of 1763 presumably disposed of the French danger, the English colonies by no means felt safe. Napoleon's recovery of Louisiana in 1800 may be said to have vindicated English fears in 1770. The French government continued mischievous intrigues with its former Indian allies, and kept its finger on the pulse of colonial discontent.

The Indian danger was more immediate. Pontiac's conspiracy of 1763 was the most formidable Indian outbreak of the century. Goaded to desperation by the tactics of the English traders and trappers, affronted by the refusal of the English to continue the French practice of annual gifts, and foreseeing the future crowding by English settlers, the Indians of the Ohio valley formed a grand confederacy under the leadership of Pontiac, chief of the Ottawa. Every Western fort except Detroit and Pittsburgh was captured, and the frontier from Niagara to Virginia was ravaged. Virginia and Maryland struck back, but Pennsylvania, the worst sufferer, failed to provide adequate defense for her frontiersmen. The uprising was not crushed by Americans, but by British red-coats. If the colonies could not even co-operate for their own defense against the Indians, could there be any doubt that stronger imperial control was needed?

Nor was the Indian question merely one of suppressing a rebellion. How were Indians to be treated after being brought to terms? Should their hunting grounds be reserved for them in the interests of humanity and the fur trade, or, if not, by what means were they to be secured against speculators and land-hungry frontiersmen? It was imperative to provide not only for present emergency but for future developments, a task necessitating centralized control.

Closely connected with the Indian problem was the fur trade. Peltry still dominated the economies of Canada and West Florida, and was a leading interest in New York, South Carolina, and Louisiana. This fur trade was not merely an international rivalry, but a ruthless competition among people of the same country, in a business which knew no ethics. As fast as the peltry of one region was exhausted, the trappers and traders moved further west, where they competed with the Spaniards for an Indian clientele; or by their aggressiveness they stirred up the nearer Indians, who retaliated on the closest white family. Here was another ungrateful task for the harassed officials in London: regulation of a group of unprincipled traders who by antagonizing the Indians endangered frontiersmen and jeopardized the supply of fur.

Even more perplexing was the problem of territorial administration and land policy. Should the extensive domain acquired from France be conserved as an Indian reserve, or opened in whole or part to white settlement? If the latter, should land be regarded as a source of revenue, and assessed with quit-rents, or should quick settling be encouraged? And if so, how? By ceding it to land companies in large tracts, or in small farms to individual settlers? Furthermore, almost every colony had claims. The rights of some, such as Virginia, were well-founded; those of others, such as New York, were tenuous. Any policy Great Britain adopted would step on someone's corns. But the land question was essentially imperial; land policy had to be administered by a central authority.

Finally, there was the political problem. If new settlements were to be established in the West, what degree of self-government should be permitted them, and what should be their relation to the older colonies and to the mother country? The Treaty of 1763 had also given England jurisdiction over some 60,000 French Canadians, men alien in race and faith, and unaccustomed to English traditions of law and administration. Some general scheme of government had to be provided for these habitants and some method discovered to gain the support of their Church.

The Colonies in 1763–73

Let us now briefly survey the British continental colonies, starting at the southern end. West Florida, defined in 1763 as old Spanish Florida west of the Apalachicola and a section of French Louisiana including Mobile, Biloxi, and Natchez, had very few European inhabitants. But an energetic governor set up civil government at Pensacola, summoned an elective assembly in 1766, and advertised for English settlers; within ten years the population had risen to 3700 Europeans and 1200 slaves. The only settlements in East Florida in 1763 were St. Augustine and St. Marks at the mouth of the Apalachicola. The people of St. Augustine, though granted toleration, chose to leave when England took over; no Spaniard could imagine living under alien heretics. South of St. Augustine lived only Indians, mostly of the Seminole branch of the Creek nation; no white man had yet penetrated the Everglades. One Robert Turnbull recruited 1500 settlers from Minorca, Greece, and Italy, and established them at New Smyrna to grow indigo; and their descendants are still there, known as 'Minorcans.' In addition to these, the census of 1771 showed only 288 whites and 900 Negroes in all East Florida, not enough to warrant the calling of an assembly.

Charleston, South Carolina. Though by 1783 it had a population of only 16,000, Charleston was regarded as a 'metropolis' as early as 1762, when this engraving was published, for, with the finest harbor between Chesapeake Bay and the Gulf of Mexico, it was the leading city in the South. (*Library of Congress*)

Georgia had passed her heroic period. No longer was General Oglethorpe drilling kilted Highlanders to pounce on the dons; evangelists like Whitefield and Wesley had gone on to richer fields. An estimated population of 10,000, including a good proportion of slaves, was scattered along or near the coast, planting indigo and rice. However, South Carolina, having gone beyond the 100,000 mark, had become very prosperous. The powerful Cherokee nation, decisively beaten when they went on the warpath in 1759, had been forced to cede more land, and the back-country was opened to settlement. Charleston had become a gay little city, the only town in America north of Mexico that had a permanent theater. North Carolina, by contrast, seemed more of a social democracy, though its democratic manners concealed the fact that there was a large proportion of landless whites.

The more patrician colony of Virginia was still a congeries of individual plantations. Towns there were none, except Williamsburg and the growing seaport of Norfolk. With only 200 houses and fewer than 1000 permanent residents, Williamsburg was a capital of distinction, with a brick state house, governor's palace, and William and Mary College. While the assembly was in session, Williamsburg was gay with balls, dinners, and assemblies; and the taverns did a roaring business. During the rest of the year most Virginians lived on their plantations. The Virginia aristocracy, now fairly stable, dominated the politics of the province. Political power was diffused among the members of the leading families by intermarriage. As Bernard Bailyn has written, 'The unpruned branches of these flourishing family trees, growing freely, met and intertwined until by the Revolution the aristocracy appeared to be one tangled cousinry.' Three families—Robinson, Randolph, and Lee—provided most of the leaders of the House of Burgesses.

From Baltimore to Philadelphia, travelers found the aspect of the country changing. In Delaware, fifteen or twenty miles from Philadelphia, farms became smaller, more frequent, and better cultivated. An Englishman crossing the Schuylkill and entering Philadelphia felt at home; the capital of Pennsylvania, remarked Lord Adam Gordon, was 'a great and noble city,' like one of the larger towns in England, but with a Quaker primness and regularity. Some of the neatly laid-out streets were paved, lined with sidewalks, lighted by whale-oil lamps, and policed at night. Philadelphia, with 18,766 people in 1760, was the largest and most prosperous town in English America. In another ten years it increased by another 10,000 and acquired some fine public buildings, including the handsome Carpenters' Hall, where the First Continental Congress would meet in 1774, and the Old State House, where independence was declared and the Federal Constitution drafted.

Pennsylvania had always been faithful to the religious liberty ideas of her founder, but the 'brotherly love' idea had not worked very well. There were many tensions between the English Quakers, who had the highest social standing, the Germans, whom they regarded as uneducated boors, and the tough Scots-Irish of the back-country, who had not been given their due weight in the assembly. Philadelphia was run by an oligarchy of lawyers and merchants, kept in power by a high property qualification for voting which shut out the lower middle class and the working people.

Proceeding northeastward across New Jersey, our traveler of 1763 would reach New York City, a compactly built little town, third in population in the English colonies, still bearing marks of the Dutch regime. A few blocks away from the stately mansions of merchants facing the Bowling Green or the river were evil slums where day laborers, dockhands, and free blacks lived. There were already enough Irish in New York to celebrate St. Patrick's Day, enough Jews to maintain a synagogue, enough Scots to support a Presbyterian church, and enough Germans to maintain four churches with services in their language. The two Anglican churches, Trinity and St. Paul's, worshipped according to the Book of Common Prayer, praying daily for 'George, our most gracious King and Governour.' In the Province of New York, most aristocratic of the continental colonies, the landed gentry controlled politics. Up-river the Livingston and Van Rensselaer manors comprised almost a million acres; four families owned 200 square miles of Long Island, and on Manhattan Island, hundreds of acres were owned by the Stuyvesant, Bayard, De Lancey, and De Peyster families, to the subsequent enrichment of their descendants.

The New England colonies owed their prosperity largely to fishing, shipbuilding, and maritime commerce. Boston with 17,000 inhabitants was the largest town, but no metropolis; there were a dozen little seaports along the coast from Bridgeport to Portland, each with some maritime specialty; and off-shore Nantucket had already gone in for deep-sea whaling in a big way. All these towns had comfortable brick and wooden houses built in the Georgian style, with excellent interior decoration and well-kept gardens. The shipowning merchants who owned them shared top status with the clergy, a few lawyers, and the physicians. New England as yet had no landed aristocracy. New Englanders were mostly members of one of the Congregational churches. Some were strictly Calvinist, having been stirred up during the Great Awakening; others, especially in the larger towns, had become liberal almost to the point of Unitarianism. Every village had a meetinghouse which served as town hall and church; and all churches, except in Boston and in Rhode Island, were supported by public taxation. In addition, there were in 1763 about a hundred Anglican and Baptist churches and Quaker meetings in New England. Every village had a free school, the towns supported grammar schools (roughly equivalent to our present high schools), and most of the people knew how to read and write.

New England had a more democratic social and political organization than any other section, in large part because land was distributed more equally. In the average country town, almost every adult male could participate in town government. The tory governor of Massachusetts, Thomas Hutchinson, complained of his own colony: 'In most of the public proceedings of the town of Boston persons of the best character and estates have little or no concern. They decline attending town meetings where they are sure to be outvoted by men of the lowest order, all being admitted and it being very rare that any scrutiny is made into the qualifications of voters.' Yet even in New England, the electorate deferred to the leading personages who held offices almost as though they were hereditary prerogatives. Despite Connecticut's republican form of government, two-thirds of the top offices were held by men bearing but twenty-five surnames of 'ancient' families, precisely the same pattern as in 'aristocratic' Virginia.

British Politics and George III

British politics were important in the American Revolution because Parliament initiated the new colonial policy and passed the laws which precipitated the War of Independence. In 1760–70 whigs had successfully eliminated tories by fastening on them the stigma of rebellion in 1745. Even King George called himself a whig, and all the ministries with which the colonists had to deal were whig ministries. But the dominant party was breaking up into factions.

Of the different whig factions, the one which showed most sympathy for the Americans was the 'old whig,' so called because its members claimed to inherit the traditions of 1688. These included the Duke of Richmond, General Conway, the Marquess of Rockingham, his secretary Edmund Burke, Lord Camden, and Isaac Barré; names given to American towns and counties in recognition of their efforts. Usually allied with them were the 'Pittites,' William Pitt and his large personal following. These were the most liberal groups in British politics, and also the most conservative; they opposed taxation of the colonies as much because it was new as because it was unfair. Pitt's following included the Duke of Grafton, who succeeded him as Prime Minister in 1767, and Lord Shelburne, who had a broader vision of colonial problems than any English statesman of his time, especially of the Western question. Unfortunately the old whigs, though rich in talents, were poor in leadership. Rockingham, a young man better known on the turf than in politics, was well-meaning but weak, and a halting speaker in the Commons. Pitt, a peerless leader in time of war, became inept in time of peace; and some strange malady thrust him out of the picture in 1767 almost as soon as he became premier. Next, there were a number of factions following such political free-lances as George Grenville and the Duke of Bedford, whose 'Bloomsbury gang' was notorious for being on hand when the plum-tree was shaken; and finally there was the king, and his friends.

George III, only 22 years old at his accession in 1760, had been brought up under the tutelage of his mother, a strong-minded German princess. 'George, be a *king!*' was his mother's frequent injunction, which he appears to have interpreted as 'George, be a politician!' The young man knew what he wanted, and got it, though it cost him an empire. He wished to beat the whigs at their own game, and restore the power of the Crown by creating and eventually governing through a party of his own. After ministries under men who would not do his bidding had crumbled, George III obtained exactly the government he wanted under his subservient friend, Lord North; and it was this ministry that drove the colonists into revolt, and lost the war.

For the first ten years of his reign, George III was conciliatory toward the colonists. He ordered his friends in Parliament to vote for the repeal of the Stamp Act. When Lord Hillsborough in 1769 proposed to punish Massachusetts by altering her charter, the king refused. But the Boston Tea-Party, the first challenge to his personal rule, aroused his liveliest resentment. In great measure he may be held responsible for the Coercive Acts of 1774, and for the inefficient conduct of the war. If George III, for all his private virtues and well-meaning patriotism, is a pitiable figure in history, it is largely for the opportunities he lost. He might have been a patriot king indeed, by reaching out over the heads of the politicians to his colonial subjects, who were devotedly loyal and attracted by his youth and personality. He did his best for the empire according to his lights; but his lights were few and dim.

George III's ministers were no gang of unprincipled villains, subservient to a royal tyrant. Lord Dartmouth, for instance, who sponsored the Coercive Acts, was a kind and pious gentleman, patron of Dartmouth College and protector of the poet Cowper. Almost every ministry meant well toward the Americans, but almost all were incompetent. The situation called for statesmanship of the highest order; and the political system which George III manipulated to his advantage put statesmanship at a discount, political following at a premium. In the end it was ignorance, confusion, and unresponsiveness to crying needs, rather than corruption or deliberate ill will, which convinced the Americans that their liberties were no longer safe within the British empire. And these three factors—ignorance, confusion, and irresponsiveness—have brought down more governments than we can count, and will continue to do so in the future unless replaced by knowledge, order, and sensitivity.

The Organization of the West

The chain of events that led to the American rebellion began with the situation confronting the Crown in 1763. To cope with the immediate task, the administration and defense of new acquisitions, the Grenville ministry adopted emergency measures for what was thought to be a temporary situation. The ministry decided that settlers must be excluded from the trans-Allegheny country until the Indians were pacified, and a definite land policy worked out. The Royal Proclamation of 7 October 1763 reserved all lands between the Appalachians, the Floridas, the Mississippi, and Quebec for the Indians. Thus at one stroke the Crown swept away every Western land claim of the Thirteen Colonies, and drew a 'Proclamation Line' along the crest of the Appalachians.

In the following year, 1764, an elaborate plan for the regulation of Indian affairs was advanced. As early as 1755 General Braddock had laid the foundations of an imperial Indian policy by appointing two highly capable colonists, Sir William Johnson and John Stuart, superintendents respectively of the Northern and Southern Indians. The 'Plan of 1764' recommended a well-organized Indian service under the control of these superintendents; licenses, regulations, and fixed tariffs for traders; and repeal of all conflicting colonial laws. This was too ambitious a program for immediate fulfillment, but it looked in the right direction.

Before opening the country west of the Proclamation Line to white settlement, it was necessary to purchase territory from the Indians and establish a new boundary west of the Alleghenies. In 1763 Stuart negotiated with the Cherokee nation a treaty establishing the Indian boundary line west of Georgia and the Carolinas. A 1768 treaty extended this boundary north to the Ohio at the confluence of that river with the Great Kanawha. This line called forth a storm of protest from Virginia land speculators and was subsequently adjusted to meet their views. In the same year, Johnson established the line north of the Ohio when by treaty the Iroquois ceded for some £10,000 their rights to a large part of central New York and Pennsylvania as well as their claims to territory south of the Ohio.

Intimately associated with Indian affairs was the pressing question of defense. 'What military establishment will be sufficient? What new forts to be erected?' inquired the secretary of state of the Board of Trade. Pontiac's rebellion made the issue acute. The Board of Trade proposed establishing a chain of garrisons from the St. Lawrence to Florida, and from Niagara to Michilimackinac, with 10,000 soldiers required to garrison these forts and maintain the military establishment in America. An effort to force the colonies to pay for this costly, in fact excessive, military establishment, met stout resistance. But for the time being adequate defense had been provided, the frontiers sufficiently garrisoned, the Indians pacified, the malpractices of Indian traders stopped, and an Indian demarcation line drawn.

Colonial fur traders and British military men wished to keep the West beyond the treaty lines an Indian reservation for the use of the fur traders. Opposed to this policy were the promoters of several big speculative companies. Of these the most important was the Vandalia Company, promoted by Benjamin Franklin, George Croghan, and Thomas Wharton of Philadelphia. The Vandalia aimed to acquire 10 million acres in the Ohio valley, for which it proposed to pay the Crown £10,000. It did, to be sure, promise to assume the cost of administration, and of satisfying the Indians, who of course were not consulted. The Vandalia let in leading English politicians on the ground floor to enlist their active interest, and bribed freely when it thought bribery would do good. Another scheme pressing for a Crown grant was 'Charlotiana,' embracing most of Illinois and Wisconsin, promoted by Franklin and Sir William Johnson. But the Board of Trade and Plantations reported against big land companies on the ground that they would make trouble with the Indians, and that 'inland colonies in America' were contrary to British interests. Let the restless Americans fill up Nova Scotia and the Floridas, where they will export directly to England, and buy British goods! This policy became official in a Royal Proclamation of 1774. It doubtless contributed toward making the big land speculators favor an independent America, which might look more kindly on their schemes, and did.

Two Attempts To Tax the Colonies

The annual cost to Great Britain of maintaining the civil and military establishments in America had risen from some £70,000 in 1748 to well over £350,000 in 1764. In the light of this situation, George Grenville, Chancellor of the Exchequer, felt that it was both necessary and just to extract revenue from the colonies. Parliament greeted this proposition with enthusiastic approval, and even the level-headed Franklin anticipated no trouble from America.

The exact extent of colonial contributions to the upkeep of the empire is not easy to determine. English landowners, paying an income tax of 20 per cent, felt that the colonists could well afford to shoulder some of their burden. But the Americans insisted that they were already carrying their full share, and contributing, directly and indirectly, to the maintenance of the imperial government to the limit of their capacities. The colonies had incurred a debt of over £2.5 million for the prosecution of the war, and, notwithstanding the generosity of Parliament in assuming a part of that debt, a large portion remained. Indirect contributions in the form of English port duties and the monopoly of colonial trade were considerable; William Pitt estimated that colonial commerce brought an annual profit of not less than £2 million to British merchants. Whatever the right of these new revenue measures may have been, events proved their inexpediency quickly enough.

The Revenue Act of 1764—often known as the Sugar Act—was the first of these measures. The preamble stated frankly its purposes: 'That a revenue be raised in your . . . Majesty's dominions in America for defraying the expenses of defending, protecting and securing the same.' It was also designed to plug leaks in the Acts of Trade and Navigation. The law cut the duty on foreign molasses in half, but levied additional duties on foreign sugar and on luxuries such as wine, silk, and linen. It 'enumerated' more colonial products such as hides, which could be exported only to England; and it withdrew some earlier exemptions that the colonies had enjoyed, such as free importation of madeira. That favorite beverage of well-to-do Americans now became subject to a duty of £7 per double hogshead, as against 10*s* on port wine imported through England—an obvious attempt to change the drinking habits of the colonial aristocrats to profit the British exchequer. Colonial leaders promptly seized on the declared revenue-raising purpose of this act as a constitutional point. If Parliament got away with taxing their trade for revenue purposes, it might proceed to tax their lands, or anything. This seemed prophetic when Parliament on 22 March 1765 passed the Stamp Act.

The Stamp Act levied the first direct, internal tax ever to be laid on the colonies by Parliament; indeed, the first tax of any sort other than customs duties. It provided for revenue stamps to be affixed to all newspapers, broadsides, pamphlets, licenses, commercial bills, notes and bonds, advertisements, almanacs, leases, legal documents, and a number of similar papers. All the revenue was to be expended in the colonies, under the direction of Parliament, solely for the purpose of 'defending, protecting and securing the colonies.' Offenses against the law were to be tried in admiralty courts with no jury. As a sugar-coating to the pill only Americans were to be appointed as agents, and a number of unsuspecting colonials such as Richard Henry Lee applied for such positions.

The reaction to the Stamp Act everywhere in the Thirteen Colonies was violent, for it was the peculiar misfortune of the Act to offend the most powerful and articulate groups in the colonies: the merchants and businessmen, lawyers, journalists, and clergymen. Business came to a temporary standstill; trade with the mother country fell off £300,000 in the summer of 1765. Respectable men organized as 'Sons of Liberty' coerced

The Stamp
(*Library of Congress*)

stamp distributors into resigning, burned the stamped paper, and incited people to attack unpopular local characters. On the very day (1 November 1765) that the Stamp Act came into operation, a howling New York mob forced Lieutenant-Governor Colden to take refuge on board a British warship. The mob then attacked the fort at the Battery, broke into the governor's coach house, destroyed his carriages, and compelled the officer in charge of stamped paper to burn the lot. In Charleston, Henry Laurens, wrongly suspected by the local mob of hiding stamped paper in his house, was pulled out of bed at midnight while the house was searched by his friends, whom he recognized under black-face and sailor disguise. In Boston a mob turned its attention to the royal customs collectors and Chief Justice Hutchinson, gutting their houses, burning their furniture, and tossing their books and papers into the street.

The law was completely nullified by violence. Courts reopened, vessels cleared and entered, and business resumed without the use of stamps. All this on the assumption that the law was unconstitutional and void. Virginia led the way in expressing that view. On 30 May, Patrick Henry made his 'Caesar had his Brutus, Charles I his Cromwell' speech, after which the assembly passed a set of resolves declaring that it had 'the only and sole exclusive right and power to lay taxes . . . upon the inhabitants of this Colony,' who were 'not bound to yield obedience to any law' of Parliament attempting to tax them.

A few days after Henry had stirred up Virginia, Massachusetts invited all continental colonies to appoint delegates to a congress to consider the Stamp Act menace. This congress, which met at New York in October 1765, drew delegates from nine colonies. Christopher Gadsden of South Carolina sounded the keynote: 'We should stand upon the broad common ground of natural rights. . . . There ought to be no New England man, no New Yorkers, known on the continent, but all of us Americans.' After the debate the congress adopted a set of resolutions asserting once more that 'no taxes ever have been, or can be constitutionally imposed on them, but by their respective legislatures.'

In August 1765, even before the Stamp Act Congress met, the Grenville ministry fell. An 'old whig' ministry led by the Marquess of Rockingham now came into power. Parliament, encouraged by the king, repealed the Stamp Act in mid-March 1766. The law was repealed simply because it could not be enforced against united opposition, and because English merchants and manufacturers suffered from a boycott of British goods promoted by the Sons of Liberty. Parliament did not thereby renounce the right to tax the colonies, as proved by the fact that on almost the same day as the repeal, it passed a Declaratory Act affirming Parliament's right, as the sovereign legislature of the British empire 'to bind the colonies . . . in all cases whatsoever.' Americans showed their fundamental loyalty to the Crown by taking no notice of the fact that the Revenue Act of 1764 was not repealed, and no notice of the Declaratory Act. Although the colonists rejoiced in their victory, in reality the British government had taken three steps forward—Proclamation of 1763, Revenue Act, Declaratory Act; and only one back, repeal of the Stamp Act.

The Townshend Acts

During the jubilation that followed repeal of the Stamp Act, no serious effort was made by the British government to find out what, if anything, could be done to raise defense funds through colonial assemblies. No royal commission was sent to America to study and report. Instead, a fresh attempt was made by Parliament to tax the colonists, and a plan of imperial reorganization was placed in effect without consulting them.

The audacious new British initiative came from Charles Townshend, brilliant, ambitious, and unprincipled, who, taunted by George Grenville in the Commons that he dared not try to tax America, retorted, 'I will, I will!' and did. He proposed to reduce the British income tax by one-quarter and meet part of the resulting deficit by obtaining revenue from the colonies. This was to be done by collecting import duties in the colonies on English paint, lead, and paper; and on tea. As the colonies had always paid some customs duties, how could they object to these? For more efficient collection a Board of Commissioners of the Customs was established at Boston, and new vice-admiralty courts were created. Writs of assistance, whose legality had been challenged by James Otis in 1761, facilitated entry into private premises. Most important of all, the money thus raised in the colonies, instead of going to support the garrisons, was to be used to pay the salaries of royal governors and judges and thus render them independent of colonial assemblies.

The Townshend Acts took Americans by surprise, but colonial leaders were hard put to find a legal argument against the duties. They wished to deny Parliament's power to tax them, yet to acknowledge Parliament's power to regulate their commerce, for they were not prepared to break loose from the protective system of the Acts of Trade and Navigation.

The colonial leader who came closest to resolving this dilemma was John Dickinson of Pennsylvania, who styled himself 'the Pennsylvania Farmer,' but actually was a conservative Philadelphia lawyer. Neither agitator nor politician, Dickinson was a public-spirited citizen, devoid of ambition or vanity, who abhorred violence and hoped to settle all pending disputes with England by persuasion. His twelve 'Farmer's Letters,' which began coming out in colonial newspapers at the end of 1767, were exactly what Americans wanted; and the loyal, respectful tone of them appealed to many in England. Dickinson conceded that Parliament had the right to regulate, even to suppress commerce, but he denied that it had the right to levy internal taxes or even port duties. Nonetheless, he counselled restraint:

> Let us behave like dutiful children, who have received unmerited blows from a beloved parent. Let us complain to our parent; but let our complaints speak at the same time the language of affliction and veneration.

Samuel Adams of Boston, boss of the town meeting and leader in the assembly, had already reached conclusions that went well beyond those of Dickinson. He believed that Parliament had no right to legislate for the colonies on any subject. But he was too clever a politician to let that out now. An austere, implacable member of Boston's

Samuel Adams (1722–1803), firebrand of the American Revolution. This 1771 portrait by his fellow Bostonian John Singleton Copley (1738–1815), often regarded as the first important American painter, was commissioned by John Hancock. Pointing to the Massachusetts charter, Sam Adams protests to the lieutenant-governor of the colony against the stationing of red-coats in Boston. (*Museum of Fine Arts, Boston*)

middle class, this 'Matchiavel of Chaos' was a typical revolutionary. A master of propaganda, he realized that people want entertainment with their politics, and Adams provided it in highly agreeable forms. There was dancing around the Liberty Tree, a big elm near Boston Common selected for that purpose; unpopular characters were hanged in effigy from its branches, and those whom the radicals wished to become popular were serenaded. His favorite motto was *principiis obsta*, 'Take a stand at the start,' lest by one appeasement after another you end in complete subjection. No orator, Adams let other Sons of Liberty like Joseph Warren and the firebrand Otis make the speeches while he wrote provocative articles for the newspapers and organized demonstrations.

In February 1768 Adams and Otis drafted (and the Massachusetts assembly adopted) a circular letter to the lower houses of all continental colonies to call their attention to the Townshend laws. The assembly, stated this letter, has 'preferred a humble, dutiful and loyal petition to our most gracious sovereign . . . to obtain redress.' The language of this circular letter was as moderate and loyal as that of Dickinson, but the Grafton ministry decided to make it the occasion for a showdown. Lord Hillsborough, the new secretary for the colonies, ordered the Massachusetts assembly to rescind the letter, and Governor Bernard to dismiss them if they refused. The assembly did refuse, by a vote of 92 to 17. And it was supported by a set of Virginia resolves introduced by the burgess from Fairfax County, Colonel George Washington, and signed, among others, by the new burgess from Albemarle County, Thomas Jefferson. Adams and the Sons of Liberty everywhere made heroes of the patriotic '92,' who refused to rescind.

In Boston the chief contributor to the Sons of Liberty war chest for free rum at Liberty Tree rallies was a 31-year-old merchant, John Hancock. The new Commissioners of the Customs therefore determined to put him out of business. He was 'framed' by a prosecution of his sloop *Liberty*, falsely charged with smuggling madeira. A Boston mob rescued him and his vessel, and gave the royal customs officials a very rough time. Governor Bernard asked for protection, and two regiments of the Halifax garrison were sent to Boston.

The presence of British red-coats in Boston was a standing invitation to disorder. It did not take long for antagonism between citizens and soldiery to flare up. In the so-called 'Boston Massacre' of 5 March 1770, snowballing of the customs house guard swelled into a mob attack, someone gave the order to fire, and four Bostonians, including a black named Crispus Attucks, lay dead in the snow. Although provocation came from civilians, Samuel Adams and Joseph Warren seized upon the 'massacre' for purposes of propaganda. The British soldiers were courageously defended by young John Adams, Sam's cousin, and Josiah Quincy, and acquitted of the charge of murder; but the royal governor was forced to remove the garrison from the town to the castle, and the strategic advantage lay with the radicals.

On the very day of the 'Boston Massacre,' the new British ministry headed by Lord North repealed all the Townshend duties except the one on tea. A tax of three pence per pound was kept on this article primarily as an assertion of parliamentary authority. 'A peppercorn in acknowledgment of the right is of more value than millions without it,' George Grenville had said; and easy-going Lord North acquiesced in this glib fallacy.

Except for that teasing little duty on tea, all outward grievances of the colonists had been removed by the summer of 1770. The radicals found themselves without an issue. Sam Adams did his best to keep up the agitation, with annual exhibits of bloody relics of the 'Boston Massacre,' but the people showed what they thought of him by defeating him for registrar of deeds in his home county. In New York soldiers of the garrison could promenade their girls on the Battery without being insulted. Prosperity reigned, imports into New England alone jumping from £330,000 to £1.2 million. It looked as if colonial agitation were at an end.

But Sam Adams was simply waiting for some unwise move by the North ministry to revive it.

Back-country Turmoil

Parts of the 'back-country' were full of turmoil during the years of agitation against the Stamp and Townshend Acts; but this turmoil had nothing to do with the America versus England controversy. It was caused by discontent with local governing classes. In Pennsylvania, in 1764, a band of frontier hoodlums known as the 'Paxton Boys,' furious at their lack of protection during Pontiac's rebellion by the Quaker-dominated assembly, took a cowardly revenge by massacring some peaceful members of the Conestoga tribe in Lancaster County. The 'Paxton Boys' then threatened to wipe out the so-called Moravian Indians, an Algonquian tribe which had been converted by Moravian missionaries and settled on a reservation near Bethlehem. These Indians fled to Philadelphia where the government quartered them in barracks, protected by British regulars. The 'Boys,' 1500 strong, heavily armed and uttering 'hideous outcries in imitation of the war whoop,' marched on the capital in February 1764, bent on killing every redskin refugee. Philadelphia was in a panic, and it took Ben Franklin to talk the ruffians into returning home, by promising more frontier protection and legislative bounties for scalps. The Pennsylvania back-country then quieted down, but bided its time to obtain more weight in the assembly.

This situation became most explosive in the Carolinas, where back-country society differed in origin, religion, and even race from that of the seaboard. In North Carolina the separation between coastal region and interior was very sharp. Here the Western grievances were not lack of government, but bad government—unequal taxation, extortion by centrally appointed judges and corrupt sheriffs, greedy lawyers, uncertainty of land titles, scarcity of hard money to pay taxes, refusal of the assembly to provide paper money or to allow taxes to be paid in produce, consequent tax levies 'by distress,' and sheriffs taking over poor men's farms.[1] A particular complaint was a province law which allowed only Anglican clergymen to perform marriage ceremonies, when there were no such clergy in the back-country! The Regulators marched on Newbern, site of the royal governor's palace, but being untrained and partly unarmed, they were easily defeated by half their number of loyal militia, 16 May 1771, at the so-called Battle of the Alamance. Casualties were only nine men killed on each side, since the Regulators ran away after the first volley. But fifteen of them were captured and tried for treason, and six were hanged. Governor Tryon and his army then made a triumphal progress through Regulator country and exacted an oath of allegiance from every male inhabitant.

That was the end of the 'War of the Regulation,' the most serious internal rebellion in the English colonies since Nat Bacon's. It was put down largely by whigs who later became patriots, though Martin Howard, the hanging judge, became a prominent loyalist. The next assembly passed some remedial legislation, but the North Carolina back-country was still so full of discontent in 1776 that many former rebels emigrated to Tennessee to avoid taking part in the war, and others became tories.

Back-country brawls from New Hampshire to South Carolina seem never to have interested the British government, which thereby missed a golden opportunity to win support from frontiersmen against the silk-stockinged Sons of Liberty and their 'wharf-rat' confederates. But London was involved in another Western problem. In 1774 the British government ordered royal governors to grant no land, and permit no new settlements, except after prior survey, allotment, and sale by auction. Although not put into effect outside Canada, this order called forth Thomas Jefferson's bold *Summary View of the Rights of British America*, denying the Crown's right to dispose of any Western land. It furnished one more grievance for the Declaration of Independence. Yet the United States public land system was based on exactly the same concept.

1. Note similarity of these grievances to those of Shays's rebels in Massachusetts in 1786. And it is significant that Herman Husband, leader of the North Carolina Regulators, turns up 25 years later as a Whiskey rebel in Pennsylvania.

The Issue Joined

Samuel Adams's genius was for agitation and destruction. Yet he was no mere rabble-rouser, greedy for power. He believed (and the Lees of Virginia, the New York Sons of Liberty, and Gadsden of South Carolina agreed) that 'every day' in the calm period of 1770–73 'strengthens our opponents and weakens us.' They were right. Prosperity dulled vigilance, and the efficiency of the Commissioners of the Customs brought in such ample revenue even after the Townshend duties were repealed that the British government put one royal governor and judge after another on the Crown payroll. The radicals fumed against this in vain—the average colonist thought it fine to be relieved of paying his governors and judges! Adams felt that if this system were allowed to go on, Americans would wake up some day and find that they were helpless under royal officials. But he needed a spectacular, emotional issue to bring home this danger before it was too late. In the tea affair, he found it.

The powerful East India Company, being in financial straits, appealed to the British government for aid and was granted a monopoly on all tea exported to the colonies. The Company decided to sell tea through its own agents, thus eliminating the independent merchants, and disposing of the tea at less than the usual price. This monopoly aspect aroused the colonial merchants and threw them again into alliance with the radicals. Burke, in his speech on conciliation, gauged well the American temper. 'In other countries, the people . . . judge of an ill principle in government only by an actual grievance; here they anticipate the evil. . . . They augur misgovernment at a distance, and snuff the approach of tyranny in every tainted breeze.'

Colonial reaction to the tea monopoly took various forms. In Charleston the tea was landed, but not offered for sale; at Philadelphia and New York the consignments were rejected and returned to England. But in Boston the ingenious Sam Adams brought about a dramatic showdown. Here, on the night of 16 December 1773, Sons of Liberty disguised as Mohawks boarded the three tea ships and dumped the offending leaves into the water. The radicals had called the ministerial bluff. They had refused even the peppercorn in acknowledgment of right.

The Boston Tea-Party accomplished just what Sam Adams wanted. The destruction of property—and tea at that—aroused John Bull more than mobbing officials and beating up redcoats. 'The die is now cast,' wrote George III to Lord North. 'The Colonies must either submit or triumph.' The House of Commons, now obedient to the king and Lord North, passed in May-June 1774 a series of Coercive Acts. These closed the port of Boston until the tea was paid for, drastically changed the provincial government in Massachusetts, and provided for the transportation of certain offenders to England for trial. These laws threatened the very life of Boston. To exclude her from the sea, the element that made her great, was a punishment comparable to the destruction of Carthage.

These 'Intolerable Acts,' as the colonists called them, were quickly followed by the Quebec Act of 1774. This statute of Parliament, the outcome of a carefully thought-out plan to give a permanent government to Quebec, was received by the colonists as yet another punitive measure. They viewed the provisions of the law, which extended the boundaries of Quebec to embrace the vast country west of the Appalachians and north of the Ohio, as a deliberate attempt to discourage expansion by the colonists beyond the mountains and to ignore their land claims. They were even more disturbed by a statement of the privileges of the Catholic Church in Canada. Young Alexander Hamilton warned that 'priestly tyranny' might 'find as propitious a soil in Canada as it ever has in Spain and Portugal.' The Quebec Act, aimed at conciliating the French habitants, had the unanticipated consequence of feeding North American rebellion, and the Coercive Acts rallied the other English colonies to Massachusetts. On 27 May 1774 members of the Virginia Assembly, meeting in the Raleigh Tavern at Williamsburg, called for a congress of all continental American colonies. 'Clouds, indeed, and darkness,' said Edmund Burke, 'rest upon the future.'

The First Continental Congress which as-

Americans throwing the Cargoes of the Tea Ships into the River,
at Boston

(*Library of Congress*)

sembled in Carpenters' Hall, Philadelphia, on 5 September 1774, had been summoned not for independence but for liberty, as Americans understood that word. They expected Congress to take steps to ward off parliamentary wrath, vigorously to assert colonial rights, and happily to restore imperial relations to their former agreeable status. The Continental Congress was an extra-legal body chosen by provincial congresses, or popular conventions, and instructed by them. This meant that the patriot party was in control of the situation, and that extreme conservatives who would have nothing to do with resistance to the laws were not represented. Otherwise, the membership of the Congress was a fair cross-section of American opinion. Here were extremists like the Adamses of Massachusetts, Richard Henry Lee and Patrick Henry of Virginia, and Christopher Gadsden of South Carolina; moderates like Peyton Randolph (chosen president of the Congress) and George Washington of Virginia, John Dickinson of Pennsylvania, and the Rutledges of South Carolina; conservatives like John Jay of New York and Joseph Galloway of Pennsylvania. Every colony except Georgia sent at least one delegate, and the total number was fifty-five—large enough for diversity of opinion, small enough for genuine debate and effective action.

Able as this Congress was, it faced a distressing problem. It must give an appearance of firmness to persuade or frighten the British government into concessions, but at the same time avoid any show of radicalism that might alarm conservative Americans or encourage the spirit of lawlessness and leveling that was already abroad in the country.

Lawlessness, as the conservatives called it, got in the first lick. While Congress was discussing a statesmanlike plan of union presented by Joseph Galloway, Paul Revere came galloping from Boston to Philadelphia with the radical Suffolk Resolves in his saddlebags. These resolutions, as drafted by Joseph Warren and adopted by a convention of the towns around Boston, declared the Coercive Acts to be unconstitutional and void, urged Massachusetts to arm and act as a free state until these 'attempts of a wicked administration to enslave America' were repealed, and called on Congress to adopt economic sanctions against Great Britain. Congress, by a majority of one colony, shelved Galloway's plan (similar to the Albany Plan of 1754) and endorsed the Suffolk Resolves, which Galloway considered 'a declaration of war against Great Britain.' Congress then proceeded to adopt new and more stringent non-importation, non-exportation, and non-consumption agreements. In practice, by denying the colonists needed supplies, these sanctions hurt the Americans more than the British.

Having agreed upon this counteroffensive, Congress passed a Declaration of Rights and Grievances addressed to the people of Great Britain and the colonies; and, as a sop to the moderates, a petition to the king. These papers, taken together, led the Earl of Chatham to declare in the House of Lords: 'For genuine sagacity, for singular moderation, for solid wisdom, manly spirit, sublime sentiment and simplicity of language . . . the Congress of Philadelphia shines unrivalled.' The Declaration of Rights anticipated in many particulars the Declaration of Independence, but did concede parliamentary regulation of commerce.

This concession did not please the radicals. Independently of one another, James Wilson of Pennsylvania, Thomas Jefferson, and John Adams had reached the conclusion that Parliament had no rightful jurisdiction over the colonies. 'All the different members of the British Empire,' said Wilson, 'are distinct States, independent of each other, but connected together under the same sovereign in right of the same Crown.' Wilson's *Considerations on the Authority of Parliament*, Jefferson's *Summary View*, and Adams's *Novanglus* papers published this startling theory between August 1774 and February 1775. Historically they found no ground for Parliament's authority, although they admitted that the colonies had weakly accepted it; logically there was no need for it, since the colonial legislatures were competent. The colonists should honor and obey the king, follow his lead in war, observe the treaties he concluded with other princes; but otherwise govern themselves. They demanded for the Thirteen Colonies the same dominion status which is now the official basis of the British Commonwealth of Nations. But these doctrines had no remote chance of acceptance. Very few Englishmen could understand how a community could be in the empire, unless parliamentary authority over it were complete.

The most important work of the Congress was an agreement called 'The Association.' This provided for committees of inspection in every town or county, whose duties were to supervise the non-importation, non-exportation, and non-consumption agreements. The Association was charged to publish the names of merchants who violated these sanctions, to confiscate their importations, and to 'encourage frugality, economy, and industry.' Congress also voted to give up imported tea and wines. Rum, however, was still a patriotic beverage. Thus the Congress called to protest against parliamentary usurpation ended by creating extra-legal machinery for supervising American daily life. The Association caused many moderates to draw back in alarm. 'If we must be enslaved,' wrote the loyalist Samuel Seabury, 'let it be by a king at least, and not by a parcel of upstart, lawless committeemen.' Having done all this, Congress rose on 22 October 1774, resolving to meet again the following May if colonial grievances had not been redressed by then.

Hostilities Begin

Before Congress reconvened, fighting broke out. Inevitably, when war came, it began in Massachusetts. Since the previous autumn Massachusetts, as suggested by the Suffolk Resolves, had become

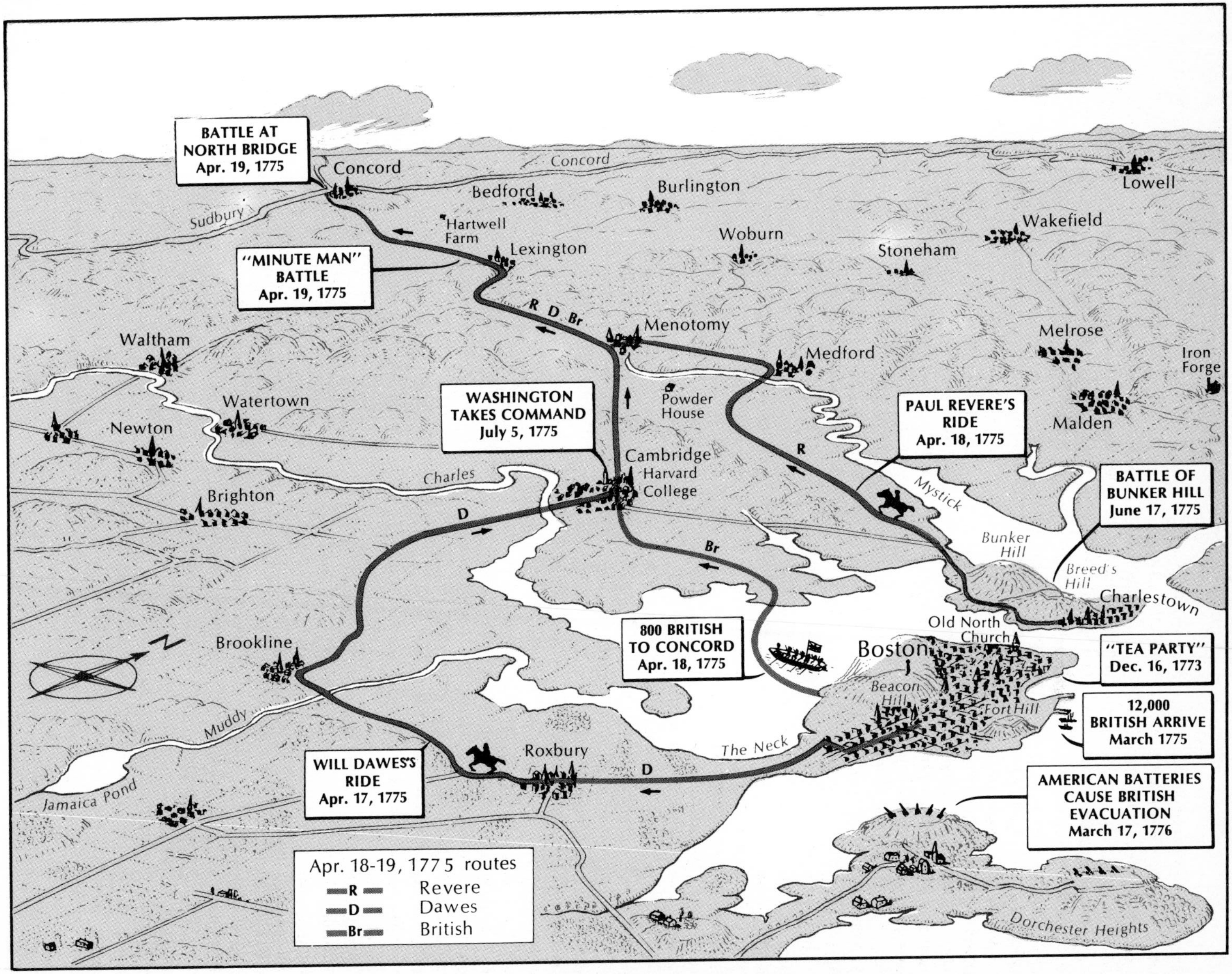

The Boston Region at the Opening of the War of Independence, 1773–1776

a free state, governed by a popularly elected provincial congress and a committee of safety which organized armed resistance. On 18 April 1775, the British general, Thomas Gage, on hearing that the revolutionary committee was collecting military stores at Concord, sent a strong detail of his garrison to destroy them. A rude surprise awaited the red-coats, for sounding the alarm 'through every Middlesex village and farm,' Paul Revere and Will Dawes aroused the whole countryside. When Major Pitcairn, after a night of marching, led his column of light infantry into the village of Lexington, he saw through the early morning mists a grim band of minute-men lined up across the common. There was a moment of hesitation, cries and orders from both sides, and in the midst of the confusion somebody fired. Then firing broke out along both lines and the Americans dispersed, leaving eight of their number dead on the green. The first blood of the War for American Independence had been shed. Who first fired, American or Englishman, is one of the unsolved riddles of history; but the patriots managed to circulate their own view of it as a brutal and wanton attack on peaceful villagers.

The British continued their march to Concord, where the 'embattled farmers' at the bridge 'fired the shot heard round the world.' Their purpose partially accomplished, the British regiments began their return march. All along the road, behind stone walls, hillocks, and houses, the minute-men made targets of the bright red coats. When the weary column finally stumbled into Boston it had lost 247 in killed and wounded. Inside of a week Boston was a beleaguered city.

On 10 May 1775, while the country was still resounding with the 'atrocities' of Lexington and Concord, the Second Continental Congress assembled in Philadelphia. The prophetic words of Patrick Henry were still ringing in the ears of the delegates: 'It is vain, sir, to extenuate the matter. Gentlemen may cry "peace, peace" but there is no peace. The war is actually begun! The next gale that sweeps from the north will bring to our ears the clash of resounding arms! Our brethren are already in the field! Why stand we here idle?' Even as Congress met questions, Ethan Allen and his Green Mountain Boys were crashing into Fort Ticonderoga and raising the standard of revolt in the North. Control of events was rapidly drifting out of the hands of law-abiding men, and Congress was forced to recognize accomplished facts.

The delegates to this second Congress, a very distinguished group, have achieved historical immortality as the 'signers.' John Hancock, the wealthy Boston merchant, was chosen president after the death of Peyton Randolph. Young Thomas Jefferson was there, fresh from composing his *Summary View;* and the venerable Dr. Franklin, so discouraged by his vain search for conciliation in London as to have become an exponent of independence. Yet the radicals did not push through their program of accepting war and declaring independence without a severe struggle. John Dickinson again raised his voice in favor of conciliation, and persuaded his reluctant colleagues to adopt another petition to the king.

Even as Congress was debating, it took the militia besieging Boston into its service, and then appointed Colonel George Washington commander-in-chief of the armed forces of the United Colonies. On 23 June Washington rode off from Philadelphia to take charge of the army. En route he heard the stirring story of Bunker Hill. On 17 June 1775 the British garrison in Boston made a frontal assault on a hill in near-by Charlestown, which the patriot militia had fortified. They won the hill, but it cost them 1054 killed and wounded out of 2200 troops engaged. As the first real stand-up battle between New England troops and British red-coats, it was a strategic victory for the Americans. Shortly after, Congress authorized a project which the British could only consider wantonly aggressive: an overland expedition to Quebec under Benedict Arnold, to bring Canada into the Union as the fourteenth colony. In October 1775 Congress began organizing a navy, in November it created the Marine Corps, and in December it sent the Continental fleet of eight converted merchantmen to raid Nassau in the Bahamas.

Independence

Nevertheless, over a year elapsed after Bunker Hill before Congress could make up its mind to declare independence. The very idea was repug-

The Battle of Bunker Hill, 17 June 1775. Historians have yielded to the popular impression in identifying this encounter which actually took place not on Bunker's Hill but on Breed's Hill on Charlestown peninsula. This illustration shows the Hill raked by British ships and land batteries. (*National Gallery of Art*)

nant to many members of Congress and to a large part of the American people. Magna Carta, Drake, Queen Elizabeth, the Glorious Revolution, the Bill of Rights, Marlborough, Wolfe—these were British memories in which the colonies had shared. Must they break with all that?

On 8 July 1775, after the news of Bunker Hill had reached Philadelphia, Congress adopted, at Dickinson's urgent request, the 'Olive Branch Petition' to George III, assuring His Majesty in most loyal and respectful terms of the 'ardent' desire for 'a happy and permanent reconciliation.' This petition was signed by almost every subsequent signer of the Declaration of Independence. As late as the autumn of 1775, the legislatures of North Carolina, Pennsylvania, New Jersey,

New York, and Maryland went on record against independence, and in January 1776 the king's health was toasted nightly in the officers' mess presided over by General Washington.

Yet the colonies could not forever remain half in, half out of the empire, professing allegiance while refusing obedience. The popular theory that they were not fighting the king or the mother country but a 'ministerial' army made little sense. Many, however, still hoped for a political crisis in England that would place the friends of America in power. But King George refused to receive the 'Olive Branch Petition,' and proclaimed the colonies to be in a state of rebellion (23 August 1775). On 22 December 1775, Parliament interdicted all trade and intercourse with the Thirteen Colonies.

Early in January 1776, before news of that vital step toward severance reached America, Thomas Paine's pamphlet *Common Sense* presented in popular form the natural rights philosophy that was to be embodied in the Declaration of Independence. 'Society in every state is a blessing, but Government, even in its best state, is but a necessary evil; in its worst, an intolerable one.' With ruthless disregard for tradition and sentiment Paine attacked the monarchy and the British Constitution. Monarchy, he argued, was a ridiculous form of government; one honest man worth 'all the crowned ruffians that ever lived'; and 'the Royal Brute of Great Britain,' George III, the worst of the lot. How absurd, too, that a continent should be governed by an island! This unnatural connection subjected the colonies to exploitation, and involved them in every European war. Independence would bring positive benefits, such as a world market for American trade. Anticipating the policy of isolation, Paine announced it to be 'the true interest of America to steer clear of European contentions, which she can never do while, by her dependence on Great Britain, she is made the make-weight in the scale of British politics.' Thus with persuasive simplicity Paine presented the alternatives: continued submission to a tyrannical king, an outworn government, and a vicious economic system; or liberty and happiness as a self-sufficient republic. Within a month this amazing pamphlet had been read by or to almost every white American. It rallied the undecided and the wavering. 'Every Post and every Day rolls in upon us Independence like a Torrent,' observed John Adams exultantly.

In each colony a keen struggle was going on between conservatives and radicals for control of its delegation in Congress. As yet only a few delegations were definitely instructed for independence; it was the task of the radicals to force all into line. In Pennsylvania the struggle was particularly bitter, coinciding with the ancient feud of Scots-Irish frontiersmen and city artisans against Quakers and the wealthier Germans. The radicals here achieved success by overthrowing the old government, establishing a new one with full representation of their frontier counties, and drawing up a new constitution. This new government promptly instructed the Pennsylvania delegates for independence. The effect on the Congress sitting in Philadelphia was overpowering.

Events now moved rapidly toward independence. In January 1776 patriots burned Norfolk to prevent its falling into the power of Governor Dunmore. In March the North Carolina legislature instructed its delegates to declare independence and form foreign alliances. Congress then threw American ports open to the commerce of the world, and sent an agent to France to obtain assistance. In early May news arrived that George III was sending over 12,000 German mercenaries to dragoon his American subjects. On 10 May, Congress advised the colonies to establish independent state governments; Virginia and others proceeded to do so. On 7 June Richard Henry Lee rose in Congress and moved 'That these United Colonies are, and of right ought to be, Free and Independent States.' After a terrific debate, Lee's motion carried on 2 July. In the meantime Congress had appointed a committee which consisted of Thomas Jefferson, John Adams, Benjamin Franklin, Roger Sherman, and Robert Livingston to prepare a formal declaration 'setting forth the causes which impelled us to this mighty resolution.' This Declaration of Independence, written by Thomas Jefferson, was adopted 4 July 1776.

The Great Declaration

The Declaration of Independence announced not only the birth of a new nation; it expressed a theory which has been a dynamic force throughout the world. Out of a 'decent respect to the opinions of mankind,' Jefferson summed up, not only the reasons which impelled Americans to independence, but the political and social principles upon which the Revolution itself rested. The particular 'abuses and usurpations' charged against the king are not advanced as the basis for revolution, but merely as proof that George III's objective was 'the establishment of an absolute tyranny over these states.' The Declaration rests, therefore, not upon particular grievances but upon a broad basis which commanded general support in Europe as well as in America. Some of the grievances, examined in the candid light of history, seem distorted, others inconsequential. One of the strongest, an indictment of British support of the African slave trade, was struck out at the insistence of Southern and New England delegates. But Jefferson was not writing history; he was trying to influence its course.

The indictment is drawn against George III. The only reference to Parliament is in the clause, 'He has combined with others to subject us to a jurisdiction foreign to our constitution and unacknowledged by our laws, giving his assent to their acts of pretended legislation.' Thus the odium of parliamentary misdeeds is transferred to the hapless George III. The main reason for fixing all the blame on poor George was to undermine traditional American loyalty to the Crown. Government, according to the theory which almost everyone then believed, was the result of a compact between ruler and people to protect 'life, liberty, and the pursuit of happiness.' And, to quote the Declaration, 'Whenever any form of government becomes destructive to these ends, it is the right of the people to alter or abolish it, and to institute new government, laying its foundation on such principles and organizing its powers in such form, as to them shall seem most likely to effect their safety and happiness.' By breaking the compact, the king had released his subjects from their allegiance.

Whatever the origin of government may have been in prehistoric times, in America it often arose just as Jefferson described. As in the Mayflower Compact of 1620, so in countless frontier settlements from the Watauga to the Willamette, men came together spontaneously and organized their own governments. Jefferson's philosophy seemed to them merely the common sense of the matter.

The Loyalists

The Declaration of Independence divided those who hoped to solve the problem of imperial order by evolution from those who insisted on revolution. By calling into existence a new nation it made loyalty to King George treason; and in most colonies patriot committees went about forcing everyone, on pain of imprisonment and confiscation of property, to take an oath of allegiance to the United States. Thus it gave to the loyalists or tories the unpleasant alternative of submission or flight.

There were loyalists in every colony and in every walk of life. In New York, New Jersey, and Georgia they probably comprised a majority of the population. Although it is impossible to ascertain their number, the fact that some 80,000 loyalists left the country during the war or after, and that everyone admitted these to be a minority of the party, gives some index of their strength. Most loyalists took the required oaths and paid taxes, while praying for the defeat of the American cause, simply because they had no place to go. As late as 1830 there were old ladies in New York and Portsmouth, N.H., who quietly celebrated the king's birthday, but drew curtains and closed shutters on the Fourth of July.

The American Revolution was a civil rather than a class war, with tories and whigs finding supporters in all classes. Outside Virginia and Maryland, most of the greatest landowners were tory, although many remained passive during the war to save their property. Yet the loyalists also won the allegiance of many back-country farmers in New York and the Carolinas. Officials went tory as a matter of course; so, too, most of the Anglican clergy, whose church prescribed loyalty to one's lawful sovereign as a Christian duty. The merchants in the North, except in Boston and the smaller New England seaports, were pretty evenly divided; and many lawyers remained faithful to the Crown. In general the older, conservative, established, well-to-do people were inclined to oppose revolution, but there were countless exceptions. Jonathan Trumbull, though an arch-conservative, was nonetheless the only colonial governor to repudiate his oath of allegiance to the king and throw in his lot with the rebels. Many families were divided. Gouverneur Morris's mother was a tory; so too was Benjamin Franklin's son, William, the royalist governor of New Jersey.

Although most of the prominent leaders of the Revolution were gentlemen, they could not carry their entire class into a revolution which involved not merely separation from the mother country but the stability of society. The question of home rule in the empire could not be divorced from the question of who would rule in America. When the conservatives realized that liberty could be won only by opening the floodgates to democracy, many drew back in alarm. Even some of the radical patriots had their bad moments. John Adams, riding home from the Continental Congress, was accosted by a horse-jockey, who declared that he hoped there would never be another court of justice in Connecticut. 'Is this the object for which I have been contending? said I to myself. . . . If the power of the country should get into such hands, and there is a great danger that it will, to what purpose have we sacrificed our time, health and everything else?' To what purpose indeed! This question forced itself upon the consideration of every thoughtful man, and when independence was achieved, it became a burning question.

The loyalist minority played a variety of roles in the war. Some did very effective fighting for the king. New York furnished more soldiers to George III than to George Washington. Loyalist marauders quartered in New York City frequently harried the shores of Long Island, and tory 'partisans,' often allied with Indians, committed atrocities on civilians of the other side. But for the most part the loyalists were good people of respectable principles. The attitude of those Americans who fought to hold the empire together in 1776 was no different from that of Southern Unionists like General Thomas and Admiral Farragut in 1861; and the difference between success and failure, more than that of right and wrong, explains the different 'verdict of history' toward these two great civil wars.

5

The War of Independence

*

1775–1783

A Divided Effort

The surprising thing about the War of Independence when you compare it with other wars of liberation is not that the Americans won, but that they did not win more easily. All they had to do to gain independence was to hold what they had. The British, on the contrary, had to reconquer a vast territory in order to win. To get troops in action against the 'rebels' of 1775–83, the British government had to send them by bulky, slow-moving sailing vessels which never took less than four weeks (and often ten) to cross the Atlantic. Moreover, those who 'came three thousand miles and died, to keep the Past upon its throne,' had to be armed, clothed, and even partly fed from England, which meant more shipping, more delays, more losses at sea, and such expense as had never been known in English history.

The direction of the war came under the Colonial Secretary of the North ministry, Lord George Germain, who is represented in the savage political cartoons of the day as wearing a white feather. He had been dismissed from the army after the Battle of Minden for something that looked like cowardice, yet had risen in politics through a combination of personal effrontery, family influence, and royal favor. His field commanders objected that he issued fussy orders but would not accept responsibility. 'For God's sake, my Lord, if you wish me to do anything, leave me to myself,' protested Sir Henry Clinton. 'If not, tie me down to a certain point and take the risk of my want of success.' Yet Germain's real shortcoming was that he never grasped the revolutionary character of the uprising.

However, the Revolutionary War was fought with such peculiar want of enthusiasm that in America it took the form of civil war. Many people were loyalists, many were simply apathetic. Washington wrote in the fall of 1775, 'Such a dearth of public spirit, and want of virtue, such stock-jobbing, and fertility in all the low arts to obtain advantages of one kind or another . . . I never saw before and pray God I may never witness to again. . . . Could I have foreseen what I have, and am likely to experience, no consideration upon Earth should have induced me to accept this command.' He was to experience less virtue and more politics as the war went on; but his own steadfast patriotism never wavered.

Raising an army presented formidable difficulties. Americans were not eager for sustained warfare. They preferred turning out under a popular local leader like John Stark or Francis Marion to repel an invasion or do a little bushwhacking, then go home to get in the hay. Steady service in an army so ill-fed, paid, and clothed was distasteful; and the average American, though he wished his side to win, saw no need of continuous fighting. When New England was cleared of the enemy, it was difficult to get Yankees to go to the aid of the Middle States or the South; after the first enthusiasm of 1775 it was equally difficult to get Southerners to serve in the North; and the people of the Middle States, where most of the fighting occurred, hung back even there. It proved necessary to offer bounties to raise troops, and the value of the bounties had to be increased steadily. The total who served and counted as veterans, and as ancestors for members of patriotic societies, was several hundred thousand. But Washington's army reached its peak of strength with a little over 20,000 in mid-1778. No provision was made for the families of men in service, and no pensions were paid to the dependents of those who fell; so enlistments were largely restricted to the very young, the adventurous, the floating population, and the super-patriotic.

Although the spokesmen of Irish-Americans, German-Americans, and other minorities like to claim that the American army was largely composed of themselves, there is no evidence of ethnic groups favoring either side. Negroes served in every line regiment of the Continental army and in John Paul Jones's ships. Virginia slaves in the armed forces were liberated at the end of the war. Yet the large numbers of blacks who escaped to British lines to gain their freedom gave a note of doubt to the claim of the patriots that they were fighting for liberty. After the war the British refused to repatriate refugee slaves, and it is possible that as many blacks as white tories departed America.

The weakness of the American government contributed to slackness in the fight. The Continental Congress had no legal authority. It passed resolutions, not laws; it issued requisitions, not orders. In providing arms and munitions, Congress did rather well, but in raising troops and in coping with feeding and clothing the army, it did very ill. War finance was so unstable that by 1780 Continental currency was worth only one-fortieth of its specie value; within a year it ceased to pass. 'Not worth a Continental' was a phrase for complete worthlessness well into the nineteenth century. The government depended heavily on loans from Europe, especially from France, but also in later years from Spain and private bankers in the Netherlands. There was great improvement after February 1781, when Congress appointed Robert Morris, a wealthy Philadelphia merchant, superintendent of finance. He stopped waste and corruption in spending, placed government finances on a specie basis, organized the first American bank of deposit and issue (the Bank of North America), and reformed military purchasing; during the last year of the war, after Yorktown, the army was much better paid, clothed, and fed. But he did not and could not improve revenue; and a financial collapse was just around the corner when the war ended.

Military Operations, 1775–77

Even before the Declaration of Independence there were military operations which affected the outcome of the war. The colonists did not hesitate to assume the offensive. Richard Montgomery, with a little over a thousand men, taking the classic route of the Hudson and Lake Champlain, captured Montreal on 12 November 1775. About six hundred of Benedict Arnold's equal force got through the wilderness of Maine to Quebec, after incredible hardships. They poled, pushed, and dragged their way in flat-bottomed boats up the Kennebec, across a twelve-mile carry, through a complicated chain of ponds and small streams, across a snow-covered mountain pass, and—those who had boats left—down the rapids of the Chaudière river, while the rest, cold and starving, stumbled north along deer trails. Rendezvous was made with Montgomery near Quebec. As many of the troops' terms of enlistment expired on New Year's Day 1776, Montgomery and Arnold delivered a premature assault on Quebec, the strongest fortress in America, in a blinding snowstorm on

Phillis Wheatley. This engraving is the frontispiece of *Poems on Various Subjects, Religious and Moral,* published in London in 1773. A Senegalese-born slave, she was encouraged by her master, a Boston tailor, to pursue her talent for writing verse. Doubts were raised about whether work of such high quality could have come from a black woman, and Jefferson had to vouch for the originality of her poetry. But instead of being resentful at her plight, Phillis Wheatley was thankful that 'young in life, by seeming cruel fate *[she]* was snatched from Africa's fancy'd happy state.' (*Library of Congress*)

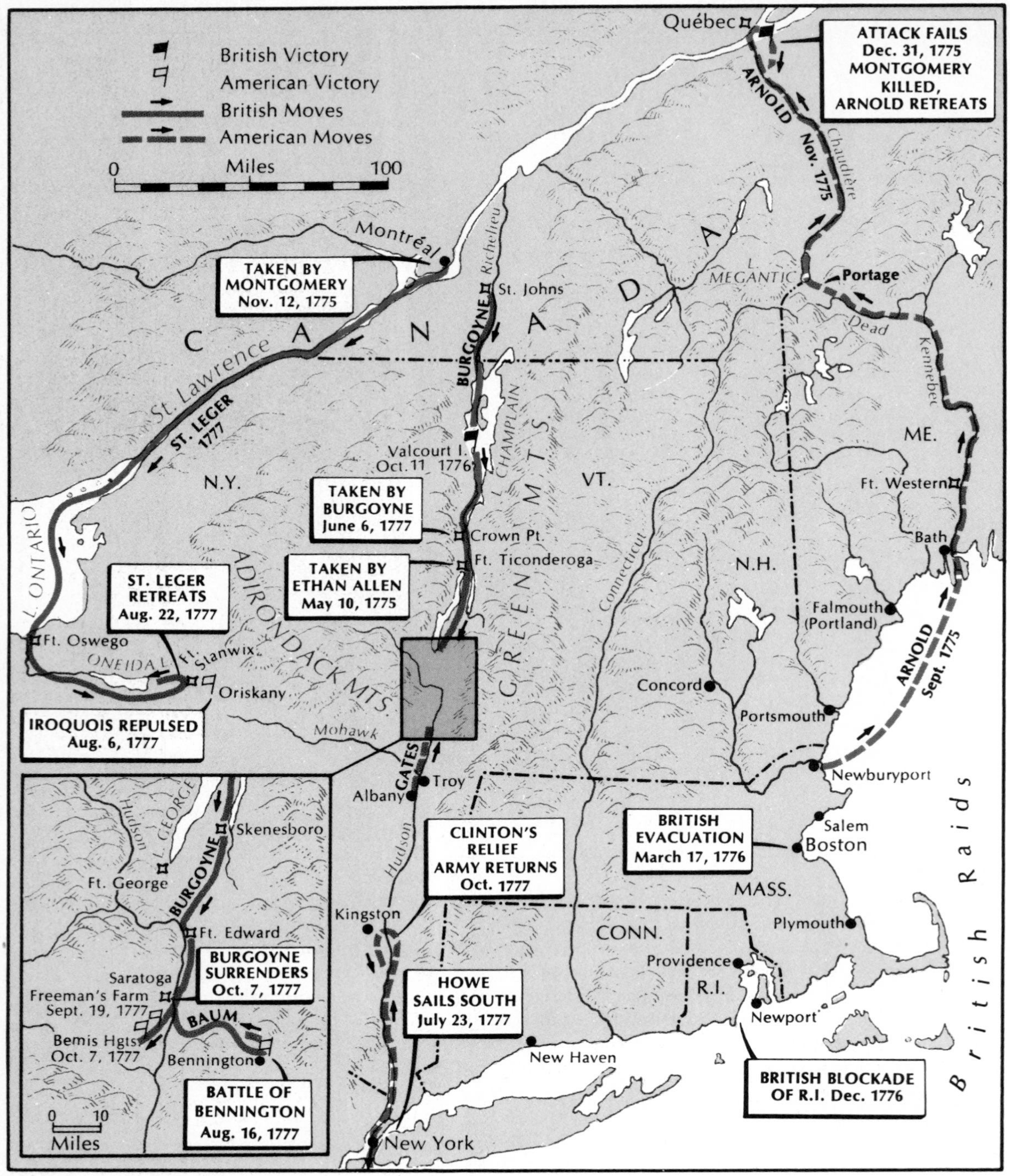

British Victory
American Victory
British Moves
American Moves
0 Miles 100
Québec
ATTACK FAILS Dec. 31, 1775 MONTGOMERY KILLED, ARNOLD RETREATS
ARNOLD Nov. 1775
Chaudière
Montréal
TAKEN BY MONTGOMERY Nov. 12, 1775
Richelieu
St. Johns
L. MEGANTIC
Portage
Dead
Kennebec
C A N A D A
St. Lawrence
BURGOYNE
ST. LEGER 1777
L. CHAMPLAIN
GREEN MTS.
Valcourt I. Oct.11 1776
N.Y.
VT.
ME.
Ft. Western
TAKEN BY BURGOYNE June 6, 1777
Crown Pt.
TAKEN BY ETHAN ALLEN May 10, 1775
Ft. Ticonderoga
Connecticut
Bath
N.H.
L. ONTARIO
ST. LEGER RETREATS Aug. 22, 1777
ADIRONDACK MTS.
Falmouth (Portland)
ARNOLD Sept. 1775
Ft. Oswego
ONEIDA L.
Ft. Stanwix
Oriskany
Concord
IROQUOIS REPULSED Aug. 6, 1777
Mohawk
Portsmouth
GATES
Troy
Albany
Newburyport
Hudson
L. GEORGE
Skenesboro
Ft. George
BURGOYNE
Ft. Edward
BURGOYNE SURRENDERS Oct. 7, 1777
Saratoga
Freeman's Farm Sept. 19, 1777
BAUM
Bemis Hgts. Oct. 7, 1777
Bennington
BATTLE OF BENNINGTON Aug. 16, 1777
0 10 Miles
CLINTON'S RELIEF ARMY RETURNS Oct. 1777
BRITISH EVACUATION March 17, 1776
Salem
Boston
MASS.
Kingston
CONN.
Plymouth
Providence
R.I.
HOWE SAILS SOUTH July 23, 1777
Newport
New Haven
BRITISH BLOCKADE OF R.I. Dec. 1776
British Raids
New York

The Northern Campaign of 1775–1777

the last night of 1775. Montgomery was killed, Arnold wounded; and although Congress sent reinforcements, the expeditionary force was compelled to retreat, and Canada remained British. The Arnold-Montgomery campaign had an important bearing on the war. It alarmed the British government for the safety of Canada and caused it to divide the largest force of regulars yet dispatched across the Atlantic and to send almost half of it to Quebec. This ultimately would result in the most decisive American victory of the entire war at Saratoga, but the immediate impact was disheartening.

The colonists had better success in defensive actions. At Moore's Creek Bridge in North Carolina on 27 February 1776 patriot militia badly defeated a band of loyalists led by Donald McDonald, kinsman of Bonnie Prince Charlie's guide Flora, who tried to cut their way through to the coast with a great skirling of pipes and flashing of claymores. A new expeditionary force from Ireland commanded by Lord Cornwallis, with a detachment of British regulars from Boston under Sir Henry Clinton, was forced to try Charleston, S.C., instead. Charleston is a remarkably hard nut to crack, as Spaniards, British, and Yankees have discovered to their cost. Local patriots drove off the ships, and Clinton and Cornwallis, baffled, retired. So the British were denied a Southern base in 1776. About the time of the Moore's Creek fight, Washington, still besieging Boston, resolved to finish up. Seizing and fortifying Dorchester Heights, he placed his artillery in a position to blast the enemy out of Boston. General Billy Howe decided it was time to leave, and, happily for modern Boston, chose St. Patrick's Day 1776 to evacuate his army.

Howe arrived at his next objective, New York, on 2 July 1776. The Howe brothers, liberal in politics and friendly to America, brought an olive branch as well as a sword. All they had to offer (so Ben Franklin drew from them at a conference on Staten Island) was royal clemency to the rebels if they would stop fighting. Franklin refused to negotiate except on the basis of independence. It would have been well for both countries if the British had accepted this condition then, instead of six years later. But national honor forbade the British to relinquish the Thirteen Colonies without a fight, and with 30,000 men and a navy to oppose Washington's land force of 18,000, it seemed as if the contest would soon be over.

Washington, on his side, felt that he could not honorably abandon New York City without a struggle. He promptly fortified Brooklyn Heights, and prepared to defend them; but Howe quickly shifted his army to the Americans' rear. In the ensuing Battle of Long Island (27 August 1776) Washington's plan was faulty, his generals did not carry out their assignments, all the breaks went against him, and British numbers were overwhelming. On 29 August Washington executed a masterly retreat in small boats to the Manhattan shore. Howe now occupied New York City, and during the remainder of the war that city remained a British base and a tory refuge.

Washington, his army weakened in morale and in men, retreated into New Jersey. This strategy was to save the army to save the cause. By the end of 1776 his army was hardly five thousand strong. The rest had simply dwindled away: deserted, gone absent without leave, or left when terms of enlistment were up. These were 'the times that try men's souls,' wrote Tom Paine. Howe, in that dreary autumn, lost several chances to capture Washington's army; for Howe waged war in the dilatory manner of European campaigns. There seemed to be no hurry. Every month the Americans grew weaker; Jersey loyalists were hospitable; gentlemen did not fight in winter. So Washington reached the far bank of the Delaware before Howe's outposts reached the near bank. But in March 1777, when the roads began to thaw, Washington had only 4000 men, and the British appeared to have everything their way. They could even contemplate an ambitious grand strategy to extinguish the rebellion.

General Burgoyne now mounted his bold tripartite campaign to cut off New England from the rest of the states, and seize Philadelphia. His idea was to march south by the line of Lake Champlain and the Hudson to Albany. Sir John Johnson, son of old Sir William of the Mohawks, promised to bring thousands of Mohawk valley tories and Iroquois braves to help. Howe, after detaching a force to meet Burgoyne up-river,

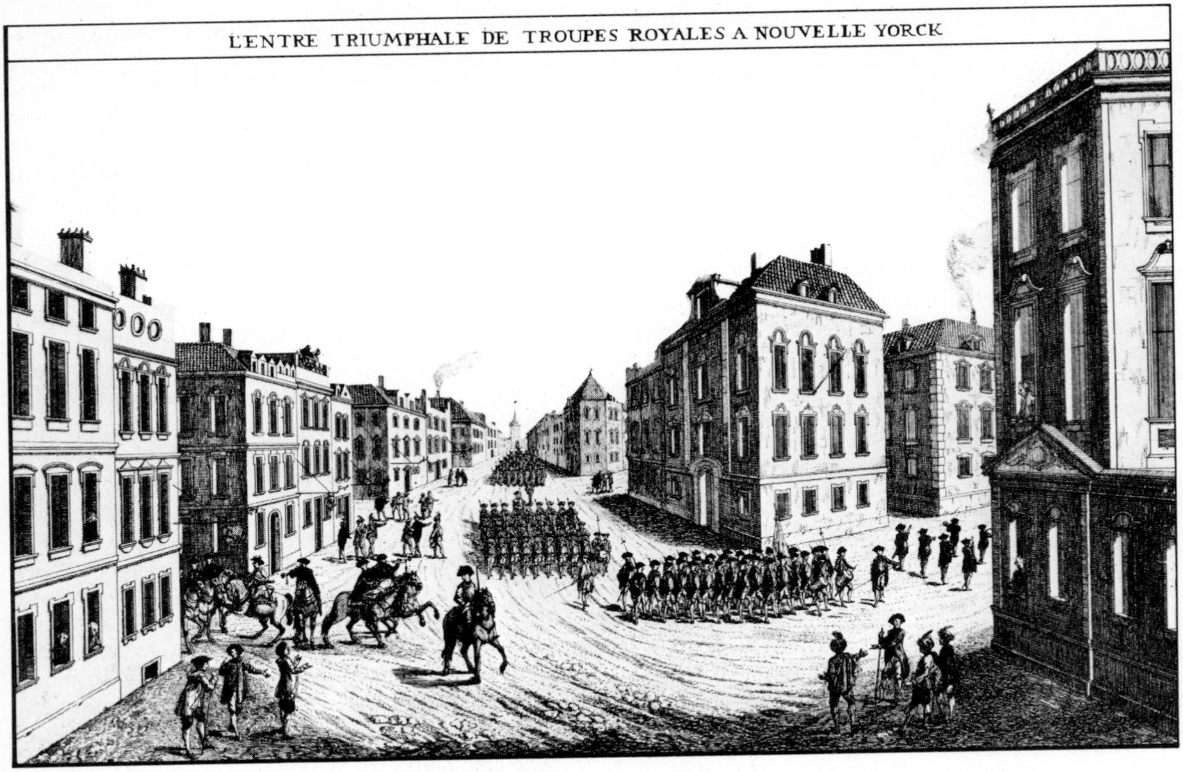

The red-coats march through New York City, 1776. This *vue d'optique,* or 'peep-show' print, was shown in Europe as a sort of newsreel in mirrored boxes; hence the reverse title at the top of the picture. (*Eno Collection, New York Public Library*)

would himself capture Philadelphia, and perhaps proceed farther south. The weakness of the plan lay partly in the difficulty of obtaining coordination at such a distance. Howe did not learn that he was expected to help Burgoyne until 16 August, when the bulk of his force was embarked in transports in Chesapeake Bay. But the fatal British mistake was to ignore the conditions of warfare in America. The several transfers between Lake Champlain, Lake George, and the Hudson meant an enormous apparatus of baggage and portable boats, ample delays, and plenty of warning to the enemy. European tactics were helpless against a countryside in arms: for the countryside in Europe never rose; warfare there was a professional game.

In the summer of 1777, General Howe advanced on Philadelphia. All Washington could do against greatly superior forces was to retard his advance at the Brandywine Creek (9 September 1777). Howe occupied Philadelphia on 26 September, and Washington's gallant attack on the British forces at Germantown (3–4 October) failed completely. The British settled down to a comfortable winter at the former seat of Congress, while Washington went into desolate winter quarters at Valley Forge, only a few miles away.

In the meantime the greatest American victory

of the war had been won, on the line of the Hudson. The British army in Canada, some seven thousand strong with a thousand Canadian militia and Indians, jumped off from the St. Lawrence on 1 June, and advanced southward with bright prospects. On 6 July, Burgoyne took Fort Ticonderoga. By 29 July he had reached Fort Edward on the upper Hudson. Here he waited for more supplies from Canada. 'Gentleman Jack' Burgoyne would make no concession to wilderness conditions; he must have his service of plate, his champagne, and thirty wagons for his personal baggage. Burgoyne imagined it would be an easy matter for a raiding force to march across Vermont to Bellows Falls, down the Connecticut river to Brattleboro, and back 'by the great road to Albany' in two weeks. For this exploit he chose 375 dismounted German dragoons, the slowest marchers in his army, and about 300 tories, Canadians, and Indians. They did not even reach the Vermont line. John Stark and his Green Mountain Boys marched out from Bennington to meet them; and after that battle, on 16 August, very few of the Germans returned. Much the same fate met Colonel Barry St. Leger, who commanded a raid from Oswego to Fort Stanwix. He and Sir John Johnson's forces were no match for the Mohawk valley militia under General Herkimer, when reinforced by a column under Benedict Arnold; St. Leger retreated to Canada on 22 August.

In militia fighting, nothing succeeds like success. The Battle of Bennington brought a general turnout of the fighting population of northern New England, and Burgoyne's delay at Fort Edward enabled Washington to dispatch regulars from the lower Hudson. When in early September Burgoyne finally got his unwieldy force in motion, he marched into a hornets' nest of Yankee militia, flushed with the success of their fellows, and stiffened by regulars. The American Northern army, which now outnumbered Burgoyne's two to one, was commanded by Horatio Gates, a timid general who fortunately had Benedict Arnold as his second in command. At Freeman's Farm (19 September) Arnold's audacious leadership and tactical skill won the day. On 7 October Burgoyne lost another fight at Freeman's Farm, and retreated to Saratoga. Americans were now in front, rear, and flank in overwhelming numbers. So on 17 October 1777, at Saratoga, Burgoyne surrendered his entire army, still over five thousand strong, to General Gates.

This was the decisive blow of the war, for it brought England's hereditary enemy to the American side.

Enter France

France had been waiting for *revanche* since 1763, and America provided the occasion. In the spring of 1776 Congress sent Silas Deane to France to procure clothing, munitions, and supplies. These he obtained secretly from the government of Louis XVI. After July 1776 Franklin and Arthur Lee were sent to join Deane, with instructions to obtain covert or open assistance, and to offer a treaty of amity and commerce. John Adams then, and always, was against an 'entangling alliance,' but the American military situation became so desperate toward the close of 1776 that Congress authorized Franklin to conclude an alliance if necessary to obtain France as a full-fledged ally.

Here indeed was a spectacle to delight the gods—smooth Ben, sleek Silas, and suspicious Arthur selling a revolution to the most absolute monarch in Europe. Actually the sale was not difficult. The French intellectual world hated feudalism and privilege, and admired republican simplicity. Washington seemed a new Cincinnatus; and ardent young men, of whom the Marquis de Lafayette was easily the first, hastened to place themselves under his command.[1] Moreover, the government had practical reasons. England must be humbled and the balance of power redressed in favor of France. French manufacturers were eager for a new market in America, closed to

1. Other foreign officers who greatly helped the American cause were Baron von Steuben, who introduced a modified Prussian drill and discipline in the Continental army; Thaddeus Kosciuszko of Poland, an admirable artillery officer; Count Casimir Pulaski of Poland, mortally wounded at Savannah; the Baron de Kalb, who died of his wounds at the Battle of Camden; and the Chevalier du Portail, an accomplished officer of engineers.

them by the British Acts of Trade. Still, though the French gave the United States unneutral aid in the shape of munitions and supplies, and welcomed Yankee privateers to French seaports, Vergennes shrank from the expense of direct intervention.

This 'short of war' policy lasted until after the news of Burgoyne's surrender at Saratoga. It then changed because Vergennes feared lest this disaster induce the English government to make such liberal concessions as would reunite the empire. He was not far wrong. Lord North was eager to recognize American independence as soon as he heard of the defeat at Saratoga; but the king refused, though he would concede everything short of independence in order to keep the American states nominally under his sovereignty. A bill introduced by North appointed a peace commission with authority to make an amazingly broad offer: parliamentary taxation of the colonies to be renounced; no military forces to be kept in the colonies without their consent; the Coercive Acts of 1774 and all other Acts of Parliament to which Congress objected—even the Acts of Trade—to be repealed, if America would but acknowledge the sovereignty of the king; these concessions to be guaranteed by treaty. This was more than Congress had wanted in 1775, all that Adams, Wilson, and Jefferson suggested in their pamphlets, almost all that Canada enjoys today. If the peace commission had reached America before news of the French alliance, its terms might well have been accepted; but, as usual, the British offer came too late.

On 6 February 1778, eleven days before the conciliatory bill passed Parliament, Franklin signed treaties of commerce and of alliance with Vergennes. Each nation promised to make common cause with the other until American independence was recognized. It was a generous treaty, in which America obtained everything and promised nothing except to defend French possessions in the West Indies. Great Britain promptly declared war on France, and the War of Independence became world-wide. Spain entered as an ally of France in 1779, and proved useful by opening New Orleans as a base for privateers and by capturing British posts in West Florida.

So, by 1780 there were naval operations on the Atlantic Ocean, the Mediterranean, the Caribbean, the North Sea, the English Channel, even the Indian Ocean. The shot at Concord bridge literally had been heard around the world.

Military Operations 1778–82

The year 1778 was one of incompetence and failure on both sides, redeemed only by the indomitable patriotism of Washington. While his troops suffered in frigid Valley Forge, Sir William Howe's men reveled in Philadelphia. Howe was recalled in the spring of 1778, and his successor, Sir Henry Clinton, was ordered to evacuate the city and to concentrate on New York in preparation for a new campaign. On 28 June, Washington attacked Clinton's retiring army at Monmouth Court House, New Jersey, a confused battle in which an American disaster was barely averted by Washington. Clinton's army reached New York safely; and all that Washington could do was to encamp at White Plains, fortify West Point, and look on. The only successful American campaign of 1778 was that of George Rogers Clark, acting for the state of Virginia. He shot the rapids of the Ohio, and led his little force across the wilderness to take the British post of Kaskaskia in Illinois, first in a series of bloodless victories. When the British struck back, the intrepid Clark in the dead of winter marched his men 180 miles through icy floods, until sick, sodden, and weary they arrived at Vincennes to surprise the disbelieving British.

At the end of that dismal year, the British turned the war in a new direction. An amphibious operation captured Savannah from its weak Continental garrison on 29 December 1778, then overran the settled part of Georgia, reinstated the royal governor, summoned an assembly, and virtually restored that state to the British empire. From Savannah an augmented force marched overland against Charleston, burning plantations and kidnapping slaves en route. Charleston was successfully defended by its small Continental garrison, and Savannah was attacked by a formidable expedition under the commander of the French fleet, Admiral the Comte d'Estaing. But in

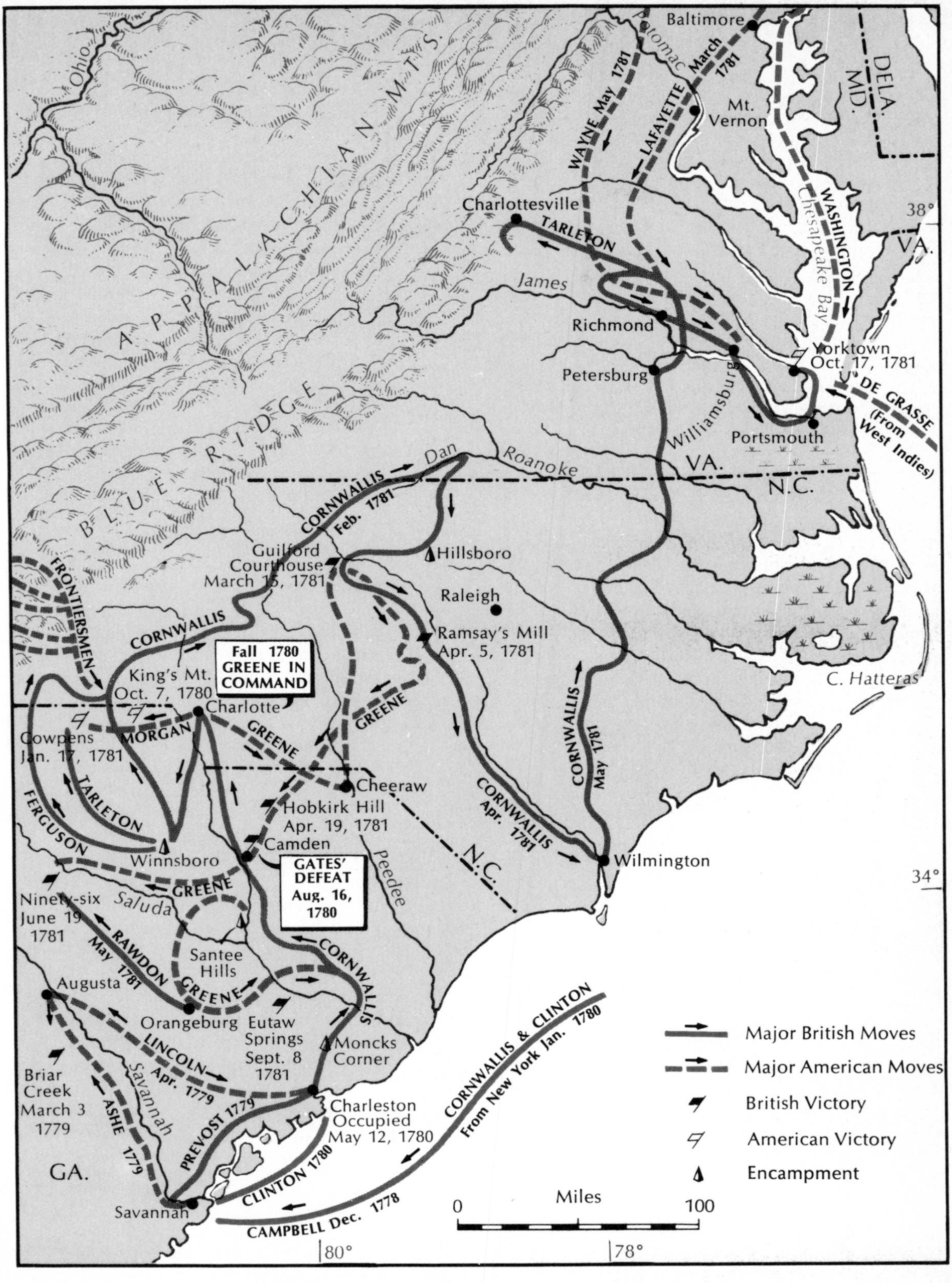

The Seat of War in the South, 1779–1781

the assault (9 October 1779) Count Pulaski was killed at the head of his legion. D'Estaing, twice wounded, re-embarked his landing force and sailed for France. A year and a half had elapsed since the French alliance, and so far it had produced little but disappointment.

The recovery of Georgia and the repulse of D'Estaing gave the British a bold strategic idea: a big amphibious expedition to capture Charleston, and with the aid of local tories set up loyal governments in the Carolinas, roll up all American fighting forces into Virginia, then secure that pivotal state, and Chesapeake Bay. There was nothing wrong with the plan, but the Carolina tories were not formidable enough, the British army treated the people so savagely as to drive even loyal men into rebellion, and the French navy intervened at a crucial moment. The Southern campaign opened brilliantly for Britain when a massive amphibious operation compelled the surrender on 12 May 1780 of Charleston and 5500 men, the worst disaster of the war for American arms. Washington now detached all Southern line regiments from his army which was watching New York, and sent them on the long march south, to stiffen local militia and form a new army. However, Congress, against Washington's advice, appointed to this command Horatio Gates and placed him over the able and courageous Baron de Kalb. Lord Cornwallis, an excellent soldier, beat Gates badly at Camden, S.C., on 16 August, Gates leading the rout on his fast thoroughbred. And Baron de Kalb was mortally wounded.

Cornwallis now had South Carolina pretty well in hand, but cavalry leader Patrick Ferguson went a bit too far when he threatened the 'hillbillies' of the Watauga country to pay them a visit and hang their leaders. They completely wiped out his tory force at its position on Kings Mountain on 7 October 1780. Kings Mountain proved that the British were not invincible, and thousands of small farmers enlisted under partisan leaders like Francis Marion, 'the swamp fox,' Andrew Pickens, and Thomas Sumter.

Congress now shelved galloper Gates for good, and let Washington choose a general for the Southern army, Nathanael Greene. This gifted son of a Rhode Island farmer, generally conceded to be the ablest general officer after Washington on the American side, found the defeated army in a terrible state. 'Nothing can be more wretched and distressing than the condition of the troops,' he wrote to Washington, 'starving with cold and hunger, without tents and camp equipage. Those of the Virginia line are literally naked, and a great part totally unfit for any kind of duty.' Only about a thousand men were effective. Somehow, Greene instilled a new spirit in them, obtained food and clothes (not uniforms, nobody ever saw a Continental uniform on anyone under a colonel in the Carolina campaign) from the countryside; and in a brilliant, shifty campaign inflicted so many losses on Cornwallis at Cowpens (17 January 1781) and Guilford Courthouse (15 March) that the British army had to retire to the coast.

However, after being reinforced and refreshed by his ocean supply line at Wilmington, N.C., Cornwallis marched north into Virginia. On 1 August 1781 Cornwallis occupied Yorktown and began turning that little town into a military base, to help the Royal Navy control Chesapeake Bay, Maryland, and Virginia.

Sea power was decisive in the War of Independence, but it was not until 1780 that the allies were able to challenge British sea supremacy. An American navy was improvised from Marblehead fishing schooners during the siege of Boston, and at least 2000 privateers were commissioned. The most successful warships were those fitted out or operated in European waters with the co-operation of French and Spanish authorities. Captain John Paul Jones raided English shipping in the narrow seas, and spiked the guns at Whitehaven near his old home in Scotland. Subsequently Franklin got him command of a small fleet in France, of which the flagship was an old French Indiaman, which Jones renamed *Bonhomme Richard*. She won a desperate battle with H.M. frigate *Serapis* off Flamborough Head on 23 September 1779. Jones's exploits made him the hero of countless ballads, chapbooks, and folk tales. Yet the Royal Navy continued to command American waters and enabled the British army to be moved from place to place by sea at will, while Washington's army had to walk if it wanted to get any-

Commodore John Paul Jones (1747–92). This bust of America's greatest naval hero was executed by Jean Houdon, the foremost French sculptor of the eighteenth century. Houdon's talent won wide recognition when he was only twelve, and at twenty he was awarded the coveted Prix de Rome. Houdon made busts of Rousseau, Voltaire, and Napoleon and carved 'Diana the Huntress' for Empress Catherine of Russia. In 1785 Franklin brought him to America where he did a bust of Washington that has been widely reproduced. (*Museum of Fine Arts, Boston*)

where. Fortunately for America, the French navy was at a high point of morale and efficiency, whilst the British navy was full of dry rot and grossly mismanaged.

When the French decided to intervene, they did so in grand style. Persuaded by Lafayette to make a real effort to bring the war to an end, Louis XVI sent over a splendid expeditionary force of 6000 men under General Rochambeau, which occupied Newport in the summer of 1780. For a year, in want of naval support, it did nothing except enrich Rhode Island farmers and amuse their daughters. But in May 1781 a powerful fleet under the command of a first-rate seaman, Admiral Grasse, arrived at Cape Haitien. The military-naval campaign of Yorktown was one of the most smoothly executed operations in the history of warfare, considering that it involved coordinated movements between two French fleets, an American and a French army, all widely separated, and with no faster means of transport or communication than sailing ships and horses.

In July 1781 Grasse decided to strike Cornwallis's army at the Chesapeake. On 5 August he sailed with his grand fleet and 4000 men of the Haiti garrison under General the Marquis de Saint-Simon. Precisely one month later, as the forces of Washington and Rochambeau were marching southward to join him, Grasse inflicted a bad beating on a portion of the British fleet in the Battle of the Capes of the Chesapeake. The French were now masters of Chesapeake Bay and able to boat Washington's and Rochambeau's armies to positions about Yorktown. The combined allied armies under Washington, Rochambeau, and Saint-Simon, together with Virginia militia, totaled 15,000 men; Cornwallis had about half that number, but his position was well fortified. Two of his redoubts were carried by American and French assaulting parties, and an attempt to escape across the York river was unsuccessful. On 17 October 1781 Cornwallis surrendered his entire force. As the British passed through the allied lines to stack arms, the military bands played 'The World Turned Upside Down.'

Lafayette joyfully wrote the news to Paris, concluding, 'The play is over; the fifth act has just come to an end.'

It was not quite that simple. Grasse's fleet sailed for the Caribbean (where it was badly beaten by the British on 12 April 1782); Rochambeau's army went to the West Indies; and Washington at the close of 1781 found himself back at White Plains watching Clinton, with no French allies at hand. During the summer of 1782 British warships and privateers based in New York were sweeping the waters off the coast. Washington felt this to be the most critical moment of the war. On 18 July he wrote, 'At present, we are inveloped in darkness.' Fortunately, the British will to victory, feeble at best, had completely evaporated. The only fighting on American soil in 1782 was in the West. British-allied Indians raided deep into Pennsylvania, western Virginia, and Kentucky. But George Rogers Clark collected 1100 mounted riflemen and on 10 November 1782 routed the Shawnee near Chillicothe, Ohio. That was the last land battle of the War of American Independence.

The Peace of Paris

If the soldiers had spoken all their parts, the sailors still had something to say; and the diplomats were just warming up behind the scenes.

Before Cornwallis's surrender, it rather looked as if the United States could only obtain peace and independence on the basis of an *uti possidetis* truce—'keep what you have'—which would have meant that Great Britain would retain the principal seaports from New York to Savannah, and Spain (France's ally but not ours) would hold both banks of the Mississippi and the shores of the Gulf of Mexico. No progress had been made toward peace when news of the victory at Yorktown reached Europe. George III still insisted he would never sanction 'getting a peace at the expense of a separation from America.' When Lord North finally threw in the sponge, George III went so far as to draft a message of abdication. But he thought better of it, and in March 1782 called Rockingham to form a ministry, together with Shelburne, Charles James Fox, and others who were traditional friends of America. Shelburne at once sent Richard Oswald to Paris to sound out Dr. Franklin.

Franklin was not to be the sole negotiator, only one of a commission of five appointed by Con-

Washington as lackey. In this contemporary British cartoon, the leader of the American rebellion is depicted in a servile role. (*Library of Congress*)

Washington as victor. This nineteenth-century American lithograph presents him as the triumphant commander, 'first in war' as well as 'first in peace and first in the hearts of his countrymen.' (*Library of Congress*)

gress. Their instructions were intended to place the United States completely under the guidance of Vergennes in the negotiations, but John Jay, one member of the peace commission, was by nature suspicious and had witnessed intrigues of the French minister at Philadelphia. John Adams shared his suspicions. Franklin, too, was converted to a separate negotiation with England, though this was contrary to the instructions from Congress. On 30 November 1782 the preliminary treaty was signed with the proviso that it not take effect until France reached agreement with Great Britain. Definitive peace was only concluded on 3 September 1783.

This Peace of Paris gives the lie to the epigram that 'America never lost a war, or won a peace conference.' Considering that the British still held New York, Charleston, Savannah, Detroit, and several other posts in the Northwest, that Washington's army was almost incapable of further effort, and that the British navy had recovered command of the sea, it is surprising what wide boundaries and favorable terms the United States obtained, though precise location of boundaries occasioned controversy for a long time. Americans also retained fishing privileges in the territorial waters of British North America. Article IV provided that 'creditors on either side shall meet with no lawful impediment' to the recovery of pre-war debts, including several million pounds owed by Americans to English merchants, but this article the United States found itself powerless to enforce for many years. Nor did the agreement that Congress should 'earnestly recommend' to the several states to restore tory property amount to much. Despite all these disadvantages from a British perspective, George III brought himself to accept 'the dismemberment of America from this Empire.' But he remained in character to the last. He would be even more miserable about the loss of America, he wrote to Shelburne, 'did I not also know that knavery seems to be so much the striking feature of its Inhabitants.'

6

From Colonies to Confederation

*

1775–1789

Forming New Governments

At the same time that the Americans were winning independence from Great Britain they were transforming colonies into commonwealths. The Revolution furnished Americans an opportunity to give legal form to their political ideals, or, as John Adams put it, to 'realize the theories of the wisest writers.' As James Madison could write, 'Nothing has excited more admiration in the world than the manner in which free governments have been established in America; for it was the first instance, from the creation of the world . . . that free inhabitants have been seen deliberating on a form of government, and selecting such of their citizens as possessed their confidence, to determine upon and give effect to it.' Americans are so accustomed to living under written constitutions that they take them for granted; yet the institution of a written constitution came out of America.

As early as 10 May 1776 Congress passed a resolution advising the colonies to form new governments 'such as shall best conduce to the happiness and safety of their constituents.' Some, such as New Hampshire and South Carolina, had already done so, and Massachusetts had established a provisional government in the fall of 1774. Within a year after the Declaration of Independence every state except Massachusetts, Connecticut, and Rhode Island had drawn up a new constitution. Massachusetts labored under her provisional government until 1780, while the two others retained their colonial charters, with a slight change in the preamble, until well into the nineteenth century.

The Pennsylvania constitution thanked God for 'permitting the people of this State, by common consent, and without violence, deliberately to form for themselves such just rules as they shall think best for governing their future society.' Yet a method of adopting new constitutions was not easily found. Three were framed by legislative bodies without any specific authorization, and promulgated by them without popular consent. In five others, the legislative bodies or provincial congresses which framed the constitutions did so by express authority, but failed to submit the finished product to popular approval. In Maryland, Pennsylvania, and North Carolina the constitutions framed by authorized legislatures were in some manner ratified by the people. Only Massachusetts (1780) and New Hampshire (1784) had constitutional conventions specifically elected for that purpose, and a popular referendum on the result. This has become the standard method of constitution making.

Massachusetts illustrates the most deliberate and effective transition from colony to commonwealth. The process took five years and the delay was fortunate, for in Massachusetts the sort of people who made John Adams wince by shouting 'no courts, no taxation' were numerous. The first step was for the colonial assembly to resolve itself into a provincial congress. On 5 May 1775 this congress deposed Governor Gage and ordered the election of a new assembly, which drafted a state constitution and submitted it to the people. It was a poor sort of constitution and the voters showed good sense in rejecting it by a five-sixths majority. The chastened assembly then put into effect a new method, which asked the people to decide in town meetings whether or not they wanted a constitutional convention. They so voted. The convention, its delegates elected by manhood suffrage, chose a committee to draft a constitution; on that committee John Adams did almost all the work. His draft, adopted by the convention, was submitted to the people. Citizens were invited to discuss the constitution in town meeting, to point out objections and suggest improvements, to vote on it article by article, and to empower the convention to ratify and declare it in force if two-thirds of the men aged 21 and upward were in favor. This complicated procedure was followed. After town meetings discussed the constitution clause by clause, and voted a two-thirds majority for every article, the convention declared the entire constitution ratified and in force on 15 June 1780.

It would be difficult to devise a more deliberate method of securing a government by popular consent. At every step the rights of the people were safeguarded, and their views consulted. By the constitutional convention, the written constitution, and popular ratification, Americans had discovered a way to legalize revolution.

Most of the new constitutions showed the impact of democratic ideas, but none made any drastic break with the past, and all but two were designed to prevent a momentary popular will from overriding settled practices and vested interests. They were built by Americans on the solid foundation of colonial experience, with the timber of English practice, using Montesquieu as consulting architect. A few men did the main work of drafting. That of New York, one of the best, was written by three young graduates of King's College: John Jay, Robert Livingston, and Gouverneur Morris, of whom the first two were just over 30 and the third, 24 years old.

Most of the constitutions began with a 'Declaration' or 'Bill' of Rights. That of Virginia, framed by George Mason of Gunston Hall, served as a model. It enumerated the fundamental liberties for which Englishmen had been struggling ever since Magna Carta—moderate bail and humane punishments, militia instead of a standing army, speedy trials by law of the land with judgments by one's peers, and freedom of conscience—together with others, based on recent experience, which Englishmen had not yet secured: freedom of the press, of elections, of the right of a majority to reform or alter the government, and prohibition of general warrants. Other states enlarged the list by drawing upon their own experience, or upon English documents such as the Bill of Rights of 1689—freedom of speech, of assemblage, of petition, of bearing arms, the right to a writ of habeas corpus, inviolability of domicile, equal operation of the laws. State governments were generally forbidden to pass *ex post facto* laws, to define treason in such a way as to 'get' undesirables, to take property without compensation, to imprison without warrant, to apply martial law in time of peace, or to force people to testify against themselves.

In other respects, too, the Americans had long English memories. The English people in the seventeenth century had tasted absolutism under Charles I, the Long Parliament, Cromwell, and James II. This experience impressed the English mind with the need for a balance among those who make laws (the legislative), those who execute the laws (king, governor, or executive council), and those who interpret the laws (the judiciary). Accordingly, all state constitutions paid allegiance to the theory of separation of powers brilliantly expounded by Montesquieu's *Spirit of Laws.* But this principle was less well observed in the first round of constitution-making in 1776. The Virginia framers, impressed by Locke's dictum, 'The legislative is the supreme power of the commonwealth,' allowed the legislature to elect governor, council, and all judges except justices of the peace. The classical education of leading men, who knew what Julius Caesar did to the Roman Republic, was reflected by a weakening of the executive power in every state but three. The judiciary in most states was appointed by the legislature, and in three states for a limited term; but every state endeavored to make the judiciary independent by protecting the judges from arbitrary removal or pressure through reduction of salaries.

Although the people were everywhere recognized as sovereign, every constitution but that of Vermont attempted to place control of the government in the hands of persons possessing more or less property. It was accepted that the body politic consisted of those who had a 'stake in society.' Even the democratic Franklin declared that 'as to those who have no landed property . . . the allowing them to vote for legislators is an impropriety.' There were property qualifications—usually meager—for voting, and proportionately higher ones for office-holding. In most states, too, religious qualifications for office-holding or test oaths of office were designed to keep out former loyalists and Roman Catholics. But these state constitutions were incomparably the most liberal and democratic of any in the eighteenth-century world and provided for a degree of self-government unknown elsewhere.

In spite of the haste with which many were drafted, five of these constitutions lasted over half a century, and that of Massachusetts is still in effect, although amended out of all resemblance to John Adams's constitution of 1780. Mistakes were made; but these amateur constitution-makers fully proved themselves worthy of their trust, and their states ripe for self-government.

In most of the states a struggle between democratic and conservative elements started during the war, but did not break out in the open until after it was over. In states such as New York, Massachusetts, South Carolina, and Maryland, where the conservative classes had taken the lead before 1775, they were in a position to direct the course of events and stem the democratic tide. In Pennsylvania and Georgia, where the initial decision in favor of independence had been a radical victory, the democratic elements had things much their own way.

The constitutional history of three typical states, Pennsylvania, Virginia, and South Carolina, illustrates the clash of classes and the essential continuity of this period with the prewar years.

In the Quaker commonwealth the struggle between east and west culminated early in 1776 in a reapportionment of representation, a smashing victory for the western counties. The radicals then produced a democratic constitution that did away with governor and upper chamber, and provided for a council of censors to examine the operation of the government every seven years. There were no qualifications for voting or for office-holding, except the payment of a state tax and the touching proviso that membership in the House should consist of 'persons most noted for wisdom and virtue.' Vermont copied this constitution almost verbatim, and in that frontier democratic community it worked well enough. But in Pennsylvania, where there were deep class, ethnic, and religious divisions, it established the nearest thing to a democracy anywhere on the globe. 'You would execrate this state if you were in it,' wrote a Pennsylvanian to Jefferson. 'The supporters of this government are a set of workmen without any weight of character.' During the war, the Assembly expended more energy in plundering tories, cracking down on profiteers, and persecuting conscientious objectors than in supporting the Revolution. James Wilson made himself so unpopular by opposing the state constitution that his house was attacked by a radical mob. The legislature annulled the charter of Philadelphia College, the most liberal in the United States, because the provost and trustees were anti-constitutionalists, and handed over the college property to the University of Pennsylvania, but gave that university very little support. Eventually the people of Pennsylvania turned against this constitution, and in 1790 obtained the election of a convention which drafted a new one with a bicameral legislature.

In Virginia the gentry who led the patriot party wanted a conservative constitution but got a moderate one. Modest property qualifications for voting and office-holding remained unchanged, and the eastern counties retained their control of the legislature through the device of giving each county exactly two members. As the western counties were large, populous, and growing fast, this disproportion became greater every year. In 1790 the five valley counties with an average white population of 12,089 had two representatives each; so did five tidewater counties with an average white population of 1471. Yet the Virginia constitution was distinguished for its noble Declaration of Rights, which served as a model for other states and even for France. Although the Virginia gentry were unyielding in matters threatening their political supremacy, they went further in reform legislation than the governing class of any other state, not excepting Pennsylvania. Within a few years, under the driving leadership of Jefferson, Madison, and Mason, quit-rents, primogeniture, and entail were abolished, church and state separated, the legal code revised, and the slave trade abolished.

The South Carolina constitution of 1778 continued those class and sectional inequalities that made trouble in the colonial period. Suffrage was limited to men with a 50-acre freehold, and property qualifications for office-holding were almost prohibitory. A state senator had to hold an estate worth £2000, while the governor, lieutenant governor, and councillors had to own property to the value of £10,000. The coastal region continued to be grossly over-represented. The Anglican Church was disestablished, but only Protestants were guaranteed civil rights. Much of this was abandoned or liberalized in the constitution of 1791. Yet even this constitution left the state under the control of low-country planters, who made it the stronghold of Southern conservatism until it blew up in 1865.

Social Progress

Although democracy had little to do with starting hostilities, the war released it as a major force in American life. Tory estates were confiscated, land reforms adopted, and relics of feudalism such as titles of nobility, quit-rents, and tithes swept away. Progress was made in achieving an incomparably greater degree of religious freedom and separation of church and state than anywhere else in the world, and a concerted attack was made on slavery and the slave trade.

During the Revolution the Crown lands, extensive domains of proprietors such as the Penns and Calverts, and the princely estates of loyalists such as Lord Fairfax of Virginia were confiscated. This was done not to equalize landholding but to punish the recalcitrant and to raise money. Confiscated lands were sold to the highest bidder. In cities like New York and Annapolis, speculators acquired most of the valuable property. Rural estates, however, were frequently subdivided so that in areas like Dutchess County, New York, manor tenants were able to become freeholders. The abolition of entail and primogeniture, chiefly of symbolic importance, indicated a determination to wipe out the remnants of feudalism and create a more egalitarian society.

The fight for separation of church and state won a series of notable victories. In Maryland, the Anglican Church was separated from the state in 1776 and in North Carolina the feeble establishment completely disappeared. In South Carolina, though the Church was firmly entrenched in the affections of the ruling class, the constitution of 1778 provided that all Protestant churches should enjoy equal liberties. The Middle Colonies, where religious liberty already existed, embodied the principle in the new constitutions as a matter of course. In Virginia the arduous struggle against religious privileges took ten years. Not until 1786 did the legislature enact the Statute of Religious Liberty which Jefferson had introduced seven years earlier, and which he accounted one of his three great contributions, the others being the Declaration of Independence and the establishment of the University of Virginia. The statute roundly declares that 'No man shall be compelled to frequent or support any religious worship, place or ministry whatsoever.'

Only in New England did this principle fail of complete recognition. Here the Congregational clergy had been early and eloquent on the winning side; the Reverend Thomas Allen of Pittsfield even led his parishioners into action at Bennington. It was argued that the town church, like the town meeting and the town school, had made New England great. Rhode Island had always enjoyed religious liberty, Vermont adopted it at once; but the other three states set up a sort of quasi-establishment, according to which everyone had to pay a religious tax to the Congregational church of the parish within which he lived, unless he belonged to a recognized dissenting church. In that case the dissenting pastor received the tax. This system lasted in New Hampshire until 1817, in Connecticut until 1818, and in Massachusetts until 1833.

Several sects seized the opportunity afforded by the war to sever ties with churches in Europe. Francis Asbury, who had been John Wesley's superintendent before the war, organized the Methodist Episcopal Church of America in 1784, with himself as first bishop and premier circuit rider—his horseback mileage averaged 5000 annually for the next five years. The Anglican communion organized itself as the Protestant Episcopal Church of America at a series of conventions between 1784 and 1789. A constitution giving far more power to the laity than in England was adopted, and references to English royalty were deleted from the Book of Common Prayer. At a series of synods between 1785 and 1788 the Presbyterian Church in the United States approved a form of government and discipline, a confession of faith, a directory of worship, and two catechisms. The several German and Dutch sects also broke loose from their old-world organizations.

There was a lively struggle among English, French, and Irish Roman Catholics for control of that Church in the United States, which in 1785 counted only 24 priests and as many thousand souls, mostly in Maryland and Philadelphia. The London vicar apostolic made no effort to exercise jurisdiction after 1776; but in France a movement led by that Bishop of Autun who is better known in history as M. de Talleyrand sought to place American Catholics under a French vicar apostolic and provide a seminary at Bordeaux for training American priests. This did not please the faithful in America, who persuaded Pope Pius VI to grant them episcopal government. The Reverend John Carroll was consecrated Bishop of Baltimore, a diocese that covered the entire country until 1804.

The inconsistency of demanding life, liberty, and happiness for themselves while denying those 'natural rights' to a half million Negro slaves was apparent to Americans even before unfriendly English criticism called it to their attention.[1] The first point of attack was the African slave trade. Time and again the American colonies had protested against this traffic, maintained chiefly for the benefit of the Royal African Company, but their protests had been in vain and their prohibitory laws had been disallowed by the Privy Council. Even the pious Lord Dartmouth denounced the colonies for their attempts 'to check or discourage a traffic so beneficial to the nation.' One of the first acts of the Continental Congress was to conclude a non-importation agreement interdicting the slave trade. Soon the states took separate ac-

1. It is impossible to ascertain the exact number of slaves in the American colonies in 1776. The table below gives the approximate number in 1776 and the actual number according to the census of 1790.

	1776	1790
New Hampshire	700	157
Rhode Island	4,000	958
Connecticut	6,000	2,648
Massachusetts	5,249*	0
New York	20,000	21,193
New Jersey	10,000	11,423
Pennsylvania	6,000	3,707
Delaware	?	8,837
Maryland	70,000	103,036
Virginia	200,000	292,627
North Carolina	70,000	100,783
South Carolina	100,000	107,094
Georgia	10,000	29,264
Kentucky	?	12,440
Southwest Territory	?	3,417
	501,949	699,374

*Including free Negroes.

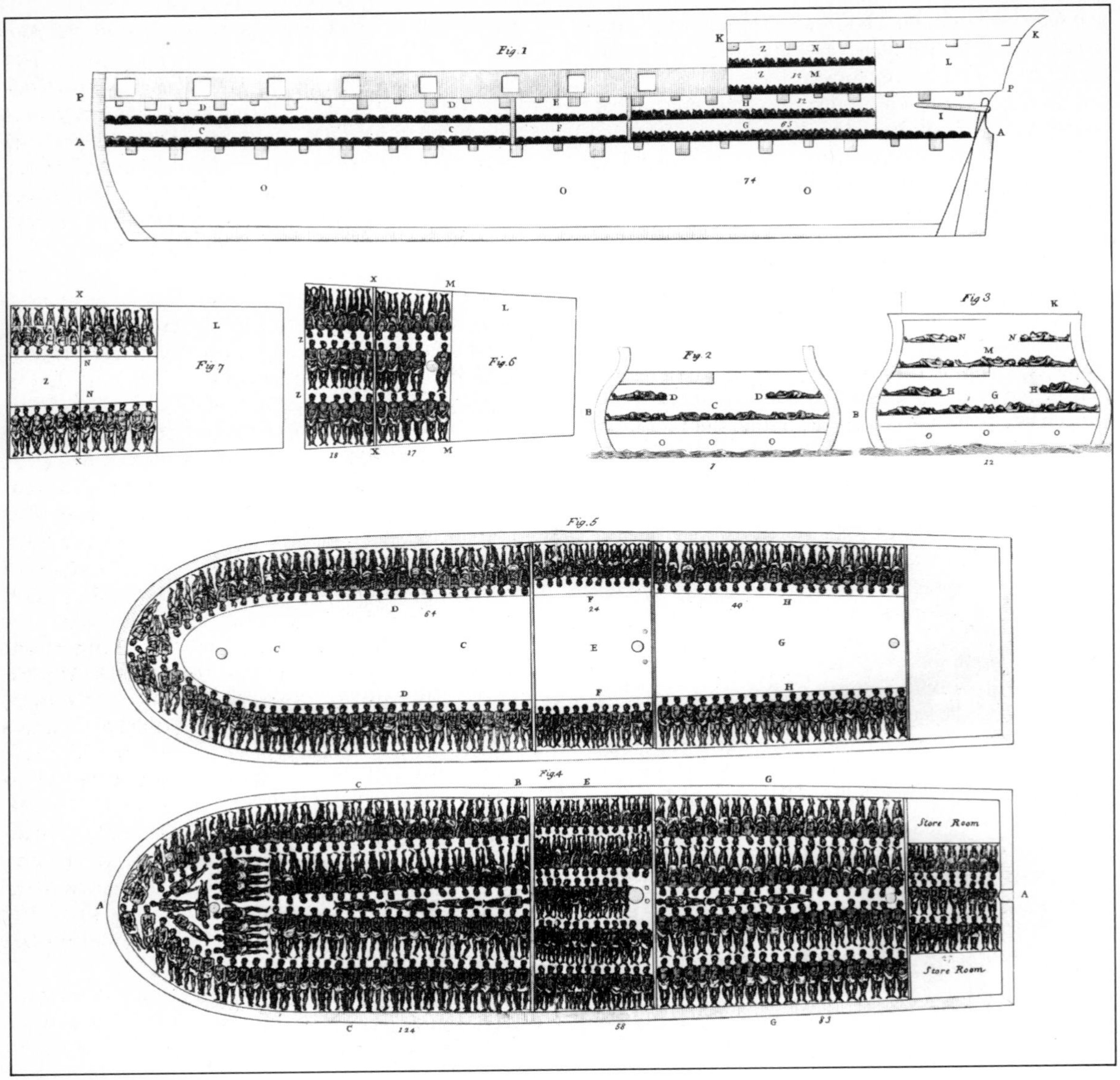

Slave ship. This diagram is of the loading plan for an English slave vessel on a voyage in the late eighteenth century. On its previous run it carried 609 passengers; a reform reduced the number this time to 'only' 450 passengers, but the ship was still so crowded that in some sections the headroom was less than three feet. (*New York Public Library*)

tion. Within ten years after independence every state except Georgia had banned or severely restrained the traffic, and Georgia followed tardily in 1798 with an absolute prohibition. But a good many ships from New York and New England continued to bring slaves illegally from Africa and sell them in the West Indies and the lower South.

The struggle for Negro emancipation proved more difficult. The Revolution and its aftermath put slavery well on the way to extinction north of the Mason-Dixon Line, but in the South slaves were so numerous that to free them would have shaken the economic and social system. 'I tremble for my country,' Jefferson wrote, 'when I reflect that God is just; that his justice cannot sleep forever.' Yet proposals for gradual emancipation were defeated in Virginia and every Southern state. Several states, however, encouraged voluntary manumission by the masters, and thousands of Negroes obtained their freedom by this means. Practically every Southern gentleman looked upon slavery as an evil, but a necessary one; in time it seemed so necessary that it ceased to appear evil.

An unintended consequence of the Revolution was to diffuse political power. Rarely has a revolution been led by men so conservative. James Otis responded to a call for reform of the Massachusetts government in 1776 by sneering: 'When the pot boils, the scum will rise.' Yet the Revolutionary era saw a modest growth in political democracy. To emphasize the right of the electorate to supervise legislators, New Hampshire and Massachusetts erected public galleries in their assemblies. In Williamsburg in 1774, the electors ended the patrician practice of being treated to strong drink by the candidates, and announced that, as befitted free men, they would entertain the candidate instead. In 1775, New Hampshire and Georgia abolished the freehold qualification for voting.

If the American Revolution had some social consequences, its main significance was unquestionably political. Although there had been small-scale revolts earlier in Geneva and Corsica, it was the American rebellion that touched off the explosion that shook the world. A war of liberation, it set an example of how to achieve both decolonization and constitutional republican government, and the force of it is not yet spent. In a Fourth of July address in 1787 Benjamin Rush declared: 'There is nothing more common than to confound the terms American Revolution with those of the late American War. The American War is over, but this is far from being the case with the American Revolution. On the contrary but the first act of the great drama is closed.'

Arts, Letters, and Education

The American Revolution also stimulated intellectual movements. The Presbyterians founded at least four new colleges in the 1780's, including Transylvania Seminary, the first institution of secondary education beyond the mountains. The Lutherans and Dutch Reformed Church established the German-speaking Franklin College at Lancaster, Pa., in 1787; and the Protestant Episcopal Church between 1782 and 1785 founded Washington College at Chestertown, Maryland, St. John's at Annapolis, and the 'Citadel' at Charleston. Bishop Carroll opened Georgetown, the first Roman Catholic college, in 1789. Within the same period the legislatures of Georgia, Maryland, and North Carolina took the initiative in providing state universities. All the older colleges were injured by the war, but most of them picked up rapidly thereafter. King's College, closed during the British occupation of New York, reopened as Columbia College in 1784, and Benjamin Rush made the Pennsylvania Medical School the best in the country. It was also during the war that William and Mary students founded the Phi Beta Kappa Society.

In other branches of arts, letters, and learning this era was prolific. The versatile Judge Francis Hopkinson, signer of the Declaration of Independence, also excelled as poet, painter, pamphleteer, musician, organist of Christ Church, Philadelphia, and designer of the American flag—even though Betsy Ross may have put it together. David Rittenhouse, a Philadelphia mathematician and astronomer, was the first man of science in America at this time; but everywhere ingenious people were seeking out the secrets of nature. In Massachusetts the Rev. Manasseh Cutler during

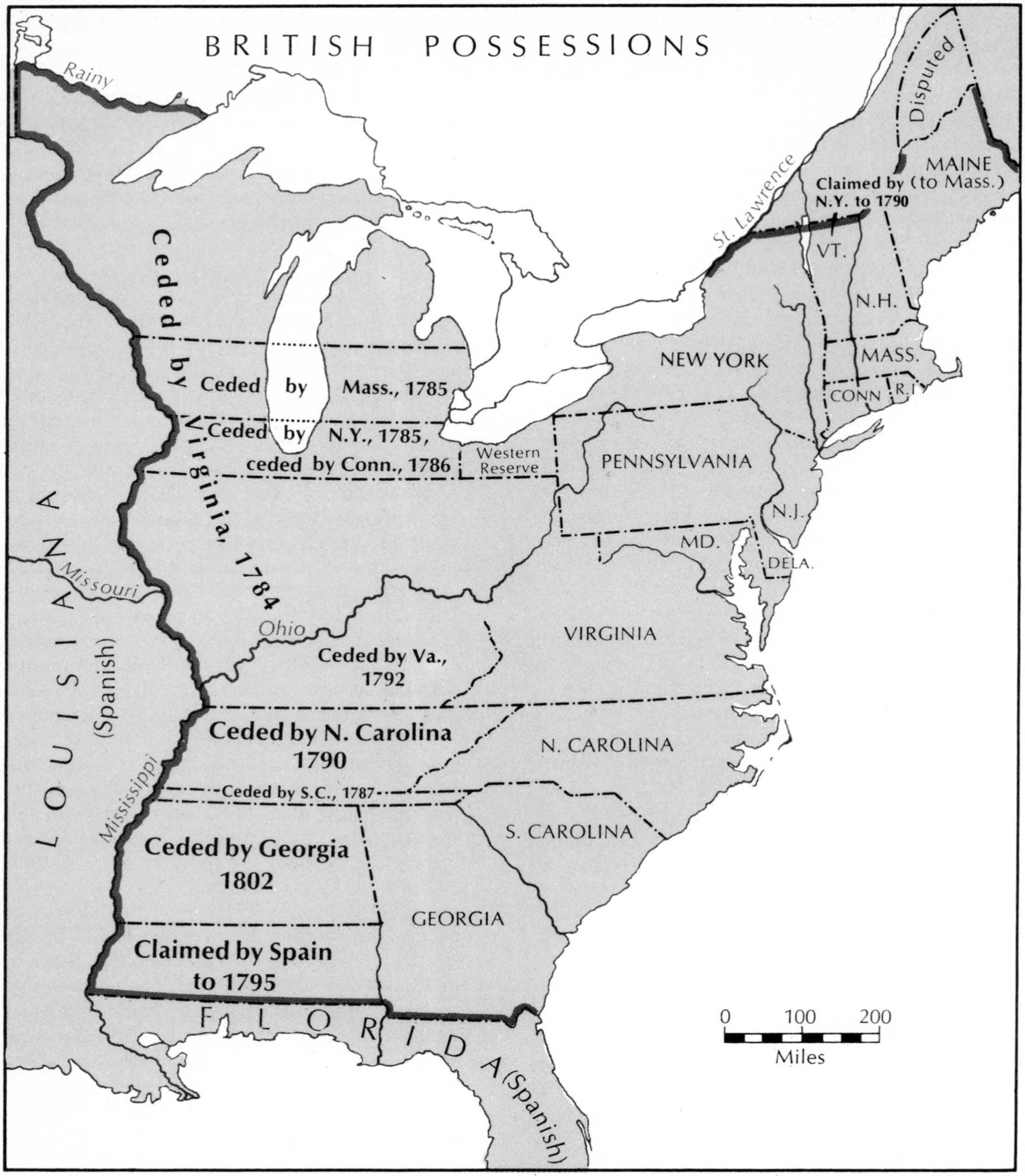

Cessions of State Claims, 1783–1802

the war prepared the first systematic account of New England flora, measured (very inaccurately) the height of Mt. Washington, and observed eclipses. Philadelphia even before the war had her learned academy, the American Philosophical Society; in 1780 Boston and Salem virtuosi founded the American Academy of Arts and Sciences.

A 25-year-old schoolmaster named Noah Webster declared in 1783, 'America must be as independent in *literature* as she is in *politics*, as famous for *arts* as for *arms*.' He did more than his share to make her so. His blue-backed speller, the first edition of which appeared in 1783, sold over 15 million copies in the author's lifetime, 60 million in a century. Joel Barlow, who was Webster's classmate at Yale, wrote his epic *Vision of Columbus* in the intervals of preaching, fighting, and teaching. John Trumbull, son of the governor of Connecticut but educated at Harvard, served in the war, studied painting at London under the expatriated Pennsylvanian Benjamin West, and there in 1786 completed his paintings, *The Battle at Bunker's Hill near Boston*, and *The Death of General Montgomery*. St. John de Crèvecœur's *Letters of an American Farmer* were published in 1782; and four years later appeared the first collected edition of the poems of Philip Freneau. The concluding stanzas of one of them, 'On the Emigration to America and Peopling the Western Country,' well express the spirit of this age:

> O come the time, and haste the day,
> When man shall man no longer crush,
> When Reason shall enforce her sway,
> Nor these fair regions raise our blush,
> Where still the *African* complains,
> And mourns his yet unbroken chains.
>
> Far brighter scenes a future age,
> The muse predicts, these States will hail,
> Whose genius may the world engage,
> Whose deeds may over death prevail,
> And happier systems bring to view,
> Than all the eastern sages knew.

Western State-Making

While the thirteen seaboard colonies were being metamorphosed into states, new commonwealths were being created in Vermont and in the trans-Appalachian country.

Ethan Allen was the first leader of the Vermonters. Patriot and speculator, he typified those frontier leaders who directed the expansive forces of that era. Defying a pre-war decision of the British Privy Council allotting the Green Mountain country to New York, defying also Congress and Governor Clinton and General Washington, who regarded this decision as valid, the Allens and their party created and defended the independent commonwealth of Vermont. Although the Allen brothers used the language of patriotism, they were primarily interested in land. To keep control of over 300,000 acres in central Vermont, they carried on intrigues with the Governor of Canada, looking to a guarantee of independence in return for neutrality during the war, or even to a return to the British empire after the war. The people of Vermont, who knew naught of these intrigues, actively supported the American cause, but Congress was estopped from recognizing their claims to statehood in fear of antagonizing New York. In 1790 New York finally relinquished her claims, and on 18 February 1791 Congress admitted Vermont as the fourteenth state.

The creation of new commonwealths west of the Appalachians was attended with even greater difficulties than in Vermont. Lured by the finest hunting and some of the richest land yet spied out in America, the pioneers poured into the 'dark and bloody ground' of Kentucky and Tennessee. As early as 1769 settlers from western Virginia, defying the royal proclamation, established a small community on the upper waters of the Watauga. In the following years James Robertson and John Sevier led a body of 80 men from North Carolina to the Watauga settlements; by 1775 several thousand settlers were west of the mountains. In 1784, frontier leaders organized the state of Franklin, elected John Sevier governor, and adopted a constitution. Taxes were payable in beaver skins, well-cured bacon, clean tallow, rye whiskey, or peach and apple brandy. After a few years Franklin became part of the state of Tennessee, which was admitted to the Union in 1796.

Central Kentucky, the blue-grass country, began to be settled shortly after the Watauga. This region was the scene of a colossal land speculation that assumed the full panoply of sovereignty—the

Daniel Boone (1734–1820). This nineteenth-century engraving from a painting suggests the romantic manner in which the Kentucky backwoodsman came to be perceived. An Indian fighter and trail blazer of the 'dark and bloody ground,' he served as the prototype for James Fenimore Cooper's Leather-Stocking and was apostrophized in Byron's *Don Juan*. (*New York Public Library*)

Transylvania Company, of which the leading spirit was Judge Richard Henderson of North Carolina. On 17 March 1775 this company purchased from the Cherokee for a few thousand pounds all lands lying between the Kentucky, the Ohio, and the Cumberland rivers, although they had no authority from king or colony, and the Cherokee had no right to make the sale. A few bold pioneers had already found their way into the blue-grass and founded Harrodsburg. Henderson and the celebrated scout Daniel Boone now conducted a few dozen more men to a place on the Kentucky river that they named Boonesborough; and there in May 1775, under a great elm in the clover-carpeted meadow, a meeting of delegates from all settlements in the Transylvania domain organized Transylvania Colony, and petitioned the Continental Congress for recognition. But not for another fourteen years was Virginia ready to surrender jurisdiction over her Western territory. On 1 June 1792 Kentucky was admitted to the Union as the fifteenth state.

At the end of the war the Kentucky and Tennessee settlements attracted a flood of emigration from the older states. Settlers from North Carolina and Virginia pressed through the Cumberland Gap, while another stream of settlers from Maryland and Pennsylvania sailed down the Ohio river into the promised land. The trans-Appalachian population, only a few thousand on the outbreak of the war, numbered well over 120,000 by 1790. In the year ending November 1788, some 967 boats containing 18,370 men, women, and children floated down the Ohio, while almost equal numbers were spilling over the mountain barriers to the South.

The most striking features of this migration were its spontaneity and the intense individualism of its members. No government provided the pioneers means of transport, or protected them at their destination. Liberty was restrained only by voluntary organizations to secure defense, and to protect property from the lawless. Some twenty or thirty families lived within a wood palisade, with blockhouses at the corners, encircled by a swath cleared from the surrounding forest as a precaution against surprise. Thus, ten centuries before in England, countless 'stokes' had looked out on unbroken fen and forest. But the American 'stations' were fortuitous and temporary. Some vague instinctive fear, perhaps, that village life would mean serfdom to them as to their Saxon ancestors, broke up the stations before it was safe to do so, and each pioneer made haste to satisfy his ambition for a wilderness farm with log cabin. Nor were the instinct for self-government and the yearning for improvement ever lost. It was typical of West as well as East when the Watauga leaders of 1784 declared: 'If we should be so happy as to have a separate government, vast numbers from different quarters with a little encouragement from the public, would fill up our frontier, which would strengthen us, improve agriculture, perfect manufactures, encourage literature and everything laudable.'

Articles of Confederation

The Articles of Confederation and Perpetual Union, drafted by John Dickinson but altered by Congress, were adopted by that body on 15 November 1777. All states but one had ratified by early 1779. Maryland held out for two years more, until the states which had Western land claims ceded them to the United States. After Virginia made a tentative cession of her claims, Maryland ratified the Articles of Confederation on 1 March 1781, and the same day Congress proclaimed that they were in effect.

The change of government did little more than legalize what Congress had been doing since 1775. The Congress of the Confederation was organized in the same way and had the same powers as the Continental Congress. Each state had one vote. The new provisions were these: (1) assent of nine out of thirteen states was required for decisions in important matters such as making war or concluding treaties, borrowing money, raising armed forces, and appointing a commander-in-chief. (2) Congress acquired the power to appoint executive departments, and shortly created five—foreign affairs, finance, war, a board of admiralty, and a post office department. (3) The Articles provided for a Committee of the States, consisting of one delegate from each state, to sit between sessions of Congress and exercise all powers except those that required the consent of nine out of the thirteen. The essence of federalism is the distribution of national and local powers between governments, and in the Articles of Confederation this distribution was not well done. But the Articles did outline a federal system, and marked an improvement over the constitution of any previous confederation in modern history.

The Articles of Confederation sought to preserve the sovereignty of the states. The Federal Government received only those powers which the colonies had recognized as belonging to king and parliament. Thus, Congress was given all powers connected with war and peace, as well as power to establish post offices and charge postage, to set standards of weights and measures, and to coin money. These were powers which the king had exercised without question. But it lacked power of taxation to support a war, and it could conclude no commercial treaty limiting the states' rights to collect customs duties. The main defects in the Articles—failure to give Congress control over taxation and trade, want of a national executive or judiciary, and lack of any sanction for national powers—resulted from the unwillingness of the states to grant to a national legislature what they had refused to Parliament. Even when the inadequacies of the Articles became glaringly apparent, unanimous consent for amendments was impossible to obtain. Rhode Island defeated a proposal in 1781 to provide Congress with a 5 per cent customs duty; and when Rhode Island was later induced to part with this 'most precious jewel of sovereignty,' the proposal was rejected by the New York Assembly.

Requisition worked as ill as under the colonial system. Payments were to be apportioned according to the value of real estate in each state, but as Congress never had the money to make any property assessment, requisitions were allocated by guess-work. Naturally some states claimed they were unfairly treated and refused to pay, and several used their requisition money to meet federal debts due to their own citizens, leaving little or nothing for the Federal Government. Thus, it was not so much *powers* that the Confederation wanted as *power*. Requisitions might have served in lieu of taxes had Congress possessed authority to enforce them. As James Madison observed in a paper written in 1787:

> A sanction is essential to the idea of law, as coercion is to that of government. The federal system being destitute of both, wants the great vital principles of a political constitution. Under form of such a constitution, it is in fact nothing more than a treaty of amity of commerce and of alliance, between independent and Sovereign States.

A New Colonial System

Despite its circumscribed power, Congress coped remarkably well with all those pesky Western problems of land, Indians, fur trade, settlement, and government of dependencies which had troubled British ministers for half a century. In view of the land cessions by the states to Congress, a strange oversight was the failure to give the new government power over federal territories; but as somebody had to see to that, Congress went ahead and did, and the greatest permanent success of the Confederation was in working out a new territorial policy.

A good precedent had been created by the Continental Congress's passage of a resolution on federal lands in October 1780:

> The unappropriated lands that may be ceded or relinquished to the United States . . . shall be disposed of for the common benefit of the United States, and be settled and formed into distinct republican States, which shall become members of the Federal Union, and have the same rights of sovereignty, freedom and independence as the other States.

By virtue of successive state cessions, Congress by 1786 was in possession of all land south of Canada, north of the Ohio, west of the Alleghenies, and east of the Mississippi. This common possession of millions of acres was the most tangible evidence of nationality that existed during these troubled years.

Though Congress got into bitter strife with frontiersmen and Indians over Western land claims, it made a notable contribution with the Land Ordinance of 1785, reported by Thomas Jefferson, chairman of a committee of Congress. This Ordinance provided for a rectangular survey of public lands and a division into townships six miles square, each to consist of 36 sections of 640 acres each. Land offices were to be established at convenient points in the West and lands sold in orderly progress at a price of not less than one dollar an acre. Four sections of every township were to be set aside for the United States government, and one section reserved for the maintenance of public schools. This land system, largely modeled on that of New England, looked forward to using the national domain as a source of revenue rather than granting it free, or on easy terms, to settlers. And as no less than one section could be sold, and $640 was too much for a pioneer farmer to pay, private land companies did most of the land-office business for many years. Although there were numerous changes in detail in later years, the Ordinance of 1785 remained the basis of public land policy until the Homestead Act of 1862.

The activities of private land companies forced Congress to make provision for the political administration of its Western territory. In the summer of 1787 General Rufus Putnam and the Reverend Manasseh Cutler appeared before Congress requesting the sale of millions of acres north of the Ohio river on highly favorable terms. The prospect of money for the impoverished federal treasury attracted Congress, and the purchase was agreed upon at a bargain price. The Ohio Company of Associates obtained 1.5 million acres at an average price of less than nine cents an acre, reserving one section in each township for education and one for religious purposes. With this immediate prospect of settlement in the Ohio country, Congress had to make some provision for government.

The Northwest Ordinance of 13 July 1787, the most momentous act in the Confederation's history, bridged the gap between wilderness and statehood by providing a system of limited self-government, the essence of which has been repeated for all continental and most insular possessions. The Northwest Territory was first organized as a single district and ruled by a governor and judges appointed by Congress. When this territory should contain 5000 free male inhabitants of voting age it could elect a territorial legislature, with the status of a subordinate colonial assembly, and send a non-voting delegate to Congress. No more than five nor less than three states were to be formed out of the Northwest Territory, and whenever any part had 60,000 free inhabitants it could be admitted to the Union 'on an equal footing with the original States in all respects whatever.' Six 'articles of compact' guaranteed the customary civil rights and liberties, and declared 'Religion, morality, and knowledge, being necessary to good government and the happiness of mankind, schools and the means of education shall forever be encouraged.' Further, 'There shall be neither slavery nor involuntary servitude in the said territory.'

Thus the time-honored doctrine that colonies existed for the benefit of the mother country and were politically subordinate was repudiated. In its stead was established the principle that colonies were but extensions of the nation, entitled, not as a privilege but by right, to equality. The Ordinance of 1787 is one of the great creative contributions of America, for it showed how to get rid of friction in the relations of colony to metropolis. The enlightened provisions of the Land Ordinance of 1785 and the Northwest Ordinance of 1787 enabled the United States to expand westward to the Pacific, and from thirteen states, with relatively little trouble.

Liquidating the Treaty of Paris

The terms of the Treaty of Paris provoked quarrels between England and the United States over several issues, especially the vexing problem of treatment of the loyalists. Congress in January 1783 made the required 'earnest recommendation' to the states to restore confiscated loyalist estates, and a few complied to some extent. Pennsylvania, for instance, paid the Penn family $650,000 in compensation for their proprietary rights, but most of the states failed to act. The treaty requirement that loyalists should be free to reside for a year in any part of the United States, in order to endeavor to recover their property, was not always respected; tory raiders or partisan troops who returned to the districts they had ravaged were fortunate to get off with a term in jail. The treaty requirement, 'that there shall be no future confiscations made,' nor fresh prosecutions commenced against loyalists, was generally obeyed, however. American tories were less harshly treated than royalists in the French Revolution, or than bourgeois, Jew, Catholic, and other dissidents in more recent upheavals. And the 80,000 tories who departed during the war, or left voluntarily afterwards, were but a minority of the loyalist party. None was forcibly expelled after 1776. Even in New York most of the tories remained, and many of the exiles drifted back—men such as Henry Cruger, elected to the New York senate while still a member of Parliament.

The obligation placed on the Thirteen States by the peace treaty to open their courts freely to British subjects seeking to recover their pre-war debts was violated blatantly. Virginia, where the debts were heaviest, led the way in passing laws hampering the recovery of British debts. Congress sent a circular letter to the states, requesting the repeal of these acts, and most had complied by 1789, when the Constitution superseded all state laws contrary to treaty obligations and opened the new federal judiciary to British litigants. The matter, however, was not finally resolved until 1802.

The treaty of peace required all British garrisons on American soil to be withdrawn 'with all convenient speed.' New York was completely evacuated by December 1783, but seven military and fur-trading posts on the American side of the new Canadian boundary remained. The British claimed they were retaining the posts because the United States had not complied with the peace treaty. In fact, they were motivated by desire to control the fur trade and manipulate the Indians. Within a decade of the Quebec Act of 1774, Scots-Canadian fur merchants had so developed the fur trade that peltry to the annual value of £200,000 passed through Montreal on its way to London. In the peace treaty, this immense imperial asset, the land between the Lakes and the Ohio river, was ceded to the new republic, and when Canadian fur merchants remonstrated, the Home Office gave orders to retain the Northwest posts until further notice. This decision exacerbated Anglo-America relations until 1815.

The war also ended America's favored economic position within the British empire. Lord Sheffield argued that England could now absorb the commerce of America without the expense of governing her.

> Parliament should endeavor to divert the whole Anglo-American trade to British bottoms. America cannot retaliate. It will not be an easy matter to bring the American States to act as a nation. . . . We might as reasonably dread the effects of a combination among the German as among the American States.

By a series of orders in council of 1783 American vessels were excluded absolutely from Canada and the West Indies. In British ports they were placed on the same footing as the ships of any European country, in carrying the produce of other European countries. American raw materials, provided they came directly from America, were admitted to British ports in American or British bottoms, practically on a colonial footing. This privilege was a great concession: no European country enjoyed as much from Great Britain. It was, however, revocable at pleasure. Anglo-American trade was so largely triangular that the exclusion of American vessels from the West Indies, and from all but a direct trade in American products with England, threw the traffic into British bottoms. The Confederation of 1781–89 had no jurisdiction over commerce, and all efforts of the states to retaliate separately were completely futile. For all its apparent liberality, the orders in council of 1783 were carefully designed for 'strangling in the birth' American shipping, as its loyalist author boasted. It might well have done so, if the American states had not formed an effective combination somewhat more promptly than those of Germany.

American relations with Spain were no more satisfactory than those with Great Britain. Alarmed by the expansive tendencies of the United States, and the danger of republican institutions to the Spanish empire, Spain sought to acquire a satellite state between the Appalachians and the Mississippi. To accomplish this, Spain retained posts on United States territory, choked the southern outlet of the West, corrupted some of its leading citizens, and allied with near-by Indian nations.

Natchez, on the left bank of the Mississippi and within the boundary of the United States as recognized by Great Britain, had been captured in 1779 by the Spaniards, who now refused to give it up to the United States. Natchez and New Orleans gave Spain control of the lower Mississippi—a powerful means of pressure on the West. The people of Kentucky, Tennessee, western Virginia, and even western Pennsylvania, discovered that the long river journey south was their only practical way to market. Their cheap and bulky products could not stand the cost of being sweated over the Appalachian passes. The Mississippi led to natural markets in lower Louisiana, and New Orleans was the natural port of trans-shipment for the New York and European markets. Permission to navigate the lower Mississippi, and to enjoy a 'right of deposit' or free trans-shipment at New Orleans, was for the West a question of life and growth, or strangulation.

Although formally denied to the United States as a right, both navigation and deposit were frequently accorded as a privilege, by the dispensing power of the Spanish governor, in favor of such Westerners as would promise to serve Spain's ambition to detach their communities from the United States. General James Wilkinson of Kentucky, who accepted favors and bribes to make his state a 'bastion of Mexico,' was the most notorious of these conspirators. When John Jay, secretary of the Confederation for foreign affairs, proposed in 1786 to waive the right of deposit temporarily in return for privileges to American shipping in Spanish ports, Spain's Western following increased. A surprising number of backwoods politicians accepted Spanish gold and intrigued for secession because they had lost hope of obtaining their outlet from the United States. To make matters worse, many leading Easterners, disliking frontiersmen as political bedfellows, wished the West well out of the Union.

The Day of the Debtor

The radical weakness of the Confederation was its complete dependence upon the good will of member states. Government starved upon the meager rations delivered by state legislatures. The sum paid into the federal treasury by the states was hardly sufficient to meet the running expenses of government, let alone war costs and the interest on foreign loans. So hopeless had the financial situation become by 1783 that Robert Morris, the able finance minister, resigned in despair, confessing 'it can no longer be a doubt . . . that our public credit is gone.'

At the close of the war most of the states tried to collect long over-due taxes, at a time when districts were burdened by an increase in debt to merchant-bankers and storekeepers. A currency famine made matters worse. Debtors began to press state legislatures for relief in the form of 'tender acts' making land or produce at fixed prices a legal discharge, 'stay laws' postponing the collection of debts, and laws providing cheap money. Seven states issued paper money in 1786, when the depression, brought on by the loss of markets, was at its worst. This virtual confiscation seemed intolerable to creditors. 'They are determined,' wrote General Knox to Washington, 'to annihilate all debts, public and private, and have agrarian laws, which are easily effected by the means of unfunded paper money.' North Carolina purchased tobacco from farmers at double its sale value. In Charleston young radicals formed the Hint Club, which made a practice of sending sections of rope to planters who would not receive state paper for their rice. Rhode Island, where the debtors put through their whole program, furnished an example of what gentlemen might expect elsewhere. The state lent large sums of paper money to landowners, and forced it on others by heavy penalties. If a creditor refused to accept state paper, the debtor could discharge his obligation by depositing the currency with the nearest judge. Hundreds of creditors fled the state to escape implacable debtors seeking to make the legal proffer of paper money! It was this radical movement within the states, threatening the property interests, which, according to James Madison, 'contributed more to that uneasiness which produced the Constitution, and prepared the public mind for a general reform' than any political inadequacies of the Articles of Confederation.

In Massachusetts, where desperate farmers lacked the political power to obtain relief, civil war broke out. Farm produce was a glut on the market, owing to the stoppage of West Indian trade, and

John Jay (1745–1829). The foremost diplomatist of his generation, Jay served as peace commissioner to England, minister to Spain, and secretary of foreign affairs under the Articles of Confederation, and wrote five of the Federalist papers, mainly dealing with foreign policy. While first Chief Justice of the United States, he negotiated Jay's treaty. This portrait was painted in 1786 by Joseph Wright, son of a waxworks proprietress and a secret American agent in Europe during the Revolution. Wright's career was tragically cut short when he and his wife died during the yellow fever epidemic of 1793 in Philadelphia. (*New-York Historical Society*)

taxes were heavier than elsewhere. Courts were clogged with suits for debt, the cost of justice was exorbitant, and lawyers were grasping. All through the summer of 1786 popular conventions and town meetings petitioned in vain for reform in the state administration, the removal of the capital from Boston, and an issue of fiat money as in Rhode Island. Some yeomen faced debtors' prison, many others were sold into servitude for a term to pay off their debt. That many resorted to violence is not so surprising as the sense of law and order that prevented the majority of sufferers from following them.

In the autumn of 1786 mobs of farmers, under the unwilling lead of a former army captain, Daniel Shays, began forcibly to prevent the county courts from sitting. The object appears to have been to prevent further judgments for debt, pending the next state election. They met with stout resistance from the state government. The mobs were ordered to disperse, the leaders declared outlaws, and a price placed upon their heads. Shays and his comrades then resolved to become rebels indeed. For a few days there was danger that the state government might be besieged in Boston by an infuriated yeomanry, as had happened to the last royal government in 1775. But the rebels lacked firearms, and their attempt to capture the federal arsenal at Springfield was repulsed with grape-shot. Loyal militia, financed by forced contributions of merchants, was set in motion from the eastern counties, and college boys formed a cavalry regiment to terrify the country folk. The rebel bands, armed for the most part with staves and pitchforks, were scattered into the barren hills of central Massachusetts, where they were hunted like game in the heavy snow. Many fled to the western wilderness; cold and hunger forced the remnant to surrender.

Fortunately the state government acted with wisdom and mercy. Fourteen leaders were captured and sentenced to death, but all were either pardoned or let off with short prison terms. The newly elected legislature, in which a majority sympathized with the rebels, granted some of their demands, such as allowing soldiers' notes to be tendered for taxes. And the return of prosperity in 1787 caused the eruption to simmer down.

Nevertheless, Shays's Rebellion had a great consequence. 'But for God's sake tell me what is the cause of all these commotions?' Washington implored. 'I am mortified beyond expression that in the moment of our acknowledged independence we should by our conduct verify the predictions of our transatlantic foe, and render ourselves ridiculous and contemptible in the eyes of all Europe.' When Massachusetts appealed to the Confederation for aid, Congress was unable to do a thing, since it had neither armed forces nor money. That was the final argument to sway many in favor of a stronger federal government. Thus, the net effect of Shays's Rebellion was to arouse an emotional surge—without which nothing great can be accomplished in America—toward a new Federal Constitution.

7

The Federal Convention and Constitution

*

1786–1789

The Philadelphia Convention

Though it would be too much to say that the Confederation was falling apart in 1786, there was enough evidence of growing disunion to alarm thinking men. George Washington, John Adams, and others of the generation who had won independence had come to the conclusion that the Union of the States could not endure without a major operation. All attempts to give the government a limited taxing power by amendment had failed. In foreign affairs, an offer by John Adams to the British to negotiate a new treaty which would settle disputes left over in 1783 was met by the sarcastic comment that, since the Confederation was unable to enforce existing treaties, His Majesty's government could only negotiate with each of the Thirteen States. Individual states could not cope with a depression caused largely by the dislocation of foreign trade, and the credit of the Confederation was at a low ebb. Shays's Rebellion revealed the impotence of Congress. Finally, there was grave disquiet concerning interstate brawls over commerce. This last consideration led Virginia's assembly to invite all the states to send delegates to a convention at Annapolis, 'to take into consideration the trade of the United States.'

Only five states sent delegates to the Annapolis Convention, which met in September 1786. Two of its youngest members, Alexander Hamilton and James Madison, took the lead in persuading their colleagues that nothing could be accomplished by so slim a body, and to adopt a report which Hamilton drafted. This report proposed that all thirteen states choose delegates to a convention, 'to devise such further provisions as shall appear to them necessary to render the constitution of the federal government adequate to the exigencies of the Union.'

That was the genesis of the Federal Convention. On 21 February 1787, Congress invited the states to send delegates to a convention at Philadelphia in May, 'for the sole and express purpose of revising the Articles of Confederation,' to 'render the federal constitution adequate to the exigencies of government, and the preservation of the Union.'

Twelve states (Rhode Island having sulkily declined) were represented in the Federal Convention by 55 delegates. Of these, thirty-one, including all who took leading parts in the debates, were college-educated. Two were college presidents; three were or had been professors, and a dozen or more had taught school. Four of the delegates had read law at the Inns of Court in London; nine, including James Wilson, the most useful member after Madison, were foreign-born. Twenty-eight had served in Congress, and most of the others in state legislatures. The surprising thing about the delegates, however, was their youthfulness. Five members, including Charles Pinckney, were under thirty; Alexander Hamilton was thirty-two or thirty-three; and the next oldest group, James Madison, Gouverneur Morris, and Edmund Randolph, were within a year of thirty-five. Practically every American who had useful ideas on political science was there. Notable exceptions were John Jay, busy with the foreign relations of the Confederation; and John Adams and Thomas Jefferson, absent on foreign missions. Samuel Adams, Patrick Henry, and others whose political talents had proved to be on the destructive side were not elected.

It is always a temptation to read present interest into past events. Richard Hildreth, when writing about the Federal Convention in 1849, featured the slavery issue. George Ticknor Curtis and George Bancroft, writing in 1854 and 1882, stressed state rights against nationalism. Charles A. Beard's *Economic Interpretation of the Constitution* (1913) sounded the note of economic determinism; and several writers of that school, with even less reverence for fact than Beard showed, have pictured the Convention as preoccupied with the protection of property and the exploitation of the common people. Another school, building upon Jefferson's qualification of the framers as 'demi-gods' (a phrase he lived to regret), regards the document as almost of divine sanction. A careful reading of Madison's and Yates's notes on the debates—an exercise in which popular writers seldom indulge—reveals that slavery interested the members only as an aspect of sectional balance and that there was substantial agreement on the extent to which the states should yield powers to the Federal Government. The determining consideration throughout the debates was to erect a government that would be neither too strong nor too shocking to popular prejudices for adoption, and yet be sufficiently strong and well-contrived to work.

The temper of the Convention, in marked contrast to that of the French Constituent Assembly of 1789, was realistic rather than theoretical. 'Experience must be our only guide. Reason may mislead us,' was the keynote struck by Dickinson. Most of the members were public creditors, who stood to lose personally by a dissolution of the Union, and to gain by a restoration of public credit; but it would be unjust to attribute their views to property alone, as it is absurd to pronounce them superior to forces that move the best of men. All hoped to remedy the proved defects of the Articles of Confederation. A few saw that something more was at stake. As Madison said from the floor, 'They were now to decide the fate of republican government.' No fair-minded person can read their debates without wonder that a country of just 4 million people could produce so many men of vision.

The Convention opened on 25 May 1787 in the Old State House in Philadelphia. Though the Convention had been authorized merely to draft amendments to the Articles of Confederation, the well-prepared nationalists decided to bring in a plan for a new national government. On the 29th Randolph presented the Virginia or large-state plan. It provided a 'National Executive,' a 'National Judiciary,' and a 'National Legislature' of two branches, with members of both House and Senate apportioned according to population, empowered 'to legislate in all cases to which the separate States are incompetent.' As to the basic question of how the states could be persuaded to abide by these Articles of Union, the Virginia plan offered three solutions: an oath of office, a negative on all state laws contravening the Constitution, and power to call forth the forces of the Union to coerce recalcitrant states. All this was not essentially different from the methods that prevailed under the British connection. The Virginia plan did not get at the root of the problem of maintaining a federal state.

After two weeks of discussion, William Paterson presented a counter-project, the New Jersey or small-state plan, containing almost every feature of the Articles of Confederation that made for weakness and uncertainty. Yet it did contain one clause of far-reaching importance. 'All Acts of the United States in Congress made in pursuance of the powers hereby and by the articles of confederation vested in them, and all Treaties made and ratified under the authority of the United States shall be the supreme law of the respective States . . . and the Judiciary of the several States shall be bound thereby in their decisions, anything in the respective laws of the individual states to the contrary notwithstanding.' Here we see the germ of the doctrine that the Constitution is supreme law, that acts contrary to it are void, and that the courts are the proper agents to enforce it.

By using their superior voting power, the large states were able to shelve the New Jersey plan on 19 June and make that of Virginia again the order of the day. But the small states were unappeased. July brought hot weather, bad temper, and deadlock. Dr. Franklin was moved to suggest that the sessions be opened henceforth with prayer; his motion was lost, not because the members disbelieved in prayer, but because the Convention had no money to pay a chaplain! Fortunately the large states met the small ones halfway. After all, it was not the best possible constitution that must be drafted, but the best that the people would be likely to accept. The same practical consideration ruled out Hamilton's plan for a centralized unitary constitution that would have made the states mere counties—a plan that revealed how completely Hamilton failed to grasp the value of federalism. The deadlock was finally broken by the appointment of a grand committee of one member from each state to deal with the vexatious problem of representation. This committee brought in a report distinctly favorable to the small states. By the terms of this Connecticut or Great Compromise (adopted 16 July), every state was conceded an equal vote in the Senate irrespective of its size, but representation in the House was to be on the basis of the 'federal ratio'—an enumeration of the free population plus three-fifths of the slaves. At the same time it was also provided that all money bills should originate in the popularly elected House of Representatives.

Other questions raised new disputes. Certain members wished no branch of the Federal Government to be popularly elected, whilst others, like Wilson, thought that the 'federal pyramid' must be given as broad a basis as possible in order that it might be 'raised to a considerable altitude.' In the end the qualifications for voting for the House of Representatives were left to each state to decide for itself. Gouverneur Morris struggled to exclude the growing West from statehood, arguing that 'if the Western people get the power into their hands they will ruin the Atlantic interests.' Fortunately, others had a vision of future expansion, and eventually Congress was given full discretion in the matter.

But there was a distinct balancing of sectional economic interests. Charles Pinckney remarked that there were five distinct commercial interests. (1) The fisheries and West Indian trade, which belonged to the New England states. (2) Foreign trade, the interest of New York. (3) Wheat and flour, staples of New Jersey and Pennsylvania. (4) Tobacco, the staple of Maryland and Virginia, and partly of North Carolina. (5) Rice and indigo, the leading exports of South Carolina and Georgia. Madison, in reply to the South Carolinian's contention that a two-thirds majority must be required for all commercial subjects to avoid sectional discrimination, made one of the most prophetic speeches. He observed that the larger the political unit the less likelihood of class or sectional injustice; he pointed out that Rhode Island was the place where one class and interest had been riding roughshod over the others. 'All civilized Societies,' he said, were 'divided into different sects, factions, and interests, as they happened to consist of rich and poor, debtors and creditors, the landed, the manufacturing, the commercial interests, the inhabitants of this district, or that district. . . . The only remedy is to enlarge the sphere, and thereby divide the community into so great a number of interests and parties, that . . . a majority will not be likely . . . to have a common interest separate from that of the whole or of the minority.' Nevertheless, the Southern delegates long contended for a two-thirds majority of both houses for laws such as a navigation act or regulating commerce. They were persuaded to abandon this demand by the Northern states' agreeing to prohibit export taxes (which would have fallen largely on the South) and to cease meddling with the slave trade for twenty years. The only two-thirds requirements embodied in the Constitution were for overriding a presidential veto, for proposing constitutional amendments, and for senatorial consent to treaties.

On 17 September 1787, the finished Constitution was engrossed and signed. The members 'adjourned to the City Tavern, dined together, and took a cordial leave of each other.' Yet the crucial part of the struggle for a more perfect union had not begun. For the document upon which the Federal Convention had expended so much thought and labor required the consent of popularly elected conventions in at least nine states to become a constitution.

The Nature of the Federal Constitution

The essence of the Constitution, and a secret of its success, was the complete and compulsive operation of the central government upon the individual citizen, within the scope of its limited powers. Whereas the old government depended upon the sanction of state governments, and, in the last resort, upon the coercion of sovereign states by force of arms, the new Federal Government could create its own sanctions and enforce them by its own courts and officials and, in the last resort, by the coercion of individuals.

> Congress shall have power . . . to make all laws which shall be necessary and proper for carrying into execution the . . . powers vested by this constitution in the Government of the United States. (Art. I., Sec. viii, § 18.)
>
> This Constitution, and the laws of the United States, which shall be made in pursuance thereof, and all treaties made, or which shall be made, under the authority of the United States, shall be the Supreme Law of the land; and the judges in every State shall be bound thereby, anything in the Constitution or laws of any State to the contrary notwithstanding. (Art. VI, § 2.)

Further, state legislators and executive and judicial officers are 'bound by oath or affirmation to support this Constitution' (Art. VI). Thus, the police power of every state is required to enforce the laws of the Union as well. State authorities, in these national aspects, are under the oversight of the federal courts, which have jurisdiction over 'all cases . . . arising under this Constitution, the laws of the United States, and treaties made . . . under their authority.' As a last resort, Congress has power 'to provide for calling forth the militia' under the President's command 'to execute the laws of the Union.'

These are the central clauses of the Constitution. They went far to solve the more perplexing problems of the period following the Revolution. They provide the Federal Government with means for a peaceful enforcement of its laws in normal times, and for coercion of organized law-breaking in abnormal times.

Yet the system is not a unitary one, for although the national government is supreme within its sphere, that sphere is defined and limited. As the Tenth Amendment made clear in 1791, 'The powers not delegated to the United States by the Constitution, nor prohibited by it to the States, are reserved to the States respectively or to the people.' And the supremacy of federal laws is limited to such as 'shall be made in pursuance of the Constitution.' The states are in no legal sense subordinate corporations. To the states belong, not by virtue of the Federal Constitution but of their own sovereign power, control of municipal and local government, chartering of corporations, administration of civil and criminal law, supervision of religious bodies, control of education, and general 'police power' over the health, safety, and welfare of the people. Nor can the Federal Constitution be amended without the consent of three-fourths of the states.

Article IV of the Constitution, copied almost word for word from the Articles of Confederation, has an international flavor. Each state shall give 'full faith and credit' to the public acts, records, and judicial proceedings of its sister states, shall extend to their citizens every privilege of their own, shall extradite criminals and return fugitive slaves. The United States guarantees to every state its territorial integrity, a republican form of government, and protection against invasion or domestic violence—another reflection of Shays's Rebellion. The Supreme Court is open to suits by states and has appellate jurisdiction over disputes between citizens of different states. As the Supreme Court later held, 'For all national purposes embraced by the Federal Constitution, the States and the citizens thereof are one, united under the same sovereign authority, and governed by the same laws. In all other respects the States are necessarily foreign to and independent of each other.'

In conferring powers on the new government, the Convention included all those of the Confederation, such as the conduct of war, foreign and Indian relations, and administering the Western territories. To these were added a limited taxing power, the judiciary, general supervision over state militia, copyright, patent, naturalization, and bankruptcy laws, and regulation of foreign and interstate commerce. The power to pass all necessary and proper laws for executing these defined powers rendered the Federal Government sufficiently elastic to meet the subsequent needs of a greatly expanded body politic.

Some aspects of the Constitution are anti-majoritarian. The Senate was intended both to defend the interests of the small states and to protect property against numbers, as Madison freely admitted, and the six-year term of senators, expiring biennially by thirds, was meant to be a brake on hasty action. It is not, however, correct to say that the sentiment of the Convention was 'undemocratic.' Members insisted on giving democracy its share in what they intended to be a 'mixt' government, with the democratic, aristocratic, and authoritative elements properly balanced. That was the recipe of all leading political writers since Polybius for the successful constitution of a state, whether republican or monarchical. There was no question that the United States should be a republic. Hamilton might think monarchy the best form of government, but he realized that it was wholly unsuited to America. Washington, it was believed, had refused to assume a crown during the war, and who could be king if not Washington?

Apart from setting up the Senate, as Madison said, 'to protect the minority of the opulent against the majority,' the delegates did not insert any safeguards to property in the Constitution. Certain confiscatory practices of the states during the immediately preceding years, for example, breaking contracts and issuing paper money, were forbidden to them, but not to the Federal Government—as the Civil War period and our own have learned. The Constitution gave Congress power to pay the national debt but did not require it to do so, as Elbridge Gerry and others demanded it should. And in one respect the Constitution was more democratic than that of any state except Pennsylvania. No property qualifications were imposed for any federal office, although George Mason wished congressmen to have the same landed requirements as those imposed on members of the House of Commons during the reign of Queen Anne and Charles Pinckney wanted a property qualification of at least $100,000 for the President, and $50,000 for federal judges, congressmen, and senators.

The curious method adopted of indirectly choosing a President of the United States was the result of several compromises, especially between the large and small states. It was assumed that Washington would be the first President, and the number of presidential terms was not limited; but the Convention, not anticipating the rise of a two-party system, expected each state to vote for a 'favorite son,' so that seldom would one candidate obtain a majority of electoral votes. That is why it provided for a final election by the House of Representatives where the voting would be by states, a majority of states being necessary to elect. Thus, the large states would nominate popular leaders, but the small states would have a preponderant share in electing them. Madison thought this would happen 'nineteen times out of twenty'; but the two-party system has allowed it to occur but twice, in 1801 and 1825. Political parties have made the nominations since 1792, and presidential electors almost always merely register the will of the state pluralities.

If the method of electing the President was clumsy, his powers were clean-cut. This was the boldest feature of the new Constitution, for most of the states had a mere figurehead of a governor, chosen by the legislature. The example of Massachusetts, where a strong and popularly elected chief magistrate had put down rebellion, encouraged the Convention to clothe the President with ample powers. He is not only the responsible head of the executive branch but also supreme war chief. He has the power to appoint all federal judges, and by virtue of his suspensive veto over acts of Congress, is a part of the legislative process too.

However, in keeping with the principles of the separation of powers and of checks and balances, Congress is also independent of him. He cannot dissolve Congress, and the Constitution requires Congress to assemble every year, whether the President wants it or not. Congress may re-enact laws over his veto, and the Senate has a check on his appointing and treaty-making powers. Both houses share the power of impeachment and removals of officials, including the Chief Executive.

Article III on the judiciary does not explicitly stipulate the power of the Supreme Court to declare acts of Congress unconstitutional, but this power of judicial review is implied. Article III, sec. 2 declares that the judicial power shall extend to all cases arising under the Constitution and the laws and treaties of the United States; and Article VI, sec. 2 declares that the Constitution, laws 'made in pursuance thereof,' and treaties 'shall be the Supreme Law of the land.' Though President and Congress have a number of ways of shaping the judiciary to their will, including altering the size of the Supreme Court, life tenure for judges has been an important guarantee of the independence of the judicial branch.

The Ratification Contest

The Convention, anticipating that many state politicians would be hostile, provided for the ratification of the Constitution by a popularly elected convention in each state. Suspecting that Rhode Island, if not other states, would prove recalcitrant, it declared that the Constitution would go into effect as soon as nine states ratified. The convention method had the further advantage that judges, ministers, and others ineligible to state legislatures could be chosen to such a body. The nine-state provision was, of course, mildly revolutionary. But the Congress of the Confederation, still sitting in New York to carry on federal government until relieved, formally submitted the new Constitution to the states and politely faded out before the first presidential inauguration.

In the contest for ratification the Federalists (as the supporters of the Constitution called themselves) had the assets of youth, intelligence, something positive to offer, and, absolutely invaluable, the support of Washington and Franklin. However, only 39 of the 55 delegates signed the Constitution, and all delegates who opposed, except Randolph, who changed his mind, took leading parts against the Constitution. The Federalist-Antifederalist lineup was not by class, section, or economic interest. Some of the wealthiest men were in opposition. George Mason, who looked down his nose at Washington as an upstart surveyor, and James Winthrop, scion of New England's most aristocratic family, wrote pamphlets against the Constitution. Delegates to the Virginia ratifying convention from the old tidewater region were mostly Antifederalist; those from the recently settled valley, Federalist. Among the Antifederalists were Patrick Henry and the Lees of Virginia, George Clinton of New York, and (for a time) Samuel Adams and John Hancock of Massachusetts. The warmest advocates of the Constitution were eager young men such as the thirty-two-year-old Rufus King.

Opponents of the Constitution appealed to the popular sentiment, announced by Tom Paine: 'That government is best which governs least.' They viewed with alarm the fact that two popular principles, annual elections and rotation in office, were not embodied in the Constitution. Old radicals such as General James Warren and his gifted wife Mercy, who thought that the states were the true guardians of 'Republican Virtue,' predicted that the Constitution would encourage speculation and vice, and that America would go the way of imperial Rome.

The Federalists, however, believed that the slogans of 1776 were outmoded; that America needed integration, not state rights; that the immediate peril was not tyranny but disorder or dissolution; that certain subjects such as commerce were national by nature; that the right to tax was essential to any government; and that powers wrested from king and parliament should

Portrait of Chief Justice Oliver Ellsworth and his wife Abigail Wolcott. As one of Connecticut's original senators, Ellsworth was mainly responsible for the act organizing the federal judiciary, and from 1796 to 1799 he served as Chief Justice of the United States. This painting by Ralph Earl suggests the wealth and social position of the squire of Windsor who, as a leader of the Connecticut bar, accumulated a sizable fortune. A conservative Federalist, he held his opinions tenaciously. Aaron Burr said of him, 'If Ellsworth had happened to spell the name of the Deity with two d's, it would have taken the Senate three weeks to expunge the superfluous letter.' (*Wadsworth Atheneum, Hartford*)

not be divided among thirteen states, if the American government were to have any influence in the world. Most effective of the Federalist presentations was the series of essays that came out in a New York newspaper, written by Madison, Hamilton, and Jay over the common signature 'Publius,' later republished as a book under the title *The Federalist*.

Despite the power of this remarkable treatise, the struggle for ratification was tough. There is little doubt that most sentiment was Antifederalist. Only in the small state of Delaware was there no contest, since their leaders knew that with an equal vote in the Senate and two extra votes for presidential electors they had got more than their fair share. The Delaware convention ratified unanimously in December 1787. In Pennsylvania, supporters of the Constitution rushed through approval before the Antifederalists could organize. Next came Massachusetts, where the situation was critical, since Shays's Rebellion had only lately been suppressed. Shortly after the ratifying convention met on 9 January 1788, a straw vote polled 192 members against the Constitution and only 144 in favor. But Samuel Adams was reached through a backfire kindled by the Federalists among his old cronies, the ship caulkers of Boston. After some leading merchants had promised to build new ships as soon as the Constitution was ratified, the shipwrights and other artisans passed strong Federalist resolutions, and Sam listened to *vox pop*.

The most important piece of strategy by the Bay State Federalists was to propose a bill of rights to supplement the Constitution. This had not been provided by the Federal Convention, partly because the Constitution was one of limited and specific powers for which it was felt no bill of rights was necessary; but mostly because when the members got around to the subject, they were worn out and wanted to go home. Lack of a bill of rights, however, was a strong Antifederalist talking point. After the Federalists agreed to support one to be recommended to the states as a set of amendments, the Massachusetts convention ratified, 6 February 1788, by the close vote of 187 to 168. The Maryland convention, also proposing bill-of-rights amendments, ratified on 28 April by an emphatic vote; partly, it seems, because the members became weary of listening to Luther Martin's three-hour Antifederalist speeches. In South Carolina Charles Pinckney made strong arguments in favor of union, which he lived long enough to regret; and on 23 May his state ratified the Constitution by a strong majority. New Hampshire had the honor of being the ninth state, whose ratification put the Constitution into force.

But four states, with about 40 per cent of the total population, were still outside, including Virginia without whom no union could be a success. Here took place the most ably and bitterly contested struggle. On the Antifederalist side were George Mason, Richard Henry Lee, and Patrick Henry, who objected that the new Constitution 'squints toward monarchy.' Their withering blasts of oratory were patiently met with unanswerable logic by Madison, Edmund Pendleton, and thirty-two-year-old John Marshall. The Virginia convention ratified unconditionally on 23 June by a vote of 89 to 79. At the same time it adopted a list of amendments similar to those proposed by Massachusetts, which the new Congress and the states were asked to ratify.

Virginia made the tenth state, but New York was still out; and in New York, as Washington remarked, there was 'more wickedness than ignorance' in Antifederalism. The party led by Governor Clinton opposed the Constitution, as did most of the big landowners, who feared heavier land taxes if the state lost her right to levy customs duties. John Jay and Alexander Hamilton led the Federalist forces in the state convention with great skill; but it was only through their threat that if New York as a state failed to ratify, New York City would secede and join the Union as a separate state, that the convention finally voted to ratify by the narrow margin of three, out of 57 voting. Only two states remained outside. The North Carolina convention refused to take a vote at its first session, but met again in November 1788 and decided to join. Rhode Island, still controlled by the debtor element, called no convention until 1790, when it tardily came into the Union.

The Congress of the Confederation, still sitting in New York, declared the new Constitution duly

Hail Columbia. In the Federal Procession, 23 July 1788, by which New York celebrated the ratification of the Constitution, the Society of Pewterers carried this silk banner. (*New-York Historical Society*)

ratified, arranged for the first elections, and decided on New York as the first capital of the new government. Under the heading 'Ship News—Extra,' the New York *Public Advertiser* noted the entrance of the good ship *Federal Constitution*, Perpetual Union master, from Elysium. Her cargo included thirteen large parcels of Union, Peace, and Friendship; on her passenger list were Messrs. Flourishing Commerce, Public Faith, and National Energy. Below is noted the clearance of *Old Confederacy*, Imbecility master, with a cargo of paper money, legal-tender acts, local prejudices, and seeds of discord; and the total loss with all hands of the sloop *Anarchy*, wrecked on the Rock of Union.

The Young Republic

America was attempting simultaneously three political experiments, which the accumulated wisdom of Europe deemed likely to fail: independence, republicanism, and federal union. While the British and the Spanish empires touched the states on their north, west, and south, it looked as if independence could only be preserved with more of that European aid by which it had been won, perhaps even by becoming a satellite state. Since the Renaissance, the uniform tendency in Europe had been toward centralized monarchy; federal republics had maintained themselves only in small areas, such as the Netherlands and Switzerland.

Even with the Mississippi as its western boundary, the United States equaled the area of the British Isles, France, Germany, Spain, and Italy. The population of a little less than four million, including 700,000 Negro slaves, was dispersed over an expanse of coastal plain and upland slightly more extensive than France. Agriculture was the main occupation of nine-tenths of the people, and in 1790 only six cities (Philadelphia, New York, Boston, Charleston, Baltimore, and Salem) had a population of 8000 or more; their combined numbers included only 3 per cent of the total. Americans had not yet conquered the forest. Volney wrote that during his journey in 1796 through the length and breadth of the United States, he scarcely traveled for more than three miles together on open and cleared land. The difficulties of communication were so great that a detour of several hundred miles by river and ocean was often preferable to an overland journey of fifty miles. It was almost as difficult to assemble the first Congress of the United States as to convene church councils in the Middle Ages. Twenty-nine days were required for the news of the Declaration of Independence to reach Charleston from Philadelphia. Less than half of the national territory had yet come under the effective jurisdiction of the United States or of any state. But if the trans-Appalachian country were ever settled, it would surely break off from the Thirteen States. So at least believed the few Europeans who gave the matter a thought.

Yet Americans dwelt in a land of such plenty that possibilities seemed infinite. There was nothing to match the poverty of a European city; and even the slave population of the Carolina rice-fields was less wretched than the contemporary Russian peasant. The ocean and its shores yielded an abundance of fish; the tidal rivers teemed with salmon, sturgeon, herring, and shad, and the upland streams with trout; game ranged from quail and raccoon to wild turkey and moose; and flights of wild pigeon darkened the air. Cattle and swine throve; Indian corn ripened quickly in the hot summer nights; even sugar could be obtained from the maple, or honey from wild bees. The American of the interior, glutted with nature's bounty and remote from a market, had no immediate incentive to produce much beyond his own actual needs; yet the knowledge that easier life could be had often pressed him westward to more fertile lands. Hence the note of personal independence that was, and in the main still is, dominant in American life. Although the ordinary American recognized the claims of social rank, he was no longer so willing to defer to the gentry. 'The means of subsistence being so easy in the country,' wrote an English observer in 1796, 'and their dependence on each other consequently so trifling, that spirit of servility to those above them so prevalent in European manners, is wholly unknown to them; and they pass their lives without any regard to the smiles or the frowns of men in power.' Yet however independent of those above him the average American might be, he depended on those about him for help in harvest, in raising his houseframe, and in illness. In a new country you turn to your neighbors for many things that, in a more advanced community, are performed by the government or by specialists. Hence the dual nature of the American: individualism and community spirit, indifference and kindliness.

The United States of 1789 was not, by any modern standard, a nation. Materials of a nation were present, but cohesive force was wanting. The English origin of the bulk of the people made for cultural homogeneity; the Maine fisherman could understand the Georgia planter much more readily than a Kentishman could understand a Yorkshireman, or an Alsatian a Breton. Political institutions were fairly constant in form through the land. But there was no tradition of union, and it was difficult to discover a common interest upon which union could be built. Most citizens, if asked their country or nation, would not have answered

American, but Carolinian or Jerseyman, or the like. A political nexus had been found, but unless a national tradition were soon established, the states would develop rivalries similar to those of the republics of Latin America. It would require the highest statesmanship to keep these new commonwealths united. The Federal Constitution made it possible; but few observers in 1789 thought it probable.

Still, if most European commentators believed that the history of the American Union would be short and stormy, the friends of liberty in Europe had high expectations. The French statesman Turgot wrote in 1778:

> This people is the hope of the human race. It may become the model. It ought to show the world by facts, that men can be free and yet peaceful, and may dispense with the chains in which tyrants and knaves of every colour have presumed to bind them, under pretext of the public good. The Americans should be an example of political, religious, commercial and industrial liberty. The asylum they offer to the oppressed of every nation, the avenue of escape they open, will compel governments to be just and enlightened; and the rest of the world in due time will see through the empty illusions in which policy is conceived. But to obtain these ends for us, America must secure them to herself; and must not become, as so many of your ministerial writers have predicted, a mass of divided powers, contending for territory and trade, cementing the slavery of peoples by their own blood.

Yet there was one dominant force in United States history that neither Turgot nor anyone foresaw in 1785: expansion. For a century to come, the subduing of the temperate regions of North America was to be the main business of the United States. In 1790 the boundaries of the republic included 800,000 square miles, in 1860 3 million. In 1790 the population was 4 million; in 1970 203 million. This folk movement, comparable in modern history only with the barbaric invasions of the Roman Empire, gives the history of the United States a different quality from that of Europe; different even from that of Canada and Australia, by reason of the absence of exterior control. The advancing frontier, with growing industrialism, set the rhythm of American society, colored its politics, and rendered more difficult the problem of union.

8

The Federalist Era

*

1789–1801

Organizing an Administration

The prospect for America seemed fair enough on that bright morning of 30 April 1789, when Washington, a picture of splendid manhood, stepped out onto the balcony overlooking Wall Street, New York, and took the oath: 'I do solemnly swear that I will faithfully execute the office of President of the United States and will, to the best of my ability, preserve, protect, and defend the Constitution of the United States.' His progress from Mount Vernon to New York had been a triumphal procession. His reception in the federal capital was tremendous—ships and batteries firing salutes, militia parades, civilians' cheers, triumphal arch, houses decorated. Not a single untoward note—no unrepentant tory raised a cheer for the king, no Antifederalist spat in the gutter as the President passed, no students paraded with signs saying 'George, go home!'

Yet Washington faced formidable problems. Every revolutionary government of Europe, even the Communist ones, has taken over a corps of functionaries and a treasury; but the Confederation left nothing but a dozen clerks, an empty treasury, and a burden of debt. No monies were coming in, no machinery for collecting taxes existed. The new Congress quickly imposed a customs tariff; but months elapsed before an administration could be created to collect it. Until a federal judiciary could be established, there was no means of enforcing any law. England and Spain controlled spheres of influence on United States territory, and a secession movement in the West threatened to split the Union along the crest of the Appalachians. The American army consisted of 672 officers and men; the navy had ceased to exist. However, economic conditions were vastly improved since the panic year 1786; and though that had been effected by good fortune and individual energy before the new government came into operation, the Federalists were quick to claim credit for the tide on which their ship was launched.

It is unlikely that the Constitution would have so soon acquired American loyalty if Washington had not consented to serve. The qualities that made him the first farmer and the first soldier in America also made him the first statesman. As landed proprietor no less than as commander-in-chief, he had shown executive ability; but we shall

George Washington (1732–99), by Edward Savage. On 21 December 1789, Washington wrote in his diary: 'Sat from ten to one o'clock for a Mr. Savage, to draw my Portrait for the University of Cambridge, in the State of Massachusetts.' *(Courtesy of Harvard University)*

underestimate the difficulties of his task if we forget that his superiority lay in character, not in talents. He had the power of inspiring trust, but not the gift of popularity; fortitude rather than flexibility; the power to think things through, not quick perception; dignity, but none of that brisk assertiveness which has often given inferior men political influence. The mask of reserve that concealed his inner life came from humility and stoical self-control, but a warm heart was revealed in numerous kindly acts. And beneath his cool surface there glowed a fire that under provocation would burst forth in immoderate laughter, astounding oaths, or Olympian anger.

Washington's character and prestige counted heavily in establishing the relationships of executive departments, a matter the Constitution purposely left vague. The heads of departments had to be appointed by the President with the consent of the Senate. But Congress, according to colonial usage, might have made them responsible to itself, and removable by the Senate. Instead, it made the secretaries of state and of war responsible to the President alone. Moreover, the Senate admitted that the President could remove officials without its consent. The effect was to make the entire administrative force and diplomatic service responsible to the chief magistrate.

For Secretary of State, Washington chose Thomas Jefferson, who had been a superb minister to France, and for the treasury Alexander Hamilton. Henry Knox, Washington's chief of artillery and Secretary of War under the Confederation, continued as such; and Governor Edmund Randolph of Virginia was appointed Attorney-General. The first President was unwilling to come to any vital decision without taking the advice of people in whom he had confidence. Hence arose the American cabinet. In 1793 there were some 46 meetings of the three secretaries and the Attorney-General at the President's house. These officials were already known collectively as the President's cabinet; but not until 1907 was the cabinet officially recognized as such by law. Washington made minor appointments conscientiously too. The federal civil service began with principles of efficiency and honesty that were in sharp contrast to the jobbery and corruption in Europe and in several states.

Although the first Senate of only 22 members was friendly to the administration, their chamber early developed that *esprit de corps* which has been the bane of willful presidents. 'Senatorial courtesy,' the practice of rejecting any nomination not approved by the senators from the nominee's own state, soon began. In the matter of treaties, however, the Senate's sense of its own dignity defeated its ambition. The Constitution grants the President power, 'by and with the advice and consent of the Senate, to make treaties, provided two-thirds of the senators present concur.' On one memorable occasion Washington appeared before the Senate, like the Secretary of Foreign Affairs in the House of Commons, to explain an Indian treaty and see it through. Hampered in freedom of debate by the august presence, the senators voted to refer the papers in question to a select committee. The President 'started up in a violent fret.' 'This defeats every purpose of my coming here,' he said. After that he dispensed with advice until a treaty was ready for ratification, a practice generally followed by his successors.

The Constitution left the judicial branch even more inchoate than the others. It remained for Congress to create and organize the inferior federal courts, to determine their procedure, and to provide a bridge between state and federal jurisdiction. All this was done by the Judiciary Act of 24 September 1789, the essential part of which is still in force. It provided for a Supreme Court consisting of a chief justice and five associate justices, for thirteen district courts, each consisting of a single federal judge, and three circuit courts, each consisting of two Supreme Court justices and the federal judge of the district where the court sat. One section of the law stipulated that a final judgment in the highest court of a state where the constitutionality of a treaty or statute of the United States is questioned 'may be re-examined and reversed or affirmed in the Supreme Court of the United States.' Without this section, every state judiciary could put its own construction on the Constitution, laws, and treaties of the Union. On 2 February 1790 the Supreme Court opened its first session, at New York. The judges assumed gowns of black and scarlet, but honored Jefferson's appeal to 'discard the monstrous wig which makes the English judges look like rats peeping through bunches of oakum.' Under Chief Justice John Jay the federal judiciary assumed its place as the keystone to the federal arch.

Hamilton's System

To attend to his relations with Congress, Washington found the right man, Alexander Hamilton, in the right office, the treasury. For the primary problems of Washington's first administration were fiscal. If the character of Washington fortified the new government, the genius of Hamilton enabled it to function successfully. No American equaled him in administrative genius; few surpassed him in maturity of judgment. As an undergraduate at King's (Columbia) College he had brilliantly defended the rights of the colonists. At 22 he had earned a place on Washington's staff. In his twenty-sixth year he wrote a remarkable treatise on public finance and commanded a storming party at Yorktown. Admitted to the New York bar at the conclusion of peace, he quickly rose to eminence in the law. With Madison he dominated the Annapolis convention; in the Federal Convention he played a spectacular though hardly a useful part. His contributions to *The Federalist* helped to obtain the ratification of a constitution in which he did not strongly believe. One of the greatest of Americans, he was the least American of his contemporaries: a statesman rather of the type of the younger Pitt, whose innate love of order and system was strengthened by the lack of those qualities among his fellow citizens. Intellectually disciplined himself, Hamilton was eager to play political schoolmaster.

The Constitution, he believed, could only be made an instrument for good and a guarantee of order by 'increasing the number of ligaments between the government and interests of individuals.' The old families, merchant-shipowners, public creditors, and financiers must be welded into a loyal governing class by a straightforward policy favoring their interests. As Thomas Cromwell fortified the Tudor monarchy by distributing confiscated land, so Hamilton would strengthen the Federal Government by giving the people who then controlled the country's wealth a distinct interest in its permanence. The rest, he assumed, would go along, as they always had.

In September 1789, ten days after he took office, the House of Representatives called upon Hamilton to prepare and report a plan for the 'adequate support of public credit.' The report was laid before the House at its next session in January 1790. Based on the tried expedients of English finance, it was worthy of an experienced minister of a long-established government. Hamilton first laid down principles of public economy, and then adduced arguments in support of them. America must have credit for industrial development, commercial activity, and the operations of government. Her future credit would depend on how she met her present obligations. Precise recommendations followed. The foreign debt and floating domestic debt, with arrears of interest, should be funded at par, and due provision should be made by import duties and excise taxes to provide interest and amortization. The war debts of the states should be assumed by the Federal Government in order to bind their creditors to the national interest. In a subsequent report, he urged the creation of a Bank of the United States, on the model of the Bank of England, but with the right to establish branches in different parts of the country.

This daring policy could not have been carried out by Hamilton alone. Every proposal was matured by the cool judgment of the President; and in House and Senate he found eager co-operation. Congress had already passed a customs tariff, with tonnage duties discriminating in favor of American shipping—both essential parts of Hamilton's system—and his other projects were altered and in some respects improved in the process of legislation. The foreign and domestic debt was funded at par, largely through loans from Dutch bankers. Most of the debts of the states were assumed by Congress, after a bitter struggle not unmixed with intrigue. The Bank of the United States was chartered, and its capital subscribed in four hours after the books were open. By August 1791, United States 6 per cents were selling above par in London and Amsterdam; and a wave of development and speculation had begun. 'Our public credit,' wrote

Alexander Hamilton (1755–1804). This portrait is by John Trumbull (1756–1843), son of a Connecticut governor and aide to Washington in the Continental army, who studied art in London under Benjamin West. He painted Hamilton several times. (*Library of Congress*)

Washington, 'stands on that ground, which three years ago it would have been considered as a species of madness to have foretold.'

At the end of that year Hamilton presented to Congress his Report on Manufactures. Alone of his state papers, this report fell flat; later it became an arsenal of protectionist arguments on both sides of the Atlantic. Hamilton believed that the government should intervene to strengthen the economy by fostering industry. He was addressing a country preponderantly rural, where manufactures were still in the household or handicraft stage, where only a few experimental factories existed, and not a single steam engine. Free trade, in view of the dearness of labor and the scarcity of capital, would mean very few American manufactures. Hamilton wished the government to protect infant industries, in order to induce artisans to emigrate, cause machinery to be invented, and employ woman and child labor. His aim here, too, was to brace the new republic by giving yet another interest group a stake in the government. He perceived that merchants and public creditors were too narrow a basis for a national governing class. He believed that manufactures might prosper in the South as well as in the North; the report was a distinct bid for Southern support over the heads of Jefferson and Madison. The South, however, regarded protection as another tax for Northern interests. Hamilton's argument would have been sound, nevertheless, had not Eli Whitney's invention of the cotton gin the following year made the culture of upland cotton a far more profitable employment for slave labor than manufactures.

All Hamilton's other plans were adopted. He turned dead paper into marketable securities and provided for their redemption by taxes that the nation was well able to bear. He set standards of honesty and punctuality that were invaluable for a people of crude financial conceptions. His youthful country, so lately on the verge of bankruptcy, acquired a credit such as few nations in Europe enjoyed. Yet Hamilton failed to achieve his ultimate end of consolidating the Union. Although he created an interested government party, his measures encountered a dangerous opposition. Instead of attaching new interests to the Federal Government, he endowed with fresh privileges those who were already attached to it.

To understand wherein Hamilton failed, we have only to glance at the effect of his measures on two commonwealths: Massachusetts and Virginia. The interests of Massachusetts were primarily maritime: fishermen who benefited by new bounties on dried codfish; foreign traders who benefited by the low tariff; and shipyards which were favored by discriminating tonnage duties. Merchants had invested heavily in government paper that gained enormously in value by the funding system. Since Massachusetts had the largest war debt of any state, she profited most from the assumption of state debts by the Federal Government. Maritime prosperity, percolating from the market towns to the interior, raised the price of country produce and healed the wounds of Shays's Rebellion. Boston, once the home of radical mobs, was now carried by the new Federalist party. The 'Essex Junto' of Massachusetts—Cabots, Higginsons, Lowells, and Jacksons, who had been to sea in their youth and viewed politics as from a quarter-deck—hailed Hamilton as their master and kept his flag flying in the Bay State long after his death. Allied with them were the solid men of Connecticut, New York City, and seaports to the southward. But Hamilton's policy did not touch the great mass of the American people. It would have been otherwise had the public debt remained in the hands of its original possessors; but farmers, discharged soldiers, petty shopkeepers, and the like who held government securities had been forced to part with them at a ruinous discount during the hard times that followed the end of the war. By 1789 the bulk of the public debt was held by the 'right people' at Philadelphia, New York, Charleston, and Boston; and the nation was taxed to pay at par for securities purchased at a tremendous discount.

By the same economic test, a system that appeared statesmanlike in Massachusetts seemed unwarrented in Virginia. The Virginia planter knew little of business and less of finance. A gentleman inherited his debts with his plantation, why then should debt trouble the United States? Why not pay it off at market value, as a gentleman compounds with his creditors? Some Virginians had sold their government I.O.U.'s as low as 15; why should they be taxed to pay other states' debts at 100? To men such as these, in love with 'republican virtue' and ignorant of the simplest principles of accounting, Hamilton's system looked like jobbery and corruption, as in England; might not it lead to monarchy as in England?

Patrick Henry drafted a remonstrance against the federal assumption of state debts which the Virginia Assembly adopted. Therein were expressed the misgivings of plain folk throughout the country, as well as those of the Virginia gentry:

> In an agricultural country like this, . . . to erect, and concentrate, and perpetuate a large monied interest, is a measure which your memorialists apprehend must in the course of human events produce one or other of two evils, the prostration of agriculture at the feet of commerce, or a change in the present form of federal government, fatal to the existence of American liberty. . . . Your memorialists can find no clause in the Constitution authorizing Congress to assume the debts of the States!

A vision of civil war flashed across Hamilton's brain as he read this remonstrance. 'This is the first symptom,' he wrote, 'of a spirit which must either be killed, or will kill the Constitution of the United States.'

Virginia could hardly form an opposition party without aid from some of her citizens who were highly placed in the Federal Government. Washington, national in his outlook, signed every bill based on Hamilton's recommendations. Richard Henry Lee, elected to the Senate as an Antifederalist, became a convert to Hamilton's views. Thomas Jefferson, Secretary of State, and James Madison, leader of the House, wavered—but found the Virginia candle stronger than the Hamiltonian star.

Enter Jefferson

When Jefferson took up his post as Secretary of State, ambition to found a political party was remote from his mind. 'If I could not go to heaven but with a party, I would not go there at all,' he wrote. Yet his name and reputation are indissolubly bound up with the party that he was destined to lead.

Jefferson was twelve years older than Hamilton, much more experienced, and far more versatile. He was easily the first American architect of his generation. Monticello, his Virginia mansion, designed by him and superbly located on a hill-top facing the Blue Ridge, has remained one of the most admirable country estates in America. The best group of collegiate buildings in the country, at nearby Charlottesville, was designed by him. Jefferson wrote upon Neo-Platonism, the pronunciation of Greek, Anglo-Saxon, the future of steam engines, archaeology, and theology. But there was one subject of which he was ignorant, and that was Hamilton's specialty, finance.

Hamilton wished to concentrate power; Jefferson, to diffuse it. Hamilton feared anarchy and cherished order; Jefferson feared tyranny and cherished liberty. Hamilton believed republican government could only succeed if directed by a governing class; Jefferson, that republicanism required a democratic base. Hamilton took the gloomy Hobbesian view of human nature; Jefferson, a more hopeful view: the people, he believed, were the safest and most virtuous, though not always the wisest, depository of power; education would perfect their wisdom. Hamilton would encourage shipping and manufactures; Jefferson would have America remain a nation of farmers. All those differences were bracketed by two opposed conceptions of what America was and might be. Jefferson shared the idealistic conception of the new world to which Turgot had paid homage—an agrarian republic of mild laws and equal opportunity, asylum to the oppressed and beacon-light of freedom, renouncing wealth and commerce to preserve simplicity and equality. To Hamilton this was mischievous nonsense. Having assimilated the traditions of the New York gentry into which he had married, he believed that the only choice for America lay between a stratified society on the English model and a squalid 'mobocracy.' Jefferson, who knew Europe, where every man was 'either hammer or anvil,' wished America to be as unlike it as possible; Hamilton, who had never left America, wished to make his country a new Europe.

Their appearance was as much of a contrast as their habits of mind. Hamilton's neat, lithe, dapper figure, and air of brisk energy, went with his tight, compact, disciplined brain. He could not have composed a classic state paper such as the Declaration of Independence; yet Jefferson's mind in comparison was somewhat untidy, constantly gathering new facts and making fresh syntheses. 'His whole figure has a loose, shackling air,' wrote Senator Maclay in 1790. 'I looked for gravity, but a laxity of manner seemed shed about him.' His discourse 'was loose and rambling and yet he scattered information wherever he went, and some even brilliant sentiments sparkled from him.' His sandy complexion, hazel eyes, and much-worn clothes played up this impression of careless ease; whilst Hamilton glowed with vigor and intensity. Women found him irresistible, but they did not care much for Jefferson.

Jefferson assumed his duties as Secretary of State in March 1790, when Hamilton's financial policy was almost a year old and government circles were ringing with his praises. Jefferson approved the payment of the domestic and foreign debt at par, and he secured adoption of Hamilton's program for the assumption of the state debts by making a deal by which the federal capital would be removed southward to the new city of Washington, after a ten-year interval at Philadelphia. Jefferson persuaded two Virginia congressmen to vote for assumption, and Hamilton rounded up Yankee votes for the Potomac. But from the date of Hamilton's report recommending a national bank (13 December 1790), Jefferson's attitude began to change. When the President called on his cabinet for opinions on the constitutionality of the bank bill, Jefferson, foreshadowing the 'strict construction' school, declared that it was unconstitutional. He contended that the congressional power 'to make all laws necessary and proper for carrying into execution' its delegated powers did not include laws merely convenient for such purposes. A national bank was not strictly necessary—the existing state bank at Philadelphia could be used for government funds. Hamilton replied with a nationalistic, 'loose construction' interpretation:

> Every power vested in a government is in its nature sovereign, and includes by force of the term, a right to employ all the means requisite . . . to the attainment of the ends of such power. . . . If the end be clearly comprehended within any of the specified powers, and if the measure have an obvious relation to that end, and is not forbidden by any particular provision of the Constitution, it may safely be deemed to come within the compass of the national authority.

A bank, he said, has a relation to the specified powers of collecting taxes, paying salaries, and servicing the debt. This opinion satisfied Washington, and he signed the bank bill; it only needed the clarifying process of Chief Justice Marshall's brain to become the great opinion of 1819, which read the doctrine of implied powers into the Constitution.

Jefferson was neither silenced nor convinced. The Federal Constitution, from his point of view and Madison's, was being perverted into a consolidated, national government. To what end? Before many months elapsed, the two Virginians thought they knew. Hamilton was simply juggling money out of the pockets of the poor into those of the rich, building up through financial favors a corrupt control of Congress; and 'the ultimate object of all this was to prepare the way for a change from the present republican form of government to that of monarchy, of which the English constitution is to be the model.' Jefferson's suspicions were deepened by the brisk speculation in lands, bank stock, and government funds that began in 1790. Northern speculators combed the countryside for depreciated paper, and several associates of Hamilton's were implicated in shady transactions. Jefferson did not, however, create an opposition; he joined and organized the elements of opposition.

The Birth of Parties

Political parties were in bad odor at the end of the eighteenth century. No provision for party government had been made in the Constitution, although parties or factions existed in all states as in all the colonies. Ought Jefferson to resign from the cabinet, leaving Hamilton in undisputed con-

Thomas Jefferson (1743–1826). This portrait is by the English-born Thomas Sully (1783–1872), who studied with the great American artist Gilbert Stuart. Sully, who not only painted four American Presidents but Queen Victoria, was said to perceive an aristocrat in every subject who sat for him. (*American Philosophical Society*)

trol? Was it proper for him openly to support opposition to a policy that Washington had accepted? The President, believing that every month and year the government endured was so much gained for stability, endeavored to keep the smouldering fire from bursting forth. Both were entreated to remain in office, and both consented. But Jefferson, believing Hamilton's policy to be dangerous, used every means short of open opposition to check it; while Hamilton spared no effort to thwart Jefferson.

The first national parties developed out of contests in Congress over Hamilton's financial program. Hamilton's partisans became known as 'Federalists.' (They should not be confused with the Federalists who had supported the Constitution in the ratification struggle; divisions over Hamilton's policies did not coincide with those over ratification.) Madison raised an opposition to Hamilton's system, and for the next seven years Madison, not Jefferson, would lead the 'Republican' interest. Disagreement over the Hamiltonian program broke on sectional lines. On the proposal to establish the Bank, southern members of the House voted 19–6 against, northern members 33–1 for. In February 1791, Jefferson wrote: 'There is a vast mass of discontent gathered in the South, and how and when it will break God knows.' Yet if Madison and Jefferson hoped to build an effective opposition, they needed backing outside their section.

A very important step toward forming an opposition party was an understanding between Virginia malcontents and those of New York. That large state was still divided into two factions. The one that interested Jefferson was led by Governor George Clinton (son of an Irish immigrant), the Livingston clan, and Attorney-General Aaron Burr. Opposed was the 'aristocratic' party of De Lanceys, Van Rensselaers, and General Schuyler, whose daughter Hamilton had married. Clinton, having bet on the wrong horse in opposing the Federal Constitution, obtained neither the vice-presidency, to which he felt he was entitled, nor any federal patronage. He wanted Virginia's support, and the Virginians needed his. On a 'botanizing excursion' that led Jefferson and Madison up the Hudson in the summer of 1791, they undoubtedly found occasion to study *Clintonia borealis*. In 1792 Republican leaders took a significant stride toward party organization in agreeing on Clinton as their vice-presidential choice, and Virginia, North Carolina, and New York gave their second electoral votes to him for Vice-President, as against John Adams. In that same election, the President was unanimously re-elected.

Washington began his new term in March 1793, in the shadow of the revolution in France, which soon precipitated all floating elements of political dissension into two national parties. For a long time America looked upon the French Revolution with the keenest sympathy. Lafayette, Tom Paine, and the Declaration of Rights seemed to make that revolution a continuation of ours. But in April 1793 came long-delayed news that brought the danger of war to America's shores and made the French Revolution an issue in American politics. France had declared war on Great Britain and Spain; the king had been guillotined; and Citizen Genet was coming over as minister plenipotentiary of the French Republic. America was still, formally, an ally of France. In the treaty of 1778 the United States had guaranteed France possession of her West Indian islands. As the British navy was certain to attack them, it was difficult to see how America could honorably refuse to defend them, if France demanded it. But how defend them without a navy? And did one want to?

On 18 April 1793 the cabinet met at Philadelphia. Washington, though dismayed at the turn of events, still wished the French well, but thought of his own country first. Hamilton loathed the French Revolution. It was disconcerting, just when there seemed some hope of America's settling down, to have America's favorite nation blow up and invite everyone else to follow suit! He wished to declare the treaty of 1778 in suspense now that the king was dead, declare American neutrality, and reject the French minister. Jefferson considered the French Revolution 'the most sacred cause that ever man was engaged in,' but was equally anxious to keep America out of the war. However, he opposed an immediate declaration of neutrality, mainly because he regarded

American neutrality, without some equivalent, as a free gift to England that she would receive only with contempt. To Washington such bargaining seemed unworthy of a self-respecting nation. Accordingly, on 22 April 1793, the President issued a neutrality proclamation. It declared the 'disposition of the United States' to 'pursue a conduct friendly and impartial toward the belligerent powers,' and warned citizens that 'aiding or abetting hostilities,' or unneutral acts committed within the country, would render them liable to prosecution.

In the meantime Citizen Genet, quaintest of the many curious diplomatists sent by European governments to the United States, had landed at Charleston. Genet's instructions called upon him to use the United States as a base for privateering; and before presenting his credentials he undertook to fit out privateers against British commerce. He was instructed to recruit forces for the conquest of Florida and Louisiana, 'and perhaps add to the American constellation the fair star of Canada.' Several land speculators like George Rogers Clark, who had some dubious claims to Western land still held by Spain, showed great enthusiasm for war with that country. To them Genet distributed military commissions, forming the nucleus of an *Armée du Mississippi* and an *Armée des Florides*. In other words, France expected the same sort of aid from her sister republic that she herself had given, aid which was as certain to embroil the giver with Britain. But even Jefferson, though he welcomed the arrival of Genet as a sort of refresher for the opposition party, enforced Washington's neutrality policy with even-handed justice.

When Genet found he could do nothing with the government, he conceived the brilliant notion of turning it out. His official notes became inconceivably truculent. In Charleston he had presided at the birth of a local Jacobin club, whose legitimacy was recognized by the parent organization at Paris; and his progress through the states was marked by similar progeny. After a few weeks of him, Jefferson concluded that Genet was likely to become the Jonah of the Jeffersonian party. In August 1793 the cabinet unanimously voted to request his recall. Robespierre gladly consented, and in return asked for the recall of Gouverneur Morris, whose intrigues at Paris had been almost as mischievous as Genet's in Philadelphia. Early in 1794 a new French minister arrived in the United States, with an order for his predecessor's arrest. Instead of returning to feed the guillotine, Genet married the daughter of Governor Clinton and settled down to the life of a country gentleman on the Hudson.

That year, 1794, witnessed a marked acceleration in the trend toward the emergence of two national parties, a development which almost everyone viewed with dismay. Each party thought the other seditious, and even treasonable, because in a well-ordered society there could be no place for a party system. The nation was alarmed at feelings so intense that congressmen would not live in the same boarding house with a member of the opposite party, and a Republican had to take care not to stop at a Federal tavern. Not for a generation would the country recognize that parties were a medium for the expression of the popular will, that they encouraged voters to make use of the franchise, and that they enabled groups out of power to channelize their grievances.

Party divisions sharpened in Congress before they did in the states, where in 1792 party organization was still so rudimentary that only New York and Pennsylvania offered slates. But in Congress, party discipline was much more marked. In January 1793 the Federalist Fisher Ames wrote: 'Virginia moves in a solid column, and the discipline of the party is as severe as the Prussian. Dissenters are not spared. Madison is become a desperate party leader.' At the end of 1793, Jefferson retired, pleased to be rid of the 'hated occupations of politics,' and Madison, 'the great man of the party,' now took full responsibility for leading the opposition. In 1794, John Taylor of Virginia observed: 'The existence of two parties in Congress, is apparent. . . . Whether the subject be foreign or domestic—relative to war or peace—navigation or commerce—the magnetism of opposite views draws them wide as the poles asunder.'

By 1794, party warfare, which had originated over the domestic problem of Hamiltonian finance, was coming increasingly to center on for-

Thomas Paine (1737–1809), the revolutionary pamphleteer. This portrait, by A. Millière after George Romney, includes, lower left, two of Tom Paine's most influential works, *Common Sense* (1776) and *The Rights of Man* (1791–92). (*National Portrait Gallery, London*)

eign affairs. The French Revolution seemed to some a clear-cut contest between monarchy and republicanism, oppression and liberty, autocracy and democracy; to others, simply a new breaking-out of the eternal strife between anarchy and order, atheism and religion, poverty and property. The former joined the Republican party; the latter, the Federalist. In reverse order to expectation, democratic New England and the Eastern seaports, rivals to Liverpool and Bristol, became the headquarters of pro-British Federalists; whilst the landed interest, particularly in slave-holding communities, became gallomaniacs. For in New England the clergy had been worrying over the younger generation: students who preferred Voltaire to Jonathan Edwards. Tom Paine's *Age of Reason* appeared in 1794. That scurrilous arraignment of the Bible sent liberal Christians hotfoot to the standard of reaction, eager for anything to exclude 'French infidelity.' Paine himself, by a nasty attack on Washington the next year, completely identified Jeffersonianism with Jacobinism in the mind of the average New Englander and Middle-State Presbyterian.

Federalism flourished in sight of salt water. In the older seaboard communities, social cleavages were more marked. Moreover, to merchant shipowners of the coastal towns, British capital was indispensable and commerce with Britain the first condition of prosperity. Like Hamilton, they did not care to risk a quarrel with the power that could give or withhold credit. During the entire period of the French war, shipowners could make immense profits by submitting to British sea-power when they could not evade it; whilst French attacks on neutral commerce tended to destroy the only traffic that the British navy permitted.

Thus it came about that great Virginia planters of English race and tradition—men like John Randolph of Roanoke who would wear no boots unless made in London and read no Bible printed outside Oxford, men whose throats would have been the first cut and whose lands the first divided if Jacobinism had really infected America—screamed for the Rights of Man and railed at Britain. Thus it came about that Boston Unitarians, like William Ellery Channing, whose creed was more subversive of traditional Christianity than the crude outbursts of the Paris commune, rang the tocsin against French impiety and anarchy. Around these two poles American opinion crystallized in 1793–95. It was not Britain and France corrupting American opinion, but American merchants and farmers stretching out to Europe for support. As a French observer wrote, 'Each party will use foreign influence as it needs, to dominate.'

Neutral Rights, the West, and Jay's Treaty

Late in 1793, just as Genet's antics had cooled American ardor for France, Britain took two actions that threw fresh, dry timber on the hot embers of Anglo-American relations. Lord Grenville informed the American minister in London that the British government proposed to hold the Northwest posts indefinitely, abandoning all pretense that they would be evacuated when the United States gave full satisfaction for the debts. Washington's patience, Jefferson's forbearance, and Hamilton's long, uphill pull toward good understanding had apparently come to naught. What was left but war? At the same time the burning issue of Atlantic commerce was flaring a like signal. The weaker naval powers had long endeavored to safeguard neutral rights in wartime, with the doctrines of effective blockade, limited contraband, and 'free ships make free goods.' As a neutral in the war of the French Revolution, America hoped to benefit by these principles. But on 6 November 1793 a British order in council of unprecedented severity directed the detention and adjudication of all ships laden with French colonial produce, whether French or neutral property, and all vessels carrying provisions to the French colonies. If a Maine schooner laden with lumber and salt fish ventured into the harbor of St. George's, Bermuda, she would be boarded by a gang of ruffians, stripped of her rudder and sails, her seamen consigned to a calaboose or impressed into the Royal Navy, and the vessel condemned.

Incensed at these developments, Congress began preparations for war. In the midst of the crisis, news leaked of a truculent speech by Governor Lord Dorchester of Canada to an Indian delegation, encouraging them to look for the king's aid shortly in driving the 'long knives' across the Ohio for good and all. In Congress the Republican party was not eager for war, but favored Jefferson's and Madison's favorite plan of commercial retaliation, which would surely have led to war. Matters were prevented from going further by a timely British gesture—revocation of the order in council. This information was communicated to Congress on 4 April 1794; and on the 16th, Washington nominated Chief Justice Jay as envoy extraordinary to Great Britain.

An American military victory expedited the achievement of a main object of Jay's mission: to obtain British evacuation of the Northwest posts. In August 1794 at the Battle of the Fallen Timbers, United States forces under 'Mad Anthony' Wayne overwhelmed an alliance of Indians, who had been incited by the British. Fort Wayne was built at the forks of the Maumee, and on 3 August 1795 the General signed the Treaty of Greenville. By this treaty the Indians ceded the southeastern corner of the Northwest territory, together with sixteen enclaves such as Detroit, and the site of Chicago, in return for annuities to the value of some $10,000. So ended almost twenty years of fighting—the last phase of the War of Independence. Peace came to the border from the Genesee country of New York to the Mississippi. Pioneers began to swarm up the valleys of the Scioto and the Muskingum, and in ten years' time their insatiable greed for land made the Treaty of Greenville a scrap of paper.

The Battle of the Fallen Timbers occurred while John Jay was negotiating in London. Jay's treaty, signed on 19 November 1794, obtained the prime objects of the mission—a promise to evacuate the Northwest posts by 1796, and a limited right of American vessels to trade with the British West Indies. It preserved the peace, secured America's territorial integrity, and established a basis for Western expansion. Other pending questions were referred to mixed commissions, in accordance with which a beginning was made of settling the Maine-New Brunswick boundary. Some £600,000 was eventually paid by the United States in satisfaction of pre-war debts, and £1,317,000 by Great Britain for illegal captures of American ships.

Yet when the terms of this treaty were printed in Philadelphia (March 1795) a howl of rage went up from all sections, especially from the West, that Jay had sold them down-river. It is difficult now to understand why, unless the treaty provided an emotional outlet for varied discontents. A good part of the opposition was simply the French 'party line' being repeated by Republican journals, for the pact prevented a war on which the French were counting. A bare two-thirds majority for the treaty was obtained in the Senate, but the House of Representatives threatened to nullify it by withholding funds for the mixed commissions.

The fight over appropriations for the Jay Treaty in the House marked the crystallization of the party system. The Federalist administration appealed to the more substantial classes to bring pressure on their representatives, and petitions from merchants in support of the treaty had a telling effect. Washington's popularity also served the Federalists well. A member of the Virginia legislature cried: 'Gracious heaven, is this the return which you are about to make to a man who has dedicated his whole life to your service?' By the narrow vote of 51–48, the House agreed to carry out the treaty, and Michilimackinac, the last frontier post, was evacuated on 2 October 1796, thirteen years after the treaty of peace.

Jay's treaty also came as a clearing breeze to American relations with Spain, which had been carrying out intrigues in the West. In the Treaty of San Lorenzo (27 October 1795), known as Pinckney's treaty after the American minister, His Catholic Majesty granted the right to navigate the lower Mississippi, as well as the 'right of deposit' at New Orleans so ardently desired by the West; and recognized the thirty-first parallel to the Chattahoochee as the southern boundary of the United States. In 1798, after exhausting all its rich resources in procrastination, Spain evacuated the posts it held north of lat. 31°. Thus, fifteen years in all elapsed before the United States obtained control of her own territories from European powers.

The Whiskey Rebellion

In the very week that Wayne crushed the Indians, President Washington was calling out 15,000 militia to put down pale-faced rebels in western Pennsylvania. This 'Whiskey Rebellion' of 1794 tested the ability of the Federal Government to enforce federal law. Hamilton's Excise Act of 1791 appeared as tyrannical to the Westerners as had the Stamp Act to the colonists. Beyond the mountains distillation was the practical way to dispose of surplus corn. Whiskey also did duty as currency—one-gallon jugs of 'moonshine' passing for a quarter in every store on the western slope of the Alleghenies. Covenants were formed never to pay the hated tax. Led by two backwoods firebrands, the people appointed a committee of public safety and called out the militia of the four western counties to protect spirituous liberties. The governor of Pennsylvania, an old Anti-federalist, minimized the affair and long refused to lend the aid of state forces.

Washington, on Hamilton's urgent plea, decided to make a test case of the defiance of federal law. Everything worked smoothly. The militia of four states, including Pennsylvania, turned out upon the President's proclamation. They were given a good stiff hike across the Alleghenies in the glorious Indian summer. The more violent leaders of the rebels fled, and the covenanters promptly caved in. Two of the ringleaders were apprehended and convicted of treason. But they were pardoned by the President, thereby ending the final episode in the only armed challenge to the authority of the new government.

Public Land Act of 1796

Now that Jay's treaty and Wayne's victory had caused the gates of the frontier to swing open, it was time to decide how land ceded by the Indians should be disposed of. An American colonial policy had been determined once and for all by the Northwest Ordinance of 1787, but the land policy blocked out in the Ordinance of 1785 was not binding on the Federal Government. Hamilton wanted to slow migration to the West because you could not develop manufactures with labor running off to the backwoods. If the demand for Western land could not be resisted, speculators wished to have it sold in large blocks. But others urged that land be within the reach of all, and that an orderly system of disposition be established to encourage compact settlement that would enable pioneers to obtain good schools and social intercourse. For the most part, those who favored the pattern of the Ordinance of 1785 prevailed.

In the Public Land Act of 1796 the township, six miles square, surveyed in compact 'ranges' or columns, starting on the western boundary of Pennsylvania, became the standard unit of public land, divided into thirty-six sections of one square mile (640 acres) each, no land to be surveyed prior to extinguishing the Indian title of occupancy, or placed on sale until surveyed. This system set the pattern of the American West. Ranges, townships, and sections marched across the continent with the pioneer, imposing their rigid rectangles on forest, plain, and mountain. The question of whether to sell the land in large plots or small was determined by a compromise. The Act of 1796 required alternate townships to be sold in blocks of eight sections each, intervening townships in single sections of 640 acres each. Both large and small lots were sold at public auction for the minimum price of two dollars an acre and one year's credit. The smallest unit, 640 acres, turned out to be too large and the minimum price too high for the ordinary pioneer. So Congress lowered the unit of sale in certain areas to 320 acres (in 1804 to 160 acres), and gave four years' credit. As thus amended the 1796 law was copied for every new acquisition from the Indians in the Northwest Territory until 1820. When Ohio, the first 'public land state,' was admitted in 1803, the Federal Government adopted the precedent of retaining title to all ungranted land within the state boundaries, excepting a donation of one section in each township to a state fund for education.

Until 1825 the Northwest frontier was advanced not so much by settlers as by adventurers. The pioneers seldom acquired a land title, and remained in one spot only long enough to kill off the game, or exhaust their clearings by crude cropping with rude implements, before moving farther west. They acted as a shock battalion for the permanent settlers who followed and provided the trained scouts and sharpshooters for Indian wars. Their wild, free life gave America much of its gusto and savor. They left two legacies—a taint of lawlessness and violence, and the robust tradition of individual prowess which has created America's favorite 'image' of herself.

Pater Patriae

Organizing a government, establishing national credit, fostering maritime commerce, recovering territory withheld under the Confederation, crushing red rebels and white, creating a land policy which set the rhythm of American society, and preserving peace: these were the notable achievements of the two administrations of President Washington. By refusing to run for a third term he established the two-term tradition, and on 17 September 1796, he summed up his political experience in a farewell address to his countrymen. An eloquent plea for union was followed by a pointed exposition of disruptive tendencies, including the 'baneful effects of the spirit of party.' As to foreign policy, the United States should not indulge 'habitual hatred or an habitual fondness' toward any nation and ought to 'steer clear of permanent alliances, with any portion of the foreign world.'

Washington's valedictory, which Hamilton had played an important part in drafting, served as a Federalist campaign document in 1796. For all his abhorrence of parties, Washington was a shrewd political strategist, and the passages in the Address on foreign affairs were aimed at the Republicans' fondness for the French alliance. To succeed Washington, the Federalists informally settled on Vice-President John Adams. Early in 1796, Adams wrote to his wife: 'I am, as you say, quite a favorite. . . . I am heir apparent you know, and a succession is soon to take place.'

The national leaders of the Republican party, centered in Congress, nominated Thomas Jefferson as their standard bearer, without consulting him. Jefferson reported: 'My name . . . was again brought forward, without concert or expectation on my part; (on my salvation I declare it).' Most of the Republicans' second choice votes went to Aaron Burr, but party lines were still so slack that ballots for the second place were widely scattered. Republicans, many of whom wore the tricolored cockade, sought to rally pro-French sentiment in a campaign in which the French ministry actively intervened. The result was a narrow Federalist victory, with the Federalists strong in the Northeast and the Republicans in the South. Adams obtained the Presidency with 71 electoral votes. Jefferson's 68 votes made him Vice-President by the curious method of choice that prevailed prior to the adoption of Amendment XII. After the election, Federalists rejoiced that the 'French party is fallen.' How wrong they were!

'Washington and Liberty.' As this primitive oil painting of the first decade of the nineteenth century reveals, Washington had already become an icon. Miss Liberty places a wreath upon his bust as she treads on the crown, symbol of the old monarchical order. (*New York State Historical Association*)

A generation passed before Washington's services in time of peace were adequately appreciated. As his personality faded into legend, it became clothed in military uniform. Yet Washington's unique place in history rests not only on his leadership in war and his influence in organizing the Federal Government; not merely on his integrity, good judgment, and magnanimity, but also on his courageous stand for peace when his countrymen were clamoring to embark on an unnecessary war with England. This quiet, plain-speaking gentleman of Virginia glimpsed a truth hidden from more talented contemporaries: that the means by which a nation advances are as important as the ends which it pursues.

The Quasi-War with France

Washington left the country one final legacy: an example of the peaceful transfer of power in a new nation. After the inauguration of John Adams on 4 March 1797, a South Carolinian wrote: 'The change of the Executive here has been wrought with a facility and a calm which has astonished even those of us who always augured well of the government and the general good sense of our citizens. . . . John Adams was quietly sworn into office, George Washington attending as a private citizen. A few days after he went quietly home to Mt. Vernon; his successor as quietly took his place.'

This peaceful transition contrasted especially favorably with the turbulence in France, where all political leaders friendly to the United States had been guillotined or were in exile. The Directory, a five-headed executive, regarded Jay's treaty as evidence of an Anglo-American entente; for by accepting the British view of neutral rights, the United States had to order French privateers out of her harbors and to permit the British to capture provision ships destined for France. In retaliation, the Directory loosed its corsairs against the American merchant fleet, refused to receive the new American minister, and employed insolent official language toward the United States. President Adams declared that he would submit to no further indignities, but hoped to maintain Washington's policy of neutrality. To assure the Republicans that he was not seeking a quarrel, Adams appointed Elbridge Gerry to a mission to France; and in order to keep Gerry out of mischief, John Marshall and C. C. Pinckney were joined with him.

In the meantime, party cleavage deepened. When Jefferson arrived in Philadelphia to take the oath of office as Vice-President in March 1797, he noted that party animosity was so intense that 'men who have been intimate all their lives, cross the streets to avoid meeting, and turn their heads another way, lest they should be obliged to touch their hats.' Jefferson, who had played a relatively passive role in party contests since 1794, now took over the reins of party leadership from Madison and Gallatin. Fearing that Adams intended war with France, he used his influence in Congress to frustrate the President.

While the Republicans refused to believe that the French government had changed its character since 1792, the Federalists regarded France as a menace, subversive to moral order and aggressive in intent. Though the fears of the Federalists were exaggerated, French designs on Canada, Louisiana, and Florida were actually more dangerous than even the Federalists suspected. The Directory sought to surround the United States with French territory and push back her boundaries to the Appalachians by coercing Spain to cede the Floridas and Louisiana to France and by seizing Canada. Not only the Federalists but Republicans too were outraged by the French response to Adams's diplomatic mission. When the American peace commission arrived in Paris, Talleyrand, the Directory's minister of foreign affairs, sent some hangers-on (referred to in dispatches as X, Y, and Z) to play on the fears of the American envoys and sound their pockets. A substantial bribe for Talleyrand and a $10 million loan on doubtful security as compensation for President Adams's 'insulting' message were prerequisites to negotiation. Pressed for an alternative, Monsieur Y hinted at the power of the French party in America, and recalled the fate of other recalcitrant nations.

The envoys' dispatches, rendering a detailed account of their Paris contacts, were submitted by President Adams to Congress and published in April 1798. On the Republicans the effect was

stupefying. 'Trimmers dropt off from the party like windfalls from an apple tree in September,' wrote Fisher Ames. Jefferson 'thought it his duty to be silent.' 'Millions for Defence, but not One Cent for Tribute' became the toast of the day.

President Adams's object was to teach the Directory good manners. He would accept war if declared by France, but hoped to avoid it. The bulk of his party agreed. Hamilton and the New England Federalists, on the contrary, regarded the French imbroglio not as an affair to be wound up, but as a starting-point for spirited measures that would strengthen the Federal Government, discipline the American people, and discredit the Republicans. For this reason, no less than to meet an expected French invasion, the regular army was increased, and Washington was appointed Lieutenant-General, with Hamilton his second in command. Congress created a navy department, and in a quasi-war at sea the French picaroons were fairly swept out of West Indian waters.

Repression and High Ambition

While organizing defense and drumming up war enthusiasm, the Federalists did not neglect their enemies at home. The Naturalization, Alien, and Sedition Acts of 1798 were aimed at domestic disaffection as much as at foreign danger. These laws provoked the first organized state-rights movement under the Constitution and helped promote the election of Jefferson to the presidency.

Gouverneur Morris had remarked in the Federal Convention that he wanted none of 'those philosophical gentlemen, those citizens of the world as they call themselves, in our public councils.' The French Revolution, however, sent a good many of them to America; and one who came earlier, Albert Gallatin of Geneva, was leading the congressional minority in 1798. Dr. Joseph Priestley, accused of trying 'to decompose both Church and State' with his chemical formulas, had found refuge in Pennsylvania after being mobbed as pro-French in England. Thomas Cooper, who followed him, founded a Republican newspaper. At the height of excitement in 1798, the Directory requested passports for a delegation

John Adams (1735–1826). He had the honor of serving as the first Vice-President of the United States, but, with characteristic acerbity, he wrote his wife Abigail: 'My country has in its wisdom contrived for me the most insignificant office that ever the invention of man contrived or his imagination conceived.' This portrait is by Mather Brown (1761–1831), a descendant of the Puritan Mathers who won renown in England as well as in America. (*Boston Athenaeum*) from the Institute of France under Du Pont de Nemours to visit the United States 'with the view of improving and extending the sciences.' John Adams replied, 'We have too many French philosophers already, and I really begin to think, or rather to suspect, that learned academies . . . have disorganized the world, and are incompatible with social order.' As these were the persons whom super-patriots wished to expel in 1798, it is interesting to note that Gallatin became one of our greatest statesmen, Priestley a notable figure in the history of science, Cooper a college president; whilst the Du Ponts settled in Delaware and have since engaged in the highly respectable manufacture of plastics and explosives.

Immigrants who were neither philosophers nor gentlemen troubled the Federalists even more. French agents were stirring up sedition in the West, and Irish refugees from the rebellion of '98 lost no time in becoming citizens and joining the anti-British party. Congress responded with the Naturalization Act of 1798, which increased the required period of residence for citizenship from five to fourteen years, and the Alien Act, which gave the President power to expel foreigners by executive decree. Adams never availed himself of the privilege; but two shiploads of Frenchmen left the country in anticipation that he would.

The Sedition Act of 1798 declared a misdemeanor, punishable by fine or imprisonment, any speech or writing against President or Congress 'with the intent to defame' or to bring them 'into contempt or disrepute.' Federalists never recognized the legitimacy of party opposition; from their quarterdeck view the Republicans were little better than mutineers. In the Sedition Act prosecutions, every defendant was a Republican, every judge and almost every juror a Federalist. About twenty-five persons were arrested and ten convicted, most of them Republican editors who were conveniently got out of the way by heavy fines or jail sentences.

Akin to the sedition prosecutions was the severe action taken against John Fries, a Pennsylvania German auctioneer who headed an 'insurrection' against the direct tax. This real estate tax, laid to pay for the new army and navy, was the most unpopular feature of the Federalist defense program. 'Captain' Fries, armed with sword and pistol and wearing a French tricolor cockade, led a company of about fifty countrymen who chased all the federal tax collectors out of Bucks County and liberated prisoners from the Bethlehem jail. He was tried for treason in Philadelphia and sentenced to death, but pardoned by the President.

All this was labeled by the Jeffersonians 'The Federalist Reign of Terror.' Looked at in the perspective of history, it was nothing of the sort; the phrase itself was mere humbug. Nobody was drowned, hanged, or tortured, nobody went before a firing squad. A few scurrilous journalists were silenced, a few received terms in jail; but the rest went right on attacking the government, defending the French, and sneering at the United States Navy. Nobody was prevented from voting against the Federalists in the next elections, state or national.

Two startling protests to the Alien and Sedition Acts came from state legislatures: the Virginia Resolves drafted by Madison, and those of Kentucky drafted by Jefferson. Both declared the objectionable laws unconstitutional. As to the Alien Act, undoubtedly the power of expelling aliens belongs to the Federal Government, not to the states. The Sedition Act stands in a different light, for the Constitution (Amendment I) forbids Congress to pass any law abridging the freedom of speech, or of the press. The Resolves developed the 'compact' or 'state rights' theory of the Constitution that Jefferson had adumbrated in his opinion on the bank bill in 1792. Kentucky declared that whenever Congress palpably transcends its powers, as in the Sedition Act, each state 'has an equal right to judge for itself, as well of infractions as of the mode and measure of redress.' She called upon her 'co-states' to 'concur . . . in declaring these acts' void, and to unite 'in requesting their repeal.' Virginia hinted at 'interposing' state authority between the persecuted citizen and his government. Exactly what Madison meant by 'interposing' is uncertain; he later explained that he meant nothing more than strong protest.

In the spring of 1799 Adams made a startling move to ease the crisis by attempting to bring the quasi-war with France to an end. The President had become increasingly alarmed by the acts and the ambitions of Hamilton and the 'High' Federalists. Hamilton, the power behind Adams's administration, was mulling over a grandiose plan. He would lead the new American army overland against New Orleans and march into Mexico while the South American patriot Miranda, helped by the British, would liberate the Spanish Main. Hamilton would return laurel-crowned, at the head of his victorious legion, to become the First Citizen of America, as Bonaparte was already the First Citizen of France. But the Hamiltonians reckoned without the President. John Adams, in no sense a democrat, regarded Jefferson's belief in the common man's innate virtue as sentimental nonsense; but he was equally hostile to anything resembling plutocracy or militarism. In March 1799 he suddenly awoke to the dangers into which the ship of state was drifting; and, taking the country completely by surprise, the President nominated a minister plenipotentiary to France. Little came of the mission, which ultimately involved three envoys, but, to the fury of Hamilton and the High Federalists, Adams's move stalled the war program completely.

The Election of 1800–1801

If the French had been so accommodating as to land even a corporal's guard on American soil, or a 'seditious alien' had been caught in a real plot, the presidential election of 1800 might have gone very differently; but as time went on, and no enemy appeared, and the new direct tax was assessed, the patriotic fervor of 1798 faded. As a result, the Republican ticket of Jefferson and Burr triumphed over the Federalist slate of John Adams and Charles Cotesworth Pinckney of the XYZ mission. However, since not one of the electors dared throw away his second vote, Jefferson and Burr tied for first place with 73 votes each, as against 65 for Adams and 64 for Pinckney. The tie vote was an unwelcome tribute to the degree of party regularity that had been achieved by 1800.

In 1801 the House of Representatives, voting by states, had to choose between Jefferson and Burr, a majority of one state being necessary for election. The Federalists saw an opportunity to thwart their enemies by supporting Burr, thus electing a cynical, pliant, and corrupt politician over a 'dangerous radical.' Party division was so close that during thirty-five ballots, and until 17 February 1801, the House was deadlocked. There was talk of civil war. Not until two weeks before the inauguration did several Federalists cast blank ballots, which led to Jefferson's being elected.[1] In the congressional elections of 1800, the Republicans obtained emphatic majorities in House and Senate. Thus, in 1801 the Federalists went out of power in every branch of government except the judiciary, an exception that proved very important.

So passed into minority the party which contained more talent and virtue, with less political common sense, than any of its successors. The character of Washington, the genius of Hamilton, and the disciplined, intelligent patriotism of their colleagues and lieutenants saved the American union from disintegration before its colors were set; but the events of 1798–1800 proved that the Federalists had little more to contribute. Their chosen basis, an oligarchy of wealth and talent, had helped to tide over a crisis, but was neither broad nor deep enough for a permanent polity.

1. The Twelfth Amendment to the Constitution (1804) removed the possibility of a tie between two candidates on the same ticket.

9

Jeffersonian Democracy

*

1801–1809

The 'Revolution of 1800'

Thomas Jefferson, ruminating years later on the events of a crowded lifetime, thought that his election to the Presidency marked as real a revolution as that of 1776. He had saved the country from monarchy and militarism, and brought it back to republican simplicity. But there never had been any danger of monarchy; it was John Adams who saved the country from militarism; and a little simplicity more or less cannot be deemed revolutionary. Fisher Ames predicted that, with a 'Jacobin' President, America would be in for a reign of terror. Yet the four years that followed were one of the most tranquil of olympiads, marked not by radical reforms or popular tumults, but by the peaceful acquisition of territory as large again as the United States. The election of 1800–1801 brought a change of men more than of measures. For the next quarter of a century, a Virginian would rule in the White House; Jefferson, Madison, and Monroe each served eight years, and each was succeeded by his Secretary of State.

Yet if it marked no revolution, the election of Jefferson did harbinger the beginning of an era of greater democracy. Although in the Federalist period the right to vote was widely held, many had not chosen to exercise it, and politics were largely controlled by the gentry. In the Jeffersonian era, an astonishing expansion of the electorate took place in part because to many Jefferson symbolized the striving for liberty and equality. In the last letter of his life, he wrote: 'The mass of mankind has not been born with saddles on their backs, nor a favored few booted and spurred, ready to ride them legitimately, by the grace of God.'

Jefferson was no social democrat, but a slaveholding country gentleman with a classical education, exquisite taste, a lively curiosity, and a belief in the perfectibility of man. His kind belonged to the eighteenth rather than the nineteenth century. Christian but no churchman, he had the serenity of one to whom now and then the Spirit has not disdained to speak. The hold that he enjoyed on the hearts of plain people was attained without speech-making, military service, or catering to vulgar prejudice. The secret of Jefferson's power lay in the fact that he appealed to and expressed America's better self: her idealism, simplicity, youthful mind, and hopeful outlook, rather than the material and imperial ambitions which Hamilton represented. 'We are acting for all mankind,' Jefferson wrote to Priestley. 'Circumstances denied to others, but indulged to us, have imposed on us the duty of proving what is the degree of freedom and self-government in which a society may venture to leave its individual members.'

Jefferson's inaugural address of 4 March 1801 was eighteenth-century idealism rubbed through the sieve of practical politics. Instead of denouncing the Federalists as monarchists, he invited them to rejoin the true republican church: 'We are all republicans—we are all federalists. If there be any among us who wish to dissolve this Union, or to change its republican form, let them stand undisturbed as monuments of the safety with which error of opinion may be tolerated where reason is left free to combat it.' This government, 'the world's best hope,' must not be abandoned 'on the theoretic and visionary fear' that it is not strong enough. 'Sometimes it is said that Man cannot be trusted with the government of himself. Can he, then, be trusted with the government of others?' 'Separated by nature and a wide ocean from the exterminating havoc of one quarter of the globe,' 'possessing a chosen country, with room enough for our descendants to the hundredth and thousandth generation' practicing the social virtues, the only thing 'necessary to close the circle of our felicities' is 'a wise and frugal government, which shall restrain men from injuring one another, shall leave them otherwise free to regulate their own pursuits of industry and improvement.'

The new capital city of Washington, to which the Federal Government had been transferred from aristocratic Philadelphia, offered an appropriate setting for Republican simplicity. Washington was still little more than a cleared space with scattered buildings between wilderness and river. Members of Congress, forced to leave their wives at home and live in crowded boarding houses, finished the public business in annual sessions of three to five months. Written presidential messages were substituted for the annual 'speech from the throne,' and the answers from both houses were omitted. Jefferson also established a new code of republican etiquette. Anthony Merry, in full uniform as British minister plenipotentiary, was received by the President in morning undress of faded threadbare coat, red waistcoat, corduroy breeches, and slippers.

Jefferson's inaugural pledges to pay the public debt, and to preserve 'the general government in its whole constitutional vigor,' created joy in the Federalist camp. Hamilton viewed the inaugural message 'as virtually a candid retraction of past misapprehensions, and a pledge to the community that the new President will not lend himself to dangerous innovations, but in essential points will tread in the steps of his predecessors.' That, in the main, was what Jefferson did. Both he and his Secretary of the Treasury, Albert Gallatin, regarded the national debt as a mortgage to be paid off without delay. Gallatin would even have retained the excise on distilled liquors, which his former constituents in Pennsylvania had resisted; but Jefferson insisted on removing this detested relic of Federalism, and so made his name immortal in the mountains. This rendered the government even more dependent than formerly on customs revenues, so that the stoppage of foreign trade seriously embarrassed federal finances on the eve of the War of 1812.

The new administration made other changes too. Jefferson signified the coming of party government when he replaced the whole Adams cabinet with prominent Republicans. In his appointments to higher federal offices, Jefferson made a modest departure in the direction of naming men of merit irrespective of social class, although most of them were from the 'top drawer' socially. Jefferson also carried into practice the Republican dislike of a standing army and a large navy. The army was reduced by a 'chaste reformation,' as Jefferson called it, and all new naval construction was stopped. Yet, strangely enough, the most brilliant achievements of Jefferson's first administration were in war and diplomacy.

A Small War and a Big Purchase

By the time Jefferson became President, almost $2 million had been paid for gifts, ransom, and tribute to the Moslem states of Morocco, Algiers, Tunis, and Tripoli, in order to permit American merchant ships to sail in the Mediterranean. Jefferson, after reducing the navy, looked around for

Building the *Philadelphia*. In 1798, during the undeclared war with France, construction was begun in a Philadelphia yard on this frigate, a type of vessel smaller and less heavily armed than a ship of the line but swifter. When Tripolitan pirates captured the *Philadelphia*, Stephen Decatur, in a daring raid in 1804, recaptured her and burned her so that she could not be used by the enemy. (*Prints Division, New York Public Library*)

profitable employment of warships remaining afloat. He found it against the Bashaw of Tripoli, who, feeling he was not getting enough cut on the tribute money, declared war on the United States in May 1801. This naval war dribbled along until 1804, when Commodore Edward Preble appeared off Tripoli in command of a respectable task force, U.S.S. *Constitution* flagship, which delivered a series of bombardments. Before his arrival, frigate *Philadelphia* had grounded on a reef off Tripoli, from which the enemy floated her free. The Bashaw imprisoned Captain Bainbridge and his crew and would have equipped the frigate for his own navy, had not Lieutenant Stephen Decatur, in a captured lateen-rigged schooner named *Intrepid,* entered the harbor at night, boarded and captured *Philadelphia,* and, after setting fire to her, made a safe getaway. Thanks to such exploits by Decatur and others, the war ended in a favorable treaty with Tripoli.

While Tripoli was being taught a lesson, the boundary of the United States advanced from the Mississippi to the Rocky Mountains. The whole of that vast territory, Louisiana, had been under Spanish sovereignty since the peace of 1763, and the retrocession of this great province from Spain to France, in October 1800, completed a policy aimed at creating a new French empire in North America and checking the expansion of the United States. In May 1801 Jefferson got wind of the secret treaty of retrocession, and another event revealed its implications. Bonaparte dispatched an expeditionary force to Hispaniola, with orders to suppress the Negro insurrection there, and then to take possession of New Orleans and Louisiana. The prospect of a veteran French army at America's back door was not pleasant. On 18 April 1802 Jefferson wrote the American minister at Paris: 'The day that France takes possession of New Orleans . . . we must marry ourselves to the British fleet and nation.' Astounding as this letter may appear, it was a logical development of Jefferson's policy for the preceding twelve years. The President's earlier experience convinced him that as long as a foreign country controlled the mouth of the Mississippi, the United States was in danger of being drawn into every European war. Isolation was not a fact but a goal; and to attain it Jefferson was ready to adopt Washington's formula of 'temporary alliances for extraordinary emergencies.'

Late in 1802 the Spanish governor at New Orleans, who still exercised authority, withdrew the 'right of deposit' from American traders. This privilege had been guaranteed only for three years by Pinckney's treaty of 1795; but the indignant inhabitants of the Ohio valley, who were annually trans-shipping a million dollars' worth of produce at New Orleans, believed they had secured it forever. The West exploded with indignation, and Congress voted $2 million for 'expenses in relation to the intercourse between the United States and foreign nations.' Jefferson remained unperturbable, but in March 1803 he commissioned James Monroe as envoy extraordinary to France, with interesting instructions to himself and to the resident minister, Robert Livingston.

First they were to offer anything up to $10 million for New Orleans and the Floridas, which would give the United States the whole east bank of the Mississippi, and the Gulf coast to the eastward. If France refused, three-quarters of the sum should be offered for the Island of New Orleans alone; or space on the east bank should be purchased for an American port. Failing here, they must press for a perpetual guarantee of the rights of navigation and deposit. That was Jefferson's ultimatum. If this were refused, Monroe and Livingston were ordered to 'open a confidential communication with ministers of the British Government,' with a view to 'a candid understanding, and a closer connection with Great Britain.' A mutual promise not to make a separate peace with France could not 'be deemed unreasonable.' More than even Hamilton had dared suggest!

Livingston began the negotiation before Monroe sailed, and for a time made little progress. But on 11 April 1803, when Livingston approached the minister of foreign affairs to repeat his usual offer for New Orleans, Talleyrand suddenly asked, 'What will you give for the whole of Louisiana?' On 30 April the treaty of cession was signed. Twelve million dollars was paid for Louisiana. The United States guaranteed the inhabitants the rights of American citizens and eventual admission to the Union.

We owe this amazing opportunity to two factors—the blacks of Haiti and the British navy. Napoleon had poured 35,000 troops into Hispaniola, the Vietnam of 1800, and lost almost all; the natives under Toussaint l'Ouverture killed those who invaded the interior, and yellow fever finished off the rest. Without Haiti, Louisiana lost most of its value to France. Second, Napoleon had decided to renew war with England, whose navy would certainly blockade and probably capture New Orleans. So Napoleon deemed it best to sell the whole of Louisiana to fatten his war chest.

UNDER MY WINGS EVERY THING PROSPERS

New Orleans, 1803. Everything was indeed prospering in the Crescent City in the year of the Louisiana Purchase, which had a galvanizing effect on commerce. Flatboat trade with the Ohio valley increased sharply, dockhands unloaded cargoes from ocean-going vessels, and above the *vieux carré* a new business center began to emerge. (*Chicago Historical Society*)

This greatest bargain in American history, the Louisiana purchase, put a severe strain on the Constitution, which said nothing about acquiring foreign territory, much less promising it statehood. Jefferson at first wanted an amendment to the Constitution, but decided to take a broad view when Livingston warned him that Napoleon might change his mind. The Senate promptly consented, not without sarcastic grumblings by the Federalists, and on 20 December 1803 the French prefect at New Orleans formally transferred Louisiana to the United States.

Even before the purchase, Jefferson had ordered his secretary, Captain Meriwether Lewis, and Lieutenant William Clark, officers of the regular army, to conduct an exploration. Their first object was to find 'water communication across this continent' in United States territory. Other aims were to secure American title to the Oregon country, and impress upon the Sioux and other Indians that their 'Great White Father' lived in Washington, not Windsor. The expedition started from St. Louis on 14 May 1804 with 32 soldiers and ten civilians, embarked in a 55-foot keelboat and two periaguas. These, propelled by sails and oars, took them up the Missouri as far as the South Fork, in

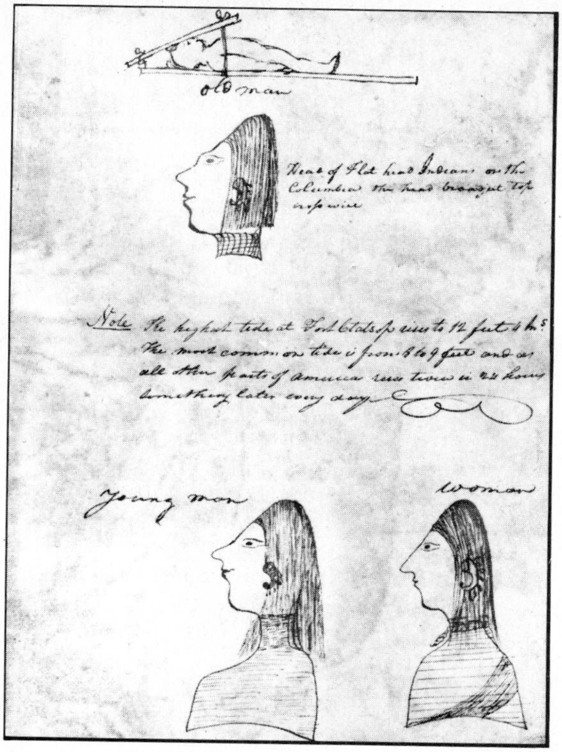

This sketch from Clark's journal shows the way Chinook Indians flattened the skulls of their infants in order to achieve the straight line from the top of the head to the tip of the nose that they admired in both men and women as an indication of a cultured upbringing. In the midst of these drawings, the explorer has taken advantage of unused space to record information on the tides at Fort Clatsop on the Oregon coast. (*Missouri Historical Society*)

The Lewis and Clark expedition came upon this canoe of the Columbia river tribes, with grotesque figures at each end. This sketch is from the journal of William Clark. (*Missouri Historical Society*)

what is now Montana. The winter of 1804–5 they spent among the Mandan in North Dakota. A fleet of dugout canoes took them to the foothills of the Rocky Mountains in what is now Idaho, where their interpreter, the Snake Indian girl Sacajawea, made friendly contact with the Shoshone. These furnished horses for the men and squaws to carry the baggage. In the Nez Percé country the expedition reached the Clearwater, a turbulent but navigable branch of the Snake, flowing westward. They entered the Columbia river, and after many difficulties with rocks and rapids, reached tidewater on 7 November 1805. 'Great joy in Camp,' wrote Clark in his diary, 'we are in view of . . . this great Pacific Ocean which we have been so long anxious to see.' And they built Fort Clatsop within sound of the great Pacific surges, there to spend another winter.

Lewis and Clark learned that New England trading vessels had visited the Columbia, through the coastal Indians' use of such elegant phrases as 'heave the lead' and 'sun-of-a-pitch.' But as months passed and no ship called, the explorers decided to return overland. The expedition reached St. Louis 23 September 1806. They had found no water route through the Rockies, since there was none; but the land and river route they discovered served later pioneers, and their Indian relations were beyond praise.

'Never was there an administration more brilliant than that of Mr. Jefferson up to this period,' said John Randolph in later years. 'We were indeed in the "full tide of successful experiment." Taxes repealed; the public debt amply provided for, both principal and interest; sinecures abolished; Louisiana acquired; public confidence unbounded.'

Crumbling Federalism

Even in this euphoric period, there was one group that could not abide Jefferson's success—the leaders of New England Federalism. Jefferson's reign, they believed, would lead to terror, atheism, and autocracy. Their power was waning, and they knew it. Ohio, admitted to the Union in 1803, looked to Virginia for guidance, although largely settled by Yankees. New states to be formed from Louisiana would follow the same light; and their political weight would be increased by the federal ratio of representation. The annexation of Louisiana, upsetting the balance of power within the Union, absolved New England from allegiance to the Union; at least so the Federalists reasoned. Before 1803 was out the 'Essex Junto' of Massachusetts and the 'River Gods' of Connecticut began to plan a Northern Confederacy with New England as a nucleus. The British minister at Washington gave this conspiracy his blessing, but Hamilton would have none of it.

The conspirators then turned to Aaron Burr. He had carried New York for Jefferson in 1800, and without that state Jefferson would not have been elected. Yet Jefferson, once safe in office, ignored the Vice-President in distributing patronage and dropped him from the presidential ticket in 1804. Burr then decided to contest the governorship of New York with the regular Republican candidate. In return for Federalist aid, Burr appears to have agreed, if successful, to swing New York into a Northern Confederacy and become its president. But most Federalist leaders opposed the scheme, Burr was defeated, and the Federalist conspiracy dissolved. How remote was its chance of success the presidential election of 1804 proved. Jefferson carried every state but Connecticut and Delaware, with 162 electoral votes to 14 for Pinckney.

At the age of forty-eight, Burr was a ruined politician. He had broken with the Republicans and failed the Federalists. Hamilton was responsible. It was not the first time that Hamilton had crossed his path; it must be the last. On 18 June 1804, six weeks after the New York election, Burr wrote to his rival, demanding 'a prompt and unqualified acknowledgment or denial' of a slur upon his character reported in the press. Hamilton refused to retract, and answered, 'I trust on more reflection you will see the matter in the same light with me. If not, I can only regret the circumstances, and must abide the consequences.' According to the 'code of honor' observed by the gentry of the South and of New York, such language was an invitation to a challenge; and the challenge came quickly. Hamilton had no business to accept. He did not need to prove his courage;

he had a wife and a large family dependent on him. Moreover, he believed it murder to kill an adversary in a duel. Yet the infirmity of a noble mind forced him to accept the challenge.

Poor Hamilton had become enmeshed in a double net of theory and ambition. He might differ from the New England Federalists as to the cure for democracy, but he judged the future by their gloomy formula. A crisis was impending, he thought. The year 1804 in America corresponded to 1791 in France. Jefferson would disappear like Mirabeau and Lafayette, dissolution and anarchy would follow; then America would demand a savior. Hamilton intended to be ready at the call—but no one under suspicion of cowardice could save his country. So Hamilton resolved to prove his courage and yet not to kill, to reserve and throw away his first fire, in the hope that Burr would miss and honor be satisfied. Aaron Burr did not intend to miss.

At six o'clock on a bright summer morning, 11 July 1804, Hamilton and his second were ferried across the Hudson to a grove of trees under the Palisades. The distance agreed upon was ten paces. When the signal *present* was given, the Vice-President raised his arm slowly, took deliberate aim, and fired. Hamilton fell mortally wounded. So perished one of the greatest men of the age, for his little faith in the government he had helped to form and in the people he had served so well.

The Assault on the Judiciary

Aaron Burr fled to Washington, where the President received him amiably and conferred upon his friends the three best offices in Louisiana Territory. It was not that Jefferson wished to reward the slayer of Hamilton, but that he wanted something of Burr. For as Vice-President he must preside over the United States Senate, sitting as a court of impeachment to try Justice Chase of the Supreme Court.

This trial was part of a Republican attempt to rid the federal judiciary of partisan Federalists. Under Chief Justice Jay the federal courts had exercised their constitutional powers without much opposition. They had, however, made two false steps. In Chisholm *v.* Georgia (1793), a case involving confiscations contrary to the peace treaty, the Supreme Court ordered that state to appear before the bar as defendant and entered judgment against it by default. State susceptibilities, thus aroused, produced the Eleventh Amendment, forbidding suits against states by citizens of other states or nations. It was ratified in 1798. That same year certain federal judges, excited by the supposed Jacobin menace, enforced the Sedition Act with unholy zeal and delivered political harangues to grand juries. In February 1801, when Congress increased the number of federal courts, President Adams filled the new places with members of his party and conferred the chief justiceship on John Marshall, a kinsman whom Jefferson hated bitterly and wished to humiliate.

The feud was intensified when Chief Justice Marshall defied the new President in the case of Marbury *v.* Madison. Marbury was a justice of the peace for the District of Columbia, a 'midnight appointment' by President Adams in the last hours of his administration. Madison, the new Secretary of State, refused to deliver his commission to Marbury, who applied to the Supreme Court for a writ of mandamus, under section 13 of the Judiciary Act of 1789. Chief Justice Marshall, delivering the opinion of the Court (February 1803), stated that Madison had no right to withhold the commission of a properly appointed official. But Marbury's hopes were dashed by the rest of the opinion. The Federal Constitution, in defining the original jurisdiction of the Supreme Court, had not included the issue of writs to executive officers. Hence, section 13 of the Judiciary Act was unconstitutional and the Court could not take jurisdiction. A nicer sense of propriety might have suggested to Marshall that if the Court had no jurisdiction it should not announce how it would have decided the case if it had. But Marshall was bent on rebuking Jefferson and Madison for what he considered an arbitrary act. In so doing, he firmly enunciated the doctrine of judicial review—the right, indeed the duty, of the Supreme Court to invalidate statutes that are 'contrary to the Constitution.'

Jefferson now incited some of his henchmen in the House to move against certain federal judges. A district judge who had become intemperate to

Aaron Burr (1756–1836). Although some historians believe that Burr's contributions to the republic merit greater recognition, the third Vice-President of the United States seems doomed to be remembered as an intriguer and as the man who killed Alexander Hamilton in a duel. Grandson of the Puritan divine Jonathan Edwards, Burr has been chided by biographers for his 'ingrained amatory habits.' This portrait is by Burr's protégé, John Vanderlyn, the first American to study painting in Paris. Vanderlyn's nudes were so realistic that viewers were shocked, but Napoleon was so impressed by his work that he had a gold medal conferred on him. (*New-York Historical Society*)

the point of insanity was impeached and removed. The next victim was to be Justice Samuel Chase, a signer of the Declaration of Independence, who on the bench had made himself peculiarly obnoxious to the Republicans. By a straight partisan vote, the House of Representatives impeached him on several counts. But since there was no evidence to substantiate the serious charges against him, enough Republican senators joined the Federalists to acquit the Justice of 'crimes and misdemeanors.'

Had Chase been found guilty, the entire Supreme Court would have been purged. As it was, this trial proved to be the high-water mark of Jefferson's radicalism. Under Chief Justice Marshall conservatism rallied, and the Supreme Court mounted a subtle offensive of ideas—the supremacy of the nation and the sanctity of property. 'The Federalists,' wrote Jefferson bitterly, 'defeated at the polls, have retired into the Judiciary, and from that barricade they hope to batter down all the bulwarks of Republicanism.' To a large measure they succeeded.

Domestic Intrigue and Foreign Complications

Thomas Jefferson, returned to the presidency by an overwhelming majority, started his second term on 4 March 1805, expecting to pursue the 'wise and frugal' policy of 1801 to its logical conclusion. But peace in Europe had been the condition of Jefferson's earlier success, and there was to be no peace in Europe for ten years. His second term was compared by John Randolph to Pharaoh's dream of the seven lean kine that ate up the seven fat kine. Many old Virginia Republicans like Randolph felt that Jefferson had deserted his own principles. In his first term he had broken with strict construction to acquire Louisiana, and in his second inaugural address, he recommended spending federal money on internal improvements. In Jefferson's second term, trouble accumulated. He confronted not only the defection of Old Republicans but something much more serious—nothing less than a threat to dismember the country in the shape of the Burr conspiracy.

Before leaving Washington at the expiration of his term as Vice-President, Burr approached the British minister with an offer to detach Louisiana from the Union for half a million dollars, provided the Royal Navy would co-operate. Mr. Merry thought well of it and urged his government to pay, but Downing Street was not interested in promoting American secession. Burr then proceeded to the headwaters of the Ohio and, with a few friends, sailed down-river in a luxury flatboat, stopping here and there to propose a different scheme. The Westerners, duelers themselves, were charmed by the polished gentleman from New York. Harman Blennerhasset, a romantic Irish exile, was fascinated with a plan to conquer Mexico, make Burr emperor and himself a grand potentate. General Wilkinson, still in Spanish pay while governor of Louisiana Territory and ranking general of the United States Army, had already discussed with Burr a project to 'liberate' Mexico from Spain and make Louisiana an independent republic. At New Orleans Burr got in touch with certain creoles who disliked being sold by Napoleon and with an association of American filibusters who were eager to invade Mexico. The Catholic bishop of New Orleans and the mother superior of the Ursuline convent gave him their blessing. Returning overland, Burr found Westerners everywhere eager for war with Spain. In Washington again, Burr obtained $2500 from the Spanish minister, ostensibly for the purpose of capturing the United States naval vessels then in the Potomac and embarking a filibustering expedition to 'liberate' Louisiana!

In the summer of 1806 the former Vice-President established headquarters at Lexington, Ky., and began active recruiting. What was his real object? Ostensibly it was to take up and colonize an enormous land claim he had purchased in western Louisiana. Those supposedly 'in the know' expected him to move into Texas and 'liberate' Mexico. Evidence is strong that Burr did have his eye on Mexico, but that, first, he would promote a secession of Louisiana Territory and become its president. At this juncture General Wilkinson, deciding that Burr was worth more to betray than to befriend, sent a lurid letter to President Jefferson denouncing 'a deep, dark, wicked, and wide-spread conspiracy' to dismember the Union. Similar warnings reached Washington from loyal Westerners. In the late autumn of 1806 the President issued a proclamation ordering the arrest of Burr. He was brought to Richmond for trial, on a charge of treason.

Fortunately for the prisoner, Chief Justice Marshall, who presided at his trial, took care that the constitutional definition of treason, 'levying war against the United States or adhering to their enemies,' and the constitutional safeguard of 'two witnesses to the same overt act,' should be strictly observed. Hence it followed that merely recruiting with treasonable intent was not treason. Burr was acquitted and sought exile in France. In 1812 he managed to obtain a passport and return to New York, where he built up a good law practice; and in 1833, at the age of 77, he married an attractive widow, Madame Jumel, who used to boast that she was the only woman in the world who had slept with both George Washington and Napoleon Bonaparte.

No sooner had the Burr trial ended than Jefferson faced a no less vexing problem in Europe, where Napoleon and Britain sought to starve or strangle each other by continental or maritime blockade and to levy tolls on neutral traders. Furthermore, as soon as the Royal Navy considered the renewal of war with France inevitable, it resumed the practice of impressing British subjects from American vessels on the high seas; men were plucked off American ships even outside New York harbor. Britain never claimed the right to take native-born Americans, but to impress her own subjects from foreign vessels wherever found. British seamen were constantly deserting. The U.S.S. *Constitution* in 1807 had 149 avowed British subjects, and only 241 who claimed American citizenship, in her crew of 419. And neither country then admitted the right of expatriation. When a short-handed man-of-war visited an American merchantman, the boarding officer was apt to impress any likely looking lad who had the slightest trace of an Irish or English accent. Mistakes were difficult to rectify, and there were enough instances of brutality and injustice to create indignation.

An impressment outrage brought the two countries to the verge of war. A British squadron, stationed within the Capes of the Chesapeake to watch French frigates up the Bay, lost many men by desertion, and had reason to believe that Jenkin Ratford, the ringleader, had enlisted in the United States frigate *Chesapeake*. That was true; and she had other British-born tars too. On 22 June 1807 the *Chesapeake*, flying the pennant of Commodore Barron, encountered H.M.S. *Leopard* about ten miles outside the Capes. When the *Leopard* signaled 'Dispatches,' Barron supposed that she wished him to carry mail to Europe, a common courtesy between the two navies, so he invited the British captain to board his vessel. But the dispatches proved to be an order to search for and remove deserters. Barron, ignorant of Ratford's presence, replied that the only deserters from the Royal Navy in his crew were three Americans who had escaped after impressment, and that he would permit no search. *Leopard* fired three broadsides into the *Chesapeake*, which had few of her guns mounted. After three men had been killed, Barron struck his flag. His crew were then mustered by the *Leopard*'s officers, and three Americans and Ratford were impressed.

News of this insult to the flag brought the first united expression of American feeling since 1798. Even the Federalists, who had hitherto defended every move of British sea power, were confounded. If Jefferson had summoned Congress to a special session, he could have had war at the drop of a hat. Instead, he instructed Monroe to demand apology and reparation in London, and ordered British warships out of American territorial waters. But no suggestion of war, or of preparation for war, came from the President. For he imagined that he had England by the throat and could strangle her by a mere turn of the wrist.

Jefferson's Embargo

For years Jefferson had been wanting an opportunity to try commercial exclusion as a substitute for war. He reasoned that since the United States was the world's largest neutral carrier and the chief market for British manufactures, Britain could be brought to terms. The President urged: 'Let us see whether having taught so many other useful lessons to Europe, we may not add that of showing them that there are peaceable means of repressing injustice, by making it to the interest of the aggressor to do what is just.' Under the Embargo Act of December 1807, American or other vessels were forbidden to sail foreign, all exports from the United States whether by sea or land were prohibited, and certain specified articles of British manufacture were refused entrance.[1] For fourteen months every American ship that was not already abroad, or could not escape, lay in port or went coasting.

The embargo struck a staggering blow to foreign trade, the most important source of America's economic growth in these years. After the outbreak of war in Europe in 1793, ships of every belligerent save England had vanished from the seas, leaving the enormous colonial trade of Europe to neutrals, and especially the United States. To avoid being intercepted, ships with tropical products—sugar, coffee, tea, pepper, cocoa—sailed to the United States, and their cargoes were then reshipped. From 1790 to 1807 domestic exports had doubled; re-exports in that same period grew from $300,000 to more than $59 million. The war also proved a boon for grain and cotton growers when Europe's sources of these staples were cut off. During this period of flourishing commerce, the population of Philadelphia more than doubled, Boston nearly doubled, and Baltimore and New York almost tripled. Much of the increase came from shipping and shipbuilding, and their effect on dependent industries such as ropewalks, sailmaking, lumbering, provisioning, marine insurance companies, and even banks. The embargo snuffed out this profitable trade and threw thousands of sailors and shipwrights out of jobs. To the Yankees it seemed as outrageous for Congress to decree 'Thou shalt not sail!' as it would have to the South, had Congress said 'Thou shalt not plant!'

It is true that between British orders in council and French decrees, American vessels could visit no part of the world without rendering themselves liable to capture by one belligerent or the other. But the American merchant marine throve on such treatment; shipowners wanted no protection other than that which the British navy afforded them. European restrictions merely increased the profit with the risk. Hence the embargo was detested by the very interest it was supposed to protect. Many small shipowners were ruined, and some of the lesser seaports such as Newburyport and New Haven never recovered their earlier prosperity. The embargo also hurt the South, where cotton prices were almost halved, but New England spoke out most loudly against the policy, because it was the stronghold of the Federalists, who viewed the embargo as a sectional and partisan conspiracy.

To succeed as a weapon of diplomacy, commercial retaliation requires an unusual combination of circumstances—which very seldom occurs, and did not occur in 1807–9. The embargo caused a shortage of provisions in the French West Indies and of colonial produce in France; but Napoleon confiscated every American vessel that arrived at a French port, on the ground that he was helping Jefferson to enforce the measure! In the English manufacturing districts the embargo caused some distress, but the usual exports soon found their way into the United States through Canada, and British shipowners loved a measure that removed American competition.

Jefferson's mistake was the Federalists' opportunity. Their strength had been dwindling, even in New England, where in 1807 every state government except Connecticut's went Republican. The Federalists had been unable to overcome the stigma of monarchism and militarism the Republicans had fastened on them, and they were handicapped by a late start in developing effective party organization. Now, unexpectedly, Jefferson had handed them an issue on which they might make a popular appeal. The Federalists approached the 1808 election with high hopes. Northern Republicans were restive under a measure that turned their constituents Federalist; and in New York City the embargo produced a schism in the Republican party. When Madison was nominated for the presidential succession by a congressional caucus, the New York legislature placed George Clinton in

1. The last measure was not, strictly speaking, a part of the embargo of December 1807, but the Non-importation Act of 16 April 1806, which did not go into effect until the embargo was adopted.

Salem sea captain. In the generation after the American Revolution, brightly painted ships from the little Massachusetts port of Salem sailed to every quarter of the globe, and prosperous captains commissioned leading artists to depict them and their handsome vessels. The identity of the painter of this portrait of John Carnes is unknown, but many of the best works of the period came from the brush of George Ropes, the deaf and dumb son of a Salem mariner who was taught by a refugee from the Napoleonic wars. (*Peabody Museum of Salem*)

nomination as an anti-embargo Republican. In Virginia John Randolph's sect of 'pure Republicans' nominated Monroe. If a union could have been effected between these factions and the Federalists, Madison might have been defeated. But the Federalist candidate, C. C. Pinckney, carried little but New England, save Vermont, and Delaware, and Madison was elected President by a comfortable majority, 122–47.

Jefferson intended to maintain the embargo until the British orders or the French decrees were repealed. In January 1809 Congress passed the 'Force Act,' permitting federal officials without warrant to seize goods under suspicion of foreign destination and protecting them from legal liability for their actions. Watchmen patrolled Atlantic wharves, and revenue officers seized sails and unshipped rudders. George III and Lord North had been tender in comparison. The people of New England, now in their second winter of privation and distress, began to look to their state governments for protection; and by this time all state governments of New England were Federalist again. The legislatures hurled back in the teeth of Jefferson and Madison the doctrines of the Kentucky and Virginia Resolves of 1798. Connecticut resolved that 'whenever our national legislature is led to overleap the prescribed bounds of their constitutional powers,' it becomes the duty of the state legislatures 'to interpose their protecting shield.' Northern Republicans revolted; and Jefferson was shaken by a volley of protests from New England town meetings, some of them threatening secession. A bill for the repeal of the embargo was rushed through Congress and, on 1 March 1809, approved by Jefferson. Three days later his term ended and he retired to Monticello.

The embargo was intended to be the crowning glory of Jefferson's second administration, as Louisiana had been of his first, but it proved a dismal failure. It neither influenced the policy of Britain or of Napoleon nor protected the merchant marine. It wasted the fruit of Jefferson's first administration: the creation of a broad, country-wide party in every state of the Union. It convinced many good people that the 'Virginia dynasty' was bound to that of Bonaparte, that the Republican party was a greater enemy than British sea power to American shipping. Whatever President Madison might do or neglect to do, he would never have such united support as Jefferson had enjoyed in 1807.

Yet despite the failure of the embargo, Jefferson was one of the greatest of Presidents and the most tolerant of revolutionists. Few men have combined in like degree a lofty idealism with the ability to administer a government. He preferred the slow process of reason to the short way of force. By his forbearance, even more than by his acts, Jefferson kept alive the flame of liberty that Napoleon had almost quenched in Europe.

10

The Second War with Great Britain

*

1809–1815

The Coming of War

Owing to James Madison's labors on the Federal Constitution he must be accounted a great statesman, but he was a very poor politician; and a poor politician usually makes a bad President, although a good 'pol' does not necessarily make a good chief magistrate. Slight in stature and unimpressive in personality, eager to please but wearing a puzzled look as though people were too much for him, 'Jemmy' Madison had few intimate friends, and among the people at large he inspired little affection and no enthusiasm. He had a talent for writing logical diplomatic notes; but logic was not much use in dealing with Europeans locked in a deadly struggle. He was negative in dealing with Congress, allowing Jefferson's system of personal influence with members to fall apart. And Madison was stubborn to the point of stupidity.

Yet, within six weeks of his inauguration on 4 March 1809, Madison was being greeted as a great peacemaker. Congress, when repealing Jefferson's embargo, substituted a non-intercourse act aimed at both Britain and France, with the promise of recommencing commercial relations with whichever nation first repealed its decrees injuring American commerce. Madison, eager to reach an understanding with England, arranged a treaty with David Erskine, the British minister in Washington, by virtue of which His Majesty's government would rescind orders against American shipping, and the United States would resume normal trading relations with Britain but maintain non-intercourse against France. Touchy subjects such as impressment and the *Chesapeake* affair were postponed. If this draft treaty had been accepted by George Canning, the British minister of foreign affairs, there would have been no second war with England. But Canning brutally repudiated both Erskine and the treaty, and Aglo-American relations returned to a state of mutual recrimination.

The Congress that assembled in December 1809 had no idea what to do, and received no lead from Madison. On 16 April 1810 it voted to reduce both the army and the navy, weak though they already were. And on 1 May Congress reversed the principle of the earlier Non-Intercourse Act by passing Macon's Bill No. 2. This law restored intercourse with both Britain and France, but promised to the first power which recognized neutral rights to stop trading with her enemy. American ships promptly resumed making juicy profits under British license, and merchant tonnage reached figures that were not again attained for another twenty years.

Madison took advantage of this interlude in commercial warfare to take a bite out of West Florida. In 1810 the inhabitants of that portion of West Florida bordering on the Mississippi 'self-determined' for the United States and seized Baton Rouge. Madison promptly incorporated them, by presidential proclamation, into the Territory of Orleans, which two years later became the state of Louisiana. In May 1812 a second bite was taken, when the district between the Pearl and Perdido rivers was annexed to Mississippi Territory.

While Madison was devouring West Florida, Napoleon was becoming aware that Macon's Act offered him an opportunity to incorporate the United States into his Continental system, a scheme for getting the European continent under his control in order to impoverish England. America could help this strategy by adding a sea-power component. For five years Napoleon had treated American shipping harshly, but in the summer of 1810 Napoleon's minister of foreign affairs informed the American minister to France that 'His Majesty loves the Americans,' and as proof of his solicitude had declared that his decrees against neutral shipping after 1 November would be revoked; 'it being understood that the English are to revoke their orders in council.'

John Quincy Adams, minister to Russia, warned Madison that this note was 'a trap to catch us into a war with England.' But the President, searching desperately for an effective policy, fell into the trap. By proclamation on 2 November 1810 he announced that France had rescinded her anti-neutral system, hence non-intercourse would be revived against Britain, if within three months she did not repeal the orders in council. Almost every mail for the next two years brought news of fresh seizures and scuttlings of American vessels by the French. But Madison, having taken his stand, obstinately insisted that 'the national faith was pledged to France.' On 2 March 1811 he forbade intercourse with Great Britain, under authority of Macon's Act. This time, economic sanctions really worked against England—but too late to preserve the peace. The winter of 1811–12 was the bitterest that the English people experienced between the Great Plague of 1665 and the German blitz of 1940–41. Warehouses were crammed with goods for which there was no market, factories were closing, workmen rioting. Deputations from the manufacturing cities besought Parliament to repeal the orders in council to recover their American market.

During these critical months several accidents postponed repeal, which, had it taken place in time, would have maintained peace. Spencer Perceval, the prime minister, was assassinated just after he had made up his mind to repeal the orders in council, and the business of finding a successor brought another and fatal delay. Finally on 16 June 1812, Castlereagh announced that the orders in council would be suspended immediately. If there had been a transatlantic cable, this would not have been too late. But Congress, having no word of the concession, declared war against Great Britain on 18 June 1812.

Congress so acted in response to a message from President Madison recommending war with Britain on four grounds—impressment of seamen, repeated violations of American territorial waters by the Royal Navy, declaring an enemy coast blockaded when it was not blockaded in fact, and the orders in council against neutral trade. Yet six senators and a large majority of the congressmen from the New England states, and a majority in both houses from New York, New Jersey, and Maryland voted against the declaration of war; whilst representatives of the inland and Western states from Vermont to Tennessee, and of the states from Virginia south, were almost solidly for war. New England, where three-quarters of American shipping was owned, and which supplied more than that proportion of American seamen, agitated against war to the brink of treason; whilst back-country congressmen who had never smelled salt water screamed for 'Free Trade and Sailors' Rights.'

The explanation? Republican party leaders believed that they had tried to prevent war by diplomacy and economic sanction and, since both had failed, they had no choice left but capitulation or war. If they did not choose war, they feared they would jeopardize both the confidence of the nation in the strength of republican institutions and the future of the Republican party. The South and West also had economic grievances. Worried over the declining prices of staple exports like cotton, tobacco, and hemp, they blamed their troubles, unjustifiably, on the British.

Some of the newer Republican leaders were much more ardent for war than was Madison. The elections of 1810–11 had sent to Congress a remarkably able group of newcomers, who quickly assumed positions of leadership. There were thirty-four-year-old Henry Clay and Richard M. Johnson from Kentucky; equally young Felix Grundy and aged but very bellicose John Sevier from Tennessee; Peter B. Porter, also in his thirties, from Buffalo, N.Y.; and twenty-nine-year-old John C. Calhoun from the back-country of South Carolina. These men, dubbed 'war hawks' by John Randolph, combined with other new members to elect Henry Clay Speaker of the House; and Clay named his friends chairmen of the important committees. The war hawks believed that national honor demanded a fight. Furthermore, they sought to conquer Canada, end the Indian menace on the Western frontier, and throw open more forest land for settlement. John Randolph of Roanoke, leader of the 'pure' Republicans who wished to keep the peace, poured his scorn on this 'cant of patriotism,' this 'agrarian cupidity,' this chanting 'like the whippoorwill, but one monotonous tone—Canada! Canada! Canada!'

Western concern over the Indian menace was a major cause of war. The 1795 Treaty of Greenville ended a period in which the Northwest Indians had usually been the aggressors, and put them on the defensive. Although the Indians faithfully fulfilled their treaty stipulations, whites in the Northwest committed the most wanton murders of Indians, for which it was almost impossible to obtain a conviction from a pioneer jury. From time to time a few hungry and desperate chiefs were rounded up by government officials and plied with oratory and whiskey until they signed a treaty alienating forever the hunting grounds of their tribe, perhaps of other nations as well. Jefferson encouraged this process; and William Henry Harrison, superintendent of the Northwest Indians and governor of Indiana Territory, pushed it so successfully that during the fourteen years following the 1795 treaty the Indians of that region parted with some 48 million acres. In 1809 this process came to a halt, owing in part to renewed efforts by British authorities in Canada to stiffen Indian resistance. Their efforts, as much as land hunger and far more than indignation over sailors' rights, contributed to war fever west of the Appalachians.

The determination of Indians not to yield to white expansionism actually owed less to the British than to the leadership of the twin brothers Tecumseh and Tenskwatawa, sons of a Shawnee chief. The former, a lithe, handsome, and stately warrior, had been one of those who defeated St. Clair in 1791; Tenskwatawa, better known as The Prophet, was a half-blind medicine man who won ascendancy over his people by such simple means as foretelling an eclipse of the sun. The two, around 1808, bravely undertook the task of saving their people. They sought to reform their habits, stop the alienation of their land, keep them apart from the whites, and to weld all tribes on United States soil into a confederacy. It was a movement of regeneration and defense, a menace indeed to the expansion of the West but not to its existence. The Indians has so decreased in the last decade that scarcely 4000 warriors could be counted on in the region bounded by the Great Lakes, the Mississippi, and the Ohio. Opposed to them were at least 100,000 white men of fighting age in the Ohio valley.

For a time the partnership of warrior and priest was irresistible. The Prophet kindled a religious revival among the tribes of the Northwest, and induced them to give up intoxicating liquor. All intercourse with white men, except for trade, ceased. In 1808 the two leaders, forced from their old settlement by the palefaces, established headquarters at a great clearing in Indiana, where Tippecanoe creek empties into the Wabash river. The entire frontier was alarmed, for The Prophet's moral influence extended as far south as Florida, and northwest to Saskatchewan. Governor Harrison met the situation with an act that Tecumseh could only regard as a challenge. Rounding up a few score survivors of tribes whom he frankly described as 'the most depraved wretches on earth,' the governor obtained from them several enormous tracts cutting up both banks of the Wabash into the heart of Tecumseh's country. This deprived Tecumseh of his remaining hunting grounds and brought the white border within fifty miles of the Tippecanoe. With justice Tecumseh declared this treaty null and void. In July 1811, Governor Harrison decided to force the issue by encamping hard by Tecumseh's village. The Prophet had been strictly enjoined by his brother to avoid hostilities; but instead of retiring he allowed himself to be maneuvered into battle by a few reckless young braves. Harrison drove the Indians into a swamp and destroyed their village. This Battle of Tippecanoe (7 November 1811) made Harrison a hero of the West and helped to elect him President in 1840.

Throughout the West it was believed that Britain had backed Tecumseh's confederacy. In fact, Tecumseh's league was the result of two Indian leaders trying to counteract an American policy which threatened to wipe out their people; as eventually it did. After Tippecanoe, however, the new governor general, Sir George Prevost, decided that war with the United States was inevitable, and his agents welcomed Tecumseh and 1800 warriors in June 1812. Thus many, if not most, Westerners were keen for war with England in order to annex Upper Canada and wipe out the assumed source of Indian troubles.

The War of 1812

Everyone knew that this war for 'Free Trade and Sailors' Rights' would be fought largely on land, preferably in Canada, the only part of the British empire that Americans could get at dry-shod. The population of British North America was less than half a million; that of the United States, by the census of 1810, 7.25 million. In the States the enrolled militia totaled about 700,000; and the regular army, by the time war broke out, had been recruited to about 7000 officers and men. There were fewer than 5000 British regulars in North America, and little chance that Britain, deeply engaged in the Peninsular Campaign, could spare reinforcements. Canada, however, could count on Tecumseh's braves.

Moreover, the war was far from popular in the United States. Every Federalist vote in Congress was cast against the declaration of war, which was greeted in New England by mournful tolling of church bells. Federalists approved neither the Westerners' land-hunger for Canada, nor the Southerners' lust for the fertile acres of the Creek nation. Jefferson's embargo had convinced them of the administration's insincerity in claiming to protect commerce; and Madison's acquiescence in Napoleon's deceptive diplomacy suggested that the Emperor had nudged America into war. And the fact that the British offered an unconditional armistice which Madison contemptuously refused convinced doubters in the party that the administration was bent on conquest. Federalists were incensed when Cognress adjourned 6 July 1812 without making any provision to increase the navy. To refuse to increase one's naval force in a war with the world's greatest sea power for 'Free Trade and Sailors' Rights' seemed gross hypocrisy. The governors of Massachusetts, Rhode Island, and Connecticut refused to call state militia into national service, and Federalist merchants would neither subscribe to war bonds nor fit out privateers. Opponents of the war sometimes met with violence. At Baltimore the plant of a Federalist newspaper was demolished by a mob. The friends of the editor, lodged for safety in the city jail, were dragged out by a waterfront mob and beaten to a pulp; the editor and General Henry Lee were badly injured, and General James M. Lingan, another Revolutionary veteran, was killed.

Chief Justice Marshall wrote that he was mortified by his country's base submission to Napoleon and that the only party division henceforth should be between the friends of peace and the advocates of war. That was indeed the division in the presidential election of 1812. The Federalists supported De Witt Clinton, who had been placed in nomination by an anti-war faction of the New York Republicans, and carried every

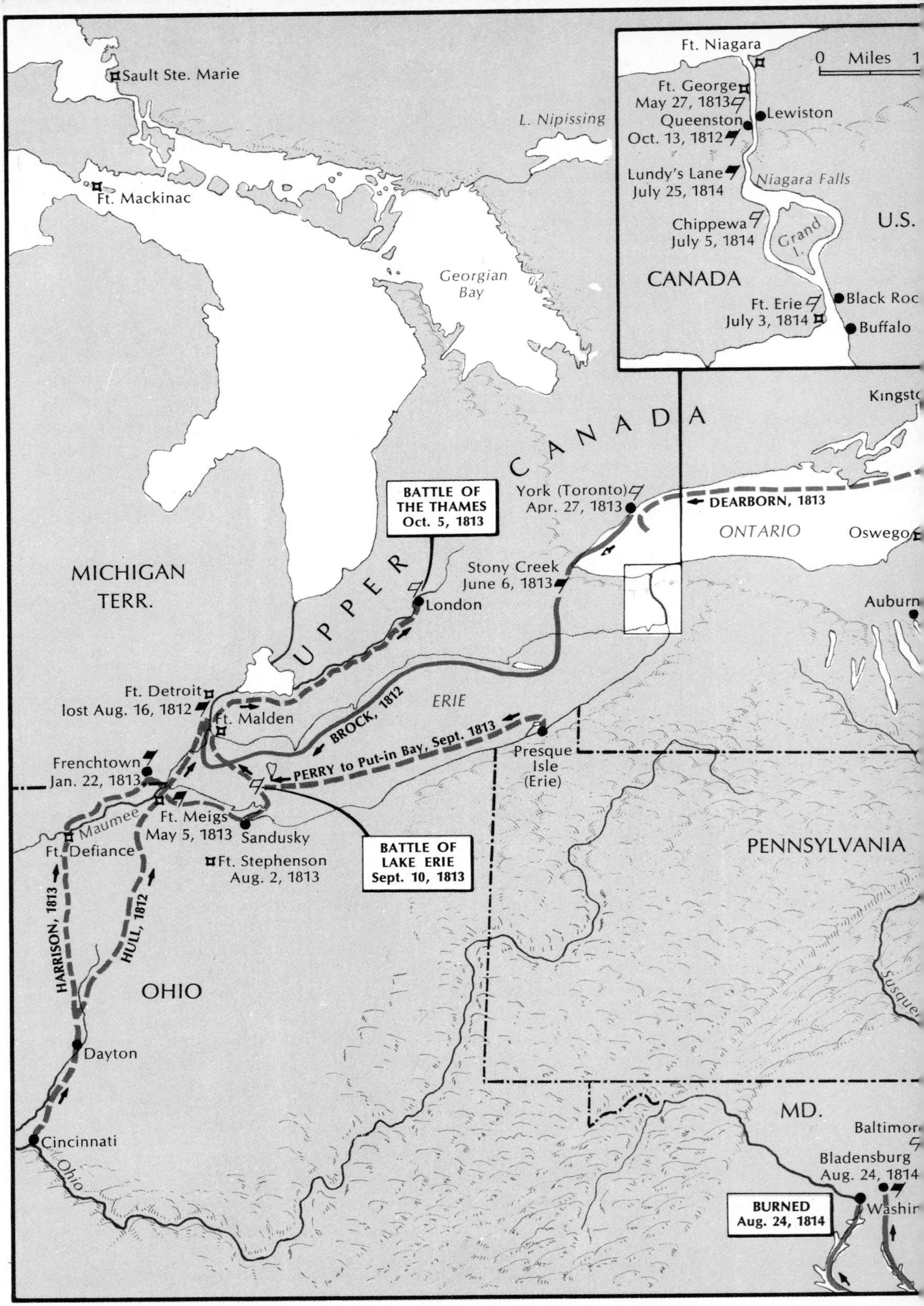

Sault Ste. Marie
L. Nipissing
Ft. Mackinac
Georgian Bay
Ft. Niagara
0 Miles 1
Ft. George
May 27, 1813
Queenston
Oct. 13, 1812
Lewiston
Lundy's Lane
July 25, 1814
Niagara Falls
Chippewa
July 5, 1814
Grand I.
U.S.
CANADA
Ft. Erie
July 3, 1814
Black Roc
Buffalo
Kingsto
UPPER CANADA
BATTLE OF THE THAMES Oct. 5, 1813
York (Toronto)
Apr. 27, 1813
DEARBORN, 1813
ONTARIO
Oswego
MICHIGAN TERR.
Stony Creek
June 6, 1813
London
Auburn
Ft. Detroit
lost Aug. 16, 1812
Ft. Malden
ERIE
BROCK, 1812
PERRY to Put-in Bay, Sept. 1813
Presque Isle (Erie)
Frenchtown
Jan. 22, 1813
Maumee
Ft. Meigs
May 5, 1813
Sandusky
Ft. Defiance
Ft. Stephenson
Aug. 2, 1813
BATTLE OF LAKE ERIE Sept. 10, 1813
PENNSYLVANIA
HARRISON, 1813
HULL, 1812
OHIO
Susque
Dayton
MD.
Baltimor
Bladensburg
Aug. 24, 1814
Cincinnati
Ohio
BURNED Aug. 24, 1814
Washin

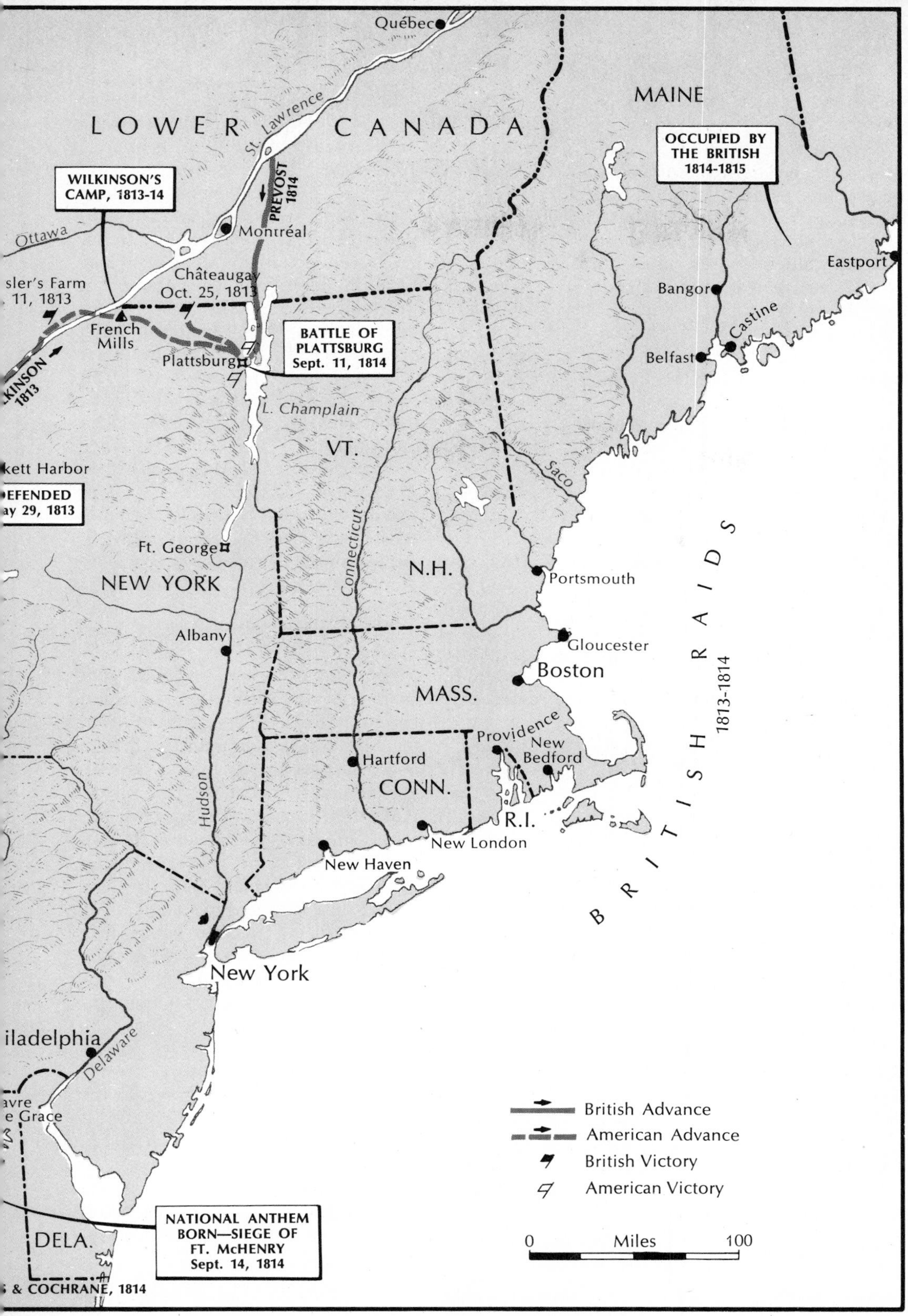
Québec
LOWER CANADA
St. Lawrence
MAINE
OCCUPIED BY THE BRITISH 1814-1815
WILKINSON'S CAMP, 1813-14
PREVOST 1814
Ottawa
Montréal
Eastport
sler's Farm
11, 1813
Châteaugay
Oct. 25, 1813
Bangor
French Mills
Castine
BATTLE OF PLATTSBURG Sept. 11, 1814
Belfast
Plattsburg
KINSON 1813
L. Champlain
VT.
kett Harbor
EFENDED
ay 29, 1813
Saco
Ft. George
Connecticut
N.H.
Portsmouth
NEW YORK
Albany
Gloucester
Boston
MASS.
BRITISH RAIDS 1813-1814
Providence
New Bedford
Hartford
CONN.
Hudson
R.I.
New London
New Haven
New York
iladelphia
Delaware
avre
e Grace
British Advance
American Advance
British Victory
American Victory
DELA.
NATIONAL ANTHEM BORN—SIEGE OF FT. McHENRY Sept. 14, 1814
0 Miles 100
& COCHRANE, 1814

War of 1812 in the North

state north of the Potomac except two. But Madison was re-elected.

In addition to having to cope with internal disaffection, the United States had a further disadvantage: the administration's military strategy was stupid. Instead of striking at Montreal or Quebec and severing the St. Lawrence, Madison attempted several feeble blows at less important points. Three weeks before war was declared, Governor William Hull of Michigan Territory, a sixty-year-old veteran of the War of Independence, was ordered to invade Upper Canada. Hull crossed into Canada on 12 July, but the British capture of the American post at Michilimackinac caused him to fall back on Detroit. Hull ordered the American commander at Fort Dearborn (Chicago) to come to his assistance; but the Indians captured a part of that small force and massacred the rest. General Isaac Brock, the British commander in Upper Canada, having transported to Detroit the few troops he could spare from the Niagara front, paraded them in red coats in sight of General Hull and summoned him to surrender. A broad hint in Brock's note, that the Indians would be beyond his control the moment the fighting began, completely unnerved the elderly general. Dreading massacre and deserted by some of his militia, Hull surrendered his army on 16 August 1812. So ended the first invasion of Canada. The effective military frontier of the United States was thrown back to the Wabash and the Ohio.

On 13 October 1812 the Americans crossed into Canada again, on the Niagara front. Captain John E. Wool led a small detachment to a successful attack on Queenston heights, in which General Brock was killed. But the New York militia under General Stephen Van Rensselaer refused to support him. They had turned out to defend their homes, not to invade Canada. In vain the Patroon exhorted them. They calmly watched their countrymen on the other bank being enveloped, shot down, and forced to surrender.

On the ocean there was a different story. The United States Navy was vastly outnumbered, but the Royal Navy was so deeply engaged in war with France that at first it could spare few vessels for this war. The pride of the United States Navy were frigates *Constitution*, *United States*, and *President*, which threw a heavier broadside than the British frigates, and were so heavily timbered and planked as to deserve the name 'Old Ironsides'; yet with such fine, clean lines and great spread of canvas that they could outsail almost anything afloat. The crews were volunteers, and the officers, young and tried by experience against France and Tripoli, were burning to avenge the *Chesapeake*. On the other hand, the compatriots of Nelson, conquerors at Cape St. Vincent, Trafalgar, and the Nile, were the spoiled children of victory, confident of beating any vessel not more than twice their size. Hence, when U.S.S. *Constitution* (Captain Isaac Hull, a nephew of the General) knocked H.M.S. *Guerrière* helpless in two hours and a half on 19 August 1812; when sloop-of-war *Wasp* mastered H.M.S. *Frolic* in 43 minutes on 17 October; and U.S.S. *Hornet* (Captain James Lawrence) in a hot fight off the Demerara river, on 24 February 1813, sank H.M.S. *Peacock* in fifteen minutes, there were amazement and indignation in England, and rejoicing in the United States. The moral value of these victories to the American people, following disaster on the Canadian border, was beyond all calculation, but the military value was slight. Most of the American men-of-war that put into harbor during the winter of 1812–13 never got out again because of the British blockade, and the British were able to raid the Chesapeake country at will.

In the meantime, naval history was being made on the Great Lakes. During the winter of 1812–13, Captain Oliver H. Perry constructed a fleet of stout little vessels. That same winter, General William Henry Harrison advanced from the Ohio river toward Detroit, in three divisions. The British General Procter did not wait for them to unite, but beat two separately in fierce wilderness fights in which the American wounded were massacred by Indian auxiliaries. Harrison then decided to await a naval decision on Lake Erie. On 10 September 1813, at Put-in-Bay among the islands at the western end of the lake, Perry won a notable victory. His laconic report, 'We have met the enemy, and they are ours,' was literally true. It was the only surrender of a complete squadron in British naval history.

The prudent course for General Procter was to abandon Detroit and fall back on the Niag-

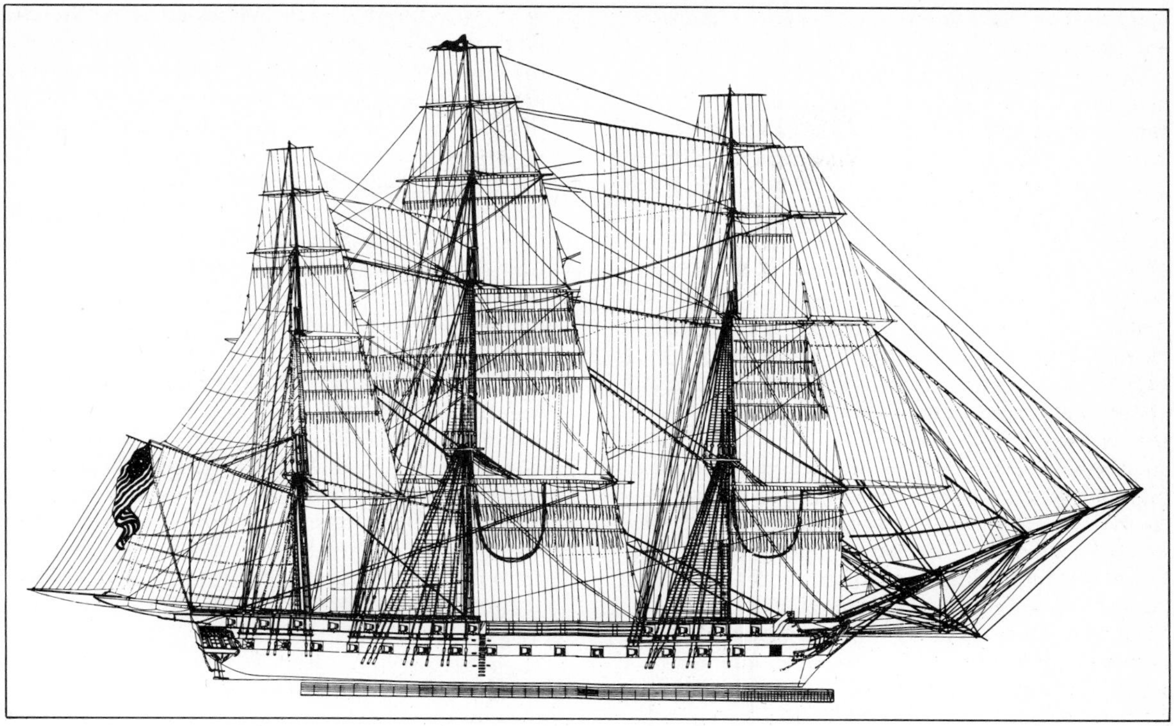

'Old Ironsides.' A 44-gun frigate launched at Boston in 1797, the U.S.S. *Constitution* earned her official nickname in a battle with the British vessel *Java* off Brazil. Oliver Wendell Holmes's poem 'Old Ironsides' sparked a campaign in 1830 that saved her from dismantling, and she is today, at Boston, the oldest ship in the American Navy still in commission. (*Library of Congress*)

ara front. But Tecumseh persuaded his ally to make a stand at an Indian village near the center of the Ontario peninsula. Thither General Harrison pursued him. The Battle of the Thames (5 October 1813) was a victory for the Kentucky mounted rifles. Tecumseh died on that field, his Indian confederacy broke up, Procter fled, and the American military frontier in the Northwest was re-established.

Perry's squadron had obtained valuable cannon from a raid on York (Toronto), the tiny capital of Upper Canada, on 27 April 1813. When the Americans were advancing into the village, a large powder magazine exploded, killing General Zebulon M. Pike and about 300 men. As a result of this incident, or of general indiscipline, the American troops got out of hand after the British surrendered the town, and burned the two brick parliament houses, the governor's residence, and other buildings. The Americans also burned Newark and as much as they could of Queenston, turning the inhabitants out of their houses on a cold winter's night. For this act the innocent inhabitants on the United States side paid dear. On 18 December Fort Niagara was taken by surprise, the Indians were let loose on the surrounding country, and the villages of Black Rock and Buffalo were destroyed. The second year of war closed with Canada cleared of American troops, and the Canadians in possession of Fort Niagara and ready to assume the offensive.

After Napoleon's abdication on 6 April 1814, Britain was able to provide Canada with an adequate army to carry the war into the United States and to intensify the naval blockade. The war office planned to invade the United States from three points successively: Niagara, Lake Champlain, and New Orleans; and simultaneously to raid the Chesapeake.

On the Niagara front America took the initiative before British reinforcements arrived. On 3 July 1814 General Jacob Brown boated his army of about 5000 men across the Niagara river and forced Fort Erie to capitulate. On the 5th, his subordinate, Winfield Scott, after giving his brigade a Fourth of July dinner that they had been too busy to eat the day before, was about to hold a holiday parade on a near-by plain when three regiments of British regulars appeared. The parade became the Battle of Chippewa, a European-style stand-up fight in open country. Both lines advanced in close order, stopping alternately to load and fire; when they were about 60 paces from each other, it was the British who broke. On 25 July, in the Battle of Lundy's Lane, the most stubbornly contested fight of the war, both American generals were badly wounded, and the casualties were very heavy for a battle in that era: on the American side, 853 out of fewer than 2000 engaged; on the British side, 878 out of a somewhat larger force. These actions prevented an invasion of the United States from the Niagara front and gave the United States Army a new pride and character.

By mid-August General Sir George Prevost commanded some 10,000 British veterans encamped near Montreal, ready to invade the United States by the classic route of Lake Champlain and the Hudson. It was the strongest, best equipped army that had ever been sent to North America. Prospects for the United States were grim. Prevost's army reached Plattsburg on 6 September 1814. Facing them were only 1500 American regulars, and a few thousand militia. Before attacking, Prevost wished to secure control of the lake. Early in the morning of 11 September there began a murderous engagement between two freshwater fleets, which anchored gunwale to gunwale at pistol range and attempted to pound each other to pieces. After the British flagship had killed one-fifth of the crew of the American flagship *Saratoga,* Captain Thomas Macdonough forced the British flagship and three other vessels to surrender. Prevost was so discouraged by the loss of this supporting fleet that he retreated to Canada. This naval Battle of Plattsburg—'Macdonough's Victory' it was then called—proved to be decisive. But it was not the last battle of the war.

In June 1814 a British expeditionary force had begun a diversion in the Chesapeake. The campaign that followed reflected little credit to the one side, and considerable disgrace on the other. General Robert Ross, British commander of the land forces, was instructed by Admiral Cochrane 'to destroy and lay waste such towns and districts upon the coast' as he might find assailable. A fleet of American gunboats, retreating up the Patuxent river, led Ross's army from Chesapeake Bay to the back door of Washington. For five days the British marched along the banks of the Patuxent, approaching the capital of the United States without seeing an enemy or firing a shot. In Washington about 7000 militia, all that turned out of 95,000 summoned, were placed under an unusually incompetent general and hurried to a strong position behind the village of Bladensburg, athwart the road over which the invaders must advance. President Madison and some of the cabinet came out to see the fight. After the militia had suffered only 66 casualties they broke and ran, and Ross pressed on to Washington (24 August 1814). Some officers arrived at the White House in time to eat a dinner that had been prepared for the President, who fled to the Virginia hills. Most of the public buildings of the capital were deliberately burned, partly in retaliation for the American burning of York and Newark, partly to impress the administration with the uselessness of further resistance. General Ross personally superintended the piling up of furniture in the White House before it was given to the flames.

Fortunately, the destruction of Washington only illustrated the strategic truth that hit-and-run raids achieve little. The British army withdrew to its transports, and proceeded to the next objective, Baltimore. Here the Maryland militia showed a very different spirit. A naval bombardment of Fort McHenry accomplished nothing for the British, but gave America a stirring national anthem. Francis Scott Key, a prisoner on board one of the bombarding vessels, gained his inspiration for 'The Star Spangled Banner' from seeing the flag still flying over Fort McHenry 'by the dawn's early light.' General Ross fell at the head of a landing party (12 September) one day after 'Macdonough's Victory,' and that ended the Chesapeake campaign.

Before the third British expeditionary force reached New Orleans, the West had produced a great military leader, General Andrew Jackson. He had emigrated to Tennessee as a young man, represented that state in the United States Senate, and as commander of its militia had been winning laurels in warfare against the Upper Creeks. That Indian nation endeavored to remain neutral, but some of Tecumseh's warriors stirred it up. A series of raids took some 250 white scalps. This news found Andrew Jackson in bed at Nashville, recovering from a pistol wound received in a street brawl with Thomas H. Benton, the future senator from Missouri. Within a month Jackson at the head of 2500 militia and a band of Choctaw and Lower Creek auxiliaries was in the Upper Creek country. The Tennessee militia showed the same disposition to panic and flee as their Northern brethren, but after Jackson had executed a few militiamen to encourage the others, discipline improved. At the Tohopeka or Horseshoe Bend of the Tallapoosa river (27 March 1814), the military power of the Creek nation was broken; 557 warriors were left dead on the battlefield, while Jackson lost only 26 of his own men and 23 Indian allies. This campaign not only had immediate strategic impact in depriving the British of a powerful ally; the subsequent treaty with the Upper Creek nation opened an immense territory—about two-thirds of Alabama, the heart of the future cotton kingdom—to white settlement and Negro slavery. In early August, a small British force landed at Pensacola in Spanish Florida; its leader proceeded to drill Creek refugees with a view to renewing the war in that quarter. Jackson invaded Florida on his own authority and crushed this diversion by taking Pensacola in November.

Two months later, the most formidable British expedition of the war threatened New Orleans. On the morning of 8 January 1815 Major General Sir Edward Pakenham directed a foolhardy frontal assault of some 5300 men in close column formation against Andrew Jackson's 3500 on a parapet so well protected that the British could not get at them. The result was more of a massacre than a battle. General Pakenham and over 2000 of all ranks were killed, wounded, or missing. Exactly thirteen Americans were killed and 58 wounded before the attacking columns melted. Ten days later the only surviving British general officer withdrew the army to its transports.

This Battle of New Orleans had no military value, since peace had already been signed at Ghent on Christmas Eve; but it made a future President of the United States, and in folklore wiped out all previous defeats, ending the 'Second War of Independence' in a blaze of glory.

Disaffection and Peace

One of the many anomalies in this curious war is the bitter opposition by the New England states, despite the fact that war built up their economy. Permanently important for New England was the war's stimulus to manufacturing. Unreliable estimates of the number of cotton mills in New England range from 57 in 1809 to as many as 113 in 1810. While John Lowell, leader of the extreme Federalist Essex Junto, was advocating a New England Confederation, his brother Francis C. Lowell was picking up information in England about power looms. After his return to the United States in 1814, Lowell invented a new power loom with which, at Waltham, Massachusetts, he equipped the first complete American cotton factory, where every process of manufacture from the raw material to the finished cloth was performed under one roof.

Though the War of 1812 was enriching New England, Federalists cried that their section was being ruined and complained that the Republican administration left it defenseless against raids by the Royal Navy. On 5 October 1814 Massachusetts summoned a New England Convention at Hartford, for the express purpose of conferring upon 'their public grievances and concerns,' upon 'defence against the enemy . . . and also to take measures, if they shall think proper, for producing a convention of delegates from all the United States, in order to revise the Constitution thereof.' This language showed a compromise between the moderate and the extreme Federalists. The former, led by Harrison Gray Otis, were not disunionists, but wished to obtain concessions for their section. Alarmed by the rising tide of secession sentiment, they hoped the Convention would act as safety valve; their desire to concert defensive measures against the enemy was sincere. But the violent wing of the Federalist party, led by Timothy Pickering and John Lowell, had other objects in view. It was their belief that the British invasion of New Orleans would succeed, and that Aaron Burr's secession plot for Louisiana and the West would then bear fruit. They wished the Hartford Convention to draft a new federal constitution, with clauses to protect New England interests, and present it as a pistol to the original Thirteen States only, not to the democratic West. If these accepted, well and good; if not, New England would make a separate peace and go it alone.

At the Hartford Convention, meeting in secret session on 15 December 1814, the moderates gained control and issued a calm report on 5 January 1815. An element of their caution was the strength of the Republican party in New England; the Federalists controlled all five states, but only by small majorities outside Connecticut, and there would probably have been civil war had the extremists persuaded the states to adopt ordinances of secession. Madison's administration and the war were severely arraigned by the Convention; 'but to attempt upon every abuse of power to change the Constitution, would be to perpetuate the evils of revolution.' Secession was ruled out as unnecessary, since the causes of New England's calamities were not permanent but the result of bad administration and of partisanship in the European war. The New England states were invited to nullify a conscription bill then before Congress, if it should pass, and it was suggested that the administration might permit them to assume their own defense, applying to that purpose the federal taxes collected within their borders. But there was no threat of a separate peace.

Presently the good news from Ghent and New Orleans put Madison's administration on a high horse, and made New England the scapegoat for government mismanagement of the war. A stigma of unpatriotism, from which it never recovered, was attached to the Federalist party, and rightly so, since the leaders could not or would not see that the war had become defensive. Yet no stigma was attached to the doctrine of state rights; and within a few years it was revived by states like Virginia, which with one voice had denounced the Hartford Convention as treasonable.

In the Treaty of Ghent, signed on Christmas Eve 1814, both sides agreed to disagree on everything important except the conclusion of hostilities, and restoring pre-war boundaries. Madison's announced reasons for declaring war— impressment and neutral rights—were not even mentioned. But the treaty did bear good fruit in the shape of four boundary commissions to settle the line between Canada and the United States. And, before the next maritime war broke out, impressment had been given up as a means of recruiting for the Royal Navy.

So ended an unnecessary war, which might have been prevented by a little more imagination and broader vision. Casualties at least were relatively 'light'—1877 American soldiers and sailors killed in action. Moreover, the war had a good effect on relations between the two governments. The United States was never again denied the treatment due an independent nation, and Americans began to grasp a basic fact of North American sovereignty: that Canada was in the British empire for as long as she wanted, not as long as we wanted. The war had yet another important consequence—Jackson's incursion into Florida indicated that the Spanish empire in North America was ready to fall apart, and the United States had an opportunity to expand to the southeast.

Most of the wartime fleet was maintained after peace, and within three months of the Treaty of Ghent it found profitable employment. The Dey

In this contemporary cartoon, the Hartford Convention Federalists are identified with Lucifer, incendiarism, and the British crown while their opponents associate themselves with the pristine symbols of the young republic. (*Prints Division, New York Public Library*)

of Algeria had taken advantage of hostilities to capture American merchant ships. On 2 March 1815 Congress declared war on Algeria, and in May Commodore Decatur commanded a squadron that captured the pirates' 44-gun flagship, then sailed to Algiers, where the Dey signed a treaty at gun-point. This time *he* had to pay. Similar 'stick-up' negotiations were held at Tunis and Tripoli. From that time on, the United States has maintained a naval squadron in the Mediterranean.

For the United States, it had been for the most part an inglorious war. Part of the nation's capital lay in ashes, and the President had had to flee. Two days before the treaty of peace, Daniel Webster, noting that the administration could not recruit troops, collect taxes, or borrow money, wrote: 'The Govt. *cannot last*, under this war & in the hands of these men, another twelve month.'

Yet, paradoxically, the country came out of the war with an exhilarating sense of the triumph of republican institutions. It had dared a second time to wage war with the mightiest power on earth, and it had come out whole. Humiliating setbacks were quickly forgotten in the recollection of thrilling victories. One ironic consequence of this divisive war was to intensify American nationalism. With national honor vindicated, with a new conviction of national power, the young republic now looked toward the vast continent to the west which, as Henry Adams wrote, lay before the American people 'like an uncovered ore-bed.'

11

Good Feelings and Bad

*

1815–1829

A Nationalist Era

The year 1815 is a turning-point in American as in European history; and a point of divergence between the two. Hitherto the development of the United States had been vitally affected by Old World brawls. With the Peace of Vienna, Europe turned to problems that had little interest for America; and with the Peace of Ghent, America turned her back on Europe—although she kept looking at the Old World over one shoulder, as the Monroe Doctrine indicates. Most of the difficulties under which the republic had labored since the War of Independence now dropped out of sight, and there opened a serene prospect of peace, prosperity, and social progress. No one suspected that expansion would also bring its problems, and that within half a century Americans would be slaughtering one another.

The nationalism kindled by the war shaped the direction of politics in the next decade. In 1815 Madison startled the country by calling for adequate military and naval forces, direct internal taxation, a protective tariff, and a new national bank. The Federalists were astonished by this volte-face, since the Republicans had long deplored peacetime armies and internal taxes and had let the first national bank expire in 1811. In his final annual message in December 1816, Madison recommended both a 'comprehensive system of roads and canals' and the creation of a national university in Washington. A Federalist governor wrote: *'The Administration have fought themselves completely on to federal ground.'*

The Republicans encountered little partisan opposition to their program, not only because the Federalists had long espoused such nationalist doctrine, but even more because the party had been all but destroyed by its role in the war. The Federalists, who lacked an appreciation of the importance of the presidential contest in party warfare, ran electoral slates in only three states in 1816. The Republicans further weakened the Federalists by denying their rivals any public office under their control. James Monroe, once the turbulent crown prince but now the accepted heir of the Virginia dynasty, succeeded to the presidency in 1817 almost unopposed, and in 1821 obtained every electoral vote but one. Contemporaries called this period the 'era of good feelings,' but it was, in fact, an interval of stagnant politics in which it became increasingly hard for the Republicans to maintain party discipline and party zeal, and in which voting in presidential elections declined precipitously.

Politics did not long continue in this placid pattern. New forces were transforming the sections; and while readjustment was taking place, everyone acquiesced in nationalism of a sort. Manufacturing was becoming the dominant interest in New England and Pennsylvania; democracy had invaded New York; King Cotton's domain was advancing into the new Gulf states; and the Northwest acquired new aspirations. By 1830 the sections had again become articulate, defining the stand they were to take until the Civil War.

With new interests came a complete reversal in sectional attitudes toward the Constitution. Daniel Webster of Massachusetts, who in 1814 had warned Congress that his state would not obey conscription, in 1830 was intoning hymns to the Union; whilst John C. Calhoun of South Carolina, leader of the war hawks in 1812 and of nationalist legislation after the war, began in 1828 to write textbooks of state rights. Of all publicists and statesmen whose careers bridged the War of 1812, only five were consistent, and three were Virginians: Chief Justice Marshall refused to unlearn the nationalism he had been taught by Washington; John Taylor and John Randolph went on as if nothing had happened since 1798. Clay and Adams never changed their nationalist ideas of 1812.

Both Clay and Calhoun, the nationalist leaders in Congress at this period, feared the growing particularism of the sections. Like Hamilton, they could imagine no stronger binding force than self-interest; and their policy was but a broader version of his reports on public credit and manufactures. Their formula, which Clay christened the 'American System,' was protection and internal improvements: a protective tariff for the manufacturers, a home market and better transportation for the farmers.

It was a propitious moment to raise the tariff. National pride had been wounded by dependence on smuggled British goods. After 1815, infant industries sustained a setback when British manufactures flooded the American market. As a consequence, the 1810–20 decade was the only one in our history in which urbanization declined. Cries from industries for protection came from interests in almost every section: New England cotton mills, experimental mills in the Carolinas, Pittsburgh iron smelters, Kentucky's new industry of weaving hemp into cotton bagging, the shepherds of Vermont and Ohio, and the granaries of central New York. Even Jefferson wrote 'We must now place the manufacturer by the side of the agriculturist.' Congressmen from states that a generation later preferred secession to protection eagerly voted for the tariff of 1816; maritime New England voted against it. Webster was 'not in haste to see Sheffields and Birminghams in America.' Yet New England and Pennsylvania were destined to pocket the earliest benefits of protection.

'Internal improvements'—public works at federal expense—complemented protection. Immediately after the War of 1812 emigrants rushed to the West, eager to exploit the lands conquered from Tecumseh and from the Creek nation. Between 1810 and 1820 the population west of the Appalachians more than doubled. Four new states, Indiana (1816), Mississippi (1817), Illinois (1818), and Alabama (1819), were admitted, as well as Louisiana in 1812. Owing to the difficulty of ascending the Mississippi and Ohio rivers, Western supplies of manufactured goods came by wagon road from Atlantic seaports. But in 1817 a steamboat managed to reach Cincinnati from New Orleans, and two years later 60 light-draught stern-wheelers were plying between New Orleans and Louisville. Their freight charges were less than half the cost of wagon transport. To preserve and expand their stake in the Western trade, Eastern states set out to forge new East-West links; most notable was New York's decision to construct the Erie Canal, which was started in 1817.

Clay and Calhoun, believing that improved transportation was a responsibility of the federal government, induced Congress to push through a national road from Cumberland on the upper Potomac to Wheeling on the Ohio.[1] Connected with Baltimore by a state road, this 'national pike' became the most important route to the Northwest until 1840. In 1817 Congress proposed to

1. This National or Cumberland road was later built to Vandalia, Illinois, by successive appropriations between 1822 and 1838; but the Federal Government relinquished each section, upon its completion, to the state within which it lay.

Chicago in 1820. This lithograph reveals the primitive quality of the settlement at that date. Four years before, the United States army had rebuilt Fort Dearborn here, but as late as 1833, when Chicago was incorporated as a village, it had about 200 inhabitants. Within a generation it would be a city of 300,000. (*Stokes Collection, New York Public Library*)

earmark certain federal revenues for bolder projects. Madison so far had accepted every item in the nationalist program; but here he drew the line, and vetoed this internal improvement bill. Monroe had similar constitutional scruples; and by the time J. Q. Adams reached the White House, with even more ambitious plans, Congress proved disappointingly stubborn. The Appalachians were destined to be crossed and tunneled by private enterprise under state authority.

To provide the financial ligaments for the American system, Congress in 1816 chartered a Second Bank of the United States. The B.U.S. began operations in 1817 as a bank of deposit, discount, and issue, with the government as principal client and holder of one-fifth of the capital stock, differing from the Bank of England mainly in the power to establish branches. This feature, necessary for the fiscal operations of a federal government, hampered lesser banks operating under state charters. In Maryland the legislature levied a heavy tax on the notes issued by the Baltimore branch of this 'foreign corporation.' When the B.U.S. refused to pay, McCulloch *v.* Maryland reached the Supreme Court.

Chief Justice Marshall's opinion became a milestone in American nationalism. First, he offered a classic definition of national sovereignty that undercut the argument that the general government held only such power as the states vested in it. Secondly, the Court disposed of the argument that the act was unconstitutional since the power to charter corporations is not expressly granted to Congress by the Constitution and cannot be inferred from the 'necessary and proper' clause. A national bank, Maryland argued, was not necessary, as the want of one since 1811 proved. 'The government of the Union, though limited in its powers, is supreme within its sphere of action,' Marshall responded. 'Let the end be legitimate, let it be within the scope of the Constitution, and all means which are appropriate, which are plainly adapted to that end, which are not prohibited, but consist with the letter and spirit of the Constitution, are constitutional.' Finally, Marshall denied that a state might, by virtue of its reserved power of taxation, levy a tax upon the operations of the B.U.S.

During Marshall's thirty-four-year tenure as Chief Justice, the Supreme Court handed down a number of other rulings giving judicial sanction to the doctrine of centralization of powers at the expense of the states. In Martin *v.* Hunter's Lessee (1816), the Court upheld the constitutionality of the Judiciary Act of 1789 that gave it the power to review and reverse decisions of state courts where they conflicted with rights guaranteed by the Constitution. In Cohens *v.* Virginia (1821) Marshall not only vigorously reasserted this principle, but partially nullified the purpose of the Eleventh Amendment by accepting appellate jurisdiction over a suit against a state provided the state had originally instituted the suit. In Martin *v.* Mott (1827) the Court denied to a state the right, which New England had asserted during the previous war, to withhold militia from the national service when demanded by the President. In Gibbons *v.* Ogden (1824), perhaps the most far-reaching of his decisions, Marshall mapped out the course that Congress would follow most of the time from that day to this in regulating interstate commerce. In speaking for the Court in a decision which smashed a state-chartered monopoly of steamboat traffic, Marshall boldly insisted that Congressional power over commerce 'is not to be confined by state lines, but acts upon its subject matter wherever it is to be found.'

During these same years, another historic line of decisions by the Marshall Court threw the protective veil of the Constitution over property interests. In Fletcher *v.* Peck (1810), the so-called Yazoo land fraud case, Marshall prohibited the state of Georgia from rescinding a grossly corrupt sale of Western lands on the principle that such action impaired the obligation of a contract. In the Dartmouth College case of 1819 the Court invalidated a New Hampshire statute abolishing the pre-revolutionary charter of the college and placing it under state control. Marshall's decision that a charter to a corporation was a contract within the meaning of the Constitution, and so beyond the control of a state, was of far-reaching importance, both for good and ill. On the one hand, it protected privately endowed colleges, schools, and the like from political interference, and encouraged endowments for education and charity. On the other, in conjunction with the Yazoo decision, it gave corporations an immunity from legislative interference that was only gradually modified through judicial recognition of the police power of the states. Marshall's opinions, and those of Associate Justice Joseph Story (Martin *v.* Hunter's Lessee and Martin *v.* Mott), worked with the spirit of the times in fostering nationalism, but worked against it in opposing democracy and majority rule.

Western Panic and Missouri Compromise

The West, which deeply resented the McCulloch opinion, found other occasions for grievances with the B.U.S. The new settlers, tempted by rising crop prices, purchased land far beyond their capacity to pay; for the Public Land Act of 1800 extended long credit. Much of the best land was engrossed by speculators. When cotton rose to 34 cents a pound in 1818, planters paid up to $150 an acre for uncleared land in the black belt of Alabama. All this led to a wide dispersal of settlers, instead of the orderly progression along a definite frontier that the Act of 1796 had planned. Until vacant spaces were settled, the scattered frontier farmers found themselves without

schools, means of communication, or markets, yet deeply in debt to the Federal Government or to 'wild-cat' Western banks. These in turn were indebted to the B.U.S. and to Eastern capitalists, who at the same time were setting up new corporations far in advance of the country's needs. The Bank of the United States, which might have put a brake on inflation, encouraged this mad scramble, until late in 1818, when the directors took steps to curtail credit. This hastened the inevitable panic, and in 1819 it broke. Many state banks collapsed, and enormous amounts of Western real estate were foreclosed by the B.U.S. in the very year that the McCulloch decision forbade the states to tax the 'Monster.' The West raged against the Eastern money power, and hard times, which lasted until 1824, afforded an ideal culture-bed for the movement afterwards known as Jacksonian Democracy.

While debt, deflation, and hard times were producing these preliminary symptoms of a vertical cleavage between East and West, another Western question, that of slavery extension, threatened to cut the Union horizontally into North and South. Ever since the Federal Convention of 1787 there had been a tacit political balance between these great sections. In 1789 North and South were approximately equal in numbers; but in 1820 the free states had a population of 5,152,000 with 105 members in the House of Representatives, while the slave states had 4,485,000 people with 81 congressmen. An even balance had been maintained in the Senate by the admission of free and slave states alternately; the admission of Alabama in 1819 gave eleven to each.

In the territory of the Louisiana purchase, Congress had done nothing to disturb slavery as it existed by French and Spanish law. Consequently, in the westward rush after the War of 1812, several thousand slaveowners with their human property emigrated to the Territory of Upper Louisiana, establishing plantations in the rich bottom lands of the lower Missouri river, or on the west bank of the Mississippi near St. Louis. When the people of this region demanded admission to the Union as the state of Missouri, slavery was permitted by their proposed state constitution.

In 1819 the House approved a bill admitting

John Marshall (1755–1835). Chief Justice of the United States from 1801 to 1835, he did more than anyone in the nation's history to give stature to the Supreme Court and to shape constitutional jurisprudence. Of the 11,000 opinions of the Court during his long tenure, Marshall wrote no fewer than 519. Chester Harding, a self-taught American artist who executed this portrait, said, 'I had such great pleasure in painting *the whole* of such a man.' (*Boston Athenaeum*)

Missouri but with an amendment prohibiting the further introduction of slaves into Missouri, and requiring that all children subsequently born therein of slave parents should be free at age 25. The bill was put down in the Senate, and a bitter national debate ensued concerned not with the morality of slavery but with sectional power. Northerners regarded the proposed admission of Missouri, which lay almost wholly north of the then dividing line between freedom and slavery, as an aggressive move toward increasing the voting strength of the South; and many threatened secession if slavery were not defeated. Southerners did not yet defend the rightfulness of slavery, but asserted their right to enjoy human property in the trans-Mississippi West, and threatened secession if that were denied. When Congress again took up the question, in January 1820, enough Northern Republicans were detached from the anti-slavery bloc by fear of a Federalist renaissance to get a compromise measure through. Missouri was admitted as a slaveholding state, but slavery was prohibited in United States territory north of lat. 36° 30′. As part of the compromise, Maine, which had detached herself from Massachusetts, was admitted as a free state, making twelve of each.

This Missouri Compromise put the question of slavery extension at rest for almost a generation, but a veil had been lifted for a moment, revealing a bloody prospect ahead. 'This momentous question, like a fire bell in the night, awakened and filled me with terror,' wrote Jefferson. 'I considered it at once as the knell of the Union.' And J. Q. Adams recorded in his diary: 'I take it for granted that the present question is a mere preamble—a title-page to a great, tragic volume.'

Anglo-American Adjustments

While Monroe was coping with the explosive slavery issue he also had to contend with portentous questions in diplomacy that would affect American foreign affairs for generations to come. Almost a century of diplomacy was required to clear up all controversies between Britain and America left by the Treaty of Ghent. J. Q. Adams wrote before the year was out that the treaty was 'a truce rather than a peace' because nothing was settled. 'All the points of collision which had subsisted . . . before the war were left open.' In particular, Canada, with a long and vague boundary, rival peltry and fishing interests, and a fresh-water naval force, promised many points of friction between the two countries.

The three statesmen who did most to preserve peace were Presidents Madison and Monroe, and Lord Castlereagh, the first British statesman since Shelburne to regard friendship with America as a permanent British interest. Madison and Monroe met him halfway, but not John Quincy Adams. He, too, hoped to preserve the peace, but he was suspicious and irascible; as Monroe's Secretary of State his notes needed softening by the now mellow President. But Adams's perception was abnormally keen, and alone of contemporaries in either hemisphere he foresaw his country's future place in the world, and the independence of colonies everywhere.

Disarmament on the Great Lakes was the first fruit of Anglo-American diplomacy after the war, and the most lasting. Peace found each side feverishly building ships against the other on Lake Ontario. The Canadians, apprehensive of further American aggression, looked for large outlays by the British treasury to complete this building program. The Americans, on the contrary, hoped to avoid a fresh-water building contest. In 1815 Congress provided for the sale or laying up of all the Lake fleet not necessary for enforcement of the revenue laws. The army was reduced to 10,000 men, and in 1820 to 6000. But it was President Madison who made the momentous proposal of naval disarmament on the Lakes, and in 1817 an agreement was effected by an exchange of notes at Washington. The Rush-Bagot agreement, named for the American and British ministers, limited naval force on the Lakes, an agreement still in operation, although modified in detail. Not until the 1840's was the boundary line finally settled, but despite periods of severe friction, mutual respect and good will have kept the American-Canadian border undefended and unfortified.

The Treaty of Ghent also provided that the contracting parties 'use their best endeavors' to

(Library of Congress)

abolish the African slave trade. Congress had outlawed the traffic in 1808, and in 1820 declared it to be piracy, punishable by death. But the United States refused to enter any international agreement for joint suppression, because, owing to recent memories of impressment and the like, Adams refused to allow American ships to be searched for slaves by British men-of-war. A squadron of the United States Navy was maintained off the African coast, to watch for slavers flying the American flag; but plenty of 'black ivory' got by under the flag of freedom, into Cuba or the Southern states.

Meantime, on the southeastern border, Anglo-American amity was gravely endangered. East Florida was a Spanish province, but Spanish authority was little exercised beyond the three fortified posts of Pensacola, St. Marks, and St. Augustine. On the American side of the boundary, there was meddling with Indians, not by Spaniards but by two British traders, an elderly Scot named Arbuthnot, who cultivated the Seminole, a branch of the Creek nation, and a young adventurer named Ambrister, who joined a group of Seminoles under a chief whom the whites called Billy Bow-legs. In 1817 the Seminoles on the American side of the border defied settlers to enter upon the Creek lands which had been ceded three years before, and scalped some of those who did. General Andrew Jackson was ordered by President Monroe to raise a force of Tennessee militia, chastise the offenders, and pursue them into Spanish Florida if necessary. While Jackson was destroying Seminole villages, an army detachment on the way to join him, with women and children, was ambushed by other Seminoles and destroyed. Jackson burst into Florida like an avenging demon. Two Seminole chiefs fled to St. Marks, where they were relieved to find a gun-boat flying the Union Jack. With mock honors they were received, and promptly clapped into irons. The gun-boat was American and the Union Jack a ruse. Next day (7 April 1818) Jackson entered St. Marks against the protest of the Spanish governor, hauled down the Spanish flag, hanged the two chiefs without trial, and arrested Arbuthnot. But when he pushed eastward to surprise

Billy Bow-legs, the Seminole chief eluded him. Furious and baffled, Jackson learned the cause of his escape when Ambrister blundered into his camp. On one of his men was found a letter from Arbuthnot, warning Billy of Jackson's approach, and offering him ten kegs of gunpowder. Following a quickly constituted court-martial, Arbuthnot and Ambrister, both British subjects, were put to death.

Jackson was not through yet. After overcoming the Seminoles, he took Pensacola, ejected the Spanish governor, and garrisoned the fortress with Americans. On his return, he was acclaimed once more a hero by the West, but in Washington, Henry Clay reminded the Senate that 'it was in the provinces that were laid the seeds of the ambitious projects that overturned the liberties of Rome.' In Monroe's cabinet, Adams alone insisted that Jackson's every act was justified by the incompetence of Spanish authority to police its own territory; and Adams had his way. When the news reached London in the autumn of 1818, the press rang with denunciation of America and the 'ruffian' who had murdered two 'peaceful British traders.' War would have been declared 'if the ministry had but held up a finger,' wrote the American minister, Richard Rush; but Lord Castlereagh's firmness preserved the peace.

From Madrid came a response of long-lasting significance. Fearful that Jackson's invasion portended an American seizure of Florida, Spain resigned herself to getting out with something to show for it. In 1819 Spain sold all her lands east of the Mississippi, together with her claim to the Oregon country, in return for $5 million. In addition, the boundary between the United States and Mexico was defined. Two years later ratification of the treaty filled out the southeastern domain of the United States to the farthest reach of the Florida Keys.

Canning Proposes, Monroe Disposes

Important as was the acquisition of Florida, Monroe had an even more historic role to play in Latin America. In 1815, two years before he took office, there were only two completely independent nations in the New World, the United States and Haiti. The next seven years saw an eruption of new republics in Latin America. By the autumn of 1822, continental America from the Great Lakes to Cape Horn was independent. European nations maintained sovereignty only in Belize, Bolivia, and the Guianas. In 1822 the United States extended formal recognition to the new republics, but the Continental powers would not accept the outcome as final. After France invaded Spain in 1823, with the avowed object of delivering Ferdinand VII from a constitution that had been forced upon him by the liberals, it was common talk that a Franco-Spanish expeditionary force to South America would follow, with the blessing of the Holy Alliance.

In London George Canning, who had succeeded Castlereagh, sought a way out of a dilemma. Despite substantial interest in South American trade, Britain was not ready to admit rebel republican colonists to the family of nations. On the other hand, if England did not do something, Canning feared that Monroe and Adams would obtain exclusive commercial advantages, and a Pan-American republican alliance. He came up with a brilliant plan. A joint Anglo-American protest against intervention would thwart the Holy Alliance, maintain England's new markets, establish England as co-protector of Latin America and, at the same time, throw America's weight onto the British scale of power. So, on 16 August 1823, the British foreign minister put a question to Richard Rush, American minister at London. What would he say to joining England in warning France to keep hands off South America?

Canning's astounding overture appealed to a number of American leaders, but J. Q. Adams knew that there was slight danger of armed intervention in Latin America, and that the British navy had the power to prevent it in any case. What could be Canning's game? The clue, he thought, was a proposed pledge, in Canning's note of 20 August, against either power's acquiring a part of Spanish America. That pledge might be inconvenient if Cuba voted herself into the United States. Furthermore, Canning was unwilling to deny Spain the right to reconquer its former colonies.

At the next cabinet meeting Adams declared, 'It would be more candid, as well as more dignified, to avow our principles explicitly to Russia and

France, than to come in as a cockboat in the wake of the British man-of-war.' For Adams, moreover, the question had a larger aspect. While the Holy Alliance seemed to threaten South America, Russia was pushing her trading posts from Alaska southward even to San Francisco Bay. In September 1821 Emperor Alexander I issued a ukase extending Alaska to latitude 51° N, well within the Oregon country and declaring *mare clausum* the waters thence to Bering Strait. Adams believed that the New World should be considered closed to further colonization by European powers.

Monroe vacillated between the extremes of doing nothing, for fear of the Holy Alliance, and of carrying the war into Turkey to aid Greece, whose struggle for independence had been followed in the United States with an even greater interest than was shown for South America. Against this meddling in European affairs Adams argued for the better part of two days, and in the end had his way. The passages on foreign relations in Monroe's annual message of 2 December 1823, although written by the President in more concise and dignified language than Adams would have used, expressed exactly the concepts of his Secretary of State. We may summarize the original Monroe Doctrine in the President's own words:

Positive principles: (*a*) 'The American continents . . . are henceforth not to be considered as subjects for future colonization by any European powers.' (*b*) 'The political system of the allied powers is essentially different . . . from that of America. . . . We should consider any attempt on their part to extend their system to any portion of this hemisphere as dangerous to our peace and safety.'

Negative principles: (*a*) 'With the existing colonies or dependencies of any European power we have not interfered and shall not interfere.' (*b*) 'In the wars of the European powers in matters relating to themselves we have never taken any part, nor does it comport with our policy so to do.'

Monroe's message was well received, but few appreciated its significance. Polk was the first President to appeal to Monroe's principles by name; and not until after the Civil War did these principles become a doctrine. Critics of Monroe have pointed out that his message was a mere declaration; that European intervention had already been thwarted by the threat of the British navy; that in view of the exclusive power of Congress to declare war, a mere presidential announcement could not guarantee Latin American independence. True, but irrelevant. What Adams accomplished was to raise a standard of American foreign policy for all the world to see, and to plant it so firmly in the national consciousness that no later President would dare to pull it down.

The Second President Adams

In December 1823 America was much more interested in the coming presidential election than in Latin America. The large number of candidates in 1824 signified the collapse of the old party system. With no outstanding member of the Virginia dynasty available, the burden of finding a nominee proved too much for the congressional caucus at a time when party discipline was weak. William H. Crawford, Secretary of the Treasury, was heir apparent of the Virginia dynasty, but he had suffered a paralytic stroke, and, as an Old Republican, he did not command a national following. A congressional caucus dutifully nominated him, but only one-quarter of the Republicans attended. Two other members of Monroe's cabinet also aspired to the succession. John Quincy Adams was the most highly experienced, but Henry Clay, 'Gallant Harry of the West,' made a wide appeal as an advocate of the American system. However, Clay had a Western rival, General Andrew Jackson, now Senator from Tennessee. All the candidates were Republicans. Jackson carried Pennsylvania, the Carolinas, and most of the West, with a total of 99 electoral votes. Adams took New England, most of New York,[2] and a few districts elsewhere, making 84. Crawford was a poor third, and Clay last. Since no candidate had a majority of the electoral vote, the choice among the top three went to the House—the only such instance since the adoption of the Twelfth Amendment.

2. There was no uniformity at this time in methods of choosing presidential electors. In eleven states the voters chose them on a general ticket, as nowadays. In seven states they were chosen by the voters in districts; in eleven by state legislatures.

When Congress convened in January 1825, backers of Jackson and Adams tried to work up a majority for their candidates. Jackson would presumably hold the eleven states which had declared for him in November, but he needed two more for a majority. Adams had only seven states secured, and needed six more. Clay, no longer a candidate, controlled the votes of three states. He opposed the elevation to the presidency of a military leader like Jackson, because he doubted 'that killing two thousand five hundred Englishmen at New Orleans' qualified a man for the chief magistracy. After it was half understood, half promised, that if Adams were elected he would appoint Clay Secretary of State, Clay threw all three of his states to Adams. The lone congressmen who represented Missouri and Illinois, states which had voted for Jackson, were 'conciliated' (Jackson men said 'bought') by Adams. New Yorkers and doubtful Marylanders who still called themselves Federalists were assured that Adams, if elected, would not take revenge on that dying party for what it had done to him and his father. And so it was that on 9 February 1825 the House on its first ballot elected John Quincy Adams President of the United States, by a majority of one state.

It was a barren victory, although perfectly legal. The charge of robbery at once went up from the Jackson forces, and active electioneering for 1828 began. Adams's election, said Senator Benton, with a wild plunge into what he believed to be Greek, violated the *demos krateo* principle. When Adams defiantly gave Clay the state department, the cry 'corrupt bargain' was raised. Jackson wrote: 'So you see the *Judas* of the West has closed the contract and will receive the thirty pieces of silver.'

John Quincy Adams was a lonely, friendless figure, unable to express his burning love of country in any way that would touch the popular imagination. Short, thick-set, with a massive bald head and rheumy eyes, his port was stern and his manners unconciliatory. A lonely walk before dawn, or an early morning swim across the Potomac in summer, fitted him for the day's toil, which he concluded by writing in his diary. The uncomfortable labor of compiling a massive report on weights and measures during a hot summer in Washington, when he might have been playing with his children on the coast of Massachusetts, was a relaxation to Adams. 'I am a man of reserved, cold, austere and forbidding manners,' he once wrote. 'My political adversaries say a gloomy misanthrope; and my personal enemies an unsocial savage. With a knowledge of the actual defects in my character, I have not the pliability to reform it.'

As President, Adams was not only so anxious to be upright that he was often disagreeable, but he made the grave political error of trimming his sails to the nationalism of 1815 after the wind had changed. He would transcend the nationalism of Hamilton and use the ample revenues of the Federal Government to increase the navy, build national roads and canals, send out scientific expeditions, and establish institutions of learning and research. Unhappily, Adams presented his ideas at a time of anti-national reaction, especially in the South which feared that a strong national government might meddle with slavery, and he offered them maladroitly. He antagonized Old Republicans by stating that he hoped no 'speculative scruple' about constitutional limitations would trouble them, and he told Congress not to give the world the impression 'that we are palsied by the will of our constituents.' Adams made many sound recommendations—a national astronomical observatory, a naval academy—that were adopted years later, but they were rudely rejected by Congress at the time.

The Second Party System

As a consequence of the renewal of the contest for the Presidency in 1824, political leaders created a new party system. Unlike the first party system, it did not originate in Congress. Nor was it the result of a popular groundswell. The new two-party system was the deliberate creation of politicians who built cross-sectional alliances in order to capture the presidency. Established not at one time but over a period of some sixteen years, it appeared first in the Northeast, then in the Old South, and finally in the new states. The second party system did not continue the political align-

General Jackson. In this painting by Ralph E. W. Earl in 1833, the year Jackson began his second term, the President's military glory is accentuated. The son of one of the most prominent artists of the late eighteenth century, Earl, who married Mrs. Jackson's niece, lived at the White House, and, in the age of 'King Andrew,' was called 'the King's painter.' Old Hickory was a favorite subject of artists of this generation; Hawthorne, standing before a representation of Pope Julius, regretted that Raphael was not alive to do justice to Jackson. (*Brooks Memorial Art Gallery, Memphis*)

Helpless orphans piteous cries
Scalding tears from widows eyes
Cool'd with tyrants daintiest food
Murder'd soldiers clotted blood
Methought the souls of all that I had murder'd came to my tent. Act. 5 Sc. 3.
RICHARD III.

Jackson as Richard III. In this engraving D. C. Johnston, called 'the American Cruikshank,' draws upon episodes from the General's military past to liken him to the English monarch, accused of murdering the two young princes in the Tower. (*American Antiquarian Society*)

ments of the Jeffersonian era. Republicans and Federalists could be found in both the new parties: the 'friends of the Administration' who subsequently became the National Republicans and then the Whigs, and the 'Jackson men,' who would later call themselves Democrats. If Daniel Webster won former Federalists to the Adams-Clay 'Coalition,' Martin Van Buren commissioned Alexander Hamilton's son to write campaign tracts for the Jackson-Calhoun alliance. In New England, Federalists joined Adams's party; in the South, Jackson's; in the Middle States, they divided.

Changes in voting procedures and the expansion of the suffrage helped shape the second party system. In 1800, only two states chose electors by popular vote; by 1832, voters cast ballots for electors in every state but South Carolina. By 1824, almost every adult white male could vote in presidential elections, save in Rhode Island, Virginia, and Louisiana. Since parties had to mobilize not a few legislators but a mass electorate, these changes revolutionized political warfare. In 1824, voting increased 130 per cent over the previous national election; in 1828, it jumped another 133 per cent. This growth resulted less from the abolition of suffrage restrictions than from the stimulus of the renewal of party competition. The transportation revolution made it possible to organize politics on a national basis, with wide-ranging campaign tours and 'monster' rallies, and the proliferation of newspapers enhanced the role of the partisan editor who fanned the flames of party feeling. As the new party system spread, the gentry yielded to professional politicians who viewed party management as a vocation.

In 1828 national leaders of the Jackson forces mobilized support for the Hero. Although the new party contained elements of a South-West alliance, the most important aspect of the future Democratic party was the renewal of the New York-Virginia understanding. The Jackson forces in 1828 tended to be more suspicious of centralized government and more favorably disposed toward unhampered capitalism than were their rivals. The South, now in full tide of reaction against nationalism, was assured that Jackson would defend state rights. For the first time, a majority of states held conventions which endorsed a national candidate, but politicians in 1828 seemed less interested in democratizing politics than in manipulating the electorate. General Jackson's frontier brawls and alleged premarital relations with Mrs. Jackson were described in detail. Nonetheless, Jackson polled 56 per cent of the popular vote; no candidate would do so well for the rest of the nineteenth century.

John Quincy Adams never understood why he was spurned by the country he loved with silent passion. In the four sad months between the election and the end of his term, there kept running through his head the refrain of an old song he had first heard at the court of Versailles:

> O Richard, O mon Roi,
> L'univers t'abandonne.

Yet the noblest portion of his long career lay ahead.

12

The Jacksonian Era

*

1829–1844

Jacksonian Democracy

We are now in an age of great political figures. Adams, Clay, Webster, Van Buren, and Calhoun were statesmen of whom any country could be proud; but the man who towered above them in popularity and gave his name to an era was Andrew Jackson. Old Hickory 'reigned,' as his enemies said, for eight years. He practically appointed his successor, Martin Van Buren; and, after one term of Whig opposition, Jacksonian Democracy returned to the saddle in the person of James K. Polk, 'Young Hickory.' After another brief interim came two Democratic Presidents who had been spoon-fed by Jackson—Franklin Pierce and James Buchanan. Thus Andrew Jackson and the brand of democracy associated with him dominated the political scene for a third of a century, from 1828 to the Civil War.

Jacksonian Democracy was a national movement in that it opposed disunion and knew no geographical limits; Jackson men in Maine and Louisiana uttered the same clichés. But it was anti-national in rejecting Clay's 'American System.' The Democracy wanted roads, canals, and (in a few years) railroads to be chartered and aided by the states, but no Federal Government messing into the operations. Jacksonians spoke for the men on the make who resented government grants of special privileges to rival entrepreneurs and who distrusted the positive state. Opponents of artificial distinctions and advocates of greater popular participation in politics, the Jackson men identified themselves with the movement toward more equality. Yet they believed in equality only for white men; they were far less charitable toward the Indian and the Negro than their 'aristocratic' foes. Jacksonian Democracy was not 'leveling' in the European sense, having no desire to pull down men of wealth to a common plane; but it wanted a fair chance for every man to level up. In the states, Jackson Democrats sometimes, but not invariably, favored free public education and a somewhat cautious humanitarianism, but dissociated themselves from most of the 'isms' of the period, such as abolitionism and feminism. In general, they shared that contempt for intellect which is one of the unlovely traits of democracy. There was no contact between political democrats like Jackson and democratic philosophers such as

Emerson, and Old Hickory cared not a whit. The jackass as symbol of the Democratic party was first used by the Whigs as a satire on Jackson's supposed ignorance; the party not only joyfully accepted this emblem, but has retained it to this day.

Andrew Jackson was no champion of the 'common man,' but they loved him because he proved that a man born in a log cabin could get rich and become President; and, perhaps most of all, because his victory at New Orleans transformed the War of 1812 from a rout to a glorious vindication of American valor. Washington had never held such crowds as assembled there on 4 March 1829 to see the people's champion installed. General Jackson, a tall, lean figure dressed in black, with the hawk-like frontier face under a splendid crest of thick white hair, walked from Gadsby's Hotel up Pennsylvania Avenue, unescorted save by a few friends, to the Capitol. There, at the top of a great stone stairway, he took the presidential oath and read his inaugural address. With difficulty he pushed through the shouting masses, all eager to shake his hand, to where his horse was waiting; then rode to the White House at the head of an informal procession of carriages, farm wagons, people of all ages, colors, and conditions. The White House was invaded by a throng of men, women, and boys who stood on chairs in their muddy boots, fought for the refreshments, and trod glass and porcelain underfoot. 'The reign of King "Mob" seemed triumphant,' said one observer.

Jackson felt that his first task was to 'cleanse the Augean stables,' for even frontier-educated boys in those days knew about the labors of Hercules. Long before Jackson, the Republicans had followed the principle of rotation in office. In a democratic nation it served a number of commendable purposes: denying the claims of officeholders to consider their posts private property; replacing superannuated officials; preventing holdovers from frustrating the policies of a new administration; and affording the citizenry greater direct participation in government. In eight years in office, Jackson removed only a small number of federal officeholders, and his own appointees were mostly college graduates at a time when comparatively few Americans attended college. Yet there is no doubt that Jackson, by stepping up the tempo of removals, seriously impaired the politically neutral career system which had developed in the first forty years of the republic and fastened the spoils system on the Federal Government, from which, despite civil service reform, it has never been wholly eradicated.

Eaton Malaria

A woman made the first and the most lasting trouble for Jackson. She was Mrs. John H. Eaton, wife of the Secretary of War. Born Peggy O'Neale, daughter of the principal tavern keeper at the Georgetown end of Washington, she was a luscious brunette with a perfect figure and a come-hither in her blue eyes that drove the young men of Washington wild, and some of the old ones too. Married at an early age to a purser in the navy, she became, during his long absences at sea, the mistress of John H. Eaton, bachelor senator from Tennessee and her father's star boarder. At least so 'all Washington' said, except Jackson. The Senator even bought the tavern when Papa O'Neale went broke, in order to continue this pleasant arrangement, and persuaded the navy department to give the purser plenty of sea duty. About the time of the presidential election, the complaisant cuckold, caught short some $14,000 in his accounts, died or committed suicide, nobody quite knew which; and shortly after the news arrived, on New Year's Day 1829, his bonny widow, still only thirty-two years old, married Eaton.

Scandal made Jackson the more determined to champion Mrs. Eaton, and to insist that official society should receive her, but Mrs. Vice-President Calhoun and the other secretaries' wives would give the 'hussy' no countenance. They refused to call, and at official receptions or White House dinners failed to speak. Neither would the ladies of the diplomatic corps, nor the wives of senators and congressmen. The President refused to surrender. He scoffed at the rumors about Peggy; after all, both Eaton and the purser had been Masons, and neither could have had 'criminal intercourse with another mason's wife, without being one of the most abandoned of men.'

Jackson actually held a cabinet meeting about Mrs. Eaton, where he pronounced her 'as chaste as a virgin'; but the female rebellion continued. This 'Eaton malaria,' as Van Buren and the gossips called it, was not only making a breach between the administration and respectable society, but making a fool of the President.

Still, there was some use to be made of the affair by Van Buren, who coveted the presidential succession. This sly fox from New York was burrowing into the heart of the old hero. As a widower, he could afford to show Peggy marked attention, which was not difficult, for she had both wit and beauty. And it was 'little Van' who bound up the wounds of the disappointed office-seekers, who arranged the diplomatic appointments, and directed the negotiations which brought prestige to the administration. His plump figure could be seen every fair day bobbing up and down on horseback, beside the lean, easy-seated President, on his daily constitutionals. Many a time they must have discussed the Eaton affair. Jackson, unable to account for the solid female phalanx against Mrs. Eaton, was sure there must be politics behind it. And we may be sure that Van Buren, oh! so gently and discreetly, would have eliminated one plotter after another until Jackson burst out, 'By the e-tar-nal! it's that proud aristocrat Calhoun' (for did not Mrs. Calhoun start the snubbing game, and were not all the recusant ministers Calhoun's friends?). And how Van Buren would protest that it could never, never be that high-souled pattern of chivalry! And how, if Jackson seemed too easily convinced, he would remind him of an ugly rumor that in Monroe's cabinet, at the time of the Arbuthnot and Ambrister affair, it was Calhoun who said General Jackson should be arrested and tried for insubordination! Calhoun, it will be remembered, was in his second term as Vice-President, and heir apparent.

Were all this merely a question of whether Martin or John should succeed Andrew, it would not be worth our attention. But the 'Eaton malaria,' as treated by Dr. Van Buren, was a symptom of the sectional and economic ills that presently isolated Calhoun and his adherents in a state-rights ward.

The Nullification Controversy

Andrew Jackson's high place in history derives from the way he confronted the two great issues of his presidency: the nullification that threatened the Union and the war on the Bank of the United States that arrayed the Jacksonians against the 'money power.' The first issue arose in South Carolina, a state that had changed from ardent nationalism to extreme wariness of the Federal Government. The protective tariff of 1816 was largely the work of two South Carolinians, Lowndes and Calhoun. Like New England, their native state had water-power, and unlike New England she had cotton; then why not manufactures? But the next few years proved these expectations hollow. Competent managers were rare in the South, and Yankee mill superintendents were unable to handle slave labor, which could be employed with more immediate profit in growing cotton. While the benefits of protection went to Northern manufacturers, Southern planters bore the burden of higher prices. As tariff schedules rose by successive acts of Congress, and the country as a whole grew richer, South Carolina declined in wealth. When the cotton-growing area expanded into the black belts of Alabama and Mississippi, cotton which had sold for 31 cents a pound in 1818 fetched only 8 cents in 1831. Actually, the tariff only aggravated distress for which the land-destroying system of cotton culture was fundamentally responsible; but the planters would not accept this. Furthermore, the South Carolina aristocracy was beginning to squirm over race relations, and rice planters joined cotton growers in wanting to curb the power of the national government.

In 1828 Congress gave new cause for grievance with the 'tariff of abominations.' It was a politicians' tariff, concerned mainly with the manufacture of a President. Pro-Jackson congressmen had introduced a bill with higher duties on raw materials than on manufactures, hoping that New England votes would help defeat it and the onus fall on Adams, but the strategy misfired, to the South's chagrin. At a great anti-tariff meeting in Columbia, S.C., President Cooper of South Carolina College asked, 'Is it worth our while to continue this Union of States, where the North demands to be our masters and we are required to be their tributaries?' More and more South Carolinians answered this question with a thumping 'No!'

Calhoun, once an enthusiastic nationalist, now believed that he had made a grave mistake, for protection had turned out to be an instrument of class and sectional plunder. In a document called the South Carolina Exposition, approved in 1828 by the legislature of that state, he set forth a new doctrine—nullification, though his authorship was secret. The Constitution, he asserted, was established not by the American people, but by thirteen sovereign states. Sovereign in 1787, they must still be sovereign in 1828. Since the Federal Government was merely the agent of the states, a state convention, the immediate organ of state sovereignty, could take measures to prevent the enforcement within state limits of any Act of Congress it deemed unconstitutional. Calhoun, however, recognized one constitutional authority superior to the interpretation of a single state, an interpretative federal amendment adopted by three-fourths of the states. Under the nullification doctrine, South Carolina insisted on the right to disobey the laws of the Union while claiming the privileges of the Union. Calhoun's sincerity and intelligence cannot be doubted, but as the aged Madison declared, 'For this preposterous and anarchical pretension there is not a shadow of countenance in the Constitution.'

A ringing rebuttal to Calhoun's dialectic came two years later in the midst of a classic debate over Western lands, when on 26 January 1830 Daniel Webster of Massachusetts replied for the second time to Senator Hayne of South Carolina. Webster was the most commanding figure in the Senate, a swarthy Olympian with a craggy face and eyes that seemed to glow like dull coals under a precipice of brows. It has been said that no man was ever so great as Daniel Webster looked. Ponderous he was at times, but he carried to perfection the dramatic, rotund style of oratory that America learned from the elder Pitt.

In his historic response to Hayne, Webster, in blue-tailed coat with brass buttons and buff waistcoat, speaking hour after hour, thrilled his audience with rich imagery, crushed his opponents with a barrage of facts, passed from defense of his state to criticism of the 'South Carolina doctrine,' and concluded with an immortal peroration:

> I have not allowed myself, Sir, to look beyond the Union, to see what might lie hidden in the dark recess behind. I have not coolly weighed the chances of preserving liberty when the bonds that unite us together shall be broken asunder. . . . Nor could I regard him as a safe counsellor in the affairs of this government, whose thoughts should be mainly bent on considering, not how the Union may be best preserved, but how tolerable might be the condition of the people when it should be broken up and destroyed. While the Union lasts we have high, exciting, gratifying prospects spread out before us, for us and our children. Beyond that I seek not to penetrate the veil. God grant that in my day at least that curtain may not rise! God grant that on my vision never may be opened what lies behind! When my eyes shall be turned to behold for the last time the sun in heaven, may I not see him shining on the broken and dishonored fragments of a once glorious Union; on States dissevered, discordant, belligerent; on a land rent with civil feuds, or drenched, it may be, in fraternal blood! Let their last feeble and lingering glance rather behold the gorgeous ensign of the republic, now known and honored throughout the earth, still full high advanced, its arms and trophies streaming in their original lustre, not a stripe erased or polluted, not a single star obscured, bearing for its motto, no such miserable interrogatory as 'What is all this worth?' nor those other words of delusion and folly, 'Liberty first and Union afterwards'; but everywhere, spread all over in characters of living light, blazing on all its ample folds, as they float over the sea and over the land, and in every wind under the whole heavens, that other sentiment, dear to every true American heart,—Liberty *and* Union, now and forever, one and inseparable!

That peroration, declaimed from thousands of school platforms by lads of the coming generation, established in the hearts of the Northern and Western people a new, semi-religious conception of the Union. One of its earliest readers was a dreamy, gangling youth on the Indiana frontier, Abraham Lincoln.

Webster's reply to Hayne went home instantly to the old patriot in the White House. Jackson counted himself a state-rights man, but he never doubted the sovereignty of the nation. At a Jefferson's birthday dinner on 13 April 1830, when his turn came for a toast, the old soldier arose to his

Daniel Webster (1782–1852). This portrait from the studio of Mathew Brady, America's premier photographer, conveys 'Black Dan's' scowling mien, his piercing eyes, and the majestic presence of the 'god-like Daniel.' (*Library of Congress, Brady Collection*)

full height, fixing his glaring eyes on Calhoun, and flung out a challenge:

> Our Federal Union—it must be preserved!

Calhoun took up the challenge with another:

> The Union—next to our liberty, the most dear!

For two years after the dinner, Calhoun and the nullifiers were held in check by the unionists of their own state, and Jackson reconstituted his entire cabinet, thereby ridding the administration of the Calhoun influence. But in 1832 Clay precipitated a showdown. With the aid of Western votes, attracted by his scheme to forge a North-West alliance by distributing the proceeds from land sales to the states, Clay pushed through a new tariff bill. Some of the 'abominations' of the 1828 tariff were removed, but high duties on iron and textiles were maintained; and the new act had an air of permanence which acted upon South Carolina as a challenge. In November 1832 the South Carolina legislature declared that the tariff act was 'null, void, and no law, nor binding upon this State, its officers or citizens.' This nullification ordinance forbade federal officials to collect customs duties within the state after 1 February 1833, and threatened instant secession from the Union if the Federal Government attempted to use force. Jackson gave a prompt answer. Forts Moultrie and Sumter were reinforced, revenue cutters were ordered to collect the duties if the customs officials were resisted, and on 10 December the President issued a ringing proclamation calling 'the power to annul a law of the United States, assumed by one State, incompatible with the existence of the Union,' and attacking Calhoun's theory of the 'right of secession.'

South Carolina could not be cowed by proclamation. Her legislature hurled defiance at 'King Jackson' and raised a volunteer force to defend the state from 'invasion.' The President, in turn, prepared to throw an army into South Carolina at the first show of resistance to the customs officers. But could he afford to? Though Virginia regarded nullification as a caricature of her Resolves of 1798, the majority in all the Southern states probably believed in the constitutional right of secession.

Extremists aside, everyone wished to avoid bloodshed. Jackson understood the need to mix conciliation with firmness, and what the nullifiers really wanted was to reduce the tariff. Within three weeks of the President's proclamation, the House committee on ways and means proposed to lower duties. Charleston then resolved to suspend the nullification ordinance until the new tariff bill became law, and not to molest the federal customs officials. On 2 March 1833 Jackson signed two bills—the Force Act, authorizing him to use the army and navy to collect duties if judicial process were obstructed, and Clay's compromise tariff, providing a gradual scaling down of all schedules. The South Carolina convention then reassembled, repealed the nullification ordinance, but saved face by nullifying the Force Act, for which there was no longer any need. South Carolina had proved that a single determined state could have her way, but Jackson saw that beyond nullification lay secession. The 'next pretext,' he predicted, 'will be the Negro, or slavery question.'

The U.S. Bank and Biddle

In the midst of these alarums and excursions came the presidential election of 1832, memorable in the history of political organization. Jackson men, now organized as the Democratic party, sent delegates to a national party convention which renominated Old Hickory for the presidency and Martin Van Buren for the vice-presidency. The opposition, organized as the National Republican party (for which the name Whig, of happy memory, was shortly substituted), nominated Henry Clay.

The Democrats and Whigs were the two major parties of the future, but in 1832 a third party took the field. The Anti-Masonic party arose in 1826, out of the disappearance of a New York bricklayer named Morgan, who had divulged the secrets of his lodge. A corpse found floating in the Niagara river could not be proved to be Morgan's; but, as a politician said, it was 'good enough Morgan until after election.' Both the event and the Masons' efforts to hush it up revived an old prejudice against secret orders, which in a mobile, swiftly changing society appeared especially threatening to democratic institutions.[1] Furthermore, the Masons seemed to stand for all the forces of special privilege that might thwart the aspirations of ordinary men. Several young politicians, such as William H. Seward, Thurlow Weed, and Thaddeus Stevens, threw themselves into the Anti-Masonic movement. In 1831 it held a national convention and nominated William Wirt of Maryland, who next year robbed Henry Clay, a Mason,

1. One aspect of this feeling was the suppression of all fraternities in American colleges except Phi Beta Kappa, which became an 'honor' organization to save its life. Not until after the Civil War did college fraternities revive.

of thousands of votes, and carried Vermont. In a few years the Anti-Masons faded out; but the sort of people who were quick to believe that democracy was being subverted by foreign conspirators were later to be found in another one-idea party, the anti-Catholic Know-Nothings.

This presidential election decided the big issue of 1832: Andrew Jackson *v.* the Bank of the United States. Since 1819 the Bank had been well managed, to the profit alike of the government whose funds it handled, the business community which it served, and the stockholders; but it was unpopular in the South and Southwest. Jackson shared this dislike, together with a conviction that the money power was the greatest enemy to democracy. As the election of 1832 approached, Nicholas Biddle, president of the B.U.S., believing that Jackson would not dare risk making an issue of the Bank in an election year, precipitated a 'war' by asking for recharter immediately, four years before expiration. Biddle's action demonstrated to the President that he had been right in believing that the Bank was meddling in politics, and that, as a consequence, the 'Monster of Chestnut Street' constituted a menace to democracy. When Congress voted a recharter bill in July 1832, Jackson vetoed it. The bill, he declared, was not only an unconstitutional invasion of state rights; it proposed to continue a monopoly, the profits of which must come 'out of the earnings of the American people,' in favor of foreign stockholders and 'a few hundred of our own citizens, chiefly of the richest class.' Biddle called Jackson's message 'a manifesto of anarchy such as Marat or Robespierre might have issued to the mobs.' After a fiercely fought campaign, in which the Bank was the outstanding issue, Jackson won an emphatic electoral victory with 219 votes to Clay's 49.

The election persuaded Jackson that he had to go farther than the veto and deprive the Bank of federal money. One Secretary of the Treasury got himself promoted to the state department in order to duck the issue; his successor was dismissed by Jackson for refusing to obey, but a third Secretary, Roger B. Taney, did; and after 1 October 1833 no more government money was deposited in the expiring 'Monster.' Biddle refused to admit defeat. 'This worthy President thinks that because he has scalped Indians and imprisoned judges, he is to have his own way with the Bank. He is mistaken.' By constricting bank loans, Biddle helped to precipitate a panic. Yet once again his actions succeeded only in demonstrating that his enemies were correct in believing he wielded too much power.

This financial war came in the midst of a period of unparalleled speculation. Clay contributed to it by winning enactment of his 'distribution' scheme in 1836. Some states used the money from the federal surplus for public works, others as a fund for education, one even made a *per capita* distribution; but mostly the money fed speculation. Jackson then administered a severe astringent; the 'specie circular' of 1836 ordered the treasury to receive no 'folding money' for public lands. Shortly after, the panic of 1837 burst upon the country; and Van Buren's four years were spent in seeking a substitute for the B.U.S.; none was found comparable with it for service and efficiency until the Federal Reserve system was established in 1913.

Although Democracy won the battle with the Bank, it lost the war. Jackson, who was right in thinking no private institution should have so much uncontrolled power as this 'hydra-headed monster' held, failed to appreciate the economic functions the Bank performed and the kind of vacuum its departure would create. Out of the war the poor farmer, mechanic, and frontiersman gained nothing. Wall Street picked up the pieces of the shattered institution on Chestnut Street, Philadelphia; and a new 'money power' in New York soon had more money and power than Nicholas Biddle ever dreamed of.

Indian Removal

Presidents of a liberal persuasion have often in our history disregarded the interests of men of a different race, as Jackson demonstrated by carrying out a policy suggested by Jefferson: the removal of all Indian tribes to the West. Between 1829 and 1837, many thousand Indians were more or less unwillingly transferred west of the Mississippi. Tribesmen with well-developed farms, especially influential half-breeds, were given the option of

Les Natchez by Delacroix. The scene derives from Chateaubriand's tale *Atala*, subtitled *Les amours de deux sauvages dans le désert.* In Chateaubriand's work, published in the first year of the nineteenth century, the Indian is depicted in the romantic mode as the melancholy victim of the march of progress, and Delacroix expands upon this theme. Hugh Honour has observed: 'This great painting, with its exquisitely tender figures by a wide expanse of river inexorably flowing past them, even goes beyond Chateaubriand to become a poignant lament for the passing of a whole race.' The experience of the Natchez, who in the eighteenth century were decimated by the French in the Mississippi valley, served as a prelude to the dispersal of the Cherokee and other tribes during the Age of Jackson, the period when Delacroix was painting this canvas. (*Collection Lord Walston*)

staying where they were and becoming American citizens. Those who preferred to leave exchanged their property for new lands in the West, and were promised travel expenses and the value of improvements on their relinquished property. The 'assent' of the Indians was often nominal; federal officials stole what was due to the Indians; and on the journey west thousands died.

Most of the tribes were too feeble to resist, but at three points there was trouble. Chief Black Hawk of the Sauk and Fox tried to retain his ancient tribal seat at the mouth of Rock river, Illinois, but squatters encroached on his village, enclosed the Indians' cornfields, and even plowed up the graves of their ancestors. So in 1831 Black Hawk withdrew into Missouri Territory. There famine followed, and hostile Sioux threatened. Hoping to find a vacant prairie in which to plant a corn crop, Black Hawk returned the following spring with about a thousand of the tribe. Misinterpreting this move as a hostile expedition, the Illinois militia turned out—Abraham Lincoln commanding a company—and pursued the starving Indians up the Rock river into the Wisconsin wilderness. It was a disgraceful frontier frolic, stained by a wanton massacre of Indians, including women and children, when they attempted to recross the Mississippi. The only redeeming feature was the chivalrous consideration of Black Hawk by Lieutenant Jefferson Davis of the regular army, when the captured chief was placed in his charge. Forty years later, Davis referred to Black Hawk's rear-guard action at Wisconsin Heights as the most gallant fight he had ever witnessed.

In the South the Creek, Chickasaw, and Choctaw nations, after much prodding, removed to the Indian Territory (Oklahoma), where the descendants of their survivors still live, but the Cherokee and Seminole were refractory. It had always been a grievance against the Indians that they would not settle down to civilized ways, but in Georgia the Cherokee had built neat houses and good roads, preserved the peace, received Christian missionaries, published books in an alphabet invented by their tribesman Sequoya, and adopted a national constitution. However, in plain derogation of treaty rights, the state of Georgia claimed the Cherokee as her subjects and tenants-at-will. An unfortunate discovery of gold in the Cherokee country in 1828 brought in a rough class of whites. By violating a treaty, Georgia raised as clear a challenge to federal supremacy as had South Carolina; but President Jackson let Georgia have her way. Regulars sent in by President J. Q. Adams to protect the Indians were withdrawn; and when the Supreme Court decided in Worcester *v.* Georgia that the laws of Georgia had no force in Cherokee territory, Jackson probably never said 'John Marshall has made his decision. Now let him enforce it,' but these sentences, often attributed to him, did reflect his views. A portion of the Cherokee were bribed to exchange the lands of the whole for a section of the Indian Territory, and $5 million. The rest held out for a few years; but in 1838 they too were driven westward from the lands of their ancestors. The Cherokee lost one-quarter of their number in the removal. Emerson protested in vain: 'Such a dereliction of all faith and virtue, such a denial of justice, and such deafness to screams for mercy were never heard of in time of peace and in the dealing of a nation with its own allies and wards, since the earth was made.'

A similar controversy with the Seminole of Florida had an even more tragic outcome. A tricky treaty of removal, negotiated in 1832 with a few chiefs, was repudiated by the greater portion of the tribe, led by its brave chieftain Osceola. Secure in the fastnesses of the Everglades, Osceola baffled the United States Army for years, and was only captured by treachery when bearing a flag of truce. His people kept up the fight until 1842, costing the United States some $20 million and 1500 lives. A few thousand remained in the Everglades, where their descendants are waging a losing battle against 'progress,' represented by the bulldozer.

By the end of Van Buren's administration all but a few tribes of Eastern Indians had been removed beyond a 'permanent' barrier that ran from Lake Superior to the Red river. A chain of military posts, garrisoned by the regular army, was established to keep whites and reds apart. Jackson declared in 1835 that the nation was pledged to keep this barrier permanent. All but the southern limb of it was torn up within twenty years.

President Jackson

Andrew Jackson, by word and action, expanded the importance of the presidential office. He vetoed more bills than his predecessors had in forty years. He was the first President to insist on his right to disallow bills not for constitutional reasons but simply because he disapproved of them, and he was the first to use the pocket veto. He refused to permit the Senate to encroach on his powers, and he strengthened the unity of the executive branch by ending the ambiguous status of the Secretary of the Treasury, who, he made clear, was in no way an agent of Congress but merely a subordinate of the President. He conducted an aggressive foreign policy, and in concluding agreements with the king of Siam and the sultan of Muscat, his administration negotiated the first treaties between the United States and an Asiatic nation. Jackson also enhanced the political prestige of the presidency by leading a national party with a mass appeal. Although after he left office no President until Lincoln, save Polk, proved a strong executive, Jackson left an indelible mark on the office.

Yet Jackson had so many limitations that it is doubtful whether he should be included in the ranks of the really great Presidents. His approach to problems was too personal and instinctive; his choice of men, at times, lamentably mistaken; and, unlike the Roosevelts, who have been compared with him, he had little perception of underlying popular movements. Still, he also had admirable qualities, and he dealt swiftly and severely with the one disruptive movement whose significance he did perceive.

The Expansion of the Second Party System

The controversies that revolved around Andrew Jackson stimulated the formation of a new party system. In the second year of Jackson's presidency the National Republicans joined with dissenting Democrats to create the Whig party. The name suggested that, as the Whigs of the 1770's had stood up against King George, so the Whigs of the 1830's were fighting for liberty against 'King Andrew I.' The new party appealed to disparate elements united only by their opposition to Jackson: Bank Democrats and others hurt by the war with the B.U.S.; old-fashioned state-righters offended by Jackson's stand on nullification; New England and Middle State Yankees; owners of factory stock who wanted more protection; and Westerners attracted by Clay's economic policies.

The Whigs wished to use the national government to further capitalistic enterprise. They favored internal improvements, rechartering the Bank, and a protective tariff. Somewhat paradoxically, although advocates of strong national government, they believed in weak Presidents, in part as a consequence of their struggle with 'King Andrew.' Yet many who gravitated to the Whigs did so for non-ideological reasons. As the Democrats attracted Irish Catholic immigrants, the Whigs drew British Protestants. While free-thinkers flocked to the Democrats, the Whigs made a home for Protestant clerics who wished to use the State to wipe out 'moral' blemishes like the liquor traffic.

If the Democrats had the 'best principles,' wrote Emerson, the Whigs had the 'best men,' notably Henry Clay. Intelligent, upright, magnetic, and with a quarter-century's experience of Congress, Clay ran for the White House more often than any major party candidate in history, but never successfully. Lincoln called Clay 'my beau ideal of a statesman, the man for whom I fought all my humble life.' Dennis Hanks, Lincoln's illiterate cousin, explained that Lincoln became a Whig because he 'always Loved Hen Clays Speaches I think was the Cause Mostly.' The insouciant 'Prince Hal' gambled for high stakes, fought a duel, enjoyed good whiskey, and attracted women. Presented by Whig orators as 'the mill-boy of the Slashes,' Clay was in fact a prosperous Kentucky planter, identified with conservative interests. 'I would rather be right than President,' he said in a speech in 1850, and he had to be content with being right.

In 1836 the Whigs by-passed Clay to run three candidates, each strong in his own section: Webster in New England, General William Henry Harrison in the West, and Hugh White in the South. They expected that these three 'favorite sons' would carry enough states to deny any one candidate a majority in the electoral college and thus throw the election into the House, where the Whigs might prevail. To counter the Whig strategy Jackson placed Democratic party fortunes in the hands of the affable Martin Van Buren. Never before had a professional politician reached so high; for thirty years, from the age of 25, he had lived largely by politics. His home, at Old Kinderhook near Albany, in its abbreviated form 'O.K.' gave a new word to the language.[2] 'Little Van' earned the nickname 'The Red Fox' from his slyness, and 'The Little Magician' from his ability to turn everything into gold.

The two-party system now took hold in areas of the South, which in recent years had been a one-party (Democratic) reserve, and in the New West, which had been conducting politics on a 'no party' basis. Since Van Buren lacked Jackson's regional appeal, the South split. Yet Van Buren did well enough. With less than 51 per cent of the popular vote, he captured 170 electoral votes to 124 for his three rivals. Harrison polled 73 electoral votes, but the regional strategy broke down, for White carried only Tennessee and Georgia, and Webster only the Bay State. Van Buren thereby became the first President born under the Stars and Stripes, the first of Dutch stock, the first from New York, and the first to step from the governor's mansion at Albany into the White House at Washington.[3]

In 1835 Tocqueville wrote that 'the political activity which pervades the United States must be seen in order to be understood. No sooner do you set foot upon American ground, than you are stunned by a kind of tumult . . . almost the only pleasure which an American knows is to take a part in the government, and to discuss its measures.' The national party organization quickly reflected constitutional developments in the states. Between 1830 and 1850 religious tests and property qualifications for office were generally swept away, manhood suffrage was adopted, and many appointive offices became elective. These constitutional changes were effected by the democratic method initiated by Massachusetts in 1780: a popularly elected constitutional convention, with a popular referendum on the result. Both parties used the device of the nominating convention, which may have increased popular control, but also made possible greater party discipline.

National politics had another important consequence—muffling the growing divergence between North and South. Churches might split, social differences might deepen, and extremists revile one another; but, so long as the Whig and Democratic parties remained national in scope, the Union was safe.

The Panic of 1837

Van Buren in the White House reaped the whirlwind that Jackson had helped to sow. The twelve-year boom in the West resulted in overextension of credit, to which Jackson unwittingly contributed by putting government deposits in 'pet banks' which used them as a base for further speculation. When English banks insisted on payment in gold of short-term loans to American enterprises, these demands precipitated a panic, for they came at an unpropitious time. In pursuance of Jackson's specie circular, banks had been depleted of hard money to pay for purchases of government land in the West. In addition, the price of cotton fell from 20 to 10 cents and the wheat crop of 1836 failed.

Van Buren was no sooner in the White House than mercantile houses and banks began to collapse, and there were riots in New York over the high cost of flour. In the panic of 1837 almost every bank in the country suspended specie payments, and the government lost $9 million on deposit in 'pet banks.' A severe four-year depression caused widespread suffering, with no government assistance other than the town or

2. O.K., meaning Old Kinderhook (the home of Van Buren), was the secret name for Democratic clubs in New York in the campaign of 1840. The Whigs, unable to penetrate the meaning, invented this conversation between Amos Kendall and Jackson. ' "Those papers, Amos, are all correct. I have marked them O.K. (oll korrect)." The Gen. never was good at spelling.'

3. Since his running mate, Richard M. Johnson, failed to obtain a majority in the electoral college, he was chosen Vice-President by the Senate, according to Amendment XII of the Constitution—the only time that has been done.

county poorhouse for the desperate; cold and hungry people in the cities had to depend on private charity for fuel and food. A special session of Congress accomplished nothing except to authorize a large issue of temporary treasury notes, which started the national debt once more. It has been growing ever since. As a permanent fiscal measure Van Buren proposed an 'independent treasury,' a depository for government funds located in several cities, devised to divorce government from private banking interests so that no one group or class would enjoy an advantage. Not until 1840 did it become law. The Independent Treasury Act was repealed by the Whigs the next year, re-enacted under Polk, and remained the basis of the federal fiscal system until the Civil War.

The Taney Court

Van Buren inherited a virtually new Supreme Court. A number of deaths, including that of Chief Justice Marshall, disposed of all but two of the judges appointed by John Adams and the Virginia dynasty. Jackson was able to designate a new Chief Justice and four associate justices and Van Buren named three more in 1837. This new blood dominated the Court until the Civil War. Marshall's successor, Roger B. Taney, came from a Federalist family, but Jackson's war with the B.U.S. taught him the potential danger of organized finance, and his first service to the country was to provide an important limitation on Marshall's definition of the contract clause in the Dartmouth College case.

An old corporation which operated a toll bridge leading out of Boston sought to invalidate a recent state law which had provided a rival and parallel free bridge. Justice Story, following what would probably have been the opinion of his former chief, believed the state's action to be confiscatory and a breach of contract; the new Chief Justice, speaking for the majority, upheld Massachusetts, on the ground that no corporate charter could confer implied powers against the public. In addition to stating the modern doctrine of the social responsibilities of private property, the Charles River Bridge decision of 1837 helped expedite the transportation revolution by freeing railroads of the obligation to buy up every competing stagecoach, canal, or turnpike company.

Taney also limited the consequences of earlier decisions related to interstate commerce. Marshall had implied that federal power to regulate commerce was not only full but exclusive, voiding state regulations even if they filled a need that the Federal Government had not yet recognized. Taney posted a different thesis in the license cases (1847):

> The controlling and supreme power over commerce with foreign nations and the several states is undoubtedly conferred upon Congress. Yet, in my judgment, the state may nevertheless, for the safety or convenience of trade, or for the protection of the health of its citizens, make regulations of commerce for its own ports and harbors, and for its own territory; and such regulations are valid unless they come in conflict with a law of Congress.

Though in many respects, the Taney Court reflected the reaction in favor of state rights, the new Court had the same views, in general, of the relation between state and nation as its predecessor. Despite the egregious mistake he would later make in the Dred Scott case, Taney, for luminous perception of those social and economic realities upon which judicial statesmanship rests, must be considered one of the three or four really great Chief Justices of the United States.

Tippecanoe and Tyler Too

In 1840 the Whigs fought the Democrats by their own methods. They adopted no platform, nominated a military hero, and ran a jolly campaign that ignored real issues. Clay, the logical Whig candidate, did not get the nomination, which went to old General Harrison, the 'Hero of Tippecanoe.' Harrison was not politically inexperienced, having served as congressman and senator from Indiana, but unlike Clay he was not associated with any particular measures. Harrison's nomination set the pattern that Jackson's had begun—a nationally known figure, uncommitted on controversial issues. The Whig convention even appointed a committee to supervise the General's correspondence lest he write something incau-

In this Whig campaign song of 1840, a soldier, symbolic of General Harrison, is employed for the treble clef while the bass signature is a barrel, to represent the theme of hard cider. (*Library of Congress*)

tious and be quoted! For Vice-President the Whigs named John Tyler, twenty years younger than Harrison but with views as old-fashioned as those of the late John Randolph.

'Tippecanoe and Tyler too' was the slogan. The Whigs had so far abandoned patrician values that Van Buren was pictured with cologne-scented whiskers, drinking champagne out of a crystal goblet at a table loaded with costly viands and massive plate. An unlucky sneer in a Democratic newspaper, to the effect that Harrison would be content with a $2000 pension, a log cabin, and plenty of hard cider, gave opportunity for effective contrast. It became the log-cabin, hard-cider campaign. Huge balls, supposed to represent the gathering majority, were rolled by men and boys from village to village and state to state, singing as they rolled:

> What has caused this great commotion, motion, motion,
> Our country through?
> —It is the ball a-rolling on, for
> (*Chorus*) TIPPECANOE AND TYLER TOO:—
> Tippecanoe and Tyler too.
> And with them we'll beat little Van, Van, Van,
> Oh! Van is a used-up man.

Tippecanoe and Tyler rolled up 234 electoral votes, a four-to-one majority, but the popular vote was much closer, Harrison winning less than 53 per cent in an election in which almost four-fifths of the eligible electorate went to the polls.

By 1840, American politics had reached a remarkable equilibrium in which every state boasted a competitive two-party system. For the next twelve years, and for the only time in our history, both parties were national organizations with strong followings everywhere. This unusual situation could persist only at the expense of ignoring divisive sectional feelings.

On 4 April 1841, after one month in office, the Hero of Tippecanoe died, and John Tyler succeeded him. By his actions Tyler established the precedent that a Vice-President in such a situation inherits all the powers, as well as the title, of President. His administration also had one notable achievement. Tyler signed the 'log cabin' bill which made permanent in public land policy the pre-emption principle first incorporated in an Act of 1830. Any American not already an owner of 320 acres or more could now buy 160 acres in the public domain, and pay later at the rate of $1.25 an acre. This Pre-emption Act of 1841 was probably the most important agrarian measure ever passed by Congress.

But in most respects, the Tyler administration broke down in political squabbling, for the new President was a state-rights ideologue who disapproved of a strong Democratic chief executive like Jackson and who was out of place at the head of a Whig government. To be sure he fulfilled Whig expectations by taking over Harrison's cabinet intact and accepting an upward revision of the tariff as a necessary measure for the revenue. But whereas Clay, who expected to be 'mayor of the palace,' wished to cater to substantial interests, Tyler believed it his mission to strip the Federal Government of its 'usurped' power. He vetoed all bills for internal improvements and harbor works, and vetoed Clay's bill for a new bank as well as a second bill especially drafted to meet his constitutional scruples. From that date (9 September 1841) there was open warfare between Tyler and Clay. Four days later the cabinet resigned—except Webster who wished to appear independent of Clay—and the President was read out of the Whig party.

Here was Calhoun's chance to count in the sectional balance of power. For three years (1841–43), while Tyler attempted to form a party with a corporal's guard of faithful Whigs, Calhoun played a waiting game, repressing a secession movement among his hot-headed followers in South Carolina, intriguing to obtain the Democratic nomination for the presidency in 1844. Webster left the cabinet in 1843; and in March 1844 Calhoun became Tyler's Secretary of State. The new combination was extraordinary. Tyler had gone over to the Democrats, and Calhoun had returned to the fold. The loss of Tyler inclined the internal balance of the Whig party slightly, but definitely, northward; Calhoun tipped the internal balance of the Democratic party very definitely southward. Significantly, the Democrats, in adopting their 1844 platform, neglected to reaffirm their faith, as had been their wont, in the principles of the Declaration of Independence.

Anglo-American Relations

Both Van Buren and Tyler faced a troublesome situation on the northern border. In the autumn of 1837, rebellion broke out in Canada. Van Buren issued a neutrality proclamation, but most Americans hailed the uprising as a new American Revolution. For over a year, the Ontario rebel William L. Mackenzie and his followers were able to recruit money, supplies, and men in the United States and return to loot and burn in Canada. In response, on the night of 29 December 1837, a picked band of loyal Canadians performed the hazardous feat of rowing across the Niagara river to the United States side just above the head of the falls and setting afire the *Caroline*, an American steamer that had been supplying the rebels. In 1840, a Canadian named McLeod boasted in a New York barroom that he had killed an American in the affray; he was promptly indicted for murder. Prime Minister Palmerston, while belatedly admitting that the *Caroline* had been destroyed under orders, as a necessary means of defense against American 'pirates,' demanded the immediate release of McLeod. His execution, so he wrote to the British minister at Washington, 'would produce war, war immediate and frightful in its character, because it would be a war of retaliation and vengeance.' Tyler, now President, was as eager as Van Buren had been to preserve the peace, but Governor Seward of New York insisted that the justice of his state should take its course. In the trial, fortunately, McLeod sober found an alibi for McLeod drunk, and was acquitted.

Lord Durham, who had been sent to Canada to report on conditions, saw the real significance of the crisis. Protracted discontent in Canada must lead to Anglo-American war, or to liberals in Canada seeking annexation to the United States. At his suggestion, the British government granted responsible government to Quebec and Ontario in 1841, and to Nova Scotia and New Brunswick several years later. Canada owes this, in some measure at least, to the disturbing presence of her neighbor.

Tyler, who did especially well in foreign relations, not only finished the work that Van Buren had begun of pacifying the New York-Ontario border, but he and Secretary Webster settled the smoldering Northeastern boundary dispute. The Webster-Ashburton treaty of 1842 established the present boundary between Maine and Canada; rectified the frontier on Lake Champlain, where the United States had inadvertently built a fort on Canadian territory; and extended the international lake and river boundary from Sault Ste. Marie to the Lake of the Woods. Skillful diplomacy thereby averted war between the United States and Great Britain at two points on the Canadian-American border, but one final test of wills between the great powers remained to be resolved—in the Oregon country.

13

The Two Sections

*

1820–1850

The Cotton Kingdom

South of the border states of Delaware, Maryland, Virginia, and Kentucky, cotton ruled from 1815 to 1861; and the principal bulwark of his throne was slavery. Almost 60 per cent of the slaves in the United States in 1850 were employed in growing cotton. In 1820 the cotton crop of 160 million pounds was already the most valuable Southern interest. As more and more people in the Western world switched from linen and wool to cotton, its production doubled by 1830, and more than doubled again in the next decade. New Orleans, which in 1816 received 37,000 bales of cotton, counted almost a million in 1840. By 1850 the crop had passed a thousand million pounds; and the crop of 1860 was almost 2300 million pounds in weight, and in value two-thirds the total exports of the United States.

This growth was brought about by a rapid extension of the cotton-growing area. Like typical pioneer farmers, exploiters rather than conservers of the soil, the cotton planters advanced from South Carolina and Georgia across the 'black belts' and Indian cessions of Alabama and Mississippi, occupied the great valley up to Memphis, pushed up the Red river of Louisiana to the Indian Territory, and passed the boundary of Mexico into Texas. On the march King Cotton acquired new subjects: moneyed immigrants from the North, and ambitious dirt farmers who purchased a slave or two on credit and with luck became magnates. The white population of Arkansas jumped from 13,000 in 1820 to 324,000 in 1860; the number of slaves rose from 1600 to 111,000. The richest lands were sooner or later absorbed by planters, while poor whites settled on pine barrens, abandoned fields, and gullied hillsides.

Cotton plantations differed greatly both in size and character. One of the better sort in Mississippi, described by Olmsted, covered several square miles. The mansion house, which the absentee owner had not seen for two years, was four miles distant from the nearest white neighbor. The cleared portion, about 1400 acres, was tilled by a plough-gang of 30 men and a larger hoe-gang, mainly women, who were encouraged by a black driver, whip in hand. Enough corn and pork were usually raised to feed the cattle and the 135 slaves, who included three mechanics, two seamstresses, four teamsters and cattle-tenders, a midwife, and a nurse who had charge of a day nursery. The overseer also maintained a pack of hounds to hunt runaways. He kept the field hands working from sun to sun, but gave them most of Saturday as well as Sunday off, except in the picking season. They cut their fuel in the master's woods and were allowed to make boards for sale in their free time. Everywhere in the South slave families were allotted land to raise vegetables and poultry to eke out their rations of corn and pork.

A 'middle-class plantation,' which did not produce enough surplus to enable the owner to travel or reside elsewhere, would have 100 to 400 acres under cultivation and 10 to 40 slaves. A planter of this class might be a younger son, a self-made pioneer, an ex-overseer, or a professional man using his plantation to enhance his dignity in the community. In few instances did he enjoy comforts or amenities superior to those of the poorest farmers in the North: a bare house without conveniences, a diet largely of 'hog and hominy,' no literature but a weekly paper, no diversion but hunting and an occasional visit to the county seat. That sort of planter belonged to the governing class and had things much his own way in Alabama, Mississippi, and Arkansas.

A large part of the cotton crop was made by small farmers with one to half a dozen slaves, and below these yeomen farmers came a class called 'pore white trash,' 'crackers,' 'peckerwoods,' and other opprobrious nicknames. Constituting less than 10 per cent of the white population, these sallow, undernourished illiterates, whose only pride was their color, envied successful white men and hated the blacks. Very different were the mountain men, the 'hillbillies' who lived in the secluded valleys and on the steep slopes of the Appalachians and the Ozarks. These upstanding, independent people were expert hunters and fishermen. Almost isolated from the rest of the South, they were encountered only when they drove ox teams to market to sell moonshine whiskey made in illicit stills, and pork cured from acorn-fed pigs.

For more than a century writers have carried on a strenuous debate over the profitability of slavery, and the argument is as vigorous today as ever. Some historians contend that as a result of the high cost of slaves even planters opulent in nominal wealth found it difficult to keep out of debt, and the poorer ones depended on the money-lender for maintenance between crops. Thus, it is said, the system was uneconomical even for large planters in the long run; and for small farmers the first cost of labor became prohibitive. Furthermore, it has been argued that slavery retarded industrialization because the purchase of slaves absorbed an inordinate amount of capital; because slavery limited the development of a home market with widespread purchasing power; and because, by keeping the bondsmen in ignorance, the South denied itself the benefits of an educated, skilled working class. Other historians question whether the slow pace of industrialization was the consequence of slavery or of the fact that the South was an agricultural society in which capital could be more profitably employed in planting. Moreover, some historians who concede that slavery was not viable as an economic system argue that it was often very profitable as a business enterprise. There is no reason to suppose that slavery would have died out if it had not been ended by war, since even the most hopelessly inefficient master acquired status from owning slaves, even if the slave did not earn his keep.

It is often forgotten that the slave trade was begun by Negroes in Africa before Europeans reached the 'Dark Continent,' that every black bought by a slave trader was sold by one of his own race, and that victims of the system who were shipped to North America were better off than those who remained in bondage in Africa;[1] better off, in some respects, than many poor workers and peasants in Europe. John Randolph's slave valet, who accompanied his master to Ireland in 1827, 'looked with horror upon the mud hovels and miserable food' of the Irish peasantry. But these 'white slaves,' as the scornful Virginian called them, could emigrate to America as free men, their sons could become congressmen and

1. Compare Saint-Exupéry's account in *Wind, Sand and Stars* (1939) of an old and useless slave being turned out in the desert by his Moslem master to die of starvation—this around 1928.

In this unusual photograph, slaves are arranged by order of rank. They stand at the rear of the house on the occasion of Captain James Rembert's seventy-fifth birthday. The foreman, Nero, is at the left of the group of field hands; the second yard boy is middle front, the first yard boy middle forefront, the cook right forefront. The picture was taken at Stirrup Branch Plantation, Bishopsville, South Carolina, in 1857. (*Library of Congress, Courtesy Frank Des Champs, Bishopsville, S.C.*)

bishops, and their grandsons governors and even Presidents; whilst the children of Negro slaves were born into bondage.

Social gradations divided the slaves. Between a Virginia slave major-domo, whose ancestors had been American for two centuries, and a Gullah Negro of the Carolina sea islands who had been smuggled over from Africa within a year, there was an immense gap. Many a black butler or maid occupied a status similar to those confidential slaves that we meet in Greek and Roman literature, but field hands constituted the majority of slaves. A third and intermediate class were those who learned a trade such as carpentry, and often were hired out by their masters. In 1820 slaves made up 20 per cent of the population of Southern cities; by 1860, a half million slaves labored in factories or in pursuits like railroad construction.

The distinctive aspect of slave society in the United States was the resistance offered to the bondsman who sought to escape the system. The master who contemplated freeing his slaves faced unusually great impediments. To a far less extent than in countries like Brazil, some slave artisans were allowed to purchase their freedom out of earnings; but state laws made that increasingly difficult, since every successful free black was a living argument against keeping the rest of his race enslaved. The Romans usually freed their talented slaves, and in any case their progeny went free. But America subjected a writer like Frederick Douglass to the caprice of a white owner who might be his inferior in every respect.

Until around 1822 the planter class apologized for slavery as something forced on them by circumstances, but thereafter there was a defiant adoption of the theory that slavery was a positive good, sanctioned by history and the Bible. The starting point for this change of sentiment was the report that Denmark Vesey, a free mulatto, with the help of Gullah Jack, an aged African witch doctor, had hatched a plot in Charleston in 1822 involving thousands of blacks bent on slaughter and rape. In retrospect it appears that the plot was at most a vague notion in the minds of a few men given to loose talk, and it is possible that no conspiracy existed. But in a city in which Negroes outnumbered whites, and in which, as urban blacks, they were more advanced, less servile, and free from constant surveillance, rumors of insurrection bred panic. Betrayed by one of the 'conspirators,' loyal to a kind master, the 'revolt' was suppressed before it really started, and 37 blacks, including Vesey, were executed. A system of control, then adopted in the Lower South, gradually spread to Virginia and the border states. Blacks were forbidden to assemble or circulate after curfew, and night patrols policed the roads. Whites were forbidden to teach slaves to read or write in every Southern state except Maryland, Kentucky, and Tennessee. Nonetheless, in tidewater Virginia in 1831, a pious slave named Nat Turner enlisted a number of others who in August killed 57 whites before they were rounded up; between 40 and 100 Negroes were killed, and Turner was hanged.

Southern Society

Slavery and cotton preserved in the South a rural, almost feudal, society.[2] The eighteenth-century social contempt for trade persisted. Agriculture, the army, the church, and the law were the only proper careers for a planter's son. Northern and

2. The following statistics roughly indicate the social classes in the South as a whole (including the District of Columbia) and in the cotton states (South Carolina, Georgia, Florida, Alabama, Mississippi, Louisiana, Arkansas, and Texas) in 1850:

	All Slave States	*Cotton States*
Number of slaveholding families	347,525	154,391
Number of families owning 1 to 9 slaves	255,258	104,956
Number of families owning 10 to 49 slaves	84,328	43,299
Number of families owning 50 or more slaves	7,939	6,144
White population	6,242,418	2,137,284
Free Negro population	238,187	34,485
Slave population	3,204,077	1,808,768

Century of Population Growth, p. 136; J. D. B. De Bow, *Statistical View of the U.S.* (1854), pp. 45, 63, 82, 95, 99. Slaveholding families are counted more than once if they owned slaves in different counties.

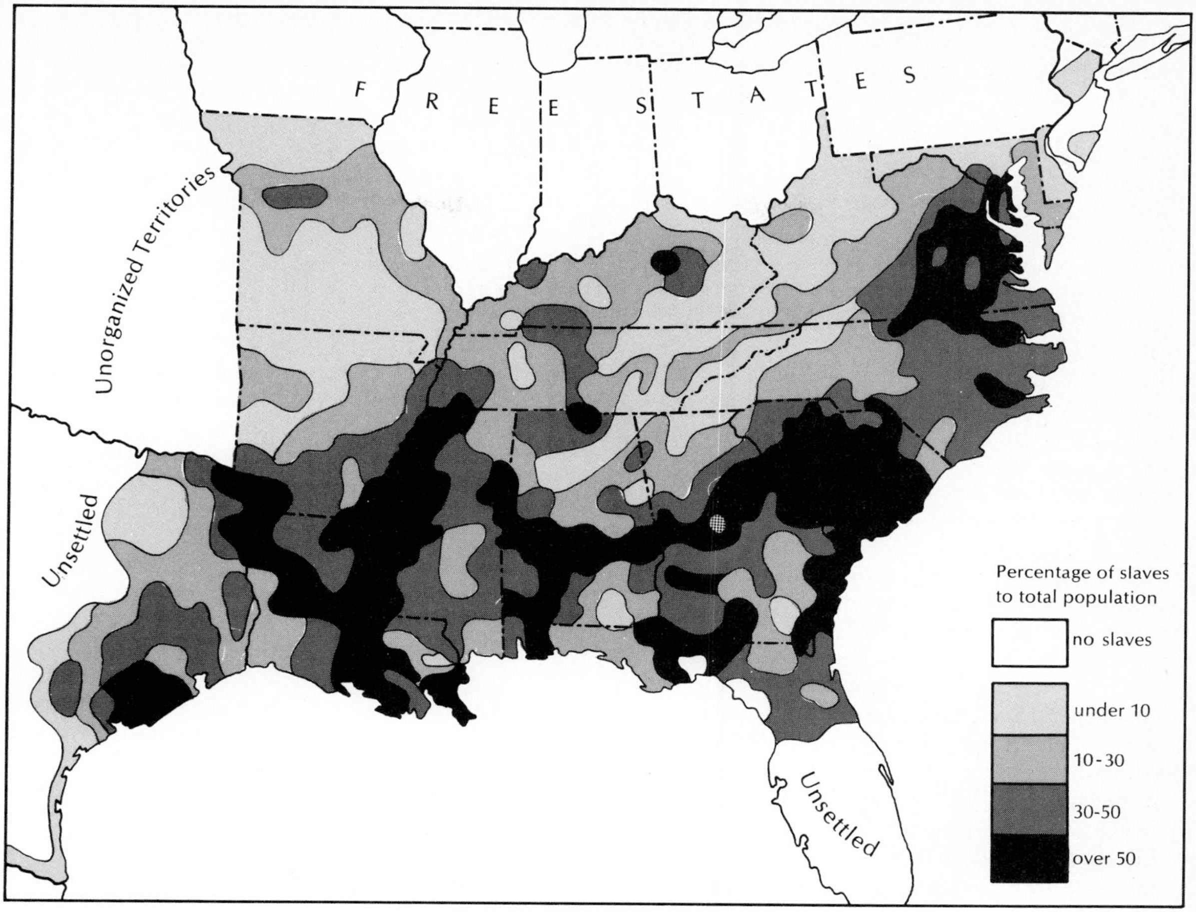

Proportion of Slaves in 1850

European merchant-bankers and shipowners handled the cotton crop, and kept most of the profits. Shopkeepers in the market towns were often Yankees, Germans, or Jews. Of the 15 largest cities in 1860, only one (New Orleans) was in the South. European immigrants, overwhelmingly from Northern countries, shunned a region where manual labor was regarded as unfit for a free man, and where the warm climate made adjustment difficult. Frontier conditions still prevailed through the greater part of the Lower South in 1850, combined with a turbulence and ignorance that seldom lingered in the Northern frontier beyond the first generation.

Theology, which had been neglected in the South when the section was liberal and anti-slavery, was much cultivated after it became conservative and pro-slavery. The influence of the evangelical sects among the planters increased in proportion as their ministers 'discovered' pro-slavery arguments in the Bible. The Catholic and Episcopalian churches remained neutral on the slavery question, and stationary in numbers. Thomas Jefferson, dying, saluted the rising sun of Unitarianism as destined to enlighten the South; but it sent only a few feeble rays beyond the Mason-Dixon Line. Horace Holley, the gifted young Unitarian who had made of Transylvania University in Lexington, Ky., a southern Harvard, was driven from his post and the university almost completely ruined by an alliance between Presbyterian bigotry and Jacksonian Democracy. Thomas Cooper, a victim of the 1798 Sedition Act, who had moved south, was 'tried' for atheism, and ejected, at the age of 75, from the presidency of South Carolina College.

The dominant religious mode was evangelical. Presbyterians and Episcopalians appealed to the upper classes, but Methodists and Baptists were more successful among middle classes, poor whites, and blacks. For a time these churches were a bond of union between North and South; but when the Northern Methodists unreasonably insisted that a Southern bishop emancipate slaves which he had inherited and could not conscientiously get rid of, the Southern members seceded and formed the Methodist Church South (1844). The Baptists followed, and doubled their membership in fifteen years. Though these Southern evangelicals condoned slavery, they banned card-playing and dancing; by 1860 the bastard puritanism of the age was more prevalent in Alabama and Mississippi than in Massachusetts and Connecticut.

The finest product of the plantation regime was the Southern gentleman. Numbering but few, the gentry ruled the older Southern states by virtue of personality even more than property, and governed them honorably and efficiently, although not with enlightenment. Discriminatingly hospitable, invariably gracious to women, endowed with a high sense of personal honor and civic virtue, they yet lacked the instinct for compromise that, time and again, has preserved the English aristocracy from annihilation.

Of this ruling class, only a small fraction belonged to the eighteenth-century aristocracy of Maryland, Virginia, and the Carolinas. The type of colonial gentleman that Washington was, appeared undiminished in his Lee kinsmen; but the old Huguenot families of Charleston were declining, and the creoles of Louisiana were easy-going and unambitious. Apart from these three persistent types, the mass of the greater planters in 1850 were self-made men like Jefferson Davis, whose parents had lived in log cabins. If not well educated themselves, their sons and daughters were. The South, despite poverty in elementary education, had good secondary schools, especially of the military type, and more students in college than the North.

Life on a resident plantation of the better sort was neither sordid as the abolitionists asserted, nor splendid as the novelists have depicted it. The mansion house, seated on rising ground, was generally a well-proportioned wooden building of neo-classic style, with a columned portico or veranda that gave dignity to the elevation and afforded shade to the ground floor and front chambers. The rooms, seldom more than fifteen in number, were high-ceiled and simply furnished. There were plenty of flowers, and masses of native flowering shrubs. Simplicity rather than ostentation was the dominant note in the planter's life. He enjoyed little leisure. On a Virginia plantation visited by Olmsted, not ten consecutive minutes

'Leaving the Manor House.' This canvas, painted on the eve of the Civil War, gives a stylized and romanticized view of the Southern plantation gentry. (*National Gallery of Art*)

elapsed even during dinner when the proprietor was not interrupted by a servant. The owner's wife had to guard against pilferers, serve out supplies, bind up wounds, and nurse the sick.

Such a life was a continuous exercise of tact, self-control, and firmness; yet the condition of unlimited power was a constant temptation to passion. The sort of bluster considered gentlemanly in the eighteenth century remained so in the South at a time when smoother and more reticent manners had become the mark of good breeding in England and the North. Alexander H. Stephens, future Vice-President of the Confederacy, was unable to take part in the political campaign of 1848 because he had been disabled by stabs received in an 'affray.'

The 'Southern chivalry' tradition was created in the generation of 1820 to 1850. In *Ivanhoe* and the flood of imitative literature that followed, the cotton lord and his lady found a romantic mirror of their life and ideals. A generalizing French traveler, Michel Chevalier, assumed that all Northerners were descended from Cromwell's Roundheads, and all Southern whites from King Charles's Cavaliers. Every owner of two Negroes, however dubious his origin or squalid his existence, became a 'cavalier,' entitled to despise the low-bred shopkeepers, artisans, and clerks of the North. The rage to establish *Mayflower* ancestry in the North, 50 years later, was a compensation of the same sort for descendants of colonial families who were being crowded by newcomers.

To comprehend the psychology of the Southern planter we must remember that his social system was on the defensive against most of the Western world. Under the leadership of Wilberforce and Clarkson in England, Parliament in 1833 passed an act emancipating all slaves in the British West Indies, allowing compensation to the owners. The Second Republic did the same in the French West Indies in 1848; Denmark and all other colonial powers in the West Indies, with the important exception of Spain, had already done so. The white Southerner's proud assertiveness was the sign not of confidence but of fear. Just as New England in 1800 refused every quickening current from France or Virginia, for fear it might bear the seeds of Jacobinism, so the South, a generation later, rejected a literature and philosophy which might conceal abolitionist sentiment. At a time when Bryant, Longfellow, and Whittier were redeeming Northern materialism with cheerful song, Southern silence was broken only by the gloomy and romantic notes of Edgar Allan Poe. The most distinguished and prolific man of letters of the antebellum South, William Gilmore Simms, wrote in 1855, 'All that I have *[done]* has been poured to waste in Charleston.'

Southern men of letters were compelled to write in glorification of the 'Southern way of life.' A pro-slavery theory of society was provided by Thomas R. Dew, a bright young Virginian who returned from study in Germany to a chair at William and Mary College. In a pamphlet of 1832, he argued that slavery had been the condition of classical culture, that the Hebrew prophets and St. Paul admitted its moral validity, that civilization required the many to work and the few to think. George Fitzhugh, in a tract entitled *Cannibals All*, argued that the Negro was something less than man, and in his *Sociology for the South* scoffed at the 'glittering generalities' of a century of enlightenment.

John C. Calhoun gave pro-slavery doctrine the sanction of his name and character, and so cunningly combined it with American prepossessions that slavery appeared no longer the antithesis, but the condition, of democracy. Calhoun began with the axiom that no wealthy or civilized society could exist unless one portion of the community lived off the labor of others. Chartism in England and trade-unionism in the United States proved that social stability could not be maintained where labor was free. It was too late to re-establish serfdom in Europe and the North. But to the South a beneficent providence had brought a race created by God to be hewers of wood and drawers of water for His chosen people. In return, kind masters provided for all reasonable wants of their slaves, and saved them from the fear of destitution that haunted the white proletariat. The masters themselves, relieved from manual labor and sordid competition, would reach that intellectual and spiritual eminence of which the founders of the Republic had dreamed.

Such was the nonsense that became orthodox in the South by 1850. Yet it is doubtful how wide or deep this folly really went. It was never accepted by the great Virginians who fought so valiantly for the Confederacy.[3] There was no place in the system for poor whites, from one of whom, Hinton R. Helper, came the first prophecy of disaster: *The Impending Crisis* (1857) which was suppressed throughout the South. Still, many non-slaveholding whites who disliked slavery agreed with the planters that it would never do to eman-

3. Robert E. Lee emancipated the few slaves he inherited from his mother, and owned no others. Stonewall Jackson purchased two slaves at their own request, and allowed them to earn their freedom. J. E. Johnston and A. P. Hill never owned a slave, and disliked slavery. J. E. B. Stuart owned but two slaves, and disposed of them for good reasons, long before the war. M. F. Maury, who called slavery a 'curse,' owned but one, a family servant.

New York in 1849. At the birth of the republic, it was already regarded as a metropolis, though it had but 33,000 souls. By the 1850 census, New York numbered 515,000, crowded into the southern sector of Manhattan Island, with settlement extending northward only to about 20th Street. In the year of this illustration, a free academy was chartered that became the City University of New York, and an argument over whether an English tragedian or the native-born Edwin Forrest was the better actor led to a nativist riot that resulted in 200 casualties. (*Eno Collection, New York Public Library*)

cipate the slave, since the South must be kept a 'white man's country.' By 1850 the Cotton Kingdom, closing in on itself, had excluded every means of saving reform, and had resolved to make Negro slavery, in an ever-increasing radius, a permanent basis of American society.

The Industrious North

Though statesmen and parties had done much in these years to preserve the Union, social and economic forces were pulling North and South apart. Both were progressing, but divergently. To be sure, both North and South were affected by common experiences: nationalism, capitalism, evangelicalism, and the westward movement. But Northern society was being transformed by the industrial revolution, by cheap transportation, and by educational, humanitarian, and migratory movements that touched the border slave states very little, and the Lower South not at all. In this same period Southern society was readjusting itself to the cotton plantation, tilled by slaves. By 1850 two distinct civilizations had evolved.

The most striking aspect of Northern society was egalitarianism, a feature that some foreign observers approved and others lamented. Harriet Martineau noted that in America 'the English insolence of class to class, of individuals toward each other, is not even conceived of, except in the one highly disgraceful instance of people of colour.' The 'sweet temper' of Americans she attributed to the 'practice of forbearance requisite in a republic.' Yet forbearance Americans carried to excess in their uncritical attitude toward their own books, customs, institutions, and abuses. Almost every European visitor denounced their acceptance of majority opinion and deplored their fear of expressing unpopular notions, for Americans were becoming less independent and more gregarious. On the other hand, so complex was the American character that the excess of one quality was balanced by its reverse. Intolerance appeared in the persecution of unpopular groups such as blacks, immigrants, abolitionists, and Catholics; and in hot resentment of unfavorable criticism. Nor was distinction wanting in a country that produced in one generation Clay, Calhoun, Webster, Poe, Hawthorne, and Irving; and in the next, Emerson, Longfellow, Whitman, Lee, and Lincoln.

It was a busy age. Each Northern community was an anthill, intensely active. Every man worked, or at least made a semblance of it. The Northern American had not learned how to employ leisure; his pleasure came from doing things. Yet the Northern and Western states were a land where dreams of youth came true; where the majority were doing what they wished to do, without class or official restraint. 'We were hardly conscious of the existence of a government,' wrote a Scandinavian immigrant in New York. The fun of building, inventing, creating, in an atmosphere where one man's success did not mean another's failure, gave American life that peculiar gusto that Walt Whitman caught in his poetry. And the resources of a new country, exploited by the inhabitants under laws of their own making and breaking, had brought a degree of comfort and security to the common man that he had not known since the days of good Queen Bess.

Transportation and Migration

The westward movement developed new momentum in the age of Jackson. New Englanders, who a generation before had settled the interior of New York and Ohio, were pressing forward into the smaller prairies of Indiana and Illinois, where the tough sod taxed their strength but repaid it in the end with bountiful crops of grain; where shoulder-high prairie-grass afforded rich pasturage for cattle, and groves of buckeye, oak, walnut, and hickory furnished wood and timber. A favorite objective was southern Michigan, a rolling country of 'oak openings,' where stately trees stood well-spaced as in a gentleman's park. Others were hewing farms from the forests of southern Wisconsin and venturing across the Mississippi into land vacated by Black Hawk's tribe.

Improved transportation was the first condition of this quickening life. Canals, roads, and railways took people west, and connected them with a market when they got there. By bringing the Great Lakes within reach of a metropolitan market, the Erie Canal, completed in 1825, opened up the hitherto neglected northern regions of Ohio, Indiana, and Illinois and made New York City the principal gateway to the farther West. Ohio linked the Great Lakes with the Mississippi valley by canal in 1833–34. By 1850 Cleveland rose from a frontier village to a great lake port; Cincinnati, at the other end of the state canal system, sent pickled pork down the Ohio and Mississippi by flatboat and steamboat, shipped flour by canal boat to New York, and in 1850 had a population of 115,000—more than that of New York City in 1815. Three hundred lake vessels arrived at Chicago in 1833, although its permanent population was about 200. An English traveler pronounced Chicago in 1846 to be a city of 'magnificent intentions,' and predicted that after being burned down once or twice it might amount to something. In 1856 the city was connected by railway with New York, and by 1860 it was almost as large as Cincinnati. During the 1840's, while the population of the United States increased 36 per cent, that of towns and cities of 8000 or more grew 90 per cent. Measured by numbers, the urban movement was stronger than westward migration, and its effect on the American character equally important.[4]

Only gradually did railroads replace the canals. In 1828 the first spadeful was turned on the Baltimore and Ohio, but the line did not reach the Ohio river until 1853. In the early '50's the completion of the Hudson River Railway from New York to Albany (where it was connected with the New York Central for Buffalo) and of the Pennsylvania Railroad from Philadelphia to Pittsburgh caused such an astounding transfer of freight from canals to railroads, particularly in the winter season, as to prove the superiority of rail for the long haul, and to suggest that the steam locomotive was the proper instrument for penetrating the continent.

Though American shipbuilders lagged behind England in applying steam to ocean navigation, their sailing vessels largely captured the freight and passenger traffic between Liverpool and New York. 'The reason will be evident to any one who will walk through the docks at Liverpool,' wrote an Englishman in 1824. 'He will see the American ships, long, sharp built, beautifully painted and rigged, and remarkable for their fine appearance and white canvas. He will see the English vessels, short, round and dirty, resembling great black tubs.' One consequence of the transportation revolution was the development of a safe and inexpensive ocean crossing. Shippers encouraged the emigrant trade in order to have a return freight on their westward voyage.

In the century after 1815 some 30 million people migrated from Europe to America. The country was staggered by the wave of nearly 600,000 immigrants in the 1830's, four times as many as in the previous decade, but in the 1850's a startling 2,314,000 newcomers would step ashore. The number of immigrants who came to the United States between 1815 and 1860 was greater than the total population of the country in 1790. Americans liked to believe that migrants were attracted to their country by admiration for the unique political institutions of the United States, but, in truth, most came for economic reasons. Cycles of prosperity in America drew them; periods of depression discouraged their coming. They responded both to the 'pull' of the burgeoning American economy and the 'push' of the population explosion and hard times in Europe. After the terrible Great Famine due to the potato blights of 1845–49, the Irish peasant came to view migration as a release instead of a banishment. Many arrived penniless; others often fell prey to waterfront sharpers. But as soon as they recovered their shore legs the immigrants were well able to defend themselves. As early as 1835 Irishmen were driving the Whigs from the polls in New York with showers of 'Irish confetti.' Despite suffering and homesickness, most of the immigrants prospered and sent for their friends.

Almost all of the 5 million immigrants in these years came from northwestern Europe, two million from Ireland, over a million and a half from Germany, three-quarters of a million from England, Scotland, and Wales. All but a small fraction of the newcomers arrived in seaports in the Northeast and settled in the northern half of the country. Although mostly country folk, the Irish congregated in cities where thousands of them were recruited for construction work and domestic service. The impoverished Irishman lacked the cash to acquire land, had no experience of farming other than potatoes, and distrusted the land after

4. Table showing populations of principal cities:

	1790	1800	1810	1820	1830	1840	1850
Boston	18,038	24,937	33,250	43,298	61,392	93,383	136,881
New York	33,131	60,489	96,373	123,706	202,589	312,710	515,547
Philadelphia	42,520	69,403	91,874	112,772	161,410	220,423	340,045
Baltimore	13,503	26,114	35,583	62,738	80,825	102,313	169,054
Charleston	16,359	20,473	24,711	24,780	30,289	29,261	42,985
New Orleans			17,242	27,176	46,310	102,193	116,375

his bitter experience in Ireland. He was too gregarious for life on the isolated American farm, and needed a community large enough to support a Catholic Church. Peasant also were a majority of the Germans, but not in like degree; among them were thousands of artisans, a few thousand political refugees from the revolutions of 1830 and 1848 such as Carl Schurz, and a sprinkling of intellectuals. German colonies were formed in cities such as Milwaukee, but the greater number acquired Western land, as did the Scandinavians.

This wave of immigration enhanced the wealth of the country, yet encountered bitter opposition. In part, the antagonism was religious, since most of the Irish and many of the Germans were Roman Catholics. In part it was political, for most immigrants to the cities became Jackson Democrats, largely because the politicians of that party were the first to give them help. In part it was due to the widespread belief among native Americans that the immigrants were paupers. Most immigrants only wanted an opportunity to work, but their need for jobs was so desperate that by cutting wages they displaced some laborers, especially free Negroes. Yet the main consequence of immigration was an acceleration of economic growth that benefitted native Americans as well as the newcomers.

Factory and Workshop

In the generation after 1815, textiles propelled the American economy. The South grew cotton, the Northeast converted it into cloth and supplied manufactured goods to the South, which obtained a large part of its food from the Midwest. From 1820 to 1840, the number of cotton spindles increased from 191,000 to two and a quarter million, two-thirds of them in New England. Farmers' daughters were attracted to the new factory city of Lowell by relatively high wages, and the scruples of their pious parents were overcome by the provision of strictly chaperoned boarding houses. For a generation the Lowell factory girls, with their neat dresses, correct deportment, and literary weekly, were a wonder. Never, unfortunately, were they typical. Yet it is also true that because of wide opportunities in a new country, no permanent proletariat was created. Lawrence, a woolen counterpart to Lowell, was established on the Merrimack, the same river, in 1845. The woolen industry developed more slowly, but by 1850 the Northern states boasted over 1500 woolen mills.

Of the many industries that were still in the domestic stage at this period, the most significant was shoemaking, for which no machine process of any importance was invented until 1850. In New England it was a winter occupation of farmers and fishermen, who, when the harvest was gathered, or the vessel hauled out for the winter, formed a 'crew' to make boots and shoes in a neighborhood workshop, from stock put out by some local merchant. Every man was master of his own time, and there was no clatter of machinery to drown discussion. A boy was often hired to read to the workers. It was said that 'every Lynn shoemaker was fit to be an United States Senator'; and Henry Wilson 'the cordwainer of Natick' became Vice-President. The shoemakers of New York and Philadelphia, more hard-pressed than their Yankee brethren by the capitalist and the immigrant, were pioneers in the first political labor movement in America.

In England the industrial revolution turned mainly on coal and iron; not so in the United States, where the iron industry lagged. Suitable coal for coking was not found east of the Appalachians, but wood for making charcoal was abundant. Even Pittsburgh used charcoal for smelting prior to 1840, rather than the bituminous coal which was plentiful in the neighborhood. And Pittsburgh, although it commanded the iron market of the Mississippi valley, could not sell its products in the East until it obtained through railroad connection with Philadelphia. Eastern Pennsylvania was the principal coal- and iron-producing region until 1860. The production of pig-iron increased from 54,000 tons in 1810 to 564,000 tons in 1850; but by that time Great Britain's output was almost 3 million tons. Very little steel was produced in America before 1870, and the engineering trades were undeveloped.

Textiles and iron do not exhaust the list of factory industries in the United States at this time, nor had mass production become a necessary condition of American industrial success. Connecticut, in particular, was famous for small, water-driven workshops where specialized articles were produced by native ingenuity. Connecticut

Passenger Pigeon by John James Audubon (1785–1851). Audubon, who arrived in America from France in 1803, painted in the 1820's in Pittsburgh this watercolor and pastel of a male passenger pigeon being fed by his mate. When Audubon's work was exhibited in Europe, critics were astonished by the fidelity to detail and by the vivid sense conveyed of the creatures of the New World. 'Who would have expected such things from the woods of America?' asked a Parisian artist. So plentiful were passenger pigeons that in 1813 in Kentucky Audubon estimated that a billion birds passed overhead in three hours, and they were but a small segment of a three-day migration. 'The air was literally filled with pigeons,' he wrote; 'the light of noon-day was obscured as by an eclipse.' But so great was the slaughter of these birds that by the end of the century they were nearly extinct, and in 1914 the last known passenger pigeon died. (*New-York Historical Society*)

tinware and wooden clocks were carried by Yankee peddlers far and wide. One of the most popular exhibits at London's Crystal Palace in 1851 was the array of reapers, ranges, sewing machines, and other 'Yankee notions.'

Science, Technology, and Education

Comparatively little scientific advance was made in the United States during this era because the stress was on practice rather than theory. Benjamin Franklin started the trend; his American Philosophical Society was dedicated to 'useful knowledge,' and his loyalist contemporary Benjamin Thompson founded the Rumford professorship at Harvard in 1816 'on the Application of Science to the Useful Arts.' Alexis de Tocqueville, in his *Democracy in America* (1835), observed that in a democratic society short cuts to wealth, labor-saving gadgets, and inventions catering to the comfort of life 'seem the most magnificent effort of human intelligence.'

The one American 'pure' scientist of this era was Joseph Henry. After inventing the electromagnet, he produced a rudimentary motor which he regarded as 'a philosophical toy.' His studies of induced currents, begun independently of his English contemporary Michael Faraday who first announced the discovery, led Henry to discover step-up and step-down transformers and to formulate theories of intensity (voltage) and quantity (amperage) of currents. In 1846 Henry became the first director of the Smithsonian Institution at Washington. This earliest American foundation for scientific research was established by a bequest of over £100,000—greater than the then endowment of any American university—from a British chemist named James Smithson, for founding at Washington 'an Establishment for the increase and diffusion of knowledge among men.' Congress expected the Institution to comprise a library, art museum, and collection of scientific curiosities that would amuse congressmen and their friends, but Henry saw to it that the Smithsonian became an indispensable agency for the financing and wide distribution of original research. Henry also helped Samuel F. B. Morse to invent the electric telegraph in 1837. It was typical of mid-century piety that the first message sent over this line on 24 May 1844 between Morse in the Supreme Court chamber in the Capitol, and Alfred Vail in Baltimore, was 'What hath God wrought!' (Numbers xxiii:23).

The branches of science that made good progress in the generation after 1830 were natural history, chemistry, and geology. John Audubon had to visit England in order to obtain subscriptions for his classic *Birds of America* (1827), but he was acclaimed a hero on his return. In 1835 Benjamin Silliman of Yale, who founded and edited the first American scientific periodical, delivered a series of lectures at Boston on geology which, pious Congregationalist though he was, made the first important dent on the Biblical account of creation. A year or two later his friend the Reverend Edward Hitchcock, a science professor of Amherst College, discovered dinosaur tracks in the red sandstone of the Connecticut valley: a new proof of the antiquity of life on this planet. When in 1848 Louis Agassiz left his native Switzerland and occupied a chair of zoology and geology in the new scientific school at Harvard, America found a leader in natural science who was at once an original investigator, a great teacher, and one who could appeal to the popular imagination. No American, native or adopted, was Agassiz's equal in stimulating both popular and scholarly interest in that segment of natural science which stretched from biology to paleontology.

The most tangible social gain during this period of ferment was in popular education. Since the Revolution, education had been left largely to private initiative and benevolence, but almost all secondary academies charged fees. Most of the Northern states had some sort of public primary school system, but only in New England was it free and open to all. In some instances only parents pleading poverty were exempted from fees. Consequently a stigma was attached to free schools. In New York City, around 1820, nearly half the children went uneducated because their parents were too poor to pay fees and too proud to accept charity.

Opposition to free public education came from people of property, who thought it intolerable that they should be taxed to support schools to which they would not dream of sending their children. To this argument the poor replied with votes, and reformers with the tempting argument that education was insurance against radicalism. New York City in 1832, and Philadelphia in 1836, established elementary public schools free from the taint of charity; but the growth of public schools did not keep pace with the increase of population by birth and immigration. There were half a million white adult illiterates in the country in 1840; almost a million in 1850.

In the New England states free elementary schools, maintained by the townships and taught by birch-wielding pedagogues or college students during their vacations, were much in need of improvement. When Horace Mann became chairman of the Massachusetts Board of Education (1837), he insisted that control of the schools should rest not with professional schoolmen but with popularly elected legislatures and school committees composed of laymen. At Lexington, in 1839, the first American teachers' college was established. After a struggle with the older teachers, who insisted that mental discipline would be lost if studies were made interesting, the elementary school ceased to be a place of terror. New England also set the pace in free public high schools; but until after the Civil War most pupils following a secondary course attended an endowed academy.

Outside New England, public schools were generally supported by the interest on a fund set up out of the proceeds of public lands or earmarked taxes, administered by a specially appointed state board. In Pennsylvania a terrific fight took place over free schools which were opposed by not only the well-to-do but the Germans, who feared the loss of their language and culture. Ohio was fairly well provided with free public elementary schools by 1830, and six years later the state sent Calvin E. Stowe, professor of Biblical literature in Lane Theological Seminary at Cincinnati (better known as husband of the author of *Uncle Tom's Cabin*) to Europe to investigate public school systems. His *Report on Elementary Instruction in Europe* (1837) had an influence not inferior to the reports of Horace Mann. Among other things, it resulted in dividing public education in Ohio into elementary, grammar, and high school grades. By 1850 the modern system of grades one through twelve had been adopted in places where the number of pupils allowed it. Indiana established a free public school system in 1848, but opposition of the Southern element in the population prevented the Illinois legislature from enacting a state-wide public school law until 1855. However, by 1860, the Midwest had a larger proportion of its children in public schools than any other region.

It was long before the free blacks of the North had any benefit from free public education. Philadelphia opened the first school for black children in 1822 with an apology for doing something for 'this friendless and degraded portion of society.' In northern New England where blacks were few, they were admitted to the public schools without question; but in urban centers both reformers and the blacks themselves favored separate schools, to avoid the stigma of charity and give the children more congenial companionship. The move against segregation began with the anti-slavery agitation of the 1830's. Massachusetts in 1855 was the first state to enforce integration of all races and religions in her public schools, but segregation was not legally ended in New York City schools until 1900.

American schools of the nineteenth century reflected Protestant thinking. They aimed to cultivate qualities of character, such as thrift and industry, appropriate to the Puritan tradition and the cult of the self-made man, and William H. McGuffey's moralistic readers reflected the values of evangelical ministers. Increasingly the community expected the school to take over the roles of church and family. As the school committee of Springfield, Massachusetts, explained: 'The school-master is for the time being during school hours *in loco parentis*; sustaining a relation to his pupils parallel to that of a father to his children.'

This period saw an amazing multiplication of small denominational colleges; and a somewhat less surprising mortality among them. In sixteen Eastern and Midwestern states (both North and South) 516 colleges and 'universities' were founded before the Civil War; but only 104 of these were still in existence in 1929. Yale alone begat sixteen Congregationalist colleges before

(*Prints Division, New York Public Library*)

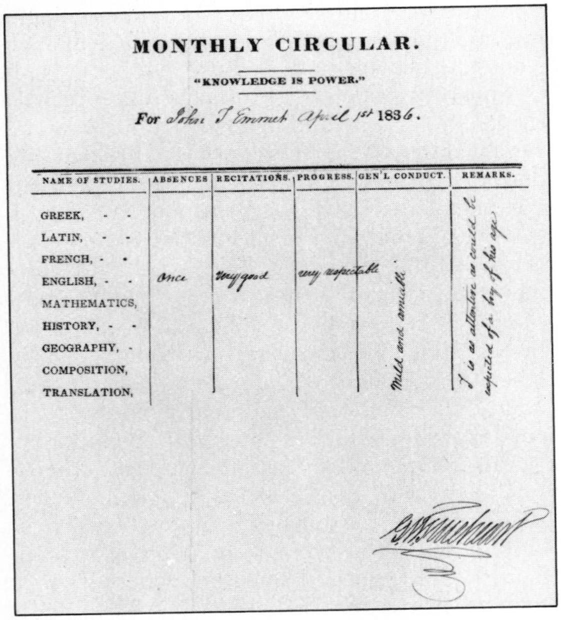

MONTHLY CIRCULAR.

"KNOWLEDGE IS POWER."

For John T Emmet April 1st 1836.

NAME OF STUDIES.	ABSENCES	RECITATIONS.	PROGRESS.	GEN'L CONDUCT.	REMARKS.
GREEK,					
LATIN,					
FRENCH,					
ENGLISH,	Once	Very good	very respectable	Mild and amiable	J is as attentive as could be expected of a boy of his age
MATHEMATICS,					
HISTORY,					
GEOGRAPHY,					
COMPOSITION,					
TRANSLATION,					

Report card. His mother wrote of the recipient of this assessment, who would grow up to be a West Point cadet and a physician: 'Little John is at my elbow and expressly desires me to tell you that he is a very good boy, that he has gotten a new spelling book from his Grandmother Patten, and that he will take care and get his lessons well. All this I am sure he has sincere intentions of performing tho I must confess that in his old spelling book he is not very brilliant.' Still, she added of John Patten Emmet's schooling, 'he does not learn any bad habits and is fond of it. At home he would be apt to grow sluggish.' (*Henry E. Huntington Library*)

1861, and Princeton 25 Presbyterian ones. It was the heyday of the small, rural college with six to a dozen professors and 100 to 300 students. During a good part of this period, Amherst, Dartmouth, and Union colleges had as many or more students than Harvard, Yale, and Princeton. The average statesman and professional man of the Northern states completed his formal education at a small college.[5]

In the same period the movement for public and secular state universities, which had begun just before the Revolution, received a new impetus, in part from the founding of the University of Virginia. The earliest of the Western state universities was founded at Detroit in 1817, but the University of Michigan remained a mere secondary school until 1837, when it was rechartered and removed to Ann Arbor. The University of Wisconsin, second of the state universities to become famous, was founded at Madison in 1848, on a wilderness site crossed by Black Hawk's warriors only sixteen years before.

Harvard was the first of the older universities after the War of 1812 to feel the new spirit of progress; and the source of her inspiration was Germany. Between the years 1815 and 1820 four young Harvard graduates—George Ticknor, Edward Everett, Joseph G. Cogswell, and George Bancroft—studied at the Universities of Göttingen and Berlin. The young Americans admired the boundless erudition, critical acumen, and unwearied diligence of German scholars, marveled at the wealth of the university libraries, and envied the *Lernfreiheit* or academic freedom. They returned with an ambition to transform their little brick colleges into magnificently equipped universities. All four upon their return received posts at Harvard. Everett gave prestige, by his graceful delivery and easily worn mantle of scholarship, to the lecture method of instruction; Bancroft applied German thoroughness to early American history; Cogswell is memorable in library history; and Ticknor remained professor of belles lettres long enough to establish a worthy school of Romance and Germanic languages, and to secure the principle that undergraduates might elect them as a substitute for traditional subjects. And it was in part the influence of American scholars who had caught the flame in Germany, in part the liberal tendency of Unitarianism, that made Harvard, as early as the 1830's, a steadfast defender of the scholar's freedom from political and religious pressure.

Though many of the colleges of mid-century had high standards in the subjects they professed to teach, the university law and medical schools of the period were not even respectable. Yet the application of anesthesia to surgery was discovered independently by three graduates of American medical schools around 1842. And, just as Jefferson wished to live as the founder of a university, so Dr. O. W. Holmes, author of *The Autocrat of the Breakfast Table,* considered his best title to fame the discovery in 1843 that puerperal fever could be prevented by the use of antiseptics.

Adults were not neglected in this educational awakening. Mechanics' institutes provided vocational courses and night schools; free public libraries were widespread; and lyceums offered popular lectures, scientific demonstrations, debates, and entertainments. Mechanical improvements in printing made possible the penny press; the New York *Tribune,* Baltimore *Sun,* and Philadelphia *Ledger* began as penny newspapers in the 1840's. The *Tribune,* under Horace Greeley's editorship, became a liberal power of the first magnitude.

By 1850, then, in the Northern and Western states there had been formulated, and to some extent established, the basic principles of American education today: (1) that free public primary and secondary schools should be available for all children; (2) that teachers should be given professional training; (3) that all children should attend school up to a certain age, but not necessarily the free public school, religious and other bodies having complete liberty to establish their own educational systems at their own cost; (4) that a liberal higher education, and professional training schools for law, medicine, divinity, and engineer-

5. Oberlin in Ohio became the first co-educational college in 1833, but had very few imitators. Wesleyan College in Georgia was the first college to give degrees to women. Mary Lyon established Mount Holyoke Female Seminary in Massachusetts in 1836, but it was some years before it offered a course of college grade.

ing be provided. However, the research function of modern universities was hardly yet thought of.

Reformers, Revivalists, and Utopians

'The ancient manners were giving way. There grew a certain tenderness on the people, not before remarked,' wrote Emerson of these years. 'The key to the period appeared to be that the mind had become aware of itself. . . . The young men were born with knives in their brain.' One of these young men was Thomas H. Gallaudet, who before he was 30 established the first American school for the deaf at Hartford, Connecticut. Samuel Gridley Howe of Boston fought for Greek independence in his early twenties, and returned to found the Perkins Institute for the Blind. Elihu Burritt, the 'learned blacksmith' of New Britain, Conn., in his early thirties threw himself heart and soul into the peace movement. Neal Dow, a prominent Maine businessman with Quaker antecedents, started a brisk campaign against Demon Rum.

Young women, too, were 'born with knives in their brain.' In 1848 Elizabeth C. Stanton and Lucretia Mott launched at Seneca Falls, N.Y., a movement for women's suffrage, which, carried forward by the eloquence of Lucy Stone and the energy of Susan B. Anthony, eventually bore fruit in Amendment XIX to the Constitution (1920).

Most remarkable of these pioneer women was Dorothea Lynde Dix, a New England gentlewoman who at the age of 33 began a life-long crusade on behalf of the insane. These unfortunates were then largely treated as criminals, 'chained, naked, beaten with rods and lashed into obedience,' as she described their plight in her *Memorial to the Legislature of Massachusetts* (1843). This amazing woman—beautiful, naturally timid and diffident—visited all parts of the United States on behalf of the mentally ill. She persuaded Congress to establish St. Elizabeth's Hospital, and, the only New England reformer to penetrate the South, secured the establishment of public hospitals for the insane in nine Southern states. Off then she went to Europe, where she enlisted the support of the Duke of Argyll and Queen Victoria, and in Rome told Pope Pius IX that the local asylum was 'a scandal and disgrace'; the Pope listened to her and did something about it.

The great breeding ground of mid-century 'isms' was not New England itself, but an area peopled by Yankees in the rolling hills of central New York and along the Erie Canal. These folk were so susceptible to religious revivals and Pentecostal beliefs that their region was called 'The Burned-over District.' Anti-Masonry began there, and, at Palmyra, N.Y., Mormonism. At Hampton, N.Y., William Miller evolved the theory that the Second Coming of Christ would take place on 22 October 1843. The Millerite or Adventist sect persuaded thousands to sell all their

(*Prints Division, New York Public Library*)

"BLOOMERISM,"
OR THE
NEW FEMALE COSTUME OF 1851,
As it has appeared in the various Cities and Towns.
BOSTON: S. W. WHEELER 66 Cornhill—1851.

Dorothea Dix (1802–87). The outstanding humanitarian reformer of the nineteenth century, she left home at ten, was teaching school at fourteen. 'I never knew childhood,' she said. She worked indefatigably on behalf of the insane, who as she told Congress, she had seen 'bound with galling chains, . . . lacerated with ropes, scourged with rods, and terrified beneath storms of profane execrations and cruel blows.' Her intercession brought changes on two continents, including new mental hospitals in Scotland and in Italy. Not until she was eighty did she retire, and in her last years she was saying, 'I think even lying in my bed I can still do something.' (*Library of Congress*)

goods and, clothed in suitable robes, to await the Second Coming on roofs, hilltops, and haystacks, which they felt would shorten their ascent to Heaven. Mother Ann Lee (at New Lebanon, N.Y.) and Jemima Wilkinson (at Jerusalem, N.Y.) attempted to sublimate sexual urges by founding Shaker and 'Universal Friend' communities on the basis of celibacy. John H. Noyes, on the contrary, sought catharsis in sexual indulgence at his Oneida Community. It seemed appropriate that spirits from the other world seeking means to communicate with this should have chosen Rochester, metropolis of the Burned-over District. There the Fox sisters' spirit-rappings and table-turnings had the whole country agog in 1848. Out of their performances issued the cult of spiritualism which within ten years had 67 newspapers and periodicals devoted to culling messages from 'angel spheres.'

This exuberant generation believed a man could take action not only to change society but to save his soul. Charles Grandison Finney, probably the greatest American evangelist, carried out most of his work in the final decade of the Second Great Awakening that began in 1795 and ended about 1835. Finney, who had felt God come to him 'in waves of liquid love,' struck one of the last blows at orthodox Calvinism and helped substitute a liberal Calvinism which found a place for man's effort to achieve his own salvation. By 1855 the evangelical Methodists and Baptists accounted for nearly 70 per cent of all Protestant communicants. Both sects rebelled against such Calvinist ideas as man's depravity, predestination, and unconditional election. Although evangelical Protestantism eventually tended to be conservative in political outlook and divided in its attitude toward slavery, in the years of the Second Great Awakening it gave powerful support to the thrust for social reform.

The first labor movement in America was initiated by urban handicraftsmen rather than factory operatives. When merchant-capitalists organized trades such as tailoring on a larger scale, with long credits, division of labor, and wholesale marketing, the master workman who employed a few journeymen and apprentices was degraded to a foreman under an entrepreneur. Minute specialization broke down the apprentice system. With the introduction of gas in the cities, the old working hours of sun to sun were lengthened in the winter, making a twelve-hour day the year round. The ranks of labor were so constantly replenished by immigrants and women[6] that native male artisans were alarmed over their declining status. In 1828 a group of Philadelphia artisans organized a 'Workingmen's party,' and parties with the same name sprang up in other Eastern cities. They were not proletarian, but largely middle-class. Mechanics and small shopkeepers wanted local and practical reforms like free schools and laws giving workers such as carpenters liens on buildings to prevent their being cheated by contractors. The Workingmen's parties, with their moderate programs of social betterment, were making progress in the cities of Pennsylvania and New York when they made a costly alliance with utopian idealists.

Robert Owen, the earliest foreign radical who imagined that because America had achieved political liberty she would be receptive to every type of libertarianism, came to reform, and remained to scold. In 1825 he purchased a settlement at New Harmony, Indiana, and experimented in a form of communism. His son Robert Dale Owen took it over, and in two years New Harmony became new discord. Young Owen then joined forces with Frances Wright (Madame d'Arusmont), a vigorous Scotswoman who had founded a community in Tennessee for the purpose of emancipating slaves. When that, too, came to an untimely end, 'Fanny' Wright became a lecture-platform apostle of woman's rights, free inquiry in religion, free marital union, birth control, and a system which she called 'National, Rational, Republican Education, Free for All at the Expense of All, Conducted under the Guardianship of the State,' apart from the contaminating influence of parents.

These 'Free Enquirers' had already attracted much unfavorable attention from the Northern press in 1829, when the artisans of New York City

6. Although women were not generally employed in shops or in offices until after the Civil War, they were in over a hundred different occupations in 1835, even in trades such as printing from which the unions later excluded them.

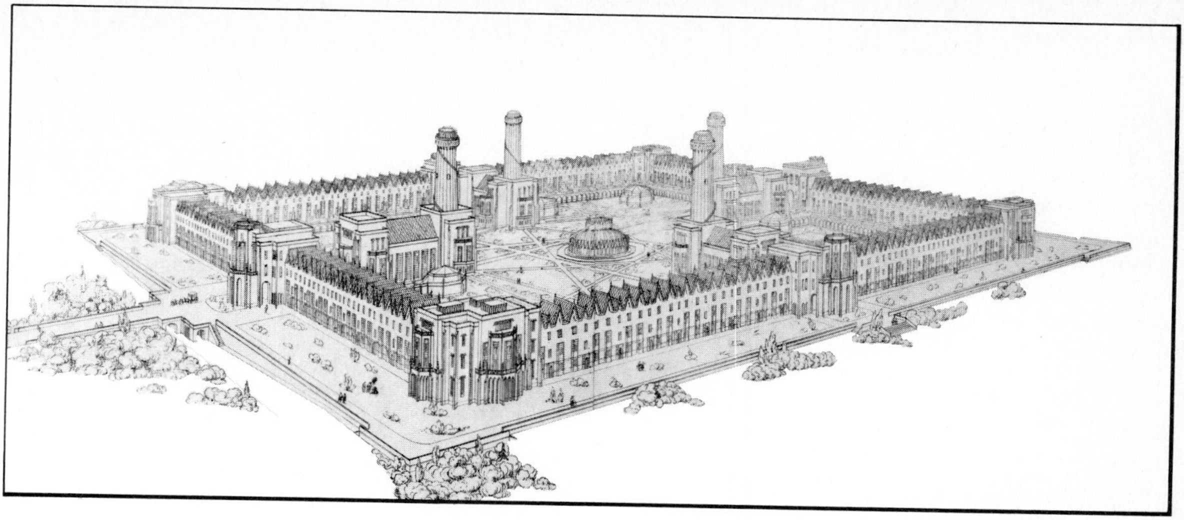

New Harmony, Indiana. *Above,* as it was envisioned by British mill-owner Robert Owen (1771–1858). But the reality fell well short of this architect's fantasy of turreted towers, and an enclosed botanical garden. Owen did attract about a thousand settlers to his communal experiment, but, his son later reflected, they turned out to be 'a heterogeneous collection of radicals, enthusiastic devotees of principle, honest latitudinarians and lazy theorists, with a sprinkling of unprincipled sharpers thrown in.' (*Library of Congress*). *Below,* New Harmony, as it actually was. This sketch by Lesueur, a French naturalist who spent ten years at the colony, makes it possible to contrast New Harmony with the original ideal. (*Muséum d'Histoire Naturelle, Le Havre*)

organized a Workingmen's party. Grateful for intellectual leadership, they accepted the aid of George Henry Evans, a young editor recently arrived from England, who was also an ardent admirer of Owen and of Fanny Wright, both of whom promptly joined the workingmen in the hope of capturing their support for 'National, Rational Education.' To the consternation of conservatives, the 'Workies' polled 30 per cent of the city vote in the autumn election. A press campaign then began, denunciatory toward Fanny Wright, the 'bold blasphemer and voluptuous preacher of licentiousness.' The printers' union repudiated this 'band of choice spirits of foreign origin,' and led a secession from the party, which promptly broke up. Small groups of the party joined the Democrats, who rewarded them by obtaining a mechanics' lien law and the abolition of imprisonment for debt.

In 1833, when a period of prosperity began, the labor movement abandoned politics in favor of trade organization, the closed shop, and the strike. Trades' unions—federations of all the organized trades in a single community—were formed in twelve Northern cities; and in 1837 delegates from these cities organized a National Trades' Union. Strikes on several occasions included not only the organized workers but the unskilled

A shoemakers' strike in Lynn, Massachusetts. Eight hundred women operatives march in a snowstorm, followed by four thousand workmen and preceded by the band of the Lynn City Guards. (*Collection Judith Mara Gutman*)

laborers of an entire city. Wages improved, and the ten-hour day was established in several cities for municipal employees, and in the navy yards by order of President Jackson. Harriet Martineau, visiting the Northern states at that time, took note of the well-dressed, well-fed, and even well-read 'dandy mechanics.'

But the panic of 1837 brought unemployment and misery to the landless artisans. Wages fell 30 to 50 per cent and the 'dandy mechanics' were glad to sell their 'gay watch guards and glossy hats' for a bit of bread. A promising labor movement collapsed; the 300,000 trade unionists of 1837 (about half the urban skilled workers in the United States) could no longer pay their dues. Hard times followed, with long hours; the Lowell factory girls petitioned the Massachusetts legislature in vain to reduce their twelve-hour day to ten. Immigrants took their places, and by 1850 these show workers, with their white gowns and literary journal, were no longer found in the cotton mills.

Disappointed in his experience both with political action and with unionization, the artisan once again lent an ear to the utopians. Almost every known panacea was applied, with meager or negative results. Robert Owen in 1845 summoned a 'World Convention to Emancipate the Human Race from Ignorance, Poverty, Division, Sin, Misery.' Josiah Warren, the first American anarchist, devised a system of 'time stores' and 'labor notes,' inspired by Owenite 'labor bazaars.' Many unions went in for producers' co-operation; others began consumers' co-operatives. The typical experiment was some sort of association or community. Brook Farm, the transcendentalist community described in Hawthorne's *The Blithedale Romance*, became one of forty Fourierite 'phalanxes' in the Northern states.

Horace Greeley kept the columns of the New York *Tribune* hospitable to all these movements; but his best advice was: 'Go West, young man, go West!' Here was a point of contact with national politics. Public land at $200 the quarter-section was not for those who needed it most, but for those who had the price, or for squatters who defied all comers to dislodge them. Greeley insisted that every man had the same natural right to a bit of land as to air and sunlight. George Henry Evans advocated a free homestead from the public domain to every settler; limitation of individual holdings; and no alienation of the homestead, voluntary or otherwise. 'Vote yourself a farm' was his slogan. In 1846 Andrew Johnson introduced the first free homestead bill in Congress, but Northern Whigs and Southern Democrats combined to defeat it.

For all the paucity of results, the labor movement did score some modest gains. Unionization made a beginning, and in 1842 Chief Justice Lemuel Shaw of Massachusetts, in the memorable case of Commonwealth *v.* Hunt, declared that a trade union was a lawful organization, the members of which were not collectively responsible for illegal acts committed by individuals. Yet there was still no national federation of labor, and the first state provision for factory inspection did not come until 1867. Instead of trying to humanize the new industrial order, both workers and thinkers had dissipated their energy in efforts to escape it.

Transcendentalism and Literature

Transcendentalism, which coursed through the Northern states between 1820 and 1860, embraced so wide a spectrum of ideas that the term almost defies definition. Optimistic about human nature, these romantic 'enthusiasts' deplored religious and literary formalism and believed that by relying on intuition Man and Society could be renovated. The new spirit appeared in some men as intense individualism, in others as a passionate sympathy for the oppressed. It gave to Hawthorne his deep perception of the beauty and the tragedy of life, to Walt Whitman his robust joy in living. But it was Emerson who perfectly embodied the essential spirit, a belief in the soul's inherent power to grasp the truth. Remarkably, this outburst of intellectual activity occurred largely within a 50-mile radius of Boston during a single generation.

The soil had been prepared by Unitarianism, which with its sister Universalism took a great weight off the soul of New England. The Unitarians not only denied that God was a member of a trinitarian Godhead but had an optimistic faith in man's capacity for good and rejected the Calvinist

The New England literati. In this clever composite photograph, the great figures of nineteenth-century letters are grouped as though actually in the same library. From left to right, they are John Greenleaf Whittier, Oliver Wendell Holmes, Ralph Waldo Emerson, John Lothrop Motley, Bronson Alcott, Nathaniel Hawthorne, James Russell Lowell, Louis Agassiz, and Henry Wadsworth Longfellow. *(Concord Free Public Library)*

view that men predestined for damnation cannot achieve salvation. Longfellow's *Psalm of Life,* which seems so trite nowadays,

> Life is real! life is earnest!
> And the grave is not its goal;
> Dust thou art, to dust returnest,
> Was not spoken of the soul.

came as a message of hope to thousands of young people reared in the fear of everlasting damnation. Yet something was lacking in mere Unitarianism. A faith in the essential goodness of human nature might be a theological counterpart to democracy; but it failed to supply the note of mysticism that democrats no less than aristocrats seek in religion.

Emerson in 1832, at the age of 29, gave up his pastoral office in a Unitarian church because it no longer interested him. In his next four years of reading and travel, he found God again in nature; and settled down as 'lay preacher to the world' in the placid village of Concord, which harbored during one generation Emerson, Hawthorne, Thoreau, and the Alcotts. If Jefferson was the prophet of democracy, and Jackson its hero, Emerson was its high priest. Like Jefferson, he believed ardently in the perfectibility of mankind; but he knew what Jefferson never learned, that free institutions would not liberate men not themselves free. His task was to induce Americans to cleanse their minds of hatred and prejudice, to make them think out the consequences of democracy instead of merely repeating its catchwords, and to seek the same eminence in spirit that they had reached in material things.

Henry Thoreau, whose *A Week on the Concord and Merrimack Rivers* came out in 1849, was the best classical scholar of the Concord group and the most independent of classic modes of thought. Concord for him was a microcosm of the world. Thoreau's *Walden* (1854) has had a pervasive influence on writers as different as Proust and Tolstoy, and translations have appeared from South America to the Orient. When bumbling county commissioners in 1959 tried to turn the shores of Walden Pond into a beach resort, a blast of protests from all over the world halted the desecration. In Emerson, Thoreau, and Hawthorne, in Herman Melville, who was half Yankee, and in the timeless Emily Dickinson of the next generation, the New England that had slowly matured since the seventeenth century justified itself.

In New York the 'Knickerbocker School' was declining. Bryant's last spurt of poetical activity ended in 1844; during the rest of his long life he was a leading figure in journalism. Washington Irving's *Sketch Book* came out as early as 1818; seven years later he turned to Spain for inspiration and to history for expression; returning to New York a literary hero, he visited the West for material, but his *Astoria* and *Adventures of Captain Bonneville* lack the authenticity of Francis Parkman's *Oregon Trail* (1849). For the rest of his life, Irving at 'Sunnyside' on the Hudson and at Madrid well played the roles of diplomat, host, and sage. James Fenimore Cooper's 'Leather-Stocking' and 'Sea Tales' started in the 1820's, after which he embarked on a crusade to put everybody right both in England and in America, and succeeded in making himself the most unpopular person in the English-speaking world.

New England intellectuals had more to say than their New York contemporaries, but they, too, conveyed it in traditional forms. 'We all lean on England,' wrote Emerson. Not until 1851 did a distinctive American literature, original both in form and content, emerge, with Melville's *Moby-Dick.* Four years later, with Emerson's blessing, *Leaves of Grass* began to sprout. Walt Whitman, half Yankee, half New York Dutch, had grown up outside the ambit of New England respectability, in intimate contact with the crude realities of American life. In the 'barbaric yawp' that so deeply influenced twentieth-century poetry, Whitman sang of the common American and his life in seaport, farm, and frontier.

Whitman was the poet of democracy, but Henry Wadsworth Longfellow was democracy's favorite poet. Longfellow's verse was tuned to catch the ear of a busy and unlearned people. And, until Lincoln's prose poem, 'The Gettysburg Address,' was delivered, no poem had a greater effect in creating that love of the Union which made young men fight to preserve it than the peroration to Longfellow's 'Building of the Ship' (1849):

Thou, too, sail on, O Ship of State!
Sail on, O Union, strong and great!
Humanity with all its fears,
With all the hopes of future years,
Is hanging breathless on thy fate!

Anti-Slavery and Abolition

Of all reform movements, the one that shook the Union to its foundation sought the abolition of slavery. An earlier anti-slavery agitation won its last victory in 1807 when Congress passed an act against the slave trade, but in 1817 the American Colonization Society was founded with the aim of doing for American Negroes what the Republic of Israel later did for Jews—to give them back a part of their homeland, though with the frank admission that the Negro, free or slave, had no place in American society. To further this enterprise, the A.C.S. purchased from native tribes several tracts along the Grain Coast of West Africa; and several thousand American blacks had been settled by 1847, when they organized the Republic of Liberia, with a capital named Monrovia after President Monroe, and a constitution modeled on that of the United States. However, when the A.C.S., having scraped the barrel of private benevolence, appealed to Congress for federal aid in 1827, Southerners opposed the movement as jeopardizing the supply of slaves and abolitionists denounced it as a subtle attempt to increase the value of the remaining slaves in America. The A.C.S., though discouraged, continued its work to the Civil War, but without congressional backing for colonization, moral suasion against slavery appeared to have spent its force.

Apathy could hardly have been more complete, when on 1 January 1831 the first number of *The Liberator* appeared in Boston, published by William Lloyd Garrison. On the first page he announced:

> I shall strenuously contend for the immediate enfranchisement of our slave population. . . . On this subject I do not wish to think, or speak, or write, with moderation. . . . I am in earnest—I will not equivocate—I will not excuse—I will not retreat a single inch—AND I WILL BE HEARD.

Therein spoke the Old Testament, not the New. Garrison's policy was to hold up the most repulsive aspects of Negro slavery to the public gaze; to castigate the slaveholders and all who defended them as man-stealers, torturers, traffickers in human flesh. He recognized no rights of the masters, acknowledged no racial animosities, tolerated no delay. Blackguarding the slaveholders would have made few converts in the South at any time, but least of all in the very year of the Nat Turner slave insurrection. Prominent Southerners at once asserted that Garrison was responsible (although only four copies of *The Liberator* had reached the South), and demanded that the Northern states, if they valued the Union, suppress this incendiary agitation.

Many efforts short of press censorship were made in the North to satisfy the South on this point. Garrison wrote that he 'found contempt more bitter, opposition more stubborn, and apathy more frozen' in New England than among slave-owners. Elijah Lovejoy, who persisted in printing an abolitionist paper, had his press twice thrown into the river, and in 1837 was murdered by a mob at Alton, Ill. Two years earlier Garrison was paraded around Boston with a rope around his neck, by what was called a 'broadcloth mob'; and on the same day delegates who met at Utica to organize an anti-slavery society were dispersed by a mob of 'very respectable gentlemen' led by a congressman and a judge. Yet the abolition movement grew, and made converts at every mobbing: of Gerrit Smith, for instance, at the Utica affair; of Wendell Phillips in Boston; of Cassius M. Clay, a cousin of Henry Clay, in Kentucky. In 1836 there were more than 500 anti-slavery societies in the Northern states, and by 1840 their membership was over 150,000.

Garrison, driven by a fierce passion for righteousness to write words that cut and burned, personified this new and dreadful force to the white South, but Theodore D. Weld of New York was the most effective abolition leader. A great bear of a man, Weld could subdue a mob or whip an assailant, and often had to. In 1833 Weld and two wealthy New York merchants, Arthur and Lewis Tappan, organized the American Anti-Slavery Society. Weld then tried teaching at Lane Seminary, Cincinnati, and when the trustees or-

Harriet Tubman (1821–1913). Born a slave, she escaped to Philadelphia and became so effective a 'conductor' on the Underground Railroad that John Brown called her 'General Tubman.' (*Schomburg Center for Research in Black Culture, New York Public Library*)

dered discussion of slavery by the students to cease, he and his student converts seceded to Oberlin, which became the first college in the United States to admit both blacks and women. Owing perhaps to their Quaker connection, the abolitionists preceded other reformers in permitting women to address their meetings and serve on committees. Lucretia Mott of Philadelphia, and the Grimké sisters, gentlewomen of South Carolina who freed their slaves and came north to obtain freedom of speech, were counted among the leaders; Angelina Grimké married Weld, and it was perhaps her influence which kept hatred of the slaveholder out of Weld's agitation for freedom and which made him favor gradual, compensated emancipation.

The abolitionists took special pride in the 'Under Ground Railroad' which carried Negroes to liberty. Slaves who had the courage to strike out for freedom would take cover in the woods or swamps near their master's plantation until the hue and cry died down, then follow the North Star to Mason and Dixon's line, or the Ohio river. Once across, the 'U.G.' took them in charge. They were transferred from one abolitionist household to another, hidden by day in attics, haystacks, or corn shocks; piloted by night through the woods, or concealed in farm wagons; sometimes driven in a Friend's carriage, disguised in women's clothes and a deep Quaker bonnet. Others were smuggled north by sea, and made their way into Canada through New England. Most famous of all 'conductors' on the 'U.G.' was Harriet Tubman, an illiterate field hand from the Eastern Shore of Maryland, who not only escaped herself but repeatedly returned southward and guided more than 300 slaves from bondage to freedom, taking some as far as Canada. The number thus rescued in proportion to the total slave population was infinitesimal. Moreover, many of the slaves who escaped did so largely through their own devices; the runaways often fled to other parts of the South where they found refuge in swamps or in cities, among Indians, or as deckhands on ships. Yet if measured by the stimulus it gave the abolitionist cause, the 'Under Ground' was a brilliant success.

By a federal statute of 1793, a master, or his agent, who caught a runaway in a free state could repatriate him forcibly after swearing to his identity before a magistrate. A professional slave-catcher whom the right Negro eluded was apt to conclude that 'any nigger' would answer. Kidnapping became so frequent that Northern states passed 'personal liberty laws' to protect their free colored citizens. The abolitionists cleverly turned local resentment against kidnapping, and Northern dislike of domineering Southerners, into opposition to the return of genuine fugitives. Gradually the personal liberty acts were strengthened to a degree that made a runaway's identity almost impossible to establish. The Supreme Court invalidated such a law in Prigg *v.* Pennsylvania (1842). But if the states had no right to obstruct, by the same token they had no obligation to assist the federal authorities; and without such assistance the slave-catchers began to receive the attention of mobs. The abolitionists for the first time voiced a popular sentiment when Whittier declared:

> No slave-hunt in our borders—no pirate on our strand!
> No fetters in the Bay State—no slave upon our land!

The most famous case involving slavery, until eclipsed by Dred Scott's, was that of the *Amistad*, in 1839. She was a Spanish slaver carrying 53 newly imported slaves from Havana to another Cuban port. Under the leadership of an upstanding young Negro named Cinqué, the 'cargo' mutinied and killed captain and crew; but, ignorant of navigation, the mutineers had to rely on the white owners who were on board to sail the ship. The owners stealthily steered north until the *Amistad* was picked up off Long Island by U.S.S. *Washington* and taken into New Haven, where the Negroes were jailed. Spain demanded that they be given up to be tried for piracy, and President Van Buren attempted to do so. Southern senators insisted that, if not surrendered to Spain, the blacks be tried for murder and piracy by a federal court. John Quincy Adams, persuaded by abolitionists to act as attorney for the mutineers, argued for their liberty on the ground that the African slave trade was illegal by Spanish law and by the natural right of mankind to freedom. The Supreme Court, with a majority of Southerners, was so impressed by the old man's eloquence that it ordered the Negroes set free, and they were returned to their native Africa. The ironic epilogue is that Cinqué, once back home, set himself up as a slave trader.

To the right of the abolitionists were the anti-slavery men. They opposed the extension of slavery into more territories, but did not propose to interfere with slavery in the slave states. However, almost all these moderate anti-slavery men were eventually forced by Southern intransigence into more radical views. The South made three tactical errors in combating abolition. It assumed that every anti-slavery person was an inciter of Negro insurrection. It enacted laws making it increasingly difficult for masters to liberate slaves, and for free Negroes to make a living. And by frantic attempts to suppress all discussion of the subject, and to expand slavery, the South ended in persuading the North that every man's liberty was at stake. William Jay, son of the Chief Justice, said in 1836, 'We commenced the present struggle to obtain the freedom of the slave; we are compelled to continue it to preserve our own.'

The most notorious attempt to suppress discussion of slavery arose from indignation at the slave trade in the District of Columbia. Washington was then a shipping point for slaves from Virginia and Maryland to the cotton states. Even from the windows of the Capitol one could watch coffles of Negroes marching by in clanking chains. Abolitionists protested, but at the insistence of Southern members the House in 1836 adopted a

John Quincy Adams (1767–1848). Denied a second term as President, he humbly sought election to the U.S. House of Representatives where for seventeen years 'old man eloquent' served his constituents in Quincy and fought against the slavocracy. This 1847 daguerreotype captures his forbidding integrity. A year later, at eighty, he collapsed at his desk and was taken to the Speaker's office, where he died. (*Metropolitan Museum of Art*)

'gag resolution,' to the effect that all petitions relating 'in any way' to slavery be laid on the table. John Quincy Adams, now a member of the House, was not an abolitionist; but the gag rule awakened in him ancestral memories of royal tyranny. Session after session he fought for the right of petition. Every attempt short of personal violence was made to silence, to censure, or to expel Adams; but the tough old puritan persisted, and in 1844 the gag rule was finally repealed. It made no difference to the slaves. But on the day when the news reached South Carolina, the leading Whig newspaper of Columbia discontinued printing installments from Washington's Farewell Address, and substituted an appeal for secession.

More than a century has elapsed since Lincoln's Emancipation Proclamation and Amendment XIII to the Constitution destroyed chattel slavery on United States soil. We now know that the slavery question was but one aspect of a race and class problem that is still far from solution. The grapes of wrath have not yet yielded all their bitter vintage.

14

Western Empire

*

1820–1848

The Great Plains

Since 1806, when Lewis and Clark returned from their journey to the Oregon Country, the United States government had not taken much interest in the Far West. Major Long's expedition of 1819 reported the Great Plains 'almost wholly unfit for cultivation,' and laid down on the map of that region, which now supports a thriving population of several millions, the legend 'Great American Desert.'

Over this area of grassland and sagebrush roamed the Kansa, Pawnee, Sioux, Cheyenne, Blackfoot, Crow, and Arapaho. Countless herds of buffalo supplied the plains Indians with every necessity of life, and they had long since domesticated the wild mustang, offspring of those set free by the Spanish conquistadors. These Indians seldom practiced agriculture, and knew little or nothing of pottery, basketry, or weaving; but they were marvelous horsemen and in warfare, once they had learned the use of the rifle, proved more formidable than the Eastern tribes that had yielded so slowly to the white man.

The only whites who penetrated this region before 1830 were explorers, fur traders, and trappers. Every river, valley, mountain, and waterhole of the Far West was known to the trappers before 1830, and without their guidance transcontinental emigration would have been impossible. It was they who discovered the South Pass of the Rockies in Wyoming, a wide valley that takes one to the transcontinental divide by easy gradients. A party of trappers led by Jedediah Smith and William Sublette took the first covered wagons from the Missouri to the Rockies in 1830. Six years later Captain Bonneville, whose adventures provided literary material for Washington Irving, led the first loaded wagons through the South Pass and down the Snake valley to the Columbia river.

The Oregon Country

The climate, timber, and salmon-teeming rivers of the Oregon Country, which included not only the present state of Oregon, but Washington, Idaho, part of Montana, and British Columbia, invited settlement. But how to get at it? And would the pioneer who braved the transcontinen-

'Watching the Cargo' by George Caleb Bingham. In 1853 Bingham wrote, 'I am getting quite conceited, whispering to myself . . . that I am the greatest among the disciples of the brush my country has ever produced.' If he was less than that, Bingham undoubtedly ranks as the most important delineator of the American political process of his day, and, as in this 1849 painting, of the Missouri river country. (*State Historical Society of Missouri, Columbia*)

tal journey or the 200-day voyage around Cape Horn find himself on United States soil when he got there?

Every diplomatic negotiation between the United States and Great Britain since 1815 had agreed to disagree on the Oregon question. The only thing settled upon was a temporary joint occupation, north of lat. 42° N, where Spanish California stopped, and south of lat. 54° 40′, where Russian Alaska ended. When John Jacob Astor's trading post of Astoria at the mouth of the Columbia river was sold to a Canadian fur trading company, which in 1821 amalgamated with the Hudson's Bay Company, the only American foothold in Oregon was relinquished. Three years later, the Hudson's Bay Company constructed on the north bank of the lower Columbia Fort Vancouver, which Dr. John McLoughlin, the company factor, a shrewd, stalwart, and humane British subject, built up to be an efficient imperial outpost. His hospitality to early American immigrants is memorable, and eventually he became a citizen of the United States; but the flag flown at Fort Vancouver was the company's British banner, not the Stars and Stripes.

In the meantime the Pacific coast was being visited by Boston fur traders and 'hide droghers.' Many of these vessels also traded with Hawaii, where the American Board of Foreign Missions had established a native Congregational church in 1820 under a great missionary, the Reverend Hiram Bingham. He kept urging Easterners to do something about the free-for-all Oregon Country, and in 1831 Hall J. Kelley founded 'The American Society for Encouraging the Settlement of the Oregon Territory.' Kelley stirred up Nathaniel J. Wyeth, a 28-year-old man of action whose zest for oceanic trade had been whetted by successfully exporting ice from Fresh Pond, Cambridge, to the West Indies and South America. Wyeth organized expeditions in 1832 and 1834 that led to the establishment of an American colony in the Willamette valley and did more than anything else to win Oregon for the United States.

In 1842 'Oregon fever' struck the frontier folk of Iowa, Missouri, Illinois, and Kentucky. Backwoodsmen who had no use for treeless prairies or arid high plains, they wanted wood, water, and game, which the Oregon Country had in abundance. Independence, Mo., was their jumping-off place. 'Prairie schooners,' as the canvas-covered Conestoga wagons were nicknamed, converged there in May, when the grass of the plains was fresh and green. Parties were organized, a captain appointed, an experienced trapper or fur trader engaged as pilot; and amid a great blowing of bugles and cracking of long whips, the caravan, perhaps a hundred wagons strong with thousands of cattle on the hoof, moved off up the west bank of the Missouri. At Fort Leavenworth, the emigrants for the last time enjoyed the protection of their flag.

For a long time there was neither road nor trail. Near Council Bluffs, where the Missouri is joined by the Platte, the route to Oregon turned west to follow the Platte over the Great Plains.[1] Until a road had been beaten into the sod, it was easy to lose the way. Numerous tributaries of the Platte, swollen and turbid in the spring, had to be forded or swum, to the great damage of stores and baggage. Every night the caravan made a hollow square of wagons round its fire of cottonwood or buffalo chips. The horses and mules were kept inside, for protection, and the howling of prairie wolves was drowned by a chorus of hymns and old ballads. At dawn the horsekind were let out to graze for an hour or two, the oxen were rounded up and hitched to the wagons, bugles blew, and another start was made toward 'the sunset regions.'

Until the forks of the Platte were reached, near the present northeastern corner of Colorado, the herbage was luxuriant, and the grades easy. Following the north fork, the trail became hilly, then mountainous, as one turned north to avoid a spur of the Rockies. Beyond the South Pass came the worst part of the journey—a hard pull across the arid Wyoming basin, where grass was scanty, and alkali deposits made the water almost undrinkable. Between the Gros Ventre and Teton ranges, the Oregon-bound emigrant found westward-flowing waters, and took heart; but there were still 800 miles to go to the lower Columbia, following the meanderings of the Snake river. As there was no good road in early days through the heavily forested country along the Columbia, wagons were often rafted down the stream; and with fair luck a party that left Independence in May might celebrate Thanksgiving Day in the Willamette valley. But it was a lucky caravan indeed that arrived with the same number of souls that started; and some of the weaker parties disappeared—whether by starvation after losing the trail, or at the hands of Indians, no one ever knew.

This sizable immigration of 1843–45, 4000 to 5000 strong, strained the provisional territorial organization that the settlers established, and convinced Congress that something must be done to

1. Later, the Oregon trail cut straight across the prairie from Independence to the southernmost bend of the Platte, near the site of Kearney, Nebraska.

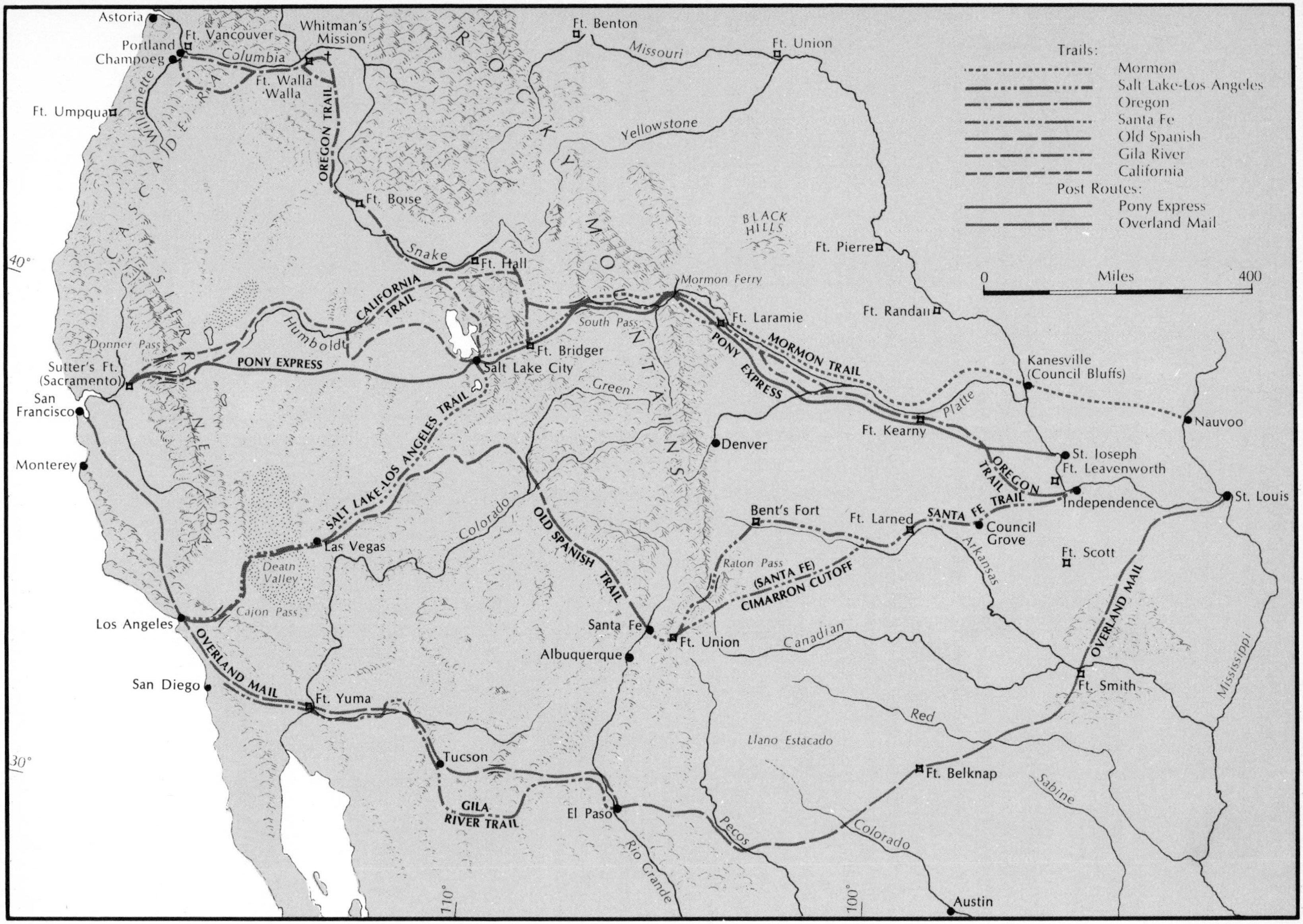

Routes to the West

reach a settlement with Great Britain and provide this remote colony with government, law, and land titles. Secretary Calhoun opened negotiations in 1844 with the British minister at Washington and repeated a proposal, thrice made by J. Q. Adams, to divide the territory along latitude 49°. But Aberdeen, like Castlereagh and Canning, refused to abandon the north bank of the Columbia. If the question were to be decided by extent of actual occupation, the British claim was just; and it would be difficult to discover any other basis of division. North of the Columbia, about Fort Vancouver and along Puget Sound, were living over 700 British subjects, and only half a dozen American citizens. The United States, however, could well afford to wait. A decline in the Columbia river fur trade was making Fort Vancouver unprofitable, and the menacing attitude of the latest American immigrants threatened its security. At Dr. McLoughlin's suggestion the company abandoned Fort Vancouver to the Americans in 1845, and erected a new post at Victoria on Vancouver Island.

By this time the expansionist James K. Polk had become President. He defiantly asserted that the American title to the whole of Oregon, up to lat. 54° 40′, was 'clear and unquestionable,' and asked Congress for authority to terminate the joint occupation agreement of 1818. Polk, however, never intended to risk a war to acquire the whole of Oregon. His ambition was to annex California, which probably meant war with Mexico; he did not care to fight England and Mexico at the same time. Thus, when Lord Aberdeen formally proposed to extend the international boundary along latitude 49° N to Puget Sound, thence to the ocean through Juan de Fuca Strait, leaving Vancouver Island to Canada, Polk accepted. He submitted the British offer to his cabinet and to the Senate. During the Senate debate some Western expansionist coined the slogan '54–40 or fight!' but few agreed, and on 15 June 1846 the Oregon treaty was ratified. Thus was completed the last section of the 3000-mile frontier between Canada and the United States.

The Mormons

Before the Oregon question was finally adjusted came the hegira of the Church of Jesus Christ of the Latter-day Saints, commonly called the Mormons, to the Great Salt Lake.

Joseph Smith was the offspring of a family of New England frontier drifters, who had made at least ten moves in nineteen years, ending at Palmyra, N.Y., in the midst of the Burned-over District. At the age of fifteen he began to see visions and dig for buried treasure. An angel of the Lord, he avouched, showed him the hiding-place of a package of inscribed gold plates, together with a pair of magic spectacles which enabled him to read the characters. The resulting Book of Mormon (first printed in 1830), a mixture of personal experiences, religious notions, and disputed history, gave the story of certain Lost Tribes of Israel (the Indians), whom the Saints were commanded to redeem from paganism. Joseph Smith then organized the Church of the Latter-day Saints, a co-operative theocracy in which all power emanated from Smith the Prophet.

Persecutions drove the Mormons to a spot on the east bank of the Mississippi which the Prophet named Nauvoo. The settlement grew rapidly—even faster than Chicago; by 1844, with 15,000 citizens, Nauvoo was the largest and most prosperous city in Illinois. Following Brigham Young's visit to Liverpool, almost 4000 English converts reached Nauvoo. It was at Nauvoo that Joseph Smith received the 'revelation' sanctioning polygamy, which he and the inner circle of 'elders' were already practicing. Although supported by Isaiah iv:1, 'And in that day seven women shall take hold of one man,' this revelation split the church. The monogamous 'schismatics' started a paper at Nauvoo, but Smith caused the press to be broken up after the first issue. He and his brother were then arrested by the authorities for destruction of property and lodged in the county jail, whence, on 27 June 1844, they were pulled out by a mob and lynched. Brigham Young, who succeeded to the mantle of the Prophet, and to five of his 27 widows, directed retaliation; and for two

Building the Mormon tabernacle, Salt Lake City. This illustration shows the skeleton turtle above and the completed edifice below. An unusual feature of this structure is that there are no interior supports for the roof. Nor were metal nails used. Workers, supervised by the builder Williams Folsom and the architect Henry Grow, fashioned wooden pegs which they glued into place. The beams are held together by strips of rawhide dipped in water and wrapped around the timbers. (*Utah State Historical Society*)

years terror reigned in western Illinois. The Mormons were a virile, fighting people, but the time had come for them to make another move, before they were hopelessly outnumbered.

Under their new Moses the Mormons abandoned their homes in Nauvoo, and in 1846, several thousand strong, began their westward journey. In July 1847 they reached the promised land, the basin of the Great Salt Lake. By the end of 1848, 5000 people had arrived in the future state of Utah, which Young named Deseret. Young chose this dry and inhospitable land in the hope that his Saints would no longer be molested by Gentiles, and also because it was Mexican territory; but the Mexican War would change that.

The Mormons soon demonstrated that they had resourceful leaders and a genius for disciplined community life. Brigham Young caused irrigation canals and ditches to be dug, and appointed committees to control water for the public benefit. He set up a system of small farms, intensively cultivated and carefully fertilized. He forbade speculation in land, but respected private property. He kept the Indians quiet by a judicious mixture of firmness and justice. He repressed heresy and schism with a heavy hand. He organized foreign and domestic missions and financed migration.

Yearly the community grew in numbers, strength, and wealth, a polygamous theocracy within a monogamous and democratic nation. Congress organized Deseret as Utah Territory in 1850, but since President Fillmore appointed Brigham Young the territorial governor, government in the hands of the Prophet continued. The Latter-day Saints brought comfort, happiness, and self-respect to thousands of humble folk; and Brigham Young must be included among the world's most successful commonwealth builders.

The Spanish Borderlands

While one column of pioneers deployed into the prairies of Illinois and Iowa, and another wound over the Oregon trail, a third crossed into Mexican territory where it came into contact with a proud and ancient civilization, no longer upheld by a dying empire but by the young Republic of Mexico. Upper California, New Mexico, and Texas, frontier provinces of the old viceroyalty, spread out fanwise toward the United States. Explored as early as the sixteenth century by the Spaniards, they had been thinly colonized after a long interval, and in the Roman rather than the English sense. Missions had been planted among the Indians; *presidios* or frontier garrisons established to protect the fathers in their work; and such few colonists as could be persuaded to venture so far were generously endowed by the Spanish government with lands and Indian serfs.

Weak, distracted, lacking expansive energy, the new Mexican government did not know how to use the frontier provinces, and eyed nervously the influx of men of ambition from the United States. Upper California, a province the size of Asia Minor, was sparsely settled by Mexicans, but by 1840, hundreds of Americans had 'left their consciences at Cape Horn' to live and trade in this delightful country, and in that year overland emigrants began to trickle in from a branch of the Oregon trail through the passes of the Sierra Nevada. Each year an armed caravan of American traders assembled at Independence, Mo., and followed the Santa Fe trail with pack-mule and wagon through the country of the Osage and Comanche to the capital of New Mexico, returning with silver and peltry.

But it was in Texas that the first compact wedge of English-speaking people was thrust across Mexico's borders. The tenuous claim of the United States to Texas, a land larger than France, had been renounced in the Florida Treaty of 1819, but both J. Q. Adams and Jackson pressed Mexico to sell the whole or a part of Texas. The mere offer was considered insulting; its repetition aroused suspicion. Yet, with strange inconsistency, Mexico encouraged emigration from the United States to Texas. The most important grant was made in 1821 to Moses Austin, and on his death confirmed to his son in 1823. This gave Stephen F. Austin the privilege of *empresario.* The Austin colony was a great success. By 1834 it comprised 20,000 white colonists and 2000 slaves, outnumbering the native Mexicans in Texas four to one. Austin, a grave and gentle young man, chose recruits for his colony with care, and ruled it with autocratic power until 1829. Texas was more law-abiding and better governed than any nineteenth-century American frontier.

Although anti-slavery by preference, Austin faced the same choice as every colonist with capital: pioneer poverty or using some form of forced labor. There were no Indian peons in that part of Mexico, and Southern planters would not come unless permitted to bring their slaves, and could not prosper without them. Mexico enacted laws or issued decrees abolishing slavery throughout the Republic. But Austin was always able to obtain some 'explanation' which allowed the Americans to hold their slaves in fact, if not by law.

Insecurity of slave property was but one of many factors pulling toward the separation of Texas from Mexico. Austin and the older American *empresarios* tried to be good Mexicans; but it was difficult to respect a government in constant turmoil. The American colonist admired the horsemanship of his Mexican neighbor and adopted his saddle and trappings, but his attitude toward the 'natives' was condescending, and toward their government, impatient. This irritation became mutual. There was trouble about the tariff, representation, and immigration; conflicts with Mexican garrisons whose proud officers resented the crude and boisterous settlers. For in the 1830's, quiet law-abiding pioneers of Austin's type began to be outnumbered by swashbucklers like Sam Houston, former governor of Tennessee, Indian trader on the Texas frontier, and adopted Cherokee; the Bowie brothers of Louisiana, slave-smugglers who designed the long and deadly knife that bears their name; Davy Crockett, a publicity-mad professional backwoodsman from Tennessee; and many others who had left their country for their country's good.

I leave This rule, for others
when I am dead Be always Sure,
you are right, then go, a head

David Crockett

David Crockett (1786–1836). This painting has been dated 'about 1835,' when the 'coonskin Congressman' served his final term in the House. Nettled at being defeated in his bid for re-election, Davy moved to Texas where in the following year he died at the Alamo, and rapidly became a legend. 'Everything here is Davy Crockett,' observed an English visitor in 1839. 'He picked his teeth with a pitchfork—combed his hair with a rake—fanned himself with a hurricane, wore a cast-iron shirt, and drank nothing but creosote and aquafortis. . . . He could whip his weight in wildcats—drink the Mississippi dry—shoot six cord of bear in one day—and, as his countrymen say of themselves, he could jump higher, dive deeper, and come up dryer than anyone else.' (*New-York Historical Society*)

The Lone Star Republic

The break came in 1835, when President Santa Anna of Mexico proclaimed a unified constitution for Mexico that made a clean sweep of state rights. The American settlers of Texas set up a provisional government and expelled the Mexican garrison from San Antonio. Over the Rio Grande came Santa Anna with 3000 men. In the Alamo, the fortified mission at San Antonio, a garrison of fewer than 200 Texans refused to retreat or to surrender. For ten days, the defenders turned back assaults on the adobe walls. At dawn on 6 March 1836 Santa Anna assaulted the Alamo again, captured it after every Texan, including Crockett, Jim Bowie, and Colonel William Travis, had been killed or wounded, and put the wounded to death.

Already a convention elected by the American settlers had proclaimed the independent Republic of Texas, and adopted a flag with a single star. Santa Anna quickly advanced eastward, and for a few weeks it looked as if the Lone Star Republic would be snuffed out. Generalissimo Sam Houston managed to keep a force together, acquired volunteers from across the border, and awaited the Mexicans in an ilex grove by the ferry of the San Jacinto river, not far from the site of the city that bears his name. On 21 April, shouting 'Remember the Alamo!' the Texans and their allies burst on Santa Anna's army, scattered it, and took the general prisoner. The Battle of San Jacinto proved decisive. The Texans ratified their new constitution, legalized Negro slavery, elected Sam Houston President, and sent an envoy to Washington. On Jackson's last full day of office (3 March 1837), the Lone Star Republic won recognition.

Texas would have preferred annexation to the United States, but annexation would affect the balance of power between the sections. The South was beginning to realize that it had received the thin end of the Missouri Compromise of 1820, which prohibited slavery in federal territory north of 36° 30′. Arkansas and Michigan had just been admitted to the Union, making thirteen free and thirteen slave states. Florida was the only slave territory left; but three free territories, Wisconsin, Iowa, and Minnesota, would soon be demanding admission, and more might well follow if the Indian barrier to the Great Plains were broken. Texas, greater in area than nine free states of the Northeast, might be carved into several slave states to balance New England. However, since the North wanted to halt the expansion of slavery, the campaign for annexation foundered.

Southern insistence on annexation became more intense when it appeared that Texas might agree to abolish slavery in return for British support of her independence. The prospect of Texas becoming a second Canada, a refuge for fugitive slaves, alarmed the South to the point of panic. Abel P. Upshur, President Tyler's Secretary of State, at once began to negotiate a treaty of annexation with the Texan minister at Washington, and informed him that the abolition project was inadmissible.

At this juncture there occurred a fatal accident on a United States warship which influenced political history. On a gala trip of U.S.S. *Princeton* down the Potomac on 28 February 1844, with President Tyler, cabinet ministers, diplomats, senators, and numerous ladies on board, one of its 12-inch wrought iron guns, 'Peacemaker,' burst. Secretary of State Upshur, the Navy Secretary, and a New York state senator were killed; Senator Thomas H. Benton and nineteen others were severely wounded. The explosion virtually threw into President Tyler's arms the fair Julia Gardiner, daughter of the slaughtered state senator; shortly she became the second Mrs. Tyler and mistress of the White House. And the loss of the two secretaries gave the President an opportunity to reconstruct his cabinet without a single Northerner or even a Whig, although it was that party which had elected him. John C. Calhoun was brought back as Secretary of State—to put Texas into the Union, and to get Tyler the Democratic (not the Whig) nomination for the presidency in 1844. Like several later Vice-Presidents who have succeeded through death, 'Tyler too' wanted to be elected President 'in his own right.' Calhoun accepted because he hoped to be able to link the Texas question with Oregon, and so forge an alliance of South and West under the Democratic aegis, and become President after Tyler. However, Calhoun's effort to annex Texas got nowhere, because it was perceived as a pro-slavery maneuver.

But President Tyler had another card up his sleeve. After the election of 1844 had 'pronounced' in favor of annexation, he recommended that Texas be admitted to the Union by joint resolution of both houses, which did not require a two-thirds vote. The deed was done on 28 February 1845. President Tyler on his last day of office had the satisfaction of sending a courier to inform President Houston that only the consent of the Lone Star Republic was necessary to make Texas the twenty-eighth state of the Union, and that consent was promptly given.

President Polk and His Maneuvers

While Tyler and Calhoun were rushing Texas into the Union, wiser politicians had been trying to keep it out of politics. In 1842 Martin Van Buren, who expected the Democratic nomination in 1844, and Henry Clay, who had an equally firm expectation for the Whig nomination, agreed to issue a letter opposing the immediate annexation of Texas. Van Buren warned that to rush the affair would mean war with Mexico, and Clay declared that he would welcome Texas to the Union if it could be done 'without dishonor, without war, with the common consent of the Union, and upon just and fair terms.' These praiseworthy efforts to preserve the peace lost Van Buren the nomination and Clay the election.

At the 1844 Democratic convention, Van Buren had a majority of the delegates, but the Southern expansionist delegates put over the two-thirds rule,[2] which Little Van was not strong enough to surmount, and the nomination went to the first 'dark horse' in presidential history: James K. Polk. Clay, now 67 years old, received the Whig nomination by acclamation, and he felt confident of election. But Clay's open letter offended the annexationists and lost him votes in the South. Enough anti-slavery Whigs in New York voted for

2. First adopted in 1836, but not used in 1840; after this it continued in Democratic national conventions until 1936.

Birney, the Liberty party (abolitionist) candidate, to give Polk a slight edge, and New York's electoral vote was pivotal. Save for the unusual four-way race in 1824, the 1844 outcome marked the first time that a President had been elected with less than 50 per cent of the vote. Hence, Polk's triumph was hardly a mandate for expansion. Yet it permitted the Democrats to claim that a firm conviction of America's 'manifest destiny' to extend west to the Pacific and south at least to the Rio Grande lay behind the defeat of the popular Clay.

James Knox Polk, though not yet 50 years of age, looked 20 years older by reason of bad health. He was a stiff, angular person, with sharp gray eyes in a sad, lean face, and grizzled hair overlapping a black coat-collar. He had majored in mathematics and the classics at the University of North Carolina to train his mind, and the event proved that he succeeded. His working day in the White House was nearer eighteen than eight hours, and in four years he was absent only six weeks from Washington. His will controlled a cabinet of experienced and distinguished men. Determined and tenacious, seldom smiling and never relaxing, Polk recalls that other presidential scholar and diarist, J. Q. Adams, rather than Jackson, with whom his political supporters were apt to compare him. Their domestic policies were as wide apart as the poles, but Polk adopted the same foreign policy as Adams, and he had a way of getting things done. He aspired not only to reduce the tariff and re-establish Van Buren's independent treasury, but to settle the Oregon question, and acquire California. Within four years all of his ambitions were fulfilled.

About California almost nothing was known in the United States until after Frémont's exploration of 1843. John C. Frémont, a 28-year-old second lieutenant in the topographical corps of the United States Army, wooed and won sixteen-year-old Jessie, daughter of Senator Thomas Hart Benton. Papa Benton, equally devoted to hard money, western expansion, and daughter Jessie, conceived the idea of sending sonny-boy on an expedition, with competent guides like 'Kit' Carson to take care of him. That was not difficult for an important senator to arrange. On Frémont's second trip, he struck political pay dirt. Turning south from Oregon into the future Nevada and then into the Sacramento valley, he passed through central and southern California and returned via Santa Fe. His report on this journey (largely written by Jessie), published in the fall of 1844, gave Washington its first knowledge of the feeble Mexican hold on California and the limitless possibilities of that romantic land. Incidentally, it made Frémont a presidential candidate, and, later, one of the most inefficient generals on either side of the Civil War.

War with Mexico

Shortly after Polk entered office, Mexico protested against the annexation of Texas, and broke diplomatic relations. From her point of view, Texas was still a rebellious province. In July 1845 Polk ordered a detachment of the regular army under General Zachary Taylor to take up a position on the Nueces river, the southwestern border of Texas, to protect the new state against a possible Mexican attack. If Polk had been content with Texas and had not reached out for something besides, there is no reason to suppose that Mexico would have initiated hostilities. But Polk desperately wanted to acquire California, because he feared, not without reason, that if the United States did not, England or France would. On 24 June 1845 the Secretary of the Navy sent secret orders to Commodore Sloat, commander of the Pacific station, to seize San Francisco if he should 'ascertain with certainty' that Mexico had declared war on the United States.

On 10 November 1845 the President commissioned John Slidell minister plenipotentiary to Mexico, with instructions to offer that the United States assume the unpaid claims of its citizens against Mexico, in return for Mexican recognition of the Rio Grande as the southern boundary of Texas and of the United States. In addition, $5 million would be paid for the cession of New Mexico, and 'money would be no object' if California could also be bought. Mexico refused to receive Slidell. On 13 January 1846, the day after

A native New Mexican religious figure. (*Index of American Design, Smithsonian Institution*)

he received word of Mexico's decision, Polk ordered General Taylor to cross the Nueces and occupy the left bank of the Rio Grande, though that river had never been the southern boundary of Texas.

On 25 April Polk began to prepare a message to Congress urging war on the sole grounds of Slidell's rejection as minister and the unpaid claims—which amounted to only $3.2 million when adjudicated by a United States commission in 1851. On that very day Mexican cavalry crossed the Rio Grande, engaged in a skirmish with United States dragoons, killed a few troopers, and captured the rest. 'The cup of forbearance has been exhausted,' the President told Congress on 11 May. 'After reiterated menaces, Mexico has passed the boundary of the United States, has invaded our territory and shed American blood upon the American soil.' Two days later Congress declared that 'by act of the Republic of Mexico, a state of war exists between that Government and the United States.' The record is clear: Polk baited Mexico into war over the Texas boundary question in order to get California.

Outside the Mississippi valley the war was highly unpopular. The Whig party opposed the war, although with more shrewdness than the Federalists of 1812 they voted for war credits and supplies in the hope that the Democrats would be hanged if given plenty of rope. Anti-slavery men and abolitionists regarded the war as part of an expansionist conspiracy of slave-owners. Henry Thoreau made his own protest against the war by refusing to pay his state poll tax. After he had spent a night in the Concord lock-up, his aunt paid the tax and he went back to his cabin on Walden Pond. It sounds petty and futile, as one tells it. Yet the ripples from that Concord pebble, like the shot of 19 April 1775, went around the world; Thoreau's *Essay on Civil Disobedience*, which he wrote to justify his action, became the best-known work of American literature to the peoples of Asia and Africa struggling to be free.

Glory and Conquest

California, the main objective, lay beyond the principal seat of war, and became the scene of confusing conflicts. A few dozen American squatters in the Sacramento valley proclaimed the 'Republic of California' and waved a white flag with a bear and star painted on it (14 June 1846). Three weeks later Commodore Sloat raised the Stars and Stripes at Monterey and declared California a part of the United States. The Spanish-speaking Californians rose in arms, but by the end of 1846 resistance had been quelled.

In the main theater of war, General Zachary Taylor pushed across the Rio Grande and captured the Mexican town of Monterrey (21–23 September 1846). Polk was not too pleased. 'Old Rough and Ready' Taylor, blaspheming veteran of the Jackson breed, was becoming dangerously popular, and the Whigs began to talk of running him for President in 1848. So Polk turned to Major General Winfield Scott, a Whig but a dandy swashbuckler whose airs and foibles were unlikely to win golden opinions from democracy. On 27 March Scott captured Vera Cruz, and then started for Mexico City along the route that Cortés had followed three centuries earlier.

It was a brilliant campaign. At the fortified pass of Cerro Gordo, Captain Robert E. Lee found a way to outflank the Mexicans, an impressive operation in which Captain George B. McClellan and Lieutenant Ulysses S. Grant took part. On 10 August Scott's army reached the divide 10,000 feet above sea level, with the wonderful Valley of Mexico stretching before, and the towers of Mexico City rising through the mist. At Churubusco (20 August) the American forces lost one in seven; most of these casualities were inflicted by a Mexican outfit made up of Irish and other deserters from the United States Army. But 3000 Mexican prisoners (including eight generals!) were captured, and the victory was overwhelming.

In the meantime Polk had provided Mexico with a leader. General Santa Anna, in exile at Havana when the war broke out, was able to persuade Polk that, once in possession of the Mexican government, he would be pliable. So he was allowed to enter Mexico City in triumph in September 1846, to assume dictatorship and take command of the army facing Taylor in the north of Mexico. Taylor beat him badly at Buena Vista (22–23 February 1847)—a picture-book battle on a sun-soaked plain; a fight that advanced in politics both General Taylor and his son-in-law, Colonel Jefferson Davis, who distinguished himself and his regiment (uniformed in red shirts, white pants, and slouch hats) by breaking up a Mexican cavalry charge. To the South, Scott's army, refreshed by a fortnight among the orchards and orange groves of the Valley of Mexico, marched forward to a bloodbath at Molino del Rey (8 September), and five days later stormed its last obstacle, the fortified hill of Chapultepec, heroically defended by the boy cadets of the Mexican military school. At dawn 17 September a white flag came out from Mexico City, and a vanguard of doughboys[3] and marines swung along to the main plaza, where they gazed with wonder on the great baroque cathedral and the lofty pink-walled palace—the Halls of the Montezumas at last. In the meantime the Gulf Squadron under Commodore Matthew C. Perry and the Pacific Squadron under Commodore Robert F. Stockton had established a tight blockade of both coasts of Mexico, preventing munitions and supplies, previously ordered from Europe, from reaching the Mexican army.

3. This term for infantrymen began in the Mexican War and lasted until World War II, when it was replaced by 'GI.'

Polk attached to the American army as peace commissioner Nicholas Trist, chief clerk of the department of state, and though he was recalled by the President and hence had no authority, and though there was for some time no Mexican government with which he could deal, Trist stayed on and negotiated the Treaty of Guadalupe Hidalgo (2 February 1848) in accordance with his original instructions. Mexico ceded Texas with the Rio Grande boundary, New Mexico, and Upper California to the United States. The region embraced what would become the states of California, Utah, and Nevada, large sections of New Mexico and Arizona, and parts of Colorado and Wyoming. The victor assumed unpaid claims, and paid $15 million to boot. It remained to be seen whether these immense and valuable acquisitions would be settled peacefully, or become a bone of contention between pro- and anti-slavery interests, leading to civil war.

15

Peaceful Interlude

*

1846–1854

The Wilmot Proviso

John C. Calhoun was right, for once. He foresaw that the acquisition of new territory would bring the question of slavery expansion into the open. The man who opened the door was an obscure Democratic congressman from Pennsylvania, David Wilmot. On 8 August 1846, about twelve weeks after the war began, the President asked Congress for a secret appropriation of $2 million as a down payment to bribe Santa Anna into ceding California. Wilmot proposed an amendment to the $2 million bill that in any territory so acquired 'neither slavery nor involuntary servitude shall ever exist,' a phrase copied from the Northwest Ordinance of 1787.

The question of slavery extension was no mere abstract principle, though many believed that the geography of the West erected a barrier against the spread of slavery. 'What do you want?—what do you want?—you who reside in the free States?' Clay would ask shortly. 'You have got what is worth more than a thousand Wilmot provisos. You have nature on your side.' Nor was the question immediately practical; even when they had a legal right to do so, few slaveholders would go West in the next decade. The 1860 census numbered only two slaves in Kansas. Yet, in truth, there was no climatic or natural bar to slavery extension, or to the Negro race—after all, a black was one of the two men who accompanied Admiral Peary to the North Pole in 1909. If slavery could flourish in Texas, why not in New Mexico, Arizona, and points west? In southern California, black slaves, if introduced, would undoubtedly have thrived and multiplied, just as the Chinese and Mexicans did who later filled the demands of ranchers and fruit growers for cheap labor.

The Wilmot proviso provoked bitter sectional animosity. To many Northerners it seemed monstrous for the 'land of the free' to introduce slavery, even in principle, where it had never previously existed. Yet it should be noted that while Northern anti-slavery men were pressing for adoption of the proviso, the Illinois constitution of 1848 excluded free blacks, and Iowa in 1851 stipulated severe penalties for any black who dared enter that state. To Southerners the proviso was alarming. They had watched anxiously as population gains gave the North control of the House;

soon the admission of new free states would upset the balance in the Senate. Now Wilmot was proposing to seal off the South so that it could never hope to add even one more slave state to the Union, unless Texas split up.

The Wilmot proviso did not pass, nor did any measure to organize the newly acquired territory. Settlers in the Far West lacked law and government, because Congress could not decide whether or not they could have slaves. Oregon in 1848 was finally organized as a territorial government without slavery, but Polk's term ended on 4 March 1849 before anything had been done about California, New Mexico, or Utah.

Election of 1848; Gold Rush of 1849

At a time of mounting crisis, both parties in 1848 turned to men with military backgrounds, since generals have a useful talent for blurring issues and winning votes. The Democrats named Senator Lewis Cass of Michigan, an ardent expansionist, veteran of 1812, and Jackson's Secretary of War. The Whigs nominated General Zachary Taylor, hero of the Mexican War. A third party, the Free-Soil, was formed by a coalition of three elements—the abolitionist Liberty party, 'conscience' or anti-slavery Whigs, and Northern Democrats alienated by Polk's policies on patronage, the tariff, or rivers and harbors. 'Free soil, free speech, free labor, and free men' was the slogan. Van Buren, convinced that only slavery restriction could save the Union, accepted the Free-Soil presidential nomination, with the 'conscience' Whig, Charles Francis Adams, as his running mate. Among the former Democrats who rallied to the Free-Soil standard was David Wilmot.

Although the Free-Soil party carried not one state, it rolled up an impressive 10 per cent of the popular vote, and by taking Democratic votes from Cass in states like New York and Pennsylvania, made possible Taylor's victory. Since little was known of Taylor's views, the Whigs had been able to offer him to voters in different sections according to which posture would draw the most support. In the South, they pointed out that 'Old Rough and Ready' was a Louisianan who held more than a hundred slaves on a Mississippi plantation; Northern voters heard that Taylor was friendly to the Wilmot proviso. The strategy worked; Taylor, with only 47 per cent of the popular vote, received 163 electoral votes to Cass's 107. But the Whigs bought victory at too high a cost; for once in office they would inevitably alienate a large section of their followers. The Southern Whigs were especially vulnerable for they were tied to a leader said to be committed to an extreme Northern position. The Whig party was living on borrowed time.

A simple, honest soldier, who detested the sophistries of politicians and regarded the slavery question as an artificial abstraction, Taylor was ready to sign any bill Congress might pass for organizing new territories; but before Congress could resolve the deadlock, California proposed to skip the territorial stage altogether, and to become a free state of the Union. On 24 January 1848, shortly before peace was signed with Mexico, a workman in the Sacramento valley discovered gold in Sutter's millrace. By the end of 1849 thousands of Argonauts from every part of Europe, North America, and the antipodes, had made their way to the gold fields and were living in a state of nature that would have made Rousseau a tory. Owing to neglect by Congress the government was still military in theory, though impotent in fact; *alcaldes* and *ayuntamientos* appointed by the military governor administered any sort of law they pleased—the code of Mexico or of Napoleon, or of Judge Lynch. So California went ahead and made herself a state, with the blessing of President Taylor. A state constitution prohibiting slavery was ratified by a popular vote of over 12,000 ayes to 800 noes. Without waiting for congressional sanction, the people chose a governor and legislature which began to function in 1850. Only formal admission to the Union was wanting; and on that issue the Union almost split.

Up to this time the most extreme Southerners had admitted the right of a state to prohibit slavery—for slavery was emphatically a state matter, but during 1849 the temper of the South had been steadily rising. South Carolina only hesitated from secession because it hoped to unite the entire South on that program. Though the South

Miner at sluice box in California's gold country. This early photograph was taken in Auburn Ravine in 1852, four years after gold was discovered in the Sacramento valley. Only recently have historians recognized the role of blacks in the development of the American West. (*Wells Fargo Bank History Room*)

had achieved disproportionate strength in the national government, it felt insecure. From every side—England and New England, Jamaica and Mexico, Ohio and the Northwest, and now California—abolition seemed to be pointing daggers at her heart. Still, it was not wholly fear that moved the South. What Benét called 'the purple dream,' the vision of a great slaveholding republic stretching from the Potomac into the tropic seas, monopolizing the production of cotton and so dictating to the world, was beginning to lift up the hearts of the younger and more radical Southern leaders.

The Union Preserved

Though Zachary Taylor was a large slaveholder, he saw no reason why the South should be bribed to admit California as a free state. Hence he recommended immediate admission of California with her free constitution and organization of New Mexico and Utah territories without reference to slavery. To protesting Georgia senators, the old soldier declared his determination to crush secession wherever and whenever it might appear, if he had to lead the army personally. Others were less willing to risk war. On 27 January 1850 Henry Clay advanced compromise resolutions: (1) immediate admission of free California to the Union; (2) organization of territorial governments in New Mexico and Utah, without mention of slavery; (3) a new and stringent fugitive slave law; (4) abolition of the domestic slave trade in the District of Columbia; (5) assumption of the Texan national debt by the Federal Government.

These resolutions brought on one of those superb Senate debates that did so much to mold public opinion. Clay defended them in a speech that lasted the better part of two days. Haggard in aspect and faltering in voice, he spoke with such passionate devotion to the Union as to bring back all the charm and fire of 'Young Harry of the West.' He asked the North to accept the substance of the Wilmot proviso without the principle and honestly to fulfill her obligation to return fugitive slaves. He reminded the South of the great benefits she derived from the Union and warned her against the delusion that secession could be peaceful. For Clay was old enough to remember the excitement in Kentucky when Spain and France had attempted to stop the river outlet of the Middle West. 'My life upon it,' he offered, 'that the vast population which has already concentrated . . . on the headwaters and the tributaries of the Mississippi, will never give their consent that the mouth of that river shall be held subject to the power of any foreign State.'

Calhoun, grim and emaciated, his voice stifled by the catarrh that shortly led to his death, sat silent, glaring defiance from his hawk-like eyes, while his ultimatum was voiced for him by Senator Mason of Virginia. The North must 'do justice by conceding to the South an equal right in the acquired territory'—which meant admitting slavery to California and New Mexico—returning fugitive slaves, restoring to the South through constitutional amendment the equilibrium of power she once possessed in the Federal Government.[1] And the North must 'cease the agitation of the slave question.' Note well this imperative as to free speech, even in the North.

Three days later Webster rose for his last great oration. His voice had lost its deep resonance, his massive frame had shrunk, and his face was lined with suffering and sorrow. But in his heart glowed the ancient love of country, and the spell of his personality fell on Senate and galleries with his opening words: 'I speak to-day for the preservation of the Union. "Hear me for my cause."' He attacked both the abolitionists and the Wilmot proviso. 'I would not take pains to reaffirm an ordinance of nature, nor to re-enact the will of God,' he said. Viewing the situation eye to eye with Clay, Webster restated in richer language the points made by his old-time rival. The North could never have been induced to swallow a new fugitive slave law, had not Webster held the spoon, and the Seventh of March speech permitted Union sentiment to ripen until it became irresistible.

Senator Seward of New York, in opposing the compromise, spoke for the 'conscience' Whigs. He admitted that Congress had the constitutional power to establish slavery in the territories. 'But there is a higher law than the Constitution which regulates our authority over the domain': the law of God, whence alone the laws of man can derive their sanction. The fugitive slave bill would endanger the Union far more than any anti-slavery proposal. 'All measures which fortify slavery or extend it, tend to the consummation of violence; all that check its extension, and abate its strength, tend to its peaceful extirpation.'

For all the skill of Clay, the omnibus bill stalemated. Southern firebrands denounced it, and Northern abolitionists called Webster a lackey of the slavehounds; a Mississippi senator confronted Senator Benton with a cocked and loaded revolver. With the older generation stymied, the young men took over. One of the youngest in the Senate was Stephen A. Douglas of Illinois, a sturdy five-footer, chock-full of brains, bounce, and swagger. In August, with the struggle in its eighth month, the 'Little Giant' put together a winning combination; his fellow Democrats proved sturdier than the Whigs.

In early September 1850 the essential bills passed: admission of California; a more stringent fugitive slave law; organization of New Mexico and Utah as territories free to legislate on slavery and to enter the Union with or without slavery when sufficiently populous; curbing of the slave trade in Washington; adjustment of the Texas boundary; assumption of the Texas debt. The Compromise of 1850 did not repeal the Missouri Compromise; the 1820 enactment dealt with the Louisiana purchase land, the 1850 law exclusively with the territory acquired from Mexico. The act

1. Calhoun's proposed amendment would have taken the form of a dual executive, one President elected by the North and one by the South, each armed with a veto.

Henry Clay addresses the Senate in the debate on the Compromise of 1850. As 'the Great Pacificator' speaks, Calhoun (standing third from the right, steel-gray hair falling loosely) stares at him intently. Seated two rows behind Clay (front left), Webster, head on his left hand, looks away. The man with the bulbous nose seated second from right is Thomas Hart Benton. (*Library of Congress*)

had some disappointing consequences. The Fugitive Slave Law failed to bring sectional peace; the free state of California added a surprising element to the argument over sectional balance when it sent pro-slavery men to the Senate; and the slave trade continued to flourish in the District. Still, the law gave both North and South something each badly wanted. Once more the Union was preserved by the same spirit of compromise that created it; but for the last time. It took another year to stop the secession movement in the cotton states, and in the North, which was committed by the law to returning runaway slaves to bondage, Emerson, the serene philosopher who had advised the abolitionists to love their white neighbors more and their colored brethren less, wrote in his journal, 'This filthy enactment was made in the nineteenth century, by people who could read and write. I will not obey it, by God!'

The Compromise of 1850 came at a time of transition in American leadership. On 9 July 1850 'Old Rough and Ready' succumbed to a combination of concern over misconduct in his cabinet, Washington heat, and doctors. The death of Taylor, denounced in the South as a Southern man of Northern principles, helped make possible the adoption of the Compromise, for his successor, Vice-President Millard Fillmore, shared the outlook of Webster and Clay. Giants of other days had already passed. Calhoun died on 31 March 1850; Andrew Jackson had died peacefully in his 'Hermitage'; John Quincy Adams, stricken at his seat in the House, had been carried out of the chamber to die. Clay and Webster, the one denounced as traitor by Southern hotspurs, the other compared with Lucifer by New England reformers, had only two years to live; but that was time enough to teach them grave doubts whether their compromise could long be maintained and whether their party could survive their departure. With their death the second generation of independent Americans departed. The galaxy of 1812 that had seemed to bind the heavens together was extinguished.

Calm Before Storm

Passage of the Compromise of 1850 caused the slavery question to subside for a short time, while other matters occupied the nation. Not that slavery was forgotten. *Uncle Tom's Cabin*, published in 1852, served to keep it in the back of people's minds; but everyone save Northern abolitionists and Southern 'fire-eaters' wished to let it remain there.

The country enjoyed the fruits of its flourishing economy. In the 1850's steam engine and machinery output shot up 66 per cent, coal mined 182 per cent, hosiery goods 608 per cent. By 1860 New York City's population would exceed one million. Craft unions were negotiating agreements with their employers; the National Typographic Union (1852), the United Hatters (1856), and the Iron Moulders' Union of North America (1859) were the first permanent federations. In the Cotton Kingdom, Kentucky backwoodsmen, who in the 1830's had taken up land in the black belts, were now gentleman planters, and their sons were attending the University of Virginia, with hounds and hunters and black servants. Georgia built a railroad across the southern end of the Appalachians, which helped to make Atlanta and Chattanooga great cities, and by 1860 there was through rail connection between New York and New Orleans.

The promise that America would fulfill her destiny through quality rather than quantity was never brighter. Consider the great books of that decade. In 1850–51, Hawthorne's *Scarlet Letter* and *House of the Seven Gables*, Melville's *White Jacket* and *Moby-Dick*, Emerson's *Representative Men* and *English Traits*. In 1852, Melville's *Pierre*; in 1854–56, Thoreau's *Walden*, Whitman's *Leaves of Grass*, and Melville's *Piazza Tales*. In 1857 the *Atlantic Monthly* was founded, with James Russell Lowell, satirist of slavery and the Mexican War, as editor, and Longfellow, Whittier, and Dr. Holmes (whose *Autocrat* appeared in 1858) as contributors. This was Longfellow's most productive decade, with *The Golden Legend* (1851), *Hiawatha* (1855), and *The Courtship of Miles Standish* (1858). Whittier published his *Songs of Labor* in 1850 and his 'Maud Muller' and 'Barefoot Boy' in 1856. And Parkman's *Conspiracy of Pontiac* (1851) opened a great historical series that required 40 years to complete.

The presidential election of 1852 proved that an overwhelming majority of Americans were disposed to regard the Compromise of 1850 as final and that economic questions were predominant once again. Since both parties endorsed the Compromise, party lines were drawn not on slavery but on such old economic issues as the tariff and internal improvements. The Democratic party nominated Franklin Pierce of New Hampshire, whose only apparent qualifications were a winning smile and a fair military record in the Mexican War. No more were needed. The New York 'barnburners,'[2] starved for four lean years with the Free-Soilers, returned to their Democratic allegiance; and thousands of Southern Whigs, disgusted by the anti-slavery tendencies of Northern Whigs, went over to their opponents. Although Pierce won less than 51 per cent of the popular vote, he handed the Whigs a drubbing in the electoral column, where General Winfield Scott carried only four states. The Whigs would never recover from this defeat.

More 'Manifest Destiny'

Republicanism and democracy appeared to be sweeping the western world. After the revolution of 1848, France adopted a constitution which was a centralized edition of that of the United States. Within the Democratic party, a 'Young America' movement sprang up, devoted at first to creating ideals of service and duty, then to enlisting Young America's aid for democrats beyond the seas, and finally to electing Stephen A. Douglas to the presidency. There had been wild talk in 1848 of annexing Ireland and Sicily to the United States, as certain revolutionists in those countries requested; and when the news came that Hungary had fallen and had been forcibly incorporated with Austria, the legislatures of New York, Ohio, and Indiana called for action. Louis Kossuth, brought to New York as guest of the nation in 1851, was given an overwhelming ovation, and a Harvard professor who exposed Hungarian humbug was forced to resign.

American diplomacy was particularly truculent when directed by Southern gentlemen who wanted new slave territory, as compensation for the 'loss' of California. Certain Southern statesmen professed to fear lest Cuba fall to England, or become a black republic like Haiti. Others had an eye on the large and redundant slave population there. Polk, still in the market for new territory after the vast acquisitions from Mexico, proposed to buy Cuba in 1848 for $100 million, but Spain rejected his offer with contempt. Then came filibustering expeditions, frowned upon by Taylor, tolerated by Fillmore and Pierce; and consequent interference by the Spanish authorities with Yankee traders. One such instance, the case of the *Black Warrior* (1854), seemed a good opportunity to provoke Spain into war. The Secretary of War, Jefferson Davis, urged President Pierce to take that line; but the Secretary of State, William L. Marcy, kept his head; and Spain disappointed the annexationists by apologizing. Nonetheless, in October 1854 the American ministers to Spain, France, and Great Britain, meeting at Ostend, drafted a serious recommendation to Marcy pontificating that if Spain refused to sell Cuba, then, 'by every law, human and divine, we shall be justified in wresting it from Spain if we possess the power.' The New York *Herald* made a 'scoop' of this secret document and published it as the 'Ostend Manifesto.' Its only effect was to lower American prestige in Europe and that of Pierce at home. The Cubans' consent to being annexed was never asked; and it is interesting to reflect whether, if it had been, a José Martí or a Fidel Castro would have arisen to demand *Cuba Libre* from the United States.

In these same years, American diplomacy was crossing the Pacific. In 1844 Caleb Cushing, as the first United States minister to China, negotiated a treaty by which American ships obtained access to certain Chinese seaports, and American merchants acquired extraterritorial privileges. The 'opening' of Japan proved more difficult. Japan had been closed for two centuries to all foreign intercourse, save a strictly regulated trade with the Dutch and Chinese at Nagasaki. Her government was feudal, her economy medieval—no factories, no steamships or steam engines, only small junks allowed to be built in order to keep the Japanese at home. Foreign sailors wrecked on the shores of Japan were not allowed to leave, and Japanese sailors wrecked on foreign coasts were not permitted to return. Commodore James Biddle USN tried to open relations at Tokyo Bay in 1845, but was surrounded by small guard boats and forced to leave.

Largely to protect castaways from the growing American whaling fleet, President Fillmore decided to make another try. He entrusted the mission to Commodore Matthew C. Perry, brother of

2. The radical wing of the New York Democrats who opposed the expansion of slavery was likened to the Dutchman who set fire to his barn to rid it of rats.

Commodore Matthew Perry (1794–1858). Japanese officials, including the imperial court of Kyoto and the Shogun's court at Edo, dispatched artists to depict the 'hairy barbarians' from America on parchment scrolls and woodblocks, and news sheets with illustrations of Perry's expedition proved immensely popular. (*Library of Congress*)

the hero of Lake Erie. The Commodore, who had had diplomatic experience dealing with Turkey, Naples, and several African kings, studied every available book on Japan. On 8 July 1853 his armed squadron anchored in the mouth of Tokyo Bay. Perry's orders forbade him to use force, except as a last resort; but the Kanagawa Shogun who then ruled Japan was so deeply impressed by the Commodore's show of force that, contrary to all precedent, he consented to receive the President's letter to the Emperor. Perry tactfully sailed to Macao, in order to give the elder statesmen time to make up their minds; and by the time he returned (February 1854), with an even more impressive squadron, they had decided to yield. At the little village of Yokohama they exchanged gifts: lacquers and bronzes, porcelain and brocades, for a set of telegraph instruments, a quarter-size steam locomotive complete with track and cars, Audubon's *Birds* and *Quadrupeds of America*, an assortment of farming implements and firearms, a barrel of whiskey, and several cases of champagne. Thus old Japan first tasted the blessings of Western civilization! Progressive Japanese leaders, who wished to put an end to isolation, persuaded the Shogun to sign the Treaty of Kanagawa allowing the United States to establish a consulate, assuring good treatment to castaways, and permitting American vessels to visit certain Japanese ports for supplies and repairs. Such was the famous 'opening' of Japan, and it was Perry's proud boast that without firing a shot he had effected what European nations had failed to do by using force.

To shorten the route from Atlantic ports to the Orient and to improve communications between the older United States and her new Pacific territories, the government gave serious consideration to an interocean canal. President Polk in 1846 obtained right of transit over the Isthmus of Panama by treaty with Colombia, in return for guaranteeing to that republic her sovereignty over the Isthmus, and undertaking to defend its neutrality. But an alternative route via Lake Nicaragua brought on a sharp controversy with Great Britain. When the Monroe Doctrine was first announced, the British had two bases in Central America: the old logwood establishment of Belize or British Honduras, and a shadowy protectorate over the Mosquito Indians of Nicaragua. Owing in part to indifference at Washington, British influence in Central America increased between 1825 and 1845. In 1848 the British government declared the sovereignty of 'Mosquitia' over San Juan or Greytown, the eastern terminus of the proposed Nicaragua ship canal.

All this created a very ticklish situation, from which the United States and United Kingdom emerged by negotiating the Clayton-Bulwer treaty in 1850. It was agreed that neither government would ever fortify, or obtain exclusive control over, the proposed Isthmian canal. Later generations of Americans regarded the treaty as a sellout; but at the time it was a fair compromise between the concessions that Britain had obtained in Central America when the American government was indifferent, and the new interest that the United States had acquired by becoming a Pacific power.

As American capitalists showed no enthusiasm for building a ship canal, the Clayton-Bulwer treaty might have caused no embarrassment for many years, but for ambiguous clauses. The United States government supposed that they meant British withdrawal from the Bay Islands, Greytown, and the Mosquito coast. The British government insisted that the treaty merely forbade future acquisitions. This dispute became dangerous in 1854, when President Pierce and the Democrats were looking for an issue to distract the country from the slavery question. The game then began of 'twisting the lion's tail' to cater to native and Irish-American voters. But the game recessed in 1859–60 when Britain ceded the Bay Islands to Honduras and the Mosquito coast to Nicaragua.

In the meantime, a curious episode occurred in Nicaragua. Cornelius Vanderbilt, 'commodore' of the Hudson river steamboat fleet, organized a company to compete with the Panama railway. It ran steamers up the San Juan river and across Lake Nicaragua, whence freight was forwarded to the Pacific by muleback. Wanting political stability in that region, this company financed William Walker, a professional filibuster, to overthrow the existing government of Nicaragua. Walker, 'the gray-eyed man of destiny,' in 1856 succeeded in

Flying Cloud. This splendid clipper ship, launched in 1851 in East Boston, established its designer, Donald McKay, as America's master builder. 'What ships they were!' Alan Villiers has written of these greyhounds of the sea. 'Man had never before and has never since been hurtled along by the elemental force of the wind at sea at such a speed.' In this 1855 Currier lithograph, *Flying Cloud* leaves another clipper ship astern while a flying fish leaps from the water off her port bow. (*Peabody Museum of Salem*)

making himself President of Nicaragua. He planned (with the approval of Pierce's Secretary of War, Jefferson Davis) to introduce Negro slavery and to conquer the rest of Central America. But he had the bad judgment to quarrel with Vanderbilt and seize his ships. The 'commodore' then supported a Central American coalition that invaded Nicaragua, and Walker surrendered. Twice more this prince of filibusters tried; on his last attempt, in 1860, he was seized and executed by a Honduran firing squad.

Midway in the Isthmian negotiations there was established a landmark in North American commerce and diplomacy, the Canadian Reciprocity Treaty of 1854. Britain's repeal of the corn laws had abolished the preference for colonial grain and flour that had given Canada the business of milling American wheat for the British market and prostrated the industry. At the request of the Canadian legislature the British foreign office negotiated at Washington a reciprocity treaty, but it was a difficult matter to put through concurrent acts of Parliament, of Congress, and of four Canadian legislatures, especially since the Maritime Provinces were loath to admit Yankees to their offshore fisheries. Secretary of State Marcy greased the way at Halifax, Fredericton, and St. John by a judicious expenditure of secret service funds; and Lord Elgin, a hard-headed but genial Scot, is said to have floated the treaty through the United States Senate on 'oceans of champagne.' If true, both served their respective countries well. The treaty opened the United States market to Canadian farm produce, timber, and fish, and Canada to American rice, turpentine, and tobacco; the bait for Southern support is obvious. Yankee fishermen got new privileges in Canadian waters, and the American merchant marine obtained the right to navigate the Great Lakes, the St. Lawrence, and their connecting canals. Thus Britain maintained her political dominion over Canada by sanctioning a partial economic union with the United States.

While the diplomats were wrangling over future canals to the Pacific, the shipwrights of New York and New England were engaged in cutting down the time of ocean passage around Cape Horn. In one month of 1850, 33 sailing vessels from New York and Boston entered San Francisco

A clipper ship sailing card. The *Hornet* once raced the redoubtable *Flying Cloud* from New York to San Francisco and, after 105 days out, finished ahead by forty minutes. (*Seamen's Bank, New York*)

bay after an average passage of 159 days. Then there came booming through the Golden Gate the clipper ship *Sea Witch* of New York, 97 days out. At once the cry went up for clipper ships at any price.

This new type of sailing vessel, characterized by great length in proportion to breadth of beam, an enormous sail area, and long concave bows ending in a gracefully curved cutwater, had been devised for the China-New York tea trade. The voyage of the *Sea Witch* showed its possibilities, and in 1851 the *Flying Cloud* of Boston made San Francisco in 89 days from New York, a record never surpassed. As California then afforded no return cargo except gold dust, the Yankee clippers sailed in ballast to the Chinese treaty ports, where they came into competition with the British merchant marine. Crack East-Indiamen humbly waited for cargo weeks on end, while one American clipper after another sailed off with a cargo of tea at double the ordinary freights. When the *Oriental* of New York appeared at London, 97 days from Hong Kong, crowds thronged the dock to admire her beautiful hull, lofty rig, and patent fittings, and *The Times* challenged British shipbuilders to set their 'long practised skill, steady industry and dogged determination' against the 'youth, ingenuity and ardour' of the United States.

Nightingale and *Witch of the Wave*, *Northern Light* and *Southern Cross*, *Young America* and *Great Republic*, *Golden Age* and *Herald of the Morning*, *Red Jacket* and *Westward Ho!*, *Dreadnought* and *Glory of the Seas*—no sailing vessel ever approached them in power, majesty, or speed. Yankee ingenuity, with its latent artistic genius, had at last found perfect and harmonious expression. Yet the clipper fulfilled a very limited purpose: speed to the goldfields at any price or risk. When that was no longer an object, no more were built. Meantime the British, leaving glory to their rivals, were quietly evolving a more useful type of medium clipper and perfecting the iron screw steamer. By 1857 the British empire had an ocean-going steam tonnage of almost half a million tons, as compared with 90,000 under the American flag. England had won back her maritime supremacy in fair competition, and civil war turned the Yankee mind to other objects.

16

The Irrepressible Conflict

*

1854–1861

Prairie Settlement and Pacific Railways

In the 1850's economic change had an enormous impact on political events. Increasingly the lines of force in the economy moved on an East-West axis rather than on a West-South axis. To be sure, the Mississippi trade flourished; the Illinois Central Railroad linked the South and the Northwest; and cotton still played a significant role in North-South trade. But cotton was no longer king. The Northeast, which now did not raise enough food for its own needs, provided the most important market for the Western farmer. And the Northwest, no longer so dependent on the South, turned its gaze away from the slave-tilled plantations and toward the empire of rolling prairie and Great Plains.

In the 1850's the prairie farmer came into his own. New agricultural machinery, especially the reaper, helped to cope with the labor shortage. Even greater impetus to prairie farming came from the rising price of wheat (from $0.93 a bushel in 1851 to $2.50 in 1855 at the New York market) and from the transportation revolution. The value of merchandise shipped to the West over the Erie Canal soared from $10 million in 1836 to $94 million in 1853. Railways linked the East with the farms and burgeoning cities of the Northwest. In 1850 railroads had hardly penetrated the Middle West; by 1860 their network covered it. The prairie farmer, hitherto dependent on long wagon hauls over execrable roads, could at last market his grain and livestock to advantage. As the Illinois prairie filled up, the state moved away from its Southern ties. One Illinois politician ruined his political future in an attempt to preserve the old alliance, and another led a new North-and-West political party which caused the South to seek safety for slavery in secession.

A struggle over the route of the first transcontinental railway promoted the same result. Of the many schemes projected since 1845, the four most important were (1) the Northern, from the upper Mississippi to the upper Missouri and by Lewis and Clark's trail to the Columbia river; (2) the Central, from St. Louis up the Kansas and Arkansas rivers, across the Rockies to the Great Salt Lake and by the California trail to San Francisco; (3) the Thirty-fifth Parallel route from Memphis, up the Arkansas and Canadian rivers, across the

Rockies near Santa Fe, and through the Apache and Mojave country to Los Angeles; (4) the Southern, from New Orleans up the Red river and across Texas and by the Gila valley to Yuma and San Diego.[1] Either of the first two would bind the Far West to the old Northwest; but the unorganized Indian country was an obstacle. The Southern route was the shortest, with the best contours, and led through states and territories already organized.

Congress, in March 1853, authorized surveys of these four routes under the direction of Secretary of War Jefferson Davis of Mississippi. He saw that the Southern route might well be the means of the South's recovering all she had lost by the Compromise of 1850; and, although a state-rights man, he advocated its construction by the Federal Government under the war power. As soon as the survey showed that a Southern railway would have to pass through Mexican territory south of the Gila river, Davis induced President Pierce and Congress to buy the land for $10 million. The Gadsden treaty of 30 December 1853 effected this purchase.

The stage was now set for Congress to sanction the Southern route.

The Kansas-Nebraska Bill

Stephen A. Douglas, the senior senator from Illinois, was the best orator in the Northwest and the idol of Northern Democrats. As an Illinoisan, he was sensitive to the demands of prairie folk for the organization of the trans-Missouri country and opening it to settlement. He wished to erase the 'barbarian wall' of Indian tribes impeding migration to the plains and 'to authorize and encourage a continuous line of settlements to the Pacific Ocean.' A heavy speculator in Western lands, including the city site which he expected to be the eastern terminus of the railroad, he favored a Central route for the transcontinental railway. To contest Davis's Southern route, he had to find a way to extend law and government over, and invite settlers into, the region through which the Central route must pass. Douglas and fellow Democrats in Washington sought a promising political issue for 1856. For these reasons, and probably for others known to themselves, the 'Little Giant' reported a bill to organize the Great Plains as the Territory of Nebraska, in January 1854. Earlier bills of this nature had been defeated by Southern senators. So Douglas baited this one for Southern votes by incorporating the principle of popular sovereignty. At the insistence of Southern leaders, he made clear that his bill would render the Missouri Compromise 'inoperative and void.' Furthermore, the bill, as amended, divided the region into two distinct territories: Kansas and Nebraska.

Douglas miscalculated grievously. He thought reopening the slavery question a minor matter; personally opposed to slavery, he believed the Plains would be inhospitable to it. But Northerners were incensed at a proposal to permit the slave power to extend its domain into a virgin land which more than 30 years before the Missouri Compromise had closed to the slaveholder 'forever.' Anti-slavery men raged at the Northern apostate; as Douglas himself said, he could have traveled from Boston to Chicago by light of his burning effigies. Nor did Douglas realize how passionate the South had become over maintaining prestige.

For three months the bitter debate dragged on. President Pierce whipped his party into line, except for a few Northern Democrats. Old Sam Houston of Texas reminded the Senate that by solemn treaties it had confirmed most of Kansas and Nebraska to the Indians 'as long as grass shall grow and water run,' but no one else thought of the aborigines. Federal agents were already bullying them into renouncing their 'perpetual' titles. The once powerful Delaware accepted a small reservation with an annual bounty. Others, like the Shawnee and Miami, who had once terrorized the Kentucky frontier and beaten a Federal army, were removed to the Indian Territory, which fortunately lay between the rival railway routes.

Democratic discipline triumphed. On 25 May 1854 the Kansas-Nebraska bill passed the Senate

1. These, in order, were followed in part by (1) the Northern Pacific; (2) the Missouri Pacific, Denver & Rio Grande, and Southern Pacific; (3) the Rock Island and the Santa Fe; and (4) the Texas Pacific and Southern Pacific.

This advertisement for McCormick's reaper appeared in May 1846 in a monthly agricultural journal *The Cultivator,* which explained: 'The machine is warranted to cut from 15 to 20 acres in a day, and at a great saving of expense over the common mode of harvesting.' (*State Historical Society of Wisconsin*)

by a comfortable majority. 'It is at once the worst and best Bill on which Congress ever acted,' declared Senator Charles Sumner. The worst, inasmuch as it is a present victory for slavery. The best, for 'it annuls all past compromises with slavery, and makes all future compromises impossible. Thus it puts freedom and slavery face to face, and bids them grapple. Who can doubt the result?'

'If the Nebraska bill should be passed, the Fugitive Slave Law is a dead letter throughout New England' wrote a Southerner in Boston. 'As easily could a law prohibiting the eating of codfish and pumpkin pies be enforced.' It did pass; and the very next day a Boston mob led by a Unitarian minister tried to rescue a fugitive slave from the courthouse where he was detained for examination. They did not succeed. Anthony Burns, the slave, was identified by his master and escorted to the wharf by a battalion of United States artillery, four platoons of marines, and the sheriff's posse, through streets lined with silent spectators and hung with crepe, every church-bell tolling a funeral dirge. It cost the United States some $40,000 to return that slave to his master; and he was the last to be returned from Massachusetts.

The Break-up of Parties

The first palpable result of the Kansas-Nebraska Act was the creation of a new anti-slavery party. A convention held under the oaks at Jackson, Mich., on 6 July 1854, resolved to oppose the extension of slavery, and 'be known as "Republicans" until the contest be terminated.' Many places, especially

Ripon, Wisconsin, claim the birthplace of the G.O.P., but Jackson at least made the happy suggestion of adopting Jefferson's old label. The new party, however, was slow in gathering momentum outside the Northwest. Seward sulked in his Whig tent; 'Anti-Nebraska Democrats' were loath to cut all connection with their party; Free-Soilers could not see why a new party was needed. With the old parties breaking up, many people hearkened to a new gospel of ignorance.

Know-Nothingism was a No Popery party. Protestants suspected that the Pope had his eye on America, for who would dwell in decaying Rome when he could live in the Mississippi Valley? Anti-Catholics thrived on volumes like Maria Monk's *Awful Disclosures of the Hotel Dieu Nunnery of Montreal*. Nativists were alarmed too by the rising flood of immigrants. In 1845, the immigrant tide passed the 100,000 a year mark for the first time; only two years later it had reached 200,000 and by 1854 had more than quadrupled. It was charged that the newcomers corrupted the nation's morals; one observer complained, 'They bring the grog shops like the frogs of Egypt upon us.' Even more important, nativists believed that the immigrants were sapping republican institutions. Between 1850 and 1855 in Boston, native-born voters increased 15 per cent, foreign-born 195 per cent. The declining Whigs attributed Pierce's victory in 1852 to the immigrant vote.

Accordingly, native-born Protestants formed a secret 'Order of the Star-Spangled Banner,' with elaborate ritual and rigid discipline. Members, when questioned by outsiders, answered 'I know nothing.' Candidates nominated secretly developed surprising strength at the polls, and many politicians joined up, thinking that this was the wave of the future. In the state elections of 1854 the Know-Nothings almost won New York and did win Massachusetts, electing a new legislature that passed some good reform laws but also conducted a clownish investigation of Catholic schools and convents. The new party sent some 75 congressmen to Washington; especially strong in New England and the border states, it also found a considerable following in the South. At Baltimore where the white working class was still largely native-born, the Know-Nothings organized 'plug-uglies,' gangs who attended the polls armed with carpenters' awls to 'plug' voters who did not give the password, and a series of pitched battles between native Americans and Irish Catholics in St. Louis in 1854 took many lives.

In the summer of 1855 the American party, as the Know-Nothings now called themselves, held a national convention; the Southern members obtained control, passed pro-slavery resolutions, and nominated for the presidency old Millard Fillmore. Northerners then lost interest, and by 1856 the movement was no longer able to offer the nation an escape from the slavery question.

Bleeding Kansas, 'Black' Republicanism

'Bleeding Kansas' soon diverted attention from the 'Popish peril.' Most of the settlers who came to Kansas went there to build a new life and live in peace, not to agitate the slavery question. Yet the new territory also witnessed a savage conflict over slavery which helped to plunge the nation into civil war. In the elections for the territorial legislature in March 1855, several thousand 'border ruffians' crossed over from Missouri to stuff ballot boxes. The legislature elected by such fraudulent means then put through a drastic slave code. The free-state men responded by setting up their own rump government, and by 1856 Kansas had two governments, both illegal. Since popular sovereignty was to settle the question of slavery in Kansas, sectional rivals dispatched settlers into the state. The New England Emigrant Aid Company sent some 1240 migrants. After Missourians had sacked their first settlement at Lawrence, the Company started arming its forces with a new breech-loading weapon, the Sharps rifle, or 'Beecher's Bible,' so called after the abolitionist preacher who advised its use. Parties of Northern 'Jayhawkers' battled with organizations from Missouri and points south. 'Now let the Southern men come on with their slaves,' wrote Senator Atchison of Missouri. 'Ten thousand families can take possession of and hold every acre of timber in the Territory of Kansas, and this secures the prairie. . . . We are playing for a mighty stake; if we win, we carry slavery to the Pacific Ocean.'

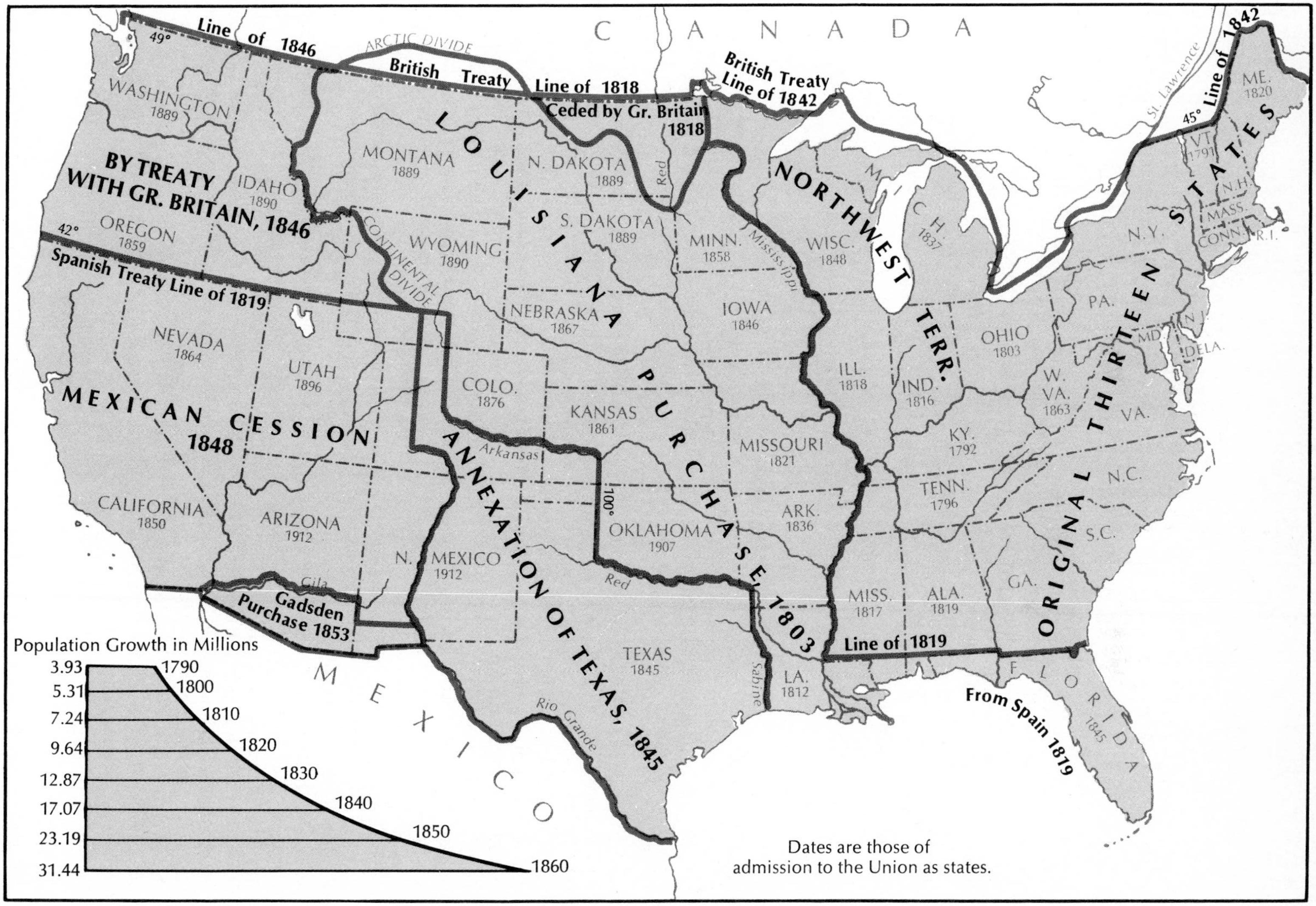

Territorial Growth of the United States

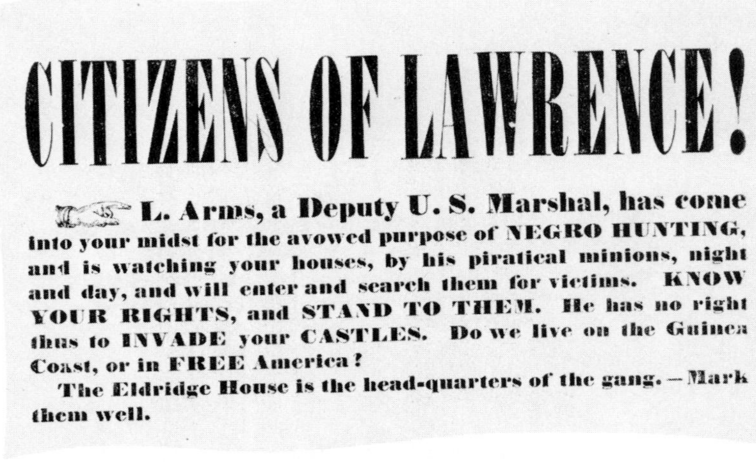

CITIZENS OF LAWRENCE!

☞ **L. Arms, a Deputy U. S. Marshal, has come into your midst for the avowed purpose of NEGRO HUNTING, and is watching your houses, by his piratical minions, night and day, and will enter and search them for victims. KNOW YOUR RIGHTS, and STAND TO THEM. He has no right thus to INVADE your CASTLES. Do we live on the Guinea Coast, or in FREE America?**

The Eldridge House is the head-quarters of the gang.—Mark them well.

(Kansas State Historical Society, Topeka)

Few Southerners, however, cared to risk valuable property in such a region, and free-state settlers came in with the spirit of crusaders. One of the newcomers, a fanatic named John Brown, was responsible for the murder of five men at the 'Pottawatomie massacre.' Such were the workings of popular sovereignty.

On 19 May 1856 Senator Sumner of Massachusetts delivered a speech on 'The Crime against Kansas,' which contained some unpalatable truth, much that was neither truthful nor in good taste, and some disgraceful personal invective against Senator Andrew Butler of South Carolina. Three days later, a kinsman of Butler, Preston Brooks, attacked Sumner as he sat at his desk in the Senate chamber and beat him senseless with a stout cane, while Stephen Douglas and Robert Toombs looked on. He was following the code of a Southern gentleman in dealing with an enemy unworthy of a duel. 'Towards the last he bellowed like a calf,' Brooks reported. 'I wore my cane out completely but saved the Head which is gold.' Returning to South Carolina, the assailant was feted from place to place and presented by admirers with suitably inscribed canes. From Louisiana, Braxton Bragg wrote, 'You can reach the sensibilities of such dogs only through their heads and a big stick.'

A few days after this episode, the new Republican party held its first national convention. The Republicans embraced diverse elements: anti-slavery radicals like Sumner; former Whigs, many of a conservative stripe; Free-Soil Democrats like Chase and Lyman Trumbull; and dissatisfied Know-Nothings. Glamorous John C. Frémont, the 'Pathfinder,' won the first Republican presidential nomination. The platform proclaimed it 'both the right and the duty of Congress to prohibit in the territories those twin relics of barbarism, polygamy and slavery.' The Democratic convention in Cincinnati met for the first time west of the Appalachians. James Buchanan, for twenty-five years disappointed at not getting the Democratic presidential nomination, now wrested it from pleasant Mr. Pierce, the first man elected President to be denied a second term by his own party.

The Republicans conducted a lively campaign for 'Free soil, free speech, and Frémont,' but Buchanan won—though with only 45 per cent of the popular vote. He swept the South and every border state but one, and took five Northern states too. Frémont polled only 33 per cent, not much more than Fillmore received. The ominous aspect to Frémont's 1.3 million votes was that all but 1200 came from non-slaveholding states.

No previous candidate had so nearly united

North and West against the South. Party divisions were approaching dangerously close to the Mason-Dixon Line; and the Lower South, even in this campaign, made it perfectly clear that it would secede if a purely Northern party elected its presidential candidate.

Dred Scott

On 6 March 1857, two days after Buchanan's inauguration, the Supreme Court published its decision in Dred Scott *v.* Sandford. Dred Scott was a slave who had been taken by his master to Illinois, thence to the unorganized territory north of lat. 36° 30′, where slavery had been forbidden by the Missouri Compromise, and finally back to Missouri, where he sued for freedom on the ground of having twice been resident of free soil. Chief Justice Taney and the four Southerners among the associate justices hoped through this case to settle the question of slavery by extending it legally to all territories of the United States. President-elect Buchanan slipped a clause into his inaugural address declaring that the Supreme Court was about to determine 'at what point of time' the people of a territory could decide for or against slavery, pledging his support to this decision, and begging 'all good citizens' to do likewise.

Poor, foolish Buchanan! He had hoped for a peaceful term of office, but the Dred Scott case unleashed the worst passions of pro- and antislavery when his administration was less than a week old. The nine justices filed nine separate opinions. Taney, speaking for the Court, declared against Scott's claim for freedom on three grounds: (1) as a Negro he could not be a citizen of the United States, and therefore had no right to sue in a Federal court; (2) as a resident of Missouri the laws of Illinois had no effect on his status; (3) as a resident of the territory north of lat. 36° 30′ he had not been emancipated because Congress had no right to deprive citizens of their property without 'due process of law.' The Missouri Compromise, it followed, was unconstitutional.

On all these points the Chief Justice's opinion was either vulnerable or mistaken. As Justice Curtis asserted in his vigorous dissent, Negroes had always been considered citizens in most of the Northern states, and thus had the right to sue in the Federal courts. Under the rule of interstate comity, Missouri had in seven earlier cases recognized the claim to freedom of a slave who had resided in free territory. And congressional authority over slavery in the territories had been acknowledged for 70 years. As for 'due process of law,' that term in the Constitution referred to the method of enforcing the law, not to its substance.

Only once before, in Marbury *v.* Madison (1803), had the Supreme Court declared an act of Congress unconstitutional. In that case the law directly concerned the Federal judiciary; but the Missouri Compromise was a general law, resting on the precedent of the Ordinance of 1787, on the statute books for 34 years. By its ruling the Court had sanctioned Calhoun's doctrine that slavery was national, freedom sectional. Oregon and Nebraska, as well as Kansas, were opened to the slaveholder. Squatter sovereignty thenceforth was no sovereignty; slavery was theoretically legal in every territory.

Buchanan reeled from disaster to disaster. The conclusion of the Crimean War, which deprived the farmer of a prime market in Europe, came at a time when the North was feeling the effects of the collapse of the Western land boom and paying the price for a weak banking structure and an overbuilt railway system; by October, the panic of 1857 had hit with full force. Congressmen returned to Washington at the end of 1857 to cope with the Kansas question in an atmosphere of anxiety over the economy and in the midst of a religious revival which intensified sectional sensitivity about slavery.

Events in Kansas pointed toward civil war. A convention chosen by a minority of the voters had adopted the 'Lecompton constitution,' an out-and-out pro-slavery charter, subsequently ratified in a bogus referendum. The free-state faction then drafted its own constitution and got it ratified in an extra-legal referendum. Each group appealed to Washington for statehood. Despite the travesty of the fraudulent elections, Buchanan insisted on pushing the Lecompton constitution through Congress. He asserted that Kansas was 'as much a slave state as Georgia,' and warned that refusal to admit Kansas as a slave state would be 'keenly felt' by the South. At this, Stephen Douglas decided he had had enough. Embarrassed by the way popular sovereignty had worked out, he broke with Buchanan and the Southern Democrats and fought the Lecompton proposal. In the end the Democrats were compelled to submit the constitution to a new referendum, and in August 1858 in an honest election the voters of Kansas rejected it overwhelmingly. But by then both sections had found new cause for grievance, and the Democratic party, badly split between the Buchanan and Douglas factions, was rapidly losing its function as a unifier of the nation.

The Lincoln-Douglas Debates

Before the Kansas struggle Abraham Lincoln had been distinguished from hundreds of Northwestern lawyer-politicians only by a high reputation for integrity and a habit of prolonged, abstracted contemplation. Slavery he had long regarded as evil; but the abolitionist agitation seemed to him mischievous and unrealistic.

About the time of the Kansas-Nebraska Act an unseen force began to work on Lincoln's soul and to prepare him for the most arduous and distressing responsibility that has ever fallen to an American. He began to preach a new testament of anti-slavery, without malice or hatred toward slave-owners. In 1858 he had become a rival candidate to Stephen A. Douglas for election to the Senate from Illinois. His opening speech in the campaign gave the ripe conclusions to his meditations during the last four years and stuck the keynote of American history for the seven years to come.

> 'A house divided against itself cannot stand.'[2]
>
> I believe this government cannot endure permanently half slave and half free.
>
> I do not expect the Union to be dissolved—I do not expect the house to fall—but I do expect it will cease to be divided. It will become all one thing, or all the other.
>
> Either the opponents of slavery will arrest the further spread of it, and place it where the public mind shall rest in the belief that it is in the course of ultimate extinction; or its advocates will push it forward till it shall become alike lawful in all the States, old as well as new, North as well as South.

2. Matthew xii:25.

Lincoln and Douglas engaged in seven joint debates, covering every section of the state, through the summer and autumn of 1858. Imagine some parched prairie town of central Illinois, set in fields of rustling corn; a dusty courthouse square surrounded by low wooden houses and stores blistering in the August sunshine, decked with flags and party emblems; shirt-sleeved farmers and their families in wagons and buggies and on foot, brass bands blaring out 'Hail! Columbia' and 'Oh! Susanna,' wooden platform with railing, perspiring semicircle of local dignitaries in black frock coats and immense beaver hats. The Douglas special train (provided by George B. McClellan, superintendent of the Illinois Central) pulls into the 'deepo' and fires a salute from the twelve-pounder cannon bolted to a flatcar at the rear. Senator Douglas, escorted by the local Democratic club in columns of fours, drives up in an open carriage and aggressively mounts the platform. His short, stocky figure is clothed in the best that Washington tailors can produce. Every feature of his face bespeaks confidence and mastery; every gesture of his body, vigor and combativeness. Abe Lincoln, who had previously arrived by an ordinary passenger train, approaches on foot, his furrowed face and long neck conspicuous above the crowd. Wearing a rusty frock coat the sleeves of which stop several inches short of his wrists, and well-worn trousers that show a similar reluctance to approach a pair of enormous feet, he shambles onto the platform. His face, as he turns to the crowd, has an air of settled melancholy.

In their debates, Douglas accused Lincoln of advocating doctrines which would lead to fratricide, while Lincoln sought to show the inconsistency of the Dred Scott decision and Douglas's popular sovereignty. At Freeport, Lincoln asked Douglas whether the people of a territory could, in any lawful way, exclude slavery from their limits. Apparently, Douglas must either accept the Dred Scott decision and admit popular sovereignty to be a farce, or separate from his party by repudiating a ruling of the Supreme Court. But this clever statesman had already found a way out of the dilemma: the principle of 'unfriendly legislation.' 'Slavery cannot exist a day or an hour anywhere, unless it is supported by local police regulations, said Douglas. If a territorial legislature failed to pass a black code, it would effectually keep slavery out, for no slaveholder would take valuable property into a territory unless he were sure of protection. No doubt Douglas was right. Congress could invalidate a positive enactment of the territorial legislature, but not force it to pass a law against its will. It is probable that this 'Freeport doctrine' won Douglas his re-election to the Senate. But by saying that popular sovereignty gave slaveholders no protection, Douglas, who had already antagonized them by his role in the Lecompton affair, made himself 'unavailable' for the Democratic nomination in 1860.

If Lincoln had the more principled argument, Douglas had a more sensible position at the moment. Kansas was safe for freedom; and if theoretically slavery were legal in all the territories, there was slight chance of any except New Mexico and Arizona, not even a territory until 1863, becoming slaveholding states. Yet the long-run practicality of Douglas's stand hinged on the extreme unlikelihood that the South would rest content with the Dred Scott principle, any more than it had rested content with the compromises of 1787, 1820, and 1850. As early as 1848 four Southern states had endorsed the 'Alabama platform' which called for positive action by Congress to protect slavery in the territories, and the majority platform of the national Democratic convention at Charleston in 1860 would demand that Congress enact a 'black code' and impose it on the Western settlers. The South was becoming increasingly insistent, too, that Northern states silence the abolitionists, and that Congress agree to reopen the African slave trade. Some writers have assumed that the institution of slavery would have withered away because it was unprofitable, and hence regard the Civil War as an unmitigated tragedy. The profitability of slavery is an issue hotly debated by historians. But even if one concludes that slavery was unprofitable, and many historians would disagree, one still confronts the fact that slavery was not merely an economic matter but was valued as a social necessity for keeping the South 'a white man's country.' There is less reason to suppose that slavery would have been abandoned than that the South would have demanded that its 'peculiar institution' be extended further and further afield until the world cried out, 'Away with this foul thing!'

Northern Aggression and John Brown

In 1859 came two startling portents of what Seward called the 'irrepressible conflict.' The Anthony Burns fugitive slave case was followed by a new crop of state 'personal liberty laws.' These penalized citizens for helping federal officials to perform this unwelcome duty. A certain Booth of Wisconsin, convicted in a federal court of having rescued a runaway slave from his captors, was released by the state supreme court on the ground that the Fugitive Slave Act of 1850 was unconstitutional. After the Supreme Court of the United States had reversed this decision, in Ableman *v.* Booth (1859), the Wisconsin legislature, quoting the Kentucky Resolves of 1798 which Southern men considered canonical, declared 'that this assumption of jurisdiction by the federal judiciary . . . is an act of undelegated power, void, and of no force.' The Federal Government vindicated its power by rearresting and imprisoning Booth; but the deeper significance lies in the fact that Calhoun's nullification had been enunciated in a new quarter.

If the Booth case aroused bitterness, the next episode of the year brought the deeper anger that comes of fear. John Brown, 'of Pottawatomie,' formed a vague project to establish an abolitionist republic in the Appalachians and wage guerrilla war on slavery with fugitive Negroes and a few determined whites. To this wild scheme he rallied support from many of the leading abolitionists. On the night of 16 October 1859, leading an army of thirteen whites and five Negroes, Brown seized the federal armory at Harpers Ferry, Virginia, killed the town's mayor, and took prisoner some of the leading townspeople.

Governor Wise called out the entire state militia and implored the Federal Government for aid. John Brown retreated to the engine-house of the armory, knocked portholes through the brick wall, and defended himself. One of his prisoners has left us a graphic description of the scene: 'Brown was the coolest and firmest man I ever saw in defying danger and death. With one son dead

John Brown of Osawatomie (1800–1859). An avid foe of slavery, Brown viewed himself as an instrument of the Lord's vengeance. In the spring of 1856 in 'bleeding Kansas' he executed reprisal for the sack of Lawrence by pro-slavery elements by leading a party of six, four of them his sons, to the Pottawatomie country where they brutally murdered five men. Though many viewed him as a fanatic, anti-slavery men hailed 'Brown of Osawatomie' as a hero. This photograph was taken in 1856, the year of the 'Pottawatomie massacre.' (*Library of Congress*)

by his side, and another shot through, he felt the pulse of his dying son with one hand and held his rifle with the other, and commanded his men with the utmost composure, encouraging them to be firm and to sell their lives as dearly as they could.' In the evening, when Colonel Robert E. Lee arrived with a company of marines, only four of Brown's men were alive and unwounded. The next day the marines forced an entrance and captured the slender remnant.

Eight days after his capture the trial of John Brown began. From the pallet where he lay wounded the bearded old fighter rejected his counsel's plea of insanity. The jury brought in a verdict of murder, criminal conspiracy, and treason against the Commonwealth of Virginia. John Brown, content (as he wrote to his children) 'to die for God's eternal truth on the scaffold as in any other way,' was hanged on 2 December 1859.

Southerners thought of Haiti and shuddered, although not a single slave had voluntarily joined their would-be liberator. Keenly they watched for indications of Northern opinion. That Christian burial was with difficulty obtained for John Brown's body they did not know. That every Democratic or Republican newspaper condemned his acts they did not heed so much as the admiration for a brave man that Northern opinion could not conceal. And the babble of shocked repudiation by politicians and public men was dimmed by one bell-like note from Emerson: 'That new saint, than whom nothing purer or more brave was ever led by love of men into conflict and death . . . will make the gallows glorious like the cross.'

The Election of 1860

An unfortunate vote of the Democratic national convention of 1856 had decided on Charleston, the headquarters of secession sentiment, as the seat of the next national convention in 1860. Southern Democrats believed that they had been duped by Douglas. They had 'bought' popular sovereignty in 1854, expecting to get Kansas; but Kansas slipped the other way. Its territorial legislature was now in the hands of anti-slavery men, encouraged by Douglas's Freeport doctrine to flout the Dred Scott decision. Nothing less than active protection for slavery in every territory would satisfy the Southerners. Northerners on the platform committee were willing to go along with Southerners in supporting the Dred Scott decision, condemning personal liberty laws, and proposing annexation of Cuba. But the Southerners insisted that Congress must adopt a black code for all territories to override 'popular sovereignty.' The Democratic party must affirm 'that slavery was right,' said Yancey of Alabama. 'Gentlemen of the South,' replied Senator Pugh of Ohio, 'you mistake us—you mistake us—we will not do it.'

The minority report of the Northern delegates was adopted by the convention on 30 April as the Democratic platform. Thereupon the Alabama delegation, and a majority from South Carolina, Georgia, Florida, Louisiana, and Arkansas, withdrew. This symbolic secession was even more rash and foolish than the actual secession which developed from it as inevitably as vinegar from cider. For the best possible way for the South to protect slavery was to elect a Democrat President; and this split in the party made it impossible to elect any Democrat.

After the Southern rights men bolted the Charleston convention, balloting started for the presidential nomination. Although Douglas led, neither he nor anyone could obtain the required two-thirds majority. So the convention adjourned, to meet again in the calmer atmosphere of Baltimore on 18 June. At Baltimore a second split occurred over re-admitting the bolters. It was decided in the negative, and another secession took place. The convention then nominated Stephen A. Douglas, who thus became the official Democratic candidate. The seceders nominated Vice-President John C. Breckinridge of Kentucky for President, an action later endorsed by the original seceders from Charleston.

In the meantime, old Whigs, Know-Nothings, and moderate men of both North and South had held a convention of what they called the Constitutional Union party, and nominated Senator John Bell of Tennessee for President and Edward Everett of Massachusetts for Vice-President. They avowed no principles other than the Constitution, the Union, and the enforcement of the laws. This praiseworthy attempt to found a middle-of-the-road party, pledged to solve the slavery extension issue by reason rather than violence, came at least four years too late.

The Republicans were no longer a party of one idea, but a party of the North. Their 1860 platform stipulated: no more slavery in the territories, no interference with slavery in the states. So there was no place in the party either for the slavocracy or for the abolitionists. John Brown was condemned in the same breath with the 'border ruffians' of Missouri. The platform also promised settlers a free quarter-section of public land and revived Clay's 'American system' of internal improvements and protective tariff, representing Northern desires that had been balked by Southern interests. Abraham Lincoln received the presidential nomination; not for his transcendent merits, which no one yet suspected, but as a matter of political strategy. His humble birth, homely wit, and skill in debate would attract the sort of Northerners who had once voted for Andrew Jackson; and no one else could carry the doubtful states of Indiana and Illinois.

Lincoln triumphed in the four-way race by capturing every free state, save New Jersey, whose vote was divided. In his camp were two newly admitted free states, Minnesota and Oregon. But in ten Southern states he did not receive one vote. Breckinridge carried every cotton state, together with North Carolina, Delaware, and Maryland. Douglas, although a good second to Lincoln in the total popular vote, won only Missouri and three electoral votes in New Jersey. Virginia, Kentucky, and Tennessee went for Bell, although his popular vote was the least. Lincoln would have won even if

Stephen A. Douglas (1813–61). This illustration, which comes from a 'propaganda envelope,' an artifact of the popular culture of the era, gives a stamp of approval to the 'Little Giant.' In 1860 Douglas ran as the presidential candidate of Northern Democrats. Though he opposed Lincoln in this campaign, as he had for some time before in Illinois, Douglas proved loyal to Lincoln and the Union when war broke out. He traveled through the border states to stir up enthusiasm for the Union cause and sought in other ways to be of service to his country. But two months after Fort Sumter fell, Douglas was stricken with typhoid fever and died. (*Library of Congress*)

John Breckinridge of Kentucky (1821–75). In 1856 he was elected Vice-President of the United States and in 1860 he polled seventy-two electoral votes as the presidential candidate of the pro-slavery Democrats. Although he had resisted disunion before the war, he helped organize a Confederate government in Kentucky after the fighting began. In November 1861 he was indicted for treason in a federal court, and in the following month the Senate formally expelled him. In the North, Breckinridge, as this propaganda envelope indicates, was branded a 'traitor,' but in the South he was respected as a statesman and as a brigadier-general in the Confederate army. (*Library of Congress*)

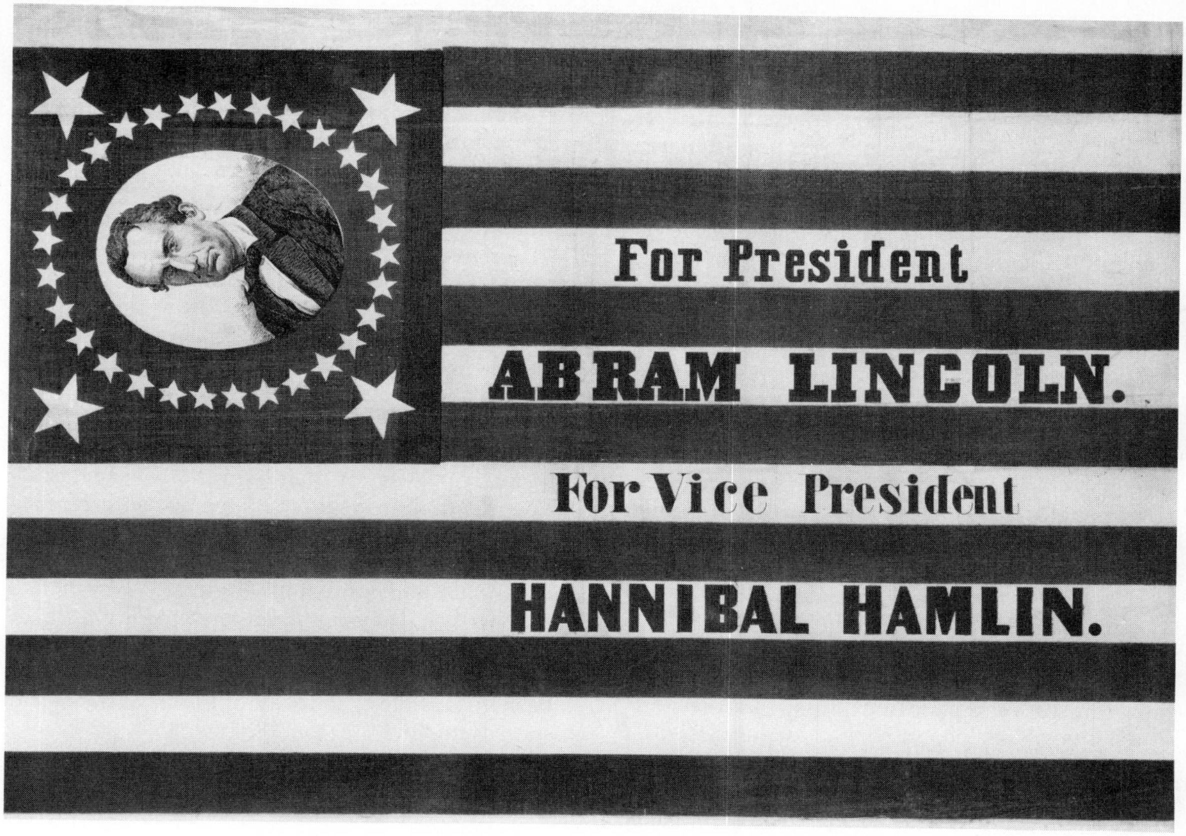

Cloth banner for the Republican party ticket, 1860. (*Library of Congress*)

the opposition to him had been united, because he rolled up a large majority in the electoral college.[3]

Secession

It was a foregone conclusion that South Carolina would secede if Lincoln were elected. As soon as the result of the election was certain, the South Carolina legislature summoned a state convention. On 20 December 1860 it met at Charleston and unanimously declared 'that the Union now subsisting between South Carolina and other states under the name of "The United States of America" is hereby dissolved.'

In the other cotton states Union sentiment was strong. Men like Jefferson Davis, who had traveled in the North, wished to give Lincoln's administration a fair trial. Outside South Carolina secession was insisted upon by small planters, provincial lawyer-politicians, journalists, and clergymen, but they met stout opposition. After Mississippi, Alabama, and Florida seceded, the key struggle took place in Georgia, trapped between states which had pulled out of the Union.

3.

Candidates	*Popular vote*	*Per cent*	*Electoral vote*
Lincoln	1,866,432	39.9	180
Douglas	1,375,197	29.4	12
Breckinridge	845,763	18.1	72
Bell	589,586	12.6	39

These figures include no popular vote in South Carolina, where Breckinridge electors were chosen by the legislature. In the other states that seceded the popular vote was Breckinridge 736,592; Bell, 345,919; Douglas, 72,084.

Alexander H. Stephens declared: 'This government of our fathers, with all its defects, comes nearer the objects of all good government than any other on the face of the earth.' But Senator Robert Toombs cried: 'Throw the bloody spear into this den of incendiaries!' On 19 January 1861 Georgia voted secession by a 2 to 1 plurality at its convention, but only after a motion to defer action had been narrowly defeated.

By 1 February 1861, these five states had been joined by two more: Louisiana, where the vote for secessionist delegates had totalled only 20,448 to 17,296 Unionists, and Texas, over the opposition of old Sam Houston, subsequently deposed as governor for refusing to swear fealty to the Confederacy. On 4 February, delegates from the seven seceded states met at Montgomery, Alabama, and on the 8th formed the Confederate States of America. The next day this Congress elected Jefferson Davis provisional President and A. H. Stephens Vice-President of the Southern Confederacy, and proceeded to draft a constitution.

The causes of secession, as they appeared to its protagonists, were plainly expressed by the state conventions. 'The people of the Northern states,' declared Mississippi, 'have assumed a revolutionary position towards the Southern states.' 'They have enticed our slaves from us,' and obstructed their rendition under the fugitive slave law. They claim the right 'to exclude slavery from the territories,' and from any state henceforth admitted to the Union. They have 'insulted and outraged our citizens when travelling among them . . . by taking their servants and liberating the same.' They have 'encouraged a hostile invasion of a Southern state to excite insurrection, murder and rapine.' To which South Carolina added, 'They have denounced as sinful the institution of slavery; they have permitted the open establishment among them' of abolition societies, and 'have united in the election of a man to the high office of President of the United States whose opinions and purposes are hostile to slavery.' On their own showing, then, the states of the Lower South seceded as the result of dissatisfaction respecting the Northern attitude toward slavery. There was no mention of any other cause, neither the tariff nor state rights. A strong minority regarded Southern independence as an end in itself.

Even for the purpose of protecting slavery, secession was a colossal act of folly. Southerners and Democrats combined would have possessed a majority in both houses of Congress. Lincoln could have done nothing without their consent. At worst Republicans might eventually gain strength to outlaw slavery in the territories, but secession would immediately lose the cotton states all rights of any sort in the territories. Northern states were not enforcing the fugitive slave law, but secession would make that law a dead letter. Abolitionists were disagreeable fellow-countrymen; but their propaganda could not be stopped by international boundaries. And as Lincoln asked, 'Can enemies make treaties better than friends can make laws?' The Republicans contemplated no interference with slavery in the Southern states, and those in Congress early in 1861 actually proposed a constitutional amendment to that effect. Even had they wished, they could not have freed the slaves in unwilling states except as an act of war. To free them by constitutional amendment would have been impossible even today, if the slave states had stayed united.[4]

Confusion and Attempted Compromise

During the awkward four months' interval between Lincoln's election in November 1860 and his inauguration on 4 March, a period in which the Confederacy was formed, the timid Buchanan was President. Buchanan had the same power to defend federal property and collect federal taxes within states that obstructed federal law as President Jackson possessed in 1832, but the President did nothing. 'Vacillating and obstinate by turns, yet lacking firmness when the occasion demanded firmness, he floundered about in a sea of perplexity, throwing away chance after chance.'[5] In his annual message of 8 December, Buchanan had an opportunity to sound the Jacksonian trumpet note to recall loyal citizens to their duty. Instead, he querulously chided the abolitionists for the fact

4. There were fifteen slave states in 1860, enough to prevent the ratification of a constitutional amendment a century later.
5. J. F. Rhodes, *United States*, III, 150.

that 'many a matron throughout the South retires at night in dread of what may befall herself and her children before the morning.' And he did a notable shilly-shally on secession, which Seward not unfairly paraphrased thus: 'It is the duty of the President to execute the laws, unless somebody opposes him; and that no state has a right to go out of the Union, unless it wants to.'

Yet Buchanan confronted a situation which appeared to spell defeat no matter what course he pursued. He hoped by a policy of conciliation to encourage the seceding states to return. But he found little support for his policies in any section. Washington was a Southern city. Congress, cabinet, and all the federal departments were riddled with secessionists. Secretary of the Treasury Howell Cobb resigned in December to organize secession in Georgia. To onlookers like young Henry Adams, the Federal Government seemed to be dissolving; soon there would be nothing left to secede from. Northern opinion was indistinct. Horace Greeley may have struck the key-note with the phrase, 'Wayward sisters, depart in peace!'

'Why not?' we may ask, in an era that has seen more than fifty new nations created. 'Why not have let the cotton states form their own republic?' With the best will in the world, redistribution of federal power would have been difficult,[6] and good will was notably wanting. Peace could not have been maintained for a year between the United States and the Confederacy. Fugitive slaves, adjustment of the national debt, and of each government's share in the territories would have raised problems only solvable by force; once the right of secession had been admitted, other states would have broken away.

The issue came to a head in Charleston harbor. When South Carolina seceded, Major Robert Anderson, who commanded the small U.S. Army detachment at Charleston, shifted his command from the mainland to the incomplete Fort Sumter, on an island commanding the harbor entrance. An 'embassy' from South Carolina to Washington almost bullied Buchanan into ordering Major Anderson out, or home; but at the turn of the year Attorney-General Jeremiah H. Black managed to put a little ginger into the President, and he refused. Buchanan also reconstructed his cabinet, with Black as Secretary of State, and made a half-hearted attempt to reinforce Fort Sumter with 200 men and arms and ammunition in an unarmed passenger steamer which retired after gunfire from a fort flying the palmetto flag had straddled her.

Buchanan did not retaliate, because he continued to hope that one of the compromise movements might succeed. None did, though when Senator John J. Crittenden of Kentucky proposed to extend the old 36° 30′ line between free and slave territories to the California boundary, the Republicans were willing to go so far as to admit New Mexico as a slave state if the people there chose slavery. A Peace Convention summoned by the Virginia legislature also broke on the rocks of Southern intransigency. Even the adoption of a 'never-never' proposition to the effect that neither by law nor constitutional amendment could Congress ever interfere with slavery in the states or the District of Columbia proved unavailing. All formal compromises failed to bring back the 'wayward sisters.' The repeal by several Northern states of personal liberty laws, and the breaking up of an abolition meeting in Boston to commemorate John Brown, seemed insufficient evidence of a change of heart. Nothing further had been done toward compromise by 4 March 1861, when Abraham Lincoln was inaugurated President of the no longer United States.

Fort Sumter and Seward

Buchanan had flinched from defending those coigns of vantage, the federal forts in the Southern states; and we shall judge him less harshly when we reflect that it took Lincoln a month to meet the issue bravely. By the time he was inaugurated, all the forts and navy yards in the seceded states, except Fort Pickens at Pensacola, Fort Sumter at Charleston, and two minor posts off the

6. The matter of breaking up the federal postal service, for instance, was so difficult that the Confederacy permitted United States mails to run their usual course through the South until 30 June 1861, six weeks after the Civil War had begun, and almost six months after South Carolina had 'resumed her separate and equal place among nations.'

Florida coast, had fallen unresisting to the Confederate authorities. So, too, had a string of post offices and custom houses and the mint at New Orleans. From the extreme Southern point of view, the jurisdiction of such places passed with secession to the states, and their retention by the Federal Government was equivalent to an act of war. Confederate commissioners came to Washington to treat for their surrender, a few days after Lincoln's inauguration. Although Seward refused to receive the gentlemen, he assured them indirectly that no supplies or provisions would be sent to the forts without due notice, and led them to expect a speedy evacuation.

William H. Seward, as Lincoln's chief rival for the nomination, and as the most experienced statesman in the Republican party, had been given the department of state, where he was playing a deep and dangerous game. Lincoln he regarded as an inexperienced small-town lawyer; and Confederate leaders, he thought, were merely using secession as a way of obtaining concessions to Southern rights. If a collision could be avoided, they would sneak back into the Union. If they did not, Seward would rally the Southern people to their old flag by a foreign war. But events were rapidly overtaking him.

Major Anderson, commanding Fort Sumter, notified the war department that his supplies were giving out, and that new Confederate batteries commanded his position. Fort Sumter had no strategic value in case of civil war. Why, then, risk war by holding it? The Confederacy made it clear that any attempt to reinforce or even to supply Sumter would be regarded as a hostile act, which would probably pull Virginia into the Confederacy. In the middle of March, five of the seven members of Lincoln's cabinet opposed supplying Fort Sumter. If, however, the forts were tamely yielded, would not the principle of union be fatally compromised? Could a recognition of the Confederacy thereafter be avoided?

Lincoln delayed decision, not from fear, but because he was watching Virginia. Jefferson Davis, too, was watching Virginia. The Old Dominion was a stake worth playing for. Her sons were the ablest officers in the United States Army, and her soil was almost certain to be the theater of any war between the sections. The 'panhandle' of western Virginia thrust a salient between Pennsylvania and Ohio to within 100 miles of Lake Erie. If Virginia seceded, she must carry North Carolina with her; and other states would probably follow.

Virginia showed her union sentiment in 1860 by voting for Bell rather than Breckinridge; but unionism in Virginia meant a voluntary association of sovereign states. A majority of the delegates to a Virginia state convention that met at Richmond in February were union men, but the secessionist minority was united, aggressive, and clever; it kept the convention in session week after week, until many unionist delegates left for their homes in the western part of the state. Delegations of unionist members besought Lincoln to let Fort Sumter go. Twice the President offered to do so if the Virginia unionists 'would break up their convention without any row or nonsense'; but they were not strong enough to promise that. Finally Lincoln came to see that to yield Fort Sumter would not bring the 'wayward sisters' back; and Virginia would join them the moment he raised his hand to strike. If Virginia would not accept the Union as it was, she must abide the consequences.

Toward the end of March Lincoln, determined to face the issue squarely, ordered a relief expedition to be prepared for Fort Sumter. Seward then showed his hand. On April Fools' Day 1861, he presented Lincoln with a paper, 'Thoughts for the President's Consideration.' The most startling proposal was that the United States should at once pick a quarrel with France and Spain, possibly with England and Russia as well, as a means of reuniting North and South for glory and conquest! And Lincoln was invited to appoint Seward his prime minister to execute this mad policy! Lincoln did not take him up on this wild proposal, but Seward pressed ahead. On 6 April, when the President ordered the Sumter expedition to sail, Seward by deception obtained Lincoln's signature diverting the capital ship of the expedition to Fort Pickens.

Jefferson Davis, who was also troubled by divided counsel, ordered General P. G. T. Beauregard to fire on Sumter only if absolutely necessary to prevent its reinforcement. On the night of 11–12 April Beauregard sent four staff officers to Fort Sumter demanding surrender. Major Anderson, a Kentuckian who loathed the idea of civil war, had no desire for the sort of fame that would come from being the occasion of it. Nothing as yet had been seen or heard of the relief expedition. So, at a quarter past three in the morning, he offered to surrender as soon as he might do so with honor—in two days' time, when the garrison's food would be exhausted. The Confederate staff officers peremptorily refused this reasonable stipulation, and on their own responsibility gave orders to open fire. For, as one of them admitted in later life, they feared that Davis would clasp hands with Seward, and the chance of war would slip away forever.

On 12 April 1861, at 4:30 a.m., the first gun of the Civil War was fired against Fort Sumter. The relief expedition appeared, but for lack of its capital ship was unable to pass the batteries. All day Major Anderson replied as best he could to a concentric fire from four or five Confederate forts and batteries, while the beauty and fashion of Charleston flocked to the waterfront as to a gala. At nine o'clock the next morning, 13 April, the barracks caught fire; in the early afternoon the flagstaff was shot away, and a few hours later, although his situation was by no means desperate, Major Anderson accepted terms of surrender. On the afternoon of Sunday, 14 April, the garrison marched out with drums beating and colors flying.

Walt Whitman caught the spirit of that occasion in his

Beat! beat! drums!—blow! bugles! blow!
Through the windows—through doors—burst like a ruthless force,
Into the solemn church, and scatter the congregation,
Into the school where the scholar is studying;
Leave not the bridegroom quiet—no happiness must he have now with his bride,
Nor the peaceful farmer any peace, ploughing his field or gathering his grain.
So fierce you whirr and pound you drums—so shrill you bugles blow.

Secession Completed

On 15 April President Lincoln issued a call for 75,000 volunteers to put down combinations 'too powerful to be suppressed by the ordinary course of judicial proceedings,' and 'to cause the laws to be duly executed.' Already the Virginian secessionists were organizing attacks on the Norfolk navy yard and the arsenal at Harpers Ferry. The state convention was in a state of high-strung emotion bordering on hysteria when Lincoln's call precipitated matters. On 17 April it voted, 88 to 55, to submit an ordinance of secession to the people. Without awaiting that verdict, the governor placed his state under Confederate orders.

The western part of Virginia refused to leave the Union;[7] but three more states did. Arkansas seceded on 6 May; Tennessee on 7 May concluded an alliance with the Confederacy, which a month later the people approved; North Carolina, having previously voted down secession, was in the impossible position of a Union enclave until 20 May, when she ratified the Confederate constitution. The attitude of Maryland was crucial, for her secession would isolate the Federal Government at Washington. The first Northern troops on their way to the capital were mobbed as they passed through Baltimore (19 April), but the danger of disunion in Maryland passed. In Kentucky, opinion was evenly divided, but by the end of the year the state threw in its lot with the Union. Missouri was practically under a dual regime throughout the war; Delaware never wavered in her loyalty. In California Unionists won a fierce struggle with Southern sympathizers; but California was too remote to give the Union cause other than pecuniary aid, in which she was generous. The Indians of the Indian Territory, many of them slaveholders, mostly threw in their lot with the South.

Before Lincoln's call for troops, a number of states in the Upper South had, in different ways, voted their sentiments against secession, but the Upper South was drawn to the Lower by a determination to keep that region a 'white men's country.' This emotion was rationalized by the theory that any state had a right to secede; hence Lincoln's call for coercion was illegal. And it forced the issue: everyone had to choose between defending the Confederacy or helping to put it down.

7. West Virginia was admitted as a state in 1863, but gave comparatively little aid to the Union cause.

Robert E. Lee (1807–70). His nobility of character has made him a hero not just of the former Confederacy but of the nation. 'I have met many of the great men of my time,' Viscount Garnet Wolseley observed, 'but Lee alone impressed me with the feeling that I was in presence of a man who was cast in a grander mold and made of different and finer metal than all other men.' (*Library of Congress, Brady Collection*)

Yet throughout the Civil War, lines were never strictly drawn between the states that seceded and those that did not. The majority of men went with their neighbors, as most people always do. But there were thousands who did not. The Confederate army contained men from every Northern state, who preferred the Southern type of civilization, and the United States Army and Navy contained loyal men from every seceded state, Americans who knew that the break-up of the Union would be the worst blow to the cause of self-government and republicanism since the day that Bonaparte assumed the purple. Samuel P. Lee commanded the Union naval forces on the James river while his uncle, General Robert E. Lee, was resisting Grant in the Wilderness. Senator Crittenden of the attempted compromise had two sons, Major General T. L. Crittenden, USA, and Major General G. B. Crittenden, CSA. Three brothers of Mrs. Lincoln died for the South, whilst near kinsmen of Mrs. Davis were in the Union army. In a house on West 20th Street, New York, a little boy named Theodore Roosevelt prayed for the Union armies at the knee of his Georgia mother, whose brothers were in the Confederate navy. At the same moment, in the Presbyterian parsonage of Augusta, Georgia, another little boy named Thomas Woodrow Wilson knelt in the family circle while his Ohio-born father invoked the God of Battles for the Southern cause.

Robert E. Lee abhorred the methods of the abolitionists, but agreed with them that slavery was wrong and emancipated his few inherited slaves. He did not believe in a constitutional right of secession, and severely criticized the action of the cotton states. In January 1861 Lee wrote to his son, 'I can contemplate no greater calamity for the country than a dissolution of the Union. . . . Still, a Union that can only be maintained by swords and bayonets, and in which strife and civil war are to take the place of brotherly love and kindness, has no charm for me.' To a cousin and brother officer of the United States Army, who determined to remain faithful to the flag, Lee expressed sympathy and respect. But, 'I have been unable to make up my mind to raise my hand against my native state, my relatives, my children and my home.' With deep regret Colonel Lee resigned his commission in the United States Army; a sense of duty induced him to accept a commission in the Confederate cause. What anguish that decision cost him we can never know. What it cost the United States we know too well.

17

The Civil War: An Overview

*

1861–1865

The Union and the Confederacy

From a distance of more than a century many wonder at the rash gallantry of the Southern war for independence. A loose agrarian confederacy of 5 or 6 million whites and 3.5 million slaves challenged a federal union of 19 or 20 million freemen with overwhelming financial and industrial advantages.[1] Yet, futile as the effort proved, the Southern cause was not predestined to defeat.

The Confederacy, in order to win, needed merely to defend her own territory long enough to weary the Northerners of war. The United States, in order to win, had to conquer an empire almost as large as the whole of western Europe and crush a people. A negotiated peace, or any less emphatic result than unconditional surrender of the Southern armies and total collapse of the Confederate government, would have meant some sort of special privilege to the Southern states within the Union, if not independence without the Union: in either event a Southern victory.

These considerations go a long way toward explaining the military advantages of the Confederacy. Since the South would be fighting on home soil, it had all the advantages of familiar terrain. The South was on the defensive, and it takes far larger armies and more formidable equipment to mount an offensive; the North would have to maintain long lines of communication deep into hostile territory. Furthermore, the South had an immense coastline, with innumerable inlets and harbors, and might expect to defy a Northern blockade and import military necessities. As Southerners were more inclined than Northerners to make a profession of arms, the officers with the longest experience were Southern. Finally, Southerners were convinced that 'Cotton was

1. By the census of 1860 the white population of the eleven seceded states was 5,449,467; the white population of the nineteen free states, 18,936,579. Both figures leave out of account the white population (2,589,533) of the four border slave states (Delaware, Maryland, Kentucky, and Missouri), which did not secede, but which probably contributed as many men to the Confederacy as to the Union. Subtracting the loyal regions of Virginia and Tennessee would reduce the Confederacy's white population to about 5 million. By the census of 1860 there were 3,521,111 slaves in the Confederate states, and 429,401 in the four border states, and from those the Union recruited about 100,000 troops.

King.' The Confederacy believed that Great Britain and France would be forced to intervene to stop the war or to aid the South in order to keep cotton supplies flowing across the Atlantic. In these circumstances there was a good reason to expect that the South would win. The Thirteen Colonies, the Netherlands, and in recent memory the South American and the Italian states had achieved their independence against great odds.

With the one crucial exception of slavery the moral scales seemed weighted in favor of the South. From their point of view, Southerners were fighting for everything that men hold dear: liberty and self-government, hearth and home. They could abandon the struggle only by sacrificing the very bases of their society; and defeat for them involved the most bitter humiliation. The Northern people, on the contrary, could have stopped the war at any moment, at the mere cost of recognizing what to many seemed an accomplished fact. They were fighting for the sentiment of Union, which, translated into action, seemed to tender souls scarcely different from conquest. Negro emancipation, itself an ideal, came more as an incident than as an object of the war. It was not the abolitionist 'Battle-Hymn of the Republic' that stirred the North in those years of trial, but the simple sentiment of:

The Union forever, hurrah! boys, hurrah!
Down with the traitor, up with the star,
While we rally round the flag, boys, rally once again,
Shouting the battle-cry of Freedom.

When we look to material factors, the position of the South was less favorable. In the secession winter, a Virginia editor had warned, with only some exaggeration, that so dependent was the South on Europe and the North that if secession came, 'we should, in all the South, not be able to clothe ourselves; we could not fill our firesides, plough our fields, nor mow our meadows.' New York state alone turned out manufactures worth four times more than the output of all the seceded states, and the North manufactured 97 per cent of the nation's firearms. The Union commanded an immense superiority in men, money, railroads, industrial potential, navy and merchant marine.

The Confederacy also labored under political disadvantages. Its constitution had one fateful flaw; it took seriously the dogma of state rights. Bounties, protective tariffs, and 'internal improvements' were forbidden. Federal officials and even judges could be impeached by the legislatures of the state in which their functions were exercised. No 'law denying or impairing the right of property in negro slaves' could be enacted by the Confederate Congress, and in all new territory acquired 'the institution of negro slavery' was protected. The executive branch proved to be distressingly weak. Nor were the other departments more successful. The pull of the army operated to discourage first-rate statesmen from service in the Confederate Congress. Finally, although the Confederate Constitution provided for a Supreme Court, this provision was never implemented, and the Confederacy fought the war without an effective judicial system.

The Southern Confederacy was weakened by faction and shaken by the vice of localism. Davis and most of the Southern leaders had been talking state rights but thinking Southern nationalism; yet many important men loved state rights more than Southern unity and feared a tyranny at Richmond no less than they had at Washington. No Union general ever had to write, as Lee did of the Lower South when contemplating an advance: 'If these states will give up their troops, I think it can be done.' The Confederacy suffered, too, from the absence of a two-party system, which could restrain petty personal politics and link leaders in state and nation.

At the outset of the war few doubted that Davis was abler than Lincoln. Lieutenant of dragoons, colonel of volunteers, congressman, senator, and Secretary of War, Davis brought to his post experience such as Lincoln had never had. Courage, sincerity, patience, and integrity were his; only tact, perception, humility, and inner harmony were wanting. Isolated from the Southern democracy out of which he had sprung, Davis moved as to the manner born among the whispering aristocracy of Richmond; yet he had a perverse knack of infuriating the gentlemen who tried to work under him, in part because of his meddling in military operations. An unstable amalgam, the Davis cabinet in four years had five attorneys-general and six secretaries of war. Nor did Davis win the affections of the plain people as Lincoln did. In the last years of the war his health and nerves gave way, and his state papers show an

Jefferson Davis (1808–89), President of the Confederate States of America. Carl Schurz, who met him when he was Secretary of War in the Pierce cabinet, recalled: 'His slender, tall, and erect figure, his spare face, keen eyes, and fine forehead, not broad, but high and well-shaped, presented the well-known strong American type. There was in his bearing a dignity which seemed entirely natural and unaffected—that kind of dignity which does not invite familiar approach, but will not render one uneasy by lofty assumption.' (*Library of Congress, Brady Collection*)

increasing querulousness which contrasts sharply with the dignity and magnanimity of all that Lincoln wrote.

At the beginning of Lincoln's administration the members of his cabinet showed scant respect for him. After the firing on Sumter, Seward assumed the role of premier—as he liked to be called, and several months elapsed before the President was really master in his own house. However, his feeling for the democratic medium in which he had to work, for its limitations, imperfections, and possibilities, proved to be akin to that of a great artist. If Lincoln was slow to direct the conduct of the war, he never faltered in his conception of its purpose: to preserve the Union. The Union, which for Hamilton was a panoply of social order, had become, in the hands of Jackson, Clay, and Webster, a symbol of popular government. Lincoln drove home this conception in his every utterance, and gave it classical expression in the Gettysburg Address. He made the average American feel that his dignity as a citizen of a free republic was bound up with the fate of the Union, whose destruction would be a victory for the enemies of freedom. Because Lincoln raised the Union standard at the beginning and kept it flying, the Union was preserved. Lincoln never forgot that those whom he liked to call 'our late friends, now adversaries' must, if his object were attained, become fellow citizens once more. He could never bring himself to contemplate the South with feelings other than sorrow and compassion.

The Two Armies

In military preparations the Confederacy had a start of several months. It secured many of the ablest officers of the United States Army then in active service—Lee, both Johnstons, Beauregard, J. E. B. Stuart, and A. P. Hill; as well as Thomas 'Stonewall' Jackson and D. H. Hill, who were teaching in Southern military colleges. While Virginia-born Winfield Scott and George Thomas and David G. Farragut of Tennessee remained loyal to the nation, most Southern officers went with their states. In the regular army of the United States—only 16,000 strong—many brilliant young officers like Philip Sheridan were confined to small units until late in the war. Until mid-April no attempt was made to enlarge or even to concentrate the small United States fleet, for fear of offending the Virginia unionists. In the meantime the Confederate States had seized the United States arsenals and navy yards within their limits, had obtained munitions from the North and from Europe, and had organized state armies; by the end of April 1861 President Davis had called for and quickly obtained 100,000 volunteers for twelve months.

Winfield Scott, general-in-chief of the United States Army, infirm in body but robust in mind, advised the President that at least 300,000 men, a general of Wolfe's capacity, and two or three years' time would be required to conquer even the Upper South. No one else dared place the estimate so high; Seward believed with the man in the street that one vigorous thrust would overthrow the Confederacy within 90 days. The President, in his proclamation of 15 April 1861, called for only 75,000 volunteers for three months. Militia regiments fell over one another in their alacrity to aid the government; within two weeks 35,000 troops were in Washington or on their way. The government should have taken advantage of this patriotic outburst to create a national army for the duration of the war. Instead, Lincoln on 3 May called for 40 more volunteer regiments of 1050 men each and 40,000 three-year enlistments in the regular army and navy, leaving the recruiting, organization, and equipment of all volunteer regiments to the states, as had been done in past wars.

As a basis for the new army, every Northern state had some sort of volunteer militia force which was mobilized for an annual 'muster' and 'Cornwallis' (sham battle)—usually not much better than a frolic. Many militia units volunteered en masse. But for the most part, the volunteer regiments that made up the bulk of the United States Army during the war were created on the spot. A patriotic citizen would receive a colonel's commission from his state governor, and raise and even equip a regiment by his own efforts and by those who expected to be officers under him. When the regiment was reasonably complete and partially equipped, it was forwarded to a training camp and placed under federal control. The Federal Government in practice had to respect state

Confederate soldiers. These are Richmond militiamen of the First Virginia Regiment. Notice the soldier (upper left) brandishing a bowie knife. (*Valentine Museum, Richmond, Virginia*)

appointments until they were found wanting in action; its own were scarcely better. This system did give an unmilitary country a stake in the war. But something better was wanted before a year had elapsed.

By much the same system was the first Confederate army raised, though the Southern respect for caste was more manifest. Indeed the first Southern armies were embarrassed by a plethora of officer material. J. E. B. Stuart remarked of one unit, 'They are pretty good officers now, and after a while they will make excellent soldiers too. They only need reducing to the ranks!' The Southern troops had the advantage of being accustomed to the use of arms—for every slaveholder kept weapons by him in case of insurrection, and the non-slaveholders were good marksmen. Both classes were lovers of horseflesh, and it was a poor white indeed who did not own a horse or a mule. Northern troops, unless from the West, had outgrown the hunting and horseback-riding frontier, and the Northern gentry had not yet adopted field sports or fox-hunting for recreation. Discipline, to which the more primitive individualistic Southerners were averse, soon outweighed these differences. The two armies became as nearly equal in fighting capacity, man for man, as any two in history; and they took an unprecedented amount of punishment. If the Confederates won more battles, it was due to their better leadership, which gave them tactical superiority on the field of battle, against the strategical superiority of their enemies on the field of operations. As the North had the greater immigrant population, it had a far larger proportion of foreign-born soldiers, in particular German, Irish, and Scandinavian.[2] Throughout the war the Union army was the better equipped in shoes and clothing, and more abundantly supplied with munitions. Yet though the Union at all times had greater fire power than the Confederacy, the South never lost a major battle for want of ammunition.

Lincoln had appealed to the states to raise 'three hundred thousand more' on 2 July 1862. The New York abolitionist James Gibbons responded with a song, 'We are coming, Father Abraham, three hundred thousand more,' but that was almost the only response; for the states, even by drafting from their own militia, produced but 88,000 men. Yet not until 3 March 1863 did Congress pass the first United States Conscription Act. The law was a travesty. All men between the ages of 20 and 45 had to be registered. As men were needed, the number was divided among the loyal states in proportion to population and subdivided among districts, giving credit for previous enlistments. In the first draft (1863) these credits wiped out the liability of most of the Western states, which had been most forward in volunteering. You could commute service in a particular draft upon payment of $300; or evade service during the entire war by procuring a substitute to enlist for three years—no matter if the substitute deserted the next day. The system was inequitable to the poor, and in the working-class quarters of New York the first drawing of names in 1863 was the signal for terrible riots. On 13 July the provost marshal was driven from his office by a mob of irate Irish-Americans, and for four days and nights marauders sacked shops, gutted saloons, burned mansions, and lynched or tortured Negroes who fell into their clutches. Not until troops poured into the city was order restored, after the loss of hundreds of lives.

Conscription provided only a very small proportion of the Union army. In the fall of 1863, of 88,000 men drafted in New York, only 9000 went into the army; more than 52,000 paid fees, the rest hired substitutes. As recruits were credited to the district where they enlisted, and not to that of their residence, several wealthy communities escaped the draft altogether by purchasing cannon-fodder in the poorer country districts. Professional bounty-brokers often induced the recruits they furnished to desert at the first opportunity and re-enlist elsewhere. 'Bounty jumpers' enlisted and deserted, ten, twenty, and even thirty times, before being apprehended. Federal officials were bribed to admit cripples, idiots, and criminals as recruits. The success of conscription, however, is not to be measured by the very small number of draftees or the large proportion of deserters, but by the number of volunteers obtained under pressure. Unquestionably the quality of both armies

2. And many foreign-born officers like the Germans Franz Sigel and Carl Schurz, the Irish generals Corcoran and Meagher, the French Philippe de Trobriand, and the Norwegian colonels Hans Christian Heg and Hans Mattson.

deteriorated as the war dragged on; but the men who followed Grant through the Wilderness compare well with any soldiers of modern times.

The slaves were, as Lincoln later said, 'somehow the cause of the war,' but at the beginning they were denied any part in it, as were free Negroes. It is not surprising that until the last days of the war Confederate authorities rejected all proposals to use slaves as soldiers, opening the door to freedom; but it is strange that for almost two years Washington followed much the same policy. Congress was so sensitive to the feelings of the border states, and so indifferent to those of the Negroes, that it refused to enlist even free blacks. And when slaves found their way to the Union armies in Virginia or Tennessee federal officers frequently returned them to their former owners. However, the irrepressible General Benjamin F. Butler decided upon a different course. Commanding in New Orleans in the summer of 1862, he found his ranks depleted and informed the Secretary of War, 'I shall call on Africa to intervene, and I do not think I shall call in vain.' Within a few weeks the First Regiment Louisiana Native Guards was mustered into the federal service. Soon there were Negro regiments in all theaters. The First South Carolina, recruited from fugitive slaves who had escaped to the sea islands, was commanded by the preacher-soldier Thomas Wentworth Higginson, whose *Army Life in a Black Regiment* is one of the classics of Civil War literature.

After the Emancipation Proclamation it was thought logical to let any and all Negroes into the ranks. About 180,000 Negro soldiers enlisted in the Union armies, and almost 30,000 served in the navy; most of these were recruited from among the free Negroes of the North. Boston witnessed the stirring spectacle of the 54th Massachusetts Infantry swinging down its flag-decked streets—William Lloyd Garrison in the reviewing stand—to the very wharf whence less than ten years earlier the fugitive Anthony Burns had been returned to slavery. Some 50,000 of the black soldiers, refugees from slavery, fought under special handicaps. As Higginson tells us:

> They fought with ropes around their necks, and when orders were issued that the officers of colored troops

Union volunteer, 1861, photographed by Mathew Brady. When on 15 April 1861, Lincoln issued a call for 75,000 volunteers, the response was overwhelming. In Iowa some men walked for ten days to reach the recruiting center, and twenty times as many volunteers offered themselves as could be accepted. Those who were rejected would not return home, and the state had to plead with Washington to expand its quota. (*Library of Congress, Brady Collection*)

The 107th U.S. Colored Infantry. (*Library of Congress*)

should be put to death on capture, they took a grim satisfaction. It helped their *esprit de corps* immensely.

Black soldiers took part in every theater of the war—at Battery Wagner guarding the harbor of Charleston, where Robert Gould Shaw fell at the head of his regiment; in the bayous of Louisiana; along the Missouri borderlands; and at Nashville, where they helped shatter Hood's command. In part because they were more susceptible to such diseases as dysentery and tuberculosis, their losses—66,000 deaths—were proportionately higher than those suffered by white troops.

Liberty in Wartime

Lincoln wielded a greater power throughout the war than any English-speaking ruler between Cromwell and Churchill. If Lincoln was the ideal tyrant of whom Plato dreamed, he was nonetheless a dictator from the standpoint of American constitutional law and practice. The war power of the President as commander-in-chief of the army and navy is, in practice, limited only by public opinion and the courts. At the very beginning of the war, Lincoln of his own authority called for enlistments not yet sanctioned by Congress, proclaimed the blockade, and suspended the writ of habeas corpus in parts of Maryland. The first assumption of power was shortly legalized by Congress, the second by the Supreme Court; but Chief Justice Taney protested in vain against executive suspension of the writ (*ex parte* Merryman). At the same time military officers, acting under orders from the state or the war department, began to arrest persons suspected of disloyalty or espionage, and to confine them without trial in military prisons for indefinite terms. Lincoln thought it unwise to indulge a meticulous reverence for the Constitution when the Union was crumbling. He asked, 'Must I shoot a simple-minded soldier boy who deserts, while I must not touch a hair of the wily agitator who induces him to desert?' Lincoln himself counseled moderation, but the power he wielded was grossly abused by subordinates.

Simultaneously with the Emancipation Proclamation, the President announced that all persons resisting the draft, discouraging enlistment, or 'guilty of any disloyal practice affording aid and comfort to rebels' would be subject to martial law, tried by court-martial, and denied the writ of habeas corpus. Under this proclamation, over 13,000 persons were arrested and confined by military authority, for offenses ranging from the theft of government property to treason. Earlier in 1862 President Davis, who was open to the same charge of behaving on occasion like a dictator, obtained from his Congress the power to suspend the writ of habeas corpus, and promptly did so in Richmond and other places, where arbitrary and unjust proceedings occurred.

Undoubtedly the provocation was great, especially in the North, where opposition to the war was open and active. The copperheads, as the Northern opponents of the war were called, worked ceaselessly to discourage recruiting and to hamstring the government. In the Confederacy, the 'Heroes of America' gave aid and comfort to the enemy. In Ohio, Indiana, and Illinois, where treason flourished side by side with the most stalwart loyalty, General Burnside attempted repression in 1863 with slight success. For violating Burnside's order against 'declaring sympathy for the enemy,' the prominent copperhead Clement Vallandigham was arrested, tried by a military commission, and sentenced to confinement for the duration of the war. Lincoln altered the sentence by having Vallandigham escorted within the military lines of the Confederacy. He received *in absentia* the Democratic nomination for governor of Ohio and conducted a campaign for peace and reunion from Canadian soil. In 1866 the Supreme Court took cognizance of a similar case (*ex parte* Milligan), and ruled that neither the Constitution nor any custom of war could sanction the military trial of a civilian in districts where the civil courts were open. But this decision, coming after the war, helped nobody.

Owing to unchecked acts of over-zealous military officers, personal liberty was subject to a more arbitrary, if spasmodic, control during the Civil War than during the two world wars. Yet on the whole pacifists, conscientious objectors, and critics of the government fared better under Lincoln than under Wilson, and the 'relocation' of Japanese-Americans in World War II was more outrageous than anything that happened under Lincoln. Throughout the Civil War there was no general censorship of the press, and hardly a Northern community lacked a few 'unterrified Democrats' who maintained with impunity that Jeff Davis was a better man than Abe Lincoln, secession was legitimate, and the Union forever dissolved.

Although in the field of civil and political liberties, the Confederate record was better than that of the Union, the habits of command bred in a slave society expressed themselves in aggravated form. Military commanders like General Braxton Bragg established martial law and ruled their areas with an iron hand. Hordes of provost marshals infested the land, demanding credentials from all who attracted their suspicion. Loyalty oaths were exacted indiscriminately—even from aliens—and neutrals and Unionists were badly treated. These practices, however, proved futile either to put down Unionism or arrest defeatism in the Confederacy.

Northern Industry and Westward Expansion

It was an article of faith among subjects of King Cotton that Northern industry, cut off from its Southern markets and its supply of fiber, would collapse. On the contrary, Northern industry grew fat and saucy during the war. Union sea power maintained the routes to foreign markets; the waste of war stimulated production. The government, generous in its contracts and lavish in expenditure, helped to create a new class of profiteers, who became masters of capital after the war.[3] The North, prepared to endure the deprivation of war, was startled to find it was enjoying a

3. The foundations of the Armour (meat packing), Havemeyer (sugar), Weyerhaeuser (lumber), Huntington (merchandise and railroads), Remington (guns), Rockefeller (oil), Carnegie (iron and steel), Borden (milk), and Marshall Field (merchandise) fortunes were laid during the war.

war-boom, an experience which would be a common phenomenon in the twentieth century. After the middle of 1862 enough cotton was obtained from the occupied parts of the South, and even brought from Liverpool, to re-open many cotton mills. Indeed the only essential Northern industry that suffered from the war was the carrying trade.

In many ways the war served as a stimulus to economic growth in the North. The drain of men into the army and navy was compensated for by immigration, which during the five war years amounted to almost 80,000, and labor-saving devices, invented before the war, were now generally applied. The Howe sewing machine proved a boon to the clothing manufacturer, though a curse to the poor seamstress, and the Gordon McKay machine for sewing uppers to shoe-soles speeded up that process one hundredfold and revolutionized the industry. Petroleum, discovered in Pennsylvania in 1859, developed so rapidly that kerosene lamps had begun to replace candles and whale oil by 1865. New industries sprang up to meet the army's insatiable demand for food: Gail Borden supplied condensed milk, the packing houses of Armour and Morris provided meat, and the Van Camp Company experimented with canned vegetables to frustrate the threat of scurvy.

Like causes speeded up the revolution in agriculture. The mechanical reaper came into general use, giving every harvest hand fivefold his former capacity with scythe and cradle. The annual pork pack almost doubled, the annual wool clip more than tripled between 1860 and 1865. The opening up of new prairie wheatfields was greatly stimulated by the Homestead Act of 1862, which supplemented the Pre-emption Act of 1841 by offering a settler title to 160 acres of public land after five years' residence and use, for a nominal fee. To be sure, the government disposed of most of the best prairie land to corporations and speculators and when the settler reached the Great Plains he usually found that if he wanted to buy a farm with fertile soil and that was near transportation he required to take his crops to market, he had to deal with a land jobber. Nonetheless, the wartime enactment did serve to expedite the advance of the trans-Mississippi frontier.

Development of the West continued. Colorado, the goal of the 'Pikes Peak or Bust' gold rush in 1859, was organized as a territory in 1861; and with the reorganization of Dakota and Nevada territories the same year, no part of the United States, on paper at least, was any longer outside the dominion of law. Kansas became a state in 1861; and Nevada was admitted prematurely in 1864, because the Republicans thought they needed its electoral vote. At least 300,000 emigrants crossed the plains during the war—some to farms, others to seek gold, and many to escape the draft.

The normal growth and activity of a civilized community carried on in the North. Enrollment in the universities hardly decreased beyond the loss of Southern students, although in some of the Western colleges the undergraduates enlisted in a body for short tours of service. Fifteen new institutions of higher learning, including Cornell University, Swarthmore College, and the Massachusetts Institute of Technology, were founded in wartime. The Harvard-Yale boat-races, interrupted in 1861, were resumed in 1864 while Grant was besieging Petersburg, and not a single member of either crew enlisted.

Paying for the War

To finance the war, Secretary Chase resorted to three methods: taxes, loans, and paper money. Congress doubled the customs duties, laid a direct tax of $20 million, and imposed numerous excise taxes. Most important for the future was the decision to levy an income tax. The merchant prince A. T. Stewart paid $400,000 on an income of $4 million, yet the income tax brought in only a meager $55 million during the entire war. And all taxes raised under $675 million in four years, less than the cost of one year of fighting. Inevitably Chase had recourse to borrowing. Altogether the government borrowed some $2.6 billion, enough to pay for three-fourths of the cost of the war. Secretaries Chase and Fessenden (who succeeded Chase when he went to the Supreme Court) relied on banks to take up most of their bonds on terms that brought rich rewards. Even at that Chase had difficulty in disposing of bonds until the Philadelphia banker Jay Cooke—who played a role analogous to that of Robert Morris in the Revolution—undertook to sell them directly to the public.

Casting about for a method of easy financing, Congress, in 1862, authorized the treasury to issue $150 million of legal tender. Before the war was over the treasury had issued some $450 million of these 'greenbacks.' Because they were not redeemable in gold, and the government itself refused to accept them in payment of customs duties, greenbacks speedily depreciated. In midsummer 1864 they fell to 39 on the gold dollar; and though they rose to 74 after Appomattox it was not until the treasury 'resumed' specie payments in 1879 that they finally reached par.

Chase's banking policy was more constructive. At the beginning of the war some 1500 banks with charters issued by 29 states operated under a bewildering variety of privileges and restrictions. No fewer than 7000 different kinds of bank notes were circulating, alongside another 5000 varieties of fraudulent notes. To bring some order out of this chaos, to provide a national currency, and to assure a regular market for government bonds, Chase recommended a national banking system. Under the National Bank Acts of 1863 and 1864 member banks were required to invest one-third of their capital in government bonds (on which they were paid a handsome interest); they could then issue notes up to 90 per cent of the value of these bonds (on which they could earn handsome profits). The scheme was useful to the government, profitable to the banks, and convenient to the public. Competition from state banks ended in 1865 when Congress taxed their notes out of existence, and by October 1865 over 1500 banks had joined the new national banking system.

The South in Wartime

Compared with the Union, the Confederacy was more nearly a nation in arms. During four years war was its only business. Fighting for independence and the supremacy of the white race, Southerners gave their government more, and asked of it less, than did Northern people. Yet the Southern cause met hostility and indifference too. In the mountainous regions of North Carolina and Tennessee no Confederate conscription officer dared show his face. Much more costly were the inveterate provincialism and widespread ignorance, the stiff-necked insistence on the rights of states and of social position, and withal a certain shrewd instinct on the part of the poor whites that it was 'a rich man's war and a poor man's fight.'

The history of conscription illustrates these attitudes. The Confederate system was, in theory, a mass levy of manhood between the ages of 18 and 35. Yet, instead of prompting solidarity, it fomented class antagonism and doubts about its constitutionality. There was no answer to Senator Foote's question, 'If agents of the Confederate Government had the right to go into any state and take therefrom the men belonging to that state, how were state rights and state sovereignty to be maintained?' The Chief Justice of North Carolina even discharged two deserters who killed a man when resisting capture, on the ground that a state had nothing to do with enforcing Confederate conscription! In Georgia, Governor Joseph E. Brown openly defied conscription, withholding Georgia soldiers for the defense of the state. A week before the fall of Atlanta, as Sherman poised for his march to the sea, Brown recalled 10,000 men he had 'loaned' to General Hood and sent them home for 30 days to harvest the crops. When the Confederate Congress exempted plantation overseers, at the rate of one to every twenty slaves, there arose a great clamor from the democracy. Deeply resented too was substitution, which was stopped toward the close of 1863 when the price of a substitute reached 6000 paper dollars. Though no Southern city was disgraced by draft riots like those of New York, fraud and evasion were widespread, and remoter districts were terrorized by armed bands of deserters and draft-dodgers who waged a successful guerrilla warfare against the troops sent to apprehend them.

Even when the South had resources it was rarely able to exploit them, and as Union armies penetrated ever more deeply, the resource base of the Confederacy shrank dangerously. Union advances imperilled food supplies and cut the Confederacy off from key cities like New Orleans. Inadequate railways also segmented the nation. At the outbreak of the war the Confederacy boasted some 9000 miles of rails, compared to 22,000 miles in the North, turned out only 4 per cent of the country's locomotives, and had in-

'The Walking Wounded' by Winslow Homer. In 1861 *Harper's Weekly* sent the twenty-three-year-old artist to the front, where he was appalled by what he witnessed. This drawing, in pen and brown ink on paper, James Thomas Flexner has observed, 'expressed horror with a spare misery of line that presaged the World War I protests of the Expressionist George Grosz.' (*Cooper-Hewitt Museum, Smithsonian Institution*)

adequate repair facilities. Through traffic hardly existed; at 'bottle-necks' like Knoxville, freight had to be carted from one station to another. Between Danville, Va., and Greensboro, N.C., a 40-mile gap interrupted a main line into the interior. Without an engineering tradition, the Confederacy was unable either to organize the transportation it had or to rebuild it when shattered. That is why there were bread riots in Richmond when the barns of the valley of Virginia were bursting with wheat.

The Confederacy also mismanaged finances. Deluded by faith in the indispensability of cotton, the government deliberately withheld its most valuable single asset from foreign markets, and restricted cultivation. Too late did the government change its policy and buy cotton for export or for security against foreign loans. The Confederacy raised only about one per cent of its revenue from taxation. Tax receipts did not exceed \$27 million, while expenditures ran to a couple of billion dollars. The gap between income and outgo was

Clara Barton (1821–1912), in a photograph by Mathew Brady. In 1862 she gained permission 'to go upon the sick transports in any direction, for the purpose of distributing comforts for the sick and wounded, and nursing them.' Though the 'Angel of the Battlefield' won renown for her courage under fire in ministering to the wounded, her significance lies less in her role as a nurse than as an organizer of relief. On returning from the Franco-Prussian war, where her service earned her the Iron Cross of Merit, she led a campaign that resulted in the establishment of the American Red Cross and became its first president. Her experience spanned much of the history of the republic, for her father fought under Mad Anthony Wayne and she lived well into the twentieth century. (*Library of Congress, Brady Collection*)

bridged by bonds and by treasury notes payable in gold on the acknowledgment of independence by the United States. By January 1864 Confederate paper was worth five cents on the dollar, and even before Lee's surrender it had become practically worthless. As a consequence of the resort to paper money and a shortage of certain staples, prices rose to fantastic levels: by 1864 flour was $500 a barrel. The government in vain tried to fix maximum prices, and blockade runners often imported luxuries for profiteers rather than necessities for the army. In desperation the Confederate government resorted to a form of confiscation, bitterly antagonizing the farmers on whom it bore unfairly.

After noting these many instances of selfishness, indifference, incompetence, and defeatism on both sides, we must remember that both the Union and Confederate governments were sustained by popular suffrage in 1862 and 1864, and that no earlier war in modern history drew out so much sacrifice, energy, and heroism. Vice-President Stephens divined the situation in 1863 when he wrote, 'The great majority of the masses both North and South are true to the cause of their side. . . . A large majority on both sides are tired of the war; want peace. . . . But as we do not want peace without independence, so they do not want peace without union.' The average American loathed army life and only acquiesced because of patriotism and social compulsion. Union soldiers sang 'When This Cruel War Is Over,' while their enemies in gray sang the equally sentimental 'Lorena,' and both rejected the 'fighting' ballads printed by patriots behind the lines. Yet both fought gallantly to the end.

Casualties

In the Union army 67,058 were killed on the field of battle, and 43,012 died from wounds; 224,586 died from disease and 25,566 more from accidents and miscellaneous causes—a total of 360,222. Confederate losses from battle probably reached 80,000 or 90,000 and deaths from disease 160,000 to 180,000.

Illness took an appalling toll from both armies. The average soldier was sick enough two or three times a year to be sent to a hospital, which was often more dangerous than the battlefield: deaths from disease were more than twice as high as deaths from battle—but we should remember that in the Mexican War the ratio was ten to one! Poor sanitation, impure water, wretched cooking, exposure, lack of cleanliness, and sheer carelessness exposed soldiers on both sides to dysentery, typhoid, malaria, and consumption—the chief killers. Care for the wounded was haphazard and callous: after Shiloh and Second Bull Run the wounded were allowed to lie for two or three days on the battlefields without relief. Antisepsis was unknown and anesthetics were not always available; abdominal wounds and major amputations meant probable death. Out of a total of 580 amputations in Richmond in two months of 1862 there were 245 deaths. Katherine Wormeley, later a distinguished literary figure, wrote of one of the hospital transports to which the wounded were brought during the Peninsular campaign:

> We went on board; and such a scene as we entered and lived in for two days I trust never to see again. Men in every condition of horror, shattered, and shrieking, were being brought in on stretchers borne by contrabands who dumped them anywhere, banged the stretchers against pillars and posts, and walked over the men without compassion. There was no one to direct what ward or what bed they were to go into. Men shattered in the thigh, and even cases of amputation, were shovelled into top berths without thought or mercy.

It was thought not quite respectable for women to nurse soldiers, and the armies relied at first on male nurses and orderlies, mostly untrained. The heroic Dorothea Dix was appointed Superintendent of Nurses at the beginning of the war, and over 3000 intrepid women volunteered to work under her, but the army did not welcome their services. Clara Barton, 'Angel of the Battlefield,' nursed the wounded. Confederate medical skill was no worse than that of the Union, but lack of drugs, anesthetics, and surgical instruments imposed pitiful difficulties and losses.

18

The Civil War: The Test of Arms

*

1861–1865

Terrain, Tactics, and Strategy

Civil War battles were fought in rough, forested country with occasional clearings—Antietam, Gettysburg, Fredericksburg, Shiloh, and Vicksburg were the only big battles in open country. The defending infantry is drawn up in a double line, the men firing erect or kneeling. Preceded by a line of skirmishers, the attacking force moves forward by brigade units of 2000 to 2500 men, covering a front of 800 to 1000 yards, in double rank; captains in the front rank, the other officers and non-coms in the rear to discourage straggling. Normally the attack moves forward in cadenced step and is halted at intervals to fire and reload—a slow business with old-fashioned muzzle-loading rifles—the enemy returning fire until one or the other gives ground. Occasionally the boys in blue, more often the boys in gray, advance on the double-quick, the former shouting a deep-chested 'Hurrah!', the latter giving vent to their 'rebel yell,' a shrill staccato hunting cry. An attack of this sort generally ends in a bayonet encounter; but both sides, ill-trained in bayonet work, prefer to club their muskets. There was slight attempt at concealment, and so little entrenchment until 1863 that the moments of actual combat were more deadly to officers and men than the battles of World War I; but as soon as contact was broken the men were comparatively safe. Between encounters, picket guards, and even whole units of men, fraternized.

Union strategy, aggressive by the nature of the cause, took a form dictated by the geography of the Confederate States. The Appalachians and the Mississippi river divided the Confederacy into three nearly equal parts: the eastern, western, and trans-Mississippi theaters of war. The most spectacular campaign came in that part of the eastern theater bounded by North Carolina, the Appalachians, the Susquehanna, and Chesapeake Bay. Here were the two capitals, Washington and Richmond, and between them a rough wooded country, crossed by numerous streams and rivers. Although destruction of the enemy's army, not occupation of the enemy's capital, is considered the proper object in warfare, in a civil war, especially, possession of the enemy capital is of immense moral value. The Union expended more effort in trying to capture Richmond than on all its

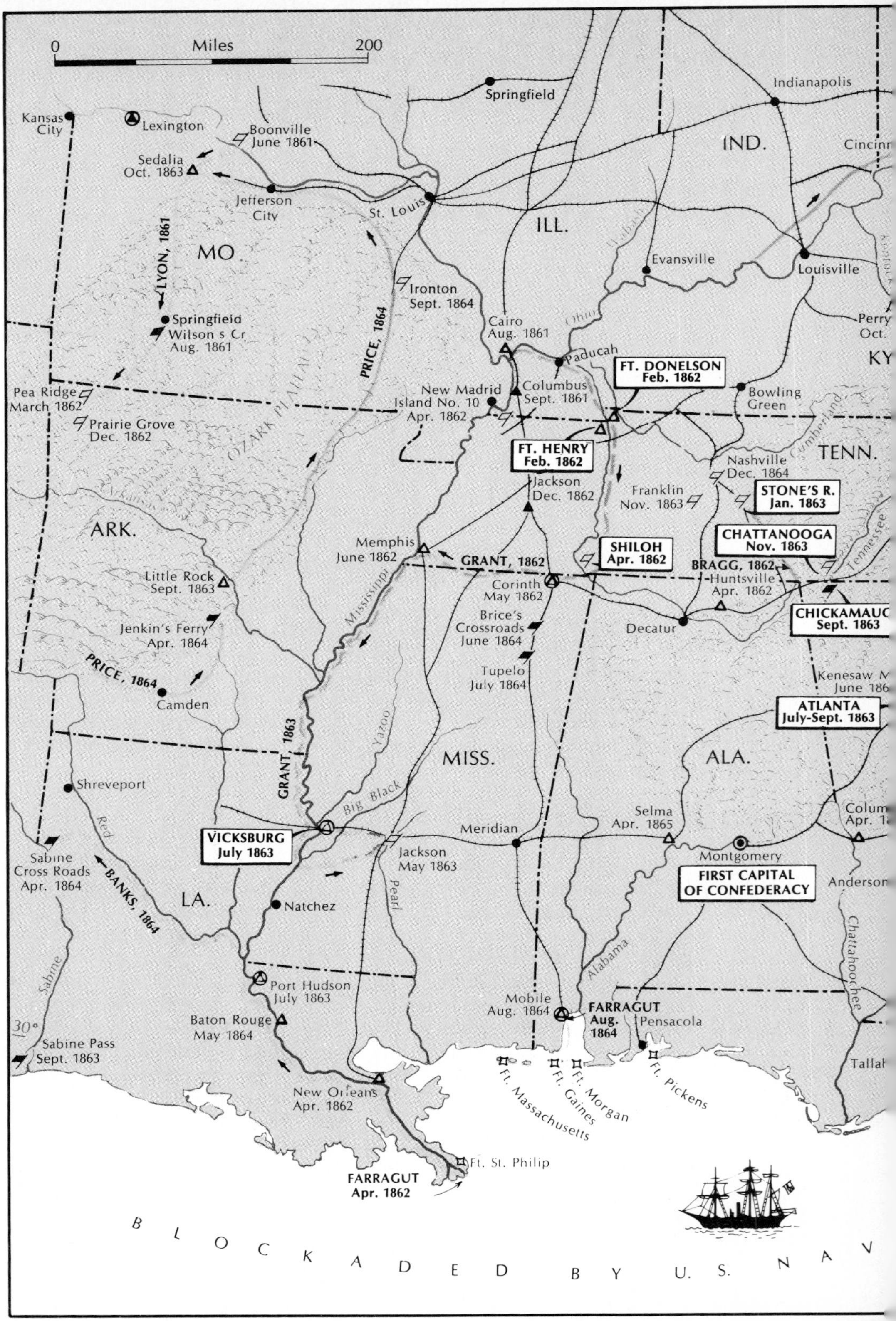

0 Miles 200
Springfield
Indianapolis
Kansas City
Lexington
Boonville June 1861
IND.
Sedalia Oct. 1863
Jefferson City
St. Louis
ILL.
LYON, 1861
MO
Evansville
Louisville
Ironton Sept. 1864
Springfield Wilson s Cr Aug. 1861
PRICE, 1864
Cairo Aug. 1861
Ohio
Paducah
Perry Oct.
FT. DONELSON Feb. 1862
OZARK PLATEAU
New Madrid Island No. 10 Apr. 1862
Columbus Sept. 1861
Bowling Green
Pea Ridge March 1862
Prairie Grove Dec. 1862
FT. HENRY Feb. 1862
Nashville Dec. 1864
Cumberland
TENN.
Jackson Dec. 1862
Franklin Nov. 1863
STONE'S R. Jan. 1863
Arkansas
ARK.
Memphis June 1862
GRANT, 1862
SHILOH Apr. 1862
CHATTANOOGA Nov. 1863
BRAGG, 1862
Huntsville Apr. 1862
Tennessee
Little Rock Sept. 1863
Corinth May 1862
Mississippi
Brice's Crossroads June 1864
Decatur
CHICKAMAUGA Sept. 1863
Jenkin's Ferry Apr. 1864
PRICE, 1864
Tupelo July 1864
Kenesaw M June 186
Camden
ATLANTA July-Sept. 1863
Yazoo
GRANT, 1863
MISS.
ALA.
Shreveport
Big Black
Selma Apr. 1865
Colum Apr.
Red
VICKSBURG July 1863
Meridian
Jackson May 1863
Montgomery
FIRST CAPITAL OF CONFEDERACY
Anderson
Sabine Cross Roads Apr. 1864
BANKS, 1864
LA.
Pearl
Natchez
Chattahoochee
Sabine
Alabama
Port Hudson July 1863
Mobile Aug. 1864
FARRAGUT Aug. 1864
Pensacola
30°
Baton Rouge May 1864
Sabine Pass Sept. 1863
Tallah
New Orleans Apr. 1862
Ft. Massachusetts
Ft. Gaines
Ft. Morgan
Ft. Pickens
Ft. St. Philip
FARRAGUT Apr. 1862
BLOCKADED BY U.S. NAV

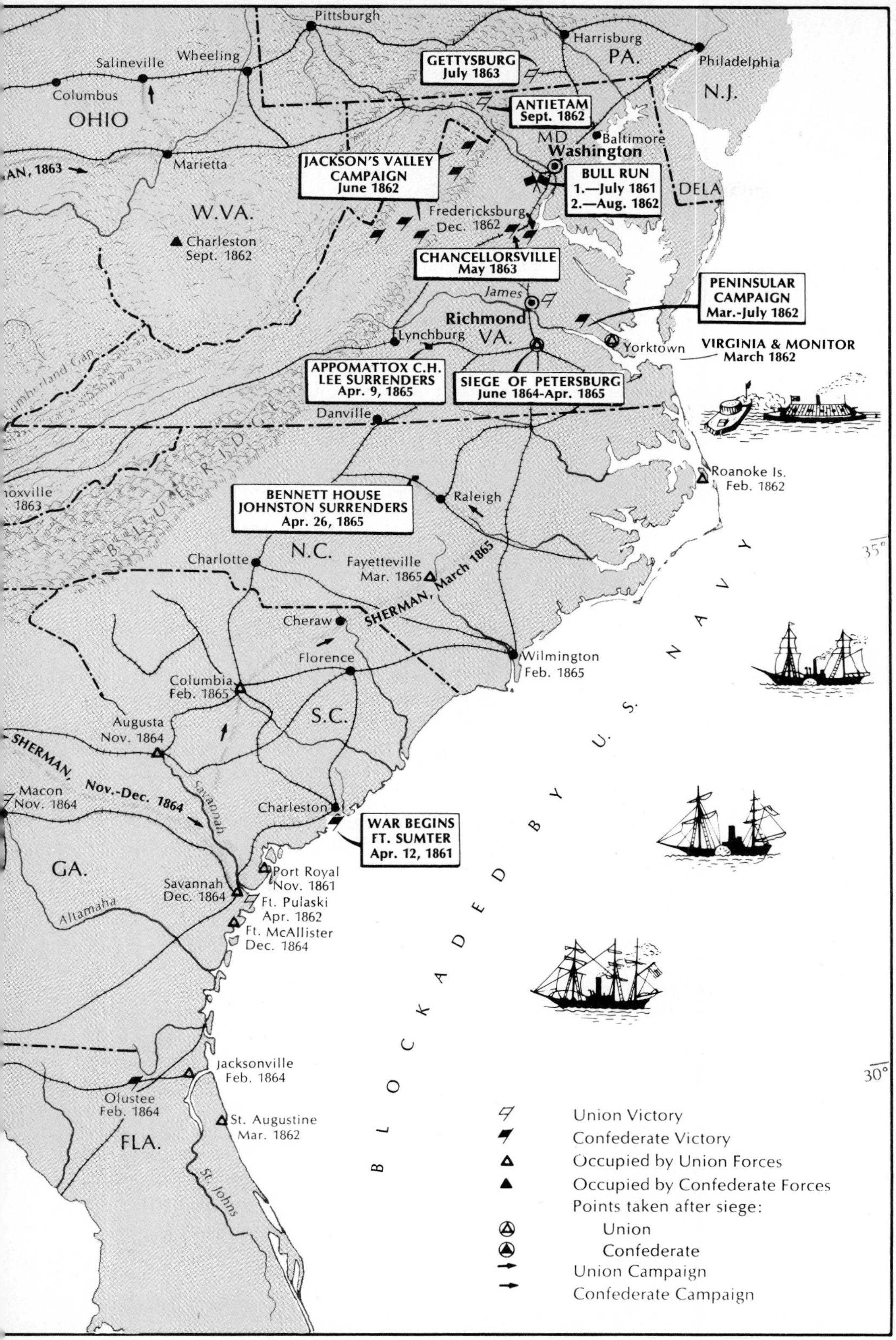

Pittsburgh
Harrisburg
PA.
Philadelphia
N.J.
Salineville
Wheeling
Columbus
OHIO
GETTYSBURG
July 1863
ANTIETAM
Sept. 1862
Baltimore
MD
Washington
AN, 1863
Marietta
JACKSON'S VALLEY
CAMPAIGN
June 1862
BULL RUN
1.—July 1861
2.—Aug. 1862
DELA
W.VA.
Charleston
Sept. 1862
Fredericksburg
Dec. 1862
CHANCELLORSVILLE
May 1863
James
PENINSULAR
CAMPAIGN
Mar.-July 1862
Richmond
Lynchburg
VA.
Yorktown
VIRGINIA & MONITOR
March 1862
Cumberland Gap
APPOMATTOX C.H.
LEE SURRENDERS
Apr. 9, 1865
SIEGE OF PETERSBURG
June 1864-Apr. 1865
Danville
BLUE RIDGE
Roanoke Is.
Feb. 1862
BENNETT HOUSE
JOHNSTON SURRENDERS
Apr. 26, 1865
Raleigh
N.C.
Charlotte
Fayetteville
Mar. 1865
SHERMAN, March 1865
35°
Cheraw
Florence
Wilmington
Feb. 1865
Columbia
Feb. 1865
S.C.
Augusta
Nov. 1864
SHERMAN,
Nov.-Dec. 1864
Savannah
Macon
Nov. 1864
Charleston
WAR BEGINS
FT. SUMTER
Apr. 12, 1861
GA.
Port Royal
Nov. 1861
Savannah
Dec. 1864
Ft. Pulaski
Apr. 1862
Altamaha
Ft. McAllister
Dec. 1864
BLOCKADED BY U.S. NAVY
Jacksonville
Feb. 1864
30°
Olustee
Feb. 1864
St. Augustine
Mar. 1862
FLA.
St. Johns
Union Victory
Confederate Victory
Occupied by Union Forces
Occupied by Confederate Forces
Points taken after siege:
Union
Confederate
Union Campaign
Confederate Campaign

The Civil War, 1861–1865

other operations combined, while the Confederacy in turn allowed its military strategy to be determined by the supposed necessity of defending its capital. In the retaliating threats to Washington, the Shenandoah-Cumberland valley, pointing like a long cannon at the heart of the Union, became the scene of dashing raids and military exploits. Military operations beyond the Mississippi had little effect on the result. But the western theater of war between the Mississippi and the Appalachians was as important as the eastern. Lee might perform miracles in Virginia, and even carry the war into the enemy's country; but when Grant and the gunboats had secured the Mississippi, and Sherman was ready to swing round the southern spurs of the Appalachians into Georgia, the Confederacy was doomed. Control of the sea was a priceless asset to the Union. The navy maintained communications with Europe, cut off those of the South, captured important coastal cities, and on the Western rivers—and as Lincoln put it, 'wherever the ground was a little damp'—co-operated with the army. A threefold task lay before the Union forces: constriction, scission, and defeat of the Southern armies. Both the nature and the magnitude of the task were imperfectly apprehended in 1861, except by Winfield Scott, whose 'anaconda policy' of constriction was dismissed as the ravings of an old fogey, but eventually adopted, in principle, by Grant.

The War in 1861

The Union plan for 1861 was to blockade the Southern coast and occupy strategic points along its edge; to mobilize a volunteer army in regions convenient for invading the South; and to capture Richmond. By July some 25,000 three-month volunteers were at Washington, spoiling for a fight, and the Northern press and people clamored for action. Against Scott's advice, President and cabinet yielded to the cry of 'On to Richmond.' General Irvin McDowell, with a 'grand army' of 30,000, crossed the Potomac to seek out Beauregard's army of some 22,000 near Manassas Junction, Virginia. A throng of newspaper correspondents, sight-seers on horse and foot, and congressmen in carriages came out to see the sport.

On 21 July McDowell attacked Beauregard near a small stream called Bull Run. The troops on both sides were so ill-trained, the officers so unused to handling large numbers, the opposing flags so similar, and the uniforms so varied that extraordinary confusion ensued. For hours it was anyone's battle, but the timely arrival of 9000 Confederate reinforcements and the stand of General Thomas Jackson (who thereby earned the sobriquet Stonewall) won the day. Union retreat turned to rout. All next day, soldiers straggled into Washington, dropping down to sleep in the very streets; rumors were flying that Beauregard was in hot pursuit, that the Capitol would be abandoned; treason was preached openly. But Lincoln did not flinch, and Beauregard did not pursue. 'The Confederate army was more disorganized by victory than that of the United States by defeat,' wrote General Johnston. There was no more talk of a 90-day war. From the dregs of humiliation the Union was nerved to prepare for a long war; while the South, believing her proved superiority would dissolve the Northern 'hordes' and procure foreign recognition, indulged in an orgy of self-applause.

At this point, on 24 July 1861, Lincoln summoned General McClellan to Washington and gave him command of the army in that department. George B. McClellan was only 34, a graduate of West Point on the eve of the Mexican War, in which he had distinguished himself. His subsequent business experience accustomed him to deal with large affairs; his personal magnetism and some easy successes in western Virginia made him a popular hero. The Northern states provided him plenty of three-year volunteers, Congress was generous with money and equipment, and the President supported him fully. No untried general in modern times has had such abundant means as McClellan enjoyed during the nine months that followed Bull Run; and few used them to so little profit when the time came to fight. McClellan's methodical mind, his appetite for work, and his attractive personality and genuine interest in his men were exactly the qualities needed to form an army from a mob. But he lacked perception of the democratic medium. His love of display, the French princes on his staff, frequent mention of 'my army,' a curt way with politicians, and his contempt for Lincoln seemed out of place in a republican soldier. ('Never mind,' said Lincoln of the affronts he received, 'I will hold McClellan's horse if he will only bring us success.') McClellan forever dreamed of the future in terms of self: victorious McClellan, dictator McClellan, President McClellan. Yet no Union general was so beloved by the untrained volunteers whom his talent turned into a superb instrument of war, the Army of the Potomac.

Weeks stretched into months, and 'All quiet along the Potomac' appeared so often in the headlines as to become a jest. When McClellan estimated the enemy's number at 150,000, the Confederate army in northern Virginia was less than 50,000 strong and wretchedly equipped. Still, Lincoln refused to let the politicians worry him into ordering an advance. In fact on 1 November he appointed McClellan general-in-chief of all the armies of the republic. But McClellan continued to mark time. 'If General McClellan does not want to use the army,' said the President, 'I would like to *borrow* it.' A mere victory, McClellan believed, would be indecisive; but one dramatic coup such as the capture of Richmond, if accompanied by satisfactory assurances as to slave property, would win back the South. 'I shall carry the thing *en grande*, and crush the rebels in one campaign,' he wrote his young and adoring wife. If McClellan's 'one big victory' concept was mistaken, his strategy of delay was correct. The Union needed to postpone offensives until its superior resources were organized for a war of attrition and constriction; the Confederacy needed to force an issue promptly.

On the Confederate side, Lee, and probably J. E. Johnston, had the right instinct of aggression; but they were overruled by President Davis's policy of defense and delay.

Naval Action

In naval strategy, the policy of constriction was so obvious that it was consciously applied from the first. On 19 April 1861, Lincoln proclaimed a blockade of the Southern ports. But the following day brought a naval counterpart to Bull Run. The navy yard at Norfolk, which the United States government had not reinforced for fear of offending Virginia, was captured without a blow by the troops of that state, together with enormous stores of ordnance, munitions, and the hull of the frigate *Merrimac*—promptly rebuilt and christened *Virginia*.

The navy department then awoke, and Gideon Welles gave the navy much more efficient direction than the army received. However, the problem of blockading 3550 miles of coastline seemed at first insoluble. Congress had begun to build a new steam navy in 1850; but as yet only 24 steamers had been placed in commission, and only two were actually available to guard the Atlantic coast in April 1861. Without waiting for Congress to assemble, the administration undertook a large construction program, and side-wheelers, screw steamers, clipper ships, tugboats, and even ferryboats were purchased. Before the end of the war the navy totaled almost 700 ships, manned by over 50,000 seamen. And in David Glasgow Farragut, with 50 years of service, the nation found a naval hero in the tradition of John Paul Jones.

It was a paper blockade for two or three months and not wholly effective for more than two years; but by the end of July 1861 four blockading squadrons were stationed off the seven or eight enemy ports that were commercially important. About 800 vessels entered and cleared from Confederate ports during the first year of the blockade; but the last year of peace had seen more than 6000. In the last half of 1861 the navy captured Cape Hatteras and Hilton Head on the sea islands off Port Royal, S.C., the only important Union victory of that year.

The achievement of the hastily improvised Union navy on inland waters was no less important. Mississippi and Ohio river steamboats were converted to transports for Union campaigns, and Western energy and ingenuity created an effective fleet suited to the special needs of Western warfare. James B. Eads, an engineering genius from St. Louis, launched a fleet of armored gunboats, and Charles Ellet built a fleet of ironclad rams which, in the summer of 1862, destroyed the entire Confederate river defense fleet guarding Memphis and captured that city. Captain Andrew H. Foote, commander of naval operations on the

The intrepid Confederate blockade-runner *Nashville* sets afire the *Harvey Birch*, a captured Union merchant vessel, in the English Channel. (*Peabody Museum of Salem*)

Mississippi, built some 40 mortar-boats. These ugly little rafts carrying mortar-guns capable of hurling a 230-pound shell over two miles did terrible damage to the river towns that stood high on the bluffs above the Mississippi.

The Attitude of Europe

The British and French had an avid interest in the Civil War. They divided, on the whole, along class lines. The plain people of Europe for the most part were convinced that destruction of the Union would be a mortal wound to democracy. To the ruling classes, however, the United States had long been obnoxious for the encouragement its success afforded to radicals and democratic reformers. 'An involuntary instinct, all-powerful and unconquerable,' wrote the Comte de Montalembert, 'at once arrayed on the side of the pro-slavery people all the open or secret partisans of the fanaticism and absolutism of Europe.' Many Englishmen even outside that category favored the South for, as Henry Adams wrote, 'the English mind took naturally to rebellion—when foreign.' Most liberals supported the North, but some, like the historian Lord Acton, could see no difference between the Southern struggle for independence and the nationalist movements in

Europe with which they had sympathized. Humanitarians, who would have welcomed a war against slavery, were put off for nearly two years by the repeated declarations of Lincoln and Seward that slavery was not the issue. Shipping interests hoped for the ruin of their most formidable competitor and approved a new cotton kingdom for which they might do the carrying trade. However, the efforts of statesmen like Bright and Cobden, intellectuals like John Stuart Mill, and American emissaries such as Henry Ward Beecher and Archbishop Hughes, as well as the march of events, rallied British opinion eventually to the support of the Union.

Southern expectations of victory were based in good part upon the belief that Britain and France would break the blockade to get cotton. By the decade of the 1850's over 80 per cent of British cotton came from America. No wonder Senator Hammond of South Carolina could boast that 'you dare not make war upon our cotton. No power on earth dares make war upon it. Cotton is King.' Yet, as it turned out, this was short-sighted. By April 1861 there was a 50 per cent oversupply of cotton in the English market. Furthermore Britain was able to get cotton from Egypt and India. So instead of demanding intervention to get more cotton, the big textile interests of England and France welcomed the opportunity to work off surplus stocks and to free themselves from dependence on the American supply. It was the workingmen of Lancashire and Yorkshire who suffered most from the cotton blockade; by the winter of 1862 some 330,000 operatives were out of work. The South had assumed that these would join with the manufacturers in demanding that Britain break the blockade, but they rallied instead to the support of the Union. That winter the workingmen of Manchester assured President Lincoln that 'our interests are identified with yours. . . . If you have an ill-wishers here, be assured they are chiefly those who oppose liberty at home, and that they will be powerless to stir up quarrels between us.' Moreover, the Civil War years saw poor wheat and corn harvests in Europe and exceptionally good harvests in the United States. If Britain's looms depended on Southern cotton, her dinner tables depended on American grain; British imports of American wheat rose from 17 million bushels in 1860 to 62 million in 1862. It was evident that any attempt to break the blockade, and consequently fight the United States, would bring the British Isles face to face with starvation. 'Old King Cotton's dead and buried, brave young Corn is King,' went the refrain of a popular song.

The South also ignored the traditional British doctrine of naval warfare. As Lord John Russell wrote, the American blockade satisfied principles that the Royal Navy had always observed; and in view of England's dependence on sea power, it would be highly imprudent for her to insist on different principles which might hamper her in the future. Lord Palmerston's government issued a proclamation on 13 May 1861 which declared 'strict and impartial neutrality' in the contest between 'the Government of the United States of America and certain states styling themselves the Confederate States of America.' This proclamation was greatly to the advantage of the Union, but its unprecedented mention of a rebel government by its chosen name seemed unfriendly to the North and raised false hopes of recognition in the South. In fact the British position was, and remained throughout the war, technically correct. There was no recognition of the South; Southern emissaries were never officially received; and delivery of ships built or under construction in British shipyards for the Confederacy was stopped—on protest from the American minister.

Yet there were episodes that threatened a serious break. The first was the *Trent* affair. The British mail steamer *Trent* was conveying to Southampton two Confederate diplomatic agents, J. M. Mason and John Slidell, when on 8 November 1861 she was boarded from the U.S.S. *San Jacinto,* Captain Charles Wilkes commanding, and the two Confederates seized and jailed. When the news reached England, the British clamored for a showdown, the government sent reinforcements to Canada, and Lord John Russell drafted a demand for apology and reparation in terms so offensive as to be unacceptable. Fortunately Prince Albert, then in his last illness, toned down Russell's dispatch, and Queen Victoria made it clear that she wanted peace. And by a notable dispensation of Providence the Atlantic cable had ceased to function. Seward from the first saw that Mason and Slidell must be surrendered; but Lincoln, fearing the political effect of yielding to Britain, required persuasion. Seward's note to the British minister, designed more to placate the American public than the British, contained no apology; but Mason and Slidell were released and forwarded to their uncomfortable posts. In the end the *Trent* episode cleared the air. Seward now appeared in the new role of conciliator—and found that he liked it; an Anglo-American war had been faced and ruled intolerable to both governments; and the British cabinet was stiffened in its policy of neutrality.

Plans and Personalities

Day by day McClellan's inaction increased Lincoln's political difficulties. The united spirit forged by the guns that fired on Fort Sumter had disintegrated. Lincoln was challenged in his own party by conservatives and by the radicals led by 'Ben' Wade, 'Zach' Chandler, and 'Thad' Stevens. A diverse group which differed on many issues, the Radicals were united in their hatred of the insolent slave power. By their zeal they helped transform the war from a struggle to put down an insurrection to a crusade for human rights, but their politics were often maladroit and even nasty. The policy they wished to force upon the President was immediate emancipation and arming of the slaves—a policy which, if adopted in 1861, would have alienated the Northern Democrats and driven the border slave states into secession. General Frémont's pretense to free the slaves in Missouri by proclamation, an act which Lincoln sternly rebuked, received their hearty approbation, whilst McClellan, even more conservative than Lincoln on the slavery question, was the particular object of their jealousy and suspicion.

To the Radical standard surged the uncompromising, who dominated the Joint Committee on the Conduct of the War created by Congress on 20 December 1861. Throughout the war their inquisitorial activities, *ex parte* investigations, and missions to the front hampered the executive, undermined army discipline, and encouraged less

Ulysses S. Grant (1822–85). Critics disparaged his slovenly appearance, and when he came to Washington in 1864 to confer with the President he seemed to Richard Henry Dana 'a short, round-shouldered man, in a very tarnished . . . uniform . . . no station, no manner . . . and rather a scrubby look withal.' But Lincoln said, 'I can't spare this man. He fights.' (*National Archives, Brady Collection*)

competent generals. Yet the Radicals differed in one crucial respect from Jefferson Davis's gadflies. While Davis's opponents often valued particularist interests more highly than winning the war, the Radicals energetically supported the war and indeed wished to enlarge its aims.

Owing to the efforts of another House committee, corruption on a gigantic scale was uncovered in the war department, and the scandal smirched Secretary Cameron. Lincoln sent him on a foreign mission and appointed a 'War Democrat,' Edwin M. Stanton, Secretary of War. Gloomy, ill-mannered, and vituperative, Stanton was another cross for Lincoln to bear. Ignorant of military matters and contemptuous of military science, intolerant of delay and harsh to subordinates, he was hated by almost every officer with whom he came in contact; and with several he dealt injustly. Yet for all that, Stanton's determination and thoroughness made him a fit instrument for Lincoln's purpose.

The first substantial victory for the Union came in an unsuspected quarter, from an unknown general. Ulysses S. Grant, an officer who disliked war and loathed army routine, had fallen on evil days since the proud moment before Mexico City. After promotion to a captaincy he resigned from the army to avoid a court-martial for drunkenness. Unable to extract a living from 'Hardscrabble Farm' near St. Louis, he attempted to sell real estate, and failed again. His father bestowed a clerkship in the family leather store at Galena, Illinois. Brothers condescended, fellow townsmen sneered. Only after many rebuffs did he obtain a colonelcy of volunteers in 1861. His regiment was promptly ordered to dislodge a Confederate regiment under a Colonel Harris. Approaching the reported position, so Grant relates, fear gripped his heart; but he had not the moral courage to halt and consider what to do. Suddenly there opened a view of the enemy's encampment—abandoned! 'It occurred to me at once that Harris had been as much afraid of me as I had been of him. This was a new view of the question I had never taken before; but it was one I never forgot afterwards.'

In August 1861 Grant received a brigadier's commission and in late autumn was stationed at Cairo, Ill., at the junction of the Ohio with the Mississippi. Less than 50 miles up the Ohio from Cairo the Tennessee and Cumberland rivers opened parallel routes into Tennessee, Alabama, and Mississippi. Grant observed that capture of Fort Henry and Fort Donelson, the two Confederate earthworks which closed these rivers, would open navigable waterways into the enemy's center and drive in his flanks. On 7 February 1862 a gunboat flotilla reduced Fort Henry. A week later, Grant made exactly the right tactical disposition in the fierce battle to wrest control of Fort Donelson. The result justified Grant in asking and the Confederate generals in agreeing to 'unconditional surrender'[1] of army and fortress. Grant had practically restored Tennessee to the Union; and, if his victory were followed up, the whole area would be open from Chattanooga to the Mississippi. Equally important was the moral gain to the then dispirited North. The prairie boys of the new Northwest had tried their mettle, and the legend of Southern invincibility collapsed.

But 'Unconditional Surrender' Grant's jealous and pedantic superior, General Halleck, instead of allowing him to pursue Albert Sidney Johnston, held up his advance and withdrew his troops to attack the northernmost Confederate strongholds on the Mississippi. On 6 April Johnston caught Grant napping, encamped in an ill-chosen position at Pittsburg Landing. His rear to the swollen Tennessee and his front unprotected by entrenchments, Grant had the Battle of Shiloh forced upon him. If the Union army was not routed in the first twelve hours, it was due less to Grant's steadfast coolness than to the fiery valor of divisional commanders like William Tecumseh Sherman and to the pluck of individual soldiers. By the end of the day the Confederates had captured a key position and thousands of stragglers were cowering under the bluffs. But Albert Sidney Johnston was mortally wounded, leaving the Confederates leaderless. After ten hours of desperate fighting the next day, the Confederate army withdrew.

Shiloh was a Union victory at a dreadful price. Out of 63,000 Union troops, the loss was 13,000; the Confederates lost 11,000 out of 40,000. Pres-

1. Actually it was the astonishing Ben Butler, at Hatteras Inlet in August 1861, who first used this term, which has become a controversial one since World War II.

Sailors on the deck of the U.S.S. *Monitor,* James river, Virginia, July 1862. The cylindrical structure is the revolving gun turret, which was introduced in the first battle between armored naval vessels four months before when the *Monitor* encountered C.S.S. *Virginia,* formerly U.S.S. *Merrimac,* at Hampton Roads. (*Brady Collection, Library of Cogness*)

sure was put upon the President to remove Grant, but Lincoln replied: 'I can't spare this man; he fights.' However, Halleck took command of his army in person, and in consequence little more was accomplished by the army during 1862 in this western theater of the war.

While Halleck temporized, Captain Farragut had to force his way up the Mississippi from the Gulf without a single ironclad, but in the small hours of 24 April Farragut's column of eight steam sloops-of-war and fifteen wooden gunboats, with chain cables secured as a coat of mail abreast the engines, crashed through a log boom and ran a gantlet of armored rams, fire-rafts, river defense fleet, and two forts. Two days later United States forces took possession of New Orleans, largest and wealthiest city of the Confederacy. Farragut then proceeded up-river to join the gunboat fleet above Vicksburg. But as Halleck could not be induced to provide troops for a joint attack on Vicksburg, that 'Gibraltar of the Mississippi' held out for a year longer, enabling Richmond to maintain communication with Arkansas, Missouri, and Texas.

The Confederacy was tightly pinched along its waistline; but the blood could still circulate. Thanks to the fumbling of Halleck the Union offensive in the West had failed in its great purpose, yet thanks chiefly to Grant it accomplished much of value. That was more than could be said of the grand campaigns of this year in the eastern theater of war.

The Peninsular Campaign

'In ten days I shall be in Richmond,' declared General McClellan on 13 February 1862. It was one of those rash boasts that made men doubt either his judgment or his sincerity. All he actually did was march his men to the deserted Confederate headquarters at Manassas, which he found abandoned, then march them back again to Washington. For Lincoln this was all but the last straw. Still, when McClellan proposed a wide flanking movement by the York peninsula, the President reluctantly acquiesced. But he stripped McClellan of his superior command and left him with forces inadequate for his ambitious plans. Nonetheless, the Army of the Potomac, well armed and 110,000 strong, was greatly superior to anything the Confederacy could organize.

McClellan's peninsular plan had one obvious advantage, that it enabled the Union army to be supplied and reinforced by sea. The navy could protect the army's right flank as it advanced up the peninsula. On its left flank the James was a better line of approach; but C.S.S. *Virginia* (ex U.S.S. *Merrimac*) closed it to the Union navy during the first weeks of the campaign. The *Virginia* met her equal in the *Monitor* in Hampton Roads on 9 March 1862, when a new principle of naval armament, the revolving turret, proved its worth. But so long as the *Virginia* was afloat she protected the mouth of the James.

McClellan intended to take Richmond and crush the rebellion that summer. Splendid visions were in his brain. Himself, on prancing charger, entering Richmond in triumph. Magnanimous terms to the gallant enemy: civil rights restored, slave property guaranteed. Discomfited administration not daring to refuse ratification. Grand review at Washington. Modest savior of his country resigns sword to Congress and returns to wife and baby at Cincinnati. Nominated by acclamation for President in 1864. Yet he did not employ the only methods that had the slightest chance of realizing these dreams: mobility and dash. His caution allowed the Confederates to withdraw in good order to the defense of Richmond.

Still it was difficult to see how Richmond could be saved. McClellan with over 100,000 men would soon be advancing up the York peninsula, and J. E. Johnston had less than 60,000 to oppose him. McDowell with 40,000 was before Fredericksburg with only 11,000 Confederates between him and McClellan's right flank. The repulse of Stonewall Jackson near Kernstown had apparently corked up the Shenandoah valley. Frémont with 15,000 was approaching the upper valley through the Appalachian passes, where only 3000 Confederates faced him. Upon Lee's advice President Davis on 16 April adopted the strategy of delaying McClellan until Jackson could frighten the Union government into recalling McDowell's corps from its advanced position. On the same day the Confederate Congress adopted conscription. Of doubtful constitutionality, this courageous act drove a wedge between Davis and his state-rights critics, who feared that their precious theory was being done to death in the house of its friends. But conscription retained in the ranks the men who saved Richmond.

By 14 May McClellan was within three days' march of Richmond. Lee, instead of recalling the scattered legions of the Confederacy to her capital, had the audacity to use Jackson to break up McClellan's plans by threatening Washington. Jackson returned to the upper valley, got around behind Banks, crushed his outposts (Front Royal, 22 May), administered a stinging defeat at Win-

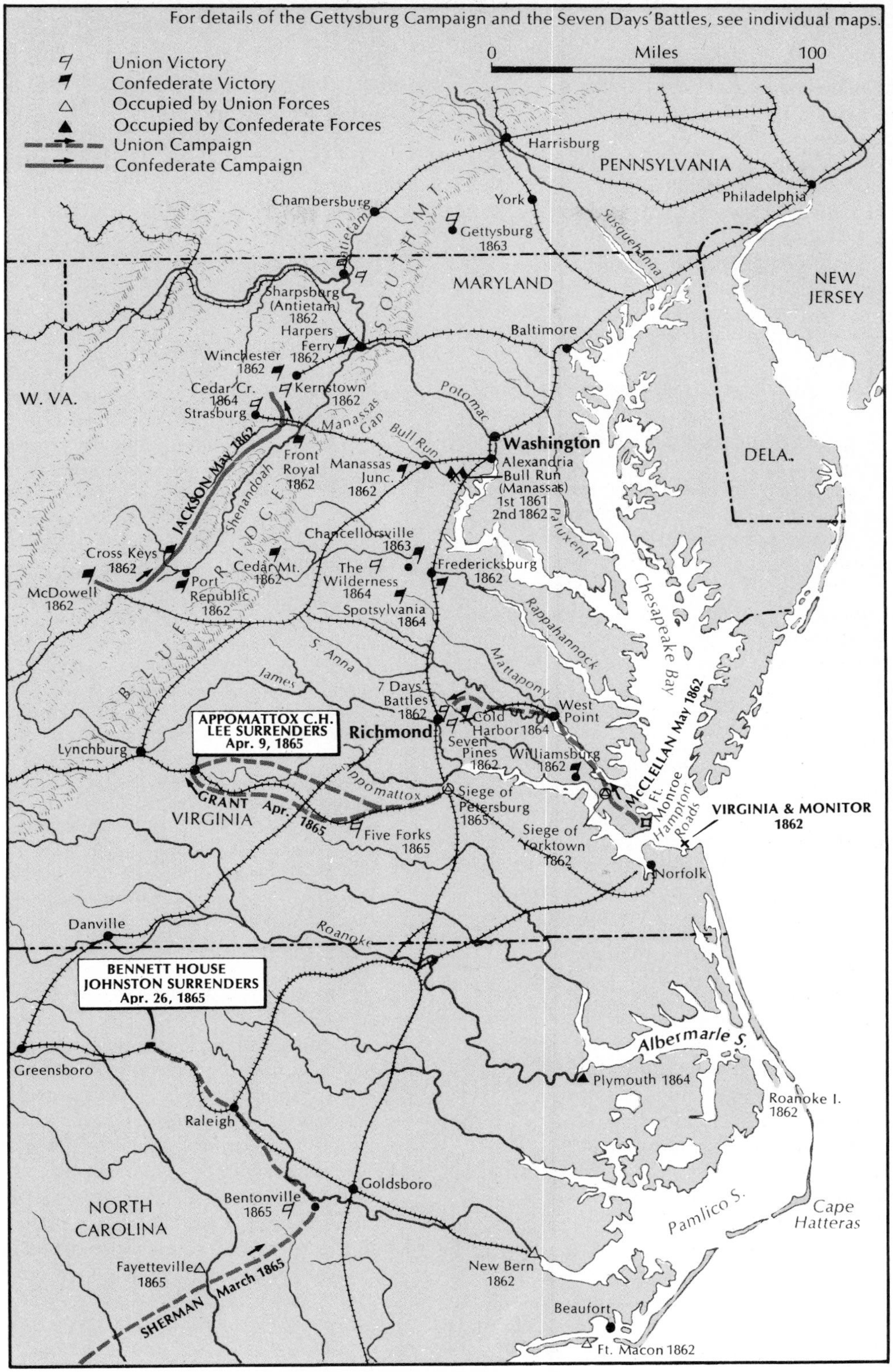
For details of the Gettysburg Campaign and the Seven Days' Battles, see individual maps.
Union Victory
Confederate Victory
Occupied by Union Forces
Occupied by Confederate Forces
Union Campaign
Confederate Campaign
0 Miles 100
Harrisburg
PENNSYLVANIA
Philadelphia
York
Chambersburg
Gettysburg 1863
SOUTH MT.
Antietam
Susquehanna
MARYLAND
NEW JERSEY
Sharpsburg (Antietam) 1862
Harpers Ferry 1862
Baltimore
Winchester 1862
Kernstown 1862
Cedar Cr. 1864
Strasburg
W. VA.
Potomac
Manassas Gap
Bull Run
Washington
Alexandria
Bull Run (Manassas) 1st 1861 2nd 1862
DELA.
JACKSON May 1862
Front Royal 1862
Manassas Junc. 1862
Shenandoah
BLUE RIDGE
Patuxent
Chancellorsville 1863
Cross Keys 1862
Cedar Mt. 1862
The Wilderness 1864
Fredericksburg 1862
McDowell 1862
Port Republic 1862
Spotsylvania 1864
Rappahannock
Chesapeake Bay
S. Anna
Mattapony
James
7 Days' Battles 1862
West Point
APPOMATTOX C.H.
LEE SURRENDERS
Apr. 9, 1865
Richmond
Cold Harbor 1864
Seven Pines 1862
Williamsburg 1862
McCLELLAN May 1862
Lynchburg
Appomattox
Siege of Petersburg 1865
Ft. Monroe
Hampton Roads
VIRGINIA & MONITOR 1862
GRANT Apr. 1865
VIRGINIA
Five Forks 1865
Siege of Yorktown 1862
Norfolk
Danville
Roanoke
BENNETT HOUSE
JOHNSTON SURRENDERS
Apr. 26, 1865
Albemarle S.
Greensboro
Plymouth 1864
Roanoke I. 1862
Raleigh
Goldsboro
Bentonville 1865
NORTH CAROLINA
Pamlico S.
Cape Hatteras
Fayetteville 1865
SHERMAN March 1865
New Bern 1862
Beaufort
Ft. Macon 1862

The Eastern Theater of War, 1862–1865

chester, and sent him whirling north to the safe side of the Potomac (25 May). Washington was panic-stricken by Jackson's rapid advance, although shielded by double his numbers. Lincoln did exactly what Lee intended him to do: on 25 May he recalled McDowell's corps, on the point of marching to join McClellan. Jackson, after winning successive victories on 8 and 9 June, was then ready to transfer his army to the Richmond front, while large Union forces remained immobile in the valley to protect Washington from another attack of nerves.

After this Battle of Fair Oaks (or Seven Pines), McClellan dug himself into a stronger position and waited for fair weather to advance on Richmond under cover of superior artillery. On 1 June Robert E. Lee succeeded Johnston, who had been wounded, and named his force the Army of Northern Virginia. He saw that McClellan must win Richmond if he were permitted to choose his own 'species of warfare' and that the closing cordon must be broken. Lee seized the offensive and threw McClellan upon the defensive.

On 26 June Lee took the initiative, and the great Seven Days' battles[2] began. Lee's strategy was superb, but too ambitious for his army to execute. McClellan, outnumbered in effective force at the beginning of the Seven Days, inflicted a superior loss on his adversaries[3] and executed a brilliant withdrawal to the James river. To be sure, he had to give up his cherished plan to capture Richmond. Yet his army was still full of fight and ready to resume the advance on Richmond if properly reinforced. The summer was still young. McClellan entreated Lincoln to give him an opportunity to attack Richmond via Petersburg. But General Halleck (who had replaced Stanton in control of operations) pronounced this plan, by which Grant subsequently brought the war to an end, impracticable; and Lincoln feared he could no longer carry McClellan. The country could see nothing except that Richmond was still in rebel hands after a costly campaign. Accordingly, on 3 August, Halleck ordered the Army of the Potomac back to the river that gave it birth; and all the gains of the Peninsular campaign were thrown away. Not for over two years did another Union army approach so near Richmond.

2. Mechanicsville (26 June), Gaines's Mill or first Battle of Cold Harbor (27th), Savage Station (29th), Frayser's Farm or Glendale (30th), Malvern Hill (1 July).

3. Union effectives engaged, 91,169; Union loss (killed, wounded, and missing), 15,849. Confederate effectives engaged, 95,481; Confederate loss, 20,614. T. L. Livermore, *Numbers and Losses*, p. 86.

The Emancipation Proclamation

For Lincoln the slavery question was complicated. He always remembered what it seemed all the world had forgotten, that he was President of the United States—not of the Northern States. His policy was explained in a letter to Horace Greeley, editor of the New York *Tribune*, of 22 August 1862:

> As to the policy I 'seem to be pursuing,' as you say, I have not meant to leave any one in doubt. I would save the Union. I would save it the shortest way under the Constitution. The sooner the national authority can be restored, the nearer the Union will be 'the Union as it was.' If there be those who would not save the Union unless they could at the same time save slavery, I do not agree with them. If there be those who would not save the Union unless they could at the same time destroy slavery, I do not agree with them. My paramount object in this struggle is to save the Union, and is not either to save or to destroy slavery. If I could save the Union without freeing any slave, I would do it; and if I could save it by freeing all the slaves I would do it; and if I could save it by freeing some and leaving others alone, I would also do that. What I do about slavery, and the colored race, I do because I believe it helps to save the Union; and what I forbear, I forbear because I do not believe it would help to save the Union.

From the first advance into Southern territory, slaves of rebel owners had flocked into the Union lines, embarrassing both government and commanders, until the ingenious Ben Butler declared them 'contraband of war.' The 'contrabands' were organized in labor battalions, and school teachers were provided to look after their welfare. When Union forces captured the sea islands between Charleston and Savannah in November 1861, the cotton planters fled, and their plantations and some 10,000 slaves came under the jurisdiction of the Treasury, which conducted an 'experiment in

Private Edwin Francis Jennison, Georgia Infantry, killed at Malvern Hill. A Wisconsin soldier wrote of this 1862 engagement in the Seven Days which cost Lee's army more than 20,000 casualties: 'Charge after charge is made on our artillery . . . till they lie in heaps and rows. . . . The slaughter is terrible, and to add to the carnage, our gun boats are throwing their murderous missiles with furious effect.' (*Library of Congress*)

reconstruction.' Betrayed by their enemies and sometimes by their friends, the blacks nonetheless demonstrated that they could participate in a free society in which they owned property and earned wages. After the war some of the returning planters found themselves borrowing money from their former slaves.

Lincoln moved cautiously but deliberately toward emancipation, though against stout resistance. The border states blocked proposals for compensated emancipation on which the President had set his heart, and not until April and June 1862 did Congress finally carry out a party pledge by abolishing slavery in the District of Columbia and the territories. 'The moment came,' said Lincoln, 'when I felt that slavery must die that the nation might live.' In the cabinet meeting on 22 July he proposed to declare that on the next New Year's Day all slaves in rebel territory would be free. Seward pointed out that such a proclamation at such a time would be interpreted as 'our last shriek on the retreat' from Richmond. Emancipation was then put aside to be a crown to the first victory.

Yet if the decisive moment had to be postponed, Lincoln had attained new stature. Resolute in purpose and sure of vision he had always been; but often vacillating and uncertain in performance. From those anxious vigils at the White House during the Seven Days the perplexed, over-advised, and humble Lincoln emerged humble only before God, but the master of men. He seemed to have captured all the better qualities of the great Americans who preceded him, without their defects: the poise of Washington without his aloofness, the astuteness of Jefferson without his indirection, the conscience of J. Q. Adams without his harshness, the forthrightness of Jackson without his ignorance, the magnetism of Clay without his vanity, the lucidity of Webster without his ponderousness; and fused them with a magnanimity peculiarly his own. Lincoln would have full need of all these qualities, for his time of troubles had already begun.

After overwhelming the Army of the Potomac under the headstrong and inept General John Pope at the second Battle of Bull Run, or Manassas (29 August–1 September 1862), thereby undoing the Union gains of an entire year in Virginia, Lee prepared to carry the war onto Northern soil. With Virginia clear of invaders, Lee early in September crossed the Potomac above Washington into Maryland. Of many crises for the Union, this was the most acute. In the West a Confederate offensive was unraveling the work of Grant; if it succeeded, Kentucky would be secured for the Confederacy, and a Southern invasion of Ohio might follow. Lee expected to win Maryland for the Confederacy; but his prime objective was capture of the railway bridge over the Susquehanna at Harrisburg, Pa. That would come perilously near cutting the Union in two, leaving Washington connected with the West only by the roundabout Atlantic Ocean, Hudson river, and Great Lakes route. The victorious Southern army would be in a central position to attack Washington, Baltimore, or Philadelphia. President Davis, on Northern soil, would propose peace on the basis of Southern independence; and if Lincoln's government refused they would have to reckon with the people in the November election and face the likelihood of foreign intervention. On 7 September the French minister at Washington informed Seward that it was time to recognize the independence of the Confederacy. Napoleon III was only waiting for English approval, which might well have come after another Confederate victory.

But Lee underestimated McClellan, whom Lincoln had put in 'command of the forces in the field.' On 13 September a soldier brought McClellan Lee's Order No. 191 setting forth in detail the whole plan of the campaign. It was one of those strokes of chance that changes the course of history. Moving decisively, McClellan caught the outnumbered Confederate forces in a cramped position between Antietam Creek and the Potomac, where Lee had no room to perform those brilliant maneuvers that were his delight and the enemy's confusion. The Battle of the Antietam or Sharpsburg (17 September) exhausted Lee's army, but when McClellan refused to renew the battle the next day, Lee was able to recross the Potomac into Virginia. McClellan had missed the opportunity for a knockout. Yet by restoring morale to the army, and through the lucky break of the lost

Union prisoners at Salisbury, North Carolina, 1862. They are playing baseball, appropriately enough, for the man usually credited with inventing the game, Abner Doubleday, was a Union general who distinguished himself in the first years of the War. *(Stokes Collection, New York Public Library)*

order, he had frustrated Lee's campaign and parried the most serious thrust at his country's heart. Antietam averted all danger of foreign recognition of the Confederacy; and by giving Lincoln the opportunity he sought to issue the Emancipation Proclamation, it brought the liberal opinion of the world to his side.

On 22 September 1862, five days after Antietam, Lincoln opened a momentous cabinet meeting. He had not summoned his cabinet for advice, he said. He had made a covenant with God to free the slaves as soon as the rebels were driven out of Maryland; God had decided on the field of Antietam. Cabinet members from border slave states thought the moment inopportune; the President reminded them that for months he had urged their states to take the initiative in emancipation. In the Preliminary Emancipation Proclamation the President, by virtue of his power as commander-in-chief of the army and navy, declared that upon the first day of January 1863 all slaves within any state or district then in rebellion against the United States 'shall be then, thenceforward, and forever free.' This proclamation, potentially more revolutionary in human relationships than any event in American history since 1776, lifted the Civil War to the dignity of a crusade. Though at the outset it did not actually free any slaves—for it did not apply to loyal border states—it did indicate that slavery would not survive Union victory.

Yet it was slow to influence public opinion at home or abroad. The South, indignant at what was considered an invitation to the slaves to cut their masters' throats, was nerved to greater effort. The Northern armies received from it no new impetus. The Democratic party, presenting it to the Northern people as proof that abolitionists were responsible for the duration of the war, made signal gains in the autumn elections. Julia Ward Howe saw in it the glory of the coming of the Lord; but in England and Europe the proclamation was greeted by conservatives with contempt, as a flat political maneuver, though by liberals with joy. However, Antietam and its aftermath did convince Palmerston's ministry that the moment was inopportune for intervention. So passed the second great crisis in foreign relations.

The Diplomatic Front

A third round of foreign crises resulted from the failure of Union generalship. Public opinion in the North was not so much grateful to McClellan for what he had done as indignant because he had let Lee escape. When Lincoln ordered McClellan to 'cross the Potomac and give battle to the enemy, or drive him South,' the General clamored for supplies and clothing and bandied words. The prospect of another winter of bickering and procrastination was more than the President could bear; and the fall elections had begun. Lincoln decided that if McClellan permitted Lee to get between him and Richmond, McClellan must go. Lee did just that; and on 7 November the President relieved McClellan of command of the Army of the Potomac and appointed Burnside in his place.

Distinguished chiefly for his flowing side-whiskers, Burnside proved monumentally incompetent. Learning nothing from experience, he reverted to the old plan of a 'covering advance' on Richmond, only to have Lee post a mighty army of 75,000 men and over 300 guns on the south bank of the Rappahannock, on the wooded heights above Fredericksburg. There, on 13 December, Burnside, with an army of 113,000, ordered a frontal attack on Lee's center, strongly entrenched on Marye's Heights. Six times the Union infantry—long double lines of blue, bright national and regimental colors, bayonets gleaming in the sun—pressed across an open plain completely covered by the Confederate artillery and entrenched riflemen. Six times the survivors were hurled back, leaving the dead and wounded lying in heaps. The slaughter was appalling and one-sided: Burnside lost 12,700 men, Lee 5400. 'It is well that war is so terrible,' said Lee as he watched the battle, 'or we should grow too fond of it.'

The interventionist forces in Europe, encouraged by Fredericksburg, began to make trouble again in 1863. In June a French army took Mexico City, and the next year the unfortunate Maximilian of Austria accepted the imperial crown of Mexico from France. Thus the Civil War gave Napoleon III an opportunity to perform the feat of which Talleyrand had dreamed: to re-establish European influence in North America. Slidell, the Southern agent in Paris, offered Confederate support to the Emperor in Mexico, and in January 1863, Napoleon III proposed a peace conference between North and South, with the object of establishing the Confederacy. Spain in a small way was pursuing a similar policy in Santo Domingo. France in Mexico, Spain in Santo Domingo, meant a counter-stroke of monarchial Europe against republican America, an after-clap of the Holy Alliance. Though the rally of liberal sentiment to the Union in England, France, and Spain as the meaning of the Emancipation Proclamation sank in was a powerful deterrent, Confederate partisans persisted. The British-built *Alabama* and *Florida* were destroying United States shipping; another English-built commerce-destroyer, the *Alexandria*, was almost ready for sea; and the Lairds were building two armored rams to break the Union blockade. But on 4 April Lord Russell ordered the detention of the *Alexandria*, and the prospects of the slave power dimmed.

Vicksburg to Gettysburg

In the end recognition of the Confederacy would be determined by military events. During the winter of 1862–63 all eyes were fastened on the struggle for the Mississippi. At Vicksburg and more than 100 miles to the south at Port Hudson, Louisiana, the Confederates had strongly fortified the bluffs bordering the river, and between them troops and supplies reached the heart of the Confederacy from Arkansas, Louisiana, and Texas.

A Confederate army camp in Louisiana. Note the orderly at the left of the picture approaching with liquid refreshment. (*Louisiana State University Archives, Baton Rouge*)

Vicksburg was a hard nut to crack, but the resolute Grant, with the aid of the audacious fresh-water navy, penned the enemy army. After a six-week siege, the 'Confederate Gibraltar' surrendered on 4 July. Five days later Port Hudson capitulated. Within a week a steamboat arrived at New Orleans from St. Louis, having passed the entire course of the Mississippi undisturbed by hostile shot or challenge. 'The Father of Waters,' Lincoln rejoiced, 'again goes unvexed to the sea.'

In the eastern theater 'Fighting Joe' Hooker, brave, vain, and unreliable, relieved Burnside after the Fredericksburg disaster. One hundred and thirty thousand strong, the Army of the Potomac was indeed 'the finest army on the planet.' Hooker did much to restore its morale, but on 27 April 1863, at Chancellorsville, Lee outsmarted him in one of the bloodiest battles of the war. The South, though, paid a heavy price for this victory—the loss of Stonewall Jackson, mortally wounded by his own men when reconnoitering between the lines. Lee had lost 'his right arm.'

Lee was soon ready for another spring at the enemy's throat, and by 27 June his entire army was in Pennsylvania. Lee anticipated that he could compel Lincoln to open peace negotiations on the basis of independence for the Confederacy. Chance placed the crucial battle where neither Lee nor General George Gordon Meade, who had replaced Hooker, wanted it. On 30 June a Confederate unit happened to come upon a Union cavalry division in a quiet little market town, Gettysburg. There, on 1 July, the great three-day battle began.

The first day went ill for the Union, until in the nick of time Winfield Scott Hancock, the greatest fighting general in the Army of the Potomac, rallied the men in blue on Cemetery Ridge. On the next evening (2 July) the Confederacy had a great opportunity when Jubal Early broke the Union defenses on Cemetery Ridge and Ewell stormed up a slope on the Union right, but both were hurled back. The following afternoon (3 July) Lee, against Longstreet's protest, ordered a direct attack on the strongest part of the Union center with Pickett's, Pettigrew's, and Trimble's divisions, 15,000 strong. Pickett rode up to Longstreet and asked, 'General, shall I advance?' Longstreet, unwilling to give the word, bowed his head. 'Sir, I shall lead my division forward,' said Pickett.

From Cemetery Ridge the Union troops saw three gray lines of battle issue from the wooded ridge three-quarters of a mile away and march with bayonets glittering and the colors of 47 regiments fluttering in the breeze into the valley below. When less than halfway across, the Union artillery opened up on them; a little nearer they

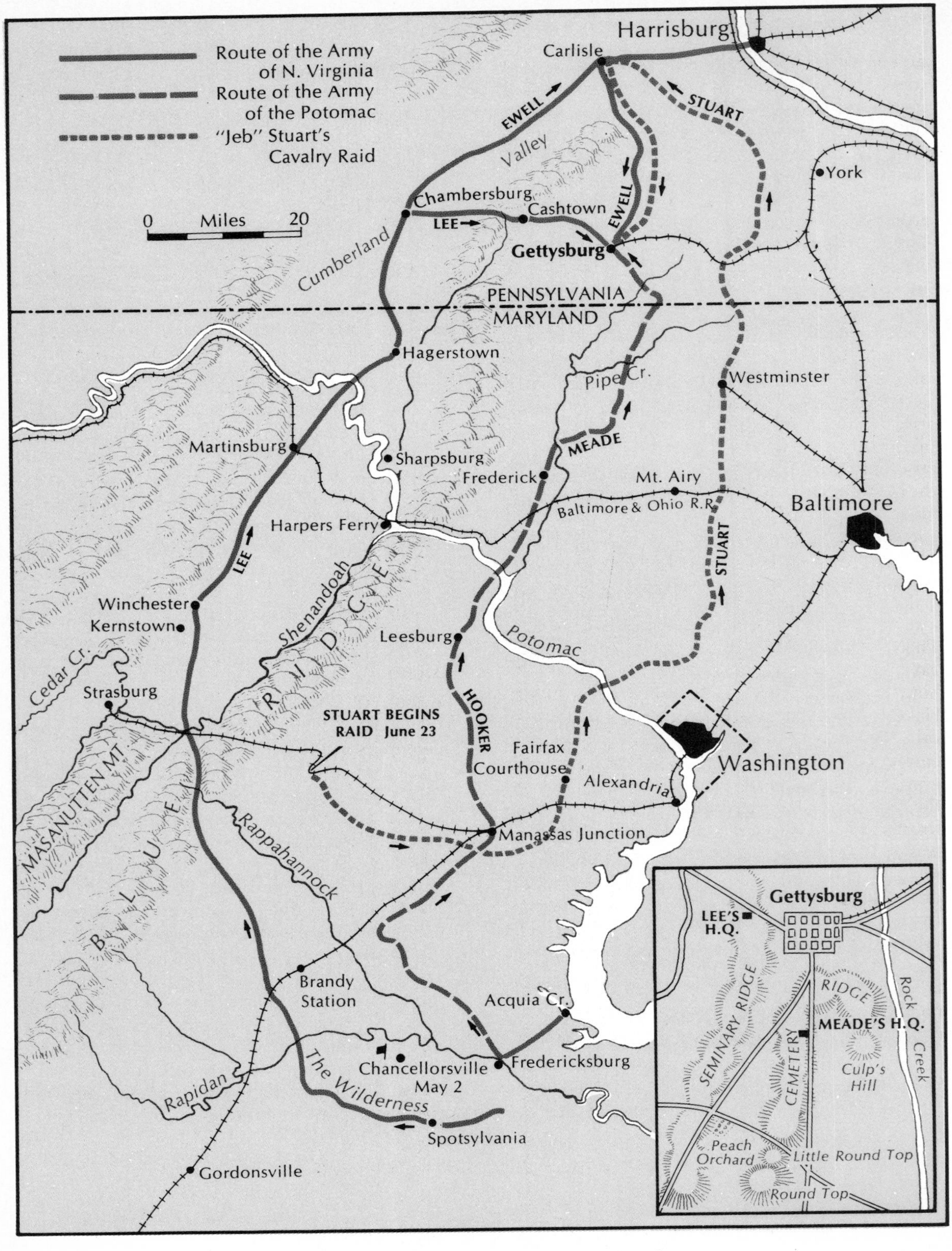
Route of the Army of N. Virginia
Route of the Army of the Potomac
"Jeb" Stuart's Cavalry Raid
0 Miles 20
Harrisburg
Carlisle
York
EWELL
STUART
Valley
Chambersburg
Cashtown
LEE
Gettysburg
Cumberland
PENNSYLVANIA
MARYLAND
Hagerstown
Pipe Cr.
Westminster
MEADE
Martinsburg
Sharpsburg
Frederick
Mt. Airy
Baltimore & Ohio R.R.
Baltimore
Harpers Ferry
Shenandoah
BLUE RIDGE
Winchester
Kernstown
Leesburg
Potomac
Cedar Cr.
Strasburg
STUART BEGINS RAID June 23
HOOKER
Fairfax Courthouse
Washington
Alexandria
MASANUTTEN MT.
Rappahannock
Manassas Junction
Brandy Station
Acquia Cr.
Chancellorsville May 2
Fredericksburg
Rapidan
The Wilderness
Spotsylvania
Gordonsville
Gettysburg
LEE'S H.Q.
SEMINARY RIDGE
CEMETERY RIDGE
MEADE'S H.Q.
Rock Creek
Culp's Hill
Peach Orchard
Little Round Top
Round Top

The Gettysburg Campaign, 27 June–4 July

came under raking fire from the batteries on Round Top. The flank divisions melted away; but the Northern troops, peering through the smoke, could see Pickett's men still coming on, merged in one crowding, rushing line. Lost for a moment in a swale, they emerged so near that the expression on their faces could be seen. 'The line springs,' wrote Frank Haskell of Meade's Second Corps. 'The crest of the solid ground with a great roar heaves forward its maddened load, men, arms, smoke, fire, a fighting mass. It rolls to the wall—flash meets flash, the wall is crossed, a moment ensues of thrust, yells, blows, shots, and undistinguishable conflict, followed by a shout universal, and the last and bloodiest fight of the battle of Gettysburg is ended and won.' Two of Pickett's brigadiers and fifteen of his regimental commanders were killed. General Armistead, with cap raised on point of sword, leaped the stone wall into the Union lines, a hundred men followed him, and for a brief moment the battle cross of the Confederacy floated on the crest of Cemetery Ridge. Then the Union lines closed in relentlessly and all Armistead's men were shot down or captured.

The next evening, 4 July, the climactic battle lost, Lee retired to a position west of Sharpsburg. There the flooded Potomac stopped his retreat and gave Meade an opportunity that Lincoln begged him to seize. 'Call no council of war,' telegraphed Halleck. 'Do not let the enemy escape.' Meade called a council of war, the Potomac fell, and the enemy got away. But Lee was too candid to congratulate himself for having escaped. He had seen the flower of his army wither under the Union fire. He knew that all hope for peace that summer was gone, and he must have felt that slight hope for Southern independence remained. Yet his soldiers gathered only confidence and resolution from the placid countenance of their beloved 'Marse Robert.' To President Davis Lee wrote, 'No blame can be attached to the army for its failure to accomplish what was projected by me, nor should it be censured for the unreasonable expectations of the public. I am alone to blame.' On 8 August he submitted his resignation as commander of the Army of Northern Virginia. 'To ask me to substitute you by some one more fit to command,' Davis answered, 'is to demand an impossibility.'

Four months later, when a national cemetery was dedicated on the battlefield of Gettysburg, Lincoln delivered his immortal address:

> Fourscore and seven years ago our fathers brought forth on this continent a new nation, conceived in liberty, and dedicated to the proposition that all men are created equal.
>
> Now we are engaged in a great civil war, testing whether that nation, or any nation so conceived and so dedicated, can long endure. We are met on a great battle-field of that war. We have come to dedicate a portion of that field as a final resting-place for those who here gave their lives that the nation might live. It is altogether fitting and proper that we should do this.
>
> But, in a larger sense, we cannot dedicate—we cannot consecrate—we cannot hallow—this ground. The brave men, living and dead, who struggled here, have consecrated it far above our poor power to add or detract. The world will little note nor long remember what we say here, but it can never forget what they did here. It is for us, the living, rather, to be dedicated here to the unfinished work which they who fought here have thus far so nobly advanced. It is rather for us to be here dedicated to the great task remaining before us—that from these honored dead we take increased devotion to that cause for which they gave the last full measure of devotion; that we here highly resolve that these dead shall not have died in vain; that this nation, under God, shall have a new birth of freedom; and that government of the people, by the people, for the people, shall not perish from the earth.

Gettysburg and Vicksburg had momentous consequences. Lord John Russell impounded the Laird armored rams, from which the Confederacy hoped much, and Napoleon III, who now had second thoughts, ordered vessels destined for the Confederacy to be sold to foreign governments. The military results of these two great victories were even more important than the diplomatic. For with Lee's invaders repulsed and the Mississippi liberated, the North could concentrate all of its energies on a final strategy of conquest.

From Chattanooga to the Wilderness

The advance of the Army of the Cumberland toward Chattanooga in July 1863 began a campaign that ended only with Sherman's march to the sea and a division of the Confederacy. Chattanooga, after Richmond and Vicksburg, was the most vital point in the Confederacy—a key railway junction and the place where the Tennessee river breaks through the parallel ridges of the southern Appalachians. Once in possession of Chattanooga, the Union armies might swing round the Great Smoky mountains and attack Atlanta, Savannah, Charleston, or even Richmond from the rear. When Lincoln made Grant supreme commander in the West, Grant ordered the loyal Virginian, George H. Thomas, 'the rock of Chickamauga,' to hold Chattanooga, which had been occupied in September, and on 24 November launched an offensive against the rebels. The capture of Missionary Ridge was perhaps the most gallant action of the war. Thomas's men, after driving the Confederates from the rifle-pits at the foot, were ordered to halt. Refusing to obey, they kept straight on up the steep rocky slope, overrunning a second and a third line of defense, rushed the Confederate guns on the crest, and turned them on the enemy; then, with Phil Sheridan leading, pursued the fleeing gray-coats down the eastern slope.

This Battle of Chattanooga placed the combined armies of the Tennessee and the Cumberland (Sherman and Thomas) in a position to advance into Georgia in the early spring. In May 1864 Sherman, in command of 100,000 men, opened his campaign, and by 2 September had captured Atlanta. On 17 October, after sending Thomas back to Nashville to cope with the fighting John B. Hood, who was imperilling the long, thin line of Union communications, the imperturbable Sherman cut loose in the opposite direction toward the sea, marching 62,000 men without supplies into the 'garden spot of the Confederacy.' The march to the sea was one of deliberate and disciplined destruction. Sherman's army cut a swath 60 miles through central Georgia, destroying stores of provisions, standing crops and cattle, cotton-gins and mills, railways and bridges, everything that could be useful to the Confederacy and much that was not. Many a Georgia family was stripped of its possessions; but outrages on persons were surprisingly few. It was the sort of campaign that soldiers love—maximum of looting and destruction, minimum of discipline and fighting: splendid weather, few impedimenta; broiled turkey for breakfast and fried chicken for supper. For a month the North lost sight of Sherman. He emerged at Savannah on 10 December 1864 and was able to offer Lincoln the city as a Christmas present. Before the month was out, Thomas had added to the jubilation in the North by inflicting on Hood at Nashville the most smashing defeat of the war.

While Sherman and Thomas were carrying on this brilliant scission of the Confederacy, Grant was having rough going with Lee, whose prowess very nearly conquered the Northern will to victory in the summer of 1864.

On 9 March 1864 Grant was appointed general-in-chief of the armies of the United States. Summoned to Washington, where he had never been, to confer with Lincoln, whom he had never seen, this slightly seedy individual, perpetually smoking or chewing a cigar, caused some misgivings among those used to the glittering generals of the Army of the Potomac. Keener observers were impressed with Grant's rough dignity. He was the first of all the commanders in the East who never doubted the greatness of his President; and Lincoln knew that he had a general at last 'who would take the responsibility and act.'

Grant assumed personal direction of the Virginia campaign against Lee. 'I determined,' wrote Grant himself, 'to hammer continuously against the armed force of the enemy and his resources, until by mere attrition, if in no other way, there should be nothing left to him but submission.' On 4 May 1864 Grant marched his army of 102,000 through the tangled Wilderness. In the first Battle of the Wilderness (5–7 May), which cost Grant 17,700 men, Lee fought him to a draw. Grant then tried to outflank the enemy; but clouds of dust from his marching columns warned Lee of his intention and by the time his van reached Spotsylvania Court House, Lee was there to check him. Both armies threw up field entrenchments, and the five-day battle that followed (Spotsylvania, 8–12 May) was the first based on trench warfare. Grant lost 31,000 more men and a cry went up for his removal. He declared, 'I . . . propose to fight it out on this line if it takes all summer' and Lincoln stood by him. On 1–3 June came the Battle of Cold Harbor, a bloody Union assault upon the entire line of Lee's trenches.

General William Tecumseh Sherman (1820–91). This photograph was taken in 1865, the year of final Union victory following his 'march to the sea' of 1864 that made him a hero to the North but anathema to the South. (*National Archives, Brady Collection*)

Before going over the top the Union soldiers pinned papers on their backs, giving their names and addresses to identify their corpses. Eight or nine thousand men fell in a few hours, but hardly a dent was made on the Confederate lines.

War had now acquired many of the horrors that we associate with World War I. The wounded, unattended between the lines, died of thirst, starvation, and loss of blood. Corpses rotted on the ground. Sharpshooters kept up their deadly work.

Officers and men fought mechanically without hope. The war had begun so long ago that one could hardly remember what it was about.

In one month Grant had advanced from the Rapidan to the Chickahominy, the exact spot where McClellan had stood two years before, and he had lost from 55,000 to 60,000 men as against Lee's 25,000 to 30,000; but he could count on a continuous flow of reinforcements, and Lee could not. On 12 June Grant began a change of base to the James. With immense skill he ferried his vast army across that broad river, unmolested by Lee. But an opportunity to push into undefended Petersburg and thus outflank Richmond was lost. Lee slipped in by the interior lines, entrenched in time, and three assaults cost the Union 8000 more men (15–18 June). Grant's army sat down to besiege Petersburg and remained there for nine months.

A war of position had arrived. Lee, with an army that despised digging as unsoldierly and hated fighting from entrenchments, had developed the technique of trench warfare to a point that Europe reached only in 1916. He had saved his army and saved Richmond. Grant, after making mistakes and suffering losses that would have broken any of his predecessors, was still indomitable. But how long would the country suffer such stupendous losses with no apparent result? The country could not then appreciate what we now know, that Grant had brought the end near and had forced the Confederate government to concentrate its best efforts on supporting Lee, thereby denying Joseph Johnston the necessary reinforcements to stop Sherman's march to the sea. But in the summer of 1864 the appalling toll of casualties seemed to have brought the war no nearer conclusion, and through the presidential campaign that year there ran an undercurrent of doubt and despair.

The Presidential Election

Alone of democratic governments before World War II, the United States carried out a general election in wartime. Lincoln said, 'We cannot have free government without elections; and if the rebellion could force us to forego or postpone a national election, it might fairly claim to have already conquered and ruined us.' In June 1864 Lincoln was renominated for the presidency by acclamation by a National Union convention of Republicans and War Democrats; the 'Union' of the two groups was dramatized by the nomination of Andrew Johnson of Tennessee, a life-long Democrat, to the vice-presidency.

Yet within a few weeks a movement developed against Lincoln within his own party. Sherman was stalled in front of Atlanta; things were going badly in Virginia; Chase resigned from the cabinet and struck an alliance with political adventurers and marplots like General Butler, Roscoe Conkling, and Horace Greeley who had concluded that Lincoln could not win and it was necessary to name another ticket. In July the President and the radicals split over how to reconstruct the Union after the war. When Lincoln pocket-vetoed a bill embodying the radical views of reconstruction, Senator Wade and Representative Henry Davis issued a public manifesto denouncing the President. Greeley published this Wade-Davis Manifesto in the *Tribune* on 5 August; two weeks later, he and the radicals began to circulate a call for a new Republican convention to reconsider Lincoln's candidacy.

It was an alarming situation. Some of Lincoln's staunchest supporters thought the election already lost, and Republican leaders implored the President to make a peace move. Lincoln sent them away satisfied that he cared nothing for himself, but that so palpable a confession of weakness as an overture to Jefferson Davis, at that juncture, would be equivalent to surrender. What Lincoln really thought is clear from the paper he wrote and sealed on 23 August:

> It seems exceedingly probable that this administration will not be re-elected. Then it will be my duty to so co-operate with the President-elect as to save the Union between the election and the inauguration, as he will have secured his election on such ground that he cannot possibly save it afterward.

A week later the Democratic national convention adopted a resolution drafted by the Ohio copperhead Vallandigham calling for an end to hostilities and nominated General McClellan for President. He repudiated the peace plank but was willing to ride into the White House on a wave of opposition to war.

However, the wave soon subsided. Jefferson Davis by bluntly insisting on recognition of Southern independence as the price for peace, the Democrats by their defeatism, and Sherman by capturing Atlanta knocked the bottom out of the schemes of Lincoln's opponents. Lincoln's election, so doubtful in August, was conceded on every side in October. After Sheridan had devastated the Shenandoah valley, the Northern people, on 8 November, chose 212 Lincoln electors and only 21 for McClellan. Still, Lincoln's popular majority was only 400,000 in 4,000,000 votes.

'The election,' said Lincoln two days later, 'has demonstrated that a people's government can sustain a national election in the midst of a great civil war.'

The Collapse of the Confederacy

The re-election of Lincoln, the failure to obtain foreign recognition, the increasing pinch of the blockade, Sherman's march to the sea, and Grant's implacable hammering at the thin lines around Petersburg took the heart out of the South. By the start of 1865 the Confederacy was sinking fast. Even slavery was jettisoned—in principle. President Davis sent an envoy to Europe, in January 1865, to offer abolition in exchange for recognition, and on 25 March the Richmond Congress authorized arming black slaves. Sherman, as he marched northward, was proving his sulphurous synonym for war. 'Columbia!—pretty much all burned; and burned *good.*' Yet the doughty Sherman passed some anxious hours when he learned that Lee and his grim veterans were on the loose again.

For nine months Grant and Lee had faced one another across long lines of entrenchment in the outskirts of Petersburg. At the beginning of the siege their forces were not disparate; but by the middle of March 1865 Grant had 115,000 effectives to Lee's 54,000. Lee had to move out of his trenches before Grant enveloped him, though if Petersburg were abandoned, Richmond must fall. Lee's only hope was to retreat westward and unite with Johnston, who commanded the remnants of his former army in North Carolina. On the night of 2–3 April Lee's army slipped out of the Petersburg lines; and the next evening the Union forces entered Richmond. Without pause Grant pursued. Sheridan blocked the Confederates' escape southward and westward. Lee's last hope was gone.

Lee ordered a white flag to be displayed and requested an interview with his opponent. The scene that followed, in a house of the little village of Appomattox Court House, has become a part of American folklore. Lee, in new full-dress uniform with jewel-studded sword, Grant in his favorite private's blouse, unbuttoned, and without a sword, 'his feelings sad and depressed at the downfall of a foe who had fought so long and valiantly.'

Formal greetings. Small talk of other days, in the old army. . . .

Grant writes the terms of surrender in his own hand. . . . Officers and men paroled . . . arms and matériel surrendered . . . not to include the officers' side-arms, and—

'Let all the men who claim to own a horse or mule take the animals home with them to work their little farms.'

'This will do much toward conciliating our people.'

The conference is over. Lee pauses in the doorway, looking out over a field blossoming with the stars and stripes. Thrice, and slowly, he strikes a fist into the palm of his gantleted hand. He mounts his horse Traveller and is gone.

A sound of cheering spreads along the Union lines.

Grant orders it to cease:

'The war is over; the rebels are our countrymen again.'

General Joshua Chamberlain, who received the surrender on behalf of Grant, recalled the moving scene:

> Before us in proud humiliation stood the embodiment of manhood: men whom neither toils and sufferings, nor the fact of death, nor disaster, nor hopelessness could bend from their resolve; standing before us now, thin, worn, and famished, but erect, and with eyes looking level into ours, waking memories that bound us

A troubled Lincoln. This photograph by Mathew Brady was taken in May 1861, a month when the President felt compelled to call for a huge increase in the armed forces. As Benjamin P. Thomas has written, 'Lincoln's face began to reveal his inner torment as lines of travail etched his features.' (*Library of Congress, Brady Collection*)

together as no other bond;—was not such manhood to be welcomed back into a Union so tested and assured?

When the head of each division column comes opposite our group, our bugle sounds the signal and instantly our whole line from right to left, regiment by regiment in succession, gives the soldier's salutation, from the 'order arms' to the old 'carry'—the marching salute. Gordon at the head of the column, riding with heavy spirit and downcast face, catches the sound of shifting arms, looks up, and taking the meaning, wheels superbly, making with himself and his horse one uplifted figure, with profound salutation as he drops the point of his sword to the boot toe; then facing to his own command, gives word for his successive brigades to pass us with the same position of the manual—honor answering honor. On our part not a sound of trumpet more, nor roll of drum; not a cheer, nor word nor whisper of vain-glorying, nor motion of man standing again at the order, but an awed stillness rather, and breath-holding, as if it were the passing of the dead! . . . How could we help falling on our knees, all of us together, and praying God to pity and forgive us all![4]

The Last Days of Lincoln

. . . With malice toward none; with charity for all; with firmness in the right, as God gives us to see the right, let us strive on to finish the work we are in; to bind up the nation's wounds; to care for him who shall have borne the battle, and for his widow, and his orphan—to do all which may achieve and cherish a just and lasting peace among ourselves, and with all nations.

Thus closed the second inaugural address of President Lincoln on 4 March 1865. The struggle over reconstruction was already on. Truculent Ben Wade with his fierce hatred of the slaveholders, Democrats eager for revenge on the President, Charles Sumner with his passionate conviction that right and justice required the South to pass under the Caudine forks, were certain to oppose the terms with which Lincoln proposed to bind up the nation's wounds. But Congress would not meet until December. It might be confronted with the established fact of a restored nation, if the South were wise, if nothing happened to Lincoln.

On 11 April, two days after Lee's surrender, Lincoln delivered his last public address. In unfolding his reconstruction policy, he announced the most magnanimous terms toward a helpless opponent ever offered by a victor. For Lincoln did not consider himself a conqueror. He was, and had been since 1861, President of the United States. The rebellion must be forgotten, and every Southern state re-admitted to full privilege in the Union as soon as 10 per cent of the whites had taken the oath of allegiance and organized a state government.

On Good Friday, the 14th, the President held his last cabinet meeting. He urged his ministers to turn their thoughts to peace. There must be no more bloodshed, no persecution. Grant, who attended the meeting, was asked for late news from Sherman, but had none. Lincoln remarked that it would soon come and be favorable,[5] for last night he had had a familiar dream. In a strange indescribable ship he seemed to be moving with great rapidity toward a dark and undefined shore. He had had this same dream before Sumter, Bull Run, Antietam, Murfreesboro, Vicksburg, and Wilmington. Matter-of-fact Grant remarked that Murfreesboro was no victory—'a few such fights would have ruined us.' Lincoln looked at him curiously and said, however that might be, his dream preceded that battle.

Secretary Welles, who records this incident, may be our guide to the fearful events of that night. He had gone to bed early and was just falling asleep when someone shouted from the street that the President had been shot. After checking on the condition of Secretary Seward and his son, who had also been shot, he hurried down to 10th Street: The dying President had been carried across that street from Ford's Theatre to a poor lodging-house, where he was laid on a bed in a narrow back room. He never recovered consciousness. 'The giant sufferer,' writes Welles, 'lay extended diagonally across the bed, which was not long enough for him. . . . His slow, full respiration lifted the clothes with each breath that he took. His features were calm and striking.'

A little before half-past seven the great heart ceased to beat.

4. Joshua Chamberlain, *The Passing of the Armies*, pp. 258ff.

5. Johnston surrendered his army to Sherman 26 April. Jefferson Davis was captured 10 May. The last Confederate force surrendered 26 May.

The assassination of Abraham Lincoln, 14 April 1865. After firing his one-shot derringer point-blank at the President, John Wilkes Booth leaps from the balustrade upon the stage of Ford's Theatre and, brandishing a dagger, heads for the wings. In the box above, Lincoln slumps, mortally wounded, while the stunned audience, many of whom recognize Booth, gesticulate at him. (*New-York Historical Society*)

Welles continues, 'I went after breakfast to the Executive Mansion. There was a cheerless cold rain and everything seemed gloomy. On the Avenue in front of the White House were several hundred colored people, mostly women and children, weeping and wailing their loss. This crowd did not appear to diminish through the whole of that cold, wet day; they seemed not to know what was to be their fate since their great benefactor was dead, and their hopeless grief affected me more than almost anything else, though strong and brave men wept when I met them.'

The Heritage of War

Bow down, dear land, for thou has found release!
  Thy God, in these distempered days,
  Hath taught thee the sure wisdom of His ways
And through thine enemies hath wrought thy peace!
  Bow down in prayer and praise!

No poorest in thy borders but may now
Lift to the juster skies a man's enfranchised brow;
O Beautiful! My Country! Ours once more!

Thus James Russell Lowell, at the Harvard commemoration service of 1865, saluted, as he believed, a reunited nation purged by war of all grossness that had accompanied its rise to power. But the fierce passions of warfare had burned good with evil; and in the scorched soil the new growth showed tares as well as wheat. 'The Civil War marks an era in the history of the American mind,' wrote Henry James fourteen years after Appomattox. From the war, the American had gained a sense 'of the world being a more complicated place than it had hitherto seemed, the future more treacherous, success more difficult.'

The North had fought the war for three purposes: Union, freedom, and democracy. At the outset, preservation of the Union had been the main goal, but after 1862 the abolition of slavery came to be a second acknowledged objective. And to many, in Europe as in America, the maintenance of a 'government of the people, by the people, for the people' was a third.

Union had been preserved, but it could not be said that the old Union had been restored. The long dispute over the nature of the Union had been settled, at last, in favor of the nationalist contention, but it had required force to bring that about. Nor had sectionalism disappeared. In the generation after the war, to the North and South was added a third powerful section—the trans-Mississippi West. Until well into the next century American political life was to be conditioned by this division of North, South, and West.

Slavery, to be sure, was gone, but emancipation, too, had been brought about by violence. Perhaps this was the only way slavery could have been ended, but even the most ardent champions of freedom were forced to admit that the method was painful for white and black alike. Moreover, slavery gave way not to freedom but to a kind of peonage. Not for another hundred years after the breakdown of Reconstruction were most Negroes to enjoy even in part those rights which the war and the new constitutional amendments had attempted to assure them.

What shall we say of the third objective—government of, by, and for the people? Democracy, indeed, had not 'perished from the earth,' yet for a brief interval Americans witnessed what they had never known before: military government in time of peace. The Civil War had destroyed slavery and the slaveholding class; but within a few years corporate industry would wield excessive power. Twenty years after the attack on Fort Sumter the railroads alone represented a greater investment and concentration of power than the slave interest ever had. Justice John M. Harlan of the Supreme Court, looking back upon this period, remembered that 'there was everywhere among the people generally a deep feeling of unrest. The nation had been rid of human slavery . . . but the conviction was universal that the country was in real danger from another kind of slavery, namely the slavery that would result from aggregations of capital in the hands of a few.'

The cost of the war had been colossal. Deaths from all causes in the two armies totaled some 620,000, and thousands more were wounded. How many lives were lost because of malnutrition, disease, and the chaotic conditions of 1865 and 1866, it is impossible to say, nor can we count the lives shattered by destruction and demoralized by defeat. The money cost of the war was staggering; proportionally higher, indeed, than that of World War I. Loans and taxes raised by the Federal Government came to nearly $3 billion, and the interest on the Civil War debt an additional $2.8 billion. The Confederacy floated loans of over $2 billion, but the total financial loss of the South, in property confiscated, depreciated, and destroyed, in the losses of banks and insurance companies and businesses, and in the expense of reconstruction, was incalculable. Many states, North and South, went heavily into debt for the prosecution of the war. And the country continued to pay for the war well into the twentieth century: United States government pensions amounted to almost $8 billion, and Southern states doled out additional sums to Confederate veterans. The total cost of the war to North and South may be estimated at well over $20 billion—five times all the expenditures of the Federal Government from 1789 to 1865!

The material problems of the war could be met;

the moral devastation was never wholly repaired. During the war violence and destruction and hatred had been called virtues; it was a long time before they were again recognized as vices. The war had brutalized combatants and non-combatants alike. Ruthlessness and corruption had accompanied the conflict, and they lingered on to trouble the postwar years. Above all, the war bred animosities that affected men, Northern and Southern, for over a generation.

But the revolution wrought by the war also offered the nation an opportunity to right the grievous wrongs done to the blacks and to make this country one truly dedicated to the principles of equality. In the years after the war, for the first time, the power of the national government was employed to extend the civil rights of the Negro. One may well doubt whether, had it not been for the war and Reconstruction, even a century later there would be constitutional guarantees of these rights. Only at this unique juncture in history, when the South was subjugated and the North felt some of the equalitarian spirit of the war, was it possible to write provisions into the Constitution designed to achieve these ends. If Reconstruction ultimately failed, it at least left a legal foundation for subsequent struggles against inequality.

19

Reconstruction

*

1865–1877

The Prostrate South

Four years of warfare had devastated the South. Over large sections of the country, Union and Confederate armies had tramped and fought. From Atlanta to Savannah and from Savannah to Raleigh, Sherman had left a broad belt of blackened ruin: 'where our footsteps pass,' wrote one of his aides, 'fire, ashes, and desolation follow in the path.' Sheridan had swept down the fertile Shenandoah valley like an avenging fury. 'We had no cattle, hogs, sheep, or horses or anything else,' wrote a native of Virginia. 'The fences were all gone... the barns were all burned; chimneys standing without houses and houses standing without roofs, or doors, or windows ... bridges all destroyed, roads badly cut up.' In the West, conditions were just as bad. The Governor of Arkansas wrote of his state: 'The desolations of war are beyond description.... Besides the utter desolation that marked the tracks of war and battle, guerilla bands and scouting parties have pillaged almost every neighbourhood.'

Some of the cities presented a picture as appalling as the countryside. Charleston had been bombarded and partially burned; a Northern visitor painted it as a city of 'vacant houses, of widowed women, of rotting wharves, of deserted warehouses, of weed-wild gardens, of miles of grass-grown streets, of acres of pitiful and voiceless barrenness.' The business portion of Richmond, the capital of the Confederacy, lay in ruins 'all up and down, as far as the eye could reach.... Beds of cinders, cellars half filled with bricks and rubbish, broken and blackened walls, impassable streets deluged with *débris*.' In Atlanta, brick and mortar, charred timber, scraps of tin roofing, engine bolts and bars, cannonballs, and long shot filled the ruined streets. Mobile, Galveston, Vicksburg, and numerous other cities of the South were in a similar plight.

With the collapse of the Confederacy, civil administration all but disappeared throughout the South. There was no money for the support of government and no authority which could assess or collect taxes. There were few courts, judges, sheriffs, or police officers with any authority, and vandalism went unrestrained except by public opinion or by lynch law. 'Our principal danger,' observed George Cary Eggleston, 'was from lawless bands of marauders who infested the country, and our greatest difficulty in dealing with them

Ruins of Charleston, South Carolina, 1865. (*Library of Congress, Brady Collection*)

lay in the utter absence of constituted authority of any sort.' Fraud and peculation added to the universal distress. United States Treasury agents seized hundreds of thousands of bales of cotton, and other property as well. The Federal Government subsequently reimbursed no fewer than 40,000 claimants because of illegal confiscation of their property.

The economic life of the South was shattered. Manufacturing had been all but destroyed. Few Southern banks were solvent, and it was years before the banking system was even partially restored. Confederate securities into which the people had sunk their savings were now as worthless as Continental currency. Shops were depleted of goods, and almost everything had to be imported from the North on credit. Even agriculture was slow to revive. Not until 1879 did the seceding states raise a cotton crop as large as that of 1860. In 1870 the tobacco crop of Virginia was one-third that of 1860, and the corn and wheat crop one-half. Farm land that had once sold for $100 an acre went begging at $5, and in Mississippi alone almost 6 million acres of land were sold for non-payment of taxes.

The transportation system had mostly collapsed. Roads were all but impassable, bridges destroyed or washed away, river levees broken. Railroad transportation was paralyzed, and most of the railroad companies bankrupt. Over a stretch of 114 miles in Alabama 'every bridge and trestle was destroyed, cross-ties rotten, buildings burned, water-tanks gone, ditches filled up, and tracks grown up in weeds and bushes.'

The cultural life of the South did not recover for over a generation. Schools, colleges, libraries, and churches were destroyed or impoverished, and the intellectual life of the South was paralyzed by the preoccupation with sheer survival and by obsession with the past and with defeat. 'You ask me to tell you the story of my last year,' wrote the poet Henry Timrod. 'I can embody it all in a few words: beggary, starvation, death, bitter grief, utter want of hope.' Young men of family who had interrupted their education to fight for Southern independence had to labor in the fields to keep their kinfolk from starving; and a planter's family which still had young men was deemed fortunate. General Anderson worked as a day laborer in the yards of the South Carolina Railroad. George Fitzhugh, the philosopher of slavery, lived in a poor shanty among his former slaves. William Gilmore Simms, the South's leading man of letters, lost not only his 'house, stables, barns, gin house, machine and threshing houses, mules, horses, cattle, wagons, ploughs, implements, all destroyed' but what was probably the finest private library in the South. 'Pretty much the whole of life has been merely not dying,' wrote the Southern poet Sidney Lanier, himself dying.

The fall of the Confederacy dealt an extremely heavy blow to the planter aristocracy that had long guided the destinies of the South. Some of this class was excluded for a time from any participation in the government, and for such able leaders as Davis and Lee the disability was never removed. Slave property valued in 1860 at over $2 billion evaporated, and the savings and sacrifices represented by Confederate securities were lost. A labor system which was the very basis of the Southern economy was overthrown, the agricultural regime which it sreved was disarranged, and a new system, no less wasteful and scarcely less oppressive, was established in its stead.

The planter aristocracy suffered especially severely; for if the war had been 'a poor man's fight,' the poor white had nothing to lose, and his condition was no worse in 1870 than it had been in 1850. Many planters gave up the struggle to maintain themselves on the land. A few fled to England, Mexico, or Brazil; others migrated to the Northern cities or started life anew in the West; many moved to the towns and adapted themselves to business or professional life. The small farmers and poor whites took advantage of this exodus to enlarge their farms and elect men of their own kind to high office. A little while and the Tillmans, Watsons, and Longs would sit in the seats of the Calhouns, the Cobbs, and the Clays.

The Triumphant North

To the North the war brought not only victory but unprecedented prosperity, a sense of power, a spirit of buoyant confidence, and exuberance of energy that found expression in a thousand out-

The Richmond and Petersburg Railroad Depot, 1865. This Mathew Brady photograph of a demolished locomotive and a gutted station in the former Confederate capital of Richmond, Virginia, reveals how little was left of the railroad system of the South after the devastation of the Civil War. (*Brady Collection, Library of Congress*)

lets. To the generation that had saved the Union everything seemed possible. 'The truth is,' wrote Senator Sherman to his brother, the General, 'the close of the war with our resources unimpaired gives an elevation, a scope to the ideas of leading capitalists far higher than anything ever undertaken in this country before. They talk of millions as confidently as formerly of thousands.' Men hurled themselves upon the continent as if to ravish it of its wealth. Railroads were flung across mountain barriers, and settlers crowded into half a continent, while cattle swarmed over the grasslands of the High Plains. Forests were felled, the earth gutted of coal, copper, iron ore, and precious metals; petroleum spouted from untended wells. Telegraph wires were strung across the country and cables stretched from continent to continent; factories sprang up overnight; speculators thronged the floors of stock and produce exchanges, inventors flooded the patent office with applications for new devices with which to conquer nature and create wealth.

The census of 1870 revealed that, despite four years of war, the per capita wealth of the North had doubled in ten years. The war, while depressing some industries, created new opportunities for amassing private wealth. Supplying the armies with food and clothing and munitions proved immensely profitable. More profitable still was the business of financing the war, and many a fortune was founded upon speculation in government bonds and on the banking expansion encouraged by the National Banking Act. Banks which held government bonds received an estimated aggregate of 17 per cent interest annually upon their investment. The rewards of railroad organization, financing, construction, and operation were even greater. In the ten years after the war, the country doubled its railroad mileage, and the profits went, often by devious means, to establish the fortunes of Vanderbilt and Gould, Huntington and Stanford, and other multimillionaires.

No less spectacular was the exploitation of natural resources. After oil was struck in western Pennsylvania in 1859, thousands of fortune-hunters stampeded into the oil-soaked triangle between the Allegheny river and Oil Creek. During the war oil production increased from 21 million to 104 million gallons, and the capitalization of new companies was not far from half a billion dollars. In 1860 silver production was a paltry $150,000; by the end of Reconstruction annual output had reached $38 million, and the silver barons of the West had come to exercise an influence in politics comparable to that of industrialists in the East. In the postwar years coal production trebled, and iron ore output in the Lake Superior region alone increased more than tenfold.

In the 1860's the number of manufacturing establishments increased by fully 80 per cent. Four times as much timber was cut in Michigan, four times as much pig iron was smelted in Ohio, four times as much freight was handled by the Pennsylvania Railroad, four times as many miles of railroad track were laid, in 1870 as in 1860. After the war, the woolens, cotton, iron, lumber, meat, and milling industries all showed a steady and even a spectacular development. And while property values in the South were suffering a cataclysmic decline, total property value of the North and West increased from $10 billion in 1860 to over $25 billion a decade later.

Accompanying this extraordinary development of business was a steady rise in the population of cities and in immigration. New York and Philadelphia, Boston and Baltimore, continued the growth which had begun back in the 'forties, and newer cities such as Chicago and St. Louis, Cleveland and Pittsburgh, St. Paul and San Francisco, more than doubled their population in ten years. Even during the war some 800,000 immigrants had entered the United States, and in the ten years after Appomattox some 3.25 million immigrants flooded into the cities and the farms of the North and the West.

These developments all contributed to the growth of income, and observers were already remarking upon the concentration of wealth in certain fortunate areas and favored groups. In 1870 the wealth of New York State alone was more than twice that of all the ex-Confederate states. Every business grew its own crop of millionaires, and soon the names of Morgan and Armour, Swift and Pillsbury, came to be as familiar to the average American as the names of his statesmen. A new plutocracy emerged from the war and Reconstruction, masters of money who were no less self-conscious and powerful than the planter aristocracy of the Old South.

While the old patterns were being rearranged in the South, a different kind of transformation was effected in the North. With the representatives of the planter class out of Congress, the spokesmen of industry, finance, and of free Western lands no longer had to contend with their most powerful opponent. During the war they pushed through legislation to fulfill the arrested hopes of the 'fifties, and after victory they garnered the fruits.

The moderate tariff of 1857 gave way to the Morrill tariff of 1861, and that to a series of war tariffs with duties scaling rapidly upward. By the National Banking Acts of 1863 and 1864, the Independent Treasury system of 1846 was swept away, and an act of 1865 imposed a tax of 10 per cent on all state bank notes, a fatal blow which none would regret. To ensure an ample labor supply, Congress in 1864 permitted the importation of contract labor from abroad, and though this act was soon repealed, the practice itself was not discontinued until the 'eighties. Internal improvements at national expense found expression in subsidies to telegraph and cable lines and in generous grants of millions of acres out of the public domain to railroad promoters.

Western farmers achieved a century-old ambition with the Homestead Law of 1862. This act, limited temporarily in its application to those who 'have never borne arms against the United States Government,' granted a quarter-section (160 acres) of public domain to anyone who would undertake to cultivate it. The Morrill Act, passed the same year, subsidized agricultural education through public lands. At the same time easier access to the West was assured through the government-subsidized railroads. By carrying out the promise of the Republican platform, this legislation strengthened that party in the agricultural West.

Finally, the Civil War had an important political consequence. The Republicans came out of the war with an aura of legitimacy, for they could claim to be the party that had saved the Union, while the Democrats had the odium of secession. For a generation Republican orators rang the changes on Fort Sumter and Andersonville prison, and 'waved the bloody shirt of the rebellion,' and presented themselves as the liberators and defenders of the former slaves.

The Freedman

In Reconstruction the Negro was the central figure. Upwards of a million blacks had in one way or another become free before the end of the war; victory and the Thirteenth Amendment liberated about 3 million more. Never before in the history of the world had civil and political rights been conferred at one stroke on so large a body of men. Many thought that freedom meant no more work and proceeded to celebrate an endless 'day of jubilee'; others were led to believe that the property of their former masters would be divided among them. 'Emancipation having been announced one day,' wrote Tom Watson about his Georgia home, 'not a Negro remained on the place the next. The fine old homestead was deserted. Every house in "the quarter" was empty. The first impulse of freedom had carried the last of the blacks to town.' Thousands took to the woods or to the road, or clustered around the United States army posts, living on doles or dying of camp diseases. As the most famous of black leaders, Frederick Douglass, said, the black 'was free from the individual master but a slave of society. He had neither money, property, nor friends. He was free from the old plantation, but he had nothing but the dusty road under his feet. He was free from the old quarter that once gave him shelter, but a slave to the rains of summer and the frosts of winter. He was turned loose, naked, hungry, and destitute to the open sky.' Deaths among blacks from starvation, disease, and violence in the first two years of freedom ran into the tens of thousands. Yet despite the deprivations of a slave society, the freedmen contributed leaders who faced these harsh realities with uncommon good sense.

To the average Southerner emancipation changed only the legal position of the Negro. Few whites were willing to acquiesce in anything approaching race equality. Some of the former slaveholders tried sincerely and with some success

Frederick Douglass (1817–95). So eloquent was he as a speaker and so independent was his spirit that some who heard him on the lecture platform refused to believe that he had been reared as a slave. He married twice, the second time to a white woman. He answered critics of his second marriage by pointing out that his first wife 'was the color of my mother, and the second, the color of my father.' (*Art Museum, University of New Mexico*)

Freedmen in Richmond, Virginia. (*Library of Congress, Brady Collection*)

to assist the black in adjusting himself to his new status. But the small farmers and the poor whites were determined to 'keep the Negro in his place,' by laws if possible, by force if necessary. J. T. Trowbridge, writing shortly after the war, remarked that 'there is at this day more prejudice against color among the middle and poorer classes . . . who owned few or no slaves, than among the planters, who owned them by the hundred.'

Most planters sought to keep their former slaves as hired help or as tenant farmers, or on the sharecrop system, and every Southern state but Tennessee attempted to assure this by a series of laws collectively known as the 'black codes.' The codes of Virginia and North Carolina, where the whites were in secure control, were mild; those of South Carolina, Mississippi, and Louisiana, where blacks outnumbered whites, severe. These black codes conferred upon the freedmen fairly extensive privileges, gave them the essential rights of citizens to contract, sue and be sued, own and inherit property, and testify in court, and made some provision for education. In no instance, however, were the freedmen accorded the vote or made eligible for juries, and for the most part they were not permitted to testify against white men. Because of their alleged aversion to work they were required to have some steady occupation, and subjected to penalties for violation of labor contracts. The especially stringent vagrancy and apprenticeship laws lent themselves readily to the establishment of peonage. The penal codes provided harsher and more arbitrary punishments for blacks than for whites, and some states permitted individual masters to administer corporal punishment to 'refractory servants.' Negroes were not allowed to bear arms, or to appear in certain public places, and there were special laws governing their domestic relations.

Southern whites, who had never dreamed it possible to live side by side with free blacks, professed to believe that these laws were liberal and generous. But every one of the codes confessed a determination to keep the freedmen in a permanent position of inferiority. This Old South point of view was succinctly expressed in the most influential of Southern journals, *De Bow's Review:*

> We of the South would not find much difficulty in managing the Negroes, if left to ourselves, for we would be guided by the lights of experience and the teachings of history. . . . We should be satisfied to compel them to engage in coarse common manual labor, and to punish them for dereliction of duty or nonfulfillment of their contracts with sufficient severity to make the great majority of them productive laborers. . . . We should treat them as mere grown-up children, entitled like children, or apprentices, to the protection of guardians and masters, and bound to obey those put above them in place of parents, just as children are so bound.

It was scarcely surprising that Northerners regarded the black codes as palpable evasions of the Thirteenth Amendment, which had abolished slavery, and conclusive evidence that the South was not prepared to accept the 'verdict of Appomattox.' In response to the black codes the North demanded that the Federal Government step in to protect the former slaves. This object, eventually embodied in the Fourteenth and Fifteenth Amendments and the various civil rights bills, was first pursued through the agencies of the Freedmen's Bureau and the military governments.

The Freedmen's Bureau of the War Department was created by Congress 3 March 1865, with powers of guardianship over Negroes and refugees, under General O. O. Howard, the 'Christian soldier.' The bureau extended relief to both races, administered justice in cases involving freedmen, and established schools for colored people. During its brief existence the Freedmen's Bureau set up over a hundred hospitals, gave medical aid to half a million patients, distributed over 20 million rations to the destitute of both races, and maintained over 4000 schools for black children. Yet, as the failure of the Freedmen's Bureau Bank—wiping out the savings of thousands of former slaves—revealed, the bureau also offered an opportunity for men of low character to enrich themselves.

The bureau's most important work was educational. As rapidly as schools were provided, the freedmen took advantage of them. 'It was a whole race trying to go to school,' wrote Booker T. Washington. 'Few were too young and none too old to make the attempt to learn. As fast as any kind of teachers could be secured, not only were day schools filled, but night schools as well. The great ambition of the older people was to try to learn to read the Bible before they died.' Most of these freedmen's schools were taught by Northern women who volunteered for what W. E. B. Du Bois called the Ninth Crusade:

> Behind the mists of ruin and rapine waved the calico dresses of women who dared, and after the hoarse mouthings of the field guns rang the rhythm of the alphabet. Rich and poor they were, serious and curious, bereaved, now of a father, now of a brother, now of more than these, they came seeking a life work in planting New England schoolhouses among the white and black of the South. They did their work well. In that first year they taught one hundred thousand souls and more.

By the end of Reconstruction there were 600,000 blacks in elementary schools in the South; the Federal Government had set up Howard University in the national capital, and private philanthropy had founded industrial schools like

Freedman's Bureau, Memphis. A long line of blacks wait to hear their cases heard. This particular office of the Bureau distributed more rations than most. (*Library of Congress*)

Hampton Institute in Virginia and Fisk in Tennessee.

Progress in land-ownership, the other great ambition of the freedmen, proved slow and halting, one of the most egregious failures of reconstruction. Northern statesmen had encouraged the Negro to look to the Federal Government to provide 'forty acres and a mule.' But in the end nothing was done to help the black man become an independent landowner. The Federal Government still owned enough public land in the South to have given every Negro family a 40-acre farm, while the cotton tax of some $68 million would have provided the mule. A Congress that was able to give 40 million acres of land to a single railroad might have done something to fulfill its obligation to the freedmen. Without effective assistance from federal—or state—governments, the vast majority of blacks could not purchase even small farms and were forced to lease land on such terms as whites were prepared to grant. And when the Negro did set up as an independent landowner he was severely handicapped by his unfamiliarity with farm management and marketing, and his lack of capital for farm animals and implements. In 1888 Georgia farmlands were valued at $88 million; the blacks, who were half the population, owned land to the value of $1.8 million.

Emancipation altered the form rather than the substance of the Negro's economic status for at least a generation after Appomattox. The transition from slave to independent farmer was long and painful, made usually through the medium of tenancy, and for many it was never completely made. Without the requisite capital, without credit except such as was cautiously extended by white bankers or storekeepers on usurious terms, and without agricultural skills, most freedmen were unable to rise above the sharecropper or tenant class. They continued to work in the fields, to live in the shacks provided by the former master or by his children, and to exist on credit provided by the same hands. A very few achieved something more—a business or a profession which brought them social standing as well as livelihood. After 1890 some blacks became laborers in the coal mines or steel mills or tobacco factories of the New South; others headed northward to work in industrial centers while their wives and daughters became 'domestics.' But the majority remained on land that belonged to others, plodding behind the plow in spring and picking cotton in the fall, reasonably sure of food and shelter and clothing, a Saturday afternoon in town, a Sunday at revival meetings, continuing in the ways of their fathers.

Reconstruction during the Civil War

Reconstruction had been debated in the North ever since the beginning of the war. As usual with American political issues involving sectional balance, the argument took place on the plane of constitutional theory. It turned largely on two questions: whether the seceded states were in or out of the Union when their rebellion was crushed and whether the prerogative of restoration lodged with President or Congress. From the Northern premise that secession was illegal, strict logic reached the conclusion that former states of the Confederacy had always been and were now states of the Union, with all the rights and privileges pertaining thereto. If, on the contrary, secession was valid, the South might consistently be treated as conquered territory, without any legal rights that the Union was required to respect. Both sides adopted the proper deductions from the other's premise. Radical Republicans, the most uncompromising nationalists, managed to prove to their satisfaction that the Southern states had lost or forfeited their rights, while former secessionists insisted that their rights in the Union from which they had seceded were unimpaired!

But the question of the status of the Southern states was to be decided in accordance not with theory but with political necessities. Lincoln, with his customary clarity, saw this, and saw, too, how dangerous was any dogmatic approach. In his last speech, on 11 April 1865, he insisted that the question whether the Southern states were in or out of the Union was 'bad as the basis of a controversy, and good for nothing at all—a merely pernicious abstraction. . . . Finding themselves safely at home, it would be utterly immaterial whether they had ever been abroad.' Obviously, these states were 'out of their proper practical relation with the Union'; the object of all should be to 'get them into their proper practical relation' again.

Lincoln had been pursuing this eminently sensible policy since the beginning of the war. As early as 1862 he had appointed provisional military governors in Tennessee, Louisiana, and North Carolina whose duty it was to re-establish loyal governments. The North Carolina experiment came to naught, but in Tennessee Governor Andrew Johnson and in Louisiana General Banks made impressive progress toward restoring federal authority, and after the fall of Vicksburg, Arkansas was similarly reclaimed. Encouraged by this success, Lincoln, in a proclamation of 8 December 1863, formulated what was to be the presidential plan of reconstruction.

The object of this plan was to get the seceded states back into their normal relations with the Federal Government as quickly and as painlessly as possible; the means was the presidential power to pardon. The plan itself provided for a general amnesty and restoration of property other than slaves to most of those who would take a prescribed oath of loyalty to the Union. Furthermore, whenever 10 per cent of the electorate of 1860 should take this oath, they might set up a state government which Lincoln promised to recognize as the true government of the state.

This magnanimous 10 per cent plan was very promptly adopted in Louisiana and Arkansas. Thousands of voters, many of them cheerfully perjuring themselves, swore that they had not willingly borne arms against the United States; they were then duly registered. They held constitutional conventions, drew up and ratified new constitutions abolishing slavery, and their states then prepared to reassume their place in the Federal Union. But all was not to be such easy sailing. Congress, which was the judge of its own membership, refused to admit the representatives of these reconstructed states, and in the presidential election of 1864 their electoral votes were not counted.

The congressional leaders had a plan of their own which carefully retained control of the entire process of reconstruction in congressional hands. The Wade-Davis Bill of 8 July 1864 stipulated that Congress, not the President, was to have jurisdiction over the processes of reconstruction, and that a majority of the electorate, instead of merely 10 per cent, was required for the reconstitution of legal state governments. When Lincoln averted this scheme by a pocket veto, he brought down upon himself the bitter excoriation of the Wade-Davis Manifesto. 'The President . . . must understand,' said the two Congressmen, 'that the authority of Congress is paramount and must be respected . . . and if he wishes our support he must confine himself to his executive duties—to obey and execute, not make the laws—to suppress by arms armed rebellion, and leave political reorganization to Congress.' Here was the real beginning of the rift between the President and the Radicals. The term refers to those who were determined to employ the power of the national government to ensure the freedmen's rights and establish the supremacy of the Republican party in national politics and of Congress in the federal administration. Though at first small, the Radical faction included such formidable leaders as Thaddeus Stevens of Pennsylvania, Ben Wade of Ohio, Zachariah Chandler of Michigan, and Charles Sumner of Massachusetts, and it would eventually come to dominate the Republican party.

With the publication of the Wade-Davis Manifesto, an issue had been raised that would not be settled until a President had been impeached, a Supreme Court intimidated, and the Constitution altered. Congressional opposition to Lincoln's plan was due in part to legislative *esprit de corps*, in part to concern for the black, in part to the hatreds engendered by the war, and in part to persuasive constitutional considerations, for it seemed only logical that Congress, which had the power to admit new states and was the judge of its own membership, should control reconstruction. Moreover, the Radicals thought it monstrous that traitors and rebels should be readmitted to full fellowship in the Union they had repudiated and tried to destroy. It would be the Union as in Buchanan's time, administered by 'rebels' and 'copperheads' for the benefit of an unrepentant slavocracy. Even Northerners who were quite willing to admit that Davis and Stephens were honorable men did not care to see them at their old desks in the Senate, shouting for state rights. Moreover, party interests were at stake. As Thaddeus Stevens put it, the Southern states 'ought never to be recognized as capable of acting in the Union, or of being counted as valid states, until the Constitution shall have been so amended . . . as to secure perpetual ascendancy to the party of the Union.' That was the nub of the matter. If the Southern states returned a solid Democratic counterpart to Congress, as appeared inevitable, a reunited Democratic party would have a majority in both houses of Congress. The amendment which Stevens had in mind was that providing for Negro suffrage, which would fulfill the moral obligation to the freedmen and create a flourishing Republican party in the South.

If the partisan considerations seem narrow, we should ask ourselves what other nation in history has ever turned over control of the government and of the spoils of victory to the leaders of a defeated rebellion.

For about six weeks after Lincoln's assassination there was a petty 'reign of terror,' directed by

Secretary Stanton and supported by President Johnson, who had always been in favor of hanging 'traitors.' Only the stern intervention of Grant prevented the seizure of Lee and other Confederate generals. Large rewards for the apprehension of Davis and his cabinet, as alleged promoters of the murder of Lincoln, resulted in their capture and temporary imprisonment. But the charge of complicity in the murder was quickly seen to be preposterous, and it was obviously impossible to get a Virginia jury to convict Davis of treason. Thirst for vengeance appeared to be slaked by the shooting or suicide of the assassin Booth, by hanging his three accomplices and the unfortunate woman who had harbored them, after an extra-legal trial by a military tribunal, and by hanging the miserable Henry Wirz, commander of the infamous Andersonville prison, for the 'murder' of Union prisoners.

All this was cause for shame, but no other great rebellion of modern times has been suppressed with so little loss of life or formal punishment of the vanquished. Not one of the rebel leaders was executed, none was brought to trial for treason. There were no mass arrests, not even of those officers of the United States who took up arms against their government. Even the civil disabilities imposed were mild; by 1872, only some 750 ex-Confederates were still barred from office-holding. For generations Southerners have rung the changes on the theme of Northern ruthlessness during the Reconstruction years, and many historians have concluded that the North imposed upon the South a 'Carthaginian peace.' Yet we have only to recall the suppression of the Peasants' Revolt in Germany in the sixteenth century, the ravages of Alva in the rebelling Low Countries, the punishments inflicted on the Irish by Cromwell and on the Scots after Culloden, or the Russian, Nazi, and Spanish revolutions of our own time, to appreciate how moderate was the conduct of the triumphant North after 1865.

Andrew Johnson Takes Charge

Lincoln's assassination and the accession to the presidency of Andrew Johnson drastically altered the political situation.[1] Like Tyler in 1841, Johnson was the nominal head of a party of which he was not really a member. Of origin as humble as Lincoln's, in early life a tailor in a Tennessee mountain village and unable to write until taught by his wife, he possessed many of Lincoln's virtues but lacked his ability to handle men. Self-educated and self-trained, he had a powerful though not well-disciplined mind. United with these intellectual qualities were the virtues of integrity, devotion to duty, and courage. But at a time when tact was called for, he was stubborn and inflexible; Johnson 'had no budge in him.' And he misunderstood the revolution brought by the war.

No President ever faced a more difficult situation. He had no personal following either in the South or in the North, none of the prestige that came to Lincoln from the successful conduct of the war, and no party organization behind him, for he had broken with the Democrats and had not been accepted by the Republicans. Seward and Welles were loyal to Johnson, but Stanton, with his customary duplicity, used the machinery of the War Department against him and kept the Radicals posted on cabinet secrets. Yet at the outset the Radicals were a minority, and they were generally well disposed toward him. It was Johnson's own blunders that isolated him not only from the Radicals but from the moderates.

At first Johnson appeared to be willing to cooperate with the Radicals. 'Treason is a crime and must be punished,' he said; 'treason must be made infamous, and traitors must be impoverished.' Bluff Ben Wade exclaimed exultantly, 'Johnson, we have faith in you. By the gods, there will be no trouble now in running this government.'

1. Some of the Radicals rejoiced in the removal of Lincoln and the accession of Johnson. 'I spent most of the afternoon in a political caucus,' wrote Representative George Julian of Indiana, 'and while everybody was shocked at his murder, the feeling was nearly universal that the accession of Johnson to the Presidency would prove a godsend to the country. Aside from Mr. Lincoln's known policy of tenderness to the Rebels . . . his . . . views of the subject of Reconstruction were as distasteful as possible to radical Republicans.'

But soon there was trouble enough. When Congress was not in session, Johnson swung around to a sharply different course. He proceeded to appoint provisional civil governors in all Confederate states where Lincoln had not already done so. These governors were enjoined to summon state constitutional conventions, which were to be elected by the 'whitewashed rebels'—former citizens of the Confederacy who took the oath of allegiance required by the presidential proclamation. Fourteen specified classes, assumed to be inveterate rebels, were excluded from this general amnesty and required to make personal application for pardon. Although many of those thus proscribed did receive special pardons from President Johnson, the general effect was to exclude many experienced statesmen from participation in the task of establishing the new state governments. The ensuing constitutional conventions invalidated the ordinances of secession, repudiated the state war debts—which they could not in any event have paid—declared slavery abolished, and wrote new state constitutions. Not one granted the vote to any class of blacks. Elections were promptly held under these new or amended constitutions, and by the autumn of 1865 regular civil administrations were functioning in all former Confederate states except Texas.

This speedy process of reconstruction excited distrust in the North. That distrust was exacerbated by the enactment of black codes, and by the understandable but impolitic alacrity with which Southern voters elected their former Confederate leaders to high offices. As James G. Blaine later wrote, 'If the Southern men had intended, as their one special and desirable aim, to inflame public opinion of the North against them, they would have proceeded precisely as they did.' Many Northerners came to believe that reconstruction had been accomplished before the South had either repented its sins or become reconciled to defeat. To meet this criticism Johnson, in the fall of 1865, sent a number of observers to survey conditions in the South. They returned with reports that the South had fairly 'accepted defeat,' but many continued to doubt that Southerners were willing to accord the Negro equal rights. 'Refusing to see that a mighty cataclysm had shaken the profoundest depths of national life,' says Professor Coulter, Southerners 'did not expect that many things would be made anew but rather looked for them to be mended as of old,—that Humpty Dumpty might after all be put back on the wall.'

Congress Intervenes

The Congress which met for the first time on 4 December 1865 appointed a joint committee of both Houses with authority to investigate and report on the title of Southern members-elect. This Joint Committee of Fifteen, a resurrection of the old Committee on the Conduct of the War, formulated the theory and set the pace of congressional reconstruction. The committee was not controlled by the Radicals, and many of the crucial measures came from moderates like Lyman Trumbull.

The most influential member of the committee was Thaddeus Stevens of Pennsylvania, leader of the Republicans in the House. A sincere democrat, lifelong spokesman for the poor and the oppressed, and tireless champion of public education, Stevens was now an embittered old man of seventy-four nursing an implacable enmity toward the Southern slavocracy and President Johnson, who, he thought, stood between them and their just deserts. 'The punishment of traitors,' he declared, 'has been wholly ignored by a treacherous Executive and a sluggish Congress. To this issue I desire to devote the small remnant of my life.' And he did. 'Strip a proud nobility of the bloated estates,' he demanded; 'reduce them to a level with plain republicans; send them forth to labor and teach their children to enter the workshops or handle a plow, and you will thus humble the proud traitors.' Partly out of passionate devotion to the Negro, partly out of conviction that the welfare of the Union was identical with the triumph of the Republican party, Stevens was determined to impose black suffrage on the South. 'I am for Negro suffrage in every rebel State,' he said. 'If it be just it should not be denied; if it be necessary it should be adopted; if it be punishment to traitors, they deserve it.' He insisted that Congress should treat the Southern states as nothing but conquered provinces.

Charles Sumner of Massachusetts, Republican leader in the Senate, was not on the Joint Committee, but next to Stevens he was the most powerful figure in congressional reconstruction. An idealist by conviction, and a reformer by training, he was a pedantic dogmatist, but in his way quite as sincere as Stevens. Against the ex-Confederates he held no vindictive feelings, but he was committed to giving Negroes the vote. Sumner advanced the theory that the Southern states had committed political suicide, had extinguished their standing as states, and were in the position of territories subject to the exclusive jurisdiction of Congress. Vain, humorless, and irritable, Sumner nevertheless had a distinguished record as a champion of good causes: the New England intellectuals looked to him for leadership, his polished orations impressed the commonalty, and he infused the Radical movement with altruism.

The Joint Committee propounded the theory of reconstruction upon which Congress ultimately acted. It announced that 'the States lately in rebellion were . . . disorganized communities, without civil government and without constitutions or other forms by virtue of which political relation could legally exist between them and the federal government,' that they had 'forfeited all civil and political rights and privileges under the federal Constitution,' and that they could be restored to their political rights only by Congress. In other words, the states were intact, but the state governments were, for most but not for all purposes, in a condition of suspended animation. Under this interpretation it was possible for Congress at once to deny representation to the Southern states and to accept the ratification of the Thirteenth Amendment by the legislatures of these same states.

The Radical program can be summarized:

1. To keep the ex-Confederate states out of the Union until they had set up governments that could be regarded as 'republican' in nature.
2. To require them, as prerequisites for readmission, to repeal their black codes, disqualify those who had been active in rebellion from holding state office, guarantee the Negro his civil rights and give him the right to vote and to hold office. Furthermore, they advocated constitutional amendments to protect the civil rights of the blacks.
3. To ensure a larger role for Congress in the process of reconstruction.

The Radicals did not, as is often said, share a common attitude on economic policy. They frequently held diametrically opposite views on currency and the tariff, and businessmen, who had diverse interests and attitudes, were as likely to be against them as for them. Some of the Radicals, however, wished to assure permanence to that body of tariff, agricultural, and money legislation which had been written into the statute books during the war years, and were prepared to exploit the Reconstruction crisis to achieve their ends.

The bitter conflict between the Radicals and President Johnson erupted over a proposal that represented the ideas not merely of the Radicals but of most Republicans and was, in fact, sponsored by the moderate Lyman Trumbull. Opposition to legislation to enlarge the scope of the Freedmen's Bureau bill centered in the Democrats, who exploited race prejudice; not one Democrat in either house of Congress voted for the bill. But on 19 February 1866 Johnson opened war on the advocates of civil rights by vetoing the measure.[2] In a shocking speech three days later, he denounced the campaign for Negro rights and cried that Stevens, Sumner, and Wendell Phillips were planning to assassinate him. Many Northern Republicans read Johnson out of the party.

Yet most Republicans still wanted conciliation with Johnson, and they hoped to win his approval for a second measure sponsored by Trumbull, a Civil Rights bill which sought to protect the rights of the freedman in the courts rather than through such institutions as the army. Congress enacted the bill, again without a single Democratic vote, but Johnson stunned his party by vetoing this measure too. The President announced that he opposed 'the Africanization of half the United States.' After this veto most Republicans broke with the President, and Congress passed the bill

2. A second Freedmen's Bureau bill was subsequently passed over the presidential veto, 16 July 1866.

Andrew Johnson had the misfortune to be the first political figure singled out by Thomas Nast, the greatest cartoonist of his day, for caricature. In this illustration (which depicts the atrocities suffered by blacks in the early Reconstruction period), Nast portrays the President as Iago and a wounded but proud black Union veteran as the scornful Othello. (*Harper's Weekly, 1 Sept., 1866*)

over his veto. Not Sumner nor Stevens but Johnson himself had turned the men of moderation in the party against the administration.

By now the Republicans were determined to write new guarantees into the Constitution and to insist that the Southern states accept them before they were readmitted into the Union. On 30 April 1866 the Committee of Fifteen reported the Fourteenth Amendment, the most important ever added to the Constitution. It was designed to guarantee the civil rights of the Negro against unfavorable legislation by the states, reduce congressional representation in proportion to the denial of suffrage to Negroes, disqualify ex-Confederates who had formerly held office, invalidate the Confederate debt, and validate the federal debt. Section I of the amendment was particularly significant. It first defined citizenship, and then provided that 'No State shall make or enforce any law which shall abridge the privileges or immunities of citizens of the United States; nor shall any State deprive any person of life, liberty, or property, without due process of law; nor deny to any person within its jurisdiction the equal protection of the laws.' It thus for the first time clearly threw the protection of the Federal Government around the rights of life, liberty, and property which might be invaded by the states, reversing the traditional relationships between these governments which had from the beginning distinguished our federal system. Designed to protect the Negro, this stipulation came increasingly to be construed as extending the protection of the Federal Government to corporations whose property rights were threatened by state legislation, although the framers of the amendment did not anticipate any such interpretation.

There was ample evidence that the freedman needed national protection. The conservative General Jefferson C. Davis reported that in Kentucky 19 blacks had been killed, 233 maltreated, and none of the offenders had been prosecuted. In Texas, one black was murdered for not doffing his hat; in Louisiana, a black who answered a white boy 'quickly' was 'taken thro' the town and across the Levee, and there stripped and terribly beaten, with raw-hides.' In May 1866 a mob of whites, aided by some of the police, burned and pillaged the Negro quarter of Memphis and killed 46 freedmen. In New Orleans on 30 July, a mob, numbering many police and former Confederate soldiers, assaulted a convention of Negroes and white Radicals, and killed and wounded scores in cold blood.

Everything now turned on the election of a new Congress in the autumn of 1866, one of the most critical contests in our history. A National Union Convention of moderates from both sections pledged support of the President but did not form a new party or create party machinery. Hence in most congressional districts in the North voters had to choose between a Radical Republican and a Copperhead Democrat. Faced with this prospect many moderate Republicans went over to the Radical camp. Johnson apparently sought a political realignment in which, with the Radicals driven from the party, he could lead a union of Republicans with War Democrats and Southern loyalists. Instead, he cut himself off from the mass of his own party. Southerners, he said, 'cannot be treated as subjugated people or vassal colonies without a germ of hatred being introduced, which will some day or other, though the time may be distant, develop mischief of the most serious character.' But the President proved to be an immoderate advocate of moderation. His 'swing around the circle,' a stumping tour of the Middle West, became in many instances an undignified exercise in vituperation. 'I would ask you,' the President shouted on 3 September 1866 in Cleveland, 'Why not hang Thad Stevens and Wendell Phillips?' The outcome was a smashing victory for the Republicans, who picked up a margin in Congress large enough to override a presidential veto.

Johnson saw himself as the champion of the Constitution, and he was a stubborn man, but Congress was no less determined. When ten of the former Confederate states refused to ratify the Fourteenth Amendment, they left Congress with no alternative save more drastic measures or acquiescence in denying equality to the Negro. In February 1867 Congressman James Garfield cried, 'The last of the sinful ten has, with contempt and scorn, flung back into our teeth the magnanimous offer of a generous nation. It is now our turn to act.'

Congressional Reconstruction

The Radicals took the results of the fall elections as a vindication of their 'thorough' policy, and under the implacable leadership of Stevens whipped through a series of measures of far-reaching importance. This program undid the whole of presidential reconstruction, placed the Southern states back where they had been in April 1865, and temporarily revolutionized the political system by substituting a quasi-parliamentary for a presidential system of government.

The most important legislation of the entire period was the First Reconstruction Act of 2 March 1867. This act declared that 'no legal government' existed in any Southern state except Tennessee, and divided the rest of the South into five military districts subject to army commanders. Escape from this military regime and restitution of state rights were promised on condition that a constitutional convention, chosen by universal male suffrage, set up governments based on black and white suffrage and that the new state legislatures ratify the Fourteenth Amendment. Johnson returned the bill with a scorching message, but to no avail.

In March 1867 military rule replaced the civil governments that had been operating in the South for over a year. The military governors ruled with a firm hand, sometimes with flagrant disregard for the rights of white inhabitants, at the same time that they secured rights for Negroes that these whites had denied them. Thousands of local officials were removed to make way for Northern 'carpetbaggers' or Negroes; the governors of six states were displaced and others appointed in their place; civil courts were superseded by military tribunals; the legislatures of Georgia, Alabama, and Louisiana were purged of conservatives; state legislation was set aside or modified; and an army of occupation, some 20,000 strong and aided by a force of Negro militia, kept order. The relatively brief rule of the major generals was harsh but had the merits of honesty and a certain rude efficiency. Particularly important were the efforts to cope with economic disorganization and to regulate the social life of their satrapies. Thus in South Carolina, General Sickles abolished imprisonment for debt, stayed foreclosures on property, made the wages of farm laborers a first lien on crops, prohibited the manufacture of whiskey, and softened racial discrimination.

The main task of the military commanders was to create new electorates and establish new governments. In each of the ten states they enrolled a new electorate; in South Carolina, Alabama, Florida, Mississippi, and Louisiana black voters outnumbered white. This electorate chose in every state a constitutional convention which, under the guidance of carpetbaggers, drafted new state constitutions enfranchising blacks, disfranchising ex-Confederate leaders, and guaranteeing civil and political equality to the freedmen.

These new state constitutions represented, in almost every instance, a definite advance upon the older constitutions. The Constitution of South Carolina, for example, set up a far more democratic, humane, and efficient system of government than that which had obtained during the antebellum regime. In addition to providing for universal manhood suffrage it abolished property qualifications for office-holding, reapportioned representation in the legislature, drew up a more elaborate Bill of Rights, abolished all 'distinctions on account of color,' reformed local government and judicial administration, outlawed dueling and imprisonment for debt, protected homesteads from foreclosure, enlarged the rights of women, and provided—on paper—for a system of universal public education.

By the summer of 1868 reconstructed governments had been set up in eight Southern states: the other three—Mississippi, Texas, and Virginia—were reconstructed in 1870. After the legislatures of the reconstructed states had duly ratified the Fourteenth Amendment, as well as the Fifteenth Amendment which stipulated that 'the right of citizens of the United States to vote shall not be denied or abridged by the United States or by any State on account of race, color, or previous condition of servitude.' Congress formally readmitted them, seated their elected representatives and senators, and, as soon as the new governments appeared reasonably secure, withdrew the army.

Ambitious as their program for Reconstruction

was, the Radicals had an even larger ultimate aim—modifying the American governmental system by establishing congressional supremacy. The majority of Congress, not the Supreme Court, was to be the final judge of the powers of Congress; the President a servant of Congress. This new dispensation was implicit in the Reconstruction Act of 2 March 1867 and in two other pieces of legislation adopted the same day. First, the Command of the Army Act virtually deprived the Executive of control of the army by requiring that he issue all military orders through the General of the Army, who was protected against removal or suspension from office. Second, the Tenure of Office Act, by denying the President the right to remove civil officials, including members of his cabinet, without the consent of the Senate, made it impossible for him to control his own administration. The Radicals put it through in order to prevent Johnson from continuing to wield the patronage weapon against them and to stop him from ousting Secretary of War Stanton, the last Radical sympathizer left in the cabinet. The next move in the game was to dispose of Johnson by the impeachment process, whereupon Benjamin Wade, president *pro tem.* of the Senate, would succeed to his office and title.

Impeachment had been proposed by Benjamin Butler in October 1866, and all through the following year a House committee had been trying to gather evidence which might support such action, but without success. Now Johnson furnished the House with the excuse for which it had waited. Convinced that the Tenure of Office Act was unconstitutional, he requested and then ordered Secretary Stanton to resign. Stanton himself thought the act unconstitutional and had even helped write the veto message, but when General Lorenzo Thomas, the newly appointed Secretary of War, sought to take possession of his office, Stanton barricaded himself in the War Department. On 24 February 1868, the House voted to impeach the President for 'high Crimes and Misdemeanors,' and within a week eleven articles of impeachment were agreed upon by the Radicals. Ten of the articles dealt with the removal of Stanton; the other consisted of garbled newspaper reports from the President's speeches. A monstrous charge to

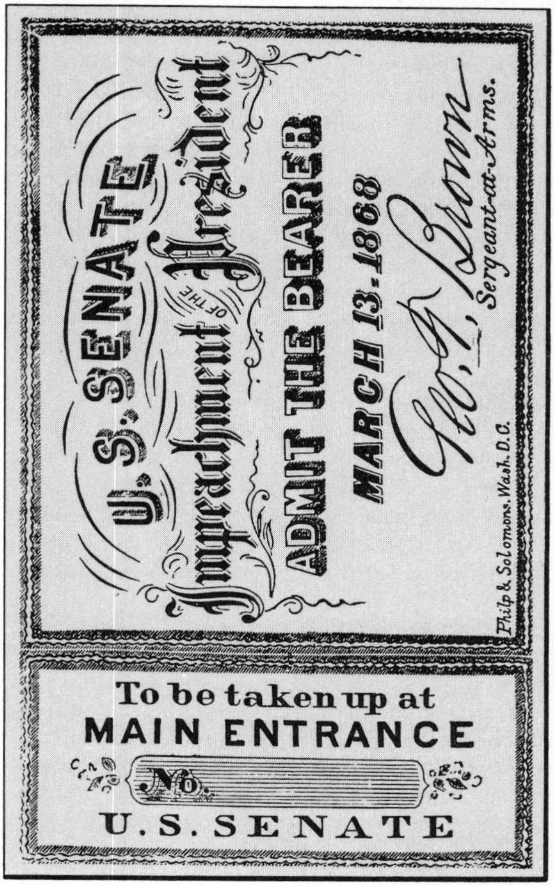

the effect that Johnson was an accomplice in the murder of Lincoln was finally excluded.

The impeachment of Johnson was one of the most disgraceful episodes in the history of the Federal Government, one that barely failed to suspend the presidential system. For had impeachment succeeded, the Radicals would have established the principle that Congress may remove a President not for 'high Crimes and Misdemeanors,' as required by the Constitution, but for purely political reasons. The managers of impeachment themselves admitted this; Johnson's crime, they asserted in their report, was 'the one great purpose of reconstructing the rebel states in accordance with his own will.' The President was defended by able counsel including William M. Evarts, leader of the American bar, and Benjamin R. Curtis, formerly a justice of the Supreme Court. These tore the allegations to shreds, and it was soon apparent to all but the most prejudiced that there was no valid case. Even the Tenure of Office Act charges proved groundless, for the law restrained a President from removing a cabinet officer he had appointed, and Stanton had been named not by Johnson but by Lincoln. Yet the Radicals would have succeeded in their object but for Chief Justice Chase, who insisted upon legal procedure, and for seven courageous Republican Senators who risked their political future by voting for acquittal.[3] One more affirmative vote and Ben Wade—who himself voted for conviction—would have been installed in the White House. Then, in all probability, the Court would have been battered into submission.

President Grant

Even as the Senate sat in solemn judgment on President Johnson, the triumphant Republicans met in party convention to nominate his successor, General Grant. Before the Civil War he had seldom taken the trouble to vote, and such political principles as he professed had inclined him toward the Democrats. He had been to Lincoln a faithful subordinate but to Johnson less than faithful, and after his break with Johnson he had been captured by the Radical politicians who saw in him an unbeatable candidate.

The campaign that followed was bitterly fought. To Republicans success promised an indefinite tenure of power, during which the party might be given a national basis through the extension of suffrage to the Southern blacks. To the Democrats, who nominated the former governor of New York, Horatio Seymour, whose wartime record had associated him with the Copperheads, victory would spell the end of federal backing for the Negro, and the restoration of the remaining Southern states. The Republicans waved the 'bloody shirt of the rebellion' effectively. Grant carried all the states but eight, although his popular majority was only 300,000. The Negro vote of some 450,000 gave him his popular margin, and the exclusion of three Southern states (Mississippi, Texas, Virginia) and the control of six others assured him his large electoral college majority. With less equipment for the presidency than any predecessor save Harrison and a temperament unfitted for high political office, Grant was unable to overcome his deficiencies. Although a leader of men, he was not a good judge of men, and the very simplicity which had carried him safely through the intrigues of the Civil War exposed him to the wiles of politicians whose loyalty to himself he mistook for devotion to the public weal. It came as a shock that he seemed to have lost the qualities he had shown in the war—a sense of order and of command, resoluteness, and consistency. The magnanimous victor of Appomattox revealed himself in office petty, vindictive, and shifty. He was naïve rather than innocent, and his simplicity, as Henry Adams remarked, 'was more disconcerting than the complexity of a Talleyrand.' He regarded the presidency as a personal prerogative, a reward for services rendered rather than a responsibility.

Grant's only hope lay in the wisdom and integrity of his advisers, but his choices were bizarre. Altogether, during his eight years of office, Grant appointed no less than twenty-six men to his cabinet. Six—Hoar, Cox, Creswell, Jewell, Bristow, and Fish—proved to be men of intelligence and integrity, and of these Grant managed to dismiss all but one, Secretary of State Fish. It was fortunate that Grant was able to command, throughout the eight years of his administration, the talents of Hamilton Fish. A New York patrician, Grant's third choice for the State Department, and relatively unknown when he took office, Fish proved himself one of the shrewdest men who have ever directed the foreign affairs of the nation. He had what most of his colleagues in Grant's cabinet lacked—honesty, disciplined intelligence, learning, experience, urbanity, and a

3. Fessenden, Grimes, Trumbull, Ross, Van Winkle, Fowler, and Henderson. Fessenden died in 1869; none of the others was re-elected to the Senate; yet they did not suffer as severely as the legend of their martyrdom would suggest.

tact and patience sufficient to win and retain the confidence of his chief.

Yet for all his defects, Grant retained the devotion of millions. 'The plain man,' as Allan Nevins observes, 'had not elected Grant; he had elected an indestructible legend, a folk-hero.' It was well for Grant that he brought to the presidency this imperishable glamor, for he brought little else.

Radical Reconstruction in the South

The election of 1868 strengthened the position of the Radicals. To be sure, 'Let us have peace,' the concluding phrase of Grant's letter accepting the presidential nomination, had led the country to believe that Grant would abandon Radical reconstruction and adopt toward the white South a more conciliatory policy, and in the beginning this belief seemed justified. The President suggested to his cabinet a sweeping amnesty proclamation and urged Congress to complete the reconstruction process in Virginia, Mississippi, and Texas. By 1870 representatives from these states again sat in Congress. But it was soon clear that Grant was still in the Radical camp. He took the lead in a drastic reconstitution of the legislature of Georgia, and in South Carolina, Alabama, Mississippi, Louisiana, and Arkansas, he authorized the use of federal troops to overthrow duly elected Democratic governments and keep these states in the Radical Republican ranks.

Inevitably Radical reconstruction aroused determined opposition, which took both legal and illegal form. In states such as Virginia and North Carolina, where whites greatly outnumbered blacks, the Democrats recaptured control of the state governments by regular political methods almost at once. Elsewhere it was thought necessary to resort to a much greater degree of intimidation to destroy the combination that made Radical success possible. Whites who took part in Reconstruction soon felt the heavy weight of economic pressure or the sharp sting of social ostracism. Negroes were dealt with more ruthlessly, by employing terror.

Much of this violence was perpetrated by secret societies, of which the most famous, though not the largest, was the Ku Klux Klan. In 1867 a social *kuklos* (circle) of young men in Pulaski, Tennessee, organized as the 'Invisible Empire of the South,' with elaborate ritual and ceremonial. The KKK described itself as an institution of 'chivalry, humanity, mercy and patriotism,' but it was in fact simply an institution for the maintenance of white supremacy. During the next three or four years the KKK and other secret societies—notably the Knights of the White Camellia and the White Leagues of Louisiana and Mississippi—policed 'unruly' Negroes in the country districts, discouraged blacks from serving in the militia, delivered spectral warnings against using the ballot, and punished those who disregarded the warnings. The Ku Klux Klan investigation of 1871 reported 153 Negroes murdered in a single Florida county that year; over 300 murdered in parishes outside New Orleans; bloody race riots in Mississippi and Louisiana; a reign of terror in parts of Arkansas; and in Texas, 'murders, robberies and outrages of all kinds.' Not all of this could be laid at the doors of the Klan or the White Leaguers, or even of the whites, but groups like the KKK were responsible for most of the violence that afflicted the South during these turbulent years. Under the impact of all this, Negro participation in politics declined sharply, and the Radical cause was put in jeopardy.

The Radicals had no intention of acquiescing tamely in the undoing of reconstruction. Their answer was first a series of state laws which sought to break up the secret societies and, when these proved unavailing, an appeal to Washington for help. The Grant administration responded with renewed military occupation of evacuated districts, the unseating of Democratic administrations on the ground of fraud, and a new crop of supervisory laws of which the most important were the Force Acts of 1870 and 1871 and the drastic Ku Klux Klan Act of 1871 authorizing the President to suspend the writ of habeas corpus and suppress violence by military force. Altogether some 7000 indictments and over 1000 convictions were found under these acts, but they did not fulfill their purpose. In large areas of the South—notably in South Carolina, Louisiana, and Mississippi—violence flourished throughout the entire reconstruction period.

From 1868 to 1877 the Radicals controlled, for

The KKK. This engraving is from a photograph of Mississippi Klansmen who were caught wearing these disguises after they attempted to murder a family. (*Library of Congress*)

varying periods, most of the reconstructed states of the South, but it was not, as it is sometimes called, 'Black Reconstruction.' In no state did the blacks ever control the government, and only in South Carolina—where blacks outnumbered whites four to three—did they have even a temporary majority in the legislature. There were no black governors, and very few Negroes in high positions in the executive branch or in administration. At no time did Negroes have a representation proportional to their numbers in any branch of any government.

Radical control of Southern states was exercised by an uneasy coalition of three groups—Negroes, 'carpetbaggers,' and 'scalawags.' Both of the latter words are heavily loaded. The one conjures up the image of an impecunious Yankee adventurer descending on a prostrate South with a carpetbag to be stuffed full of loot; the other was a word commonly applied to runty cattle and, by implication, to the lowest breed of Southerner. There were, in truth, disreputable adventurers among the carpetbaggers, but most were Union veterans who had returned to the South to farm, businessmen looking for good investments, government agents who for one reason or another decided to stay on in the South, schoolteachers who thought of themselves as a kind of 'peace corps' to the freedmen. As for the 'scalawags'—the largest single element in the Radical coalition—these were the men who had opposed secession in the first place and were now ready to return to the old Union and to take in the blacks as junior partners in the enterprise of restoration.

The Radical governments were, in many cases, incompetent, extravagant, and corrupt. The corruption was pervasive and ostentatious. In Florida, for example, the cost of public printing in 1869 exceeded the total cost for all of the state government in 1860; in South Carolina the state maintained a restaurant and barroom for the legislators at a cost of $125,000 for a single session, and under the head of 'legislative supplies' provided Westphalia hams, Brussels carpets, and ornamental cuspidors; and in Louisiana the youthful Governor Warmoth managed to garner a fortune of half a million dollars during four years of office, while bartering away state property and dissipating school funds. But corruption did not begin with the advent of the Radicals, nor did it cease when they were forced from office. The land and railroad legislation of some of the 'Redeemer' governments was no less corrupt and considerably more expensive than anything that the Radical governments achieved. Corruption was confined to no class, no party, and no section: larceny by the Tweed Ring in New York City and the Gas Ring in Philadelphia made the Southern Radicals look like feckless amateurs, as most of them were.

Radical reconstruction was expensive, and taxes and indebtedness mounted throughout the South, but we should keep in mind mitigating circumstances. The task of repairing the damages of the war was herculean and made unprecedented demands on government; with emancipation the population requiring public services had almost doubled and Radical governments for the first time tried to set up public schools for all children; much of the property that had customarily borne the burden of taxation—banks, railroads, and industries—had been destroyed by the war, leaving almost the whole burden to fall on real estate. Some two-thirds of the total new indebtedness was in the form of guarantees to railroads and other industries. In this extravagant and often corrupt policy of underwriting railroads, the conservative governments which succeeded the Radicals spent, or pledged, more money than had the Radicals. Of the situation in Alabama, John Hope Franklin has observed, 'Corruption was bisectional, bipartisan and biracial.'

More important was the constructive side of Radical reconstruction—progressive legislation. In South Carolina the Radical legislature reformed the system of taxation, dispensed relief to the poor, distributed homesteads to Negroes, established numerous charitable and humane institutions, encouraged immigration, and, for the first time in the history of the state, provided free public schools and compelled attendance of all children from six to sixteen. It was in the realm of public education that the Radical governments made their most significant contribution. In general the Radical legislatures advanced political democracy and inaugurated social reforms, and these contributions go far to justify a favorable judgment upon them. So, too, does the consideration that the Radical legislatures enacted no vindictive legislation against the former slaveowners.

Notwithstanding these accomplishments, the Negro was unable to make any serious dent on Southern white hostility or prejudice. Convinced that he was incompetent politically, Southern whites blamed him for all the ills and burdens and humiliations of reconstruction. And because the experiment of black participation in politics had been associated with the Republican party, Southerners concluded that Democrats were the party of white supremacy and fastened upon the South a one-party system. Because some progressive laws were identified with carpetbag and Negro rule, they came to distrust such legislation. Because high taxes had accompanied Radical rule, they concluded that economy and good government were synonymous. Even many of their quondam

Northern champions reached the unhappy conclusion that black participation in politics had been premature.

Reconstruction and the Constitution

At no time in American history has the Constitution been subjected to so severe or prolonged a strain as during the era of reconstruction. There arose at once a number of knotty problems concerning the legal status of the seceded states after Appomattox and the status of persons who had participated in the rebellion. Throughout the war President Lincoln maintained the legal principle that the states were indestructible. This theory, though vigorously controverted by the Radical leaders, received judicial support in *Texas v. White* in 1869, in which Chief Justice Chase, speaking for the majority, said:

> The Constitution, in all of its provisions, looks to an indestructible Union composed of indestructible States. . . . Considered, therefore, as transactions under the Constitution, the ordinance of secession . . . and all the acts of her legislature intended to give effect to that ordinance, were absolutely null. They were utterly without operation in law. The obligations of the State, as a member of the Union, remained perfect and unimpaired. . . . Our conclusion therefore is, that Texas continued to be a State, and a State of the Union.

Upon what theory, then, could reconstruction proceed? If the states were still in the Union, it was only the citizens who were out of their normal relations with the Federal Government, and these could be restored through the pardoning power of the President. This was Lincoln's theory, and Johnson took it over from him; when, in a series of proclamations, Johnson declared the insurrection at an end, the Supreme Court accepted his proclamations as legally binding.

But if the insurrection was at an end, by virtue of what authority did Congress proceed to impose military government upon Southern states and set up military courts? The Supreme Court had already passed upon the question of military courts in *ex parte Milligan.* In this case involving the validity of military courts in Indiana, the Court laid down the doctrine that 'martial rule can never exist where the courts are open, and in the proper and unobstructed exercise of their jurisdiction'; and to the argument of military necessity the Court said, 'No doctrine involving more pernicious consequences was ever invented by the wit of man than that any of the [Constitution's] provisions can be suspended during any of the great exigencies of government. Such a doctrine leads directly to anarchy or despotism.' Yet within a year, in clear violation of this decision, Congress established military tribunals throughout the South; and when the validity of this legislation was challenged, in the McCardle case, Congress rushed through a law depriving the Court of jurisdiction over the case, while the Supreme Court sat idly by.

Radical leaders sought to legitimize their policies by relying upon the clause in the Constitution that 'the United States shall guarantee to every State a Republican Form of Government.' For three-quarters of a century this clause had been interpreted to mean that Congress would sustain the pre-existing governments, but now the Radicals insisted that—for the Southern states at least—a 'republican' form of government included Negro suffrage, despite the fact that at the beginning of the Reconstruction era only six Northern states permitted the black man to vote. The Court supported the Radicals to the extent of declaring that 'the power to carry into effect the clause of guarantee is primarily a legislative power, and resides in Congress.'

Some of the reconstruction acts were palpably unconstitutional, but the attitude of the Radicals was well expressed by General Grant when he said of this legislation that 'much of it, no doubt, was unconstitutional; but it was hoped that the laws enacted would serve their purpose before the question of constitutionality could be submitted to the judiciary and a decision obtained.' This hope was well founded, for the validity of some of the reconstruction measures never came before the courts, and others were not passed upon until long after they had 'served their purpose.' When Mississippi asked for an injunction restraining President Johnson from carrying out the reconstruction acts, the Supreme Court refused to accept jurisdiction. Georgia then brought suit against Secretary of War Stanton and General Grant, but once again the Court refused to intervene in what it termed a political controversy.

Individuals fared somewhat better. In *ex parte Garland* the operation of the federal test oath to exclude lawyers who had participated in the rebellion from practicing in federal courts was declared unconstitutional because *ex post facto;* and in *Cummings v. Missouri* similar state legislation was held invalid on the same grounds. For practical reasons it proved almost impossible to challenge the constitutionality of the confiscation of cotton or other property seized from those who were assumed to be rebels, but one notable case vindicated the right of the individual against lawless action even when committed in the name of the United States government. During the war Robert E. Lee's splendid estate at Arlington, Virginia, had been seized for nonpayment of taxes and bid in by the Federal Government, which then used it as a national cemetery. Long after the war the heirs of Lee brought suit. By a five to four vote the Supreme Court held that it would hear a suit against a sovereign—or its agents—and that the original seizure was illegal. Constitutionally, the significance of the decision lies in the assertion that no official of the government may cloak himself in the immunity of sovereignty for his illegal acts.

The Grant Administration

While Grant was wrestling with the difficult problems of Reconstruction he also had to concern himself with diplomatic and economic issues that were often altogether unrelated to the question of what policy to pursue toward the South. Thanks to Seward the Johnson administration was at its best in the realm of foreign affairs. Thanks to Hamilton Fish the Grant administration likewise won its most notable successes in this area. Both administrations had to cope with vexatious foreign questions which had grown out of the Civil War. Seward, by his firm attitude toward the French in Mexico and the Spaniards in Santo Domingo, sustained the Monroe Doctrine, and by strokes of diplomacy advanced imperialism in the Pacific. Spain's attempted conquest of Santo Domingo broke down of its own accord, but the Spanish withdrawal from the island in 1865 appeared to be a diplomatic victory for Seward. Two years later Seward persuaded Napoleon III he must abandon the Mexican venture: in June 1867 the puppet-Emperor Maximilian slumped before a firing squad and the cardboard empire collapsed. Russia had long been eager to get rid of Alaska, and in 1867 Sumner in the Senate and a well-oiled lobby in the House permitted Seward to buy that rich domain, known at the time as 'Seward's Folly,' for $7,200,000. To round out his expansionist policy Seward annexed the Midway Islands west of Hawaii, and, with a view to the construction of an isthmian canal at some future date, acquired the right of transit across Nicaragua.

President Grant was enormously interested in another of Seward's projects—the annexation of Santo Domingo. This hare-brained proposal had originated with two Yankee fortune-hunters who planned to secure for themselves half the wealth of the island. They managed to draw into their conspiracy powerful economic interests and bought the support of such men as Ben Butler, John A. Rawlins, and Grant's personal secretary, Orville Babcock; these in turn won over the President. But when Grant submitted a treaty of annexation to the Senate, it encountered the implacable hostility of Charles Sumner and Carl Schurz and failed of ratification, a severe defeat for the administration.

The Santo Domingo episode, in itself minor, had important consequences. It revealed how easily Grant could be taken in and how naïve was his understanding of foreign affairs. It led to the deposition of Charles Sumner as chairman of the Senate Committee on Foreign Affairs, which widened the rift in the Republican party. And by distracting the attention of Grant and the Radicals from the Cuban situation, it enabled Fish to preserve peace with Spain.

A Cuban rebellion had broken out in 1868 and dragged on for ten dreadful years before it was finally suppressed. The sympathy of most Americans was with the rebels, but a movement to recognize Cuban belligerency encountered the firm opposition of Fish. Recognition would have been a serious mistake, for it would have gravely com-

A ripening pear. In this 1868 *Harper's Weekly* engraving, a covetous Secretary of State, William H. Seward, advocates annexation of Cuba, which had just raised the standard of rebellion against Spain, while a sage Uncle Sam counsels patience—but with the same end in view. Seward, who roved the Caribbean from Santo Domingo to the Danish West Indies in search of acquisitions, aimed at nothing less than 'possession of the American continent and the control of the world,' but Congress restrained his ambitions. From the presidency of James K. Polk to that of John Fitzgerald Kennedy, 'the Pearl of the Antilles,' only ninety miles off the Florida coast, tempted and vexed American administrations. (*Library of Congress*)

promised pending American claims against Great Britain for premature recognition of the belligerency of the Confederacy. As it was, the United States and Spain came to the very brink of war in 1873 over the curious *Virginius* affair. The *Virginius*, a ship flying the U.S. flag and carrying arms for the Cuban insurgents, was captured on the high seas by a Spanish gunboat; fifty-three of her seamen, including eight Americans, were summarily executed for 'piracy.' When Spain disowned the barbarous deed and paid an indemnity, and when it was discovered that the ship had no right to her American papers or to fly the American flag, the danger of war evaporated.

To the northward, too, relations were strained. During the war Canada had furnished a base for

Confederate raids on Vermont and New York. In time of peace the Fenians, or Irish Revolutionary Brother-Republics, took similar liberties in the United States. Two rival Irish republics were organized in New York City, each with its president, cabinet, and general staff in glittering uniforms of green and gold. Each planned to seize Canada with Irish veterans of the Union army, and hold it as hostage for Irish freedom. The first invasion, in April 1866, was promptly nipped by federal authorities at Eastport, Maine. But the ensuing outcry from Irish-Americans, who carried heavy weight at the polls, frightened the Johnson administration. Before it could decide who should take on the onus of stopping him, 'General' John O'Neil led 1500 armed Irishmen across the Niagara river. The next day, 2 June 1866, the Canadian militia gave battle, and fled; but the Fenians fled farther—to New York State, where they were promptly arrested and as promptly released. In the spring of 1870 tatterdemalion armies moved once more on Canada from St. Albans, Vermont, and Malone, New York. United States marshals arrested the Fenian leaders, and the armies disintegrated. Ridiculous as they were, the Fenian forays caused Canada much trouble and expense for which she was never reimbursed by the United States.

The greatest achievement of the Grant administration was the liquidation of outstanding diplomatic controversies with Great Britain. The sympathy of the English ruling classes for the Confederacy and the lax enforcement of neutrality by the British government had aroused deep resentment in the United States, and for some years no calm adjudication of American claims was possible. The most important of these claims had to do with the alleged negligence of the British in permitting the Confederate cruisers *Alabama*, *Shenandoah*, and *Florida* to be armed in, and escape from, British ports. Seward's persistent advocacy of these claims was finally rewarded in the last months of Johnson's administration by a convention for their adjudication. In April 1869 the Senate rejected this convention as insufficient, after Sumner had charged Great Britain with responsibility for half the total cost of the war: a mere $2,125 million! Sumner's speech shocked his English friends who so faithfully had sustained the Union cause; nor were they much comforted by his explanation that the cession of Canada would be an acceptable form of payment.

After Sumner was eliminated as a result of his recalcitrance on Santo Domingo, negotiations went forward more successfully, for England was now ready to make amends. So the Canadian Sir John Rose staged with Hamilton Fish a diplomatic play of wooing and yielding that threw dust in the eyes of extremists on both sides. The covenant thus arrived at, the Treaty of Washington (8 May 1871), provided for arbitration of boundary disputes, the fisheries question, and the *Alabama* claims; determined rules of neutrality that should govern the arbitral tribunal (which subsequently assessed the British for damages wrought by the three cruisers); and contained an expression of regret for the escape of the *Alabama*.

Although the United States was thereby vindicated, the greater victory was for arbitration and peace. Never before had questions involving such touchy matters of national honor been submitted to a mere majority vote of an international tribunal. The English accepted the verdict with good grace. Charles Francis Adams never forgot that he was judge not advocate, and President Grant by his unwavering support of peaceful methods showed a quality not unusual in statesmen who know war at first hand. In a later message to the Arbitration Union of Birmingham, Grant set forth his guiding principle: 'Nothing would afford me greater happiness than to know that . . . at some future day, the nations of the earth will agree upon some sort of congress which will take cognizance of international questions of difficulty, and whose decisions will be as binding as the decisions of our Supreme Court are upon us. It is a dream of mine that some such solution may be.'

If the Grant administration, for all its shortcomings, was at its best in diplomatic affairs, the hero of Appomattox came off most poorly in coping with domestic issues such as the 'money question' and civil service reform. Like the Southern question, the money question was inherited from previous administrations. During the war the government had issued $450 million of legal tender notes, and at the close of the war some $400 million of these 'greenbacks' were still in circulation. The presence of greenbacks gave rise to two divisive issues. The first involved the medium of payment of the interest and principal of government bonds. Since these bonds had been purchased with depreciated greenbacks, farmers and workingmen reasoned that they should be redeemable in greenbacks unless otherwise specified, while bondholders insisted on payment in gold. The Democrats endorsed the proposal to redeem government securities in greenbacks, and Johnson went even further and urged that future interest payments be applied to liquidating the principal of the debt. But in his first inaugural address Grant committed himself to paying all government obligations in gold, and the first measure passed by the new Congress (18 March 1869) pledged the faith of the United States to such payment.

The second question concerned government policy toward the contraction of greenbacks and the resumption of specie payments. The inflation of the currency through greenbacks had tended to raise commodity prices, make credit easier and money cheaper. The farmer and the debtor therefore regarded with dismay any proposal to contract the currency by calling in these greenbacks. Business interests were divided; most wanted a stable currency, and hence opposed both currency expansion and abrupt resumption. But some businessmen, such as those who had gone into debt, favored expansion, while conservative bankers and others of the creditor class demanded that the government pledge itself to redeem greenbacks with gold and thus bring this paper currency to par.

A powerful argument for stabilizing the currency was that constant fluctuation in the value of greenbacks invited speculation. Because greenbacks were not legal tender for all purposes and because it was uncertain whether the government would ever redeem them in gold, they circulated at a discount which varied from month to month. In September 1869 two notorious stock gamblers, Jay Gould and Jim Fisk, took advantage of this fluctuation in the value of money to organize a 'corner' in gold. With the passive connivance of persons high in the confidence of the President and the Secretary of the Treasury, the nefarious scheme almost succeeded. On 'Black Friday,' 24 September 1869, the premium on gold rose to 162, and scores of Wall Street brokers faced ruin. Then the government dumped $4 million in gold on the market, and the 'corner' collapsed. 'The worst scandals of the 18th century,' wrote Henry Adams, 'were relatively harmless by the side of this which smirched executive, judiciary, banks, corporate systems, professions, and people, all the great active forces of society.' Yet the episode reflected not so much upon Grant's character as upon his judgment, which vacillated.

In 1870 the greenback question came before the Supreme Court. When Chief Justice Chase—who as Secretary of the Treasury had originally issued them—announced that greenbacks were not legal tender for obligations entered into prior to the emission of the notes, and even made the alarming suggestion that they were completely invalid,[4] the government promptly moved for a rehearing. Two vacancies on the Supreme Court afforded Grant a propitious opportunity. In Joseph P. Bradley and William Strong, Grant found jurists upon whose faith in the constitutionality of the greenbacks he could rely. He was not disappointed. In the second Legal Tender decision, *Knox v. Lee,* the Court in 1871 reversed itself and sustained the constitutionality of the Civil War greenbacks. Thirteen years later, in an even more sweeping decision, *Juilliard v. Greenman,* it proclaimed the government's right to issue legal tender even in time of peace. When, in 1874, Congress attempted to do this, Grant interposed his veto and the threat of inflation passed. In 1875 Congress finally provided for the resumption of specie payments on 1 January 1879. This act settled, for the time being, the legal tender question, but the money question remained to plague the next generation.

The tariff question also vexed the Grant administration. The skyhigh Civil War tariffs were originally accepted as emergency revenue measures; protected industries soon came to regard them as permanent. After Appomattox, Western farmers

4. *Hepburn v. Griswold* 8 Wallace 603 (1870).

and Eastern reformers joined hands in demanding tariff reduction, but the protected interests would not yield. The Grant administration set itself against tariff reform. Secretary Cox was forced out of the cabinet in part because of his sympathy for it, and David A. Wells, the able economist who was a special commissioner of revenue, had to resign for the same reason.

Nor did civil service reform fare better. In no area was the record of Grant's administration more discreditable. Grant's appointment of Jacob Cox to the Interior Department was a gesture toward reform, and when in 1871 a Civil Service Commission, headed by George William Curtis, submitted a list of desirable reforms, Grant promised a fair trial. But Cox was shoved out, and Grant soon scuttled the commission and packed the civil service with party henchmen. Curtis, wearied of shadow-boxing with the spoilsmen, resigned in disgust, and in 1875 the commission itself was discontinued.

The Liberal Republican Movement

Within less than a year after Grant's assumption of office, a revolt within the Republican party was in full swing. The full measure of administrative corruption was as yet unknown, but enough was suspected to outrage men who cherished standards of political decency. Grant's Southern policy was controversial, his Caribbean policy an affront, while his repudiation of reformers troubled even some of his own followers. Above all there was a growing distrust of Grant himself, which found expression in Senator Sumner's speech of May 1872 scoring him for taking and giving bribes, nepotism, neglect of duty, and lawless interference with the other departments of the government. Grant's abuse of the civil service alienated Cox and Schurz, his Southern policy antagonized Lyman Trumbull and Gideon Welles, his tariff policy cost him the support of David A. Wells, and such men as Chief Justice Chase, Horace Greeley, Charles Francis Adams, and E. L. Godkin came to regard the President as unfit for high office.

This revolt against Grant was started by liberals and reformers, but old-line politicians and disappointed factional leaders soon flocked to it in embarrassing numbers. In the end it consisted of a group even more heterogeneous than usual in American parties. The one idea that animated them was distrust of President Grant. It was a movement of opposition rather than of positive reform; and therein lay its chief weakness. When the Liberal Republican convention met at Cincinnati 1 May 1872, this weakness became apparent. It was impossible for the discordant elements to agree upon a satisfactory platform or a logical candidate. The platform called for the withdrawal of troops from the South, civil service reform, and a resumption of specie payments; as for the tariff, the convention 'recognizing that there are in our midst honest but irreconcilable differences of opinion' remanded 'the discussion of the subject to the people in their congressional Districts.' Nor could the convention unite on a presidential candidate like Charles Francis Adams or Lyman Trumbull, the latter for almost 20 years one of the ornaments of the party. Intrigues and jealousies defeated them, and in the end the convention stampeded to Horace Greeley.

No man in the country was better known than Greeley, for over thirty years editor of the powerful New York *Tribune*, but he was renowned as an editor not as a statesman. A Vermont Yankee who had kept his homespun democracy and youthful idealism, Greeley persistently championed the cause of the underprivileged, the worker, and the farmer. Yet for all his intellectual abilities and idealism, Greeley lacked the first qualifications for responsible political position. He was impulsive, intriguing, vain, and vindictive, and his carefully cultivated idiosyncrasies laid him open to caricature. A familiar figure on the streets of New York, he wore a crumpled white coat, its pockets stuffed with newspapers, and crowning his bewhiskered face was a tall white hat. He reminded some of Mr. Pickwick, others of the Mad Hatter.

The nomination of Greeley came as a shock to the reformers who had organized the Liberal Republican movement. *The Nation* reported that 'a greater degree of incredulity and disappointment' had not been felt since the news of the first battle of Bull Run. But the discomfort of the reformers was as nothing to the dismay of Southern Dem-

Election Night, 1872. A New York City crowd peers up at the rooftop of a building at Broadway and 22nd Street where a stereopticon projects a bulletin showing Pennsylvania giving Grant a 100,000-vote lead. Final returns increased Grant's margin in the Keystone State to a whopping 138,000. Rock-ribbed Republican Pennsylvania voted for Buchanan in 1856 but did not wind up in the Democratic column again until Franklin D. Roosevelt's landslide in 1936. (New-York Historical Society, *Frank Leslie's Illustrated Newspapers, 23 Nov. 1872*)

ocrats. For thirty years Greeley had castigated the South and the Democratic party, and much of the responsibility for anti-slavery, and later for Radical reconstruction, could justly be laid at his door. Yet the Democrats had no choice but to make Greeley their nominee, for he offered the only alternative to the continuation of Radical reconstruction. But it was hard to work up enthusiasm for a candidate who had said: 'May it be written on my grave that I was never the Democratic party's follower and lived and died in nothing its debtor.'

Greeley proved himself an excellent campaigner, but the odds against him were insuperable. Grant could command the support of rank and file Republicans, veterans of the Union armies, the blacks North and South, and most of the German vote alienated by Greeley's temperance views. Grant carried all but six states; Greeley, with less than 44 per cent of the vote, failed to win a single state in the North or West. Three weeks later Horace Greeley died, broken-hearted. The Liberal Republican party did not long survive him, but many of the men who took part in that campaign would be active in the 'Mugwump' wing of the Republican party for the next generation.

Scandal and Stagnation

While the 1872 campaign was still under way, the country was startled by charges of wholesale corruption in connection with the construction of the Union Pacific Railroad, charges which reflected upon men high in Republican councils. The promoters of the Union Pacific, in order to divert the profits of construction to themselves, had organized a construction company, the Credit Mobilier of America. To this company the directors of the Union Pacific awarded fantastically profitable contracts. As a result of this corrupt arrangement the Union Pacific was forced to the verge of bankruptcy while the Credit Mobilier paid in a single year dividends of 348 per cent. Fearing Congress might interpose, the directors placed large blocks of Credit Mobilier stock 'where they would do most good.' Exposure of the scheme brought disgrace to a number of representatives, and to Vice-President Schuyler Colfax, while others such as Henry Wilson of Massachusetts and James A. Garfield of Ohio were never able to explain away their connection with the unsavory affair.

Scarcely less excusable was the so-called Salary Grab. In 1873 Ben Butler pushed through a bill doubling the President's salary and increasing by 50 per cent the salary of Congressmen. This could be justified; what particularly affronted public opinion was that the increases granted to Congressmen were made retroactive for two years: thus each Congressman voted himself $5000 in back salary out of public funds. The bill was an evasion if not an outright violation of the Constitution, but Grant signed it without demur. A storm of indignation against this 'steal' swept the country, and in the following session Congress hastened to restore the old salary scale.

The Credit Mobilier and the Salary Grab were merely the most sensational of the exposures. In the Navy Department, Secretary Robeson accumulated a fortune of several hundred thousand dollars during his tenure of office. The Department of the Interior worked hand in glove with land speculators. The Treasury farmed out uncollected taxes to one J. D. Sanborn who promptly proceeded to highjack some $425,000 out of corporations, one-half of which he took for himself. The U.S. minister to England, Robert Schenck, lent his prestige to the Emma Mine swindle, and the minister to Brazil, J. W. Webb, defrauded the Brazilian government of $50,000 and fled to Europe, leaving the United States Government to refund the money, with apologies. The Custom House in New York was a sink of corruption, but when Collector Thomas Murphy was finally forced out, Grant accepted his resignation 'with regret.' In the national capital 'Boss' Shepherd ran up a debt of $17 million, a large part of which was graft, and found himself appointed by a grateful President to be chairman of the Board of Public Works. It was Shepherd, too, who was largely responsible for the failure of the Freedmen's Bank, a cruel hardship for thousands of trusting blacks.

Worse was still to come. After the Democrats carried the congressional elections of 1874, a Democratic House, the first since the Civil War, set

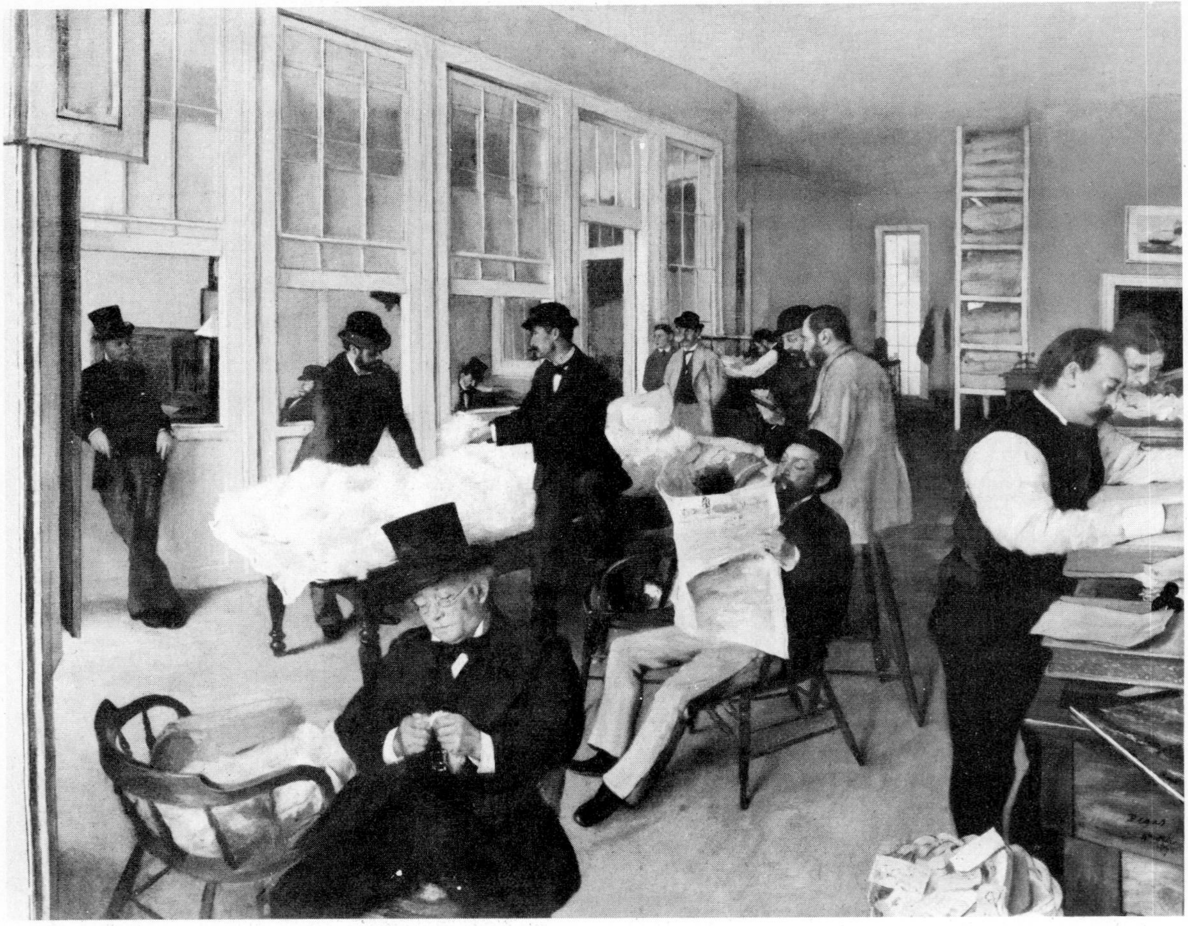

'The Cotton Exchange at New Orleans.' This painting by the French artist Edgar Degas entitled 'Le Bureau de coton de la Nouvelle-Orleans' shows that though the war devastated trade in the South, cotton continued to be 'King.' In 1872 Degas visited the Crescent City, where his brothers were cotton brokers. 'One does nothing here,' he wrote. 'It's in the climate, so much cotton, one lives for and by cotton.' From the sketches he made he painted this picture on his return to France in 1873. The following year he helped organize the first exhibition of the Impressionists. (*Musée des Beaux Arts, Pau. Photo Giraudon*)

The "Brains."

That achieved the Tammany victory at the Rochester Democratic Convention.

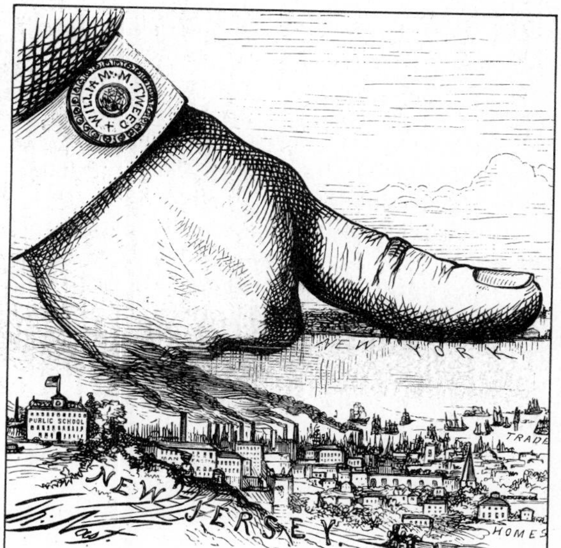

Under the Thumb.

THE BOSS. "Well, what are you going to do about it?"

The Tweed Ring. Nast, who invented the tiger as the symbol of Tammany Hall, caricatured the Tammany boss, William Marcy Tweed, so effectively that the Ring's lawyers offered him $500,000 to desist. New York voters might not be able to read, Tweed said, but they could 'look at the damn pictures,' in which he was depicted as obese and corrupt, wearing an ornate diamond stickpin. To evade imprisonment, Tweed, disguised as a sailor, fled to Spain, but he was identified from a Nast cartoon, arrested, and returned to America, where he died in a New York jail. (*Harper's Weekly, 19 Aug. 1871*) afoot a series of investigations. In the Treasury and War departments, investigators uncovered sensational wrongdoing. For years a 'Whiskey Ring' in St. Louis had systematically defrauded the government of millions in taxes on distilled whiskey. The Ring had operated with the collusion of Treasury officials and of the President's private secretary, Babcock. When Grant was apprised of the situation he said, 'Let no guilty man escape.' But most of them did escape, Babcock with the President's connivance. No sooner had the 'Whiskey Ring' been exposed than the country confronted a new scandal. Secretary of the Treasury Benjamin H. Bristow found irrefutable proof that Secretary of War Belknap had sold Indian post traderships. Faced with impeachment, Belknap hurried to resign, and his resignation was accepted 'with great regret' by the President whom he had betrayed. Impeachment proceedings were instituted, but the Secretary was finally acquitted on the technical ground that the Senate no longer had jurisdiction over his case.

Corruption was not confined to the national government. It could be found in local governments, in business, and even in the professions. There was almost everywhere a breakdown of old moral standards. The industrial revolution, the building of transcontinental railroads, and the exploitation of new natural resources had called into existence a class of new rich untrained to the responsibilities of their position. Never before and only twice since—after World War I and in the 1970's—have public morals fallen so low.

State legislatures, too, were guilty of gross corruption. In the fierce struggle between Daniel Drew and Cornelius Vanderbilt for control of the Erie Railroad the legislature of New York State was auctioned off to the highest bidder, and both bar and bench proved that they too were for sale. In Pennsylvania the Cameron machine bought and sold legislation with bare-faced effrontery. In Wisconsin, Minnesota, and California, railroads controlled the legislatures; in Iowa the money for the Agricultural College realized from land-grant sales was stolen. Cities also presented a sorry spectacle. The brigandage of the Tweed Ring cost New York City not less than $100 million.

At a time when the Grant administration was reeling from reports of corruption, the panic of 1873 struck an even heavier blow. Reckless speculation and wholesale stock watering helped precipitate the panic. Other causes were perhaps equally important. Europe, too, felt the hard times, and overseas investors proceeded to call in their American loans. The unfavorable balance of trade, which had persisted all through the war and the postwar years, mounted during the early 'seventies. Too rapid expansion of the agricultural West produced surplus crops which could not be marketed abroad at satisfactory prices. Credit was overextended, currency inflated, and public finances deranged by the conflicting claims of greenbacks and of gold. With an immense self-confidence the country had mortgaged itself to the future; now it found itself unable to pay either interest or principal.

The crash came 17 September 1873 with the failure of the great banking house of Jay Cooke and Company—the house that had helped finance the war and the Northern Pacific Railroad. Soon one substantial business firm after another toppled, and the New York Stock Exchange took the unprecedented step of closing its doors for ten days. Industrial plants shut down, railway construction declined sharply, and over half the railroads defaulted on their bonds. Long bread lines began to appear in the larger cities, and tramps swarmed the countryside. Such a crisis was bound to have political consequences; it not only lead to the birth of a farmer-labor party, but put the chances of the Republicans in the 1876 election in serious jeopardy.

The Disputed Election of 1876

Republican defeat seemed certain in 1876 as the bankruptcy of the Grant administration became increasingly apparent. To give the party respectability, the Republicans chose the honest if uninspiring Rutherford B. Hayes, thrice Governor of Ohio. The Democrats, determined to make reform the issue of the campaign, nominated Samuel J. Tilden, who had broken the notorious Tweed Ring and then, as Governor of New York, smashed the 'Canal Ring.'

When the first reports came in, Tilden appeared

to have won a sweeping victory. He carried New York, New Jersey, Connecticut, Indiana, and apparently all the South while piling up a popular plurality of over 250,000. But, scanning the returns, the Republican campaign managers became convinced that the election might yet be swung to their candidate. Four states—South Carolina, Florida, Louisiana, and Oregon—were apparently in doubt. Without these states Tilden had only 184 electoral votes; 185 were necessary to win. On the morning after election Zach Chandler wired each of the doubtful states, 'Can you hold your state?'—and that afternoon he announced, 'Hayes has 185 electoral votes and is elected.'

The situation was highly precarious. In all three Southern states there had been intimidation and fraud on both sides. Hayes appeared to have carried South Carolina, but in Florida and Louisiana Tilden seemed to have a safe majority. Republican returning boards threw out about 1000 Democratic votes in Florida and over 13,000 in Louisiana, and gave certificates to the Hayes electors. In Oregon a Democratic governor had displaced a Republican elector on a technicality and appointed a Democrat in his place. From all four states came two sets of returns.

The Constitution provides that 'The President of the Senate shall, in the presence of the Senate and House of Representatives, open all the certificates, and the votes shall then be counted.' But counted by whom? If the Republican President of the Senate did the counting, the election would go to Hayes; if the Democratic House counted, Tilden would be President. And if the two houses could not agree on the procedure, there would be no President. Was the nation then to drift, distraught and confused, without a chief executive?

Conservatives, North and South, hastened to head off such a crisis. The solution was hinted at by Representative Garfield in a letter to Hayes. Some of the extremists on both sides, he wrote, were prepared to make trouble, but 'in the meantime two forces are at work. The Democratic businessmen of the country are more anxious for quiet than for Tilden; and the old Whigs are saying that they have seen war enough, and don't care to follow the lead of their northern associates.' Garfield suggested that 'if in some discreet way, these southern men who are dissatisfied with Tilden and his violent followers, could know that the South is going to be treated with kind consideration,' they might acquiesce in Hayes's election. If Southern conservatives secured an end to military reconstruction, restoration of 'home rule,' some voice in the Hayes administration, and generous subsidies for internal improvements, particularly railroads, they were prepared to concede the presidency. The Hayes forces were prepared to make these concessions.

With this understanding and with Tilden's reluctant consent, Congress was able to act. On 29 January 1877 it set up an Electoral Commission of fifteen members (five from the House, five from the Senate, and five from the Supreme Court) to pass on the disputed credentials. It was originally planned to appoint to this committee seven Democrats and seven Republicans and, as the fifteenth member, the non-partisan Judge David Davis of Illinois. At the last moment, however—and not by inadvertence—the legislature of Illinois elected Davis to the U.S. Senate and, with the approval of both parties, Judge Bradley was named in his place. As it turned out it was Bradley who named the next President of the United States. For on all questions the Electoral Commission divided along strict party lines, and Bradley voted invariably with the Republicans. By a straight 8-7 vote the Commission awarded all four states to Hayes, and thus the presidency—electoral count: 185 to 184.

Would the Democrats accept a solution which seemed so partisan and so unfair? For a time it was touch and go. Northern Democrats were prepared to filibuster long enough to prevent Congress from opening and counting the votes. But in the end wiser counsels prevailed. With renewed assurances from Hayes that he would abide by the sectional understanding, enough Southern Democrats deserted the Northern intransigents to permit Congress to count the ballots, and on 2 March 1877, only two days before Inauguration Day, Hayes was declared elected. This compromise worked well for those who contrived it. The real victim of the compromise was the Southern Negro, for it had been made at his expense and delayed for three generations the enforcement of those guarantees written into the Fourteenth and Fifteenth Amendments.

The Undoing of Reconstruction

Even before the Compromise of 1877, the country had wearied of the 'Southern question.' No longer would opinion molders in the North sustain military rule. In 1874 the Democrats captured the lower house, and the repudiation of Radicalism was all but complete. Meantime all the Southern states had been readmitted, and by the Amnesty Act of 1872 almost all Southern whites who were still disfranchised were restored to full political privileges. When the Radicals, their power waning, called for more military intervention, Grant rebuffed them. 'The whole public,' he protested, 'are tired out with the annual autumnal outbreaks in the South, and the great majority are ready now to condemn any interference on the part of the government.'

In state after state conservative whites recaptured control of the political machinery, until by the end of 1875 only South Carolina, Louisiana, and Mississippi were still under Radical control, and even in these states that control was precarious. Negores were eliminated from politics, carpetbaggers scared out, scalawags won over—and 'home rule' was restored. The Redeemer governments then proceeded to reduce expenditures and taxes—often at the expense of school children—and to erase a good deal of progressive legislation from the statute books. Acting on the assumption that the Radicals had saddled their states with fraudulent debts, and on the fact that in some instances the railroads, for whose benefit the debts had been contracted, had not carried out their part of the bargains, the Redeemers proceeded to repudiate a good part of the state obligations. By this convenient method Southern states rid themselves of perhaps $100 million of debts.

When Rutherford B. Hayes was inaugurated President, 4 March 1877, the carpetbag regime had been overthrown in all the states save South Carolina and Louisiana, where it was still upheld by federal bayonets. In South Carolina Confederate veterans known as Red Shirts organized white voters, kept blacks away from the polls, and elected the beloved Confederate General Wade Hampton governor and a Democratic legislature. A Republican returning board, however, sustained by federal soldiers, threw out the ballots of two counties, canceled thousands of others, and declared the carpetbag Governor D. H. Chamberlain duly re-elected. The Democratic members then organized their own House, and with Speaker, clerks, and sergeant-at-arms forced their way into the representatives' chamber where the Radicals were sitting. During three days and nights the rival Houses sat side by side, every man armed to the teeth and ready to shoot if the rival sergeant-at-arms laid hands on one of his colleagues. At the end of that time the Democrats withdrew, leaving Chamberlain in possession of the state house, but for four months the people of the state paid their taxes to Hampton's government. Chamberlain hastened to Washington to appeal for aid, but in vain. Faithful to the compromise by which he had been elected, President Hayes broke the deadlock by withdrawing the troops from Columbia, and the Democrats took possession. Two weeks later, when federal troops evacuated New Orleans, conservative white rule was completely restored throughout the South.

The withdrawal of troops by President Hayes in 1877 marked the abandonment not only of reconstruction, but of the Negro, who paid the price of reunion. There were three parts to the unwritten agreement: that President, Congress, and the North generally, would hereafter keep hands off the 'Negro problem'; that the rules governing race relations in the South would be written by whites; and that these rules would concede the Negro limited civil rights, but neither political nor social equality. The principle underlying this relationship was set forth succinctly by Henry Grady of the Atlanta *Constitution*: 'The supremacy of the white race of the South must be maintained forever, and the domination of the Negro race resisted at all points and at all hazards, because the white race is superior.' It was as simple as that.

The Negro's sole remaining hope lay with the courts. When, in 1873, the Supreme Court was called upon for the first time to interpret the phrases of the Fourteenth Amendment, Justice Samuel Miller, speaking for the Court, reviewed the history of the three Civil War Amendments and observed:

> No one can fail to be impressed with the one pervading purpose found in them all, lying at the foundation of each, and without which none of them would have been even suggested; we mean the freedom of the slave race, the security and firm establishment of that freedom, and the protection of the newly made freedman and citizen from the oppressions of those who had formerly exercised unlimited dominion over him.

At the time this seemed the common sense of the matter, and no judge challenged this interpretation.

Each of these Amendments contained an unusual provision, 'Congress shall have power to enforce this article by appropriate legislation.' And, beginning with the ill-fated Civil Rights Act of 1866, Congress enacted a series of laws designed to do just that. The most important were the Enforcement Acts of 1870 and 1871 which threw the protection of the Federal Government over the Negro's right to vote; the Ku Klux Klan Act of 1871 which made it a federal offense to conspire to deprive Negroes of the equal protection of the laws; and the Civil Rights Act of 1875 which undertook to secure the Negro 'full and equal enjoyment of the accommodations, advantages, facilities, and privileges of inns, public conveyances on land or water, theatres, and other places of public amusement,' as well as the right to serve on juries.

Abandoned by Congress and the President, the Negro was now repudiated by the courts. If the 'one pervading purpose' of the Amendments was to protect the freedman, then it failed. Beginning with the Slaughterhouse case of 1873 the Supreme Court proceeded systematically to riddle the structure of Negro rights. In the Slaughterhouse case the Court asserted that all the important privileges and immunities derived not from national but from state citizenship and that the Fourteenth Amendment did not extend federal protection over these. The Cruikshank opinion of 1875, which involved a mob attack on blacks who were trying to vote, deliberately restricted the reach of the Fourteenth Amendment to state—not private—interference with rights, and to such interference as was clearly directed against blacks on account of their race or color. When an election official in Kentucky refused to receive a black's vote, the Court held that Congress did not have authority to protect the right to vote generally, but only where that right was denied by the *state*, and on grounds of *race* or *color*. In 1878 the Court provided the legal foundation for segregation by striking down a Louisiana statute forbidding discrimination in transportation as an unlawful interference with congressional authority over interstate commerce! In the *United States v. Harris*, a case in which a Tennessee mob had lynched four black prisoners, the Court returned to the theme that the national government could protect the black only against acts by the state, and that for protection against violence by individuals or mobs the victim must look to state authorities. The crucial test came with the Civil Rights Cases of 1883, where the Court, in effect, wiped off the statute book the Civil Rights Act of 1875.

> It would be running the slavery argument into the ground *[said Justice Bradley]* to make it apply to every act of discrimination which a person may see fit to make as to the guests he will entertain, or as to the people he will take into his coach or cab or car, or admit to his concert or theatre, or deal with in other matters of intercourse or business.

And the Court added, that

> When a man has emerged from slavery and by the aid of beneficent legislation has shaken off the inseparable concomitants of that state, there must be some stage in the progress of his elevation when he takes the rank of a mere citizen, and ceases to be the special favorite of the laws, and when his rights as a citizen, or a man, are to be protected in the ordinary modes by which other men's rights are protected.

This was the thesis, too, of the crucial *Plessy v. Ferguson* decision of 1896 which, by accepting the doctrine of 'separate but equal accommodations,' threw the mantle of judicial approval over segregation.[5]

This jettisoning of the civil rights program did not go without protest from within the Court itself. Justice Harlan of Kentucky spoke for a con-

5. Reversed some sixty years later in the even more crucial decision of *Brown v. Board of Education of Topeka.*

'Twenty Years After Independence.' This photograph of a Fourth of July celebration in Richmond suggests that two decades after the Emancipation Proclamation blacks still had a long way to go, but it also indicates reverence toward the Great Emancipator. (*Valentine Museum, Richmond, Virginia*)

struction of the Constitution broad enough to embrace the rights of all citizens. And, observing that the 'separate but equal' doctrine of the Plessy case would, in time 'be quite as pernicious as the decision in the Dred Scott case,' Harlan wrote prophetically:

The destinies of the two races in this country are indissolubly linked together, and the interests of both require that the common government of all shall not permit the seeds of race hate to be planted under the sanction of law. What can more certainly arouse race hate, what more certainly create and perpetuate a feeling of distrust between these races, than state enactments which in fact proceed on the ground that colored citizens are so inferior and degraded that they cannot be allowed to sit in public coaches occupied by white citizens.

The end of Reconstruction and the nullification of the Enforcement Acts exiled the Southern Negro to a kind of no-man's land halfway between slavery and freedom. No longer a slave, he was not yet free. He was tied to the soil by the sharecrop and crop-lien systems, excluded from most

The Negro exodus. In 1879 some 50,000 blacks from Mississippi and other Deep South states migrated to the Western prairie out of discontent with the violent aftermath of Reconstruction, bad crops, and yellow fever, and with great expectations of 'sunny Kansas.' Many died during the bitter winter of 1879–80, and the 'Exodusters' found that racial discrimination was not confined to the South but was endemic in the old abolitionist havens too. This sketch by James H. Moser depicts a scene on the wharves at Vicksburg. (*Collection Judith Mara Gutman*)

professions and from many jobs, and fobbed off with 'separate' accommodations that were rarely 'equal.' He was expected not only to accept a position of social inferiority without protest, but to rejoice in it by playing the role of 'Uncle Tom.' At first gradually, then with dramatic speed, he was rendered politically impotent: 'grandfather' clauses, literacy tests, poll taxes, and—where these failed—naked intimidation, deprived him of the vote. In 1885 the Louisiana novelist, George Washington Cable, wrote:

One of the marvels of future history will be that it was counted a small matter, by a majority of our nation, for six millions of people within it, made by its own decree a component part of it, to be subjected to a system of oppression so rank that nothing could make it seem small except the fact that they had already been ground under it for a century and a half. . . . It heaps upon him

> in every public place the most odious distinctions, without giving ear to the humblest plea concerning mental or moral character. It spurns his ambition, tramples upon his languishing self-respect, and indignantly refuses to let him either buy with money or earn by any excellence of inner life or outward behavior, the most momentary immunity from these public indignities.

Southerners generally congratulated themselves that they had persuaded the North to concede them almost complete control of their domestic institutions. Yet the cost of the restoration of white rule was high, for white as well as for black. By sanctioning the use of fraud and coercion to deny the black his legal rights, they weakened moral standards. By restricting Negro voting they limited white suffrage, and thus struck a heavy blow at democracy. By identifying white supremacy with the Democrats they saddled a one-party system upon the South, and threw that party into the hands of the least enlightened elements of their society.

Reconstruction left deep physical and moral scars upon the South. A century later, the apostles of white supremacy were able to ring the changes on the evils of Reconstruction whenever even modest alterations in racial patterns were suggested. For decades after 1877, race relations were poisoned by an annual crop of outrages. Politics were forced into an unnatural groove, and the one-party system, a hostage to white supremacy, proved inhospitable to the introduction of new issues. Southern society remained relatively static, immune to modern movements in education and social regeneration. But Reconstruction also left another legacy: the civil rights amendments to the Constitution. In years to come, although much too tardily, Americans would begin to give to these provisions the meaning their framers intended.

20

The Economic Revolution

*

1865–1914

Industrial America

It was the dream of Jefferson that his country—'with room enough for our descendants to the hundredth and thousandth generation'—was to be a great agrarian democracy. 'While we have land to labor,' he wrote, 'let us never wish to see our citizens occupied at a work bench, or twirling a distaff,' for 'those who labor in the earth are the chosen people of God.' But within two generations of Jefferson's death the value of manufactured products was almost treble that of agricultural, and by 1910 the United States had progressed so far in the direction Alexander Hamilton wished that it had become the leading industrial power in the world. When the census of 1920 recorded over 9 million factory wage-earners producing commodities to the value of some $62 billion, and over 50 per cent of the population crowded into towns and cities, surely Hamilton was able to collect some bets from Jefferson in the Elysian Fields!

This economic revolution was a consequence of the creation of a national market, made possible by a railway network which linked farms to commercial centers and spurred the growth of cities. As population tripled between 1860 and 1920, and incomes rose at an even more rapid pace, mass demand encouraged industrial expansion, which was further accelerated by the application of electric power and the introduction of the internal combustion engine. By the early 1900's many firms were operating on a national scale and not a few were turning out producers' goods for other industries rather than for the consumer. By then, too, the great corporation had established itself as the basic unit, and the main industries were dominated by a few huge enterprises which maintained extensive national organizations for buying and marketing.

This revolution enhanced national wealth, raised standards of living, and produced cycles of prosperity and depression with periodic unemployment. It speeded up urbanization, encouraged immigration, stimulated rapid growth of population, and modified social institutions such as the family. It helped plunge America into world affairs, shifted the balance of international payments, and made the United States a creditor nation. It led also to a concentration of wealth and control, creating, in a nation brought up on Jeffersonian principles, a whole series of difficulties which the teachings of the Fathers did little to illuminate.

The Age of Invention

The United States Patent Office was created in 1790 largely through the efforts of one of the greatest American inventors, John Stevens of Hoboken, New Jersey. So numerous were the patents granted to ingenious Americans in the following years that in 1833, it was said, the head of the Patent Bureau decided to resign because he felt that everything of importance had been invented! Yet the 36,000 patents granted before 1860 were but a feeble indication of the flood of inventions that was to inundate the Patent Office after the Civil War. From 1860 to 1890 no less than 440,000 patents were issued. The average number of inventions patented in any one year since 1900 equals or exceeds the total number patented in the entire history of the country before 1860.

Though the beginnings of many important inventions can be traced to the late eighteenth and early nineteenth centuries, their application on a large scale came only after the Civil War. In the eighteenth century Franklin, Galvani, and Oersted had experimented with electricity, and as early as 1831 Michael Faraday in England and Joseph Henry of the Smithsonian Institution had developed the principle of the dynamo. But it was not until after 1880 that the genius of Thomas A. Edison, William Stanley, Charles Brush, and a host of others put the dynamo to use on the streetcar, the elevated train, and the subway. Elias Howe invented the sewing machine in 1846, but it did not have general use until popularized by Isaac Singer after 1860, and was first applied to the making of shoes by Gordon McKay in 1862. Eli Whitney adapted for firearms the revolutionary principles of standardization and interchangeability of parts as early as 1798, but mass production did not come until after the achievements of Kelly, Holley, and Bessemer ushered in the age of steel. Dr. N. A. Otto of Germany invented the internal combustion engine in 1876, but it meant little to the average American until Henry Ford in 1908 placed a motorcar on the market that was not a rich man's toy but a poor man's instrument. By 1920 Ford was making more than 6000 cars a day in his Detroit factories, and the automobile industry ranked first in the country in value of finished products. Transportation was affected by invention in yet another way when around 1908 the vision of Samuel P. Langley and the perseverance of the Wright brothers and Glenn Curtiss lifted the airplane out of the experimental stage.

Invention radically changed communication too. In 1856 the Western Union Company was organized and soon the whole country was crisscrossed with a network of telegraph wires. In 1858 the duplex telegraph was invented, and in 1896 an Italian, Guglielmo Marconi, discovered the secret of wireless telegraphy. In the centennial year of 1876, Emperor Dom Pedro of Brazil, attending the Philadelphia Exposition, sauntered up to the booth of young Alexander Graham Bell; he picked up the cone-shaped instrument on display there, and as he placed it to his ear Bell spoke through the transmitter. 'My God, it talks!' exclaimed His Majesty; and from that moment the telephone became the central feature of the Exposition. Within half a century 16 million telephones had profoundly affected the life of the nation. The invention in 1867 of the typewriter by an erratic printer, Christopher Sholes, proved a boon to the writer as well as the business office. The linotype composing machine invented by Ottmar Mergenthaler, Hoe's rotary press, the web press, and folding machinery made it possible to print as many as 240,000 eight-page newspapers in an hour; and the electrotype worked a comparable change in printing magazines and books. This revolution—plus the benevolent policy of the postal authorities in allowing cheap postal rates—made it possible for new magazines to reach a mass market heretofore unsuspected.

Meantime a host of inventions were transforming daily life, especially in the towns. The 'Wizard of Menlo,' Thomas Edison, gave the world the incandescent lamp in 1880, and within a few years millions were supplied with better, safer, and cheaper light than had ever been known before. It was Edison, too, who perfected the talking machine—which was in time to become a music-

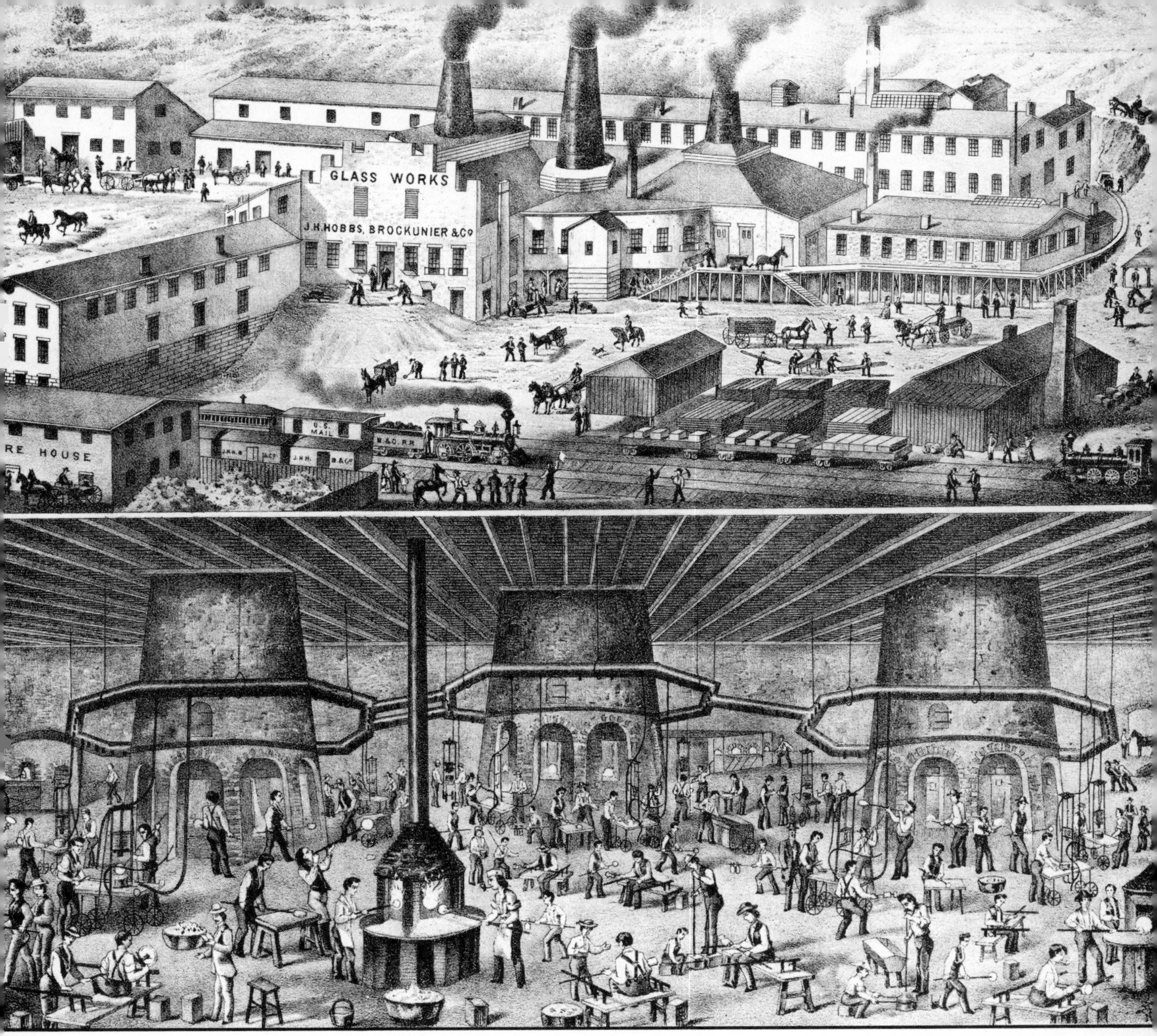

Glass Works, Wheeling, West Virginia. This lithograph is from *The Illustrated Atlas of the Upper Ohio River Valley*, published in 1877. (*Library of Congress*)

playing machine—and in conjunction with George Eastman developed the motion picture.

Machinery, science, and invention enabled man to increase his productivity a thousandfold. Under primitive conditions of weaving it required 5605 hours of labor to produce 500 yards of cotton sheeting; by 1900 manufacturers were able to turn out the same amount with only 52 hours of human labor. Two centuries ago Adam Smith celebrated the efficiency of machine production by observing that without machinery a workingman would need a full day to make a single pin, whereas machinery enabled him to manufacture 5000 pins in a day. A century later the great economist might have pointed his moral even more effectively, for by then a single worker could supervise the manufacture on automatic machines of 15 million pins each day.

The New South

Although the economic revolution continued to center in the Northeast, its impact was felt in every region, even the South. New cities like Birmingham, Chattanooga, and Durham sprang into existence, and Atlanta rose from her ashes to boast a population in 1880 four times as large as at the outbreak of the war. 'Chicago in her busiest days,' wrote a visitor, 'could scarcely show such a sight as clamors for observation here.' Here was the 'New South'—the South of cities, factories, and blast furnaces. 'Think of it,' said Henry Grady in a rapturous outburst—

> In cotton a monopoly. In iron and coal establishing swift mastery. In granite and marble developing equal advantages and resources. In yellow pine and hard woods the world's treasury. Surely the basis of the South's wealth and power is laid by the hand of Almighty God!

Before the South could achieve wealth and power, it needed more capital and better transportation. Capital presented the more difficult problem. The South itself had no surplus, and the fiscal policies of the Reconstruction governments, Radical and Redeemer alike, were not calculated to inspire confidence in Northern or foreign investors. But gradually the South attracted, or accumulated, money. The Freedmen's Bureau and the army spent large sums; the government appropriated millions for internal improvements; Northerners bought up farms and plantations, and Northern capital went into railroads, timberlands, coal and iron. Gradually, too, the South re-entered the world market with her exports, and lifted herself by her financial bootstraps. By the 'eighties money was pouring into the South from the North and from abroad. Much of this went to rebuilding the railroads. During the 'seventies the South added 5000 miles to her railroad network, and in the 'eighties no fewer than 23,000 miles.

For two generations Southerners had sent their cotton to the mills of Old and New England where the manufacturing establishments, labor, capital, and facilities for world marketing were well organized. The 'fifties had seen the beginnings of a textile industry in Georgia and South Carolina, but not until the 'seventies did the South seriously challenge the monopoly of New England mills. Proximity to raw materials and to water power, cheap labor, freedom from legal restraints, low taxes, and eager community support all gave Southern mills an advantage. By the end of Reconstruction over 100 Southern mills had almost half a million spindles; twenty years later some 400 mills boasted over 4 million spindles. Yet this was only a beginning. By 1920 the textile industry had moved south, and North Carolina, South Carolina, and Georgia ranked second, third, and fourth among the textile states of the nation.[1]

The pattern of the Southern textile industry differed in important ways from that of New England. Small mills sprouted on the outskirts of scores of little Carolina and Georgia towns, financed by local capital, managed by local enterprise, supported by local pride, and worked by white labor recruited from the neighborhood. The mill-workers, mostly from the poor-white class, welcomed the opportunity to exchange their drab and impoverished existence for the questionable attractions of the mill village. The great majority were women, and children between the ages of ten and fifteen; these worked an average of seventy hours a week for a wage of about three dollars. No

1. In 1957 each of these states had more spindles than all the New England states combined.

laws limited the hours of labor of women, and such child labor laws as were enacted remained unenforced.

The mill village gathered around the factory as a medieval village clustered about a feudal castle, and the mill manager ruled his community as a feudal lord ruled his manor. The company ordinarily owned the entire village—houses, stores, streets, the school, the church; needless to add, it effectively owned the workers, the shopkeepers, the teachers, and the preacher as well. Labor organizers could be denied access to the village, trouble-makers could be evicted, and teachers or preachers who indulged in criticism of the system could be sent packing. By the opening of the twentieth century the New South had gone a long way toward substituting industrial autocracy for the old agrarian feudalism.

The New South proved hospitable to a variety of industries. As with textile manufacturing, the tobacco industry enjoyed the advantages of the proximity of raw material, low transportation costs, and cheap labor; unlike textiles, it concentrated in large cities such as Richmond and Louisville, and used Negro labor. Two circumstances account in large part for its great prosperity: the invention, in 1880, of a cigarette-making machine by James Bonsack, and the organizing genius of James Buchanan Duke. Starting as a boy peddling his father's tobacco to North Carolina farmers, young Duke rose to be the Rockefeller of the tobacco industry, made his native town of Durham, North Carolina, the tobacco capital of the world, and in 1890 welded together the gigantic American Tobacco Company, whose operations—conducted in New York City—stretched from Southern tobacco fields to the Orient. The 'eighties saw, too, the beginnings of a flourishing coal and iron industry concentrated in Birmingham, Alabama, which quickly became the Pittsburgh of the South, and a lumber industry which exploited and devastated the pine forests of Louisiana and Mississippi. And after the opening of the new century the plains of Texas and Oklahoma, once the domain of Indians and cattlemen, became part of the empire of oil.

The industrialization of the South carried with it changes in political outlook. The 'Bourbons' who ruled the South from Reconstruction to the turn of the century were committed to industrialization; before long the South, as well as the North, could boast its 'railroad Senators' and its 'coal and iron Senators.' The three men who controlled Georgia politics, General Alfred Colquitt, General John Gordon, and Governor Joseph E. Brown, were all deeply involved in railroad promotion, manufacturing, real estate, and speculation. Through Milton Smith and General Basil Duke the Louisville and Nashville Railroad manipulated Kentucky politics for over twenty years; when in 1900 a reformer, Governor William Goebel, threatened that control, he was assassinated.

Yet for all the talk of a 'New South,' old patterns persisted. The South of 1900 accounted for a smaller proportion of the total manufacturing product of the country than did the South of 1860. Far more than other sections, the South escaped those two concomitants of industry—urbanization and immigration. The South was still, in 1900 as in 1860, predominantly rural, and the population of the Southern states remained almost entirely native-born. Furthermore, the South continued to be almost wholly a staple-crop—and even a one-crop—section; if King Cotton had been deposed he was still a lively pretender. Nonetheless, the South was changing, and as, with the passing years, the contrast between the dream of the Old South and the reality of the New—between the myth of plantation and slavery and the reality of tenant-farming and the mill villages—became ever more visible, white Southerners grew more defiantly insistent upon the old magnolia legend. Perhaps most remarkable is that in the end the South imposed this myth not only on itself, but on the North as well.

Iron and Steel

'The consumption of iron,' wrote the great ironmaster, Abram S. Hewitt, 'is the social barometer by which to estimate the relative height of civilization among nations.' By this gauge, the progress of civilization in the United States from the Civil War to World War I was remarkable. The works of man in the United States of 1860 were constructed of wood and stone, with a little brick and iron; by 1920 America had become a nation of iron, steel, and concrete. The United States of 1860 produced less than one million tons of pig iron; 60 years later output approached 36 million tons and the United States easily led the world in iron and steel manufacturing. This transformation resulted from the exploitation of new resources of iron, the discovery of new processes for converting it into steel, the indirect subsidy that was contributed by the government in the form of a prohibitive tariff, and the rise of a group of ironmasters with a genius for organization and production.

In the late 1840's enormous iron-ore deposits were discovered in the northern Michigan peninsula, and the year of the rush to the California gold diggings witnessed a rush to the iron-ore fields around Marquette scarcely less spectacular. Superior, that greatest of lakes, proved to be rimmed by iron. In the mid-1880's Charlemagne Tower opened up the rich Vermilion iron range on the north side of the lake, pushed a railroad through from Duluth, and within a few years was shipping one million tons annually through the Soo Canal. To the west and north lay even richer fields. The Mesabi iron range west of the lake, the greatest ore producer in the world, made possible the supremacy of the American steel industry for half a century.

The ore fields of the Lake Superior region are hundreds of miles distant from coal deposits, but cheap lake and railway transportation brought the two together. Ore and coal met in smelters of Chicago where the first American steel rails were rolled in 1865, and in Cleveland, Toledo, Ashtabula, and Milwaukee. Much of the ore was carried to Pittsburgh, center of the great Appalachian coal fields and strategically located with reference to water and rail transportation. In the 'eighties the iron and coal beds of the southern Appalachians were first exploited, and soon Birmingham became a southern rival to Pittsburgh and Chicago; in the twentieth century Colorado with apparently inexhaustible resources of minerals emerged as the Western center of the steel industry.

The Bessemer and open-hearth processes were as fundamental to steel making as the new ore beds. The Bessemer process, which consists in blowing air through molten iron to drive out the impurities, was anticipated in America by William Kelly, a prophet without honor in his own country; for it was not until Henry Bessemer had demonstrated the utility of his method in England that American manufacturers adopted it. The Bessemer process gave U.S. steel producers one incalculable advantage: it was effective only where the phosphorus content of the iron ore was very low; comparatively little of the English iron ore was free from phosphorus, but practically all the Lake Superior ore was. By 1875 Andrew Carnegie had adopted the Bessemer process in his great J. Edgar Thomson steel works. Shortly after the Civil War, Abram Hewitt had introduced to this country the more costly Siemens-Martin open-hearth method of smelting, and the superiority of the steel it produced was soon apparent. In 1880 ten times as much steel was manufactured by the Bessemer as by the open-hearth process, but by 1910 the latter method accounted for twice the tonnage of the Bessemer process. The Bessemer and open-hearth processes not only made steel of fine quality and in enormous quantities but reduced the price from $300 to $35 a ton.

The application of chemistry to steel making introduced further economies and solved many technical problems. 'Nine-tenths of all the uncertainties were dispelled under the burning sun of chemical knowledge,' affirmed Andrew Carnegie. The introduction of electric furnaces made it possible to produce hard manganese steel for automobiles and machines and 'high-speed' steel for tools. By 1900 American furnaces turned out as much steel as those of Great Britain and Germany combined; and this supremacy in iron and steel manufacture, once attained, was never surrendered.

An important element in the growth of the iron and steel industry was the tariff, which enabled American manufacturers to compete successfully with their English and German competitors and to pile up fabulous profits. Abram Hewitt put the matter succinctly: 'Steel rails . . . were subject to a duty of $28 a ton. The price of foreign rails had advanced to a point where it would have paid [the

Andrew Carnegie (1835–1919). This painting by H. R. Butler suggests the benevolent serenity of the magnate who entered the mills at the age of thirteen, working from sunrise to sunset, and ended his days a multi-millionaire philanthropist. 'How much have I given away?' he asked his secretary. Informed that the sum had reached $324,657,399, Carnegie replied, 'Wherever did I get all that money?' (*Teachers Insurance and Annuity Association, Photo Jean Shapiro*)

manufacturer] to make rails without any duty, but of the duty of $28 a ton he added $27 to his price and transferred from the great mass of the people $50 million in a few years to the pockets of a few owners who thus indemnified themselves in a very short time, nearly twice over, for the total outlay which they had made in the establishment of their business.' Even Carnegie, when his company showed a profit of $40 million in a single year, felt that the time had come to abandon protection.

Andrew Carnegie was the greatest leader in the iron and steel industry and the archetype of the industrial age. A poor immigrant boy from Scotland, he followed and helped perpetuate the American tradition of rising from poverty to riches, and his success he ascribed entirely to the democracy which obtained in this country. By dint of unflagging industry and unrivaled business acumen, and especially through his extraordinary ability to choose as his associates such men as Charles Schwab, Henry Frick, and Henry Phipps and to command the devotion of his workmen, Carnegie built up the biggest steel business in the world, and retired in 1901 to chant the glories of 'Triumphant Democracy' and to give away his enormous fortune of $450 million. This was made possible by the sale of his holdings to a rival organization, directed by the Chicago lawyer Elbert Gary and the New York banker J. Pierpont Morgan. The result was the United States Steel Corporation, a combination of most of the important steel manufacturers, capitalized at the colossal sum of $1400 million. Half of this capitalization was 'water,' but by 1924 the company had earned aggregate net profits of $2,108,848,640.

Trusts and Monopolies

The organization of U.S. Steel in 1901 brought to a climax a movement which had been under way for a generation: the concentration of business in large units—pools, trusts, corporations, and holding companies. Combination had many advantages. It tended to eliminate competition, diminishing the hazard that unregulated production would drive prices below costs and facilitating economies in manufacture, transportation, marketing, administration, and finance. Through combination, capital reserves could be built up to stabilize or expand industry. Where combination was along horizontal lines—the combination, for example, of all manufacturers of typewriters—it was easy to control production and price. Where combination was along vertical lines—the control, by one corporation, of the entire process from raw materials through manufacture to marketing of a single product, like the Ford car—it gave a degree of independence and power that no isolated industry could enjoy. In steel and oil, combination was both horizontal and vertical and created industrial sovereignties as mighty as states.

The primary legal instrument of combination was incorporation, which became widespread after the Civil War. Incorporation gives permanence of life and continuity of control, elasticity and easy expansion of capital, limited liability for losses in case of disaster, concentration of administrative authority with diffusion of responsibility, and the 'privileges and immunities' of a 'person' in law and in interstate activities.

The concentration of industry developed swiftly in the years after the Civil War and reached a climax around the turn of the century. The trust movement grew out of the fierce competition following hard upon the Civil War. Competing railways cut freight rates, in the hope of obtaining the lion's share of business, until dividends ceased and railway securities became a drug on the market. The downward trend of prices from 1865 to 1895 put a premium on greater units of mass production and led, in the 1870's, to pooling—'gentlemen's agreements' between rival producers or railroad directors to maintain prices and divide business, or even to pro-rate profits. But it was found so difficult to maintain these rudimentary oligopolies that a 'gentlemen's agreement' came to be defined as one that was certain to be violated.

In the 1880's pools were superseded by trusts—a form of combination in which affiliated companies handed over their securities to be administered by a board of trustees. The trust device was 'invented' by a Standard Oil lawyer in 1882; first adopted by the great oil combination, it quickly became the pattern others followed. The term itself shortly outgrew its purely technical meaning, and came to be used as a description of all large-scale combinations. According to the economist Eliot Jones, 'a trust may be said to exist when a person, corporation, or combination owns or controls enough of the plants producing a certain article to be able for all practical purposes to fix its price.' How much is 'enough' is something that not even the courts have been able to determine, and in some ways Mr. Dooley's definition of a trust is more accurate: 'A trust,' he said, 'is somethin' for an honest, ploddin', uncombined manufacturer to sell out to.'

The Standard Oil Company was not only the first trust and—as Allan Nevins observes—'the largest and richest industrial organization in the world'; it was also the most characteristic, and it provides the classic example of the advantages and dangers of this form of organization. It was built on the exploitation of a great natural resource; it prospered by the astute application of technology and of scientific management; it combined control of almost every activity that affected its welfare—raw material, transportation, wholesale and retail trade, and finances; it was deeply involved in overseas operations; it influenced, perhaps corrupted, political processes; it inspired, and frustrated, anti-trust legislation and litigation; and it piled up unparalleled fortunes for its founders and beneficiaries, most of which were poured back into philanthropy.

In 1858 Edwin Drake, prospecting along Oil Creek, near Titusville, Pennsylvania, sank a shaft some 70 feet into the ground and struck oil. The word echoed through the East like the cry of 'Gold' in 'forty-eight. Within two years tens of thousands of prospectors were sinking wells along the hillsides and in the gullies of the forsaken countryside. The life of the 'Regions' was like that of a Western mining camp. When a prospector struck oil at Pithole Creek, a town of almost 15,000 grew up overnight, with hotels, theaters, and concert halls, dance halls and brothels, newspapers and churches; five years more and the place was deserted. As prospectors denuded the hills of trees they erected a forest of derricks; the open wells sometimes caught fire, and a pall of smoke hung over the valley. Railroads pushed their way in, and enterprising oil men ran miniature pipelines to the swollen Allegheny, where the barrels were filled and floated down to Pittsburgh.

In nearby Cleveland a young commission-merchant, John D. Rockefeller—he was not yet twenty-five—watched the birth of the oil industry with shrewd understanding; in 1863 he sold out his commission business and acquired an oil refinery. Two years later his was the largest refinery in Cleveland, and in 1870 he and his partners incorporated as the Standard Oil Company of Ohio. Two years later he organized the South Improvement Company to do battle with, or absorb, his competitors in Pittsburgh and Philadelphia. With ample financial backing he bought up weaker competitors or forced them to their knees; entered into arrangements with shippers that put him in an invulnerable position; and achieved a virtual monopoly on the pipelines of the East. Within a decade he was master of the oil business of the nation.

What accounts for this spectacular achievement? Rockefeller's own explanation might apply to almost any one of the major monopolies of the day:

> I ascribe the success of the Standard to its consistent policy to make the volume of its business large through the merits and cheapness of its products. It has spared no expense in finding, securing, and utilizing the best and cheapest methods of manufacture. It has sought for the best superintendents and workmen and paid the best wages. It has not hesitated to sacrifice old machinery and old plants for new and better ones. It has placed its manufactories at the points where they could supply markets at the least expense. It has not only sought markets for its principal products, but for all possible by-products. . . . It has not hesitated to invest millions of dollars in methods of cheapening the gathering and distribution of oil by pipe lines, special cars, tank steamers and tank wagons. It has erected tank stations at every important railroad station to cheapen the storage and delivery of its products. It has spared no expense in forcing its products into the markets of the world among people civilized and uncivilized. It has had faith in American oil, and has brought together millions of money for the purpose of making it what it is, and holding its markets against the competition of Russia and all the many countries which are . . . competitors against American oil.

What Rockefeller failed to mention in this testimony was what made Standard Oil feared and hated. By playing competing railways one against another, he obtained rebates from their published freight rates, and even forced them to pay to the Standard rebates from competitors' freight payments. If competing oil companies managed to stagger along under such handicaps, they were 'frozen out' by cutting prices in their selling territory until the Standard had all the business.

The Standard Oil trust was soon followed by other combinations. The most important, besides Standard Oil and U.S. Steel, were the Amalgamated Copper Co., the American Sugar Refining Co., the American Tobacco Co., the United States Rubber Co., the United States Leather Co., the International Harvester Co., and the Pullman Palace Car Co., no one of which had a capitalization under $50 million. In no field was concentration more significant than in transportation and communication. By the turn of the century the major part of the railroad business was in the hands of six groups; the expressing business was apportioned between three companies which by their influence prevented the United States mails from taking parcels until 1912; the Western Union, until the rise of the Postal Telegraph, had a virtual monopoly on the telegraph business; and the American Telephone and Telegraph Company, capitalized in 1900 at one-quarter of a billion dollars, was already on its way to becoming the greatest of modern combinations.

The role of New York City bankers in putting together many of these combinations led to the fear that the most fearsome of all trusts was in the making—the 'money trust.' The House of Morgan was exhibit A in this concern. In 1864 Junius Spencer Morgan, long a leader in marketing U.S. securities in England, placed his son John Pierpont in charge of the American branch of the firm. Within a few years young Morgan had tied up with the old banking house of Drexel in Philadelphia, and soon was challenging the supremacy of Jay Cooke and Company. The failure of Cooke in the panic of 1873 put Morgan in a position of immense power. In the 1880's the House of Morgan formed a close association with the New York Central Railroad, and through that decade and the next organized and reorganized

J. P. Morgan (1837–1913). This 1903 portrait of the financial titan is by Edward Steichen, who over a lengthy career did so much to win recognition for photography as an art form. Steichen's picture of Morgan with his 'bead-bright eyes, ferocious eyebrows, and rubescent nose' conveys the enormous personal power of the man who ruled over the great house at Broad and Wall. It suggests what George Bernard Shaw meant in writing of the 'terrible truthfulness' of the camera. *(Metropolitan Museum of Art)*

railroads, extending its influence through the South and even into the Far West where, after the turn of the century, it formed an alliance with the Hill group. Meantime Morgan interests had spread into many other fields, until in the new century there was scarcely an important business which they did not touch except those in the orbit of the rival Rockefeller interests. In 1901 the House of Morgan put through the gigantic deal that created the United States Steel Corporation. Morgan brought together the warring manufacturers of agricultural instruments, and emerged with the International Harvester Company, and he helped finance American Telephone and Telegraph, General Electric, and a dozen other giants. The House of Morgan controlled a dozen large banks—Hanover, Chase, First National, Bankers' Trust, and others; more important, it had tied up with three of the greatest insurance companies—New York Life, Mutual Life, and Equitable.

Trust Regulation

In the 1880's the public began to demand effective regulation of the trusts; but the problem of regulation was seriously complicated by the federal form of government. Corporations are chartered by the states, not the nation. The constitutions of many states contained general prohibitions of monopolies or conspiracies in restraint of trade, but most state prohibitions were ineffective, especially after the federal courts began to interpret broadly the congressional authority over interstate commerce and to limit severely the kind of regulation permitted the states under the Fourteenth Amendment. A corporation chartered by one state has the right to do business in every other state. Hence it was easy for corporations to escape the restrictions or limitations of strict state laws by incorporating in states such as New Jersey, West Virginia, or Delaware where the laws as to issuing stock, accountability of directors, and the right to hold stock in other corporations were very lax.

To make up for the deficiencies of state legislation, Congress enacted the Sherman Anti-Trust Act in 1890. Its central provisions are found in the first two articles:

> 1. Every contract, combination in the form of trust or otherwise, or conspiracy, in restraint of trade or commerce among the several States, or with foreign nations is hereby declared to be illegal. . . .
>
> 2. Every person who shall monopolize, or attempt to monopolize . . . any part of the trade or commerce among the several States, or with foreign nations, shall be deemed guilty of a misdemeanor. . . .

It is difficult to determine the precise purpose of this law. At the time it was alleged that the act sought to give the federal courts common law jurisdiction over the crime of monopoly and conspiracy in restraint of trade; if so the law should have been interpreted in accordance with common law precedents to the effect that only *unreasonable* restraints of trade, or monopolies contrary to public interest, were illegal. But there were no such qualifications in the provisions of the act itself. Nor were there any definitions of the terms 'trust,' 'conspiracy,' and 'monopoly,' while the phrase 'in the form of trust or otherwise' left much to the imagination. In all probability the provisions of the law were purposely couched in indefinite terms, leaving to the courts the task of interpreting and applying them. By thus placing responsibility upon the courts the legislators evaded the problem, and put off its solution indefinitely, for judicial regulation proved singularly ineffective.

In *United States* v. *E. C. Knight and Company*, the Court in 1895 held that the mere control of 98 per cent of the sugar refining of the country did not in itself constitute an act in restraint of trade. In a vigorous dissenting opinion, Justice Harlan warned:

> Interstate traffic . . . may pass under the absolute control of overshadowing combinations having financial resources without limit and audacity in the accomplishment of their objects that recognize none of the restraints of moral obligations controlling the action of individuals; combinations governed entirely by the law of greed and selfishness—so powerful that no single State is able to overthrow them and give the required protection to the whole country, and so all-pervading that they threaten the integrity of our institutions.

This is just about what happened. Attorney-General Richard Olney wrote complacently, 'You will observe that the government has been defeated in the Supreme Court on the trust question. I always supposed it would be, and have taken the responsibility of not prosecuting under a law I believed to be no good.'

In case after case the courts emasculated or nullified the act; yet the disappointment of the anti-trust law should not be charged exclusively to the judiciary. The legislature failed to amend the act; the executive failed to enforce it. Altogether only seven suits under the Sherman Act were instituted by Harrison, eight by Cleveland, and three by McKinley, and all these suits were ineffective. More business combinations were formed during the McKinley administration than ever before. Only when the law was applied to labor unions—embraced in the ambiguous term 'or otherwise'—did the government win a series of victories.

The failure of the machinery of enforcement inevitably gave rise to the suspicion that the whole trust-busting movement was something of a sham. Americans were, in fact, caught on the horns of a dilemma. On the one hand their traditions exalted individualism and idealized the independent entrepreneur. On the other hand all those forces of technology which Americans so deeply admired advertised the advantages of large-scale organization. Had the people really wished to strike down trusts, they could have done so easily enough by taxing them out of existence. But wanting the best of both worlds—the pastoral world of the eighteenth century and the technological world of the twentieth, they contented themselves with ceremonial gestures. They satisfied their moral scruples by undertaking, from time to time, ritualistic skirmishes against the trusts.

Big Business and Its Philosophy

The age was memorable not for statesmen, as in the early years of the Republic, or for reformers and men of letters, as in the middle years, but for titans of industry. Schoolchildren today who have difficulty in remembering the names of any President between Grant and Theodore Roosevelt identify readily enough John D. Rockefeller. Few novelists of these years blunted their pens on the political scene, but the world of business was portrayed in distinguished novels, from Mark Twain's *The Gilded Age* and William Dean Howells's *The Rise of Silas Lapham* to Theodore Dreiser's *The Titan* and Henry James's *The Ivory Tower*.

Gold and silver, copper and oil, forest and stream, all the bounties of nature which in the Old World had belonged, as a matter of course, to crown or commonwealth, were allowed to fall into the hands of strong men. Willing legislators gave them first chance, and amiable judges confirmed them in what they had won or seized. No income tax impeded the swift accumulation of fortunes; no government official told them how to run their business; public opinion never penetrated the walls of their conceit.

Political power and social prestige naturally gravitated to the rich. They controlled newspapers and magazines; subsidized candidates; bought legislation and even judicial decisions. The greatest of them, such as J. P. Morgan, treated state governors as servants, and Presidents as equals. The new rich hired architects to build French châteaux or English country houses in Newport, Washington, New York, Cleveland, and San Francisco, and undertook to indulge themselves in luxuries which Thorstein Veblen designated as 'conspicuous waste.' They filled their houses with paintings and tapestries from the Old World; built enormous yachts; staffed their palaces with hordes of servants; gave parties which they imagined were like those of Versailles before the Revolution.

Business even fostered a philosophy which drew impartially on history, law, economics, religion, and biology to justify its acquisitiveness and its power. At its most full blown Social Darwinism was made up of four not wholly harmonious ingredients. First, the principle drawn from Jeffersonian agrarianism and Manchester liberalism, that that government was best which governed least, a doctrine vigorously enunciated by Professor William Graham Sumner of Yale. Second, the principle of the peculiar sanctity of property—including, of course, corporate charters and franchises. This principle, presumed to be written into the Fourteenth Amendment's prohibition of the deprivation of life, liberty, and property without due process of law, was applied with uncompromising rigor by jurists like Justice Stephen J. Field. Third, the principle that the acquisition of wealth was a mark of divine favor, and that the rich therefore had a moral responsibility both to get richer and to direct the affairs of society. Fourth, perhaps most persuasive of all, was the pseudo-scientific principle of 'the survival of the fittest,' derived from Darwinian biology and applied to the affairs of mankind by the English philosopher Herbert Spencer and his many American disciples. All this added up to the conclusion that America itself was a business civilization—and should be kept that way.

21

Workers and Immigrants

*

1865–1920

The Machine Tenders

During most of the nineteenth century the benefits of the mechanization of industry redounded to the advantage of society as a whole, but more especially to capital than to labor. Machinery made enormous savings in manufacturing costs, but only a small proportion of these savings was passed on to workers in the form of higher wages, and the decrease in hours of labor did not keep pace with the gains in productivity. In addition the workingman suffered from the fatigue and nervous strain of monotonous machine labor which devalued the experience of the skilled worker by eroding the creative instinct of craftsmanship.

As machinery represented a large part of capital investment, it was thought necessary to accommodate the worker to machinery rather than machinery to the worker. If efficiency required that machines be run twenty-four hours a day and seven days a week, workers were expected to adjust themselves. Furthermore machinery constituted a fixed capital charge which could not well be reduced; when economies were necessary there was a temptation to effect them at the expense of labor. The introduction of machinery also resulted in throwing laborers out of work. While most were eventually absorbed in other industries, and while in the long run mechanization more than balanced losses in factory jobs by the growth of clerical and service positions, the process worked severe hardship on the individual employee. Moreover, the increasing efficiency of machinery sometimes resulted in the production of more commodities than the public could or cared to buy, leading to unemployment and lower wages. Industrial unemployment, a product of the machine age, grew proportionately with the development of the machine economy.

The rise of the giant corporation had consequences for labor almost as serious as those which flowed from mechanization. The fiction that a corporation was a person had a certain legal usefulness, but every worker knew that the distinguishing characteristic of a corporation was its impersonality. A person was responsible for his

'Bell-Time.' Winslow Homer's 1868 drawing shows workers, carrying their lunch buckets, streaming out of the mills in Lawrence, Massachusetts, at 7 p.m. at the end of a thirteen-hour day that began before dawn. Notice the range of ages and the large proportion of female employees. (*Library of Congress*)

acts to his own conscience; a corporation was responsible to its stockholders. As individuals, corporation directors might be willing to make concessions to labor, even at personal sacrifice; but as directors their first duty was to maintain dividends.

The change from individual employer to mammoth corporation sharply lessened the worker's bargaining power. It was one thing for an iron-puddler in the mid-nineteenth century to strike a bargain about wages and hours with the owner of a small ironworks; it was a very different thing for a 'roller' in the twentieth century to negotiate with the United States Steel Corporation. Theodore Roosevelt put the matter clearly:

> The old familiar relations between employer and employee were passing. A few generations before, the boss had known every man in his shop; he called his men Bill, Tom, Dick, John; he inquired after their wives and babies; he swapped jokes and stories and perhaps a bit of tobacco with them. In the small establishment there had been a friendly human relationship between employer and employee.
>
> There was no such relation between the great railway magnates, who controlled the anthracite industry, and the one hundred and fifty thousand men who worked in

'Steel Workers—Noontime.' This study by Thomas Anshutz, dated at about 1882, is said to be the first 'labor' painting in America. Anshutz, a pupil of Thomas Eakins, succeeded his mentor as director of the Pennsylvania Academy. Like Eakins, he anticipated twentieth-century artists in portraying urban America.

their mines, or the half million women and children who were dependent upon these miners for their daily bread. Very few of these mine workers had ever seen, for instance, the president of the Reading Railroad. . . . Another change . . . was a crass inequality in bargaining relation between the employer and the individual employee standing alone. The great coal-mining and coal-carrying companies, which employed their tens of thousands, could easily dispense with the services of any particular miner. The miner, on the other hand, could not dispense with the companies. He needed a job; his wife and children would starve if he did not get one. What the miner had to sell—his labor— was a perishable commodity; the labor of today—if not sold—was lost forever. Moreover, his labor was not like most commodities—a mere thing; it was part of a living, breathing human being. The workman saw that the labor problem was not only an economic but also a moral, a human problem.[1]

When in response to this situation laborers organized, giant corporations could afford to fight a strike for months, import strike-breakers, hire

1. *Theodore Roosevelt: An Autobiography*, Scribners, pp. 470–71.

Pinkerton detectives, carry their battle through the courts with highly paid lawyers, buy the press and influence politicians, and, if necessary, close down their plants and starve the workers into submission. In some places—Southern textile towns, Appalachian mining communities, lumber camps—industrial feudalism reigned. In 1914 a United States congressman testified that he had to have a pass to enter a Colorado town situated on the property of the Colorado Fuel and Iron Company.

The late nineteenth century had a double standard of social morality for labor and capital. Combination of capital was regarded as in accordance with natural laws; combination of labor as a conspiracy. Government had a duty to protect corporation interests, but government aid to labor was socialism. Appeals to enhance property interests were reasonable, appeals to protect labor interests demagogic. The use of Pinkerton detectives to protect business property was preserving law and order, but the use of force to protect the job was violence.

Corporations benefited, too, from widespread disapproval of the very idea of unionization, for in a land of equal opportunity, there were not and never would be classes, and any laboring man could rise by his own efforts. Even so openminded a man as President Eliot of Harvard could assert that the closed shop was un-American, and in 1886 the New York banker, Henry Clews, identified the strike with treason. 'Strikes may have been justifiable in other nations,' he said, 'but they are not justifiable in our country. The Almighty has made this country for the oppressed of other nations, and therefore this is the land of refuge . . . and the hand of the laboring man should not be raised against it.'

The Rise of Organized Labor

American labor failed to build a successful union movement during the years following the Civil War largely because it was unable to agree about the nature of industrial society. Throughout the nineteenth century and well into the twentieth, labor debated whether to accept or reject capitalism, whether to trust laissez-faire or seek government patronage, whether to organize on a broadly industrial or on a narrow craft basis, whether to embrace unskilled as well as skilled, black as well as white workers. Two rival approaches—reform unionism and trade unionism—vied for the allegiance of the workingman. The reform unionists rejected the factory system, with its division of labor and its sharp differentiation of interests of employer and employee, and sought to restore a society which valued the independent artisan. Determined not to become machine tenders assigned to a small part of the process of production, they strove to preserve their status as craftsmen. To safeguard equality of opportunity, they fought those forces of monopoly, especially in finance, which they believed aimed to shackle the worker. They viewed themselves as members of a 'producer class' which embraced master as well as journeyman, farmer as well as artisan. Yet as early as 1850, when the National Typographical Union was founded, some workers had abandoned the hope of escaping the factory system, or of becoming entrepreneurs, and accepted their role as wage-earners. Instead of looking for ways to be self-employed, they organized trade unions to bargain with employers, whose interests, they recognized, differed from their own. At the outset, the reform unionists had the larger following, but as the factory system colonized the city and the countryside, the trade union analysis came to seem more appropriate.

In 1866, under the guidance of William Sylvis of the iron molders, labor leaders set up the first national labor federation in America—the National Labor Union. Although it welcomed trade unions, the National Labor Union reflected the reform unionist outlook, for it included various middle-class reform organizations, including women's suffrage leagues. Moreover, it was hostile to the strike weapon and experimented with co-operatives as an alternative to the wage system. The National Labor Union also plunged into politics; in 1872, it sponsored the country's first national labor party, the Labor Reform party. But when both presidential and vice-presidential candidates turned down the nominations, the Labor Reform party looked ridiculous; that same year, the National Labor Union collapsed.

The fiasco of the Labor Reform party proved to

be only the first in a series of such episodes. In 1876, when Eastern labor reformers joined with Midwestern soft money men to create the National Independent party, more popularly known as the Greenback party, they chose, as their presidential candidate, Peter Cooper, who suffered the handicap of being 85 years old, and who attracted almost no working-class votes. In 1880, the Greenback-Labor party nominee, James Baird Weaver of Iowa, found little support in the factory towns of the industrial Northeast. In 1884, reform unionists sank to nominating the notorious Ben Butler on an Anti-Monopoly party ticket, although Butler may well have been in the race as an agent of the Republicans. Trade unionists concluded from these disasters that the attempts of reform unionists to find political solutions for the workers' problems were doomed to failure.

By far the most important organization of reform unionism was the Noble Order of the Knights of Labor, founded in 1869 by a Philadelphia tailor, Uriah S. Stephens, a Mason with a smattering of Greek who contributed his knowledge of ritual to the secret order. Native American in leadership and largely in personnel, it attempted to unite workers into one big union, under centralized control. Membership was open to men and women, white and black, skilled and unskilled, laborers and capitalists, merchants and farmers. Only liquor dealers, professional gamblers, lawyers, and bankers were excluded!

The growth of the Knights of Labor was phenomenal. When a Pennsylvania machinist, Terence V. Powderly, became Grand Master in 1878, the membership was under 50,000. A vain man, Powderly acted 'like Queen Victoria at a national Democratic convention.' Opposed to the tactics of combative unionism, he said: 'Strikes are a failure. Ask any old veteran in the labor movement and he will say the same. I shudder at the thought of a strike, and I have good reason.' Powderly emphasized co-operatives, and even more the land question, because 'we must free the land and give men the chance to become their own employers.' Yet under his leadership the Order made spectacular gains, especially after it shed its secrecy and thus overcame the hostility of the Catholic Church, and, ironically, after it won a great railroad strike on the Gould lines in the Southwest in 1885. Capital then, for the first time, met labor on equal terms, when the financier, Jay Gould, conferred with the Knights' leaders and conceded their demands. The prestige of this victory lifted the Order's membership to over 700,000 the following year, an increment of more than half a million members in 14 months.

In May 1886 local units of the Knights took part in a strike for the eight-hour day, which inadvertently associated the Order with violence. On 3 May Chicago police killed and wounded half a dozen labor demonstrators. The following day when the police broke up a protest meeting at Haymarket Square, someone threw a bomb into their midst; seven persons were killed and over sixty injured. Though the actual perpetrator of the outrage could not be found, a Cook County judge held that those who incited the deed were equally guilty with those who committed it. Under this ruling the jury found eight anarchists guilty of murder and sentenced one to imprisonment and seven to death. Of these seven, one committed suicide, four were executed, and the other two had their sentences commuted to life imprisonment. Six years later Governor John Peter Altgeld, alleging that 'the judge conducted the trial with malicious ferocity,' pardoned the three anarchists still in prison. Although these men were clearly innocent, Altgeld was denounced as an aider and abetter of anarchy. The Knights of Labor was in no way responsible for the Haymarket massacre and Powderly had even attempted to disassociate the Order from the eight-hour movement, but the revulsion against radicals embraced the Knights too. Indiscriminate strikes, all failures, mismanagement by Powderly, and the difficulty of holding skilled and unskilled labor in the same union also made serious inroads. By the end of the decade membership in the Order had dwindled to about 100,000, and the Knights soon all but disappeared.

As the Knights of Labor declined, its place in the van of the labor movement was usurped by a new organization, the American Federation of Labor. This body, which was to dominate the labor scene for the next half-century, rejected the idea of one big union in favor of craft unions of skilled workers. The two organizations differed in other respects as well: where the K. of L. had been idealistic and vague in its aims, the A.F. of L. was opportunistic and practical; where the old Order embraced farmer-labor parties and theoretically discouraged strikes, the new organization abjured third parties and relied on the strike and the boycott. The Knights had looked forward to a co-operative republic of workers, whereas the Federation accepted capitalism and chose to work within the established economic order.

The A.F. of L. issued from the brain of a foreign-born worker. In the late 'sixties a bullet-headed young man named Samuel Gompers, a London-born Jew of Flemish ancestry, was working in a highly unsanitary cigar-making shop in the Lower East Side, and speaking at union meetings. As he rose in the councils of his fellow workers, Gompers determined to divorce unionism from independent political action, which dissipated its energy, and from radicalism, which aroused the fear of the public and the fury of the police. By 1881 he and other local labor leaders had thought their way through to a national federation of craft unions, and five years later the A.F. of L. was established. Animated by the philosophy of the job, the Federation concentrated on tangible objectives like shorter hours and better wages. 'We have no ultimate ends,' testified one of Gompers's co-workers. 'We are going on from day to day. We are fighting only for immediate objects—objects that can be realized in a few years.'

By the turn of the century the A.F. of L. boasted a membership of over half a million; by 1914 it would reach 2 million. This rapid growth was in great part due to the leadership of Gompers who for 40 years guided its destiny, impressed it with his personality, permeated it with his ideas, inspired it with his stubborn courage, and held it steadily to the course of aggressive self-interest. The A.F. of L. opposed creating a separate labor party nor would it divide its ranks by giving allegiance to either of the major parties. Instead, it used its power to persuade legislators to adopt specific demands and judged them accordingly. It hewed to a simple line: 'Reward your friends and punish your enemies.' Nor did the A.F. of L. ever try to organize the great mass of unskilled workers in the factories.

The void was only partially filled by ragged unions that sprang up in the turbulent mining camps of the West and eventually coalesced in 1905 into the Industrial Workers of the World, the first labor organization formally committed to class warfare. The I.W.W. (or 'Wobblies,' as they came to be known) set out to organize the migratory farm workers of the Great Plains, lumbermen of the Far Northwest, copper miners in Arizona, and dock hands along the Pacific waterfront. In 1912 it ventured east to take charge of a textile strike in Lawrence, Massachusetts, where mill-owners had slashed wages. It won this strike, as well as an astonishingly large number of others. But when its activities threatened to interfere with the war in 1917 and 1918, it was destroyed.

Industrial Conflict

As labor shifted its objectives from social reform to the job, it resorted with increasing frequency to the strike and the boycott, and business retaliated with the lockout, the blacklist, the injunction, and company police or the National Guard. The result was uninterrupted industrial conflict, often violent, that assumed the ominous character of warfare.

The great majority of strikes after the 1870's involved hours or wages. As late as 1910, only 8 per cent of industrial workers were on an eight-hour day. In many industries hours were shockingly long: steel had a twelve-hour day and a seven-day week, a schedule maintained for many steel workers until 1923. Hours in textiles ranged from 60 to 84 a week, even for women and little children, who constituted a large part of the working force. Furthermore, from 1880 to 1910 the unskilled laborer commonly earned less than $10 a week and the skilled worker rarely more than $20, while earnings of women ranged from $3.93 a week in Richmond to $6.91 in San Francisco. During the whole of this 30-year period the average annual family income of industrial workers was never more than $650, or of farm laborers more than $400, sums considerably below a decent living standard. Moreover, unemployment averaged 10 per cent and was often higher, and even those employed rarely enjoyed continuous work, at a

The Great Strike of 1877. An angry mob watches Pittsburgh's Union Depot and Hotel go up in flames. Many workingmen and militia lost their lives in civil strife in which rioters raided the armory of the Pittsburgh militia, stole a cannon, marched on the gunshops, and set fires that razed large quantities of railroad property and nearly levelled the city. (*Library of Congress*)

time when with the growth of cities the vegetable garden, fruit trees, chicken-coop, and family cow disappeared.

The first great industrial conflict came in 1877 when the Eastern trunk railroads jauntily announced a wage-cut of 10 per cent, the second since the panic of 1873. Without adequate organization railway employees struck, and with the support of a huge army of hungry and desperate unemployed, the strike flared up into something that seemed to respectable folk like rebellion. During one week in July traffic was entirely suspended on the trunk lines, and every large industrial center was in turmoil. In Baltimore, Pittsburgh, Chicago, Buffalo, San Francisco, and elsewhere, there were battles between militia and the mob, and order was restored only by federal troops. Pittsburgh was terrorized for three days; fatalities ran into the scores, and a wall of three miles of flame destroyed every railroad car, including 160 locomotives, and every railroad building, and almost levelled the city.

Not until 1892 was the nation again to witness so menacing an outbreak. That year a strike in the Homestead works of the Carnegie Steel Company culminated in a pitched battle between infuriated strikers and an army of Pinkerton detectives hired by the president of the Carnegie Company, Henry C. Frick. The strikers won the sanguinary battle, but the attempted murder of Frick alienated public opinion and militia broke the backbone of the strike.

Two years later a strike erupted against the Pullman Palace Car Company in the model town of Pullman, Illinois. The strike resulted originally from the arbitrary refusal of Mr. Pullman to discuss grievances with representatives of his employees, but it came eventually to involve far larger issues. The cause of the Pullman workers was taken up by the American Railway Union, a powerful body under the leadership of the magnetic Eugene V. Debs. When this union voted to boycott all Pullman cars, the cause of the Pullman Company was championed by the newly organized General Managers' Association of Railroads. The result was paralysis of transportation throughout the North and widespread disorder. The railroads succeeded in enlisting the sympathies of President Cleveland and Attorney-General Olney, a former railroad lawyer. On 1 July, Olney appointed as special counsel for the United States a prominent railway attorney, at whose suggestion the federal circuit court at Chicago served on the officers of the American Railway Union a 'blanket injunction' against obstructing the railroads and holding up the mails. Hooligans promptly ditched a mail train and took possession of strategic points in the switching yards. Cleveland declared that he would use every dollar in the Treasury and every soldier in the army if necessary to deliver a single postcard in Chicago. On 4 July he ordered a regiment of regulars to the city. The effect was like that of sending British regulars to Boston in 1768.

Cleveland's antagonist in this conflict was not so much Debs as Governor John P. Altgeld. This honest and fearless statesman had already been marked for destruction by big business because he had helped Jane Addams to obtain factory regulations in Illinois and because he had pardoned the Haymarket prisoners. During the Pullman strike Altgeld was ready and able to maintain law and order with state militia. But his eloquent protest against gratuitous interference by the Federal Government and his demand for the withdrawal of U.S. troops were cavalierly disregarded. When Debs defied the injunction, he was given six months' imprisonment for contempt of court. By early August the strike was smashed.

The Supreme Court of the United States, to which Debs appealed his sentence, upheld the government, declaring that even in the absence of statutory law it had a dormant power to brush away obstacles to interstate commerce—an implied power that would have made Hamilton and Marshall gasp. Yet the whole affair was not without a certain educational value. Debs, in his prison cell, studied socialism and in time became the organizer and leader of the Socialist party; the workers learned the real meaning of the Sherman Anti-Trust Act; business awoke to the potentialities of the injunction; and the country at large was taught a new interpretation of the sovereign powers of the Federal Government. Only George Pullman emerged innocent of new ideas.

Scarcely less spectacular than the Pullman strike was the outbreak in Pennsylvania's anthracite coal fields in 1902. In 1898 the youthful John Mitchell had become president of the United Mine Workers, which then numbered some 40,000 members. Within two years he whipped it into shape, invaded the anthracite fields, where the railways controlled the operators, and wrested favorable terms from the powerful coal companies of eastern Pennsylvania. Two years later the operators abrogated this agreement, and the miners struck for recognition of their union, a nine-hour day, and a wage rise. For four tense months the strike dragged on while the strikers maintained an unbroken front. In the course of this struggle President George F. Baer of the Philadelphia and Reading Railroad announced that 'the rights and interests of the laboring man will be protected and cared for, not by the labor agitators, but by the Christian men to whom God in His infinite wisdom, has given control of the property interests of the country.' In October, with both a congressional election and a coal-less winter looming, Roosevelt brought pressure on miners and operators to arbitrate. The miners were willing, but not Mr. Baer, who rebuked the President for 'negotiating with the fomenters of anarchy.' Outraged, Roosevelt threatened to take over the mines and run them with militia. This

The Ludlow Massacre. In the winter of 1913–14 miners at the Rockefeller-owned Colorado Fuel and Iron Company in Ludlow, Colo., walked out of the pits and, abandoning the oppressive company town, set up tent colonies with their families. The worst episode of the prolonged and violent strike came when state militia machine-gunned the tent colony and set it afire; two women and eleven children burned to death or suffocated. (*State Historical Society of Colorado*)

threat, and the force of public opinion, persuaded the mine-owners to arbitrate, and the strike ended in a signal victory for the miners, enhancement of the prestige of John Mitchell and of President Roosevelt, and a triumph for the cause of arbitration.

Labor unrest in the coal industry was chronic. The murderous activities of the Molly Maguires in the eastern Pennsylvania coal fields in the early 'seventies had given the first premonition of class warfare. In 1903–04 came a violent outbreak in the Rockefeller-owned coal fields of Colorado which was crushed by the military. Ten years later the United Mine Workers tried to unionize the Colorado Fuel and Iron Company; armed guards broke up the miners' camps, and the militia attacked a tent village in the 'Ludlow massacre,' which took the lives of several men, women, and children. The ensuing battle between outraged miners and soldiers plunged parts of Colorado into something like civil war, aroused nation-wide sympathy for the strikers, and led, eventually, to far-reaching reforms.

Labor Legislation and the Courts

Until the 1930's American social legislation lagged a generation behind that of European states like Denmark and Germany and such Commonwealth nations as Australia and New Zealand, for the role of the Federal Government was sharply circumscribed. Yet as early as 1868 Congress established an eight-hour day on public works, and in 1892 an eight-hour day for all government employees; the Adamson Act of 1916 extended this boon to all railway workers. In 1898 Congress passed the Erdman Act providing for arbitration of labor disputes on interstate carriers, and in 1908 an Employers' Liability Act, likewise confined to railway employees. A Bureau of Labor, created in 1884, was elevated to cabinet rank in 1913. The La Follette Seaman's Act of 1915 gave seamen for the first time the full status of free men. Twice Congress attempted to outlaw child labor—in 1916 under the guise of a regulation of commerce, and again in 1919 through the medium of taxation, but both laws were nullified by the Court.

Before the 1930's, most social legislation lay in the domain of the states, but progressive reforms ran the constant danger of judicial nullification. It is forbidden in most state constitutions and in the Fourteenth Amendment to deprive persons of liberty or property without due process of law. As no reform can be effected without depriving someone of something he may deem a liberty or a property right, American courts (following English precedents) early elaborated the doctrine of a superior 'police power'—the reserved right of the state to protect the people's health, safety, morals, and welfare. However, when labor laws began to appear on the statute books, corporation lawyers persuaded courts that such laws were not a proper exercise of the police power but a violation of the 'due process' clause of the Fourteenth Amendment.

For half a century after Reconstruction judges such as Field and Sutherland, and their disciples in the state courts, turned the bench into a dike against the surging tides of welfare legislation. They interpreted the Constitution as a prohibition rather than an instrument, and, insisting that they were without discretion and that their functions were purely mechanical, struck down hundreds of state police laws. In truth, the judges were writing into law their fears that labor statutes constituted 'the first step towards socialism.' In 1913 Justice Holmes observed, 'When twenty years ago a vague terror went over the earth and the word socialism began to be heard, I thought and still think that fear was translated into doctrines that had no proper place in the Constitution or the common law.' In 1905 the Supreme Court drew a vigorous dissent from Holmes in *Lochner* v. *New York* when in a split decision it invalidated a New York law prescribing hours of labor in bakeries. 'The Fourteenth Amendment does not enact Mr. Herbert Spencer's *Social Statics*,' Holmes protested.

Yet the conservatives did not always prevail. As early as 1898 the Supreme Court, in *Holden* v. *Hardy*, accepted a Utah law limiting to eight the hours of labor in mines. An Oregon Act of 1903 limiting to ten the hours of employment for women was upheld by the Supreme Court in 1908 in the notable case of *Muller* v. *Oregon*—notable especially because the mass of sociological, economic, and physiological data introduced by the counsel for Oregon, Louis D. Brandeis, was admitted as evidence. Thus the principle was established that the courts could take cognizance of the circumstances that demonstrated the reasonableness of the exercise of the police power. Following Australian and British precedents, fifteen states, beginning with Massachusetts in 1912, enacted minimum wage laws for women and children, and in 1916 Brandeis and Felix Frankfurter persuaded the Supreme Court to accept the Oregon act.[2] Seven years later, however, in a remarkable reversal, the Court, in the *Adkins* case, found a District of Columbia minimum wage law unconstitutional, and on this rock of judicial intransi-

2. *Stettler* v. *O'Hara* 243 U.S. 629 (1916). On this case the Court divided four to four, thus sustaining the act.

gence the campaign for minimum wage legislation was temporarily grounded.

In no other industrial nation were the hazards of industry so great. In 1917 fatal accidents in manufacturing establishments amounted to 11,338 and non-fatal to the astonishing total of 1,363,080. Statutes required the installation of safety devices and provided for sanitary and fire inspection, but not until inspection was entrusted to civil servants was there any perceptible improvement. To secure compensation for the injured or incapacitated victims, it was necessary to get rid of the monstrous common law doctrines which stipulated that if the worker had willingly assumed the risks of his job, if his accident resulted from his own negligence or that of a fellow worker, the company was not responsible. Alone of major industrial nations the United States lacked workmen's compensation legislation at the turn of the century. Congress provided workmen's compensation for interstate railroad workers, but when the states enacted similar laws, the courts declared them void. Not until 1917 when the Supreme Court sustained New York's new compensation act were the states able to go ahead. Within a few years most states outside the South had legislated workmen's compensation. Advanced European countries also provided unemployment and old-age pension programs, but here, too, the United States lagged behind. Although a few companies experimented with pension plans and Wisconsin adopted pathbreaking unemployment insurance, not until the New Deal did the nation begin to take appropriate action.

A Nation of Nations

Unionists viewed with alarm the tidal wave of immigration which spilled almost 18 million persons on American shores in the single generation from 1880 to 1910. When unions attempted to organize these 'new' immigrants, as the United Mine Workers did, they succeeded. But in part because of ethnic and religious antagonisms, partly because much of organized labor was by this time committed to the craft principle, most unions made no serious effort to enlist the immigrants. Almost inevitably labor experienced its most serious difficulties in those industries where the proportion of foreign-born workers was highest—meat-packing, iron and steel, and mining. Although some of the most important labor leaders were foreign-born, many unions became champions of immigration restriction.

The transfer of peoples from the Old World to the New was the most extensive and successful experiment of its kind in history, carried out on a larger stage and over a longer period and with fewer convulsive reactions than any comparable enterprise. The disruptive agricultural revolution in Europe, persistent poverty for the peasants, recurrent hard times for workers, war and the constant threat of military service for young men, political oppression, religious persecution, a class system which closed the door of opportunity to the vast mass of the poor and denied education to their children—these were, for 200 years, the main motivations for the emigration of 40 million Europeans to the United States. As for the magnetic attraction of America, that is even more easily explained: open land, work for almost all who were willing to work, a higher standard of living for ordinary folk than was known in Europe, religious freedom, political democracy, greater social equality, a second chance for the young.

Men and women foregathered in the mill towns of Scotland or the fishing villages of Norway, or along the sanguinary banks of the Danube, to sing some new ballad about America or listen to the latest America-letter: in America you eat meat every day; in America you do not pull your forelock to the priest or take your hat off to the mayor—he takes his hat off to you; in America women do not work in the fields; in America all the children go to school; in America no one makes you serve in the army. When Andrew Carnegie was a little boy in Dumfermline, Scotland, he used to hear his father and mother sing

> To the West, to the West, to the land of the free,
> Where the mighty Missouri rolls down to the sea;
> Where a man is a man if he's willing to toil,
> And the humblest may gather the fruits of the soil;
> Where children are blessings, and he who hath most
> Has aid for his fortune and riches to boast.
> Where the young may exult and the aged may rest,
> Away, far away, to the land of the West.

It was this song that induced the elder Carnegie to

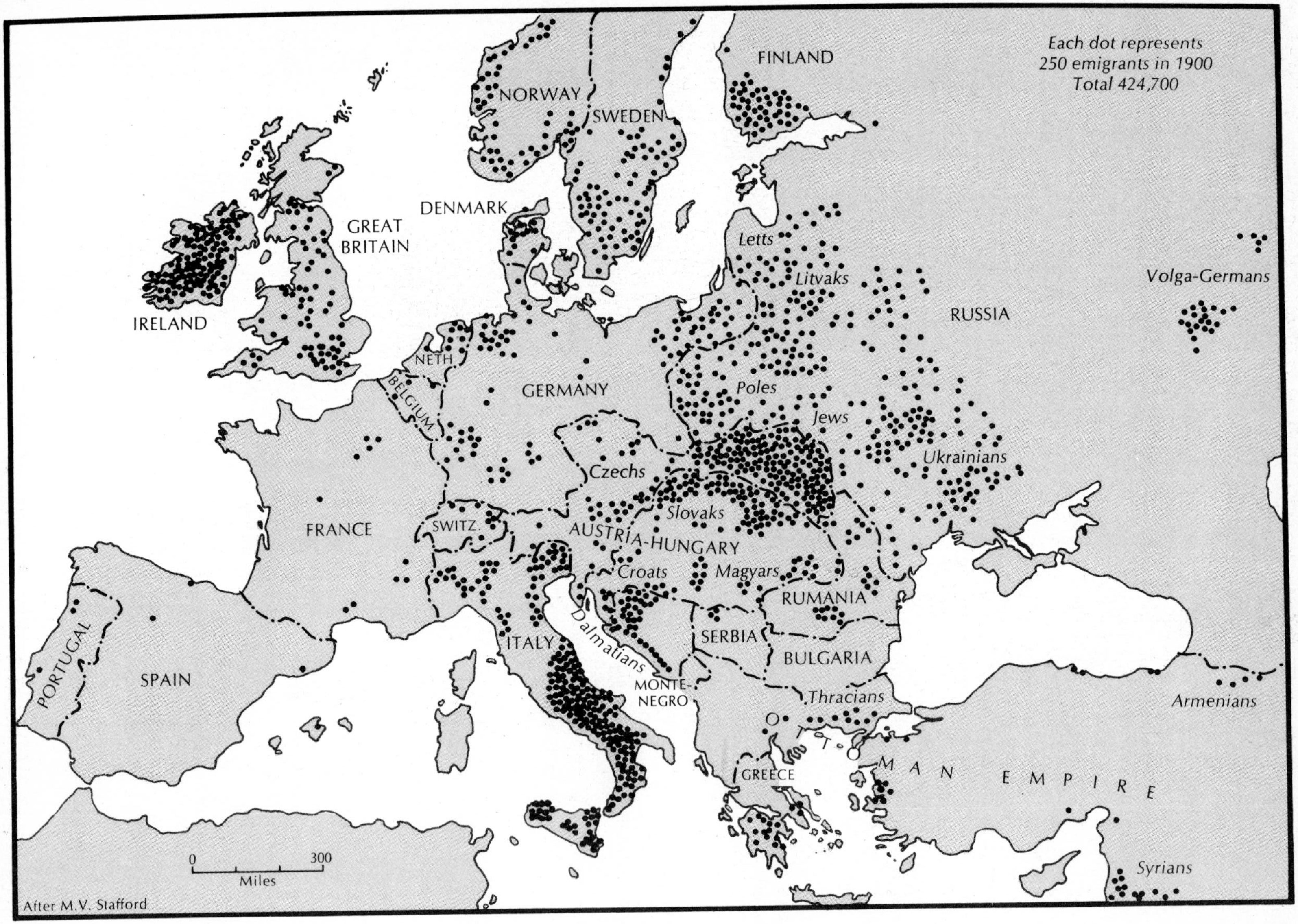

Emigration from Europe to the United States in 1900

'In the Land of Promise—Castle Garden.' Charles Ulrich painted this scene of the entrance way for throngs of Hungarians, White Russians, Croats, and other 'New Immigrants' from the European continent in 1884. This picture has a saccharine quality typical of much of American art in the Gilded Age. (*Corcoran Gallery of Art*)

migrate to America, where his son amassed a fortune.

In the three-quarters of a century after Appomattox some 33 million emigrants sought American shores, swarming out onto the rich prairie lands of the West, transforming the cities into enormous cosmopolitan beehives, performing the back-breaking labor that made possible the economic expansion of the nation, creating new problems of assimilation and adaptation, and bringing to the United States the richest cultural heritage vouchsafed any modern nation—though one all too often dissipated. After a century and a half of colonization and unprecedented natural increase, the population of the English colonies in America was but slightly over 2 millions; every decade from 1850 to 1930 witnessed an immigration large enough to replace this entire population.

In attempting to interpret the significance of the greatest folk movement in history, it may be well to dispose of certain misconceptions. Neither immigration nor racial heterogeneity is a recent development; immigration was as large, proportionately, in the later colonial period as in the latter part of the nineteenth century, and the population of the colonies on the eve of the Revolution, though predominantly English and African, represented six or seven nationalities and three or four languages. Nor was there ever any ground for fearing that the 'native stock' would succumb to the alien invasion. Despite the fecundity of many of the immigrant groups, the number of Americans of foreign or mixed parentage constituted only one-fifth of the population in 1920, and declined steadily thereafter. And though the number of foreign-born in the country more than doubled in the 50 years after 1880, so, too, did the population, and the foreign-born made up a smaller percentage of the population in 1930 than in 1880.

Of the 35 million who migrated to America between 1850 and 1930, the largest number were from the United Kingdom—some 8.5 million in all—of whom over 4.5 million came from Ireland. Germany accounted for approximately 6 million, Canada for almost 3 million, and the three Scandinavian countries for 2.25 million. The largest number of immigrants from northern and western Europe arrived in the generation immediately after the Civil War—there was a notable decline in immigration from Germany and the United Kingdom after 1890 and from Scandinavia after 1910.

The ingredients that made up the American population in 1870 did not differ markedly from those which had made up the population a century earlier, but in the 1870's there began to appear new types among the thousands who swarmed in at Castle Garden, New York: Austrians and Hungarians from the valley of the Danube, Bohemians from the river Moldau, Poles from the Vistula, and Serbs from the river Save, blue-eyed Italians from the banks of the Arno and olive-skinned Italians from the plains of Campania or the mountains of Sicily, Russian Jews from the Volga and the Dnieper and the steppes of Ukraine. By the 'eighties this trickle from southern and eastern Europe had become a stream, by the 'nineties a torrent, and in the early years of the new century a veritable flood. Altogether in the 50 years between 1880 and 1930, Italy sent over 4.5 million emigrants, Austria, Hungary, and the succession states over 4 million, Russia and Poland perhaps another 4 million—a total from these countries alone of 13 million. In 1860 southern and eastern Europe made up only 1 per cent of the foreign-born population; in 1910, 38 per cent. While the 'old' immigration was predominantly Protestant, the 'new' arrivals were for the most part Catholic, Greek Orthodox, or Jewish. The United States, in short, had become a much more heterogeneous country.

Immigrants from northern Europe tended to go west and take land. Though numbers of Germans congregated in cities such as Cincinnati, St. Louis, and Milwaukee, Norwegians and Swedes showed a marked tendency to go out to the land. The great agricultural states of Minnesota, Illinois, North and South Dakota, Nebraska, and Iowa still have substantial Scandinavian population, and Minnesota displays no less than 400 Swedish place names, while the influence of these industrious and intelligent farmers was felt south to Texas and west to California. However, most of the Irish remained in the cities of the Eastern seaboard, where their group loyalty and talent for politics in a democratic medium made them the first and most enduring of ethnic blocs in American politics.

Like the Irish, the immigrants from southern and eastern Europe chose the cities. Most of them were far too poor to buy a farm or invest in the machinery and stock necessary for modern agriculture, and peoples whose language, customs, and religion were very different from those of the older stock naturally tended to live together in colonies rather than isolate themselves on farms or in small towns. For many, too, migration to America was their urban movement—inspired by the same notions that took native Americans from the farms to the cities. In 1900 two-thirds and in 1930 three-fourths of the foreign-born were liv-

Immigrants arriving, New York harbor. This picture was taken about 1900 by Frances Benjamin Johnston, one of several distinguished women photographers whose work, long neglected, is now highly valued. (*Coll. Judith Mara Gutman*)

ing in towns and cities. The proportion of foreign-born in such large cities as New York and Detroit was impressive, but the concentration in the smaller industrial cities, such as Paterson, New Jersey, or Fall River, Massachusetts, was even more notable. American cities came to have their 'ghettos,' their 'little Italy' or their 'Chinatown,' and 'slum' became a familiar word in the American vocabulary. In 1890 two-thirds of the population of New York City was crowded into tenements. Desperately poor, without industrial or mechanical skills, the immigrants from southern and eastern Europe became, for the most part, unskilled laborers in mine, in factory, or on the railroad. Jews congregated in the garment trade, Finns in mining, Portuguese in the textile towns.

Two other groups of immigrants came in increasing numbers after the turn of the century: Canadians and Mexicans. It was easy for Canadians to drift into the United States, and after the

Civil War many found their way to northern New England, the Great Lakes states, and the Far Northwest. Canadian immigration first took on major proportions after 1910; in the next 20 years 1.5 million Canadians, one-third French and about two-thirds English-speaking, crossed the border, cementing the strong ties already binding the two neighboring democracies. The census of 1930 revealed that not far from 750,000 Mexicans were domiciled in the United States, the majority of them in the border states of Texas, New Mexico, Arizona, and California. For the most part poor and illiterate, these casual laborers worked under shocking conditions in the cotton, rice, and beet-sugar fields of Colorado and the Southwest.

Toward the assimilation of these millions of immigrants, the United States held inconsistent attitudes. The predominant expectation was that the newcomer, no matter what his place of origin, would conform to Anglo-Saxon patterns of behavior and cherish those institutions transported to the New World from the British Isles. Competing with this view was the conviction that in this hemisphere a new type was being fused out of a variety of ethnic elements. In 1845 Emerson predicted:

> In this continent,—asylum of all nations,—the energy of Irish, Germans, Swedes, Poles, and Cossacks, and all the European tribes,—of the Africans, and of the Polynesians,— will construct a new race, a new religion, a new state, a new literature, which will be as vigorous as the new Europe which came out of the smelting-pot of the Dark Ages.

Still a third conception came from the experience of the settlement-house workers: respect for the cultural heritage of the new arrivals. Those who saw at first hand the tragic alienation of first from second generation Americans feared that attempts to 'Americanize' the immigrants would lead to ethnic self-hatred and would deprive the country of a variety of distinct cultural contributions.

Most newcomers were quick to abandon their Old World loyalties and profess those of the New. Everything conspired to root out old attachments and supplant them with new: the vastness of the country which broke up compact settlements; the economy which rewarded speedy acquisition of the American language; the political system which encouraged naturalization and voting; the habit of voluntary association which welcomed most newcomers into political parties, granges, and a hundred other organizations; and perhaps most effective of all, the public schools. The Russian Jew, Mary Antin, recalled:

> Education was free. That subject my father had written about repeatedly, as comprising his chief hope for us children, the essence of American opportunity, the treasure that no thief could touch, nor even misfortune or poverty. It was the one thing that he was able to promise us when he sent for us; surer, safer than bread or shelter. On our second day I was thrilled with the realization of what this freedom of education meant. A little girl from across the alley came and offered to conduct us to school. My father was out, but we five between us had a few words of English by this time. We knew the word school. We understood. This child, who had never seen us till yesterday, who could not pronounce our names, who was not much better dressed than we were; was able to offer us the freedom of the schools of Boston! No application made, no questions asked, no examinations, rulings, exclusions; no machinations, no fees. The doors stood open for every one of us. The smallest child could show us the way.[3]

The immigrant contribution of muscle and brawn is obvious; the contribution to public affairs, industry and labor, science and education, arts and letters, is scarcely less apparent. To remember the achievements of Carl Schurz and John Peter Altgeld in politics, Jacob Riis in social reform, E. L. Godkin in journalism, Andrew Carnegie, James J. Hill, and Henry Villard in business, Samuel Gompers in unions, Alexander Graham Bell in the field of invention, Louis Agassiz in science, Augustus Saint-Gaudens in sculpture, and Jascha Heifetz in music, is to realize the extent to which the foreign-born have enriched American life.

Putting Up the Bars

Despite these contributions, many Americans took a hostile attitude toward the newcomers and demanded that immigration, especially of Orientals, be restricted or ended altogether. For well-

3. Mary Antin, *The Promised Land,* Houghton Mifflin Co.

nigh a century, Congress had left the regulation of immigration to the states, but in the 1880's it felt called upon to act, largely because California settlers expressed alarm over the mass migration of Chinese coolies. The discovery of gold in 1849 and the consequent demand for cheap labor had first brought the Chinese to California, and their numbers were augmented in the 'sixties by the demand for laborers on the Central Pacific Railroad; by the end of the 'seventies there were almost 150,000 Chinese in California alone. Their low standards of living, long hours of labor, and tractability were said to constitute a serious menace to native labor. At the same time they aroused racial prejudice by their exotic appearance, customs, religion, and language, and their obvious intention to return to China with their savings. As a result an anti-Chinese movement developed in the 'seventies under the leadership of an Irish agitator, Denis Kearney. Taken up by the California Workingmen's party, it culminated in discriminatory legislation and a demand for the prohibition of further Oriental immigration. In response to this demand Congress, in 1882, enacted a law excluding Chinese laborers for a period of ten years—a prohibition that was extended in 1890 and again in 1902 until it became permanent.

By then the West Coast was demanding that the policy of exclusion be extended to embrace the Japanese, who arrived in large numbers in the first decade of the twentieth century. To avoid an international crisis, President Roosevelt, in 1907, reached a 'gentlemen's agreement' with the Japanese government whereby it pledged itself to continue 'the existing policy of discouraging emigration of its subjects of the laboring classes to continental United States.' Despite this agreement a small stream of Japanese continued to trickle in, and between 1911 and 1913 California and other Western states enacted a series of laws designed to prevent Japanese from owning or even leasing real estate. In 1924 Congress went out of its way to ban Japanese immigration completely, a deliberate affront to a wartime ally. 'Our friends in the Senate have in a few minutes spoiled the work of years,' said Secretary of State Charles Evans Hughes, 'and done lasting injury to our common country.' By its long record of racial prejudice, segregation in schools, prohibition of land-holding, and discrimination in immigration, the United States managed to stockpile for itself a formidable arsenal of ill-will among the Japanese people.

Once embarked upon a policy of regulation, Congress faced two basic alternatives: selection or exclusion. The first general immigration law, that of 1882, was based upon the theory of selection; it imposed a head tax of 50 cents on each immigrant admitted, and excluded convicts, idiots, and persons likely to become public charges. From this time on a long series of federal acts elaborated the policy of selection; Congress increased the head tax, prohibited contract labor, and considerably extended the classes excluded. The new statutes excluded the sick and diseased, paupers, polygamists, prostitutes, anarchists, alcoholics, and—by the Act of 1917—persons with constitutional inferiority complexes!

Though this policy of selection afforded protection against some unwelcome additions to the population, it made no response to the rising clamor for a plan designed to reduce the total number who would be admitted and to select those thought to be best. Agitation came from three disparate groups. First, and most powerful, was organized labor, which had long looked upon the immigration of unskilled workers as a major threat. Second were social reformers who had come to the conclusion that there could be no solution of the problems of slums, public health, and the exploitation of the poor as long as illiterate immigrants poured into the great cities. Third were the traditionalists who had been taken in by the doctrines of Nordic supremacy and who deplored the

> Accents of menace alien to our air,
> Voices that once the Tower of Babel knew.[4]

The criterion of selection was to be literacy, and an historic battle was waged over this issue. A bill incorporating a literacy test passed one of the two Houses of Congress no less than 32 times, and on four occasions it was approved by both Houses and

4. Thomas Bailey Aldrich, 'Unguarded Gates.'

went to the President, only to be vetoed each time. In 1917, however, a bill was enacted over Wilson's veto. By its terms no alien over 16 years of age who could not read English or some other language was to be admitted to the United States. Since in the first decade of the century less than 3 per cent of the 'old' immigrants were illiterate, but over half of those from Sicily and southern Italy, the literacy test provided a method of discrimination on ethnic lines.

After the First World War a new wave of immigration led Congress to abandon the policy of selection for one of absolute restriction. By the Immigration Act of 1921, the number of aliens admitted from any European, Australasian, Near Eastern, or African country[5] was to be limited to 3 per cent of the total number of that nationality residing in the United States in 1910, a system designed to reduce the proportion of immigrants from southern and eastern Europe. The act also severely restricted the total number that could be admitted in any one year. In 1924 Congress framed a new law which provided for parcelling out the immigration quotas from the various European countries in proportion to the 'national origins' of the American people. Immigration from Western Hemisphere nations was left undisturbed, except by a Department of Labor ruling that no immigrants should be admitted who might become public charges.

The enactment of the first quota law of 1921 ended an era. In a hundred years the tide of immigration had risen to a flood, engulfing the whole country and depositing millions of people from every land and the cultural accretions of centuries. Then suddenly it ebbed. The Statue of Liberty still stood guard over New York harbor, its beacon light held proudly aloft, the inscription on its base not yet erased:

> Give me your tired, your poor,
> Your huddled masses yearning to breathe free,
> The wretched refuse of your teeming shore,
> Send these, the homeless, tempest-tost to me:
> I lift my lamp beside the golden door.

But it was a symbol of things strange, and faintly remembered.

5. The Act of 1917 created a Barred Zone, including India, Siam, Indo-China, and other parts of Asia, from which no immigrants were to be admitted.

22

The Passing of the Frontier

*

1865–1890

The Last West

The roaring vitality, the cascading energy of the American people in the postwar years, is nowhere better illustrated than in the history of the West. The generation after the Civil War witnessed the most extensive movement of population in our history; a doubling of the settled area; rapid transition from primitive society to contemporary civilization; the subjugation of the Indian; the rise and fall of the mineral empire and of the cattle kingdom; the emergence of new types of economic life articulated to the geography of the High Plains and the Rocky Mountains; and the organization of a dozen new states with a taste for political experiment.

The most notable of these developments was the conquest of the Great Plains—that region extending from about longitude 98 to the Rocky Mountains, and from Texas to the Canadian border. This vast area, comprising roughly one-fifth of the United States, had long interposed a hazardous barrier to settlement. In the 1840's the frontier had reached the edge of the Plains. Then, instead of moving progressively westward as it had always done, the frontier leaped 1500 miles to the Pacific coast. For 30 years the intervening territory was practically uninhabited except by Indians and Mormons; not until the decade of the 'seventies did settlers begin to close in on the Plains and Mountain regions; then the process went on with unprecedented rapidity until by 1890 the frontier line had been erased.

The environment of the Great Plains required a radical readjustment. Here was an immense grassland, sparsely wooded, with few navigable streams, and with a rainfall seldom sufficient for farming as practiced in the East. When pioneer farmers tried to apply here the experience they had gained and the tools they had developed in the wooded East, they failed. Before white settlers could establish themselves permanently on the Plains, four things were necessary: the suppression of the Indian; new methods of farming to cope with inadequate rainfall; a substitute for traditional wooden fencing; and transportation to take the crops to market. The army and the destruction of the buffalo undid the Indian; barbed wire solved the fencing problem; the windmill, dry farming, and irrigation went far to overcome the effect of insufficient rainfall and intermittent droughts; and the railroad furnished transportation. In the course of this arduous struggle with the Plains environment, the miner, the cattleman, and the farmer evolved institutions that differed markedly from those which had obtained in the woodlands of the East—a modification not only of the tools and methods of farming, but of social attitudes, economic concepts, and political and legal institutions as well.

The Railway Key

For almost fifty years after the Civil War the railroad dominated industry and politics. There were 35,000 miles of steam railway in 1865, practically all east of the Mississippi; during the next eight years the country doubled its rail network. By 1900, with just under 200,000 miles, the United States had a greater railway mileage than all Europe. Railroad expansion touched American life at countless points. It closely interacted with western migration, with iron and steel, and with agriculture; it greased the way for big business and high finance, helped pollute politics, and gave birth to new problems of constitutional law and government policy. By widening the market for manufactured goods, it helped trigger a revolution in the economy.

Immediately after the war came mechanical improvements such as the coal-burning expansion-cylinder locomotive, the Pullman sleeping car (1864), and the safety coupler. The Westinghouse air brake (1869) did more than any other invention to transform the original string of boxes on tracks into the modern train and to make possible safe operation at high speeds. But it was the old wood-burning, spark-belching 'bullgine,' gay with paint and sporting a name instead of a number, tugging unvestibuled coaches with swaying kerosene lamps and quid-bespattered wood stoves, which first wheezed across the Great Divide and linked the Atlantic to the Pacific.

On 1 July 1862 President Lincoln signed the first Pacific Railway Act. This law provided for the construction of a transcontinental railroad by two corporations—the Union Pacific which would build westward from Council Bluffs, Iowa, and the Central Pacific, which was to build eastward from Sacramento, California. It pledged liberal aid in the form of alternate sections of public lands to the depth of ten miles (and later twenty) on either side of the road, and loans ranging from $16,000 to $48,000 for every mile of track completed. Active construction, which began in 1865, confronted almost insuperable obstacles, including the constant struggle with mountain blizzard and desert heat, and—in the mountains—with the Indians as well. That the obstacles were overcome must be attributed not only to the indomitable perseverance of engineers like the U.P.'s General Grenville Dodge and of entrepreneurs like the C.P.'s Collis Huntington but also to the endurance of the thousands of laborers—ex-soldiers, Irish immigrants, and Chinese coolies—upon whose brawny shoulders the heaviest part of the task rested.

> When I think *[*wrote Robert Louis Stevenson*]* of how the railroad has been pushed through this unwatered wilderness and haunt of savage tribes . . . ; how at each stage of construction, roaring, impromptu cities full of gold and lust and death sprang up and then died away again, and are now but wayside stations in the desert; how in these uncouth places pigtailed Chinese pirates worked side by side with border ruffians and broken men from Europe, talking together in a mixed dialect mostly oaths, . . . how the plumed hereditary lord of all America heard in this last fastness the scream of the 'bad medicine wagon' charioting his foes; and then when I go on to remember that all this epical turmoil was conducted by gentlemen in frocked coats, and to nothing more extraordinary than a fortune and a subsequent visit to Paris, it seems to me . . . as if this railway were the one typical achievement of the age in which we live.[1]

Both the Union and the Central Pacific roads were pushed forward in record time, 20,000 laborers laying as much as eight miles of track a day in the last stages of the race. When, amidst universal rejoicing, the two sets of rails were joined with a golden spike at Promontory Point, Utah, 10 May 1869, the Union Pacific was regarded as the winner, but the Central Pacific promoters had made enough to enable them to buy the state government of California.

Within a few years Congress chartered and endowed with enormous land grants three other

1. *Across the Plains*, pp. 50–52.

'The First Transcontinental Train Leaving Sacramento, California—May 1869.' This rare example of Western folk art, painted by Joseph Becker in 1869, shows snow still on the tracks, though the month is May, and Chinese workmen waving the train through. The 'C.P.R.R.' on the coal car stands for Central Pacific Railroad. (*The Thomas Gilcrease Institute of American History and Art, Tulsa*)

lines: (1) the Northern Pacific—from Lake Superior across the Badlands of Dakota to the headwaters of the Missouri, and by an intricate route through the Rockies to the Columbia river and Portland; (2) the Southern Pacific—from New Orleans across Texas and through the territory of the Gadsden Purchase to Los Angeles, up the San Joaquin valley to San Francisco; (3) the Sante Fe—following closely the old Santa Fe Trail, from Atchison, Kan., to Sante Fe and Albuquerque, through Apache and Navajo country and across the Mojave desert to San Diego. By 1883 all three links had reached the Pacific. Thus within 20 years of the Pacific railway legislation there were four transcontinentals; a fifth, the Great Northern, was pressed through in the next decade by the dynamic James J. Hill.

The transcontinental railways drastically altered population patterns in the West. At the end of the Civil War, the Plains and the Rocky Mountain regions were virtually unpeopled, and the Overland Stage Line required at least five days

Slaughtering buffalo. This scene along the line of the Kansas-Pacific Railroad appeared in Frank Leslie's illustrated periodical in 1871. It has been estimated that sixty million bison roamed the land in 1800; by 1895, there were fewer than a thousand. (*Library of Congress*)

to transport passengers and mails from the Missouri river to Denver, where potatoes sold for $15 a bushel. The railways brought a dramatic change. They pushed out into the Plains far in advance of settlers, advertised for immigrants in the Eastern states and Europe, transported them at wholesale rates to the prairie railhead, and sold them land at from $1 to $10 an acre. Henry Villard of the Northern Pacific employed almost a thousand agents in England and continental Europe, and the Union Pacific's advertising painted the Northwest in such roseate colors that U.P. lands were popularly known as Jay Cooke's banana belt. The Santa Fe Railroad attracted to Kansas, in 1874, 10,000 German Mennonites whose ancestors had colonized the Ukraine, and these brought with them not only piety and industry but the Red Turkey wheat which made Kansas prairies bloom like a garden. Thousands of section-hands entered a free homestead right, saved their wages to buy farm equipment and a team of horses, built a sodhouse or cabin, and became permanent settlers. The termini and eastern junction points of these lines—like Omaha, opposite the old Council Bluffs of the Indians; Kansas City, hard by the former jumping-off place for the Oregon Trail; Duluth, the 'Zenith City of the Unsalted Seas'; Oakland on San Francisco bay; Portland, Oregon; Seattle, Washington—places non-existent or mere villages before the Civil War—became in thirty years metropolitan cities.

The new Northwest was the domain of James J. Hill, the 'Empire Builder,' and the Great Northern Railway his path of empire. St. Paul was a small town on the edge of the frontier when he migrated thither from eastern Canada just before the Civil War, and Minneapolis a mere village at the Falls of St. Anthony on the Mississippi. Such importance as they had was due to their position at the end of a trail from the Red river of the North, which connected Winnipeg with the outside world. Long trains of two-wheeled ox-carts transported the peltry and supplies in 40 or 50 days' time. In the winter of 1870 Donald Smith, resident governor of the Hudson's Bay Company, started south from Winnipeg, and James J. Hill north from St. Paul, both in dog-sleds. They met on the prairie and made camp in a snowstorm; from that meeting sprang the Canadian Pacific and the Great Northern railways. In the panic of 1873 a little Minnesota railway with an ambitious name, the St. Paul and Pacific, went bankrupt. Hill watched it as a prairie wolf watches a weakening buffalo, and in 1878, in association with two Canadian railway men, wrested it from Dutch bondholders by a mere flotation of new securities.

The day of land grants and federal subsidies was past, and Hill saw that the Great Northern Railway, as he renamed his purchase, could reach the Pacific only by developing the country as it progressed. So he introduced scientific farming, distributed blooded bulls free to farmers, supported churches and schools, and assisted in countless ways the development of the communities of the 'Hill country.' In constructing his railroad Hill showed equal forethought and shrewdness, and by 1893 the Great Northern had reached tidewater at Tacoma. Ten years more, and Hill had acquired partial control of the Northern Pacific, had purchased joint control of a railway connecting its eastern termini with Chicago, and was running his own fleets of steamships from Duluth to Buffalo, and from Seattle to Japan and China.

The Indian Barrier

The Indians of the Great Plains and the Rocky Mountains, perhaps 225,000 in number, presented a formidable obstacle to white settlement. Strongest and most warlike were the Sioux, Blackfeet, Crow, Cheyenne, and Arapahoe in the north; the Comanche, Kiowa, Ute, Southern Cheyenne, Apache, and Southern Arapahoe in the south. Mounted on swift horses, admirably armed for Plains warfare, and living on the millions of buffalo that roamed the open range, these tribes for generations had successfully resisted white penetration.

The fate of the California Indians after the gold rush was prophetic of what was to happen elsewhere. There were 100,000 Indians in California in 1850, ten years later only 35,000; the Commissioner of Indian Affairs wrote that 'despoiled by irresistible forces of the land of their fathers; with no country on earth to which they can migrate; in the midst of a people with whom they cannot assimilate; they have no recognized claims upon the government and are compelled to become vagabonds—to steal or to starve.' The advance of the miners into the mountains, the building of the transcontinental railroads, and the invasion of the grasslands by cattlemen threatened other tribes with the same fate. Most serious was the wanton destruction of the buffalo, indispensable not only for food but for hides, bowstrings, lariats, fuel, and a score of other purposes. Scarcely less ruinous were two other developments: the perfection of the Colt repeating revolver, fearfully efficient in Plains warfare, and the spread of smallpox, cholera, and venereal diseases among the Indians.

The story of Indian relations from 1860 to 1887, the year of the passage of the Dawes Act, is a melancholy tale of intermittent and barbarous warfare, greed, corruption and maladministration, of alternating aggression and vacillation on the part of the whites, of courageous defense, despair, blind savagery, and inevitable defeat for the Indians. President Hayes observed in his annual message of 1877, 'Many, if not most, of our Indian wars have had their origin in broken promises and acts of injustice on our part.'

Until 1861 the Indians of the Plains had been relatively peaceful, but in that year the invasion of their hunting grounds by thousands of ruthless miners, and the advance of white settlers along the upper Mississippi and Missouri frontier, together with dissatisfaction at their treatment by the government and the breakdown of the reservation system, resulted in numerous minor conflicts. In 1862 the Sioux of the Dakota region devastated the Minnesota frontier and massacred and imprisoned almost a thousand white men, women, and children. Retribution was swift and terrible and fell indiscriminately upon the innocent and the guilty. For the next 25 years warfare was constant, each new influx of settlers driving the Indians to acts of desperation which brought on renewed outrage and punishment. In 1864 the Cheyenne, banished from their hunting grounds to the wastes of southeastern Colorado, attacked Ben Halliday's stages and harried mining settlements to the north; they were persuaded to abandon their depredations and concentrate at Indian posts, and at one of these posts Colonel Chivington ordered a savage slaughter of the Indian men, women, and children which sent a thrill of horror through the nation. General Nelson Miles called the Sand Creek Massacre the 'foulest and most unjustifiable crime in the annals of America,' but Denver hailed Chivington, a former Methodist minister, who exhibited his collection of a hundred scalps at a local theater. Two years later a small force under Colonel Fetterman was in turn massacred by the embittered Sioux. The climax came in 1876 when gold-seekers overran the Sioux reservation in the Black Hills. Under Sitting Bull and Crazy Horse the Sioux ambushed the impetuous 'glory-hunter,' General George Custer, on the Little Big Horn, and annihilated his whole command of 264 men. Punishment was quick; the Sioux were scattered and Crazy Horse captured and murdered by his guard.

In the mountains, as on the plains, the Indians were driven from their ancient homes. In Montana the Crow and the Blackfeet were ejected from their reservations; in Colorado the vast holdings of the Utes were confiscated and opened to settlement; in the Southwest the Navajo were herded onto a bleak reservation, and ten years of warfare ended in the capture of the intractable Geronimo and the practical destruction of the Apache. The discovery of gold on the Salmon river in western Idaho precipitated an invasion of the country of the peaceful Nez Percés. Chief Joseph struck back, but in vain, and in 1877 there began a retreat eastward over 1500 miles of mountain and plain that remains the most memorable feat in the annals of Indian warfare. In the end the feeble remnant of the Nez Percé tribe was captured and exiled to Oklahoma. Chief Joseph spoke for all his race:

> I am tired of fighting. Our chiefs are killed. Looking-Glass is dead. Too-hul-hut-sote is dead. The old men are all dead. It is the young men now who say 'yes' or 'no.' He who led the young men is dead. It is cold and we have no blankets. The little children are freezing to death. My people, some of them, have run away to the hills and have no blankets, no food. No one knows where they are, perhaps freezing to death. I want to have time to look for my children and see how many of them I can find. Maybe I can find them among the dead. Hear me, my chiefs. My heart is sick and sad. I am tired.

Authority over Indian affairs was divided between the Departments of War and of the Interior, and both departments vacillated, the one failing to live up to treaty obligations, the other failing to protect the Indians on their reservations from the aggressions of white settlers. By fraud and chicanery large areas of Indian lands were alienated by 'treaty' or by 'sale.' One railroad acquired 800,000 acres of Cherokee lands in southern Kansas by methods that the governor of the state denounced as 'a cheat and a fraud in every particular,' but nothing was done to cancel the arrangement, and the railroad resold the lands to settlers at 100 per cent profit.

If most frontiersmen believed that the only good Indian was a dead Indian, Easterners, removed by a century from the Indian menace, had a different attitude. Statesmen like Carl Schurz, religious leaders such as Bishop Whipple, and

Major-General George Armstrong Custer (1839–76). Only two years after graduating from West Point in 1861, he was brevetted major-general and during the Civil War he earned a brilliant reputation as a cavalry officer. 'Custer's Last Stand' at the Battle of the Little Big Horn, 25–26 June 1876, was one of the memorable episodes in the waning years of the Wild West. Vain, cocksure, Custer has been denounced as a glory-hunter who led his men into a massacre, but more recent scholarship has placed the blame for the disaster on his subordinate commanders and on a feckless policy toward the Indians. (*Library of Congress*)

Sioux Indian camp. This photograph of the Villa of Brule, 'the great hostile Indian Camp' on the River Brule near Pine Ridge, South Dakota, was taken in about 1891, shortly after the appalling 'Battle' of Wounded Knee of 29 December 1890 in which United States troops killed two hundred Dakota Sioux, including women and children. (*Library of Congress*)

literary figures like Helen Hunt Jackson, whose *A Century of Dishonor* stirred the nation's conscience, effected important changes in Indian policy.

In 1887 Congress adopted the Dawes Severalty Act, which set Indian policy for the next half-century. The Dawes Act was the first serious attempt to teach Indians the practices of agriculture and social life and merge them in the body politic of the nation. It provided for the dissolution of the tribes as legal entities and the division of tribal lands among individual members. To protect the Indian in his property the right of disposal was withheld for 25 years; upon the expiration of this probationary period, the Indian was to become the unrestricted owner and to be admitted to full citizenship in the United States. In October 1901 the Five Civilized Nations of Oklahoma, already well assimilated, were admitted to citizenship and in 1924 Congress granted full citizenship to all Indians.

The Dawes Act was hailed at the time as an Indian Emancipation Act; it might better have been compared to Appomattox. Under the operation of this misguided law, Indian holdings decreased in the next half-century from 138 to 48 million acres, half of these arid or semi-arid. Whites deprived Indians of their lands by various kinds of deceit and even by murder, in one case the bombing of two sleeping children. Indian timber land was seized by speculators; in 1917 the Indian commissioner explained that 'as the Indian tribes were being liquidated anyway it was only sensible to liquidate their forest holdings as well.' Tribal funds amounting to more than $100 million were diverted from their proper use to meet the costs of the Indian Bureau—including the costs of despoiling the Indians of their lands. Not until the New Deal did the government adopt a more responsible policy, and even then glaring injustices remained.

The Mining Frontier

The vast territory between the Missouri and the Pacific, first explored by fur traders, had been crossed and recrossed by emigrants along the great trails, but it was the miners who first revealed the possibilities of this country. In 1849 the lure of gold had drawn to California a heterogeneous throng of miners who later formed the nucleus of a large permanent population and who developed the varied agricultural resources of the state. This process was to be repeated time and again in the 'sixties: in Colorado, Nevada, Arizona, Idaho, Montana, and Wyoming. In each state precious metals attracted the first settlers; then, as the big pay dirt was exhausted, the mining population receded, and its place was taken by ranchers and farmers who established, with the aid of the railroads and the government, the permanent foundation of the territory.

In 1859 the discovery of gold in the foothills of the Rockies, near Pike's Peak, drew thousands of eager prospectors. Denver City, Golden, Boulder, and Colorado City arose almost overnight, and the Territory of Jefferson—changed later to Colorado—was organized. The mining boom soon spent itself; not until the silver strikes of the 1870's, the advent of the railroads, and the influx of farmers was the basis for a sounder development laid. By 1880 Leadville, the second city of Colorado, had 13 schools, 5 churches, and 28 miles of streets; its annual silver production soon outdistanced that of any foreign country save Mexico.

In the same year that gold was discovered in Colorado came the announcement of a rich strike of silver on the eastern slopes of the Sierra Nevada. Here was located the Comstock Lode, one of the richest veins in the world. Within a year roaring towns like Virginia City sprang up in the desert waste, the Territory of Nevada was carved out of Utah, and 10,000 men were digging frantically in the bowels of the earth for the precious ore. Nevada furnishes the most extreme example of a mining community; nowhere else in history do we find a society so completely and continuously dependent upon minerals. However, very little of the enormous riches remained there. The change from placer mining to more efficient quartz mining required expensive machinery, engineering skill, and the organization of mining as a big business. So outside capital took over; the miners became day laborers working for wages, and the profits went to stockholders scattered throughout the United States and Europe. Mining added nothing to the wealth of the state. It did not create permanent industries or cities, nor provide foundations for healthy growth. This was the history of Comstock, and to a greater or less extent of most of the mines of the West in the following decade.

The story of Idaho runs parallel to that of Nevada. After gold was discovered in 1860 on the Nez Percé reservation in the extreme eastern part of Washington Territory, a wave of prospectors rolled in. Lewiston and Boise City sprang into existence, and in 1865 the Territory of Idaho was carved out of Washington and Montana. But mining furnished a most insubstantial foundation, and the census of 1870 showed a population of only 15,000. Gold was discovered east of the Con-

Albert Bierstadt, 'Storm in the Rocky Mountains—Mt. Rosalie' (1866). Bierstadt (1830–1902) was the most successful member of the second generation of the Hudson River school, painters of grand landscapes in the romantic tradition. Born in Germany, Bierstadt painted Rocky Mountain vistas out of memories of the Swiss and Italian Alps. (*The Brooklyn Museum*)

tinental Divide, too, but the mines along the Sweetwater were soon played out, and after 1865 the future of Wyoming Territory depended almost wholly upon cattle and sheep.

Although Montana produced over $100 million in precious metals in the first decade, the mining kingdom was short-lived and scarred by violence. For a brief time the notorious Henry Plummer and his gang of cutthroats threatened the prosperity of the Montana camps, and it required a vigilante organization such as that which had arisen in California fifteen years earlier to restore law and order. Virginia City, Montana, which typified the mining towns of the West, was thus described by N.P. Langford in his book *Vigilante Days and Ways:*

This human hive, numbering at least ten thousand people, was the product of ninety days. Into it were crowded all the elements of a rough and active civilization. . . . Nearly every third cabin in the town was a saloon where vile whiskey was peddled out for fifty cents a drink in gold dust. Many of these places were filled with gambling tables and gamblers, and the miner who was bold enough to enter one of them with his day's earnings in his pocket, seldom left until thoroughly fleeced. Hurdy-gurdy dance-houses were numerous, and there were plenty of camp beauties to patronize them. . . . Not a day or night passed which did not yield its full fruition of fights, quarrels, wounds, or murders. The crack of the revolver was often heard above the merry notes of the violin. Street fights were frequent, and as no one knew when or where they would occur, everyone was on his guard against a random shot.

But it would be a mistake to picture the mining camps as mere nests of lawlessness. They had, to be sure, few of the institutions taken for granted in the East—churches, schools, newspapers, theaters—but they hastened to establish these institutions as quickly as they could. Moreover, they showed ingenuity in developing a legal system appropriate to their circumstances. Each miners' camp was an administrative and a judicial district. It had its own executive officers, judges, recorders; voted laws and regulations suited to its own peculiar needs; and enforced these laws through public opinion and police officers. The legal codes and practices of these mining communities were eventually recognized in the American courts and incorporated into U.S. statutes and the constitutions and laws of the western states.

Not gold and silver but copper proved the chief resource of Montana, and of Arizona too. In the 1870's Marcus Daly, once an impoverished Irish immigrant, bought an option on a small silver mine in Butte, the Anaconda. In the next half-century he and his associates took over two billion dollars' worth of copper out of this 'richest hill in the world.' To control this and other mines, Daly, William Clark, and other 'copper kings' corrupted the public life of the state for a generation. Clark got a senatorship, $100 million, and a mansion on New York's Fifth Avenue with 121 rooms and 31 baths. After the turn of the century, copper mining shifted to Arizona where the Phelps-Dodge interests dominated the economy of the state, and where a single copper mine at Bisbee yielded more money than all the gold and silver mines of the Territory.

The gaudy last gold rush belongs as much to Canadian as to American history. The discovery of gold along the Klondike, which flows from Yukon into Alaska, came in 1896; soon 30,000 fortune-hunters were washing the icy waters of the Klondike and its tributaries. The Klondike strike furnished material for a dozen red-blooded novels which gave Jack London an international reputation; inspired Robert Service to write and a million hams to recite 'The Shooting of Dan McGrew'; and provided the background for Charlie Chaplin's wonderful movie *The Gold Rush.* More important, it marked the beginnings of modern Alaska.

Ephemeral as it was, the mining frontier had a great impact. The miners forced a 'solution' of the Indian 'problem,' dramatized the need for railroads, and laid the foundations for a permanent farming population. Out of the necessities of their situation they contributed much of value to the legal and political institutions of the West. They produced, in the 30 years from 1860 to 1890, $1,241,827,032 of gold and $901,160,660 of silver, enabled the government to resume specie payments, and precipitated 'the money question' which was for well-nigh twenty years the main political issue before the country. They added immeasurably to folklore, enriched the American idiom, and in the stories of Bret Harte and Mark Twain inspired lasting contributions to literature.

The Cattle Kingdom

One of the most dramatic shifts in the screen-picture of the West was the replacement of millions of buffalo that had roamed the Great Plains by cattle, and of the Indian by the cowboy and the cattle king. The territory between the Missouri and the Rockies, from the Red river of the South to Saskatchewan—an area comprising approximately one-fourth of the United States—was the cattle kingdom, the last American frontier. Here millions of cattle—Texas longhorns, full-blooded Herefords, Wyoming and Montana steers—fatted on the long luscious grasses of the public lands, and cowboys and their liege lords, the cattle barons who ruled this vast domain, developed a unique society.

The emergence of the cattle industry on a large scale was due to a combination of causes: the opening up of the public domain after the Civil War, the elimination of the Indian danger and the annihilation of the buffalo, the extension of railroads into the High Plains, the decline in cattle-raising in the Middle West and the East, increased consumption of meat here and abroad, the invention of the refrigerator car, and the growth of great packing centers.

Since the days when the American Southwest belonged to Spain, the sturdy Texas longhorn, descendant of Spanish *toros* from the plains of Andalusia, had grazed on the limitless prairie, but not until the middle 'sixties did the 'long drive' north to the region of rich grasses and good prices cease to be an experiment. On the first of the organized long drives, 35,000 longhorns pounded up clouds of dust all along the Chisholm Trail, across the Red and Arkansas rivers and into the land of the Five Nations, to Abilene, Kansas. Two years later no less than 350,000 longhorned kine made their way along the Chisholm and Goodnight trails to fatten on the tall northern grasses and find a market at one of the several roaring cattle towns on the Kansas and Pacific Railroad: Abilene, Dodge City, or Newton. Later the 'long drive' extended north to the Union Pacific and even to the Northern Pacific.

> In after years [writes the historian of the cattle kingdom] the drive of the Texas men became little short of an American saga. To all who saw that long line of Texas cattle come up over a rise in the prairie, nostrils wide for the smell of water, dust-caked and gaunt, so ready to break from the nervous control of the riders strung out along the flanks of the herd, there came a feeling that in this spectacle there was something elemental, something resistless, something perfectly in keeping with the unconquerable land about them.[2]

Between 1866 and 1888, cowboys, who first learned their art from Mexican *vaqueros*, drove some 6 million cattle from Texas to winter on the High Plains of Colorado, Wyoming, and even Montana. Every spring they rounded up the herds in designated areas, all the way from Texas to Wyoming and the Dakotas, identified their owners' cattle by the brands, and branded the calves, dividing up pro rata the strays or 'mavericks.' The breeding cattle were then set free for another year while the likely three- and four-year-olds were driven to the nearest cow town on a railway. Each 'outfit' of cowboys attended its owner's herd on the drive, protecting it from wolves and rustlers, sending scouts ahead to locate water and the best grazing.

The long drive seems romantic in retrospect, but to the cowboys it was hard and often hazardous work. Andy Adams, later one of the cattle barons of Texas, describes a dry drive along the Old Western Trail:

> Good cloudy weather would have saved us, but in its stead was a sultry morning without a breath of air, which bespoke another day of sizzling heat. We had not been on the trail over two hours before the heat became almost unbearable to man and beast. Had it not been for the condition of the herd, all might yet have gone well; but over three days had elapsed without water for the cattle, and they became feverish and ungovernable. . . . We threw our ropes in their faces, and when this failed, we resorted to shooting; but in defiance of the fusillade and the smoke they walked sullenly through the line of horsemen across their front. Six-shooters were discharged so close to the leaders' faces as to singe their hair, yet, under a noonday sun, they disregarded this and every other device to turn them, and passed wholly out of our control. In a number of instances wild steers deliberately walked against our horses, and then for the first time a fact dawned upon us that chilled the marrow in our bones—*the herd was going blind.*[3]

In Wyoming, where cattlemen seized most of the public and much of the Indian lands, the great cattle companies ruled supreme. For almost 20 years the Wyoming Stock Growers' Association was the *de facto* government of the Territory; it formulated laws and regulations governing land and water rights, the round-up, and similar matters, and enforced them on members and non-members alike; it agitated ceaselessly for revision of the land laws and for recognition of the prior rights of cattlemen; it attempted, by fraud, intimidation, and violence, to keep Wyoming the exclusive preserve of the ranchers.

This proved impossible. The most dangerous threat to the cattle kingdom, in Wyoming as elsewhere through the West, was not, at first, the farmer but the lowly sheepherder. Sheep, like cattle, could graze free on Uncle Sam's inexhaustible lands; labor costs were negligible; and the wool clip, protected by high tariffs, was increasingly valuable. The cattlemen, convinced that sheep ruined the grass by close cropping, waged open war on their rivals. The Tonto Basin War in northern Arizona, like Kentucky feuds, dragged on for years and ended only when ranchers and

2. E. S. Osgood, *The Day of the Cattleman*, p. 26.

3. Andy Adams, *The Log of a Cowboy*, Houghton Mifflin Co., pp. 63–64.

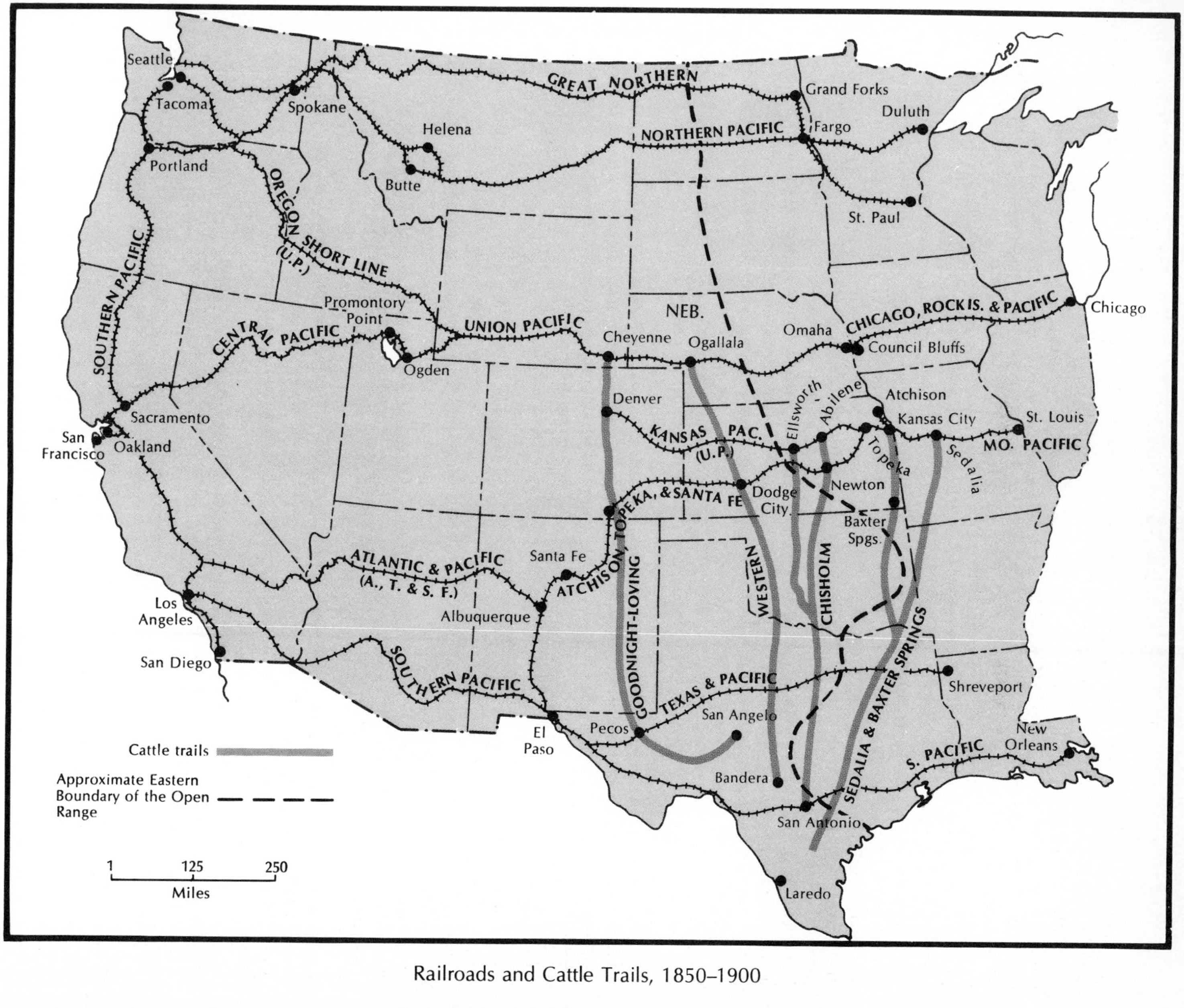

Railroads and Cattle Trails, 1850–1900

sheepherders had wiped each other out. But in the end the sheepmen triumphed, even in Wyoming where sheep came to outnumber cattle ten to one. Oddly enough, though the sheepherder is an older and more beloved figure than the rancher, and one with many Biblical associations, sheep raising never caught the American imagination or acquired a folklore or a literature.

The cattle boom reached its height about 1885. By that time the hazards of ranching had increased enormously. The appearance of cattle diseases and the enactment of state quarantine laws, the conflict between cattlemen and sheepherders, between northern and southern cattlemen, and between cattlemen and homesteaders, the decline of prices because of overproduction, the destruction of the range by overgrazing, and the determination of the Federal Government to enforce its land laws—all these presaged the decline of the cow kingdom. Then came the two terrible winters of 1885–86 and 1886–87 which almost annihilated the herds on the open ranges. Cattle owners began to fence off their lands. Almost in a moment the cattle range replaced the open ranges. The cowboy, now a cattleman or ranch employee, was penned in behind wire and no longer knew the joys and dangers of the long drive.

The Disappearance of the Frontier

The picturesque 'Wild West' fell before the pressure of farmers, swarming by the hundreds of thousands onto the High Plains and into the mountain valleys. During the Civil War, dangers and uncertainties, especially in the border states, induced many to try their luck in the new regions, while the liberal provisions of the Homestead and later land acts, the low cost of railroad lands, and the high rewards of farming proved an irresistible magnet for thousands of others. From Council Bluffs, Iowa, eastern terminus of the Union Pacific, the Reverend Jonathan Blanchard wrote in 1864:

> When you approach this town, the ravines and gorges are white with covered wagons at rest. Below the town, toward the river side, long wings of white canvas stretch away on either side, into the soft green willows; at the ferry from a quarter to a half mile of teams all the time await their turn to cross. Myriads of horses and mules drag on the moving mass of humanity toward the setting sun; while the oxen and cows equal them in number.

All this seems incredibly remote from Shiloh and the Wilderness; one of the great pulses of American life went on beating amid the din of arms.

The close of the war brought a sharp acceleration of this movement. It was in part the absorbing power of the West that enabled a million soldiers to resume civilian life without serious economic derangements. Southerners by the tens of thousands, despairing of recouping their fortunes in the war-stricken South, migrated westward although excluded temporarily from the privileges of the Homestead Act. Immigrants, mostly from northern Europe, found their way to the prairies of Iowa and Minnesota and eastern Dakota by the hundreds of thousands. The railroads provided transportation, ensured markets, and were active colonizing agents.

But it was not enough to provide land and transportation for the migrants. Some method had to be found to overcome the natural handicaps to agriculture in the semi-arid Plains. In the Plains, where lumber had to be imported, the cost of timber-fencing a quarter-section of land was prohibitive. Yet if cattle were to be controlled, crops protected from the ravages of cattle, and water holes preserved, fencing was essential. In 1874, J. F. Glidden discovered a solution: barbed wire. By 1883 Glidden's company was turning out 600 miles of barbed wire daily, and fencing had been reduced to a mere fraction of its former cost. The importance of barbed wire to the development of the Great Plains was comparable to that of the cotton gin in the South.

Fencing made farming on the High Plains possible, but not necessarily profitable. There was still the menace of drought. For a time irrigation promised to solve the problem. The Pueblo Indians were familiar with irrigation, and the Mormons had reclaimed millions of acres by this ancient method. In 1894 the Carey Act turned over to the Western states millions of acres of public lands to be reclaimed through irrigation. When the law proved ineffective, the Federal Government took charge; under the Reclamation

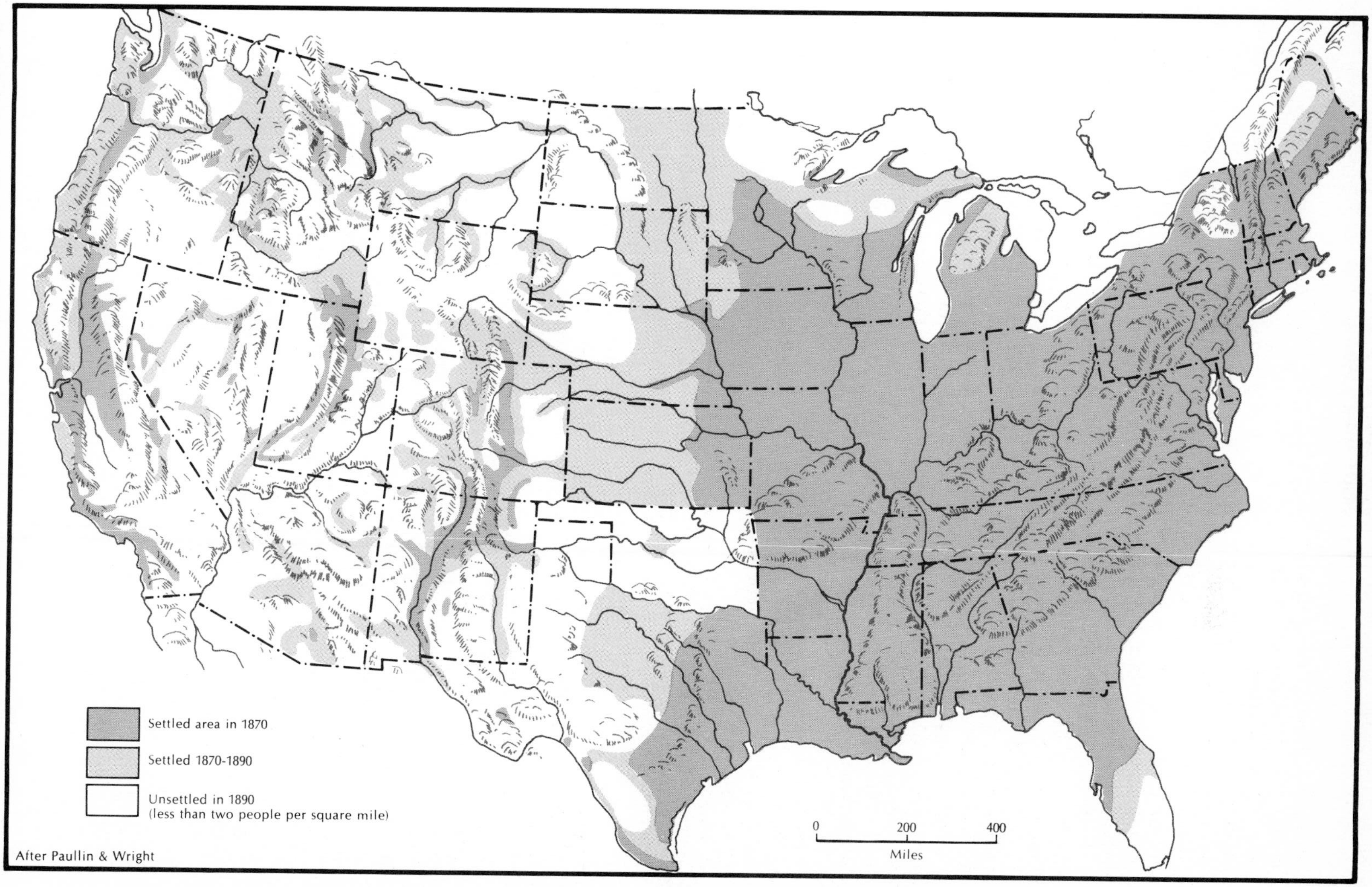

The Passing of the Frontier

Act of 1902 acreage under irrigation was multiplied fourfold. Yet irrigation was not an unqualified success, and its effects were limited to a comparatively small area of the mountainous West and to California.

Far more effective was the use of deep-drilled wells and of the windmill, and the practice of dry farming. By drilling from 100 to 500 feet below the surface it was possible to tap ground water and bring it to the surface in slender metal cylinders lowered and raised by never failing windmills. Dry farming—the conservation of moisture in the soil by creating a dust blanket to prevent evaporation—made it possible to grow cereal crops successfully over large parts of the Plains.

As a result of all these factors—transportation, immigration, the growth of domestic and foreign markets, new methods of fencing and of cultivation—the settlement of the last West went on with unprecedented rapidity. In the 20-year period from 1870 to 1890 the population of Nebraska increased eightfold, Washington fourteenfold, and Dakota Territory fortyfold. In his annual report for 1890, the Superintendent of the Census made an historic announcement:

> Up to and including 1880 the country had a frontier of settlement, but at present the unsettled area has been so broken into by isolated bodies of settlement that there can be hardly said to be a frontier line.

The 'disappearance of the frontier' was shortly marked by a great historian, Frederick Jackson Turner, as the close of a movement that began in 1607 and the start of a new era in American history.

Yet if the frontier line had been obliterated, Western settlement continued at a brisk pace. Indeed, more land was patented for homestead and grazing purposes in the generation after 1890 than in the previous generation. The westward movement of population, too, continued unabated. While from 1890 to 1930 population grew in the flourishing Middle Atlantic and North Central States by about 90 per cent, in the Mountain and Pacific States it increased threefold, and the greatest era in the westward movement was still to come.

Political Organization

In 1860 something over one-third of the area of the United States consisted of Territories. From Minnesota to Oregon, from Texas to the Canadian border, there were no states. Nevada was admitted in 1864 to obtain its three electoral votes for Lincoln, and Nebraska in 1867 over President Johnson's veto (in time to cast its vote for his impeachment), but few of the remaining Territories showed promise for early admission into the Union. Yet within a generation all this region, comprising something over a million square miles, was organized politically, and the major part included in states.

The transcontinental railroads proved crucial to state-making in the West, for they brought to the Territories a permanent farmer population and a solid economic foundation. This became apparent first in the northernmost tier. In 1870 the population of the Dakota, Idaho, and Washington Territories was only 75,000; by 1890, after the Northern Pacific had been completed and the Great Northern almost finished, their population had increased to one million. However, statehood was held up for a full decade by political differences in Congress. The decisive influence of Colorado, admitted in 1876 as the Centennial State, in the disputed presidential election of that year brought the statehood question into party politics. Furthermore, there was fear in the East of Western radicalism, and resentment over the repudiation of railway bonds. By playing politics with the futures of the Territories, both parties forfeited the confidence of these embryo states and made them the more willing to follow the banner of Populism in the early 1890's.

The so-called blockade came to an end abruptly in 1888, with the prospect of complete Republican control of the government. Both parties and both Houses then strove to get credit for the admission of the Western states. Hence, the Omnibus Bill of 1889 provided for the admission of North and South Dakota, Montana, and Washington. No provision was made for Wyoming and Idaho, but in both Territories constitutional conventions met without specific authority, and a few months later

Cherokee Strip. At high noon on 22 April 1889 Oklahoma 'Boomers' race to stake their claims. By nightfall nearly two million acres had been settled in a madcap fashion, and Oklahoma City boasted a population of 10,000. (*Oklahoma Historical Society*)

both were admitted by a debate-weary and vote-hungry Republican Congress.

With the admission of these six states there existed for the first time a solid band of states from the Atlantic to the Pacific, but not for another two decades would the rest of the continental United States achieve statehood. The same year that the Omnibus Bill passed, the government purchased a large part of the lands of the Five Civilized Tribes and threw Oklahoma open to settlement under the homestead laws. At high noon on 22 April 1889 a gun was fired, and settlers raced pell-mell across the prairie to stake their claims. By November, Oklahoma had 60,000 settlers; within a decade almost 800,000, and in 1907 Oklahoma and Indian Territory were admitted as one state. When in 1890 the Mormon government in Utah promised to abandon polygamy, it removed the last objection to its admission to statehood. Under the able administration of the Mormon Church the Latter-day Saints had prospered amazingly, and when Utah was finally admitted in 1896, it was with a flourishing population of some 250,000. In 1912 Arizona and New Mexico entered the Union too.

Thus was completed a process inaugurated by the Northwest Ordinance of 1787. Since then the United States had grown from 13 to 48 states, embracing the whole continental domain.[4] Texas came in as an independent republic; Maine and West Virginia were separated from other states; Vermont and Kentucky entered without previous Territorial organization. But all the others, after passing through a Territorial stage, were admitted as states in a Union of equals, in the greatest experiment in colonial policy and administration of modern times.

4. The non-contiguous Territories of Alaska and Hawaii achieved statehood half a century later.

23

The Politics of Dead Center

*

1877–1890

Masks in a Pageant

There is no drearier chapter in American political history than that which records the administrations of Hayes, Garfield, Arthur, Cleveland, and Harrison. Civil War issues were dead, though politicians continued to flay the corpses. National politics became little more than a contest for power between rival parties waged on no higher plane than a struggle for traffic between rival railroads. 'One might search the whole list of Congress, Judiciary, and Executive during the twenty-five years 1870–1895 and find little but damaged reputations,' wrote Henry Adams. 'The period was poor in purpose and barren in results.'

At first glance it would appear that this was an era of Republican supremacy. No Democrat had entered the White House with as much as 50 per cent of the vote since Franklin Pierce in 1852, and none would again until Franklin D. Roosevelt 80 years later. The Republicans came out of the war as the party of the Union, while the Democrats were tarred with secession and even treason. As the Grand Old Party that had stood by the flag, Republicans for a generation counselled: 'Vote the way you shot.' The Grand Army of the Republic, the leading veterans' organization, mobilized the vote of old soldiers for the Republicans, and for nine of ten campaigns beginning in 1868 the G.O.P. chose a military figure as their presidential nominee; during that same period, the Democrats did so only once. The G.O.P.'s stronghold was New England and the belt of New England migration across northern New York, the Old Northwest, and sweeping west to Oregon, the region which had been the center of antislavery sentiment. Since this sector was rural and Protestant, the party was strongly inclined toward temperance, nativism, and anti-Catholicism.

As a legacy of the Civil War era, the Republicans won the allegiance of black voters, but this did not prevent the party from playing a double game in the South. Some leaders wanted to use federal force to protect the freedman's right to vote, either out of solicitude for the black or in order to prevail at the polls. But others attempted to create a 'lilywhite' Republican party in the South. This policy was pressed by Northern industrialists, who hoped to find allies in the New South for their tariff policies; by merchants in border cities like Cincinnati who feared that agitating the Negro question jeopardized North-South trade; and by publicists who had come to share the racial outlook of the old slavocracy. Neither strategy succeeded in breaking the Democratic hold on the South, and after the abortive attempt to push through a Force bill in 1890, most Republicans gave up. By the end of the century, the South, with Northern acquiescence, had virtually completed black disfranchisement.

Outside the South, the Republicans commanded the support of the wealthy and were accepted by many others as the party of culture and respectability. Along the elm-lined streets of New England and the Old Northwest, not a few thought of the Democratic party as an almost illegitimate organization. Frederic Howe recalled: 'There was something unthinkable to me about being a Democrat—Democrats, Copperheads and atheists were persons whom one did not know socially. As a boy I did not play with their children.'

Despite these disadvantages, the Democrats showed impressive strength, largely because they were less of a sectional party than the Republicans. Powerful not only in the 'Solid South' but in the border states and the Southern belt of migration in the Midwest, the Democrats could capitalize, too, on their following in Northern cities. In 1880 the Democrats had a plurality of 24,000 in the twelve largest cities; by 1892, the margin had reached 145,000. The Democrats enlisted the support of most Irish Catholics, while the Republicans recruited the natural enemies of the Irish, especially British immigrants and French Canadians. Burton K. Wheeler remembered that to win Democratic nomination in Butte 'it was best to claim nativity in County Cork and second best to claim birth in some county in Ireland with slightly less prestige in Montana.'

By 1874 the two parties had struck an equilibrium, and for the next two decades each election turned on a very few votes. In the five presidential contests from 1876 to 1892, the Republicans failed to win a popular majority even once, and in three of these elections the difference between the major party candidates was less than 1 per cent. From 1877 to 1897 the Democrats controlled the presidency and Congress at the same time for but two years; the Republicans achieved this for four years, but in only two did they have a working majority.

Since the parties were roughly equal, political leaders were wary about introducing disturbing new issues that might break up their coalitions. In the South, Democrats agitated the race question and clamped a lid on economic questions that might prove divisive. In the North, Republicans kept alive Civil War memories to distract attention from economic difficulties that could split their party. 'Our strong ground,' Hayes wrote Blaine when he was campaigning for the presidency, 'is the dread of a solid South and rebel rule. I hope you will make these topics prominent in your speeches. It leads people away from hard times, which is our deadliest foe.'

During this entire period the electorate played a game of blind man's buff, for no consequential issue divided the major parties. Questions of currency and the tariff broke on sectional rather than party lines. Although America was emerging from her isolation, there was little appreciation of world responsibilities. Big business was growing bigger, and thoughtful men recognized the conflict of 'wealth against commonwealth' which Henry D. Lloyd would soon dramatize; but political leaders showed little awareness of the implications. The farmer was threatened by forces over which he could exercise no effective control; but politicians lacked the imagination to understand even the existence of a farm problem until it was called to their attention by political revolt.

Behind the colorless titular leaders were the real rulers—men who sat in committee rooms listening to the demands of the lobbyists, 'boys' who 'fried the fat' out of reluctant corporations. At the head of their ranks were great bosses such as Roscoe Conkling of New York. Next were the representatives of special interests—Standard Oil, sugar trust, steel, and railroad men known by business rather than political affiliations. Yet there was always a small group who preserved integrity and a sense of responsibility, men such as Lyman Trumbull of Illinois.

James G. Blaine of Maine, Congressman, Senator, twice Secretary of State, and perpetual aspirant to the presidency, typified this era, as Calhoun and Webster did an earlier one. A man of intellectual power and personal magnetism, Blaine was the most popular figure in American politics between Clay and Bryan. Year after year thousands marched, shouted, and sang for 'Blaine of Maine' pictured as the 'Plumed Knight,' defender of the true Republican faith. A magnificent orator, he could inspire a frenzy of enthusiasm by twisting the British lion's tail or solemnly intoning the platitudes of party loyalty. Yet he made no impression upon American politics except to lower its moral tone. He was assiduous in cementing a corrupt alliance between politics and business and in fanning the flames of sectional animosity. His name is connected with no important legislation; his sympathies were enlisted in no forward-looking causes. Nevertheless, he was rewarded with votes, office, power, and almost with the presidency.

Business had no party favorites except insofar as it preferred to invest in successful rather than unsuccessful candidates. Democratic senators such as Gorman of Maryland could command business support quite as effectively as Republicans like Cameron of Pennsylvania. In a number of states, a single corporation dominated political life; as in Montana under Anaconda Copper. The California railroad king, Collis Huntington, conceded: 'Things have got to such a state that if a man wants to be a constable he thinks he has first got to come down to Fourth and Townsend streets to get permission.' But even when party leaders were most sympathetic to business, they frequently had institutional interests which were not identical with those of the corporations. Politicians, far from being unfailingly subservient to business, often preyed on merchants and importers; and in cities like New York, businessmen played a prominent role in the campaign for civil service reform to curb the spoilsmen.

Glimmerings of Reform

In an era of generally issueless politics, one group sought to introduce reforms: the patrician dissenters who advocated a civil service system. Members of the older gentry who were being pushed aside by the newly rising industrialists resented a rude new world which did not accord them the deference they had been led to expect. Henry Adams later wrote of the return of his family to the United States in 1868 after a decade abroad: 'Had they been Tyrian traders of the year 1000 B.C., landing from a galley fresh from Gibraltar, they could hardly have been stranger on the shore of a world, so changed from what it had been ten years before.' They looked back to a golden age just beyond their memory. Charles Eliot Norton thought the ideal community 'New England during the first thirty years of the century, before the coming in of Jacksonian Democracy, and the invasion of the Irish, and the establishment of the system of Protection.' They loathed the industrialization of America and what it was doing not only to politics but to culture. 'Between you and me and the barber, I like it not,' wrote Richard Watson Gilder. 'The steam whistle attachment which you can see applied nowadays even to peanut stands in the winter streets; the vulgarizing of everything in life and letters and politics and religion, all this sickens the soul.'

These genteel reformers sought to emulate the British M.P. and were disappointed that America would not afford them the same recognition their friends in Parliament enjoyed. They were convinced that the hope of the republic lay in the conquest of politics by an educated elite. Like classic British liberals, they favored free trade, hard money, and civil service reform, and opposed both business and labor union monopolies. Most were Republicans, but they had bolted their party in 1872 to help launch the Liberal Republican movement and in 1884, as 'Mugwumps,' would leave their party again. In 1876, they found the Republican choice, Rutherford B. Hayes, acceptable, chiefly because they knew him to be honest. Joseph Pulitzer of the Democratic New York *World* cried: 'Hayes has never stolen. Good God, has it come to this?'

A well-educated lawyer, Union officer, twice elected to Congress and for three terms governor of Ohio, Hayes was experienced and able, but he was seriously handicapped as President in his efforts to effect constructive measures. Not only the Democrats but even many of his own party re-

The assassination of James A. Garfield. On 2 July 1881, the President went to the Baltimore and Potomac Railroad Depot in Washington, D.C., to board a train that would take him to a college reunion in Williamstown, Mass. At the station he was fatally wounded by a political factionalist, Charles A. Guiteau. On 19 September 1881, Garfield died, and on 30 June 1882, Guiteau was executed. (*Library of Congress*)

fused to recognize his election as legitimate; they referred to him as 'His Fraudulency.' Factional disputes also plagued him. Hayes incurred the animosity of Blaine, leader of the 'Half Breeds,' and the implacable hostility of Conkling, chieftain of the 'Stalwarts.' The 1876 elections had preserved Democratic control of the House, and two years later the opposition party captured the Senate too. At one point Haye was reduced to the sorry state of having only three supporters in the Senate, and one of these was a relative. In such circumstances it is a tribute to Hayes that his administration was not a total failure.

That it was not a complete failure can be credited to the courage with which Hayes set out to cleanse his party of the corruption which had so seriously damaged it during the Grant administrations. He named a cabinet of moderates: as Secretary of State, William Evarts of New York who had defended Andrew Johnson at the impeachment trial; the able John Sherman as Secretary of the Treasury; the paladin of the patrician reformers, Carl Schurz, to be Secretary of the Interior. He broke with the principle of vindictive sectional rule by appointing a former Confederate officer, David Key of Tennessee, Postmaster General. Hayes also tried, somewhat quixotically, to reform the party system and lessen the control by local politicians of the national government. He issued an executive order which forbade federal office-holders to manage politics. 'Party leaders,' said Hayes to the astonishment of the politicians, 'should have no more influence in appointments than other equally respectable citizens.' Hayes was combatting a system under which senators, responsive to local machines, controlled the national party and in turn the Federal Government.

But Hayes quickly found that if he was to govern he also had to be a leader of his party. He was soon dispensing patronage to the men who had put him in office like any other politician; especially scandalous was the way he rewarded every member of the notorious Louisiana returning board which had been instrumental in giving him the presidency. John Hay commented acidly: 'Not Pomeroy or Butler or Boss Tweed himself ever attempted to run an administration in the interests of his own crowd as this model reformer has done.' Although he thereafter removed some of Grant's most offensive appointees and cleaned up the New York custom house, he was never able to win the full confidence of the civil service reformers.

Indecisive as it was, Hayes's struggle with the spoilsmen had considerable consequence. That encounter was precipitated by Hayes's ouster of Chester A. Arthur and Alonzo B. Cornell from the New York custom house, which was mismanaged and corrupt. Senator Conkling, alarmed at the assault on his organization, persuaded the Senate to reject the nominations of those whom the President appointed to succeed Arthur and Cornell. This squabble involved not merely a falling-out between two Republican factions and 'Senatorial courtesy,' but a larger issue of the form of government. By such devices as the profligate use of legislative riders, Congress, since the Civil War, had so largely eaten into the presidential prerogative that the chief executive was by way of becoming a mere figurehead. The Republican Senate sought, as one writer noted, to turn the presidency 'into an office much like that of the doge of Venice, one of ceremonial dignity without real power.' President Hayes took up this challenge, and in the end, with the support of the Democrats, he won out. His appointees were renominated and confirmed, and the normal constitutional relationship between President and Congress began to be restored.

For the larger task of articulating the government to new economic forces, Hayes was not prepared. He responded to the 'Great Strike' of 1877 by sending troops to put down the strikers. When Congress approved the Bland-Allison Silver Act in 1878, Hayes interposed his veto unsuccessfully. To the problems of railroad malpractices, trusts, and land frauds he gave no attention. He later confessed that 'the money-piling tendency of our country . . . is changing laws, government and morals, and giving all power to the rich, and bringing in pauperism and its attendant crimes and wickedness like a flood,' but when President he did not even hang out danger signals. His administration, for all its political drama, was largely negative.

As the election of 1880 approached, the Stalwarts proposed Grant for a third term, but he was blocked by the Half Breed leader, Blaine. One of the 306 Stalwarts who stood by Grant to the end had 306 medals struck bearing the legend, 'The Old Guard,' thereby coining a new name for Republican regulars. A 'dark horse' from Ohio, General James A. Garfield, got the nomination, and to placate Conkling, who had supported Grant, the convention named his henchman, Chester A. Arthur, to the vice-presidency. The Garfield-Arthur ticket won with a popular plurality of less than 10,000 in a total of over 9 million votes.

Four months after his inauguration, at the climax of another bitter patronage struggle with Conkling, Garfield was shot in the back by a disappointed office-seeker who boasted, 'I am a Stalwart and Arthur is President now.' After a gallant struggle, Garfield died on 19 September 1881. The murder of Garfield, and the assassin's admission he killed the President in order to replace him with a factional leader, brought the nation to its senses on the extremism of spoils politics and promoted a civil service reform law.

Yet politicians fought the bill sponsored by 'Gentleman' George Pendleton of Ohio bitterly, some out of desire to preserve their control of patronage, others from a Jacksonian fear that a permanent civil service would produce an overbearing Prussian bureaucracy or haughty Mandarins. Others objected that a competitive examination was a class device which would discriminate against those too poor to afford a college educa-

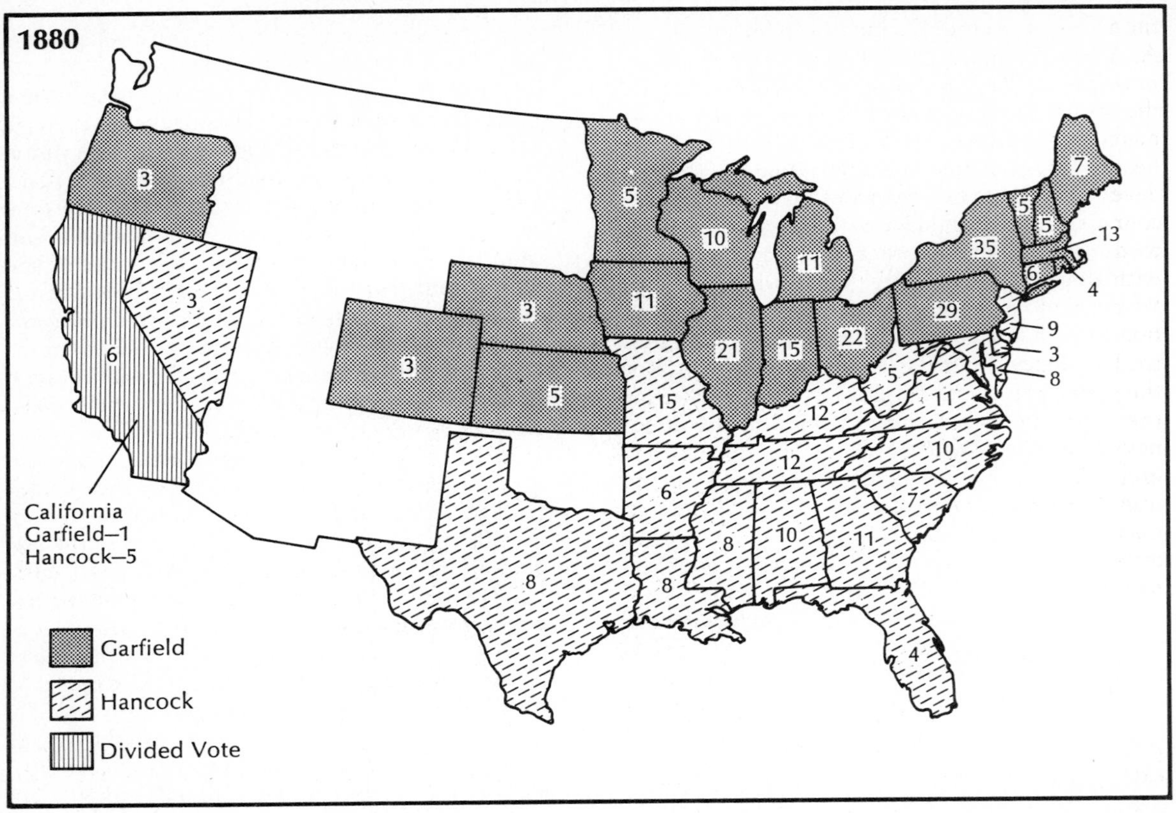

Presidential Election, 1880

tion. Restricting entrance to college graduates, observed one critic, would open doors to a Pierce but exclude a Lincoln, while a Mississippi Congressman objected that if government jobs were to be based on competence, his constituents would not qualify. Under other circumstances, such appeals would have carried the day. But the country had had enough of unrestrained factionalism. A rapidly industrializing society wanted to place government on a more businesslike basis. In enacting the Pendleton bill in 1883, Congress wrote the demands of the patrician reformers, the protests of the importers, and the public outcry at Garfield's death into law.

The Pendleton Act created a Civil Service Commission to administer a new set of rules which required appointments to be made as a result of open competitive examinations and prohibited assessments on office-holders for political purposes. By law these new rules were applied only to some 14,000 positions, about 12 per cent of the total, but the President was empowered to extend them at his discretion. At the turn of the century there were not far from 100,000 in the classified civil service; at the end of Theodore Roosevelt's administration the number had more than doubled, and when Wilson left the White House it had increased to almost half a million. At the same time most states were passing civil service laws. It was fortunate that the merit principle was adopted before the twentieth century when administrative expansion greatly increased the need for honest and expert service.

To the surprise of many, civil service reform had

the ardent support of Garfield's successor, Chester A. Arthur. A satellite of the corrupt Conkling, the new President had nothing in his record to justify the hope that he would make more than a mediocre executive and much to arouse fear that he would be a very bad one. Unexpectedly he developed genuine independence. He severed his connections with the worst of the spoilsmen, vetoed a lavish river and harbor bill, and prosecuted, with some vigor, the 'Star Route' frauds in the Post Office Department. The Arthur administration brought one other change too. The War of the Pacific involving Peru, Bolivia, and Chile, and the rising interest in an isthmian canal, awakened the nation to a realization of the decrepitude of its navy,[1] inferior to that of Chile, and in 1882 Congress authorized 'two steam cruising vessels of war . . . to be constructed of steel of domestic manufacture.' The *Chicago* and the *Boston* entered active service in 1887, and a new era in U.S. naval history began.

The Administrations of Cleveland and Harrison

Arthur's placid administration ended in the most exciting presidential campaign since the Civil War, although the only real issue between the parties was possession of the government. The Republicans, disappointed in Arthur, turned to the magnetic Blaine. But Blaine was more than conscientious Republicans could swallow. The principal charge against him was prostitution of the speakership to personal gain; in that connection he could not explain his missive to a certain Fisher with the damning postscript, 'Burn this letter.' Even Conkling, when asked to campaign for Blaine, replied, 'I don't engage in criminal practice.' Under the leadership of Carl Schurz and George William Curtis the reform wing bolted from the convention, promised to support any decent nomination the Democrats might make, and proudly accepted the name 'Mugwump' which was given them in derision.[2]

With the Promised Land in sight, the Democrats nominated Grover Cleveland, a self-made man who as reform mayor of Buffalo and governor of New York had distinguished himself for firmness and integrity, to the disgust of Tammany Hall. 'We love him for the enemies he has made,' said General E. S. Bragg. Powerful journals such as *Harper's Weekly*, with Nast's telling cartoons, shifted over to Cleveland, as did the Mugwumps.

The 1884 campaign was noisy and nasty. Cleveland was charged, among other things, with fathering an illegitimate child, which he admitted, to the consternation of his supporters. But, as one of them concluded philosophically, 'We should elect Mr. Cleveland to the public office which he is so admirably qualified to fill, and remand Mr. Blaine to the private life which he is so eminently fitted to adorn.' Democratic torchlight processions paraded the streets, shouting,

> Blaine, Blaine, James G. Blaine,
> The continental liar from the State of Maine
> *Burn this letter!*

To which Republican processions retorted: 'Ma! Ma! Where's my pa?' The contest was bitterly fought throughout the North, but New York was the decisive state. Here Blaine had a strong following among Irish-Americans, which was weakened at the eleventh hour by the tactless remark of a supporter, a hapless parson named Burchard, who described the Democracy as the party of 'Rum, Romanism, and Rebellion.' Blaine neglected to rebuke this insult to the faith of his Celtic friends; Cleveland carried New York by a plurality of 1149 in a vote of over a million; and New York's electoral votes gave him the presidency. Yet the crucial point about the 1884 outcome is that the net shift compared to the previous election was the smallest of any in American history. The politics of dead center had reached almost exact equilibrium.

For a person of such generous bulk, Grover

1. '"I don't think I should like America."—"I suppose because we have no ruins and no curiosities," said Virginia, satirically.—"No ruins! no curiosities!" answered the Ghost; "you have your navy and your manners."' Oscar Wilde, *The Canterville Ghost*.

2. Mugwump, a term applied on this occasion by the New York *Sun*, is the word for 'great captain' in Eliot's Indian Bible.

Grover Cleveland (1837–1908). This etching by Anders Zorn suggests the hefty bulk of the twenty-second and twenty-fourth President of the United States. *(National Portrait Gallery, Smithsonian Institution)*

Cleveland was remarkably ungenial. He showed steadfast devotion to duty, but was singularly lacking in imagination and in understanding of the problems of farmers and urban workers. Cleveland hated paternalism in all forms: the tariff, land grants to railroads, pensions, social welfare legislation. He reflected his party's suspicion of strong government, a consequence in part of Southern resentment of Reconstruction, in part of the long period out of power which taught the Democrats to act as opposers. They were so much the party of state rights and limited government that Republican Tom Reed asked: 'Are they but an organized "no"?'

Cleveland's attitude toward government action is exemplified by his veto of the Texas Seed bill in 1887, with a message that was frequently quoted later by opponents of the Welfare State. In reply to requests from sufferers of a severe drought, Congress had voted the small sum of $10,000 for seed grain. When Cleveland vetoed the measure, he declared:

I do not believe that the power and duty of the General Government ought to be extended to the relief of individual suffering which is in no manner properly related to the public service or benefit. Though the people support the Government, the Government should not support the people. Federal aid in such cases encourages the expectation of paternal care on the part of the Government and weakens the sturdiness of our national character. The friendliness and charity of our countrymen can always be relied upon to relieve their fellow-citizens in misfortune.

Character made Cleveland's administration the most respectable between Lincoln's and Theodore Roosevelt's. He alone of the titular leaders had sufficient courage to defy the groups that were exploiting the government and to risk his career in defense of what he thought right. He advanced civil service reform, challenged the predatory interests that were engrossing the public lands, denounced the evils of protection, and called a halt to raids on the Treasury by veterans. If the total achievements of his administration were negative, even that was something of a virtue at a time when too many politicians were saying 'yes' to the wrong things.

The main drama of Cleveland's first term centered on the tariff problem. The high tariff contributed, in Cleveland's opinion, not only to increases in the prices of protected goods, but to the development of trusts. Furthermore, when government revenues showed a consistent surplus over ordinary expenses of almost $100 million annually all through the 'eighties, this surplus offered a standing temptation to extravagance of the pork barrel and pension grab variety. In 1887, Cleveland, despite warnings to avoid the explosive subject, startled the nation by devoting his annual message exclusively to the tariff. 'Our progress toward a wise conclusion,' he wrote, 'will not be improved by dwelling upon theories of protection and free trade. It is a condition which confronts us, not a theory.' The *Nation* called the message 'the most courageous document that has been sent from the White House since the Civil War.' But Blaine denounced it as pure 'free trade,' and the Republicans prepared joyously to make capital out of it in the forthcoming campaign. Cleveland, though, had accomplished his purpose. He had brought the tariff question sharply to the attention of the country, and he had forced his own party to espouse tariff reform as the paramount issue.

In 1888 the Democrats renominated Cleveland, and the Republicans picked the grandson of the hero of Tippecanoe, Benjamin Harrison of Indiana. In a campaign marked by pronounced ethnic appeals, the Irish vote was turned against Cleveland. A naturalized Anglo-American was inspired to inquire of the British Minister, Sir Lionel Sackville-West, how he should vote in order to serve the mother country. Sir Lionel, with incredible stupidity, advised him by letter to vote for the Democrats, a piece of counsel that hurt Cleveland with the Anglophobic Irish. Though Cleveland's popular vote exceeded Harrison's by 100,000, the Republicans carried New York State by a few thousand votes, and again New York was decisive. Harrison made a dignified figurehead in the presidency. Honest and conscientious, he lacked the insight to comprehend the problems of a new day.

With the autocratic 'Czar' Thomas B. Reed as Speaker of the House, and with a majority in both Houses, the Republicans used their newly regained power to benefit their followers. Within a year Postmaster-General Wanamaker had removed over 30,000 postmasters, more than twice as many as Cleveland had dismissed in the same period. The McKinley tariff bill of October 1890 was pushed through as the result of a bargain between Western Republicans who wanted silver legislation and Eastern Republicans who wanted a high tariff.[3] Its provisions were formulated chiefly by William McKinley of Ohio and Nelson W. Al-

3. The year 1890 saw the passage of the McKinley tariff, the Sherman Silver Purchase bill, the Sherman Anti-Trust Act, the Disability Pension Act, and the admission of the last of the 'omnibus' states.

Benjamin Harrison (1833–1901). Eastman Johnson's charcoal drawing heightened with chalk is believed to have been executed in 1889, the year Harrison entered the White House. Johnson (1824–1906) was one of the leading portrait and genre artists of the day. In 1849 he had gone to Europe to study, and he proved so successful that he was invited to be court painter at The Hague. His best known work is 'Old Kentucky Home.' (*National Portrait Gallery, Smithsonian Institution*)

drich of Rhode Island, but the important schedules were dictated by such interested groups as the National Association of Wool Manufacturers.[4] During his campaign Harrison had announced that 'it was no time to be weighing the claims of old soldiers with apothecary's scales,' and he lived up to the implications of that statement. 'God help the Surplus,' said Harrison's Pension Commissioner, whose openhandedness cost the Treasury millions. The total expenditures of the Fifty-first Congress, 2 December 1889 to 3 March 1891, reached the unprecedented sum of almost a billion dollars. 'This is a Billion Dollar country,' was the retort attributed to 'Czar' Reed.

4. The unpopularity of the McKinley tariff was largely responsible for the big turnover in the congressional elections of 1890. Only 88 Republicans were elected to the new House, as against 235 Democrats and nine Populists; McKinley himself failed of re-election.

Government and the Railroads

At a time when railroads were looked upon as an unmixed blessing and their promoters were regarded as public benefactors, the Federal Government aided them with a liberality which at the time seemed commendable but which a later generation came to regard as excessive. Besides granting charters and rights of way across the territories, Congress gave land, loans, subsidies, and tariff remission on rails. The Northern Pacific alone obtained the enormous total of 44 million acres of public lands, an area equal to the entire state of Missouri. Altogether the Federal Government gave the railroads 131,350,534 acres. Furthermore, the states—notably Texas and Minnesota—granted the railroads an additional 48,883,372 acres.

While disposing briskly of their agricultural and grazing lands to obtain ready cash, the railroads reserved mineral and timber lands and potential town sites for speculative purposes, a policy encouraged by amiable interpretations of the law by successive land commissioners. Some of these holdings proved fabulously rich. It cost about $70 million to build the Northern Pacific, but in 1917 that road reported gross receipts from land sales of over $136 million, with substantial valuable acreage still unsold.

The Federal Government received substantial benefits in return for its largess. Land-grant railroads were required to carry government mail at a reduced price, and also to transport military personnel and supplies at less than normal charges, an arrangement of considerable importance during the First World War. Spokesmen for the railroads estimated the accumulated value of these benefits at more than the total worth of the land grants, but those who have ventured into the labyrinths of this accounting have never been known to emerge. However one may assess such claims, it does seem that short of government construction and operation—something unimaginable to Americans of that generation—subsidy was probably the only way to get the Western railroads built, and for all its shortcomings the system did achieve its purpose of spanning a continent. Yet, given all the chicanery in which the railroads indulged, it is not surprising that many Americans were more shocked by the corruption than impressed by the achievements.

Within a few years after the extension of the railroads, the Western farmers, who had initially welcomed them as an unmitigated boon, now blamed them for the hard times of the 1870's, which they traced to abuses by the railroads. To the farmer the most grievous abuses were the high freight rates charged by the Western roads, rates so exorbitant that the farmers at times burned their corn for fuel rather than ship it to market. The railway masters argued that they were barely able to maintain dividend payments, and it is true that in periods of depression, such as those following upon the panics of 1873 and 1893, a good many roads went into receivership. Furthermore, on some routes vigorous competition drove rates below cost. Yet it is equally true that profits were often exorbitant, and that both the extortionate freight rates and the financial troubles of the roads were traceable to excessive construction costs, fraudulent purchase of other properties at inflated prices, stock manipulation, and incompetent management.

Construction costs ran so high chiefly because costs were artificially increased by dummy construction companies in order to provide profits for the directors. In the East, Jay Gould and Jim Fisk systematically milked the Erie Railroad, which did not finally recover until the 1940's. This technique of using dummy construction corporations is illustrated by the short-lived Southern Pennsylvania Railroad, a little road started by Vanderbilt in order to force the Pennsylvania Railroad to buy it. A contractor offered to construct it for $6.5 million, but instead Vanderbilt organized a corporation consisting of his clerks, which received $15 million to build the road; the syndicate who furnished this money was paid with $40 million in railroad shares. The Pennsylvania, which eventually had to buy this property, not unnaturally expected to earn dividends on the cost of acquiring all this. No wonder Poor's Railroad Manual for 1885 estimated that approximately one-third of all railroad capitalization that year represented water.

Complaint was loud and persistent against other abuses too. Railroad 'pools' eliminated competition in large areas by fixing prices and dividing up profits. By granting secret rebates to powerful shippers, railroads put small shippers at a hopeless disadvantage. The Standard Oil Company was granted a rebate on each barrel of oil shipped to Cleveland, and an additional drawback on each barrel shipped by a competitor. The long-and-short-haul evil consisted in slashing freight rates at competitive points and making up the losses at noncompetitive points. Goods traveling from Boston to Denver direct paid $1.70 a hundredweight, but if they traveled from Boston to San Francisco

'The Senatorial Round-House.' Thomas Nast's satirical cartoon, which appeared in *Harper's Weekly* in 1886, depicts a Senate so dominated by special interests that the nation has been reconstituted as 'The Rail-Road States of America.' As he blows off steam, the filibustering Senator treads on a copy of a bill 'to prevent members of Congress from accepting fees from subsidized railroads.' In the very next year Congress instituted the first federal regulation of railroads. (*Coll. Judith Mara Gutman*)

and then back to Denver, they went for $1.50. Farmers bridled also at railroad domination of all the great grain elevators in Chicago; through them the roads fixed the price they would pay for wheat from the hinterland. Railroads also owned the Union stockyards which enabled them pretty well to determine the price of beef in the Mid-West. Protests were voiced as well against the corrupt activities of railroads in politics. In New Hampshire, as in California, a 'railroad lobby,' ensconced in an office near the state capitol, acted as a chamber of initiative and revision; and, as the novelist Winston Churchill tells us in his *Coniston* and *Mr. Crewe's Career,* few could succeed in politics unless by grace of the Boston and Maine.

A movement to curb these abuses gained new strength during the postwar deflation and the panic of 1873. Centered in the Mid-West, it won support from Massachusetts to California. It took several forms: denial of further state aid, as in the constitutions of California, Kansas, and Missouri; recovery of land grants; prohibition of practices such as rebates and passes; and regulation of rates and services. The Eastern state governments inclined to supervision by special railway commissions, and that of Massachusetts, under the leadership of the gifted Charles Francis Adams, Jr., became the conservative model for numerous states.

The Mid-Western states adopted more direct methods. The Illinois Constitution of 1870 instructed the legislature to 'pass laws to correct abuses and to prevent unjust discrimination and extortion in the rates of freight and passenger tariffs.' Pursuant to this charter the legislature outlawed discrimination, established a maximum rate, and created a Railway and Warehouse Commission to regulate roads, grain elevators, and warehouses. At the demand of farmers, and of businessmen who had suffered from railroad discrimination, the example of Illinois, denounced as socialist in the East, was followed in 1874 by Iowa and Minnesota, and by Wisconsin with its drastic Potter law. Within a few years the railroads of the Middle West found their independence severely circumscribed by a mass of restrictive legislation.

The Supreme Court validated this legislation in the 'Granger' cases. The first and most important of these, *Munn* v. *Illinois* (1876), involved the constitutionality of a statute regulating the charges of grain elevators. In one of the most far-reaching decisions in American law, Chief Justice Morrison R. Waite, pointing to the historical right of the state in the exercise of its police power to regulate common carriers, announced:

> When private property is affected with a public interest it ceases to be *juris privati* only. . . . When, therefore, one devotes his property to a use in which the public has an interest, he . . . must submit to be controlled by the public for the common good, to the extent of the interest he has created.

The warehouse owners not only challenged the right of the state to regulate their business but contended further that rate-fixing by a legislative committee violated the Fourteenth Amendment by denying 'due process of law.' To this contention the Court responded:

> The controlling fact is the power to regulate at all. If that exists, the right to establish the maximum charge, as one of the means of regulation is implied. . . . We know that this is a power which may be abused; but that is no argument against its existence. For protection against abuses by legislatures, the people must resort to the polls, not to the courts.

On the same day that the Court validated the Illinois statute, it handed down decisions on Granger laws establishing maximum rates in the important cases of *Peik* v. *Chicago & Northwestern R.R.*, *Chicago, Burlington & Quincy R.R.* v. *Iowa*, and *Winona & St. Peter R.R.* v. *Blake*. The Court sustained these laws against charges that they violated not only the Fourteenth Amendment but the exclusive authority of Congress over interstate commerce. The railroad, said the Court,

> is employed in state as well as interstate commerce, and until Congress acts, the State must be permitted to adopt such rules and regulations as may be necessary for the promotion of the general welfare of the people within its own jurisdiction, even though in so doing those without may be indirectly affected.

Thus the Court announced three major principles: first, the right of government to regulate all business affected with a public interest; second, the

Union Stockyards, Chicago, 1889. Above is the main portal and below are the cattle pens. At a time when litigation over the regulation of marketing facilities provided the most important items on the docket of the Supreme Court, farmers and ranchers focused much of their attention on these huge stockyards, covering 360 acres and with 40 miles of railway track linked to all of the railroads entering the great city. One awe-struck observer wrote: 'If for ten hours of every working day in the year, a constant stream of cattle at the rate of ten per minute, of hogs at the rate of thirty per minute, with the small addition of four sheep every minute, passed through these yards, it would fall short of the actual numbers brought to this market for sale, slaughter, or distribution!' (*Chicago Historical Society*)

right of the legislature to determine what is fair and reasonable; third, the right of the state, in areas of concurrent authority, to act where Congress has failed to act.

Within a decade the composition of the Supreme Court became more conservative, and two of the three Granger principles were duly modified. In 1886, in the Wabash case, the Court retreated from the third principle by holding invalid an Illinois statute prohibiting the 'long-and-short-haul' evil, on the ground that it infringed upon the exclusive power of Congress over interstate commerce. That same year, in *Stone* v. *Farmers' Loan Co.*, the Court intimated that the reasonableness of the rate established by a commission might be a matter for judicial rather than legislative determination. Three years later, in *Chicago, Milwaukee and St. Paul Railroad Co.* v. *Minnesota*, this obiter dictum became the basis for a decision invalidating rate regulation by a legislative commission. These decisions dealt a heavy blow to state regulation of roads and rates, and placed the burden squarely upon the Federal Government.

Congress responded with the Interstate Commerce Act of 1887, which represented a compromise between the Massachusetts or supervisory type of regulation and the Granger or coercive type of regulation. It specifically prohibited pooling, rebates, discrimination of any character, and higher rates for a short haul than for a long haul. It provided that all charges should be 'reasonable and just' but failed to define either of these ambiguous terms. Perhaps most important, it established the first permanent administrative board[5] of the Federal Government, the Interstate Commerce Commission, to administer the law. Enforcement was left to the courts, but a large part of the burden of proof and prosecution was placed upon the commission. Although the bill was popularly regarded as a victory for the public, it had the support of the railroads, and railway stocks rose in the market upon its passage.

Administrative regulations were still so foreign to the American conception of government that the federal courts insisted upon their right to review orders of the Interstate Commerce Commission, and by a series of decisions took the teeth out of the act. In the *Maximum Freight Rate* case (1897), the Supreme Court held that the commission did not have the power to fix rates, and in the *Alabama Midlands* case of the same year it practically nullified the long-and-short-haul prohibition. It was found almost impossible to require agents of the railroads to testify about railroad malpractices, and witnesses would introduce into the court new testimony which had been withheld from the commission, thus requiring an entirely new adjudication. Reversals of the commission's rulings were frequent; by 1905 fifteen of the sixteen cases appealed to the Supreme Court had been decided adversely to the commission. Furthermore, down to 1897 shippers had succeeded in collecting refunds from recalcitrant roads in only five out of 225 cases. Indeed, the roads evaded the provisions of the act so successfully that Justice Harlan declared the commission to be a 'useless body for all practical purposes,' and the commission itself, in its annual report for 1898, confessed its failure. Nevertheless, the principle of federal regulation of railroads had been established, and the machinery for such regulation created. It remained for a later administration to apply the principle and make the machinery effective.

5. The Civil Service Commission, established in 1883, came four years earlier, but it was not involved directly in regulation of the economy.

24

The Embattled Farmer

*

1860–1897

The Agricultural Revolution

While manufacturing was advancing rapidly in the half-century following the Civil War, agriculture remained the basic industry, the one which engaged the largest number of people. But agriculture itself was undergoing a revolution, featuring expansion of its domain, application of machinery and science to farming, use of modern transportation to convey products to world-wide markets, and intervention by the Federal Government. This revolution exposed the farmer to the vicissitudes of the industrial economy and the world market and brought a vast increase in productivity which did not always yield comparable returns. From 1860 to 1910 the number of farms in the United States and the acreage of improved farm land trebled. More land was brought under cultivation in the 30 years after 1860 than in all the previous history of the nation. Yet in 1900 the farmers' share of the national wealth was less than half that of 1860. Farm population grew absolutely, but the proportion of people living on farms declined; while the agricultural domain expanded, the relative political and social position of the farmer contracted.

In the half-century after the Civil War farming was subjected to a series of shocks. First, war and its aftermath partially destroyed the plantation system and fostered the crop-lien and sharecrop systems. Second, opening up the High Plains and the West depressed farming in the Middle West and the East and required drastic readjustments. In 1860 Ohio led the nation in the production of wool; by 1900 Wyoming and New Mexico were the leading woolen states. A third shock was the rapid growth of world markets, and of world competition, as the productivity of the American farm outstripped the nation's capacity to consume. American wheat competed with the wheat of the Argentine, Australia, and Russia; beef and wool with the products of Australia, New Zealand, and the Argentinian pampas; cotton with Egypt and India. Fourth, and scarcely less disturbing to the agricultural equilibrium, was the impact of new machinery, new crops, and new techniques. Except in isolated regions like the Southern highlands or the rich Pennsylvania and Maryland country, the average farm ceased to be a self-sufficient unit, where a man and his family raised most of what they needed, and became instead a cog in an industrial system.

'Residence of Mr. E. R. Jones,' Dodgeville, Wisconsin, 1881. This watercolor and tempera rendering of a Midwestern farm was done by the self-taught 'naïve' artist Paul Seifert, who revealed a talent for composition and precise detail and who achieved unusual shading by painting on colored paper. The Dodgeville area had been settled sixty years earlier by lead miners, and as farmers tilled the soil they could hear 'the rumble of blasts deep beneath the earth' under their furrows. (*New York State Historical Association*)

One thing, however, did not greatly change. American agriculture continued to be extensive rather than intensive, robbing the land of its fertility and leaving desolation behind. Not until the sharp rise in farm land values in the early years of the new century dramatized the passing of cheap good land did the government realize the need for conservation, or the farmer the necessity for scientific farming. Then it was almost too late. When economists came to count the cost, they found that 100 million acres—an area equal to Illinois, Ohio, North Carolina, and Maryland—had been irreparably destroyed by erosion; that another 200 million acres were badly eroded; that over large areas the grasslands of the Great Plains had been turned into dust, and that the forest resources of the Eastern half of the country were rapidly disappearing.

The Use and Abuse of the Homestead Act

Under the Homestead Act any citizen, except one who had served in the Confederate army, could obtain 160 acres on the public domain by living on it or cultivating it for five years. Recognizing that the neat little rectangular farm of the East was not really suitable to the West, Congress added a complex series of other laws: the Timber Culture Act of 1873, the Desert Land Act of 1877, the Timber and Stone Act of 1878, the Carey Irrigation Act of 1894, and the Enlarged Homestead Act of 1909. These statutes broadened the areas that could be patented, facilitated entry and final acquisition, and provided government aid to enterprises like reclamation.

All of this should have meant that the immense public domain—perhaps 1 billion acres in 1860—would go into the hands of the independent yeoman. In fact, only one-sixth to one-tenth of the public domain went to Homesteaders, and the rest was not given away but sold—or held off the market by speculators, or by the government itself. By the end of the century Homesteaders had patented about 80 million acres, but the railroads had received—from federal and state governments—180 million acres, the states had been given 140 million acres, and another 200 million acres—much of it Indian lands—had been put up for sale to the highest bidders. The Homestead policy was never suited to the needs of the landless workingman or immigrant; after all, how was he to move himself and his family to the West, build a house and barn, buy farm equipment and cattle, and keep going for a year until the money for his crops came in? Moreover, for all their professed concern for the independent yeoman, Congress and the states proved far more interested in satisfying the demands of business and speculator groups. Railroads and lumber companies, ranchers' associations, emigration and colonization companies, and individual speculators like Ezra Cornell of New York or Amos Lawrence of Boston got princely domains.

The disposition of public lands in the South illustrates the unhappy history of the Homestead Act. In 1866 Congress set aside some 47 million acres of public lands in five Southern states for 80-acre homesteads. Ten years later the pressure of Northern lumber interests forced a repeal of these arrangements, and the land was thrown open to purchase by speculators. One congressman acquired 111,000 acres in Louisiana; a Michigan firm got 700,000 acres of pine lands. One English company bought 2 million acres of timberland in Florida, and another got 1.5 million acres in Louisiana for 45 cents an acre. In 1906 a government expert concluded that the exploitation of the South by these and other companies was 'probably the most rapid and reckless destruction of forests known to history.'

Cleveland instituted some far-reaching reforms, and these were carried further under Harrison. An act of 1889 put an end to all cash sale of public lands, and the next year the government limited land acquisitions to 320 acres; in 1891 came the first act setting aside forest reservations on public lands. But these modifications were both too little and too late.

Machinery and Scientific Agriculture

The application of machinery to agriculture lagged fully a century behind the application of machinery to industry. Mechanization of agriculture began in the 'thirties and 'forties, when Obed Hussey and Cyrus McCormick experimented

The 'Holt combine.' Drawn by thirty-three mules, this harvester, which first appeared in 1886, marked the culmination of the era of animal power just before the gasoline engine revolutionized agricultural machinery. (*Caterpillar Tractor Co.*)

with a reaper, A. D. Church and George Westinghouse with a thresher, and John Lane and John Deere with a chilled plow. Agricultural machinery, however, remained relatively unimportant before 1860. The Civil War, robbing farms of their laborers and raising grain prices, induced farmers to adopt machines such as the reaper, which enabled a woman or a boy to perform the work of several men. Over 100,000 reapers were in use by 1861 and during four years of war the number grew by a quarter of a million. After the war almost every operation in the North from seeding to harvesting was mechanized. The Oliver chilled plow, perfected in 1877, meant an enormous saving in time and money; within a few years the wonderfully efficient rotary plowed and harrowed the soil and drilled the grain in a single operation. George Appleby's twine binder greatly increased the amount of grain a farmer could harvest, and the steam threshing machine was perfected. Within twenty years the bonanza farms of California were using 'combines' which reaped, threshed, cleaned, and bagged the grain in a single operation. During these same years the mowing machine, the corn planter, corn binder, husker and sheller, the manure spreader, the four-plow cultivator, the potato planter, the mechanical hay drier, the poultry incubator, the cream separator, and innumerable other machines entirely transformed the ancient practices of agriculture.It took 21 hours to harvest a ton of timothy hay in 1850; half a century later, four hours. This vast saving in labor made it possible for a proportionately smaller number of farmers to feed an ever-increasing number of city-dwellers and have a surplus left for export.

In the twentieth century came the application of steam, gasoline, and electricity to the farm. Huge combines, formerly drawn by 20 or 30 horses, were propelled by gasoline tractors. The value of farm implements and machines increased from about $246 million in 1860 to $750 million in 1900, and then, swiftly, to $3595 million in 1920. This growth was distinctly sectional. Mechanization did not profit much of New England, with its rolling topography and little specialties, or the South where cotton and tobacco farming did not take readily to machines. But the Middle West and the Far West absorbed reapers, mowers, tractors, harvesters, and threshers at a great rate. In 1920 the average value of farm implements and machinery on each South Dakota farm was $1500; on each farm in the Cotton Belt $215.

Farming as a way of life gave way to farming as a business. The small diversified farm of the 1860's, with fields of grain, orchard and vegetable garden, pasture mowing and woodlot, gave way to the large farm specializing in staple crops which could be produced with one kind of machinery and sold for cash. Rising land values, heavy costs of machinery, and the substitution of chemical fertilizer for manure required capital and commonly involved the farmer in heavy indebtedness. One result was an ominous increase in farm mortgages and in tenancy: by 1930 almost every second farmer was a tenant, and one-fifth of the total value of farms was mortgaged.

As long as there was abundant cheap land and a shortage of labor, conditions which obtained until some time after the Civil War, it was more economical for farmers to abandon wornout soil and move on to virgin land than to cultivate intensively and invest in expensive fertilizers. It was the passing of these conditions that led to scientific agriculture, conservation, and reclamation. Scientific agriculture in the United States has depended largely upon government aid. A number of states subsidized agriculture even before the Civil War, and as early as 1839 Congress made its first appropriation, $1000, for agricultural research, although the Constitution gives Congress no explicit jurisdiction over farming. In 1862 Congress created a Department of Agriculture, under the direction of a commissioner with the happy name of Isaac Newton, and in 1889 this department was raised to executive grade with a secretary of cabinet rank. The Department of Agriculture grew steadily until by 1930 it embraced some 40 subdivisions and bureaus and spent almost $100 million.[1] Its Bureau of Plant Industry introduced over 30,000 foreign plants including alfalfa from Liberia, short-kernel rice from Japan, seedless grapes from Italy, and grass from the Sudan to cover the High Plains; its Bureau of Entomology fought plant diseases; its Bureau of Animal Husbandry conquered hog cholera, sheep scab, and Texas fever in cattle. The first government department to undertake extensive research, it was, for a time, the country's leading research institution.

The Morrill Land-Grant College Act of 1862 not only had a great impact on education but was the most important piece of agricultural legislation in American history. This far-sighted law, which provided for the appropriation of public land to each state for the establishment of agricultural and industrial colleges, discriminated heavily in favor of the more populous states of the

1. In 1968 the Federal Government spent $5.9 billion on agriculture. In 1973 the Federal Government spent $6.2 billion on agriculture.

Winslow Homer, 'Country School,' 1871. Homer's painting, though realistic in its portrayal of peeling walls and cracked floorboards, conveys a romantic innocence of the rural setting and the idealized young woman teacher. Through such a scene, writes Marshall Davidson, move 'Whittier's barefoot boys and Howells' summertime idlers.' Though the locus of the painting is interior, one has a pervasive awareness of nature immediately beyond the sun-bright windows. (*City Art Museum of St. Louis*)

East—where farming was of less importance—and against the agricultural states of the West. New York State got almost a million acres of Western lands, while Kansas, which depended entirely on agriculture, got 90,000 acres. Seventeen of the states, including Illinois, Wisconsin, and Minnesota, turned the Morrill land-grant money over to the existing state universities; others, like Iowa, Indiana, and Oregon, chose to set up independent agricultural and mechanical colleges. At first agricultural colleges were looked upon by the farmer with suspicion, but in time farmers learned their value and came to take pride in them. Scarcely second to the Morrill Act in importance was the Hatch Act of 1887. Influenced by the valuable work performed by the experimental station of Wesleyan University in Middletown, Connecticut, Congress provided in this act for agricultural experiment stations in every state; since that time Congress has steadily expanded the work of education and experimentation in agriculture.

Scientific agriculture has its roll of heroes. Mark Alfred Carleton, who experienced on the Kansas plains the devastations of wheat rust and rot and the vagaries of Kansas weather, scoured Asia for a wheat strong enough to withstand the rust, the droughts, and the frosts of the Middle West. He returned with the Kubanka wheat and later introduced the Kharkov wheat to the American farmer; by 1919 over one-third of U.S. wheat acreage was sown with Carleton's varieties. Niels Ebbesen Hansen of the South Dakota Agricultural College brought back from the steppes of Turkestan and the plateaus of inner Mongolia a yellow-flowered alfalfa that would flourish in the American Northwest. From Algeria and Tunis and the oases of the Sahara came white Kaffir corn, introduced by Dr. J. H. Watkins, and admirably adapted to the hot dry climate of the great Southwest. Dr. Stephen M. Babcock saved the dairy farmers of the nation millions of dollars through the Babcock milk test, which determined the butter fat content of milk; he gave the patent to the University of Wisconsin. Seaman Knapp found in the Orient varieties of rice wonderfully adapted to the Gulf region today. Luther Burbank, in his experimental garden at Santa Rosa, California, created a host of new plants by skillful crossing, and George Washington Carver of the Tuskegee Institute developed hundreds of new uses for the peanut, the sweet potato, and the soy bean.

The Agricultural Revolution in the South

The Civil War and Reconstruction shattered the old plantation regime in the South and brought about a widespread redistribution of land and revolutionary patterns of land-tenure. The crippling of the planter class led to the most far-reaching transfer of land-ownership since the Revolution, as yeoman farmers, small merchants and businessmen, Northern soldiers, carpetbaggers, and investors snapped up what looked like bargains in land. On the surface this meant the breakup of plantations into small farms and a striking increase in land-ownership. In 1860 there were 55,128 farms in Alabama; twenty years later there were 135,864. Between 1860 and 1880 in nine cotton states the number of farms under ten acres jumped almost twentyfold.

But these figures are misleading. The years after the war saw a revolution not in land-ownership but in farm labor. The number of large farms (or plantations) remained about the same, but now they were divided up into small 'holdings' and farmed not by slaves but by sharecroppers and tenants. In Louisiana the percentage of farms over 100 acres actually went up in the two decades after secession from 34 to 70. As C. Vann Woodward concludes, 'The evils of land monopoly, absentee ownership, soil mining, and the one-crop system, once associated with and blamed upon slavery, did not disappear, but were instead, aggravated, intensified, and multiplied.'[2]

The explanation was to be found in the sharecrop and crop-lien systems. These twin evils emerged as a response to the breakdown of the old labor system and the collapse of credit after the war. Sharecropping was an arrangement whereby planters could obtain labor without paying wages and landless farmers could get land without paying rent. Instead of an interchange of money, there was a sharing of crops. The planter furnished his tenant with land and frame cabin, and, generally, with seed, fertilizer, a mule, a plow, and other implements; in return he received at the end of the year one-half of the crop which the tenant raised. The tenant furnished his labor, and got, in return, the rest of the crop as well as whatever he could raise for himself in his vegetable garden. At the end of the war most freedmen and many poor white farmers entered into such an arrangement. This system, which appeared at first to be mutually advantageous, was really injurious to all. The sharecropper was rarely able to escape into the farm-owning class; the planter could seldom farm efficiently with sharecrop labor. With every year the number of tenant farmers increased, farm profits and soil fertility decreased. In 1880, one-third of the farmers of the Cotton Belt were tenants; forty years later, two-thirds.

The crop-lien system was perhaps even more disastrous. Under this system the farmer mortgaged his ungrown crop in order to obtain supplies for the year. Rates of interest were usurious, and the merchant who supplied food, clothing, seed, and other necessities customarily charged from 20 to 50 per cent above the normal price. Because cotton and tobacco were sure money crops, creditors generally insisted that most of the land be planted to one of these, which accelerated soil exhaustion. As early as 1880 two-thirds of the farmers of South Carolina had

2. *Origins of the New South*, pp. 179–80.

mortgaged their ungrown crops, and by 1900 this proportion was applicable to the entire cotton belt. Sharecrop and crop-lien systems served to keep the poorer farmers of the South in perpetual bondage to the large planters, country storekeepers, and bankers—a condition from which few were ever able to extricate themselves. For when the farmer's share failed to meet the inflated charges against him at the country store, he was forced to renew the lien on next year's crop to the same merchant—and often on more onerous conditions. The result was increasing impoverishment of the farm population, growing class stratification, and a determination to seek political redress.

The 'Farm Problem'

When we've wood and prairie land,
Won by our toil,
We'll reign like kings in fairy land,
Lords of the soil.

So sang Richard Garland and the 'trail-makers of the Middle Border' as they pushed hopefully westward from the forests of Maine to the coulees of Wisconsin, the prairies of Iowa, and the sun-baked plains of Kansas, Nebraska, and the Dakotas. They won their wood and prairie land, but often won it for others—for absentee landlords, railroads, banks, and mortgage companies, who became the real lords of the soil. Within a generation the 'marching song of the Garlands' gave way to a different tune:

There's a dear old homestead on Nebraska's fertile plain,
There I toiled my manhood's strength away:
All that labor now is lost to me, but it is Shylock's gain,
For that dear old home he claims today.

And when young Hamlin Garland wrote his *Main-Travelled Roads* he dedicated it to 'my father and mother, whose half-century of pilgrimage on the main travelled road of life has brought them only pain and weariness.'

The conquest of a continent had resulted not in the realization of Jefferson's dream of a great agrarian democracy but in a 'farm problem.' There was the physical problem of soil exhaustion and erosion, drought and frost and flood, plant and animal diseases; the economic problem of rising costs and declining returns, exploitation in the domestic market and rivalry in the world market, mortgages and tenancy; the social problem of isolation and drabness, inadequate educational, religious, medical, and recreational facilities, narrowing opportunity and declining prestige. Finally, there was the political problem of wresting remedial legislation from intransigent governments, which were much more responsive to the demands of business than to the appeals of the farmer.

Of all these problems, the physical difficulties were the most intractable. By 1930 almost 100 million acres in the South—approximately one-sixth of the total—had been hopelessly lost or seriously impaired through erosion, and in some sections of the Piedmont as much as half of the arable land had been swept of its topsoil. Early travelers in the South recorded that the streams were as clear as those of New England, but by the twentieth century the rivers of the South, which every year carried to the ocean over 50 million tons of soil, were mud-black or clay-red. Southern farmers tried to replenish their worn-out soil with fertilizer, but that meant an intolerable financial burden. Not until the Tennessee Valley Authority began to produce cheap fertilizer and the New Deal to provide low-cost farm loans was the South able to inaugurate a program of restoration.

In the grasslands of the West, too, the farmer confronted the ravages of insect pests. Before the attack of the chinch bug and the corn borer, the boll weevil and the alfalfa weevil, the average farmer was all but helpless, and what reader of Rölvaag's *Giants in the Earth* can forget how the grasshoppers destroyed not only the wheat but the morale of the farmers of the West:

> And now from out the sky gushed down with cruel force a living, pulsating stream, striking the backs of the helpless folk like pebbles thrown by an unseen hand. . . . This substance had no sooner fallen that it popped up again, crackling and snapping—rose up and disappeared in the twinkling of an eye; it flared and flittered around them like light gone mad; it chirped and buzzed through the air; it snapped and hopped along the ground; the whole place was a weltering turmoil of raging little demons. . . . They whizzed by in the air; they literally

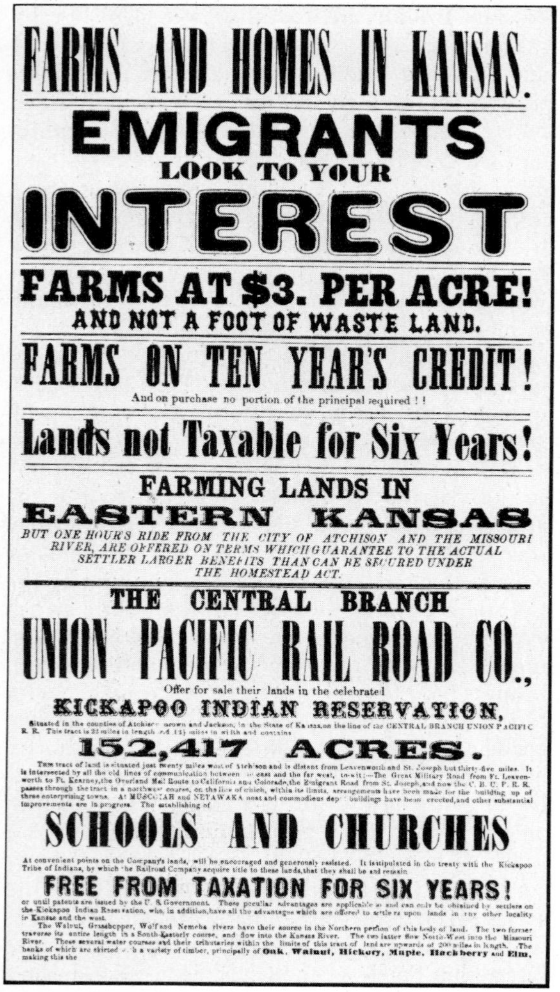

Railroad lands for sale, May 1867. This poster announces the availability of a huge tract in northern Kansas purchased by the Union Pacific from the Kickapoo Indians. The placard boasts of the presence of coal and points out that the land, bisected by the old Overland Mail Route to California, is watered by tributaries of the Kansas and Missouri rivers along which are stands of oak, walnut, hickory, maple, hackberry, and elm. (*Union Pacific Railroad Museum*)

covered the ground; they lit on the heads of grain, on the stubble, on everything in sight—popping and glittering, millions on millions of them. The people watched it stricken with fear and awe.[3]

More complex, but more susceptible to remedial action, was the farmer's economic problem: rising costs and falling prices, a situation exacerbated by the rapid expansion of the agricultural domain. This expansion westward brought ruin to the farmers of New England and the seaboard South and placed the Western farmer in a precarious position, because his future rested on unrealistic assumptions about the land, the weather, the market, and the credit system. Even official reports of the Kansas Board of Agriculture told prospective settlers: 'Kansas agriculture means a life of ease, perpetual June weather, and a steady diet of milk and honey.' One Kansas newspaper urged:

> Do not be afraid of going into debt. Spend money for the city's betterment as free as water. Too much cannot be spent this year, if properly applied. Let the bugaboo of high taxes be nursed by old women. Do all you can for Belle Plaine regardless of money, and let the increase of population and wealth take care of the taxes. Double, treble, quadruple our expenditures, and do it in the right manner, and before the year 1886 is passed Belle Plaine will be able to pay them and much more—and Belle Plaine will boom with a double pica black face B.

This boom spirit was exacerbated by the eagerness of Eastern banks and loan companies to lend money without discretion. *Rhodes Journal of Banking* estimated that the savings banks of New Hampshire and Vermont had invested 40 per cent of their funds in Western mortgages. So great was the desire of Easterners to speculate that competition existed not among borrowers but among lenders. The manager of one loan company reported: 'During many months of 1886 and 1887 we were unable to get enough mortgages for the people of the East who wished to invest in that kind of security. My desk was piled high every morning with hundreds of letters each enclosing a draft and asking me to send a farm mortgage from Kansas or Nebraska.'

This feverish optimism overlooked the fact that

3. *Giants in the Earth*, Harper & Bros., pp. 342–43.

the opening up of the West was paralleled by a no less remarkable expansion of the agricultural domain of Canada, the Argentine, Australia, Russia, and Brazil. When the American farmer grew more than the American market could absorb—a condition with which the cotton planter was long familiar—he had to sell his product in the world market, which determined the price he received, at home as abroad. Industry, which could regulate its production and which operated behind tariff walls, bought in a world market and sold in a protected market; agriculture, which could not effectively regulate its production and had little to gain from tariffs, bought in a protected market and sold in a world market. The cost of the farmer's transportation was fixed by the railroads, his manure by a fertilizer trust, his farm implements by the McCormick Harvester Company, his fencing by a barbed wire trust. The prices he paid for daily necessities—for furniture and clothing, for lumber and leather goods—were artificially raised by the operation of protective tariffs.

The expansion of agriculture into the West meant an absolute dependence upon railroads, and freight charges came to consume an increasingly large share of the farmer's income. The *Prairie Farmer* asserted in 1867 that Iowa corn cost eight or ten times as much at Liverpool as the farmer received for it at the local grain elevator. In 1880 wheat fetched almost a dollar in the Chicago pit, but it cost 45 cents to ship a bushel of wheat from central Nebraska to Chicago. Furthermore, railroads came to control the warehouse facilities of the West, fixed the price for storage, and controlled grading.

Above all, the price the farmer paid for money was prohibitively high. Some states attempted, through usury laws, to fix low interest rates, but such laws were flouted or evaded, and interest rates in the farm belts of the South and West were seldom below 10 per cent and in the 'nineties much higher. Inadequate banking facilities were in part responsible. In 1880 the per capita banking power of the Eastern states was $176, of the Central states $27, and of the Southern states $10. Furthermore, with the rise in the value of money after the Civil War, the farmers' debt appreciated steadily. It took about 1200 bushels of wheat, corn, oats, barley, and rye to buy a $1000 mortgage in the years 1867 to 1869; between 1886 and 1888 it required approximately 2300 bushels to repay that mortgage.

During most of the thirty years after the Civil War the farmer of the South and West was the victim not only of rising costs but of falling prices. Wheat which netted the farmer $1.45 a bushel in 1866 brought only 49 cents in 1894. Corn which brought 75 cents at Chicago in 1869 fell to 28 cents in 1889. Cotton sold at 31 cents a pound in 1866 and 6 cents in 1893. Agriculture, which represented not quite half of the national wealth in 1860, accounted for but one-fifth half a century later. The value of manufactured products was 50 per cent higher in 1870 than the value of all farm products; by 1910 it was over twice as large. The farmer received 30 per cent of the national income in 1860, 19 per cent in 1890, 13 per cent in 1920, and after the collapse of the early 'thirties, 7 per cent in 1933.

Farming yielded not only decreasing economic returns but also decreasing social returns. Before the coming of the automobile, the telephone, and the radio, the isolation of the farm was fearful. Thousands of families were cut off from companionship and conviviality, church and school. Thousands of mothers died in childbirth, thousands of children died through lack of simple medical care. It was the women who suffered most from the narrowness of farm life. The confession of Benét's John Vilas might have been that of a whole generation of pioneers:

> I took my wife out of a pretty house,
> I took my wife out of a pleasant place,
> I stripped my wife of comfortable things,
> I drove my wife to wander with the wind.[4]

No wonder the wives and the mothers inspired the revolt against the farm, and encouraged their sons and daughters to try their fortunes in the cities.

City life offered opportunities and conferred a social prestige that no longer attached to farm life. The farmers, who had once been regarded as 'the chosen people of God,' came to be looked upon as 'hayseeds' and 'hicks,' fit subjects for the comic strip or the vaudeville joke. An ever increasing number of young people, unwilling to accept the

4. *John Brown's Body*, p. 143.

Sod-house frontier. In this photograph, taken about 1886, the Chrisman sisters pose in their finest before their sod home on Lillian Creek north of Broken Bow, Custer County, Nebraska. In *Old Jules,* Mari Sandoz has written a moving memoir of the experiences of a girl raised in a sod house in Nebraska's Niobrara river country northwest of Broken Bow. (*Nebraska State Historical Society*)

drudgery and frustration that their parents had suffered, left the farms for the cities. Between 1870 and 1930 the rural population declined from over 80 to less than 40 per cent of the total, and the drop in the actual farm population was even more precipitous.

It must not be supposed that the farmer made no effort to save himself. For almost every problem he had a solution, one that was usually reasonable and intelligent. But solutions generally required legislative action, and the farmer was seldom in a position to obtain such action. From Jefferson to Jefferson Davis the politics of the nation had been guided chiefly by those who were responsible to the farmers. But with the shift in population from the farm to the city, the rise of giant corporations, and the concentration of financial power in the East, this situation changed. Farmers wanted railroad regulation, but the railroad interest was too powerful, except for the brief Granger interlude. The vast majority of farmers wanted cheap money and a more flexible banking system, too, but they got neither. Farmers still constituted the largest single economic group in 1870, but they could not bridge the sectional gulf. Although the Southern planter and the Middle Western farmer shared similar problems, they failed to forge an effective alliance. Nor were the farmers successful in placing their representatives in state legislatures or in Congress. Lawyers and businessmen constituted the majority of the legislatures even in such states as Georgia and Nebraska, while in the halls of Congress a 'dirt' farmer was something of a curiosity.

Agrarian Revolt

When the bubble of Civil War prosperity burst in 1868, the collapse of crop prices resulted in the first agrarian revolt, which featured the organization of farmers' societies. The first of the societies was the Patrons of Husbandry, commonly known as the Grange. In 1866 President Johnson sent Oliver H. Kelley, a clerk in the Bureau of Agriculture, on a tour of investigation through the South. Kelley returned deeply impressed with the poverty, isolation, and backwardness of the farmers of that section, and determined to establish a farmers' society which might ameliorate these evils. In 1867 he and a group of government clerks in Washington, D.C., founded the Patrons of Husbandry, and in the following year the first permanent Grange of this society was born in Fredonia, New York. When the panic of 1873 burst, the Grange had penetrated every state but four. Two years later it boasted a membership of over 800,000 in some 20,000 local Granges, most of them in the Middle West and the South. The major function of the Grange was social. One secret of its success was that it admitted women to membership, and for farmers' wives the Grange, with its meetings and picnics, lectures and entertainments, offered an escape from the loneliness and drudgery of the farm.

The Grange was formally non-political, but almost from the beginning the movement took on a distinctly political character. In Illinois, Iowa, Wisconsin, Minnesota, Kansas, California, and elsewhere, the farmers elected their candidates to legislatures and judgeships, and agitated for regulatory statutes. The result was the so-called Granger laws limiting railroad and warehouse charges and prohibiting some of the grosser railway abuses.

The Grangers also embarked upon business ventures. To eliminate the middleman, they established hundreds of co-operative stores on the Rochdale plan, whereby profits were divided among shareholders in proportion to their purchases. They set up co-operative creameries, elevators, and warehouses, organized farmers' insurance companies, and constructed their own factories, which turned out excellent reapers, sewing machines, and wagons for half the price charged by private concerns. But owing to relentless opposition by business and banking interests, the individualism of the farmers, overexpansion and mismanagement, most of the co-operative enterprises failed. Yet some good resulted. Prices were reduced, thousands of farmers saved money, and with the establishment of Montgomery Ward and Company in 1872 specifically 'to meet the wants of the Patrons of Husbandry' the mail-order business came into existence. By 1880 Grange membership had fallen to 100,000. Chastened, the Grange confined itself thereafter largely to social activities.

The Grange gave way to the more aggressive Farmers' Alliances, and the history of farm revolt during the 'eighties and 'nineties is largely that of the Alliance movement. There were, at the start, several Alliances, but by the late 'eighties consolidation had resulted in the creation of two powerful groups, the Northwestern Alliance, and the Farmers' Alliance and Industrial Union, commonly known as the Southern Alliance. The Northwestern Alliance was particularly strong in Kansas, Nebraska, Iowa, Minnesota, and the Dakotas, and during the hard times of the late 'eighties it became a major influence in the politics of the Middle Border. The Southern Alliance dated back to a cattlemen's association in Lampasas County, Texas, in the middle 'seventies. By the early 'nineties the Southern Alliance boasted a membership of from one to three million and was the most powerful farmers' organization in the country. It had three times as many members as the Northwestern Alliance, and was much more

Granger meeting. This engraving is of a gathering near Winchester in Scott County, Illinois, in 1873. Notice the presence of women, who were organized in Grange auxiliaries. One placard protests against a scandal of the Grant administration, 'No More Mobilier Swindle,' while another reads, 'President $50,000 a Year, Congressmen $7000 a Year, Farmers 75 cts. a Week?' (*Library of Congress*)

radical. Despite an obvious community of interest between the Northwestern and the Southern Alliances, all efforts to amalgamate the two organizations foundered on the rocks of sectionalism.

The activities of the Alliances were more diverse than those of the Grange. Social affairs included not only the customary meetings and picnics, but farmers' institutes, circulating libraries, and the publication of hundreds of farm newspapers and dozens of magazines, so that the Alliance became, in the words of one observer, a farmers' national university. The economic enterprises of the Alliance were more substantial than those of the Grange. The North Dakota Alliance underwrote co-operative insurance, the Illinois Alliance organized co-operative marketing, and thousands of farmers' 'exchanges' were established; it was estimated that in 1890 the various Alliances did a business of over $10 million.

But historically the significance of the Alliance lies in its political rather than its social and economic activities. From the first the Alliances entered more vigorously into politics than had the Grange. Their programs embraced demands for strict regulation or even government ownership of railroads and means of communication, currency inflation, abolition of national banks, prohibition of alien land ownership and of trading in futures on the exchange, more equitable taxation, and progressive political reforms. An original contribution was the sub-treasury scheme, which provided for government warehouses where farmers might deposit non-perishable produce, receiving in exchange a loan of up to 80 per cent of the market value of the produce, which might be redeemed when the farmer had sold his produce. This scheme had the triple advantage of enabling the farmer to borrow at a low rate of interest, sell his produce at the most favorable market price, and profit by an expanded and flexible currency. When first advanced, it was regarded as a socialistic aberration, but the Warehouse Act of 1916 and the Commodity Credit Corporation of 1933 adopted a similar proposal as national policy. By 1890, the Alliances, with an ambitious set of legislative demands, were prepared to plunge into national politics to launch the Populist movement, the most far-reaching farm protest in the history of the nation.

Populism

In 1890 American politics lost its steady beat and began to dip and flutter among strange currents of thought that issued from the caverns of discontent. Many Americans had come to feel that something was radically wrong and groped for a remedy. Industrial unrest was acute; 1890 witnessed the most strikes in any one year of the nineteenth century. Money was tight, credit inflexible, and banking facilities inadequate. Vital political institutions were undemocratic: the Senate, chosen not by popular vote but by state legislatures, was a stronghold of special interests; the Supreme Court increasingly reflected the ideas of the privileged.

Dissatisfaction was most acute on the farms of the South and the West. The Middle Border was suffering the devastating effects of deflation following a land boom. After several years of excessive rainfall there came in 1887 a summer so dry that crops withered all along the border of the Plains. Eight of the next ten years in western Kansas and the Dakotas were too arid, and the region suffered also from chinch bugs, high winds, and killing frosts. From 1889 to 1893 more than 11,000 farm mortgages were foreclosed in Kansas alone and in fifteen counties of that state over three-quarters of the land fell into the hands of mortgage companies. The West was literally in bondage to the East. During these years the people who had entered that El Dorado trekked eastward again; on their wagons they scrawled, 'In God we trusted, in Kansas we busted.' Whole sections of the West were left without a single person. Half the people of western Kansas deserted the country between 1888 and 1892. Little wonder that Oliver Goldsmith's 'The Deserted Village' was the favorite work of Populist orators. The misery of the Middle Border was more than matched in the South where cotton growers struggled from year to year against a falling market, while mortgage indebtedness and tenancy grew at an ominous rate.

In the 1890 elections the angry farmer struck back. The Southern Alliance, spurning third party tactics, launched a campaign to capture the Democratic party, and scored a series of stunning victories. It won control of the legislatures in eight states, and elected six governors and more than 50 Congressmen. In South Carolina, 'Pitchfork Ben' Tillman pushed a series of reforms through the legislature and created a political machine to do his bidding. That same year the Alliance helped launch a series of state third parties in the West. These new parties elected five of seven Congressmen and a U.S. Senator in Kansas and won the balance of power in South Dakota and Minnesota. Kansas called its organization the People's party, which two years later was to be the name of the national party. A generation which knew its Latin found it an easy transition from People's party to calling its followers Populists.

The new party had some remarkable leaders. Davis H. Waite, Governor of Colorado, friend of all the underprivileged of the earth, was called by his admirers the 'Abraham Lincoln of the Rockies' and by his critics 'Bloody Bridles Waite' because he had said it was better 'that blood should flow to the horses' bridles rather than our national liber-

'I Feed You All!' This lithograph perceives the farmer as the fulcrum of American society as the nation celebrates its centennial. The other figures—the lawyer, the statesman, the soldier, the preacher—are peripheral while the broker, who appears over the caption 'I Fleece You All,' is viewed with contempt. The picture suggests, not altogether correctly, a society still pre-industrial—the age of sail rather than steam, the noble yeoman not at his tractor but at his plow. (*Library of Congress*)

ties should be destroyed.' Minnesota boasted the inimitable Ignatius Donnelly, discoverer of the lost Atlantis, advocate of the theory that Bacon wrote Shakespeare's plays, author of the prophetic *Caesar's Column*, undismayed champion of lost causes and desperate remedies. Kansas, where, as William Allen White remembered, the farm revolt became 'a religious revival, a crusade, a pentecost of politics in which the tongue of flame sat upon every man and each spake as the spirit gave him utterance' was most prolific of leadership. Here the sad-faced Mary Lease went about advising farmers to 'raise less corn and more Hell.' Here Jerry Simpson, the sockless Socrates of the prairie, espoused the doctrines of Henry George and exposed the iniquities of the railroads. Here Senator William A. Peffer of the hickory-nut head and long flowing beard, whom Roosevelt denounced as 'a well-meaning, pin-headed, anarchistic crank,' presented with logic and learning *The Farmer's Side, His Troubles and Their Remedy*.

The Populist convention that met in Omaha on Independence Day of 1892 approved a platform, drawn up by the eloquent Ignatius Donnelly, that raked both the major parties and painted a melancholy picture of the American scene:

> We meet in the midst of a nation brought to the verge of moral, political, and material ruin. Corruption dominates the ballot-box, the legislatures, the Congress, and touches even the ermine of the bench. The people are demoralized; . . . The newspapers are largely subsidized or muzzled; public opinion silenced; business prostrated; our homes covered with mortgages; labor impoverished; and the land concentrating in the hands of the capitalists. The urban workmen are denied the right of organization for self-protection; imported pauperized labor beats down their wages; a hireling standing army, unrecognized by our laws, is established to shoot them down, and they are rapidly degenerating into European conditions. The fruits of the toil of millions are boldly stolen to build up colossal fortunes for a few, unprecedented in the history of mankind; and the possessors of these in turn, despise the republic and endanger liberty. From the same prolific womb of governmental injustice we breed the two great classes—tramps and millionaires.

Specifically, the platform demanded the free and unlimited coinage of silver; a flexible currency, controlled by the government and not by the banks, with an increase in the circulating medium; a graduated income tax; the subtreasury scheme; postal savings banks; public ownership and operation of railroads, telegraph, and telephones; prohibition of alien land ownership and reclamation of railroad lands illegally held; immigration restriction; the eight-hour day for labor; prohibition of the use of labor spies; the direct election of Senators, the Australian ballot, the initiative and referendum. The platform was regarded throughout the East as little short of communism, yet within a generation almost every one of the planks was enacted in whole or in part. The People's party was a seed-bed of American politics for the next half-century.

The Populist standard bearer, James Baird Weaver, received over a million popular votes, better than 8 per cent of the national total, and 22 electoral votes, all west of the Mississippi. The Populists were the only third party to break into the electoral column between 1860 and 1912. Save for the Republicans, no new party had ever done so well in its first bid for national power. The Populists ran reasonably well in the Middle Border, where they elected governors in North Dakota and Kansas, but their new stronghold was the Mountain states, where they captured almost twice as many counties as both major parties combined, and in a single election established themselves as the majority party. However, this new strength threatened to drive the Populists even farther in the direction of an obsession with one issue, silver.

No party could hope to forge a winning combination if its sectional alliance was limited to the sparsely populated Middle Border and Mountain West. In 1892 the Populists failed completely to crack the South, where Alliance leaders were reluctant to divide the white vote by abandoning the one-party system. In Tillman's South Carolina, the Populists fielded no candidates at all, and Weaver, as a former Union general, was, as Mrs. Lease observed wryly, 'made a regular walking omelet by the Southern chivalry of Georgia.' The new party made almost no impression on the Old Northwest. The Populists took only one county north of the Ohio and east of the Mississippi. Weaver, a native son of Iowa, got only 5 per cent of the vote of that state. Donnelly, who ran third as Populist candidate for governor of Minnesota, wrote in his diary: 'Beaten! Whipped! Smashed! . . . Our followers scattered like dew before the rising sun.'

In a three-cornered race, Cleveland rolled up the biggest victory for the Democrats in forty years. But the outcome proved deceptive, for it encouraged Cleveland and his supporters to adopt policies which would lead to the disruption of their party.

The Money Question

Grover Cleveland, a little stouter and more set in his ideas, was inaugurated President on 4 March 1893, and promptly confronted the money question. Investor classes entertained the classical bullion theory, which held that the value of money was determined by the bullion which was held as security for its redemption. It required that all money in circulation have behind it some substantial metallic value, and that government confine itself to issuing money on security of bullion actually in the treasury vaults, either directly or indirectly through banks. As long as the ratio between gold and silver remained relatively stable, the bullion theorists accepted a bimetallic standard; when the decline in the value of silver disrupted that long-established ratio, orthodox economists turned to the single gold standard.

This classical view was disputed by those who regarded money as a token of credit rather than of bullion, and maintained that it was the proper business of the government to regulate money in the interests of society. They pointed out that bullion, especially gold, did not provide a sufficiently large or flexible basis for the money needs of an expanding nation, and that tying the whole monetary system to gold placed it at the mercy of a fortuitous gold production. They insisted that bullion security for money was unnecessary or necessary only in part; that the vital consideration was the credit of the government, and that 'the promise to pay' of the United States was sufficient to sustain the value of any money issued by that government. These proponents of credit money demanded that currency be expanded whenever essential to meet the needs of the country. Enthusiastic support for this viewpoint came from the farmers of the South and the West and from debtor groups everywhere—groups who had favored easy money since the days of Shays's Rebellion.

After the middle 'seventies the inflationists transferred their zeal from greenbacks to silver. Silver satisfied the requirement that there should be some substantial security behind money. Furthermore, dependence upon both silver and gold would ensure a reasonable expansion of the currency but guard against any such reckless inflation as might result from the use of mere legal tender notes. Silver had behind it, too, the powerful silver-mine owners and investors. In 1861 the mines had produced approximately $43 million worth of gold but only $2 million of silver. The coinage ratio between silver and gold of 15.988 to 1 undervalued silver, and in consequence silver was sold for commercial purposes and only gold was carried to the mints for coinage. But as the result of the discovery of immense deposits of silver in the West, by 1873 the value of silver mined had increased to $36 million while the value of gold had declined to the same figure; the price of silver had consequently slumped to approximately the legal ratio. The next year, for the first time since 1837, it fell below that ratio, and it became more profitable to sell silver to governments for coinage than to sell it for commercial purposes.

But when the silver-mine owners turned to governments, they found their market gone. Germany in 1871 had adopted a gold standard, and the rest of Europe hastened to suspend the free coinage of silver. Still worse, from the point of view of the silver interests, the United States had, by the Coinage Act of 1873, demonetized silver by the device of omitting from the act any specific provision for coining silver dollars. Silverites hotly charged a trick, and the act became known as 'the Crime of '73.' The schoolmaster in *Coin's Financial School*—a book which was to the free silver crusade what *Uncle Tom's Cabin* was to the anti-slavery crusade—wrote:

> It is known as the crime of 1873. A crime, because it has confiscated millions of dollars worth of property. A crime, because it has made tens of thousands of tramps. A crime, because it has made thousands of suicides. A crime, because it has brought tears to strong men's eyes and hunger and pinching want to widows and orphans. A crime because it is destroying the honest yeomanry of the land, the bulwark of the nation. A crime because it has brought this once great republic to the verge of ruin, where it is now in imminent danger of tottering to its fall.

From the middle 'seventies to the middle 'nineties, silver interests and inflationists joined in demanding the free and unlimited coinage of silver. In 1878 the silverites pushed through, over a presidential veto, the Bland-Allison Act which required the government to purchase each month not less than $2 million nor more than $4 million worth of silver, to be coined into silver dollars at the existing legal ratio with gold. Successive secretaries of the treasury chose the minimum amount, and the addition to the currency was not sufficient to increase appreciably the per capita circulation of money. The hard times of the late 'eighties intensified the silver agitation. Domestic and world production of the white metal soared, further depressing the price of silver. At the same time per capita circulation of money barely held its own, and in some sections declined sharply. The connection between low commodity prices and high gold prices, between low per capita circulation of money and high interest rates, was not lost upon the farmers.

Yet silver agitation might have come to nought had it not been for the admission of the 'omnibus' states. When the enabling acts of 1889 and 1890 brought into Congress representatives from six new Western states, the Senate at once became the stronghold of silver sentiment. The result was the Sherman Silver Purchase Act of 1890. This measure stipulated that the Treasury Department purchase each month 4.5 million ounces of silver at the market price, paying for such silver with Treasury notes of the United States. It contained further the fateful provision that 'upon demand of the holder of any of the Treasury notes . . . the Secretary of the Treasury shall . . . redeem such notes in gold or silver coin, at his discretion, it being the established policy of the United States to maintain the two metals on a parity with each other upon the present ratio.'

The Sherman Act proved a futile and dangerous compromise. It neither raised the price of silver, nor increased the amount of money in circulation, nor halted the steady decline in crop prices. The failure of the Sherman Act to effect these ends was variously explained by two opposing schools of thought. Gold monometallists insisted that the act demonstrated that the price of silver could not be raised artificially by government action. Silverites argued that the law proved the futility of compromise and the necessity for free and unlimited coinage. The act provided, to be sure, for the purchase of practically the entire domestic production of silver. But the world output was almost three times the domestic production, and as long as there were huge quantities of silver seeking a market, the price would be sure to slump. The solution, said the gold forces, was to abandon silver to its fate and return to the gold standard. The solution, said the silverites, was to open our mints to unlimited coinage of silver, and peg the price at the traditional ratio of 16 to 1. The bimetallists reasoned that if the United States stood ready to exchange, with all comers, one ounce of gold for sixteen ounces of silver, no one would sell silver for less than that sum. That is, if the United States could absorb all the silver that would be brought to her mints, she could peg the price, and bimetallism would be an established fact. But that *if* was crucial. The success of the operation depended upon the ability of the United States to pay out gold for silver until speculators were convinced of the futility of trying to break the price, or until the increased demand for silver raised its commercial value.

The silver question aroused intense emotions. 'Gold-bugs' smugly denounced their opponents as cheats, while silverites branded the monometallists as 'Shylocks.' We can see now that the issue was both deeper and less dangerous than contemporaries realized. It was deeper because it involved a struggle for the ultimate control of government and economy between the business interests of the East and the agrarian interests of the South and the West. It was less dangerous because none of the calamities so freely prophesied would have followed the adoption of either the gold or the silver standard. When the country committed itself to the gold standard in 1900, the event made not a ripple. When the gold standard was abandoned a full generation later, the event led to no untoward results.

The President and the Panic

The Cleveland administration was just two months old when it was struck by the panic of 1893. The agricultural depression which began in 1887 had seriously curtailed the purchasing power of one large group of consumers, and had similarly affected railway income. The collapse of markets abroad, owing to business distress in Europe and Australia, had serious repercussions on American trade and manufacturing. Overspeculation attendant upon the organization of trusts endangered stability, while industrial disorders like the Homestead strike reduced profits and cut purchasing power. Finally the Government's silver policy impaired business confidence and persuaded European creditors to dump American securities on the market and drain the nation of its gold.

By midsummer of 1893 the panic was in full swing. The Reading Railroad had failed in the spring. In July came the failure of the Erie, and soon the Northern Pacific, the Union Pacific, and the Santa Fe were all in the hands of receivers. Banks everywhere called in their loans, often with consequences fatal to firms and individuals unable to meet their obligations; over 15,000 failures were recorded for the year 1893. 'Men died like flies under the strain,' wrote Henry Adams, 'and Boston grew suddenly old, haggard, and thin.' In rural areas banks toppled like card-houses; of the 158 national bank failures in 1893, 153 were in the South and the West. By the summer of 1894, four million jobless walked the streets of factory towns in a vain search for work.

Convinced that monetary uncertainty was the chief cause of the panic, President Cleveland summoned a special session of Congress to repeal the Sherman silver law and enact legislation which should 'put beyond all doubt or mistake the intention and the ability of the Government to fulfill its pecuniary obligations in money universally recognized by all civilized countries.' Cleveland's discreet manipulation of the patronage provided enough Democratic votes to help the Republicans repeal their own silver-purchase act at the request of a Democratic President and a bimetallist Secretary of the Treasury! Wall Street breathed more freely, but the farmers cried betrayal, and 'Silver Dick' Bland warned the President that Eastern and Western Democrats had finally come to 'a parting of the ways.'

Nor did repeal of the Sherman Act bring about that restoration of prosperity so confidently predicted. The Treasury was freed of its obligations to purchase silver but Secretary of the Treasury John Carlisle's troubles had just begun. Distrust of the monetary policy of the government was by no means allayed, and there began a steady raid on the gold reserves of the Treasury. Holders of silver certificates, fearful for the future, began to bring them to the Treasury and ask for gold. The resultant drain on the gold reserve not only carried that reserve below the established mark of $100 million, but threatened to wipe it out altogether. To the frightened President it seemed that the hour was fast approaching when the government would be unable to meet its legal obligations in gold and would therefore be pushed onto the silver standard. Hence he decided to sell government bonds for gold; in desperation he turned to a banking syndicate headed by the House of Morgan. This bond sale did not permanently help the Treasury, because purchasers of the bonds simply drew from it the gold with which to pay for their bonds, thereby depleting the gold supply of the Treasury at one end as fast as it was replenished at the other. More bond sales thus became inevitable, and twice again Cleveland turned to the bankers. This convinced the farmers that there was a traitor in the White House and a Judas in the Treasury Department. Finally in 1896, the Treasury floated a $100 million bond issue through popular subscription. With the success of this fourth and last bond issue, the crisis passed.

The financial difficulties of the government were ascribable not only to the gold drain, but to a sharp decline in revenues. The McKinley tariff had actually reduced income from customs duties, and the depression cut into internal revenues, while the 'billion dollar Congress' had committed the government to heavy expenditures. As a result the surplus of 1890 became a deficit of $70 million by 1894. In the face of this situation Cleveland tried to force the Democratic party to redeem its pledge of tariff reduction. But vested interests had been built up under Republican protection, and Democratic Senators from the East were no less averse to tariff reduction than their Republican colleagues. The Wilson tariff in the House sought to reduce duties, but when it emerged from the joint committee of the House and Senate the

Coxey's army. Leading the marchers on horseback is Carl Browne, a religious mystic who believed that he and Coxey shared an unusually large quantity of the soul of Christ. A painter of Western panoramas, Browne designed a banner for the army with a picture of the head of Christ (who, it was remarked, bore a striking resemblance to Browne) and with the inscription: 'Peace on Earth Good Will to Men. He Hath Risen, but Death to Interest on Bonds.' (*Library of Congress*)

reduction was no longer recognizable. Protectionist Democrats like Gorman of Maryland had introduced no fewer than 634 changes, most of them upward. Cleveland, who had insisted that 'a tariff for any other purpose than public revenue is public robbery,' denounced the bill as smacking of 'party perfidy and party dishonor.' Believing, however, that the Wilson-Gorman tariff was some improvement on the McKinley Act, he allowed it to become law without his signature.

Since the sponsors of the Wilson bill anticipated a reduction in customs receipts, they had wisely added a provision for a tax of 2 per cent on incomes above $4000. However, this tax was declared unconstitutional by a five to four decision of the Supreme Court which fifteen years earlier had unanimously validated the war income tax. As some of the opinions, notably that of Mr. Justice Field, were characterized by gross prejudice and as one judge had changed his mind at the eleventh hour, the Pollock decision seemed further proof to farmers and workingmen of the class bias of the government.

While Congress was making futile gestures toward tariff reform and free silver, a more constructive proposal came from 'General' Jacob Coxey, a wealthy quarry owner of Massillon, Ohio, who with his wife and infant son, Legal Tender Coxey, would shortly lead an army of unemployed on a march to Washington. Coxey's legislative attack on the depression and the money question was double-barreled. One bill authorized any county or town desiring to undertake public improvements to issue non-interest-bearing bonds which should be deposited with the Secretary of the Treasury in exchange for legal tender notes. Public improvements thus financed were to guarantee employment to any jobless man at not less than $1.50 for an eight-hour day. The Good Roads bill called for $500 million of legal tender notes to construct a county road system throughout the country at the same rate of pay. These measures were designed to inflate the currency, bring down interest rates, inaugurate much-needed public improvements, and provide work for the unemployed. The program was not unlike that later inaugurated by Franklin D. Roosevelt, but at the time it excited only contempt or amusement.

This year, 1894, was the darkest that Americans had known for thirty years. Everything seemed to conspire to convince the people that democracy was a failure. Ragged and hungry bands of unemployed swarmed over the countryside, the fires from their hobo camps flickering a message of warning to affrighted townsfolk. Coxey's army of broken veterans of the armies of industry, inspired by the pathetic delusion that a 'petition on boots' might bring relief, marched on Washington, only to be arrested for trespassing on the Capitol grounds. When Pullman workers struck for a living wage, every agency of government was enlisted to smash the strike. When Congress passed an anti-trust law, it was enforced not against the trusts but against labor unions. When Congress enacted an income tax, it was voided in the highest court. Tenant farmers cheered lustily as 'Pitchfork Ben' Tillman demonstrated how he would stick his fork into the ribs of Grover Cleveland, and on the plains the 'Kansas Pythoness' Mary Lease warned the East that 'the people are at bay, let the bloodhounds of money beware.' There was intellectual ferment too. Everywhere people were discussing the revelations of Lloyd's *Wealth against Commonwealth,* the first great broadside against the trusts, and Edward Bellamy's Utopian novel, *Looking Backward;* while Jacob Riis told the sordid story of *How the Other Half Lives.*

Bryan, Bryan, Bryan, Bryan

The party in power is always blamed for hard times. The 1894 elections, in which the G.O.P. won over numbers of urban voters who had previously been in the Democratic camp, ended the 20-year period of party equilibrium and began an era of Republican supremacy. For the next 16 years the Republicans would control both houses of Congress, and during the next 36 years, the Democrats would win only three Congressional elections.

The silver issue portended still more trouble for the Democratic party. Either the silver forces would capture control of the party, or the silverites would secede and make the lusty young Populists one of the great major parties. In 1893–94 silver Democrats effected a fusion with the Populists, and in many Western states it was difficult to distinguish between the two parties. But the silver leaders were unwilling to abandon the Democrats without a final effort to seize control of the party organization, and a fierce struggle ensued.

While the Democratic party was being torn apart, the Republicans concluded that in 1896 any Republican could be elected—a boast that Mark Hanna made a prophecy. Marcus Alonzo Hanna was a businessman satiated with wealth but avid for power, naturally intelligent though contemptuous of learning, personally upright but tolerant of corruption, cynical in his management of

'A Man of Mark!' This 1896 cartoon in William Randolph Hearst's New York *Journal* shows McKinley, wearing a syndicate collar, dangled by his sponsor, Marcus Alonzo Hanna (1837–1904). Hearst had hired the cartoonist Homer Davenport for his San Francisco *Examiner* and brought him to New York for the 1896 campaign, during which Davenport created his image of Hanna covered with dollar signs, an impression that 'Uncle Mark' was not able to shake off for the rest of his life. (*Library of Congress*)

men but capable of abiding friendships; he was the nearest thing to a national 'boss' that had ever emerged in this country. Convinced that the business interests should govern the country, Hanna believed ardently in the mission of the Republican party to promote business activity, whence prosperity would percolate to the farmers and wage-earners. Since 1890 he had been grooming for the presidency his friend William McKinley, and at the 1896 G.O.P. convention McKinley was nominated on the first ballot. Only one untoward event marred the jollity of the occasion: as the convention committed itself to the gold standard, the venerable Senator Henry Teller of Colorado bade

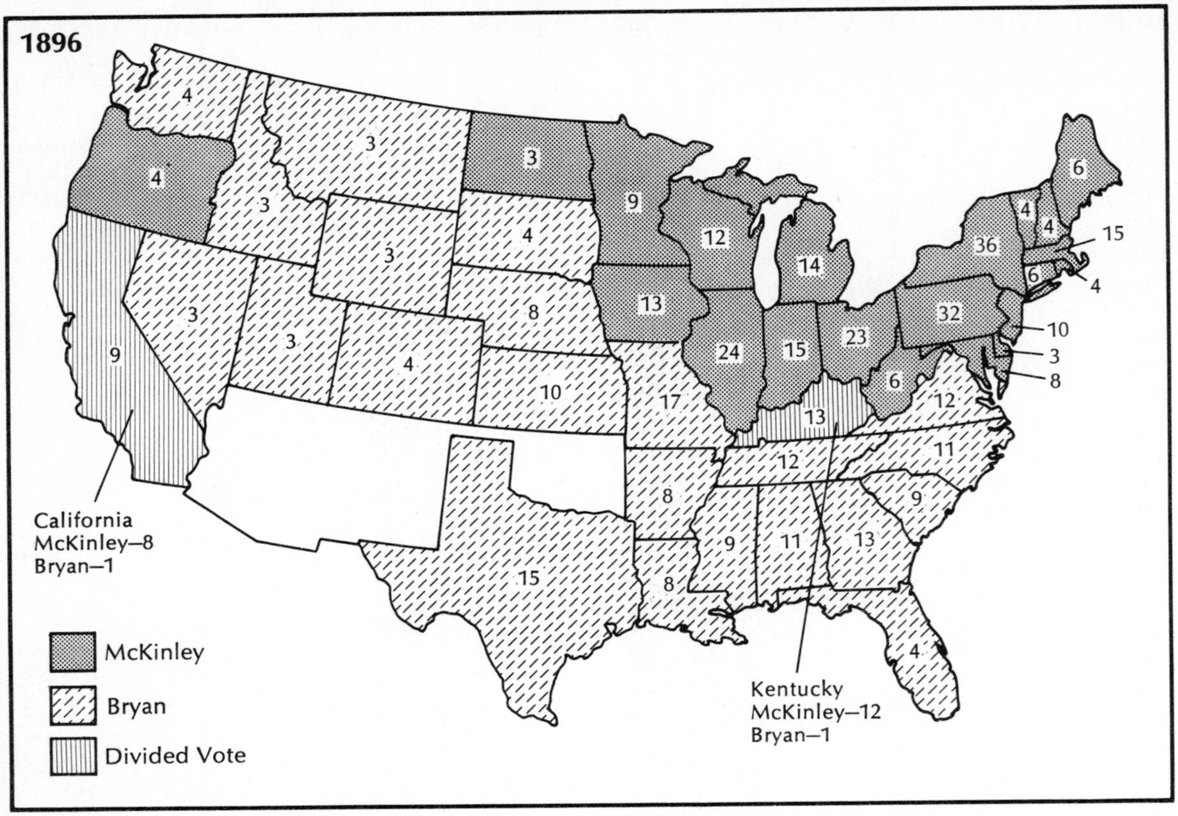

Presidential Election, 1896

farewell to the party which forty years earlier he had helped to found. And up in the press gallery William Jennings Bryan looked on with palpitating interest as Teller led a grim band of twenty-two silver delegates from the convention hall.

Three weeks later, when the Democratic convention met at Chicago, the silverites, instead of going over to the Populists, captured control of the party organization. Trainload after trainload of enthusiastic delegates swarmed into the streets of the Windy City, silver badges gleaming from their lapels. 'For the first time,' wrote one Eastern delegate, 'I can understand the scenes of the French Revolution!' The Democratic party had been taken over by spokesmen for the farmers of the South and the West who had long since decided to repudiate their own President. Champ Clark of Missouri called Cleveland one of the three great traitors of our history, linking him with Benedict Arnold and Aaron Burr, while Altgeld had put it even more bluntly: 'To laud Clevelandism on Jefferson's birthday is to sing a Te deum in honor of Judas Iscariot on Christmas morning.'

'All the silverites need,' said the New York *World* on the eve of the Convention, 'is a Moses. They have the principle, they have the grit, they have the brass bands and the buttons and the flags, they have the howl and the hustle, they have the votes, and they have the leaders, so-called. But they are wandering in the wilderness like a lot of lost sheep, because no one with the courage, the audacity, the magnetism and the wisdom to be a real leader has yet appeared among them.' The lament was premature. In the person of William

Jennings Bryan of Nebraska, the silver forces found their leader. Only 36 years of age, Bryan had already distinguished himself as the most aggressive and eloquent spokesman of silver in the country.

Bryan's opportunity arrived with the debate on the platform. The champions of gold had made impressive appeals, 'Pitchfork Ben' Tillman had failed to do justice to silver, and the sweltering throng of 20,000 was anxious and impatient. Bryan's was the closing speech, and as he made his way nervously down the aisle a great shout went up. The silver forces came, he said, not as petitioners, but as a victorious army.

> We have petitioned, and our petitions have been scorned; we have entreated and our entreaties have been disregarded; we have begged, and they have mocked when our calamity came. We beg no longer; we entreat no more; we petition no more. We defy them.

The delegates had found their champion, and every sentence was received with a frenzied roar of applause. Bryan's rousing peroration drew the class and sectional lines:

> You come to us and tell us that the great cities are in favor of the gold standard; we reply that the great cities rest upon our broad and fertile prairies. Burn down your cities and leave our farms, and your cities will spring up again as if by magic; but destroy our farms and the grass will grow in the streets of every city in the country. . . . Having behind us the producing masses of the nation and the world, supported by the commercial interests, the laboring interests and the toilers everywhere, we will answer their demand for a gold standard by saying to them: You shall not press down upon the brow of labor this crown of thorns, you shall not crucify mankind upon a cross of gold.

Bryan's 'Cross of Gold' speech helped make him the choice of the Democrats to wage the Battle of the Standards.

Not only on silver, but on banks, trusts, the injunction, and other issues, the Democrats had stolen the Populist thunder, although they failed to adopt the full Populist program. When the People's party met, the fusionists were in complete control, to the distress of those like Henry Demarest Lloyd who charged that the social emphases of their party were being superseded by the single questionable issue of silver. The Populists endorsed Bryan, but balked at accepting the Democratic vice-presidential nominee, a banker, and named the Georgia firebrand Tom Watson instead, thereby giving Bryan two different running mates. Within a short time silver Republicans bolted to Bryan; Gold Democrats named a separate ticket but actually threw their support to McKinley. For the first time in 30 years the country divided roughly along class and sectional lines, and the electorate was confronted with a clear-cut choice.

In Bryan the agrarians had an ideal leader:

> Prairie avenger, mountain lion,
> Bryan, Bryan, Bryan, Bryan,
> Gigantic troubadour, speaking like a siege gun,
> Smashing Plymouth Rock with his boulders from the West.[5]

Radical only on economic questions of money, banks, and trusts, strictly orthodox in matters of morality and religion, Bryan justified his title, 'the Great Commoner.' Born in a small farming town in southern Illinois, he came from mixed Scotch, Irish, and English stock from both North and South. One of his parents was Baptist, one Methodist; he himself joined the Presbyterian church. For generations his family had participated in the westward movement—from the Virginia tidewater to the Mississippi valley; he continued the process by moving out to the frontier in Nebraska. He attended a small denominational college, studied law, dabbled in politics, and finally became champion of a great popular cause. He was well equipped for politics, but it was qualities of character rather than of mind that won for him such loyalty as no other leader of his generation could command. Conservatives responded as though the Hun were thundering at the gates. The New York *Tribune* denounced 'the wretched rattle-pated boy, posing in vapid vanity and mouthing resounding rottenness.' But this seems not to have disturbed Bryan. Mark Sullivan wrote: 'Bryan used to repeat what his enemies said, with a smile and manner that was subtly designed as half-way between Christ forgiving his

5. Vachel Lindsay, 'Bryan, Bryan, Bryan, Bryan,' *Collected Poems*, Macmillan.

The railroad Senator. This caricature shows Chauncey Depew (1834–1928) wearing the ball and chain of the New York Central. In 1866, after being confirmed as the first United States minister to Japan, Depew was offered a place as attorney for the Vanderbilt interests. When he wavered, Commodore Vanderbilt told him: 'Railroads are the career for a young man; there is nothing in politics. Don't be a damned fool.' Depew resigned his ministerial appointment to accept Vanderbilt's offer, and by 1885 was president of the New York Central and Hudson River lines. But he did not have to give up his political aspirations. In 1899, when this caricature appeared, the New York legislature sent him to the U.S. Senate where progressive reformers immediately branded him a lackey of the special interests. (*Library of Congress*)

persecutors and John L. Sullivan showing himself a good sport.'

In the 1896 election Bryan received more votes than had ever before been cast for a presidential candidate and more than any Democratic nominee would get for another twenty years. But McKinley not only outpolled him by half a million but won a big edge in the Electoral College. Bryan carried the late Confederacy and most of the Middle Border and the Mountain West; but the electoral votes of the populous East and the Middle West together with five trans-Mississippi states gave McKinley an emphatic victory. In the silver region, Bryan won by prodigious margins—Montana, 4–1; Colorado, 6–1. In the East, he met disaster; he lost every county in New England, all but one in New York. The Eastern worker was repelled by a Western rural movement which, by spurring inflation, threatened his real wages. As Daniel De Leon said, labor feared it might be crucified 'upon a cross of silver.' McKinley ran so well in the cities that the Democratic plurality of 145,000 in the twelve largest cities in 1892 became a Republican advantage of 352,000 in 1896.

But Bryan lost chiefly because he failed to carry the old Granger areas. The more settled the Midwestern states became, the less they were dependent on outside forces they could not control. Since farmers there had nearby city markets for many of their crops, which were carried by a well-developed railroad system, they were not as subject to the whims of the world market and their operations were less speculative than they had been at the outset. Furthermore, this section was much more industrialized and urbanized. The election demonstrated that the industrial Northeast had extended its empire to embrace all of the Old Northwest, and the Republicans would hold this region for most of the next generation.

The election of McKinley constituted a triumph for a manufacturing and financial rather than an agrarian order. 'For a hundred years,' Henry Adams observed, 'the American people had hesitated, vacillated, swayed forward and back, between two forces, one simply industrial, the other capitalistic, centralizing, and mechanical. . . . The issue came on the single gold standard, and the majority at last declared itself, once and for all, in favor of a capitalistic system with all its necessary machinery. All one's friends, all one's best citizens, reformers, churches, colleges, educated classes, had joined the banks to force submission to capitalism; a submission long foreseen by the mere law of mass.'

McKinley left no doubt that he regarded the election as a mandate for the policies industry wanted. He named a lumber baron Secretary of War, the president of the First National Bank of Chicago Secretary of the Treasury, a New York banker Secretary of the Interior, a post that had been conceded to the West. He summoned Congress into special session to rush through the mountain-high Dingley Tariff Act. In the 1898 elections the Populists were all but wiped out. 'For the first time in twenty years the silver menace is cleared away from the financial horizon,' wrote *The Nation*. With the silver forces routed, McKinley was able to push through the Gold Standard Act of 1900, and the enormously increased production of gold in Australia and the Klondike soon muted the cry for free silver. Yet Bryan's campaign had significance not only as the last protest of the old agrarian order against industrialism, but as the first attempt to create a new order. Bryan was the bridge between Andrew Jackson and Franklin D. Roosevelt.

25

The American Mind

*

1865–1910

The Gilded Age

Historians agree that the Civil War and its aftermath devastated Southern culture and coarsened Northern society. Of the destructive impact on the South, there can be no doubt. The Kentucky-born scientist, Nathaniel Shaler, wrote:

> Not only did the Civil War maim the generation of Kentuckians to which I belonged, it also broke up the developing motives of intellectual culture of the commonwealth. Just before it I can see that while the ideals of culture were in a way still low and rather carnal, there was an eager reaching-out for better things; men and women were seeking, through history, literature, the fine arts, and in some measure through science, for a share in the higher life. Four years of civil war, which turned the minds of all towards what is at once the most absorbing and debasing interest of man, made an end of all this. . . .[1]

Many of the South's intellectual leaders—the novelist Simms, the poet Paul Hamilton Hayne, the sociologist George Fitzhugh—retired to live with poverty and bitterness for the rest of their lives. Others fled the South for the more prosperous or hospitable North and West: Frederick Barnard left the University of Mississippi to become president of Columbia University; the LeConte brothers gave up their scientific work in South Carolina and went to the new University of California; the novelist George W. Cable of Louisiana took refuge in Massachusetts; the brilliant young architect, Henry Hobson Richardson, moved from New Orleans—via Paris—to Boston and New York.

Such intellectual energies as the South was able to summon up went chiefly into the elegiac celebration of the Lost Cause. The dream of the Old South was a phantasmagoria of the wide-spreading plantation and the white-pillared manor house, of families always old and distinguished, of aristocratic colonels and great ladies and girls who were lovelier and purer than girls elsewhere, of happy slaves singing in the cotton fields or dancing in the quarters on Saturday nights, of an independent yeomanry and picturesque mountaineers given to Elizabethan speech, of a special grace, a special hospitality, and sense of chivalry and code of honor, a Cause forever right

1. Shaler, *Autobiography*, pp. 76–77.

and forever Lost. The Old South was, in short, mankind before the Fall, but it was Southern mankind, not Yankee—a unique experience which Providence had vouchsafed to Southerners and which set them apart.

In the meantime a lusty and arrogant North, its wealth enhanced by the war, was pushing forward to ever greater power. The decade after Appomattox was a period of relentless tawdriness and vulgarity. It was the era of lachrymose novels and the pious tales of Horatio Alger; of Rogers's plaster-cast statues and Currier and Ives lithographs and massive choruses of 10,000 voices shouting the Anvil Chorus to the accompaniment of cannon fired by electricity. The editor of *The Nation*, E. L. Godkin, called this a 'chromo civilization,' and in 1871 in *Democratic Vistas* Walt Whitman pronounced it:

> Cankered, crude, superstitious, and rotten. . . . Never was there, perhaps, more hollowness of heart than at present, and here in the United States. . . . I say that our New World democracy . . . is so far an almost complete failure in its social aspects, and in really grand religious, moral, literary and esthetic results.

All true enough, yet we must not accept these verdicts uncritically. Next year after *Democratic Vistas* came Whitman's 'Thou Mother with Thy Equal Brood'—the most exultant tribute to America that any poet has ever penned:

> Thou wonder world yet undefined, unform'd, neither
> do I define thee, . . .
> Land tolerating all, accepting all, not for the good alone,
> all good for thee,
> Land in the realms of God, to be a realm unto thyself,
> Under the rule of God to be a rule unto thyself.

Whitman had recognized that along with so much that was vulgar there was, in these years, an immense vitality. For if the war had coarsened the characters of some, it had refined the spirits of others, and there was truth in the noble words of Justice Oliver Wendell Holmes, who bore the wounds of three battles:

> The generation that carried on the war has been set aside by its experience. Through our great good fortune, in our youth our hearts were touched with fire. It was given to us to learn at the outset that life is a profound and passionate thing. . . . We have seen with our own eyes, beyond and above the gold fields, the snowy heights of honor, and it is for us to bear the report to those who come after us.

Literary Currents

And bear the report they did. The literary record of the war was varied and rich. No public man of the nineteenth century wrote more eloquently than Lincoln, and a handful of his public papers can be ranked as world literature. The memoirs of the great captains like Grant and Longstreet are unfailingly interesting but rarely possess the literary qualities found in the recollections of some of the lesser figures: Joshua Chamberlain's *The Passing of the Armies*, or Thomas W. Higginson's *Army Life in a Black Regiment*, or General Taylor's brilliant *Destruction and Reconstruction*. Nor has any American war produced more memorable poetry. In Walt Whitman's poems we can read much of the history and meaning of the war, from 'Eighteen Sixty-one':

> Arm'd year—year of the struggle,
> No dainty rhymes of sentimental love verses for you
> terrible year, . . .

to the lovely elegy for President Lincoln: 'When Lilacs Last in the Dooryard Bloom'd.' Whitman spanned the whole period from the 'fifties to the 'eighties, linking the romanticism of the Golden Day and the naturalism of the Gilded. In the years after the war he wrote many of his greatest poems.

These years, too, saw the emergence of three great writers who were to dominate the literary scene for almost half a century—Mark Twain, William Dean Howells, and Henry James—as well as Emily Dickinson, whose exquisite genius awaited later recognition. Though Twain, Howells, and James had very different backgrounds, they had much in common: a revolt against the pervasive romanticism which plagued so much of the style of the time; an obsession with the relations between the New World and the Old—all three lived much of their lives abroad; disillusionment with many aspects of American society; and a common concern for moral values.

Born in frontier Missouri where North meets South and East meets West, Sam Clemens spent his boyhood on the banks of the river whose epic he was to write under the name Mark Twain. Before he was twenty-five he had served an apprenticeship as a Mississippi pilot, learning the great river and the varied country it traversed and the society that floated on its muddy waters. When the war came he enlisted, briefly, in a volunteer Confederate company, then—like his own Huck Finn—lit out for the Territory. It was there, in Nevada and California, that he found the material for *Roughing It,* the first full-length novel about the Far West. In 1867 he sailed to the Mediterranean and the Holy Land. *Innocents Abroad* (1869), which gave him a reputation as a 'humorist' which he never quite lived down, struck the familiar note of American innocence and Old World corruption. *The Gilded Age* (1874) drew on his acquaintance with the frontier and with the Washington of Grant's administration. Thereafter it was the Mississippi that provided inspiration for his greatest books. From the steamboat leadsmen's cry at two fathoms, 'by the mark, twain!' he took his literary name, and on the river were born his three immortal characters, Tom Sawyer, Huck Finn, and the Negro Jim. These early books—*Roughing It, Innocents Abroad, Old Times on the Mississippi* (later *Life on the Mississippi*), and *Tom Sawyer,* all written before 1877—were, as Van Wyck Brooks observed, 'germs of a new American literature with a broader base in the national mind than the writers of New England had possessed. By his re-creation of the frontier life in the great central valley, by his skill in recapturing its speech and its turns of mind, Mark Twain pre-empted for later writers a realm that was theirs by right of birth but might never have been theirs for literature if he had not cleared the way.'[2]

Mark Twain published *Tom Sawyer* in 1876; thereafter he entered into the era of his greatest productivity and his highest achievement. In the course of the following twenty years he wrote *The Prince and the Pauper,* an enlarged version of *Life on the Mississippi, A Connecticut Yankee in King Arthur's Court, Pudd'nhead Wilson, Joan of Arc,* and, of course, the immortal *Adventures of Huckleberry Finn.*

2. *The Times of Melville and Whitman,* p. 297.

Huckleberry Finn (1884) is, by common consent, the greatest of Mark Twain's books and one of the two or three greatest of American novels. The wonderful device of the raft floating down the Mississippi through the heartland of America enabled Mark Twain to pass in review American society at mid-century. All modern American literature comes from *Huckleberry Finn,* said Ernest Hemingway, for it is the first novel so unmistakably American in subject matter, setting, characters, idiom, and style that it could not have been written elsewhere. 'Emerson, Longfellow, Lowell, Holmes, I knew them all, and all the rest of the sages, poets, seers, critics, humorists,' said Howells. 'They were like one another and like other literary men. But Mark Twain was sole, incomparable, the Lincoln of our literature.'

William Dean Howells wrote, at the age of 23, an undistinguished campaign biography of Lincoln and was rewarded with the consulship at Venice. There he had time to immerse himself in European letters, and to study America from the vantage point of the Old World. Returning home at the close of the war, he wrote critical essays for *The Nation* and in 1871 the Ohio printer's devil became editor-in-chief of the *Atlantic,* that house-organ of the Brahmins. Somehow he found time to carry on his editorial and critical work, while a steady stream of novels and stories flowed from his pen. As with Mark Twain's, Howells's early books anticipate his later themes: the conflict in manners, and in standards, of Boston and the hinterland (*A Chance Acquaintance,* 1873), the impact of the Old World on unsophisticated Americans (*A Foregone Conclusion,* 1875, and *The Lady of the Aroostook,* 1879), and the morality of the commonplace and the immorality of what passed for 'romance.'

The first major critic to recognize that Mark Twain was not just a humorist but an authentic genius, just as he was the first to recognize talent in his young friend Henry James, Howells functioned for almost half a century as Dean—or Pope—of American letters. Not the greatest novelist of his generation, nor the most profound critic, nor the most talented editor, nor the most perspicacious biographer, he combined these roles more successfully than any other individual. In

Mark Twain *[Samuel Langhorne Clemens]* (1835–1910). He appears here in his Connecticut home dressed in the robe he wore when he was awarded an honorary degree from Oxford in 1907. On that occasion a large cheering crowd escorted him from the site of the ceremony to the college gates. 'I came in with Halley's Comet in 1835,' he said, 'and I expect to go out with it.' And so he did—with the reappearance of the comet in 1910. (*Mark Twain Memorial, Hartford, Conn.*)

some forty novels, thirty plays, a dozen books of criticism, and a score of biography and travel recording 'the more smiling aspects of American life,' Howells provided the most comprehensive description of middle-class Victorian America to be found in our literature. Howells was the American Balzac, fascinated by the homely details of social relationships. *The Rise of Silas Lapham* drew a classic portrait of the self-made man; *A Modern Instance* interpreted a Victorian marriage and its breakdown; *A Hazard of New Fortunes* dramatized industrial conflict in New York City; and *Dr. Breen's Practice* dealt with the new woman. In all of this, as James wrote, 'he adores the real, the natural, the colloquial, the moderate, the optimistic, the domestic, and the democratic.'

Gradually the 'optimistic' note died out as Howells came up against 'the riddle of the painful earth.' More and more he got caught up in the conflicts of the day. 'After fifty years of optimistic content with civilization and its ability to come out all right in the end,' he wrote, 'I now abhor it, and feel that it is coming out all wrong in the end, unless it bases itself anew on a real equality.' Yet while Howells criticized the America of his day more sharply than did Mark Twain, he never suffered the desperate bitterness that ravaged the author of *The Man that Corrupted Hadleyburg*. Thus, Howells wrote *A Traveller from Altruria* to show what men could do to save themselves, while Mark Twain wrote *The Mysterious Stranger* to show that man was not worth saving. Still, if realism triumphed over romanticism, much of the credit goes to Howells. He did more than anyone else to obtain a hearing for the rebellious younger novelists who were coming to the fore: he found a publisher for Stephen Crane's *Maggie, A Girl of the Streets,* wrote an introduction to Hamlin Garland's *Main-Travelled Roads,* championed Thorstein Veblen and Edward Bellamy, and welcomed a host of European naturalists like Émile Zola.

Where Mark Twain wrote of rivermen and miners and smalltown boys and slaves, and Howells of the proper middle classes, Henry James took for his theme the sophisticated relationships of an aristocratic—or sometimes merely a very rich—international society. Unlike the Old World, America he found thin and arid, lacking color, drama, intensity, and the marrow of literature. After 1875 James lived mostly abroad, and though a few of his novels—*The Bostonians,* for example—have an American setting, generally he set his stories in the great houses, the hotels, or the boulevards of London, Paris, and Rome. He was fascinated by the trappings and machinery of society—houses, gardens, teas, ceremonies—but only because these reflected, or concealed, values with a deeper moral significance. A long shelf of novels and stories—and James wrote almost as voluminously as Howells—elaborates on two basic themes. The first of these—the interaction of New World innocence and Old World sophistication—is the theme of the greatest of his books—*The American* (1877), *The Portrait of a Lady* (1881), *The Ambassadors* (1903), *The Wings of the Dove* (1903), *The Golden Bowl* (1904). The second—the interaction of the artist and fashionable society—permeates much of these books as well as *Roderick Hudson* (1876), *The Aspern Papers* (1888), and others. Because James wrote of subjects and characters far removed from the interest of the average American, and in an intricate style, he had few readers in his own lifetime. Like Melville, he has been rediscovered in our time, and is now generally acknowledged to be one of the great masters of the modern novel.

These three novelists grew to literary maturity during the period of the Darwinian controversy, but their writings do not reflect the new philosophy, which had a much greater impact on younger men of letters, born after the Civil War. These were especially fascinated by the principle of the survival of the fittest. In Frank Norris's *Vandover and the Brute,* the central character reverts to a kind of animal brutality, and Jack London's Wolf Larsen argues crudely 'that life is a mess' in which 'the strong eat the weak.' In Theodore Dreiser's writings, man was less animal than fool, victim of his own vagrant impulses, pitiful vanities, insatiable lusts and greeds. Dreiser was obsessed with power; the city provided his background, and his characters pitted their cunning and ruthlessness against their fellow men in the desperate battlefields of business or of love. Frank Cowperwood, the protagonist of *The Titan* and *The*

Financier, is a far more sophisticated creature than Wolf Larsen, but not therefore more admirable. Through a quarter-century of writing, from *Sister Carrie* (1900) to *An American Tragedy* (1925), Dreiser played variations on the theme of determinism, a salient feature of Darwinian thought. The Norwegian-American O. E. Rölvaag, in *Giants in the Earth* (1927), wrote the epic story of the immigrant farmer in the Dakota country. *Giants in the Earth* caught the spirit of the westward movement, but instead of being the proud story of man's conquest of the earth, it is the record of earth's humbling of man.

Philosophy and Religion

The year 1859, when Darwin published his *Origin of Species*, began a revolution in thought as in science. The leaders of practically every Christian sect fought hard for the book of Genesis and special creation, and Louis Agassiz of Harvard University attacked evolution of species on scientific grounds. But with the support of scientists like Asa Gray and of popularizers like Edward Youmans and John Fiske, the doctrine of evolution spread rapidly, and by the 'eighties had triumphed in most intellectual circles, and was making heavy inroads on the popular consciousness.

This doctrine of evolution was chiefly responsible for the abandonment of transcendentalism and the formulation of pragmatism. Rooted in the eighteenth century, transcendentalism celebrated many things dear to the romanticists: Nature, individualism, spontaneity, the imagination. It rested upon primal intuitions not susceptible to proof, such as the benevolence of God and of Nature, and preferred *a priori* principles to the findings of the laboratory. Such a philosophy was clearly irrelevant to the kind of universe unveiled by Darwin. Truth could no longer be something plucked from the inner consciousness of man, nor yet what God revealed to man; any hypothesis must stand up under laboratory tests. Moral standards, when discovered to be the product of social evolution and environment, could no longer be thought absolute. Laws, by the same test, were neither eternal nor cosmic; they derived from the social needs of the day. Fixed ideas were as out of place in politics and economics as in science and religion.

Pragmatism was elaborated by a remarkable group of philosophers who came to maturity in the last third of the nineteenth century: Chauncey Wright, Charles Peirce, William James, and John Dewey—all from New England. Although European philosophers cried out that its concern with consequences was a piece of American sordidness, it may yet be admitted that pragmatism was one of the really important innovations in the history of thought through the ages. It is not easy to define pragmatism; the Italian Papini observed that pragmatism was less a philosophy than a method of doing without one. James certainly, and Dewey probably, would have conceded this, for they insisted that pragmatism was less an independent system of thought than a way of thinking about philosophical questions. They intended pragmatism not for the schoolroom but for the world of affairs. 'Better it is,' wrote Dewey, 'for philosophy to err in active participation in the living struggles and issues of its own age and times than to maintain an immune monastic impeccability.' The pragmatists regarded truth not as an absolute, but as something that each society and each thinking individual had to make for himself. 'The truth of an idea,' wrote James, 'is not a stagnant property inherent in it. Truth *happens* to an idea. It becomes true, it is *made* true by events.' The test of truth was to be found in its consequences; the business of the philosopher was to find out what worked best. 'The ultimate test of what a truth means,' wrote James, 'is the conduct it dictates or inspires.' The pragmatists conceived of our world as still in the making, a conception admirably suited to a nation so oriented to progressive changes as the United States.

The effect of such an attitude on politics, law, economics, social institutions, education, art, and morals was little less than revolutionary. Progressive teachers abandoned the idea that education consisted of acquiring a body of information, and tried to make it a function of society. Political scientists talked less about abstractions such as 'sovereignty' and more about the political process. Jurisprudents ceased to regard the law as a body of

William James (1842–1910), in a portrait by Ellen Emmet. Few thinkers had a greater influence on his age than this Harvard philosopher who pioneered in making psychology a laboratory science, expanded on C. S. Peirce's conception of pragmatism, and in works like *The Varieties of Religious Experience* (1902) sought to harmonize faith and science. (*Houghton Library, Harvard University*)

changeless truth and accepted the doctrine that every generation must make its own precedents. Economists reluctantly surrendered 'laws' which they had long regarded as inviolable, and sociologists came to reject the dour doctrine that man is the creature of his environment, and taught instead that man could transform his environment. Even historians submitted that historical truth was relative to each generation.

Protestant fundamentalism suffered most from the new philosophy. Theological scholars applied to the Bible critical standards long accepted in other fields of scholarship, testing the Scriptures by the facts of history, philology, geology, archaeology, and other sciences, but the Protestant churches were more afraid of Darwinism than of the 'higher criticism,' and several Southern states actually passed laws forbidding the teaching of evolution. Orthodox defenders of the faith quoted with approval Disraeli's declaration, 'Is man an ape or an angel? I, my Lords, am on the side of the angels.' Stout champions of science countered with vigorous attacks upon what they denominated religious bigotry: John William Draper's *History of the Conflict Between Religion and Science* (1874) and Andrew D. White's 'Warfare of Science' (1876)[3] ran through innumerable editions, while the professional agnostic, Colonel Robert Ingersoll, lectured on 'Some Mistakes of Moses' to rapt audiences.

Moderates on both sides, meantime, attempted to effect a reconciliation. John Fiske, a very behemoth of a scholar, who wrote on history, ethnology, and sociology, expounded a reconciliation of science and religion as early as the 'sixties, published his elaborate *Outlines of Cosmic Philosophy* in 1874, and thereafter, by books and lectures, spread his message that evolution was simply God's way of doing things. Soon the most popular of American preachers, Henry Ward Beecher, announced his conversion, and shortly thereafter such distinguished clergymen as President McCosh of Princeton came over to the side of the evolutionists.

While 'higher criticism' and Darwinism caused some churchmen to do battle for their faith, others chose to meet a third challenge, that of the industrial revolution which was making it increasingly difficult for people to lead the life that Christ commanded. They were troubled by the conviction that class divisions had fractured the nation and atrophied the capacity of people of different social groups to feel toward one another, and they were especially concerned that the ministers had become alienated from the poor in the great cities. The social gospel movement discarded all but the essentials of the gospel and concentrated on making the Church an instrument of social reform. From his parsonage in Columbus, Ohio, Washington Gladden championed the cause of industrial peace, and millions of copies were sold of Charles Sheldon's *In His Steps*, describing a congregation which followed consistently the teachings of Jesus.

Probably the most influential books came from the pen of the gifted Walter Rauschenbusch. Upon graduation from seminary, he was sent to the Second German Baptist Church of New York, a small, impoverished congregation on the fringe of Hell's Kitchen. Here, in the depression of the 1890's, he saw good men go 'into disreputable lines of employment and respectable widows consent to live with men who could support them and their children. One could hear human virtue cracking and crumbling all around.' This experience convinced Rauschenbusch that evil was the consequence not of individual frailty but of environment. When Rauschenbusch went as professor to the Rochester Theological Seminary, it was to train a generation of preachers in the social gospel and to produce a series of books, the most notable of which was *Christianity and the Social Crisis* (1907).

While many of the Protestant churches sought to come to terms with the new forces, the Roman Catholic Church was under no pressure to conform to the new science. It specifically repudiated 'modernism' in the papal encyclical *Pascendi Dominici Gregis* of 1907, although in the encyclical *Rerum Novarum* of 1891 the Church had sharply attacked the evils of unregulated capitalism and encouraged far-ranging reforms.

Perhaps in the long run the most important

3. Elaborated later (1896) into the two-volume *History of the Warfare Between Science and Theology*.

religious development of these years was the growth of Catholicism. In 1890 the Roman Catholic Church counted some 9 million communicants in the United States; thirty years later the number had doubled, and every sixth person and every third church member was Catholic. This growth resulted in large part from the flood of immigration which brought 16 million people to the New World during these years; well over half came from the Catholic countries of central and southern Europe. No church that had been in the Americas a century before the Jamestown plantation could be called an immigrant church, but probably the majority of Catholic communicants were first- or second-generation Americans, while the Church hierarchy was long dominated by the Irish—thus Cardinal Gibbons of Baltimore and Archbishop Ireland of St. Paul. As in the past the growth of Catholicism gave rise to anti-Catholic movements. Most prominent of these was the American Protective Association which flourished, chiefly in the Middle West, during the 'nineties. Like the Know-Nothings of the 'fifties and the Klan of the 1920's, the A.P.A. was wholly negative in character; unlike them it did comparatively little damage.

Social and Legal Thought

Though Darwinism deeply affected social and legal thinking, a number of theorists challenged the view that progress could come only as a result of the survival of the 'fittest' at the end of a struggle that would require several thousand years to work itself out. Frank Lester Ward, the father of American sociology, formulated a philosophy which, while fully accepting Darwinian evolution in the realm of Nature, resolutely rejected its authority in the realm of human nature. Man, he argued—and he was a distinguished zoologist and paleontologist—is not subject to the same iron laws that govern the animal world, for while environment, or Nature, masters and transforms the animal world, man masters and transforms Nature. What is more, he does this not by a blind struggle for existence, but by co-operation and applied intelligence. In book after book—*Dynamic Sociology, Applied Sociology, Psychic Factors in Civilization*—Ward emphasized that survival of the fittest required the application of organized intelligence, and the institution best qualified to organize man's intelligence was government.

The same forces that shaped sociology shook the study of economics to its foundations. Economists, like sociologists, had acquiesced passively in a series of iron laws that were said to control the economy. The full-throated attack upon this notion came from a new generation of academic economists, most of them trained in Germany where they were taught that the State should be an agency to produce a more humane social order. In 1885, a group of young men, all of whom had studied in Germany—Simon Patten, Herbert Baxter Adams, John Bates Clark, Edwin James, and E. R. A. Seligman—founded the American Economics Association. They boldly asserted: 'We regard the state as an educational and ethical agency whose positive aid is an indispensable condition of human progress. . . . We hold that the doctrine of laissez faire is unsafe in politics and unsound in morals.'

Men such as these wished to place the American university at the service of government. At the University of Wisconsin, they played an important role in aiding the administration of Governor Robert M. La Follette. The university, especially the School of Economics, Politics and History under Richard T. Ely, trained students for careers in public administration; it even offered a course in bill drafting. Wisconsin is only the most spectacular example of what was happening across the country in these years. A similar relationship existed in New Jersey between Governor Woodrow Wilson and a group of reformers with close ties to Princeton and Columbia. On the national level, government commissions looked into problems of conservation, rural life, and industrial strife. By the time America entered World War I, it was accepted as a matter of course that professors like Felix Frankfurter would man the wartime agencies.

No economist did more to change old ways of viewing society than Thorstein Veblen. A Norwegian farm-boy who had grown up in the Middle West, Veblen was all his life something of an outsider, and able therefore to look at institutions and practices of the American economy without emotional or intellectual commitments. This he did in *The Theory of the Leisure Class* (1899), *The Theory of Business Enterprise* (1904), and a long series of other volumes. Veblen emphasized the irrational element in the economy; the role of conspicuous leisure, conspicuous consumption, and conspicuous waste; the conflict between the instinct for craftsmanship and the instinct for pecuniary gain, the engineer and the price system. He called for an economy which would be controlled by engineers, subject to the discipline of tools and the machine, rather than by businessmen, who valued profits rather than production.

Evolution and pragmatism profoundly affected the interpretation of politics and history as well. There was a widespread revolt against Newtonian concepts of government—against the tyranny of abstract concepts like the state, and the illusion that there could be such a thing as 'a government of laws and not of men.' Instead scholars turned to the analysis of constitutions and governments as they actually functioned: to the Constitution as a mechanism that often broke down and had to be tinkered with rather than as a sacred Covenant. They analyzed what presidents and judges did rather than abstractions called The Executive Power or The Judiciary; explored the battlefields of party politics or the misty fogs of public opinion rather than the formal documentary record. Woodrow Wilson, who was a professor of politics at the time, explained:

> Government is not a machine but a living thing. It falls not under the theory of the universe, but under the theory of organic life. It is accountable to Darwin, not to Newton.

History, in many ways closer to literature than to the social sciences, responded somewhat more sedately to the new teachings. In the 'nineties the elder statesmen who had dominated the historical stage for two generations were passing from the scene. The venerable George Bancroft completed the Author's Last Revision of his great history just in time to have it go out of date on publication. In 1892 the indomitable Francis Parkman published the final panel of his great historical series on the struggle between the French and English for the control of North America—the most impressive achievement of the era of historical romanticism. With the death of Bancroft in 1891 and of Parkman in 1893 the golden age of American history came to an end and the iron age set in. Three names dominate the new generation. In 1890 Captain Alfred Mahan published the remarkable *Influence of Sea-Power upon History;* the next year Henry Adams completed his brilliant nine-volume study of the administrations of Jefferson and Madison and turned to the study of historical forces; in 1893 young Frederick Jackson Turner announced a frontier interpretation that was to bemuse the imagination of American historians for another half-century. Turner and Charles A. Beard both were deeply influenced by the Populist revolt and the Progressive movement, but they developed very different formulas. Turner argued that what chiefly differentiated America from the Old World was the frontier, which took a European and transformed him into an American. Beard's emphasis, too, was environmental; in a prodigious flow of books and articles he read an economic interpretation into much of American history from the making of the Federal Constitution to American participation in two world wars. A crusader as much as an historian, Beard used scholarship as a weapon in the struggle for Progressivism and reform, and eventually for isolationism.

Of all the social sciences, the study of law responded most decisively to evolution and pragmatism. Under the compelling pressures of the new exegesis Natural Law gave way to historical jurisprudence, and this in turn to sociological jurisprudence. The concept of the law as a living, growing organism owes much to the most distinguished American jurist of his generation, Oliver Wendell Holmes, Jr., who sat on the Supreme Courts of Massachusetts and the United States for half a century, from 1882 to 1932. A product of Harvard and of the Union Army, Holmes had early associated with members of the Metaphysical Club of Cambridge, and he took in pragmatism as naturally as his father, the famous Dr. Holmes, accepted the new teachings about antisepsis. From

Oliver Wendell Holmes, Jr. (1841–1935). For half a century, from 1882 to 1932, 'the Great Dissenter' graced the bench first of the Massachusetts Supreme Court, then of the U.S. Supreme Court. 'If there is any principle of the Constitution that more imperatively calls for attachment than any other it is the principle of free thought—not free thought for those who agree with us but freedom for the thought that we hate,' he said. This portrait by Charles Hopkinson was painted a few years before Holmes retired in 1932. Presidents never pay calls, but in 1933 the newly elected Franklin D. Roosevelt courteously broke precedent to visit the former judge. 'Why do you read Plato, Mr. Justice,' FDR asked. 'To improve my mind, Mr. President,' the ninety-two-year-old man replied. (*Photograph by ACKAD, Washington, D. C.*)

the beginning he confessed the pragmatist's distrust of absolutes. 'The life of the law has not been logic,' he wrote in *The Common Law,* which he published in 1881, 'it has been experience. The felt necessities of the time—the prevalent moral and political theories, intuitions of public policy, avowed or unconscious, even the prejudices which judges share with their fellow men—have had a good deal more to do than the syllogism in determining the rules by which men should be governed. The law embodies the story of a nation's development through many centuries and cannot be dealt with as if it contained only the axioms and corollaries of a book of mathematics.'

Scientific Interests

Tocqueville observed that a democracy almost inevitably addressed itself to what was practical and immediate in science, a generalization largely valid for this period. These years witnessed a series of ambitious explorations of the Far West; the organization of research at the Lawrence and Sheffield scientific schools and at government bureaus; far-reaching developments in geology, paleontology, botany, and ethnology; and the popularization of science by men like John Fiske and Edward Youmans.

With settlement ready to penetrate the Last West, the need for knowledge of its geology and geography, its flora and fauna, was urgent, and in the decade after the war the Federal Government undertook to fill the need. The Wilkes Exploring Expedition of the 'forties, the Railroad Surveys and Boundary Surveys and Coastal Surveys of the 'fifties, provided the pattern. First in the field was the army-sponsored Geological Survey of the Fortieth Parallel led by the gifted Clarence King of the Sheffield Scientific School, whom John Hay called 'the best and brightest man of his generation.' Meanwhile the Corps of Engineers launched a large-scale expedition to explore the territory west of the 100th meridian, which yielded 40-odd volumes of scientific reports of immense value. The Hayden Geological Survey of the Territories mapped much of the *terra incognita* of the Far West. Easily the most dramatic of the expeditions were those headed by the remarkable John Wesley Powell, a one-armed veteran of the Civil War who had already piloted four boats down the 900 miles of the Green and Colorado rivers. Out of all this came not only discoveries but, in 1879, the creation of the United States Geological Survey headed first by Clarence King and then by Powell.

A more scientific interest in native races emerged. Lewis Morgan, having led the way with his work on the Iroquois, turned his attention to the Indians of the West and the Southwest, and in 1877 published *Ancient Society,* an argument for the common origin and evolution of all races which owed a great deal to Darwin. During these same years Hubert Howe Bancroft published his five-volume *History of the Native Races of the Pacific Coast,* and the Swiss-born Adolphe Bandelier launched his pioneering studies of the archaeology of the pueblo Indians of the Southwest which led to his fascinating novel, *The Delight Makers.* The year 1879 saw both the establishment of the United States Bureau of Ethnology and the founding of the Archaeological Institute of America.

Notable contributions were also coming from the universities. At Harvard Asa Gray completed his *Flora of North America.* In the midst of the war James Dwight Dana, dean of academic geologists, published his *Manual of Geology,* which reflected the evolutionary findings of Charles Lyell in England. Dana's Yale colleague, the paleontologist Othneil Marsh, organized a series of scientific expeditions into the West and published his *Vertebrate Life in America,* which placed the study of fossils on a scientific basis. At the Smithsonian Institution the zoologist Spencer Baird brought to completion his *History of North American Birds.*

All this work revealed the urgent need to conserve resources. Pioneer in alerting the American people was the versatile George Perkins Marsh, diplomat, historian, philologist, and scientist. From observing the waste of soil and forest in his native Vermont, and from experience in Turkey and Asia Minor, he came to appreciate the consequences of these violations of nature's laws. In 1864 he published his masterpiece, *Man and Nature* (later published as *The Earth as Modified by Human Action*), the most influential American geographical work of the nineteenth century. It dealt with 'man as a disturbing agent,' described the destruction of animal and vegetable life by men, and emphasized the need to conserve forests. John Wesley Powell applied Marsh's central thesis to the problem of land and water on the High Plains. In 1878 Powell's memorable *Report on the Arid Regions of the West* warned against using Eastern techniques of farming on the High Plains, argued for farm units of not less than 2500 acres, stressed the paramount importance of water and access to water supplies, and insisted that the right to water should inhere in the land.

These fermenting years were distinguished by contributions to both pure and popular science. In 1876 Edward Pickering, director of the astronomical observatory at Harvard, began a photographic record of the stellar universe. At Yale Willard Gibbs, the most gifted mathematician of his generation, made fundamental advances in mathematical physics with papers on the equilibrium of heterogeneous substances. William James opened America's first psychological laboratory in the early 'seventies, and there began studies that culminated in his epoch-making *Principles of Psychology*. In the meantime, John Fiske was engaged in reconciling Darwinian evolution, Spencerian sociology, and liberal religion in the *Outlines of Cosmic Philosophy*, a work that sprawled through four volumes, and Edward Youmans fed it to the public through the *Popular Science Monthly* and the many volumes of his International Scientific Series.

Journalism

In the eighteen-sixties and 'seventies New York City was the newspaper center of the nation. Although local papers such as the *Springfield Republican*, *Boston Transcript*, *Toledo Blade*, and *Cincinnati Commercial* were influential, the great New York dailies—the *Tribune*, *Sun*, *Evening Post*, and *Times*—held a commanding position.

William Cullen Bryant, since 1826 editor of the *Evening Post*, was dean of America's journalists. Few more vigorous, discriminating, and far-sighted critics have dealt with the American scene than this poet-editor who combined respectability with a zeal for righteousness. He lifted American journalism to a higher literary and ethical plane than it had heretofore occupied, and gave not only his editorial column but his entire paper a dignity that assured it the leading place in American journalism. But he lacked the talent to appeal to a broad popular audience, and his following was limited almost entirely to the intellectual elite.

Horace Greeley of the *Tribune*, greatest of American editors, was spokesman for the plain people, of the entire North. Practical, liberal, open-minded, fearless, and with boundless faith in democracy, he was a social reformer who fashioned a great paper as an instrument for social purposes. He founded the *Tribune* in 1841, drove its circulation up over the hundred thousand mark, and until the close of the Civil War exerted a larger influence over public opinion north of the Mason-Dixon Line than any other editor—and possibly than any other private citizen in the country. Throughout a long career Greeley found room in his paper for the liveliest literary intelligence, the most varied points of view, and the most extreme reforms. His thirty years' editorial leadership of the *Tribune* still constitutes the greatest achievement of personal journalism in our history.

A very different paper was *The Sun*, after 1868 under the control of Charles A. Dana, graduate of Harvard College and of Brook Farm. Dana had been trained to journalism under Greeley; he had seen service in the war under Grant, and was close to the center of power. By attracting to his staff some of the most skillful journalists of the day, he made *The Sun* the most popular paper in the country. With the passing of years, however, Dana grew increasingly cynical and even capricious, equally hostile to corruption and to civil service reform, to organized capital and to organized labor; in the end he frittered away his influence and condemned his paper to sterility.

The most powerful newspaper in the country outside New York City was probably the *Springfield Republican*, edited from 1844 to 1915 by three generations of Samuel Bowleses. Like the *Tribune*, the *Republican* issued a weekly edition, which had a much wider circulation, spreading liberal principles throughout New England and into the Ohio and Mississippi valleys. The second

Samuel Bowles advocated a magnanimous policy toward the defeated South, fought corruption under Grant, and held fast to principles of independence and honesty.

More powerful than many daily papers were weekly journals of opinion such as *The Nation, The Independent,* and *Harper's Weekly.* Of these *The Nation,* under the Irish-born E. L. Godkin, was for the thirty years after 1865 easily the most influential. A great editor, incisive and vigorous, with high literary and intellectual standards, Godkin enlisted the best minds in the country: Henry James and William James, Henry Adams, James Russell Lowell, William Dean Howells, C. W. Eliot and Daniel C. Gilman, Asa Gray and John Fiske. Yet for all his high-mindedness, Godkin found himself increasingly out of touch with the political and economic realities of his adopted country. His liberalism was doctrinaire; he had no understanding either of the farmer or the workingman. 'He couldn't imagine a different kind of creature from himself in politics,' wrote William James shrewdly, and it is significant that the most fervent appreciation of Godkin came from his New England and English friends who, like him, often mistook good taste for good sense.

Securely in the American tradition was *Harper's Weekly,* long edited by the versatile and scholarly George William Curtis. A family magazine, designed for entertainment rather than agitation, it was a force for political decency, and Curtis came in time to occupy the position previously held by Bryant. *Harper's Weekly* is chiefly remembered for its lively coverage of the Civil War, Winslow Homer's early drawings, and Thomas Nast's political cartoons.

The *Atlantic* and *Harper's Monthly,* high-minded but somewhat parochial, had for some time almost pre-empted the field of the monthly magazine. After the war they were joined by a number of newcomers. First arrival was *The Galaxy,* designed to compete with the *Atlantic* and ultimately absorbed by it. Mark Twain, Henry James, and many of the most popular English authors wrote for the new magazine, and it gave extensive space to new developments in science. More interesting was California's bid for literary attention, the *Overland Monthly,* edited by Bret Harte, whose 'Luck of Roaring Camp' and 'Outcasts of Poker Flat' first appeared in its pages. Harte abandoned the magazine at the end of a year, and it never lived up to its initial promise. A happier fate was reserved for that best of all children's magazines, the beloved *St. Nicholas.* Founded in 1873 by Mary Mapes Dodge who had already written *Hans Brinker and the Silver Skates, St. Nicholas* managed to attract to its pages almost every distinguished author on both sides of the Atlantic, and many of the most talented artists and engravers as well.

The late eighteen-seventies and 'eighties marked a dividing line in American journalism. First there developed the subordination of politics to 'news,' with a consequent development of the highly efficient machinery of reporting and news-gathering, and the organization of news-gathering agencies like the United Press and the Associated Press. Second, we note the passing of the personal element in journalism and the growth of editorial anonymity. Third, the creation of chains, with elimination of competition, and the use of syndicated material. Fourth, an enlargement and improvement in the appearance of the newspapers, accomplished in large part through the immense growth of advertising, which gave newspaper-owners the money to install expensive machinery like the linotype. And last, the Federal Government co-operated by providing low postal rates for newspapers and magazines, and rural free delivery.

No one better represented the new journalism than Joseph Pulitzer. A Hungarian-German Jew, trained under Carl Schurz, he first made a respectable newspaper of the St. Louis *Post-Dispatch,* which he took over in 1878, then moved on to New York where he acquired the almost defunct *World* from the speculator Jay Gould. By elaborating on the sensationalism of James Gordon Bennett, Pulitzer pushed the circulation of the *World* up to unprecedented figures, passing the million mark during the hectic days of the Spanish-American War. His paper, popular in appeal, played up sensational news in screaming headlines and illustrations, while its bold political program recommended it to the poor. Yet the *World* under Pulitzer was never merely a 'yellow' journal.

'The Yellow Kids.' This savage cartoon depicts the publishers Joseph Pulitzer and William Randolph Hearst in 1898 as childish irresponsibles playing at war. Two years earlier they had brawled over a comic strip character, 'The Yellow Kid,' who gave the name of 'yellow journalism' to the sensationalist press. The cartoonist, in a heavy-handed way, represents the Hungarian-born Pulitzer as talking with a thick Continental accent. 'Vatch de Tome' translates as 'Watch the Dome,' symbol of Pulitzer's newspaper, the New York *World*. (*Library of Congress*)

There was a wide gap between the news stories and the editorial page, conducted on a high intellectual and moral plane. After the retirement of Pulitzer and the accession of Frank I. Cobb to the editorship, the *World* became the leading Democratic organ in the country, a position which it maintained under the able direction of Walter Lippmann until its demise in 1931.

The success of Pulitzer in tapping substrata of newspaper readers was contagious. William Randolph Hearst, who had inherited a vast mining fortune, bought the New York *Journal* in 1896. Soon Hearst was outsensationalizing Pulitzer, and there ensued a fierce struggle which sent the circulation of both papers soaring, but degraded the press. Hearst, in the *Journal* and in the nationwide chain of papers he acquired, brought 'yellow' journalism to its most extreme development, but without the editorial compensations offered by the *World*. Lavish use of enormous black leaders, colored paper, blaring full-page editorials, and colored cartoon strips assured the Hearst papers an extraordinary popularity, but sensationalism became a national menace when, in order to boost circulation, Hearst whipped up popular demand for war with Spain. E. L. Godkin, in one of his last editorials, hotly denounced 'a regime in which a blackguard boy with several millions of dollars at his disposal, has more influence on the use a great nation may make of its credit, of its army and navy, of its name and traditions, than all the statesmen and philosophers and professors in the country.'

Pulitzer and Hearst, for all their faults, were real journalists; not so Frank A. Munsey, who in 1882 came to New York City from Portland, Maine, and began to deal in magazines and newspapers the way Daniel Drew had dealt in stocks. An entrepreneur, who at one time owned more valuable newspaper properties than anyone else in the country, Munsey subscribed to no ascertainable policies beyond an uncritical attachment to the status quo and recognized no responsibility to the public.

At one time or another Munsey owned six New York papers, two in Baltimore and one each in Philadelphia, Washington, and Boston; most of these he merged or killed, for he believed in the survival of the fittest, by which he meant, of course, the most profitable. 'Frank Munsey,' wrote William Allen White in one of the bitterest of obituaries, 'contributed to the journalism of his day the talent of a meat packer, the morals of a money changer, and the manners of an undertaker. He and his kind have about succeeded in transforming a once-noble profession into an eight per-cent security.'

Despite this vulgarization of the press, the professional standards and ethics of journalism were on the whole improving as a result of the establishment of schools of journalism—of which those at Columbia and the University of Missouri were the most influential—and the example of such papers as the *New York Times*. When Ochs bought the *Times* in 1896, it was on the verge of collapse; by printing only the news 'that's fit to print,' and building up a staff of skillful correspondents, Ochs made the *Times* the American counterpart of *The Times* of London. The vigorous growth of such papers as the St. Louis *Post-Dispatch*, the Baltimore *Sun*, and the Chicago *Daily News* also helped to offset the low standards of the mass circulation press.

The 'eighties saw something of a revolution in magazines as well. The magazine field had long been dominated by respectable family journals like *Harper's*, content with a modest circulation and catering to middle-class readers whose tastes were primarily literary. In 1886 came the *Forum*, designed—as its title announced—for discussion of controversial issues. Three years later Benjamin Flower launched the lively *Arena*, which opened its pages to radicals, reformers, and heretics of all stamps. Then came a flood of weekly and monthly magazines devoted to agitation rather than to entertainment—Bryan's *Commoner*, for example, and *La Follette's Weekly*. In 1912 Oswald Garrison Villard obtained control of *The Nation*, and transformed it into a radical weekly. The *New Republic*, launched two years later under the auspices of Herbert Croly, and with an editorial staff that included Walter Lippmann and Randolph Bourne, was designed 'to start little insurrections,' and assumed at once a commanding position among the magazines of opinion.

Education

The effect of the war on education in the South was disastrous. Schoolhouses had fallen into ruin; teachers were killed or scattered; the impoverished South, less able to bear heavy taxes than at any time, now faced the additional burden of providing a public education for white and Negro alike. The University of North Carolina closed its doors for some years during reconstruction; the University of Louisiana was kept alive only by the heroic self-denial of a few professors who refused to abandon the stricken institution. Southern education did not fully recover until the twentieth century.

In the North, by contrast, education progressed at almost every level. By mid-century the responsibility of the community to provide schooling for all its children was generally acknowledged, but that obligation was faithfully discharged only in elementary education. In 1870 there were only 200 public high schools in the entire country; a decade later the number had increased to some 800. As late as the 1870's it was still possible to challenge the legality of public support to high schools; not until 1874 was this question forever laid to rest by Justice Thomas Cooley of the Michigan Supreme Court in the Kalamazoo case.

During the decades after Reconstruction, education made even more spectacular gains. No nation was ever more fully committed to the ideal of education, free, universal, and comprehensive, than the United States. Yet in 1870 there were only 6,871,000 pupils enrolled in the public schools of the country, and of these only 80,000 were in the high schools.[4] By 1920, however, enrollment had leaped to 21,578,000,[5] of whom over two million were in the high schools. In the same half-century the percentage of children between five and seventeen who were in school increased from 57 to 78, while the average daily attendance grew fivefold. In 1870 Americans spent some $63 million on their public schools; by 1920 expenditures had passed the billion mark.

Most pupils went to a 'little red schoolhouse'—more picturesque than efficient—where some student working his way through a nearby college, or a girl too young to marry, taught all subjects and all grades, largely by rote. Discipline was capricious but severe, corporal punishment taken for granted, and extracurricular activities were limited to marbles or crack-the-whip on a muddy school ground. The backbone of the curriculum was the 'three R's'—reading, 'riting, and 'rithmetic. Children learned spelling, and many other things, out of Noah Webster's Blue Backed Spellers, which had already done service for three generations, and 'spelling-bees' were as exciting a part of school life as basketball games today. McGuffey's Readers, which sold over 100 million copies between 1836 and the end of the century, introduced children to 'selections' from the best of English and American literature. The novelist Hamlin Garland, who went to country schools in Iowa during these years, remembered that 'from the pages of McGuffey's Readers I learned to know and love the poems of Scott, Byron, Southey, Wordsworth, and a long line of English masters, and got my first taste of Shakespeare.' The McGuffey Readers, with their pious axioms and their moral tales, made a somewhat heavy-handed contribution, too, to 'molding character.'

By 1870 almost two-thirds of public schoolteachers were women—a number which increased through the rest of the century. With only twelve normal schools in the country at the outbreak of the Civil War, the great majority of teachers were untrained, and it was generally supposed that any respectable girl was competent to teach school. In due course states created boards of education designed to establish minimum requirements, and gradually teaching took on some of the characteristics of a profession. During the reconstruction years nine states provided for compulsory school attendance for at least part of the year, and some even enforced these laws.

In 1867 Congress created the office of United States Commissioner of Education to 'collect statistics and facts concerning the conditions and progress of education' and 'to diffuse information regarding the organization and management of schools and methods of teaching.' Though the office was reduced to the status of a bureau and systematically starved by Congress, it managed nevertheless to attract distinguished educators: first Henry Barnard, founder and editor of the *American Journal of Education*; then the learned philosopher, William T. Harris, for a long time superintendent of schools of St. Louis. Under Harris's auspices the first public kindergarten was opened in 1873, and it was Harris, too, whose long series of annual reports on public schools did for his generation what Horace Mann's reports had done for an earlier generation, providing a rationalization of public education in an industrial age.

What was later known as 'progressive' education received its formulation and earliest application during these years. The doctrines of the Swiss Johann Pestalozzi and of the German Friedrich Froebel had been introduced to America just before the war; now they triumphed in the work of Edward A. Sheldon of the Oswego State Normal School, whose graduates carried the new gospel throughout the East and the Middle West. Almost equally important was the work of Colonel Francis

4. Compare, however, Great Britain, which had a population roughly two-thirds that of the United States; only 1,450,000 children were enrolled in schools, and the number who attended was much smaller.

5. Non-public school enrollment for 1900 was 1,334,000 and for 1920 was 1,700,000.

Parker who had studied pedagogy in Germany, returned to be the superintendent of schools in Quincy, Massachusetts, where he quietly carried through a revolution in education whose philosophy and techniques anticipated, and deeply influenced, John Dewey two decades later.

In the next generation progressive education came into its own. The leaders in the transformation of the school were Lester Ward, who thought education the mainspring of progress; William James, whose *Principles of Psychology* provided inspiration for the new dispensation; G. Stanley Hall, first professional psychologist in America, the author of a pioneer work on *Adolescence;* Edward L. Thorndike of Columbia University's new Teachers' College, whose experiments shattered orthodox assumptions about the learning process; and above all John Dewey, philosopher and symbol of the whole progressive education movement. Dewey believed that the school was a legatee institution which had to carry on functions previously attended to by other groups in the community. In *The School and Society* (1899) he wished to use the school as a lever for reform to make society more 'worthy, lovely, and harmonious.' In *Democracy and Education* (1916) he argued that in an 'intentionally progressive' society, culture could not be divorced from vocation.

The 'revolution' that these men and their disciples carried through involved a shift in emphasis from subject matter to learning by experience, from education as a preparation for life to education as life itself. It called for participation in the learning process by the children themselves—the original principle of the *Kindergarten*—through such activities as woodworking and cooking; did away with much of the formality of the classroom; greatly broadened the curriculum, often at the expense of thoroughness and discipline; encouraged children to play an active role in such affairs as student government; and attempted to make each school, in the words of Dewey, 'an embryonic community life, active with types of occupations that reflect the life of the larger society.' Within a short time Dewey and his associates at Teachers' College succeeded in imposing their educational outlook on much of the country.

Higher education in the North, meantime, experienced a renaissance which can be traced to a number of factors: the Morrill Land-Grant Act of 1862; the demand of business and the professions for specialized knowledge and skills; new pressures for educational facilities for those heretofore neglected; and the emergence of a remarkable group of educational statesmen, most of them deeply influenced by German ideas and practices.

Agitation for the Morrill Act began as early as 1850, and in 1859 a bill looking to federal support for agricultural education passed both houses of Congress only to be vetoed by Buchanan. Three years later Lincoln gladly signed a more generous bill sponsored by Justin Morrill of Vermont. The Morrill Land-Grant Act of 1862 gave each state 30,000 acres of public land for each Congressman, to be used as endowment or support of a college of agricultural and mechanical arts. Under provisions of the Morrill Act, undoubtedly the most important piece of educational legislation in nineteenth-century America, land grant colleges were founded in every state. Some states gave their lands to existing institutions; others to private universities; most established new agricultural and mechanical schools.

The scientific revolution and the growing complexity of economic life resulted in the encouragement of the natural sciences and the establishment of numerous professional and vocational schools. Soon schools of law, medicine, architecture, and engineering were turning out graduates fitted by special training to meet the demands of the economy. Some of the older states assigned their Morrill funds to schools of science or engineering at existing institutions: Massachusetts turned her money over to the new Institute of Technology, and New York's princely grant of one million acres provided a large part of the endowment of the new Cornell University. Private philanthropy created a series of engineering schools: Columbia's School of Mines in 1864, Lehigh University in 1865, Stevens Institute in 1870, and a School of Mines in Colorado as early as 1874—two years before that Territory was admitted as a state.

In these years, too, educational leaders sought to provide in America the kind of facilities for graduate study that had long flourished abroad.

Ever since George Ticknor and George Bancroft had led the way to Göttingen University in the second decade of the century, eager graduates of American colleges had streamed to Berlin, Jena, Halle, Leipzig, and Munich, bringing back with them admiration for German scholarship, the seminar, and the Ph.D. degree. Yale awarded the first Ph.D. granted in America in 1861 and ten years later organized a graduate school; Harvard followed in 1872; and President Andrew D. White, who had studied at Berlin, made provision for graduate studies on the German model at Cornell. With the opening of the Johns Hopkins University in 1876 the German model was firmly transplanted in the New World.

The third influence—a quickened sense of equalitarianism—required provision for higher education for women and for Negroes. Wesleyan Academy for girls had opened at Macon, Georgia, as early as 1836, and the gallant Mary Lyon had persevered against heavy odds to found Mount Holyoke College at South Hadley, Massachusetts, in 1837, while Oberlin—pioneer in this as in so many things—adopted coeducation in the late 1830's. The postwar years saw the founding of Vassar, the gift of a rich brewer of Poughkeepsie, New York, which opened its doors in 1867; Wellesley College and Hunter College in 1870 and Smith College in 1871. Meantime Iowa led the way among state universities in adopting coeducation, and most of the state and municipal universities in the North followed its example. At a time when Englishmen were debating the propriety of establishing their first college for women, the United States could boast a dozen flourishing women's colleges, and a growing acceptance of coeducation as the common sense of the matter.

Oberlin College had admitted blacks almost from the beginning, and before the Civil War blacks had founded a university of their own at Wilberforce, Ohio. Institutions for blacks in the South were largely industrial training colleges. General Clinton Fisk, who had been a colonel of a black regiment during the war, opened a training school for blacks in Nashville in 1866 which eventually evolved into Fisk University. In 1868 General Samuel Armstrong, who also had led a black regiment, established Hampton Institute in Virginia; a few years later its most distinguished graduate, Booker T. Washington, was to found Tuskegee Institute in Alabama.

A fourth contribution to the educational renaissance was the emergence of the most remarkable group of statesmen in the history of American higher education. In 1869 Harvard elected a 35-year-old chemist, Charles W. Eliot, to the presidency. Eliot, who had spent some time observing German universities, was a scientist prepared to accept the teachings of Darwinian evolution, and he was peculiarly sensitive to the changes brought about by the industrial revolution. He signalized his advent to the presidency by a revolution in academic policies. Though Eliot was not the first to advocate the elective system, his tireless championship of freedom of choice helped popularize the system. Of greater ultimate significance was Eliot's rehabilitation of the schools of law and medicine, which he placed upon a sound professional basis. So significant was his achievement and so widespread his influence that he came to be regarded as the first citizen of his country.

While Eliot was transforming Harvard, Andrew Dickson White was pioneering far above Cayuga's waters, at Ithaca, New York. The new Cornell University, based on income from the Morrill Land Grant and on gifts from the industrial philanthropist Ezra Cornell, was both public and private and thus established a new pattern of higher education. Graduate of Yale, student at Paris and Berlin, professor at the University of Michigan, chairman of the New York State committee on education, White had long dreamed of a university that should be the equal of those of Germany and France, and now he had his chance. He decided that Cornell would have no barriers of color, sex, or faith; it would treat students like adults, encourage mature scholarship, maintain professional standards for the study of engineering and agriculture, and be a stronghold of academic freedom. Opened in 1868, Cornell set a pattern, later followed by Hopkins and Chicago, of springing to life full-panoplied in academic armor.

An even more important educational statesman was Daniel Coit Gilman, who had helped found the Sheffield Scientific School at Yale, and in 1871 became president of the new University of California. In 1874 a Baltimore philanthropist, Johns Hopkins, left $7 million to found a university and a hospital; when the trustees of the university turned to Eliot of Harvard, White of Cornell, and Angell of Michigan for advice, each recommended that they make Gilman president and give him a free hand. They did. Gilman created a university largely on the German model, with emphasis on graduate study and scholarship. He put his money in men, not buildings, and collected not only a distinguished faculty but an exceptional group of younger 'Fellows'—among them the future President Woodrow Wilson, Josiah Royce and John Dewey, leaders of two schools of philosophy, J. Franklin Jameson and Frederick Jackson Turner, historians, Walter Hines Page and Newton D. Baker, prominent in the public life of the next generation. Wilson said later of Gilman that he was 'the first to create and organize in America a university in which the discovery and dissemination of new truth were conceded a rank superior to mere instruction.'

In the half-century after the Civil War, higher education underwent an immense expansion: the 52,000 students who attended some five hundred colleges in 1870—all of them financially and most of them intellectually impoverished—increased to 600,000 students in 1920—more than in all the universities of the Old World. The habit of building new universities overnight, from the ground up, proved contagious. In 1889 John D. Rockefeller made his first munificent gift to create the new University of Chicago, which promptly took its place among the foremost institutions of learning. In the 1880's, too, the railroad magnate, Leland Stanford, endowed a university at Palo Alto, California, in memory of his son. Supported by an initial gift of some $20 million, this Stanford University became at once the leading private institution of learning west of the Mississippi. A third major creation of private benevolence was Clark University in Worcester, Massachusetts, which, under the guidance of the eminent psychologist G. Stanley Hall, undertook to be a New England version of the Johns Hopkins University. From these new universities came many innovations: the quarter system, the summer session, extension divisions, the university press, and above all the creation of new graduate and professional schools. More prophetic of future developments was the rapid growth of state universities after the turn of the century; California, which attracted only 197 students in 1885, enrolled over six thousand in 1915. Many of the best state institutions, such as Michigan, Wisconsin, Illinois, and California, could hold their own academically with the older private universities.

New educational statesmen came to the fore. William Rainey Harper, a Hebrew scholar from Yale, gathered about him on Chicago's Midway perhaps the most remarkable group of scholars to be found in America in the 1890's and inaugurated far-reaching experiments that contrasted sharply with the traditional Gothic architecture of the institution. Nicholas Murray Butler was elected president of Columbia University in 1901, and for over forty years directed the destinies of that institution, changing it from a small residential college to the leading center for graduate research in the country. Influenced by the German example, these men were interested primarily in graduate and professional training and in the university as a center for research. Woodrow Wilson, who came to the presidency of Princeton just as Butler took over the helm at Columbia, preferred the English model. He toughened the intellectual fiber of the college and introduced something like the Oxford tutorial system, with marked success; when he was defeated in his attempt to add on top of this a great graduate school, he resigned to become Governor of New Jersey.

An essential instrument of education, and of popular culture, was the library. The first of the great modern public libraries was founded in Boston in the 'fifties, and soon attracted both public support and generous private bequests. The Chicago Public Library was developed around the gift of 7000 volumes presented after the great fire of 1871 by Thomas Hughes of England, author of *Tom Brown at Rugby*, the New York Public Library, which quickly became the largest of its kind in the Western world, was formed by the merger of three privately endowed libraries with the library resources of the city, while the Library of Congress, built around the nucleus of Thomas Jefferson's private library, is the largest and most effective library in the world. The major impulse to the public library movement came from the generosity of Andrew Carnegie. Inspired by a passion for education, persuaded that the public library was the most democratic of all highways to learning, and mindful of his own debt to books and his love of them, the Pittsburgh iron-master devoted some $45 million of his vast fortune to the construction of library buildings throughout the country. By requiring a guarantee of adequate support to the libraries he built, he laid the foundation for healthy growth of library facilities after his own gifts had served their initial purpose.

If, as most Americans from Jefferson to John Dewey confidently believed, education could be counted on to provide a sound basis for 'a happy and a prosperous people,' Americans at the turn of the century had reason to be cautiously optimistic. The principle of universal free public education from kindergarten through the university had been established; it would take only another half century or so for the practice to catch up with the principle.

The Fine Arts

Even before the Civil War the architectural renaissance sponsored by Thomas Jefferson and Benjamin Latrobe, and its offspring the Greek Revival, had petered out, and the most promising architects, James Renwick and Richard Upjohn, had turned to Gothic. Renwick's Grace Church and St. Patrick's Cathedral, and Upjohn's Trinity Church and Church of the Ascension, all in New York City, gave promise of a Gothic revival like that which flourished in the England of Ruskin and Gilbert Scott. What came instead was pseudo-Gothic. Used in many large public buildings, such as the Smithsonian Institution in Washington, it had a peculiar fascination for college trustees, who littered the academic landscape with grotesque structures. The enraptured John Fiske of Harvard urged that 'we honestly confess our stupidity and show some grain of sense by copying the Oxford and Cambridge buildings literally.' Harvard did not accept this advice but Trinity College in Hartford, Connecticut, did, and Knox College on the Illinois prairie; and a few years later the new University of Chicago reproduced Oxford, 'battlemented towers' and all. Spires and buttresses, stained glass windows and gargoyles, jigsaw scroll work, endless bric-a-brac—all of this proclaimed the emptiness and insincerity of the architects and confessed the decline in taste since the simplicity and dignity of Jefferson and Bulfinch.

Out of all this welter two distinguished architects emerged: Henry Hobson Richardson and Richard Morris Hunt. As a student in Paris, Richardson fell under the influence of the medievalist Viollet-le-Duc, and he set out to transplant Romanesque architecture to the United States. Such was Richardson's power that he enjoyed a success greater than any other architect before Frank Lloyd Wright. 'To live in a house built by Richardson,' wrote one art historian, 'was a cachet of wealth and taste; to have your nest-egg in one of his banks gave you a feeling of perfect security; to worship in one of his churches made one think one had a pass key to the Golden Gates.' Richardson's greatest monuments were Trinity Church, Boston, for which John La Farge did the stained-glass windows, and the fortresslike Marshall Field warehouse in Chicago. Although it was these public buildings that contemporaries most prized, later critics have been more impressed by Richardson's influence on domestic architecture, particularly his use of shingles to create low, rambling houses which adapted to the landscape of the New England seacoast, and anticipated some of the innovations of Frank Lloyd Wright.

Contemporary with Richardson was Richard Morris Hunt, the favored architect of the plutocracy. He introduced to America the beauty and lavishness of the French Renaissance and built for millionaires magnificent country houses patterned after châteaux, or palatial town houses that resembled hôtels-de-ville. Viollet-le-Duc had prophesied an architecture of metal and glass, and even as Richardson and Hunt wrought in their derivative styles, these materials were working a revolution in architecture, notably in the work of the bridge-builders, John Roebling and his son Washington, who all through the 'sixties and 'seventies supervised the construction of that *stupor mundi,* the Brooklyn Bridge.

These years saw the beginning also of the pro-

Stanford University. Opened at Palo Alto, California, in 1891 with an initial gift of $20,000,000, the Leland Stanford Junior University erected twenty-seven buildings of buff sandstone and red tile connected by long colonnades in a Romanesque mode around two quadrangles. In the beginning, Stanford had more female students than male, until Mrs. Stanford limited the number of women to five hundred. *(Los Angeles County Museum)*

fessionalization of art and architecture. The American Institute of Architects had been founded in the late 'fifties, and the National Academy of Design in the early 'sixties when the Massachusetts Institute of Technology, and then Cornell University, offered the first formal training for architects. In the early 'seventies Boston opened her Museum of Fine Arts; a group of New York philanthropists chartered the Metropolitan Museum of Art; and in the national capital William Corcoran—son of an Irish immigrant—built and endowed the gallery that bears his name. Important, too, was the development of landscape architecture and of city planning associated so largely with the work of Frederick Law Olmsted. He laid out Central Park, Prospect Park in Brooklyn, the Capitol grounds in Washington, the park system of Boston and, eventually, the Chicago

World's Fair of 1893, and was chiefly instrumental in preserving Yosemite valley as a national park and in protecting Niagara Falls from the worst ravages of commercialization.

The advance in American aesthetics in the post-Reconstruction era might be measured by comparing the buildings of the Centennial Exposition of 1876 with those of the Columbian Exposition at Chicago in 1893. The first had been a helter-skelter of frame and iron structures without either design or harmony—doubtless the ugliest collection of buildings ever deliberately brought together at one place in the United States. The Chicago Exposition, by contrast, was elaborately designed by Richard Morris Hunt, who enlisted the most distinguished artists and architects in the country: Daniel Burnham of Chicago, Stanford White, and Louis Sullivan among the architects; Augustus Saint-Gaudens, Daniel Chester French, and Frederick MacMonnies among the sculptors; Mary Cassatt as one of the painters; while Frederick Law Olmsted was put in charge of landscaping.

Though these artists created along the shores of Lake Michigan the best designed and most beautiful exposition of modern times, the design was conventional and the beauty mostly derivative, for the overall plan was classical. Hunt's Administration Building was a brilliant copy of St. Paul's Cathedral in London; Charles Atwood's Art Building had been unequalled—so Burnham said—since the Parthenon. Louis Sullivan's exquisitely decorated Transportation Building did reveal originality, but almost everything else reminded the visitor of something he had read about or heard about. Americans had not yet developed an indigenous architectural style.

To the despair of Louis Sullivan, the classical style spread over the whole United States. Washington adopted the classical as the official style; soon most public buildings, railroad stations, libraries, banks, and college dormitories were being constructed in this mode. Sullivan resisted the vogue. The most gifted architect of his generation—he built the great Auditorium Building in Chicago, and the Carson, Pirie, and Scott store with its daring use of glass and metal and its rich ornamentation—Sullivan failed in the end to sustain this early promise. It remained for his student and disciple, Frank Lloyd Wright, to vindicate his philosophy and realize his vision.

Trained in the architectural office of Adler and Sullivan, Wright had taken to heart Sullivan's guiding principle that function determines form and form follows function. He conceived a building not as something superimposed upon the landscape, but as part of an organic whole embracing the structure and its furnishings, the grounds and gardens about it, the people who use it or live in it. He began to apply these ideas in the 'nineties as soon as he set up on his own, in such early prairie-style buildings as the Isabel Roberts House at River Forest, Illinois, as well as in the first Taliesin House at Spring Green, Wisconsin, where he worked and taught. In 1906 he built the Unity Temple in Oak Park, Illinois, which helped to revolutionize ecclesiastical architecture in the United States. At the same time he was putting up office buildings and factories, among them the dazzling Larkin Building in Buffalo. Later there came masterpieces—houses like Falling Waters near Pittsburgh where the rocks and waterfalls were incorporated into the house itself; the Imperial Hotel in Tokyo, built to withstand earthquakes; office buildings such as the futuristic Johnson Wax works in Racine, Wisconsin; desert residences like his own Taliesin West in Arizona. Wright's artistic life spanned two generations; he tied together the world of Louis Sullivan and the world of Mies van der Rohe and Walter Gropius.

Three major figures dominated American painting during the transition years: Winslow Homer, Albert Ryder, and Thomas Eakins.

Homer was a product of the Civil War. Trained as a lithographer, he had been sent to the battle lines by *Harper's Weekly;* his work was the best to come out of the war—'Prisoners from the Front' and 'The Sharpshooter,' or some of his Negro sketches. In the postwar years Homer lifted genre painting to the highest level it had attained in America: 'Morning Bell' (1866), 'High Tide at Long Branch' (1869), the beloved 'Snap-the-Whip' (1872), 'The Carnival' (1875). Homer's greatest period, however, was still ahead. In one great canvas after another—'The Life Line, 'Fog Warning,' 'Lost on the Banks,' 'The Undertow,'

Portrait of Walt Whitman by Thomas Eakins. A splendid teacher who stressed anatomical study, a gifted mathematician, a pioneer in photography, Eakins (1844–1916) was above all the greatest American painter of his age. As early as 1871, the Philadelphia artist had painted 'Max Schmitt in a Single Scull,' and in 1875 he did his stark 'The Gross Clinic.' But Eakins's uncompromising naturalism proved unacceptable. At the Centennial Exhibition of 1876, 'The Gross Clinic' was hung in the medical display rather than with art works, and when in 1886 he stripped the loincloth from a male model in a class that included female students, he was forced out of the Pennsylvania Academy. The following year he met Walt Whitman (1819–92), who was living out his days, a crippled man, across the Delaware in Camden, and Eakins painted this classic portrait of 'the Good Grey Poet.' (*Pennsylvania Academy of the Fine Arts*)

John Singer Sargent (1856–1925) in his Paris studio. The painting is his full-length portrait of 'Madame X,' who was, in fact, Mme. Gautreau, the wife of a French banker. Sargent's oil, exhibited at the Paris Salon of 1884, shocked the *haute monde* because of his candid rendering of the décolletage, the lavender make-up, and scarlet hair of the free-living New Orleans-born beauty. So great was the outcry that Sargent had to relocate in London, where his stylish, and more circumspect, portraits earned him fat fees and comparison to Reynolds and Gainsborough. Sargent himself, however, regarded 'Madame X' as his masterpiece. (*Archives of American Art, Smithsonian Institution*)

'Eight Bells,' and 'Gulf Stream'—he was to portray the struggle of man against the elements.

Ryder, like Herman Melville, lived obscurely in New York. Like Melville, too, he lived, as Lewis Mumford has observed, 'in a dark, moon-ridden world, stirring with strange beauty that indicated unexplored realities, deeper than the superficial levels of being.' Ryder's imagination was lyrical and mystical. He transferred to his varnish-covered canvases a mysterious world of clouds flitting across the moon, ships forever lost scudding before the wind, dim figures out of the mythological past—thus his 'Death on a Pale Horse,' 'The Flying Dutchman,' 'Jonah,' 'Siegfried and the Rhine Maidens,' which make us fancy for a moment, in Justice Holmes's phrase, 'that we heard a clang from behind phenomena.'

In these years, too, the most original genius among American painters was experimenting with new techniques and new subjects. Thomas Eakins had studied at the École des Beaux Arts, but that artistic finishing school left little impression on him. Back in Philadelphia in 1870 he began to turn out pictures whose unashamed realism forfeited the popularity his talent merited: paintings of swimmers, fishermen, oarsmen, and professional men and women busy with their work. A kind of Thorstein Veblen among artists, Eakins had no use for the salon or the academy; he brought to his art a scientific knowledge of the human body and portrayed it with an intimacy that shocked many of his contemporaries. When he painted President Hayes it was at his desk, working, and in shirt sleeves; as Presidents were not supposed to have shirt sleeves, the painting was rejected. 'I never knew but one artist, and that's Tom Eakins, who could resist the temptation to see what they think ought to be rather than what is,' said Walt Whitman, whose portrait is one of Eakins's masterpieces.

In the first decade of the new century, a group of Eakins's disciples launched the 'Realistic' movement. Robert Henri, George Luks, Everett Shinn, William Glackens, and John Sloan had all studied at the Philadelphia Academy under Eakins's disciple, Thomas Anshutz. Most of them had worked as pictorial reporters on the old Philadelphia *Press*, where they had come to know the seamy side of life in the great city, and most had studied in Paris. During the 'nineties they drifted to New York where they formed a loose-knit brotherhood joined by other young rebels and independents like George Bellows and Maurice Prendergast. The leader of the group was the gifted Robert Henri. Affectionately and sensitively they painted the color of the great city—McSorley's Bar, boys swimming off East River piers, children dancing in the teeming streets of the Five Corners; Bowery bums lounging under the 'El'; Yeats dining at Petipas; girls drying their hair on the roofs of tawdry tenements; a prize-fight at Sharkey's; the Staten Island ferry. In 1908 these Manhattan realists gave their first exhibition and were promptly dubbed the 'Ash-Can School.' When two years later they presented an exhibition, two thousand visitors tried to crash the gates on opening day. These exhibits mark the beginnings of modern art in America as truly as the Armory Show of 1913.

In the meantime another group of painters took up impressionism, that new technique, vision, and philosophy of painting which artists like Monet were revealing to an astounded world. The most distinguished landscape painter of the prewar era, George Inness, had anticipated something of impressionism, and so, too, John La Farge, who was equally talented in oils, water colors, murals, and stained glass. He returned from Paris in the 'sixties determined that his paintings 'indicate very carefully in every part the exact time of day and circumstance of light.' In 1874 Mary Cassatt settled in Paris, where she studied with Degas, exhibited with the Impressionists, bought their paintings, and herself experimented both with impressionism and with techniques of Japanese art with notable success. Others who revealed the influence of Impressionists were Childe Hassam, who painted the New England countryside in shimmering light and New York City in its gayer and more colorful moods, and the frail Theodore Robinson, who had studied with Monet and whose early death deprived his country of its most promising Impressionist.

Modern American sculpture begins with Augustus Saint-Gaudens, who for a generation towered over all of his artistic contemporaries. Born in Ireland of Irish and French parentage, he nevertheless recorded the American genius with rare sympathy and understanding. His Lincoln, in Lincoln Park, Chicago, with its intuitive comprehension of the combination of rugged shrewdness and spirituality, is so convincing that 'no one, having seen it, will conceive him otherwise thereafter.' The Farragut Monument (1881), its base executed by Stanford White, and the Shaw Memorial (1897) in Boston established him as the foremost monumental sculptor of his day. But the loveliest of Saint-Gaudens's statues is the figure he made for the tomb of Mrs. Henry Adams. 'From Prometheus to Christ, from Michael Angelo to Shelley,' wrote Henry Adams, 'art had wrought on this eternal figure almost as though it had nothing else to say.'

26

Imperialism and World Power

*

1876–1906

The United States in World Affairs

Writing in 1889 Henry Cabot Lodge observed that 'our relations with foreign nations today fill but a slight place in American politics, and excite generally only a languid interest.' From the settlement of the *Alabama* claims and the successful weathering of the *Virginius* affair to the eruption of the Hawaii and Venezuela crises, foreign relations were singularly placid. The change came in the 1890's, and it synchronized with the passing of the frontier, the shift from the 'old' to the 'new' immigration, the rise of the city, and the coming of age of our industrial system. Almost every year before 1876 the United States suffered an unfavorable balance of trade; almost every year thereafter the balance was decidedly in its favor. In 1865 foreign trade had been $404 million; by 1890 it had reached $1635 million.

America's longstanding interest in the Pacific came increasingly to center on the Hawaiian islands, 2300 miles southwest of California. Hawaii, or the Sandwich Islands, had been discovered by Captain Cook in 1778, and early served as a convenient port of call in the China trade and recruiting station for Yankee whalers. By 1840 Honolulu, with whalemen and merchant sailors rolling through its streets, shops filled with Lowell shirtings, New England rum, and Yankee notions, missionaries living in frame houses brought around the Horn, and a neo-classic meeting house built of coral blocks, was a Yankee outpost. In the 1850's and 1860's efforts toward annexation aborted, but in 1875 the United States concluded with the Hawaiian monarch a reciprocity treaty which granted exclusive trading privileges to both nations and guaranteed the independence of the islands against any third party; twelve years later the Senate approved a treaty renewing these privileges and ceding Pearl Harbor on the island of Oahu to the United States.

These treaties greatly stimulated the sugar industry, which the sons of thrifty missionaries had established in Hawaii. American capital poured in, sugar production increased fivefold within a decade, and by 1890, 99 per cent of Hawaiian exports went to the United States. Native Hawaiians became increasingly disturbed by the growing determination of the American government to establish a protectorate, the ambitions of American

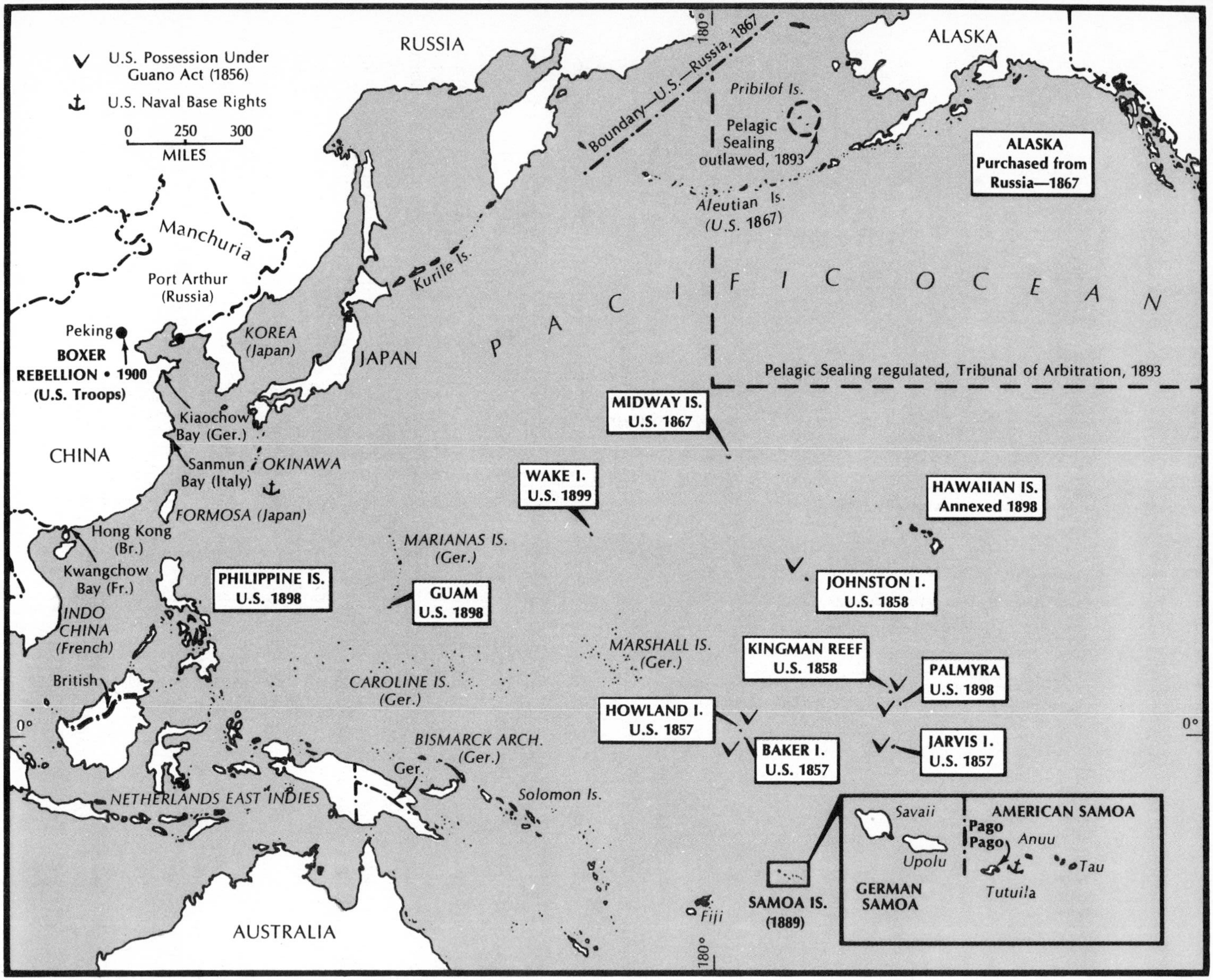

United States in the Pacific

settlers, and the overdependence on the American economy. Then came the McKinley tariff of 1890, which by providing a bounty of 2 cents a pound to domestic sugar dealt a catastrophic blow to the Hawaiian economy; sugar fell overnight from $100 to $60 a ton, and property values collapsed. American planters and industrialists who had opposed annexation out of fear that it would hamper their importation of Asiatic labor, now concluded that only annexation could restore to sugar interests in Hawaii their American market on equal terms.

They were even more alarmed when, in 1891, Queen Liliuokalani inaugurated a policy looking to the elimination of American influence and the restoration of autocracy. This threat excited a prompt counteroffensive. After marines had been landed from the U.S.S. *Boston* with the connivance of the American minister John L. Stevens, a Committee of Safety consisting largely of missionaries' sons deposed the hapless Queen on 17 January 1893. A provisional government under Chief Justice Sanford B. Dole promptly opened negotiations for annexation to the United States. 'I think we should accept the issue like a great Nation,' wrote Minister Stevens, 'and not act the part of pigmies nor cowards.' President Harrison, in full sympathy with this 'white man's burden' attitude, precipitately accepted a treaty of annexation on 14 February; but before the Senate got around to it, Grover Cleveland became President and hearkened to the appeal of 'Queen Lil.' 'I mistake the Americans,' he said, 'if they favor the odious doctrine that there is no such thing as international morality; that there is one law for a strong nation and another for a weak one.' He withdrew the treaty from the Senate and sent out a special commissioner to investigate. When the commissioner reported that the Hawaiian revolution was the work of American interests, aided by Minister Stevens, he denounced the affair. But the provisional government would not step down, and Cleveland was forced to recognize the Republic of Hawaii.

Between 1893 and 1898 two developments in the Far East sharpened the demand to annex the Hawaiian islands. The first was the rise of Japan to world power, and the fear of a Japanese inundation of the islands; the second was the prospective annexation of the Philippines, which gave Hawaii new significance as a naval base. Toward annexation McKinley had no such scruples as had animated his predecessor, but there was still sufficient opposition in the Senate to necessitate action by a Joint Resolution, on 7 July 1898, instead of through the normal method of a treaty. An organic act of 1900 conferred American citizenship on all subjects of the short-lived republic and the full status of a Territory of the United States, eligible for statehood, on the islands.

The Samoan, or Navigators', Islands were to the South Pacific what the Hawaiian were to the North Pacific, and from the 1830's on they had offered refuge to whalers and a virgin field for missionaries. In 1878 a treaty granted the United States trading privileges and the right to build a coaling station at Pago Pago in the island of Tutuila. Shortly thereafter Great Britain and Germany secured comparable concessions, and there followed ten years of ridiculous rivalry for supremacy among the three powers, each supporting a rival claimant to the native kingship. The danger of involving the United States in serious international complications was averted by the establishment in 1890 of a tripartite protectorate guaranteeing the independence and neutrality of the islands and confirming American rights to Pago Pago. Unimportant as this episode was, it constituted nevertheless, in the words of Secretary of State Gresham, 'the first departure from our traditional and well established policy of avoiding entangling alliances with foreign powers in relation to objects remote from this hemisphere.' After another embarrassing native civil war, and intensified bad feeling between the United States and Germany, the tripartite agreement was abrogated in 1900, and the islands divided between Germany and the United States, Great Britain obtaining compensation elsewhere.

Well before, this policy toward Latin America took a new direction under the vigorous leadership of Secretary of State James G. Blaine. Since 87 per cent of Latin American exports to the United States entered duty free, Blaine threatened to clamp a tariff on them unless the Latin American countries lowered their duties on U.S. prod-

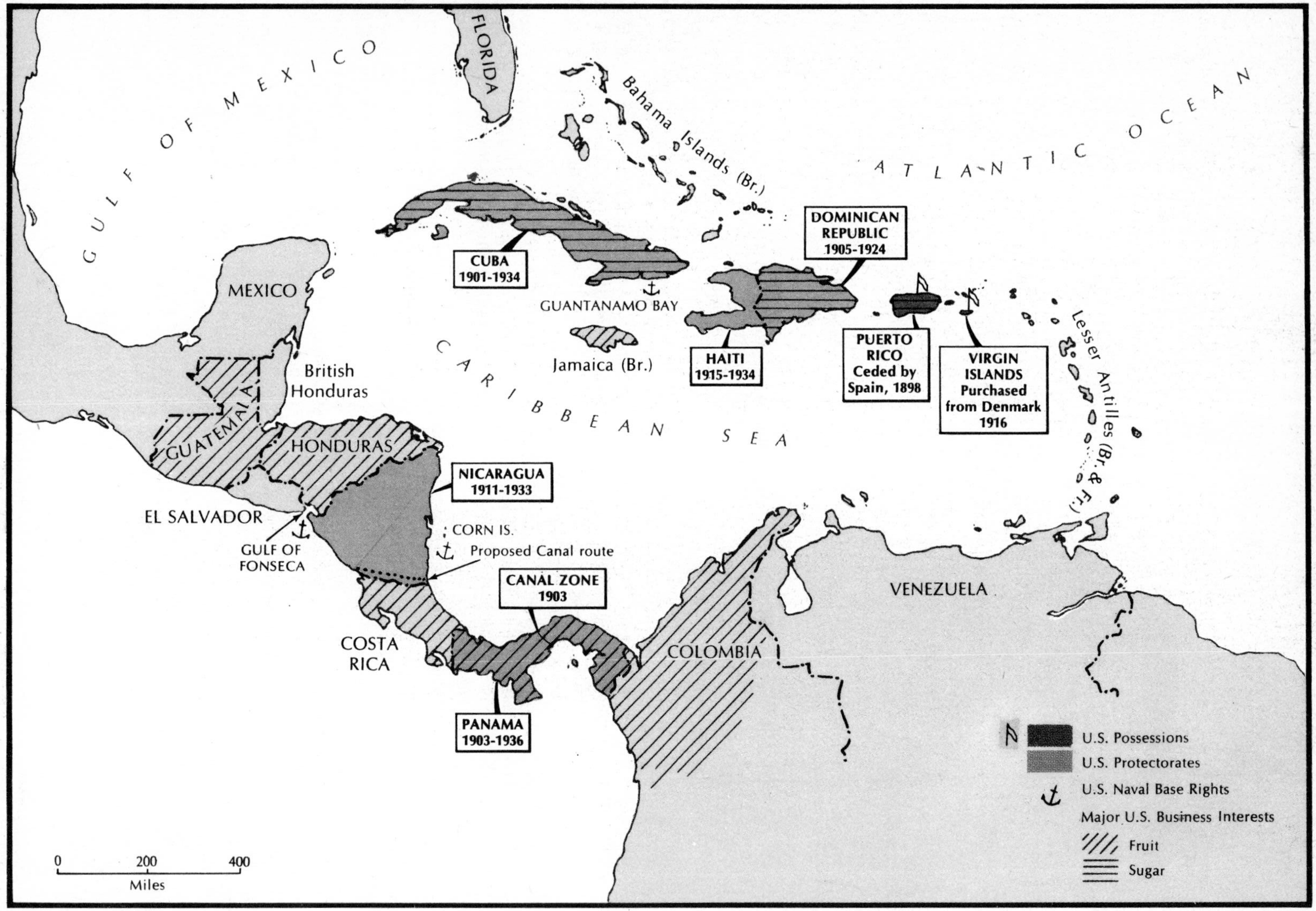
GULF OF MEXICO
FLORIDA
Bahama Islands (Br.)
ATLANTIC OCEAN
MEXICO
CUBA
1901-1934
GUANTANAMO BAY
DOMINICAN REPUBLIC
1905-1924
HAITI
1915-1934
PUERTO RICO
Ceded by Spain, 1898
VIRGIN ISLANDS
Purchased from Denmark
1916
Lesser Antilles (Br. & Fr.)
Jamaica (Br.)
CARIBBEAN SEA
British Honduras
GUATEMALA
HONDURAS
EL SALVADOR
GULF OF FONSECA
NICARAGUA
1911-1933
CORN IS.
Proposed Canal route
CANAL ZONE
1903
COSTA RICA
PANAMA
1903-1936
COLOMBIA
VENEZUELA
U.S. Possessions
U.S. Protectorates
U.S. Naval Base Rights
Major U.S. Business Interests
Fruit
Sugar
0
200
400
Miles

United States in the Caribbean

ucts. To promote a Pan-American customs union, a series of uniform tariffs which would give reciprocal preference to American products or goods in all American countries, he called a Pan-American Conference in 1881. President Garfield's death was followed by a change in the State Department, and President Arthur revoked the invitations. Eight years later President Harrison placed Blaine once more in a position to advance his cherished project. In October 1889 the first International American Conference, representing eighteen countries, convened at Washington to consider Blaine's proposals for a Pan-American customs union and the arbitration of international disputes. To the Latin Americans both seemed like the invitation of the spider to the fly, and were politely rejected. But the Conference resulted in the creation of a Commercial Union of American States, renamed the Pan American Union in 1910, which served as a clearinghouse for the dissemination of scientific, technical, and economic information and set a precedent for future inter-hemispheric meetings.

Although the Pan-American Conference did not accept arbitration as a formal policy, American statesmen served as arbiters of several boundary disputes in Latin America, and the principle of arbitration won a notable victory in the Bering Sea controversy. Eager to prevent extermination of the seal in Alaskan waters, mainly by Canadian sealers, Blaine proclaimed American jurisdiction over the Bering Sea, and excluded all Canadian fishing vessels from these waters. The controversy took an ugly turn, but in 1891 the United States and Great Britain had the good sense to resort to arbitration. The tribunal decided all points of law adversely to the United States, but implicitly admitted the wisdom of Blaine's efforts by drawing up regulations to save the seal.

Far more dangerous was a boundary dispute in South America. British Guiana and Venezuela had long quarreled over their boundary line, a disagreement that suddenly took on new importance with the discovery of gold in the hinterlands of both countries. Both Britain and Venezuela advanced ambitious claims, but Venezuela's was especially extravagant; Lord Salisbury, refusing to submit the question to arbitration because, not unreasonably, he feared arbiters would split the difference, sent troops to the disputed area. Secretary of State Olney promptly dispatched a note which gave a definition of the Monroe Doctrine that alarmed Latin America, insulted Canada, and challenged England:

> Today the United States is practically sovereign on this continent, and its fiat is law upon the subjects to which it confines its interposition. . . . Distance and three thousand miles of intervening ocean make any permanent political union between a European and an American state unnatural and inexpedient.

Lord Salisbury allowed four months to go by before acknowledging this cheeky note—and rejecting it. On 17 December 1895 President Cleveland informed Congress of Salisbury's refusal, asked it to set up a commission to determine the proper boundary line, and added that any attempt by Britain to assert jurisdiction beyond that line should be resisted by every means in the nation's power. No facts of the controversy could justify these extreme claims and provocative language, but Olney and Cleveland had become disturbed by British encroachments in Latin America, including the seizure of Belize (British Honduras), and Congressmen had put Cleveland on the defensive by insisting that after having refused to take a strong line on Hawaii and Samoa he could not permit an Old World monarchy to discipline a New World republic.

Only the felt necessity for friendship with the United States induced the Salisbury government to let this challenge lie. The British navy's numerical strength over the American was at least five to one, but Britain, as Bayard wrote, 'has just now her hands very full in other quarters of the globe.' In early January 1896 came Jameson's raid in the Transvaal and Kaiser Wilhelm's congratulatory telegram to the Boer leader Kruger. The South African crisis reinforced Britain's determination to avoid war. After some secret diplomacy at London and Washington, Great Britain and Venezuela concluded a treaty submitting the boundary question to an arbitral tribunal, to be governed by the rule that 'adverse holding or prescription during a period of fifty years shall make a good title.' Thus Cleveland and Olney

Twisting the lion's tail. In this 1888 cartoon, which appeared in *Judge*, Cleveland, by his tariff policies, is depicted as a pawn of England, an allegation designed to appeal to both American nationalists and Irish-American Anglophobes. As the President kneels before John Bull, he is joined by Secretary of State Thomas Bayard, Speaker of the House John Carlisle, and Rep. Roger Q. Mills, sponsor of tariff reform legislation. Behind them George William Curtis, the patrician editor of *Harper's* magazine, surrenders American prosperity while 'Marse Henry' Watterson, editor of the Louisville *Courier-Journal*, strikes the colors. (*Library of Congress*)

secured their principle that the whole territory in dispute should be subject to arbitration, and Salisbury his, that the British title to *de facto* possessions should not be questioned. The tribunal, which included the Chief Justices of Great Britain and the United States, gave a unanimous decision in 1899, substantially along the line of the original British claim. So the Monroe Doctrine was vindicated, arbitration triumphed, and Anglo-American friendship was restored.

Manifest Destiny and Cuba Libre

In the eighteen-nineties, the spirit of 'manifest destiny,' long dormant, was once more abroad in the land. Captain A. T. Mahan, the naval philosopher of the new imperialism, demonstrated in his brilliant series on the history of sea power that not the meek, but those who possessed big navies, inherited the earth, and his teachings were heeded. The Reverend Josiah

Strong, author of the enormously popular tract, *Our Country*, asked rhetorically, 'Does it not look as if God were not only preparing in our Anglo-Saxon civilization the die with which to stamp the peoples of the earth, but as if he were massing behind that die the mighty power with which to press it?' The Washington *Post* stated on the eve of the Spanish War:

> We are face to face with a strange destiny. The taste of Empire is in the mouth of the people even as the taste of blood in the jungle. It means an Imperial policy, the Republic, renascent, taking her place with the armed nations.

In 1880 the U.S. Navy ranked twelfth in the world; by 1900, with 17 battleships and 6 armored cruisers, it was third.

The Cuban revolution of 1895 brought this latent imperialism to a head. From the days of Jefferson, Cuba had been regarded as properly within the American sphere of influence, and the possibility of ultimate acquisition was never out of the minds of American statesmen. Yet curiously enough, when the opportunity came, during the Ten Years' War of 1868–78, the United States was coy. That Ten Years' War was characterized by all the disorder, cruelty, and affronts to American interests and honor that later marked the course of the revolution of 1895. However, in the first instance the murder of the crew of the *Virginius* in 1873 did not create a demand for war, while the explosion of the *Maine* in 1898 was followed by a wave of war hysteria.

How did it happen that the destiny which necessitated American control of the Caribbean in the eighteen-nineties was not manifest in the eighteen-sixties? Americans of the eighteen-nineties had come to share with the British, Germans, and French a willingness to take up 'the white man's burden.' Editors of journals like the New York *World* and *Journal* found that circulation responded to atrocity stories. For three years, from 1895 to 1898, mongering of sensations went on until the country was brought to the point where it demanded intervention on behalf of 'humanity.' The economic stake of the United States in Cuba had increased enormously during these thirty years. As the American minister to Spain said, 'The sugar industry of Cuba is as vital to our people as are the wheat and cotton of India and Egypt to Great Britain.' Even more important than the $50 million invested in Cuban sugar and mining was trade with Cuba, which by 1893 had passed the $100 million mark, and the business and shipping interests dependent upon that trade. Finally, the United States had developed world interests which made it seem necessary to control the entire Caribbean. American interests in the Pacific enhanced the importance of an isthmian canal and made the islands that guarded the route to the canal strategically important, especially to provide harbors and coaling stations for a big navy.

These concerns would lead the United States in 1898 to fight a war to liberate Cuba, but by then the Cubans had already struggled three years for their own liberation. The fundamental cause of the revolution which broke out in 1895 was Spanish oppression; the immediate cause was the prostration of the sugar and tobacco industries which resulted from tariffs, both American and Spanish. The price of sugar which had been 8 cents per pound in 1884 fell to 2 cents in 1895. The consequent misery furnished the impetus for revolution. From the beginning the United States was inextricably involved in the revolution. When, within a fortnight of the outbreak of war, a Spanish gunboat fired upon an American vessel, an outburst of jingoism revealed the temper of the country. 'It is time,' said Senator Cullom, 'that some one woke up and realized the necessity of annexing some property.' In the face of a mounting demand for intervention, President Cleveland remained imperturbable. When Congress, in April 1896, passed a concurrent resolution recognizing the belligerency of the Cubans, Cleveland ignored it, and in the summer of 1896 he confessed that 'there seemed to be an epidemic of insanity in the country just at this time.' Yet by the end of that year even Cleveland's patience had been strained well-nigh to the breaking point by Spain's refusal to conciliate the rebels.

McKinley had been elected on a platform calling for Cuban independence, but at first he, too, moved with circumspection. 'You may be sure,' he confided to Carl Schurz, 'that there will be no

The sinking of the *Maine*, Havana harbor, 15 February 1898. This chromolithograph portrays vividly the violent explosion that took 260 lives and made a national catchphrase of 'Remember the *Maine*!' The small portraits are of Admiral Montgomery Sicard, commander of the North Atlantic Squadron, and Captain Charles Sigsbee, who survived the blast. (*Chicago Historical Society*)

jingo nonsense under my administration.' In September 1897 McKinley tendered the good offices of the United States to restore peace to Cuba, but even though a more liberal government had come to power in Spain, the American overture was rejected. Nevertheless, the Spanish government did inaugurate some long overdue reforms. General Weyler, who had earned the unenviable title of 'Butcher Weyler,' was recalled; the policy of herding Cubans into concentration camps, where many died of disease and mistreatment, was disavowed; all political rights enjoyed by peninsular Spaniards were extended to the Cubans; and a program looking to eventual home rule was inaugurated.

Home rule no longer satisfied the Cubans, who were increasingly confident that the United States would intervene. They would accept nothing but independence, the one demand Madrid felt it could not grant. Reforms which might have headed off the revolution had they been offered in 1895 had come too late, and the war of extermination went on. Yet the sincere desire of the Spanish government for peace did much to moderate the attitude of the American government if not of the American people. In his annual message of December 1897 McKinley repudiated the idea of intervention and urged that Spain 'be given a reasonable chance to realize her expectations and to prove the asserted efficacy of the new order of things to which she stands irrevocably committed.' But neutrality was not to the interest of the Cuban junta, and on 9 February 1898 the *Journal* printed a private letter to Washington from the Spanish minister, Enrique de Lôme, which had been stolen from the Havana post office. 'McKinley's message,' wrote the tactless minister, 'once more shows what McKinley is, weak and a bidder for the admiration of the crowd, besides being a would-be-politician who tries to leave a door open behind himself while keeping on good terms with the jingoes of his party.'

At this juncture the nation was horrified by the news that in the night of 15 February 1898 the battleship *Maine* had blown up in Havana harbor with the loss of 260 lives. 'Public opinion,' Captain Sigsbee wired, 'should be suspended until further report,' but when a naval court of inquiry reported that the cause of the disaster was an external explosion by a submarine mine, 'Remember the *Maine*!' went from lip to lip. Without a dissenting vote Congress rushed through a bill appropriating $50 million for national defense. McKinley continued to exercise restraint, but war fever was mounting. Redfield Proctor, a fair-minded Vermonter who had opposed war, gave the Senate on 17 March a vivid description of the horrors of the concentration camps he had seen in Cuba. Still Spain procrastinated. On 25 March McKinley sent Madrid what turned out to be his ultimatum: immediate armistice, final revocation of the concentration policy, American mediation between Spain and Cuba, and, ambiguously, independence for Cuba. Spain's formal reply was unsatisfactory, but Madrid, anxious to avoid war, moved toward peace with unusual celerity. Orders were given revoking the concentration policy and a desperate effort was made to persuade the Pope to request a suspension of hostilities—a request to which Spain could agree without loss of face. But McKinley's reply was non-committal. On 9 April the Spanish government accepted every demand but Cuban independence, and Woodford, the American minister at Madrid, thought, perhaps too optimistically, even that might be worked out. Hostilities were suspended, and Woodford cabled that if nothing were done to humiliate Spain further the Cuban question could be settled in accordance with American wishes. Any President with a backbone would have seized this opportunity for an honorable solution.

But by now McKinley's course was set. He had lost faith in Spain's ability to resolve the conflict. Nor did he have the courage to withstand public sentiment. Although Mark Hanna, much of big business, and the Republican Old Guard wanted peace, Congress, the press, and much of the country were clamoring for war. Theodore Roosevelt wrote in a private letter, 'The blood of the murdered men of the *Maine* calls not for indemnity but for the full measure of atonement, which can only come by driving the Spaniard from the New World.' By going to war, McKinley would silence such critics within his own party, and deny the Democrats the opportunity to campaign for Free Silver and Free Cuba. On 11 April the President, making only casual reference to the fact that Madrid had capitulated on almost every point at issue, sent Congress a message which could have only one consequence: war.

Exit Spain

Lightheartedly the United States entered upon a war that brought quick returns in glory, but new and heavy responsibilities that were to grow all through the next century. Although imperialistic in result, the war was not so in motive, as far as the vast majority were concerned. To the Joint Resolution of 20 April 1898, authorizing the use of armed forces to liberate Cuba, was added the self-denying Teller Amendment, declaring that 'The United States hereby dis-claims any disposition or intention to exercise sovereignty, jurisdiction or control over the said Island, except for the pacification thereof, and asserts its determination, when that is accomplished, to leave the government and control of the Island to its people.'

With what generous ardor the young men rushed to the colors to free Cuba, while the bands

Off to war. In Washington, D.C., the 1st Regiment D.C. volunteers depart for Camp Alger, May 1898. (*Library of Congress*)

crashed out the chords of Sousa's 'Stars and Stripes Forever!' And what a comfortable feeling of unity the country obtained at last, when William J. Bryan got himself commissioned Colonel and donned a uniform alongside the irrepressible T. R.; when Joe Wheeler, the gallant cavalry leader of the Confederacy, became a high commander of the United States Army in Cuba! To most Americans, the war arrayed hip-hip-hurrah democracy against all that was tyrannical, treacherous, and fetid in the Old World. And what heroes the war correspondents created—Lieutenant Rowan who delivered the 'message to Garcia,' Commodore Dewey ('You may fire when ready, Gridley'), Captain Philip of the *Texas* ('Don't cheer, boys, the poor fellows are dying'), and Teddy Roosevelt with his horseless Rough Riders!

Prince Bismarck is said to have observed, just before his death, that there was a special prov-

Frederic Remington, 'Captain Grimes's Battery Going Up El Poso Hill,' 1898. 'It was a fine sight to see the great horses straining under the lash as they whirled the guns up the hill,' wrote Teddy Roosevelt of this episode in the battle for San Juan Hill. But hardly had the Americans opened fire, he went on, when 'there was a peculiar whistling singing sound in the air, and immediately afterward the noise of something exploding over our heads.' Shrapnel from Spanish batteries wounded several of his regiment, grazed Teddy's wrist, and routed Remington, the noted Western illustrator who had been sketching Grimes's horses. Remington reported: 'It was thoroughly evident that the Spaniards had the range of everything in the country. Some gallant soldiers and some as daring correspondents as it is my pleasure to know did their legs proud there. The tall form of Major John Jacob Astor moved in my front in jack-rabbit bounds. Prussian, English, and Japanese correspondents, artists, all the news, and much high-class art and literature, were flushed, and went straddling up the hill.' (*New-York Historical Society*)

idence for drunkards, fools, and the United States of America. While Spain had almost 200,000 troops in Cuba before the war, the American regular army included less than 28,000 officers and men, scattered in small detachments from the Yukon to Key West. The American Commissary Department was disorganized, and soldiers complained that they were fed on 'embalmed beef.' Volunteers neglected even such principles of camp sanitation as were laid down in Deuteronomy, and for every one of the 286 men killed or mortally wounded in battle, 14 died of disease. Yet the little

U.S. expeditionary force was allowed to land on the beach at Daiquiri without opposition (20–25 June), and the Captain-General of Cuba, with six weeks' warning was able to concentrate only 1700 on the battlefields of Las Guasimas, El Caney, and San Juan, against 15,000 Americans.

It was the navy, however, that clinched the conquest of Cuba. On 19 May the Spanish admiral, Cervera, with four armored cruisers and three destroyers, slipped into the narrow land-locked harbor of Santiago Bay and was promptly bottled up by the American navy under Admiral Sampson and Commodore Schley. With the army closing in on Santiago, Cervera had no alternatives but surrender or escape. On 3 July the Spanish battlefleet sailed forth from Santiago Bay to death and destruction:

> Haste to do now what must be done anon
> Or some mad hope of selling triumph dear
> Drove the ships forth: soon was *Teresa* gone
> *Furór, Plutón, Vizcaya, Oquendo,* and *Colón.*[1]

Not since 1863 had there been such a Fourth of July as that Monday in 1898 when the news came through. Santiago surrendered on the 16th and except for a military promenade in Puerto Rico, which Mr. Dooley described as 'Gin'ral Miles' Gran' Picnic and Moonlight Excursion,' the war was over. Ten weeks' fighting and the United States had wrested an empire from Spain.

The most important event of the war had occurred not in the Caribbean but in the Far East. As soon as war was declared, Commodore Dewey, commander of the Asiatic Squadron, set out under full steam for the Philippines, and on the night of 30 April he entered Manila Bay, where a Spanish fleet was anchored. Gridley fired when ready; they all fired; and the Spanish fleet was utterly destroyed. But not until 13 August—one day after the signing of the peace protocol—did an American expeditionary force, with the support of Aguinaldo's Filipino army, take the city of Manila.

The collapse of her military and naval power forced Spain to sue for peace. McKinley dictated terms on 30 July—immediate evacuation and relinquishment of Cuba, cession of Puerto Rico and an island in the Ladrones (Guam, as it turned out), and American occupation of Manila pending final disposition of the Philippine Islands. Spain signed a preliminary peace to that effect on 12 August, sadly protesting, 'This demand strips us of the very last memory of a glorious past and expels us . . . from the Western Hemisphere, which became peopled and civilized through the proud deeds of our ancestors.' John Hay wrote his friend Theodore Roosevelt in a very different vein: 'It has been a splendid little war; begun with the highest motives, carried on with magnificent intelligence and spirit, favored by that fortune which loves the brave.'

The Fruits of Victory

In the formal peace negotiations which began at Paris on 1 October 1898, only the question of the disposition of the Philippines offered serious difficulties. If they had been contented under Spanish rule, there would have been no question of annexing them. However, an insurrection had just been partially suppressed when the Spanish War broke out, and Dewey had encouraged Emilio Aguinaldo, leader of the *insurrectos,* to return from exile after the battle of Manila Bay. Upon the fall of Manila the Filipino leader had organized the 'Visayan Republic' and made a bid for foreign recognition. The obvious thing to do was to turn the Philippines over to the Filipinos, as Cuba to the Cubans. But Dewey cabled that the 'republic' was only a faction, unable to keep order within its nominal sphere. Still, Aguinaldo represented government in the islands, and if the United States expected to retain the Philippines, it would first have to conquer them.

McKinley was in a quandary. In his message of December 1897 he had laid down with respect to Cuba the rule that 'forcible annexation . . . can not be thought of. That, by our code of morality, would be criminal aggression.' Did the same rule hold good for the Philippines? Already navalists were emphasizing the military importance of the islands and suggesting the danger should Germany or Japan annex them. Senator Beveridge

1. 'Spain in America' in *Poems* by George Santayana, Scribners, p. 118.

An expansive Uncle Sam. In this cartoon, which appeared in *Puck* in 1900, the anti-imperialist Carl Schurz offers anti-expansion elixir, as Joseph Pulitzer of the New York *World* and the reform Democrat Oswald Ottendorfer, proprietor of the German-language newspaper, the *New-Yorker Staats-Zeitung*, back him up, but Uncle Sam, having become accustomed to his portly shape, will have none of it. (*Library of Congress*)

was speaking hopefully of 'China's illimitable markets' and Whitelaw Reid wrote that the Philippines would 'convert the Pacific ocean into an American lake.'

Yet there were still several choices. The United States might simply guarantee the independence of the Philippines as it was to do in Cuba. It might take only the island of Luzon, leaving the rest of the archipelago to the Filipinos. It might take the Philippines in trust, as it were, with a promise of independence—the principle of the Bacon bill that was defeated only by the casting vote of the Vice-President in the Senate. Or it might annex all the Philippines.

McKinley hesitated long and prayerfully, but finally concluded to fulfill manifest destiny by taking them all. 'One night late it came to me this way,' he told his Methodist brethren, '(1) That we could not give them back to Spain—that would be cowardly and dishonorable; (2) that we could not turn them over to France or Germany, our commercial rivals in the Orient—that would be bad business and discreditable; (3) that we could not leave them to themselves—they were unfit for self-government—and they would soon have anarchy and misrule over there worse than Spain's was; and (4) that there was nothing left for us to do but take them all, and to educate the

Filipinos, and uplift and Christianize them.' So Spain was required to part with the islands for $20 million, and on 10 December 1898 the Treaty of Paris was signed and the United States became, officially, a world power.

However, the prospect of the annexation of an alien people without their consent aroused the fierce indignation of many Americans who thought it a monstrous perversion of the ideals which had inspired the crusade for Cuba. Old-fashioned Senators like Hoar of Massachusetts girded on their armor to fight for the principles of the Declaration of Independence, while others pointed out that the conquest, defense, and administration of the Philippines would cost far more than the islands would ever bring in return. Opponents warned that flouting the principles of democracy in the Philippines would impair the vitality of democracy at home. Some, though, who opposed the creation of an American empire did so out of dislike of incorporating other races and cultures in white American society. Tillman cried: 'Coming . . . as a Senator from . . . South Carolina, with 750,000 colored population and only 500,000 whites, I realize what you are doing, while you don't; and I would save this country from the injection in it of another race question.' Finally they argued that the Constitution did not permit the acquisition of extraterritorial possessions and the government of alien peoples without their consent. For two months the fate of the treaty hung in suspense. But on 6 February 1899 the necessary two-thirds majority for ratification was obtained, after what Lodge called 'the hardest fight I have ever known.'

McKinley, in 1897, had rejected a proposal to buy Cuba because he did not care to buy an insurrection; the United States now found that it had purchased, for $20 million, a first-class Filipino insurrection. The Filipinos, who had been good Catholics for over three centuries, did not wish to be 'uplifted and Christianized' by the Americans; but when, on 4 February 1899, Aguinaldo's troops disregarded the command of an American sentry to halt, the United States Army undertook to 'civilize them with a Krag.' Before the Philippine insurrection was stamped out it had cost the United States almost as many lives as the Spanish War, in hellish fighting between white soldiers and men of color. Colonel Frederick Funston boasted he would 'rawhide these bullet-headed Asians until they yell for mercy' so they would not 'get in the way of the bandwagon of Anglo-Saxon progress and decency.' The United States did in the Philippines precisely what it had condemned Spain for doing in Cuba. Soon stories of concentration camps and 'water-cures' began to trickle back to the United States, and public opinion became inflamed.

To the banner of anti-imperialism rallied people of the most diverse views. Republicans like Speaker Reed joined hands with Democrats such as Cleveland and Bryan; Samuel Gompers spoke for labor, and Andrew Carnegie paid the bills. Editors like E. L. Godkin of *The Nation*, college presidents like David Starr Jordan of Leland Stanford, philosophers like William James, clergymen like Henry Van Dyke, social workers like Jane Addams, all worked together for a common cause. Mark Twain, deeply embittered by the conquest of the Philippines, suggested that Old Glory should now have 'the white stripes painted black and the stars replaced by the skull and cross bones.' The most powerful indictment came from the young poet William Vaughn Moody in 'An Ode in Time of Hesitation':

Tempt not our weakness, our cupidity!
For save we let the island men go free,
Those baffled and dislaureled ghosts
Will curse us from the lamentable coasts
Where walk the frustrate dead . . .
O ye who lead,
Take heed!
Blindness we may forgive, but baseness we will smite.[2]

In 1900 the Democrats, determined to make imperialism the 'paramount' issue, once again named Bryan, who also got the nominations of the Silver Republicans and one wing of the Populists. Their platform warned: 'The Filipinos cannot . . . be citizens without endangering our civilization; they cannot be subjects without imperiling our form of government.' But Bryan had played such

2. William Vaughn Moody, *Selected Poems*, Houghton Mifflin, 1931.

Bryan campaign poster, 1900. This elaborate chromolithograph, by its reference to 'No Crown of Thorns' and 'No Cross of Gold,' joins the anti-trust and free silver emphases of the Commoner's 1896 campaign with the newer issue of 'No Imperialism.' (*Library of Congress*)

an ambiguous role in the treaty debate that he obscured the imperialism issue. Moreover, during the campaign he insisted that silver was still the nation's chief concern; as Tom Reed remarked, 'Bryan would rather be wrong than President.' The Republicans held all the trump cards and played them well. The end of the economic crisis that had begun in 1893 appeared to justify the claim that McKinley was the 'advance agent of prosperity.' McKinley's running mate, Colonel Theodore Roosevelt, stormed through the West crying, 'Don't lower the flag,' and even referred to Bryan as 'my opponent.' By sweeping all of the agricultural West, including the Middle Border, McKinley improved on his performance in 1896; Bryan won only the South and four silver states. Henceforth, for good or evil, America was a world power with an overseas empire.

The Open Door

Many Americans feared that the annexations of the year 1898 were only a beginning; that the United States was destined to become a great colonial power. Imperialism in the Roman sense did not, however, appeal to the American people. But if the United States had no more than a passing desire to acquire an overseas empire, the country had an avid interest in developing foreign markets not only in Latin America but in Asia, where the partition of China jeopardized American prospects. The Japanese victory in the War of 1894–95 had revealed to the world the weakness of China: to forestall the Japanese, the European powers hurried to obtain spheres of influence in China. 'The various powers,' said the Dowager Empress of China, 'cast upon us looks of tiger-like voracity, hustling each other in their endeavors to be the first to seize upon our inner-most territories.' Japan had already acquired Formosa (Taiwan) and established ascendancy in the 'Hermit Kingdom' of Korea; in 1897 and 1898 Russia took Port Arthur and the Liaotung Peninsula, which gave access to the interior of Manchuria; Germany seized Kiaochow in Shantung, France consoled herself with a lease to Kwangchow bay, adjoining Indo-China; Italy got Sanmun bay, south of the Yangtze; and England added to her holdings the port of Wei-hai-wei. Along with these leases went valuable railway concessions, which promised to give European powers all but complete control over China's internal trade.

The carving up of China appeared to threaten American trade and to nullify part of the value of the Philippines. Interested parties drafted a proposal urging all the major powers to accept the principle of trade equality in China, and to refrain from violations of Chinese territorial integrity. Hay accepted these proposals and incorporated some of them into his own 'open door' policy for China. In a circular note of 6 September 1899, Hay, while recognizing the existence of 'spheres of influence,' requested from each major European power a declaration that, in its respective sphere, it would maintain the Chinese customs tariff, and levy equal harbor dues and railway rates on the ships and merchandise of all nations. The powers made ambiguous replies, with Britain most favorable, Russia least, but Hay promptly announced the agreement of all the powers as 'final and definitive.'

The 'open door' policy originally aimed solely at safeguarding American commercial interests in China, but within less than a year it was given a new and far-reaching interpretation. The brazen exploitation of China by the great powers had created deep antipathy to foreigners, and in June 1900 a secret organization called the Boxers tried to expel the 'foreign devils.' Within a short time the Boxers had massacred some 300 foreigners, mostly missionaries and their families; others were driven into Peking, where they took refuge in the British legation. An expeditionary force to rescue the beleaguered Europeans was hurriedly organized; the United States contributed some 5000 soldiers. Concerned that the situation might deteriorate into general war, Hay bent his energies to localizing the conflict. On 3 July, in a circular note to all the powers, he tried to limit the objectives of the joint intervention:

> The policy of the government of the United States is to seek a solution which may bring about permanent safety and peace to China, preserve Chinese territorial and administrative entity, protect all rights guaranteed to friendly powers by treaty and international law, and safeguard for the world the principle of equal and impartial trade with all parts of the Chinese Empire.

These were not the objectives entertained in the chancelleries of Berlin, St. Petersburg, and Tokyo, but these powers, fearful of each other and of war, concurred. The danger of war subsided, and the Chinese government permitted the joint expedition to save the legations. Punishment, however, was visited upon the guilty Boxers, and China was saddled with an outrageous indemnity of $333 million. Of this some $24 million went to the United States; half of it was eventually returned to the Chinese government which established therewith a fund for sending Chinese students to American colleges.

Now the United States was committed to maintain not only an 'open door' to China but the political integrity of that decrepit empire. Yet what did the commitment mean? Only by alliance with some European power like England could the United States have enforced this policy, and at no time did the exigencies of American politics permit an open alliance. Americans rejoiced in the spectacle of the United States teaching a moral lesson to the wicked imperialists of the Old World, but as Secretary Hay said, 'the talk of the papers about our pre-eminent moral position giving us the authority to dictate to the world, is mere flap-doodle.' And when, in 1901, Japan made cautious inquiries about the American reaction to Russian encroachments in Manchuria, Hay assured them that the United States was not prepared 'to attempt singly, or in concert with other Powers, to enforce these views in the east by any demonstration which could present a character of hostility to any other Power.' In short the United States wanted an 'open door' but would not fight for it.

Yet we cannot dismiss the 'open door' policy quite this easily. It faithfully expressed America's sentimental interest in China; delayed for a time the attack on China from Japan; and probably enhanced American prestige in China and other parts of the globe. And, like the Monroe Doctrine, it came in time to be a hallowed principle: that America would have no part in imperialistic designs on China and would discourage such designs in others. It helped build up popular support for resistance against Japan's aggression in China, and this in turn exacerbated Japanese resentment toward the United States.

The American Colonial System

The annexation of extra-continental territory, already thickly populated by alien peoples, created new problems in government. The petty islands and guano rocks that had already been annexed had never raised, as Puerto Rico and the Philippines did, the embarrassing question of whether the Constitution followed the flag. Opinions of the Supreme Court in 1901 in the 'Insular Cases,' a muddle of split decisions, left the status of the new possessions very unclear, but eventually, as in the British Empire, a theory was evolved from practice. Insular possessions are of two categories: incorporated and unincorporated; and the question of what constitutes incorporation is revealed in congressional legislation. Alaska was held to be incorporated, but Puerto Rico was unincorporated, despite the fact that after 1917 the inhabitants of the island became citizens of the United States. Unincorporated territories are not foreign, however, and their exports are not controlled by American customs duties unless by special act of Congress. But Congress may, nevertheless, impose such duties as it sees fit. This meant, according to a dissenting opinion by Chief Justice Fuller, that

> if an organized and settled province of another sovereignty is acquired by the United States, Congress has the power to keep it like a disembodied shade, in an intermediate state of ambiguous existence for an indefinite period: and more than that, after it has been called from that limbo, commerce with it is absolutely subject to the will of Congress, irrespective of constitutional provisions.

Thus the country was able to eat its cake and have it; to indulge in territorial expansion and yet maintain a tariff wall against such insular commodities as sugar and tobacco which might compete with home-grown products.

The question of the civil and political rights of the inhabitants of these new possessions proved even more perplexing. Organic acts of Congress became the constitutions of the Philippines, Hawaii, and Puerto Rico, but to what extent was Congress bound, in enacting these laws, and the courts, in interpreting them, by the provisions of the United States Constitution? How far, in short, did the Constitution follow the flag? To this question the Court returned an ingenious answer. It distinguished between 'fundamental' rights and 'formal' or 'procedural' rights. Fundamental rights are extended to all who come under the sovereignty of the United States, but mere procedural rights, such as trial by jury, extend to the inhabitants of unincorporated territories only if Congress so chooses. Like eighteenth-century London, the government at Washington was reluctant to admit the existence of an empire. Despite the legitimization of this vast accretion, no colonial office was established or colonial secretary appointed, and the imperial administration was characterized by diversity and opportunism.

Cuba was not a colony, but until 1902 the island was ruled by the United States Army, with General Leonard Wood as military governor. This regime conducted a remarkable clean-up of Havana under the direction of Major William C. Gorgas which halved the average annual death rate. In 1900 came one of the worst yellow-fever epidemics in years. A commission of four army surgeons under Dr. Walter Reed investigated the cause. Working on the theory advanced by a Cuban physician, Dr. Carlos Finlay, they proved that the pest was transmitted by the stegomyia mosquito; and two of them, Dr. James Caroll and Dr. Jesse W. Lazear, proved it with their lives. Major Gorgas then declared war on the mosquito; and in 1901 there was not a single case of yellow fever in Havana. One of the greatest scourges of the tropics was at last under control.

By the Teller Amendment the United States had disclaimed any intention of exercising sovereignty over Cuba. On the conclusion of the war General Wood provided for the calling of a constitutional convention, which drafted a constitution modeled upon that of the United States. But the American government applied discreet pressure to induce the Cubans to add a series of provisions known collectively as the Platt Amendment. The Amendment gave the United States an ultimate veto over Cuba's diplomatic and fiscal relations with foreign powers, recognized the right of the United States to intervene to preserve Cuban independence and to protect life and property, and committed Cuba to sell or lease a naval base.

Under terms of the Platt Amendment the United States leased and built a naval base at Guantánamo, which was retained even after the Amendment itself was abrogated. The right of intervention was first exercised in 1906, at the request of Cuba. President Theodore Roosevelt[3] sent his Secretary of War, William Howard Taft, to take charge of the island. When peace and stability were restored, the United States withdrew, leaving the affairs of Cuba in sound condition. At the same time Roosevelt warned the islanders that 'if elections become a farce and if the insurrectionary habit becomes confirmed . . . it is absolutely out of the question that the Island remain independent; and the United States, which has assumed the sponsorship before the civilized world for Cuba's career as a nation, would again have to intervene.'

The Philippine Islands presented peculiar difficulties, especially since from the beginning it was supposed that American tenure was temporary. The Filipino Insurrection dragged on until 1902, but as early as 1900 military government gave way to a civil Philippine Commission under William Howard Taft, first Governor-General of the islands. The Commission, entrusted with executive, legislative, and judicial powers, was authorized to reconstruct the government of the islands from the bottom up. Enlarged by the addition of three Filipinos, the Commission was instructed to 'bear in mind that the government which they are establishing is designed . . . for the happiness, peace and prosperity of the people of the Philippine Islands, and the measures adopted should be made to conform to their customs, their habits, and even their prejudices' so far as was consistent with the principles of good government. The Organic Act of 1902 recognized the islands as unincorporated territory of the United States and the inhabitants as 'citizens of the Philippine Islands' entitled to the protection of the United States, and provided for the ultimate creation of a legislature.

The United States gave the Philippines as enlightened an administration as is possible in an imperial system which, no matter how well

3. Theodore Roosevelt's accession to the presidency in 1901 is discussed in the next chapter.

intentioned, is inevitably paternalistic and self-interested. Under American rule the Filipinos made remarkable advances in education, well-being, and self-government. Through Taft's diplomacy at Rome, the United States acquired title to vast areas of agricultural land from the religious orders, and sold them on easy terms in small holdings to the peasants. 'Uncle Sam' provided the islands with honest, intelligent, and sympathetic administrators such as Taft and W. Cameron Forbes; with schools, sanitation, good roads, a well-trained native constabulary, a representative assembly, and baseball. The number of pupils attending school rose from 5000 in 1898 to over a million in 1920. The infant death rate in Manila declined from 80 to 20 per thousand between 1904 and 1920; and smallpox and cholera were practically stamped out. Although the islanders defrayed the entire cost of civil administration, their per capita taxation in 1920 was only $2.50, and their per capita debt, $1.81. But American economic policy left the islands at the mercy of the U.S. market, and as late as 1946 Congress required the Filipinos to grant special privileges to American businessmen. From the outset the islands were an American hostage to Japan, and the Filipinos sensed that some day their country might have the unhappy fate of serving as a battleground for imperial powers.

The Big Stick

'There is an old adage that says, "speak softly and carry a big stick."' This familiar quotation, from one of Theodore Roosevelt's earlier speeches, provided cartoonists with a vivid image to depict the President's aggressive foreign policy. Yet, paradoxically, it was Roosevelt who gave the Hague Tribunal its first case (a dispute with Mexico), who instructed his delegation at the second Hague Conference to work for the restriction of naval armaments, who was responsible for the return of the Boxer indemnity, who smoothed over a dangerous controversy with Japan, participated in the Algeciras Conference, and won the Nobel peace prize for successful mediation between Russia and Japan.

Roosevelt inherited from McKinley a Secretary of State, John Hay, whose experience as ambassador in London made him eager to meet halfway the new British policy of friendship. There was, in fact, an Anglo-American understanding during the entire progressive era. Downing Street readily conceded to Washington a free hand in the New World; and in return the State Department refrained from any act or expression that would unfavorably affect British interests, and supported British diplomacy in the Far East. The entente, if we may so call it, was consummated by the appointment of the author of *The American Commonwealth*, James Bryce, to the Washington embassy in 1907.

A first fruit of this understanding was the Panama Canal. The 1898 voyage of the U.S.S. *Oregon*, steaming at full speed round the Horn to be in time for the big fight, touched the popular imagination; and new island possessions in the Caribbean and the Pacific made an interoceanic canal appear vital. The Clayton-Bulwer Treaty of 1850 stood in the way of its realization, but not the government of Lord Salisbury. The Hay-Pauncefote Treaty of 1901 abrogated the earlier agreement, permitted the United States to construct a canal and control it, and provided that the canal would be open to all nations on equal terms.

The project for an isthmian canal had captivated the United States since Polk's administration. In 1876 French interests purchased from Colombia the right to build a canal across Panama, but De Lesseps, engineer of the Suez canal, failed to cut a canal through the mountains and jungles of Panama. When his company was forced into bankruptcy, a new organization was set up for the sole purpose of selling the dubious assets of the old to the United States.

With the quickening of interest in the canal project Congress became a battleground of rival groups: the Panama Canal Company, which wished to sell its concession on the Isthmus, and an American syndicate which had purchased a concession from the Republic of Nicaragua. McKinley appointed a commission to investigate the merits of the rival routes and the commission, finding that the Panama Company wanted $109 million for its concession, reported in favor of the Nicaraguan route, which had the added advantage of sea-level rather than lock construction. The

Panama Company countered by reducing its price to a mere $40 million and by engaging the services of a prominent New York lobbyist, William Nelson Cromwell, who tactfully contributed $60,000 to the Republican campaign fund and enlisted the powerful support of Senator Hanna. Heaven itself came to the aid of the Panama Company; in May 1902, while Congress was considering the rival routes, Mont Pelée in Martinique erupted with a loss of 30,000 lives. Mount Monotombo in Nicaragua followed suit, and when the Nicaraguan government denied that an active volcano existed in that republic, the Panama lobbyists triumphantly presented each Senator with a Nicaraguan postage stamp featuring a volcano in full action. Under these genial auspices Congress on 28 June 1902 passed the Spooner Act authorizing the President to acquire the French concession for $40 million if Colombia would cede a strip of land across the Isthmus of Panama 'within a reasonable time' and upon reasonable terms; if not, the President was to open negotiations with Nicaragua. On 22 January 1903 Secretary Hay induced the Colombian chargé at Washington to sign a treaty granting the United States a hundred-year lease of a ten-mile wide canal zone, for the lump sum of $10 million and an annual rental of $250,000.

The Colombian government procrastinated about ratifying the treaty in spite of a truculent warning from Hay that something dreadful would happen in case of amendment or rejection. Roosevelt was outraged. 'I do not think the Bogotá lot of obstructionists should be allowed permanently to bar one of the future highways of civilization,' he exclaimed to Hay. Neither did Cromwell nor a revolutionary Panama junta, dominated by Philippe Bunau-Varilla, a former agent for the French canal company. In July 1903 at New York an informal meeting of Panama businessmen, agents of the Panama Company, and United States army officers agreed on a way out: the secession of Panama from the Republic of Colombia. Without making any promise or receiving any of the plotters, Roosevelt and Hay let their intentions become so notorious that Bunau-Varilla advised the junta to proceed in perfect assurance of American assistance.

The revolution came off according to schedule. The Governor of Panama consented to being arrested, the Colombian admiral on station was bribed to steam away, and United States warships prevented troops from being landed by the Colombian government to restore authority. Three hundred section hands from the Panama Railroad and the fire brigade of the city of Panama formed the nucleus of a revolutionary army commanded by General Huertas, former commander in chief of Colombian troops. On 4 November a Declaration of Independence was read in the Plaza, and General Huertas addressed his soldiers. 'The world,' he said, 'is astounded at our heroism. President Roosevelt has made good.' Two days later Secretary Hay recognized the Republic of Panama, which by cable appointed Bunau-Varilla its plenipotentiary at Washington. With him, twelve days later, Hay concluded a treaty by which the Canal Zone was leased in perpetuity to the United States. As Roosevelt afterwards declared, 'I took Panama.' Colombia was hit by the big stick, but all Latin America trembled. Subsequently, in 1921, the United States paid $25 million to hush Colombia; it would have been better to have paid the sum eighteen years earlier.

Open to commercial traffic in August 1914, and formally completed six years later, the Panama Canal was a triumph of American engineering. No less remarkable was the sanitary work of Colonel Gorgas, which gave one of the world's worst pestholes a lower death rate than any American city, while Colonel George Goethals converted the spot described by Froude as 'a hideous dung-heap of moral and physical abomination' into a community of healthy workers.

Roosevelt's intervention in Santo Domingo produced the 'Roosevelt corollary' to the Monroe Doctrine. The financial affairs of that republic were in a desperate state, and in 1904 the government appealed to Roosevelt 'to establish some kind of protectorate' over the island and save it from its European creditors. Roosevelt had no desire to get involved in the affairs of the Republic—'about the same desire,' he said, 'as a gorged boa constrictor might have to swallow a porcupine wrong-end-to'—but he agreed that something had to be done to avoid anarchy and

'The Conquerors: Culebra Cut, Panama Canal.' To link the two oceans, American engineers had to create artificial lakes by damming two rivers and then connect them by wedging out an eight-mile gorge (Culebra Cut) through the Continental Divide. Despite the frustration of slides into the Cut, the Panama Canal was nearly finished when Jonas Lie (1880–1940) painted this picture in 1913. A series of paintings of the Canal by the Norwegian-born artist was presented to the U.S. Military Academy at West Point as a memorial to General Goethals. (*Metropolitan Museum of Art, George A. Hearn Fund, 1914*)

European intervention. He set forth his views in an open letter to Elihu Root: 'If a nation shows that it knows how to act with decency in industrial and political matters, if it keeps order and pays its obligations, then it need fear no interference from the United States. Brutal wrongdoing, or an impotence which results in a general loosening of the ties of civilizing society may finally require intervention by some civilized nation; and in the Western Hemisphere the United States cannot ignore this duty.' In February 1905 he signed a protocol with the Dominican Republic placing an American receiver in charge of its customs, and arranging that 55 per cent of customs receipts should be applied to the discharge of debts and 45 per cent to current expenses. The Senate refused to ratify the protocol, but Roosevelt went ahead anyway, and in 1907 the Senate came around. In little more than two years Santo Domingo was transformed from a bankrupt island to a prosperous and peaceful country, with revenues more than sufficient to discharge its debts and pay its expenses. But a dangerous precedent had been established, and within a decade the United States was deeply involved in the affairs of other Latin American nations. So burdensome did this responsibility become that a quarter-century later the Department of State officially repudiated the 'Roosevelt corollary.' But in the 1960's the United States was still meddling in Dominican affairs.

Elsewhere in the Caribbean Roosevelt moved with more restraint. In 1902 a crisis arose over the question of international intervention to collect Venezuelan debts. Great Britain, Germany, and Italy established a blockade to force the dictator, General Castro, to come to terms. Castro appealed to Roosevelt to arbitrate the claims, but inasmuch as no American rights were involved, Roosevelt properly refused. Yet he deprecated the use of force to collect debts, and looked askance at the potential threat to the Monroe Doctrine. A crisis was avoided when Germany, breaking away from the lead of Great Britain, agreed to submit her claims to arbitration. The Hague Tribunal settled the dispute satisfactorily, scaling down the demands and accepting the doctrine of the Argentinian jurist Luis Drago which denied the propriety of coercion for the collection of claims.

For the first time the United States had a President the rulers of Europe looked upon as one of themselves. In the Russo-Japanese War, the President, at the suggestion of the Japanese and the German Emperors, negotiated directly with premiers and crowned heads. He brought the two belligerents together and broke the deadlock, from which the Treaty of Portsmouth emerged. Roosevelt preserved for the time being the integrity of China, but the Treaty of Portsmouth merely substituted Japan for Russia in Manchuria and embittered the Japanese, although Roosevelt's action had been dictated by friendship for Japan.

By the conclusion of the Treaty of Portsmouth, Roosevelt established for his country a right that she did not at that time want—to be consulted in world politics. Again, in the Moroccan crisis of 1905–6, he quietly intervened to preserve peace with justice. French policy of hegemony in Morocco threatened a war with Germany that might easily have become a world conflagration. At the suggestion of the German Emperor, Roosevelt urged France to consent to a conference on the North African question, and the American representative, Henry White, was in large part responsible for the Algeciras Convention which, whatever its inadequacies, did keep peace for several years. The Senate ratified the Convention, but with the qualifying amendment that ratification did not involve any departure 'from the traditional American foreign policy which forbids participation by the United States in the settlement of political questions which are entirely European in their scope.'

27

The Progressive Era

*

1890–1916

The Promise of American Life

At the turn of the century, Americans could look back over three generations of unparalleled progress. The nation had advanced, in Jefferson's prophetic words, to 'destinies beyond the reach of mortal eye.' The continent was subdued, the frontier gone, and already Americans were reaching out for new worlds to conquer. The institution of slavery, which had threatened to destroy not only the Union but democracy, had been itself destroyed. The ideal of free public education had been substantially realized; the ideal of a free press maintained; the ideal of religious freedom cherished. Population had increased from 5 to 76 million, and in the half-century from 1850 to 1900 national wealth had grown from $7 to $88 billion. When, in 1888, James Bryce finished his survey of *The American Commonwealth,* he concluded that life was better for the common man in America than elsewhere on the globe.

Yet thoughtful Americans did not look with complacency upon their institutions. The continent had been conquered, but the conquest had been attended by reckless abuse of soil, forest, and water. The greatest of manufacturing nations, the United States permitted the exploitation of women and children and neglected the aged, the incompetent, and the infirm; cyclical depressions plunged millions into want. Wealth was gravitating rapidly into the hands of a few, and the power of wealth threatened the integrity of the Republic. In the great cities the slums grew apace. The Civil War had ended slavery but the degradation of the Negro was a blot on American civilization. Corruption poisoned the body politic. Against these crowding evils there arose a full-throated protest which demanded extension of the power of government over industry, finance, transportation, agriculture, labor, and even morals, a protest which gave to these times the name, 'the progressive era.'

The first of the many problems reformers faced on the threshold of the new century was the ethical confusion which resulted from attempting to apply the moral code of an individualistic, agrarian society to a highly industrialized and integrated social order. In a simple village society, personal and social morals were much the same, and the harm that a bad man could do was pretty well limited to crimes directly inflicted on other individuals. But in a complex industrial society personal crimes and social sins were very different. Society could be hurt in a thousand new ways, many of them not recognized by the Ten Commandments or the law codes. Those guilty of the new sins against society were often upright and well-intentioned gentlemen. The impersonality of 'social sin,' the diffusion of responsibility through the use of the corporate device, required reformers to formulate a new social ethics and to educate the people to that new code, and much of the work of the 'muckrakers' was directed toward this end. They also had to devise new administrative machinery for discovering the consequences of industrial malpractices and new legal machinery for fixing responsibility, and the effort to do this can be read in the struggle over trust, factory, pure food, and similar legislation.

A second problem—the rise of big business, the growth of trusts and monopolies—greatly concerned reformers because so many difficulties flowed from the new industrial order—unemployment, exploitation of workers, the use of natural resources for corporate aggrandizement. Political reformers learned that to cleanse politics it was necessary to regulate the business interests that controlled politics; social reformers found that to eliminate child labor or the sweatshop or the slums it was essential to curb the industrial interests that profited from these evils. Henry Demarest Lloyd concluded his analysis of *Wealth Against Commonwealth* with the observation: 'The word of the day is that we are about to civilize industry.'

No less serious was the problem of the maldistribution of wealth. Benjamin Franklin had found 'a general happy mediocrity.'

> There are few great proprietors of the soil [he wrote] and few tenants; most people cultivate their own lands, or follow some handicraft or merchandise; very few are rich enough to live idly upon their rents or incomes or to pay the high prices given in Europe for Paintings, Statues, Architecture, and other works of Art, that are more curious than useful.

The first half of the nineteenth century saw the rise of a few large fortunes, most of them either in land or in shipping, but when Moses Yale Beach of the New York *Sun* published in the 1850's a pamphlet on 'Wealthy Men of New York,' he discovered only nineteen who could be called millionaires, and the richest, John Jacob Astor, boasted a fortune of only $6 million. The industrial revolution changed all this. Men discovered a hundred new ways of making money, and many of the new fortunes carried with them no sense of responsibility. In 1896 Charles B. Spahr concluded that 1 per cent of the population owned over half the total national wealth, and that 12 per cent owned almost nine-tenths. When in 1892 the New York *Tribune* compiled figures on the millionaires, it discovered that almost 1000 had earned their fortunes in 'merchandising and investment,' over 600 in manufactures, over 300 in banking and brokerage, over 200 in transportation. The *Tribune* counted 178 millionaires in the lumber industry, 113 in coal and lead mining, 73 in gold and silver mining, and 72 in oil.

Another problem which challenged the progressives was the rise of the city. By 1890 nine of every ten people in Rhode Island clustered in towns, and Massachusetts had a larger proportion of people in towns of 10,000 than any nation in Europe. One district of New York's Eleventh Ward, with a density of 986 per acre, was probably the most crowded spot on earth; even the notorious Koombarwara district of Bombay had but 760 persons per acre. In the twenty years from 1880 to 1900 the population of New York City increased from a little less than two to almost three and a half millions; Chicago grew from half a million to a million and a half, to become the second city in the nation; such cities as Detroit, Cleveland, Buffalo, Milwaukee, Indianapolis, Columbus, Toledo, Omaha, and Atlanta more than doubled. In 1880 there were 19 cities with a population of 100,000 or more; by 1910, there were 50. Those who came to the great cities, either from the farms or from foreign lands, had to tear up their roots, and the process of transplantation was often painful.

The rapid and unregulated growth of cities created perplexing questions. How should the teeming thousands be housed? What provision could be made to guard against the diseases and epidemics that resulted from filth, congestion, and poverty? What measures should be adopted to control crime and vice; what measures to prevent the recurrence of fires such as those which devastated Chicago in 1871 and Boston in 1872? Could the cities build enough schools for their children and find room between the crowded streets for playgrounds? The burden of finding answers for these questions devolved upon the city governments, and in no field was the progressive movement more vigorous than in municipal reform, where it borrowed liberally from English and German experience. The cities were the experimental laboratories in which many of the new progressive ideas were tested.

Working within the framework of municipal, state, or federal government, reformers frequently confronted a further problem—the prevalence of corruption. Although not unique to America, corruption flourished more shamelessly in the United States than in other democratic nations. This resulted in part from America's tradition of lawlessness; in part from the unstable character of social life, especially migration from country to city, and from Old World to the New; in part from the absence of a 'patriciate'—a class with the leisure and skill for public service. Fundamentally there was a deep-rooted belief, inherited from the Jacksonian period, that any honest man could fill any office, and the fear of a permanent bureaucracy, which kept the expert out of politics. Thus incompetents brought the prestige of office so low that 'gentlemen' did not go into politics.

Too often, the fight against corruption yielded disappointing results. After the reformers had won a victory over the local 'ring' or the state 'boss,' the public lost interest in the housecleaning that followed, and permitted corrupt groups to regain lost ground. The exposure of the 'Shame of the Cities' or of dishonesty in state politics loomed large at the time, but was actually of little importance. Far more significant was the effort of progressives to devise new techniques and administrative agencies to ensure better government.

Finally, there was the race question. Since the Civil War the position of the freedman had steadily worsened. The vast majority of Southern blacks were every year more deeply sunk in the tenancy-mortgage morass, and as late as 1900 only some 8000 Negro boys and girls attended high schools in the entire South. Political and civil rights presumably guaranteed by the Fourteenth and Fifteenth Amendments were eroded. There had been little separation of the races in public facilities in the 70's and 80's, but after *Plessy* v. *Ferguson* in 1896 'Jim Crow' became almost universal. With the rise to power of the classes represented by men like Vardaman of Mississippi, racial violence became the order of the day: in the fifteen years after 1885 almost 2500 blacks were lynched. In the North, blacks were herded into ghettos, segregated in most public places, fobbed off with inferior schooling, cold-shouldered by labor unions, and consigned to the most menial and ill-paid jobs.

The Era of Muckrakers

In 1906 President Roosevelt applied to those engaged in uncovering corruption in American society the epithet 'muckrakers':

> In Bunyan's *Pilgrim's Progress,* you may recall the description of the Man with the Muck-rake, the man who could look no way but downward with the muck-rake in his hands; who was offered the celestial crown for his muck-rake, but would neither look up nor regard the crown he was offered, but continued to rake the filth of the floor.

Like many other epithets—Puritan, Quaker, Democrat—the term became in time a title of approbation. For the muckrakers exposed iniquities and stirred public opinion to the point where it was willing to support men like Roosevelt and Wilson in their reform programs.

Actually the literature of protest began some two decades earlier, the work of philosophers, and social scientists, such as Lester Ward, Thorstein Veblen, Henry George, and Edward Bellamy.[1] George's *Progress and Poverty,* published in 1879, resulted from his effort to resolve the paradox of progress and poverty through a 'formula so broad as to admit of no exceptions.' The

1. Ward and Veblen are discussed in the chapter entitled 'The American Mind.'

An escaped convict is treed and captured. (*Department of Archives and Manuscripts, Louisiana State University, Baton Rouge*)

formula which he found was the Single Tax—a tax which would wipe out unearned increment on land, ensure equal access to the land and its resources, and thus destroy monopoly, eliminate speculation, and restore equality. George's diagnosis of the causes of poverty and inequality was more profound than his single-tax cure, and a whole generation of progressives confessed their indebtedness to this 'Bayard of the Poor'—men like Hamlin Garland, Tom Johnson, Clarence Darrow, and Brand Whitlock in the United States, Sidney Webb, H. G. Wells, and Bernard Shaw in England, Tolstoy in Russia, and Sun Yat-sen in China. Nor was George's influence confined to the intellectuals. Over two million copies of his book were sold in America alone, and on the dusty plains of Kansas, in the slums of Liverpool and of Moscow, on the banks of the Ganges and of the Yangtze, poor men painfully spelled out its message. While *Progress and Poverty* envisioned a single action by the State that would liberate the forces of individual enterprise, the utopia of Edward Bellamy's *Looking Backward, 2000–1887* was a co-operative industrial society, where not only profit but even money was eliminated. The book enjoyed an enormous popularity, and hundreds of Nationalist Clubs, dedicated to the nationalization of industries and natural resources, were established.

Though late nineteenth-century periodicals also published articles of exposure, historians usually date the start of muckraking with Lincoln Steffens's 'Tweed Days in St. Louis,' in the October 1902 issue of *McClure's,* for not until then did such writing captivate the nation. By January 1903, *McClure's* was publishing an installment in Ida Tarbell's series on Standard Oil, Ray Stannard Baker's indictment of labor violence, and Steffens's 'The Shame of Minneapolis.' 'Shame' suggests that muckraking was a kind of secular Great Awakening, for, with imagery borrowed from Protestant evangelism, the journalists sought to arouse the country to a consciousness of guilt. Muckraking could not have succeeded without a public eager to hear the worst. By the end of 1903, newsstands were covered with magazines featuring muckraking articles, and the demand had not begun to be sated. 'Time was,' Mr. Dooley remarked to his friend Hennessy, when the magazines 'was very ca'ming to the mind.' But no more:

> Now whin I pick me fav-rite magazine off th' flure, what do I find? Ivrything has gone wrong. . . . All th' pomes by th' lady authoresses that used to begin: 'Oh, moon, how fair!' now begin: 'Oh, Ogden Armour, how awful!' . . . Graft ivrywhere. 'Graft in th' Insurance Companies.' 'Graft in Congress,' 'Graft be an Old Grafter,' 'Graft in Its Relations to th' Higher Life,' be Dock Eliot. . . .

Exposure of malpractices by corporations and the wealthy was a characteristic form of muckraking. Ida Tarbell's free-lancing for *McClure's* resulted in her classic *History of the Standard Oil Company,* which analyzed the methods whereby Standard Oil had crushed competitors, seized natural resources, and purchased legislative favors. Within a few years appeared a whole cluster of books of this type: Charles Edward Russell's *Greatest Trust in the World,* an attack on the beef trust; Thomas Lawson's *Frenzied Finance,* an exposé of Amalgamated Copper by a Wall Street insider; Burton J. Hendrick's *Story of Life Insurance,* which did much to create public demand for regulation of that business; and Gustavus Myers's *History of the Great American Fortunes,* which concluded that many fortunes were based on fraud or favor. Works like Myers's and Russell's series, 'Where Did You Get It, Gentlemen?', by taking much of the respectability away from accumulated wealth aided the movement to redistribute income.

The muckrakers also leveled their guns at political corruption and the alliance between corporations and politics. In a notable series published as *Shame of the Cities,* Lincoln Steffens, greatest of the muckrakers, exposed 'Philadelphia: Corrupt and Contented'; 'Pittsburgh, a City Ashamed'; and 'The Shamelessness of St. Louis.' In Minneapolis, Steffens achieved one of the great coups in the history of reporting. He obtained the ledger in which graft collectors had entered their accounts and the names of the persons to whom money was paid, and photographed its pages. In *McClure's,* he told how, under a mayor who had been elected twice by the Republicans, twice by the Democrats, the chief of detectives, an ex-gambler, had invited criminals to Minneapolis, fired 107 honest policemen, and freed prisoners to collect revenues for the gang. Steffens's writings helped Joseph Folk win the governorship of Missouri and Robert La Follette to gain re-election as governor of Wisconsin. Steffens worked out a law of municipal government: privilege controlled politics. In Colorado, Judge Ben Lindsey found the same rule applicable to state politics, and in *The Beast* told with compelling fervor the story of corporation control of the Centennial State. Nor were national politics immune from the muckraker's rake; in 'The Treason of the Senate' the novelist David Graham Phillips called the roll of Senators he found loyal to their business masters but traitors to their constituents: Depew of New York, Aldrich of Rhode Island, and others of the same stamp.

For every volume by a muckraking journalist there was a companion volume of fiction. Theodore Dreiser's *The Financier* and *The Titan* made it easier to understand *Frenzied Finance*. Frank Norris's *The Octopus* complemented Bryan's attacks on the railroad monopolies, and Norris's picture of wheat speculation in *The Pit* explained much of the agrarian protest. Russell's exposure of the meat trust was not nearly as effective as Upton Sinclair's account of life in the stockyards, *The Jungle*—a book which contributed directly to the enactment of meat inspection legislation. David Graham Phillips's best novel, *Susan Lenox: Her Fall and Rise*, found many readers for an exposure of the white slave traffic. And the story of corruption in politics was never better told than in the American Winston Churchill's *Coniston* and *Mr. Crewe's Career*.

Humanitarian Reform

Inspired by the example of Toynbee Hall in London, social workers established settlement houses in the slums of the great cities. In 1886, Stanton Coit set up the first American settlement house in New York City, and by the turn of the century almost a hundred such settlements had been founded, including the Henry Street Settlement in New York, the South End House in Boston, and Hull House, established by Jane Addams in Chicago in 1887. Designed originally to end the estrangement between social classes, they became in time elaborate social service agencies and foci for social reforms. Hull House, with its day nursery, gymnasium, drama school, handicrafts shop, and many other activities, quickly became a laboratory for social work. Jane Addams and associates like Dr. Alice Hamilton spearheaded drives for regulation of the labor of women and children, the establishment of the first juvenile court, protection for immigrant girls, improved sanitary inspection, and better schools. The proposal for a federal Children's Bureau originated with Lillian Wald of Henry Street, and social workers also helped launch city surveys modeled on Charles Booth's study of London. Presidents listened to what these women had to say, and legislatures did their bidding. Hull House became a world institution, and Jane Addams more nearly a world figure than any other woman of her day.

Settlement workers early engaged in a 'battle with the slums,' especially with the malodorous tenement house—a huge, compact structure of five or six stories, with scores and often hundreds of rooms and apartments. The rooms were small, dingy, airless, and sunless; the halls long and dark; the sanitation shockingly primitive; and many of the tenements were fire traps. By 1890 over a million New Yorkers were packed into 32,000 tenements; some of these were decent apartment houses, but many were 'crazy old buildings, rear yards, dark, damp basements, leaking garrets, shops, outhouses, and stables converted into dwellings though scarcely fit to shelter brutes.' That year a Danish immigrant, Jacob Riis, published *How the Other Half Lives*, which depicted the horrors of tenement blocks like Blind Man's Alley, Murderers' Alley, Poverty Gap, Misery Row, and Penitentiary Row. Riis sketched vividly the lives of the poor in New York's East Side:

> Cherry Street. Be a little careful, please! The hall is dark and you might stumble over the children pitching pennies back there. Not that it would hurt them; kicks and cuffs are their daily diet. They have little else. Here where the hall turns and dives into utter darkness is a step, and another, another. A flight of stairs. You can *feel* your way, if you cannot see it. Close? Yes! What

Ferreting out evil. For the progressives, the phrase had more than metaphorical significance. This nattily dressed city employee demonstrating a rat-catching ferret is the personification of the middle-class urban reformer. (*Library of Congress*)

would you have? All the fresh air that ever enters these stairs comes from the hall-door that is forever slamming, and from the windows of dark bedrooms that in turn receive from the stairs their sole supply of the elements God meant to be free, but man deals out with such niggardly hand.

Theodore Roosevelt, after reading *How the Other Half Lives*, stopped by at Mulberry Street and left his card, saying: 'I have your book and I have come to help.'

The country responded to such accounts with an outburst of humanitarian activity of a sort that had not been seen since before the Civil War. The American people suddenly discovered the poverty in their midst, for in the United States each generation has to discover all over again, with innocent surprise, that we have poor among us. Others came to feel that if they did not reform the city, it would threaten their own safety. 'The city has become a serious menace to our civilization,' warned Josiah Strong. 'Not only does the proportion of the poor increase with the growth of the city, but their condition becomes more wretched. Dives and Lazarus are brought face to face.' Even when doing humane errands at considerable personal sacrifice, some reformers were awed by an apocalyptic vision of an uprising of the ignorant poor. Riis wrote of 'the sea of a mighty population, held in galling fetters, heav*[ing]* uneasily in the tenements.' Many of the reformers responded to such warnings by seeking to impose upon the immigrants in the slums the middle-class way of life; their interest in tenement house legislation represented less humanitarianism than an effort at social control.

Despite opposition from vested interests, public opinion rallied to the reformers. A tenement house commission appointed by Governor Theodore Roosevelt recommended a series of changes, and most of these were incorporated in the model tenement house law of 1901 which did away with the old 'dumbbell' tenements and ensured more decent housing for the poor. State after state followed the example of New York, and by 1910 most of the great cities had inaugurated housing reform. Yet though the worst conditions were eliminated, new slums constantly replaced the old.

This same period witnessed the climax of the movement for the organization of charity. Almost every large city in the country had a Charity Organization Society similar to that founded in New York in 1882, designed to introduce efficiency into the haphazard administration of charity by scores of private agencies. These societies maintained shelters for homeless men, undertook the care of dependent children, 'rescued' delinquent girls, provided legal aid to the poor, fought loan sharks, and attempted in scores of ways to alleviate the burden of poverty. Professional social work started with Mary Richmond of Baltimore, who trained young women prepared to make social service a career. In 1909 the Russell Sage Foundation established a clearing house for this work and inaugurated a series of far-reaching investigations into the causes of poverty, crime, and disease.

Social workers paid particular attention to children. John Spargo, echoing *The Bitter Cry of the Children*, told of little girls toiling 16 hours a day in factories and nine-year-old 'breaker boys' working ten hours a day picking slate out of moving coal. Jane Addams, who had created the first summer camp for poor children, wrote in *The Spirit of Youth and the City Streets* the best argument yet made for playgrounds and parks. By 1915 over 400 cities had community playgrounds. Baby clinics and day nurseries were established; free milk was distributed; Visiting Nurses' Associations gave medical care to children; and eventually medical and dental examination became routine at most public schools.

Juvenile delinquency was especially vexatious. At common law, children above seven were held capable of crime, and those above fourteen had the same responsibility as an adult; as late as 1894 these common law principles were incorporated into the penal code of New York. Children were tried by the same laws as were applied to adults and, when convicted, were jailed with adult offenders, and thus schooled in a career of crime. In 1899 Miss Addams persuaded Illinois to establish special courts for children, and soon the institution spread throughout the country. Most notable of those who labored for a more humane attitude toward the juvenile delinquent was Judge Ben Lindsey of the Denver Juvenile Court, whose judicial practices and writings commanded international attention.

Everywhere efforts were made to improve prison conditions, mitigate the penalties of the law, and humanize the administration of justice. Under the leadership of Frederick Wines, the Cincinnati Prison Conference of 1870 inaugurated a new era in penal and prison reform, and within a generation many of the recommendations of that conference had been incorporated into law. Altgeld had written a slashing attack on *Our Penal Machinery and Its Victims* as early as 1884; as Governor of Illinois he did much to reform that machinery and rescue its victims. It was reading Altgeld's book that started Clarence Darrow on his life-long career as champion of the underdog. The fundamental idea that 'the supreme aim of prison discipline is the reformation of criminals' was acknowledged in principle, though rarely in practice. Reformatories were established for juvenile delinquents; first offenders were separated from hardened criminals; the indeterminate sentence and the parole system were widely adopted; state prison farms were established; convict labor and the lease system were outlawed in some states at least; some of the most barbarous features of the penal codes were repealed; and several states abolished capital punishment.

The 'emancipation' of women had proved a mixed blessing; for many, emancipation from the drudgery of the home meant a change to the worse drudgery of the sweatshop. The shift from the country home to the city apartment and the declining size of the family circumscribed the domestic activities of women, but when they turned their energies and talents into business or the professions, they encountered discrimination. Moreover, in few states did married women enjoy the same property rights as men; marriage and divorce laws worked to their disadvantage; and they were denied participation in politics where they might better their position. Furthermore, strict codes imposed a double standard of morality. But during these years the women's rights movement achieved equality in the schools, improvement in legal status, reform of marriage and divorce laws, regulation of hours and conditions of female labor, prenatal care and maternity aid, and, in 1920, the Nineteenth Amendment granting woman suffrage.

Most importunate of all the crusades was that against 'Demon Rum,' a movement which dated to the early days of the Republic. By 1851 temperance forces had established prohibition in Maine and won minor victories in other states, but between 1860 and 1880 the liquor business increased almost sevenfold, and by the end of the century large cities with heavy Irish and German populations contained about one saloon for every 200 inhabitants. Old stock, Protestant middle-class Americans, especially in rural areas and small towns, waxed indignant at the mores of urban immigrants, who flouted such values as self-control and sobriety. The churches denounced drinking as a sin; women attacked the saloon as a menace to the home; reformers exposed the unholy alliance of the liquor business with crime and the connection between intemperance and poverty; businessmen discovered that drinking affected the efficiency of workingmen and increased the dangers of industrial accidents; while Southern whites insisted on denying liquor to the Negro. For many of the progressives, prohibition was as crucial a reform as social welfare legislation. As Andrew Sinclair has written, they looked forward to 'a world free from alcohol and, by that magic panacea, free also from want and crime and sin, a sort of millennial Kansas afloat on a nirvana of pure water.'

Prohibition was furthered by three well-organized agencies: the Women's Christian Temperance Union, founded in 1874 and long dominated by Frances Willard; the Anti-Saloon League, founded in 1895; and the Methodist Church. By the turn of the century these organizations had succeeded in drying up five states, all predominantly rural. In the first fifteen years of the new century prohibition advanced with rapid strides, and by the time the United States entered World War I over two-thirds of the states were dry, and almost three-fourths of the population lived under 'local option' dry laws. The large cities, however, continued to be wet and from them supplies of liquor flowed unimpeded into thirsty dry areas. During World War I, Congress, allegedly for reasons of economy and efficiency,

Woman's suffrage day. In St. Louis on 16 May 1911, a speaker in a stylish suit, shirtwaist and rakish bonnet addresses the predominantly male crowd. (*Missouri Historical Society*)

prohibited the wartime manufacture or sale of intoxicants. While this law was still in force Congress wrote prohibition into the Constitution in the form of the Eighteenth Amendment.

The achievements of the humanitarians were impressive, yet much that they did was only palliative, as the reformers themselves recognized. Josephine Shaw Lowell, founder of the New York Charity Organization Society, active in work for dependent children, for delinquent girls, and for the insane, decided finally to withdraw from much of this work. She explained:

> If the working people had all they ought to have, we should not have the paupers and the criminals. It is better to save them before they go under than to spend your life fishing them out when they're half drowned and taking care of them afterwards.

As a result of this more realistic attitude, progressives then turned from organized charity and humanitarianism to political and legislative action.

Progressivism in Politics

The progressives achieved their most notable results in state and municipal politics. State constitutions were thoroughly revised or liberalized by amendments, over 900 of which were adopted in the first two decades of the new century. South

'McSorley's Bar.' To the prohibitionists, the saloon was the epitome of evil, but to artists like John Sloan this males-only bar was a convivial gathering place for ale-drinkers. Sloan (1871–1951) was a disciple of Robert Henri, who in 1908 formed 'the Eight,' a group of painters of the urban scene dismissed by critics as the 'Ash-Can School.' (*Detroit Institute of Arts, Gift of the Founders Society*)

Dakota in 1898, Utah in 1900, and Oregon in 1902 adopted the initiative and referendum, and by the First World War over 20 states had provided for these devices. In 1908 Oregon committed itself to the recall, and within six years its example was followed by ten states, all but one west of the Mississippi. At first confined to executive officers, the recall was extended by Arizona to judges, and by Colorado to judicial decisions. Governor La Follette, who had been twice defeated for the governorship by a boss-ridden convention, persuaded Wisconsin to adopt the direct primary in 1903; within a decade two-thirds of the states had enacted direct primary and presidential preference laws. Yet the direct primary often proved disappointing, for professional politicians found ways to control the primaries; by 1912 one advocate of the plan confessed that 'some bosses are wondering why they feared the law, and some reformers why they favored it.' No such dissatisfaction followed adoption of the Australian or secret ballot, which soon became universal. More popular still was the demand for direct election of Senators. As early as 1899 Nevada formulated a method for circumventing the constitutional requirement of election by state legislatures, and by 1912 some thirty states had provided for the expression of popular opinion in the choice of Senators. The Seventeenth Amendment, ratified in 1913, was therefore rather a recognition of an accomplished fact than an innovation.

From New York to California reform governors gave their support to enlarging the scope of government control over business. Charles Evans Hughes, elected Governor of New York after exposing spectacular corruption in the great insurance companies, obtained the establishment of a public utilities commission. In Wisconsin Robert La Follette regulated public utilities, reorganized the tax system, established an industrial commission, and made the state university an effective instrument of the regeneration of the state. Hazen Pingree in Michigan, Albert Cummins in Iowa, and Hiram Johnson in California shattered railway domination over state politics. In the South, Charles B. Aycock changed North Carolina into the most progressive of Southern commonwealths, Charles A. Culberson brought Texas into the main current of the reform movement, and 'Alfalfa Bill' Murray made Oklahoma for a brief period an experimental laboratory of Bryan democracy.

The progressives also scored gains in municipal politics. Tom Johnson, a wealthy manufacturer who had come under the influence of Henry George, rescued Cleveland from the grip of the utilities and the domination of Mark Hanna and made it, for a time, the best governed city in the country. In Toledo, 'Golden Rule' Jones guided the city in accordance with his interpretation of the Golden Rule, and after his death Brand Whitlock carried on the work of reform—including municipal ownership of public utilities—in the same spirit and with even more acute understanding. Emil Seidel, Socialist mayor of Milwaukee, gave that city efficient and honest government, and in San Francisco, Fremont Older exposed the skulduggery of a political ring controlled by the president of the Union Pacific. Even New York, under mayors like Seth Low and John Purroy Mitchel, lapsed into respectability, only to repent and reinstate the Tammany Tiger.

The reformers also tried to find permanent solutions to the vexatious problems of city government. The commission plan grew out of the Galveston flood of 1900; adopted with modifications by Houston and Des Moines, it was soon widely copied. The council-manager plan resulted from a similar crisis—the Dayton flood of 1913. By 1940, some 332 cities had adopted the commission form, and 315 cities the council-manager.

Much of this progressive zeal was naïve, some of it was misguided. Fundamentally moralists, the reformers assumed that most of the failings of government could be ascribed to Bad Men—bosses, vested interests, 'malefactors of great wealth'—and assumed, too, that if only Men of Good Will would devote themselves to public service, all would be well. Progressivism had a touching faith, too, in mechanical contrivances; Wilson once said that the 'short ballot was the key to the whole problem of the restoration of popular government in this country.' Yet progressives like Jane Addams, Louis Brandeis, and Robert La Follette were as hard-headed as any of their successors. If their faith failed to move mountains, it did eliminate many of the obstacles in the way of effective popular government. Insofar as politics was more honest, society more enlightened, in 1914 than in 1890, much of the credit goes to the indefatigable progressives.

The Struggle for Negro Rights: Washington and Du Bois

The most conspicuous failure of the progressive movement was in race relations. Many Northern liberals had wearied of the Negro issue. Worse yet, Southern progressives themselves often exploited racial prejudice; men like Josephus Daniels of North Carolina, who on most matters went along with Bryan and La Follette, readily

Booker T. Washington (1856–1915). Born into slavery, he had gone to work in a salt furnace after the Civil War, gained a hard-earned education, and built Tuskegee Institute in Alabama into a college with one hundred buildings and a two-million-dollar endowment. Yet despite all of his accomplishments, when he dined at the White House with Theodore Roosevelt in 1901 (a year before this photograph was taken), the Southern press denounced this violation of racial taboos as 'a crime equal to treason.' 'Entertaining that nigger,' said Senator Tillman of South Carolina, would 'necessitate our killing a thousand niggers in the South before they will learn their place again.' (*Library of Congress*)

sacrificed the Negro to their political ambitions. Daniels stated, 'We abhor a northern policy of catering to Negroes politically just as we abhor a northern policy of social equality.'

Left to fend for themselves, blacks developed two conflicting approaches: one represented by Booker T. Washington of Tuskegee Institute in Alabama, the other by the Massachusetts-born W. E. B. Du Bois of Atlanta University. The issues these two towering figures raised, the programs they sponsored, have dominated black thought and thought about blacks. Born in slavery, raised in abject poverty, catching an education as best he could at the new Hampton Institute in Virginia, Booker T. Washington came to be the most distinguished leader of his race after Frederick Douglass. When *Up From Slavery* appeared in 1901, William Dean Howells called Washington 'a public man second to no other American in importance.' Persuaded that blacks must win economic independence before they could expect to command social or political equality, Washington opened the Tuskegee Normal and Industrial School for Negroes in 1881, with the object of teaching students habits of work, thrift, and good citizenship.

Over a period of almost forty years Washington counseled progress by evolution rather than by violence, temporary acquiescence in policies of segregation, and co-operation with the ruling white class. 'In all things that are purely social,' he said, in a speech of 1895, 'we can be as separate as the fingers, yet one as the hand in all things essential to mutual progress.' 'The wisest among my race,' he insisted, 'understand that the agitation of questions of social equality is the extremest folly.' To win his immediate objective of economic gains, Washington told blacks to shun politics and scolded them not to forget that they were to work with their hands. This philosophy of accommodation delighted the white community, relieved to hear a Negro leader consign his brethren to an inferior status. Washington won the confidence of Presidents, influenced newspaper editors, and persuaded Northern white philanthropists to pour money into Tuskegee and other projects that had his blessing. But at the same time that Washington was playing the public role of 'Uncle Tom,' he was acting in a very different fashion behind the scenes. He lobbied against discriminatory legislation and financed litigation against disfranchisement laws, and advised Presidents Roosevelt and Taft on patronage; at his suggestion, Negroes were named to such posts as collector of internal revenue in New York and assistant attorney general, appointments not to be matched or surpassed by a black until after World War II.

Despite his dedication Washington fought a losing battle, in part because his program was irrelevant to the urban black. He trained Negroes for jobs on the land and in handicrafts at a time when America was rapidly industrializing. He told the black man to stay in the rural South, but by 1910 Washington and New York each had more than 90,000 Negroes. In the city the Negro met discrimination from most unions, an ever-tightening cord of residential segregation, and a pattern of legitimized violence. The new century began with the lynching of more than 100 Negroes in its first year, and in 1909 a Memphis newspaper reported that no white man had been hanged in Shelby County since 1890, but noted, 'Since then we have had a hanging of negroes pretty much regularly every year.'

At the beginning of the century the young W. E. B. Du Bois, trained at Harvard and Berlin, challenged the Washingtonian program of compromise and concession. Negroes, said Du Bois, could never win economic security without the vote, or achieve self-respect if they acquiesced in a position of inferiority, or attain true equality if they preferred vocational to intellectual training. Du Bois argued in *Souls of Black Folk* that the Negro would be raised by the 'Talented Tenth' who had a liberal arts education. In 1905 he and his followers met at Niagara Falls, Canada, to inaugurate what came to be called the Niagara Movement. The Niagara platform, as elaborated at subsequent meetings, called for evenhanded enforcement of the laws, and Congressional action to ensure that the Fourteenth Amendment would be carried out 'to the letter.'

This movement made slow progress until white reformers who had previously backed Washington decided that more militant action was needed. Moved by an ugly race riot in Lincoln's town of

The Niagara Movement. In this photograph of black leaders silhouetted against a backdrop of Niagara Falls, W.E.B. Du Bois is second from the right in the second row. Du Bois (1868–1963) spoke for more militant blacks who challenged Booker T. Washington's leadership. Their meeting near Niagara Falls in 1905 helped lead to the founding of the NAACP. (*Schomburg Center for Research in Black Culture, New York Public Library*)

Springfield, Illinois, in 1908, William English Walling wrote in the *Independent:* 'Either the spirit of the abolitionists, of Lincoln and of Lovejoy, must be revived and we must come to treat the Negro on a plane of absolute political and social equality or Vardaman and Tillman will soon have transferred the Race War to the North. . . . Yet who realizes the seriousness of the situation and what large and powerful body of citizens is ready to come to their aid?' Stirred by Walling's challenge, a group of Northern whites sent out a call for a National Negro Conference in 1909; the call was written by the publisher of the New York *Evening Post,* Oswald Garrison Villard, the grandson of William Lloyd Garrison. To the conference came many of the Niagara Movement participants as well as such luminaries as Jane Addams, William Dean Howells, and John Dewey.

The conferees' plans for a permanent organization led to the creation of the National Association for the Advancement of Colored People with Moorfield Storey of Boston as president, Walling chairman of the executive committee, and Du Bois director of publicity and research. The strength of the Association lay in its college-educated Negro members. With Du Bois as editor, the NAACP organ, the *Crisis,* reached a circulation of 100,000 a month by 1918. Under the leadership of Arthur B. Spingarn, white and black lawyers carried out a successful strategy of litigation. In 1915, the Supreme Court invalidated the grandfather clauses in the Oklahoma and Maryland Constitutions, and in 1917 the Court ruled unconstitutional a Louisville ordinance imposing residential segregation.

Unlike Walling and Storey, most white progressives were either indifferent to race or shared in the prejudices of their day. Theodore Roosevelt's administration was marred by an ugly episode of discrimination against black troops, and in 1912, Roosevelt, who had outraged the South by inviting Booker T. Washington to dine at the White House, insisted that the Progressive party be a lily white organization in the South. Woodrow Wilson's administration, largely Southern, appointed whites to posts previously granted to blacks and imposed racial segregation on the national government. Not until the 1940's would civil rights for the Negro take a prominent place on the agenda of American liberalism.

Theodore Roosevelt and the Square Deal

In September 1901, President McKinley was murdered by an anarchist, and Theodore Roosevelt became President of the United States. Not yet forty-three, Roosevelt was the youngest by several years in the line of Presidents; but few have been better equipped to administer the office. He had already achieved prominence as a naturalist, a man of letters, a soldier, and a statesman. He had served as a member of the New York State Assembly and as Civil Service Commissioner, and in between had found time to write the four-volume *Winning of the West,* and to win a bit of it himself as a Dakota ranchman. In 1895 he had accepted the thankless post of Police Commissioner of New York City, a post which threw him into intimate contact with social reformers. Two years later McKinley appointed him Assistant Secretary of the Navy, but this office proved too confining for his ebullient energies and with the outbreak of the Spanish War he organized the Rough Riders and fought his way to glory at San Juan Hill. Elected Governor of New York in 1898 on his return from war, he had struck at corruption with such vigor that in self-defense Boss Platt and the machine politicians had boomed him for the vice-presidency. His accession to the presidency, regarded with dismay by conservatives,[2] inaugurated a new era in American politics.

People everywhere knew Teddy as a red-blooded, democratic American of enormous vitality. Henry Adams said: 'Roosevelt more than any other man living, showed the singular primitive quality that belongs to ultimate matter—the quality that medieval theology ascribed to God—he was pure act.' He could lasso a bucking steer, turn out an historical essay, hunt lions, run a political convention, play tennis, lead a regiment, and hypnotize an audience with equal facility; he could hold his own in the company of cowboys, ward politicians, Methodist clergymen, reporters, and diplomats. Like Bryan and Wilson, Roosevelt was a moralist. It was almost impossible for him to think of a political question except in moral terms. 'Theodore,' Tom Reed said to him, 'if there is one thing more than another for which I admire you, it is your original discovery of the ten commandments.' His morality was positive, but not

2. H. H. Kohlsaat tells of riding in the McKinley funeral train with Mark Hanna. 'He was in an intensely bitter state of mind. He damned Roosevelt and said, "I told William McKinley it was a mistake to nominate that wild man at Philadelphia. I asked him if he realized what would happen if he should die. Now look, that damned cowboy is President of the United States,"' *McKinley to Harding,* p. 101.

Theodore Roosevelt as Hamlet. So irresolute was the President on the tariff issue, which he thought a matter of 'expediency and not morality,' that in this caricature in *Puck*, entitled 'Tedlet's Soliloquy,' Joseph Keppler, Jr. portrays him as the melancholy Dane. Borrowing and modifying a line from Shakespeare's drama, Keppler has T. R. saying, as in Hamlet's soliloquy, 'Thus the Tariff does make cowards of us all.' Roosevelt professed to believe in tariff reform, but no time ever seemed right for it; before an election was perilous and after an election was no better. In the end he bequeathed the whole problem to his successor, who was not so agile at evasion. Keppler, whose father, the founder of *Puck*, was an even more noted cartoonist, sold the magazine in 1914, and from then until his death in 1956 devoted himself to the cause of the American Indian. (*Library of Congress*)

subtle; and he regarded those who differed with him as either scoundrels or fools.

Roosevelt believed that as President he had two important functions: to serve as moral leader and to enforce the national interest against special interests. The country, he thought, faced two great dangers: the mob, which might be whipped up by demagogues, and the plutocracy, which, by its excessive greed, incited the mob. He sought to strengthen the government as a mediating force, for he had, as he once said, a horror of extremes. He aimed to carry out a program that would be neither populistic nor representative of the men he called 'malefactors of great wealth.'

Roosevelt's commitment to change was always qualified by his distaste for most reformers. He demanded a 'square deal' for labor, but no one in the country was more vitriolic in denouncing men like Altgeld, Debs, and Bryan who tried to inaugurate the 'square deal.' He avoided dangerous issues such as tariff and banking reform; and even on those issues he did pursue, he was usually ready to compromise rather than risk a break with the Old Guard. His chief service to the progressive cause was to dramatize the movement and make it respectable. Yet Roosevelt's dramatics often distracted attention from the big tent to the side shows. After the seven years of tumult and shouting had passed, many reformers felt they had been fighting a sham battle and that the citadels of privilege were yet to be invested.

Roosevelt believed in executive leadership and gave an exhibition of it that recalled Andrew Jackson and anticipated his cousin Franklin. According to his conception of stewardship, 'it was not only his right but his duty to do anything that the needs of the Nation demanded, unless such action was forbidden by the Constitution or by the laws,' and he soon indicated his conviction that the needs of the nation were multifarious.

Yet he responded to the outcry for regulation of corporations with circumspection. He knew he had come to power not by choice of the people but 'by act of God'; Roosevelt had the common sense to see that the problem was complicated. However, he knew, too, that the country was ready for action. At Roosevelt's behest Congress in 1903 established a Department of Commerce and Labor and authorized a Bureau of Corporations to investigate interstate corporations. At first the new bureau was innocuous, but eventually it investigated the oil, packing, tobacco, steel, and other industries and furnished material for prosecution under the anti-trust laws.

More dramatic was Roosevelt's decision to re-invigorate the Sherman law. In 1902 he shocked Wall Street by instructing his Attorney General to enter suit against the Northern Securities Company, a consolidation of the Hill-Morgan and the Harriman railways which embraced the Northern Pacific, the Great Northern, and the Chicago, Burlington and Quincy systems. By a 5–4 vote the Supreme Court in 1904 sustained the government and overruled its previous decision in the E. C. Knight case, thereby stopping a process of consolidation that Harriman proposed to continue until every important railway came under his control. Roosevelt asserted: 'It was necessary to reverse the Knight case in the interests of the people against monopoly and privilege just as it had been necessary to reverse the Dred Scott case in the interest of the people against slavery.'

In part as a consequence of the Northern Securities suit, the President grew steadily in popularity. Merely by being himself—greeting professors and pugilists with equal warmth, teaching his boys to ride and shoot, leading major-generals on a point-to-point ride, exercising with his 'tennis cabinet,' praising the good, the true, and the beautiful and denouncing the base, the false, and the ugly—Roosevelt became an institution. In 1904 the Republicans nominated Roosevelt by acclamation. When the Democrats discarded Bryan and put up a conservative New York judge, Alton B. Parker, Roosevelt polled a stunning 56.4 per cent of the vote, the greatest proportion any Republican had ever received, and on 4 March 1905 became 'President in his own right.'

Encouraged by this mandate, Roosevelt turned with new enthusiasm to the enforcement of his trust policies. Altogether there were forty-five prosecutions, and in notable instances they were successful. But they simply punished the grosser mischief after it had been committed and did not always do that. As early as 1905, Roosevelt had reached an informal gentleman's agreement with the House of Morgan. He left the impression that he would avoid court action against Morgan companies in return for their co-operation. Roosevelt came to conclude that the mere size and power of a combination did not necessarily render it illegal; there were 'good trusts' such as the International Harvester Company, another Morgan firm, which traded fairly and passed on their economies to consumers; and there were 'bad trusts,' which did not. The Supreme Court raised this moral distinction to the dignity of a legal one when, in the Standard Oil case of 1911, it accepted the common-law doctrine that only those acts or agreements of a monopolistic nature 'unreasonably' affecting interstate commerce were to be construed as in restraint of trade. Justice Harlan, in a vigorous dissent, denounced this 'rule of reason' as 'judicial legislation' and a 'perversion of the plain words of an Act in order to defeat the will of Congress.' But the 'rule of reason' became the guiding rule of decision, notably in the United States Steel Corporation case in 1920.

Roosevelt did, however, expand government supervision over business in other fields, such as labor relations. His intervention in the coal strike of 1902 revealed his determination to make full use of the authority of the Chief Executive. It was his initiative, too, that led Congress to enact factory inspection and child labor laws for the District of Columbia, and safety appliance legislation for interstate carriers. Yet despite his enthusiasm for the 'square deal,' Roosevelt failed to support Senator Beveridge in his struggle to outlaw child labor.

Government supervision of railways furnished the fireworks for the second Roosevelt administration as the trusts had for the first. Abandoned by Congress, ignored by Presidents Harrison, Cleveland, and McKinley, and emasculated by court decisions, the Interstate Commerce Act of 1887 had proved all but useless. Nonetheless, the necessity for regulation remained urgent. The railroads themselves were anxious to make the prohibition of rebates effective, and in 1903 they supported the Elkins Act, which made the published freight rates the lawful standard, substituted civil for criminal penalties, and provided that shippers were equally liable with the railroads

'Manchester Valley.' This painting by Joseph Pickett (1848–1919), a self-taught artist, indicates the centrality of the railroad to the life of the American small town. Pickett, who started his brief career in his middle years using house paint, worked very deliberately (sometimes spending years on a single canvas) behind his general store in New Hope, Pennsylvania. Only four of his paintings survive, but he was known to have done more, for he painted backdrops for his shooting gallery in the period when he traveled with a carnival. *(Museum of Modern Art, Gift of Abby Aldrich Rockefeller, oil with sand on canvas, 45½" x 60⅝")*

for obtaining rebates. Under this act the Attorney General instituted prosecutions against the Chicago & Alton and the Burlington for granting rebates and against Chicago packing houses for accepting them. Soon the government went after bigger game. In 1907 Judge Kenesaw Mountain Landis assessed a fine of $29,240,000 against the Standard Oil Company for accepting rebates, but the sentence was set aside by a higher court.

In 1904 Roosevelt pronounced railway regulation the 'paramount issue,' and in 1906 Congress responded with the Hepburn Act, which made rate regulation for the first time possible. The act authorized the ICC to determine and prescribe maximum rates. The railroads could appeal, but the burden of proof was now on the carrier, not the commission. Regulation was extended to include storage, refrigeration, and terminal facilities, sleeping car, express, and pipeline companies, and in 1910, telephone and telegraph companies. The law prohibited free passes for other than railroad employees, and required the railroads to disgorge most of the steamship lines and coal mines they had bought up to stifle competition—a requirement which they managed to evade. The Hepburn Act represented a substantial advance in railway regulation; within two years the commission heard almost twice as many complaints as in the previous nineteen years, and by 1911 it had reduced almost 200,000 rates by as much as 50 per cent. Yet the act did not get to the heart of the matter, for it failed to empower the commission to evaluate railroad properties and the cost of service by which alone it could determine reasonable rates. Not until 1913 was provision made for valuation, and another decade was to elapse before that valuation came to be used for rate-making.

Another step toward federal centralization was the extension of governmental supervision over foods and drugs. Investigations of Dr. Harvey Wiley, chief chemist of the Department of Agriculture, revealed almost universal use of adulterants and preservatives in canned and prepared foods, while the *Ladies' Home Journal* campaigned against poisonous patent medicines and misleading advertising and Samuel Hopkins Adams exposed 'The Great American Fraud.' In 1905 Roosevelt asked Congress to act, and, with the support of the American Medical Association and despite the frantic efforts of the Liquor Dealers' Association and the patent-medicine interests, Congress adopted in 1906 a Pure Food and Drugs Act, amended in 1911 to forbid misleading labeling of medicines.

The main spur for a pure food and drugs bill came from a book which, ironically, was written for a very different purpose. In March 1906 Upton Sinclair published *The Jungle*, a novel which made a frankly Socialist appeal and included an introduction by Jack London, who assured readers that the book was 'straight proletarian.' A story of the tribulations of a Lithuanian immigrant and his conversion to socialism, *The Jungle* was a startling success; but not, in Sinclair's view, for the right reasons. Instead of rising to indignation about the exploitation of the workers, the American public focused on a dozen pages vividly describing the processing of diseased cattle. When men who worked in the tank rooms fell into open vats, Sinclair wrote, 'sometimes they would be overlooked for days, till all but the bones of them had gone out to the world as Durham's Pure Leaf Lard.' As Mr. Dooley said, it was 'a sweetly sintimintal little volume to be r-read durin' Lent.' The public outcry against poisoned meat not only rescued the pure food and drugs bill from defeat but led to the adoption of federal meat inspection. Though this legislation still left much to be desired, it did give American consumers better protection than the laws of any other country then afforded.

Unquestionably Roosevelt's most important achievement came in the conservation of natural resources. As early as 1873 the American Association for the Advancement of Science had called attention to the reckless exhaustion of forest resources, but not until 1891 did Congress pass a Forest Reserve Act authorizing the President to set aside timber lands. Under this authority Harrison withdrew some 13 million, Cleveland 25 million, and McKinley 7 million acres of forest from public entry. Nevertheless, exploitation was still outpacing conservation when Roosevelt assumed office. Taking advantage of the 1891 law, Roosevelt set aside almost 150 million acres of unsold government timber land as national forest reserve, and at the suggestion of Senator La Follette withdrew from public entry some 85 millions more in Alaska and the Northwest, pending a government study of their resources. The discovery of a gigantic system of fraud by which railroads, lumber companies, and ranchers were looting and devastating the public reserve enabled the President to obtain authority to transfer the national forests to the Department of Agriculture, whose forest bureau, under the far-sighted Gifford Pinchot, administered them on scientific principles.

Realizing the necessity for arousing the public

Seeing the West. In California, this group of tourists was photographed making a pilgrimage to the natural wonders of Yosemite. This spectacular region on the western slope of the Sierra Nevada played an important part in the history of the conservation movement. As early as 1864 Congress granted land there for a state park, and in 1890 it created the Yosemite National Park, which in 1906, in Theodore Roosevelt's presidency, also acquired the state park. Under the authority of the secretary of the interior, the U.S. Army operated the park until 1916, when the National Park Service was established. The name 'Yosemite,' meaning 'grizzly bear,' derives from the clan totem of the Indians who dwelled there. (*Los Angeles County Museum*)

to the imperative need for conservation, Roosevelt took a great variety of different initiatives. He secured wide publicity for the work of the Forest Service. In 1907 he appointed an Inland Waterways Commission to canvass the whole question of the relation of rivers and soil and forest, of water-power development, and of water transportation. That same year the President invited all the state governors, cabinet members, justices of the Supreme Court, and other notables to a White House conference which focused attention upon conservation and gave the movement an impetus and a prestige that enabled it to survive later setbacks.

By sponsoring an ambitious irrigation program Roosevelt helped bring new life to barren regions of the West. The Newlands Reclamation Act of 1902 provided that irrigation should be financed out of the proceeds of public land sales under federal supervision and established a Reclamation Service. Over the next generation, the government constructed Roosevelt dam in Arizona, Hoover dam on the Colorado, Grand Coulee on the Columbia, and a dozen others. Roosevelt also put an end to the acquisition of water-power sites by private utilities and created five national parks, four game preserves, and over fifty wild bird refuges. Alone of our Presidents up to this time, Theodore Roosevelt grasped the problem of conservation as a whole. Unfortunately, until the accession of Franklin D. Roosevelt, none of his successors had the breadth of vision to carry on the work he so hopefully inaugurated.

Taft and the Insurgency

Strong-willed Presidents have generally managed to nominate their successors, and Roosevelt bequeathed his office to William Howard Taft, a man he loved as a brother and believed the ideal person to carry out his policies. In the 1908 election, Taft overwhelmed Bryan, who, in his third try for the White House, made the poorest showing, save for Parker's race, of any Democrat since the party split in 1860. Many progressives welcomed the change from Roosevelt to Taft, for except in the realm of conservation the last year ot T.R.'s administration was without achievement; as soon as the Republican leaders in Congress learned that Roosevelt would retire in 1909, they had ignored alike his recommendations and his threats. 'Big Bill' Taft, it was hoped, would apply the emollient of his good nature to the wheels of legislation.

If Roosevelt appeared to be less conservative than he really was, Taft seemed more so. Roosevelt was primarily a man of action, Taft of inaction. As a constitutional lawyer Taft did not share Roosevelt's view that the President could do anything not forbidden by law; rather, the executive could do only those things for which he had specific authority under the Constitution. Taft was by instinct cautious, by training 'regular.' Roosevelt had given the presidency an organic connection with Congress; under Taft the initiative passed to Old Guard leaders like 'Uncle Joe' Cannon of Illinois in the House and Nelson W. Aldrich in the Senate who thought reform had gone far enough, if not too far. And when Roosevelt sailed to Africa in March 1909, he left his successor with many critical problems, especially the tariff and the trusts, unsolved.[3]

The Republican platform of 1908 pledged to revise the tariff: an issue that Roosevelt had gingerly avoided. Revision was popularly understood as reduction, and Taft had specifically committed himself to this interpretation. A student of William Graham Sumner's at Yale, Taft had thereafter opposed high protection. 'Mr. Taft is a very excellent man,' wrote Senator Foraker in 1909, 'but there never was a minute since I first knew him when the tariff was not too high to suit him.' For downward revision there was, by 1909, pressing demand, especially in the Midwest, which exported many of its commodities. The tariff was blamed for the rising cost of living and was thought to be 'the mother of trusts.' In his inaugural address the new President asked that 'a

3. In August 1908, he explained, 'Well I'm through now. I've done my work. People are going to discuss economic questions more and more: the tariff, currency, banks. They are hard questions, and I am not deeply interested in them; my problems are moral problems, and my teaching has been plain morality.' John Hay noted in his diary: 'Knox says that the question of what is to become of Roosevelt after 1908 is easily answered. He should be made a bishop.'

Campaigning for the Socialist ticket, the Lower East Side, New York City, 1908. J. G. Phelps Stokes, the millionaire Socialist candidate for the state legislature, appeals to the crowd to vote for the Socialist slate headed by Eugene V. Debs. Though the Socialists had their greatest numerical strength in districts peopled by 'New Immigrants,' the party found its greatest following in proportion to population in rural Oklahoma. (*Museum of the City of New York*)

tariff bill be drawn in good faith in accordance with the promises made before the election,' and he summoned Congress into special session to act.

When Congress assembled, Sereno Payne of New York was ready with a tariff bill which placed iron ore, flax, and hides on the free list and reduced duties on steel, lumber, and numerous other items. The bill promptly passed the House, but in the Senate representatives of interested industries fell upon it. When it emerged as the Payne-Aldrich tariff, it was seen that of the 847 changes, some 600 were upward and that the free list was a joke. Accused of violating the party's promise to revise the tariff, Aldrich retorted: 'Where did we ever make the statement that we would revise the tariff *downward?*' Progressive Republicans were outraged, and La Follette, rapidly emerging as their leader, organized the Midwestern Senators to fight the proposed measure item by item. In a stirring debate La Follette attacked the woolens schedule, Beveridge the tobacco, Cummins the steel, Bristow the sugar, Dol-

William Howard Taft (1857–1930). Robert Lee MacCameron's oil portrait was painted in the year Taft became President. The new Chief Executive's girth provided the subject for jokes at his expense. Taft, it was said, once got up in a streetcar and offered his seat to three ladies. (*National Portrait Gallery, Smithsonian Institution*)

liver the cotton, and if in the end they failed, they did at least enlighten the country on the connection between tariffs and trusts, and laid dynamite for the political explosion of 1910. The insurgents urged Taft to veto the bill for violating party pledges, but after painful vacillation he signed it.

To heal this deep sectional wound in the party would require deft diplomacy. But the President promptly made a bad situation worse by deciding to tour the Middle West in the summer of 1909, to 'get out and see the people and jolly them.' He began his trip by paying tribute to Aldrich in the East; in Winona, Minnesota, in the heart of progressive discontent, he enraged insurgents by calling the Payne-Aldrich measure 'the best tariff bill that the Republican party has ever passed, and therefore the best tariff bill that has been passed at all'; and he capped the tour by having himself photographed with his arms around Speaker Cannon.

Progressive Republicans, already uneasy about Taft's performance, came to suspect him of playing traitor to Roosevelt on conservation. James R. Garfield, Roosevelt's lieutenant in conservation, was supplanted in the Interior Department by R. A. Ballinger, who was presently accused by Chief Forester Gifford Pinchot of letting a Morgan-Guggenheim syndicate obtain reserved coal lands in Alaska. The President then fired Pinchot, an act interpreted as a dramatic reversal of Roosevelt's program. Actually, Taft was not unfriendly to conservation. He was the first President to withdraw oil lands from public sale, he obtained from Congress authority to reserve the coal lands which Roosevelt had set aside without specific authority, and he made the Bureau of Mines guardian of the nation's mineral resources. Pinchot was replaced by the head of the Yale School of Forestry, and his policy was continued by the purchase, in 1911, of great timbered tracts in the Appalachians. But the Ballinger-Pinchot affair served further to alienate the insurgents from Taft.

The progressives directed their indignation not only against the President but against the Old Guard upon whom he depended. In the Senate, La Follette, Beveridge, and Dolliver excoriated Aldrich to such effect that he decided not to stand for re-election. In the House, insurgency took the form of a revolt against Speaker Cannon, 'a hard, narrow old Boeotian,' who controlled a well-oiled legislation mill which rejected progressive grist. In March 1910 George Norris offered a resolution depriving the Speaker of membership on the powerful Committee on Rules and making that committee elective, and Democrats joined with progressive Republicans to put it through. If the progressive cause gained, legislative efficiency lost. Authority was needed to enforce party discipline in a body so unwieldy as the House. Some progressives denied any right of party leaders to regularize the flow of legislation. Victor Murdock later described his attitude as 'merely reflecting Jonathan Edwards' philosophy that nothing should come between God and man, in maintaining that nothing should come between the people and their representatives.' Cannon bridled at such notions: 'The Speaker does believe and always had believed that this is a government through parties, and that parties can act only through majorities.' Although at the time the defeat of Cannon struck a blow for progressivism, many modern-day liberals find the Speaker's concept of party government more appropriate to liberal democracy than that of the insurgents who spoke for the autonomy of the Congressman.

The fights over Payne-Aldrich, Ballinger-Pinchot, and Cannonism caused an irrevocable split between Taft and the progressive Republicans, and in the 1910 campaign the President attempted to drive the insurgents out of office. Taft sent the Vice-President to campaign against La Follette in Wisconsin, and worked with the Southern Pacific crowd against Hiram Johnson in California. But the progressives handed him and the Old Guard a stunning set of defeats. Iowa Republicans howled down a resolution to endorse Taft; Johnson, who said his Republicanism came not from Washington but from Iowa and Wisconsin, overwhelmed the Taft Republicans; and La Follette won impressively. This factionalism in the primaries proved devastating for the Republicans in November. The Democrats captured the governorships of Massachusetts, Connecticut, and New York; sent Dr. Woodrow Wilson, lately president of Princeton University, to the State House in New Jersey; and won control of the House for the first time since 1894.

Taft's political ineptitude must not blind us to

'Catching the Limited,' 1910. William Harnden Foster's oil is one of the earliest paintings of the exciting new invention, the aeroplane. But unwittingly it demonstrates that the railroad still dominated American transportation, for the purpose of the flight is to enable the straw-hatted passenger with his satchel to catch up with the express train that will carry him to his destination. (*Berry-Hill Galleries*)

his achievements. The Mann-Elkins Act of 1910 strengthened the Interstate Commerce Commission by empowering it to suspend rate increases until and unless their reasonableness was ascertained, and created a Commerce Court to hear appeals from the ICC. The Department of Commerce and Labor, established in 1903, was wisely divided; and Congress set up a Children's Bureau in the new Department of Labor. A postal savings bank and a parcel post—conveniences long overdue—were provided. Approximately twice as many anti-trust prosecutions were instituted during Taft's four years as in Roosevelt's seven. The Sixteenth, or income-tax, Amendment and the Seventeenth Amendment, which transferred the election of United States Senators from state legislatures to the people, were adopted by Congress in 1909 and 1912 respectively and ratified in 1913. Alaska, peevish and discontented since the collapse of the Klondike gold bubble, at last obtained full territorial government in 1912, the same year that New Mexico and Arizona became the forty-seventh and forty-eighth states of the Union. Here again Taft antagonized the progressives by refusing to certify the admission of Arizona until it expunged from its constitution a provision for the popular recall of judges; once admitted as a state, Arizona promptly restored the device.

Even developments in foreign affairs served to lessen Taft's popularity and tear his party asunder, despite the fact that the unlucky President's foreign policy was often more sensible than Roosevelt's had been. When Japan began to consolidate her position in Manchuria, Secretary Knox countered by proposing, in 1909, that the United States and European powers lend China sufficient money to buy back all the railroads controlled by foreign interests. But his plan was rejected somewhat contemptuously by Russia and Japan. Failing in this effort to assist China, Taft insisted that American bankers be allowed to participate in a four-power consortium to finance railway construction in the Yangtze valley, 'in order that the United States might have equal rights and an equal voice in all questions pertaining to the disposition of the public revenues concerned.' But this plan, innocent enough in purpose, was repudiated by Wilson within two weeks of his accession to office.

It was fear of Japan, too, which provoked the so-called Lodge corollary to the Monroe Doctrine. In 1911 an American company proposed to sell Magdalena Bay in Lower California to a Japanese fishing syndicate. On hearing of the proposal, Senator Lodge, suspicious that the syndicate might be a cover for the government itself, introduced and the Senate passed a resolution that the purchase or control by any non-American government of any part of the American continents which had a potential naval or military value would constitute an unfriendly act. Though Taft declared that he was not bound by the resolution, it further aggravated Latin American opinion. The doctrine was strictly a one-way affair; designed to prevent foreign establishments in the Western hemisphere, it did not limit American expansion to other continents.

A comparison of the Roosevelt and Taft policies recalls the old adage that some persons can make off with a horse, while others cannot look over the stable wall. Secretary Knox signed treaties with Nicaragua and Honduras similar to Roosevelt's pact with Santo Domingo, underwriting American loans by guaranteeing bankers against revolution and defalcation. But the Knox treaties were rejected by the Senate, and Taft's policy both in Central America and the Far East was denounced as 'dollar diplomacy.' In 1911 Taft, a warm friend to international peace, concluded treaties with both England and France for the arbitration of all disputes, including those involving 'national honor.' The German-American press and professional Irish-Americans broke out into shrieks of dissent. A presidential election was approaching, and the Senate rejected the treaties.

Again it was Taft's misfortune, not his fault, that tariff reciprocity with Canada failed. In November 1910 three United States commissioners concluded with two members of the Dominion Parliament a reciprocity agreement to be adopted by identical legislative acts. The agreement provided free trade in primary food products, which would naturally flow from Canada southward, and a large reduction on manufactures, which would obviously go the other way. It was a sincere effort by Taft to cement friendly relations, but bad politics. Insurgent Republicans, most of whom represented Western

President Taft and Colonel Goethals in Panama. In 1907, two years before William Howard Taft entered the White House, George Washington Goethals (1858–1928) was appointed chief engineer of the Panama Canal. He proved a brilliant choice. By his accessibility and his grasp of detail, he created such an *esprit de corps* among his motley work crew of 30,000 that he was able to complete his arduous assignment ahead of schedule. In 1915 Congress rewarded him with an expression of gratitude and elevation to the rank of major-general. (*Library of Congress*)

agrarian states, were able to argue that reciprocity was a good bargain only for the trusts, which would gain a new market and free raw materials at the farmer's expense; yet many Eastern industrialists opposed it too. Democratic votes pushed the bill through Congress, but in the debate, Champ Clark, the new Democratic Speaker, said, 'I am for it because I hope to see the day when the American flag will float over every square foot of the British North American possessions clear to the North Pole.' Clark's words infuriated Canadians, and Sir Wilfrid Laurier, the Canadian Prime Minister, was forced to appeal to his country. Canadian manufacturers, who feared to lose their protected home market, financed the opposition, and in September 1911 the treaty and Sir Wilfrid went down to defeat.

Taft's foreign policy also widened the division between the President and his predecessor. Roosevelt disliked Taft's Latin American policy, and he fiercely denounced the President's proposal for blanket arbitration treaties as 'maudlin folly' and the product of 'sloppy thinking.' Stung by Roosevelt's attack, Taft commented privately: 'The truth is that he believes in war and wishes to be a Napoleon and to die on the battlefield.'

The Campaign of 1912

In the summer of 1910, Theodore Roosevelt, recently returned from his African safari and a triumphal progress through Europe, embarked on a speaking tour in the West which showed that shooting lions and dining with crowned heads had not dulled his fighting edge for reform. His ideas, systematized as the 'New Nationalism,' included not only the old Roosevelt policies of honest government, regulation of big business, and conservation, but a relatively new insistence on social justice. This principle led to vigorous criticism of recent Supreme Court decisions which had nullified social legislation in the states. He urged the country to rely not on the courts but on a Chief Executive who would be 'the steward of the public welfare,' and he boldly asserted the rights of the community over 'lawbreakers of great wealth.' At Osawatomie on 31 August 1910, T.R. stated: 'The man who wrongly holds that every human right is secondary to his profit must now give way to the advocate of human welfare, who rightly maintains that every man holds his property subject to the general right of the community to regulate its use to whatever degree the public welfare may require it.'

Conservative Republicans shuddered at the 'New Nationalism' and feared a split in the party. Taft was worried. 'I have had a hard time,' he confessed to his old friend. 'I have been conscientiously trying to carry out your policies, but my method of doing so has not worked smoothly.' Although still friendly, the two men were being pulled apart. Insurgents were continually telling Roosevelt that the President had surrendered to the Old Guard, and entreating him to run in 1912. Taft, on the other hand, was surrounded by friends and relatives whose advice resembled that of George III's mother: 'George, be a King!'

Roosevelt had declared in 1904 that 'under no circumstances' would he again be a Presidential candidate. Moreover, Taft was his friend and his own choice. But Roosevelt, who despised Taft's foreign policy and was uneasy about his domestic program, was infuriated when in October 1911 the Taft administration filed an anti-trust suit against U.S. Steel which, by implication, impeached Roosevelt's judgment in sanctioning a special dispensation when he was President. On 21 February 1912, Roosevelt announced, 'My hat is in the ring.' That same day, in an address which opened his campaign, he spoke of big business as 'inevitable and desirable,' but also insisted that the rich man 'holds his wealth subject to the general right of the community to regulate its business use as the public welfare requires,' and urged that the police power of the state be broadened. Further, he advocated not only the initiative and the referendum, but the recall of decisions by state courts. His radicalism alienated thousands of Republican voters, cost him the support of friends like Lodge, and made his nomination by the Republicans extremely improbable.

The contest for the Republican nomination became unseemly and bitter. In the Ohio primary campaign, Taft and Roosevelt called one another Jacobin, apostate, demagogue, and fathead. In the thirteen states which chose their delegates to party

Theodore Roosevelt on the way to the Progressive party convention, 6 August 1912. As his demeanor suggests, the Colonel was in a heroic mood. The leader of a secession from the Republican party, T.R. knew his chances for victory were slim, but he claimed that the only alternative to a triumph for progressivism was 'a general smash up of our civilization,' and he refused to let Taft have the better of him. 'I wish to Heaven I was not in this fight,' the former President wrote to Ambassador Jusserand, 'and I am in it only on the principle, in the long run a sound one, that I would rather take a thrashing than be quiet under such a kicking.' (*Chicago Historical Society*)

conventions through popular primaries, Roosevelt won 278, Taft 46, and La Follette 36 delegates. Roosevelt had the overwhelming support of rank and file Republicans, but the bosses were with Taft. Where delegates were chosen by conventions, the President was almost uniformly successful, and the Southern districts, the Republican rotten boroughs, returned a solid block of Taft delegates who represented little more than the federal office-holders in that region. With the credentials of some 200 delegates in dispute, Roosevelt, who charged that his legitimate majority was being stolen, told his enraptured followers, 'We stand at Armageddon and we battle for the Lord.' When the party organization awarded practically all the contested seats to Taft men, Roosevelt instructed his delegates to take no further part in the proceedings; and Taft was renominated easily.

Roosevelt and his followers at once took steps to found a new party. In August 1912 the first Progressive party convention met at Chicago amid scenes of febrile enthusiasm. The delegates paraded around the convention hall singing 'Onward Christian Soldiers' and

> Follow! Follow!
> We will follow Roosevelt,
> Anywhere! Everywhere,
> We will follow on.

The Progressive party welcomed social workers like Jane Addams, municipal reformers like Harold Ickes of Chicago, as well as moneyed men like George Perkins, known as Secretary of State for the House of Morgan. The new party equivocated on its trust plank, but the rest of the platform, which reflected the social justice aspirations of leaders like Jane Addams, was so radical that Gene Debs declared that the red flag of socialism had been replaced by the red bandannas of the Progressives. The convention nominated Roosevelt by acclamation, and a phrase of the beloved leader, 'I am feeling like a bull moose,' gave the new party an appropriate symbol, beside the Republican elephant and the Democratic donkey.

In the perspective of history the formation of the Progressive party appears to have been a mistake for the reformers. The bolt lost many good men their political careers and ended all chance of liberalizing the Republican party. Roosevelt's error was so contrary to his long-settled principles of party regularity that one naturally asks whether appetite for power was not his moving force. Like the elder Pitt, Roosevelt believed that he, and he alone, could save the country; unlike Pitt, he did not win the opportunity to justify his faith.

The year before Roosevelt entered Harvard and the year after Taft entered Yale, Woodrow Wilson, son and grandson of Scots Presbyterian ministers, came up to Princeton. Wilson was remembered at Whig Hall, Princeton, for having lost an interclub debating contest rather than defend protection against free trade. Before graduating from Harvard, Roosevelt wrote his first book, *The Naval History of the War of 1812,* which sounded the note of preparedness for war upon which his life closed. In his last year at Princeton, Wilson published an article exposing the irresponsibility of congressional government, which he later did so much to remedy. Roosevelt entered public life in 1881; Wilson, after a brief and unprofitable practice of law, took his doctorate at Johns Hopkins, and began a quiet career of teaching and scholarship. In 1890, the year after Roosevelt was appointed to the Civil Service Commission, Wilson became a professor of political science at Princeton; and in 1902, the year after Roosevelt became President of the United States, Wilson was chosen president of Princeton University.

As a scholar, publicist, and leader in education Wilson enjoyed a national reputation; but active politics was considered a closed sphere to professors. However, George Harvey, the arch-conservative editor of *Harper's Weekly,* was attracted by Wilson's views; an anti-Bryan Democrat, Wilson had denounced 'the crude and ignorant minds of the members of the Farmers Alliance,' and deplored the 'passion for regulative legislation.' Harvey's suggestion in 1906 that Wilson was presidential timber was greeted skeptically, but the college president took it to heart. In 1910 the Democrats of New Jersey—an amorphous state, half bedroom to New York and half to Philadelphia, under the control of corporations attracted by the laxity of its laws—thought their unsavory reputation might be sweetened by a scholar. At Harvey's suggestion the bosses nominated Wilson, and the people elected him governor. Within a year Wilson had repudiated the bosses, broken the power of the sinister 'Jim' Smith, and written more progressive legislation into the statute books than had been enacted in the previous half-century. He split with Harvey, but a silent politician from Texas, Colonel Edward M. House, took him up; and Wilson became a leading candidate for the presidential nomination. At the Democratic convention in 1912, Champ Clark of Missouri had a majority of the delegates, but, unable to muster the necessary two-thirds, on the forty-sixth ballot he lost to Wilson.

The presidential election became a three-cornered contest between Taft, Roosevelt, and Wilson; but really between the last two. Roosevelt ran on a more advanced program of social reform, while Wilson opposed both a national child labor law and minimum-wage legislation. Roosevelt believed that big business was inevitable and that it should be regulated. Wilson subscribed rather to the doctrine of Louis Brandeis that bigness was a curse and government had a responsibility to break it down. The solution, as Brandeis saw it, was regulated competition instead of regulated monopoly. While Roosevelt's 'New Nationalism' borrowed from continental experience with a directive state, Wilson's 'New Freedom' derived from British liberalism. 'The history of liberty,' Wilson asserted, 'is the history of the limitation of governmental power.' Roosevelt, with biblical imagery and voice like a shrilling fife, stirred men to wrath, to combat, and to antique virtue; Wilson, serene and confident, lifted men out of themselves by phrases that sang in their hearts, to a vision of a better world.

Wilson polled less than 42 per cent of the vote, but he won an overwhelming victory in the Electoral College. Roosevelt, with 27 per cent, carried six states. Taft, with 23 per cent, took only Utah and Vermont. Nine hundred thousand voted for the Socialist nominee, Eugene Debs. Progressives thought of 1856 and looked toward 1916. The Grand Old Party, as they saw it, had gone the way of the Whigs—killed by a great moral issue it would not face, and another bland Buchanan was in the White House. But the Old Guard neither died nor surrendered. And Woodrow Wilson, instead of playing the part of Buchanan, welded his party into a fit instrument of his great purpose 'to square every process of our national life again with the standards we so proudly set up at the beginning and have always carried at our hearts.'

Wilson and the New Freedom

Woodrow Wilson came to power at a propitious time. The progressive movement was nearing its culmination, and new men in the Democratic party were eager to transform it from a diffuse alliance of rural Southerners and machine bosses into a modern national organization. It was one of those moments in history when the situation called for a particular kind of man, and the man was there. Wilson, who had minimized the importance of the presidency in his *Congressional Government in the United States*, had come to think of the Chief Executive as 'the only national voice in affairs.' A month before his inauguration he wrote that the President 'must be prime minister, and he is the spokesman of the Nation in everything.' And more perhaps than anyone who had ever held the office Wilson understood the force of words as a political weapon. In 1909 he had cried: 'I wish there were some great orator who could go about and make men drunk with this spirit of self-sacrifice . . . whose tongue might every day carry abroad the golden accents of that creative age in which we were born a nation.'

The Democratic party for which he was now the spokesman had undergone little change since Andrew Jackson's time. The elements in it that counted were the emotional and somewhat radical Western wing represented by Bryan; Irish-Americans of the industrial states, who wanted the power and office denied them during the Republican dynasties; a large segment of labor; and the Solid South, including almost every white man in the late Confederacy, and many in the new Southwest—Oklahoma, New Mexico, and Arizona. Tradition, habit, and common suspicion of Big Business and Wall Street held these groups together. Though the Democrats had enough popular appeal to poll a plurality in five of the ten presidential elections since Reconstruction, the party wanted leadership. Cleveland's victories had proved barren, Bryan had thrice failed, and the majority leaders in Congress were elderly and timid. For the task of leadership Wilson proved himself peculiarly equipped. He had inherited a Calvinistic philosophy which placed the halo of moral necessity on expediency, and he had developed an intellectual arrogance which inclined him to rely largely upon his own judgment, while from a prolonged professional study of the science of government he had learned the necessity of executive direction of the modern state.

Portrait of Woodrow Wilson (1856–1924) by Sir William Orpen. (*White House Historical Association*)

Wilson's inaugural address, striking a note of high idealism and couched in words reminiscent of Jefferson's first inaugural, aroused hope and enthusiasm.

We have been proud of our industrial achievements, but we have not hitherto stopped thoughtfully enough to count the human cost of lives snuffed out, of energies over-taxed and broken, the fearful physical and spiritual cost to the men and women and children upon whom the dead weight and burden of it all has fallen pitilessly the years through. The groans and agony of it all had not yet reached our ears, the solemn, moving undertone of our life, coming up out of the mines and factories and out of every home where the struggle had its intimate and familiar seat. . . . The great Government we loved has too often been made use of for private and selfish purposes, and those who used it had forgotten the people.

No administration of modern times has been inaugurated with more passionate eloquence, but Wilson was neither a fighting progressive like La Follette, nor a spokesman for agrarian and labor discontent like Bryan. He was rather a nineteenth-century liberal, suspicious of special interests whether they were of Wall Street or of the Grange or the labor union, and distrustful of the new breed of intellectuals who were calling for government to intervene directly in the economy. 'I don't want a smug lot of experts to sit down behind closed doors in Washington and play Providence to me,' he said. Wilson's beliefs, noted Walter Lippmann, were 'a fusion of Jeffersonian democracy with a kind of British Cobdenism. This meant in practical life a conviction that the world needs not so much to be administered as to be released from control.' Wilson spoke for 'the man on the make,' the risk-taking entrepreneur who asked only a fair chance to gain his fortune. To foster the interests of the small capitalist, the new President offered a three-point program: a lowered tariff to deny the trusts an unfair advantage; a changed banking structure to make credit more available to the small businessman; and trust legislation to prevent big business from squeezing out the small competitor.

Wilson, who had entered politics as an admirer of J. P. Morgan, had become increasingly critical of financial interests which he believed were crushing the independent businessman. Even before he took office, Wilson attempted to build up public support by a blunt attack on Wall Street. If any tycoon dared to frustrate his program, he warned, 'I promise him, not for myself but for my countrymen, a gibbet as high as Haman—not a literal gibbet, because that is not painful after it has been used, but a figurative gibbet, upon which the soul quivers as long as there are persons belonging to the family who can feel ashamed.' Yet however radical his rhetoric, Wilson proposed to do little to disturb vested interests, and his program ignored many of the realities of life in industrial America.

On 8 April 1913, hardly more than a month after he was inaugurated, Wilson made the dramatic move of coming before Congress in person to deliver his message on tariff reform. Not since John Adams had a President appeared before Congress. One Democratic Senator protested: 'I am sorry to see revived the old Federalistic custom of speeches from the throne. . . . I regret all this cheap and tawdry imitation of English royalty.' But Wilson was determined to seize the initiative in law-making by narrowing the distance between 'the two ends of Pennsylvania Avenue.' A slight thing in itself, this act caught the popular imagination.

On the very day he took office, Wilson had summoned Congress into special session to revise the tariff. It was a dangerous issue; in the preceding twenty years only one tariff revision had not resulted in defeat at the polls. But Wilson did not hesitate. 'The tariff duties must be altered,' he said. 'We must abolish everything that bears even the semblance of privilege, or of any kind of artificial advantage, and put our business men and producers under the stimulation of a constant necessity to be efficient, economical and enterprising.' After a brief debate, the Underwood tariff, as it came to be known, passed the House by a strict party vote. The real struggle, as everyone anticipated, came in the Senate, which prepared to exercise its ancient prerogative of rewriting a House measure. In May Wilson lashed out at the sinister activities of lobbyists for special interests, and through the hot months of a Washington summer, held Congress to its appointed task. He himself set an example of ceaseless vigilance, scrutinizing every section of the measure and appearing with embarrassing frequency at Senate committee rooms. Through such adroit personal leadership, Wilson secured enactment of the measure with almost unanimous Democratic support.

The Underwood tariff was far from a free-trade measure, but it did reverse a tariff policy which had prevailed for fifty years. A London editor called it 'the heaviest blow that has been aimed at the Protective system since the British legislation of Sir Robert Peel.' The act lowered average duties from some 37 per cent to some 27 per cent; more important were reductions in specific schedules and additions to the free list. Duties were decreased on 958 articles, raised on 86, and maintained on 307. Reductions embraced important commodities such as iron and steel, while wool, sugar, coal, and many other products were to enter duty free. To meet the anticipated reduction in customs revenues, Representative Cordell Hull of Tennessee added a provision for a graduated tax on incomes of $4000 and over, ranging from 1 to 6 per cent.

While Congress was still wrestling with the Underwood tariff, Wilson presented a proposal to reorganize the banking system. The need for a thorough overhaul was almost universally recognized. The 'bankers' panic' of 1907 reflected no basic unsoundness in the economic system, but a ruinous shortage of currency and inelasticity of credit; only by hasty importations of gold from abroad and by resort to extra-legal forms of currency was business able to weather the crisis. The final report of a National Monetary Commission, created by Congress, listed no less than seventeen serious defects in the American banking system, among them the concentration of financial power in New York. The extent of that concentration was emphasized by the Pujo Committee of 1912, which revealed that the firm members or directors of two sets of New York banks, controlled by the Morgan and Rockefeller interests, held '341 directorships of 112 corporations having aggregate resources of capitalization of $22,245,000,000.'

If all agreed to the necessity of reform, they disagreed vigorously about what shape it should take. Conservatives wanted a central bank like the old Bank of the United States without its branches, with control of credit in the hands of the bankers, whereas Bryan's followers insisted that control of the new banking system should be exclusively governmental and that the system should be decentralized. In June Wilson appeared before Congress to outline his own program.

> We must have a currency, not rigid as now, but readily, elastically responsive to sound credit. . . . And the control of this system of banking and of issue which our new laws are to set up must be public, not private, must be vested in the Government itself, so that the banks may be the instruments, not the masters of business and of individual enterprise and initiative.

Carter Glass was ready with a bill which carried out these general principles, and for six months Congress wrangled over this administration measure which metropolitan bankers and Western farmers criticized with equal severity. Wilson had little to fear from the opposition of the bankers, but he could not afford to forfeit the support of Bryan and his followers. In the end the provisions of the new law recognized both of Bryan's demands: that there should be no active banker representation on the banking board and that all Federal Reserve currency should be governmental obligations. So disciplined had the party become under Wilson's leadership that not a single Democratic Senator voted against the bill.

The Federal Reserve Act of December 1913 created a new national banking system upon regional lines. The country was divided into twelve districts, each with a Federal Reserve Bank owned by the member banks, which were required to subscribe 6 per cent of their capital. These regional banks acted as agents for their members. All national banks were required to join these regional banks and state banks were permitted to join; within a decade one-third of the banks, representing 70 per cent of the banking resources of the country, were members of the Federal Reserve system. A Federal Reserve Board, consisting of the Secretary of the Treasury, the Comptroller, and six others appointed by the President, supervised the business of the regional banks. The law authorized a new type of currency: Federal Reserve notes secured by short-term commercial paper and backed by a 40 per cent gold reserve. The new system was designed to develop more elastic credit, a sounder distribution of banking facilities, and more effective safeguards against speculation. In time the bankers themselves admitted that the Federal Reserve system had added immeasurably to the financial stability of the country.

The Federal Reserve Act also aimed to provide easier credit for farmers, but the law did little to bring down farm interest rates or ease farm credit. These objects were partially achieved, however, by the Federal Farm Loan Act of May 1916 which created a Federal Farm Loan Board and 12 regional Farm Loan banks authorized to extend loans on farm property. A further step toward better credit facilities for farmers was taken in the Warehouse Act of 1916, which authorized licensed ware-

Marcel Duchamp, 'Nude Descending a Staircase, No. 2.' In 1913 the Association of American Painters and Sculptors sponsored an exhibit at the 69th Regiment Armory in New York City that turned out to be the most momentous event in the history of twentieth-century art in the United States. Nearly 300,000 people in New York, and in other cities when it went on tour, came to see the work not only of Americans like 'the Eight' but of European Post-Impressionists, Fauves, and Cubists, and often went away bewildered. The prominent critic Royal Cortissoz derided 'Ellis Island art,' and at the Art Institute of Chicago students hanged Matisse in effigy. The greatest sensation of the Armory Show was created by Duchamp's '*Nu descendant un escalier*.' The *American Art News* ran a contest challenging its readers to locate the nude, and one observer captioned the picture 'An explosion in a shingle factory.' (*Philadelphia Museum of Art, The Louise and Walter Arensberg Coll.*)

'Tariff Descending Downward.' This clever political cartoon takes advantage of the stir created by Duchamp's 'Nude Descending a Staircase' to depict President Wilson as a 'near-Futurist' artist. Looking on are the sponsors of the tariff bill, Representative Oscar W. Underwood of Alabama and Furnifold M. Simmons of North Carolina. John McCutcheon's cartoon appeared in the Chicago *Tribune* on 3 April 1913; exactly six months to the day later, Congress enacted the tariff revision Wilson sought. (*Library of Congress*)

houses to issue against farm products warehouse receipts which might be used as negotiable paper. Thus were the Populists vindicated a quarter-century after their sub-treasury scheme had been rejected with contempt.

As soon as the tariff and banking reform bills were disposed of, Wilson appeared before Congress to ask for legislation on trusts and monopolies. His address of 20 January 1914 included five recommendations: prohibition of interlocking directorates of corporations, banks, railroads, and public utilities; authority for the Interstate Commerce Commission to regulate the financial operations of railways; explicit definition of the anti-trust laws; creation of a federal interstate trade commission to supervise and guide business; and penalization of individuals, not business, for violations of the anti-trust laws. Congress responded with two bills: the Clayton bill, which prohibited numerous forms of unfair trade practices, and a measure to set up a commission with limited authority. When the Clayton bill was denounced as inadequate, Wilson embraced a proposal from Brandeis to establish a strong regulatory commission, although this was an idea that the New Nationalists had advanced and Wilson opposed in 1912. The Federal Trade Commisssion Act replaced Roosevelt's Bureau of Corporations with a new non-partisan commission. The act outlawed unfair methods of competition and authorized the commission to issue 'cease and desist' orders against any corporation found guilty of violations, and, if this failed, to bring the accused firm into court.

Once Wilson accepted the FTC approach, he lost interest in the Clayton bill, which emerged as a weak law. Senator Jim Reed complained: 'It is a sort of legislative apology to the trusts, delivered hat in hand, and accompanied by assurances that no discourtesy is intended.' The Clayton Act prohibited discriminations in price which might tend to lessen competition or create monopoly and 'tying' agreements limiting the right of purchasers to deal in the products of competing manufacturers. It forbade corporations to acquire stock in competing concerns, and outlawed interlocking directorates in large corporations and banks. In keeping with the President's recommendation, officers of corporations were made personally responsible for violations of the law.

Wilson, who opposed grants of special privilege to any group, set himself stiffly against a demand to exempt unions and farm organizations from anti-trust prosecutions. Faced by a party revolt, he agreed only to a provision that such organizations were not, per se, in restraint of trade. Unions were exempted from the terms of the act as long as they sought legitimate objectives, and the use of the injunction in labor disputes 'unless necessary to prevent irreparable injury to property . . . for which there is no adequate remedy at law' was explicitly forbidden. Samuel Gompers hailed these provisions as 'labor's charter of freedom, but the act proved to be a good deal less than that.

'With this legislation,' said Wilson optimistically, 'there is clear and sufficient law to check and destroy the noxious growth [of monopoly] in its infancy.' But the courts reserved to themselves the right to determine what constituted 'unfair methods of competition' just as they reserved the right to interpret the phrase 'irreparable injury to property,' and in the war and postwar years judicial rulings became increasingly conservative. The effort to enforce the provision making directors responsible for corporation malpractices broke down when the government failed to prove its case against the directors of the New Haven Railroad. During the war the Clayton Act was tacitly suspended, and in the postwar period of Republican ascendancy the Federal Trade Commission, by encouraging the formulation of codes of trade practices, entered into something suspiciously like an alliance with the trusts. Two decades after the enactment of the Wilsonian anti-trust legislation, the trusts were as powerful as ever. Perhaps all this merely demonstrates the validity of Thurman Arnold's theory that the function of anti-trust agitation and legislation is purely ceremonial—that it provides us the satisfaction of declaiming against the 'evil' part of a 'necessary evil' while retaining what is necessary about it. Still, if the legislation did not curb monopolies, it may well have imposed on them a pattern of good behavior.

In pushing through his three-point program, Wilson had demonstrated that he was a great leader: of his party, of Congress, of the nation. He had held the 63rd Congress in Washington for over a year and a half, the longest session in history, and he had kept relentless pressure on its members. The *New York Times* commented: 'President Cleveland said he had a Congress on his hands, but this Congress has a President on its back, driving it pitilessly. . . . Never were Congressmen driven so, not even in the days of the "big stick."' Above all, Wilson had proven what many reasonable men had long doubted—that the Democratic party could govern.

Yet by the autumn of 1914 Wilson was content to call a halt to further reforms. As spokesman for the Democratic party's Jeffersonian equal rights tradition, he rejected three types of legislation: social welfare innovations that sought to hurdle constitutional barriers; proposals aimed at benefiting special interests, including workers; and measures which reflected the New Nationalist approach of reconciling business and government. He blocked a bill to provide long-term rural credits, refused to support a woman's suffrage amendment, opposed child labor legislation, and in March 1915 almost vetoed the La Follette Seamen's bill. Until alarmed by the storm of liberal disapproval, he permitted members of his cabinet to practice racial discrimination. For all his rhetoric against big business, his appointments to government agencies were so conservative that one Senator said of his selections for the Federal Reserve Board that they looked as though they had been chosen by the head of the National City Bank.

Wilson might have continued his cautious drift to the right had it not been for the collapse of the Progressive party, which carried the threat that Roosevelt's ardent following might move back into the Republican fold. Having won less than 42 per cent of the vote in 1912, Wilson was doomed to defeat in 1916 if a reunited Republican party polled its full strength. To attract voters of a progressive inclination, Wilson decided to turn to the left. Moreover, just as his views in New Jersey had shifted, Wilson's convictions were no doubt changing as the result of his White House experience. He began the transformation with the appointment in January 1916 of the distinguished reformer, Louis D. Brandeis, to the Supreme Court, a selection that was confirmed despite an appalling outburst of anti-Semitism. In rapid succession he reversed himself to support social welfare measures, including a law excluding the products of child labor from interstate commerce and a Workmen's Compensation Act for federal employees. He gave his blessing to special interest legislation for farmers and workers, including the Rural Credits Act, which provided long-term farm loans, and the Adamson Act, imposing an eight-hour day on all interstate railways. The New Nationalist program of business-government co-operation won a partial victory with the creation of a tariff commission and the exemption of exporters from the anti-trust laws.

In four years Wilson had reasserted presidential leadership, converted a state-rights party to enlightened nationalism, and made clear that progressivism transcended party lines. If Wilson had not accepted the idea that the national government would play a directing role in the economy, or the conception of a managerial class ruling in the national interest, he could nonetheless boast that the Democrats had 'come very near to carrying out the platform of the Progressive Party' as well as their own.

28

Wilsonian Diplomacy and World War I

*

1913–1920

Moralistic Diplomacy

Wilson had not mentioned foreign affairs in his inaugural address; yet his first administration was concerned largely, his second almost exclusively, with international relations. He approached the world with the same high-mindedness with which he advanced the New Freedom, and in his two terms he succeeded in moderating American imperialism in China, the Philippines, and the Caribbean, in achieving a less vindictive peace after World War I than many wanted, and in launching an association of nations. Yet he would also learn that good intentions were not always enough. To ensure the independence of Mexico, he would intervene in that country's affairs. To achieve a peaceful world, he would lead his country into war. And, in the end, his hopes for a new world order, in which the United States would play an active role, would be shattered.

In principle and to a lesser extent in practice, Wilson reversed much of the foreign policy of his predecessors. The first hint of that reversal was a statement in March 1913 withdrawing support from the proposed bankers' loan to China as incompatible with Chinese sovereignty. This was widely interpreted as a formal repudiation of 'dollar diplomacy.' At the same time Secretary Bryan launched a program of conciliation treaties in whose success he had a touching faith. Altogether Bryan concluded thirty agreements submitting all disputes—including those involving questions of 'national honor'—to arbitration, and providing a 'cooling-off' period of one year before resort to arms; of the major powers only Germany refused to sign.

Bryan had long favored independence for the Philippines, and in 1914 a Bryan follower, Representative Jones of Virginia, introduced a bill granting immediate self-government to the Filipinos and promising complete independence in the near future. Under pressure from the War Department, which was alive to the strategic importance of the Philippines, and from Catholics who feared confiscation of church property, Wilson maneuvered for a less drastic measure, which would not stipulate a specific time-limit on American control. The Jones Act, passed in 1916, formally pledged the United States to withdraw from the Philippines 'as soon as a stable government can be established therein,' and inaugurated far-reaching political and administrative reforms, including a popularly elected legislature. At the same time Governor-General Harrison filled the civil service with native Filipinos and encouraged the Philippine government to establish state-controlled railroads, banks, mines, and industries. Under these auspices the Filipinos made such progress that President Wilson, in his last annual message, reminded Congress that the time had come to fulfill the promise of the Jones Act. But the incoming Republican administration had no sympathy with such a program, and reversed practically all of Harrison's enlightened policies. Not until 1934 did Congress finally provide for Philippine independence; not until 1946 did the law take effect.

Wilson showed even more high-mindedness in his reaction to two Panama Canal problems that he had inherited. The first was the long-standing dispute with Colombia, which still bitterly resented the part that President Roosevelt had played in detaching Panama. In 1914 Bryan negotiated a treaty with Colombia which expressed 'sincere regret' for whatever injury the United States might have inflicted, paid an indemnity of $25 million, and granted Colombia free use of the Panama Canal. That a powerful nation should apologize to a weak one was something new in international relations. To Roosevelt it was nothing less than an outrage, and his friend Senator Henry Cabot Lodge led a successful fight against ratification of the treaty, thus delaying for seven years the restoration of good relations with Colombia and getting in some practice for his more ambitious battle against the Versailles treaty a few years later. The second dispute grew out of the special exemption which Congress had granted American coastwise shipping from paying tolls on the canal. The British protested this as a violation of earlier treaty agreements. Convinced that the British were right, and anxious to have British support in Mexico, Wilson persuaded Congress to repeal the exemption.

Within two weeks of his inauguration Wilson announced that one of the chief objects of his administration would be to cultivate the friendship of Latin America. A few months later, he promised that the United States would 'never again seek one additional foot of territory by conquest.' Yet despite such sincere protestations of altruism, Wilson and Bryan continued many of the Caribbean policies of Roosevelt and Taft. Marines remained in Nicaragua, and in 1914 Bryan negotiated a treaty which so seriously infringed on Nicaraguan sovereignty that it was denounced by the Central American Court of Justice. In Santo Domingo Bryan authorized 'an enlargement of the sphere of American influence beyond what we have before exercised'; and as minister to that hapless republic he sent an ex-pugilist named James Sullivan who introduced the worst Tammany methods into Dominican politics, exploited his office for personal profit, and in the end helped precipitate a revolution. In 1916 Wilson ordered a military occupation of the Dominican Republic, which lasted for eight years. A year earlier, after civil strife had taken over 2000 lives, the United States Marine Corps occupied Haiti. Under the terms of the treaty the Wilson administration dictated to the Haitians, American control was continued until 1930.

Elsewhere in the Caribbean, relations were less troubled. Despite some mistrust, Wilson avoided any critical difficulty in Cuba. Puerto Rico, like Cuba, was governed for a time by the United States military, but in 1900 the Foraker Act had established civil government of the old crown colony type: an elective assembly, with an executive council appointed by the President acting as an upper house. This, too, was contrary to the Wilsonian philosophy, and in 1917 Congress enacted a law granting American citizenship to the inhabitants of the island, and a semi-responsible government. Not until 1947 were the islanders permitted to elect their own Governor, but in 1952 the island achieved Commonwealth status, whatever that term might mean in American constitutional law. Intervention in Nicaragua, Santo Domingo, and Haiti, then, were balanced, in a sense, by a more enlightened policy toward Cuba and Puerto Rico.

Mexico presented the real test of Wilson's policy toward Latin America. In 1911 a revolution had overthrown Porforio Díaz, dictator of Mexico for thirty-five years, during which Indian lands had been seized, peons exploited, and the masses

Bluejackets with rifles picking off snipers, Vera Cruz, 1914. Wilson, who thought that the Mexicans would welcome the American forces as liberators, was shocked at the bloodshed. When the President met with reporters, he seemed to Senator Lodge to be 'pale, parchmenty,' and 'positively shaken,' and Wilson told Admiral Grayson, 'The thought haunts me that it was I who ordered those young men to their deaths.' (*Library of Congress*)

reduced to desperation. The revolution was conducted by a small doctrinaire middle class under Francisco I. Madero, but supported by the peons in the hope of recovering their lands. Installed as constitutional President in 1911, Madero neither kept order nor satisfied the aspirations of the landless. A counter-revolution of the landowners, backed by foreign investors, displaced him by assassination in February 1913, and installed Victoriano Huerta as President. Although unable to exert his authority over the greater part of the country, which was fast falling into anarchy, Huerta was promptly recognized by Great Britain and most of the Powers. Strong pressure on President Wilson to do the same was exerted by the American ambassador and by American business interests which owned 78 per cent of the mines, 72 per cent of the smelters, 58 per cent of the oil, 68 per cent of the rubber plantations, and some two-thirds of the railroads of Mexico.

President Wilson refused to be moved by the importunities of business, for he would not recognize a government that did not rest upon the consent of the governed. Such a policy, importing moral considerations into the realm of international law, departed from the traditional practices of the United States as well as of other nations. The easier course would have been to accord the Huerta government *de facto* recognition, and leave to the Mexicans the solution of their problems of constitutional law and democracy. Wilson's policy was fraught with peril, for it placed upon the United States the responsibility of deciding which government was moral, and there was no assurance that the decision would be disinterested. Furthermore in the event that Huerta did not back down, Wilson faced the awkward alternatives of some kind of intervention or of a serious loss of prestige.

Wilson moved to a showdown with Huerta. In February 1914 he permitted American arms to go to the leader of the Constitutional forces, Venustiano Carranza. But the landed aristocracy and the Catholic Church rallied to Huerta, and the situation seemed as unsolvable as ever. At this point the zeal of a Mexican colonel made history. When the crew of an American warship landed, without permission, at Tampico, they were arrested. The Mexican commander instantly apologized and returned the men, but Admiral Mayo demanded not only an apology but a salute to the American flag, and Wilson, eagerly looking for an excuse to intervene, backed him up. On 21 April American marines landed at Vera Cruz, which they took with slight loss to themselves but at the cost of several hundred Mexican casualties. However, war with Mexico did not begin, partly because Wilson realized that his legal case was ridiculous, since he was demanding acknowledgment from a government he did not recognize, and his moral case far from strong, but chiefly because he wished above all to help the people of Mexico find themselves.

At this acute juncture, Wilson was rescued by a proposal from Argentina, Brazil, and Chile for a joint mediation, an offer the President gladly accepted, especially as he was confident that he could control the proceedings. A conference with these 'A.B.C.' powers at Niagara Falls in May 1914—the first of its kind in the history of the Americas—averted war and proposed a new constitutional government for Mexico. Huerta stood out stiffly against the terms of the mediation, but he was forced out of office, and in August, Carranza, leader of the Constitutional party, became President. Unhappily, there was to be no peace for stricken Mexico. No sooner had Carranza won Mexico City than his ablest lieutenant Francisco ('Pancho') Villa, raised the standard of revolt. With incomparable ineptitude the Wilson administration decided to back Villa, mistakenly supposing him more tractable than Carranza. But when Carranza shattered the Villa forces, the United States had no alternative save to accord him recognition.

During the five years that followed there were occasional outbreaks of peace in Mexico. The main trouble was that the underlying force of the revolution—the land hunger of the peasants—was unable to find a leader determined to adopt fundamental reforms. Meantime, Wilson adopted a policy of 'watchful waiting,' while endeavoring, without much success, to create a Pan-American machinery for dealing with a situation that was taking a heavy toll of the lives and property of both American civilians in Mexico and of Mexicans. Defeated by Carranza and abandoned by the United States, Villa resorted to banditry. Early in 1916, he took Americans from a train in Mexico and murdered them, then crossed the border in raids that, in Columbus, New Mexico, left nineteen Americans dead. Wilson, in retaliation, sent an expeditionary force under General John Pershing that pursued Villa deep into the interior of Mexico. It failed to capture him, and in violating Mexican soil, outraged Carranza and aroused the suspicion of much of Latin America. Yet, although Wilson had, as his biographer Arthur Link observes, 'embittered Mexican-American relations, for many years to come,' he had also,

> almost alone, stood off Europe during the days of the Huertista tyranny, withstood the powerful forces in the United States that sought the undoing of the Revolution, and refused to go to war at a time when it might have insured his re-election.

In Latin America, Wilson had pursued a policy of evangelical diplomacy without engaging the nation in a major war; in Europe, the difficulties in such a course were more numerous, the risks infinitely more grave.

The Struggle for Neutral Rights

On 28 June 1914 a shot was fired that closed an era of progress, liberalism, and democracy and inaugurated an age of warfare, destruction, revolutionary upheavals, and dictatorships, which is not yet ended. Archduke Franz Ferdinand, heir to the throne of Austria-Hungary, was assassinated at Sarajevo in the province of Bosnia. A month later Austria declared war on Serbia, and by early August all of the great powers of Europe were embroiled in what has come to be known as the First World War. President Wilson at once proclaimed the neutrality of the United States, and in 1914 there was an almost universal determination on the part of the American people to stay out of the European conflict, which did not appear to involve any American interests.

Nonetheless, from the very outset, American public opinion predominantly favored the Allies. It matters little how much this was due to Allied propaganda, since propaganda can be effective only on receptive minds. The majority of Americans were English-speaking, and regarded some part of the British Empire as their mother country, with whom war would have seemed immoral. Ties of language and literature, law and custom, as well as those of a more personal character, bound America to the British in a hundred ways. With France our relations were more sentimental than intimate, but the tradition of Franco-American friendship went back to the Revolution. With Germany and her allies, on the other hand, American relations were amicable but not cordial. To many Americans the posturings and saber-rattlings of William II were ridiculous when they were not odious. Suspicion was intensified by Germany's cynical violation of Belgian neutrality. Wilson himself illustrated these attitudes. Of mixed Scots and English ancestry, steeped in English literature and history, and an admirer of British political institutions, he was willing to endure almost any provocation rather than risk war with England. Though Wilson tried to be neutral, Bryan was right in protesting that the President was quicker to hold Germany than England to 'strict accountability' for violations of neutral rights.

The United States also developed an economic stake in the war. Even before 1914 a large part of American trade had been with the Allied nations, and when the Allies blockaded the Central Powers, United States trade with Germany became negligible, while trade with Great Britain and France

'Portrait of a German Officer,' 1914. This painting by Marsden Hartley (1877–1943) is suggestive of what many associated with Prussian militarism, including the emblem of the Iron Cross. Hartley, who had his first one-man show at Stieglitz's '291' gallery in 1909, painted it while he was living in Berlin, where he exhibited with the *Blaue Reiter* group at the First Autumn Salon in 1912. The initials in the lower left corner are those of a German friend. (*Metropolitan Museum of Art, Alfred Stieglitz Collection, 1949*)

4
24
Kv.F

mounted impressively. This increase in foreign trade, in full swing by the middle of 1915, rescued the United States from a commercial depression that had lasted a year. Within a year after the outbreak of war the whole fabric of American economic life was so closely interwoven with the economy of the Allies that any rupture would have been ruinous. It was the realization of this, in addition to sympathy for the Allies, that persuaded Wilson and his cabinet to reject an embargo on munitions of war.

Countenanced by international law, the munitions trade was theoretically open to all belligerents. In fact, Allied sea power prevented the Central Powers from procuring American munitions; the Allies got all they wanted; and American munitions exports increased in value from some $40 million in 1914 to $1290 million in 1916, and total trade to the Allies from $825 million to $3214 million. Germany never officially denied the legality of this trade, but protested bitterly that its one-sided nature violated the spirit of neutrality. To the suggestion that the United States place an embargo upon munitions exports, Washington replied that it could not change the rules of neutrality to the advantage of one belligerent while the war was in progress. As a technical defense this was sound; but both belligerents were changing the rules of war, and it was within the rights of Congress to stiffen neutrality requirements as the Dutch had done, by treating armed merchantmen as warships and interning them. But neither Congress nor most of the nation wished to do so.

Without credit the belligerents could not buy American goods. At the beginning of the war the United States was a debtor nation: this situation was promptly reversed as foreign investors dumped their securities on the American market. Soon the Allies found it advisable to finance their purchases in the United States through loans floated in Wall Street, a scheme Bryan opposed. 'Money,' he said, 'is the worst of all contrabands because it commands everything else.' In August 1914 the State Department announced that 'in the judgment of this Government, loans by American bankers to any foreign nation which is at war are inconsistent with the true spirit of neutrality.' Yet within a month this position was modified to permit bank credits to belligerents; by the late summer of 1915 Bryan was out of the cabinet; and in September 1915 the State Department withdrew altogether its opposition to loans. By the time the United States entered the war, over $2 billion had been lent by the American public to the Allied governments, as opposed to only $27 million to the Central Powers.

Though America's economic stake in an Allied victory no doubt inclined some people toward war, it was not the crucial consideration. The financial community as a whole preferred American neutrality, which afforded Wall Street all the profits of war without the corresponding sacrifices and taxation. Furthermore, most of the loans were secured by pledged collateral which would be unaffected by the outcome of the war. To be sure, the Wilson administration saw Germany as a threat to a stable world order in which American interests, including those of American capital, would thrive. But it was neither trade, nor munitions, nor loans, nor propaganda that persuaded the administration of the necessity of war; it was the German submarine policy.

From the beginning the United States waged a losing struggle to preserve her rights as a neutral. There were two fundamental difficulties: lack of international law to deal with unforeseen circumstances, and the immense stakes and savage fighting which made the belligerents ready to flout law or morality if that was necessary for their survival. America's first and most prolonged dispute came with Great Britain. Promptly upon the outbreak of the war, Britain instituted a new type of blockade that extended considerably the contraband list; expanded the 'continuous voyage' doctrine to justify confiscating cargoes of enemy destination in neutral ships, even when billed for neutral ports; and declared all of the North Sea and the English Channel 'military areas.' American direct trade with the Central Powers was entirely, and indirect trade largely, cut off. In addition, the Allies employed such questionable devices as rationing trade to neutrals and blacklisting firms suspected of trading with the Central Powers.

Against these palpable violations of its neutral

rights, the United States protested in vain. At any time after the middle of 1915 a real threat of an American embargo on munitions would probably have brought the Allies to heel. Their own factories were unable to supply the enormous demand of their armies for high explosives; the cutting off of supplies from America would have lost them the war. But Wilson and the State Department had no intention of taking a stand for neutral rights which, if persisted in, might land America in war on the side of autocracy, as had happened in 1812. So they chose the course of protest and persuasion in order to keep the record clear while avoiding the catastrophe of war. As a consequence, until the beginning of 1917, the British and French continued to violate neutral rights, while the State Department filed protests and the Germans fumed.

Faced with economic strangulation, Germany struck back with the only weapons at its disposal: mines and submarines. As early as August 1914 it began to mine the North Sea and the Irish Sea, and on 4 February 1915 it announced that all the waters around the British Isles constituted a war zone in which Allied vessels would be destroyed and warned neutral ships to keep out in order to preclude accidental attacks, which seemed highly likely. That the sinking of unarmed neutral ships was a clear violation of existing international law, Germany did not deny; but it insisted that its policy was justified by the equally lawless British blockade.

Wilson and most Americans distinguished between British and German violations of neutral rights. As Mr. Asquith said, 'Let the neutrals complain about our blockade and other measures taken as much as they may, the fact remains that no neutral national has ever lost his life as the result of it.' (To be sure, if the United States had insisted on full freedom of the seas, American lives might well have been lost to British mines in the North Sea.) But the U-boat warfare took a toll of 209 American lives on the high seas—twenty-eight of them on American ships. Damages to property entailed by Allied violations of American rights could be settled after the war; loss of lives could never be adequately indemnified.

Alarmed at the threat of submarine warfare, Wilson informed the German government on 10 February 1915 that 'the United States would be constrained to hold the Imperial German Government to a strict accountability' for 'property endangered or lives lost.' Thereby the Wilson administration took the stand that must inevitably lead to war, unless either the United States or Germany backed down. Soon came a test of the meaning of 'strict accountability.' On 28 March 1915 an American citizen went down on a British ship; on 29 April a U.S. merchant vessel was attacked by a German airplane; and on 1 May an American tanker was torpedoed. Germany offered to make reparations for an 'unfortunate accident' but refused to abandon submarine warfare. Matters came to a head when on 7 May the Cunard liner *Lusitania* was torpedoed off the coast of Ireland with a loss of over 1100 lives, including 128 American citizens. Germany justified the sinking as one of the hazards of war: the *Lusitania* was a 'semiwarship' carrying munitions and troops, and passengers had been duly warned. Yet the sinking violated international law as it then stood, and it was a piece of criminal folly as well. Nothing except the invasion of Belgium did so much to inflame American sentiment against Germany. Leaders like Theodore Roosevelt clamored for war.

But the country was not yet mentally prepared for war, and Wilson refused to be stampeded. On 13 May he demanded that Berlin disavow the sinking of the *Lusitania*, 'make reparation so far as reparation is possible for injuries that are without measure, and take immediate steps to prevent the recurrence of anything so obviously subversive of the principles of warfare.' Germany, persuaded that Wilson was playing to the gallery, tried to drag out the issue by a series of technical objections. Impatient of procrastination, Wilson sent, on 9 June, a second peremptory note insisting upon a formal disavowal of the outrage.

Bryan, who felt that this protest was perilously close to an ultimatum, resigned from the cabinet rather than sign the note. His own solution was to renounce responsibility for the lives of Americans who chose passage on belligerent ships. 'Germany,' he said, 'has a right to prevent contraband from going to the Allies, and a ship carrying con-

The *Lusitania* tragedy, 1915. This was one of a series of cartoons by William A. Rogers of the New York *Herald,* who taunted Wilson with being too unwilling to go to war against Germany. For his efforts, Rogers received the French Legion of Honor. (*Library of Congress*)

traband should not rely upon passengers to protect her from attack—it would be like putting women and children in front of an army.' (Subsequently, this plausible argument was embodied in the Gore-McLemore Resolutions of 1916 refusing passports to American citizens who purposed to travel on the armed ships of belligerents. Wilson moved promptly to defeat the resolutions. 'Once accept a single abatement of right,' he wrote to Senator Stone, 'and many other humiliations would certainly follow, and the whole fine fabric of international law might crumble under our hands piece by piece.' As a result of executive pressure, the resolutions were defeated, and the 'whole fine fabric of international law' was saved—for the moment.)

Despite Bryan's misgivings, Wilson persisted in taking a stern line with the Germans, for he regarded the U-boat campaign as intolerable. On 19 August 1915, before the *Lusitania* controversy had been settled, the English liner *Arabic* was torpedoed with the loss of two American lives. A diplomatic rupture seemed inescapable, but Germany pledged that in the future 'liners will not be sunk by our submarines without warning and without safety of the lives of non-combatants,' and the crisis passed.

For six months American relations with Germany were undisturbed by any new U-boat sinkings, but this peaceful interlude was rudely shattered when in February 1916 the German government announced a renewal of submarine warfare on armed merchant vessels. On 24 March the unarmed channel steamer *Sussex* was torpedoed without warning. Outraged at this violation of the pledge which had been given after the *Arabic* affair, Wilson warned Germany that unless she immediately abandoned submarine warfare against freight and passenger vessels the United States would break off diplomatic relations. Faced with this threat, Berlin capitulated, promising, on 4 May, that henceforth no more merchant vessels would be sunk without warning, provided the United States held England also to 'strict accountability.' For the next nine months American relations with Germany were less disturbed than at any time since the *Lusitania* tragedy, and, in fact, during the summer and fall of 1916 the United States had sharper differences with England than with Germany.

The Coming of War

Despite this apparent settlement of the U-boat controversy, President Wilson became more and more persuaded that the only way in which the United States could avoid war was to end the war. So eager was Wilson to achieve peace that he went to the somewhat inconsistent extreme of suggesting he might fight for it. In February 1916 Lord Grey, after a series of conferences with the ubiquitous Colonel House, was able to assure his government that 'President Wilson was ready . . . to propose that a Conference should be summoned to put an end to the war. Should the Allies accept this proposal, and should Germany refuse it, the United States would probably leave the Con-against Germany. . . . If such a Conference met, it would secure peace on terms not unfavorable to the Allies; and if it failed to secure peace, the United States would probably leave the Conference as a belligerent on the side of the Allies, if Germany was unreasonable.' But Grey did not take these overtures seriously; the British did not want to negotiate at a time when Germany held the upper hand, and like the French and Germans they wanted the spoils of an eventual victory.

Profoundly discouraged, Wilson turned early in 1916 toward a program of military preparedness, in part from conviction, in part from political expediency. A presidential campaign was in the offing, and the Democrats could not afford to permit their Republican opponents to capitalize on the popular issue of national defense. During the summer of 1916, the administration urged through Congress a series of measures strengthening military and naval forces. The National Defense Act enlarged the regular army, integrated the national guard into the National Defense system, and provided for an officers' reserve corps; the Naval Appropriation Act authorized the construction of new battleships and cruisers. To lessen the dependency on belligerent or Scandinavian merchantmen to carry exports, the United States Shipping Board Act appropriated $50 million for the purchase or construction of merchant ships. To co-ordinate industries and resources, Congress created a Council for National Defense.

Having thus made appropriate gestures toward the more militant elements, the President embarked upon a campaign for re-election under the slogan, 'He kept us out of war.' With the Republicans and the Progressives reunited behind Supreme Court Justice Charles Evans Hughes, all the portents indicated a Republican victory, but Hughes proved a disappointing candidate; Wilson's reforms were not forgotten; and hundreds of

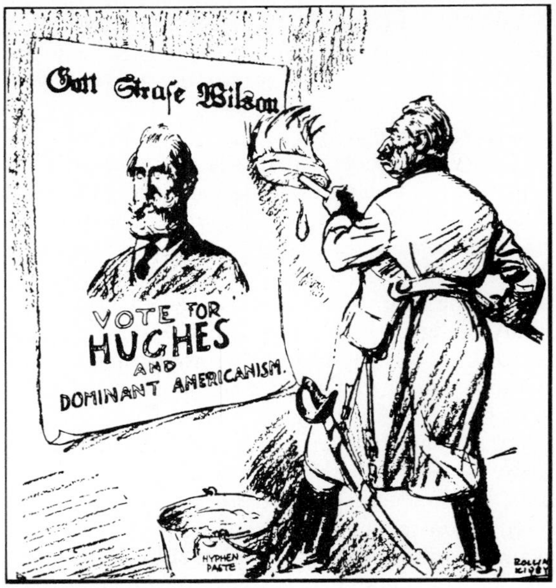

'Berlin's Candidate.' This partisan cartoon by Rollin Kirby in the Democratic New York *World* shows the Kaiser, using 'hyphen paste,' posting a picture of the Republican candidate, Charles Evans Hughes. At a time when both parties were aware that German-Americans, Irish-Americans, and other groups designated with hyphens might determine the outcome of the 1916 election, publicists frequently charged their opponents with catering to the 'hyphenate' vote. During his years on the *World* (1913–21) Kirby was America's leading cartoonist and the recipient of three Pulitzer Prizes.

thousands of Socialists, more loyal to peace than to party, gave their votes to the candidate who had kept America out of war. By forging a new alliance of the South and West, Wilson overcame the massed strength of the reunited Republican party. But the future of this coalition rested on a precarious supposition: that the President could continue to keep the country out of war.

As soon as his re-election was assured, Wilson determined to renew his overture for a negotiated peace, but without success. Faced with intransigence on the part of the belligerents, and convinced that the time had come when the United States must cooperate in securing and maintaining world peace, Wilson, in a memorable speech on 22 January 1917, formulated the conditions upon which such co-operation might be extended. Those conditions, anticipating the subsequent 'Fourteen Points,' included government by the consent of the governed, freedom of the seas, limitation of armaments, and a League to enforce peace. Fundamental to all of these principles was the requirement that the settlement must be a 'peace without victory,' an appeal that fell upon deaf ears. Increasingly, Wilson came to feel that only if America was a belligerent would he be able to win attention for his ideas at the peace table.

Even before Wilson made his 'peace without victory' speech, Berlin had made a decision that would plunge America into war. The Germans decided to embark upon unrestricted submarine warfare, knowing full well this might bring the United States into the war. Wilson promptly severed diplomatic relations, and though he still hoped that Germany would not commit the supreme folly of aggressive acts against the United States, the nation prepared for war. Wilson himself took the first step in this direction by calling upon Congress for authority to arm American merchant vessels. A Senate filibuster, led by La Follette and what Wilson described as 'a little group of willful men,' prevented congressional action until the adjournment of 4 March, when the President discovered a piracy statute of 1819 that authorized him to act. But events moved so rapidly that this controversy was soon irrelevant. Late in February the British secret service gave Washington a copy of the 'Zimmermann note' in which the German government proposed that, if the United States declared war, Mexico conclude an offensive alliance with Germany and Japan; Mexico to have Texas, New Mexico, and Arizona for its share of the loot. This note, released to the press on 1 March, immensely strengthened the popular demand for war. On the 17th came news that a revolution in Russia had overthrown the Tsar and established a provisional republican government; the last taint of autocracy in the Allied cause disappeared. When, also during March, German submarines torpedoed five American merchant vessels, Wilson decided that Germany was warring upon the United States.

So on 2 April 1917, the President appeared before Congress and read his message asking for a declaration of war:

> It is a fearful thing to lead this great peaceful people into war, into the most terrible and disastrous of all wars, civilization itself seeming to be in the balance. But the right is more precious than peace, and we shall fight for the things which we have always carried nearest our hearts,—for democracy, for the right of those who submit to authority to have a voice in their own Government, for the rights and liberties of small nations, for a universal dominion of right by such a concert of free peoples as shall bring peace and safety to all nations and make the world itself at last free. To such a task we can dedicate our lives and our fortunes, everything that we are and everything that we have, with the pride of those who know that the day has come when America is privileged to spend her blood and her might for the principles that gave her birth and happiness and the peace which she has treasured. God helping her, she can do no other.

In the small hours of Good Friday morning, 6 April 1917, Congress passed a joint resolution declaring war on the German Empire.

Industrial and Financial Mobilization

'It is not an army that we must shape and train for war,' said President Wilson, 'it is a nation.' At a time when German submarine warfare was succeeding beyond all expectations and the Allies were almost at the end of their tether, the United States not only had to raise an army but provide clothing, arms, ammunition and explosives, build a 'bridge' across the Atlantic, set up dockage facilities and arrange transportation in France, string thousands of miles of telephone wires, create a vast medical and nursing corps, and construct hundreds of hospitals in the United States and overseas. No task of similar magnitude had ever been attempted before by this country.

Spurred by necessity, Congress conferred upon the President extensive powers to commandeer essential industries and mines, requisition supplies, control distribution, fix prices, and take over and operate the entire system of transportation and communication. The President in turn delegated these powers to a series of boards, under the Council for National Defense. These boards mobilized America's industrial, agricultural, and even intellectual resources for war purposes, and gave the country an experience in government planning that went far beyond anything the prewar reformers had contemplated.

To mobilize the nation's industrial resources, the Council set up a War Industries Board in the summer of 1917, but not until the economy verged on collapse did the WIB get the sweeping powers it needed. In March 1918 Wilson made a Wall Street broker, Bernard Baruch, virtual economic dictator. Under Baruch, the board regulated all existing industries that produced war materials, developed new industries, enforced efficiency, fixed prices, determined priorities of production and delivery, and managed all war purchase for the United States and the Allies. The production of some 30,000 articles came under minute supervision. Baby carriages were standardized, and traveling salesmen were limited to two trunks. It was such a regimentation of the economy as had never before been known, and it later served as a model for the New Deal mobilization of 1933.

The United States Shipping Board Act of 1916 had already called into existence an organization to cope with the task of providing ships to replace the vessels which the submarines were destroying at the rate of over half a million tons monthly. In April 1917 Congress authorized the creation of a subsidiary of the Shipping Board, the Emergency Fleet Corporation, to build ships. This operation moved at a snail's pace; the first vessel from the

PROVIDE THE SINEWS OF WAR
BUY LIBERTY BONDS

Liberty bond poster, 1918, by Joseph Pennell. After studying briefly under Eakins, Pennell (1857–1926) became an expatriate, living much of his life in London, where he moved in the circles of Whistler and the pre-Raphaelites. When World War I broke out, Pennell, an outstanding etcher, made lithographs of British munitions-workers which the War Ministry sponsored, and was invited by the French government in the spring of 1917 to make drawings for them. But the first-hand experience of the Western front unnerved him. Pennell fled to the United States, where he regained his emotional stability by contributing more than 100 posters to the American cause and by serving as vice-chairman of a division of the Creel Committee. (*Library of Congress*)

enormous shipyard at Hog Island in the Delaware river was not delivered until after the armistice. But by seizing interned German ships, commandeering or buying neutral vessels, taking over all private shipping, and by a modest amount of new construction, the Shipping Board succeeded in increasing the available tonnage from one million to ten million and overcoming the submarine danger.

The administration also had to reorganize transport within the United States, for under the impact of war orders and troop movements the railroad system broke down. In December 1917 the government took it over, and proceeded to operate the railroads as a unified system, guaranteeing adequate compensation to the owners. Secretary of the Treasury William G. McAdoo resigned to become Director-General of the railroads. By consolidating terminal facilities, standardizing equipment, shutting down little-used lines, spending millions on sorely needed improvements, discouraging passenger traffic, and coordinating freight traffic, he succeeded in bringing the railroads to a peak of effectiveness heretofore unknown. But this experiment cost the government $714 million. During the war the government also took over other agencies of transportation and communication, including warehouses and telephone, telegraph, and cable lines.

The Food Administration really brought the war home to the American people. Under Herbert Hoover it displayed extraordinary ingenuity in stepping up production and decreasing consumption of food so that the Allies might have enough. Hoover fixed the price of wheat, established a grain corporation to buy and sell it, organized the supply and purchase of meat, and bought the entire Cuban and American sugar crop and resold it. A systematic campaign persuaded the American people to observe 'Wheatless Mondays,' 'Meatless Tuesdays,' and 'Porkless Thursdays.' As a result of 'Hooverizing,' the United States was able to export in 1918 approximately three times the normal amounts of breadstuffs, meats, and sugar.

The war spawned a great many other agencies. A fuel administration, under the direction of Harry A. Garfield, president of Williams College, introduced daylight saving and 'Fuelless Mondays,' banned electric displays, and closed down non-essential plants in order to conserve coal. A war trade board licensed exports and imports and blacklisted firms suspected of trading with the enemy. A war finance corporation supervised all security issues of $100,000 or over and in addition was empowered to underwrite loans to war industries.

The war produced unprecedented changes in the government's relationship to labor unions. A War Labor Policies Board under Felix Frankfurter standardized wages and hours and for the first time gave the government a national labor policy. A newly created United States Employment Service placed nearly four million workers in vital war jobs. But the most important new agency was the War Labor Board, headed by former President Taft and the brilliant labor lawyer, Frank P. Walsh. Many of the prewar progressives had frowned on unions as monopolies which denied equality of opportunity and threatened middle-class interests, but the WLB threw the power of government behind the right of workers to organize and bargain collectively. When the Smith & Wesson Arms plant rejected a WLB decision, the board boldly commandeered the plant. The various labor boards also made progress in imposing the eight-hour day and in protecting women and children from exploitation. When the Supreme Court overturned the Child Labor Act of 1916, Congress quickly enacted a new law using the taxing power to discourage the employment of child labor. As a result of all of these actions and of the insatiable manpower demand, the A.F. of L. gained more than a million members; hours of labor declined sharply; and real wages rose 20 per cent.

The government had to find money not only for its own but for Allied expenses. During and immediately after the war the United States Government lent some $10 billion to the Allies and associated governments, practically all of which was spent in this country. These loans, direct war expenditures of $26 billion, and indirect costs like pensions brought the total cost of the war to well over $42 billion by 1936. The country financed approximately one-third of the war cost by taxation, two-thirds by loans. To avoid a repetition of the unhappy experience of Cleveland's negotiations with Wall Street, Congress insisted that bonds be sold through popular subscription. The five loans which were floated between May 1917 and May 1919—four Liberty loans and one Victory loan—were all handsomely oversubscribed. The war also demonstrated the potential of the steeply graduated income tax as an instrument for distributing costs more equitably. In the Revenue Act of 1918 Congress not only raised the excess profits tax to 65 per cent but increased the surtax so that the total levy on the

Samuel Gompers (1850–1924). In this unusual photograph, he is togged out in an aviator's helmet looking for all the world like a war ace. The picture indicates the indefatigable support the head of the American Federation of Labor gave to America's participation in World War I at a time when the IWW and many other working-class groups opposed the war. (*Office of War Information, National Archives*)

wealthy reached 77 per cent. Although the war created new millionaires and resulted in swollen profits in some instances, it also showed that in a time of crisis the government can impose its will on the rich in a way that is rarely possible in peacetime.

Notwithstanding the many achievements, the war mobilization fell short. Despite the enormous upsurge of production, the American army depended heavily on Allied arms and supplies. By the end of the war American factories had produced only 64 tanks, the Liberty aviation engine was just getting into production, field artillery relied almost exclusively on French 75 mm. field guns, and more doughboys went to Europe in British transports than in American vessels.

Mobilizing Public Opinion

When Congress declared war, a sizable minority objected and a very large part of the public was indifferent to the issues. Millions of Americans—anti-war Socialists, German, Irish, and other ethnic groups, pacifists, 'Wobblies,' many progressives—opposed American intervention. In Oklahoma's 'Green Corn Rebellion,' tenant farmers, including Indians and Negroes, burned bridges and cut pipelines in protest against participation in the war. Anti-war progressives charged that the poor people of the country had been dragooned into war by greedy profiteers. 'We are going into the war,' George Norris asserted, 'upon the command of Gold.' Furthermore, many who did not oppose the conflict had little ideological commitment. Consequently, Congress established a Committee on Public Information, whose chairman, George Creel, undertook to mobilize the mind of America as Baruch was mobilizing industry. Creel enlisted artists, advertisers, poets, historians, photographers, and educators, who inundated the country with a flood of propaganda. Creel distributed over 100 million pieces of 'literature,' while 75,000 'four-minute men' let loose a barrage of oratory which all but paralyzed the intelligence of the country. Motion pictures displayed to horrified audiences the barbarities of the 'Hun'; pamphlets written by learned professors proved to the more skeptical that the Germans had always been a depraved people; and thousands of canned editorials taught the average man what to think about the war. School children learned to lisp the vocabulary of hatred, and foreigners were taught to be ashamed that they had not arranged to be born in America.

The administration directed its propaganda toward international opinion too. Charges by radicals that the war was being fought for imperialistic aims encouraged Wilson to enunciate a declaration of principles. He sought two ends: to establish a moral basis for peace upon which all belligerents—including the Allies—must agree, and to sow dissatisfaction among the peoples of Germany and Austria-Hungary. To achieve these goals Wilson announced, on 8 January 1918, the Fourteen Points upon which it would be possible to formulate terms of peace. They included the principle of 'open covenants openly arrived at,' freedom of the seas, the reorganization of much of Europe on the basis of self-determination, and the creation of a 'general association of nations.' Wilson's statement, assiduously circulated throughout Germany, eventually helped to drive a wedge between the people and the government, and, at the end, led to negotiations for an armistice upon the basis of the Fourteen Points.

The Wilson administration also took steps, frequently drastic ones, to deal with internal dissension. The Espionage Act of 1917 fixed a maximum penalty of a $10,000 fine and 20 years' imprisonment for anyone who interfered with the draft or encouraged disloyalty, and empowered the Postmaster General to deny the mails to any materials he thought seditious. The Sedition Act of 1918 extended these penalties to anyone who should obstruct the sale of United States bonds, incite insubordination, discourage recruiting, 'wilfully utter, print, write or publish any disloyal, profane, scurrilous or abusive language about the form of government of the United States, or the Constitution, or the flag, or the uniform of the Army or Navy, or bring the form of Government . . . or the constitution . . . into contempt . . . or advocate any curtailment of production of anything necessary to the prosecution of the war.' In addition a Trading-with-the-Enemy Act of 1917 gave the President authority to censor all international communications, and the Postmaster General power over the foreign-language press in the United States. Under these harsh laws the government instituted widespread censorship of the press and banned two Socialist newspapers from the mails. A film-producer was sentenced to ten years in jail for producing a film on the American Revolution called *The Spirit of Seventy-six*, because it was thought that it might excite anti-British sentiments; a Vermont minister was sentenced to fifteen years' imprisonment for citing Jesus as an authority on pacifism; and South

Dakota farmers went to jail for petitioning for a referendum on the war and on the payment of war costs through taxation. A drive against conscientious objectors, who were theoretically excluded from the draft, netted 4000 men, of whom more than 400 were hurried to military prisons.

Altogether, the government carried out 1500 prosecutions under the Espionage and Sedition laws. Among those convicted, the two most distinguished were Eugene V. Debs and Victor Berger. Debs, four times a candidate for the presidency of the United States, was sentenced to 20 years in jail for a speech which was held to have a tendency to bring about resistance to the draft, though there was no evidence to prove that it did. Berger, Congressman from Milwaukee, also received a 20-year sentence for editorials in his newspaper branding the war a capitalist conspiracy. Twice re-elected by his constituents he was twice refused his seat. C. T. Schenck, General Secretary of the Socialist party, was convicted on the same charge; Justice Holmes's opinion sustaining the conviction is memorable because it announced for the first time the 'clear and present danger' test as a safeguard for freedom of speech. 'The question in every case,' wrote Holmes,

> is whether the words are used in such circumstances and are of such a nature as to create a clear and present danger that they will bring about the substantive evils that Congress has a right to prevent. It is a question of proximity and degree.

Holmes's standard was not adhered to in a more controversial case where a miserable garment-worker, Jacob Abrams, was sentenced to twenty years' imprisonment for distributing a pamphlet calling on the workers of the world to rise against the American military expedition to Siberia—an expedition conceived in folly, conducted in vain, and abandoned in disorder.[1] The decision of the Court in 1919 evoked from Justice Holmes the most moving of his many eloquent dissents:

> When men have realized that time has upset many fighting faiths, they may come to believe even more than they believe the very foundations of their own conduct that the ultimate good desired is better reached by free trade in ideas—that the best test of truth is the power of the thought to get itself accepted in the competition of the market, and that truth is the only ground upon which their wishes can be safely carried out. That at any rate is the theory of our Constitution. It is an experiment, as all life is an experiment. Every year if not every day we have to wager our salvation upon some prophecy based upon imperfect knowledge. While that experiment is part of our system I think that we should be eternally vigilant against attempts to check the expression of opinions that we loathe and believe to be fraught with death, unless they so imminently threaten immediate interference with the lawful and pressing purposes of the law that an immediate check is required to save the country.

No less disturbing than this official crusade against sedition was the unofficial witch-hunting. The war offered a great opportunity to bring patriotism to the aid of personal grudges and neighborhood feuds. A non-conformist was lucky if he did not have flashes from his shaving mirror reported as signals to U-boats. German-Americans, the vast majority of them loyal to the United States, were subjected to all sorts of indignities. Schools dropped German from their curricula; Frederick Stock, distinguished conductor of the Chicago Symphony Orchestra, was deprived of his baton; and some universities revoked degrees they had conferred on distinguished Germans, thus giving academic sanction to the doctrine of retroactive guilt.

Naval and Military Operations

'Force to the utmost, force without stint or limit' had been Wilson's promise, yet neither the Germans nor the Allies expected much military and naval contribution from the United States. In fact, it was fully a year after the declaration of war before American soldiers arrived in sufficient numbers to affect the military situation on the Western front, and the Germans confidently expected to win the war in less than a year. When American military aid did come, it was decisive. But even before American troops turned the tide

1. A token force of Americans fought in the Archangel-Murmansk campaign of 1918–19 and another in an Allied expedition in Siberia that terminated in 1920. Though some historians have interpreted these interventions as attempts to destroy Bolshevism, or to check the Japanese, they appear to have been motivated largely by military concerns, which turned out to be quite ill-founded.

'The Draftee.' In World War I the draft was the main supplier of recruits for the Army, but through most of the conflict the Navy, as well as the Marines, relied upon voluntary enlistment. Not until the last three months of the war did the selective service system embrace sailors and marines too. This picture is by Lewis W. Hine (1874–1940), who succeeded Jacob Riis as the most important photographer of the New Immigrants in the urban slums. (*George Eastman House Collection*)

at Château-Thierry, the navy had cooperated to destroy the effectiveness of German submarines.

General Joffre early assured American officials that half a million soldiers was the largest number the Allies expected the United States to send to France, but the government organized its military machine upon a far more ambitious basis. Within eighteen months the United States created an effective army of 4 million men, transported over 2 million to France, and placed 1.3 million on the firing line. This was a result of the organizing genius of Newton D. Baker, who, despite pacifist inclinations, proved himself one of the ablest of all secretaries of war. Even before the actual declaration of war, Baker had been convinced of the need to raise an army by conscription rather than by the volunteer system. Under the Selective Service Act of 1917, 2,810,296 men were inducted into the army. The regular army, national guard, navy, and marine corps continued to be recruited by voluntary enlistment. Including these and 'minor branches of service,' the armed forces totalled nearly five million.

The United States Navy got into the thick of the action much sooner than the army, but only after a bad start. Although Secretary Daniels and his Assistant Secretary, Franklin D. Roosevelt, had done a great deal to build up the morale and efficiency of the fleet, new construction was still mostly in the blueprint stage. The Chief of Naval Operations had no war plan ready when war was declared, and the one he promulgated on 11 April envisioned a considerable Pacific Fleet to watch Japan—an ally! Fortunately, the President had been prevailed upon to send the gifted and energetic Rear Admiral William S. Sims to London a few days ahead of the declaration of war; and Sims's pungent dispatches described a situation so appalling that the navy almost completely altered its plans. Sims reported that England had only a three weeks' supply of grain on hand, the U-boats were increasingly devastating, and if something was not done promptly to repair the life line, the Allies would have to throw in the sponge before the end of the year.

Under Sims's influence, the Allies adopted the convoy system of operating merchant ships in groups so that they could be protected from submarine attack by an escort of cruisers and destroyers, and the convoy system enabled American troops and supplies to cross the Atlantic safely. Sims also persuaded the navy to send as many destroyers as it could spare to Ireland to be operated for escort-of-convoy and anti-submarine patrol under the British. The new convoy tactics and aggressive patrolling reduced Allied monthly shipping losses from 881,000 tons (April) to 289,000 tons (November), and these losses were more than replaced by new construction; submarine operations became very hazardous and the United States could send troops and supplies abroad with confidence that they would arrive. Not one loaded transport was lost. Finally, it was the U.S. Navy that laid the colossal mine barrage across the North Sea which, beginning in June 1918, practically closed that exit to enemy submarines. Without the work by the U.S. Navy, the Allies might have been defeated before American ground forces could have arrived. Nevertheless, it was the American Expeditionary Force which, in conjunction with the Allied armies, secured victory.

Late in 1917 the military situation turned radically against the Allies. In October the Italian army cracked at Caporetto and the Allies had to hurry troops from the Western front to stem the Austrian tide. Two months later negotiations by the new Soviet government at Brest-Litovsk released hundreds of thousands of German soldiers for the Western front. By the spring of 1918 the Germans had a clear numerical superiority in the West, and their high command prepared with confidence for a drive on Paris that would end the war.

A Macedonian cry went up for American troops, and there began a 'race for France.' Could the United States speed up her troop shipments sufficiently to redress the balance between the Allies and the Central Powers? 'Would she appear in time to snatch the victor's laurels from our brows?' asked Hindenburg. 'That, and that only was the decisive question! I believed I could answer it in the negative.' Altogether, during the critical months from March to October 1918, 1,750,000 American soldiers landed in France. 'America,' wrote German Commander-in-Chief Ludendorff, 'thus became the decisive power in the war.'

The great German offensive began on 21 March 1918, and by early June, after capturing well over 100,000 prisoners, the Germans, standing on the right bank of the Marne, threatened Paris. At this crisis of the war Pershing, who wanted the American army in France to form an independent unit, temporarily waived this claim and placed all his forces at the disposal of the new supreme commander, General Foch, who dispersed them among the Allied armies where, at engagements like Belleau Wood, they made an incalculable contribution to Allied morale. On 15 July came the fourth and last phase of the German offensive, the Second Battle of the Marne. The Germans launched their heaviest attack at the Château-Thierry salient; had they broken through, Paris could not have been saved. American troops, 275,000 strong, supported the French in stemming a tide which at first seemed irresistible. In

(*West Point Museum*)

three days the German offensive was exhausted, and on 18 July, without giving the enemy an opportunity to consolidate, Foch called upon the 1st and 2nd American and the First French Morocco Divisions to spearhead a counterattack, which was brilliantly executed. The German Chancellor later confessed that 'at the beginning of July 1918, I was convinced . . . that before the first of September our adversaries would send us peace proposals. . . . That was on the 15th. On the 18th even the most optimistic among us knew that all was lost. The history of the world was played out in three days.'

With the passing of the crisis on the Marne, Pershing won approval of his cherished plan for an independent American army. In September the new American force wiped out the strategically important St. Mihiel salient in two days, and in the Meuse-Argonne battle, which cost 117,000 American casualties, played an important role in breaking the Hindenburg line. On 3 October Prince Max of Baden addressed to President Wilson the first overture for peace—on the basis of the Fourteen Points. Wilson handled these negotiations with a skill that belied his reputation as an impractical idealist. After a month of diplomatic fencing, in which the Germans were worsted, the Allied governments instructed Foch to negotiate for an armistice. On 9 November the Kaiser fled across the border to Holland. Two days later an armistice was officially proclaimed, and the greatest and most costly war that the world had yet known came to an end.

The Peace Conference, the Treaty, and the League

Wilson was to discover that it was easier to win a war than to make a peace. The only statesman representing a major power who combined intelligence and magnanimity, he nevertheless bore some of the responsibility for creating a situation in which vindictiveness and greed would have free play. He had acquiesced in the suppression of freedom of expression in the United States; he had supported Creel's campaign to inoculate Americans with the germs of hatred for the Central Powers; and he had encouraged utopian expectations about the outcome of the war. Furthermore, it should be recognized that if no other statesman had Wilson's breadth of vision, he was not altogether disinterested, for his aims were congruent with America's stake in a stable international order in which liberal capitalism would prosper.

Even before the armistice Wilson determined to shatter precedent by taking personal charge of the peace negotiations. On 24 October 1918 he had appealed to the American electorate for a vote of confidence: 'If you have approved of my leadership and wish me to continue to be your unembarrassed spokesman in affairs at home and abroad, I earnestly beg that you will express yourselves unmistakably to that effect by returning a Democratic majority to both the Senate and House of Representatives.' Two weeks later the voters chose a majority of Republicans for both houses of Congress. By winning control of the Senate by two votes, the Republicans were able to place Henry Cabot Lodge in the chairmanship of the critically important Senate Foreign Relations Committee.

Well before the election Republican leaders like Roosevelt and Lodge had opposed Wilson's plans for a postwar association of nations. Roosevelt, who had long had an intense hatred of Wilson, was a bitter partisan who believed that casualty lists were being suppressed in order to hide the fact that two-thirds of the American war dead were Republicans. The former President insisted that the United States had gone to war strictly to seek vengeance for insults to American honor, and he demanded that the peace be dictated by 'hammering guns' instead of 'clicking . . . typewriters.' Lodge, who regarded himself as a Scholar in Politics, resented the renown Wilson had won in the same field. (In fact, Senator Depew's remark is to the point: Lodge had a mind like the New England landscape—'naturally barren, but highly cultivated.') Though the Democratic setback in 1918 resulted less from resentment at the President's appeal than from Western grievances over price regulation, Wilson left himself open to the Republican claim that, after drawing the line on foreign policy, he had been rejected. When on 13 December the President sailed for France, Roosevelt

'Signing of the Treaty of Versailles,' by John C. Johansen. The ceremony took place on 28 June 1919 which, by an odd coincidence, marked the fifth anniversary of the slaying of the Archduke Francis Ferdinand at Sarajevo, and it was held in the Hall of Mirrors in Louis XIV's palace of Versailles. The Germans, who were compelled to sign, were unreconciled. 'We must never forget it is only a scrap of paper,' said the Berlin *Vorwärts*. 'Treaties based on violence can keep their validity only so long as force exists. Do not lose hope. The resurrection day comes.' (*Smithsonian Institution*)

warned 'our allies, our enemies and Mr. Wilson himself' that 'Mr. Wilson has no authority whatever to speak for the American people at this time. His leadership has just been emphatically repudiated by them.'

In the preliminary armistice negotiations with the Allies, Wilson had been made painfully aware of the conflict in war aims between the United States and the Allied powers. Though he had clung tenaciously to his Fourteen Points, he had been forced to admit qualifications with respect to the important items of 'freedom of the seas' and reparations. Aware of the existence of secret treaties which in part nullified the Fourteen Points, he persuaded himself to ignore their significance. These secret treaties had been concluded between the major Allies and powers like Japan, Italy, and Romania, in order to induce them to join the Allied side. The treaties were contrary to the principle of self-determination, and Wilson should have tried to obtain abrogation or modification of them before sending American troops to Europe.

In the Peace Conference, which held its first formal session 18 January 1919, all the Allied and associated powers were represented, but the 'Big Four'—Britain, France, Italy, and the United States—made the important decisions. Like the conference at Brest-Litovsk, this one gave the defeated powers no part in the negotiations; they were merely called in when the treaty was ready and ordered to sign. Moreover, the jingo atmosphere of Paris and the personalities of leaders made a just peace exceedingly difficult to attain. David Lloyd George, the British prime minister, had won a general election since the armistice on the slogans 'Hang the Kaiser' and 'Make Germany Pay.' Georges Clemenceau, the 'tiger' of French politics, regarded Wilsonian liberalism with complete skepticism and assailed it with mordant wit: 'Mr. Wilson bores me with his Fourteen Points; why, God Almighty has only ten!' Many Europeans regarded Wilson as little short of a new Saviour come to bring peace on earth. But too many had been outraged, impoverished, and wounded by a war which they regarded as entirely Germany's fault to support the sort of peace that Wilson wanted. In the end Wilson was forced to agree to many compromises, but he imposed upon his colleagues something of his own ideas of a 'just' peace and wrung from them some concessions. Perhaps no one could have done more.

The Treaty of Versailles, to which the Germans affixed their signature on 28 June, was not as drastic as France wanted, nor harsh enough to keep Germany down. It required Germany to admit her war guilt, stripped her of all colonies and commercial rights in Africa and the Far East, of Alsace-Lorraine, Posen, and parts of Schleswig and Silesia, confiscated the coal mines of the Saar basin, imposed disarmament upon her, saddled her with an immediate indemnity of $5 billion and a future reparation bill of indeterminate amount, and placed practically the whole of her economic system under temporary Allied control. The Versailles treaty and collateral agreements also sanctioned the creation of a number of new states, including Czechoslovakia, Yugoslavia, and Poland. Wilson successfully resisted some of the more extreme demands of the Allies. He prevented France from detaching the entire Rhineland from Germany; denied Fiume to Italy, an action which caused Orlando to withdraw from the conference in a huff; persuaded Japan to evacuate Shantung; and refused to permit the Allies to charge Germany with the whole cost of the war. And, finally, he wrote into the treaty the covenant of the League of Nations, which, he felt, was the part that justified the whole.

The League of Nations gave every member nation an equal vote in the Assembly, which was a deliberative body, while the United States, Great Britain, France, Italy, and Japan were permanent and four other nations temporary members of the Council, which was more largely an executive body. An independent Permanent Court of International Justice was established at The Hague. The members of the League pledged themselves to 'respect and preserve as against external aggression the territorial integrity and existing political independence of all Members of the League' (Art. X); to give publicity to treaties and to armaments; to submit to inquiry and arbitration all disputes threatening international peace, breaches of treaties, and questions of international law, and refrain from war until three months after the award by the arbiters; to refrain from war with the nations complying with the award of the League;

and to employ, on the recommendation of the League Council, military, naval, financial, and economic sanctions against nations resorting to war in disregard of their covenants under the League. The Council was further authorized to exercise mandates over the former colonies of Germany and Turkey and oversee conditions of labor, traffic in women and children, drugs, arms, and munitions, and the control of health. The covenant specifically recognized 'the validity of . . . regional understandings like the Monroe Doctrine.'

The President called Congress into special session to consider the treaty and the League of Nations, but when he returned to the United States, early in June, 1919, he found the Senate in an ugly mood. Opposition to the League was compounded of diverse elements: hostility to Wilson, partisanship, and senatorial pique; resentment at the fact that the American delegation to Versailles included no senator and no prominent Republican; indignation of German-Americans who felt that their country had been betrayed, Italian-Americans angry over Fiume, and Irish-Americans stirred up against England, then engaged in trying to suppress the Sinn Fein revolution; conservative disapproval of what was alleged to be leniency toward Germany, liberal disapproval of severity toward Germany; and a general feeling that Wilson and America had been tricked, and that the country should avoid future European entanglements. In the Senate three groups could be discerned. At one extreme stood the 'irreconcilables'—Borah, Johnson, La Follette, and others who were determined to undo the whole of Wilson's handiwork; at the other extreme were the President's faithful followers who were ready to ratify the treaty as it stood. In between a large number favored reservations to protect American interests. At all times, during the prolonged debate over the treaty, more than three-fourths of the Senate was ready to accept membership in the League in some form or other.

Both opposition to the League and support of it broke on party lines. Of the 47 Democrats in the Senate, only four were outright opponents of the treaty, a remarkable record of party solidarity. With Democratic votes Wilson could easily overcome the irreconcilables like Borah. His crucial problem was how to cope with the pivotal group of Republican reservationists, especially the powerful faction of strong reservationists led by Lodge who were not only jealous of American sovereignty but wanted to deny the Democrats the opportunity to go to the country in 1920 as the party which had led the nation not only through a victorious war but to a successful peace. Lodge insisted on altering the treaty proposal so that it no longer bore Wilson's stamp; if this failed, he preferred to see it die.

Wilson, unwilling to accept any but the mildest 'interpretations,' showed himself almost as stubborn as the irreconcilables. Failing to make headway against the senatorial clique, he resorted to a direct appeal to the people. On 4 September he set out on a speaking tour which carried him through the Middle West and Far West. He spoke with passionate conviction. In Omaha, he warned: 'I tell you, my fellow citizens, I can predict with absolute certainty that within another generation, there will be another world war if the nations of the world do not concert the method by which to prevent it.' But against the rising tide of isolationism and illiberalism he made little headway, and much of the effect of his speeches was spoiled by the counter-arguments of the irreconcilables who stalked him relentlessly from city to city. On 25 September he suffered a physical collapse. And with his collapse went all the hopes of ratification.

On 19 November 1919, the Treaty of Versailles went down to defeat in the Senate, both with and without reservations. Yet a large majority of Senators favored ratification with some kind of reservations, as did a large majority of the American people. Senator Lodge would not budge; neither would Wilson. He instructed Senate Democrats to vote down the treaty with reservations, and half of them heeded him. When the treaty came up for reconsideration again on 19 March 1920, twenty-three Democrats joined the twelve Republican irreconcilables to defeat ratification with reservations by a vote of 49 to 35, seven votes less than the required two-thirds. Thus was sacrificed the fairest prospect for world order which had yet been opened to mankind.

Like a British prime minister with a balky Parliament, Wilson waited for the next general elec-

Ben Shahn, 'Bartolomeo Vanzetti and Nicola Sacco.' This is one of a number of *gouaches* that brought the painter Ben Shahn (1898–1969) into the public eye in 1932. Shahn was to become the most important social commentator in twentieth-century art in America. 'Ever since I could remember I'd wished I'd been lucky enough to be alive at that great time—when something big was going on, like the Crucifixion,' he said. 'And suddenly I realized I was. Here I was living through another crucifixion. Here was something to paint!' *(Museum of Modern Art, Gift of Abby Aldrich Rockefeller, tempera on paper over composition board, 10½" x 14½")*

tion to vindicate his policies and give him a more malleable legislature. The 1920 election, he declared, should be 'a solemn referendum' on American membership in the League of Nations. But the League question was obfuscated in the campaign, and it never again figured as a vital issue in a national election. As early as 1922 the United States began to send 'unofficial observers' to League conferences, but it never took a direct part in the League's peace-keeping machinery.

Aftermath

No sooner had the war ended than the country moved precipitately to erase all evidence of the war experience, especially the experiment of an enhanced role for government. Wilson called for a rapid liquidation of governmental activities, and legislation returning the railroads to private operation and promoting a privately owned merchant marine was enacted after the war. Nonetheless, the government continued to affect the structure of the transportation industry. The Esch-Cummins Transportation Act of 1920 differed from previous railroad regulation in that it sought to encourage rather than discourage consolidation, but with small success. More consequential were a series of actions by federal, state, and local governments which built up rivals of the railroads—trucks, buses, private cars, and airplanes. In the half-century after the experiment with federal operation of the railways in World War I, the government, instead of managing the railroads in the public interest, chose to subsidize highways which scarred the countryside and spewed traffic into crowded cities, while the railroads, which in other lands were the basis of an efficient transportation system, faced extinction.

Another legacy of the war roiled the waters of international affairs. America's efforts to collect more than $10 billion in debts from its former Allies involved it in a series of abortive enterprises in which financiers like Charles G. Dawes and Owen D. Young attempted to develop a viable relation between the debts and German reparations. The insistence by the United States that the debts be repaid proved to the Europeans that 'Uncle Shylock' was heartless, and by June 1933 only Finland was meeting its obligations in full. The whole business addled American politics and poisoned relations with Europe for more than a decade.

World War I had a still more venomous consequence: a residue of pent-up violence that found expression in a number of ugly forms. Between 1917 and 1925, some 600,000 blacks moved north, thereby jeopardizing the pattern of racial segregation in America, and black soldiers returned from the war less willing to accept second-class citizenship. Southern whites responded by using violence and intimidation to compel the Negro to acquiesce in the rituals of white supremacy. In the first year after the war, seventy Negroes were lynched, some still wearing their army uniforms. In Washington, D.C., on a sultry Sunday in the summer of 1919, gangs of whites, many of them restless unemployed ex-servicemen, set upon isolated blacks and beat them; two Negroes were mauled right in front of the White House. The next day, blacks struck back, firing shots into crowds of whites, attacking a streetcar, emptying their guns at random at whites in the street. One Negro explained: 'We have been through war and gave everything, even our lives, and now we are going to stop being beat up.'

That same year the government itself contributed to the postwar acrimony by playing an active role in the Red Scare, in which Wilson's Attorney General, A. Mitchell Palmer, tried to make political capital by persecuting alien radicals. Using private spies and *agents provocateurs*, Palmer conducted a series of lawless raids on private houses and labor headquarters, rounded up several thousand aliens, and subjected them to drumhead trials. Some five hundred aliens were deported, many of them illegally. State governments also persecuted dissenters. In 1920 the Empire State distinguished itself by expelling five Socialist members from the state legislature. It was not alleged that the party was illegal or that the Socialist members were guilty of any crime, but merely that socialism was 'absolutely inimical to the best interests of the State of New York and of the United States.' The distinguished Charles Evans Hughes, later to be elevated to the chief justiceship, was one of many to protest against this palpable violation of elementary constitutional rights, but his call for sanity fell on deaf ears.

Hostility to radicals, antipathy to foreigners, and a jealous protection of the status quo were revealed in the most sensational murder trial since that of the Haymarket anarchists—the Sacco-Vanzetti case (1920–27). Nicola Sacco and Bartolomeo Vanzetti, foreigners and philosophical anarchists, were accused of murdering a paymaster at South Braintree, Massachusetts. When they were convicted and sentenced to death there was a widespread belief that the jury had been moved more by their radical views and their evasion of military service than by the evidence. For seven years men and women of all shades of opinion and in almost every country labored to obtain a retrial, and the governor of Massachusetts appointed an investigating committee consisting of two college presidents and a judge of probate. Although this committee found the trial judge guilty of 'grave breach of official decorum,' it reported that justice had been done. When Sacco and Vanzetti were electrocuted on 23 August 1927, a cry of horror went up around the world. Citizens of Massachusetts who loved justice remembered John Adams and the Boston Massacre case and Judge Sewall's retraction in the case of the Salem witches and hung their heads in shame.

29

American Society in Transition

*

1910–1940

The New Society

In the interwar decades American society underwent far-reaching changes, many of which were foreshadowed in the years before the United States entered World War I. As early as 1908 the photographer Alfred Stieglitz had hung Matisse canvases in his Fifth Avenue gallery. In 1909 Sigmund Freud came over to lecture at Clark University, and by 1916 some 500 psychoanalysts were already practicing in New York. At Mabel Dodge's salon in Greenwich Village, writers, artists, and revolutionaries discussed the ideas of Henri Bergson and Georges Sorel, of Nietzsche and Shaw and those insurgent thinkers who stressed spontaneity, instinct, emotion, and movement, and assaulted nineteenth-century conceptions of morality and decorum. In 1913 a dance craze swept the country, symbol of a growing sense of sexual liberation. Disturbed by the intimacy of movement, Columbia University stipulated that six inches must separate the dancers. By 1915 H. L. Mencken had identified the new American woman as 'the Flapper.' In intellectual circles at least, there was a quickening awareness of taking part in an insurrection against the old order, and a vivid anticipation of the coming of great events.

The prewar rebels, for all their earthshaking manifestos, lived in an exuberant age of confidence, an era that World War I shattered beyond repair. Too many had known the young men who, in Ezra Pound's words, 'walked eye-deep in hell / believing in old men's lies,' or, as e.e. cummings wrote, had heard 'death's enormous voice,' which left 'all the silence / filled with vivid noiseless boys.' The war blighted the immense sense of promise of the Progressive period and left a sense of outrage at the killing and maiming. Hemingway caught much of the spirit of the postwar years in his story of the Oklahoma boy who returned from the war 'much too late' and who 'did not want any consequences ever again.' Although some of the old progressives remained faithful to earlier ideals, many rejected public involvement for a preoccupation with self. Like the 'Hamlet' of Archibald MacLeish, they would 'Cry I! I! I! forever.' This private vision inspirited the literature of the 1920's but impoverished the politics.

Portrait of Gertrude Stein (1874–1946) by Pablo Picasso. 'Three generations of young writers have sat at her feet,' wrote Carl Van Vechten. Writers were deeply affected by her experiments with prose style in works like *Three Lives* (1909) and *The Autobiography of Alice B. Toklas* (1933) and even more by the shelter and stimulus she provided at her salon at 27 rue de Fleurus, Paris. 'It was like one of the best rooms in the finest museum,' recalled Ernest Hemingway, 'except there was a big fireplace and it was warm and comfortable and they gave you good things to eat and tea.' (*Metropolitan Museum of Art, Bequest of Gertrude Stein, 1946*)

The socialist Norman Thomas protested: 'The old reformer has become the Tired Radical, and his sons and daughters drink at the fountain of the *American Mercury*. They have no illusions but one. And that is that they can live like Babbitt and think like Mencken.'

George Babbitt, the protagonist of Sinclair Lewis's novel, personified the materialistic aspirations of this period. During the piping years of the 'twenties, population grew by 17 millions in a decade, and the growth in national wealth was equally noteworthy. The wealth of the nation was unevenly distributed: 25 million families—over 87 per cent of the population—had incomes of less than $2500, while only about a million families—less than 3 per cent—had incomes of over $5000. Yet since advertising looked to a mass market, a large proportion of the nation was able to find more gratification of its wants. Business co-operated with these desires by providing easier credit, and the public responded by buying what it wanted on the installment plan. No longer inclined to regard thrift as a virtue, Americans speculated avidly on the stock market or in Florida real estate.

These changes contributed to significant alterations in the national character, for as Joseph Gusfield has noted, 'In an easygoing, affluent society, the credit mechanism has made the Ant a fool and the Grasshopper a hero.' The nation was swiftly moving toward a society in which styles of consumption would determine status. The New Middle Class—from the white collar clerk to the Madison Avenue executive—was captivated by the plethora of novel consumer products. In Montgomery Ward catalogues, toasters and irons made their first appearance in 1912, vacuum cleaners in 1917, the electric range in 1930, the refrigerator in 1932.

These new products first found their way in an urban market, for rural America still lacked electricity, and in this period America was becoming a predominantly urban nation. In 1890 the population was 65 per cent rural; in 1930 it was 56 per cent urban. Many cities, especially in Florida and California, grew tenfold during these years, while increases in the larger cities of the older parts of the country were spectacular.[1] Nearly half the population of the country lived within easy access of cities of 100,000 inhabitants or more; these cities became the shopping, entertainment, and cultural centers of the nation. The city promised excitement and adventure. In a Floyd Dell novel, the protagonist has a recurring image of a map at the depot 'with a picture of iron roads from all over the Middle West centering in a dark blotch in the corner. . . . "Chicago!" he said to himself.'

To this process of urbanization the automobile especially contributed. At the close of World War I there were some 9 million motor cars in use; a decade later, 26 million. The automobile broke down isolation and provincialism, promoted standardization, accelerated the growth of cities at the expense of villages and then of suburbs at the expense of cities, created a hundred new industries and millions of new jobs. It also required the destruction of large parts of the country to make way for roads, and took an annual toll of life and limb as high as that exacted by the First World War.

The radio, like the automobile, began as a plaything and became a necessity and a promoter of social change. The first broadcasting station opened at Pittsburgh in 1920; within a decade there were almost 13 million radios in American homes, and by 1940 there were close to 900 broadcasting stations and 52 million receiving sets. From the beginning radio was privately owned, not—as in Europe—in public hands, and a few great networks controlled most of the wavelengths. Government regulation was tardy, feeble, and fragmentary; not until 1927 did Congress

1. Thus, in thousands:

	1890	1930
Atlanta, Ga.	65	270
Detroit, Mich.	205	1568
Grand Rapids, Mich.	60	170
Hartford, Conn.	60	150
Indianapolis, Ind.	105	305
Kansas City, Mo.	130	400
Minneapolis, Minn.	164	464
Pittsburgh, Pa.	238	669
Rochester, N.Y.	130	320
Syracuse, N.Y.	88	209
Toledo, Ohio	81	290
Washington, D.C.	189	487

establish a Federal Radio Commission to license stations, assign wave-lengths, and supervise policies. In 1934 this commission gave way to the Federal Communications Commission, which was authorized to require that all broadcasts conform to the 'public interest, convenience and necessity,' a stipulation interpreted so loosely as to be almost meaningless.

Second only to the radio as diversion were the 'movies.' Invented by the resourceful Thomas Edison at the turn of the century, the motion picture grew steadily in popularity. David Griffith's *The Birth of a Nation,* shown to rapt audiences in 1915, introduced the spectacle film which another producer, Cecil B. de Mille, shortly made his peculiar property. Stars of the silent screen supplanted luminaries of the 'legitimate' stage: Mary Pickford, 'America's sweetheart'; Charles Chaplin, greatest of comedians; Douglas Fairbanks, handsome and acrobatic; Bill Hart, always in cowboy costume; Pearl White, whose endless escapades left her audience palpitating each week for the next installment. Sound, introduced in 1927, greatly expanded film potentialities, and the development of the cartoon movie by Walt Disney, creator of Mickey Mouse and Donald Duck, delighted adults as well as children. By 1937 the motion-picture business was eleventh in assets among the industries of the nation, and some 75 million persons visited the movies each week, while millions more were attracted to sporting events.

Few phenomena attracted so much attention as the 'emancipation' of women, though, in fact, there was less change than many thought. Woman suffrage was written into the Constitution in 1920, and increasing numbers of women took part in public life; a generation that observed Jane Addams and Eleanor Roosevelt could not seriously believe women less competent than men in public affairs. During the manpower shortage in World War I, so many women crowded into factory and office that it appeared a major shift had occurred in the position of women. In fact, patterns of employment in the 1920's remained essentially unaltered. More enduring changes came in the social and psychological realms. Labor-saving appliances liberated millions of women from the stove and the wash-tub, and knowledge of birth control from the demands of large families. As women won greater independence, they had some success, too, in replacing the old double standard of morality.

The institution of the family faced a difficult adjustment. In 1890 out of every one hundred marriages, six ended in divorce; forty years later, eighteen of every one hundred marriages were thus terminated, and that year some 200,000 couples were legally separated. In other respects, too, family life seemed less stable. Those who continued to live in the town where they were born became objects of curiosity, and the shift from roomy Victorian houses to city flats made it difficult for large families—grandparents and maiden aunts—to live together. For many Americans the Depression was to reveal that

> Home is the place where when you have to go there,
> They have to take you in.[2]

For many it was that, and nothing more. Yet for all the vicissitudes, the family continued to adapt, and to endure.

Literary Interpretations

In the 'lyric years' before the war almost everything was 'new': the new poetry, the new criticism, the new art, the 'New Freedom,' the 'New Nationalism,' the new history. Herbert Croly established the *New Republic;* the Armory Show of 1913 exploded traditional art; the Provincetown Players welcomed young Eugene O'Neill; and William C. Handy composed the 'Memphis Blues.' 'The fiddles are tuning up all over America,' wrote John Butler Yeats.

So they were, but it was in Chicago that Harriet Monroe whipped them together into a kind of orchestra. In 1912 she launched *Poetry: A Magazine of Verse,* and within six years almost all the poets who would dominate the literary scene for the next fifty years made their bow, most of them in the pages of this little magazine: the

2. Robert Frost, 'Death of the Hired Man.'

'The Leaguers.' This depiction of members of the League of Women Voters is almost certainly the first (and perhaps the only) example of a painting of women in politics by a prominent artist. It is even more surprising that it should come from the brush of Guy Pène du Bois (1884–1958), one of the leading spirits behind the Armory Show, who concentrated on painting café society. 'His canvases,' it has been noted, 'often show two or three simplified figures in frozen motion, like mannequins caught in a spotlight.' (*Goldfield Galleries, Los Angeles*)

'prairie' poets, Carl Sandburg and Vachel Lindsay; the imagists, Amy Lowell and Conrad Aiken; the lyricists, Edna St. Vincent Millay and Elinor Wylie; Freudians like Edgar Lee Masters; and Robinson Jeffers, who went his own way. In England three Americans—Ezra Pound, T. S. Eliot, and Robert Frost—were publishing their first books. Not since New England's golden day had there been anything like it.

When Carl Sandburg published 'Chicago' in *Poetry:*

Hog Butcher for the World,
Tool Maker, Stacker of Wheat,
Player with Railroads and the Nation's Freight Handler;
Stormy, husky, brawling,
City of the Big Shoulders

a jaundiced critic wrote that 'the typographical arrangement for this jargon creates a suspicion that it is intended to be taken as some form of poetry.' And so it was. A disciple of Whitman, Sandburg thought nothing too undignified for poetry. Born of Swedish parents, Sandburg was as authentically American as Lincoln, whose biography he later wrote in six huge volumes. Like Lincoln he was instinctively democratic; his most important collection of poetry is called *The People, Yes.*

Another son of Illinois, Vachel Lindsay, wandered from town to town preaching the 'Gospel of Beauty,' and 'trading his rhymes for bread.' In 1913 he brought out *General Booth Enters Heaven* with its moving tribute to Governor Altgeld, the 'Eagle Forgotten,' and thereafter the 'Congo' and 'The Chinese Nightingale.' His verse, made to be chanted rather than read, led Lindsay to a career on the lecture circuit which laid a heavy toll on his energy, and in December 1931 he took his own life.

Imagism was altogether more sophisticated, closer to abstract painting and modern music than to the kind of poetry being written by Vachel Lindsay. A revolt against the verbose pretentiousness of late nineteenth-century rhymesters, it valued the intense, concrete image. Ezra Pound, who led the movement, explained that there was to be 'no Tennysonianness of speech; nothing—nothing that you couldn't in some circumstance, in the stress of some emotion, actually say.' When Pound wearied of it, Amy Lowell assumed leadership of the group and aggressively promoted *vers libre*. The 'Amygists,' as Pound called them, not only encouraged free verse, but sought to write 'hard and clear' poetry and sometimes succeeded.

Ezra Pound and T. S. Eliot were both in London when Harriet Monroe launched *Poetry*; Pound became its London editor, and Eliot contributed to it his first important poem, 'The Love Song of J. Alfred Prufrock.' Impetuous and scholarly, adventurous and reactionary, Pound poured out a steady stream of translations, criticisms, and original verse—notably the endless series of *Cantos* composed with brilliant and calculated obscurity. Where Pound dissipated his talents, Eliot became one of the commanding figures of his age. Like Henry James he lived by preference in London, and eventually became a British citizen; like James, too, he became increasingly the champion of traditionalism. Equally distinguished as a poet, a dramatist, and a critic, Eliot did as much to change modern poetry as had Wordsworth and Whitman in earlier generations, and his *The Waste Land* (1922), subtle and profound, became the *vade mecum* of a whole generation. Yet some rebelled against the imagery of disintegration and sterility. 'After this perfection of death,' concluded Hart Crane, 'nothing is possible but a motion of some kind.'

American traditionalists looked to Henry James rather than to Eliot for inspiration, notably the three intrepid women who bridged the gap between the realism of Howells and the social protest of Dos Passos: Edith Wharton, Ellen Glasgow, and Willa Cather. In a series of novels from *The House of Mirth* (1905) to *Hudson River Bracketed* (1929), Mrs. Wharton presented complex social problems against a background of fashionable New York where Civil War profiteers and the new rich were crashing the gates of society, shattering old standards of elegance and taste, and calling in question old moralities. She was fascinated by the moral implications of the clash of cultures, and though she began as a rebel against the traditional social standards, she ended as something of an apologist for them. Ellen Glasgow, too, began by writing with ironic detachment about an old social order that she subsequently came to treat with 'sympathetic compassion.' By the 'twenties she perceived the threat to the values she cherished came less from the sentimentality of the Old South than from the absence of tradition in the New. Beginning with *Barren Ground* (1925), she expressed a mounting distaste for the emptiness of the new day and a grudging appreciation of the older virtues; with *The Sheltered Life* (1932) the appreciation was ardent; and *Vein of Iron* (1935) was an open appeal for the re-creation of the older values. Similarly, Willa Cather's novels and stories—those of the Arcadian Virginia of her childhood, the golden Nebraska of her youth, the shimmering Southwest of Bishop Latour, the Quebec of the Ursulines—were animated by a single theme: the superiority of the moral values of the past over the material interests of the present. The American West, she wrote, had been settled

> by dreamers, great hearted adventurers who were unpractical to the point of magnificence; a courteous brotherhood strong in attack but weak in defence, who could conquer but could not hold. . . .

All this now was gone; industry, business, and

speculation had destroyed it: that was the moral of the most nearly perfect of her books, *A Lost Lady*, and of *The Professor's House*.

The most popular serious poet of this generation was both traditionalist and innovator. Robert Frost made his first appearance just as the fiddles were tuning up, but he belonged to no school, took part in no movement, fitted into no pattern. For half a century he went his own way, developing a philosophy deceptively homespun and a style deceptively simple. Born in San Francisco, he was unmistakably a New Englander; raised in cities, he was a countryman to the marrow; authentically American, he did not gain recognition until he expatriated himself to England, where he published his first two volumes of poetry: *A Boy's Will* (1913), and *North of Boston* (1914), with 'Mending Wall,' 'Death of the Hired Man,' 'Home Burial'—poems not surpassed in our literature for beauty and insight. Through the 'twenties and 'thirties, Frost turned out book after book: *New Hampshire, West Running Brook, A Further Range*, until by the end of this period he was the grand old man of American letters, and with yet another quarter-century of honors ahead of him.

If the second decade of the new century had been one of affirmation, the decade of the 'twenties was one of disillusionment. The most vociferous critic of his generation, Henry L. Mencken of Baltimore, made it his special business to expose bourgeois complacency and his 'Americana' column in the *American Mercury* recorded with melancholy faithfulness the fatuousness and vulgarity of American life. His views were almost all malicious, for Mencken was catholic in his dislikes: he disapproved of the rich and the poor, the ignorant and the intelligent, the mob and the elite, fundamentalism and advanced thought, devotion to the past and confidence in the future. Still, Mencken made some positive contributions: a magazine that attracted the brightest writers of the day; an irreverent style that went far to liberate writing from pedantic pretentiousness; and three learned volumes on *The American Language*.

The 'revolt from the village' found its bards in Edgar Lee Masters and Sherwood Anderson. In *The Spoon River Anthology* (1915) Masters recorded, in the mode of the Greek Anthology, the drab existence of some two hundred victims of life in a little Illinois town, where dreamers were always defeated and idealists ended as cynics. Sherwood Anderson's grotesques revealed the unhinging experience of alienation and loneliness. *Winesburg, Ohio* (1919) was a declaration of war against the small town, the factory, industry, the ties of marriage and of family; and almost all other conventions. It was Sinclair Lewis, however, whose *Main Street* (1920) and *Babbitt* (1922) made the revolt against the small town and against business a popular preoccupation. Lewis satirized the dullness and provincialism of Gopher Prairie and Zenith City, but, like Mark Twain, he was very much a part of the world he repudiated, and he had a grudging affection for the characters he ridiculed.

American poetry ranged widely in the interwar period. Elinor Wylie and Edna St. Vincent Millay mastered the traditional sonnet form. Wallace Stevens wrote sensual, elegant poems distinguished by the vivid hues of their imagery: 'pungent oranges and bright, green wings,' 'porcelain chocolate and pied umbrellas,' and 'a dove with an eye of grenadine.' In *The Bridge* Hart Crane attempted to create an ambitious synthesis of American experience; and although he failed, his brilliant employment of symbol and myth made his failure a greater achievement than lesser men's successes. Robinson Jeffers revealed a preoccupation with violence, depravity, and death. William Carlos Williams wrote poetry spare in form, conversational in idiom, like 'The Red Wheelbarrow,' and Marianne Moore peopled 'imaginary gardens with real toads.'

The 'Harlem Renaissance' produced in quick succession Countee Cullen's *Color* in 1925, Langston Hughes's *The Weary Blues* in 1926, and James Weldon Johnson's *God's Trombones* in 1927. (Cullen's moving poem, 'Heritage,' reflected a fascination with the Negro's African origins which prompted Marcus Garvey to lead an abortive back-to-Africa movement in the 1920's.) 'I can never put on paper the thrill of the underground ride to Harlem,' Hughes wrote. 'I went up the steps and out into the bright September sun-

Langston Hughes (1902–67). This pastel by Winold Reiss was done about 1925, a year before the publication of *The Weary Blues,* the volume of poems that brought Hughes to artistic prominence. Over the next generation, Hughes published other works of poetry, including *Fine Clothes to the Jew* and *Shakespeare in Harlem,* as well as novels, short stories, drama, witty essays, and an autobiography. (*National Portrait Gallery, Smithsonian Institution*)

light. Harlem! I stood there, dropped my bags, took a deep breath and felt happy again.' The exuberant 'Negro Renaissance' resulted not only in poems but novels, plays, and social analyses by writers such as Claude McKay, Jean Toomer, Alain Locke, and E. Franklin Frazier. Yet the Harlem Renaissance often burdened the black writer with unrealistic expectations, and the white world's celebration of 'exotic' Harlem gave a distorted image of the 'laughing, swaying' black and glossed over the grim reality of slum life.

The most significant and most widely read writers of this period were those who confessed that theirs was a 'lost generation.' F. Scott Fitzgerald's *This Side of Paradise* (1920) became a guidebook to the new generation 'grown up to find all Gods dead, all wars fought, all faiths in man shaken.' Fitzgerald depicted the world of Princeton and the St. Regis roof, the Riviera and the Ritz bar in Paris, West Egg and Hollywood, of ambition that cannot be gratified, of wealth that in the end makes no difference, of pleasures that bring ennui and passion that cannot achieve lasting love. 'My millionaires,' he wrote, 'were as beautiful and damned as Thomas Hardy's peasants.' Still, his characters do not experience the nightmare that broods over the novels of a Kafka or a Camus; they differ little from the denizens of Gopher Prairie or Zenith City, and *The Great Gatsby* (1925), a melancholy account of Jay Gatsby, who put his life at 'the service of a vast, vulgar and meretricious beauty,' is a counterpart of Willa Cather's *A Lost Lady*.

The year after the appearance of *The Great Gatsby*, the 28-year-old Ernest Hemingway published his first novel, *The Sun Also Rises*. In this book, and in subsequent works like *A Farewell to Arms*, set against the background of the Italian retreat after Caporetto, Hemingway sought to work out his preoccupation with senseless, violent injury, especially the wound he had received in the war, and to develop a code whereby a man may live with honor in the face of violence and annihilation. Hemingway lived the flamboyant life which was the stuff of his novels and stories—he drove an ambulance in war-torn Italy, was a correspondent in the Spanish Civil War, and hunted big game in Africa. But his great influence came not from his manner of living but from his literary style: direct, pithy, nervous, idiomatic. No other quite mastered it, but almost every writer of his generation imitated it.

A third major literary figure of the 1920's, Eugene O'Neill, has the distinction of being the first American dramatist to approach the kind of fame accorded Ibsen, Chekhov, and Shaw. Very much a child of his age, he reflected almost all the intellectual currents of the day, responding—as he put it—to the 'discordant, broken, faithless rhythms of our time.' He indulged himself in naturalism in his early plays of the sea like *Anna Christie;* participated in the revolt from the village—particularly the New England village—in *Desire Under the Elms;* shot his arrows at Babbitry in *The Great God Brown;* confessed a brief nostalgia for a homespun past he had never known in the charming *Ah, Wilderness!;* experimented with expressionism in *Lazarus Laughed;* immersed himself in Freudianism in *Strange Interlude* and in *Mourning Becomes Electra,* where he boldly invited comparison with the Agamemnon trilogy of Aeschylus. When he died he left a searing autobiographical drama, *Long Day's Journey into Night,* which, like *The Iceman Cometh,* returned to naturalism. A note of desperation resounds in this the best of O'Neill's plays, which recapitulate his painful childhood memory of his intimidating father, his drug-addicted mother, and his alcoholic elder brother; and in his final autobiographical *cri du cœur* there is a sense of hopelessness and of doom.

The fourth major figure to emerge during these postwar years, William Faulkner, wrote of the disintegration of the values of the Old South and the failure of the New, on such eternal themes as the conflict of freedom and necessity and Man's quest to liberate himself from the burden of history. Beginning with *The Sound and the Fury* (1929), and including such masterpieces as *Light in August, As I Lay Dying,* and *The Hamlet,* Faulkner traced the pathology of the South, Old and New—the collapse of standards, the ineffectiveness of the old families—like his own Falkners—and the irredeemable vulgarity and corruption of the new—like the Snopeses and the Sutpens. The greatest of American literary experimenters, a writer of dazzling virtuosity, Faulkner had learned something from Proust, something from

James Joyce, but his use of the stream of consciousness technique, the flashback, interior monologues, tortured syntax, and jumbled time sequences is all his own.

A host of lesser writers addressed themselves to the crises that bedeviled the postwar years and made a powerful impression on their own generation. John Dos Passos's sprawling *U.S.A.* trilogy, a profoundly pessimistic work, portrays a society that is rootless and disintegrated, hurrying to wealth and pleasure without faith or purpose. James T. Farrell, Dreiser's most faithful disciple, in his *Studs Lonigan* series depicts the Chicago of the 'twenties with unrelenting bitterness. Thomas Wolfe, the promise of whose *Look Homeward, Angel* (1929) was never wholly fulfilled in his later and more popular books, belongs only marginally to this group. Gargantuan, tempestuous, capable of both bathos and beauty, Wolfe was something of a genius and something of a charlatan. John Steinbeck's early books—*Tortilla Flat, In Dubious Battle,* and the enchanting *Red Pony*—revealed a high technical skill and a deep understanding of the Mexican Americans and the migratory workers of California. His *Grapes of Wrath* (1939), a moving saga of the trek of the Joad clan from their dust-blown Oklahoma farm to the promised land of California, was the one great story to come out of the depression that caught the tragedy of the Dust Bowl, the gallantry as well as the meanness of the rural proletariat.

Painting and Music

A new chapter in American art began when the Armory Show opened its doors in February 1913. In the next month or so more than 100,000 people crowded into the vast hall in New York City to gaze at paintings by Impressionists and post-Impressionists, Fauvists and Cubists. Here for the first time Americans could see the paintings of Cézanne and Matisse, Van Gogh and Picasso as well as that forever baffling 'Nude Descending a Staircase' by Marcel Duchamp. The new sculptors were there too—figures by Epstein and Maillol and Brancusi as well as by the newly Americanized Gaston Lachaise.

Yet the triumph of the Modernists still lay well ahead, and preoccupation with the social scene became the most pronounced feature of American painting. In 1936 the artist George Biddle, reviewing an exhibition of contemporary American and French painting, found that while among the French pictures there was not one that was concerned with social problems, among the American works 'seventy-four dealt with the American scene or with a social criticism of American life; six with strikes or with strikebreakers; six with dust, sand, erosion, drought, and floods. There were no nudes, no portraits, and two still lifes. Out of the hundred not one could be said to enjoy, reflect, participate in our inherited democratic-capitalist culture.'[3] Biddle himself was preoccupied with the social scene. So, too, were those abler artists, Charles Burchfield and Edward Hopper. Burchfield spread before us a panorama of ugliness—the ugliness of the small town in Ohio or Indiana, of the factory in that Buffalo where he chose to live, of rain-swept nights on dreary streets. He set himself, writes Sam Hunter, 'the task of exploring in humble visual metaphors the failures behind the American success story, the corruption of the landscape that followed in the wake of industrial progress and which most Americans had managed to ignore.'[4] Edward Hopper painted the poignant isolation of people in the great cities, while social criticism is to be found in the political cartoons of William Gropper; in Reginald Marsh's gaudy pictures of Coney Island, the Bowery, and other gathering places of those who have nowhere to go; and in Ben Shahn's Daumier-like commentaries. Better disposed toward American institutions were the regionalists: Thomas Hart Benton, who transcribed the social history of the Mississippi, of the South and the West; John Steuart Curry, who celebrated the plains of Kansas and the cottonfields of Dixie; Grant Wood, who bathed the rolling hills and the gimcrack houses of Iowa in rich color and sentiment, though in such paintings as 'American Gothic' and 'Daughters of the Revolution' he showed that he, too, could indulge in social criticism.

In the meantime the Modernists were rebelling against representational art. During a brief transi-

3. *An American Artist's Story*, p. 292.

4. *Modern American Painting and Sculpture*, p. 111.

tion period, craftsmen like Jonas Lie and John Marin moved into new experiments in the use of color or—as with Charles Sheeler—in geometric designs. They were succeeded by modernists such as Marsden Hartley, Stuart Davis, and the brilliant Georgia O'Keeffe. And, after them, the pure abstractionists like Jackson Pollock were just around the corner.

American music was not as advanced as American art. With the notable exceptions of folk music and Negro spirituals, America had always imported its music and musicians, and the most determined efforts to cultivate a 'native' music had failed. Edward MacDowell's sonatas and concertos were applauded on two continents, but most of the music of this generation now seems second-rate and derivative. More vitality appeared in the generation of composers that came to maturity after World War I—Virgil Thomson, John Alden Carpenter, Roy Harris, and Aaron Copland. Influenced by modernists like Stravinsky and Schönberg, Carpenter and Copland explored the symphonic possibilities of jazz and translated into music the nervous and explosive character of our mechanical civilization, while George Gershwin's *Rhapsody in Blue* and *Porgy and Bess* and Jerome Kern's *Show Boat* raised popular music to an art form. America's musical genius was best revealed in folk melodies and their modern equivalents, ragtime, jazz, blues, and swing. The Negro carried jazz from New Orleans to Chicago, and by 1915, the year W. C. Handy wrote 'St. Louis Blues,' jazz had reached Harlem. In the ensuing years Benny Goodman and Duke Ellington and Louis Armstrong won a loyal following among millions of Americans ranging from 'bobby-soxers' to musical sophisticates. The totalitarian terror recruited to American shores some of the most distinguished of contemporary European composers—Stravinsky, Hindemith, Bartók, Schönberg, to mention only a few. Musical conservatories like the Juilliard flourished, and great foundations like the Guggenheim stood ready to give such patronage to budding genius as Mozart and Schubert never knew.

'The Bridge' by Joseph Stella, 1922. Born in Italy, Stella (1880–1946) came to America in 1900 and first exhibited as an Italian Futurist, but by the 1920's he was identified with American Precisionists like Charles Sheeler and Charles Demuth who were fascinated by the structures of an industrial civilization. Of the Brooklyn Bridge, which also captivated the poet Hart Crane, Stella said: 'To realize this towering imperative vision, I lived days of anxiety, torture and delight alike, trembling all over with emotion. . . . Upon the swarming darkness of the night, I rung all the bells of alarm with the blaze of electricity scattered in lightnings down the oblique cables, the dynamic pillars of my composition. . . .' (*Newark Museum*)

Science

Tocqueville had observed that 'in America the purely practical part of science is admirably understood, and careful attention is paid to the theoretical portion which is immediately requisite to application . . . but hardly any one in the United States devotes himself to the essentially theoretical and abstract portion of human knowledge.' That was still true a century later; yet by then not only universities but industry were liberally underwriting research in pure science. What is more, the United States greatly benefited from the migration of European scientists which set in with the advent of Hitler to power in 1933. Einstein was the most famous of hundreds of physicists, chemists, and medical men who found in America refuge from oppression and an opportunity to pursue their researches in the most favorable circumstances. The most striking advances came in astronomy and physics. Working with the giant telescope of Mt. Wilson Observatory, which enabled them to plot thousands of new galaxies, astronomers postulated an expanding universe. Physicists, meantime, invented the cyclotron to break down the composition of the atom and held out the hope that some elements—uranium, for example—might yield fabulous amounts of energy.

Throughout this postwar generation doctors and chemists and bacteriologists, working in the laboratories of universities, the Federal Government, or the great foundations, waged war against diseases that had baffled medical science for centuries. The results were spectacular. In the first third of the century, infant mortality declined in the United States by two-thirds and life expectancy increased from 49 years to 59 years. The death rate for tuberculosis dropped from 180 to 49 per 100,000, for typhoid from 36 to 2, for diphtheria from 43 to 2, for measles from 12 to 1. Yellow fever and smallpox were practically wiped out, the battle against malaria, pellagra, hookworm, and similar diseases was brilliantly successful, and insulin cut the death rate of diabetes from over 700 to 12 per 1000 cases. The most sensational development came in the fight against coccus infections. Sulfanilamide and its numerous derivatives were used with stunning success against a host of coccal infections—streptococcus, meningitis, gonorrhea, gangrene, pyelitis, and, above all, pneumonia.

Nevertheless, the general health of the American people was not a matter for complacency. Infant mortality was still higher than in countries such as Norway and Sweden, and the draft statistics of the early 'forties revealed that an alarmingly large proportion of American men suffered from ailments caused by poverty or neglect, and that the incidence of venereal disease was shockingly high, especially in the rural counties of the South. The clear correlation between health and income suggested the desirability of government support to public health comparable with that given to public education, a goal that America did not even begin to take seriously until the 1960's and has yet to achieve.

30

The New Era and the Old Order

*

1920–1929

Return to 'Normalcy'

In the decade after the First World War, the dominant Republican party avowed a philosophy of laissez faire, but in practice made government an instrument of large corporations. The decade saw a florid but badly distributed industrial prosperity accompanied by agricultural distress and succeeded by acute and prolonged depression. It was characterized by a decline in liberalism and an ardent nationalism. And it moved into the future with its eyes fixed on the past; as the post-Civil War decade looked back to ante-bellum days, the 1920's sought to preserve the rural values of nineteenth-century America from the rude intrusion of the great city.

After years of playing second fiddle to strong leaders like Theodore Roosevelt within their own party and to a strong-minded Democratic President, the Republican Old Guard in 1920 was determined to nominate a pliable candidate, one who would not attempt to dictate to the Senate. They had such a man in the undistinguished Senator from Ohio, Warren Harding, who announced that the country needed a return to 'not heroism but healing, not nostrums but normalcy . . . not experiment but equipoise, not submergence in internationality but sustainment in triumphant nationality.' For the party's vice-presidential nominee, the delegates selected Calvin Coolidge. Fame had recently thrust herself upon Governor Coolidge when, in the course of a Boston police strike, he declared that there was 'no right to strike against the public safety by anybody, anywhere, anytime.' This resounding declaration caught the imagination of a public jittery about the 'Red menace.'

The Republicans exploited the national mood of weariness with the tensions and discord of the Wilson years—the war, the draft, the meatless days, and Spartan life of the war economy, the League fight, the Red Scare. Since much of this dissatisfaction found a personal target in Wilson, many of the Republicans directed their fire not against the Democratic presidential nominee, Governor James Cox of Ohio, but against the President. At the Republican convention, Lodge cried: 'Mr. Wilson and his dynasty, his heirs and assigns, or anybody that is his, anybody who with bent knee has served his purposes, must be driven

Franklin D. Roosevelt accepts the vice-presidential nomination of his party, 9 August 1920. On the platform with him at his Hyde Park, New York, home are his wife, Eleanor, and his 'Chief' when he was Assistant Secretary of the Navy, Josephus Daniels, in white suit and black string tie. In his acceptance speech, at a time when Harding was enunciating isolationist themes, FDR said, 'Modern civilization has become so complex and the lives of civilized men so interwoven with the lives of other men in other countries as to make it impossible to be in this world and not of it.' Compared to Harding's performance, observed the Harvard economist F. W. Taussig, Roosevelt's acceptance address was 'like Hyperion to a satyr.' (*Franklin D. Roosevelt Library*)

from all control, from all influence upon the Government of the United States.' The Democrats, who were hurt by the difficulties of operating a war economy which splintered their coalition into antagonistic interest groups, also bungled the transition from war to peace, which resulted in severe economic dislocations. The middle class was angered by the post-war inflation, labor by the cut in take-home pay after the war and the suppression of strikes. The administration, which had lost the support of many conservatives who disliked Wilson's progressive measures, was now blamed by liberals for the Palmer raids, the compromises at Versailles, and the increasingly conservative orientation of the government.

In the 1920 election the Republicans won a crushing victory which restored them as the majority party, a position they would hold for the next twelve years. With the electorate swollen by millions of new women voters, Harding won over 61 per cent of the vote, the largest proportion ever achieved in a presidential contest up to that time. He received 16 million votes to Cox's 9 million, and took 404 electoral votes to Cox's 127 by capturing the entire North and West and breaking the Solid South by carrying Tennessee. (The Socialist Eugene V. Debs received slightly under a million votes, although he was serving a term in the federal penitentiary at Atlanta.) Harding swept every borough in New York City, and Cox won but one county in all New England and lost every county on the Pacific Coast. Although the League issue had been muddled, isolationists claimed Harding's landslide victory as a triumph for their views. Even more emphatically, the election marked an end to an era of political intensity and discouraged the forces of reform.

Save for the Washington arms conference and

the creation of the Bureau of the Budget, Harding's administration was barren of accomplishment and tarnished by scandal. If Harding found room in his cabinet for Charles Evans Hughes as Secretary of State and Herbert Hoover as Secretary of Commerce, he dismayed conservationists by naming Albert B. Fall to the Department of the Interior. Fall, with the acquiescence of Secretary of the Navy Denby, entered into a corrupt alliance with the Doheny and Sinclair interests to give them control of immensely valuable naval oil reserves. The Elk Hills reserve in California was leased to Doheny's company; the Teapot Dome reserve in Wyoming to Sinclair's; in return Fall got at least $100,000 from Doheny and $300,000 from Sinclair. Investigations conducted by Senator Thomas Walsh of Montana forced the resignations of Denby and Fall; civil prosecutions in the federal courts brought the cancellation of the oil leases; criminal prosecutions sent Fall and Sinclair to prison. Colonel Charles R. Forbes, director of the Veterans' Bureau, was charged with the corrupt sale of government property, liquor, and narcotics, and misconduct in office, and was sentenced to a term in the federal penitentiary. Colonel Thomas W. Miller, the alien-property custodian, who sold valuable German chemical patents for a song, was dismissed from office and convicted of a criminal conspiracy to defraud the government. The President's close friend Attorney-General Harry Daugherty, who had been Harding's campaign manager, was found guilty by a Senate committee of various malpractices, but on a criminal trial he escaped conviction.

Harding seems to have been innocent of participation in or profit from this orgy of corruption, but he could not have been entirely unaware of it or of the consequences when the inevitable exposures began to come shortly before his death in office on 2 August 1923. Eight years later, at the belated dedication of the Harding Memorial at Marion, Ohio, President Hoover said, 'Warren Harding had a dim realization that he had been betrayed by a few men whom he trusted, by men whom he had believed were his devoted friends. It was later proved in the courts of the land that these men had betrayed not alone the friendship and trust of their staunch and loyal friend, but they had betrayed their country. That was the tragedy of the life of Warren Harding.'

When Vice-President Coolidge succeeded Harding, Republicans breathed a sigh of relief. For Calvin Coolidge, whatever his limitations, represented probity and economy; if he displayed little zeal in tracking down the malefactors who had wrecked the Harding administration, he did not permit a continuation of their malpractices. A person of respectable mediocrity, Coolidge had little to his credit in the way of constructive legislation or political ideas and equally little to his discredit. So completely negative a man never before lived in the White House; it is characteristic that Coolidge is best remembered for his vetoes and his silence. 'Mr. Coolidge's genius for inactivity is developed to a very high point,' observed Walter Lippmann. 'It is far from being an indolent inactivity. It is a grim, determined, alert inactivity which keeps Mr. Coolidge occupied constantly.'

Yet this dour, abstemious, and unimaginative figure became one of the most popular of all American Presidents. For his frugality, unpretentiousness, and taciturnity gave vicarious satisfaction to a generation that was extravagant, pretentious, and voluble. To people who had pulled up their roots and were anxiously engaged in 'keeping up with the Joneses,' there was something comforting about the fact that Coolidge had been born in a village named Plymouth, that his first name was Calvin, that he had been content with a modest law practice and half of a two-family house in a small Massachusetts city, and that the oath of office which inducted him into the presidency had been administered in a Vermont farmhouse by his aged father, and by the light of a kerosene lamp. Actually Coolidge's frugality indicated no distrust of wealth; his taciturnity no philosophic serenity; his simplicity no depth. Coolidge lacked such Yankee traits as a desire to make the world better. Consequently, although 'Silent Cal' had a moral integrity wanting in his predecessor, his administration, more fully even than Harding's, represented a return to 'normalcy.'

Throughout this period, these conservative regimes held the progressives at bay. Even before the war some of the progressives had dropped by the way, and the war, although it brought such achievements as government labor boards, deeply divided the reformers. The aftermath was even more costly, for progressives disagreed with one another about the League, and some of them played an active role in the Red Scare. In the early 1920's a progressive element took part in the attempt to build a farmer-labor party, but the effort failed, chiefly because both farmers and workers were on the defensive throughout the decade.

During most of the 1920's, farmers were in distress, and the government did little of value to help them out. High war prices had persuaded farmers to expand, with an increase in borrowings and mortgage indebtedness, but farm prosperity did not last long enough to enable them to liquidate their debts. Even more important was the collapse of the foreign market. For a brief period, farmers took effective steps to meet their difficulties. During the Wilson administration the Non-Partisan League, organized in North Dakota, spread into fifteen states of the West. In 1916 the League captured control of the government of North Dakota and in the ensuing years enacted a far-reaching program: state-owned warehouses and elevators, a state bank, exemption of farm improvements from taxation, creation of a hail-insurance fund, a Home Building Association to encourage home ownership, and the establishment of an industrial commission to organize state-owned and state-financed industries. After the war, the more conservative American Farm Bureau Federation came to dominate farm politics. In the Harding regime a bipartisan 'farm bloc' pushed agrarian legislation through Congress. But by the Coolidge era the Non-Partisan League had disintegrated, and the farm bloc had lost much of its power. When farm leaders came up with schemes to enlist government support for agriculture as the tariff engaged its support for industry, they ran into a stone wall.

Union labor fared little better. Labor's time of troubles came right after the war when the return of millions of veterans, the threat of cheap labor and cheap products from abroad, and the cancellation of wartime contracts led to industrial unrest. More than 3000 strikes involving over 4 million workers erupted in 1919, and almost as many the following year. Business, and some elements in

'The Temple of Ceres,' Salina, Kansas. In this conceptualization, F.B. Bristow likens grain elevators on the Great Plains to a shrine of the Roman goddess of agriculture. The photograph is similar in design to that of Precisionist painters like Sheeler and Demuth. (*Smithsonian Institution*)

the government, made a concerted effort to establish the 'open shop' and to break the power of the unions, once and for all. During the 'twenties the position of organized labor deteriorated steadily; membership in unions declined from 5.1 million in 1920 to 3.6 million in 1929.

A series of spectacular strikes in steel, coal, railways, and textiles marked the beginning and the end of this decade of 'normalcy.' The most dramatic of the 1919 strikes came in the steel industry. One-third of all steel workers still labored twelve hours a day, seven days a week, and most of the rest worked a ten-hour day; when the steel workers demanded an eight-hour day, Judge Gary of the U.S. Steel Corporation refused even to discuss the matter with them. A commission of the Federal Council of Churches reported that the grievances of labor were acute: 'the average week of 68.7 hours . . . and the underpayment of unskilled labor, are all inhumane. The "boss system" is bad, the plant organization is military, and the control autocratic.' But the Steel Corporation managed to portray the strike as the entering wedge of communism, and it collapsed.

The coal industry had long been sick. The toll of accidents and deaths in the underground pits was appalling; many miners could count on only two or three days' work a week; and miners who lived in company-owned towns could call neither their homes nor their souls their own. When in 1919 West Virginia miners went out on strike, President Wilson pronounced the walkout a violation of wartime regulations, and the governor of West Virginia used state militia to smash it. Three years later another and more widespread strike exploded in the 'massacre' of imported strikebreakers at Herrin, Illinois. So devastated was the United Mine Workers by these strikes, and by hard times in the mines, that between 1920 and 1932 it declined from half a million to 150,000 members.

In 1922, to avert a slash in wages, railway shopmen, 400,000 strong, went out on strike. Harding set up a mediation board whose terms were accepted by the shopmen but rejected by the railway operators, or the bankers who controlled them, and the strike continued. At this juncture Attorney-General Daugherty invoked the law, not against the operators but against the strikers; he obtained a sweeping injunction which outlawed any word or gesture that aided the strike in any way. The injunction was probably unconstitutional, but the strike ended before this could be determined.

The textile industry, like coal mining, had chronic difficulties. Originally centered in New England, it was now shifting to the South where there was less agitation about limitations on hours of work or child labor. Southern textile companies owned not only their mills but the mill villages, and usually the local sheriffs and politicians as well. A strike in 1927, in Elizabethton, Tennessee, where girls worked 56 hours a week for 18 cents an hour, was broken by a combination of local vigilantes, company militia, and state troops. In 1929 the union tried to organize the textile workers of North Carolina and Virginia, but once again vigilantes and police smashed both strike and strikers.

Throughout this period, the government, including the courts, threw its weight to the side of management. The Supreme Court held two child-labor laws unconstitutional, struck down a minimum wage law for women, sustained yellow-dog contracts, assessed triple damages against an unincorporated union, and threw out an Arizona anti-injunction law. Not until 1932 did the Norris-LaGuardia law erect effective safeguards against the misuse of the injunction in labor disputes and against the yellow-dog contract.

Both labor unions and farm organizations looked increasingly toward the national government to redress their grievances, but both major parties turned their backs. In 1924 the Republicans nominated Coolidge for a full term at a convention dominated by eastern business elements. The leading candidate for the Democratic nomination, William McAdoo, had been besmirched by the oil scandals. Not only did this make it difficult for the Democrats to make the most of the Republican scandals but the party became a national laughing stock when it took 103 ballots to choose a presidential nominee. After the convention deadlocked between McAdoo and Governor 'Al' Smith of New York, the Democrats tried to compete with the Republicans by nominating an ultraconservative, John W. Davis. 'I have a fine list of clients,' Davis declared. 'What lawyer wouldn't want them? I have J. P. Morgan and Company, the Erie Railroad, the Guaranty Trust Company, the Standard Oil Company, and other foremost American concerns on my list. I am proud of them.' The choice of Charles W. Bryan, brother to the 'Great Commoner,' as Davis's running mate did little to remove the taint of Wall Street. 'How true was Grant's exclamation,' observed Hiram Johnson, 'that the Democratic Party could be relied upon at the right time to do the wrong thing!'

Despairing of both major parties, labor and farm leaders joined with Socialists and old Bull Moosers to run a third ticket headed by 'Fighting Bob' La Follette. For their vice-presidential nominee the Progressives chose Senator Burton K. Wheeler, Montana Democrat, who declared: 'When the Democratic party goes to Wall Street for its candidate I must refuse to go with it.' The Progressive platform stressed the ancient issue of anti-monopoly but also advocated public ownership of water power, farm relief, abolition of the injunction in labor disputes, a federal child labor amendment, the election of all federal judges, legislation permitting Congress to override a judicial veto, the abolition of conscription, and a popular referendum on declarations of war.

At a time of boom prosperity most of the nation was satisfied enough with Republican policies to give Coolidge a lopsided victory with more than 54 per cent of the vote to Davis's less than 29 per cent, the least ever registered by a Democratic presidential candidate. Davis, with 136 electoral votes to Coolidge's 382, won only 12 states, all in the South. La Follette ran ahead of Davis in much of the West, and with nearly 5 million votes (better than 16 per cent) he made a respectable showing. But his failure to win any state but his own Wisconsin shattered the movement for a farmer-labor party, and his death the following year deprived the Progressives of their commander.

Businessmen responded more ebulliently to the returns; they interpreted Coolidge's victory as a ratification of the 'New Era' in which a benevolent capitalism would develop the economy in the national interest. In the Coolidge years the nation reaped the benefits from the application of electricity to manufacturing and the adoption of the scientific management theories of Frederick Winslow Taylor. In 1914, electricity operated only 30 per cent of American factory machinery; by 1929, it sparked 70 per cent. The war nurtured a chemical industry, and the electrochemical revolution drastically altered factory procedures and improved output in industries like petroleum and steel. As a consequence of all these changes, the productivity of the worker increased rapidly and the real income of each person gainfully employed rose from $1308 in 1921 to $1716 in 1929, though prosperity was less widely diffused than many thought.

These achievements added to the stature of the businessman and encouraged Republican administrations to heed his demands, such as tax reduction. Instead of liquidating the public debt of $24 billion left by the war, Secretary of the Treasury Andrew Mellon, an aluminum magnate who held this post under all three Republican Presidents, sought to reduce taxes, especially the steep war levies. For a few years, an alliance of Democrats and Republican progressives balked him, but after the 1924 landslide Democratic conservatives outdid the Coolidge administration in urging lower taxes for the well-to-do. A series of revenue acts wiped out excess profit levies, drastically reduced surtaxes, granted rebates on 'earned income' and refunds to corporations of over $3.5 billion. Yet notwithstanding these reductions, the national debt was lowered by 1930 to $16 billion. No wonder the business community asserted that Andrew W. Mellon was 'the greatest Secretary of the Treasury since Alexander Hamilton.'

This policy of tax reduction, however, was not maintained with respect to one critical tax—the tariff. The Underwood tariff had never really been tried under normal conditions, for the war afforded protection to American manufactures and fostered the establishment of new industries. On conclusion of the war these 'infant' industries like chemicals clamored for protection. Fearful that the United States would be inundated with the produce of depressed European labor, a Republican Congress, in March 1921, pushed through an emergency tariff bill which Wilson promptly vetoed. 'If we wish to have Europe settle her debts, governmental or commercial, we must be prepared to buy from her,' he said. But this elementary logic failed to sink in.

Within a month of Harding's accession to the presidency, Congress enacted the emergency tariff of 1921, with prohibitive agricultural schedules which, though affording no relief to farmers with surplus crops to sell, did commit them to the principle of protection. More important was the Fordney-McCumber tariff of 1922, which established rates higher than ever before. The law also authorized the President to raise or lower duties as much as 50 per cent, but Harding and Coolidge used this authority only thirty-seven times. Thirty-two of these changes, involving items such as pig iron, were upward; the five articles on which duties were reduced were mill feed, bobwhite quail, paint-brush handles, cresylic acid, and phenol, but there was no Mr. Dooley to see the joke. The Fordney-McCumber act provoked a tariff war which cut seriously into our foreign trade, persuaded many manufacturers to establish branch plants abroad, and inspired among some large manufacturers and bankers their first serious misgivings about the wisdom of protection. Nonetheless, no sooner was Hoover inaugurated than he summoned Congress in special session to consider farm relief and 'limited changes in the tariff.' The Hawley-Smoot tariff bill represented increases all along the line. Objections from the American Bankers Association and from industries with foreign markets were brushed aside and a vigorous protest from 1028 economists had no effect on President Hoover, who signed the bill in June 1930. Within two years twenty-five countries established retaliatory tariffs, and American foreign trade slumped further.

Yet Republican administrations could not be impervious to considerations of foreign markets, raw materials, and investments. During the First World War the United States had changed from a debtor to a creditor nation. American private investments abroad, less than \$3 billion before the war, increased to \$14 billion by 1932. Part of this investment reflected the determination of American industry to control its own sources of raw material, and in this policy the government cooperated, just as governments had cooperated in the mercantilism of the seventeenth and eighteenth centuries. It encouraged foreign trade associations, discovered new trade opportunities abroad, and helped American oil interests obtain concessions in Latin America and in the Middle East.

Characteristically, the neo-mercantilists of the 1920's fostered large-scale combinations. Herbert Hoover, as Secretary of Commerce, inaugurated a policy of 'alliance with the great trade associations.' His sense of engineering efficiency was outraged at the spectacle of competition with its inevitable waste, and he proposed modifying the Sherman Act to permit business organizations to combine for certain purposes. He placed his department at the disposal of business, and under his auspices trade associations not only pooled information, advertising, insurance, traffic, and purchases, but drew up codes of fair practice. 'We are passing,' said Hoover, 'from a period of extreme individualistic action into a period of associational activities.'

In part as a result of this official encouragement, concentration of control grew apace. The decade from 1919 to 1929 saw 1268 combinations in manufacturing and mining, involving the merging of some 4000 and the disappearance of some 6000 firms. The same process took place in other fields. In the eight years after the war 3744 public utility companies disappeared through merger. In 1920 there were 30,139 banks; fifteen years later the number had been reduced by failures and mergers to 16,053. In 1920 the twenty largest banking institutions held about 14 per cent of all loans and investments; ten years later, 27 per cent. Chain stores ate heavily into the business of the independent shopkeeper. As the inevitable result of this process, in 1933 some 594 corporations, each capitalized at \$50 million or more, owned 53 per cent of all corporate wealth in the country; the other 387,970 owned the remaining 47 per cent.

In few fields had concentration gone further than in hydroelectric power, but not without challenge. In the years after World War I the electric light and power industry grew with extraordinary rapidity, and largely through the holding-company device, control was concentrated in the

Charles Sheeler, 'Classic Landscape.' In 1912 Sheeler (1883–1965), whose paintings appeared in the controversial Armory Show of 1913 in New York, turned to photography, and this 1931 oil is based on photographs he had taken of the Ford Motor Works at River Rouge in 1927. Sheeler's paintings have the sharply defined order characteristic of the Precisionists, who adapted Cubism to American edifices like skyscrapers and grain elevators, as well as the ascetic attitude toward color and light that led critics to describe Sheeler and Charles Demuth as 'Immaculates.' *(Collection Mrs. Edsel B. Ford, Dearborn, Mich.)*

hands of six giant financial groups. Senators Walsh of Montana, La Follette of Wisconsin, and the indomitable Norris of Nebraska led the most important contest in this sphere—for government operation of the water-power dams at Muscle Shoals on the Tennessee river, which had been constructed to furnish power for nitrate plants during World War I. After the war, conservatives wanted to turn them over to private companies, and President Coolidge vetoed a bill providing for government operation of the dams. But in 1931 Congress once more passed the Norris bill, calling for the construction of a second dam on the Tennessee river and for government manufacture and sale of fertilizer and power. President Hoover vetoed the measure. 'I am firmly opposed to the Government entering into any business the major purpose of which is competition with our citizens,' he stated. 'That is not liberalism, it is degeneration.' This *ex cathedra* statement as to the nature and purposes of government did not settle the matter. Two years later, with the creation of the Tennessee Valley Authority, the Roosevelt administration entered jauntily upon the course of 'degeneration.'

The Quest for Peace

Although all three Republican administrations followed a generally isolationist course, they co-operated with other governments for purposes like disarmament. In his first year of office Harding, pursuant to a resolution sponsored by Senator Borah, called a conference of the nine powers with interests in the Pacific area, and in November 1921 delegates heard Secretary Hughes propose an itemized plan for scrapping warships and limiting naval armaments to prevent a naval race. The United States, Great Britain, Japan, France, and Italy agreed upon maintenance of a battleship and carrier ratio of 5-5-3 for the first three countries and 1.7 for the others, the scrapping of designated ships, and a ten-year naval holiday in the construction of capital ships. At the time, this Washington Treaty of 1922 and the London Naval Treaty of 1930, which extended its provisions to other classes of ships, were regarded as outstanding victories for peace. Yet few well-meaning reforms of the twentieth century proved so disappointing as naval limitation. Despite concessions to the Japanese which rendered the defense of Guam, Singapore, and the Philippines virtually impossible, Japan was insulted rather than appeased; their militarists used the slogan '5-5-3' to discredit the liberal government which had accepted limitation, and to get into power. When that had been accomplished, at the end of 1934 Japan denounced the naval-limitation treaties and started a frenzied building program which, by the time war broke out in the Pacific, rendered the Japanese navy more powerful in every type of ship than the United States and British Pacific and Asiatic fleets combined.

The Washington conference was designed not only to achieve arms limitation but to avoid conflict in the Far East where the Japanese had been extending their power. Japan had profited greatly from World War I by seizing the German islands in the North Pacific and the German concessions in Shantung, and, taking advantage of the involvement of the European powers and the isolation of the United States, consolidating its position in Manchuria and browbeating China. Early in 1915 the Japanese government presented to China Twenty-one Demands that would establish a practical protectorate over China. The ultimatum was a clear violation of the Root-Takahira agreement of 1908 to maintain the independence and territorial integrity of China and the 'open door' for commerce. Bryan protested, but he acted from a position of weakness, for it was just at this time that California, contemptuously rejecting President Wilson's plea for moderation, forbade Japanese to own land in the state. Such discriminatory legislation outraged the Japanese, who found it difficult to distinguish between action by the United States government and an affront from one of its sovereign states. In 1917 the Wilson administration conceded Japan's 'paramount' interest in China. Though the Lansing-Ishii Agreement reaffirmed the 'open door,' pledged both nations to respect the independence and territorial integrity of China, and disclaimed any desire for 'special rights or privileges,' it specifically recognized that 'territorial propinquity creates special relations, and that Japan has special interests in China, particularly in that part to which her possessions are contiguous.' At the Paris Peace Conference Japan also succeeded in legalizing her claims to Shantung and the former German islands in the Pacific.

At the Washington Conference, the American government sought to make the best of a bad situation by converting bilateral into multilateral understandings, thus freeing the United States from sole responsibility for a policy which it could not in any event enforce. By the Four Power Treaty (1921) the United States, Great Britain, France, and Japan engaged mutually to 'respect their rights in relation to their insular possessions in the region of the Pacific Ocean' and pledged themselves to confer about any controversy that

The changing of the guard. In 1925, when this photograph was taken, Frank B. Kellogg (1856–1937) succeeded Charles Evans Hughes (1862–1948), Secretary of State under Harding and Coolidge. In 1930, the bearded Hughes became Chief Justice of the United States, a position appropriate to his Jove-like appearance. (*Library of Congress*)

might arise over these rights. By the Nine Power Treaty (1922) the same powers, plus Italy, Belgium, the Netherlands, Portugal, and China, agreed to respect China's sovereignty, independence, and territorial and administrative integrity, maintain the principle of the 'open door,' and refrain from creating 'spheres of influence,' seeking privileges or concessions, or abridging therein the rights and privileges of citizens of friendly states. The Four Power Treaty buried the Anglo-Japanese alliance, and the Nine Power pact gave treaty form to the open door. But these agreements had one serious weakness: they set up no machinery for enforcement.

Lack of enforcement machinery was also the glaring weakness of the Pact of Paris (or Kellogg-Briand Pact). When in 1927 the French foreign minister, Aristide Briand, proposed a bilateral treaty to the United States for the outlawry of war, Secretary of State Frank B. Kellogg countered with the suggestion of a multilateral treaty of the same character. In the Pact of Paris of 1928, adhered to eventually by 62 nations, the contracting powers renounced war 'as an instrument of national policy.' The most thoroughgoing commitment to peace the great powers ever made, the Pact of Paris may fairly be called an attempt to keep peace by incantation. Little more than three years after the Pact of Paris was negotiated, Japanese militarists riddled its pretensions. World War II in the Far East really began on 18 September 1931 when General Hayashi moved his army into Manchuria and overran that great Chinese province. The Japanese government, which had not authorized this 'Manchuria Incident,' was forced to acquiesce under threat of assassination, and in 1932 Japan declared Manchuria the independent kingdom of Manchukuo, under a puppet monarch. This course violated the Nine Power Treaty, the Kellogg Pact, and the Covenant of the League of Nations, by each of which Japan was bound.

Secretary of State Henry L. Stimson met the Japanese aggression by enunciating the Stimson doctrine of refusing to recognize forceful acquisitions of territory, and he edged the United States closer to cooperation with the League, which proved to be impotent throughout the crisis. Stimson was uncertain about what else to do, and Hoover, who viewed the Kellogg Pact and the Nine Power Treaty as 'solely moral instruments,' opposed both military and economic sanctions. By 1932 little remained of the treaty structure of the 1920's.

In Latin America the outlook was more promising, despite the fact that here, too, Wilson had left his successors a heritage not only of fine principles but of tough problems, especially in Mexico. Article 27 of the Constitution of 1917 had vested in the Mexican nation ownership of all mineral and oil resources, and limited future concessions to Mexican nationals. If Article 27 should be interpreted as retroactive, American investments in mining and oil amounting to about $300 million would be confiscated. Under Harding war threatened over the possibility of a retroactive interpretation, and under Coolidge the conflict deepened when the Mexican government promoted agrarian laws that jeopardized American land investments and ecclesiastical legislation that affronted Roman Catholics. But Secretary of State Kellogg was unable to enlist popular support for an aggressive defense of American oil interests, and in January 1927 the Senate voted unanimously to arbitrate the controversy.

Sobered by this rebuke, Coolidge appointed as ambassador to Mexico his Amherst classmate, Dwight W. Morrow, a member of the House of Morgan who had publicly declared opposition to 'dollar diplomacy.' Through a remarkable combination of character, intelligence, shrewdness, and charm, Morrow succeeded in repairing most of the damage that his predecessors in Mexico City and his superiors in Washington had done. In response to Mexican Supreme Court rulings, oil and mineral legislation was modified in line with American objections, while Morrow obtained an adjustment of land issues, claims, and the Church question. Throughout the 1930's this new understanding remained undisturbed, while in the United States a widespread admiration for Mexican culture (especially the paintings of Rivera and Orozco) and a growing appreciation of the social ideals of the Mexican revolution made a good base for the future.

Elsewhere in the Caribbean the United States showed more reluctance to pick up the 'big stick' that Theodore Roosevelt, Taft, and Wilson had brandished. American opinion was impatient with 'dollar diplomacy,' the Caribbean countries manifested a greater sense of order, and American investors wielded so much influence on the local governments that the old cry 'Send the Marines!' was unnecessary. In 1924 the Dominican flag displaced the American in that distracted republic. In 1925 United States Marines returned to Nicaragua to put down a revolution and supervise elections, but the acrimonious criticism which greeted this brief revival of intervention led to a more circumspect policy and eventually to a final withdrawal in 1933. Indeed, it was upon the foundation of the Latin American policy of Herbert Hoover that Franklin Roosevelt built his Good Neighbor Policy.

Nineteenth-Century America's Last Stand

In the years after World War I the older America of the Protestant, old-stock culture felt deeply threatened by the values of the burgeoning city and erected barriers against change. The census of 1920 revealed that for the first time most Americans lived in urban areas, broadly defined, a frightening statistic for those on the farms and in small towns whose way of life had prevailed for three centuries. They attributed to the metropolis all that was perverse in American society: the revolution in morals, the corner saloon, the control of municipal government by urban immigrants, and the modernist skepticism of the literal interpretation of the Bible.

Religious fundamentalism took an aggressive form after the war. Under the leadership of William Jennings Bryan, crusader for religious orthodoxy, several southern states enacted laws forbidding the teaching of evolution. In 1925 the whole country became caught up in the fun-

John Steuart Curry, 'Baptism in Kansas,' 1928. This painting is the best known of a series of Midwestern subjects by Curry (1897–1946) that helped set the style of 'regionalism.' In an age of urban-rural tension when New York City art circles responded to the latest fashion from Europe, the Kansas-born Curry, along with Grant Wood and Thomas Hart Benton, established a rival power center in the Midwest that cultivated indigenous American painting. (*Whitney Museum of American Art*)

damentalist controversy when a high-school biology teacher, John T. Scopes, was tried for violating a Tennessee statute forbidding the teaching of evolution. To Dayton, Tennessee, swarmed armies of reporters to watch Clarence Darrow, the iconoclastic attorney, subject Bryan, who joined the prosecution, to a savage examination that revealed the ignorance of the Commoner. Within a few days after his ordeal, Bryan was dead, and with him died much of the older America. The judge found Scopes guilty,[1] and the anti-evolution laws remained on the statute books. But the fundamentalist crusade no longer had the same force.

The impulse to use coercion to preserve the

1. A higher court subsequently reversed the conviction on a technicality.

The Ku Klux Klan. This KKK gathering took place in Beckley, W. Va., on 9 August 1924. (*Library of Congress*)

values of the older America took a much uglier form in the creation of the Ku Klux Klan. An organization of white, native-born Protestants, the Klan was aggressively anti-Negro, but its chief target was not the Negro but the Catholic. (The chief organ of the KKK in Illinois advertised '12 red hot anti-Catholic postcards, all different.') The Klan was also anti-Semitic and anti-foreign-born. Although the Klan was founded in Georgia, it had its greatest strength not in the Deep South but in the Midwest, where the dominant figure was the Grand Dragon of the Realm of Indiana, David Stephenson. In its war against 'metropolitan morality' the Klan opposed all the forces turning cities into 'modern Sodom and Gomorrahs.' To compel adherence to its moral code, the KKK employed social ostracism against individuals judged guilty of moral infractions, but it also sometimes resorted to violence—church burnings, lynchings, mutilations, and whippings.

Wherever it had strength, the Klan reached out for political power. In some states the KKK was so potent that elections were held in Klaverns before the regular primaries. The Klan infiltrated both major parties. In 1924 in Colorado it elected a governor, one house of the legislature, several judges and sheriffs, and the Denver chief of police. In Alabama, it ended the career of the veteran Senator Oscar Underwood, whom it denounced as the 'Jew, jug, and Jesuit candidate,' and replaced him with Hugo Black, who accepted a life membership in the KKK. In the 1924 presidential campaign it silenced the Republicans and fractured the Democrats, who voted not to mention the Klan by name, $543\frac{3}{20}$ to $542\frac{3}{20}$. No longer did the KKK hide in the shadows. On 8 August 1925, in a brazen assertion of strength, more than 50,000 Klansmen marched for $3\frac{1}{2}$ hours down Pennsylvania Avenue in the nation's capital.

But the Klan declined even more rapidly than it rose to power. It was fought by the various ethnic groups it attacked; by liberals and old-stock conservatives; by corruptionists and bootleggers; and by courageous southern governors and mayors. In Indiana in 1925, after a sordid episode, Stephenson was convicted of second-degree murder and sentenced to life imprisonment. When the governor refused to come to his aid, Stephenson made public the corruption and violence in the order. Within a year, the Klan was headed downhill, and by the end of the decade only small pockets of power remained.

Many who abhorred the Klan shared the order's conviction that the older Americans of Anglo-Saxon stock owned the United States and its fear that republican institutions were being undermined by the tidal wave of European immigrants. During the 'twenties Congress enacted laws which drastically limited immigration and set up a quota system that discriminated in favor of the 'old' and against the 'new' immigration. As a result of this legislation and, even more, of the Great Depression, immigration from the Old World fell to about 35,000 during the 1930's, while during that decade almost 100,000 more aliens returned to their homes than came to America.

At the very outset of the decade rural America had scored an emphatic victory when the Eighteenth Amendment, forbidding the 'manufacture, sale or transportation of intoxicating liquors,' went into effect in January 1920. Prohibition permitted the Protestant countryside to coerce the newer Americans in the city. One 'dry' asserted: 'Our nation can only be saved by turning the pure stream of country sentiment and township morals to flush out the cesspools of cities and so save civilization from pollution.' In the cities opposition to prohibition, once strongest among foreign-born workingmen, spread through every class of society, and the thirst for liquor was sublimated into a philosophy of 'personal liberty.' Mencken claimed that prohibition had caused suffering comparable only to that of the Black Death and the Thirty Years War, and the president of the Carnegie Institute of Technology told a Senate committee that rum was 'one of the greatest blessings that God has given to men out of the teeming bosom of Mother Earth.' States with large urban populations sabotaged prohibition laws just as Northern states had once nullified the fugitive slave acts. Agents of the Prohibition Bureau entered into corrupt alliances with bootleggers like Chicago's vicious Al Capone, and there was a breakdown not only of law but of respect for the law.

Both political parties tried to evade the troublesome issue, but without success. The Republicans, strongest in rural, Protestant communities, were inclined to stand behind what Hoover called 'an experiment noble in motive and far-reaching in purpose.' The Democrats were in a quandary. Their strength came in almost equal proportions from southern and western rural constituencies which were immovably dry and northern industrial constituencies which were incurably wet. In the Northeast Democratic leaders reflected the rage of foreign-born and second-generation Americans at the moralistic attitudes of the drys. 'The government which stands against the founder of Christianity cannot survive,' declared Senator David I. Walsh of Massachusetts. If Christ came back to earth and performed the Cana miracle again, 'he would be jailed and possibly crucified again.' But Democratic leaders like Bryan found their Methodist followers no less intensely in favor of prohibition. This division almost split the party in 1924 and deeply affected the outcome of the 1928 election.

In 1928 the Democrats, impaled on the urban-rural split four years earlier, decided to ride with the forces of urbanism by nominating Alfred E. Smith, the able governor of New York and *beau ideal* of the newer Americans from the slums of the great cities. A product of the 'Sidewalks of New York,' he was a Tammany brave, wringing wet, and the first lifetime city-dweller to receive the presidential designation of a major party. The *New Republic* observed: 'For the first time, a representative of the unpedigreed, foreign-born, city-bred, many-tongued recent arrivals on the American scene has knocked on the door and aspired seriously to the presiding seat in the national Council Chamber.'

Since the Democrats were as solicitous as the Republicans of business interests in 1928, they erased any real difference on economic issues between the candidates, permitting much of the campaign to revolve around a single fact: that for the first time in American history a major party had nominated a Roman Catholic for President. Smith's detractors whispered that if he were elected all Protestant children would be declared bastards. When bigots were not claiming that Smith's election would make the White House an outpost of the Vatican, they were depicting the election of a wet like Smith as a religious affront to rural Protestants. If 'the Christian vote' did not go to the polls, warned the *Christian Endeavor World*, 'we shall see our towns and villages rum-ridden in the near future and a whole generation of our children destroyed.' Finally, the assault on Smith was closely linked to an attack on the foreign-born in the northern cities. 'Elect Al Smith to the presidency,' declared one southern churchman, 'and it means that the floodgates of immigration will be opened, and that ours will be turned into a civilization like that of continental Europe. Elect Al Smith and you will turn this country over to the domination of a foreign religious sect, which I could name, and Church and State will once again be united.'

The objection to Smith expressed not simply anti-Catholicism but a pervasive anti-urbanism that embraced antagonism to his religion, his views on liquor, his tie to Tammany Hall, his identification with the new immigrants, and his association with the city itself. On the other hand, Smith's opponent, Herbert Hoover, had the advantage of being able to summon up the image of a pristine America. He wrote of boyhood memories of gathering walnuts in the fall, carrying grain to the mill, fishing for catfish and sunnies, and finding 'gems of agate and fossil coral' on the Burlington track. His family, he recalled, had woven its own carpets, made its own soap, preserved 'meat and fruit and vegetables, got its sweetness from sorghum and honey.'

Hoover won decisively, with over 58 per cent of the popular vote to Smith's less than 41 per cent. Whereas Cox had taken eleven states and Davis twelve, Smith took only eight. For the first time since Reconstruction, the Republicans cut deeply into the Solid South. Smith, who received a much higher proportion of the popular vote than Davis or Cox had, ran well in the large cities inhabited by newer Americans; in Irish wards in South Boston, he got as much as 90 per cent of the vote. Hoover won because he ran as a candidate of the majority party at a time of boom prosperity, but Smith's background also proved costly. 'America is not yet dominated by its great cities,' concluded a Minnesota newspaper after the election. 'Main Street is still the principal thoroughfare of the nation.'

Collapse

Herbert Hoover entered the White House with the brightest of reputations. His successful management of relief organizations in Belgium, Russia, and the Mississippi valley had earned him the sobriquet of great humanitarian; his vigorous administration of the Commerce Department won him the confidence of business, if not of Wall Street. Innocent of any previous elective office, Hoover seemed to be a new type of political leader: a socially minded efficiency expert, a world-famous mining engineer. Hoover, in short, carried into the White House with him all of the shining promises of the New Era. 'We in America are nearer to the final triumph over poverty,' he proclaimed during the campaign, 'than ever before in the history of any land. . . . We have not reached the goal, but, given a chance to go forward with the policies of the last eight years,

Thomas Hart Benton, 'City Activities with Subway.' This panel, one of a series of murals Benton was commissioned to paint for the New School for Social Research in Greenwich Village in 1930, conveys both the frenetic energy and the fragmentation of the big city. In the subjects he chooses—a prize fight, a burlesque show, a tabloid, a Salvation Army street band—and in his depiction of raw sexuality, Benton also conveys a sense of a metropolitan way of life alien to the pristine society of the American heartland that he and the other 'regionalists' were portraying. In Benton's view, 'the great cities,' dominated by Marxists and homosexual aesthetes, were 'dead.' (*New School for Social Research*)

we shall soon with the help of God be in sight of the day when poverty will be banished from this nation.'

Hoover's election was the signal for a boom on the Stock Exchange. The average value of common stocks soared from 117 in December 1928 to 225 the following September. Inspired by dazzling gains, brokers increased their borrowings from $3.5 billion in 1927 to $8.5 billion two years later, and in the single month of January 1929 no less than a billion dollars' worth of new securities were floated. Factory employment, freight car loadings, construction contracts, bank loans, almost all the indices of business, showed a marked upward swing.

Yet even as Hoover announced in his inaugural address that 'in no nation are the fruits of accomplishment more secure,' shrewd investors were pulling out of the market. The Federal Reserve Board did little to reverse the policy of easy credit it had inaugurated in 1927, but there were many reasons for concern. The world economic situation was discouraging. War debts were uncollectable, foreign trade had declined precipitously, and the interest on billions of dollars of private investments was in default. Agriculture was depressed, and industries such as coal and textiles had not shared in the general well-being. Much of the new wealth had gone to the privileged few; 5 per cent of the population enjoyed one-third of the income. Business plowed a disproportionate amount of the gains in productivity into new plants or passed them on as dividends rather than wages. So long as industry turned out mountains of goods but denied workers the purchasing power to buy them, a breakdown was inevitable. Meantime public and private debts had mounted to staggering sums; by 1930 the total debt burden was estimated at approximately one-third the national wealth. Too many Americans were living on the future. When confidence in the future disappeared, the system collapsed.

The crash came in October 1929. In less than a month stocks suffered an average decline of 40 per cent. At the outset many assumed that the Wall Street crash, although devastating, was only the latest of those familiar financial panics that America had experienced before. In fact, it helped bring about a depression which would leave an enormous fault line in the United States. 'The stock market crash,' wrote the literary critic Edmund Wilson, 'was to count for us almost like a rending of the earth in preparation for the Day of Judgment.' Before the Great Depression ended, some thirteen years later, it would alter the whole landscape of American society, terminate the long reign of the Republicans as the majority party, cut short the political career of Herbert Hoover, and bury in its ruins the bright prospects of the New Era.

31

The Great Depression and the New Deal

*

1929–1939

The Depression and the Hoover Response

The stock market crash of 1929 confronted the United States with its greatest crisis since the Civil War. Factories slashed production; construction practically ceased; millions of investors lost their savings; over 5000 banks closed their doors in the first three years of the depression. Between 1920 and 1932 total farm income declined from $15.5 billion to $5.5 billion. 'Wheat on the Liverpool market,' noted one observer, 'fetched the lowest price since the reign of Charles II.' Foreign trade declined in three years from $9 billion to $3 billion. One writer observed: 'We seem to have stepped Alice-like through an economic looking-glass into a world where everything shrivels. Bond prices, stock prices, commodity prices, employment—they all dwindle.'

As the depression wore on, unemployment mounted to staggering levels, and suffering became intense. Of New England's 280,000 textile millhands, 120,000 had no work a year after the crash. New Bedford was bankrupt; Lowell and Lawrence seemed like ghost towns. By 1933 the number of jobless was variously estimated at from 12 to more than 15 million, as factory payrolls fell to less than half the level of 1929. In a country of some 120 million people, probably more than 40 million were either unemployed or members of a family in which the main breadwinner was out of work. Blacks learned the cruel truth of the saying that they were the 'last to be hired, first to be fired.' Those who did have jobs often worked for a pittance. Young girls got $1.10 a week for sweatshop labor in progressive Connecticut, and grown men worked for 5 cents an hour in sawmills. Yet this desperate deprivation came at a time when orchards were heavy with fruit, granaries bulging with grain. Miners froze in the midst of mountains of coal, while their children lived on weeds and dandelions.

The depression seriously impaired confidence in business leadership. Nowhere else in the world had the titans of finance and the moguls of industry enjoyed such prestige, but by 1932 businessmen who in the 1920's had taken credit for prosperity now found themselves saddled with the blame for hard times. One economist wrote: 'It is easier to believe that the earth is flat than to believe that private initiative alone will save us.'

The Great Depression, Fulton Street, New York City. (*National Archives*)

Yet business leaders became discredited not merely because they were judged accountable for the depression and proved unable to restore prosperity but because so many revealed themselves to be socially irresponsible. The public learned with astonishment that the dignified House of Morgan kept a 'preferred list' of customers and influential public men to whom it sold securities below the market price. 'The belief that those in control of the corporate life of America were motivated by ideals of honorable conduct was completely shattered,' observed the millionaire Joseph P. Kennedy.

The crisis in confidence produced by the depression went far beyond a disaffection with business leadership. Throughout the Western world, men brooded over whether the great society of the West which had grown in strength since the days of Charlemagne had not begun to disintegrate. The British historian Arnold Toynbee wrote: 'The year 1931 was distinguished from previous years—in the "post-war" and in the "pre-war" age alike—by one outstanding feature. In 1931, men and women all over the world were seriously contemplating and frankly discussing the possibility that the Western system of Society might break down and cease to work.' If in Europe men wondered whether the Western world had not reached the stage of the Roman empire after Theodosius, most Americans were of a more optimistic frame of mind. Yet even in the United States the cold fear that the world Americans had known might be at a terminus could not easily be overcome.

The Hoover administration discounted the seriousness of the depression, for those who had guided the destinies of the nation through the 1920's believed that the economy was fundamentally sound and that prosperity would return as soon as there was a restoration of confidence. To this end President Hoover urged industrial leaders to maintain employment and wages and, in speech after speech, exhorted the nation to keep a stiff upper lip. But he did more than this. Assuming responsibilities no President had ever taken on before, he stepped up public works; announced a tax cut; and, through the Federal Reserve System, encouraged an easy credit policy. To support crop prices, the Federal Farm Board purchased vast quantities of wheat and cotton.

Yet these measures were largely nullified by other policies. Committed to budget-balancing, Hoover took away with one hand what he gave with the other. The increase in federal spending for public works was so modest that it was more than offset by the drastic cut in state and local spending. Although he insisted that the source of America's troubles lay overseas, he agreed to the Hawley-Smoot tariff which raised new barriers to international trade. Above all, he persisted in relying on voluntary agreements even when this faith proved misplaced.

Nothing demonstrates so well the inadequacy of voluntarism as the sad experience of Hoover's Federal Farm Board. Despite the Board's activities, cotton prices skidded from 17½ cents in October 1929 to less than 8 cents in 1930. The program failed because the Board was attempting to support crop prices without restricting production, and it was swamped by surpluses. In summer 1931, faced by a glut of millions of bales of cotton, the chairman of the Board wired cotton state governors 'to induce immediate plowing under of every third row of cotton now growing.' But Hoover continued to hold out against controls. By June 1932 cotton prices had slumped to 4.6 cents. The Board had financed the removal of 3½ million bales from the market only to see ten million bales added to the surfeit. After the collapse of these voluntary price stabilization operations, Hoover had nothing more to offer. The farmer faced ruin, and because of his importance to the economy of agrarian states, he threatened to pull the nation's banks down with him.

Despite mounting evidence of the breakdown of his program for recovery, Hoover spurned appeals for more vigorous federal action. He shared the common belief that federal spending would prolong the depression by discouraging investment and inviting inflation. A man touted as a Great Engineer, he brought to government none of the engineer's insistence on testing theories by their results. One who prided himself on his willingness to consult experts, he ignored advice which ran counter to his preconceptions. In vain did progressives like La Follette, Costigan, and Cutting plead for a large-scale program of public works, financed directly by federal funds. In vain did they present statistics proving the breakdown of private charity and the inability of municipal and state authorities to carry the burden any longer.

In 1931 European financial squalls struck the United States in full force. In June Hoover braved the displeasure of isolationists by proposing a one-year moratorium on reparations and war debt payments, a constructive move which failed to save the day. The European panic caused a fresh financial crisis in America. In August, 158 banks failed, in September, 305, in October, 522. When the Federal Reserve Board raised the rediscount rate sharply, it halted the flow of gold abroad but did untold damage. As credit tightened, production fell off, stocks plummeted, and a typhoon of bank failures swept areas that had been hardly touched before: New England, the Carolinas, the Pacific Northwest.

Hoover responded first by encouraging bankers to set up their own credit organization, and then by asking Congress for an eight-point program intended chiefly to shore up the great financial institutions. In December 1931 he called on Congress to establish a Reconstruction Finance Corporation, which was the old War Finance Corporation in new guise. The RFC, chartered by Congress in 1932, was authorized to lend money to banks, railroads, and other institutions. Congress also approved most of the rest of Hoover's requests in 1932, including the creation of such institutions as the Federal Home Loan Banks to discount mortgages.

Yet Hoover's new program proved no more successful than his original efforts, and for the same reasons: he acted on too small a scale and put too much faith in voluntarism. The RFC made so little use of its power that it frustrated the intent of Congress. The Federal Home Loan Banks neither averted collapse of the mortgage market nor helped the distressed homeowner. The credit organization fell apart when bankers refused to cooperate. As Hoover himself later wrote: 'After a few weeks of enterprising courage, the bankers' National Credit Association became ultraconservative, then fearful, and finally died. It had not exerted anything like its full possible strength. Its members—and the business world—threw up their hands and asked for government action.'

This same misplaced faith in voluntarism marked Hoover's approach to relief for the unemployed. Despite widespread hardship, Hoover claimed that federal relief was not needed, and that the traditional sources—private charity and local government—would meet the needs of the unfortunate. But neither private agencies nor municipal governments could hope to meet distress in a city like Cleveland where 50 per cent of the work force were jobless, or in Akron or East St. Louis when unemployment reached 60 per cent, or Toledo where it mounted to 80 per cent. By the spring of 1932 the country confronted a relief crisis. New York City, where the average family stipend for relief was $2.39 a week, had 25,000 emergency cases on its waiting list. Houston, Texas, announced: 'Applications are not taken from unemployed Mexican or colored families. They are being asked to shift for themselves.' In Chicago, families were separated, and husbands and wives sent to different shelters. On 25 June 1932, Philadelphia ran out of funds—private, municipal, state—and suspended aid to some 52,000 families. But Hoover, doggedly, stubbornly, continued to insist that he had the situation well in hand.

The failure of Hoover to liquidate the depression placed the Republicans in an extremely vulnerable position, and brightened the expectations of the Democrats who chose as their presidential candidate in 1932 the governor of New York, Franklin D. Roosevelt. A distant connection of T. R., and married to the former President's niece, Franklin D. Roosevelt was born to wealth and position, and as a child had learned a patrician's conviction of *noblesse oblige*. He rose rapidly in the Democratic party, served as Assistant Secretary of the Navy under Wilson, and in 1920 was nominated as Cox's running mate. The following year his promising political career was apparently ended by a severe case of infantile paralysis, but during the next seven years, he fought his way back, though he remained permanently crippled. In 1928 the voters of New York elected him governor when they rejected Smith for President, and in 1932, after a closely fought contest, he was picked as his party's presidential nominee. Running safely ahead, FDR straddled a number of important questions and was silent on others, and scolded Hoover as a spendthrift, but he also made clear that he favored unemployment relief, farm legislation, and 'bold and persistent experimentation' to give a 'new deal' to the 'forgotten man.' Furthermore, he showed a willingness to turn to the universities for counsel, since his 'Brain Trust' of speech writers and advisers included three Columbia University professors: Raymond Moley, Rexford Guy Tugwell, and Adolf A. Berle, Jr.

Hoover, laboring under the dead weight of hard times, faced a hopeless task. He made matters still worse when in the summer of 1932 he resorted to

The routing of the bonus army, 1932. The shanties of World War I veterans encamped in Washington go up in flames in sight of the Capitol dome. (*National Archives*)

force to rout a 'bonus army' that had marched on Washington to demand immediate payment of the bonuses voted to veterans of World War I. Swords in hand, cavalrymen rode down the marchers and their wives and children, burning their hovels and scattering their pitiful possessions. The smouldering ruins of Anacostia flats served to confirm the impression that the President was hostile to the dispossessed, and that the country needed a change. Roosevelt received almost 23 million votes, to fewer than 16 million votes for Hoover, and his victory was even more decisive in the Electoral College, where he carried every state but six. Hoover, with less than 40 per cent of the vote, sustained the worst defeat ever inflicted on a Republican presidential nominee in a two-party race. The Democrats also won their greatest majority in the House since 1890 and their largest margin in the Senate since before the Civil War. The Great Depression had ended the reign of the Republicans as the nation's majority party and fastened on the G.O.P. the unwelcome reputation of the party of hard times.

Franklin Roosevelt would not take office for another four months, since the Twentieth Amendment, the 'lame duck' proposal advanced by Senator George Norris, had not yet been ratified. The harsh interregnum was a time of exaggerated worry over the peril of incipient revolution, as Iowa farm rebels recalled the insurrection of Daniel Shays, but it was even more a time of lassitude and of fear. Charles M. Schwab of Bethlehem Steel was quoted as saying: 'I'm afraid, every man is afraid.' The premonitions of disaster seemed well founded when, on the eve of Roosevelt's inauguration, banks shut their doors in every section of the country and on the morning of inauguration day the Stock Exchange closed

The inauguration of Franklin D. Roosevelt, 4 March 1933. In this fanciful and highly stylized depiction of the event, the Mexican illustrator Miguel Covarrubias shows the Chief Justice of the United States, Charles Evans Hughes, placing a wreath on the President's head while the new First Lady, Eleanor Roosevelt, looks on. The tableau, which appeared in *Vanity Fair*, is in the manner of David's 'Coronation of Napoleon' and foreshadowed those observers who were soon to see in Roosevelt's reign manifestations of imperial Rome. The two men to the left of FDR in the picture are the pudgy, high-collared outgoing President, Herbert Hoover, with a high hat, and the incoming Vice President, John Nance Garner, in wrinkled trousers and carrying the Stetson cowboy hat of his native Texas. *(Copyright © 1933 (renewed 1961) by Condé Nast Publications).*

down. As the financial system collapsed, all eyes looked toward Washington.

Wall Street and Washington

When Roosevelt took the oath of office on 4 March 1933, he declared, 'This nation asks for action, and action now!' If it proved necessary, he said in his electrifying inaugural address, he would ask Congress for 'broad Executive power to wage a war against the emergency as great as the power that would be given me if we were in fact invaded by a foreign foe.' Roosevelt's first task was to rehabilitate the nation's banks. In the Treasury, lights burned all through the night as Hoover and Roosevelt lieutenants worked to-

Franklin D. Roosevelt signs the Emergency Banking Act, 9 March 1933. Behind him are the United States flag and the presidential flag and two naval prints. Some of the progressives who admired FDR's domestic policies were uneasy about the fact that he was a 'big navy man.' (*UPI (INS)*)

gether in a spirit of wartime unity to cope with the financial crisis. On the day after his inauguration, the President issued two edicts: one summoned Congress into special session; the other halted transactions in gold and proclaimed a national bank holiday. When Congress convened on 9 March, it took only seven hours to pass Roosevelt's banking bill which validated presidential powers over banks and facilitated the reopening of liquid banks under proper regulation. Three days later, in the first of his radio 'fireside chats,' the President told his listeners it was safer to 'keep your money in a reopened bank than under the mattress'; when the bank holiday ended the next morning in Federal Reserve cities, deposits exceeded withdrawals. The crisis had been ended. Although the powers of government had been greatly enhanced, the nation's financial institutions remained in private hands.

The historic 'Hundred Days' had begun. From 9 March until Congress adjourned on 16 June, Roosevelt sent fifteen different proposals to Congress and saw all fifteen adopted. In quick succession, he followed up his banking message with proposals for government economy and to amend the Volstead Act to legalize light wine and beer.[1] Within two weeks after FDR took office, the country seemed to have regained a large share of its sense of purpose, a recapture of morale, said Walter Lippmann, comparable only to the news of the second battle of the Marne.

Yet the weight of Roosevelt's early actions was deflationary, and he recognized that he must experiment with ways to raise prices, in order to alleviate the debt burden and speed recovery. In a bold series of actions, he took the United States off the gold standard.[2] That fall, the President tried to raise prices through buying gold, and he later bowed to the demand of Mountain State senators to undertake silver purchases; however, currency manipulation did not effect any appreciable increase in commodity prices. In January 1934 the President obtained authority to devalue the dollar, which he fixed at 59.06, and the nation returned to this modified gold standard. Though the goal of controlled inflation had been carried through with utmost caution, the country had taken a big stride toward a managed currency.

Roosevelt also dealt with the debt burden directly. Foreclosures of rural properties had become so numerous that in some sections farmers banded together to intimidate prospective purchasers, close courts, and terrorize judges; in late April 1933 a mob dragged an Iowa judge off his bench and came close to lynching him. The following month Congress authorized the creation of a new Farm Credit Administration which within eighteen months had refinanced a fifth of all farm mortgages in the United States. Congress also came to the aid of the distressed home owner, in the cities as well as in the country. In June 1933 it established a Home Owners' Loan Corporation to refinance small mortgages on privately owned homes; within a year this corporation had approved almost a billion dollars in loans.

Roosevelt, who had a patrician's distrust of Wall Street and a Wilsonian's memory of the machinations of the 'money trust,' was determined to discipline the financiers. The congressional investigation of banking and securities practices directed by Ferdinand Pecora, which revealed conditions characterized as 'scandalous,' and the banking collapse of 1932–33 dramatized the need and furnished the opportunity for reform. The Glass-Steagall Act of June 1933 separated commercial and investment banking, severely restricted the use of bank credit for speculative purposes, and expanded the Federal Reserve System. To prevent a recurrence of the epidemic of bank failures, the act set up a Federal Deposit Insurance Corporation to insure bank deposits up to a fixed sum. Roosevelt accepted this proposal with reservations, and the American Bankers Association denounced it as 'unsound, unscientific, unjust and dangerous,' but it turned out to be one of the most constructive devices of the New Deal era. Bank failures, which had averaged a thousand a year in the previous decade, became almost non-existent. During the 'Second Hundred Days'

1. Before the year was out, the Twenty-first Amendment repealing the Eighteenth (Prohibition) Amendment had been ratified.

2. A Joint Resolution of 5 June canceled the gold clauses in all government and private obligations and made all debts payable in legal tender. When the resolution was challenged in the courts, the Supreme Court in a 5–4 decision sustained congressional power over legal tender and held that though the cancellation of gold clauses in government contracts was both illegal and immoral the plaintiff had suffered no damage and had no grounds for suit.

William Gropper, 'The Senate,' 1935. Called 'the American Daumier,' Gropper, the son of a sweatshop worker, left high school to work at odd jobs like dishwasher, scraped enough cash together to study with the artists Robert Henri and George Bellows, became an illustrator for the radical *New Masses,* and on his return from a trip to Soviet Russia with Theodore Dreiser and Sinclair Lewis in 1927, put out a book of drawings. Like so many other painters in the Great Depresson, Gropper found employment on the Federal Art Project. In this bitter satire, a balding, pot-bellied U.S. Senator declaims to a largely empty chamber while one solon dozes and another reads a newspaper. *(Museum of Modern Art, Gift of A. Conger Goodyear, oil on canvas, 25⅛" x 33⅛")*

of the summer of 1935, Congress put the final stone in the new structure of government regulation of banking with the Banking Act of 1935 which expanded the powers of the reorganized and newly named Board of Governors of the Federal Reserve System.

The New Deal also brought the marketing of stocks and bonds under federal control. The Securities Act of 27 May 1933 stipulated that new securities must be registered with a government agency, subsequently the Securities and Exchange Commission; that every offering should contain full information to enable the prospective purchaser to judge its value; corporation officials were to be criminally liable for any misrepresentation. The following year came legislation to curb malpractices on the Stock Exchange. An act of June 1934 created a Securities and Exchange Commission and instituted regulation of stock exchanges. Joseph P. Kennedy, financier and speculator, was appointed chairman of the SEC because, Roosevelt said, he knew the tricks of the trade. Much of this legislation reflected the influence of the followers of Justice Brandeis—Felix Frankfurter of the Harvard Law School, Benjamin Cohen, Thomas Corcoran. In the Second Hundred Days, the Brandeisians scored their greatest triumph when Congress enacted legislation to level the public-utility holding company pyramids and to place these companies, too, under the SEC.

Although the New Deal left the system of private control of credit and investment intact, it markedly altered the relationship between government and finance. As early as 1934 one writer noted: 'Financial news no longer originates in Wall Street. . . . The pace of the ticker is determined now in Washington, not in company board-rooms, or in brokerage offices.' The new securities and banking legislation, the reorientation of the Reconstruction Finance Corporation under the Houston banker Jesse Jones, the enhanced powers of the Federal Reserve System, and the accelerated rate of government spending gave Washington a significantly new position as senior partner in the management of the nation's finances.

Farm Relief

In consultation with national farm leaders, Roosevelt's Secretary of Agriculture Henry A. Wallace prepared a farm relief plan of unexpected boldness. On 12 May 1933 Congress passed the Agricultural Adjustment Act, in order to reestablish 'parity' between agriculture and industry by raising the level of commodity prices and easing the credit and mortgage load. Its most important provisions authorized the Secretary of Agriculture to make agreements with staple farmers whereby, in return for government subsidies, they undertook to reduce production. Costs of payments to growers were to be met from taxes on the processing of the products involved. The Secretary could also negotiate marketing agreements for commodities like citrus fruits and dairy products. Subsequent programs made available Commodity Credit Corporation loans on crops and authorized compulsory marketing quotas for cotton and tobacco. In part because of crop reduction, in part because of government payments, and in part because of the devaluation of the dollar, farm income increased from $5,562,000,000 in 1932 to $8,688,000,000 in 1935.

On 6 January 1936 in a 6 to 3 decision the Supreme Court invalidated the AAA's processing tax as an improper exercise of the taxing power and an invasion of the reserved rights of states. 'This is coercion by economic pressure,' said Justice Owen Roberts, who conjured up the terrifying consequences that would flow from unbridled national power. Justice Harlan Fiske Stone, in his powerful dissenting opinion, protested, pointing out that 'the present levy is held invalid, not for any want of power in Congress to lay such a tax . . . but because the use to which its proceeds are put is disapproved' and observed, with some asperity, that 'courts are not the only agency of government that must be assumed to have capacity to govern.'

The Court's decision in the Butler case compelled the administration to piece together a stopgap measure: the Soil Conservation and Domestic Allotment Act of 1936. This law subsidized farmers for increasing acreage of soil-conserving crops and reducing acreage of soil-depleting crops, which, conveniently, were the surplus staples; it financed this program directly, rather than through the outlawed processing tax. Although this act speeded the development of soil conservation, it proved unsatisfactory as a price-raising device since the government had no way to compel compliance. In 1938 Congress adopted a second AAA which embraced a number of earlier programs in addition to such new approaches as the 'ever normal granary' and crop insurance; furthermore, it extended the coercive principle, which a chastened Supreme Court was now willing to sanction.

The administration also took steps to cope with

YEARS OF DUST
DUST STORM
RESETTLEMENT ADMINISTRATION
Rescues Victims
Restores Land to Proper Use

Dust Bowl blues, 1936. In 1935 the Resettlement Administration sent Ben Shahn on a three-month photographic assignment in the South and Southwest. A much admired painter who had studied with Diego Rivera, Shahn had no training with a camera, but he returned with a portfolio of photographs that were valuable in themselves and also served as the basis for murals and posters. 'Shahn,' F. Jack Hurley has written, 'had an ability few could match for capturing the torture in the body of a farm wife, old before her time, or the terror in the eyes of a drought-scarred child.' *(Museum of Modern Art, poster, 37 7/8" x 25")*

A family of 'Okies.' In this portrait of drought refugees from Oklahoma in Blythe, California, in 1936, Dorothea Lange demonstrates the stark candor, combined with a sense of dignity and compassion, that was characteristic of her work. In 1935 Roy Stryker, impressed by her pictures of the rural poor on the West Coast, had hired her for the historical section of the Resettlement Administration (later absorbed by the FSA), and in 1939 she and her husband Paul Taylor brought out the splendid *American Exodus* which drew on this experience. (*Library of Congress*)

the long-range problems of agriculture and assist the disadvantaged farmer. In 1935 the President set up a Resettlement Administration which, under the guidance of Rexford Tugwell, removed from cultivation some 10 million acres of marginal land; gave financial aid to 635,000 farm families; and built model suburban 'greenbelt' developments. The Farm Security Administration, which succeeded the Resettlement Administration in 1939, lent tenants almost $260 million to purchase farms and over $800 million in rehabilitation loans; helped organize co-operatives, including medical co-ops; and built camps for migratory workers, like the Joads of Steinbeck's *The Grapes of Wrath*. But as the spokesman for the poorer farmers, the FSA incurred the opposition of the powerful Farm Bureau Federation, and its funds were never large enough to meet the need. World War II did more than the New Deal to bail out the tenant farmer. In 1935, two-fifths of the farmers in the country were tenants; by 1950 only one state—Mississippi—reported more than half of her farms held by tenants; in the nation as a whole the figure had dropped to one-fourth.

Like the New Deal's financial operations, its agricultural program expanded the power of government while leaving property relationships essentially undisturbed. AAA subsidies gave disproportionate benefits to large farmers, and the crop reduction campaign even drove some of the tenants and sharecroppers off the land. Furthermore, the New Deal remained perpetually embarrassed by its scarcity economics, even though the plow-up of cotton and the slaughter of the little pigs were only emergency measures restricted to 1933. Yet, for all its shortcomings, the New Deal's farm program marked a great improvement on the single-interest government of the 1920's. Though net farm income in 1939 still fell well under that of 1929, the administration rescued the farmer from his desperate plight of the late Hoover period. The New Deal sent out millions of subsidy checks; saved large numbers of rural families from foreclosure; extended participatory democracy to involve thousands of local volunteers in the administration of the AAA; gave Southern Negro farmers the opportunity to vote in national crop referenda; and made at least a start toward helping the forgotten men of American agriculture.

Industry and Labor Under the New Deal

The New Deal's program for industrial recovery had multiple origins. Business groups like the U.S. Chamber of Commerce wanted government sanction for trade associations to draft agreements exempt from anti-trust prosecution. Planners such as Tugwell sought centralized direction of the economy. Labor leaders like John L. Lewis wanted guarantees for workers. Progressive senators led by 'Young Bob' La Follette had been pressing for massive public works spending. When the President told advocates of these different proposals to lock themselves in a room and stay there until they had reached agreement, they came out with an omnibus measure that had something for everybody.

The National Industrial Recovery Act of June 1933 authorized businessmen to organize their industries by drafting codes, exempt from the anti-trust laws but requiring government approval. Section 7(a) of the statute guaranteed labor the right to collective bargaining. The Recovery Act also set up a Public Works Administration with an appropriation of $3.3 billion, and the President designated his Secretary of the Interior, Harold Ickes, to head the PWA. Under the prodigiously energetic Recovery Administrator, General Hugh Johnson, administrators were familiar only with the general principles of the new program, businessmen and their legal advisers were familiar with all the details; the inevitable result was that big business generally imposed its own codes upon both government and small business. Yet out of the welter of conference and debate there emerged a pattern of industrial organization that met many of the requirements laid down by the act. To rally support, Johnson hit on the Blue Eagle as a symbol of compliance with the wage and hour provisions of the codes, and for a short time the Blue Eagle was almost as popular as the flag. Within a year some 500 codes had been adopted and some 200 more were in process of formulation. Under the NRA, industry reabsorbed unemployed workers, adopted hundreds of codes setting minimum wages and maximum hours, and went far toward abolishing child labor and the sweatshop.

But the NRA overextended itself in trying to regulate small enterprises, and it could not muster enough power to discipline the big corporations, which raised prices and persisted in monopolistic practices. During 1934 and 1935 the NRA was assailed with increasing bitterness from all sides: by large businessmen who resented government control of their labor relations; by small businessmen dismayed at the growth of monopoly; by liberals who feared the long-range consequences of a 'planned economy' dominated by business; by consumers outraged at price increases; by labor disappointed in the practical results of the codes.

The NRA was breaking down of its own weight when in May 1935 the Supreme Court destroyed it by undermining its legal foundations in a unanimous decision, the Schechter case. The Recovery Act, said the Court, involved an illegal delegation of legislative power to the Executive. Furthermore, it constituted an improper exercise of the commerce power and an invasion by the Federal Government of the realm reserved to the states, for 'if the commerce clause were construed to reach all enterprises and transactions which could be said to have an indirect effect upon interstate commerce, the federal authority would embrace practically all the activities of the people and the authority of the state over its domestic concerns would exist only by sufferance.' Never again would big business play so large a role in the New Deal, but neither would the planners like Tugwell ever have so promising, but illusory, an opportunity to impose centralized planning on the economy.

The framers of the Recovery Act hoped, too, that the $3.3 billion appropriation for public works would be an important lever for industrial recovery. However, Roosevelt, pledged to budget-balancing, was skeptical of the value of public works and repeatedly raided the grant for other projects, while Ickes, worried about the possibility of another Teapot Dome, insisted on reviewing every word of every PWA contract. The industrious, sardonic Ickes won himself the reputation of 'Honest Harold,' but neither he nor the President realized the economic potentialities of public works spending.

On the other hand, Roosevelt's labor policy, despite a period of uncertainty, proved much more successful. His appointment of Frances Perkins, the first woman cabinet member, to the post of Secretary of Labor augured well for the workingman, and Section 7(a) of the National Industrial Recovery Act showed some responsiveness to the aspirations of union leaders. Under the impetus of the NRA, organized labor more than recovered all the losses which it had suffered in the preceding decade. Using the magic name of FDR, John L. Lewis launched an organizing drive in the coal fields in the summer of 1933 which gained the United Mine Workers 300,000 members in two months, and by the tens of thousands workers signed union cards in industries that had long been resistant to organization—rubber, automobiles, textiles.

But 1934 proved considerably more troublesome. By manipulating the device of the company union, industrialists complied with the letter of the Recovery Act while keeping organizers out of their plants. At the same time the craft union leaders of the A.F. of L., hostile or indifferent to the unskilled recruits flocking to the Federation, treated their new members with such disdain that many tore up their union cards. In 1934 an epidemic of strikes by industrial workers under radical sponsorship hit cities such as Minneapolis. Most failed; in San Francisco a general strike was smashed by the militia and by self-constituted vigilantes. The Roosevelt administration, dismayed by strikes that impeded its recovery effort, fumbled for a labor policy. It antagonized employers, who resented any kind of intervention, and industrial unionists, who protested that government labor boards were powerless to cope with employer defiance. While the executive branch temporized, congressional liberals stepped in to replace the New Deal's makeshifts with legislation of a more permanent character.

In 1935, Congress, led by Senator Robert Wagner, gave labor an emphatic victory with the National Labor Relations Act, better known as the Wagner Act. This measure, which secured Roosevelt's last-minute endorsement, not only embraced some of the provisions of the recently invalidated Recovery Act but also significantly

The Memorial Day massacre, South Chicago, 1937. Philip Evergood's 'The American Tragedy' shows club-wielding police mauling workers and firing pistols at the backs of unarmed demonstrators at Tom Girdler's Republic Steel plant. For radicals, the episode amply demonstrated the brutality of the employer class, but proletarians in flight, even from overwhelming force, left an inappropriate impression; hence, Evergood also depicts, in the foreground, a heroic worker shielding his pregnant wife from officers of the law gone berserk. Though Evergood, a New Yorker who painted for the WPA's Federal Art Project, affected the crude style of an untrained dauber from the working class, he had in fact gone to Eton and Cambridge and studied art in Paris and London. (*Coll. Mrs. Gerrit Pieter Van de Bovenkamp*)

expanded the government's powers. It set up an independent National Labor Relations Board authorized to conduct plant elections and issue 'cease and desist' orders against unfair practices, including coercion of employees, discrimination against union members, and refusal to bargain collectively with employees. By stipulating that a majority of workers should have exclusive bargaining rights, the law all but destroyed the divisive tactic of the company union.

Under the umbrella of government protection, organized labor carried out a dramatic recruiting drive. In 1935 Lewis led a secession from the A.F. of L. of unions impatient with the resistance of the Federation's leadership to organizing factory workers. The C.I.O., first known as the Committee for Industrial Organization and later as the Congress of Industrial Organizations, sometimes employed the novel technique of the 'sit-down,' seizing possession of a plant and refusing to leave until demands had been granted. In February 1937 General Motors agreed to a settlement after a forty-four-day sit-down, and before the year was out such giants as U.S. Steel, Chrysler, and General Electric had surrendered, too. The C.I.O. insurrection also awakened the A.F. of L., which emerged even more powerful than its upstart rival.

The New Deal had helped make possible one of the most important developments of twentieth-century America: the unionization of the mass production industries. The benevolent neutrality of the administration (including Roosevelt's refusal to countenance force to oust the sit-down strikers), the sympathy of local leaders like Governor Frank Murphy of Michigan, and the aid of congressional liberals such as Wagner and La Follette, who headed a Senate committee that exposed employer violence, all proved immensely beneficial to the unions. By World War II even Henry Ford had recognized the worker's right, long granted in other industrial nations, to unionize and to bargain collectively.

Conservation and the TVA

No part of the New Deal was more imaginative than that which looked at the conservation of natural resources. The initial step was the creation (March 1933) of the Civilian Conservation Corps, to give work relief to jobless young men from 17 to 25. In the eight years of its existence the CCC enlisted almost 3 million young men, who, under the direction of army officers and foresters, added over 17 million acres of new forest land, checked forest fires, fought plant and animal diseases, stocked hatcheries with over a billion fish, built 6 million check dams to halt soil erosion, and by mosquito control helped stamp out malaria.

Of more lasting importance was the dramatic Tennessee Valley Authority, a vast experiment in regional reconstruction. The TVA acquired or constructed some 25 dams for flood control, nitrate production, and the generation of electric power; to these it eventually added a series of stream generator plants. The government built some 5000 miles of transmission lines and sold surplus power to nearby communities at rates low enough to ensure widespread consumption. In 1932 only two farms out of one hundred in the valley were electrified; five years later the proportion was one out of seven, and by 1960 electrification was well-nigh complete. The TVA also resettled marginal farmers, promoted public health, and encouraged local industry, all in close cooperation with the people of the valley, for the TVA was dedicated to decentralized administration. Too often, decentralized administration meant that decisions were made by wealthy white farmers and the TVA bowed to the local pattern of racial segregation. But the TVA also left a substantial record of achievement. Within a few years millions of abandoned acres were restored to cultivation, industry returned to the valley, vacationers crowded its artificial lakes, and the river, navigable now over its entire length from Knoxville to the Ohio river, was one of the busiest streams in the country. The TVA itself became a model which attracted the emulation of the whole world.

The Roosevelt administration initiated a host of new enterprises in conservation and electric power. It not only disciplined the utility-holding companies and strengthened the Federal Power Commission but set up the Rural Electrification Administration which radically changed life on the farm. At the outset of the New Deal, only one out

Moses Soyer, 'Artists on WPA,' 1936. The art projects of the New Deal helped foster a cultural nationalism that esteemed native American subjects. But Soyer, one of three brothers who were artists, warned against being 'misled by the chauvinism of the 'Paint America' slogan. Yes, paint America, but with your eyes open. Do not glorify Main Street. Paint it as it is—mean, dirty, avaricious. Self glorification is artistic suicide. Witness Nazi Germany.' Soyer's statement revealed not only the righteous provincialism of New York artists but the ubiquitous anxiety about fascism in the 1930's. (*Smithsonian Institution*)

of nine American farms had electricity; by the end of the Roosevelt era, eight out of nine enjoyed electric power. In the Pacific Northwest, construction of the Grand Coulee Dam, and of Bonneville Dam in the lower Columbia river basin, developed some 2.5 million kilowatts of electric power and made possible the irrigation and reclamation of over a million acres of farm land. The alarming spread of the 'dust bowl' on the high plains inspired the planting of a 100-mile-wide shelter belt of trees, stretching from Texas to Canada. To stop soil erosion the government enlisted one-fourth of the nation's farmers. The New Deal found a home for the brilliant head of the Soil Conservation Service, Hugh H. Bennett; for the thoughtful planner, Morris Llewellyn Cooke, who turned out landmark reports on the nation's resources; for John Collier, who, as Indian Commissioner, sought to save the Indians' lands at the same time that he preserved their culture; and Pare Lorentz, who produced such film epics as *The River* and *The Plough That Broke the Plains.* Not even in Uncle Teddy's day had the conservation movement enjoyed such brilliant leadership.

The Welfare State

Roosevelt had promised during his campaign that no one should starve, and during the Hundred Days of 1933, Congress responded to his recommendations for the unemployed by creating the Civilian Conservation Corps and setting up the Federal Emergency Relief Administration to make grants to state and local governments for public projects and, where necessary, direct grants to the needy. Under the experienced social-work administrator, Harry Hopkins, the FERA in the next two years disbursed $4 billion for relief, three-fourths from federal and one-fourth from local funds.[3] By 1934 more than twenty million people—one out of every six Americans—were receiving public assistance. In addition the Public Works Administration under Ickes was putting men to work on construction projects which helped change the face of the land. The PWA burrowed Chicago's new subway, built the Skyline Drive in Virginia, and constructed the carrier *Yorktown;* in the six years of its existence it helped build two-thirds of all new school buildings in the nation and one-third of the new hospitals.

In January 1935 Roosevelt proposed that a distinction to be made between employables and unemployables, that more satisfactory provision be made for the former, and that the burden of supporting the latter be transferred to the states. In response, Congress appropriated nearly $5 billion, and the President established a Works Progress Administration to disburse most of this huge sum. The WPA was wasteful, and the government never provided for all who were in need. Yet by 1943 when the WPA terminated its activities, it had given work to over 8 million unemployed, who were responsible for 600,000 miles of highways, 125,000 public buildings, 8000 parks, 850 airport landing fields, and thousands of hospitals, municipal power plants, and school buildings, and the achievement of the imaginative Federal Arts Project. The Federal Theatre produced the classic works from Euripides to Ibsen; offered the plays of contemporaries like Eugene O'Neill; and sponsored vaudeville troupes, marionettes, and circuses. The Federal Writers' Project gave jobs to established writers like Conrad Aiken, unknown men such as John Cheever and Richard Wright, and, mercifully, jobless historians. It turned out a thousand publications, including the immensely useful series of state guides. The Federal Music Project put together three orchestras—the Buffalo Philharmonic, the Oklahoma Symphony, and the Utah State Symphony—which became the established orchestras in their communities, while the Federal Arts Project supported such painters as Jackson Pollock and sponsored the influential *Index of American Design.* Another progeny of the relief act of 1935, the National Youth Administration, found part-time jobs for more than 600,000 college and 1.5 million high-school students, and 2.5 million who were out of school.

The New Deal's housing program joined together a number of separate aims: to create pub-

3. When Roosevelt realized that not even the FERA would get the country through the first New Deal winter of 1933–34, he named Hopkins to head a temporary Civil Works Administration, and the resourceful Hopkins quickly put four million jobless on federal projects.

lic works projects to employ the jobless; to revive the construction business; and to provide better dwellings. In 1934 Congress set up the Federal Housing Administration which insured mortgages to encourage the repair and building of private homes. Of benefit chiefly to the middle class, the FHA had by 1945 financed more than one-third of all privately constructed homes, and proved a boon to builders and savings and loan associations. On a much more modest scale the PWA constructed low-rent public housing, but the New Deal moved so slowly that, as Charles Abrams wrote, 'a great opportunity to rebuild many of America's decayed urban centers was lost.' Roosevelt was much more interested in bootless schemes to return city-dwellers to the land than in massive urban housing projects; not until 1937 did he commit himself to the public housing measure Senator Wagner had been sponsoring. With FDR's support, Congress in 1937 created the U.S. Housing Authority to assist local communities in slum clearance and the construction of low-cost housing. The USHA eventually built 165,000 family units. If the New Deal failed to take full advantage of the opportunity that housing offered, both as a humanitarian enterprise and as a lever for recovery, it did establish a new principle: federal responsibility for clearing slums and housing the poor.

As early as 1934 the President had called for a broad program of old-age and unemployment insurance. 'There is no reason,' he told Secretary Perkins, 'why every child from the day he is born, shouldn't be a member of the social security . . . cradle to grave—they ought to be in a social insurance system.' Pressure for an old-age pension scheme was also exerted by advocates of the Townsend Plan. Dr. Francis Townsend of California agitated for monthly payments of $200 to all persons over 60 years of age, on the sole proviso that they retire from work and spend the money; Dr. Townsend's plan was championed by Townsend Clubs claiming close to a million members. In August 1935 Congress enacted the Social Security law, an omnibus measure which provided for old-age insurance, unemployment insurance, benefit payments to the handicapped, aid to dependent children and their mothers, pensions to needy aged, and extensive appropriations for public health.

The United States still had a long way to go to provide adequately for the impoverished and the handicapped, but the New Deal had taken giant strides in that direction. It not only engaged in an unprecedented range of activities—vast relief programs, slum clearance, aid to tenant farmers, curbs on the sweatshop and child labor, minimum labor standards, a social security system—but had established the principle of federal responsibility for society's victims. 'Government has a final responsibility for the well-being of its citizenship,' Roosevelt declared. 'If private co-operative endeavor fails to provide work for willing hands and relief for the unfortunate, those suffering hardship from no fault of their own have a right to call upon the Government for aid; and a government worthy of its name must make fitting response.'

The Roosevelt Coalition

The Great Depression made a deeper impact on American politics than any event since the Civil War. By identifying the Republican party with the collapse, the voters in 1932 had given the Democrats an opportunity to establish themselves as the majority party for the next generation, and Roosevelt made the most of it. By 1936 he had forged a new party coalition which would prevail not only in his lifetime but for many years thereafter. From 1930 to 1976 the Republicans would win control of the House in only two elections.

The Roosevelt coalition centered in lower income groups in the great cities. In 1936 FDR captured all but two of the 106 cities of 100,000 population or more. The New Deal's urban appeal was especially marked among labor and ethnic groups. John L. Lewis, who had endorsed Hoover in 1932, opened his union treasury to Roosevelt in 1936, and voting broke sharply on class lines. A variety of ethnic elements were grateful for New Deal measures and for recognition. In 1932 the Negro had still given his allegiance to the party of Lincoln, and in the early years of the New Deal, black leaders were distressed by racial discrimination in agencies like the CCC. However, attitudes

Eleanor Roosevelt and Alice Hamilton. Mrs. Roosevelt made the most of her opportunity as First Lady to accord recognition to individuals of singular achievement who had been battling for social justice for decades before the advent of the New Deal. Alice Hamilton (1869–1970) overcame prejudice against women in medicine and against female reformers to become an outstanding authority on industrial toxicology. In the progressive era, she investigated occupational diseases and industrial poisons for the state of Illinois and the U.S. Department of Labor, and her service as assistant professor of industrial medicine at Harvard, which began just after World War I, continued into the age of FDR. *Exploring the Dangerous Trades* is a fascinating account of the long and useful career of a woman who lived to be a centenarian. (*Schlesinger Library, Radcliffe College*)

changed in response to the fact that Negroes received a lion's share of relief jobs; got one-third of the federal housing units; and won appointments to important national posts. Although the President refused to antagonize Southern committee chairmen by pressing civil rights legislation, Eleanor Roosevelt intervened repeatedly on behalf of the blacks. By 1934 Negro voters were switching to the Democrats in large numbers, and in 1936 they rolled up big majorities for FDR.

In his bid for re-election Roosevelt faced a dual challenge from the Republicans and from a third party. The G.O.P. chose as its nominee Alfred M. Landon of Kansas, who had been a fairly progressive governor. But Landon was embarrassed by the Hoover wing of the party which took the campaign away from him. His only hope lay in the possibility that a third-party candidate would draw enough votes away from FDR to let a Republican slip in. For a time Louisiana's Senator Huey Long, advocate of a popular share-the-wealth scheme, raised the formidable threat of an alliance of his forces with those of Dr. Townsend and Father Coughlin, the rabble-rousing radio priest. But in September 1935 Long was assassinated and the Union party ticket, fielded by dissidents in 1936, attracted little support.

On 2 November Roosevelt's campaign manager, Postmaster General Jim Farley, wrote the President: 'I am still definitely of the opinion that you will carry every state but two—Maine and Vermont.' Farley hit it right on the button. With 523 votes to Landon's 8, Roosevelt won the greatest electoral margin of any presidential candidate since Monroe. Never before had a major party suffered so overwhelming a defeat as the Republicans had sustained. Buoyed by this impressive vote of confidence, Roosevelt began his second term in office with high hopes.

The Constitutional Revolution

Outnumbered in Congress, humiliated at the polls, the Republicans lifted their eyes to the Supreme Court. The G.O.P. 'retired into the judiciary as a stronghold, and from that battery all the works of republicanism were to be beaten down and erased.' So Jefferson had said of the Federalists over a century earlier, and his successor in the White House had reason to echo the bitter charge. Never before had the Supreme Court worked such havoc with a legislative program as it did in 1935 and 1936 with that of the New Deal. It overthrew the NRA in part on the novel ground of improper delegation of power. It struck down the AAA through what a dissenting justice called a 'tortured construction of the Constitution,' while the Bituminous Coal Act was invalidated because the Court, in the Carter case, insisted that mining was a purely local business. It nullified the Municipal Bankruptcy Act on the assumption that such legislation invaded the domain of the states—even though the Act required state consent, which many states had already given. The Federal Government had long been denied the power to enact minimum-wage legislation; when in the Tipaldo case the Court denied this power to the states as well, it created a no-man's-land where neither federal nor state power might be applied.

What was Roosevelt to do? The process of constitutional amendment was slow and uncertain, and in the past the judiciary had been brought to acquiescence in majority will only by the process of new appointments. But Roosevelt was the first President in more than a century to serve a full term without having the opportunity to choose at least one new justice, although six of the judges were over seventy years of age. If the trouble lay not in Constitution but in the Court, that could be remedied by appointing new members. So at least Roosevelt thought, and this was the crucial part of the proposal he submitted to a startled Congress on 5 February 1937. The President proposed to obtain the 'addition of younger blood' by the appointment of one new judge, up to a maximum of six, for every justice of the Supreme Court who, having passed the age of seventy and served for ten years, failed to retire.

For months the nation reverberated to protests against the scheme as an attempt to 'pack' the Supreme Court and subvert the judiciary, but in the end it was the strategic retreat of the Court that brought about the defeat of the plan. For abruptly and unpredictably, the Court found ways of making the constitutional sun shine on legislation which had heretofore been under a judicial cloud. Nine months after the Court had struck down the New York minimum-wage law, it sustained a similar act of the state of Washington. Two weeks later came five decisions, all upholding various provisions of the National Labor Relations Act. A month later, and the controversial Social Security law was vouchsafed judicial blessing. In all but one of these decisions, the conservative 'Four Horsemen'—McReynolds, Sutherland, Butler, and Van Devanter—took an adamant stand, but they now constituted a minority, because Justice Roberts had joined the liberal triumvirate of Brandeis, Cardozo, and Stone, together with Chief Justice Hughes, whom many credited with frustrating the President by marshalling the Court in support of new interpretations. At the same time that the Court approved New Deal laws, it spiked the 'court packing' scheme, for many saw no point in altering the judiciary now that the reform legislation had been validated. As one commentator quipped: 'A switch in time saved nine.' Although the fight continued into the month of July, the opponents prevailed. The President, at the height of his power, had suffered a stinging rebuke.

Roosevelt claimed that though he had lost the battle, he had won the war. Even while the Court debate was under way, Justice Van Devanter announced his retirement, and before the President left office he would be able to name eight of the nine justices and elevate Justice Stone to the chief justiceship. Since 1937 the Court has not invalidated a single congressional statute in the realm of regulation of business, and very few laws, national or state, in any realm. In a series of decisions it swept away any lingering doubts about the power of the Federal Government over manufacturing and farming and removed the limitation imposed upon congressional spending in the Butler case. In addition the Court took a sympathetic attitude toward the exercise of police power by the states. Finally, the 'Roosevelt Court' continued even more assiduously than the Court had before 1937 to throw new safeguards around civil liberties, although even in the 1920's important gains had been made in protecting the rights of minorities. It had long been assumed that the Bill of Rights limited only the national Congress. Beginning, however, with *Gitlow v. New York* in 1925, the Court intimated that the rights of 'life, liberty and property,' guaranteed against state impairment by the Fourteenth Amendment, might be presumed to embrace many of those rights set forth in the first ten amendments. This dictum, at first only cautiously advanced, was within a decade incorporated into constitutional law.

In its decisions on property rights even more than on civil liberties, the Court had wrought a constitutional revolution that appeared to justify Roosevelt's claims that he had won the war; yet in another sense he lost the war. The Supreme Court fight, together with such other developments in 1937 as the recession and resentment at the sit-down strikes, cost the President much of his middle-class following and dealt a heavy blow at the Roosevelt coalition. The Court struggle helped weld together a bipartisan coalition of anti-New Deal legislators who soon held a pivotal position. If Roosevelt's Court proposal secured the legitimization of a vast expansion of the power of government, it also played an important role in the untimely end of the New Deal.

The End of the New Deal

Middle-class enthusiasm for Roosevelt owed much to the fact that the President appeared to be leading the country out of the depression, for in the spring of 1937 the nation had finally achieved 1929 levels of production, but in August the economy suddenly slumped. From September 1937 to June 1938, in a decline of unparalleled severity, industrial output fell 33 per cent. Middle-class support for the President, already shaken by the Supreme Court and sit-down episodes, was now even more seriously tried, for no longer did FDR seem a magic-maker who had a formula for ending the depression. Yet, ironically, the recession had been produced by Roosevelt's acquiescence in the most cherished of middle-class prescriptions for recovery: balancing the budget. Denounced as a wild spender, the President had, in fact, always viewed federal deficits with regret. As Tugwell later reflected: 'Roosevelt felt just as much convicted of sin when the budget was unbalanced as Hoover had been.' When early in 1937 the econ-

Defense industry town. Jack Delano's photograph of a Pittsburgh mill district in the winter of 1941 was taken for the historical section of the Farm Security Administration. Under the direction of Roy Stryker, this New Deal unit nurtured the talents of artists like Delano, John Vachon, and John Collier, Jr., and assisted the brilliant young black photographer Gordon Parks. Increasingly in 1941 the section turned its attention toward portraying a country preparing for war. (*Library of Congress*)

omy continued to show steady improvement, Roosevelt concluded that he could safely return to more conservative fiscal policies; the Federal Reserve Board contracted credit, and government spending was radically slashed. Since it had been the deficit spending that had been largely responsible for the gains of Roosevelt's first term, his abrupt reversal produced a convulsive reaction.

Through the winter of 1937–38, Roosevelt's advisers belabored him with conflicting advice. Secretary of the Treasury Henry Morgenthau, Jr. urged him to commit himself to orthodox finance to win business 'confidence.' But men like Harry Hopkins and Federal Reserve Chairman Marriner Eccles argued that when private investment fell off, the government should step up spending. 'In other words,' Eccles insisted, 'the Government must be looked upon as a compensatory agency in the economy to do just the opposite to what private business and individuals do.' In addition, these New Dealers believed that the government should curb monopoly, on the grounds that the inflexible 'administered' price practices of the monopolies were prolonging the depression. Some of these ideas reflected the influence of the British economist, John Maynard Keynes, but Keynes made rather little impact on Roosevelt; he served chiefly to reinforce views which the New Dealers already held.

In the early spring of 1938 the liberals won out, for Roosevelt had concluded that the recession was taking too great a toll of the unemployed and that he must spend. He asked Congress to approve a large-scale 'lend-spend' program, and Congress responded by voting nearly a billion for public works and almost three billions more for other federal activities. The President gave his liberal advisers something else to cheer about when he asked Congress for a full-dress investigation of the concentration of economic power, which led to the creation of the Temporary National Economic Committee, and when he appointed Thurman Arnold of Yale Law School to be Assistant Attorney-General in charge of the Antitrust Division. That same year Congress established the second AAA and passed a Fair Labor Standards Act which reduced child labor and put a floor under wages and a ceiling on hours for workers in industries engaged in interstate commerce. In the remainder of Roosevelt's second term, the economy painfully climbed up toward its earlier levels, but the New Dealers could not escape the fact that whatever they had done had not been sufficient to avert the recession, and that in 1939 there were still ten million unemployed. Never before had any administration been so responsive to the nation's social needs or built so many useful economic institutions, but it would require the coming of World War II to restore the country's prosperity.

After the passage of the Fair Labor Standards Act in 1938, Congress did not adopt any other reform legislation for the rest of the decade. The impetus of the New Deal came to an end not only because it failed to bring recovery, but because the forces opposed to further change were too powerful. The informal conservative bipartisan coalition forged during the Court fight showed its strength in the special session of Congress in the fall of 1937 when the President could not gain approval of a single measure. In 1938 Democratic insurrectionists joined with Republicans to bury Roosevelt's plan for executive reorganization.[4] That same spring the House set up a Committee on Un-American Activities which, under the chairmanship of the Texas Democrat Martin Dies, became a forum for right-wing forays against the Roosevelt administration. 'Stalin baited his hook with a "progressive" worm,' Dies said, 'and New Deal suckers swallowed bait, hook, line, and sinker.'

This series of setbacks exasperated New Dealers who recalled that many of the Democrats who were now attacking Roosevelt had come in on the President's coattails only a short time before. Liberal Democrats, convinced that Roosevelt still had the country with him, persuaded the President to attempt to 'purge' a number of legislators in the 1938 Democratic primaries, in particular Senators Walter George of Georgia, 'Cotton Ed' Smith of South Carolina, and Millard Tydings of Maryland. The President succeeded in eliminating a Tammany congressman, but George, Smith, and Tydings all won handily, leaving the party's con-

4. Congress did, however, approve a modified program to revamp the executive branch in 1939, the same year that it adopted the Hatch Act to restrict the political activities of government employees.

Roosevelt as captain of the ship of state. This little-known painting by the Norwegian-American artist Gulbrand Sether conveys the enthusiasm for the New Deal in FDR's first months in office. The two women in the picture are Secretary of Labor Frances Perkins and the First Lady, Eleanor Roosevelt. The figures in cap and gown may be intended to suggest the influence of the Brain Trust on the Roosevelt administration. By the end of FDR's second term, the naval craft depicted here had become increasingly important as the issues of World War II overwhelmed those of the New Deal. *(Library of Congress)*

servatives more cocksure than ever. That fall, the Republicans picked up 81 seats in the House, 8 in the Senate, and 13 governorships; all but given up for dead two years before, they introduced to the national spotlight that year such new faces as Thomas Dewey and Robert Taft.

Without enough votes to carry his program through Congress before the election, the President now faced a greatly bolstered conservative alliance. Resigned to the inevitable, Roosevelt in his annual message to Congress in January 1939 for the first time advanced no new measures. 'We have now passed the period of internal conflict in the launching of our program of social reforms,' he told Congress. 'Our full energies may now be released to invigorate the processes of recovery in order to preserve our reforms.' As an innovating force, the New Deal was at an end, and the President henceforth directed most of his attention to the critical problems of foreign policy.

The New Deal: An Evaluation

Critics of the New Deal, at the time and subsequently, have argued that it should have done more, that it should have done less, and that it should have done things differently. They emphasize that the Roosevelt administration failed in its fundamental assignment—bringing the country out of the depression, for recovery came only with the tocsins of war. In the 1970's both Right and Left have seen in the New Deal the breeding place of the 'Imperial Presidency' of the Watergate era. There can be no doubt that the New Deal was deficient in a number of respects.

Nevertheless, the accomplishments of the New Deal seem more impressive than its shortcomings. At the very outset, it brought the country through the crisis that Roosevelt had inherited, and it did a whole lot to ameliorate the worst hardships of the depression. As a result of the legislation of the Hundred Days, farm families were safeguarded from foreclosure of their lands and debt-ridden city families from dispossession of their homes. Throughout the 1930's, work was found for millions of unemployed in a series of projects from the FERA to the WPA, and the government took pains to provide rewarding jobs for novelists and essayists, muralists and sculptors, circus clowns and symphony composers. It showed particular concern for the young—from subsidizing hot lunches for grade school pupils to making it possible for college students to continue their education.

In contrast to the largely single-interest government of the 1920's, the New Deal extended benefits to groups that had been neglected, or short-changed, in the past. It encouraged unionization of factories and curbed sweatshops and child labor by stipulating minimal working conditions. AAA checks sustained millions of staple farmers, and the government made it possible for tenants to own farms and built camps for migrant workers, albeit on a modest scale. Though, unhappily, some agencies persisted in discrimination, blacks made unprecedented gains and the New Deal provided the American Indian with new opportunities for self-government. Eleanor Roosevelt and Frances Perkins gave visible evidence of the enhanced role of women in government, and the 'Brain Trust' meant a new welcome by Washington to university graduates.

The New Deal vastly expanded the scope of government in America. It fostered the Welfare State with old-age pensions, unemployment insurance, and aid for dependent children; engaged in multifarious housing ventures; created the nation's first state theater; and shot documentary films. It inaugurated ambitious regional enterprises like the TVA and the Columbia river projects, brought electricity to rural America, set up the Soil Conservation Service, dispatched the CCC boys into the forests, and, in countless other ways, changed the American landscape. For the first time, in the 1930's Wall Street was compelled to accept federal regulation, and national authority was extended to business units like public-utility holding companies. Before the decade was over, this enlargement of the orbit of government had been legitimized by the Constitutional Revolution of 1937 and the 'Roosevelt Court.'

Most significant of all was the maintenance of a democratic system in a world swept by totalitarianism. 'The only sure bulwark of continuing liberty,' Roosevelt had observed, 'is a government strong enough to protect the interests of the people, and a people strong enough and well enough informed to maintain its sovereign control over its government.' The proof that in the United States it was possible for such a government to exist and such a people to flourish was of fateful significance. For in the 'thirties it became doubtful whether liberty or democracy could survive in the modern world. It was of utmost importance to the peoples of the world that American democracy had withstood the buffetings of depression and that the American people were refreshed in their faith in the democratic order.

32

Gathering Storm

*

1933–1941

The Pacifist Mood

If there was one principle upon which the vast majority of the American people agreed in 1937, it was that what was happening in Europe was no concern of theirs; and that if Europe were so wicked or stupid as to get into another war, America would stay out of it. Yet at a time when the Fascist powers were planning to pounce on the democratic states and when the system of collective security was breaking down, it was not clear that pacifism and isolation would bring peace. Edna St. Vincent Millay wrote:

> Longing to wed with Peace, what did we do?—
> Sketched her a fortress on a paper pad;
> Under her casement twanged a love-sick string;
> Left wide the gate that let her foemen through.[1]

Such admonitions fell on deaf ears. They sounded too much like the slogans of World War I, now recalled with bitter resentment. Ostensibly fought to preserve democracy, the war had left Europe a continent where democracy appeared to have only the barest chance to survive. In 1925, Prime Minister Stanley Baldwin had asked: 'Who in Europe does not know that one more war in the West and the civilization of the ages will fall with as great a shock as that of Rome?' In America, fifteen years later, thousands of grim reminders of that conflict still lay in veterans' hospitals.

Many thought the greatest danger of war came not from Hitler but from war-mongering internationalists who would attempt to embroil the United States, an attitude that received official sanction in 1934 from a Senate investigation under Gerald Nye. The Nye committee concluded that America had intervened in World War I not to defend its own interests, nor for the altruistic purpose of saving the world for democracy, but as a consequence of the intrigues of financiers and armament interests. If Europeans had to fight, Nye scolded, 'let them pay for their own wars. If the Morgans and other bankers must get into another war, let them do it by enlisting in the Foreign Legion.' Although the Nye committee failed to prove anyone's responsibility for the war, it did reveal scandalously high profits, and, along with historians like Charles A. Beard and jour-

1. *Make Bright the Arrows,* Harper & Brothers, 1942, copyright 1939, 1940 by the author.

nalists like Colonel McCormick of the Chicago *Tribune*, converted much of the nation to the naïve view that America had been stampeded into war in order to make money for 'merchants of death,' and that the United States could go its own way oblivious of the rest of the world.

Watchfully Waiting

On the very day Roosevelt took the oath of office, the Japanese marched into the provincial capital of Jehol in China, and on the following day the last free elections in Germany consolidated the power of Adolf Hitler. Roosevelt recognized the perils of the breakdown of the world order, but isolationist and pacifist opinion left him little room to maneuver, and the crisis of the Great Depression persuaded him he must concentrate his energies on domestic affairs. 'I shall spare no effort to restore world trade by international economic readjustments,' he said in his inaugural address, 'but the emergency at home cannot wait on that accomplishment.'

In his first months in office Roosevelt encouraged the world to believe that he held out high hopes for the international economic conference scheduled for London in June. But by the time the delegates convened, he had come to fear that France and the other gold bloc countries were seeking to commit him to a policy that would destroy his efforts at price-raising at home. He not only killed a currency stabilization agreement but sent the conference a harsh message scolding the delegates for succumbing to the 'old fetishes of so-called international bankers.' Some like Keynes thought that the President was 'magnificently right,' but Roosevelt's 'bombshell message' undoubtedly reinforced the isolationists and persuaded Europe it could not count on the United States.

Despite this initial setback, Roosevelt's Secretary of State, Cordell Hull, unsympathetic to economic nationalism, persisted in exploring the possibilities for the recapture of foreign markets through reciprocity agreements. Under the terms of the Trade Agreements Act of June 1934, Hull negotiated a series of unconditional most-favored-nation reciprocity treaties. He hoped that the new commercial policy would not only operate for economic improvement but would advance international understanding. In fact, these agreements failed to have important economic consequences but did serve to win political good will. Even more illusory as a panacea for improved trade was the recognition of the Soviet Union in 1933, an event which twenty years later would be denounced as a treasonable act perpetrated by New Deal liberals. The truth of the matter is that recognition was widely applauded by businessmen avid for Russian markets, and Roosevelt's decision simply brought American practice in line with that of most of the rest of the world.

Roosevelt had the greatest leeway in foreign affairs when he sought to liquidate American commitments. 'In the field of world policy,' he said in his inaugural address, 'I would dedicate this Nation to the policy of the good neighbor.' The 'Good Neighbor policy' soon became the term for FDR's willingness to disavow America's intention to intervene in the internal affairs of Latin American nations. In 1934 the United States agreed to abrogate the Platt Amendment, thereby giving up its right to intervene at will in Cuba, and that same year it pulled the last marines out of Haiti, recognized a revolutionary government in El Salvador, and established the Export-Import Bank which extended credit to Latin American republics. Before the decade was over, the administration had ended financial controls in the Dominican Republic and resisted pressures to prevent Mexico from expropriating American oil. On the other side of the world, the Philippines won a promise of independence in 1946 when Congress passed the Tydings-McDuffie Act of 1934.

But such actions defined the limits of Roosevelt's power, for when he sought to use his influence in European affairs Congress would have none of it. In 1933 isolationists warned the President away from a proposal to co-operate in League sanctions against an aggressor, and in 1935 the Senate killed a measure to permit the United States to join the World Court. That year, too, Congress passed the first of a series of neutrality measures which prohibited private loans or credits to belligerent nations, embargoed shipments of arms or munitions to belligerents, and stipulated 'cash and carry' for any other articles. That is, belligerents who wanted to buy nonmilitary goods had to pay for them on delivery and haul them away in their own vessels or those of some country other than the United States. As Italy marched into Ethiopia in 1935 and Germany reclaimed the Rhineland the following year, Roosevelt found himself powerless to do anything effective. 'I am "watchfully waiting,"' he wrote one of his envoys, 'even though the phrase carries us back to the difficult days from 1914 to 1917.'

By August 1936, when the President spoke at Chautauqua, he appeared to have capitulated to the pacifist mood. 'We shun political commitments which might entangle us in foreign wars; we avoid connection with the political activities of the League of Nations,' he asserted. He added:

> I have seen war. I have seen war on land and sea. I have seen blood running from the wounded. I have seen men coughing out their gassed lungs. I have seen the dead in the mud. I have seen cities destroyed. I have seen two hundred limping, exhausted men come out of line—the survivors of a regiment of one thousand that went forward forty-eight hours before. I have seen children starving. I have seen the agony of mothers and wives. I hate war.

When in July 1936 anti-republican forces plunged Spain into a 'civil war' that Hitler and Mussolini soon made a testing ground for World War II, Roosevelt outdid the isolationists in his plea that Congress impose an arms embargo. Most of the nation approved, secure in the belief that the United States, by this series of steps, was avoiding the mistakes that had led to its unhappy involvement in the First World War. Claude Bowers, Roosevelt's ambassador to Spain, was unconvinced. 'My own impression,' he wrote in July 1937, 'is that with every surrender beginning long ago with China, followed by Abyssinia and then Spain, the fascist powers, with vanity inflamed, will turn without delay to some other country—such as Czechoslovakia—and that with every surrender the prospects of a European war grow darker.'

In signing the Neutrality Act of 1937, Roosevelt seemed to be endorsing all the assumptions of the isolationists; in fact, he was a troubled man. By 1937 Roosevelt's alarm at the actions of Hitler and Mussolini in Europe was matched by concern over the ambitions of the Japanese in the Far East. That year, Japan engaged in hostilities in China with a barbarity, as in the bombing of Shanghai and the sack of Nanking, that appalled American opinion. Roosevelt was still committed to peace, but he looked for some way to build a concert of powers to curb the expansion of Germany, Italy, and Japan.

In October 1937 in Chicago, the isolationist capital, the President warned that, if aggression triumphed elsewhere in the world, 'let no one imagine that America will escape, that America may expect mercy, that this Western Hemisphere will not be attacked.' Roosevelt noted that 'the epidemic of world lawlessness' was spreading, and he added: 'When an epidemic of physical disease starts to spread, the community approves and joins in a quarantine of the patients in order to protect the health of the community against the spread of the disease.' The President's 'quarantine' speech was interpreted as a new departure in Roosevelt's foreign policy—the abandonment of isolation for collective security, and advance notice to Tokyo of sanctions against Japan. Actually, Roosevelt had not yet committed himself to any project to contain the Axis powers, and though public response to the quarantine speech was generally favorable, the nation resolutely opposed any commitment of American forces abroad. On 12 December 1937 a small river gunboat of the American navy's Yangtze river patrol, U.S.S. *Panay,* was bombed and sunk by Japanese planes. When the Japanese government apologized and offered to pay indemnity to the victims, a sigh of relief passed over the length and breadth of America. In a January 1938 poll, 70 per cent of those with an opinion on the subject favored complete withdrawal from China—Asiatic Fleet, marines, missionaries, medical teams, and all.

By 1938 the Fascist powers were on the march. Hitler called Austrian Chancellor Kurt von Schuschnigg to his retreat in Berchtesgaden to bully him into submission. 'Perhaps I shall be suddenly overnight in Vienna, like a spring storm,' he warned. 'Do you want to turn Austria into another Spain?' On 11 March 1938 Schusch-

Ernest Hemingway (1898–1961). The publication of *For Whom the Bell Tolls,* centering on the Spanish Civil War, which appeared in 1940, was as much a political as a literary event. Hemingway's longest novel was hailed as a re-affirmation of democratic values by a novelist identified with the disillusionment of the post-World War I era, and the title, derived from John Donne, became a text for internationalists who argued that Americans should be as much concerned with the erosion of liberty abroad as at home, for the cause of humanity was indivisible. (*National Archives*)

nigg resigned. Immediately afterwards, Nazis swarmed into Vienna's Kärntnerstrasse; they ripped badges off Austrian officials, broke the shop windows of Jewish merchants, ran up the swastika over the Chancellery. The next morning, German tanks and troops poured over the border and, to the pealing of church bells and deafening cheers from Nazi followers, Adolf Hitler entered Austria at Braunau. In Vienna the following night, the Gestapo arrested no fewer than 76,000 people. Yet when at Munich in September 1938 Britain and France succumbed to Hitler's demand that Czechoslovakia be dismembered and the Sudetenland incorporated in the Reich, Americans had an overwhelming feeling of relief, coupled with the conviction that the European democracies were concerned only with self-interest. The New York *Post* commented: 'If this transcendental sellout does not force the Administration at Washington to return to our policy of isolation—then Heaven help us all!' Two months later, the Nazis carried out an appalling pogrom. Numbers of German and Austrian Jews came to America, but the United States, shamefully, refused to lower immigration barriers in any substantial way. Many who were denied visas later died in Hitler's gas chambers.

In September 1938, Hitler had said that once the Sudeten problem was settled, there would be 'no further territorial problem in Europe.' He added: 'We want no Czechs.' But less than six months later, on the Ides of March, Germany gobbled up most of Czechoslovakia. On the night of 15 March 1939 the Gestapo roved the streets of Prague making mass arrests; no Jewish shops opened the next day. The Fuehrer had, in a single stroke, destroyed any pretext that his ambitions were restricted to the desire to reunite Germans; had exposed appeasement as a failure; and had rendered general war all but inevitable.

At an off-the-record conference with newspaper editors in April 1939, the President confided that informants had told him that there was now an even chance of war in Europe and that it was even money on which side would win. If the totalitarian countries triumphed, Roosevelt said, the United States would face serious economic problems just as this country would have 'if Napoleon Bonaparte had won out that time that he organized the fleet to invade England.' The President concluded: 'We are not going to send armies to Europe. But there are lots of things, short of war, that we can do to help maintain the independence of nations who, as a matter of decent American principle, ought to be allowed to live their own lives.'

Roosevelt did all that he could, 'short of war.' He asked Congress for larger appropriations to rebuild the army, which in 1933 ranked seventeenth in the world, and got approval for a Naval Expansion Act. He solidified friendship with Canada by promising in August 1938 at Kingston, Ontario, 'that the people of the United States will not stand idly by if domination of Canadian soil is threatened by any other Empire.' On 14 April 1939 he sent a personal message to Hitler and Mussolini asking them to promise not to attack some twenty small countries in Europe. Hitler made an insulting reply and then bullied some of the countries (which he was about to swallow) into assuring Roosevelt that they had no cause to fear good neighbor Germany. To strengthen his hand, the President asked Congress to repeal the Neutrality Act. But on 11 July 1939 the Senate Foreign Relations Committee voted, 12–11, to postpone such action, in part out of the conviction that there would be no war. Less than two months later, on 1 September 1939, Germany attacked Poland and brought the 'Long Armistice' to an end.

And the War Came

Three weeks after the outbreak of war, the President asked Congress, called into special session, to repeal the arms embargo. He said of the Neutrality law: 'I regret that the Congress passed that Act. I regret equally that I signed that Act.' Roosevelt preferred no neutrality legislation at all, but isolationist sentiment was still too strong. 'If you try that you'll be damn lucky to get five votes in my committee,' Senator Pittman told him. The President was forced to compromise on a bill continuing the principle of cash-and-carry, and even this brought forth violent denunciations from isolationists. But after six weeks of heated debate, Congress repealed the arms embargo and applied the cash-and-carry requirement to munitions as well as raw materials. Events in Europe had moved America another step toward war. Yet the anti-war forces were still strong enough to include a provision forbidding American ships to sail to belligerent ports and, if the President stipulated, to combat zones. The Neutrality Act of 1939 abandoned the doctrine of freedom of the seas that had been maintained since the days of the Napoleonic wars and the incursions of the Barbary pirates.

The nation still did not feel that its own security

was at stake in Europe—and, so long as it did not, further commitments were stoutly opposed. Not even Russia's attack on Finland in November shook this determination. The war in the West settled down to a long siege; some Americans even complained about the lack of excitement in the 'bore' war. Since the war seemed so unreal, there was little to shake the conviction that Hitler would be defeated in a war of attrition, and the United States, without danger to itself, could be the quartermaster for the Allied forces.

Early in April 1940, the 'phony war' came to a dramatic end. Without warning Germany moved into Denmark, a nation with whom Hitler had recently concluded a non-aggression pact, and then into Norway. Denmark fell within hours, Norway in less than two months. One month later, on 10 May, the German army invaded the Low Countries. In five days the Netherlands was conquered; three days later Antwerp fell. Already the German Panzer (armored) divisions had crashed through the Ardennes Forest, enveloped a French army, and smashed ahead toward the Channel ports. On 21 May—only eleven days after the attack on Holland—the Germans reached the English Channel, cutting off the British expeditionary force which had been rushed to the aid of Belgium and France. A week later Belgium surrendered, and the British were left to their fate. Their evacuation has well been called 'the miracle of Dunkirk.' Every available warship, yacht, power boat, fisherman, barge, and tug, to the number of 848, was pressed into service; and with a suicide division holding the front and the Royal Air Force screening, 338,000 men were transported to England. But they did not bring their weapons, and evacuations do not win wars.

The German army now swung south, and in two weeks cut the French army to pieces. On 10 June 1940 Mussolini entered the war. Five days later Paris fell, and Premier Reynaud, in desperation, appealed to Roosevelt for 'clouds of planes.' But Roosevelt could give only sympathy, and a hastily formed French government under the aged Marshal Pétain sued for peace. Hitler exacted a savage price. He occupied half of France, leaving the southern part to be ruled, from Vichy, by Pétain and Premier Laval, who were forced to collaborate with the victors, even to recruit workers for German war industry and to deliver French Jews to torture and death. In one month Hitler's mechanized armies had done what the forces of William II had been unable to accomplish in four years.

The Nazi *Blitzkrieg* had shattered America's illusions about the outcome of the European war and its own impregnability. France had capitulated, Britain might soon go under. Walter Lippmann wrote: 'Our duty is to begin acting at once on the basic assumption that the Allies may lose the war this summer, and that before the snow flies again we may stand alone and isolated, the last great Democracy on earth.' For the moment even Roosevelt's severest critics rallied to him as the nation's leader in a time of crisis. Within a year after the invasion of the Low Countries, Congress appropriated $37 billion for rearmament and aid to the Allies— more than the total cost to the United States of World War I. To take advantage of the support by elements in both parties for his foreign policy, Roosevelt replaced the colorless Secretaries of War and of the Navy in his cabinet with two prominent Republicans—the 72-year-old Henry Stimson, who had been Secretary of War under Taft and Secretary of State under Hoover, and Frank Knox, the G.O.P. vice-presidential candidate in 1936.

At Charlottesville, Virginia, on 10 June the President pledged to 'extend to the opponents of force the material resources of this nation,' but Congress was less willing to approve aid to Britain than to agree to strengthening American defenses. Only 30 per cent of the country still thought the Allies would triumph, and the President's military and naval advisers warned that, with America's own stocks below the safety point, stepped-up aid to Britain would be highly precarious. If the United States extended such aid, and Britain surrendered, leaving the United States, stripped of its arms, to face an Axis invasion, Roosevelt would be hard put to justify his decision. Nonetheless, Roosevelt made available to the Allies planes, supplies of arms, and ammunition. He went even further by concluding a swap with Britain which was, as Churchill later observed, 'a decidedly unneutral act,' which by 'all the standards of history' would have 'justified the German Government in declaring war' on

Peter Blume, 'The Eternal City.' In this powerful satire of the corruption of Fascist Italy, Blume depicts a jack-in-the-box Mussolini in the ruins of Rome's once proud city. Blume, called 'the most sophisticated of [the] practitioners of Magic Realism,' explained, 'Since I am concerned with the communication of ideas I am not at all ashamed of "telling stories" in my paintings, because I consider this to be one of the primary functions of the plastic arts.' *(Museum of Modern Art, Mrs. Simon Guggenheim Fund, oil on composition board, 34" x 47⅞")*

America. In early September the President announced an arrangement whereby the United States transferred to Britain 50 World War I destroyers and received in return 99-year leases on a series of naval and air bases in the British West Indies.[2]

2. The Argentia (Newfoundland) and Bermuda bases were free gifts. The U.S. Navy also transferred ten Coast Guard cutters to Britain.

By the time the destroyer-bases deal was announced, Congress was in the closing stages of a bitter wrangle over a proposal to conscript men for military service in time of peace. Mail to Congressmen ran 90 per cent against the bill, and on Capitol Hill angry women hanged internationalist Senator Claude Pepper in effigy. But as the Nazis poised to strike across the English Channel, polls revealed a rapid shift of opinion in favor of selective service. In mid-September, Congress voted to draft men between the ages of twenty-one and thirty-five. A month later, Secretary Stimson, blindfolded, plucked from a fishbowl the first of the numbers which would determine the order men would be called into uniform.

The Election of 1940

In the midst of a heated debate over Roosevelt's foreign policy came the presidential election. The German *Blitzkrieg* made it inadvisable for the Republicans to chose an isolationist for their presidential candidate, and this gave an opportunity to a political maverick, Wendell Willkie, a Wall Street lawyer and a life-long Democrat, who had become the utility interests' most articulate critic of the New Deal and a frank proponent of aid to the Allies. When the Republican convention met in June, seasoned politicians could not hold back the rising tide of Willkie sentiment, although as late as April he had not had a single delegate. Events in Europe also assured FDR the Democratic nomination for a third term. Roosevelt, who had long since parted company with Garner, brought pressure on the delegates to accept the much more liberal Henry Wallace, a former Republican, as his running mate. The President demonstrated convincingly to people who thought he had lost control in the purge of 1938 that he still dominated the Democratic party.

Willkie looked forward to a personal battle with FDR, but the President refused to recognize him; instead, he played his role as commander in chief to the hilt. One Republican Congressman complained: 'Franklin Roosevelt is not running against Wendell Willkie. He's running against Adolf Hitler.' In such a contest, Willkie was at a decided disadvantage, especially because he shared Roosevelt's outlook on foreign policy. In his acceptance speech, Willkie warned: 'We must face a brutal but terrible fact. Our way of life is in competition with Hitler's way of life.' To be sure, before the campaign was over, both candidates had succumbed to the temptation to make extravagant appeals. Willkie said that if Roosevelt were elected 'you may expect war in April 1941,' and the President asserted, 'I have said this before, but I shall say it again and again and again. Your boys are not going to be sent into any foreign wars.' But the isolationists knew that neither candidate was their man, and the conviction that the nation had never had a fair choice between war and peace in 1940 was to poison American politics for many years to come.

In the November election Roosevelt received 449 electoral votes, Willkie only 82, but FDR's share of the popular vote had fallen to less than 55 per cent. He continued to run very well in lower income districts. In an analysis of the election, Samuel Lubell wrote: 'The New Deal appears to have accomplished what the Socialists, the I.W.W. and the Communists never could approach. It has drawn a class line across the face of American politics.'

Year of Decision

The President interpreted re-election as an endorsement of his policies. When Congress met early in January 1941 he appealed to it for support of nations who were fighting in defense of what he called the Four Freedoms—freedom of speech, freedom of religion, freedom from want, freedom from fear. Four days later he submitted a program which was the result of an urgent message the President received a month after his election to an unprecedented third term. Prime Minister Churchill had written that Britain was in 'mortal danger' and that it was fast reaching the point when it would not be able to pay cash for the vast quantities of American arms it needed. As a consequence Roosevelt unveiled a new proposal: to lend arms directly on the understanding that they would be returned, or replacements for them provided, when the war ended. 'What I am trying to do,' he explained, 'is to eliminate the dollar sign.'

The lend-lease plan aroused fierce opposition. 'Lending war equipment is a good deal like lending chewing gum,' Senator Taft grumbled. 'You don't want it back.' Montana's Senator Wheeler called lend-lease the 'New Deal's "triple A" foreign policy—to plow under every fourth American boy.' (Roosevelt told newspapermen two days later: 'That really is the rottenest thing that has been said in public life in my generation.') However, by mid-January 1941, aid to Britain even at

'Vandenberg, Dewey, and Taft' by Ben Shahn, 1941. A year earlier it had appeared all but certain that one of this trio—Senator Arthur H. Vandenberg of Michigan, New York's district attorney Thomas E. Dewey, Senator Robert A. Taft of Ohio—would be the Republican presidential nominee in 1940. But as it turned out, the G.O.P. chose a newcomer, Wendell Willkie, to contest Franklin D. Roosevelt's bid for a third term. *(Museum of Modern Art, Gift of Lincoln Kirstein, serigraph printed in color, sh; 19 3/8" x 25 3/8")*

the risk of war was favored by 70 per cent of those polled; and when the rolls were called in March, Congress voted passage of the Lend-Lease Act by sizable margins. The law authorized the President to 'sell, transfer, exchange, lease, lend,' any defense articles 'to the government of any country whose defense the President deems vital to the defense of the United States.' It also made available to such nations the facilities of American shipyards. By the end of the month Congress had voted the staggering sum of $7 billion, and this would be only the first installment in a mammoth program to arm the Allies that would total more than $50 billion.

Events now moved speedily. A few weeks after the enactment of lend-lease, the United States seized all Axis shipping in American ports. In April 1941 it took Greenland under protection and announced that the navy would patrol the sea lanes in defense zones. In May, after the sinking of an American freighter by a U-boat, Roosevelt proclaimed an 'unlimited national emergency.' In June the United States froze all Axis assets in this country and closed all Axis consulates. And on 24 June the President announced that lend-lease would be extended to a new ally—Russia. For on 22 June, Hitler broke his 1939 pact and set out to conquer that vast country, a colossal mistake which gave England and France an ally capable of pinning down the bulk of the German army on an eastern front. The Communist party in the United States, which had been denouncing the 'imperialist war,' now demanded American participation in a 'crusade.'

Roosevelt, like Wilson a generation earlier, moved to obtain a statement of war aims from the Allies. On 14 August 1941 he and Winston Churchill met afloat in Argentia Bay, Newfoundland, and there drew up the Atlantic Charter. Its principles included the already proclaimed Four

Freedoms, renunciation of territorial aggrandizement, a promise to restore self-government to those deprived of it, and a pledge of equal access to trade and raw materials.

The Atlantic also appeared likely to be the place where the United States would be drawn into World War II. On 4 September a German submarine attacked the United States destroyer *Greer* in the waters off Iceland, where American troops had been stationed some weeks earlier. The President ordered the navy to 'shoot on sight' these 'rattlesnakes of the Atlantic,' and stated indignantly: 'I tell you the blunt fact that the German submarine fired first upon this American destroyer without warning, and with deliberate design to sink her.' The President was being less than frank. The *Greer* had not only informed a British plane of the presence of the U-boat but had pursued the sub and broadcast its position for three and a half hours. During this period, the British plane had dropped four depth charges. Only then had the U-boat fired at the *Greer*. Two days after the shoot-on-sight speech, the Atlantic Fleet was ordered to protect all vessels on the run between North America and Iceland, even convoys which numbered no American ships. Since the Fleet had also been instructed to destroy any Nazi ship it sighted, the order of 13 September brought the United States Navy into all-out, even though undeclared, war in the Atlantic.

On 9 October, the President asked Congress to repeal the 'crippling provisions' of the Neutrality Act of 1939. Isolationists organized for a protracted struggle to defeat the President, but they failed to reckon on the impact of events in the North Atlantic. On 17 October, news arrived that the destroyer *Kearny* had been torpedoed southwest of Iceland; eleven sailors were lost. Three days later, the destroyer *Reuben James* became the first armed American vessel to be sunk by Germany; ninety-six officers and men lost their lives. Within two weeks Congress had voted to repeal restrictive sections of the neutrality law; henceforth, the President could arm merchantmen and send ships directly into combat areas. Little wonder that the nation's attention was focused on these reverberations of the war in Europe. But when war came to America, it would come not as the result of developments in the Atlantic but as a consequence of even more momentous events in the Pacific.

For over a year, tension had been mounting in the Far East. After the German victories of May-June 1940, it became more difficult for moderate elements in Japan to restrain the militarists. With France and Holland conquered, Indo-China and the Netherlands East Indies were ripe for the picking; Malaya, Burma, and even India looked inviting. Japan wrested permission to build airfields in Indo-China from the helpless Vichy government of France, and added Tokyo to the Rome-Berlin Axis when it signed a Tripartite Pact with the European Fascist powers. The United States struck back with a loan to China and a partial embargo on exports to Japan.

In 1941 events moved toward a final crisis. In July, Japan occupied Indo-China. President Roosevelt responded by appointing General Douglas MacArthur to command all army forces in the Far East, and froze Japanese assets in the United States; Great Britain and the Netherlands followed suit. Japan was now cut off from its American market and such vital commodities as rubber, scrap metal, oil, and aviation fuel. The Japanese war lords decided to make war on these three countries within four months unless the flow of strategic supplies was restored, for the armies had to have fuel or evacuate China and Indo-China, which the military would not countenance. The subsequent negotiations were a sparring for time by two governments that considered war all but inevitable. Japan would not get out of China, and the United States would settle for nothing less. The American government wanted to stall off war, for its armed forces were not ready, but by late autumn Tokyo's plans had hardened. On 26 November 1941 a Japanese striking force of six big carriers with 353 battle-ready planes, two battleships, two heavy cruisers, and eleven destroyers sortied for Pearl Harbor.

The Japanese carried out the covert operation with devastating effect. Oahu was in a relaxed Sunday morning mood at 7:55 a.m. 7 December, when the bombs began to drop. Despite a war warning message of 27 November, Admiral Kimmel had not canceled week-end leave; General Short had his army planes parked wing-to-wing, fearing only danger from sabotage. At the end of

(*Library of Congress*)

this sad and bloody day, 2403 American sailors, soldiers, marines, and civilians had been killed, and 1178 more wounded; 149 planes had been destroyed on the ground or in the water; battleship *Arizona* was sunk beyond repair; *Oklahoma* shattered and capsized; *Tennessee*, *West Virginia*, and *California* were resting on the bottom; *Nevada* run aground to prevent sinking; other vessels destroyed or badly damaged. Although MacArthur's Far Eastern command had ample notice of the attack on Pearl Harbor, a Japanese bomber assault from Formosa caught the army air force grounded on fields near Manila and all but wiped it out—a major disaster. Next day Congress declared a state of war with Japan; on 11 December Germany and Italy, faithful to their tripartite pact with Japan, declared war on the United States. Pacifism and isolationism had been strong enough to keep America at peace for more than two years after the invasion of Poland in September 1939, but in the end the United States, too, was embroiled in the Second World War.

33

World War II

*

1941–1945

Mobilization

Franklin D. Roosevelt led America into war, not as an Associated Power as in World War I, but as a full-fledged member of the 'United Nations,' a grand alliance that would ultimately embrace forty-six countries. In collaboration with Prime Minister Churchill, the President involved himself directly in working out military strategy and in supervising war operations. The two countries had already established one critical priority: they would concentrate first on winning the war in Europe. This concept had been arrived at because the Rome-Berlin Axis had a greater war potential than Japan, a consideration that became the more pressing after Hitler attacked Russia; for if Germany prevailed the geopolitical 'heartland' would be Hitler's dominion, from Finisterre to Vladivostok and from the North Cape to the bulge of Africa. The informal Anglo-American understanding thus formed continued throughout the war. Meeting together, the American Joint Chiefs of Staff (as the heads of army, navy, and army air force shortly became) and the British Chiefs of Staff were called the Combined Chiefs of Staff. They, under President Roosevelt and Prime Minister Churchill, initiated strategy, drafted plans, allocated forces, and directed the war.

A war of this magnitude required a massive mobilization and considerable sacrifice. All men between 18 and 45 were made liable to military service. Including voluntary enlistments, over 15 million people served in the armed forces during the war; 10 million in the army, 4 million in the navy and coast guard, 600,000 in the marine corps. About 216,000 women served as nurses, and in the auxiliary 'Waves' and 'Wacs' or as marines. There were 970,000 American casualties, including 254,000 dead and 66,000 missing.

Although at the time of Pearl Harbor only 15 per cent of industrial production was going to industrial needs, the United States truly became the 'arsenal of democracy' after entering the war. When the Allies launched their cross-Channel invasion in 1944, the armies 'lurched forward,' wrote Allan Nevins, 'like a vast armed workshop; a congeries of factories on wheels with a bristling screen of troops and a cover of airplanes.' The mobilization gave an enormous impetus to aluminum and magnesium production, enlarged

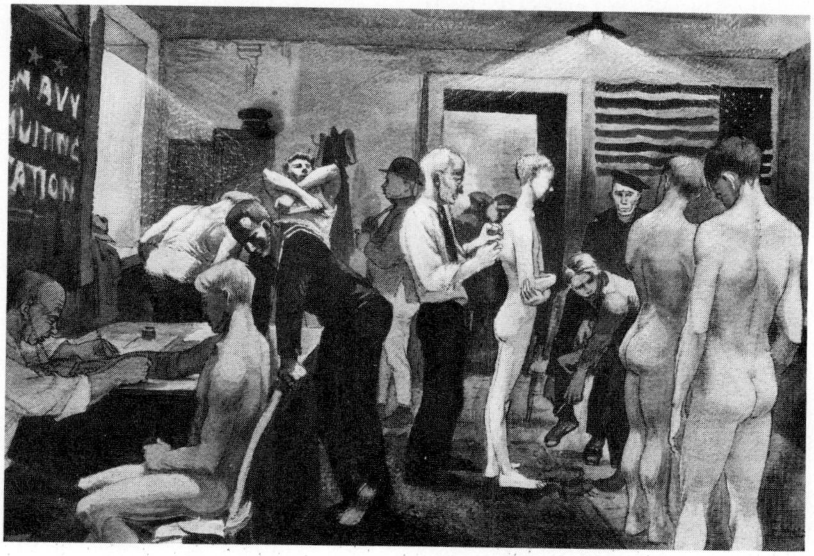

'Naval Recruiting Station, No. 1.' In 1942, Mitchell Jamieson's watercolor won a competition sponsored by the Section of Fine Arts, one of a number of New Deal experiments mobilized to serve martial purposes during World War II. (*National Archives*)

electricity output to nearly half again as much as in 1937, increased machine tool production sevenfold, and turned out more iron and steel than the whole world had produced a short time before. In 1939 America's airplane industry employed fewer than 47,000 persons and produced fewer than 6000 planes; in the peak year of 1944, the industry employed 2,102,000 workers and rolled out more than 96,000 planes. Medium tank production advanced so rapidly that it had to be cut back. By the beginning of 1944 the industrial output of America was twice that of all the Axis nations.

The genius of ship construction, Henry J. Kaiser, trimmed the time for turning out merchant ships from 105 days to 46, then 29, then 14. In mid-November 1942, Kaiser's Richmond, California, yard launched 'Hull 440,' the *Robert E. Peary*, in 4 days, 15½ hours. It went down the ways fitted out with life belts, coat hangers, electric clocks, and ink wells. By the middle of 1942, Kaiser was building one-third of the government's vessels, and his pace-setting records fixed the standard the Maritime Commission demanded of other firms. As a consequence, merchant shipping construction, which amounted to only one million tons in 1941, surpassed 19 million only two years later.

In January 1942 the President set up the War Production Board to direct the mobilization. Donald Nelson, the WPB administrator, did not have the personal force to impose priorities, and not until 1943 was an effective system of allocation developed. As a consequence of Nelson's failings, the President named 'czars' to handle the critical problems of oil and rubber, and in October 1942 appointed Supreme Court Justice James F. Byrnes to head an Office of Economic Stabilization. In May 1943 he gave Byrnes, who proved an able administrator, still greater authority as director of the Office of War Mobilization.

To curb inflation, the government not only stepped up taxes and sold nearly $100 billion in war bonds but controlled prices directly through the Office of Price Administration which

Women welders, Todd Erie Basin drydock. 'Females had demonstrated that they could do a man's work and do it well, and, as the war progressed, more and more men in the factory started treating their women co-workers as equals,' William H. Chafe has written of World War II. 'A Women's Bureau official noted after an extensive tour of a California shipyard that men barked orders at women, refused to pick up their tools when dropped. . . . After witnessing the extent to which females had become assimilated into the formerly male-dominated industries of the Connecticut Valley, Constance Green observed that "presenting a tool chest to a little girl need no longer be dubbed absurdly inappropriate."' (*Library of Congress*)

Roosevelt had set up in August 1941 under Leon Henderson, an ebullient New Deal economist. After experimenting with selective controls of prices and rents, Henderson imposed a general price freeze in April 1942. The OPA also rationed scarce commodities like meat, gasoline, and tires. But the agency ran into trouble from businessmen who resented controls, from the farm bloc which insisted on 110 per cent of parity, and from union labor which protested that even the War Labor Board's formula of a 15 per cent wage increase did not meet the rising cost of living. In 1943, to counter a strike by John L. Lewis's mine workers, the government took over the coal mines; at the same time, it rolled back food prices. By the middle of 1943, prices had reached a plateau, and for the rest of the war, the OPA, under the advertising executive Chester Bowles, held the increase in the cost of living to less than 1.5 per cent, one of the remarkable achievements of the war.

Mighty as America's effort was, it did not add up to total war. There was no firm control over manpower, no conscription of women. A few edibles were rationed, but most Americans ate more heartily than before. Gasoline and tires were rationed, but hundreds of thousands of cars managed to stay on the road for purposes remotely connected with the war. As prices of most essentials were kept down, the standard of living rose. The country was never invaded, except by U-boats penetrating the three-mile limit, and a large measure of the 'blood, sweat and tears' that Churchill promised his countrymen was spared his country's ally. Yet even for Americans it was a grim, austere war. In contrast to the Creel Committee in World War I, the Office of War Information, under the sensible newspaperman, Elmer Davis, presented the war not as a utopian struggle, but, in the President's words, simply as 'the survival war.' For the American fighting forces there were no brass bands or bugles, no 'Over There' or marching songs, no flaunting colors; not even a ship's bell to mark the watches.

Social Consequences of the War

World War II had a profound impact on American society, for good or evil. Of the many changes, none had more immediate importance than the termination of the Great Depression. The demands of the armed services and the war industries brought to an end more than a decade of unemployment. Indeed, there quickly developed a shortage of workers which gave women opportunities in aircraft plants and shipyards. Women accounted for one-third of all workers on the B-29's. Moreover, unlike World War I, the Second World War resulted in a permanent increase in the proportion of women in the labor force. The war brought unparalleled prosperity to millions of Americans. The farmers' net cash income more than quadrupled between 1940 and 1945, and the weekly earnings of industrial workers rose 70 per cent.

Wartime full employment, together with progressive tax legislation, resulted in a redistribution of income that had not been achieved in the halcyon days of the New Deal. Although tax laws hit millions of Americans for the first time, through the new device of 'withholding,' the top 5 per cent of income receivers were soaked more than at any time in our history. Their share of disposable income dropped from 26 per cent in 1940 to 16 per cent in 1944, as the federal income levy reached a maximum of 94 per cent of total net income. With a corporation income tax as high as 50 per cent and an excess profits tax stepped up to 95 per cent, few corporations enjoyed 'swollen profits.' Net corporation income in 1945 was less than in 1941.

World War II reshuffled more Americans than had any internal migration over the same span in the nation's history. During the war years, the West showed a net gain of 1,200,000 people, three-fourths of them from the South. Within a few months after Pearl Harbor, the Pacific Coast states were building one-fourth of the nation's war planes, one-third of its ships. Southern California, which ranked second only to Akron as a rubber manufacturing center, even boasted a steel plant. A nation in which 27 million people moved during the war counted the social costs of this upheaval: a critical housing shortage, lack of civic facilities in jerry-built war plant towns, and a conspicuous rise in juvenile delinquency occasioned by the uprooting of families.

'Negro Soldier,' by Thomas Hart Benton. During World War II, a half-million blacks saw service overseas. Twenty-two Negro combat units, including nine field artillery battalions and two tank battalions, fought in Europe, and eighty-two black pilots received the Distinguished Flying Cross. (*State Historical Society of Missouri*)

During the war, 60,000 Negroes moved from the Deep South to Detroit, 100,000 to Chicago, 250,000 to the West Coast, and wherever they went they encountered discrimination. When they gave their blood to the Red Cross, it was segregated from that of whites. When war plants advertised for more help, black applicants were rejected. When they got jobs, as in the Mobile shipyards, white workers organized 'hate strikes' against them. Although not confined to labor battalions, as they largely had been in World War I, blacks were generally segregated in barracks and mess halls, and often confined to menial tasks.[1]

But Negroes fought with increased militance for their rights. From 1940 to 1946 NAACP membership grew ninefold. Dismayed by the reluctance of employers to hire black labor even in boom times, A. Philip Randolph, president of the Brotherhood of Sleeping Car Porters, issued a call for 50,000 Negroes to march on Washington in protest. Randolph cancelled the call only after Roosevelt had issued Executive Order 8802 on 25 June 1941. The President's edict forbade discrimination in work under defense contracts and established a Fair Employment Practices Committee. In part as a result of the FEPC's activities, but more because of the critical labor shortage, the Negro's share of jobs in war industries increased from 3 to 8 per cent of the whole, while the number of black employees in the Federal Government jumped from 40,000 to over 300,000.

Despite such brutal episodes as a race riot in

1. However, 7000 blacks were commissioned as officers. The all-Negro 99th Fighter Squadron won distinction in Europe, and a combat team of the 93rd Infantry Division at Bougainville.

Detroit in which 25 Negroes and nine whites were killed, World War II resulted in marked advances for black Americans and for relations between the races. Georgia repealed the poll tax; the Supreme Court outlawed the white primary in Texas; and in Atlanta in 1944, Negro and white leaders sat down together to organize the Southern Regional Council. The doctrine of white supremacy met a formidable intellectual challenge. Gunnar Myrdal's *An American Dilemma* offered an imposing scholarly analysis, and Lillian Smith's novel, *Strange Fruit,* found a wide audience.

Although America's performance on civil liberties was generally better than in World War I, one dreadful blot stained this record: the relocation and internment of Japanese-Americans. The Roosevelt administration attempted to quiet demands for the evacuation of the 112,000 Japanese or Americans of Japanese descent (*Nisei*) from the West Coast, but it was overwhelmed by the outcry against them. Even men long regarded as friends of civil liberties beat the drums for evacuation: Senator Hiram Johnson, California's Attorney-General Earl Warren, Walter Lippmann. On 19 February 1942, Roosevelt, yielding to the hysteria, approved an edict surrendering control to the army, which ordered the ouster of every 'Japanese' (more than two-thirds were American citizens) from the western parts of Washington, Oregon, and California and the southern quarter of Arizona. Thousands of United States citizens were expelled from their homes and herded into relocation centers in the western deserts and the Arkansas swamplands. No such action was taken against German or Italian aliens, let alone Americans of German or Italian descent. Much of the justification for the expulsion rested on fears of sabotage. Yet in Hawaii, where people of Japanese birth were much more concentrated than on the West Coast (and where they were not interned), not one act of sabotage was committed. Nonetheless, the Supreme Court sanctioned the government's action in the Korematsu case, although Justice Murphy commented that the evacuation of Japanese-Americans bore 'a melancholy resemblance' to the Nazis' treatment of the Jews. When the army reversed its policy and recruited *Nisei,* they proved to be the toughest of all fighters in the Italian campaign. But when Japanese-Americans returned to the West Coast after the war, they still encountered gross discrimination and personal indignities.

Retreat and Resurgence in the Pacific

In the Far East in the days after Pearl Harbor, the news was calamitous. Thailand surrendered to the Japanese, who promptly began a relentless march on the British base at Singapore. On 10 December the Rising Sun flag was hoisted on Guam, which had been bravely but pitifully defended by a few hundred Americans and Chamorros. Other Japanese task forces captured Hong Kong and the Borneo oilfields. On Wake Island, lonely outpost in the Central Pacific, a small marine defense force was overwhelmed. In the Philippines, General MacArthur evacuated Manila on 27 December, and withdrew his army to the Bataan Peninsula. On 9 April the 'battling bastards of Bataan,' about 12,500 Americans and over 60,000 Filipinos, had to surrender unconditionally. Only a couple of thousand escaped to the island fortress of Corregidor before the ranks of the prisoners were thinned by the infamous 65-mile 'death march' from Bataan to Japanese prison camps. A month earlier, on orders of President Roosevelt, MacArthur had left the Philippines and set up headquarters in Australia; he vowed to return, as he did. On 6 May, General Jonathan M. Wainwright was forced to surrender Corregidor together with its 11,000 defenders, and a Philippine army of over 50,000 on the Visayas and Mindanao. There had been no such capitulation in American history since Appomattox.

In the meantime the Japanese had won all their objectives in Southeast Asia. The great naval base of Singapore, on which Britain had lavished millions of pounds, fell on 15 February. On 9 May 1942 Java surrendered. Rangoon, capital and chief seaport of Burma, had been occupied by the Japanese the day before. The Japanese now ruled East Asia, west to British India and south to the waters adjacent to Australia and Fiji. India, as threatened by nationalists within as by enemies without, and Australia trembled that their turn might come next. Never in modern history has there been so quick and valuable a series of conquests; even Hitler's were inferior. The prestige

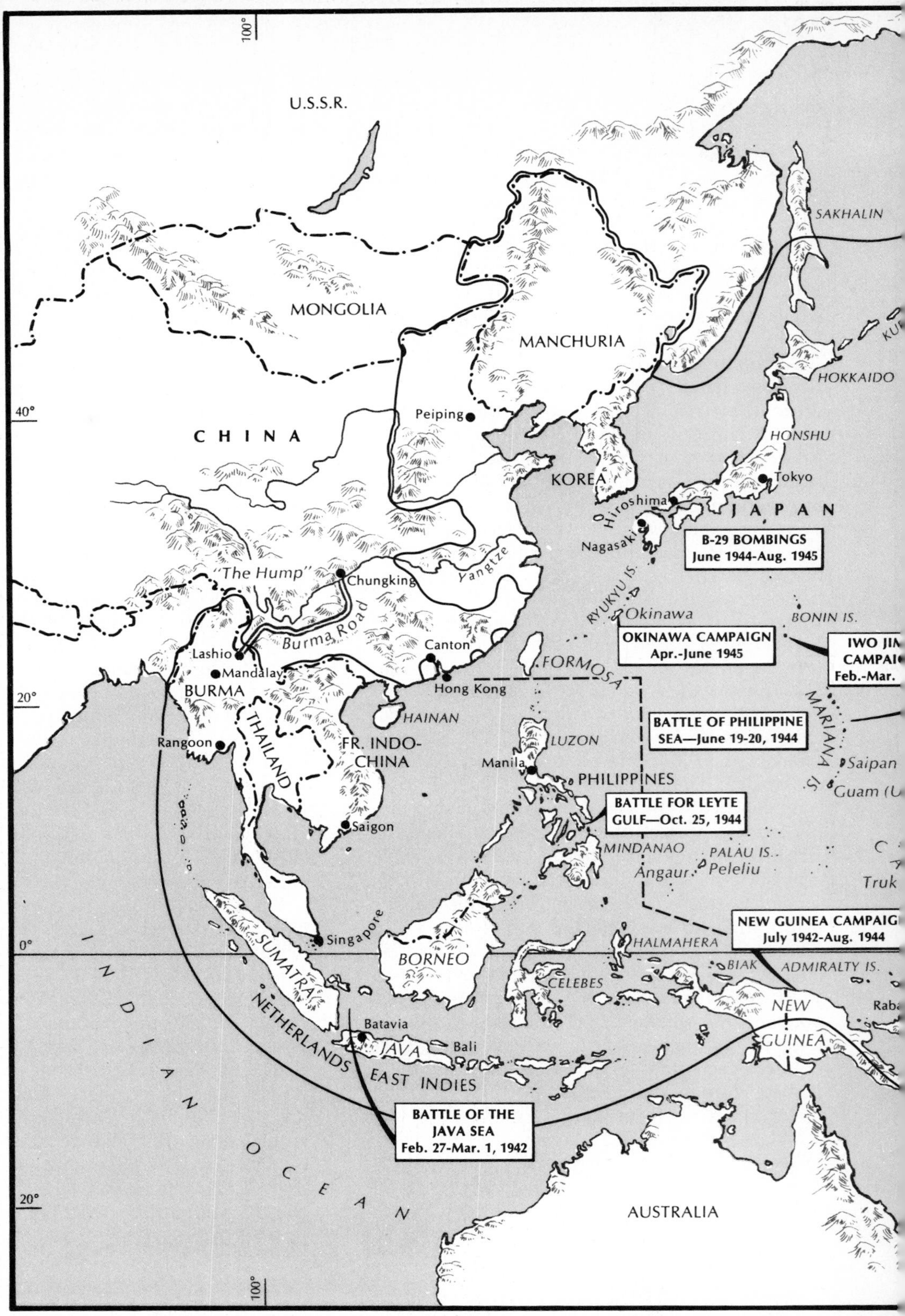

U.S.S.R.
MONGOLIA
MANCHURIA
SAKHALIN
HOKKAIDO
HONSHU
Tokyo
CHINA
Peiping
KOREA
Hiroshima
JAPAN
Nagasaki
B-29 BOMBINGS
June 1944-Aug. 1945
"The Hump"
Chungking
Yangtze
RYUKYU IS.
Okinawa
BONIN IS.
Burma Road
OKINAWA CAMPAIGN
Apr.-June 1945
Lashio
Mandalay
Canton
FORMOSA
Hong Kong
BURMA
HAINAN
MARIANA IS.
BATTLE OF PHILIPPINE
SEA—June 19-20, 1944
THAILAND
Rangoon
FR. INDO-CHINA
LUZON
Manila
PHILIPPINES
Saipan
BATTLE FOR LEYTE
GULF—Oct. 25, 1944
Saigon
MINDANAO
PALAU IS.
Angaur
Peleliu
Truk
Singapore
NEW GUINEA CAMPAIG
July 1942-Aug. 1944
SUMATRA
BORNEO
HALMAHERA
BIAK
ADMIRALTY IS.
CELEBES
NEW GUINEA
Batavia
JAVA
Bali
NETHERLANDS EAST INDIES
INDIAN OCEAN
BATTLE OF THE
JAVA SEA
Feb. 27-Mar. 1, 1942
AUSTRALIA
100°
40°
20°
0°
20°

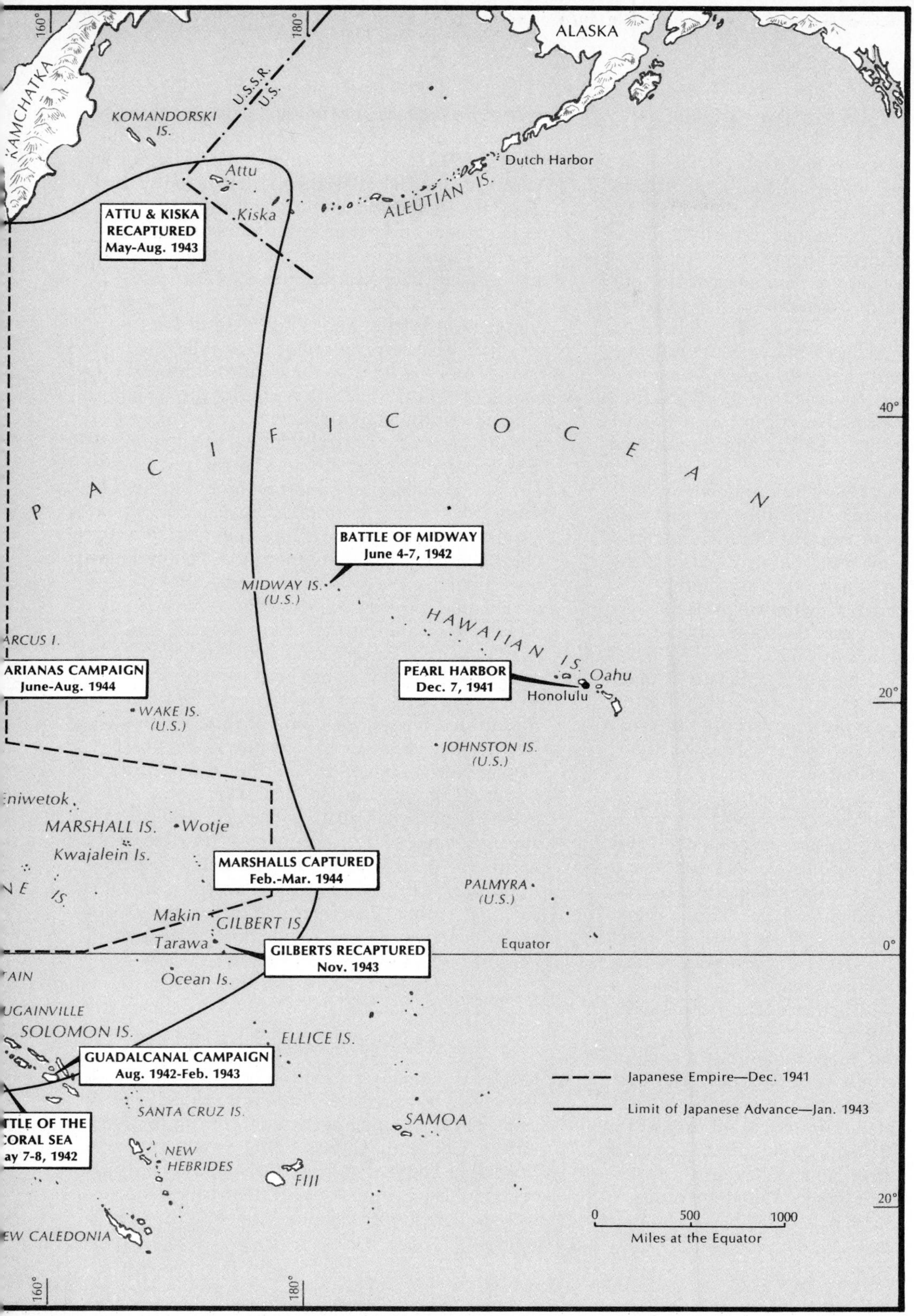
ALASKA
KAMCHATKA
KOMANDORSKI IS.
U.S.S.R.
U.S.
Attu
Kiska
Dutch Harbor
ALEUTIAN IS.
ATTU & KISKA RECAPTURED May-Aug. 1943
PACIFIC OCEAN
BATTLE OF MIDWAY June 4-7, 1942
MIDWAY IS. (U.S.)
HAWAIIAN IS.
PEARL HARBOR Dec. 7, 1941
Oahu
Honolulu
ARCUS I.
ARIANAS CAMPAIGN June-Aug. 1944
WAKE IS. (U.S.)
JOHNSTON IS. (U.S.)
Eniwetok
MARSHALL IS.
Wotje
Kwajalein Is.
MARSHALLS CAPTURED Feb.-Mar. 1944
PALMYRA (U.S.)
Makin
GILBERT IS.
Tarawa
GILBERTS RECAPTURED Nov. 1943
Equator
Ocean Is.
UGAINVILLE
SOLOMON IS.
ELLICE IS.
GUADALCANAL CAMPAIGN Aug. 1942-Feb. 1943
Japanese Empire—Dec. 1941
Limit of Japanese Advance—Jan. 1943
SANTA CRUZ IS.
SAMOA
TTLE OF THE CORAL SEA ay 7-8, 1942
NEW HEBRIDES
FIJI
EW CALEDONIA
0 500 1000
Miles at the Equator
160°
180°
40°
20°
0°
20°

The Pacific Theater of War, 1941–45

of the white races fell so low that even victory over Japan could not win it back; and the areas that the Japanese conquered, though no longer Japanese, are now also independent of Europe.

However, instead of consolidating their new conquests to make their country invincible, the Japanese succumbed to what one of their admirals after the war ruefully called 'victory disease.' They decided to wrest more Pacific territory from the Allies, and Admiral Yamamoto wished to provoke a major sea battle. A good prophet, he pointed out that the United States Navy must be annihilated, if ever, in 1942, before American productive capacity replaced the Pearl Harbor losses. But even in 1942 American forces proved to be more formidable than the Japanese anticipated.

The Battle of the Coral Sea (7–8 May 1942) frustrated the first forward lunge in the new Japanese offensive to capture Port Moresby, a strategic base in Papua, New Guinea. This was the first naval battle in which no ship of either side sighted one of the other; the fighting was done by carrier plane against carrier plane, or carrier plane against ship. Each side in this new sort of naval warfare made mistakes, but the Japanese made more; and although their losses were inferior, they dared not press on to occupy Port Moresby. For Australia, Coral Sea was the decisive battle, saving her from possible invasion.

In the next and more vital Japanese offensive, Yamamoto went all-out. Personally assuming command, he deployed almost every capital ship of his navy. His first objective was to capture Midway, a tiny atoll at the tip end of the Hawaiian chain, 1134 miles northwest of Pearl Harbor, where the United States had an advanced naval and air base, but his dearest object was to force Admiral Nimitz to give battle with his numerically inferior Pacific Fleet. He had his wish, but the battle did not go to the strong. On 4 June 1942, a Japanese four-carrier force, advancing undetected under a foul-weather front, was near enough Midway to batter the air base, but American carrier-based planes destroyed all four of the best Japanese carriers and Yamamoto had to order his vast fleet to retire. He had sustained the first defeat to the Japanese navy in modern times.

After this glorious Battle of Midway, the Joint Chiefs of Staff decided to breach the island barrier to an Allied advance toward Japan by invading the mountainous, jungle-clad Solomon Islands. On 7 August 1942, the 1st Marine Division landed at Tulagi and Guadalcanal, surprised the enemy, and seized the harbor of the one island and the airfield on the other. There then began the prolonged and bloody struggle for Guadalcanal; an island worthless in itself, like the battlefield of Gettysburg in 1863, but even more violently contested. Seven major naval battles were fought, until Iron Bottom Bay, as American sailors named Savo Island Sound, was strewn with the hulls of ships and the bodies of sailors. Every few nights the Japanese ran fast reinforcement echelons, the 'Tokyo Expresses,' down the central channel, the Solomons' 'Slot'; every few days American reinforcements came in, and daily air battles became routine. On shore, the marines, reinforced by army divisions, fought stubbornly and, in the end, successfully. On 9 February 1943, six months after the landings, the Japanese evacuated Guadalcanal. In this campaign American soldiers found that the supposedly invincible Japanese foot-soldiers, who had overrun half of Eastern Asia, could be beaten, and after this deadly island had been secured, the navy won every battle with the Japanese fleet. In the meantime the western prong of this Japanese offensive had been stopped on the north coast of Papua, New Guinea, by American and Australian troops. The fighting, in malaria-infested mangrove swamps against a trapped and never-surrendering enemy, was the most horrible of the entire war, but by early 1943 the defensive period in the war with Japan had finally come to an end, at the very time when the Allies were carrying out ambitious new designs in a more vital area of concern—the European theater.

From North Africa to Italy

While Winston Churchill was conferring with Roosevelt at the White House in June 1942, news came of the German capture of Tobruk in North Africa. Churchill confessed that he was the most miserable Englishman in America since the surrender of Burgoyne. For the fall of Tobruk opened a German road into Egypt and beyond. If Alexan-

Thomas Hart Benton, 'Prelude to Death.' Benton's painting is based on sketches he made at the loading docks in Brooklyn of the first contingent of American troops departing for the North African front. It was intended as a contribution to the war propaganda program, but government officials rejected it because, Benton explained, 'the central character is looking back home instead of "forward to duty."' (*State Historical Society of Missouri*)

dria and the Suez Canal fell, nothing short of a miracle could keep the Axis out of India, on whose eastern frontier the Japanese were already poised.

Meeting at the White House the Allied leaders debated the time and place for the first combined military operation against the Axis. The Americans wanted a cross-Channel operation in France, a beachhead in 1942 and the big invasion in 1943. The British opposed any such attempt before the Allies had overwhelming force, lest it be thrown back with heavy loss. Roosevelt was deeply impressed with the need for a second front in Europe to prevent Russia's being overrun. Something had to be done in 1942—Churchill and Roosevelt could not stand the obloquy of fighting another 'phony war.' They decided, overriding most of their military advisers, on an occupation of French North Africa. Oran and Algiers on the Mediterranean, and Casablanca on the Atlantic coast of Morocco, were selected as the three strategic harbors to be seized by amphibious forces under General Dwight D. Eisenhower, who, as he later wrote, was to occupy 'the rim of a continent where no major military campaign had been conducted for centuries.'

On 23 October 1942 General Sir Bernard Montgomery launched the second battle of El Alamein against Rommel, and on the same day Rear Admiral H. Kent Hewitt, commanding the Western Naval Task Force, sailed from Hampton Roads. Never before had an amphibious operation been projected across an ocean, but the complex operation went like clockwork. By midnight 7–8 November all three task forces (the two for Oran and Algiers under British command) had reached their destinations, unscathed and unreported. Admiral Hewitt had to fight a naval battle with the French fleet off Casablanca, and sink most of it, in order to get General Patton's troops ashore safely, but there was little resistance from the French army. Admiral Darlan, second to Marshal Pétain in the Vichy government, was so impressed by the

At the headquarters of Lieutenant-General George S. Patton, the four-star general Dwight D. Eisenhower studies a map of the Tunisian campaign. At one point in the bitter fighting in North Africa, Patton, disappointed that a certain general had twice failed to take a hill, noted in his diary: 'I believe that he is a coward. Therefore, I have ordered him to ride in the lead attack vehicle tomorrow. This will make him either a corpse or a man.' The general took the hill, and Patton concluded, 'I feel I can now put full confidence in this officer.' (*Library of Congress*)

strength of the Anglo-American landings that Eisenhower was able to persuade him to issue a cease-fire order to all French forces in North Africa on 11 November. Defended as a military expedient, this 'Darlan deal' was denounced by liberals as capitulation to a Nazi collaborator. Darlan was assassinated on Christmas eve, but not until October 1944 did the United States recognize Charles de Gaulle as the leader of the French nation.

Early in January 1943 Roosevelt and Churchill and the Combined Chiefs of Staff met at Casablanca to plan future operations. For the first time Allied prospects seemed favorable; this was, as Churchill said, 'the end of the beginning.' The Russians had turned the tide at the decisive battle of Stalingrad; the British had saved Egypt; Mussolini could no longer call the Mediterranean *mare nostrum*. Allied chiefs at Casablanca decided to invade Sicily as soon as Tunisia was secured, gave America the green light to start an offensive against the Japanese, and promised 'to draw as much weight as possible off the Russian armies by engaging the enemy as heavily as possible at the best selected point.' And they made the momentous announcement that the war would end only with 'unconditional surrender.' That formula, borrowed from General Grant's declaration before Fort Donelson, was prompted by the failure of the armistice of 1918 to eliminate the German menace, and a desire to reassure Russia that it would not be let down. The formula was subsequently criticized as helping Hitler to persuade his people to fight to the bitter end, but it is not clear that it actually had much effect.

While Roosevelt and Churchill were discussing grand strategy, the war took a critical turn. For a time Rommel's Afrika Korps threatened to cut the Allied armies in two. But this proved to be Rommel's last offensive. Hammered front and rear, pounded by a devastating aerial attack, Rommel retreated northward into Tunisia. The Allied armies, now half a million strong, closed in for the kill. As Montgomery broke the German lines in the south and raced for Tunis, Omar Bradley smashed into Bizerte. Both cities fell on 7 May 1943. Cornered, the German army, still 275,000 strong, surrendered on 13 May. It was the greatest victory that British and American arms had yet won. North Africa was cleared of the enemy, the spliced lifeline of the British Empire to India through Suez made it possible to reinforce Russia via the Persian Gulf, and the way was open at last for a blow at what Churchill mistakenly called 'the soft underbelly' of Europe.

D-day for the Anglo-American attack on Sicily was 10 July. In the biggest amphibious assault of the war, 250,000 British and American troops landed simultaneously, eight divisions abreast, and in black darkness. The 350,000 Italian and German defenders of Sicily were surprised and thrown off balance. The American Seventh Army swept across Sicily; on 22 July General Patton made a triumphal entry into Palermo and set up headquarters in the ancient palace of the Norman kings. By 17 August the great island was in Allied hands.

Italy, though not mortally wounded, was heartily sick of the war. On 25 July, six days after Allied air forces had delivered a 560-plane bombing raid on Rome, King Victor Emmanuel III summoned up enough courage to force Mussolini to resign. Marshal Badoglio, who told the king that the war was *perduto, perdutissimo* (absolutely and completely lost), now headed the government and began to probe for peace. While negotiations dragged along until 3 September, the Germans had time to rush reinforcements into Italy and to seize key points such as Rome. In early September 1943 the American Fifth Army, commanded by General Mark W. Clark, with two British and two American infantry divisions in the assault, took off from a dozen ports between Oran and Alexandria to invade the Italian mainland. En route to the objective the familiar voice of General 'Ike' was heard broadcasting news of the Italian surrender, so all hands expected a walk-over. They had a bitter surprise. Some very tough and uncooperative Germans were at the beach at Salerno on D-day, 9 September. After a week of vicious fighting, the beachheads were secured, and as the Germans started an orderly retirement northward, the Fifth Army on 1 October entered Naples.

Here the Italian campaign should have been halted. But the British contended that the battle of Italy pinned down and used up German divisions which might resist the Normandy landing in

The Yanks in Tunisia. When American troops entered a North African town, the first to greet them were swarms of Arab boys asking for candy and cigarettes. In this scene, photographed by Robert Capa, a sergeant from Mississippi and a corporal from Connecticut are besieged in their jeep by boys crying 'bon-bon' and 'shoon-gum.' (*Robert Capa—Magnum*)

1944. Actually the Italian campaign failed to draw German reserves from France, and by June 1944 the Allies were deploying in Italy double the number of the Germans in that area. Marshal Kesselring, fighting a series of delaying operations along prepared mountain entrenchments, exploited natural advantages to the full. From Naples to Rome is but a hundred miles; yet the Allies, with numerical superiority on land and in the air, and with control of adjacent waters, took eight months to cover that ground. In the mud and frost of that miserable campaign, wrote the war correspondent Ernie Pyle, GI's 'lived like men of prehistoric times, and a club would have become them more than a machine gun.' Not until midnight of 4 June 1944 did the Fifth Army enter Rome. For one brief day the American troops in Italy held the attention of the world. Then, on 6 June, came the news that the Allies had landed on the coast of Normandy, and the soldiers in Italy, their brief share of the limelight quickly ended, plodded on to meet the Germans at the Gothic line another 150 miles to the north.

The Battle of the Atlantic

Before the Allies could launch the long-awaited cross-Channel invasion, they first had to win control of the Atlantic. The Atlantic sea lanes had to be kept open for supplies and to build up a United States army in England for the eventual assault on the Continent. During the first eleven months of 1941 almost a thousand Allied or neutral merchantmen, totaling over 3.6 million tons, had been lost by enemy action, half of it by U-boats, and in 1942 Admiral Doenitz moved his wolf-packs to the American east coast, where he rightly anticipated rich pickings from non-convoyed tankers and merchantmen. The U-boat offensive opened on 12 January 1942 off Cape Cod, and frightful destruction was wrought by the submarines in coastal shipping lanes. During January-April 1942, almost 200 ships were sunk in North American, Gulf, and Caribbean waters, or around Bermuda. Doenitz then shifted his wolf-packs to the Straits of Florida, the Gulf of Mexico, and the Caribbean; and in those waters 182 ships totaling over 751,000 tons were sunk in May and June. Vessels were torpedoed 30 miles off New York City, within sight of Virginia Beach, off the Passes to the Mississippi, off the Panama Canal entrance. Since tourist resorts from Atlantic City to Miami Beach were not even required to turn off neon signs until April 1942, hapless freighters and tankers passing them were silhouetted to the benefit of the U-boats.

Fortunately Admiral Ernest J. King, commander in chief of the United States fleet, was taking energetic measures to combat the submarine menace. To supply small escort vessels, the slogan 'sixty vessels in sixty days' was nailed to the mast in April 1942, and 67 vessels actually came through by 4 May, when a second 60–60 program was already under way. Scientists were mobilized to find more efficient means of tracking and sinking U-boats (British scientists had already contributed radar and would soon give America sonar); inshore and offshore patrols were organized into a 'Hooligan Navy' of converted yachts, and an interlocking convoy system was worked out. In the second half of 1942 coastal convoys lost only 0.5 per cent of their ships; transatlantic convoys lost only 1.4 per cent in a whole year.

The crucial period in the Battle of the Atlantic came in the first half of 1943, when the Germans more than doubled the number of U-boats operating in the Atlantic. A fresh German blitz in March 1943 accounted for 108 merchant ships aggregating over 625,000 tons. These sinkings, occurring at the worst season in the North Atlantic when the temperature of the water hovers around 30° F, were accompanied by heavy loss of life. And although the United States Navy, which escorted transatlantic troop transports, lost none of those going to and from Great Britain or the Mediterranean, it lost three army transports en route to Greenland and Iceland; one of these, the *Dorchester*, on 3 February 1943, with great loss, including four army chaplains. By April, though, the Allies were definitely ahead. The increased number of convoys and escorts, improved devices and training, and the work of scientists and technicians were getting results, and merchant ship new construction was now well ahead of losses. But throughout the war the Germans were able, on

'Emmitsburgians in Service.' This photograph by Marjory Collins of a window display in a general store in Emmitsburg, Maryland, in February 1943 indicates the pervasive impact of World War II on American communities. The array of pictures includes 'boys in the service' of a wide range of ages and ranks, Army and Navy, and near the center a woman commissioned second lieutenant in the U.S. Army Nursing Corps, Camp Meade, Md. (*Library of Congress*)

occasion, to send wolf-packs full cry after transatlantic traffic; the Battle of the Atlantic did not end until Germany surrendered.

Forward in the Pacific

In the same months that the Allies were clearing the Atlantic of the U-boat menace in preparation for the assault on the Continent, the war on the other side of the globe was entering its climactic phase. Before Japan could be invaded, positions had to be taken within air-bombing distance. But how to get there? The short northern route, via the Aleutians, was ruled out by bad flying weather. In the Central Pacific, hundreds of atolls and thousands of islands—the Gilberts, Marshalls,

Carolines, Marianas, and Bonins—plastered with airfields and bristling with defenses, sprawled across the ocean like a maze of gigantic spider webs. South of the equator, Japan held the Bismarck Archipelago, the Solomons north of Guadalcanal, and all New Guinea except its slippery tail. General MacArthur wished to advance by what he called the New Guinea-Mindanao axis; but Rabaul, planted like a baleful spider at the center of a web across that axis, would have to be eliminated first. And as long as Japan held the island complex on MacArthur's north flank, she could throw air and naval forces against his communications at will. So it was decided that Admiral Nimitz must take a broom to the Gilberts, the Marshalls, and the Carolines, while MacArthur and Halsey cleaned out the Bismarcks. All could then join forces for a final push into the Philippines and on to the coast of China.

Accordingly the plans for mid-1943 to mid-1944 began with preliminary operations to sweep up enemy spider webs. The central Solomons were the first objective. After three sharp naval actions up the Solomons' Slot in July and a number of motor torpedo boat actions (in one of which John Fitzgerald Kennedy distinguished himself), the United States Navy won control of surrounding waters, and in New Guinea and on New Britain, amphibious operations secured the main passage from the Coral Sea through the Bismarcks barrier into the Western Pacific. Japan could now be approached in a series of bold leaps instead of a multitude of short hops. The essence of the 'leap-frogging' strategy was to by-pass the principal Japanese strongpoints like Truk and Rabaul, sealing them off with sea and air power, leaving their garrisons to 'wither on the vine,' while the Allies constructed a new air and naval base in some less strongly defended spot several hundred miles nearer Japan. By 25 March 1944 the Bismarcks barrier to MacArthur's advance was decisively breached, and almost 100,000 Japanese troops were neutralized at Rabaul.

Meantime, Allied forces had moved into the Gilberts and Marshalls in the first full-scale amphibious operations in the Pacific. Some 200 sail of ships, carrying 108,000 soldiers, sailors, marines, and aviators converged on two coral atolls of the Gilbert group. Makin, where the enemy had no great strength, was taken methodically, but Tarawa, a small, strongly defended position behind a long coral-reef apron, cost the lives of almost a thousand marines and sailors in disposing of 4000 no-surrender Japanese on an islet not three miles long. The Gilberts became bases from which aircraft helped to neutralize the Japanese air bases in the Marshalls, which were invaded early in 1944 at Kwajalein and Eniwetok. The Japanese troops, as usual, resisted to the last man; but the Marshalls cost many fewer casualties than tiny Tarawa. Another leap-frogging operation scored important victories in New Guinea in the spring of 1944, while an offensive against the Marianas, of which the principal islands were Saipan, Tinian, and Guam, threatened Japan's inner line of defense. When the Japanese attempted to beat back the American offensive by deploying a huge naval force, they lost over 345 planes and three carriers in the Battle of the Philippine Sea (19 June 1944). Thereafter the conquest of the Marianas proceeded apace. On 6 July, the Japanese general and his staff committed suicide, and the rest of his army jumped off cliffs or holed up in caves. By 1 August 1944 three big islands of the Marianas were in American possession, and by fall, Marianas-based B-29's were bombing southern Japan.

The more sagacious Japanese now knew they were beaten; but they dared not admit it, and nerved their people to another year of bitter resistance in the vain hope that America might tire of the war when victory was within grasp in Asia and the Allies were on the offensive in Europe.

From Normandy to the Rhine

While waiting for an appropriate moment to launch the cross-Channel invasion of Hitler's 'Fortress Europe,' the R.A.F., in conjunction with the United States Army Air Force, was doing its best to render invasion unnecessary by bombing Germany into submission. Largely British, but assisted by B-17's of the Eighth Army Air Force, was the most destructive air bombing of the European war—the series of attacks on Hamburg in July-August 1943, which, by using incendiary

D-Day, 6 June 1944. At Utah Beach, near Cherbourg, members of an American landing party help ashore soldiers whose craft was sunk by enemy action. These survivors of the Normandy invasion made their way through rough seas in a life raft to this stony beach. (*U.S. Army Photograph*)

bombs, wiped out over half the city, killed 42,600, and injured 37,000 people. This strategic air offensive never succeeded as an alternative to land invasion. The bombing almost nightly by the R.A.F. and every clear day by the A.A.F. did not seriously diminish Germany's well-dispersed war production and conspicuously failed to break civilian morale. It was also frightfully expensive. In six days of October 1943, culminating in a raid on the ball-bearing plants at Schweinfurt, deep in the heart of Germany, the Eighth lost 148 bombers and their crews, mostly as a result of battles in the air.

Yet the Allied bombing raids, much more effective in 1944, did deny many hundreds of aircraft to the enemy when he needed them most. By the spring of 1944 the Allied air forces had established a thirty-to-one superiority over the German air force. On D-day, 'Ike' told his troops, 'If you see fighting aircraft over you, they will be ours,' and so they were. The air war in Europe cost the lives of some 158,000 British, Canadian, and American aviators. In this new dimension of warfare, many mistakes were made; but the Germans made even more. Without victory in the air there could have been no victory anywhere, no expectation of success in that enormously risky continental invasion on which hinged all hopes for a final triumph in the war.

Never before in modern times had an invading army crossed the English Channel against opposition, and Hitler's coastal defenses were formidable: underwater obstacles and mines, artillery emplacements, pill boxes, wire entanglements, tank traps, land mines, and other hazards, and behind these defenses were stationed 58 divisions. Yet the Allies had reason for confidence. For six weeks Allied air forces had been smashing roads and bridges in northern France, reducing the transportation system to chaos. The Allied force of soldiers, sailors, aviators, and service amounted to 2.8 million men, all based in England. Thirty-nine divisions and 11,000 planes were available for the initial landings, and the Allied supporting fleet was overwhelmingly superior to anything the Germans could deploy; the U-boats had been so neutralized by the Allied navies that not one of the thousands of vessels engaged in the invasion was torpedoed.

The Allied command selected as target a 40-mile strip of beach along the Normandy coast. The eastern sector was assigned to the British, the western to the Americans. Shortly after midnight 5 June three paratroop divisions were flown across the Channel to drop behind the beaches. During the night the invasion fleet of 600 warships and 4000 supporting craft, freighted with 176,000 men from a dozen different ports, moved over to the Norman coast. Before naval bombardment ended, landing craft, lowered from transports over ten miles from shore, began their approach. It was D-day, 6 June.

The first assault troops, who touched down at 6:30, achieved tactical surprise. On the American right—designated Utah Beach—VII Corps got ashore against light opposition, but 1st and 29th Divisions, landing on four-mile Omaha Beach, found the going tough. Soldiers were wounded in a maze of mined underwater obstacles, then drowned by the rising tide; those who got through had to cross a 50-yard-wide beach, exposed to cunningly contrived cross-fire from concrete pill boxes. Men huddled for protection under a low sea wall until company officers rallied them to root the defenders out of their prepared positions. The numerically superior British assault force had a somewhat less difficult landing, but it bore the brunt of the next week's fighting. All in all, the D-day assault on that memorable 6th of June was a brilliant success. In a single week the Allies landed 326,000 men, 50,000 vehicles, and over 100,000 tons of supplies. 'The history of war,' said Marshal Stalin, in one of his rare compliments to his allies, 'does not know any undertaking so broad in conception, so grandiose in scale, and so masterly in execution.'

It required less than three months to reach the French capital. By early August the Allied armies had conquered Normandy and overrun Brittany, and on 15 August they invaded southern France. Toulon and Marseilles were soon taken by the French, while General Patch's Seventh American Army rolled up the Rhone valley and captured Lyons; by mid-September Patch had linked up with Patton. 'Liberate Paris by Christmas and none of us can ask for more,' said Churchill to Eisenhower. General Hodges's First Army raced for the Seine; Patton's Third boiled out onto the open country north of the Loire and swept eastward. Paris rose against her hated masters, and, with the aid of General Leclerc's 2nd Armored Division, was liberated on 25 August, four months ahead of Churchill's request. General Charles de Gaulle entered the city in triumph and assumed the presidency of a French provisional government.

With Paris freed, the Allied armies drove relentlessly toward the Rhine. Patton's spearheads reached the Marne on 28 August, pushed through Château-Thierry, overran Rheims and Verdun. To the north, Montgomery's British and Canadians drove along the coast into Belgium. By 11

General George Patton, General Omar Bradley, and General Sir Bernard L. Montgomery, France, July 1944. The two Americans confer with 'Monty' in the month following the Normandy invasion. (*Library of Congress*)

September the American First Army had liberated Luxembourg and near Aachen crossed the border into Germany. Within six weeks all France had been cleared of the enemy, and from there to Switzerland Allied armies stood poised for the advance into Germany.

On other fronts, the German position was becoming equally bad. By the spring of 1944 the Red armies had reached the Dnieper in the north and the Carpathians in the south. On 23 June Stalin launched a new offensive along an 800-mile front. In five weeks the Russians swept across the Ukraine and Poland and up to the gates of Warsaw where, despicably, they paused instead of helping Polish patriots to liberate their capital; they hoped to reduce Poland to a satellite state, and they did. Romania threw in the sponge when another Red Army crossed her borders, and by October the Russians had linked up with Tito forces in Yugoslavia. Yet in the east as well as in the west the Germans were still strong enough to force another winter's campaign on their enemies.

Political Interlude

As the Allied armed forces fought ahead, another presidential election came up—the first in wartime since 1864 although in no war had the United States ever suspended elections. In World War II America's energies were devoted not only to winning the struggle against the Axis but to political and ideological battles at home. In some respects, the war was a boon to the New Dealers. TVA, Grand Coulee, and the other public power projects proved indispensable; private utility spokesmen who had claimed there would never be a market for so much power had to eat their words. Under the approving eye of the War Labor Board, union membership rose to nearly 15 million by 1945. Inevitably, the war enhanced the powers of the President and accelerated the aggrandizement of Federal bureaus. The war resulted, too, in a revolutionary change in fiscal policy. Total Federal spending in the war years soared above $320 billion—twice the total of Federal expenditure in all the previous history of the republic. When in 1936 the government outlay totaled eight billion dollars, critics had cried that the New Deal was risking national bankruptcy. When the government spent $98 billion in 1945, few were concerned, for the country was enjoying boom prosperity. The war amply demonstrated the Keynesian hypothesis: with mounting deficits, unemployment disappeared.

Yet in other respects the war tilted politics in a more conservative direction. The President frankly confessed that 'Dr. New Deal' had given way to 'Dr. Win-the-War.' Roosevelt and aides like Hopkins became preoccupied with the grand design of military strategy and diplomatic alliances. In 1942, the Republican Congressional candidates received more votes than Democrats for the first time since 1928, and conservatives interpreted the outcome as a mandate for their policies. Ever since 1937 the coalition of conservative Southern Democrats and Republicans had been gaining power, and in World War II this alliance was cemented. The next session of Congress set out to dismantle the New Deal and drive liberals out of war agencies, and it had considerable success in both aims. As the New Deal lost its momentum, political power shifted perceptibly to what Samuel Lubell has called the 'border state Democrats': men like Jimmie Byrnes and Fred Vinson. Respected by Congress as tough legislative tacticians who were unlikely to advance 'visionary' ideas, the 'border state Democrats' headed the crucial war agencies and fixed the boundaries of what Roosevelt could hope to achieve in domestic affairs. When the 'visionary' Henry Wallace, who in 1942 proclaimed 'the century of the common man,' brawled with the business-minded Jesse Jones, Roosevelt resolved the conflict by awarding victory to the Jones faction.

In 1944 organization Democrats insisted that Roosevelt drop Vice-President Wallace as his running mate and choose instead Missouri's Senator Harry S. Truman whose able management of a Defense Investigating Committee (the 'Truman committee') had won him a national reputation. Another 'border state Democrat,' Truman satisfied the demand for a candidate who would be acceptable both to the New Dealers and the party bosses; the New York *Times* dubbed him 'the new Missouri Compromise.' With no need this time for a 'draft,' Roosevelt won his party's presidential nomination for a fourth term on the first roll call. The Chicago *Daily News* commented: 'If he was good enough for my pappy and my grandpappy, he is good enough for me.'

While the Democrats were using the vice-presidential nomination as a contest for party control, the Republican party was carrying on a similar struggle between its internationalist and isolationist wings for the G.O.P. presidential nomination in 1944. Leader of the internationalist wing was Wendell Willkie who in 1943 published an account of a trip around the globe, *One World*, that proved enormously popular. Yet isolationism was still powerful enough to drive Willkie out of the race. With Willkie out, the contest for the Republican nomination in 1944 proved a runaway for New York's competent but colorless Governor Thomas E. Dewey, a moderate.

Dewey, wanting the personal charm that made Willkie and FDR so formidable, was a poor campaigner, and the issue was never in doubt. Although the President had less than 53 per cent of the vote, his following in the big cities swung large states with big blocks of electoral votes. Roosevelt carried 36 states with 432 electoral votes; Dewey, 12 states with 99 electoral votes. Isolationists like Gerald Nye went down to defeat, and internationalists such as J. William Fulbright arrived in the Senate to strengthen the forces favoring world organization. The election marked the end of isolationism as a potent political factor, though it would re-emerge in new guises after the war.

The New Deal goes to war. From 1942 to 1945 the Tennessee Valley Authority built Fontana Dam on the Little Tennessee river in North Carolina bordering the Great Smokies. The highest concrete dam east of the Rockies, Fontana Dam generated 225,000 kilowatts. Not only the TVA but installations like Grand Coulee and Bonneville powered munitions industries in World War II. (*Tennessee Valley Authority*)

Victory in Europe, September 1944–May 1945

While Americans at home were going to the polls, GI's in Europe were trying to increase the momentum of their campaign against the Germans. In the confused fighting that stretched from October to mid-December 1944, the war settled down to what General Eisenhower called 'the dirtiest kind of infantry slugging.' At a heavy cost in casualties, the Canadians took logistically important Antwerp, and Americans seized the ancient capital of Charlemagne, Aachen, the first German city to fall to the Allies; reached the Roer river;

captured Metz; plunged into the Saar; and drove into Alsace. By mid-December the Allied armies were poised all along the border from Holland to Switzerland, ready to plunge into Germany.

Then came a dramatic change of fortune: a German counteroffensive through the Ardennes Forest. Because bad weather prevented Allied air reconnaissance, the Germans achieved surprise and success along a 50-mile front on 16 December. They concentrated on the center of the Allied line, and as they thrust toward the Meuse, maps of the Western front showed a marked 'bulge' to indicate their advance. But at Bastogne they were checked. This little Belgian town, headquarters of General Troy Middleton's VIII Corps, was a center of a network of roads essential to the Germans, and Middleton decided to hold it at all costs. For six days the enemy hurled armor and planes at them, while foul weather prevented aerial reinforcement of the defenders. On 22 December the American situation appeared hopeless, and the Germans presented a formal demand for surrender, to which General 'Tony' McAuliffe of the 101st Airborne replied 'Nuts!' Next day the weather cleared, and planes began dropping supplies; by Christmas Eve, with bomber and fighter support, the situation looked more hopeful. Meantime, Patton's Third Army had started pell-mell north to the rescue of the besieged garrison; on 26 December it broke through the German encirclement and Bastogne was saved. The Battle of the Bulge was not over, but by 15 January 1945 the original lines of mid-December had been restored. Hitler had held up the Allied advance by a full month, but at a cost of 120,000 men, 1600 planes, and a good part of his armor. Never thereafter were the Germans able to put up an effective defense.

At the end of January, Eisenhower resumed the advance toward the Rhine, while the Russians, moving off on a thousand-mile front, crossed the Vistula, and swept toward Germany in a gigantic pincer movement that inflicted over a million German casualties. The 7th of March 1945 was one of the dramatic days of the war. On that day a detachment of the 9th Armored Division of the First Army captured the bridge over the Rhine at Remagen, just as the Germans were about to blow it up. And on 22 March Patton began crossing the Rhine at Oppenheim. Moving at breakneck speed—the 3rd Armored Division covered 90 miles in a single day—Hodges's First Army swung north, Simpson's Ninth turned south, and a giant pincer closed on the Ruhr, trapping some 400,000 Germans. Encircled, pounded on all sides, hammered day and night by swarms of bombers, the German armies caught in the pocket disintegrated. Montgomery now drove toward Bremen and Hamburg, Patton raced for Kassel, and Patch sped through Bavaria toward Czechoslovakia.

As the Allied armies drove deep into Germany, Austria, and Poland, they came upon one torture camp after another—Buchenwald, Dachau, Belsen, Auschwitz, Linz, Lublin—and what they reported sickened the whole Western world. These atrocity camps had been established in 1937 for Jews, gypsies, and anti-Nazi Germans and Austrians; with the coming of war the Nazis used them for prisoners of all nationalities, men, women, and children, and for Jews rounded up in Italy, France, Holland, and Hungary. In these camps, hordes of prisoners had been scientifically murdered; other multitudes had died of disease, starvation, and maltreatment. The total number of civilians done to death by Hitler's orders exceeded 6 million. And the pathetic story of one of the least of these, the diary of the little Jewish girl Anne Frank, has probably done more to convince the world of the hatred inherent in the Nazi doctrine than the solemn postwar trials.

As German resistance crumbled and victory appeared certain, the Western world was plunged into mourning by the news that a great leader had died. President Roosevelt, returning from the Yalta conference of the Combined Chiefs of Staff in February a sick man, went to his winter home in Warm Springs, Georgia, to prepare for the inauguration of the United Nations at San Francisco, which he hoped would usher in a new era of peace and justice. On 12 April, as he was drafting a Jefferson Day address, he died suddenly. The last words he wrote were an epitome of his career: 'The only limit to our realization of tomorrow will be our doubts of today. Let us move forward with strong and active faith.'

The end was now in sight for Hitler's Germany. The Western Allies were rolling unopposed to the Elbe; the Russians were thrusting at Berlin. Ad-

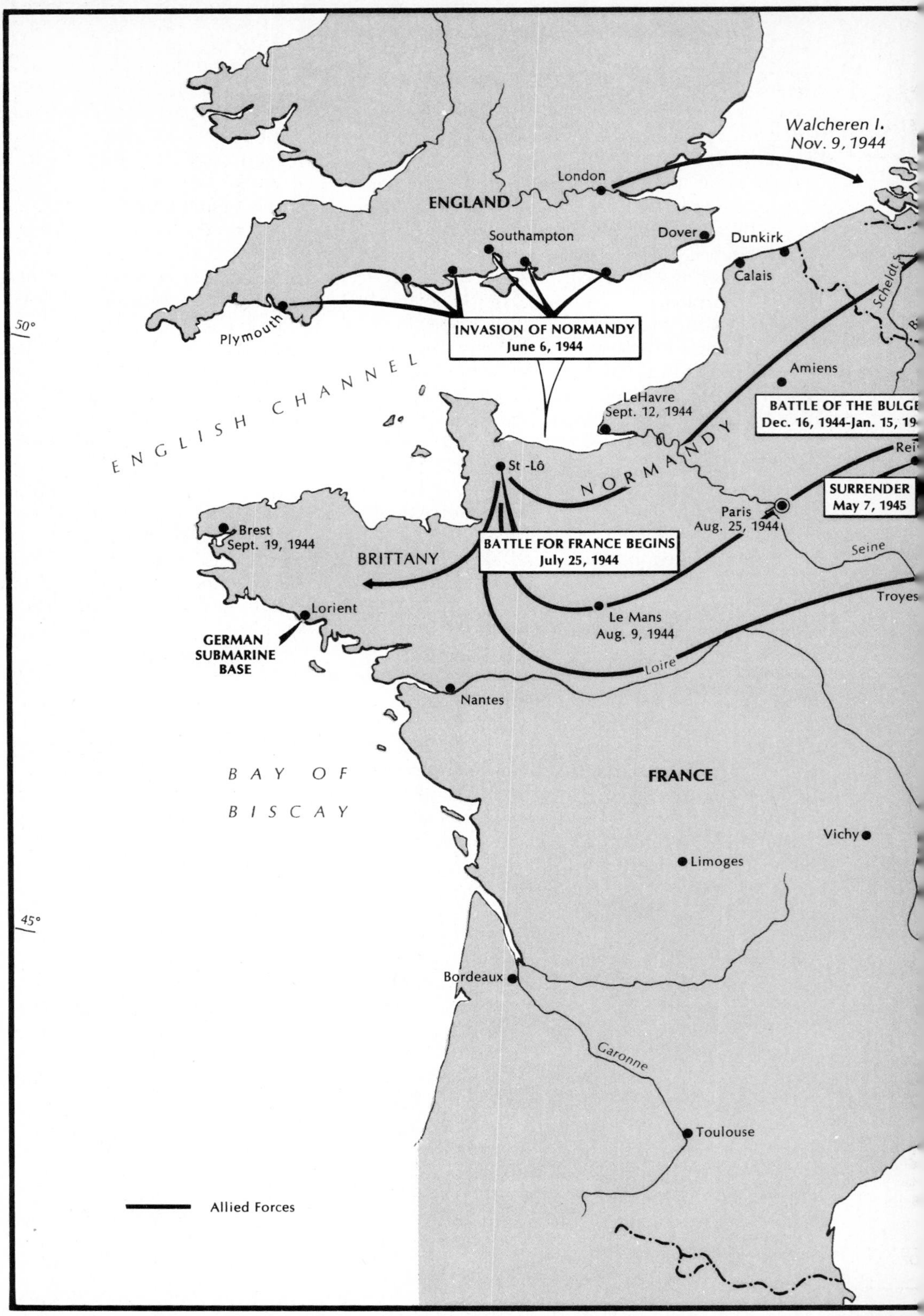
ENGLAND
London
Southampton
Dover
Plymouth
Walcheren I.
Nov. 9, 1944
Dunkirk
Calais
Scheldt
INVASION OF NORMANDY
June 6, 1944
ENGLISH CHANNEL
Amiens
LeHavre
Sept. 12, 1944
BATTLE OF THE BULGE
Dec. 16, 1944-Jan. 15, 19
NORMANDY
St -Lô
SURRENDER
May 7, 1945
Paris
Aug. 25, 1944
Brest
Sept. 19, 1944
BRITTANY
BATTLE FOR FRANCE BEGINS
July 25, 1944
Seine
Troyes
Lorient
GERMAN
SUBMARINE
BASE
Le Mans
Aug. 9, 1944
Loire
Nantes
BAY OF
BISCAY
FRANCE
Vichy
Limoges
50°
45°
Bordeaux
Garonne
Toulouse
Allied Forces

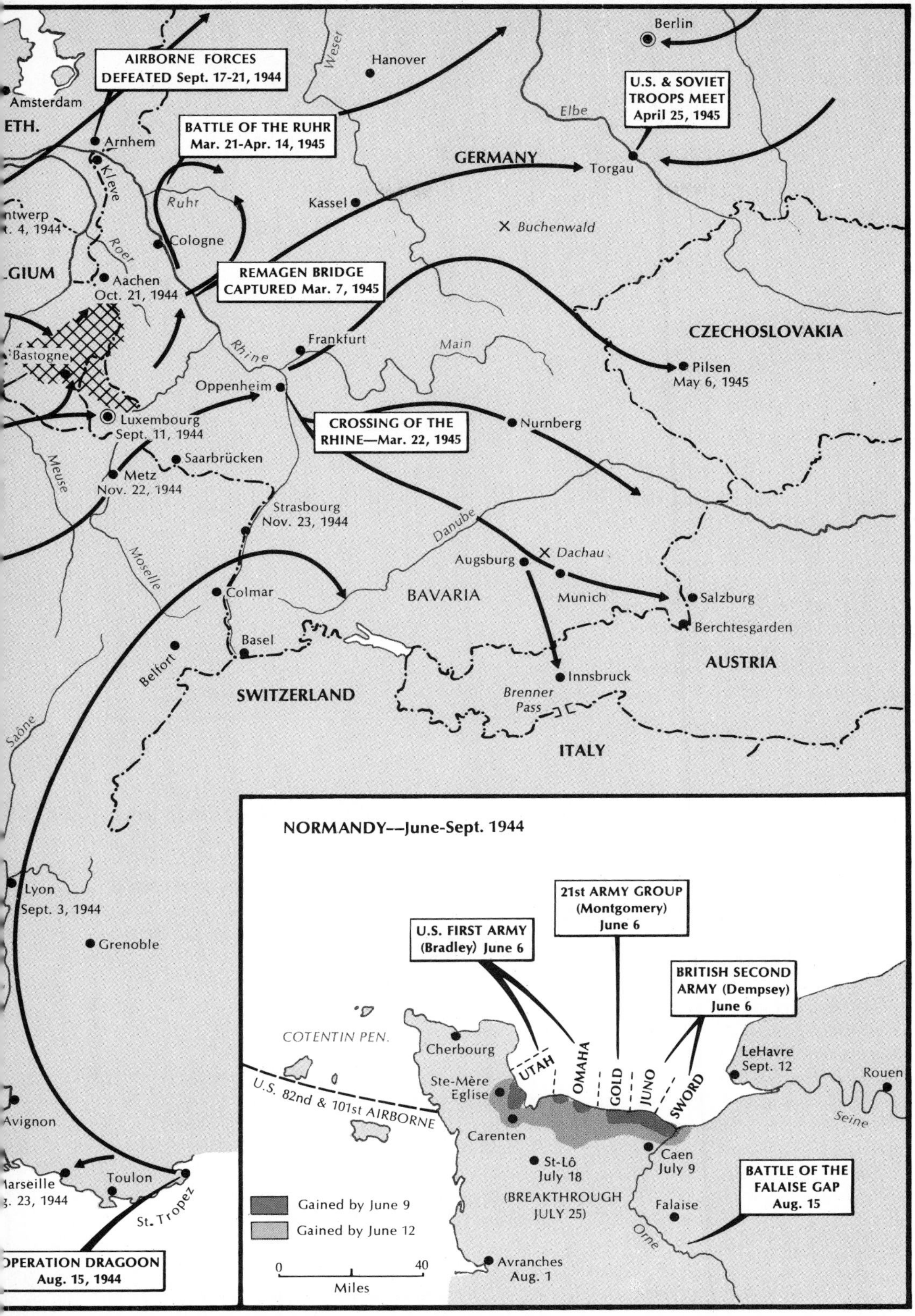

The Conquest of Germany, 1944–45

אלה אזכרה ונפשי עלי אשפכה
כי בלעונו זרים כעוגה בלי
הפוכה כי בימי השר לא
עלתה ארוכה להרוגי מלוכה

'Warsaw 1943.' Two decades later, Ben Shahn commemorated the heroic resistance of the remnants of the Jewish community in the Polish capital to the Nazis. The Hebrew inscription comes from the thirteenth-century 'ten martyrs' prayer' for Yom Kippur based on the legend of the execution of ten Jews by the Roman emperor Hadrian. The prayer begins, 'These martyrs I well remember, and my soul is melting with secret sorrow. Evil men have devoured us, and eagerly consumed us.' (*New Jersey State Museum Collection, Trenton*)

vance detachments of the two armies met at Torgau on 25 April, severing Germany. On the last day of April, Hitler died a coward's death, killing first his mistress and then himself in a bombproof bunker under Berlin. On 4 May General Mark Clark's Fifth Army, which had fought all the way up the boot of Italy, met, at the Brenner Pass, General Patch's Seventh, coming down through Austria, and next day German resistance in Italy ceased. Italian partisans had already captured and killed Mussolini. Thus ended, in ruin, horror, and despair, the Axis that pretended to rule the world and the Reich which Hitler had boasted would last a thousand years. Admiral Doenitz, Hitler's designated heir, tried desperately to arrange a surrender to the Western Allies instead of Russia, but loyalty to our Eastern ally caused General Eisenhower sternly to decline these advances. On 7 May General Jodl signed an unconditional surrender.[2] Bradley, awakened by a telephone call from Eisenhower with the news, opened his mapboard and smoothed out the tabs of the 43 divisions under his command.

'With a china-marking pencil, I wrote in the new date: D day plus 335.'

'I walked to the window and ripped open the blackout blinds. Outside the sun was climbing into the sky. The war in Europe had ended.'

Victory Over Japan

On the other side of the globe the war had entered its final phase. In the fall of 1944 MacArthur launched his cherished plan to return to the Philippines. After a three-day 'knock-down,

2. V-E Day is celebrated on 8 May because the surrender became effective at 2301 that day, Central European Time.

Franklin Delano Roosevelt, 12 April 1945. Lucy Mercer Rutherfurd, with whom FDR had conducted a long-term affair, commissioned Elizabeth Shoumatoff to paint this watercolor of the President as a gift to her daughter. As Madame Shoumatoff sketched on that April afternoon at Roosevelt's retreat in Warm Springs, Ga., Lucy watched. But the portrait was never finished, for near the end of the session, the President said, 'I have a terrific headache' and slumped over; in a short while, he was pronounced dead. (*Franklin D. Roosevelt Warm Springs Memorial Commission*)

drag-out fight,' as Halsey described it, over the Ryukyus and Formosa destroyed more than 500 planes, the Central Pacific forces and the Southwest Pacific forces were combined in one massive thrust. On 20 October 1944 General MacArthur and President Osmeña of the Philippines splashed ashore from a landing craft. MacArthur announced: 'I have returned. By the grace of Almighty God our forces stand again on Philippine soil. . . . Rally to me. . . . Let no heart be faint.'

At Tokyo the war lords decided that now was the time to commit the entire Japanese fleet, defeat American forces afloat, and isolate MacArthur, so that he would be virtually back at Bataan. From that decision there resulted, on 25 October, the battle for Leyte Gulf, greatest sea fight of this or of any other war. The Japanese divided their fleet into three forces. In a night encounter in Surigao Strait, the American navy devastated the Japanese Southern Force and killed Admiral Nishimura. A short time later, in the critical central sector, there ensued the bloodiest naval action in American history—1130 Americans killed, 913 wounded—in which, off Samar, a fleet more than ten times as powerful as the Americans in gunfire power was defeated. Up north, off Cape Engaño, all four Japanese carriers (including the last survivor of those which had struck Pearl Harbor) were sunk. This three-part battle for Leyte Gulf left the United States Navy in complete command of Philippine waters; never again could the Japanese navy offer a real threat. But months of fighting ashore were required against the no-surrender Japanese infantry before the archipelago was liberated.

After the landings at Leyte the Allies concentrated on securing island bases for a final assault on Japan. On 19 February 1945 marines landed on Iwo Jima, a desolate little island of coal-black lava, which could serve as a halfway house on the 1500-mile bomber run to Tokyo. Even before organized resistance ceased on 14 March, B-29's began using the Iwo airfields; and it is estimated that by this means thousands of American lives were saved. But Iwo, which cost the navy and marine corps some 28,000 casualties, was remembered with a special kind of horror, for the island seemed too small for all the killing it absorbed.

Two weeks after Iwo fell, four American divisions went ashore on Okinawa on Easter Sunday, 1 April. The Japanese put up a desperate resistance, exacting a heavy toll of American lives, before the island was finally conquered late in June. In the meantime the navy, which had to cover the operation and furnish fire support, took a terrific beating from the self-sacrificing kamikaze planes. Twenty-seven ships were sunk, and sixty-one others so badly damaged as to be out of the war; casualties were heavy even on the ships that survived—the carriers *Franklin*, *Wasp*, and *Bunker Hill* between them lost 2211 men killed and 798 wounded. The total cost to the United States of the invasion of Okinawa was over 12,500 killed and over 62,500 wounded; but the island as a base proved indispensable.

While the Allies were conducting amphibious operations on islands like Okinawa, they were also waging a war of attrition against Japan. The navy and the army air force redoubled the fury of their attacks on the Japanese home islands, where B-29 bombing raids directed by General LeMay of the Air Strategic Command burned large parts of Tokyo and other industrial cities. Meanwhile Allied naval forces were destroying the Japanese merchant fleet. Japan, with 10 million tons of merchant shipping by conquest and new construction, ended up with only 1.8 million tons, mostly small wooden vessels in the Inland Sea. United States forces alone sank 2117 Japanese merchant vessels of almost 8 million tons during the war, and 60 per cent of this was done by submarines, of which 50 were lost in action.

The Combined Chiefs of Staff, meeting at Quebec in September 1944, figured that it would take eighteen months after the surrender of Germany to defeat Japan. Actually, the war in the Pacific ended with a terrific bang only three months after V-E Day. President Truman and Winston Churchill, meeting with the C.C.S. at Potsdam, presented Japan with an ultimatum on 26 July 1945. The surrender must be complete, and must include a temporary Allied occupation of Japan and the return of all Japanese conquests since 1895 to their former owners. The alternative was 'prompt and utter destruction.' If Tokyo had made up its mind promptly to accept the Potsdam declaration as a basis for peace, there would have been no atomic bomb explosion over Japan. But the government was more afraid of Japanese militarists than of American power.

The fearful consequences resulted from experimentation in atomic fission. In 1939 Albert Einstein, Enrico Fermi, Leo Szilard, and other physicists who had sought refuge in the United States from tyranny in their native countries warned President Roosevelt of the danger of Germany's obtaining a lead in uranium fission. In the summer of 1940 Fermi, assisted by members of Columbia's football team, began to build an atomic pile. Using a mighty cyclotron, or 'atom smasher,' Dr. Ernest Lawrence of the University of California solved the problem of turning out fissionable material in sufficient quantities. The President assigned responsibility for further developments to the Office of Scientific Research and Development, set up in May 1941 under the direction of Vannevar Bush and James B. Conant.[3] By December Fermi and others, working in the squash court at the University of Chicago's Stagg Field, achieved the first self-sustaining nuclear chain reaction, halfway mark to the atomic bomb. Army engineers under General Leslie Groves then took over, under the code name 'Manhattan District,' and built small cities at Oak Ridge, Tennessee, and Hanford, Washington, to make plutonium. As research progressed, a special laboratory was erected at Los Alamos, New Mexico, for which J. Robert Oppenheimer was responsible.

On 16 July 1945, scientists and military men gathered before dawn on the New Mexico desert, their eyes covered with dark glasses, their faces with anti-sunburn cream, some of the young scientists unnerved by the tension, Oppenheimer holding onto a post to steady himself. With the word, 'Now!' the bomb was detonated. A blinding flash illuminated the desert, and an enormous fireball, changing colors from deep purple to orange to 'unearthly green' erupted skyward. Following the fireball, a great column rose from the ground, eventually taking the mushroom shape that was to symbolize the new age; pushing through the clouds, it reached a height of 41,000 feet. Then came a wave of intense heat and a thunderous roar; the ground trembled as though shaken by an earthquake. Oppenheimer was reminded of the passage from the *Bhagavad-Gita:* 'I am become Death, the shatterer of worlds.' Another scientist commented: 'This was the nearest to doomsday one can possibly imagine. I am sure that at the end of the world—in the last millisecond of the earth's existence—the last man will see something very similar to what we have seen.'

President Truman's committee of high officials and top atomic scientists recommended that atomic bombs be exploded over Japan at once, and without warning. At 9:15 a.m., 6 August, the bomb was toggled out over Hiroshima, the second most important military center in Japan. The bomb wiped out the Second Japanese Army to a man, razed four square miles of the city, and killed 60,175 people including the soldiers. That morning the dreadfully-burned survivors moved through the city, eerily silent, holding their arms out before them to prevent the burned surfaces from touching, hoping in vain that someone could ease their pain. Of the 1780 nurses in the city, 1654 had been killed instantly or were too badly hurt to work; most of the doctors were dead or wounded. That afternoon people who seemed to have escaped unharmed died, the first signs of the effects of radiation. At about noon 9 August, a few hours after Russia declared war on Japan, a second atomic bomb was exploded over Nagasaki, killing 36,000 more.

Should the United States have used this most terrible of weapons? Having revealed its dreadful potentialities over Hiroshima, should America have used it a second time over Nagasaki? These are

3. The OSRD supervised such developments in military technology as the proximity fuse and short-range rockets, notably the 'bazooka.' The government also fostered the achievement of the 'miracle drug,' penicillin, soon to be followed by streptomycin. DDT also proved effective during the war. The development of sulfa drugs and penicillin, the use of plasma, and new techniques reduced the death rate from wounds to less than half that of World War I.

questions men will ask for a hundred years, if the atomic weapon allows mankind another hundred years. On the one hand it can be said that if Japan had not been brought to its knees by this awful display of power, the war might have dragged on for another year, with incomparably greater loss of lives, both Japanese and American; for Japan still had more than 5000 planes with kamikaze pilots, and a million ground troops prepared to contest every beachhead and every city. The explosion over Hiroshima caused fewer civilian casualties than the repeated B-29 bombings of Tokyo, and those big bombers would have had to wipe out one city after another if the war had not ended in August. On the other hand it is asserted that destruction of the Japanese merchant marine and the blockade had brought Japan to the verge of defeat, that the empire could have been strangled without invasion. Long-range considerations are likewise surrounded by uncertainty. It is, however, fairly certain that if the war in the East had lasted six months longer, Russia would have occupied the northern part of Japan and would still be there; and that the costs in blood and bitterness of an Allied invasion of the Japanese mainland are incalculable. Honorable and humane men made the fateful decision to drop the two atomic bombs; honorable and humane men may, in time, conclude that it was the most mistaken decision in the history of warfare.

Even after the two atomic bombs had been dropped, and the Potsdam declaration had been clarified to assure the Japanese that they could keep their emperor, the surrender was a very near thing. Hirohito had to override his two chief military advisers, and take the responsibility of accepting the Potsdam terms. That he did on 14 August. Even thereafter, a military *coup d'état* to sequester the emperor, kill his cabinet, and continue the war was narrowly averted. Yet the gloom of the postwar years owed not a little to the awareness that a liberal, democratic government had not scrupled to unleash a weapon which might mean the end of mankind.

34

Cold War and Fair Deal

*

1945–1952

Organization for Peace

We seek peace—enduring peace. More than an end to war, we want an end to the beginnings of all wars—yes, an end to this brutal, inhuman and thoroughly impractical method of settling the differences between governments. . . . We are faced with the pre-eminent fact that, if civilization is to survive, we must cultivate the science of human relationships—the ability of all peoples, of all kinds, to live together and work together in the same world, at peace. . . . Today, as we move against the terrible scourge of war—as we go forward toward the greatest contribution that any generation of human beings can make in this world,—the contribution of lasting peace—I ask you to keep up your faith.

These were among the last words Franklin Roosevelt wrote, and they were eloquent of a concern that possessed him throughout the war years. Roosevelt's interest in peace went back to his service in the Wilson administration during World War I. That he had been impressed by Wilson's idealism is clear; that he was determined not to repeat Wilson's mistakes is equally clear. 'The tragedy of Wilson,' wrote Robert Sherwood, 'was always somewhere within the rim of his consciousness.'

Harsh experience had taught Roosevelt a lesson denied to Wilson of the importance of a sturdy economic foundation for the postwar world. A decade of depression had preceded World War II and had been an important cause of that war. Furthermore, the depression had undermined democratic institutions and aspirations in countries like Germany. Roosevelt recognized that foreign as well as domestic policies could be directed toward averting another collapse in the United States, and that economic aid could be used as an American weapon toward achieving an international arrangement in which Western conceptions would prosper. During the war he brushed aside ideological objections to collaboration with the Kremlin and approved a program of aid to the USSR that eventually totaled $11 billion. Yet in one respect he was as 'Wilsonian' as his predecessor, for, like the World War I President, he favored a global economic order in which American and other goods would flow freely, and this attitude would lead to discord with both the Russians and the British.

While the war was still being fought, the United States took steps both to foster a stable postwar economy and to sustain the millions of victims of the war. As early as 1944 a United Nations Monetary and Financial Conference at Bretton Woods, New Hampshire, had set up two new agencies: an International Monetary Fund to stabilize currencies and an International Bank for Reconstruction and Development to make credit available for international trade and investment. Even before that the United States had taken the lead in creating the United Nations Relief and Rehabilitation Administration (UNRRA) in 1943. Under the leadership of Herbert Lehman and Fiorello LaGuardia, UNRRA distributed food, clothing, seed, fertilizer, livestock, machinery, and medicine where the need was greatest. In four years UNRRA spent some $4 billion, of which the United States gave $2.75 billion. In addition, the U.S. Army fed large areas of occupied Europe, lend-lease continued to pour foodstuffs and other supplies into Allied countries, and private gifts and CARE supplemented governmental contributions on a generous scale. Yet if America did much for relief, it did less than its resources permitted.

Unlike Wilson, Roosevelt did not wait until the war was over to join other nations in taking first steps toward creating a new international organization designed to keep the peace. He made more effort than Wilson had to cultivate the support of prominent Republican senators, but it is also true that he benefited as Wilson had not from a change of outlook that led commentators to speak of the 'conversion' of prewar isolationists like Senator Arthur Vandenberg. Pearl Harbor, Vandenberg said later, 'drove most of us to the irresistible conclusion that world peace is indivisible. We learned that the oceans are no longer moats around our ramparts. We learned that mass destruction is a progressive science which defies both time and space and reduces human flesh and blood to cruel impotence.' Allied leaders engaged in drafting proposals for a postwar international organization, and in August 1944 their representatives met at Dumbarton Oaks, in Washington, D.C., and drew up the blueprint for the Charter of the United Nations.

All prospects for the success of this legatee of the League of Nations hinged on whether the two powers that would dominate the postwar world—the United States and the Soviet Union—could reach an accommodation. Roosevelt saw clearly the importance of Russian co-operation to assure peace after the defeat of the Axis; he did not see so clearly the forces militating against such co-operation. During the war, American publicists depicted Stalin as a lovable pipe-smoking uncle; in fact, he united, as one knowledgeable Communist said, 'the senselessness of a Caligula with the refinement of a Borgia and the brutality of a Czar Ivan the Terrible.' Still, even the most benign Russian leader might well have insisted on safeguarding his nation's western border from another German assault, and here lay the seeds of future conflict with the West. At times Roosevelt appeared to accept the idea of a Soviet sphere of influence in eastern Europe. When the leaders of the Big Three powers met at Teheran in 1943, Roosevelt told Stalin that he 'did not intend to go to war with the Soviet Union' over its subjugation of the Baltic nations, and also agreed that Russia's Polish boundary should be shifted westward. On the other hand, Roosevelt persisted in believing that the peoples of eastern Europe should also have the right to their own governments, freely chosen. Furthermore, Roosevelt had to bear in mind the possibility of a backlash at his party from voters of eastern European extraction if he made too many concessions to Stalin. The Russians, on the other hand, could not comprehend why, when America could roam all the rest of the world, it begrudged the USSR a small sphere on its borders, or why the West claimed the right to meddle in eastern Europe when it barred the Soviet Union from Italy. Roosevelt hoped that these frictions would yield to the emollient of wartime comradeship, and that particular misunderstandings could be cleared up by personal consultations, and to this end he went to Teheran and to Yalta.

The Yalta Conference of February 1945 in the Crimea appeared to have achieved the end to which Roosevelt so ardently looked. Of primary importance was Russia's agreement to enter the war against Japan 'within two or three months' of the defeat of Germany. In return the USSR was promised the Kurile Islands, the southern half of Sakhalin, and privileges in Manchuria and at Port Arthur and Dairen. Stalin acquiesced in the American formula for the admission of Latin

American states to the United Nations, withdrew his preposterous demand for 16 votes in the General Assembly, agreed to permit France a zone of occupation in Germany, accepted the reparation figure as tentative only, and—presumably—left open to further negotiation the reorganization of the Polish government. Roosevelt and Churchill conceded the Curzon line as Russia's western boundary, accepted a tentative reparations figure far beyond what they thought proper, promised the USSR three votes in the General Assembly, and left open for future negotiation such thorny questions as Soviet rights in the Dardanelles and in Iran, the future of the Baltic countries, and the disposition of Italian colonies. 'We really believed in our hearts,' said Roosevelt's aide Harry Hopkins, 'that this was the dawn of the new day we had all been praying for and talking about for so many years.'

Yet, in truth, Yalta had revealed the rudiments of much of the discord that would bedevil the postwar world. Later Yalta came to be regarded as a sellout to the Kremlin by a sick Roosevelt manipulated by pro-Communist advisers, but in reality the West conceded nothing substantial that Russian armies could not have taken anyway. Roosevelt's fault lay rather in leading the American people to expect that fundamental difficulties had been readily resolved. Eastern Europe remained a bleeding sore, especially after the Polish government in exile in London charged, with good reason, that the Russians had murdered thousands of Polish officers whose bodies were found in the Katyn Forest, and had permitted the courageous Warsaw underground fighters to be slaughtered by the Nazis when Soviet forces could have gone to their aid. Though Stalin promised 'free and unfettered elections' in Poland, he had no intention of tolerating an open choice in the eastern European nations. As he later said, 'A freely elected government in any of these countries would be anti-Soviet, and that we cannot allow.' In April 1945, shortly before his death, Roosevelt expressed to Stalin his 'astonishment,' 'anxiety,' and 'bitter resentment' over Russia's 'discouraging lack of application' of the Yalta protocols.

Roosevelt died on 12 April, but invitations had already gone out for a United Nations Conference to meet at San Francisco to draft a charter for the new organization, and late in that month delegates from 50 nations gathered at that city whose very choice suggested the new importance of the Pacific area. The conference, which lasted for two months, was marked by many sharp disagreements over such matters as the Polish delegation, but it ended on a note of surface harmony with all 50 nations signing the Charter.

The United Nations Charter provided for a General Assembly in which each nation had one vote, and whose functions were largely deliberative, and a Security Council of five permanent and six elected members, which alone had power to act in international disputes. It permitted any one of the five great powers (the United States, Britain, Russia, France, and China) to exercise a veto on any but procedural questions, and it authorized the use of force against aggressor nations.[1] So far had the United States moved away from traditional isolationism that the Senate ratified the document on 28 July 1945 with only two votes in opposition.

Launched with high hopes, the United Nations soon ran into the dangerous waters of the East-West conflict. Nonetheless, in the first few years of its existence it had some accomplishments to its credit. It succeeded in settling—after a fashion—three major disputes: that between Russia and Iran, the problems connected with the emergence of Israel as a nation, and the inflammable Indonesia issue. Furthermore, it served—in Senator Vandenberg's phrase—as a 'town meeting of the world,' and such agencies as the International Labor Organization performed useful services. Yet the United Nations unquestionably disappointed those who had hoped that it would succeed where the League had failed. The ostensible difficulty was the veto; designed for use only in

1. The Charter also created a number of other agencies: an International Court of Justice with powers comparable to those formerly exercised by the World Court; an Economic and Social Council to promote social and cultural welfare and human rights; a trusteeship system to replace the unsatisfactory mandate system of the old League; a permanent Secretariat. Under the Economic and Social Council there was a proliferation of special agencies—UNESCO, a Food and Agriculture Organization, an International Labor Organization, a World Health Organization, and eventually many others of a technical character.

President Harry S. Truman at Mackinac Island in a typically jaunty posture. (*Elliot Erwitt—Magnum*)

emergencies, it was invoked by Russia some fifty times in the first four years, often for purposes that were trivial. But the real difficulty of the United Nations was not mechanical but substantial: the division of the world into hostile camps led by the United States and the Soviet Union. For within an ominously brief period after the end of World War II, the two great powers had come to a total impasse.

Truman and the Cold War

When, on 12 April 1945, Franklin D. Roosevelt died and the Vice-President took the oath of office as President, there were some who affected to ask, 'Who is Harry S. Truman?' just as a century earlier some had asked, 'Who is James K. Polk?' Yet if Truman lacked the renown and the imposing presence of FDR, he came to the presidency with longer experience in politics than Theodore Roosevelt, Woodrow Wilson, or Herbert Hoover, and as Chief Executive revealed a continuing capacity for growth. He frequently spoke, and acted, impulsively, a quality that caused him grief in the handling of crises both at home and abroad. Intensely loyal to his friends, he was inclined to overlook even their more flagrant shortcomings. Too often he surrounded himself with men unsympathetic to the cause he espoused. But these failings were matched by corresponding virtues: boldness, decisiveness, and courage. Truman's domestic record, which seemed modest by comparison with that of his predecessor, came to seem more respectable when compared with that of his successor, and few Presidents did so much to shape American foreign policy as did this unassuming man from Missouri.

Truman came to power just as Soviet-American distrust was congealing, and he was determined to prove himself a strong President who would brook no nonsense from the Kremlin. Within a day after he entered the White House, he was telling his Secretary of State, 'We must stand up to the Russians at this point and not be easy on them.' Before the month was out, he was chewing out Molotov for not keeping pledges. 'I have never been talked to like that in my life,' said the Russian foreign minister. 'Carry out your agreements,' Truman replied, 'and you won't get talked to like that!' By January 1946 Truman was writing his Secretary of State: 'Unless Russia is faced with an iron fist and strong language another war is in the making. Only one language do they understand—"how many divisions have you?" . . . I'm tired of babying the Soviets.' Two months later he accompanied Sir Winston Churchill to Fulton, Missouri, where the former Prime Minister declared: 'From Stettin in the Baltic to Trieste in the Adriatic, an iron curtain has descended across the Continent.'

Much of the disagreement between the USSR and the West centered on policy toward their defeated enemy, Germany, despite elaborate efforts to agree on a common course. Wartime meetings of the Allies had worked out the basic principles for the treatment of Germany after the war: the destruction of German militarism and military potential; the dissolution of the Nazi party and the punishment of war criminals;[2] creation of occupation zones; readjustment of Germany's eastern border to compensate Poland for territory lost to Russia; and the payment of reparations 'to the greatest extent possible.' At the Potsdam Conference, held in July 1945, Truman, Stalin, and Clement Attlee—who had replaced Churchill as spokesman for the British government—decided that notwithstanding the division into occupation zones, Germany should be treated as an economic unit; but also provided that each occupying power should take reparations from its own zone and that, in addition, the USSR might receive reparations in the form of industrial equipment from the Western sectors in exchange for food and other products from its zone. Eastern Germany was assigned to Russia; northwestern Germany to Britain; southwestern Germany to the United States; while France received two smaller areas, Baden and the Saar. Austria, too, was carved up into four occupation zones, and both Berlin and Vienna were parceled out to the victors.

The principle of treating Germany as an economic unit broke down almost immediately. The

2. Postwar trials before an International Military Tribunal at Nuremberg resulted in death sentences for twelve high Nazi officials, including Goering and Ribbentrop, and the sentence of death was pronounced at trials of lesser Nazi leaders too.

Russians stripped their own zone and made heavy demands for factories, power plants, rolling stock, and tools in the British and American zones. But the Potsdam declaration had included a precautionary clause to the effect that the conquerors 'should leave enough resources to enable the German people to subsist without external assistance.' If Britain and the United States permitted their zones to be gutted, Germany would become a permanent burden on their taxpayers. Furthermore, if the industrial potential of the Ruhr and the Saar were destroyed, the consequences for European recovery generally would be disastrous. On 3 May 1946, almost exactly one year after the German surrender, General Lucius Clay, deputy American commander in Germany, announced an open break between the victors when he halted delivery of reparations to the Soviet zone. To the Russians it seemed unreasonable that when their country had been bled by the war (in Leningrad alone, 600,000 civilians had starved to death during a prolonged siege) the United States, which had emerged more prosperous than ever, should hamper their drive for economic reconstruction. Furthermore, the Russians were alarmed that the West was deliberately rebuilding the economy, and hence the war-making potential, of their hereditary Teutonic foe. To the West it was no less unsettling that Stalin was violating the spirit and the letter of wartime agreements, creating a permanent Communist regime in his temporary zone of occupation, and insisting on leaving Germany so impoverished that the prospects for a thriving world economy were seriously jeopardized.

In a speech at Stuttgart in September 1946, Secretary of State Byrnes enunciated the Truman administration's 'get tough' policy. Although he offered the USSR a forty-year security treaty, Byrnes plainly implied that he no longer contemplated agreement with the Russians over Germany. The United States, which had started out determined to reduce Germany's industrial potential, would henceforth seek to spur the country's economic revival. To that end, the British and American zones were fused on 1 January 1947. So within less than two years after the defeat of Hitler's Reich, Germany was being divided into two nations, one owing its allegiance to Russia, the other to the West.

In these same months, another East-West dispute erupted over the atomic bomb. Truman recognized the fact that the United States monopoly of 'the ultimate weapon' gave it a decided diplomatic advantage. Nonetheless, American officials were fully cognizant of the menace to peace that the A-bomb constituted, and were prepared to share control. In March 1946, the United States put forth a plan, formulated by two committees headed by Dean Acheson and David Lilienthal. It called for the creation of an International Atomic Development Authority, which should have exclusive control over raw materials such as uranium and over every stage of the production of atomic energy throughout the world, and should act as custodian of atomic weapons and stockpiles of fissionable materials. At its first session the General Assembly of the United Nations had created an Atomic Energy Commission to consist of representatives from all eleven members of the Security Council plus Canada. President Truman appointed Bernard Baruch as American representative on this commission, and in June 1946 Baruch presented a proposal that incorporated the main features of the Acheson-Lilienthal Plan plus provision for rigid international inspection and for the elimination of the veto in cases involving illegal manufacture of atomic bombs. Under the Baruch Plan, the proposed International Atomic Development Authority, which would control the whole field of atomic energy, would concern itself not only with the prevention of the manufacture of atomic weapons but with the production of atomic energy for peaceful purposes. If this program were adopted, the United States stood ready to destroy its stock of atom bombs, stop further manufacture of bombs, and share its scientific knowledge with the rest of the world.

The United Nations Atomic Energy Commission endorsed the American plan by a vote of 10–0; the USSR and Poland abstained. Russia rejected it for several reasons: inspection would be an intolerable invasion of national sovereignty, and the suspension of the veto would destroy the unanimity principle that was the basis of the Security Council. They also objected that the plan would give the United States the advantage of knowing how to make an atomic bomb while restricting experimentation by other countries. Fur-

Bikini, 25 July 1946, the world's first underwater blast of a nuclear weapon. Though the explosion sent up a towering column of water, neither this test nor one a few weeks earlier at the Pacific atoll seemed as awe-inspiring as had been expected. Only afterwards did scientists realize how widely dispersed was the radioactive debris. 'The most improbable objects turned out to be thoroughly charged—a ship's bell of brass, some chemicals from a first-aid locker on a deck, a bar of soap that had been caught in a stream of neutrons,' Eric Goldman has written. 'Rocks miles away were found tainted by fission products. Fish that had been near the fleet area and fish that had eaten the deadly fish spread over huge areas of the Pacific. On the ships themselves, nothing—soap, scrubbing, the best of Navy profanity—nothing short of sandblasting off the whole outer surface got rid of the deadly material.' (*U.S. Air Force Photo*)

Albert Einstein (1879–1955) and J. Robert Oppenheimer (1904–67), by Alfred Eisenstaedt. Both Einstein, whose 1905 equation $E = mc^2$ provided the theoretical foundation for nuclear fission, and Oppenheimer, who as director of the Los Alamos Science Laboratory was known as 'the father of the atomic bomb,' expressed misgivings over the race to build bigger and bigger nuclear devices. Eisenstaedt was already an established photographer in Europe before he came to America in 1935, when he almost immediately joined the staff of the new picture magazine *Life.* Although Eisenstaedt was not, as he is often said to be, 'the father of photojournalism,' a description that better fits earlier artists like Lewis Hine, he did contribute to *Life* close to two thousand picture stories, many of distinction. (*Alfred Eisenstaedt LIFE Magazine © Time Inc.*)

thermore, the United States would almost certainly control the international atomic agency. Gromyko proposed instead the immediate destruction of all atom bombs and the prohibition of the manufacture of atomic weapons. Such a scheme was unacceptable to the West, for it required the surrender by the United States of its advantage, and, in the absence of inspection, gave no corresponding assurance that Russia would not proceed secretly to make atomic weapons. With the great powers unable to agree, the United Nations Atomic Energy Commission suspended its deliberations.

When the Russians detonated an atomic device in September 1949, and the United States, a few months later, announced plans for a hydrogen bomb, a thousandfold as powerful as the atomic bomb, the quest for effective international control assumed a new urgency. Speaking with deep solemnity, the venerable philosopher-scientist Albert Einstein, who had originally called President Roosevelt's attention to the potentialities of nuclear fission, warned the world,

> The armament race between the U.S.A. and the U.S.S.R., originally supposed to be a preventive measure, assumes hysterical character. On both sides, the means to mass destruction are perfected with feverish haste, behind respective walls of secrecy. The H-bomb appears on the public horizon as a probably attainable goal. . . . If successful, radio-active poisoning of the atmosphere and hence annihilation of any life on earth has been brought within the range of technical possibilities. The ghost-like character of this development lies in its apparently compulsory trend. Every step appears as the unavoidable consequence of the preceding one. In the end, there beckons more and more clearly general annihilation.

Although the differences over weapons control and over policy toward Germany had serious repercussions, the first actual showdowns between Russia and the West took place in the Mediterranean and the Near East. In March 1946, the United States forced Russia to withdraw its troops from oil-rich Iran, but within a year there was a new crisis in Greece where Communist guerillas supported by Soviet satellites, were threatening a conservative monarchy backed by the British, and in Turkey where the USSR was exerting pressure on the Dardanelles. On 24 February 1947 the British informed the American government that they could no longer carry the burden and proposed to pull out. Rarely in history had there been so dramatic a moment when one nation turned over responsibilities of empire to another.

On 12 March, Truman sent a message to Congress embodying not only a request for appropriations for Greece and Turkey, but what came to be known as the Truman Doctrine: 'that it must be the policy of the United States to support free peoples who are resisting attempted subjugation by armed minorities or by outside pressures.' Congress voted the money—eventually close to $700 million—and American power moved into the vacuum created by Britain in the Near East. After prolonged fighting the Greek guerillas were beaten, Turkish defenses were strengthened, and the situation in the Mediterranean was stabilized. But a perilous precedent had been established—that the United States would arm any regime, no matter how reactionary, that was threatened by Communists or by forces thought to be Communist. Even more troublesome were the implications of Truman's speech—that the menace of Communism was global and that the United States was prepared to intervene anywhere in the world.

In July 1947 *Foreign Affairs* published an article under the enigmatic signature of 'X' which took a hard-headed view of Russian-American relations. 'X,' shortly revealed to be one of the State Department's veteran Russian experts, George Kennan, warned that, at least for some time to come, there could 'never be on Moscow's side any sincere assumption of a community of aims between the Soviet Union and powers which are regarded as capitalist.' In enunciating what came to be known as the 'containment' policy, Kennan argued that it must be made clear to the USSR that expansion beyond a given perimeter would be met with force. Kennan stressed:

> The United States has it in its power to increase enormously the strains under which the Soviet policy must operate, to force upon the Kremlin a far greater degree of moderation and circumspection than it has had to observe in recent years, and in this way to promote tendencies which must eventually find their outlet in

The Cold War: Soviet version. In this Russian cartoon, an armed, filthy-rich American soldier overwhelms a European continent pockmarked with U.S. bases. In his hip pocket an American propagandist, waving an olive branch at the same time that yet another American base is being established in Greece, spouts hypocritical slogans. (*Library of Congress*)

The Cold War: American version. In this cartoon by Milt Morris for the Associated Press, an avaricious Russian bear, a red star on his cap, salivates as he paws the entire globe. (*Wide World*)

either the breakup or the gradual mellowing of Soviet policy.[3]

Kennan, who thought the Truman Doctrine too negative an application of the containment doctrine, made an important contribution to a more imaginative development in American foreign policy: the Marshall Plan. In 1947 a policy-planning staff headed by Kennan recommended short-term aid to halt deterioration of the European economy and a long-range program looking to European economic integration. Speaking at a Harvard Commencement in June, Secretary of State Marshall advanced these recommendations by advising Europe to work out a joint plan for reconstruction and pledging full co-operation by the United States.

Marshall's speech came at a time when much of western Europe approached economic breakdown. By 1947 the world owed the United States $11.5 billion for goods it had acquired but could not pay for. Europe needed everything but was able to buy nothing; the United States had—or was capable of producing—almost everything, but could sell nothing to a bankrupt Europe. If the European economy collapsed, the American economy would take a tailspin. Moreover, if the United States stood idly by while western Europe plunged into economic chaos, it would be faced, in a few years, with a Soviet-dominated continent. Truman's abrupt and ill-considered termination of lend-lease in 1945 had precipitated a serious economic crisis in Britain, whose resources had been drained by the war. To ward off a catastrophe, Congress voted a substantial loan which, it was hoped, would carry Britain through the next five years. But despite heroic efforts, the money ran out in two years, and by 1947 Britain again confronted economic disaster. In March 1947, as UNRRA came to an end just when Europe was buffeted by a vicious winter, the people of western Europe faced starvation. So critical was the coal shortage in England that, for hours every day, London shut off electric power. The financial editor of Reuter's wrote: 'The biggest crash since the fall of Constantinople—the collapse of the heart of an Empire—impends.' The political consequences of the impending disaster would be as serious as the economic cost. Europe, wrote Churchill, was 'a rubble heap, a charnel house, a breeding ground of pestilence and hate.'

The invitation from Marshall found an instantaneous response. The Prime Ministers of Britain and France promptly issued an invitation to 22 nations, including Russia, to meet at Paris the following month to draw a blueprint for European recovery. Though Molotov came to Paris to discuss preliminaries, the Kremlin decided it was unwise to take part in a project that would extend American influence in Europe. Molotov withdrew, and all the Soviet satellites followed. In the end representatives of 16 nations, under the leadership of the Oxford philosopher Sir Oliver Franks, drafted an elaborate plan for European recovery, which fixed new production targets and set other economic goals.

In December 1947 President Truman asked Congress to further these ambitious aims by appropriating $17 billion over a four-year period. Opposition to the proposal, led by Senator Taft, came chiefly from those who felt that the American economy could not stand so heavy a burden. Liberals of both parties as well as powerful business, farm, and labor organizations rallied to the bill, whose leading senatorial champion was Arthur Vandenberg, architect of the bipartisan foreign policy. What finally turned the tide was not so much economic arguments as the Communist coup in Czechoslovakia in March 1948, together with new Russian demands on Finland and the fear of Communist success in the forthcoming Italian elections. A program to halt the advance of Communism appealed to many who were immune to an appeal on economic or humanitarian grounds, and the Foreign Assistance Act—providing an immediate grant of $5.3 billion for European recovery plus $463 million for China and $275 million for Greece and Turkey—passed both houses of Congress by big majorities and became law on 3 April 1948.

The Marshall Plan mounted the most effective counterattack on poverty, despair, and disintegration in modern history. Altogether Congress voted some $12 billion to carry it out. Critics had

3. *Foreign Affairs,* July 1947.

The Marshall Plan, Berlin. The German signboard announces that Marshall Plan aid is supporting the city's Emergency Works Program (*Berliner Notprogramm*). The photograph was taken in the early spring of 1952, seven years after American planes reduced much of the former German capital to rubble. (*National Archives*)

predicted that the enterprise would bankrupt the United States; instead the country enjoyed unparalleled prosperity, in part because Marshall Plan funds, like almost every cent of subsequent 'foreign aid,' had to be spent in the United States for American products. Moreover, by 1951 the administration could point to an over-all increase of production in Marshall-aid countries of 37 per cent. As the economy rebounded, so did the confidence of the peoples of western Europe, not only in their ability to fend for themselves but in their democratic institutions.

However, if the Marshall Plan succeeded in reviving western Europe, it also served to deepen divisions between the United States and Russia. In April 1947, in a speech at Columbia, South Carolina, Bernard Baruch had declared: 'Let us not be deceived—today we are in the midst of a cold war.' Increasingly, American institutions—the government, the corporation, the university, the foundation—were called into the service of the Cold War, and economic aid, too, came chiefly to be a weapon in that war. At the outset, Congress stipulated that not one penny of Marshall Plan aid was to be used for military purposes. In less than three years the United States was informing Europe that every cent of aid would be allotted so as to contribute to Western defenses.[4]

This new military posture resulted in large part from concern over Soviet aggressiveness in Germany. The Russians had been disturbed when the French fused their zone with the British and the American zones to create a 'Trizonia' with the richest industrial resources in Germany and a population of 50 million which outstripped the Soviet zone's 17 million. In the spring of 1948 the Western powers alarmed the Kremlin by inviting the Germans to elect delegates to a convention to create a new government for West Germany. (Subsequently, in May 1949, the German Federal Republic was established at Bonn.) When in June 1948 the Allies carried out a drastic currency reform that triggered a remarkable economic revival for western Germany, the Russians retaliated on 24 June by clamping a tight blockade around Berlin. Through some inexplicable oversight the Western powers had not guaranteed access to their zones of Berlin, and as a result the Russians were able to cut all land communication by erecting road blocks and stopping railroad trains.

Confronted with the alternatives of mass starvation for the 2 million Germans of the western zones of Berlin or an ignominious evacuation of that city, the American and British governments rejected both. They also spurned the temptation to ram an armored train through the Russian blockade, for this might have precipitated general war. Instead they embarked upon an 'airlift' operation to supply the beleaguered capital not only with food but with coal and other necessities. To the consternation of the Russians the airlift was a spectacular success: American and British planes dropped 2.5 million tons of provisions into the city. On 12 May 1949, outwitted by the West, Russia ended the blockade.

The Berlin crisis and the Czech coup prompted negotiations for a military alliance that would weld western Europe into a unified military force. The Brussels Pact of 1948, joining Britain, France, and the Benelux nations in a defensive alliance, provided the springboard. In April 1949 the North Atlantic Treaty brought together the United States, Canada, and ten nations of western Europe in an alliance against aggression; eventually it embraced other nations as well. The treaty pledged that an armed attack against any one member would be considered an attack upon them all. Never before had the United States gone so far in a practical surrender of part of its sovereign power, or so clearly recognized that its frontier henceforth lay overseas along the lines that divided non-Communist nations from the Soviet Union.

A military assistance program gave the North Atlantic Treaty Organization (NATO) authority to spend over a billion dollars on military needs. From 1945 to 1950 the armed services had been reduced from 12 million to well below one million. But in 1946 a peacetime draft had been instituted temporarily, and in 1948 it became a regular feature of American life. The NATO pact encouraged an increase in the size of America's armed forces, and United States troops were stationed in Europe. In 1950 the first American shipments of arms reached Europe, and within a few years West Germany's armed forces were integrated into the NATO army. Not surprisingly, Russia looked upon the creation of NATO as a declaration of hostility and upon the re-arming of Germany as an act of defiance.

Reconversion, Reaction, and Reform

Truman not only had to lead the country in the final months of the war but guide it through the difficult transition from war to peace. Fortunately, reconversion presented fewer problems than had been anticipated, and the postwar depression many had feared never materialized. Nor was there a re-enactment of the Harding melodrama. However, the political stalemate that had begun with the waning of the New Deal in 1938 persisted in the era of the Cold War and the age of affluence.

Unlike the aftermath of World War I, the Tru-

4. When the United States set up 'Point Four' (named after the fourth point of Truman's inaugural address of 1949), the program began as a modest venture in providing technological aid to underdeveloped nations, but by 1951 had been brought under the Mutual Security Act as another weapon in the Cold War arsenal.

The Berlin airlift, 1948. German children watch from a hillside as a U.S. plane approaches Tempelhof airport. A Berlin clerk wrote: 'Every two minutes a plane arrives from West Germany, loaded with food for West Berlin! The sound of engines can be heard constantly in the air, and is the most beautiful music to our ears. One could stand for hours on the Tempelhof elevated station platform and watch the silver birds landing and taking off.' Forty-eight men were killed in the joint American-British effort to provision a city which little more than three years before had been the capital of the Third Reich and the object of relentless Allied bombing. 'When the first victims of the combined airlift were reported, we grieved about these young men as much as if they had been our own,' reflected a Berliner. 'Nobody wanted to mention that perhaps it had been the same boy who had presented us with a quite different variety of cargo a few years before, and whom we then quietly cursed.' (*National Archives*)

man years saw a continuation and expansion of wartime prosperity. In the five years after the war, national income increased from $181 billion to $241 billion. In 1935 over one-half the workers of the country earned less than $1000; by 1950 only one-tenth of the workers were in this unhappy category. Farmers, too, continued to enjoy unprecedented prosperity. Total farm income in 1948 was over $30 billion as compared with $11 billion in 1941 and $5.5 billion in 1933. As a consequence, farm tenancy fell to the lowest point in the twentieth century. In 1935 only 6 per cent of American families enjoyed an income of over $3000 a year; by 1950 half of all families earned over $3000 a year, though, to be sure, a sharp increase in the cost of living qualified these statistics.

What was the explanation of this phenomenon of postwar prosperity? It was, in part, the pent-up demand for goods after five years of war; in part, the market for American surpluses assured by the program of relief and reconstruction abroad; in part, the explosive increase in private investment; in part, the continuation of heavy government spending. At the depth of the depression the Federal Government had spent about $9 billion; five years after the war the Federal budget ran over $40 billion. The government cushioned the shock of the transition from the armed services to civilian life by providing mustering-out pay, unemployment pay for one year, civil-service preferment, insurance and loans for home building and the purchase of farms or businesses. Eventually some 12 million veterans took advantage of the education subsidies of the 'G.I. Bill of Rights.'

Yet if reconversion went more smoothly than had been expected, Truman nonetheless faced one grievous problem: inflation. Manufacturers and farmers, who had bridled at wartime controls, wanted to exploit a sellers' market, and consumers, their pockets bulging, demanded goods that had been denied them during the war. The President was expected both to get rid of controls and prevent inflation, and he could anticipate political reprisals if he failed to achieve this impossible assignment. While Roosevelt in the depression years had been able to distribute benefits to interest groups as a part of his recovery program, Truman had to discipline interest groups at the very time when peace encouraged them to expect new gains. When Truman sided with John Snyder, a conservative Missouri banker whom he had named director of the Office of War Mobilization and Reconversion, against Chester Bowles, the OPA administrator who represented the consumer, he antagonized New Deal liberals who wanted to keep a tight lid on prices. FDR's followers had been impressed when in September 1945 Truman outlined a twenty-one point program of far-reaching reforms, but they were dismayed by Truman's support of Snyder and his appointment of other conservatives to his cabinet and the Supreme Court. Before long, Roosevelt stalwarts like Harold Ickes had fled the government in protest.

However, when Truman did take a firmer stand against inflation, he added to his difficulties with the liberal wing of his party because he ran into a head-on conflict with union labor. After the war, fear of rising costs of living and the prospect of a return to the 40-hour week with consequent loss of overtime pay brought a demand for substantial wage increases. Within a month after victory over Japan half a million workers were out on strike, while 1946 saw a loss of 116 million man-days of work. On 1 April 1946 John L. Lewis led 400,000 coal miners out of the pits, and for forty days the strike cut off the nation's supply of fuel and threatened European recovery. On 21 May, after a brief truce, the government took over the mines. When Lewis refused to order his men back to work, a Federal court slapped the union with a fine of $3.5 million, later reduced to $700,000. Nonetheless, Lewis eventually won almost all of his demands. If Truman did not find some way to call a halt, wages and prices threatened to chase one another up to the sky.

When in the midst of the coal crisis railway union leaders threatened the first total strike on the roads since 1894, the President seized the railroads to head it off. But in defiance of the President the rail workers walked out, marooning 90,000 passengers and stopping 25,000 freight cars, many of them loaded with perishables. On 25 May, Truman went before Congress to ask for authority to draft strikers into the army. Since the strike was settled that day, he never had an opportunity to carry out this threat, but he had shocked liberals and severed his ties with union leaders. Yet when Congress enacted a milder labor measure, Truman irked conservatives by vetoing it. The politics of inflation was costing the President support at both ends of the political spectrum.

Five weeks after Truman's threat to draft the rail strikers, he confronted a showdown on price control, for on 1 July 1946 the authority of the OPA would expire. When just before the deadline Congress passed a bill which eviscerated the OPA, Truman vetoed it, although this left the nation temporarily with no controls. In two weeks prices jumped 25 per cent, more than in the previous three years. After Congress enacted a new measure, stockmen held back their cattle, and meat all but disappeared. Truman's popularity fell from a peak of 87 per cent to 32 per cent, and Republicans jeered at 'Horsemeat Harry.' On 14 October the President announced he had no alternative but to take off controls on meat, but when meat returned to the butcher's counter, housewives were incensed to find that it commanded sharply increased prices.

At the height of national annoyance over the price control controversy, the country went to the polls in the 1946 elections. Exasperated by high prices and shortages, voters gave the Republicans their first majority in Congress since 1930. They sent to the Senate for the first time that year such conservatives as John Bricker of Ohio and the little known Joseph McCarthy, who toppled the La Follette dynasty in Wisconsin, and to the House young Richard Nixon. The election was interpreted as a brutal repudiation of Truman's leadership. Democratic Senator William Fulbright of Arkansas advised the President to name a Republican successor and resign from office. Truman rejected this gratuitous advice, but four days after the election he removed most of the remaining controls.

The 1946 elections gave the Republicans an opportunity to demonstrate that they were a party of moderation, but the 80th Congress misinterpreted the vote, which reflected a momentary impatience over reconversion, as a mandate reaction. It not only rejected Truman's recommendations to raise the minimum wage and extend social security coverage but turned down modest proposals by Republican Senator Robert Taft of Ohio for Federal action in education and housing. Bricker complained: 'I hear the Socialists have gotten to Taft.' While performing creditably on foreign affairs, the 80th Congress antagonized farmers by failing to provide adequate crop-storage facilities, Westerners by slashing funds for power and reclamation, and ethnic groups by enacting an anti-Semitic, anti-Catholic displaced persons law. When the lifting of controls resulted in a price rise from 1946 to 1947 greater than in all of World War II, people on fixed incomes were caught in the inflationary squeeze.

If Senator Taft differed with the Bricker wing of his party on some welfare measures, he shared their determination to curb organized labor. The Taft-Hartley Act of 1947 outlawed the closed shop and the secondary boycott; made unions liable for breach of contract or damages resulting from jurisdictional disputes; required a 60-day cooling-off period for strikes; authorized an 80-day injunction against strikes that might affect national health or safety; forbade political contributions from unions, featherbedding, and excessive dues; required union leaders to take a non-Communist oath; and set up a conciliation service outside the Labor Department, which was suspected of being too friendly to labor. When Truman vetoed the bill, Congress re-enacted it by thumping majorities. The Taft-Hartley law drove organized labor back into Truman's arms, and in 1948 union members returned to private life many Republican supporters of the act, including Representative Hartley.

The Republicans muffed an even more promising opportunity to capitalize on Democratic vulnerability when they failed to enact civil rights legislation and chose instead to coalesce with Southern Democrats to block reforms. It was President Truman who seized the initiative, in part because he understood that at a time when the United States was competing with Soviet Russia for the allegiance of the uncommitted nations events in Mississippi and Alabama were watched closely in Beirut and Karachi. In response to protest against a number of racial murders in the

South in 1946, Truman appointed a President's Committee on Civil Rights which in October 1947, after ten months of study, issued an historic report, 'To Secure These Rights.' In February 1948 Truman asked Congress to implement part of this report by approving a ten-point program which embraced a permanent Civil Rights Commission, a Federal Fair Employment Practices Act, and laws to protect the right to vote, do away with poll taxes, and prevent lynching. Spurned by the 80th Congress, Truman refused to back down. He increased the pace of desegregation of the armed forces and issued an executive order which stipulated that there was to be no discrimination in Federal employment. No President in at least seventy-five years had done so much for the cause of civil rights. Yet by his actions Truman infuriated Southern whites who feared that their social system was collapsing at a time when the Supreme Court was ruling restrictive covenants unenforceable and when Jackie Robinson was breaking the color line in baseball. The President appeared to have ensured his defeat in the 1948 election.

Only in the area of governmental reorganization did the 80th Congress make important contributions, and here, too, Truman played an important role. The Presidential Succession Act of 1947 provided that the Speaker of the House and the President pro tempore of the Senate should be next in line of presidential succession after the Vice-President. That same year Congress adopted a proposed Twenty-second Amendment limiting Presidents to two terms; the amendment was ratified in 1951, an indication of growing concern over presidential power. In 1947 Congress also established a commission which, headed by Herbert Hoover, pointed the way toward more effective governmental administration. Yet another act of 1947 unified the army, navy, and air force under a Secretary of Defense. The National Security Act also set up a National Security Council, a Central Intelligence Agency, and a National Security Resources Board, and gave legal status to the Joint Chiefs of Staff. That same year Congress created the Atomic Energy Commission.

The Truman years marked a transition from the informal personal presidency of the Roosevelt era to the institutionalized White House of Eisenhower. By 1947 the President was filing three separate messages to Congress: State of the Union, Budget, and Economic Report, the latter as a consequence of the Employment Act of 1946 which established a three-man Council of Economic Advisers. Although the main responsibility for economic decision-making was left in private hands, this law recognized a degree of government responsibility for the health of the economy, and in subsequent years the reports of the Council helped educate the country in the new economics. However, this innovation came only after the 80th Congress had gutted the original legislation.

Despite the generally dismal performance of the 80th Congress, the Republican victory in 1946 and subsequent rifts in the Democratic party convinced almost everyone that Truman could not win in 1948. When, over the opposition of the administration, which sought to unite the party on a moderate civil rights plank, the Democratic convention adopted a strong civil rights plank sponsored by Hubert Humphrey, the young mayor of Minneapolis, Mississippi and Alabama delegates, waving the battle flag of the Confederacy, marched out. Within a week the 'Dixiecrats' had organized a States Rights party with Governor J. Strom Thurmond of South Carolina as their presidential nominee.

At the same time that the Dixiecrats were cutting off one flank of the Democratic party, opponents of Truman's foreign policy were severing another. In September 1946 the President had dropped Henry Wallace from his cabinet because he had become too vocal a critic of the administration's Cold War tactics. In July 1948 his followers organized the Progressive party with Wallace as their candidate. Although the platform of the new party included such demands as the nationalization of basic industries, it centered its fire at the President's foreign policy. The party's uncritical attitude toward Soviet Russia deprived it of much of its potential support, but observers reckoned that Wallace would cut heavily into Truman's vote in the North.

The Republicans felt so confident as to nominate a former loser, Thomas E. Dewey, with the liberal governor of California, Earl Warren, as his

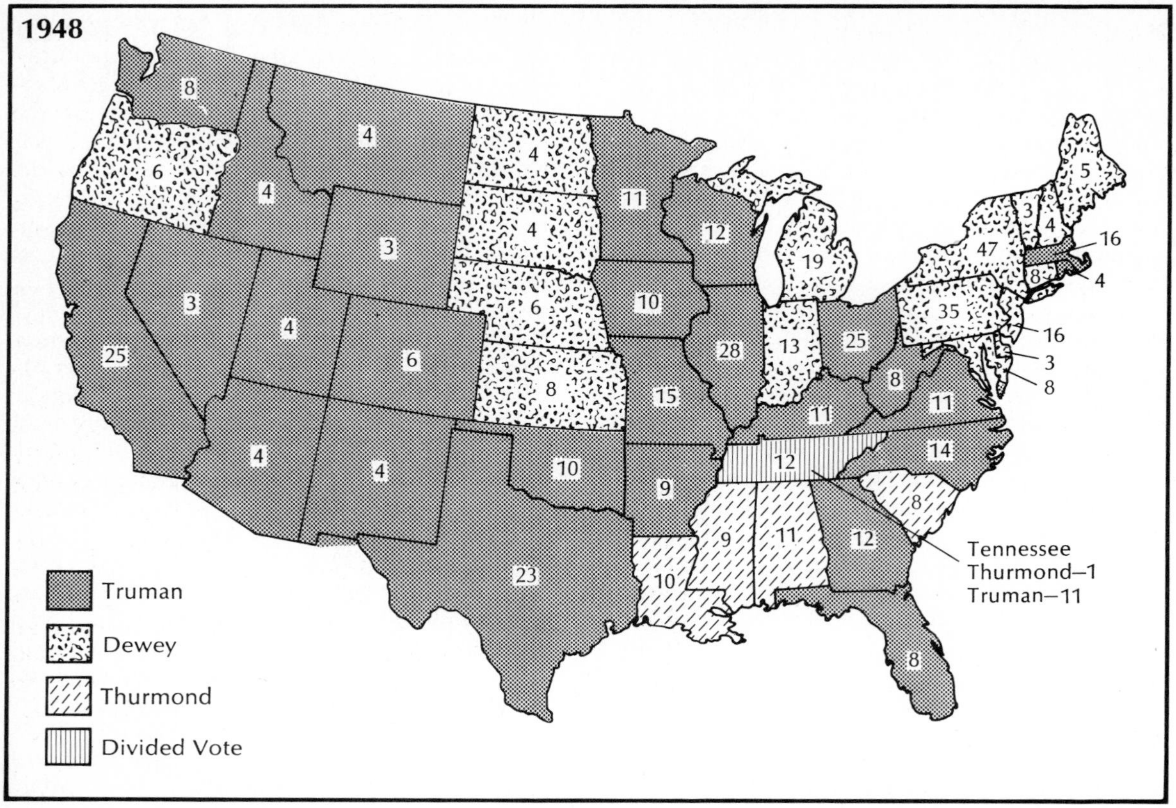

Presidential Election, 1948

running mate. Dewey ran a deliberately cautious campaign, during which he made such startling observations as 'We need a rudder to our ship of state and . . . a firm hand at the tiller,' 'Our streams should abound with fish,' and 'Our future lies before us.' Truman, on the other hand, made full use of the powers of his office to wage a vigorous campaign to remould the Roosevelt coalition. Throughout the election year he fired a series of messages to Congress calling for specific reforms, and that summer he summoned Congress back into a special session on 26 July, the day turnips are planted in Missouri. When the 'turnip Congress' did nothing, Truman was well on his way to making the issue of the campaign not Dewey's record but the performance of the 'do-nothing, good-for-nothing' 80th Congress. On a 22,000-mile 'give-em hell, Harry' whistle-stop tour, the President met an enthusiastic response. Still, almost every political expert, and pollsters like Gallup and Roper, predicted defeat for Truman.

To the astonishment of both prognosticators and the nation, Truman scored the biggest political upset of the century.[5] Thurmond captured four

5. The vote was:

	Popular	Per Cent	Electoral College
Truman	24,179,345	49.6	303
Dewey	21,991,291	45.1	189
Thurmond	1,176,125	2.4	39
Wallace	1,157,326	2.4	0

Southern states, and Wallace, while winning no electoral votes, deprived Truman of New York, Michigan, and Maryland. But the President ran well among workers, blacks, and farmers, many of whom resented the 80th Congress. Dewey had 'snatched defeat out of the jaws of victory,' while Truman, running as the candidate of the majority party in an election with a low turnout, got enough of the party faithful to the polls to prevail. The party also recaptured control of both houses of Congress; to the Senate came Humphrey of Minnesota, Estes Kefauver of Tennessee, and, by the tiny margin of 87 votes, Lyndon Johnson of Texas. The Roosevelt coalition, which had seemed shattered two years before, had taken a new lease on life.

The 81st Congress, which met for the first time in January 1949, enacted more liberal legislation than any Congress since 1938. It extended social security benefits; raised the minimum wage; expanded public power, rural electrification, soil conservation, and flood control projects; approved a more generous, but still inadequate, Displaced Persons Act; set up a National Science Foundation; and granted the President powers to cope with inflation. By adroitly exploiting middle-class dissatisfaction with the housing shortage, Truman put through a law which authorized new public housing for the slum-dweller. The National Housing Act of 1949 provided for the construction of 810,000 subsidized low-income housing units over the next six years, as well as grants for slum clearance and rural housing.

However, most of this legislation represented only extensions of New Deal measures; and when Truman tried to break new grounds for his 'Fair Deal,' he had little success. Congress bowed to the American Medical Association's campaign against the President's proposal for national health insurance, rejected a new approach to farm subsidies, and filibustered an FEPC bill to death. Federal aid to education was lost in an unhappy squabble over whether such aid should go to private and parochial schools. Truman also fought losing battles to extend the TVA principle to the Columbia and the Missouri river valleys, and was able to carry out no more than a delaying action to preserve for the United States the immensely valuable oil reserves under the 'tidelands.' He also vetoed a bill which would have raised the price of natural gas, even though the measure was supported by powerful elements in his own party.

Truman's troubles with Congress resulted largely from the insurmountable obstacles he faced, but also owed something to his own shortcomings as a legislative leader. Although genuinely interested in achieving change, he never could arouse the kind of popular enthusiasm for his proposals that a Roosevelt did. 'Alas for Truman,' wrote one commentator, 'there is no bugle note in his voice.' Nor did Truman take pains enough to cultivate good will among Congressmen. Much more significant, though, was the powerful opposition he confronted, especially the rural-based, bipartisan conservative coalition entrenched in the committee structure in Congress. In his final months in office Truman, his program frustrated, was reduced to fighting a rearguard action against those who wished to repeal the New Deal and was overwhelmed by an explosion of ill feeling that was fueled by irritation at an undeclared war in a part of the world to which most of the nation had given little heed.

The Korean War

While Americans were preoccupied with the problems of Europe, the Far East burst into flames. When Truman took over, he continued the Roosevelt policy of regarding China as the mainstay of American interests in Asia and of supporting the Nationalists against the Communists. However, the Chiang Kai-shek regime, corroded by corruption and without strong popular support, proved wholly unable to stem the tide of Chinese Communism. Efforts by the United States to reform and strengthen the Nationalist regime and to force some settlement of the Chinese civil war proved abortive. Early in 1946 General Marshall arranged a truce between the Nationalists and the Communists, but it was speedily violated by both sides. Exasperated with both factions, Marshall withdrew most of the American troops from China and washed his hands of the whole muddle. Though the United States continued to send military and financial aid to Nationalist China, Truman would not make a massive commitment to the Nationalists because he and his advisers did not believe that Chiang could be salvaged. By the end of 1949 the Communists had swept the whole of the mainland, and Chiang, with the remnant of his forces, had fled to the island of Formosa (Taiwan).

The 'fall' of China had a number of momentous consequences. By allying the 500 million Chinese with the Russians, it shifted the balance of power in the Cold War in Asia. It led to a fierce attack on the Truman administration from Republican 'Asia-firsters' and publicists like the Luce empire, fostered anxiety about subversion, helped bring the twenty-year reign of the Democrats to an end, and served to lock American policy in Asia in the matrix of an inflexible anti-Communism. The Democrats were vulnerable to criticism, for Roosevelt had led the country to believe that Nationalist China was a major power and some diplomats had misconceived the nature of the Communist threat. Yet, as John King Fairbank pointed out, 'The illusion that the United States could have shaped China's destiny assumes that we Americans can really call the tune if we want to, even among 475 million people in the inaccessible rice paddies of a subcontinent 10,000 miles away.' The administration, shocked by indignities to American consular officials and sensitive to criticism of its Asia policy, refused to recognize Red China and blocked attempts to admit Mao Tse-tung's government to the United Nations. And the 'loss' of China resulted in a dramatic reversal of American policy toward Japan.

At the end of World War II, the United States had but one aim in Japan: to make certain that the Japanese would never again constitute a military threat in Asia. To this end the American occupation authorities sought both to democratize Japan and to reduce that country to a second-rate power. Within a short time after the surrender, General MacArthur in co-operation with liberal elements in Japan destroyed Japanese military potential and inaugurated drastic reforms. Meantime an International Tribunal tried the leading war criminals and sentenced Prime Minister Tojo and a dozen of the leading generals to death for their part in war crimes and atrocities, while, as a result of action by local tribunals, no fewer than 720 high-ranking officers of the army and navy were executed. A new Diet, elected under a law permitting woman suffrage, drafted a democratic constitution that provided for popular sovereignty and parliamentary government, reduced the Emperor to a figurehead, and included a bill of rights. The United States took special pride in one provision of the constitution, written in part by Americans, which stipulated that 'the Japanese people forever renounce war as a sovereign right of the nation.'

With the fall of China, American policymakers did a complete about face. The United States now came to value Japan as a military counterweight against Red China. As a consequence, it took steps to help the Japanese win industrial supremacy in Asia. No longer did the Americans press Tokyo for a permanent renunciation of war; and when in 1951 the United States signed a treaty which formally ended World War II and the occupation, it put through another which permitted America to maintain troops and air bases on the Japanese islands.

The United States little reckoned that the focus of its attention would shortly become neither Japan nor China but Korea. After World War II that nation, which was annexed to Japan in 1910, had been divided temporarily along the 38th parallel into zones of occupation: the United States in the more populous south, and Russia in the north. All efforts at unification proved vain; the Russians set up a Communist regime in North Korea, while the Americans threw their support to the conservative Syngman Rhee, a kind of Korean Chiang Kai-shek, who in 1948 was elected President of a new republic in South Korea. However, even after the American military occupation came to an end, the nation continued to be a heavy drain on the American taxpayer, and in January 1950 when Secretary of State Acheson outlined a 'defensive perimeter' vital to national security, he included neither Korea nor Formosa.

On 25 June 1950, just five months after Acheson's 'perimeter' speech, North Korean troops launched a full-scale attack upon the South, and within three days they had seized the capital at Seoul and threatened to overrun the entire country. Once again, as at the time of the threat to

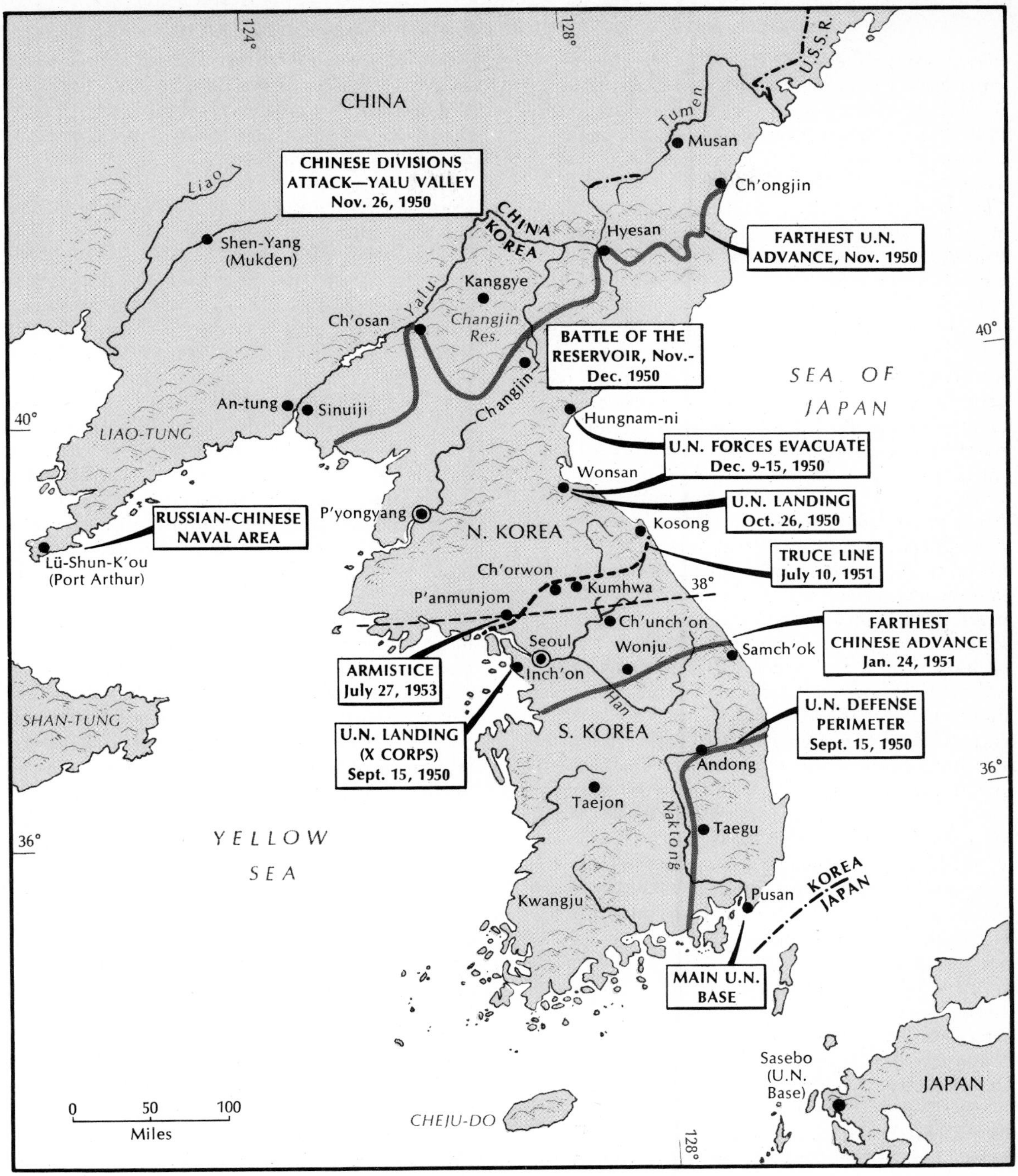
CHINA
U.S.S.R.
Tumen
Musan
Ch'ongjin
Liao
CHINESE DIVISIONS ATTACK—YALU VALLEY Nov. 26, 1950
CHINA
KOREA
Hyesan
FARTHEST U.N. ADVANCE, Nov. 1950
Shen-Yang (Mukden)
Kanggye
Yalu
Ch'osan
Changjin Res.
BATTLE OF THE RESERVOIR, Nov.-Dec. 1950
SEA OF JAPAN
An-tung
Sinuiji
Changjin
Hungnam-ni
LIAO-TUNG
U.N. FORCES EVACUATE Dec. 9-15, 1950
Wonsan
U.N. LANDING Oct. 26, 1950
P'yongyang
RUSSIAN-CHINESE NAVAL AREA
N. KOREA
Kosong
Lü-Shun-K'ou (Port Arthur)
TRUCE LINE July 10, 1951
Ch'orwon
Kumhwa
38°
P'anmunjom
Ch'unch'on
FARTHEST CHINESE ADVANCE Jan. 24, 1951
Seoul
Wonju
Samch'ok
ARMISTICE July 27, 1953
Inch'on
Han
U.N. DEFENSE PERIMETER Sept. 15, 1950
SHAN-TUNG
U.N. LANDING (X CORPS) Sept. 15, 1950
S. KOREA
Andong
Taejon
Naktong
Taegu
YELLOW SEA
Kwangju
Pusan
KOREA
JAPAN
MAIN U.N. BASE
Sasebo (U.N. Base)
JAPAN
CHEJU-DO
0 50 100
Miles
124°
128°
40°
36°

The Korean War, 1950–53

Berlin, Truman reacted decisively. The President reflected: 'I recalled some earlier instances: Manchuria, Ethiopia, Austria. I remembered how each time that the democracies failed to act it had encouraged the aggressors to go ahead. . . . If this was allowed to go unchallenged, it would mean a third world war.' On 27 June he announced that he was sending American air and naval forces to the aid of the South Koreans. That same day the United Nations Security Council—with Russia momentarily absent on a boycott—called on member nations to repel aggression in Korea, and before long the UN banner waved over a motley world army—the first of its kind in history. But since the United States sent more than five times as many troops as the rest of the world combined, most Americans regarded the conflict as a U.S. war.

For nearly six weeks North Korean armies advanced down the peninsula driving the outnumbered South Korean and American forces before them to the southernmost tip of Korea. There they held firm while reinforcements poured into the harbor of Pusan and General MacArthur, commander in chief of the United Nations forces, built up naval and air support. In mid-September, MacArthur carried out a daring amphibious landing at Inchon, the first engagement in a well-conceived counteroffensive that drove the North Koreans in full retreat to the north. On 26 September Seoul was once more in South Korean hands, and the United Nations armies were pounding on the North Korean border.

The United States had gone to war when North Koreans crossed the 38th parallel; would China go to war when South Koreans—and Americans—crossed it in the other direction? From the beginning, Truman had insisted that the intervention in Korea would be limited; he had no intention of getting bogged down in a land war in Asia, or in a direct conflict with Russia or China. Exponents of containment like George Kennan now argued that the UN had achieved its objective of expelling the North Koreans; the UN should consolidate its lines along the 38th parallel and negotiate a settlement. But MacArthur, buoyed by his success, was convinced that the only way to end the war, and unite Korea, was to conquer the North. For a brief interval both Truman and Acheson, as well as the UN, were persuaded. In the teeth of a Chinese warning that they might enter the war, the UN General Assembly authorized MacArthur to cross the parallel.

So concerned was Truman with the threat of Chinese intervention that in mid-October he flew to Wake Island to confer with MacArthur. The General assured him that the Chinese would not attack, and if they did 'there would be the greatest slaughter.' On this advice, Truman approved an advance to within a few miles from the Chinese border on the Yalu river. MacArthur predicted that enemy resistance would be ended by Christmas, and for a time it seemed he might be right. On 20 October the North Korean capital of Pyongyang fell to UN forces, and by the end of the month MacArthur was approaching the Manchurian border. Yet even as Truman and MacArthur spoke, masses of Red Chinese soldiers were streaming across the Yalu into Korea. On the night of 25 November Mao's 'volunteers' unleased a ferocious assault. Three days later MacArthur issued a chilling communiqué: 'We face an entirely new war.' An army of more than a quarter-million Chinese drove MacArthur's armies out of all the territory they had won in North Korea and sent them reeling back across the 38th parallel. That winter saw some of the cruelest warfare in American history, with shocking cold and blinding storms, a rugged terrain of jagged mountains, treacherous swamps and unbridged streams, and an enemy who gave no quarter.

MacArthur, who in September had been lauded for the Inchon success, found himself by December under fire for miscalculating Chinese intentions and for deploying his troops poorly. Never one to take reproof lightly, the proud general turned increasingly to issuing statements which intimated that the real blame lay not with him but with Washington's decision to fight a limited war. He proposed bombing China's 'privileged sanctuary' in Manchuria, pursuing MIGs across the Yalu into China, a blockade of the Chinese coast, air attacks on the cities of the Chinese mainland, and an invasion of China by the armies of Chiang Kai-shek. Truman firmly rejected these ideas. Chastened by its costly flirta-

Truman and MacArthur at Wake Island, 15 October 1950. For press photographers, the President and the General made a show of cordiality, but Truman has offered a saucy version of what took place at their private meeting, the details of which are in dispute. To Truman's dismay, MacArthur was not at the airfield to greet him. 'So, I just sat there,' Truman told Merle Miller. 'I'd have waited until hell froze over, if I'd had to. I wasn't going to have one of my generals embarrass the President of the United States. Finally, the son of a bitch walked out of one of the buildings . . . wearing those damn sunglasses of his and a shirt that was unbuttoned and a cap that had a lot of hardware. I never did understand . . . an old man like that and a five-star general to boot, why he went around dressed up like a nineteen-year-old second lieutenant.' When they were alone, he admonished the General, 'I don't give a goddamn what you do or think about Harry Truman, but don't you ever again keep your Commander-in-Chief waiting.' (*Brown Brothers*)

tion with a liberation policy, the administration returned to the policy of containment. It did not want MacArthur to lead the United States into the 'gigantic booby trap' of an all-out war with Red China. Moreover, the military situation in Korea in early 1951 offered new hope for peace. UN forces under General Matthew Ridgway blunted the Chinese offensive, and in March recaptured Seoul for the second and last time and recrossed the 38th parallel. With the Republic of Korea cleared of Communist soldiers, Truman and the UN believed the time had come to press for negotiations.

The General would have none of it. Although he had been warned repeatedly not to make statements which conflicted with UN policy, on 24

March 1951 he defiantly threatened China with an attack, a declaration which Truman believed killed any hope for an early truce. On 5 April, on the floor of the House, Republican minority leader Joseph Martin read a letter MacArthur had written him on 19 March criticizing the President and insisting, 'There is no substitute for victory.' This arrogant challenge to civilian authority was intolerable, and Truman peremptorily dismissed General MacArthur from command. He came home to receive tumultuous ovations. Herbert Hoover saw MacArthur as 'a reincarnation of St. Paul into a great General of the Army who came out of the East,' and when this new apostle addressed Congress, Republican Congressman Dewey Short declared that he had seen 'a great hunk of God in the flesh.' But enthusiasm for MacArthur died down after it was revealed that all three Chiefs of Staff backed Truman against the General. If MacArthur's counsel had been followed, the President's military advisers declared, the United States would have won the enmity of all Asia, wrecked the coalition of free nations, and diverted its strength to a costly struggle with China while Russia, which had instigated the North Korean invasion, would have been unscathed. MacArthur's policy, General Bradley observed, 'would involve us in the wrong war, at the wrong place, at the wrong time, and with the wrong enemy.'

Yet if Truman survived the MacArthur episode, the Korean War cost him and his party dearly. The President made the decision to intervene without seeking the approval of Congress, for, by treating the conflict as a 'police action,' he hoped to avoid a major war. However, this strategy deprived Congress of its constitutional authority to declare war, and proved unwise politically; when the fighting went badly, the President had to bear sole responsibility for intervention. By the spring of 1951 the Korean conflict was deadlocked; and when in June the Soviet delegate to the United Nations suggested an armistice with mutual withdrawal behind the 38th parallel, Washington welcomed the proposal. But discussions looking to an armistice dragged on interminably, and the bloodletting did not stop. When the country went to the polls in November 1952, this unpopular war still had not ended, and it was inevitable that the President's party would pay the price.

The Korean War mobilization hurt Truman in yet another way. When steel workers threatened to strike in the midst of the war, the Wage Stabilization Board recommended an increase of 18 cents an hour without corresponding rises in steel prices. The operators rejected this solution; the union called a walkout; and Truman on 8 April 1952 seized the mills. One of the mills—the Youngstown Sheet and Tube Company—challenged the constitutionality of the President's act, and the Supreme Court struck down the presidential order on the ground that it constituted executive lawmaking. The Court's decision, and the President's helplessness in the face of the ensuing 54-day strike, further impaired Truman's prestige.

The combat in Korea had other and deeper consequences. It accelerated the pace of desegregation of the armed forces. It tied American interests more closely to those of Chiang on Formosa and to the French in Indochina, and thereby moved the country a fateful step toward the subsequent disaster in Southeast Asia. It resulted in a vast increase in the military budget, which underwrote the prosperity of America in the 1950's but also occasioned alarm over whether the United States was becoming a 'Warfare State.' And it nurtured a nasty period of xenophobia rivaling the Red Scare of 1919.

The Politics of Subversion

Although the Cold War with Russia and the hot war in Korea provided most of the fuel for the era of 'McCarthyism,' anxiety over subversion preceded World War II, and although Republicans were the main agents of this new Red Scare, Democrats, including Truman and his appointees, played an important part. As early as 1938 the House established a committee on un-American activities, but HUAC was so irresponsible that its allegations were discounted. However, when a raid in 1945 on the magazine *Amerasia* turned up quantities of classified State Department documents, another House committee began a study which resulted in Truman's issuing Executive Order 9835 in March 1947. Though this order to investigate the loyalty of civil servants set up procedural safeguards, it also embraced the doctrines of guilt by intention and by association.[6] Of the 3 million persons passed on, only a few thousand were actually investigated. Of these, 212 were dismissed, but none, apparently, had committed offenses serious enough to warrant prosecution. Potentially the most ominous feature of the executive order was the one authorizing the Attorney-General to prepare lists of subversive organizations and giving these lists a quasi-legal character. 'If there is any fixed star in our constitutional constellation,' Justice Jackson had said, 'it is that no official, high or petty, can prescribe what shall be orthodox in politics, nationalism, religion or other matters of opinion, or force citizens to confess by word or act their faith therein.'

Even the executive order did not free the Truman administration from charges of being 'soft on communism,' and on 20 July 1948 it precipitately took steps to indict the eleven top Communists on the charge of violating the Smith Act of 1940, which made it a crime to conspire to 'advocate and teach' the violent overthrow of government. In the Dennis case the Supreme Court accepted Judge Learned Hand's modification of the 'clear and present danger' test: 'in each case courts must ask whether the gravity of the evil, discounted by its improbability, justifies such invasion of free speech as is necessary to avoid the danger'—and concluded that the Smith Act was constitutional and that the Communists were in fact guilty of conspiracy to advocate the overthrow of government.

The outcome of the 1948 election left the Republicans embittered (to be beaten by Roosevelt was disappointing but familiar; to be rejected in favor of Truman seemed intolerable) and shortly after the election came two prodigious events: the Communist takeover in China and the Soviet detonation of an atomic bomb. On top of this came the Korean War. How did it happen? How did we 'lose' China, and the atomic monopoly all at once, and then come close to losing the Korean War as well? To many it was unthinkable that Communism could win on its own and incredible that Soviet scientists were as clever as American or British. The answer must lie elsewhere—in subversion and treachery, perhaps by intellectuals and 'one-worlders' in the State Department who were secret sympathizers with Russia. For Republicans seeking a promising political issue, such an assumption was especially attractive. Yet though the Communists did, in fact, control a number of 'fronts' and perhaps one-third of the C.I.O., and though there were Communist cells in Washington, no hard evidence was adduced to link an important government official to actual espionage.

Then came the Hiss case. In August 1948 Whittaker Chambers, onetime editor of *Time* magazine, accused Alger Hiss, who had been a State Department official before becoming president of the Carnegie Endowment for International Peace, of having been a Communist. Since Chambers produced nothing convincing to sustain his charge, Truman decried the affair as a 'red herring' aimed at distracting the public from the failures of the 80th Congress. But in December 1948 Chambers produced microfilms of classified State Department documents—out of a pumpkin!—and asserted that Hiss had not only been a party member but a spy. When Hiss denied these allegations, a New York grand jury indicted him for perjury; since the statute of limitations had expired, Hiss could not be indicted for espionage, but everyone understood that it was treason that was really at issue. After two trials Hiss was found guilty and sentenced to five years in jail. Though Hiss was not a key policy-maker, he had been with Roosevelt in a minor capacity at Yalta where, it was contended, American interests had been 'sold out' to the Russians. Moreover, Hiss was tailor-made for the role of a villain: a graduate of the Harvard Law School, a New Dealer, a friend of Secretary Acheson, who said he would not turn his back on him, an international 'do-gooder'; even his name suggested perfidy! Two weeks after Hiss's conviction came disquieting news from England—Klaus Fuchs, an atomic physicist who had worked at the Los Alamos laboratory, had been found guilty of systematically feeding atomic information to the Russians.

This series of events provided the background for that phenomenon known as McCarthyism.

6. A supplementary executive order in April 1951 authorized the firing of Federal employees even if there was only 'reasonable doubt' as to their loyalty. That same month Julius and Ethel Rosenberg were sentenced to death for conspiring to transmit secret information on the atomic bomb to Soviet Russia.

AFTER GENERAL EISENHOWER HANGS UP HIS UNIFORM, WILL HE DON —
VICKY
AN 'ABE LINCOLN' – A 'TEDDY ROOSEVELT' – A 'WOODROW WILSON' – A 'HERBERT HOOVER' – AN 'F.D.R' – OR A 'HARRY TRUMAN'?

The fungible candidate. So popular was Eisenhower that elements in both major parties wanted to nominate him even though they knew little about what course he would follow, as this panel by the British cartoonist, Vicky, in the *News Chronicle* suggests. (*Associated Newspapers Group, Ltd., London*)

Senator McCarthy himself was a finished demagogue: brutal, unscrupulous, and cunning; his methods were wild charges, fake evidence, innuendoes and lies, appeals to ignorance, prejudice, hatred, and fear. On 9 February 1950 he alleged that he had the names of 205—or was it 57?—'card-carrying Communists' in the State Department. Five months later, a Senate committee under Senator Tydings reported that McCarthy's charges were 'a fraud and a hoax perpetrated on the Senate of the United States and on the American people. They represent perhaps the most nefarious campaign of half-truth and untruth in the history of the Republic.' Nothing daunted, McCarthy moved on to larger game. 'It was Moscow,' he cried, 'which decreed that the United States should execute its loyal friend, the Republic of China. The executioners were that well-defined group headed by Acheson and George Marshall.'

Out of the panic aroused by such accusations emerged the McCarran-Nixon Internal Security Act of 1950. This law required all Communist-front organizations to register with the Attorney-General, excluded Communists from employment in defense plants, made it illegal to *conspire* to perform any act that would 'substantially contribute' to the establishment of a dictatorship, debarred from the United States anyone ever affiliated with a totalitarian organization, or with organizations looking to the revolutionary overthrow of government, authorized deportation for aliens involved in suspect organizations, denied passports to Communists, provided for the internment of subversives in the event of war, and set up a Subversive Activities Control Board. Truman vetoed the bill, alleging that it was 'worse than the Sedition Act of 1798,' but Congress passed it over his veto by acclamation.

The subversion issue highlighted the 1950 elections in which the Republicans picked up five seats in the Senate and twenty-eight in the House. McCarthy, who received more invitations from Republican senators to speak in their states than all other senators combined, received credit for the defeat of Governor Bowles in Connecticut and of Senator Tydings in Maryland, where a fraudulent composite photograph was used. In California,

Richard Nixon, who emphasized McCarthyite issues, won a Senate seat. Actually, voters were less concerned with the Communist question than politicians believed. Nonetheless, the 1950 elections not only sealed the fate of the Fair Deal but encouraged the Republicans to anticipate that the same tactics would win them the White House in 1952.

By the spring of 1952 Americans were ready to listen to the Republicans' contention that it was 'time for a change' from twenty years of Democratic administration. Prices were too high; there was a 'mess in Washington'; anxiety about subversion was rife; and the war in Korea was at a stalemate. The Republicans also had an attractive candidate. Though right wing Republicans rallied behind Senator Taft, the more moderate, internationalist wing of the G.O.P. secured the nomination for the popular General Dwight D. Eisenhower, Supreme Commander of NATO on leave from the presidency of Columbia University, with Senator Nixon as his running mate. The Democrats faced the necessity of choosing a candidate not too closely identified with the Truman administration, which was blemished by scandals involving such agencies as the RFC. Senator Kefauver of Tennessee had won a large following by his investigation of organized crime, the first political event to attract an avid television audience, but the convention turned instead to Governor Adlai Stevenson of Illinois, a man of wit, intelligence, and eloquence, who, nonetheless, was overmatched.

Eisenhower captivated the nation in 1952. At first the General showed himself unwilling to repudiate policies of the Truman administration which he had helped to shape, but after a momentous meeting with Taft, he began to give aid and comfort to the right wing of his party. He accepted the support of demagogues like McCarthy, denounced the Truman administration for harboring subversives, and poured scorn on the 'eggheads' who had rallied to Stevenson. To no avail did Stevenson remind the country: 'No one is running on a pro-corruption ticket or in favor of treachery.' With ample funds at their command, the Republicans exploited to the full the possibilities of television which, for the first time, was important in a presidential campaign. Thus when Nixon was revealed to have been subsidized by a secret fund subscribed by California millionaires, he converted the liability into an asset by a dramatic television appearance, which critics denounced as 'soap opera' but to which the public responded favorably. However, the greatest advantage that the Republicans enjoyed was neither control of the mass media, the smoke screen of 'subversion,' nor the corruption issue, but 'Ike' himself. 'The crowd is with him,' wrote one correspondent. 'Idolatry shows in their solemn, upturned faces.' Moreover, at a time when casualties were mounting in Korea, Eisenhower struck a popular chord when he promised he would go to Korea to bring the deadlocked war to an early end.

General Eisenhower won with more than 55 per cent of the popular vote and captured 39 states with 442 electoral votes, while Stevenson carried only 9 states with 89 votes in a contest marked by a sharply increased turnout. Eisenhower even won four states of the no longer Solid South. The personal nature of this triumph was apparent when contrasted with the congressional vote. In spite of all their advantages, the Republicans barely carried the House and managed only a tie in the Senate. Clearly the election was less a triumph for the Republican party than a vote of confidence in Eisenhower; and if the support of the people is the secret of presidential power, the new President could be expected to be one of the strongest of American executives.

35

The Eisenhower Era: Tranquility and Crisis

*

1953–1960

Dynamic Conservatism

Dwight Eisenhower's conception of his office suited the mood of many Americans in the 1950's, a mood the President himself helped to set. In the 1952 campaign some backed Eisenhower because they hoped he would lead the nation in new ventures, while others did so because they wished him to repeal the past. Yet many, perhaps most, who voted for him did so because they anticipated that the General would give the country a respite from a generation of unrelieved crises: a disastrous depression, a world war, a cold war, an enervating limited war. Kept in a constant state of tension by two activist Presidents, they had reached a point of weariness with the intrusion of public issues into their lives. They expected Eisenhower not to solve problems but somehow to charm them away.

The country demanded too much of the new President; and, since he was asked to do contradictory things, he was bound to disappoint some of his followers. Those who thought the General would lead the country in new directions were quickly disillusioned, and those who favored a sharply conservative turn had to accommodate themselves to the fact that most of what the New Deal had wrought could not be undone. For a time he satisfied those who hoped he would bring a new spirit of quiescence, until the eruption of crises at home and abroad disrupted the sense of tranquility. Even then, however, Eisenhower continued to hold the affection of most of the nation.

Eisenhower belonged to the McKinley-Taft rather than the Roosevelt-Wilson tradition of the presidency. He thought of the President less as party leader or chief legislator than as a combination chief of staff, mediator, and father of his people. To be sure, Eisenhower was more active in mobilizing his party in support of his objectives, especially in foreign affairs, than many recognized at the time. But he repudiated the 'left-wing theory that the Executive has unlimited powers' and adopted the Whig view that the prerogatives of his office should be used as little as possible. His general outlook, noted Walter Johnson, was: 'What will we refrain from doing now?' Thoroughly American as 'Ike' was, he nevertheless conceived his role to be somewhat like that of a constitutional monarch: he was to be a symbol above the battle.

Dwight David Eisenhower (1890–1969). Ike's enormous popularity owed much to his self-deprecating manner, a quality not always associated with victorious generals. In the years after World War II, he spurned efforts to draft him as a presidential candidate. 'I don't believe a man should ever try to pass his historical peak,' he told reporters. 'I think I pretty well hit my peak in history when I accepted the German surrender in 1945.' Of his election to the presidency in 1952 he later wrote, 'Remembering my beginnings, I had to smile. . . . The . . . old saw had proved to be true: in the United States, any boy *can* grow up to be President.' (*Dwight D. Eisenhower Library*)

Eisenhower's long military experience predisposed him toward a staff system, which he had used successfully in Europe. He preferred to work through subordinates who would shelter him from demands on his time and protect him from personal involvement in the hurly-burly of politics. He was not disposed to probe deeply into any subject; and he liked to have every problem, even the most complex, summarized for him on a single sheet of paper. Because he insulated himself from public affairs, he was often taken by surprise on learning things that almost everyone knew—such as book burning by Department of State underlings in overseas libraries or sit-ins by black students in the South.

As his special assistant Eisenhower chose one of his original backers, Governor Sherman Adams of New Hampshire. This dour Yankee, who became a kind of unofficial alter-ego of the President, wielded a power out of all proportion to his official position. Under the Eisenhower staff system he decided who could see the President and selected letters and papers to be submitted. Increasingly, as the President took refuge on his Gettysburg farm from routine demands, the burden of running the presidential office fell on the hard-working 'Governor.' He was to Eisenhower what Colonel House had been to Wilson, who also took office after a long reign by the opposition party.

The 1952 election marked the return of the Republican party to power after twenty years; many Republicans looked forward to a complete reversal of Democratic policies which, their platform asserted, led toward socialism and the wrecking of the free enterprise system. Yet, once in power, the Republicans found they could do little more than modify past practices, for the country had become irretrievably committed to many elements of the Welfare State. In the 1952 campaign Eisenhower had displayed sympathy with the Taft conservatives; and when he took office he aimed to remove 'the Left-Wingish, pinkish influence in our life.' In his first year he fired 200,000 government workers and boasted of having 'instituted what amounts almost to a revolution' in the national government by 'finding things it can stop doing rather than new things for it to do.' But the new President also wanted to demonstrate that his party was responsible. Eisenhower's two favorite phrases were 'middle of the road' and 'dynamic conservatism.' His administration turned out to be more conservative than dynamic, but when he left office federal employment was the same as when he came in, and it was apparent that the President had not moved far from the middle of the road.

Eisenhower kept to the middle of the road mostly because the political situation left him little choice. The Democrats erased the slim Republican margin in Congress in 1954, and for six of his eight years in office Eisenhower had to work with a Congress controlled by the opposing party, a circumstance that served to modify his conservative predilection. In 1956 he once again trounced Adlai Stevenson, polling 35,590,000 votes (57.4 per cent) and sweeping 41 states with a total electoral vote of 457 to Stevenson's 26,023,000 votes (42 per cent) and only 73 electoral votes from 7 states, none in the North or West. Yet, astonishingly, despite Eisenhower's one-sided triumph, the Democrats held control of both houses of Congress. Not since Zachary Taylor had a President been elected without carrying at least one house of Congress for his party. The Eisenhower era, noted one political scientist, 'was one of almost unprecedented ambiguity in regard to partisan responsibility for the conduct of the government,' and both conservatives and liberals had to settle for a government of the center which was in keeping with the quiescent spirit of the 'fifties.

At the outset, however, Eisenhower appeared to have free rein to give government a conservative stamp. He named to his first cabinet six prominent businessmen, several of whom were multimillionaires. Secretary of Defense Charles E. Wilson, who had been head of the General Motors Corporation, achieved a kind of immortality by his statement that 'what was good for our country was good for General Motors, and vice versa.' Arthur Summerfield, also of General Motors, distinguished himself as Postmaster-General by trying to put the department on a 'businesslike footing,' regardless of the impact on postal service,

Harry Truman and Eleanor Roosevelt, 1956. One would not guess from the affectionate look the 72-year-old former President bestows on his 72-year-old companion that she has just clobbered him at a press conference. In 1956 Truman, opposed to the renomination of Adlai Stevenson, insisted that the party required a 'fighting' candidate. But, in what was called 'an adroit and ruthless performance,' the former First Lady demolished this argument at a session in which she told reporters that Stevenson was 'better equipped' in foreign affairs than Truman had been when he succeeded her husband. (*Cornell Capa—Magnum*)

while Secretary of the Interior Douglas MacKay, a third product of General Motors, had a long record of hostility to conservation and public power. Secretary of Commerce Sinclair Weeks, a Massachusetts manufacturer, began his administration by firing the head of the Bureau of Standards because he was oblivious to 'the business point of view.' Both Secretary of the Treasury George Humphrey, president of Mark Hanna's old firm, and Secretary of Agriculture Ezra Taft Benson had strong convictions about the dangers of Federal centralization. Attorney-General Herbert Brownell, a prominent New York lawyer, represented the Dewey wing of the party as did the leader of the cabinet, John Foster Dulles, the new Secretary of State. Dulles employed his energies chiefly in foreign affairs, but as a Wall Street lawyer he, too, weighted the cabinet on the conservative side. In this atmosphere it is little wonder that Secretary of Labor Martin Durkin, a Stevenson Democrat and union official, felt thoroughly out of place and resigned before the year was out; his post was filled by James P. Mitchell, a former personnel manager.

Nowhere did the conservatism of the Eisenhower administration express itself more emphatically than in its attitude toward natural resources. Truman had twice vetoed bills giving the states control of the underseas oil deposits lying off their shores, but within a few months of Eisenhower's accession he signed a Submerged Lands Act, put through by Republicans and Southern Democrats, which assigned Federal rights to the off-shore oil to the seaboard states. In the realm of atomic energy private interests also gained. The Atomic Energy Act of 1954 provided for government financing of atomic research but farmed out the operation of the new atomic energy plants to General Electric and Union Carbide. In addition, the Eisenhower administration cut the budget of Federal power administrations and jettisoned a plan for a federally built and controlled dam at Hell's Canyon on the Snake river in favor of a project of the Idaho Power Company.

Early in his administration, Eisenhower cited the TVA as an example of that 'creeping socialism' against which he so insistently warned his countrymen, and he even indicated he would like to sell the TVA to private industry. Between 1952 and 1960 appropriations for the TVA fell from \$185 million to \$12 million. It was the administration's reluctance to expand this enterprise that led in 1954–55 to the Dixon-Yates fiasco. To serve the needs of the Memphis area, the Atomic Energy Commission signed a juicy contract with two private utilities, represented by Edgar Dixon and Eugene Yates, to build a generating plant. However, a congressional investigation revealed that the contract had been written by a consultant to the Bureau of the Budget who, by an odd coincidence, was also vice-president of the corporation which would finance the operation; and the AEC had to void the contract. When Dixon-Yates sued to recoup its losses, the administration was placed in the awkward position of claiming that the contract, in which it had taken such pride, had been illegal and 'contrary to the public interest' from the very beginning.

Devotion to private enterprise, and suspicion of public, persisted throughout the Eisenhower administration. Shortly after assuming office the President ended all price and rent controls and did away with the Reconstruction Finance Corporation. He vetoed a school construction bill which he thought interfered unduly with local autonomy, acquiesced in a sharp reduction in Federal aid to public housing, and opposed medical insurance amendments to social security bills. In general, he subscribed to the Republican orthodoxy that an unbalanced budget was the road to ruin.

But he soon discovered that it was one thing to preach the virtues of economy and another to practice them, as the intractable farm question demonstrated. Disturbed by the cost of government subsidies, Eisenhower embraced Secretary Benson's recommendation for flexible agricultural price supports, but Benson's program proved a costly failure. Farm income fell drastically, surpluses mounted. In 1954 Senator Humphrey revived Henry Wallace's idea of paying farmers to take their land out of production. This 'soil bank' scheme was at first rejected by Eisenhower, but in 1956 he came around to it, and even persuaded Congress to adopt it. Although the Republican platform of 1952 had charged the Democrats with using 'tax money to make farmers dependent upon government,' federal expenditures for agriculture multiplied during Eisenhower's two terms. Indeed, overall, in only three of its eight years did the administration achieve a balanced budget.

The Eisenhower administration stayed in the 'middle of the road' not only by maintaining a significant, if restrained, role for government in the economy but by balancing conservative policies in fields like natural resources with more liberal responses in other areas. Congress extended reciprocal trade agreements; enlarged social security to embrace some ten million additional persons; raised the minimum wage; pushed through two civil-rights bills; established a new Department of Health, Education, and Welfare; admitted Hawaii and Alaska to statehood in 1959; appropriated some $887 million for student loans and the support of science and language teaching under the National Defense Education Act; provided for the admission of an additional 214,000 refugees outside the normal immigration quotas; and authorized the construction of the Great Lakes-St. Lawrence seaway, which Hoover, Roosevelt, and Truman had all urged in vain and which Canada and the United States completed within the decade. In short, Eisenhower, partly by intent, partly by inadvertence, pursued a course of moderation in domestic affairs that much of the country seemed to approve.

Liquidation of McCarthyism

For one of the long-needed accomplishments in Washington, the Senate rather than the President deserves credit: the liquidation of Senator McCarthy as an effective force. Yet in truth both performed ingloriously. Only a rare senator like Herbert Lehman dared to stand up to McCarthy, and the administration at times seemed bent on diverting the Wisconsin mountebank by outdoing him. Shortly after taking office Eisenhower extended the security system to all agencies of the government, replaced the earlier criterion of 'loyalty' with a broader and vaguer criterion of 'security risk,' and authorized the discharge of any person whose employment was not 'clearly consistent with the interests of national security.' Between May 1953 and October 1954 no fewer than 6926 'security risks' were 'separated' from their government jobs. Very few of these were even charged with subversion, and not one had committed any crime or breach of duty for which he was brought to trial in a court of law. Secretary Dulles appointed a McCarthyite as the State Department's security officer and sacrificed valued officials to appease the Senator. In December 1953 the Atomic Energy Commission, on orders from Eisenhower, withdrew security clearance from the 'father of the atomic bomb,' J. Robert Oppenheimer.

All this display of zeal, however, failed to assuage McCarthy, who now trained his guns on the administration itself. McCarthy objected to Eisenhower's new ambassador to Russia, Charles Bohlen, because he had been at Yalta, and he sent to Europe two bumbling assistants to track down and destroy 'subversive' literature (such as the works of Emerson and Thoreau) in libraries of the U.S. Information Service—a usurpation of State Department authority in which Dulles readily acquiesced. Early in 1954, McCarthy seized on the case of an obscure army dentist, a major who had been given a routine promotion and an honorable discharge from the army notwithstanding a suspicion of Communist sympathies. In the course of an investigation of this trivial episode of the 'pink dentist' McCarthy browbeat the major's superior, General Zwicker, and then turned on Robert Stevens, Secretary of the Army, who allowed himself to be cowed into signing a 'memorandum of agreement' with the Senator.

But on 11 March 1954 the army struck back with the charge that McCarthy had demanded preferential treatment in the army for one of his aides who had been drafted. The Senator counterattacked with forty-six charges against the army, and the war was on. The hearings to determine the facts were televised nationally, and the whole country watched with a kind of horrified fascination the spectacle of McCarthy as bully. Thereafter the tide of opinion turned against McCarthy. No sooner was the investigation concluded than Republican Senator Ralph Flanders moved that the Senate formally censure McCarthy for improper conduct. A Senate committee

Earl Warren (1891–1974). Appointed Chief Justice of the United States in 1953, he rapidly used his gifts as a harmonizer to achieve unanimity of the Court in the historic school desegregation decision the following year. Not regarded as a great technician, Warren nonetheless moved the judiciary onto a number of new paths by posing the question, 'Is this fair and just?' Throughout his tenure he had to cope with 'Impeach Earl Warren' placards, but when he left the bench in 1969 he was widely regarded as the most influential Chief Justice since John Marshall. This picture is by the noted photographer Karsh. (© *Karsh, Ottawa*)

headed by Watkins of Utah, another Republican, recommended censure, and on 2 December 1954 the Senate formally 'condemned' McCarthy by a vote of 67 to 22, with Republicans casting all the opposition votes. Thereafter McCarthy's influence declined rapidly. On 2 May 1957 he died, his force largely spent, his name an 'improper noun' for a guiltily-remembered episode.

Yet if McCarthy was gone, McCarthyism left as a heritage a large body of laws and practices based on the notion that there were litmus tests for Americanism, and that it was the business of governments to apply these tests to all who served in any public capacity. The elaborate apparatus improvised in the 'forties now hardened as a permanent engine of the American security system. To the Smith Act of 1940 and the Internal Security Act of 1950 was added the Communist Control Act of 1954 outlawing the Communist party. Just as in pre-Civil War days Southern hostility to abolition gradually became hostility to all liberal nineteenth-century ideas, so now hostility to 'subversion' became also a bitter opposition to those who championed the rights of Negroes, favored recognition of Communist China, and supported medical care for the aged, or even—as Arthur Schlesinger said—those who believed in the income tax, the fluoridation of water, and the twentieth century.

Constitutional questions raised by security programs sharply divided the Supreme Court, with Justice Frankfurter speaking for one group—usually the majority—and Justices Black or Douglas or Chief Justice Earl Warren for the other. The Frankfurter wing tended to support the right of the legislature to qualify or suspend some of the guarantees of the First Amendment where it felt that the security of the commonwealth was at stake; it believed that in a democratic society, popularly elected legislatures, not judicial tribunals, should strike the balance between liberty and security. The Black group believed that the constitutional prohibition against the abridgment of free speech was an absolute, and that legislatures should not be permitted to plead the necessity of security as a justification for overriding constitutional guarantees. In the Dennis case of 1951 the Court had found the balance of interest to be on the side of security, but after 1954 there was a shift toward stronger emphasis on the guarantees of the First Amendment. In 1957 alone, *Yates v. United States* curtailed the scope of the Dennis opinion and of the Smith Act by holding that even advocacy of forcible overthrow of government was not illegal if it confined itself to mere advocacy; *Watkins v. United States* curbed the authority of the Un-American Activities Committee to punish uncooperative witnesses at will; and in *Kent v. Dulles* and *Dayton v. Dulles*, the Court deprived the State Department of the right to deny passports arbitrarily. However, with the sharpening of the Cold War after 1958 there was a perceptible shift to the side of security, and the Court sustained the activities of legislative investigating committees even when these were palpably bent on exposure rather than on acquiring information.

The Civil Rights Revolution

If the Supreme Court failed to speak with a clear voice on civil liberties, it acted emphatically on behalf of blacks who, as the centenary of the Emancipation Proclamation approached, were still second-class citizens. In the South, black children were fobbed off with schools that were not only segregated but inferior, and black youths were denied entrance to the state universities they helped to support by taxation. When Negroes traveled they were forced to use segregated waiting rooms and sections of buses. They were not permitted to sit with white people in theaters, movies, restaurants, or at lunch counters; even in many churches. Their right to vote was flouted by various devices, and they were tried by Jim Crow juries. In the North urban blacks met various kinds of discrimination and were confined to slum dwellings in black ghettos. Yet changes were in the wind. Between 1940 and 1960 blacks in the North increased from 2.8 to 7.2 million, thereby markedly increasing their political leverage in a region where they could freely exercise the vote. Furthermore, the conscience of the nation had been deeply disturbed by what the great Swedish sociologist, Gunnar Myrdal, called the American Dilemma—the dilemma of commitment both to equality and to white superiority.

After a series of antidiscrimination rulings in

fields like housing and public transportation, the Supreme Court struck a heavy blow against white supremacy in the 1954 school segregation case, *Brown v. Board of Education of Topeka*. In 1896 the Supreme Court had held that the Fourteenth Amendment did not require that blacks and whites share all public facilities and that it was not illegal for such facilities to be 'separate' as long as they were 'equal.' In the Brown case a unanimous Court, speaking through Chief Justice Warren, reversed this decision and held that 'separate educational facilities are inherently unequal.' It followed this ruling with another in May 1955 which required that desegregation of the schools proceed 'with all deliberate speed'—in short, gradually but with a 'prompt and reasonable start.'

Deliberateness became more apparent than speed. In the border states, except Virginia, desegregation encountered only sporadic resistance, but in the Deep South, segregationists organized White Citizens' Councils, and whipped up opposition sentiment to fever pitch. Georgia made it a felony for any school official to spend tax money for public schools in which the races were mixed; Mississippi made it a crime for any organization to institute desegregation proceedings in the state courts; North Carolina withheld school funds from any school district which integrated its public schools. In February 1956, when Autherine Lucy became the first black to register at the University of Alabama, a howling mob of students drove her from the campus.

Out of patience with resistance in the Deep South, where not a single child attended a desegregated school at the beginning of Eisenhower's second term, a Federal court ordered a start of desegregation in the schools of Little Rock, Arkansas, a city known for racial progress, in the fall of 1957. But Governor Orval Faubus responded by creating an atmosphere of violence and then calling out the National Guard, not to protect the black children in their right to attend the public schools but to deny them that right. When these troops were withdrawn on order of a Federal district judge, a mob blocked Negro students from entering Central High School. President Eisenhower, who had not lifted a finger to enforce the Brown decision, now confronted an act of defiance that could not be permitted to go unchallenged. On 24 September he dispatched Federal troops to Little Rock. However, Faubus, re-elected to the governorship, persisted in his tactics of obstruction, and not until the Supreme Court handed down yet another decision in September 1958 was even token integration accomplished.

If desegregation was to be achieved, the President and Congress would have to assume some of the lonely burden of the Federal judiciary. But Eisenhower spurned suggestions that he use his immense prestige to educate the country on civil rights. He did take effective action in areas like the District of Columbia where Federal authority was unquestioned. But even after the Little Rock episode, he observed: 'I have never said what I thought about the Supreme Court decision—I have never told a soul.' Congress proved somewhat more responsive. In 1957, under the leadership of Lyndon Johnson of Texas, the Senate Majority Leader, it enacted the first civil rights law in 82 years. Although weakened by amendments, it provided a degree of Federal protection for Negroes who wanted to vote and set up a Civil Rights Commission. A second statute in 1960 authorized the appointment of Federal referees to safeguard the right to vote and stipulated that a threat of violence to obstruct a Court order was a Federal offense. However, Congress did nothing effective to speed enforcement of the Court's decisions. Six years after the Court had called for desegregation with 'all deliberate speed,' not a single school was integrated in South Carolina, Georgia, Alabama, Mississippi, or Louisiana.

The brightest spark for the civil rights revolution came not from the President or Congress, not even from the Supreme Court, but from the blacks themselves. The pathbreaking Court decisions would not have been possible without the carefully developed strategy of black and white attorneys in the National Association for the Advancement of Colored People under the astute leadership of Roy Wilkins. They would have had no meaning if there had not been black children with the courage to brave the wrath of ugly mobs and withstand the taunts of their fellow students.

Yet in the long run more important still may have been an occurrence on a Montgomery,

Martin Luther King (1929–1968). On the wall hangs a picture of Gandhi. From his first acquaintance at Boston University with the Mahatma's teachings through his time of testing in the Montgomery bus boycott to his climactic visit to India in 1959, King grew ever more deeply committed to the doctrines of nonviolent resistance and *Satyagraha* (soul force) and to the need to set an example of physical suffering by inviting imprisonment. In confrontations in Georgia and Alabama in the 1960's, King would recall Gandhi's experiences in Punjab and at Ahmadabad. The Negro, King wrote, must reach the point where he could say to his white brother: 'We will not hate you, but we will not obey your evil laws. We will soon wear you down by pure capacity to suffer.' (*Bob Fitch–Black Star*)

Alabama, bus on 1 December 1955. Late that day Rosa Parks, a middle-aged black seamstress riding home from work, refused to give up her seat to a white man. When she was arrested for violating the city's Jim Crow statutes, the blacks of Montgomery boycotted the buses. Led by a twenty-five-year-old Baptist minister, the Reverend Martin Luther King, Jr., who had been influenced by Gandhi and Thoreau, they employed non-violent resistance in a campaign that eventually resulted in desegregation of the city's buses. King, whose home was bombed and who was arrested (one of thirty jailings in his career) said:

> If we are arrested every day, if we are exploited every day, if we are trampled over every day, don't let anyone pull you so low as to hate them. We must use the weapon of love. We must have compassion and understanding for those who hate us. . . .

Out of this experience Dr. King emerged a national leader, and his new organization, the Southern Christian Leadership Conference, would be in the vanguard of many protests in the 1960's.

A similar small incident toward the end of Eisenhower's reign touched off a movement that shook Southern society to its foundations. On 1 February 1960, four freshmen at a black college in North Carolina sat down at a lunch counter in downtown Greensboro; when the waitress refused to serve them, they remained in their seats. Within a few weeks the sit-in movement had swept the South and soon took such forms as 'wade-ins' in motel and municipal swimming pools and 'kneel-ins' in churches. In the North the Congress of Racial Equality (CORE), which had employed the tactic of passive resistance as early as the 1940's, organized demonstrations to break racial barriers. Other blacks and whites joined in 'freedom rides' to desegregate interstate transportation. Within a brief period Northern hotels and restaurants ended their subtle forms of discrimination, Southern department stores and lunch counters were desegregated, and WHITE and COLORED signs were pulled down from waiting rooms in hundreds of Southern rail, air, and bus terminals.

The New Look and the Old View

In domestic affairs Eisenhower set the tone for his administration, but in foreign policy the dominant figure was his Secretary of State, John Foster Dulles. Grandson of one secretary of state and nephew of another, he had been a secretary at the Hague Peace Conference of 1907 and an adviser to the United States delegation at Versailles. One of the architects of the United Nations, Dulles, like Eisenhower, had been so closely identified with the programs of the outgoing administration that it seemed probable that there would be substantial continuity in policy. Yet Eisenhower had won election on a platform which attacked 'the negative, futile and immoral policy of containment' and Dulles denounced the Truman-Acheson approach as 'treadmill policies which, at best, might perhaps keep us in the same place until we drop exhausted.'

Dulles advanced as alternatives to containment a series of policies which would permit the United States to seize the initiative in world affairs. A prominent Protestant layman with a moralistic view of America's responsibilities, he objected that containment abandoned 'countless human beings to a despotism and Godless terrorism' and proposed the 'liberation' of the captive peoples of eastern Europe. The satellites were to be liberated not by force but by the intensity of our moral indignation. The mere announcement by the United States 'that it wants and expects liberation to occur would change, in an electrifying way, the mood of the captive peoples,' Dulles claimed. 'Never before,' noted one writer, 'had the illusion of American omnipotence demanded so much of American diplomacy.'

At the same time that Eisenhower and Dulles would roll back the Iron Curtain and 'unleash' Chiang to assault the Chinese mainland, they would reduce the armed forces. They shared the fear of men like Senator Taft that America's security was threatened less from abroad than by inflationary spending to meet foreign commitments. Under what Admiral Radford, chairman of the Joint Chiefs of Staff, called the 'New Look' policy, the United States cut back on expensive ground troops and placed more reliance on

John Foster Dulles (1888–1959). This photograph shows the peripatetic Secretary of State in a characteristic action—in full stride after alighting from an aircraft. (*Wide World*)

nuclear bombs, which the air force would deliver. The New Look responded to America's pride in air power and its revulsion from trench warfare. Although it reduced military spending, the administration insisted it was providing greater security by getting 'more bang for a buck.'

In January 1954 Dulles announced that henceforth the United States would rely more on 'the deterrent of massive retaliatory power . . . a great capacity to retaliate instantly, by means and at times of our own choosing.' The doctrine of 'massive retaliation' reflected the irritation of much of the country with limited war, as a result of the Korean experience. The United States, declared Secretary Humphrey, had 'no business getting into little wars.' If the country had to intervene, he said, 'let's intervene decisively with all we have got or stay out.' But the trouble with the massive retaliation doctrine was that it escalated every dispute into an occasion for a war of annihilation, and, if carried to its logical conclusion, left the country with no alternative save surrender or a nuclear holocaust. Moreover, since the threat of nuclear retaliation had not proved effective even when the United States held an atomic monopoly, it seemed even less likely to work now that Russia had its own nuclear arsenal.

In the end the Eisenhower foreign policies differed from those of Truman more in style than in substance. The President shared Dulles's faith in 'personal' diplomacy; not only was everything to be talked out in front of microphones and television lights but the participants should be principals, not subordinates. Eisenhower preferred to negotiate 'at the summit'; while Dulles, flitting from continent to continent, turned out to be the most traveled Secretary of State in American history prior to Kissinger. But despite the bustle, the new administration learned that it had far less room for maneuver in the conduct of foreign affairs than it imagined.

Elected on a platform which charged the Democrats with waging war in Korea 'without the will to victory' and with 'ignominious bartering with our enemies,' Eisenhower quickly scored one of the most important achievements of his administration by bartering with the enemy to secure a peace without victory in Korea. In obtaining a cease-fire in that stricken country, the President fixed the pattern for the remainder of his years in office: warlike rhetoric would yield to deeds of peace. The war had cost the United States some 30,000 dead and over 100,000 wounded and missing; Korean and Chinese casualties probably totalled more than two million. Korea, divided absurdly at the waist, faced an uncertain and gloomy future. It was threatened hourly by the 'People's Republic' on its northern boundary and by Communist China and Russia on its flanks; lacking a sound economic basis, it subsisted largely on the vast sums poured in by the United States, which was committed to come to its aid. Syngman Rhee, who grew more and more dictatorial with the passing years, was eventually ousted by a popular rebellion, only to be succeeded by the equally dictatorial General Park. Still, if the outcome was less than satisfactory, Eisenhower had fulfilled his pledge to go to Korea, and the fighting had stopped.

In 1954 the revolution against colonialism in Asia and Africa presented another test of administration doctrines. For almost seven years Communist guerillas known as the Viet-Minh had been waging war against the French in the jungles of Indochina. By the summer of 1953 they had overrun much of the northern half of Vietnam, largest of the three states comprising French Indochina, and threatened the neighboring state of Laos. Fearful that the Communist wave might engulf the whole of southeastern Asia, and eager to take pressure off the French so that they could fulfill their obligations toward the European Defense Community, Truman had sent a military mission to Saigon and stepped up aid. By 1954 America was paying almost four-fifths of the cost of the war. When the French position became critical that spring, Dulles insisted that Indochina could not be permitted to fall; Admiral Radford proposed an air strike to save the beleaguered jungle fortress of Dienbienphu; and Vice-President Nixon favored, if necessary, 'putting our boys in.' But the British as well as elements in America, including military advisers and such Democratic leaders as Lyndon Johnson, opposed action which might lead to another Korea. Eisenhower believed that the United States had a vital stake in Vietnam. 'You have a row of dominoes set up,' he explained. 'You knock over the first one, and what will happen to the last one is that it will go over very quickly.' But despite his attraction to this 'domino theory,' he was persuaded to veto the plan to intervene. When the United States permitted Dienbienphu to fall on 7 May, the doctrine of massive retaliation died an early death. As a consequence of a conference at Geneva of the great powers, the Kingdoms of Cambodia and Laos emerged as nominally independent new nations, while Vietnam was divided provisionally in two along the 17th parallel until free elections could be held.

To counter Communist influence in this region, Dulles took steps to create an Asiatic defense community that would parallel NATO. In November 1954, Pakistan, Thailand, and the Philippines joined with the United States, Britain, France, Australia, and New Zealand to set up a Southeast Asia Treaty Organization (SEATO). Unlike NATO, however, SEATO existed largely on paper; the signatories had no obligation save to consult, although in the 1960's it would be falsely argued that the United States was compelled by its SEATO commitment to intervene militarily in Vietnam.

At the same time that Dulles was negotiating the SEATO pact, he was fostering liberation illusions on Formosa—now called Taiwan—whither Chiang Kai-shek and the Chinese Nationalists had betaken themselves when driven by the Reds from the mainland in 1949. With the encouragement of Taft's successor as Republican leader in the Senate, William Knowland, 'the Senator from Formosa,' Dulles nurtured the unrealistic notion that Chiang, representing the true and rightful government of all China, would eventually recross the Formosa Strait and reconquer the mainland. Chiang multiplied the dangers of the Formosan problem by occupying a group of small islands—Quemoy, Matsu, and the Tachens—close to the Chinese mainland. On his accession to the presidency, Eisenhower had announced that he was lifting Truman's 'blockade' of Taiwan by the U.S. Seventh Fleet, thus 'unleashing' Chiang Kai-shek

President Eisenhower greets the Prime Minister of India, Jawaharlal Nehru, in the north portico of the White House as journalists make notes and snap pictures. In the 1950's relations between the two leaders were made more difficult by the pro-Chinese attitudes of India's supercilious special envoy, Krishna Menon, and by the hardshelled hostility to neutralism of America's sanctimonious Secretary of State, John Foster Dulles. *(Library of Congress)*

for an attack upon the mainland, an enterprise that existed largely in the minds of men like Senator Knowland, for Chiang lacked the strength to carry it out. When, in the summer of 1954, the Communists began a heavy bombardment of the off-shore islands, the President told the Congress that 'in the interest of peace the United States must remove any doubt regarding our readiness to fight.' Congress responded with a somewhat ambiguous resolution authorizing the President to use the armed force of the nation 'as he deems necessary' to defend this region, one of the few times in history that Congress formally gave the Executive power to involve the nation in war at his discretion. But Eisenhower once again pulled back from a war of liberation, and Chiang gave up the Tachens to the Communists.

In August 1958 the problem flared up again when the Communists opened another and heavier bombardment of the islands. Dulles promptly asserted that the United States stood ready to repel any attack, and the Seventh Fleet escorted troops which Chiang rushed to garrison the beleaguered islands. But public opinion at home and abroad reacted sharply to the threat of war over these islands, which were almost as close to the Chinese mainland as Staten Island is to Manhattan. Were they really worth an atomic war—or even a 'conventional' war? On 30 September, Dulles executed a stunning reversal. He stated that Chiang had been 'rather foolish' and declared that the United States had 'no commitment to help Chiang back to the mainland'; Eisenhower, who had recklessly committed himself to the ambitions of the Nationalists, now said that Chiang's build-up of troops on the offshore islands was 'a thorn in the side of peace.' On 23 October, Dulles 'releashed' Chiang by compelling him to renounce publicly the use of force to regain control of the mainland of China. So ended another experiment in 'liberation.'

In a magazine interview Dulles offered an explanation of his approach which gave birth to a new term: 'brinkmanship.' He stated:

> You have to take chances for peace, just as you must take chances in war. Some say that we were brought to the verge of war. Of course we were brought to the verge of war. The ability to get to the verge of war without getting into the war is the necessary art. If you cannot master it, you inevitably get into wars. If you try to run away from it, if you are scared to go to the brink, you are lost. We've had to look it square in the face—on the question of enlarging the Korean War, on the question of getting into the Indo-China war, on the question of Formosa. We walked to the brink and we looked it in the face.

Critics not only disputed the accuracy of Dulles's account of these incidents but asked whether, in a world of nuclear terror, such an attitude was not irresponsibly provocative.

However, the administration matched these bellicose gestures with more pacific ones, and at times, especially midway through Eisenhower's first term, the new administration displayed a more conciliatory attitude. By 1955 a series of events combined to bring about a mild thaw in the Cold War: the death of Stalin, truce in Korea, a cease-fire in the Formosa Strait, a compromise peace in Vietnam. Eisenhower himself had become a symbol of peace. In a dramatic gesture before the United Nations Assembly in December 1953 he had proposed that the major scientific nations of the world jointly contribute to a United Nations pool of atomic power to be used exclusively for peaceful purposes. On four crucial occasions—Korea, Taiwan, Indochina, and in negotiations with China over prisoners—he had thrown the weight of his influence to the side of peace. The European defense community was now a reality. A wave of prosperity surged through Western Europe, greatly diminishing fear of Communist subversion or aggression. Russia, having detonated a hydrogen bomb, showed signs of a more reasonable relationship with the West. As if to dramatize the new spirit, the Soviet Union in May 1955 ended its long and harsh occupation of Austria.

Thus the stage was set for the 'summit' conference at Geneva in mid-summer 1955, at which Eisenhower proposed a disarmament plan that caught the popular imagination. He called upon Russia and the United States to:

> give each other a complete blueprint of our military establishments, from beginning to end, from one end of our countries to the other; lay out the establishments and provide the blueprints to each other. Next to provide within our countries facilities for aerial photography to the other country, ample facilities for aerial reconnaissance where you can make all the pictures you choose and take them to your own country to study, you to provide exactly the same facilities for us, and we to make these examinations, and by this step to convince the world that we are providing as between ourselves against the possibility of great surprise attack, thus lessening danger and relaxing tension.

'What I propose,' he added, 'would be but a beginning.' As Moscow would not even consider Eisenhower's generous offer, nothing came of the Geneva conference. But the 'spirit of Geneva' still seemed to many to symbolize the change in mood that Eisenhower epitomized—from the rancorous 'thirties and 'forties to the more tranquil 'fifties.

Affluence and Apprehension

Tocqueville had predicted that American society in achieving equality would preserve the same civilization, habits, and manners. In the Eisenhower years, it appeared that this prophecy had been fulfilled. To some, this was a source of pride; to others, an occasion for dismay; while still others were more impressed by the persistence of inequality. The nineteen-fifties would be remembered as a period of placidity typified by the genial Eisenhower. But this was also a decade of discord and strife as well as dissatisfaction with a culture which conveyed the dreary sense, in the words of the novelist John Updike, of 'a climate of time between, of standoff and day-by-day.' Mobility and affluence opened greater opportunities to millions of Americans, but before Eisenhower's reign was over an accumulation of problems—the decline of the central city and the countryside, the vicissitudes of the economy, the impairment of national prestige in the 'space race', and the complacency of political leadership—would lead to questioning of whether the United States had not lost its sense of 'national purpose.'

The 'affluent society' derived from the phenomenal expansion of the economy in the postwar era. By 1955 the United States, with only 6 per cent of the world's population, was turning out half the world's goods. From 1945 to 1967 the gross national product increased from $213 billion to $775 billion a year; even when adjusted for inflation, this was an astonishing gain. In the twenty years after 1940 electrical energy surged from 150 to 800 trillion kilowatt hours. The economy was sparked by the emergence of new industries like plastics and electronics and by the huge investments of business and government in research. Not content with the vast home market, American corporations bought control of great automobile, drug, and electrical companies overseas, and economists expressed concern about the vast power of the 'multinational corporation.'

This prodigious economic growth brought a sharp rise in national income and a remarkable expansion of the middle class. From 1945 to 1970, a time when 22 million people, including a sizable segment of women, were added to the labor force, real weekly earnings of factory workers increased 50 per cent and the proportion of Americans defined as living in poverty was cut almost in half. Even more striking is the fact that the proportion of families and unattached individuals receiving an annual income of at least $10,000 (measured in 1968 dollars) had soared from 9 per cent in 1947 to 33 per cent in 1968.

The most impressive social development was the advance, rather than the decline, of equalitarianism. The expansion of the middle class, the cessation of large-scale immigration, the advent of all but universal high school education and the enormous increment in college and university enrollments, the standardization of consumer products—all of these developments tended to make American society at mid-twentieth century more equalitarian. The gap between native and foreign-born, Protestant, Catholic, and Jew, narrowed, and representatives of newer stocks like Governor DiSalle and Governor Rosellini, Secretary Ribicoff and Secretary Goldberg, moved into the seats of power. With 95 per cent of the population native-born, American society became more homogeneous, though racial distinctions remained painfully significant.

America was the first country in modern history where each generation had more education than its forebears—an elementary consideration which goes far to explain that child-centered society which puzzled foreign observers. The familiar process of enlarging both the base and the height of the educational pyramid was greatly accelerated in the years after the Second World War. Prosperity, the G.I. Bill of Rights, the urgent demands for expertise—all of these combined to give a powerful impetus to education. By 1960 the college occupied about the same position in the educational enterprise as the high school in 1920 and the junior college in 1940. Between 1920 and 1960, the total number of students at institutions of higher education grew from less than 600,000 to 3.6 million, a critical development in the enlargement of the middle class.

Automation in industry, mechanization on the farm, and labor-saving devices in the home combined to add to the hours of leisure. For thousands of years most men and women, and many children too, had worked from sun-up to sun-down; now, abruptly, the work day was cut to seven hours and the work week to five days or occasionally even less, with paid holidays and more extended vacations. Industries catering to leisure flourished: boating, golf, skiing, camping, touring, and swimming pools, and as the work ethic evaporated America became increasingly a society dedicated to play. Television, which absorbed many leisure hours each day, was in almost no homes at the start of the postwar era, became widespread in the 1950's, and was virtually universal in the 'sixties. It affected the political process, was a strong nationalizing influence, and carried the pervasive consumer culture into every section of the country.

As fewer farmers and workers were needed to produce the food and goods for an affluent society, the service industries swiftly became central to the economy, a development which also helped to obliterate class lines. In 1956 for the first time white collar workers outnumbered blue collar employees. Between 1947 and 1957, the number of factory operatives declined 4 per cent while clerical workers increased 23 per cent and the salaried middle class 61 per cent. The proportion of self-employed dropped sharply, and an increasing number of Americans spent their lives in a world of organizations, a phenomenon which many found alarming. In W. H. Whyte, Jr.'s *The Organization Man*, C. Wright Mills's *White Collar*, Vance Packard's *The Status Seekers*, and Sloan Wilson's *The Man in the Gray Flannel Suit*, a bureaucratized society discouraged the free-wheeling individual and placed a premium on conformity, and in John Hersey's *The Child Buyer* a pupil is marked down as a troublesome deviate because he scores poorly in 'followership.' The 'other-directed man' described by David Riesman, whose aptly titled *The Lonely Crowd* was the prophetic book of this generation, engaged in 'smooth, unruffled manipulation of the self' to satisfy an 'irrational craving for indiscriminate approval.'

The economy of the second half of the century created a new type of employee whose talents lay primarily in adaptability and team work rather than independence and ingenuity; and it discouraged dominant personalities, even at the top. Just as the academic system no longer produced strong presidents like Eliot, Butler, and Harper, so the new economy rarely brought to the fore new Rockefellers, Carnegies, McCormicks, and Morgans. Yet if there was social loss in the failure of innovative and strong-willed leaders to emerge, few deplored the passing of the type represented by George Baer, Tom Girdler, or Sewell Avery; if leadership was blander, it was also more responsive.

Even in organized labor, where the tradition of personal leadership was strong, warriors like John L. Lewis and idealists like Eugene Debs gave way to bureaucrats who ran large and flourishing organizations from comfortable and well-staffed offices. In the postwar years unions achieved both prosperity and stability. In 1955 when the A.F. of L. and the C.I.O. merged, they boasted a joint membership of 17 million; still only one-fourth of the entire labor force, it was well over one-half of blue collar workers who had always been the core of labor strength. By then organized labor generally had secured the 40-hour week, vacations with pay, and welfare benefits. As labor prospered, it became increasingly conservative. European union officials claimed that the only way they could tell the difference between businessmen and labor leaders in America is that the union chieftains dressed better and drove bigger cars.

Social critics who had long been disturbed by the inequalities in American life now expressed their anxiety about the trend toward a homogenized society. They drew a dismaying picture of the American suburb which displayed the same 'ranch houses' on single or split levels, with picture windows, television antennae, and a two-car garage; the same well-manicured back gardens with little swimming pools; the same country clubs and shopping centers and supermarkets, all built to a pattern. Almost all the men commuted to nearby cities, society was matriarchal, and the well-protected young gravitated from the local high or country-day school to the state university or the Ivy League college of the East.

But American society had more variety than such a portrait suggests. To be sure, in the Eisenhower years, many observers sensed that

'Office in a Small City' by Edward Hopper, 1953. 'In the inhuman surfaces of urban life,' the art critic Sam Hunter has written, Hopper 'has found metaphors for spiritual vacancy and imprisonment. . . . He is an artist of American ennui and loneliness. . . . His atmosphere . . . is stifling and curiously unreal, with a strange anxiety hovering at its edges. . . . The result of his combination of bald literalism and dramatic heightening by a mysterious alchemy of light, is to give a mood of impenetrable monotony the quality of a dream.' (*Metropolitan Museum of Art, George A. Hearn Fund, 1953*)

'the bland were leading the bland,' and the college generation of the 1950's seemed exceptionally passive. Still, not even the suburbs were uniform: in New York's Westchester County blacks in the river streets of Ossining lived different lives from bankers on Scarsdale estates, as the world of Cicero differed from that of Oak Park, and Daly City from Tiburon. No doubt standardization and conformity are tributes that a mobile, equalitarian society is often compelled to pay, but this same movement toward equality opened up new opportunities for many Americans.

Nevertheless, mobility exacted a heavy toll, and increasingly social observers asked whether the pace of change, affecting every type of community from metropolis to village, was not moving too fast. The census of 1960 revealed what had long been foreseen—the erosion of the great cities: eight of the ten largest cities had fewer people in 1960 than in 1950. The movement to the suburbs began well before the war, but after 1945 it became something like a mass migration. Driven by the urge for space and privacy, better schools and recreation facilities, by concern about status, and sometimes by the lure of all-white communities, some 40 or 50 million Americans had by 1960 found refuge in suburbia or, as the fringes came to be called, 'exurbia.' The well-to-do led the exodus to outlying areas, thus depriving the central cities of much of their tax base; city residential districts deteriorated into ghettos of the poor. As population fled to the suburbs, newcomers from the cotton fields of Mississippi, the mountains of West Virginia, and the teeming villages of Puerto Rico poured in to fill some of the void. A few cities, such as New Haven, had some success in arresting the erosion that was eating them away, but for the most part the efforts of cities to stop decay were like those of Alice in her race with the Red Queen: they found that they had to run at least twice as fast if they expected to get anywhere.

Many came to question whether the American city was governable. Efforts to raze slums through 'urban renewal' often resulted in sterile housing projects which destroyed the old neighborhoods. Strikes of municipal employees crippled essential services for weeks at a time; white policemen and black residents viewed one another with mutual suspicion; and by 1968 the welfare population of New York City had passed 900,000, with one person on welfare for every three employed in private industry. Lewis Mumford wrote mordantly: 'Lacking any sense of an intelligent purpose or a desirable goal, the inhabitants of our great American cities are simply "waiting for Godot."'

The automobile not only made it possible to live in the suburbs, or far out in the country, and do business in the city, but also, by creating insoluble traffic problems, ruining public transportation, devouring space for parking lots (two-thirds of central Los Angeles has been given over to streets, freeways, parking lots, and garages) and filling the air with noxious fumes, made it disagreeable to live in the central city. Intended as a vehicle for quick mobility, the automobile no longer served this function in many cities. In 1911 a horse and buggy paced through Los Angeles at 11 m.p.h.; in 1962 an auto moved through the city at rush hour at an average of 5 m.p.h. Yet while commuter railroads received little government aid, federal and local governments poured money into highways which funneled yet more traffic into the city.

As metropolitan areas wrestled with the problems of growth, the countryside became citified. Nearly 70 per cent of the population lived in and near cities in 1970, when the total farm population was less than in 1830. For generations farmers had taken pride in sending their children to agricultural colleges; now these schools dropped the word 'agricultural' from their names, and the students turned to everything except tilling the soil.

While some fretted about the transformation of rural and urban society, others worried about what the swift pace of change was doing to the economy, for if growth continued, so did concentration. The giant corporation came to be more and more gigantic, and the ten years after 1948 saw no fewer than 2191 mergers and combinations of corporations worth over $10 million. Between 1940 and 1960 bank deposits increased fourfold, but the number of banks declined by over one thousand and branch banking came to be almost as common in the United States as in Great Britain. Three great corporations—General Motors, Ford, and Chrysler—dominated the automobile industry, although in the 'fifties a fourth, American Motors, entered the competition. Three networks all but monopolized the air; six tobacco companies fed the insatiable appetite of Americans for cigarettes. Even in the realm of news the process seemed inexorable. In 1910 almost 700 cities and towns in the United States had competing daily newspapers; by 1967 the number had fallen to 64, and 17 states were without any locally competing newspapers. In many cities newspaper publishers held a news monopoly by owning the radio and television stations as well.

Automation increased apace, as computers stored and used information to control, adjust, and correct complex operations. Walter Reuther wrote:

> I went to work in the automotive industry back in 1927. At that time, it took us about twenty-four hours to take a rough engine block, as it was cast in the foundry, and to machine that block, ready for assembly. . . . We kept making progress. We cut it down to 18 hours, and then 14 hours, then 12, then 9 hours. If you'll go through the Cleveland Ford engine plant, which is fully automated, you will see a Ford V-engine, 8 cylinders—a very complicated piece of mechanism—in which the rough castings are automatically fed into this automated line, and in fourteen and six-tenths minutes later, it is fully machined, without a human hand touching it. . . . There are acres and acres of machines, and here and there you will find a worker standing at a master switchboard, just watching green and yellow lights blinking off and on, which tell the worker what is happening in the machine.[1]

1. Walter P. Reuther, *Selected Papers,* Henry M. Christman (ed.), pp. 178, 180.

'Supermarket' by Ben Shahn, 1957. In the postwar era, painters like Shahn and Andy Warhol, as well as poets such as Allen Ginsberg and Randall Jarrell, were captivated by the consumer culture. Shahn called this serigraph of shopping baskets, one of several works commissioned by CBS, 'among the abiding symbols of American life, to be celebrated and brought into awareness.' (*Philadelphia Museum of Art, the Print Club Permanent Coll.*)

Automation presented labor with the menace of falling employment—and industry with the peril of declining purchasing power among workers; made inevitable the shorter working day, week, and year; and gave rise to an urgent demand for the annual wage. At a time when the numbers of young and old were growing at the expense of the numbers in between, it denied employment to the young and retired the old, thus putting on the 20- to 55-year-olds an ever increasing burden of support for the rest of the community. Since the new technology raised skill requirements for jobs, the school 'dropout' was at a disadvantage, and educational opportunities assumed increased urgency.

America had never known an economy of scarcity in the Old World sense of the term, but in the past it had always been able to dispose of its abundance by a steady rise in the standard of living and by exports. Now the capacity of farm and factory to produce far more than could normally be consumed created a new series of problems. Four responses were adopted in whole or in part. One was to build obsolescence into the product itself, thus making reasonably sure that there would be a continuous demand for new models. A second was to create new consumer wants: this task was the special responsibility of the advertisers, who rose to so prominent a position that the term 'Madison Avenue' came to take on some of the connotations that 'Wall Street' had held a generation earlier. A third technique was to dump vast quantities of surplus goods abroad—to give wheat or airplanes, dynamos or books, to 'needy' nations. The fourth, government expenditures in the public area—highways, airports, the military, the exploration of outer space—helped keep the economy going.

Though the nation's space enterprise owed something to the desire to stimulate the economy, it owed more to concern about the country's prestige, and also about the state of American society. In October 1957 the Russians startled Americans by putting a satellite in orbit around the globe; a month later Sputnik II, more than six times heavier and carrying a live dog, orbited the earth;

Edward Hopper, 'Western Motel, 1957. Lloyd Goodrich, the leading authority on Hopper, has written: '*Western Motel* with its awful interior in decorator's green, beige, and crimson, its hard-faced blonde, its bright green automobile, and its bare desert landscape under a burning sun, is one of his toughest pictures of any period. It makes no concessions to accepted ideas of what is artistically admissible. Its garish colors are unsoftened by grays. It captures the quintessence of that most American of institutions, the motel. In a purely naturalistic style it is as firsthand an exposé of our mass culture as pop art.' (*Yale University Art Gallery*)

and in 1959 they fired a rocket past the moon. These achievements led to self-searching examination to explain how the Soviet Union had managed to get ahead of the United States in the 'space race.' In particular, publicists took a hard look at the American educational system. They found that Russia was spending a larger proportion of its income on education than was the United States, and Russian and Western European students who left school at eighteen were better educated than the average American of college age. Not a few blamed the inadequacies of American schools on progressive education, which valued 'adjustment' more than intellectual discipline. One consequence of the furor was that the national government became much more willing to grant funds to colleges, often to good effect but also with the less desired result of shaping the curriculum to the needs of the Department of Defense. The 'Sputnik crisis' also led to far-ranging, and often tendentious, discussion of whether the country did not have a distorted sense of values, a matter which, from a very different perspective, was also disturbing American men of letters.

The literature of these years reflected the anxiety of 'the lonely crowd.' The leader of the postwar poets, Robert Lowell, in *Lord Weary's Castle*, voiced the same absorbed interest in the quest for identity that characterized novels like Saul Bellow's *The Adventures of Augie March* and the writings of J. D. Salinger, who, one critic observed, presented 'madness as the chief temptation of modern life, especially for the intelligent young.' Salinger's *The Catcher in the Rye*, which sold almost two million copies, became the special favorite of adolescents in the 1950's. Writers persistently sounded the theme of loneliness, isolation, and the inability of people to communicate with one another. In one of Tennessee Williams's plays a character says, 'We're all of us sentenced to solitary confinement inside our own skins for life.' If America's mobile society permitted unparalleled freedom, it also cut people off from tradition and a sense of community, a rootlessness which concerned almost all of these writers. In Truman Capote's *Other Voices: Other Rooms*, one character protests, 'We go screaming round the world, dying in our rented rooms, nightmare hotels, eternal homes of the transient heart.'

In the early nineteen-fifties very few writers expressed their foreboding about the path America had taken, but in Eisenhower's second term a hornet's nest of troubles swarmed around him, and pundits raised an outcry about the country's lack of a sense of 'national purpose.' Late in 1957 a severe recession brought an abrupt and unanticipated end to the 'Eisenhower prosperity.' With the country reeling from the shock of the highest unemployment rate since 1941, it learned that Eisenhower's 'crusade' for decency in government had also turned out unhappily. 'Not one appointee of this Administration has been involved in scandal or corruption,' the President had boasted. But in his second term a series of scandals rocked the administration. The worst blow fell in September 1958 when Sherman Adams had to resign as confidential assistant to the President after a congressional committee had exposed his indiscreet relations with an industrial promoter. As a consequence of these developments, American voters in 1958 handed the Republicans their third consecutive congressional defeat, an event unprecedented in the history of a party that controlled the executive branch. The Democrats swelled their margin in the Senate from a one-seat advantage to almost 2–1 and gained the largest proportion in the House that any party had won since Roosevelt's landslide in 1936.

In the last two years of Eisenhower's tenure a conflict between the President and liberal Democrats in Congress created a virtual deadlock in Washington. Eisenhower, convinced that the Democrats were leading the country down the road to socialism, set himself obdurately against proposals for Federal action in areas like education and housing; liberal Democrats knew that they could enact such legislation only if they were able to muster a two-thirds vote to override the President's veto, an unlikely circumstance. On the other hand, Eisenhower could not impose his will on Congress since he confronted the largest opposition majority in the twentieth century. In such a situation an unusual share of the responsibility for leadership fell to such moderates as Majority Leader Lyndon B. Johnson and Speaker Sam Rayburn, both veteran Texas Democrats who pursued a course of compromise with the administration. In vain, liberal Democrats protested that the Johnson-Rayburn strategy of slicing appropriations to escape vetoes blurred the party's identity and surrendered crucial legislation to the President's 'reckless frugality spree.' Despite the large Democratic majorities, accomplishments were meager.

A World in Turmoil

In Eisenhower's last years in office he took even more direct responsibility for the conduct of foreign affairs than for domestic policy. In April 1959 Dulles, fatally ill, resigned; his successor, Christian Herter, was much less self-assertive, and, with both Dulles and Adams gone, the President grasped the reins more firmly. In the next year he made trips which rivaled Dulles's peregrinations: a 22,000-mile journey to eleven countries from Spain to India and a good-will tour of Latin America. 'There is no place on this earth to which I would not travel, there is no chore I would not undertake, if I had any faintest hope that by so doing, I would promote the general cause of world peace,' Eisenhower said. On these travels, as at the conference in Geneva, the President's personal commitment to avoid a nuclear war was unmistakable. In India people showered him with flowers until he stood a foot deep in them, and he was hailed with signs: 'WELCOME PRINCE OF PEACE.' Yet well before then he had been taught that dedication was not enough and that the world was rapidly spinning out of control.

Even before Eisenhower's first term was over, the 'spirit of Geneva,' which had inspired such high hopes, had evaporated. At the celebration of the Twentieth Communist Party Congress in February 1956, Nikita Khrushchev, the new leader of the USSR, startled the world by a fierce attack on his predecessor, Stalin; that kind of savage leadership, he implied, was a thing of the past. Seven months later the festering discontent of the Poles broke out into the open; and under the leadership of Wladyslaw Gomulka, the Poles demanded freedom from Soviet bayonets and autonomy within the Communist system. When Khrushchev accepted these demands, it looked like the dawn of a new and better day. But when that same autumn the long-suffering Hungarians rose up against Communist misrule, Khrushchev sent two hundred thousand soldiers and thousands of tanks, and while the West looked on in despair, this heroic revolt was ruthlessly stamped out. These events revealed the hollowness of 'massive retaliation' and 'liberation' when Eisenhower refrained from intervening.

The crisis in the Middle East, which erupted the very same week the Hungarian revolt was put down, had been building since World War II. Syria and Lebanon had asserted their independence; and in 1948 the British gave up their mandate in Palestine, the Israelis struck for freedom and, when invaded by the combined forces of Egypt, Lebanon, Jordan, and Syria, broke the invaders and won independence. In 1952 the King of Egypt was driven into exile, and two years later Colonel Gamal Abdel Nasser took over the government, as Arab nationalism surged through the whole Moslem world.

Into this extraordinarily complex situation Dulles jumped with both feet. When he attempted to create a regional defense against Soviet penetration, the result was the Baghdad Pact of 1954 to which Turkey, Iraq, Iran, and Pakistan adhered, but not the United States! The Pact did not in fact intimidate the Soviets; it did, however, antagonize Nasser, who saw it as a deliberate attempt to undermine his own leadership and to split the Moslem world. Nasser struck back by negotiating for the withdrawal of all British troops from the Suez Canal zone by 1956; forming a close military alliance with Syria, Jordan, and Saudi Arabia; swinging a deal with Czechoslovakia for arms, presumably to use against the Israelis; and launching a war of nerves—and of attrition—against Israel by denying Israeli ships passage through the Suez Canal, by subversion, and by ceaseless threats of destruction. Finally, he entered on the dangerous game of inviting the United States and the USSR to bid against each other for the privilege of financing a vast dam and irrigation system at Aswan on the Upper Nile. Dulles first offered to help Egypt build the dam, then abruptly withdrew the offer.

On 26 July 1956, one week after Dulles's about-face, Nasser precipitated a serious world crisis by seizing the Suez Canal in clear violation of treaty agreements. Faced with the prospect of being cut off from essential Middle East oil supplies, the British and French determined to use force to recover control of the Canal. This provided Israel with an opportunity to launch its own offensive against Egypt. On 29 October, as Russian tanks were rumbling into the streets of Budapest, Israeli troops invaded the Sinai peninsula, scattered a much larger Egyptian army, and within a few days were on the banks of the Canal. When Britain and France joined in hastily with aerial attacks, Nasser responded by sinking enough ships in the Canal to close it to traffic indefinitely. Here were the makings of another major war, for India and the Soviet bloc threatened to pile in unless there was an immediate cease-fire. A possibly fatal rift between East and West was avoided when the United Nations, too, denounced the war as aggression and the United States supported the UN position. But though hostilities ended, the Suez affair had driven a wedge between the United States and her allies, while playing into the hands of Nasser, who now presented himself as the very symbol of Arab nationalism in its struggle against Western imperialism. The peaceful settlement was a victory for Eisenhower; a few more such victories and the Western alliance would be in ruins.

The Suez dispute had created a situation favorable to the expansion of Communist influence throughout the Middle East, and in January 1957 Eisenhower asked for authority to extend economic assistance to Middle Eastern countries and to use the armed forces to protect any nation 'threatened by aggression from any country controlled by international communism.' On 9 March Congress authorized some $200 million for economic and military aid to implement this 'Eisenhower Doctrine.' When in the spring of 1958 nationalists threatened the pro-Western government of Lebanon, there was some doubt about the applicability of the Eisenhower Doctrine, but Eisenhower immediately ordered the Sixth Fleet to steam into the eastern Mediterranean and dispatched marines to Lebanon. By October the crisis had eased, but Russia hurriedly announced that it would help finance Egypt's Aswan dam, and henceforth the United States would have to cope with the fact that the Soviet Union was in the Middle East to stay.

Preoccupied with affairs across the sea, the United States failed to take note of what was happening in the Western hemisphere. The abrupt cessation of wartime purchases dealt a heavy blow to Latin American economies; the population explosion pressed implacably on existing resources which were exploited by foreign capital; the gap between rich and poor grew wider. Latin American friendship was taken for granted. Down to 1951 all the Latin American republics together had received about the same amount of foreign aid as Greece; and in the next ten years Latin America received only $3.4 billion out of a total of some $80 billion in aid: that was less than Taiwan got.

Events in Guatemala shocked the United States out of its complacency. For years that little Central American state had groaned under the dictatorship of General Jorge Castañeda; in 1954 he was overthrown and the government came under the control of Jacobo Arbenz, sympathetic to Communism. He and his followers carried through a wholesale confiscation of land, dominated the labor unions, ran the government-owned newspapers, and obtained arms from Poland. Alive to the proximity of Guatemala to the Panama Canal, Dulles shipped arms to Guatemalan rebels gathering along the Honduras border, and in June these forces, with American support, invaded Guatemala, overthrew the Arbenz government, and set up a new regime led by ultra-conservatives. What Secretary Dulles cheered as a triumph for constitutionalism, most Latin Americans, with greater logic, condemned as old-fashioned intervention in the same year that Eisenhower presented the Legion of Merit to the dictators of Venezuela and Peru. When in 1958 Vice-President Nixon visited South America on a good will tour he was showered with anti-American pamphlets in Uruguay, stoned in Peru, mobbed in Venezuela. Only tardily did the United States apply itself to mending its Latin American fences by stepping up economic aid.

Cuba provided a hard test for the new departure. In January 1959 a rebellion led by Fidel Castro succeeded in overthrowing the cruel dictatorship of General Batista. Influenced by his Argentine Communist economic adviser, 'Che' Guevara, Castro apparently planned to turn the 'Pearl of the Antilles' into the first Communist country in the New World. This was not evident for some time. Castro made a triumphant tour of eastern America in 1959, and in Washington was promised economic aid. But when Castro returned to Cuba, he dispensed with elections, threw thousands of Cubans who opposed his regime into jail, and expropriated plantations and major businesses. When the United States protested, Castro became overtly hostile and moved ever closer to the USSR, which for the first time had a foothold in the Western hemisphere.

At the same time that Eisenhower bridled at the establishment of a Communist beachhead in the Caribbean, he approached a potentially even more explosive confrontation with the Kremlin over Berlin. Under the auspices of Russia, the Communists had sought to make East Germany a showpiece of Communism which would win over the hesitant neighbors in the West. To their in-

Paul Cadmus, 'Night in Bologna,' 1958. In the cold war years large numbers of Americans, military and civilian, were stationed at posts thousands of miles from home. Cadmus's painting of an American soldier in Italy conveys a sense of yearning and foreboding in an alien land. (*Sara Roby Foundation, New York*)

tense mortification, every week thousands of East Germans escaped into West Germany, which prospered beyond any other European state, and it was West Berlin, a glittering jewel in the drab fabric of East Germany, that was the showpiece. A thriving rearmed West Germany, its economy united with that of France and other nations in the European Economic Community, its NATO forces possibly equipped by the United States with nuclear weapons, raised a threat which the Communist bloc regarded with grave misgivings. In 1958 Khrushchev delivered an ultimatum to Berlin and the Germanies: either negotiate a settlement within six months, recognizing the permanent partition of Germany, or Russia would make a separate treaty with East Germany, giving it control of East Berlin and the air lanes into West Berlin. Committed to the defense of West Germany, and of Berlin as an outpost of freedom, and dependent on West Germany's contribution to the European defense system and to the economy of the Western world, the United States refused to back down. For the rest of Eisenhower's term, the Berlin controversy smoldered.

Yet at the same time Khrushchev showed an interest in conciliation, and Eisenhower was more than willing to meet him halfway. In September 1959, at the President's invitation, Khrushchev made his first visit to the United States; he wound up his tour at Eisenhower's rural retreat, Camp David, where the two leaders appeared to get on famously. The 'spirit of Camp David' supplanted the defunct 'spirit of Geneva' as the Western world prepared for a summit meeting to resolve the problems of Berlin and nuclear weapons. Not since the beginning of the Cold War had hopes for a peaceful world run so high.

Once again everything went wrong. On 5 May 1960, only eleven days before the summit conference was to have convened in Paris, Khrushchev announced that the Russians had shot down an American U-2 reconnaissance plane in the heart of Russia. After trapping the administration in a lie, the premier gave further details: they had captured the pilot, Francis Powers, who admitted that he was employed by the U.S. Central Intelligence Agency and engaged in aerial photographic espionage. Khrushchev chose to use this incident as an excuse to wreck the summit conference, and, in a deliberate insult, withdrew his invitation to the President to visit the USSR. American 'aggressors,' he cried, should be treated as a boy handled an erring cat: 'We would catch such a cat by the tail and bang its head against the wall.' A month later, the Russians broke up the ten-nation disarmament conference in Geneva. Eisenhower's hopes for a *détente* had been shattered.

Within less than two months of the U-2 fiasco, the friendly nation of Japan told Eisenhower it would be unsafe for him to visit their country; relations with Castro's Cuba fell to a new low; and Africa burst into flame. In the vast area of tropical Africa, one former colony after another won its independence, sometimes with a minimum of unpleasantness and a maximum of co-operation. But in the Congo (as well as in Algeria) prolonged violence attended the transfer of power. When the Belgians pulled out of the Congo, civil war erupted. Under the leadership of the intrepid Secretary-General, Dag Hammarskjöld, the United Nations raised an international military force to maintain the peace. But to extend Soviet influence south of the Equator, Khrushchev disrupted the work of the UN. In the same year that Soviet Russia penetrated the Western hemisphere for the first time, the Communists made their presence felt in the jungles of Africa. Soviet bloc technicians infiltrated the Congolese government, and Red China used Guinea as a base of operations in other African countries. The UN eventually brought the war under control and set the Congo on the road to nationhood, but the negotiations cost Hammarskjöld his life, and the Congo crisis provided a dreadful example of how Cold War rivalries might envelop the whole world.

The session of the United Nations which opened in September 1960 revealed the tumultuous changes that had taken place in the Eisenhower years. When Eisenhower took office, the West dominated the UN; now the Afro-Asian nations were the largest voting bloc, and African states that did not exist in 1953—countries like Upper Volta—each had parity with the United States in the General Assembly. To New York came a group of prominent leaders none of whom held power in 1953, all antagonistic to the United

States: Khrushchev, Nasser, Castro, as well as spokesmen for the revolution of rising expectations like Sukarno of Indonesia and Nkrumah of Ghana. As Khrushchev banged his shoe on a table to show his boorish displeasure, Castro assaulted the delegates with an interminable harangue, and American blacks stormed the chambers to protest the murder of the Congolese leader, Patrice Lumumba, it seemed that the winds of violence from every quarter of the globe were racing through the sheltered corridors of the pristine buildings on the East river, once fraught with hopes for peace.

Eisenhower: An Assessment

Eisenhower's place in history will probably rest less on what he did than on what he did not do. He gave the nation a chance to consolidate past gains, take stock of itself, and renew its spirits for future struggles. The querulous partisanship of the late Truman years had been mitigated, the acerbity of the national temper had been sweetened. Yet these achievements came at a price. By the very nature of his role as a moderator of differences, he could not risk dividing the country by raising new questions. Moreover, he had a limited interest in such matters and, at times, limited strength. One writer observed: 'When he leaves office in January 1961, the foreign policies and the domestic policies of the past generation will be about where he found them in 1953. No national problem, whether it be education, housing, urban revitalization, agriculture, or inflation, will have been advanced importantly toward solution nor its dimensions significantly altered.' Critics like the Harvard economist John Kenneth Galbraith charged that America's preoccupation with the output of consumer goods was starving the public sector, and Adlai Stevenson protested that the United States had become a society characterized by the 'contrast of public squalor and private opulence.' A country with a half-trillion dollar economy permitted crowded classrooms and hospital wards, antiquated transportation systems and festering slums. If America was more tranquil, the uneasy peace in the South had been bought at the expense of the blacks. None could doubt that Eisenhower had made an important contribution toward unifying the nation, but not a few asked whether the price that had been paid was too high.

In foreign policy it seems likely that Eisenhower's place in history will rest largely on what he did not do. Above all he did not go to war: he achieved peace in Korea and resisted the temptation to intervene in Vietnam and Quemoy, in Hungary and Suez. Even the Lebanon episode was quickly ended. Elected on a platform of denouncing containment, he had gone beyond the Truman-Acheson policies to explore the possibility of peaceful coexistence with the Communist world. And he ended his tenure by warning against 'the acquisition of unwarranted influence, whether sought or unsought, by the military-industrial complex.' Yet it could fairly be asked whether Eisenhower and Dulles had not, by rhetoric and deed, often contributed to the atmosphere of violence and to the recurrent crises which brought the world to the 'brink' of war. Even in his last days in office the President was heading toward a collision with the Russians in Laos and promoting an invasion of Castro's Cuba. He went out of office with his hopes for peace unfulfilled and with America's world prestige diminished, and he left to his successor a legacy of difficulties—in Berlin, in Cuba, in the Middle East, in Southeast Asia—which might, at any moment, bring on that war of annihilation that he so conscientiously sought to prevent.

36

From Camelot to the Reagan Era

*

1960 to the Present

John Fitzgerald Kennedy

In 1960, as the elderly Eisenhower prepared to leave office, both major parties turned to younger men, each of whom had been identified with the unadventurous politics of the 1950's. The Republicans named the Vice-President, Richard Nixon; the Democrats the senator from Massachusetts, John F. Kennedy, who, to the dismay of liberals, persuaded Lyndon Johnson, the middle-of-the-road Majority Leader, to take second place on the ticket. Neither candidate aroused much enthusiasm among those who had been critical of America's failure to develop a strong sense of national purpose under Eisenhower. Nixon, who had been an ardent supporter of McCarthy, was manipulative and unimaginative. By failing to take a stand against McCarthy, Kennedy, who had won a Pulitzer Prize for his book *Profiles in Courage*, opened himself to the taunt that he should have shown less profile and more courage. But in his acceptance speech delineating a 'New Frontier,' Kennedy gave indications that his critics may have misjudged him, for he began to elaborate the theme of his campaign: the need for sacrifice, imagination, and boldness to 'get the country moving again.'

Senator Kennedy ran under a formidable handicap: he was a Roman Catholic, and Al Smith's defeat was well remembered. He met this issue directly by addressing the Greater Houston Ministerial Association and answering frankly any question the ministers chose to ask. He declared:

> I believe in an America where the separation of Church and State is absolute—where no Catholic prelate would tell the President (should he be a Catholic) how to act, and no Protestant minister would tell his parishioners for whom to vote—where no church or church school is granted any public funds or political preference—and where no man is denied public office merely because his religion differs from the President who might appoint him or the people who might elect him.

By his forthrightness he succeeded in muting, if not eliminating, the religious issue.

Polls still showed Nixon running ahead of his rival when he agreed to a series of four nationally televised debates in late September and October. Nixon, who had used television skillfully in 1952,

At a White House press conference the youthful President, John Fitzgerald Kennedy, radiates charm. (*National Archives*)

thought he would improve his advantage, but he was outpointed in the crucial first debate in which Kennedy displayed a poise and maturity that erased the impression that he was a callow upstart lacking the experience of Nixon, who had actually held the reins of government during Eisenhower's illnesses. Kennedy also improved his standing with black voters, who had been cool toward him. When, on 19 October, Martin Luther King was sentenced on a technicality to four months' hard labor in a Georgia penitentiary, from which many feared he would not emerge alive, Kennedy phoned Dr. King's wife to express concern; and Kennedy's brother, Robert, secured the minister's release. This act appears to have swung large numbers of Negro voters to Kennedy, and black ballots provided the margin of victory in several critical states.

Kennedy won, but in the closest race in this century. He gained a popular majority of only 118,000 out of a total of some 68 million votes, a mere two-tenths of 1 per cent, though he had a more comfortable majority of 303 to 219 in the Electoral College. Yet, by however small a margin, Kennedy and Johnson had ended eight years of Republican rule despite the handicaps of youth, Catholicism, a discontented South, and the immense popularity of Eisenhower.

Ten weeks later, as blustery winds and snow flurries swept across Washington, the new President announced:

> Let the word go forth from this time and place, to friend and foe alike, that the torch has been passed to a new generation of Americans—born in this century, tempered by war, disciplined by a hard and bitter peace, proud of our ancient heritage, and unwilling to witness or permit the slow undoing of those human rights to which this Nation has always been committed.

He called upon his generation

> to bear the burden of a long twilight struggle, year in and year out, 'rejoicing in hope, patient in tribulation'—a struggle against the common enemies of man: tyranny, poverty, disease and war itself.

And he concluded with an affirmation of confidence and of faith:

> And so, my fellow Americans: ask not what your country can do for you—ask what you can do for your country.

Kennedy, who so deliberately made himself the spokesman for 'a new generation of Americans,' put together an administration notable for its youth. His cabinet, which included his thirty-five-year-old brother Robert as Attorney-General, was ten years younger than Eisenhower's. The youngest man ever elected to the presidency, he appointed to key positions still younger men, who were, as one observer said, the junior officers of World War II now come to power. By the youth and 'vigor' of his administration, Kennedy contributed to that change in the national mood which saw the 'Silent Generation' of the 1950's give way to the deeply committed young people of the 'sixties.

From the very first day in the brilliant winter sunshine of the inauguration, at which Robert Frost read a poem, Kennedy gave a tone to the White House which not only contrasted sharply to that of the Eisenhower years but differed from anything Washington had seen. Kennedy and his circle developed a style that reminded some of the Whig society of early nineteenth-century Britain, others only of the 'jet set' of Palm Beach and St. Tropez. Led by a President who quoted Madame de Staël on television, Kennedy's world found a place for both Oleg Cassini gowns and Pablo Casals at the White House, even for a Postmaster-General who had published a novel.

In contrast to the Eisenhower era, in which the 'egghead' was an object of contempt, the new administration welcomed the contributions of men of ideas to public affairs. Kennedy made a point of honoring Nobel Prize winners at a White House dinner; with characteristic felicity he greeted them as 'the most extraordinary collection of talent, of human knowledge, that has ever been gathered together at the White House, with the possible exception of when Thomas Jefferson dined alone.' He also sought to encourage the arts, and to improve the appearance of Washington he invited architects like Mies van der Rohe to design Federal buildings, while his wife Jacqueline, born into the Newport plutocracy, refurbished the White House to make it a cherished 'national object.' Increasingly, Washington commentators talked of 'the Kennedy style.'

Yet no one was more impatient than Kennedy with the notion that the success of a presidency

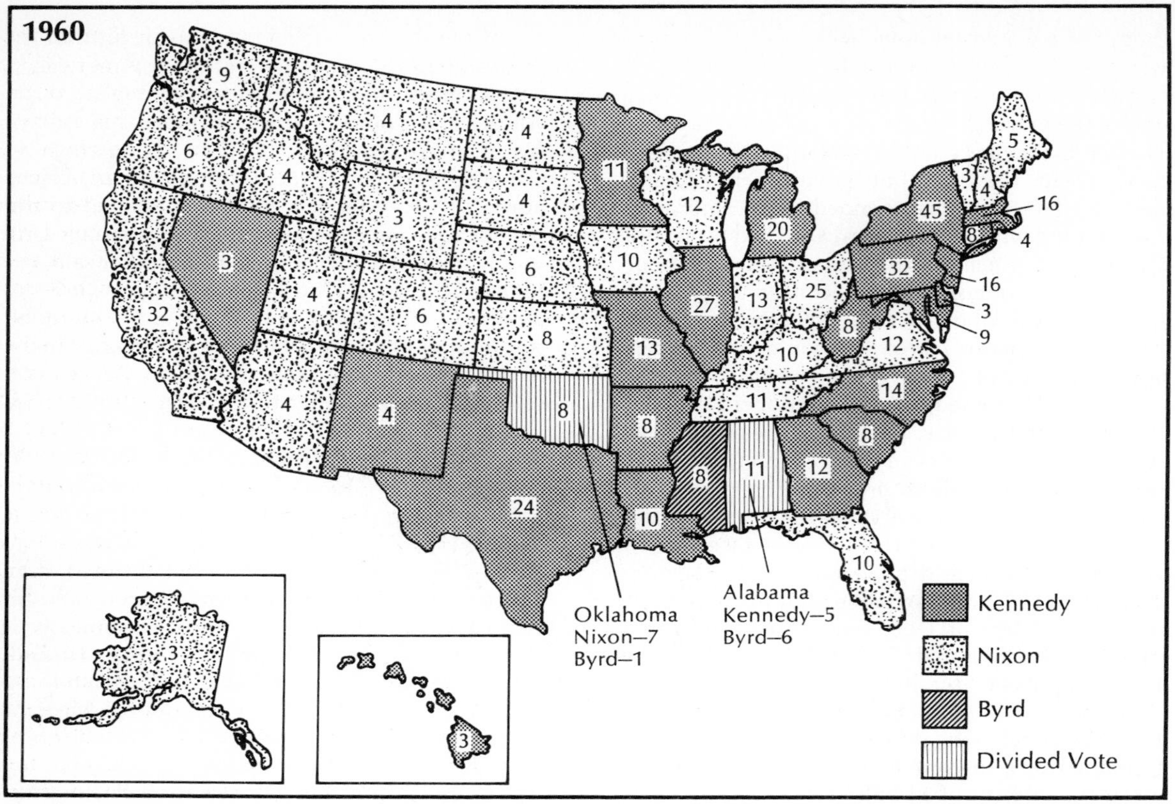

Presidential Election, 1960

could be measured by style. The real test of his administration, he knew, would be whether he could achieve significant substantive changes. 'I run for the Presidency,' he had declared, 'because I do not want it said that the years when our generation held political power . . . were the years when America began to slip. I don't want historians writing in 1970 to say that the balance of power . . . began to turn against the United States and against the cause of freedom.' He approached this task full of hope, yet soberly, and the reference to 'balance of power' gave an ominous hint of what was to be his chief preoccupation.

The End of the Postwar World

At the same time that Kennedy sought to explore the 'New Frontier' of American society, he faced the formidable task of shaping a foreign policy which would accommodate to a world in flux. The Cold War had entered its sixteenth year, yet the situation in 1961 seemed to differ dramatically from that of 1945 and commentators spoke of 'the end of the postwar world.' The bipolar alignment of 1945 was breaking apart in both East and West. Within the Communist camp, the Soviet Union confronted the rivalry of Red China. In the West a prosperous Europe no longer recognized the United States as the unchallenged leader of the free world. The emerging nations of three continents, comprising more than half of the world's population, often found the East-West conflict irrelevant to their own needs.

Kennedy comprehended these changes, but he did not respond consistently to them. Weary of Dulles's chiliastic rhetoric, the new President reminded the American people that

> the United States is neither omnipotent nor omniscient—that we are only six per cent of the world's population—that we cannot impose our will upon the other ninety-four per cent of mankind—that we cannot right every wrong or reverse every adversity—and that therefore there cannot be an American solution to every world problem.

It was a just observation but one he himself often forgot. He had charged during the campaign that under Eisenhower the United States had lost its 'position of pre-eminence,' and he intended to regain that position at the earliest opportunity. His choice for Secretary of State, Dean Rusk, shared some of Dulles's unfortunate quality of moralistic rigidity, and on more than one occasion the President's own rhetoric suggested that he anticipated a showdown with the Kremlin. For all of his emphasis on restraint, he was destined, in a number of fearful episodes, to carry brinkmanship farther than Dulles had dared, or Eisenhower permitted.

After his election, Kennedy learned the startling news that plans were far advanced for an invasion of Cuba to overthrow Fidel Castro. Since the spring of 1960 the CIA had been secretly training and arming hundreds of anti-Castro exiles in Florida and Guatemala. Kennedy gave the bizarre scheme his reluctant approval. On 17 April 1961 the invaders landed at the Bay of Pigs on the swampy southern coast of Cuba. In short order Castro's forces overwhelmed the rebels, who lacked adequate air cover. The United States was denounced for trying to destroy the government of a weaker nation and jeered for botching the attempt. The fiasco badly impaired the prestige of the Kennedy regime and put an end to the euphoria of the young administration.

Six weeks later, in a grim confrontation with Kennedy in Vienna, Khrushchev threatened to extinguish Western rights of access to Berlin. That summer the menace of nuclear war mounted dangerously. In response to appeals from Kennedy, Congress authorized the calling up of reserves and passed huge military appropriations, and a frenzy of air-raid shelter building swept the country. At border points in Berlin, American tanks eyed Soviet tanks. In August the crisis reached its peak when East Germany sealed the Berlin border and erected an ugly wall of concrete and barbed wire to halt the flow of refugees into West Berlin, a tacit admission of the Communist world's inability to compete with the West in Germany. To reassure West Berliners that the United States would not be driven out of the old German capital, Kennedy ordered a battle force of American troops down the 100-mile Autobahn from Western Germany through the Communist zone into Berlin. In another move in the war of nerves, the USSR that fall exploded some fifty nuclear devices, including a bomb nearly 3000 times more powerful than the one which had leveled Hiroshima.

By the end of the year the crisis had eased. Fallout shelter companies went bankrupt, and civil defense units folded. Critics charged that Kennedy, after behaving provocatively in Cuba, had over-reacted in Berlin. Yet just as he had resisted demands for full-scale American intervention in Cuba after the Bay of Pigs debacle, he had shown restraint as well as firmness in Berlin. In particular he had rejected counsel to smash through the Berlin Wall, for he recognized the danger of a nuclear exchange. The President told the country, 'In the thermonuclear age, any misjudgment on either side about the intentions of the other could rain more devastation in several hours than has been wrought in all the wars of human history.'

The Berlin experience reinforced Kennedy's determination to expand and diversify America's military forces. Whereas Dulles had relied inordinately on nuclear power, Kennedy and his Defense Secretary, Robert McNamara, developed a more balanced fighting capability. Kennedy won from Congress the biggest military and naval build-up in the country's history, one which increased the nuclear arsenal but placed more emphasis on mobile Polaris submarines than on overseas missile sites. The administration stressed

Adlai Stevenson and Eleanor Roosevelt at the United Nations, 2 March 1961. On Stevenson's recommendation, President Kennedy named Mrs. Roosevelt to the United States delegation to the Special Session of the General Assembly. Illness limited her service, but at a time when episodes like the Bay of Pigs elicited international distrust for American representatives, she remained a popular figure. When she dropped by the Human Rights Commission, the delegates broke into applause and the chairman invited her to speak. Near the end of the General Assembly session, she wrote the President, 'I don't think I have been very useful but I think I accomplished what Adlai wanted in just appearing at the UN.' (*The New York Times*)

The Berlin Wall. In February 1962 Robert F. Kennedy, seen here with Mayor Willy Brandt, addressed an enthusiastic crowd of 120,000 West Germans. The Wall, he told them, was a 'snake across the heart of your city.' (*Keystone Press Agency*)

the importance of conventional forces that could fight limited conflicts and special forces trained for jungle and guerilla warfare.

Even the exploration of space became implicated in the Cold War. From the moment on 20 February 1962 when Lt. Col. John Herschel Glenn, Jr., began the first of three orbits of the earth through Astronaut Gordon Cooper's landing in May 1963 'right on the money' after twenty-two orbits, the United States, which had once known little but bitter failure in its space efforts, scored a series of spectacular successes in the 'space race' with the Russians. In May 1961, Kennedy announced plans to land a man on the moon 'before this decade is out,' and Congress responded with huge appropriations for 'Project Apollo.'

In the fall of 1962 the United States came to the very brink of nuclear war. That summer, ships displaying the hammer and sickle had steamed boldly past the American base at Guantánamo, Cuba, and had unloaded missiles, patrol boats, and MIG fighters, as well as Russian technicians and instructors. This was no more than the United States had done for years in Turkey, Greece, and elsewhere, but the very fact that the Russian move was unprecedented gave it an ominous character. Hard-pressed to take action against this Soviet build-up, the President refused to risk a calamitous war so long as photographic reconnaissance showed no evidence of offensive missiles. On 16 October, however, he received shocking news: an Air Force U-2 had spotted Russian medium-range missiles in place, and the USSR, despite solemn assurances to the contrary, was rushing launching pads to completion. Missiles from these sites could deliver hydrogen warheads to targets as distant as Minneapolis.

Kennedy responded with a combination of determination and restraint. He would not permit the USSR to shift the balance of power by establishing a missile base only ninety miles from America's shores. Instead, on 22 October he quarantined arms shipments to Cuba and issued orders to intercept Russian vessels headed for the island. He warned the Kremlin that a nuclear attack from Cuba on any nation in the Western hemisphere would require a 'full retaliatory response on the Soviet Union' by the United States. Yet he rejected the advice of all his military advisers, many of his civilian aides, and even Senator Fulbright that he order an air strike, for this might lead to general war. Nonetheless, as Soviet vessels headed toward Havana where U.S. ships of war awaited them, the world shuddered at the imminence of Doomsday.

But the President's firm stand prevailed. At the end of two weeks, Kennedy, confronted by two letters from Khrushchev offering conflicting replies, chose to acknowledge the more acceptable one. Russia agreed to remove all offensive weapons and accept international inspection if the United States promised not to invade Cuba; the President consented, and the crisis ended. After a time the bases were dismantled and the missiles crated and withdrawn. Kennedy had won the war of nerves. Yet he took pains not to humiliate Khrushchev, for he recognized there were limits to 'eyeball to eyeball' diplomacy.

The missiles crisis had the ironic consequence of improving hopes for peace and permitting the President to direct his attention to more constructive programs, many of which he had initiated earlier. Kennedy appointed envoys sympathetic to the aspirations of the emerging nations in the Southern Hemisphere; expanded Food for Peace shipments of farm surpluses to almost $1.5 billion each year; and shifted the emphasis of foreign aid from military to economic assistance. The newly created Peace Corps, under the President's brother-in-law, R. Sargent Shriver, sent enthusiastic volunteers to offer educational or technical services to underdeveloped regions. Kennedy abandoned the Dulles attitude of condemning neutralism as immoral and gave his support to the attempt of the UN to build a central government in the Congo which would resist both Communist-oriented elements and right-wing secessionists. In August 1961 he proposed an ambitious program for Latin America: the Alliance for Progress. Upon agreement to basic reforms of their social structure to end the grievances Castroism might exploit, Latin American nations would be eligible for a ten-year, $20 billion program of aid, half of it provided by the United States. But the *Alianza* got off to a poor start, and in the end its contributions were negligible.

When on the morning before his inauguration Kennedy met with Eisenhower at the White House, the outgoing President pointed to a map of Southeast Asia and said: 'This is one of the problems I'm leaving you that I'm not happy about. We may have to fight.' In Laos, Kennedy, recognizing that the conservative regime backed by Eisenhower lacked popular support, abandoned the idea of an anti-Communist crusade and by an adroit use of force and diplomacy achieved his aim of 'a neutral and independent Laos, tied to no outside power,' and, at least for a time, removed from the Cold War.

Elsewhere in Southeast Asia, Kennedy showed less prudence. The Geneva settlement of 1954, which ended the Indochinese war, had stipulated the calling of free elections to unify Vietnam, but the elections were never held, and the United States backed Ngo Dinh Diem, who rapidly established authoritarian rule in the Republic of South Vietnam. When the Communist dictatorship of Ho Chi Minh in North Vietnam gave aid to the Viet Cong, the Communist guerillas of South Vietnam, Kennedy stepped up his support of Diem and sent military 'advisers' to assist the Saigon regime. In the spring of 1963 the Diem government took harsh repressive measures against dissidents, a policy which aroused the indignant opposition of many Americans to the Diem regime. In vain Kennedy urged Diem to undertake reforms to win the loyalty of landless peasants, and he expressed doubts about the extent of America's commitment to the South Vietnamese. However, he also believed that he could not afford a defeat like that of the French at Dienbienphu, and his advisers assured him that a military victory was within grasp. On 1 November 1963 the situation entered a new phase when, with the tacit approval of the American government, a military junta deposed Diem and murdered him and his brother; the United States promptly recognized the new government. At that point the American contingent in Vietnam was still less than 16,000, but Kennedy had planted the grapes of wrath which the next administration would nurture and harvest.

In Europe, President Kennedy sought to recreate the transatlantic community fractured by the independence of France's premier, Charles de Gaulle. The 'Grand Design' aimed to tie the United States into a European Common Market which would also admit the British. To make this possible, Kennedy secured from Congress the Trade Expansion Act of 1962 which empowered the President to lower tariff barriers in return for trade concessions. But when in January 1963 de Gaulle vetoed the admission of Britain to the Common Market, he ended Kennedy's dream of an 'Atlantic Partnership,' and when he insisted on developing an independent nuclear force, he jeopardized the unity of NATO. No longer could the United States count on getting its way in the Western world.

During his 1960 campaign Kennedy promised 'a supreme effort to break the log jam on disarmament and nuclear tests,' because 'the world was not meant to be a prison in which man awaits his executioner.' Though for more than two years the Russians balked, Kennedy persisted in his efforts toward achieving a test ban and a *détente* with the USSR. In June 1963 in a remarkable address at American University he stated that the United States should not see 'only a distorted and desperate view of the other side,' and urged: 'Let us reexamine our attitude toward the Soviet Union.' The President, observed one commentator, 'spoke at times of the cold war as if it hardly existed any longer.' As a consequence of Kennedy's appeal, and perhaps even more of the growing breach between the USSR and Red China, the Russians agreed to enter into negotiations toward a limited test ban in environments where physical inspection would not be required. At Moscow in July 1963 the United States, Great Britain, and the USSR signed a pact banning atmospheric and underwater testing of nuclear devices. It was a small step, but for the first time the powers had made a start, as the President said, toward getting 'the genie back in the bottle.' By the summer of 1963 there was renewed optimism about a thaw in the Cold War. The Kremlin agreed to the installation of a 'hot line' which would connect it with the White House by telephone in the event of a future crisis that might result in nuclear war, and the President approved a big sale of wheat to Russia. Yet fundamental disagreements persisted, and in Southeast Asia the Vietnam war was a running sore.

The New Frontier

The Kennedy circle hoped that the first session of Congress in 1961 would rival Roosevelt's Hundred Days, but the young President quickly found that in domestic legislation as in foreign policy he could score only limited gains. The conservative coalition of Southern Democrats and Northern Republicans which had blocked almost all innovative social reform measures for a generation had no interest in moving America toward new frontiers. Congress turned down Kennedy's pleas for medical care for the aged (Medicare) and for a Department of Urban Affairs and Housing, while Federal aid to education was blocked once again because of an inability to resolve the issue centering on the demand of Roman Catholic bishops for grants to parochial schools.

Kennedy's critics deplored his failure to take advantage of his great popularity to win support for administration measures, and his lack of finesse in dealing with congressmen. They conceded that the conservative coalition posed difficulties, but pointed out that he had top-heavy Democratic majorities in both houses and complained that the President was too unwilling to risk defeat. Kennedy, doubtful that direct appeals to the nation would find an effective response, recalled that when in Shakespeare's *Henry IV, Part I,* Owen Glendower boasts, 'I can call spirits from the vasty deep,' Hotspur retorts:

> Why, so can I, or so can any man;
> But will they come when you do call for them?

Moreover Kennedy could point to a number of accomplishments. By a narrow margin he won a tough fight to dislodge conservatives from control of the Rules Committee. He pushed through legislation which raised the minimum wage,

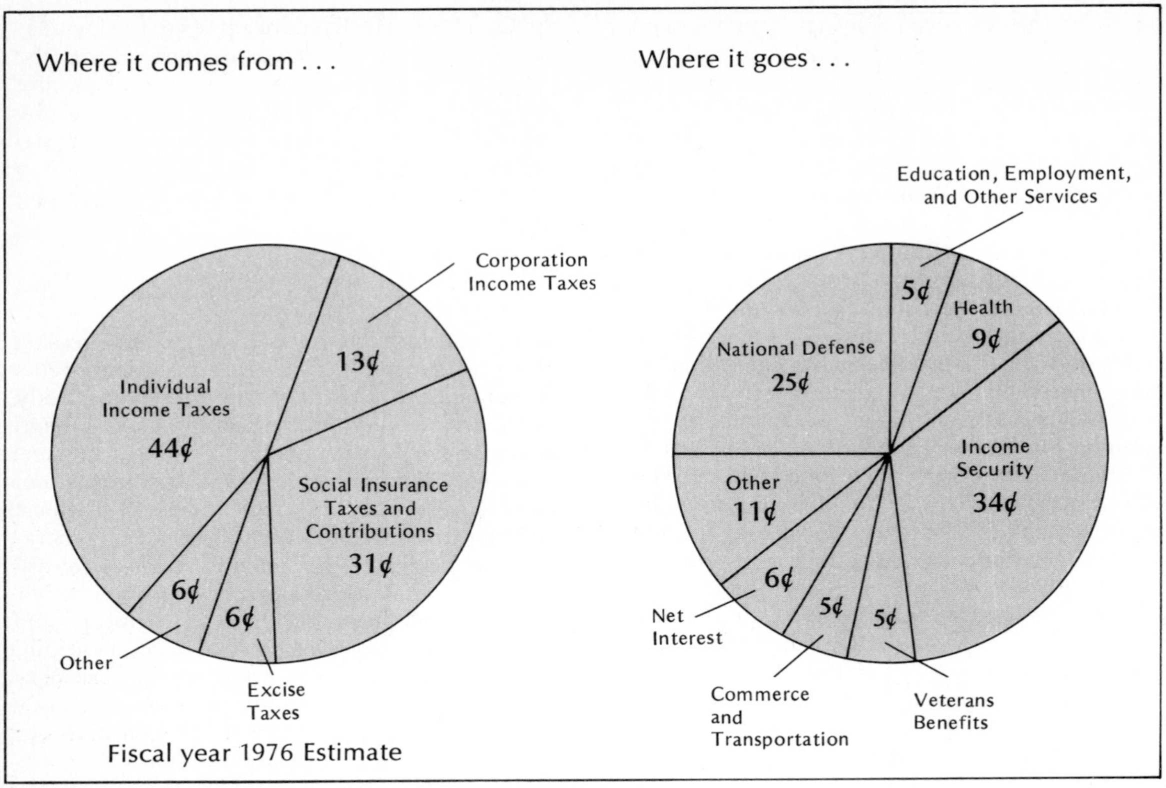

The Federal Government Dollar

liberalized social security benefits, extended emergency unemployment compensation, appropriated funds for mental health, provided new housing, and funneled public-works money into depressed areas. Kennedy won approval for a Federal Water Pollution Control Act, and Congress established three national seashores, one of them at the President's favorite vacation place, Cape Cod.

Kennedy played an important part, too, in sparking an economic revival, although at the outset he moved too cautiously. He came to office at a time when nearly 7 per cent of the working force was unemployed in the fourth recession since World War II. Some of the President's liberal advisers urged him to stimulate the economy through social spending, but in a period of near-crisis in the international balance of payments, Kennedy feared that massive expenditures might accelerate the gold drain and augment inflation. Instead, he adopted a more modest program which included easier credit. Together with stepped-up military and highway spending, these measures lifted the country out of the recession.

To preserve these gains, Kennedy emphasized the importance of maintaining the price level. The President was delighted when steel workers were persuaded to accept a non-inflationary wage contract. Ten days later he received the unwelcome news from Roger M. Blough, chairman of the

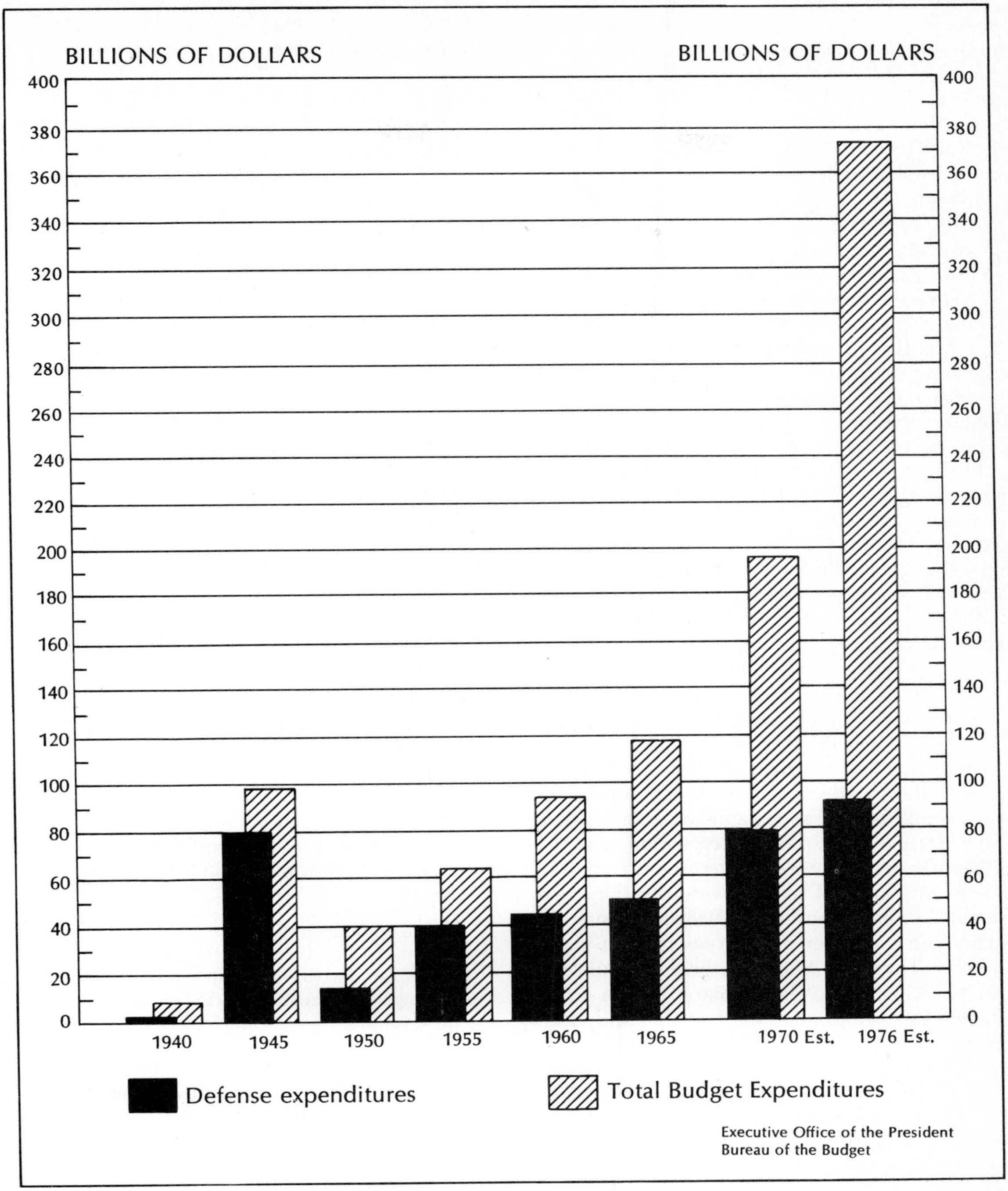

BILLIONS OF DOLLARS
BILLIONS OF DOLLARS
400
380
360
340
320
300
280
260
240
220
200
180
160
140
120
100
80
60
40
20
0
1940
1945
1950
1955
1960
1965
1970 Est.
1976 Est.
Defense expenditures
Total Budget Expenditures
Executive Office of the President
Bureau of the Budget

National Spending 1940–1976

board of U.S. Steel, that his company was raising prices six dollars a ton; other steel firms quickly followed. Believing he had been betrayed by the steel corporations, Kennedy denounced the rise angrily in public and with more vivid language in private. To compel the companies to back down, the President mobilized the power of the Federal government: anti-trust suits, a tax investigaton by the Treasury, an FTC inquiry into collusive price-fixing, a Defense Department boycott. Within 72 hours steel capitulated. After Blough surrendered, Kennedy was asked what he had said to the steel magnate. The President responded: 'I told him that his men could keep their horses for the spring plowing.'

Although Kennedy's skillful management helped promote an upturn, the President recognized the need for further measures to create more jobs, and under the tutelage of Walter Heller, chairman of the Council of Economic Advisers, he embraced the ideas of the New Economics. In keeping with the New Economics heresy that the government should deliberately create deficits at a time when indices were climbing, Kennedy asked Congress for a multibillion dollar tax cut to encourage consumer spending and business investment and thus stimulate economic growth. The President did not live to see the tax cut adopted, but the Kennedy years mark a watershed in thinking about the economy.

In the field of civil rights, too, Kennedy at first moved slowly. He sought to avoid jeopardizing the rest of his program by antagonizing Southern Democrats over civil rights legislation, and consequently relied instead on executive action to advance civil rights. Unlike Eisenhower, he left no doubt that he supported the Brown decision. He appointed a number of Negroes to high places, notably Thurgood Marshall, general counsel of the NAACP, to the United States Circuit Court, Robert Weaver to head the Housing and Home Finance Agency, and Carl Rowan as ambassador to Finland. Under Robert Kennedy the Department of Justice acted far more vigorously than in the Eisenhower administration in bringing suits on denial of voting rights. When in the spring of 1961 Alabama mobs mauled 'freedom riders' traveling through the South to challenge Jim Crow bus terminals and bombed and set afire a 'freedom bus,' the young Attorney-General dispatched hundreds of Federal marshals. Later that year, at the goading of the Department of Justice, the ICC ordered bus companies to desegregate interstate buses and to stop only at restaurants and terminals that took down their WHITE and COLORED signs.

When James H. Meredith, a black Air Force veteran, was denied admission to the University of Mississippi, a United States Circuit Court issued an injunction to compel his acceptance, an order sustained by the Supreme Court on 10 September 1962. Meredith tried to register later that month, but Governor Ross Barnett, defying the courts, physically interposed himself and used state police to rebuff Meredith. On 30 September 1962 President Kennedy sent several hundred Federal marshals to escort Meredith to the campus at Oxford. That night a howling mob engulfed the marshals, and Kennedy dispatched Federal troops and federalized national guardsmen; before the rioting ended, two were killed and seventy wounded. Under Federal bayonets, Meredith was registered.

Though the actions of the administration made the names of 'the Kennedy brothers' anathema in the Deep South, civil rights leaders castigated them for not acting more forcefully. During the campaign the President had said that discrimination in public housing could be wiped out 'tomorrow' with a stroke of the pen; but pens flooded the White House mail before he decided to act, and then administrative interpretation weakened his order of 20 November 1962. Martin Luther King stated:

> This Administration has outstripped all previous ones in the breadth of its civil rights activity. Yet the movement, instead of breaking out into the open plains of progress, remains constricted and confined. A sweeping revolutionary force is pressed into a narrow tunnel.

In the spring and summer of 1963, one hundred years after the Emancipation Proclamation had been effected, the Negro's cry for equality resounded throughout the land. Dr. King announced: 'We're through with tokenism and gradualism and see-how-far-you've-comeism.

We're through with we've-done-more-for-your-people-than-anyone-elseism. We can't wait any longer. Now is the time.' North and South, blacks came out on the streets. In one week they carried out sixty separate demonstrations. That spring in Birmingham, where King led massive protests, civil rights marchers were met with snarling police dogs, electric cattle prods, and high-pressure fire hoses that sent demonstrators sprawling; and the police commissioner, Eugene 'Bull' Connor, crowded the jails with hundreds of young marchers. But they continued to sing their freedom anthem:

> Black and white together
> We shall overcome some day.

The combination of passive resistance—'Refrain from violence of fist, tongue or heart'—and the latent threat of violence won speedy results. In the first two weeks of June 1963 all the leading hotels and motels of Nashville agreed to desegregate; Atlanta announced plans to integrate its swimming pools; and blacks teed off on the municipal golf course in Jackson, Mississippi.

By 1963 only one state in the Union, Alabama, had no Negro attending any state-supported school with white students. When in June two young blacks sought to register at the University of Alabama, Governor George C. Wallace stood in the doorway to bar their way. But it was only a charade. After the President ordered the Alabama National Guard into Federal service, the Governor submitted. In 1956 Eisenhower had done nothing to help Autherine Lucy, but seven years later Kennedy threw the full weight of Federal power behind the black students. One week after the tawdry melodrama in the doorway, the President delivered a notable message calling for far-reaching Federal legislation to curb discrimination and segregation. He said:

> Surely, in 1963, 100 years after Emancipation, it should not be necessary for any American citizen to demonstrate in the streets for the opportunity to stop at a hotel, or to eat at a lunch counter in the very department store in which he is shopping, or to enter a motion picture house, on the same terms as any other customer.

Other American Presidents, notably Harry Truman, had spoken out against discrimination, but Kennedy will go down in history as the first President to identify himself with the elimination of racial segregation.

Yet Kennedy's eloquence failed to move Congress to enact civil rights legislation that year, and his last months in office saw a rising tide of ugly rhetoric and violent deeds. A white racist murdered Medgar Evers, the head of the Mississippi NAACP, and in Jackson police used clubs, tear gas, and dogs against marchers who sought to pay tribute to their slain leader. A bomb in a Birmingham church killed four little Negro girls while they attended Sunday school. To win passage of Kennedy's comprehensive civil rights bill 200,000 people, 'black and white together,' took part in a 'March on Washington,' but it was clear that Congress would not pass the bill at that session, and on 12 November the *New York Times* wrote: 'Rarely has there been such a pervasive attitude of discouragement around Capitol Hill and such a feeling of helplessness to deal with it. This has been one of the least productive sessions of Congress within the memory of most of the members.'

Ten days later, on 22 November 1963, the President arrived in Dallas, recently the scene of displays of violence by the radical right. As the motor caravan of open cars moved through the streets of the city, the wife of Texas's governor, John Connally, remarked to Kennedy: 'You can't say that Dallas isn't friendly to you today.' An instant later the President was struck twice by rifle bullets; within minutes he was pronounced dead. Over that frightful weekend, yet another act of violence stunned a grief-stricken nation. Before a national television audience, the President's assassin, Lee Harvey Oswald, who had once expatriated himself to Russia, was murdered in a corridor of the city jail by Jack Ruby, the operator of a sleazy night club. A commission under Chief Justice Warren subsequently concluded that the assassination of the President was the work of Oswald, acting alone. The commission's findings have frequently been challenged, and though no substantial evidence of a conspiracy has been adduced, doubts remain.

Within a short time after the painful mourning

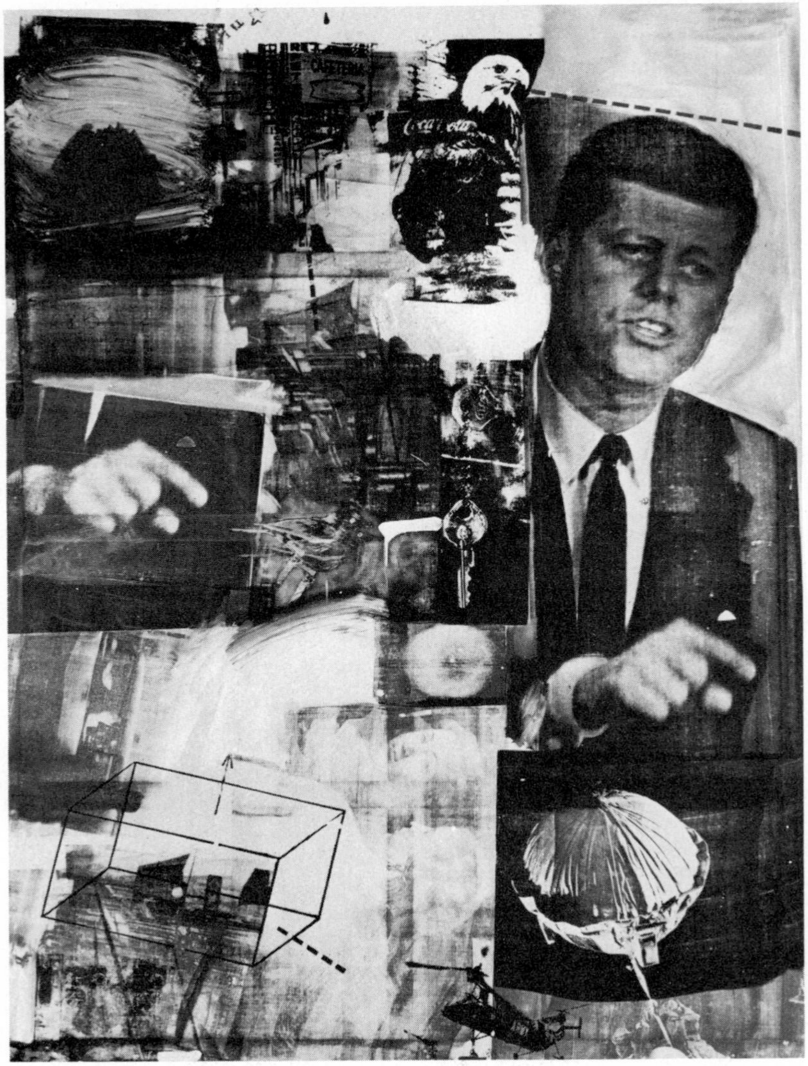

A Kennedy era retrospective. In 'Buffalo II' (1964), Robert Rauschenberg displays not only the late President at a press conference, but an American eagle, an army helicopter, an astronaut descending from outer space, and symbols of the consumer culture like a Coca-Cola sign, all caught in a swirl of paint indicative of a globe spinning out of control. Rauschenberg, born in Port Arthur, Texas, in 1925, had his first one-man show in New York in 1951, and is thought of as a New York City artist. He has adapted the Cubist innovation of collage to incorporate 'found objects' and photographs on a canvas of brushed and spilled paint reminiscent of the Abstract Expressionists. *(Coll. Mrs. Robert B. Mayer and the Estate of Robert B. Mayer)*

over the President's death, writers began to debate the meaning of his life. Some said that a President must be judged by his accomplishments, and that Kennedy's were small. Others granted that the achievements of his administration had been meager, but insisted that Kennedy, if he had lived, would have achieved much more. Kennedy, one writer observed, was a Prince Hal who died before Agincourt. Many, however, concluded that he was a man of greatness less for what he did than for what he was. They recalled his gallantry in the face of an intimate acquaintance with death and misfortune, and remembered his disarming wit: When asked how he became a wartime hero, he retorted, 'It was involuntary. They sank my boat.' At the time of his death, *Le Figaro* wrote: 'What remains as the loss . . . is a certain feeling of possibilities, of an *élan*, and—why not say it?—of an impression of beauty. These are not political qualities, but surely they are enduring legendary and mythological qualities.' It is the legend that built swiftly—of the young prince brutally dispossessed from Camelot.

But still others contended there was more to Kennedy's short presidency than the gossamer of legend. Arthur Schlesinger, Jr., who served on Kennedy's staff, wrote:

> Yet he had accomplished so much: the new hope for peace on earth, the elimination of nuclear testing in the atmosphere and the abolition of nuclear diplomacy, the new policies toward Latin America and the third world, the reordering of American defense, the emancipation of the American Negro, the revolution in national economic policy, the concern for poverty, the stimulus to the arts, the fight for reason against extremism and mythology. . . . He re-established the republic as the first generation of our leaders saw it—young, brave, civilized, rational, gay, tough, questing, exultant in the excitement and potentiality in history.

Both critic and admirer tended in retrospect to be more sympathetic toward Kennedy's reluctance to divide the nation to achieve his goals. In the summer before his death he read to White House visitors the speech of Blanche of Castile from *King John:*

> The sun's o'ercast with blood; fair day, adieu!
> Which is the side that I must go withal?
> I am with both: each army hath a hand;
> And in their rage, I having hold of both,
> They whirl asunder and dismember me.

No legacy of John F. Kennedy is more important than his championing of reason against the anarchy of Right and Left and his understanding that liberty is possible only in an ordered society. But in the end the whirling forces of violence, pulling the nation asunder, dismembered him.

The Great Society

At 2:38 p.m. on 22 November 1963, in the plane bearing the late President's body back to Washington, Lyndon Baines Johnson took the oath of office as President of the United States. A self-made man from the Texas hill country, Johnson quickly imprinted the LBJ brand on the White House. At fifty-five he was only a decade older than his predecessor; yet they seemed a generation apart, for Johnson had first come to Washington while Kennedy was a student at Choate. Intimidating, irascible, egocentric, he radiated a lust for power. 'The President,' wrote an English observer, 'comes into a room slowly and warily, as if he means to smell out the allegiance of everyone in it.' As Kennedy's patrician grace gave way to Johnson's country manners, the Eastern 'Establishment' so deplored the change in style that it frequently refused to give the new President his due.

For as chief legislator Johnson had infinitely greater experience than Kennedy. A veteran of twenty-three years in Congress, he had served in both houses and had risen to Majority Leader of the Senate, where he had won renown for his skill as a legislative tactician. Liberals, recalling his role as a moderate in the 1950's, feared he had only a lukewarm commitment to the Kennedy reforms; but Johnson, who came out of a Populist background and had been a protégé of Franklin Roosevelt's, had known hard times and the direct benefits of government as Kennedy had not, and he was determined to be a national, not a sectional, leader.

Johnson came to power at a time when political scientists were bewailing 'the deadlock of democracy,' but in short order he broke the log jam of Kennedy legislation. Within a month of his acces-

LBJ in the shadow of FDR. Lyndon B. Johnson's attitude toward Franklin D. Roosevelt was ambivalent. On the day Roosevelt died, Johnson said, 'He was a daddy to me, always,' and Johnson's Great Society clearly owed a large debt to the New Deal. Yet Johnson was not content to emulate the hero of his youth; he sought to outdo him, to have History record him as a President who had achieved more than FDR. Furthermore, Roosevelt's reign provided not only an example to be followed but a failure to be avoided. Johnson carried a vivid memory of the fact that a Chief Executive may win in a landslide, as Roosevelt did in 1936, and be in deep trouble within a year—for Johnson first entered Congress in a special election in the spring of 1937 in the midst of FDR's abortive 'Court-packing' struggle. In 1964 Johnson triumphed by an even greater margin than FDR had, and within a year discord over Vietnam was pulling his coalition apart. (Wally McNamee, *The Washington Post*)

sion to office, Congress had voted $1.2 billion for college construction projects. He quickly secured assent for a mass transit bill and legislation to protect wilderness areas. By giving an impression of fiscal responsibility, he consolidated business interests behind liberal measures and induced congressmen to approve an $11.5 billion tax cut. The economy responded immediately; in 1964 gross national product soared $38 billion over the previous year.

The first resident of a Southern state to enter the White House since Andrew Johnson a century earlier, the new President urged Congress to enact the civil rights bill as a memorial to Kennedy. With the cooperation of the Democratic whip, Senator Hubert Humphrey, and Republicans like Senator Everett Dirksen, he dislodged the bill from the House Rules Committee and broke the Southern filibuster in the Senate. The Civil Rights Act of 1964, the most sweeping since Reconstruction, and the most effective, prohibited discrimination in places of public accommodation; authorized the Attorney-General to bring suits to speed school desegregation; strengthened voting rights statutes; set up an Equal Opportunity Commission to wipe out job discrimination; and empowered Federal agencies to withhold funds from state-administered programs that discriminated against Negroes.

Johnson not only won approval for proposals that had been stymied under Kennedy but began to enunciate his own program. His State of the Union Message in January 1964 announced: 'This Administration today, here and now, declares unconditional war on poverty in America.' Starting with the Economic Opportunity Act of 1964, Congress in the next two years voted funds for such anti-poverty projects as VISTA, the domestic peace corps; a Job Corps for dropouts; Upward Bound, to encourage bright slum children to go to college; a Neighborhood Youth Corps for jobless teenagers; Operation Head Start, to give pre-school training; and a Community Action Program to permit 'maximum feasible participation' of the poor. In an address at Ann Arbor in the spring of 1964, Johnson emphasized that he wanted to achieve a 'Great Society,' which he described as 'a place where the city of man serves not only the needs of the body and the demands of commerce but the desire for beauty and the hunger for community.'

In the 1964 campaign the credo of the Great Society faced a sharp challenge from a new kind of Republican candidate, not a man of the center but of the Right, Barry Goldwater of Arizona. The Right had long argued that outside the Northeast there was a vast silent vote—conservative and isolationist—which had never been drawn to the polls. By offering 'a choice not an echo,' the Arizona senator, it was claimed, would command a huge support which 'Me Too' Republicans like Willkie had never been able to attract.

Certainly Goldwater seemed to offer a clear choice. He appealed to all those elements who were frustrated by modern America. At a time when the country was deeply troubled by extremists, he told the Republican convention, 'Extremism in the defense of liberty is no vice.' In Cleveland, a scene of racial strife, Goldwater, who had voted against the civil rights bill, exploited white 'backlash' by speaking for the freedom not to associate. In the Tennessee valley, he suggested the sale of the TVA to private interests. To the old folks of St. Petersburg he criticized social security. Such statements permitted Johnson to campaign both as the liberal candidate and as the 'safe' candidate.

In foreign affairs Goldwater, who raised uneasy feelings about whether he could be trusted with The Bomb, denounced the administration's 'no win' policy in Vietnam, which he promised to reverse. But Johnson took much of the sting out of this charge when in August he ordered air raids against North Vietnam in response to an attack by North Vietnamese gunboats on American destroyers in the Gulf of Tonkin. (Subsequently a Senate inquiry disclosed that the order for 'retaliation' had been prepared long before the Tonkin Gulf incident, and indicated that the whole 'incident' had been deliberately designed and fraudulently publicized to provoke a military response which could be used as justification for bombing North Vietnam.) The President seized advantage of the occasion to secure from Congress the 'Tonkin resolution' authorizing him 'to take all necessary measures to repel any armed attack against the forces of the United States and to prevent future aggression.' The resolution was so ambiguously worded that it could be interpreted as a blank check authorization for escalating the war, yet only two Senators, Morse of Oregon and Gruening of Alaska, had the courage to vote against it. At the same time Johnson appealed to the nation as the peace candidate. When Goldwater advocated enlarging the war, Johnson stated: 'We are not going to send American boys nine or ten thousand miles away from home to do what Asian boys ought to be doing for themselves.'

Goldwater's appeal received a sharp rebuke. The electorate exploded the theory of the silent vote and gave Lyndon Johnson a record-breaking popular majority. With 43 million votes (61.1 per cent) to Goldwater's 27 million (38.5 per cent), Johnson captured 44 states and the District of Columbia which, as a consequence of the Twenty-third Amendment ratified in 1961, voted in the national election. Negroes, once a mainstay of the G.O.P., voted better than 90 per cent for Johnson, and the Irish supported the President more strongly than they had Kennedy. The Republicans had the electoral votes only of Goldwater's Arizona and five Deep South states which backed him on the race issue. In Congress, so sizable was the Democratic margin that for the first time since 1938 the bipartisan conservative coalition would not hold the balance of power.

When the 89th Congress convened in January 1965, Johnson fired a fusillade of messages, and before Congress recessed in October he had gotten almost everything he had asked. Among the new measures were a number long deferred, including Medicare, to provide medical care for the aged under the social security system, Federal aid for elementary and secondary education, and the creation of a cabinet-level Department of Housing and Urban Development. Congress also expressed the Great Society's concern for 'quality' with the Highway Beautification Act. Throughout 1965 the United States witnessed a new national rite: the pageant of presidential bill-signing. Johnson signed the Voting Rights Act of 1965 in the President's Room of the Capitol where exactly 104 years before Lincoln had signed a bill freeing slaves impressed into the Confederate service. He

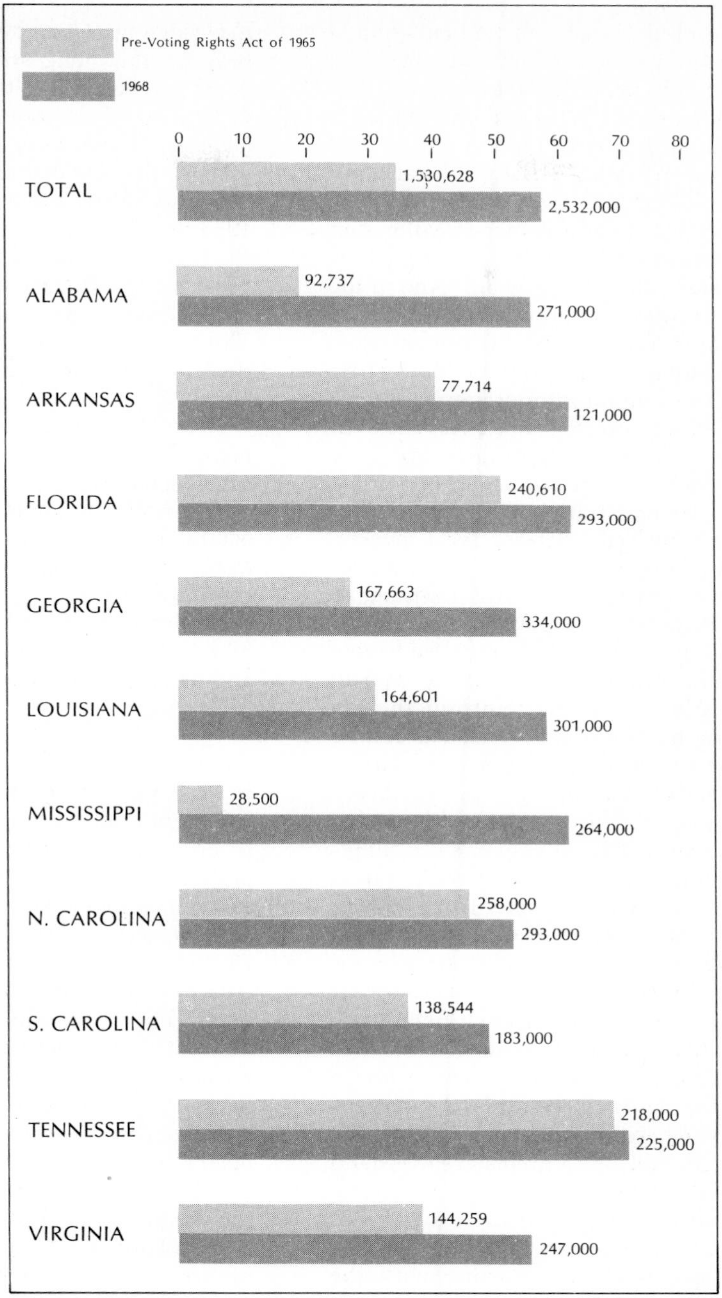

Per Cent of Black Voting Age Population Registered

put his name to a Federal aid to elementary education bill at the one-room schoolhouse in Texas he had attended as a child. At the National Institutes of Health in Bethesda, Maryland, he signed a measure authorizing a multimillion-dollar program for medical research. On a bright autumn day in the Rose Garden of the White House, attended by such luminaries as Agnes de Mille, Ben Shahn, and Katherine Anne Porter, he affixed his name to a Federal-aid-to-the-arts bill. And in the shadow of the Statue of Liberty, facing Ellis Island, he signed into law the bill which ended racist restrictions on immigration, although for the first time it placed a ceiling on immigration from the Western Hemisphere. In 1965 and 1966, the 89th Congress, the most productive since the New Deal, adopted such innovations as legislation for rent subsidies, demonstration cities, a teacher corps, regional medical centers, 'vest pocket' parks, a rescue operation for the economically depressed region of 'Appalachia,' and Medicaid to provide medical care for the poor.

The Voting Rights Act of 1965 resulted from a series of demonstrations organized by Martin Luther King early in 1965 to point out the obstacles to voting by blacks that persisted despite civil rights statutes. In Dallas County, Alabama, where Negroes of voting age outnumbered whites, there were 28 whites registered for every one black. A series of violent responses to King's demonstrations, including the murder of the Rev. James J. Reeb, a Unitarian minister from Boston, in Selma, the county seat of Dallas County, led the President to ask Congress for sweeping new legislation. He also gave Federal support to a massive civil rights march from Selma to Montgomery, the state capital, which it reached on 25 March. That August the President approved a new law providing for direct Federal intervention. In districts where 50 per cent or more of the voting-age population was unregistered, Federal examiners would enroll voters.

Together with Supreme Court decisions based on the principle of 'one man, one vote,' which struck at malapportionment (starting with the 1962 landmark case of *Baker v. Carr*), and the ratification in 1964 of the Twenty-fourth Amendment, which curbed the use of the poll tax to abridge suffrage, the Voting Rights Act of 1965 took another long stride toward democratizing American politics. In the next three years Federal voting examiners registered more than 150,000 Negroes in five Deep South states. Mississippi, with 6.7 per cent of voting-age blacks registered in November 1964, had 59.8 per cent by the spring of 1968. In 1967 a major city chose a black mayor for the first time when Carl B. Stokes triumphed in Cleveland, and Mississippi elected a black legislator. That same year the President elevated Thurgood Marshall to the Supreme Court; he was the first Negro to be appointed to the highest tribunal.

Returned to office by the greatest landslide in history, Lyndon Johnson could take pride in the achievements of the 'fabulous 89th' which opened up prospects for a new era of reform and of Democratic domination for the next generation. But in these same months Johnson had made fateful commitments in Vietnam which would snuff out hopes for reform, undo much of the work of the 89th Congress, topple the Democrats from power, and drive the President from the White House.

The Vietnam Quagmire

In his State of the Union message in January 1965 President Johnson found the international picture so bright that he was able to place his main emphasis on domestic concerns. To be sure, Southeast Asia remained troublesome, but as the President began his new term there were still only 23,000 American 'advisers' in Vietnam. In Latin America, prospects seemed the most hopeful in years. The world rejoiced that in the recent election the United States had emphatically rejected a reckless Cold Warrior and given decisive backing instead to a candidate who had scoffed at the 'illusion that the United States can demand resolution of all the world's problems and mash a button and get the job done.' Yet before the new term was four months old the President had taken initiatives in Latin America that caused world-wide apprehension and had embarked on a course in Southeast Asia that would embroil the United States in the fourth largest war in its history and the longest.

In April 1965 civil strife erupted in the Dominican Republic, which had failed to find stability after the assassination of the ruthless dictator Trujillo. From the outset the American embassy and the State Department sided with conservative generals against the forces loyal to Juan Bosch, a democratic reformer. Claiming that Bosch's movement had been taken over by Communists, Johnson, without consulting with Latin American republics, landed more than 20,000 marines on the island. Critics at home and abroad deplored Johnson's misjudgment, for there was scant evidence that Communists controlled the movement, and denounced the President's usurpation of power and his heavy-handed, unilateral action that revived memories of gunboat diplomacy. The Dominican venture ended in a compromise solution, but it raised disquieting doubts about Johnson's ability to use power with discrimination.

Some months before the Dominican affair the President had made a much more critical decision about Vietnam. Even as he was denouncing Goldwater for his belligerency, he was listening to advisers who warned him that if he did not step up America's military contribution the anti-Communist forces in South Vietnam would be overwhelmed. Prudence might have suggested a reconsideration of America's commitment if after more than a decade of U.S. aid the army of the Saigon government could not overcome the Viet Cong forces it outnumbered six to one. But Johnson was not prudent and refused to admit 'defeat' or withdraw. Two days after he took office he had told the U.S. ambassador to Saigon, Henry Cabot Lodge, 'I am not going to lose Vietnam. I am not going to be the President who saw Southeast Asia go the way China went.'

On 7 February 1965 when a mortar attack by the Viet Cong on an American camp at Pleiku killed eight Americans and wounded 108 others, Johnson retaliated by ordering carrier-based air strikes against North Vietnam, for he viewed the Viet Cong in the South only as agents of Hanoi. So quickly did the President respond that it seemed clear that the administration had planned such a strike well in advance. On 7 March two battalions of marines, the first U.S. combat units, landed in Vietnam, and by 28 June they had moved into battle in the land war on the Asian continent against which almost every military expert had warned. Month by month the war reeled farther out of control. Like the generals in World War I who thought 'one more push' on the Western front would terminate the war, the administration was confident that 'one more step' would bring an early victory; in each case it served only to raise the cost of the war. The Pentagon found it hard to believe that a little more firepower would not overcome these miserable guerillas, clad in black pajamas and supplied with ammunition carried over jungle trails on the backs of old women. As a result the war steadily became Americanized. During some weeks in the spring of 1966, U.S. casualties were greater than those of the South Vietnamese. By the middle of 1968 the total of U.S. forces had passed half a million, and by the end of the year American casualties exceeded 30,000 dead and 100,000 wounded.

The bombing, too, found new justifications. In April 1965 the President offered to begin 'unconditional discussions' to end the war and pledged a $1 billion investment in Southeast Asia including North Vietnam. When the Communists replied with a demand that the United States get out of Vietnam altogether, the administration expanded the bombing raids on the grounds that only additions to 'the quotient of pain' in North Vietnam would bring Hanoi to the bargaining table. By the end of 1968 the United States had dropped more tons of bombs on Vietnam than fell on Germany and Japan in World War II.

In the face of sharpening criticism Johnson and his associates asserted that they must persist, for if Vietnam went Communist, all Southeast Asia would tumble, the Pacific would become a 'Red Sea,' and America's defense line would fall back to California. They insisted that the Vietnamese conflict was not a civil war but a scheme by 'the Sino-Soviet military bloc' and more particularly by Red China to expand into Southeast Asia through its agents, the Communist regime of Ho Chi Minh in Hanoi and the Viet Cong. The Vietnam war represented the crucial test of the feasibility of 'wars of national liberation'; a Communist victory would lead Southeast Asian

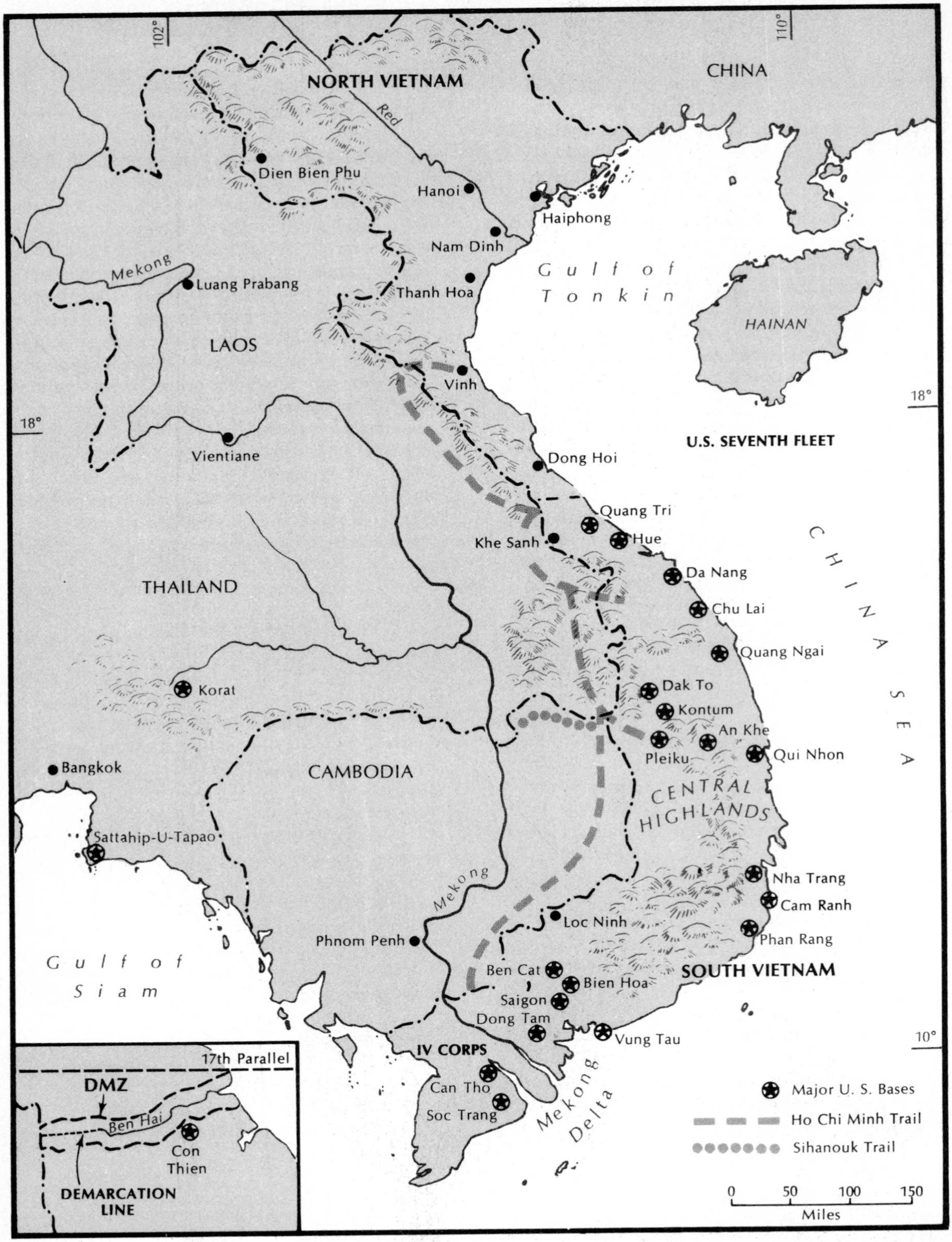

102°
110°
NORTH VIETNAM
CHINA
Red
Dien Bien Phu
Hanoi
Haiphong
Nam Dinh
Mekong
Luang Prabang
Thanh Hoa
Gulf of Tonkin
HAINAN
LAOS
Vinh
18°
18°
Vientiane
U.S. SEVENTH FLEET
Dong Hoi
Quang Tri
Khe Sanh
Hue
CHINA SEA
Da Nang
THAILAND
Chu Lai
Quang Ngai
Korat
Dak To
Kontum
An Khe
Pleiku
Qui Nhon
Bangkok
CAMBODIA
CENTRAL HIGHLANDS
Sattahip-U-Tapao
Mekong
Nha Trang
Cam Ranh
Loc Ninh
Phnom Penh
Phan Rang
Gulf of Siam
Ben Cat
Bien Hoa
SOUTH VIETNAM
Saigon
Dong Tam
Vung Tau
10°
17th Parallel
DMZ
IV CORPS
Ben Hai
Can Tho
Soc Trang
Mekong Delta
Con Thien
DEMARCATION LINE
Major U. S. Bases
Ho Chi Minh Trail
Sihanouk Trail
0
50
100
150
Miles

Vietnam

Vietnam, 1967. Men of the 1st Infantry Division, dropped from helicopters near Phuoc Vinh, dash for cover. (*U.S. Army Photograph*)

nations to turn to China as Balkan countries had sought out Nazi Germany after Munich. 'I'm not the village idiot,' Rusk said. 'I know Hitler was an Austrian and Mao is Chinese.... But what is common between the two situations is the phenomenon of aggression.'

Critics of Johnson's policy mounted a formidable assault on the administration's arguments. 'Hawks,' especially strong among conservative Republicans, urged the President to be even more bellicose; and as late as the spring of 1967 polls showed that a preponderance of opinion favored strong measures. More dangerous to the administration were the objections of the 'doves,' embracing both those who wanted to end the bombing in order to encourage negotiations and those who favored withdrawal, for the 'doves' threatened to disrupt the Johnson coalition. In the Senate the 'dove' faction, which in 1965 consisted of only a few mavericks, came by 1967 to include such respected Democratic leaders as the chairman of the Senate Foreign Relations Committee, J. William

Fulbright, Robert Kennedy of New York, Eugene McCarthy of Minnesota, and George McGovern of South Dakota.

The 'doves' denied that the United States was advancing the cause of democracy in Asia. The corrupt, repressive regime of Air Marshal Nguyen Cao Ky made a mockery of Washington's claim that it was defending the right of the Vietnamese to govern themselves. They viewed the Vietnam conflict as primarily a civil war in which the Viet Cong were an indigenous force, and they denied that the North Vietnamese, with a long history of distrusting the Chinese, were pawns of Peking. They scoffed at the Munich analogy and the domino theory; General David M. Shoup, former commandant of the Marine Corps, thought it 'ludicrous' to believe that if the Communists won in Vietnam, they would 'soon be knocking at the doors of Pearl Harbor.' Many of America's allies, it was noted, deplored the attempt of the United States to set itself up as judge, jury, and executioner for mankind, and Afro-Asian nations resented the bombing of non-white populations. Finally, the 'doves' pointed out that even if this dirty war, in which the United States employed napalm, and the South Vietnamese (as well as the Viet Cong) tortured prisoners, could be 'won,' Vietnam would be destroyed in the process, its countryside defoliated and gutted by bomb craters, its society shattered.

Such criticism fell on deaf ears. As Johnson jeered at 'nervous Nellies,' and Dean Rusk at 'the gullibility of educated men,' administration critics escalated their activities too, from 'teach-ins' on campuses and demonstrations at which draft cards were burned to more violent confrontations with authority. Johnson's policies, by reversing the apparent mandate of the 1964 election, soured many Americans, especially young people, on a political system which appeared to give them so little effective voice and put enormous strains on the bonds that held American society together. 'Our Saigon expedition,' warned Archibald MacLeish, 'may well turn out to have played the part in our ultimate destiny which the Syracusan expedition played in the destiny of Athens.'

As early as April 1965 Senator Wayne Morse predicted that Johnson's policy in Vietnam would send him 'out of office the most discredited President in the history of this nation'; but few doubted that Johnson, after his unprecedented victory in 1964, would win another four-year term in 1968. When on 30 November 1967 Senator Eugene J. McCarthy announced he would enter Democratic primaries to challenge the President over the issue of Vietnam, his decision was viewed as quixotic, for Johnson's control of his party appeared unshakable. However, liberal Democrats had become increasingly disenchanted with a war that, by draining money and energy from critical domestic problems, had brought to an abrupt halt the most promising reform movement in a generation, and, by overheating the economy, sent prices and interest rates soaring. With stunning rapidity the tide of events overwhelmed the President. On 23 January 1968 four North Korean gunboats seized U.S.S. *Pueblo*, a Navy intelligence-gathering ship (and held its officers and crew captive for the next eleven months). One week later, on 30 January, as Vietnam began to celebrate the Tet (lunar New Year) holiday, the Communists launched a massive assault on thirty provincial capitals, overran the ancient city of Hué, and in Saigon even held a portion of the American embassy compound for several hours. By demonstrating that after years of effort the United States and South Vietnam could not even safeguard Saigon, the Tet offensive shook the faith in Johnson's policy of some of the President's most stalwart supporters.

On 12 March 1968, Senator McCarthy surprised the nation by rolling up 40 per cent of the vote in the New Hampshire primary. Four days later Robert Kennedy plunged into the race for the Democratic nomination. Polls now indicated that McCarthy would carry Wisconsin against the administration (which he did), and showed only 26 per cent approved Johnson's handling of the Vietnam situation. On 31 March Johnson told a national television audience that he was restricting the areas of North Vietnam to which bombing missions would be sent and invited Hanoi to discuss a settlement, an invitation that was quickly accepted. He concluded his address with a statement that jolted the country: 'I shall not seek and I will not accept the nomination of my party for a

The President shows his scar. The ebullient LBJ created a minor ruckus when he raised his shirt and showed reporters the evidence of a recent operation. Some thought that such behavior on the part of a President of the United States was in poor taste. The episode also spawned an outrageous pun; Johnson, it was said, was the Abdominal Showman. In this 1966 caricature, David Levine has cleverly made use of the incident to suggest that the scar that the President has revealed is in the shape of the map of Vietnam, a jagged wound from which Johnson never recovered. (*The New York Review of Books*)

second term as your President.' The war in Vietnam, which had claimed so many victims, had now consumed Lyndon Johnson's ambitions too.

A Divided Nation

In the last years of Johnson's tenure, spasms of violence rocked the nation as bitterness over Vietnam, racial strife, and a series of assassinations raised doubts about the stability of American society. 'The rage to demolish,' in John Gardner's phrase, threatened the most venerable institutions and symbols; antiwar radicals rampaged through college campuses and burned the American flag. Even movements dedicated to peaceful change turned to the use of force. The Student Nonviolent Coordinating Committee chose as its leaders young men who urged blacks to use arms against whites, while in San Francisco's Haight-Ashbury, once the haunt of the flower children of the 'counter culture,' love posters were taken down and violent crime increased sharply.

On 11 August 1965, just five days after President Johnson signed the Voting Rights Act of 1965, which appeared to take the civil rights struggle out of the streets, the worst race riot in the nation's history erupted in the Watts community of Los Angeles. Six turbulent days left 34 dead, 856 injured, far more serious than any of the disturbances that had troubled Northern cities in 1964. In 1966 riots broke out in the Negro districts of Cleveland, Chicago, and other cities, and racial insurrections in 1967 took 26 lives in Newark and 43 in Detroit, where black militants set fires and sniped at police. Northern Negroes, who had long exercised such rights as the suffrage, complained that civil rights statutes did almost nothing to alleviate the hardships of the urban ghetto: unemployment, inferior education, slum housing, and hostile police.

In 1966 Negro rioters chanted a new slogan: 'black power,' which could mean anything from an expression of pride ('black is beautiful') to a determination to play the same kind of ethnic politics that groups like the Irish had found profitable, to hatred of whites, reliance on violent confrontations, or a rejection of integration in favor of separate black institutions. Black nationalism

Ben Shahn, 'I Think Continually of Those Who Were Truly Great.' Beneath the dove are the words of Stephen Spender's poem, and above are inscribed the names of those who died in the cause of civil rights or were the victims of wanton racial violence. Among the names that may be discerned are those of Jimmie Lee Jackson, a 26-year-old black youth slain in Marion, Ala.; the Rev. James J. Reeb, a white Unitarian minister from Boston clubbed to death in Selma, Ala.; Carol Robertson, 14, one of four Negro girls killed by a bomb while attending Sunday School at a church in Birmingham, Ala.; Viola Gregg Liuzzo, a white civil rights worker from Detroit, murdered on an Alabama highway on the night of the Selma-Montgomery march; Virgil Wade, a 13-year-old black boy killed as he rode his bicycle on the outskirts of Birmingham; and William L. Moore, a white postal worker who set out to walk alone from Chattanooga, Tenn., to Jackson, Miss., to show that peaceful protest against segregation was possible, and who, near Attalla, Ala., was shot to death. When Shahn was asked what his subjects were, he answered there were only three: 'aloneness, the impossibility of people to communicate, and the indestructible spirit of man.' *(Kennedy Galleries, New York)*

I THINK CONTINUALLY OF THOSE WHO WERE TRULY GREAT
NEAR THE SNOW,
NEAR THE SUN,
IN THE HIGHEST FIELDS
SEE HOW THESE NAMES ARE FETED
BY THE WAVING GRASS
AND BY THE STREAMERS
OF WHITE CLOUD
AND WHISPERS OF WIND
IN THE LISTENING SKY.
THE NAMES OF THOSE
WHO IN THEIR LIVES
FOUGHT FOR LIFE
WHO WORE AT THEIR HEARTS
THE FIRE'S CENTRE.
BORN OF THE SUN
THEY TRAVELLED A SHORT WHILE
TOWARDS THE SUN.
AND LEFT THE VIVID AIR SIGNED
WITH THEIR HONOR.
STEPHEN SPENDER
Ben Shahn

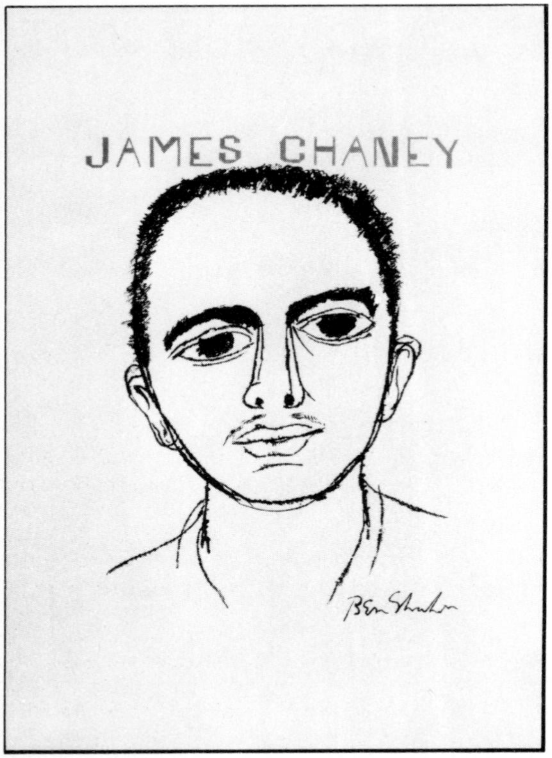

had long been espoused by the Black Muslim movement, most recently by the eloquent Malcolm X. In 1964 he defected from the organization, only to be murdered by three Black Muslims the next year. Many of his ideas, however, were taken up by the new leaders of SNCC, Stokely Carmichael and his even more militant successor, H. Rap Brown, and by such guerilla groups as the Black Panthers. Martin Luther King commented on this movement: 'In advocating violence it is imitating the worst, the most brutal, and the most uncivilized value of American life.' However, President Johnson's National Advisory Commission on Civil Disorders, headed by Governor Otto Kerner of Illinois, put the main blame for the riots on 'white racism,' and issued a grim warning: 'Our nation is moving toward two societies, one black, one white—separate and unequal.'

Reviled by vindictive racists, hounded by J. Edgar Hoover and the FBI, and regarded as a compromiser by black extremists, Dr. Martin Luther King still hoped to bridge the gulf between the two societies. As the leading apostle of nonviolence, he had been honored with the award of the Nobel Peace Prize, but in the United States he had made little headway in his recent efforts on behalf of the poor of all races. He met rebuff both in Chicago, where techniques of passive resistance encountered obdurate hostility, and in Memphis, where he came to the aid of striking garbage collectors. In the early evening of 4 April 1968, as he stood on the balcony of a Memphis motel, Dr. King was shot and killed. James Earl Ray, a white man who was an escaped convict, was imprisoned for the crime.

The nation grieved for the slain leader who in his thirty-nine years had contributed so much, but it reacted to his death in the same ambiguous

The civil rights martyrs. On 21 June 1964 James Earl Chaney, a 21-year-old black from Meridian, Miss., Andrew Goodman, a 20-year-old white from New York who was a student at Queens College, and Michael Henry Schwerner, a 24-year-old white from Brooklyn, all of whom were taking part in a project to register Negro voters in Mississippi, disappeared. On 4 August their bullet-ridden bodies were unearthed; before Chaney was murdered, he had been subjected to an 'inhuman beating.' These lithographs are by Ben Shahn. (*Philadelphia Museum of Art, Given by the Lawyers Constitutional Defense Fund of the American Civil Liberties Union.*)

way it had responded to his life. The death of a man who had so often cautioned against violence triggered race riots in a hundred cities, at the cost of thirty-nine lives. On 10 April 1968, a day after Dr. King was buried, the House of Representatives passed a 'fair housing' bill designed to ban racial discrimination in 80 per cent of housing in the United States. Yet even King's death failed to move 171 Congressmen who voted in opposition. The act also set penalties for activities in interstate commerce aimed at encouraging riots.

With King gone many looked toward Robert Kennedy as the one national leader who had the confidence of the poor of both races. A Kennedy campaign aide, Charles Evers, brother of the murdered Medgar Evers, later called him 'the only white man in this country I really trusted.' Kennedy won in Indiana, but when McCarthy upset him in Oregon, he had to capture the California primary of 5 June 1968 if he was to stay in the race. A little after midnight it became clear that Kennedy had won California and South Dakota on the same day. As he walked through a kitchen passageway at the Ambassador Hotel in Los Angeles, he was shot and fatally wounded by a Jordanian immigrant, Sirhan Bishara Sirhan, who resented Kennedy's support of Israel. At the age of forty-two, Robert Francis Kennedy was buried beside his brother in the hillside plot at Arlington National Cemetery.

The anguish over the deaths of Robert Kennedy and Martin Luther King raised probing questions about the nature of American society. Their deaths recalled other recent murders: John Kennedy, Medgar Evers, Rev. James Reeb, Malcolm X, the four Negro girls killed by a bomb in a Birmingham church, the three young men—James Chaney, Andrew Goodman, and Michael

Schwerner—brutally murdered by enemies of civil rights in Mississippi, and too many more. The rising crime rate, the casual merchandising of slaughter on television, the resort to coercion by students at Berkeley, Columbia, and other universities, and the lobbying by the National Rifle Association against effective gun control legislation caused many to ask whether violence was not the American way of life. Such assessments were often ill-balanced, for the United States had achieved notable success in developing peaceful solutions to social crises; yet in the context of the continuing warfare in Vietnam, the events of the spring of 1968 could not help but be disturbing.

The winds of violence whistled through the chinks in the American political structure in the 1968 campaign, but the party system withstood the buffeting. To the Democratic convention city of Chicago that summer came the youthful idealists of Senator McCarthy's 'Children's Crusade.' To Chicago, too, came itinerant revolutionists bent on provoking a violent confrontation. In most respects the convention was exceptionally democratic; it suspended the unit rule, seated black delegates from states like Mississippi, and provided for full debate on Vietnam. But the McCarthy enthusiasts believed the will of the people had been flouted when the presidential nomination went to Vice-President Hubert Humphrey, whose delegates had been chosen at party meetings rather than in primaries. Bitter exchanges marred the convention proceedings while in the streets anti-war demonstrators clashed with Mayor Richard J. Daley's police, some of whom ran amok. Televised accounts of the party warfare and the mayhem in the streets placed an enormous handicap on Humphrey's campaign.

Millions of Americans felt that in being asked to choose between Humphrey and the Republican nominee Richard Nixon they were offered no real choice, since both men had been identified with a 'hard' line in Vietnam and with the politics of the older generation. Humphrey countered by pointing to his outstanding record as leader of the Senate liberals and spokesman for civil rights. Moreover, he had made a fortunate move when he picked Senator Edmund S. Muskie to be his running mate. On the other hand, Nixon had selected for his vice-presidential candidate Governor Spiro T. Agnew of Maryland, who, by racial slurs and chauvinistic invective, tempted Democratic dissidents to return to the fold.

Still other Americans expressed a different kind of dissatisfaction with the presidential choices in 1968 by building the most formidable third party in a generation. Governor George Wallace's American Independent party appealed chiefly to those who resented gains for the Negro, especially in the South but also among many white workingmen in the Northern cities. Wallace's plea for 'law and order,' although largely a euphemism for racial discrimination, also struck a chord among those who blamed the upsurge of crime and the violence of college students and anti-war demonstrators on men in authority, especially 'permissive' Supreme Court justices. To exploit the sentiment of those who criticized Johnson for not prosecuting the war more unrestrainedly, Wallace chose as his running mate General Curtis Le May, former Air Force Chief of Staff who was known for his strident advocacy of bombing North Vietnam back to the Stone Age. But Le May's complaint about the country's 'phobia' concerning the use of nuclear weapons drove still more Democratic defectors back into the arms of their party.

Humphrey, who started out far behind, almost pulled even in the final five days of the campaign after Johnson announced he was halting the bombing of North Vietnam, but Nixon scored a narrow victory. With 31.8 million votes (43.4 per cent) Nixon gained a 301–191 margin in the Electoral College. Humphrey, with 31.3 million votes (42.7 per cent), continued to draw most of his support from the 'Roosevelt coalition' of lower-income voters in the big cities, including 85 per cent of the non-white vote. But his share of the ballots of manual workers fell off sharply, and the once-Solid South was so shattered that he captured only one Southern state, Texas. Wallace polled 9.9 million votes (13.5 per cent) and 46 electoral votes, all in the South. The Vietnam war and social disruption had cost the Democrats dearly. In four years a plurality of 16 million votes on the presidential line had evaporated, and for the first time a party that won a landslide victory lost control of the White House at the subsequent election.

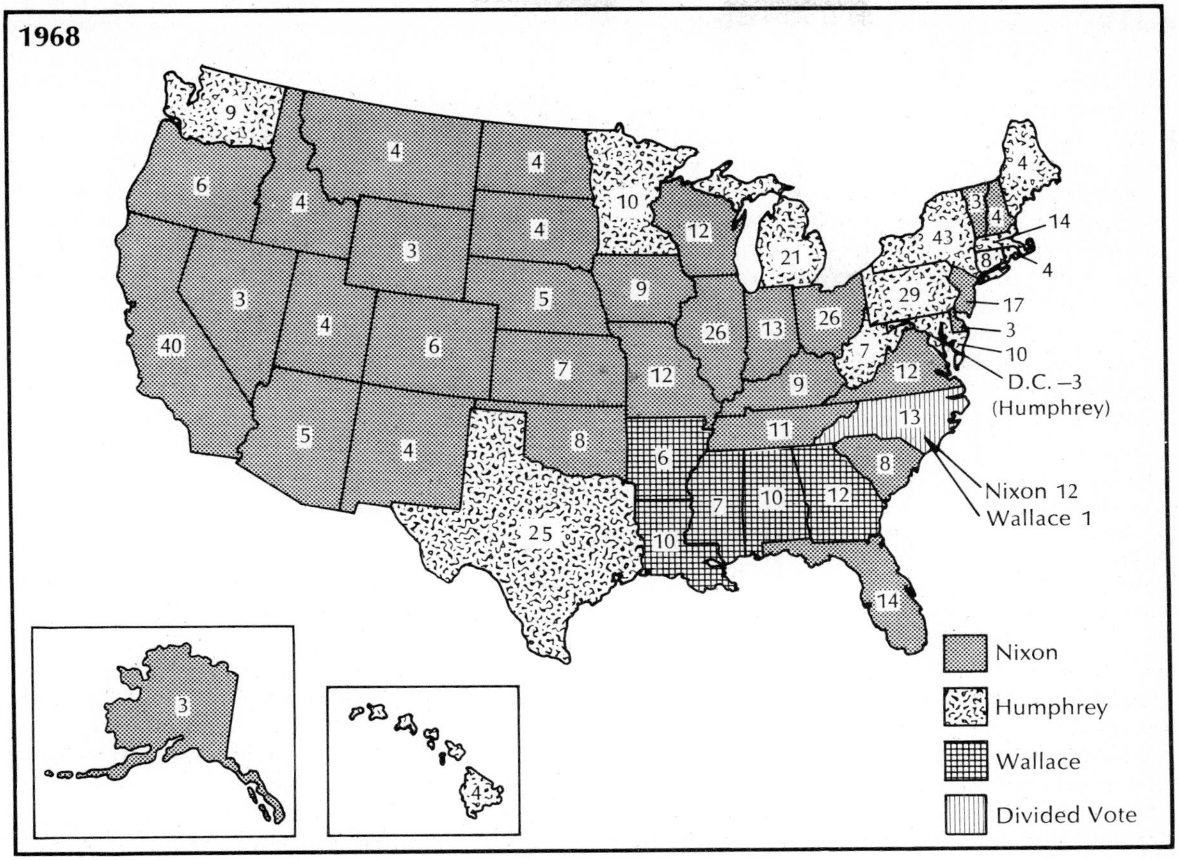

Presidential Election, 1968

As the grim year of 1968 drew to an end the country found excitement in a majestic voyage that dramatized the potentialities of American society. In Christmas week Col. Frank Borman, Capt. James A. Lovell, Jr., and Col. William A. Anders of Apollo 8 became the first mortals to see the dark side of the moon. Many wondered why the United States, capable of so spectacular an achievement in outer space, could not approach its problems on earth with the same dedication and resourcefulness. As President Johnson prepared to turn over the reins of office to a successor known neither for his imagination nor his scruples, few could be sanguine about the prospects.

The Nixon Melodrama

The outcome of the 1968 election set the ill-fated course of the Nixon presidency. Despite all that had befallen the Democratic administration, Nixon had won only a narrow triumph, with the smallest percentage of the popular vote of any victor since 1912. Long thought of as a 'born loser,' he was determined to win re-election in 1972—and by a landslide. To do so he adopted a number of strategies: moderation to appeal to the Center, divisiveness to attract the followers of George Wallace, and exploitation of the issues of cultural politics that were troubling 'Middle

America.' In the end, the Nixon 'team,' not content with these expedients, did not scruple at adopting methods that would reduce the presidency morally to its lowest point in the nation's history and bring about a crisis of confidence in the democratic process.

When analysts sifted through the 1968 returns, they found that voters were more concerned about 'law and order' than any other problem, even the Vietnam war, and Nixon made the most of this. The country had been shaken by five consecutive summers of rioting in the black ghettos; by campus violence; and by a sharp rise in crime, including assaults upon persons. In his inaugural address, the President declared:

> America has suffered from a fever of words; from inflated rhetoric that promises more than it can deliver; from angry rhetoric that fans discontents into hatreds; from bombastic rhetoric that postures instead of persuading.
>
> We cannot learn from one another until we stop shouting at one another—until we speak quietly enough so that our words can be heard as well as our voices.

Nixon had some initial success in portraying himself as a promoter of domestic peace. The ghetto turbulence abruptly ended, to a certain extent because Nixon, by raising few expectations, created less possibility of disappointment. The bloodletting in Vietnam continued (one-third of American deaths in the war would occur under Nixon), but in the process of taking as long to end the war as Lincoln had required to fight the Civil War, he did reduce United States troop levels, which had peaked at 543,000 in 1968 to 39,000 on 1 September 1972. Furthermore, a reform of the draft diminished anxiety for registrants with higher numbers. In part as a consequence of these developments, the mood of protest on college campuses became muted, if only for a time.

However, Nixon's role as a builder of bridges over troubled waters proved less congenial than that of capitalizing on apprehension about social change. Millions of Americans strongly disapproved of the ideology of the 'counter culture,' which denigrated respected institutions and values, notably the work ethic. Dislike of the counter culture was especially marked among lower income voters, long the ballast of the Democratic party. In the Johnson years the 'greening of America' had taken a bewildering variety of forms, including experimentation with psychedelic drugs, uninhibited sexual behavior, and the vogue of 'acid' rock music, a volatile mixture which in Nixon's first year in office drew hundreds of thousands of young people to the Woodstock Music and Art Fair.

At the same time the counter culture was assailing American folkways, the women's liberation movement was raising challenges to traditional perceptions of sex roles and the structure of the family. In the 1960's two-thirds of new jobs went to women, and by 1970 43 per cent of adult women were in the labor force. Advocates of equal opportunity, who succeeded in securing legislation like the Civil Rights Act of 1964 which forbade discrimination in employment on the basis of sex, sometimes asked only that women receive equal pay for equal work. But increasingly, they advanced other demands—for child care centers, an end to restrictions on abortion, and sex quotas in hiring—that defied orthodox conceptions of woman's 'place' and the nuclear family. These innovations seemed especially unsettling in a period when the stability of the family was shaken by an 80 per cent rise in the number of divorces between 1960 and 1972.

Into this highly controverted arena of cultural politics barged the Nixon administration, led by the lubberly Spiro Agnew who took to the stump to deplore the erosion of time-honored American values. 'We have gone through a debilitating, enervating age of indulgence,' the Vice-President said. Agnew barnstormed less on the old issues of economic policy than on the latest disputes about life style, although he linked the two when he blamed changing attitudes on 'a political hedonism that permeates the philosophy of the radical liberals' and when he excoriated Dr. Benjamin Spock, author of an immensely popular manual on child-rearing and an outspoken foe of the Vietnam war. Nixon, too, berated the 'Spock-marked generation,' attacked 'abortion on demand,' and denounced the latitudinarian conclusions of the Federal Commission on Obscenity and Pornography.

The disintegration of the consumer culture. Probably the best known work of 'pop art' is Andy Warhol's silk-screen of a bright array of Campbell's soup cans in cheerful order on a supermarket shelf. Such a painting could be perceived either as indifferent to the banality of its subject or even as a celebration of consumer goods. Warhol's 'Campbell's Soup Can with Peeling Label,' however, implies the decay of a consumer-oriented society. (*Kunsthaus, Zürich*)

Many of the new manifestations converged on the Supreme Court. In invalidating the censorship of *Lady Chatterley's Lover* in 1959, the Court stated that the First Amendment 'protects advocacy of opinion that adultery may sometimes be proper, no less than advocacy of socialism or the single tax,' and in defense of *Fanny Hill* in 1966, the justices ruled that a book could not be proscribed unless it was found 'to be utterly without redeeming social value.' During the same years when it was ending virtually all restrictions on pornography, the Warren Court stirred up an even sharper controversy by outlawing Bible-reading and prayer in public schools as a violation of the First Amendment. 'They've put the Negroes in the schools,' expostulated an Alabama Congressman, 'and now they've driven God out.' Many of the same people who were exercised about these decisions deplored the rulings of the Court in cases such as *Escobedo v. Illinois* (1964), which stipulated that a suspect must be informed of his right to remain silent and to have counsel present when he was interrogated. Though civil libertarians applauded decisions like *Gideon v. Wainwright* (1963), which stipulated that the state must provide a pauper charged with a felony with an attorney at public expense, others, frequently unreasonably, blamed the Warren Court for the dramatic rise in crime in the cities, and in the climactic *Miranda* case of 1966, which broadened the 'due process' requirement of the Fourteenth Amendment, the four dissenting justices warned against returning 'a killer, a rapist or other criminal to the streets . . . to repeat his crime whenever it pleases him.'

When Nixon took office, he set out to reverse this jurisprudence by appointing law-and-order judges who would be 'strict constructionists,' and he was soon given the opportunity to fill several vacancies. In 1969, Chief Justice Warren retired, and the President chose a federal judge, Warren Burger, to replace him. That selection occasioned little comment, but when he and his maladroit Attorney-General, John Mitchell, attempted to elevate judges from Southern circuits to the High Court they were twice rebuffed by the Senate, a humiliation that had not been visited on an American President in this century. Nixon and Mitchell then came up with two more names that were so unacceptable that they did not submit them. All of this greatly distressed a Republican Senator from Nebraska who said of one of Nixon's nominees: 'There are lots of mediocre judges and people and lawyers. They are entitled to a little representation aren't they? . . . We can't have all Brandeises and Frankfurters and Cardozos and stuff like that there.'

In the end Nixon, by more respectable though still conservative appointments, did succeed in modifying the stance of the Court but not nearly to the extent he desired. In a number of decisions the 'Burger Court' softened the position of the Warren Court. Nonetheless, it also broadened the orbit of cultural politics and extended the safeguards of civil liberties and civil rights. The Court elaborated the right of a woman to an abortion during the first three months of pregnancy, curbed the imposition of the death penalty, repudiated the Attorney-General's arrogant claim that he could utilize wiretaps on domestic dissenters without a court order, and held that the government could not restrain publication of the 'Pentagon Papers,' a detailed examination of Vietnam policy which a Pentagon expert, Daniel Ellsberg, leaked to the press. In a unanimous opinion in April 1971, the Court, in a Charlotte, North Carolina, case, sustained the busing of pupils out of their neighborhoods in order to foster racial integration.

The Nixon administration found this last decision especially galling, for it had been pursuing a 'Southern strategy' to wean George Wallace's followers away from him. The aborted attempt to name a South Carolina judge to the Supreme Court had been aimed at pleasing that state's arch-conservative senator, Strom Thurmond, who regarded Agnew as the greatest Vice-President America had ever had, save only for Calhoun. Toward blacks the administration pursued a policy of 'benign neglect,' in the words of Nixon's adviser Daniel Patrick Moynihan. Sometimes 'benign neglect' implied continuing to foster racial gains but doing it surreptitiously so as not to antagonize the Wallaceites. At other times it meant outright hostility to programs of the Kennedy-Johnson era, as when Mitchell's Department of Justice opposed extension of the Voting Rights Act of 1965. When the administration asked a federal court to delay the desegregation of Mississippi schools, the NAACP asked to have the United States named a defendant, for 'it no longer seeks to represent the rights of Negro children.'

The accent on 'benign neglect' came in an era when other groups besides blacks were insisting on their rights. So substantial was the migration from the Caribbean islands in the quarter-century after World War II that there were more Puerto Ricans in New York than in San Juan, and by 1970 nearly a quarter of a million Cubans in Florida's Dade County; both groups wanted greater recognition. Over one-fourth of Mexican-Americans lived below the poverty line; cultural nationalists furthered the cause of these 'Chicanos,' and Cesar Chavez led strikes of migrant workers in the vineyards and lettuce fields of California that evoked sympathy among liberal Democrats. However, the Nixon administration showed no understanding of the aspirations of Spanish-American groups or of the afflictions of American Indians who, with a rapidly growing population, had a life expectancy of only 46 years, compared with the national average of 69, and the country's highest rate of infant mortality. The increasing militance of Indian groups, beginning with an occupation of Alcatraz Island in San Francisco Bay and running through the ransacking of the Bureau of Indian Affairs headquarters in Washington, reached a climax in the Nixon period in a bloody confrontation on the Sioux reservation at Wounded Knee.

The hard-shelled indifference of the Nixon administration reflected the composition of its leadership. 'Richard Nixon's White House is a controlled, antiseptic place, not unlike the upper tier of a giant corporation,' observed an American journal, while a British commentary referred to the Nixon cabinet as 'a steering committee of the conformist middle class triumphant.' Dominating

Nixon the hardhat. On 8 May 1970 construction workers wearing 'hardhats' and shouting 'All the way USA' and 'Love it or leave it' beat up student antiwar demonstrators in New York City. 'Once the defender of economic and social justice, in the vanguard of progressive movements, we now find the AFL-CIO endorsing the war in Vietnam,' said one union official ruefully. 'It has totally alienated our youth and antagonized others as well.' By donning a hardhat, President Nixon identified himself both with the prowar stance of the construction workers and with their tactics. (*National Archives*)

the White House staff were two former 'advance men,' Harry R. Haldeman and John Ehrlichman who, with their Prussian haircuts and no-nonsense comportment, seemed so much alike that they were called the 'Rosencrantz and Guildenstern' of the administration. The President for his part frequently isolated himself behind the 'Berlin Wall' erected by his two main advisers on domestic policy.

In foreign affairs, too, despite all of the buncombe about bringing the nation together, Nixon launched periodic forays that provoked paroxysms of rage. Although Nixon had claimed during the 1968 campaign that he had a plan to move the Vietnam conflict to a speedy end, the war went on, year in, year out. In 1969 massive antiwar demonstrations shook Washington, but to no avail. The President detonated an even greater explosion in 1970 when he sent American troops and bombers into Cambodia and sought to justify the invasion by saying, 'We will not be humiliated. We will not be defeated. . . . If when the chips are down, the world's most powerful nation . . . acts like a pitiful, helpless giant, the forces of totalitarianism and anarchy will threaten free nations and free institutions throughout the world.' Nixon's expansion of the fighting ignited campuses from coast to coast. Martial law was proclaimed in a number of states, including Ohio, where Kent State demonstrators firebombed the ROTC building. The situation became more inflamed when on 4 May National Guardsmen shot to death four students at Kent State and, in an unrelated incident on 15 May, Mississippi troopers killed two students at Jackson State College. In protest, indignant students, faculty, and administrators shut down scores of colleges, some for the rest of the semester.

The unmistakable evidence that he had miscalculated caused Nixon to back-track momentarily by pulling out of Cambodia, but he soon resumed a more bellicose line, in part in order to appeal to those who favored a hawkish foreign policy. When New York's mayor, John Lindsay, ordered the flag at City Hall lowered to half-staff in respect for the Kent State victims, hard-hatted construction workers rampaged through the financial district bludgeoning long-haired students and ran the flag up again. Nixon deliberately cultivated both these 'hard hats' and the disciples of George Wallace by intervening in the case of Lt. William L. Calley, Jr., convicted of slaughtering several hundred defenseless civilians at the South Vietnamese hamlet of Mylai. In 1971 the President incited new outbursts by invading Laos, and in 1972 he risked a confrontation with Russia by saturation bombing of North Vietnam and by mining harbors used by Soviet vessels there.

Yet though Nixon embarked on inflammatory adventures in foreign policy, he also undertook initiatives which lent credence to his claim to be a sponsor of *détente*. In 1969 he proclaimed a 'Nixon Doctrine,' which implied willingness to forego any more interventions like Vietnam. He appointed as his National Security Adviser a Harvard professor, Henry Kissinger, who was regarded as a 'realist' in foreign affairs, and in 1972 the President flew to Moscow to negotiate a treaty limiting strategic missiles. He also ended the production of biological weapons. But Nixon created the greatest sensation by flying to Peking in February 1972 to confer with Premier Chou En-lai. A man who had built a career on relentless animosity to the Communist world had become the first President to contrive an opening to the People's Republic of China.

Nixon also gained stature from an extraordinary event toward which he had made no

Man on the Moon. The astronaut Col. Edwin E. 'Buzz' Aldrin, Jr. is photographed walking on the lunar surface. In Aldrin's visor are reflected the photographer, Neil A. Armstrong, civilian commander of Apollo II, and the lunar landing vehicle, *Eagle*. Notice the American flag patch, emblem of U.S. victory in the 'space race.' Aldrin's 73-year-old father, a veteran aviator who was a friend of Orville Wright and Charles Lindbergh, suggested as the text for their mission Psalm 8: 'When we behold the heavens, the work of Your fingers, the moon and the stars which You set in place; what is man that You should be mindful of him, or the son of man that You should care for him.' On 20 July 1976, on the seventh anniversary of this extraordinary event, an American spacecraft made the first successful landing on Mars, more than 212 million miles from Earth. (*NASA*)

contribution—man's first voyage to the moon. On 20 July 1969, four days after they blasted off from earth, two members of the crew of Apollo 11—Neil A. Armstrong and Col. Edwin E. Aldrin, Jr.—became the first men ever to walk on the moon. While Lt. Col. Michael Collins maneuvered their spaceship, Armstrong and Aldrin placed on the surface of the moon a plaque signed by the crew and President Nixon that read: '*Here men from the planet earth first set foot upon the moon July 1969, A.D. We came in peace for all mankind.*' Some complained that the country's resources would be better spent in coping with terrestrial problems, but more were impressed by the achievement, and Nixon, sharing the television screen with the astronauts, profited from the approbation for the journey to the Sea of Tranquility.

The President's domestic policies, too, sometimes departed from the conservatism of Mitchell's 'Southern strategy.' The proportion of pupils in all-black schools fell precipitously from 68 per cent in 1968 to 18 per cent in 1970, in large part because of longtime trends, some of which Nixon resisted, but also because of positive steps as when the administration sued the entire state of Georgia to end dual educational systems. A series of statutes starting with the National Environmental Policy Act of 1969 improved the quality of air and water, and the Environmental Protection Agency, created in 1970, enforced higher standards on the automobile industry and on municipalities and corporations. Frequently initiatives came not from the White House but from the Democratic Congress, as when plans to construct supersonic transport aircraft were frustrated. Still, either because of or despite the attitude of the White House, social advances continued in the Nixon years. Social security benefits increased more than 50 per cent from 1969 to 1972, and federal expenditures for education and health soared. Though these developments were offset by other moves in a reactionary direction, liberals found them a welcome surprise. 'Everybody is saying that Mr. Nixon is doing better than they expected,' noted James Reston, 'which proves the success of past failures.'

Nixon also showed more flexibility than anticipated in coping with the main domestic issue he confronted—the ailing economy. From Lyndon Johnson he had inherited an economy overstimulated by spending on the Vietnam war, and soon he had to deal with an unpropitious combination that liberal economists had not envisaged: skyrocketing prices accompanied by rapidly mounting unemployment. The President started out by prescribing conventional nostrums, but when these failed, he turned to deficit spending. 'I am now a Keynesian,' he said; as one commentator remarked, that was 'a little like a Christian crusader saying, "All things considered, I think Mohammed was right."' But Nixon continued to resist more direct intervention. 'Controls, Oh my God, no!' he expostulated in 1969. However, when in 1971 prices continued to rise, and the nation experienced its first trade deficit since 1893, he ordered a temporary freeze on wages, prices, and rents and devalued the dollar. Nixon's new policies enjoyed only moderate success. Nonetheless, he was able to make his bid for reelection at a time when many Americans were enjoying the benefits of the world's first trillion-dollar economy.

In the 1972 campaign Nixon had the decisive advantage of prevailing over both the Right and the Center sectors of the electorate. His main worry from the Right ended on 15 May 1972 when George Wallace, who showed conspicuous strength among blue-collar workers in Democratic primaries, was shot and so badly wounded that he had to withdraw from the presidential race. Nixon appropriated the Center when the Democrats chose as their Presidential nominee a factionalist, Senator George McGovern. An antiwar liberal who had made an admirable record, McGovern won the nomination as the result of changes in party procedure that alienated union chieftains and big city organizations and left the erroneous impression that he was the candidate of the counter culture. He had the further misfortune of picking as his running mate Senator Thomas Eagleton of Missouri and, after it came out that Eagleton had been treated for mental illness, dropping him from the ticket. Nixon overwhelmed McGovern with 47.2 million votes (60.7 per cent) to 29.2 million and a 520 to 17 triumph in the Electoral College; McGovern carried only Massachusetts and the predominantly black District of Columbia. Especially disappointing to McGovern was the performance of young people; an act of Congress and the Twenty-sixth Amendment, ratified in 1971, had given eighteen-year-olds the right to vote, but the majority of them did not trouble to go to the polls.

On the eve of the election Henry Kissinger had marshaled votes for Nixon by stating, 'Peace is at hand.' This welcome announcement proved premature, for in the month after his re-election the President celebrated the Christmas season by approving a merciless bombing of North Vietnam, especially of heavily populated Hanoi, that dismayed and disgusted large numbers of Americans and brought worldwide censure. However, Nixon did finally achieve a cease-fire in Vietnam in January 1973 and by the end of March the last United States troops had been withdrawn from the stricken country. In addition, the government proclaimed the end of the draft. Nixon boasted that he had achieved 'peace with honor.' In fact, the agreement acknowledged an unmitigated defeat and the term 'honor' was totally irrelevant. The war had cost 57,000 American lives, more than 300,000 wounded; had inflicted over one million casualties on Asians; had absorbed billions of dollars in resources; and had done incalculable damage to American society and to the effectiveness of the United States in world affairs.

Returned to office by one of the most convincing margins in history, Nixon gave up all pretense of being a man of the Center and immediately veered sharply to the Right. He had hardly begun his second administration when he precipitated a serious constitutional crisis. He flaunted the authority of Congress by dismantling the Office of Economic Opportunity that administered the War on Poverty, impounded funds Congress had appropriated for social purposes, and defied requests from Capitol Hill for information on the behavior of civil servants. Increasingly Nixon's aides, who supervised a White House staff over two-and-a-half times larger than that with which Roosevelt had run World War II, behaved less like servants of the people in a democratic republic and more like a Praetorian Guard. Nixon, wrote a British journalist, was asserting 'Robespierre's claim to personify the general will,' while other critics likened him to de Gaulle, a refractory ruler convinced that history was on his side, contemptuous of the legislature, and isolated from those he governed.

Concern about abuse of power became the leitmotif of the second Nixon administration. In the spring of 1973 the United States Attorney for Maryland launched a criminal investigation into allegations that Spiro Agnew, while county executive of Baltimore and governor of Maryland, had accepted bribes. On 10 October the Vice-President, faced with a possible prison term, pleaded *nolo contendere* (no contest) to a charge of filing a 'false and fraudulent' tax return, and resigned. A federal court fined Agnew $10,000 and sentenced him to probation for three years. Though the Department of Justice halted prosecution, it released an extensive account of Agnew's malefactions which, it stated, continued during the period when he was 'only a heartbeat away' from becoming President of the United States. Never before had so high an office in the republic been so disgraced. Under the terms of the Twenty-fifth Amendment, ratified in 1967, Nixon named as Agnew's successor the Republican Minority Leader, Representative Gerald R. Ford of Michigan, a conservative who had never been suspected of originality. But neither had he aroused suspicions of dishonesty, and so far had the reputation of the American government sunk that this qualification, which should have been taken for granted, was regarded as an exceptional mark of distinction.

Agnew's resignation occurred in a season of mounting public indignation over a matter of far graver purport: 'the Watergate affair.' On 17 June 1972 a security guard came upon intruders in the Democratic National Committee headquarters. Though the culprits, who were quickly tried and convicted, were employees of the Committee to Re-elect the President (CREEP), Nixon dismissed the burglary as a 'bizarre incident,' and for a time it seemed that no more would come of the episode. But neither Judge John J. Sirica of the U.S. District Court nor reporters for the *Washington Post* were content with this explanation, and by the spring of 1973 the Nixon administration had become enmeshed in a web of duplicity and deceit.

Investigation disclosed that wrongdoing had not been limited to the Watergate break-in. Campaign officials had engaged in political sabotage and other 'dirty tricks' in New Hampshire and Florida, and the White House had connived in rifling the office of Daniel Ellsberg's psychiatrist. Both businessmen and politicians had violated the laws governing campaign contributions, and corporations were accused of subverting the election process not only in America but in Chile and other countries. Most damaging of all was the report that some of the President's closest advisers had been involved in suborning perjury and paying 'hush money' to cover up the Watergate scandal.

A Senate investigation headed by Sam Ervin, Jr., of North Carolina, shook the Nixon administration to its foundations. When, to forestall interrogation by the Senate inquiry, Nixon sought to cloak his assistants with a mantle of Executive prerogative, Ervin responded that 'divine right went out with the American Revolution and doesn't belong to White House aides.' Under pressure from the Ervin committee, John W. Dean, III, counsel to the President, confessed to having taken part in an elaborate conspiracy to conceal the Watergate transgressions, and he implicated others. L. Patrick Gray, III, acting director of the FBI, admitted that he had deliberately destroyed documents. He resigned under fire, as on 30 April 1973 did Dean, Haldeman, Ehrlichman, and Attorney-General Richard Kleindienst. Former Attorney-General Mitchell, the champion of law and order, conceded that he had attended three meetings at which bugging the Democratic headquarters was discussed. But the most startling disclosure of the Ervin committee hearings came when it developed that Nixon had been surreptitiously tape recording discussions and telephone conversations.

The tapes spelled Nixon's doom. Until this revelation, no one had demonstrated that the President himself was culpable, though such pointed questions had been asked about his tax returns and government expenditures on his lavish residences in Florida and California that he felt compelled to say, 'I am not a crook.' (In the end, he had to pay the government nearly half a million dollars in back taxes and interest.) If he had nothing to hide about his role in the Watergate imbroglio, the tapes should clear him. But Nixon refused to turn over the tapes, even to a special prosecutor, Archibald Cox of Harvard Law School, to whom he had pledged full cooperation. When Cox went to court to obtain the tapes, Nixon ordered Attorney-General Elliot Richardson to fire him, but, to their credit, both Richardson and his assistant, William Ruckelshaus, resigned instead on 20 October 1973. The solicitor general then obliged the President by discharging Cox.

This 'Saturday night massacre,' as Washington called it, led to widespread demands for Nixon's impeachment. When the President, at bay, agreed to surrender tapes to Judge Sirica, it turned out that critical conversations were missing and that a crucial portion of one tape had been 'accidentally' erased. On 30 April 1974, to still the outcry against him, Nixon made available edited, and inaccurate, transcripts of some of the tapes, but this self-serving move backfired. The transcripts shocked the country by exposing the President's naked insensitivity to the national interest and his crude language; overnight 'expletive deleted' became a catchphrase. Cox's successor, unpersuaded by White House subterfuges about the separation of powers, subpoenaed tapes and documents of 64 additional conversations, and on 24 July, in *U.S. v. Richard M. Nixon*, the Supreme Court, while accepting the President's contention that he might invoke a claim of Executive privilege in the national security sphere, ruled unanimously that in this instance he must comply 'forthwith.'

One week later after nationally televised deliberations impressive for the evidence they gave of conscientiousness and probity, the House Judiciary Committee voted three articles of impeachment. The President was charged with betraying his oath of office by lying, obstructing justice, and manipulating the Internal Revenue Service and other agencies to breach the Constitutional rights of citizens. In desperation, Nixon played his final card. He released the transcripts of three conversations with Haldeman and, in essence, threw himself on the mercy of the Senate. But since the transcripts further incrimi-

Robert Indiana, 'The Golden Future of America.' It has been said that the work of Indiana, who named himself after his native state, 'both celebrates and chides the signs and sights of Middle America.' This 1976 serigraph captures the ambivalent attitude of many Americans as the nation marked the two hundredth anniversary of its independence in the aftermath of Watergate. At first glance the work appears to be an exultant paean to the U.S.A. But closer examination reveals that when each of the eyes is interpreted as the letter 'I' and combined with block letters in the circles, they spell out CIA, FBI, and IRS (Internal Revenue Service), all of which were implicated in the Watergate scandals. (*Trans World Art Corp., New York*)

nated him, he lost the last remnants of his support among right-wing Republicans. With no other recourse left, Richard Nixon, on 8 August 1974, brought the sordid affair to a climax by writing, 'I hereby resign the Office of President of the United States.' 'For 25 years,' wrote Bill Moyers, 'the man had massaged the baser instincts of politics.' Now he was gone, and with him went fifty-six men convicted of Watergate-related offenses, including twenty former members of the cabinet, the White House staff, and CREEP.

On the day after Nixon submitted his resignation, Gerald Ford succeeded to the presidency, the first man ever to become Chief Executive by the appointment route. Ford began with a large reservoir of good will which he quickly dissipated. On 8 September 1974 he stunned the nation by announcing that he was pardoning Nixon for all federal crimes he 'committed or may have committed or taken part in' while President. White House Press Secretary J. F. ter Horst resigned immediately as a matter of 'conscience,' and amidst a clamor of disapproval of Ford's action, which smacked of the exercise of the royal prerogative, public support for the new President dropped precipitately.

In most respects Ford's administration differed little from Nixon's. To be sure there appeared to be much less of the knavery of the Watergate era. But when Senate investigators revealed that the FBI had been involved for over a quarter of a century in more than two hundred 'black bag jobs' against 'domestic security targets' and that the CIA had not only contravened its charter by spying on American citizens but had recruited the Mafia to assassinate Fidel Castro, Ford responded not with moral outrage but by endeavoring to suppress the evidence and punish those who wished to bring it to light. He continued to rely on Kissinger in foreign affairs and, despite the lesson of Vietnam, to contemplate intervention in the civil war in Angola. In domestic matters, Ford was more reactionary and less imaginative than Nixon. At a time of tenacious unemployment and 'double-digit' inflation, he persisted in shopworn economic policies, and repeatedly vetoed legislation for public housing, federal aid to education, health care, and other social purposes. He asked regulatory agencies to give 'maximum freedom to private enterprise' and told industrialists that he wanted Washington 'out of your business, out of your lives, out of your pockets and out of your hair.' Early in 1976 a poll found that overwhelmingly the American people thought he was 'a nice guy,' but by a large margin, too, they had concluded that 'he does not seem to be very smart about the issues the country is facing.' No one summed up his performance better than the President himself when he said, disarmingly but truthfully, 'I am a Ford, not a Lincoln.'

Ford's tribulations gave the Democrats a welcome opportunity to return to power in the 1976 election, but they almost blew it. When the former governor of Georgia, James Earl Carter, Jr., emerged from the Democratic convention with his party's nomination, he held a 33-point advantage over Ford in the polls. By November, that big lead had evaporated because of a series of mishaps, such as his indiscretion in giving a frank interview to the sexually oriented magazine *Playboy*. However, in a campaign not distinguished by its concentration on serious issues, Ford made blunders of his own, especially when, in a televised debate with Carter, he made the astounding assertion that 'there is no Soviet domination of Eastern Europe,' a remark that seemed particularly odd coming from a man who had spent much of his public life warning of the Russian menace. In the end, Jimmy Carter won, but only narrowly, polling 40.8 million votes (50.1 per cent) and 297 electoral votes to Ford's 39.1 million votes (48 percent) and 240 electoral votes, the smallest winning electoral tally since 1916.

From Carter to Reagan

As President, Carter altered the domestic policies of his predecessors only moderately. To be sure, he did address the energy crisis that had first disturbed the country during the Arab oil embargo of 1973, and under his aegis Congress created a Department of Energy and a series of procedures aimed at lessening American dependence on foreign oil. Carter also carried out his campaign pledge to pardon Vietnam-era draft

Bicentennial Quilt. Though some Americans took a jaundiced view of the nation's 200th birthday, millions of others participated in observances from Maine to Hawaii. In many communities, women sewed bicentennial quilts. This especially fine example was a cooperative enterprise of the Friends of the Library of Dobbs Ferry, N.Y. The quilt details the history of a Hudson River village that was the staging area for the battle of Yorktown in the American Revolution and grew from a section of a great Dutch manor in the seventeenth century to a modern suburb in the twentieth century. (*Photo Cathleen Polgreen*)

The changing of the guard. The outgoing president, Jimmy Carter, takes his leave of the incoming chief executive, Ronald Reagan, and his wife Nancy. (*Diego Goldberg, Sygma*)

evaders, showed courage in vetoing 'pork barrel' public works legislation, and put through the first significant revision of the federal civil service laws in a century. He not only appointed two women to Cabinet posts, one of them the newly-established Department of Education, but shepherded through Congress a 39-month extension of the deadline for ratification of the Equal Rights Amendment. On the other hand, he incurred the wrath of liberals by proposing an "austere" 1980 budget that eliminated features such as the Social Security death benefit to widows, a proposal the Senate rejected, and also in the Carter years Congress doubled the military budget at the expense of social spending, and heeded the President's request to deregulate banking and transportation. In sum, Carter differed from Ford and Nixon less in substance than in style. His low-keyed manner deflated the pretensions of the imperial presidency, and, as a 'born-again' Christian, he brought to the White House a moral earnestness that had been largely absent at the start of the decade.

On racial matters, both the President and the Supreme Court took a middle path. Carter diverged from Ford and Nixon on civil rights primarily in his record on appointments, for he named blacks to such important posts as Secretary of Housing and Urban Development, Secretary of the Army, Solicitor General and ambassador to the United Nations. On the other hand, he did nothing effective to lessen the scandalously high rate of unemployment among black youth or to cope with the decay of black neighborhoods. Despite the promises of his campaign, he indicated that though he was willing to uphold rights already established, he would not move appreciably further. Similarly, the Supreme Court, when called upon to rule on the delicate issue of 'reverse discrimination,' walked a tightrope. In a landmark 5 to 4 decision in the *Bakke* case, Justice Lewis Powell joined four other judges to rule that it was permissible to consider race in determining admission to universities, but he then joined with four different judges in holding that the medical school of the University of California at Davis violated the law in setting a quota of places for blacks. The full implications of the decision remained to be elaborated in later decisions, but the Court's action was widely interpreted as placing a limit on 'affirmative action' for blacks, other minorities, and women.

In foreign affairs, too, Carter pursued a centrist course, but in this realm his performance earned him higher grades, at least in his first two years. By presenting himself as the defender of human rights throughout the world, he restored some of the moral prestige of the presidency. Furthermore, Carter demonstrated that he was not beguiled by the globalist ambitions that had led earlier Presidents astray when he committed himself to a very gradual withdrawal of American ground troops from Korea, and even more when, in a strong show of executive leadership, he won Senate approval for treaties that would acquiesce in Panamanian control over the Panama Canal and the Canal Zone by the year 2000. Throughout his administration, Carter proved responsive to the aspirations of the Third World. Despite a round robin signed by thirty-nine Senators calling for an end to sanctions against white-controlled Rhodesia, Carter encouraged the peaceful transition to a black-controlled Zimbabwe, and when leftist guerrillas ousted a right-wing dictator in Nicaragua, Carter gave the new government his support. If he frequently took a hard line toward the Soviet Union, he also sought assiduously to work out a Strategic Arms Limitation Treaty (SALT) with the Russians.

The President showed his willingness to break with Cold War patterns when, in December 1978, he caught the country by surprise by announcing a dramatic change of American policy in the Orient, though one that had been foreshadowed by Nixon. On 1 January 1979, he revealed, the United States would end three decades of refusal to accept the legitimacy of a Communist regime in Peking by establishing full diplomatic relations with the People's Republic of China. This meant that America was withdrawing recognition from Taiwan as the rightful government of China and abrogating its defense treaty with that island republic. Yet, paradoxically, it maintained the right to sell arms to Taiwan and extracted a vague promise from Peking not to invade the country. Carter's action infuriated conservative senators, despite the fact that it had been Nixon who had paved the way for recognition of Mainland China, but most Americans agreed with the White House press officer who said, 'The idea of our not having relations with nearly a billion people is just ridiculous.' Inadvertently, the President left no doubt about what he thought the popular response would be. Unaware that a microphone had not been turned off, Carter, after presenting the news to the country, was heard to murmur: 'Massive applause throughout the nation!'

Carter's most striking success, however fragile, came in the Middle East where he took the bold risk of inviting Prime Minister Menachem Begin of Israel and President Anwar el-Sadat of Egypt to meet with him in America in September 1978. It seemed highly likely that the gathering at Camp David, the presidential retreat in the Maryland hills, would end in failure, and when instead the three men emerged with the glad tidings that they had agreed in principle, Carter scored his most impressive personal triumph since entering the White House. The euphoria, though, proved to be short-lived. A revolution in Iran led by Moslem fundamentalists overthrew the Shah, and the new government, under the sway of the Ayatollah Khomeini, denounced the United States for collaborating with the Shah's tyrannical regime. In Afghanistan, the American ambassador was murdered. By then it had become painfully clear that in the Middle East Carter had many hard miles to travel.

In part as a consequence of these developments abroad, Carter experienced such severe difficulties at home in 1979 that he felt obliged to call a 'domestic summit.' His popular support, at its zenith in March after the signing of the Egyptian-Israeli pact, eroded badly that spring as prices rose to their highest level since the postwar inflation of 1946, partly because the cut-off of Iranian oil forced motorists to queue up in exasperatingly long lines at filling stations and to pay unprecedentedly high prices for gasoline. By early July, Carter's approval rating in the polls had slumped to an abysmal 28 per cent. In response the President spent ten days in retreat at Camp David, then came down from the mountain to deliver a forceful address in which he deplored America's 'crisis of confidence,' acknowledged that some faulted him for a failure of leadership, and proposed an ambitious energy program that he anticipated would restore a sense of national purpose. The speech was well received, but Carter almost immediately lost all he had gained by firing three of his most independent-minded Cabinet officials, and accepting the registration of two others, a maladroit maneuver that once again raised serious questions about the President's capacity to lead.

Before the year was out, Carter had to undergo two very different, and even more demanding, tests. In October, acting on bad advice from David Rockefeller and Henry Kissinger, he agreed to admit the seriously ill Shah of Iran to the United States for medical attention that he could have received elsewhere. On 4 November, as informed observers had predicted, Iranians retaliated by overrunning the U.S. embassy in Teheran and taking Americans there hostage. Late in the following month, Soviet troops crossed the border of neighboring Afghanistan, a move that, though it appears to have been limited in design, could be seen as a threat to the rich oil reserves of the Persian Gulf region.

Carter spent much of 1980 attempting to cope with these twin challenges, to no discernible effect. Badly overreacting, he called the Afghanistan episode 'the most serious crisis since the last World War' and issued a strident warning that any attempt to seize control of the Persian Gulf area would be 'repelled by use of any means necessary, including military force.' He embargoed grain shipments and other trade with the Soviet Union, reinstituted draft registration, requested the Senate to postpone consideration of SALT, called on Congress to sanction covert actions by the CIA, and carried out a boycott of the Olympic games in Moscow, all without persuading the Russians to leave Afghanistan. He had no more success in Iran. After adopting a series of measures such as freezing Iranian assets, Carter sought through diplomatic channels to gain the release of the hostages, but the Ayatollah told his followers to 'rub America's face in the dirt.' Despite such provocations, including threats to execute the Americans, the President showed extraordinary restraint in avoiding an intervention that might have resulted in another Vietnam, or worse. But patient diplomacy got nowhere, and in April a foolhardy attempt by commandos to spirit the captives out of Teheran aborted in the desert. Thereafter, Carter appeared to be, as the Senate majority leader observed, the fifty-fourth hostage of the Iranians.

Voters went to the polls in 1980 with two issues foremost on their minds—Iran and the economy. In a singularly unfortunate piece of timing for Carter, Election Day fell precisely on the date that the hostages began their second year of captivity, a fact that for numbers of voters epitomized Carter's incapacity to act effectively. The captivity of the hostages, observed the *New York Times*, had become "a metaphor for American decline," and the Republican nominee, Ronald Reagan, a Hollywood actor who became governor of California, made the most of it in stressing the need to restore America's pre-eminence as a world power. He gained even more from popular dissatisfaction with the performance of the economy. Although Carter had made headway on the energy problem by persuading Congress to create a costly synthetic fuels corporation and enact a $227.7 billion windfall profits tax on oil companies, his efforts to curb inflation had only succeeded in creating a recession, with rising unemployment. None of this averted the second consecutive year of double-digit inflation, the worst such record since World War I.

Despite his earnest, if often uninspired, endeavor to serve the nation faithfully, Carter could not overcome such burdens. In the November 1980 elections, Reagan's 43.9 million votes (50.7 per cent), compared to Carter's 35.5 million (41 per cent), earned him 489 electoral votes to only 49 for Carter, who carried just six states and the District of Columbia. An independent, John Anderson, received 5.7 million votes (6.6 per cent) but no electors. (In truth, the favorite candidate of millions of Americans, unhappy with Carter but distrustful of the right-wing ideologue Reagan, was 'None of the above.' Voter turnout percentage was the lowest in 32 years.) Reagan's victory helped the Republicans win the Senate and capture enough Democratic seats in the House to give control there to a bipartisan conservative coalition. Indeed, some saw in the returns evidence of a conservative Republican realignment that would leave its mark on American politics for the next generation, though careful analysis revealed not a tidal wave of reaction but rather discontent with the Carter presidency.

Reagan, however, behaved from the outset as though he had in fact received a mandate to undo the half century of history that began with the New Deal. In electing him president, Reagan claimed, the country had delivered a message: "That message was very simple. Our government is too big and it spends too much." Denying that America had entered an age of limits to which it must adjust, Reagan claimed that by scaling down federal expenditures, reducing government regulation, and cutting taxes for three successive years, he would curb inflation, put millions back to work, and launch a new era of industrial growth. Without abandoning altogether the protective devices instituted in the Roosevelt era, Reagan sought to return the United States to the world of Calvin Coolidge.

In his first year as president, Reagan surprised critics who thought of him as a movie star out of character by proving to be a masterful legislative tactician. Congress gave him nearly everything he wanted, including sharp reductions in social spending and a tax cut. In the House, he won every Republican vote for his budget, while also gaining the support of more than three score Democrats, many of them 'boll weevils'—Southern Democrats of conservative persuasion. In vain did Jimmy Carter warn that 'an enormous transfer of government benefits is now taking place from the very poor to the very rich.' In voting to remove one million Americans from the rolls of those eligible for food stamps, the Senate slashed $400 million more than Reagan had requested. Nor did Congress raise any effective objections to Reagan's relentless determination to lessen government regulation, even though the actions of his Secretary of the Interior, James Watt, seriously imperiled the environment. By late summer, Reagan could boast, 'I feel that we did just about a 180-degree turn in the course of government.'

Reagan's foreign and defense policies came from the same ideological mold. At the outset his Secretary of State, Alexander M. Haig, Jr., who, as Nixon's chief of staff, had played an inglorious role in the Watergate disaster, seemed to be an implacable Cold Warrior. But so militant were some of the President's other advisers that General Haig almost came to be seen as a moderating influence. Reagan and his aides alarmed Latin America by supporting a government in El Salvador responsible for butchering civilians and frightened America's allies in Europe by approving full production of neutron weapons and taking a sanguine view of the prospect that a nuclear war might be fought on the Continent. Carrying still further the arma-

Freed American hostages after arriving from Teheran at Rhein-Main Air Base January 21, 1981. (*United Press International*)

ments build-up that Carter had begun, Reagan proposed to spend no less than $1.5 trillion on the military over five years.

Though such policies engendered pointed criticism, Reagan elicited substantial popular enthusiasm during much of his first year in office. In part, this resulted from his genial personality; it was hard to connect so likeable a man to the mean-spirited programs with which he was too often associated, or so plausible a man to the implausible program he sponsored. But it came, too, from a series of fortuitous events. Twenty-five minutes after Reagan was sworn in, a plane carrying the American captives to freedom took off from Teheran airport, and, although the release owed nothing to Reagan and everything to Carter's painstaking negotiations, the new president benefited from the outpouring of thanksgiving that ensued. There was another surge of good feeling when on 30 March Reagan responded to being shot by a would-be assassin with a nonchalance that won him respect and affection. Moreover, although Reagan was doctrinaire on fiscal policy, he appeared to be less zealous on cultural issues than the "Moral Majority" whom he disappointed when he named as the first woman member of the Supreme Court Sandra Day O'Connor, an Arizona state judge regarded as 'soft' on abortion.

However, Reagan's popularity waned as it became increasingly clear that his economic program was not working. During the contest for the Republican nomination in 1980, George Bush, who would subsequently become vice president, characterized Reagan's dogma as 'voodoo economics,' and others warned that if reductions in social spending were neutralized by rises in military expenditure, a tax cut would unbalance the budget. In fact, only ten months after Reagan took office, the White House admitted that it anticipated a cumulative deficit of over $400 billion before the end of the term. Reagan had promised that his policies would bring boom times, but instead the economy foundered in recession. He had campaigned on a pledge to put people back to work, but before his first year was out, unemployment neared 9 per cent, the second highest monthly rate since the beginning of World War II, while high interest rates devastated the housing and automobile industries. Yet, despite this record, Reagan adamantly insisted on still more slashes in social spending, and instead of addressing himself to the problem of recession, proposed a 'New Federalism' to turn national programs back to the states. In spirit, the New Federalism was a return to the philosophy of Calhoun and Jefferson Davis; if carried into practice, it would injure the disadvantaged who were already bearing the heaviest burden of Reagan's policies.

America in the Carter and Reagan era no longer seemed confident that, in Lord Bryce's words, it 'sailed a summer sea.' Carter had been elected in the year that the United States celebrated its 200th birthday, but the bicentennial had been less an occasion for self-congratulation than for sober introspection. Pundits raised searching questions about whether the values that had served the republic well in the beginning were any longer appropriate. For much of their history Americans had been buoyed by the conviction that they dwelt in a Zion settled by Chosen People, that they were citizens of, in Jefferson's words, 'the only monument of human rights and the sole depository of the sacred fire of freedom and self-government,' from which was 'to be lighted up . . . other regions of the earth.' But critics now asked whether the myth of America's uniqueness had not led to an arrogance toward the rest of the world that culminated in imperial misadventures like Vietnam. They inquired, too, whether America's faith in perpetual progress was salutary in an era when dwindling resources and the aspirations of the Third World made it imperative to nurture the environment, discipline technology, and curb population growth, and whether the United States should not accept a sense of limits. 'For the first time in the nearly four centuries of the American experiment, America as a nation is encountering failure, the final frontier of every civilization,' commented a European observer. 'It has reached the termination of boundless potentiality.'

Yet America has repeatedly shown its capacity for self-renewal. It created a nation; peopled deserts and built great cities; cut the bonds of the

Sandra Day O'Connor with Chief Justice Warren Burger on steps of Supreme Court the day she took her oath of office. (*United Press International*)

black slave and made its industrial system more humane; resolved the baffling problem of federalism; devised political forms to permit majority rule but protect the rights of dissenters; and fostered an economic order which, for all its failings, provided more abundance than any other in history. As the United States moved toward the year 2000, it still had the resources of character and spirit to make an important contribution to meeting the problems confronting the world.

Perhaps no one stated the realities that loomed in the last years of this century so well as had John Kennedy. In his moving talk to the Irish parliament, he said: 'Across the gulfs and barriers that now divide us, we must remember that there are no permanent enemies. Hostility today is a fact, but it is not a ruling law. The supreme reality of our time is our indivisibility as children of God and our common vulnerability on this planet.' Yet no one knew better than Kennedy how difficult was the road to peace, at home as well as abroad. In the last speech he ever gave, at Fort Worth on 21 November 1963, he warned: 'This is a dangerous and uncertain world. . . . No one expects our lives to be easy—not in this decade, not in this century.'

Bibliography, Appendices, and Index

Bibliography

GENERAL WORKS

1. *Journals, Encyclopedias, and Reference Books*

The American Historical Review (1895–); *The Mississippi Valley Historical Review* (1915–), now *The Journal of American History;* U.S. Bureau of the Census, *Historical Statistics of the United States; Colonial Times to 1970,* and *Statistical Abstract of the United States* (annual); F. Freidel & R. K. Showman (eds.), *Harvard Guide to American History;* A. Johnson & D. Malone (eds.), *The Dictionary of American Biography* (22 vols.), and supplementary volumes; R. B. Morris, *Encyclopedia of American History.*

2. *Collections of Documents and Other Sources*

H. S. Commager, *Documents of American History;* R. Leopold, A. Link, and S. Coben (eds.), *Problems in American History;* M. Meyers *et al., Sources of the American Republic* (2 vols.); R. B. Morris (ed.), *Documentary History of the United States.*

CHAPTER 1

1. *The Indians and Prehistoric America*

W. N. Fenton, *American Indian and White Relations to 1830;* A. M. Josephy, Jr. (ed.), *The American Heritage Book of Indians;* G. B. Nash, *Red, White, and Black;* W. T. Sanders, *New World Prehistory;* R. Underhill, *Red Man's Religion;* W. Washburn (ed.), *The Indian and the White Man;* C. Wissler, *Indians of the United States;* H. M. Wormington, *Ancient Man in North America.*

2. *Northmen*

E. Haugen, *Voyages to Vinland;* H. R. Holand, *Westward from Vinland;* A. M. Reeves, *Finding of Wineland the Good;* E. Wahlgren, *The Kensington Stone, a Mystery Solved.*

3. *Exploration*

C. H. & K. George, *The Protestant Mind of the English Reformation;* J. H. Hexter, *Reappraisals in History;* H. M. Jones, *O Strange New World;* S. E. Morison, *European Discovery of America,* vol. i: *Northern Voyages,* vol. ii: *Southern Voyages;* J. H. Parry, *The Age of Reconnaissance,* and *The Establishment of European Hegemony, 1415–1715;* J. J. Te Paske, *Three American Empires.*

4. *Spanish and Portuguese*

H. E. Bolton (ed.), *Spanish Borderlands,* and *Spanish Exploration in the Southwest;* E. G. Bourne, *Spain in America;* C. R. Boxer, *Four Centuries of Portuguese Expansion, 1415–1825;* R. B. Cunninghame Graham,

The Conquest of New Granada; C. H. Haring, *The Spanish Empire in America;* F. W. Hodge & T. H. Lewis (eds.), *Spanish Explorers in the Southern United States;* W. Lowery, *Spanish Settlements in the United States;* D. L. Molinari, *Descubrimiento y Conquista de América;* S. E. Morison, *Admiral of the Ocean Sea* (shorter version, *Christopher Columbus, Mariner*); G. T. Northup (ed.), *Vespucci Reprints;* J. E. Olson & E. G. Bourne (eds.), *The Northmen, Columbus and Cabot;* J. H. Parry, *The Spanish Seaborne Empire;* A. Pigafetta, *Magellan's Voyage Around the World* (J. A. Robertson, ed.); W. H. Prescott, *Conquest of Mexico,* and *Conquest of Peru;* E. Wolf, *Sons of the Shaking Earth.*

5. *English and French*

J. B. Brebner, *The Explorers of North America;* H. S. Burrage (ed.), *Early English and French Voyages;* Sir William Foster, *England's Quest of Eastern Trade;* R. Hakluyt (ed.), *The Principall Navigations, Voiages, Traffiques and Discoveries of the English Nation;* M. Kammen, *People of Paradox;* W. Notestein, *The English People on the Eve of Colonization;* F. Parkman, *Pioneers of France in the New World* (selections in S. E. Morison, ed., *The Parkman Reader*); J. E. Pomfret and F. M. Shumway, *Founding the American Colonies;* D. B. Quinn, *Raleigh and the British Empire;* A. L. Rowse, *The Expansion of Elizabethan England,* and *The Elizabethans and America;* H. R. Wagner, *Sir Francis Drake's Voyage around the World;* D. W. Waters, *The Art of Navigation in England in Elizabethan and Early Stuart Times;* J. A. Williamson, *Voyages of John and Sebastian Cabot,* and *Age of Drake.*

CHAPTER 2

1. *Virginia and Maryland*

C. A. Andrews, *The Colonial Period of American History,* vols. i, ii; P. L. Barbour, *The Three Worlds of Captain John Smith;* P. A. Bruce, *Economic History* (2 vols.), and *Institutional History of Virginia in the Seventeenth Century* (2 vols.); W. F. Craven, *Dissolution of the Virginia Company, The Southern Colonies in the 17th Century,* and *White, Red, and Black;* C. H. Firth, *An American Garland;* I. N. Hume, *Here Lies Virginia;* M. W. Jernegan, *Laboring and Dependent Classes in Colonial America, 1607–1783;* R. L. Morton, *Colonial Virginia,* vol. i; H. L. Osgood, *The American Colonies in the 17th Century* (3 vols.); H. R. Shurtleff, *The Log Cabin Myth;* A. Smith, *Colonists in Bondage;* J. M. Smith (ed.), *Seventeenth Century America: Essays in Colonial History;* A. Vaughan, *American Genesis;* L. B. Wright, *First Gentlemen of Virginia,* and *Cultural Life of the American Colonies.*

2. *The Puritan Colonies*

B. Bailyn, *New England Merchants in the 17th Century;* W. Bradford, *Of Plymouth Plantation* (S. E. Morison, ed.); J. Demos, *A Little Commonwealth;* R. S. Dunn, *Puritans and Yankees;* K. T. Erikson, *Wayward Puritans;* G. L. Haskins, *Law and Authority in Early Massachusetts;* W. G. McLoughlin, *New England Dissent, 1630–1833;* P. Miller, *Orthodoxy in Massachusetts, The New England Mind: The Seventeenth Century, Roger Williams* (with T. H. Johnson), *The Puritans,* and *From Colony to Province;* E. S. Morgan, *The Puritan Family, Visible Saints,* and *The Puritan Dilemma: The Story of John Winthrop;* S. E. Morison, *The Founding of Harvard College, Harvard in the Seventeenth Century* (2 vols.), *Builders of the Bay Colony, Intellectual Life of Colonial New England,* and *Story of the 'Old Colony' of New Plymouth;* R. G. Pope, *The Half-Way Covenant;* S. Powell, *Puritan Village;* D. B. Rutman, *Husbandmen of Plymouth;* A. Vaughan, *New England Frontier;* T. J. Wertenbaker, *The Puritan Oligarchy;* O. Winslow, *Roger Williams;* L. Ziff, *The Career of John Cotton,* and *Puritanism in America.*

3. New Netherland

J. F. Jameson (ed.), *Narratives of New Netherlands;* C. Ward, *Dutch and Swedes on the Delaware;* T. J. Wertenbaker, *The Founding of American Civilization: The Middle Colonies.*

4. *New France*

M. Bishop, *Champlain;* D. Creighton, *History of Canada,* ch. 1; F. Parkman, *Pioneers of France in the New World* (selections in S. E. Morison, ed., *The Parkman Reader*); J. F. Saintoyant, *Colonisation française sous l'ancien régime.*

CHAPTER 3

1. *General*

C. A. Andrews, W. F. Craven, and H. L. Osgood, as in ch. 2; G. L. Beer, *The Old Colonial System* (2 vols.); D. J. Boorstin, *The Americans: The Colonial Experience;* W. F. Craven, *The Colonies in Transition, 1660–*

1713; O. M. Dickerson, *American Colonial Government, 1696–1765;* L. A. Harper, *The English Navigation Laws;* R. Hofstadter, *America at 1750;* D. S. Lovejoy, *The Glorious Revolution in America;* J. H. Smith, *Appeals to the Privy Council from the American Plantations;* C. L. Ver Steeg, *The Formative Years;* C. Williamson, *From Property to Democracy.*

2. *The Carolinas*

L. F. Brown, *The First Earl of Shaftesbury;* V. W. Crane, *The Southern Frontier, 1670–1732;* D. D. Wallace, *History of South Carolina,* vol. i.

3. *New York and the Jerseys*

A. C. Flick (ed.), *History of the State of New York,* vol. ii; J. H. Kennedy, *Thomas Dongan;* T. J. Wertenbaker, *The Founding of American Civilization: The Middle Colonies.*

4. *Pennsylvania*

H. Barbour, *Quakers in Puritan England;* W. W. Comfort, *William Penn and Our Liberties;* M. D. Learned, *Francis Daniel Pastorius;* F. B. Tolles, *Meeting House and Counting House.*

5. *Virginia and New England*

V. F. Barnes, *The Dominion of New England;* R. E. Brown, *Middle Class Democracy and the Revolution in Massachusetts;* R. E. & B. K. Brown, *Virginia: Democracy or Aristocracy?;* N. H. Chamberlain, *Samuel Sewall and the World He Lived In;* D. E. Leach, *Flintlock and Tomahawk;* D. Levin (ed.), *What Happened in Salem;* P. Miller, *The New England Mind: From Colony to Province;* R. L. Morton, *Colonial Virginia,* vol. i; G. W. Mullin, *Flight and Rebellion;* C. S. Sydnor, *Gentlemen Freeholders;* G. B. Warden, *Boston, 1689–1776;* W. E. Washburn, *The Governor and the Rebel;* T. J. Wertenbaker, *Torch-bearer of the Revolution;* L. B. Wright (ed.), *The Secret Diary of William Byrd of Westover, 1709–1712;* R. Zemsky, *Merchants, Farmers, and River Gods.*

6. *Canada and the West Indies*

V. W. Crane, *The Southern Frontier, 1670–1732;* C. H. Haring, *The Buccaneers in the West Indies in the Seventeenth Century;* L. W. Labaree, *Royal Government in America;* F. Parkman, *Frontenac and New France,* and *La Salle and the Discovery of the Great West* (extracts in S. E. Morison, ed., *Parkman Reader*).

7. *Social, Economic, and Religious Development*

B. Bailyn, *Education in the Forming of the American Society,* and *The New England Merchants in the 17th Century;* C. Bridenbaugh, *Cities in the Wilderness, Rebels & Gentlemen: Philadelphia in the Age of Franklin, Cities in Revolt, The Colonial Craftsman,* and *Mitre and Sceptre;* L. Cremin, *American Education: The Colonial Experience, 1607–1783;* D. S. Freeman, *George Washington,* vol. i; E. S. Gaustad, *The Great Awakening in New England;* W. M. Gewehr, *The Great Awakening in Virginia, 1740–90;* L. H. Gipson, *The British Empire before the American Revolution* (9 vols.); C. Grant, *Democracy in the Connecticut Frontier Town of Kent;* C. C. Gray, *History of Agriculture in the Southern United States;* P. J. Greven, Jr., *Four Generations;* E. Heckscher, *Mercantilism* (2 vols.); J. B. Hedges, *The Browns of Providence Plantations;* B. Hindle, *The Pursuit of Science in Revolutionary America;* K. A. Lockridge, *A New England Town;* C. H. Maxson, *The Great Awakening in the Middle Colonies;* R. Middlekauff, *Ancients and Axioms,* and *The Mathers;* P. Miller, *Jonathan Edwards;* E. S. Morgan, *The Gentle Puritan: A Life of Ezra Stiles;* R. B. Morris, *Government and Labor in Early America;* L. Morton, *Robert Carter of Nomini Hall;* R. L. Morton, *Colonial Virginia,* vol. ii; R. Pares, *Yankees and Creoles;* A. Simpson, *Puritanism in Old and New England;* A. Smith, *Colonists in Bondage;* W. W. Sweet, *Religion in Colonial America;* F. B. Tolles, *Quakers and the Atlantic Culture;* O. Winslow, *Jonathan Edwards,* and *Meetinghouse Hill;* L. B. Wright, *The Cultural Life of the American Colonies;* M. Zuckerman, *Peaceable Kingdoms.*

8. *Georgia*

V. W. Crane, *Promotion Literature of Georgia;* J. R. McCain, *Georgia as a Proprietary Province;* A. B. Saye, *New Viewpoints in Georgia History.*

9. *Wars*

J. S. Corbett, *England in the Seven Years' War* (2 vols.); D. S. Freeman, *Washington,* vol. ii; E. P. Hamilton, *The French and Indian Wars;* J. S. McLennan, *Louisbourg from Its Foundation to Its Fall;* R. Pares, *War and Trade in West Indies, 1739–63;* S. Pargellis, *Lord Loudoun in North America;* F. Parkman, *Half-Century of Conflict,* and *Montcalm and Wolfe* (extracts in Morison, ed., *Parkman Reader*); H. H. Peckham, *The Colonial Wars;* G. A. Wood, *William*

Shirley; G. M. Wrong, *The Fall of Canada,* and *The Rise and Fall of New France.*

CHAPTER 4

1. *Imperial Problems*

C. M. Andrews, *Colonial Background of the American Revolution,* and *The Colonial Period of American History,* vol. iv; G. L. Beer, *British Colonial Policy, 1754–1765, The Old Colonial System* (2 vols.), and *The Origins of the British Colonial System;* O. M. Dickerson, *The Navigation Acts and the American Revolution;* L. H. Gipson, *British Empire before the American Revolution,* vols. ii, iii, and iv; J. P. Greene, *The Quest for Power: The Lower Houses of Assembly in the Southern Royal Colonies;* L. A. Harper, *The English Navigation Laws;* M. Jensen, *The Founding of a Nation;* M. Kammen, *Empire and Interest;* L. W. Labaree, *Royal Government in America;* E. I. McCormac, *Colonial Opposition to Imperial Authority during the French and Indian War;* C. H. McIlwain, *The American Revolution;* P. Maier, *From Resistance to Revolution;* E. S. Morgan, *The Birth of the Republic;* C. Nettels, *The Money Supply of the American Colonies Before 1720;* J. Sosin, *Agents and Merchants.*

2. *The West and the Albany Plan of Union*

S. E. Morison, *Sources and Documents Illustrating the American Revolution;* H. M. Muhlenberg, *Notebook of a Colonial Clergyman;* R. Newbold, *The Albany Congress and Plan of Union;* H. Peckham, *Pontiac and the Indian Uprising;* J. Sosin, *Whitehall and the Wilderness.*

3. *The Colonies, 1763–1773*

C. L. Becker, *The History of Political Parties in the Province of New York;* P. U. Bonomi, *A Factious People;* C. Bridenbaugh, *Seat of Empire;* I. B. Cohen, *Benjamin Franklin;* E. B. Greene, *The Revolutionary Generation;* C. S. Sydnor, *Gentlemen Freeholders.*

4. *The West*

T. P. Abernethy, *Western Lands and the American Revolution;* C. W. Alvord, *The Mississippi Valley in British Politics* (2 vols.); C. Bridenbaugh, *Myths and Realities;* S. E. Morison, *Sources and Documents,* introd. and pp. 1–55.

5. *Revenue and Stamp Acts*

B. Bailyn (ed.), *Pamphlets of the American Revolution;* L. H. Gipson, *The Coming of the Revolution;* B. W. Labaree, *The Boston Tea Party;* J. C. Miller, *Origins of the American Revolution,* and *Sam Adams;* E. S. & H. M. Morgan, *The Stamp Act Crisis;* P. D. G. Thomas, *British Politics and the Stamp Act Crisis;* E. Wright, *Fabric of Freedom.*

6. *Townshend and Coercive Acts*

R. D. Brown, *Revolutionary Politics in Massachusetts;* O. M. Dickerson, *Boston Under Military Rule as Revealed in the Journals of the Times;* M. G. Kammen, *A Rope of Sand;* C. H. Metzger, *The Quebec Act;* R. B. Morris, *Studies in the History of American Law,* and *The Era of the American Revolution;* A. M. Schlesinger, *The Colonial Merchants and the American Revolution,* and *Prelude to Independence: The Newspaper War in Great Britain;* M. C. Tyler, *Literary History of the American Revolution;* H. B. Zobel, *The Boston Massacre.*

7. *Back-country Turmoil*

T. P. Abernethy, *Western Lands and the American Revolution;* J. R. Alden, *John Stuart and the Southern Colonial Frontier;* C. Bridenbaugh, *Myths and Realities;* R. M. Brown, *The South Carolina Regulators;* C. Woodmason, *The Carolina Backcountry.*

8. *Ideology*

R. G. Adams, *Political Ideas of the American Revolution;* B. Bailyn, *Pamphlets of the American Revolution;* C. L. Becker, *The Declaration of Independence;* J. P. Boyd, *Anglo-American Union;* E. C. Burnett, *The Continental Congress;* D. F. Hawke, *Paine;* D. Malone, *Jefferson the Virginian;* R. L. Schuyler, *Parliament and the British Empire;* C. P. Smith, *James Wilson.*

9. *Opening of Hostilities*

J. R. Alden, *General Gage in America;* J. Bakeless, *Turncoats, Traitors, and Heroes;* A. French, *The First Year of the American Revolution.*

10. *The Loyalists*

C. Berkin, *Jonathan Sewall;* J. B. Brebner, *The Neutral Yankees of Nova Scotia;* R. M. Calhoon, *The Loyalists in Revolutionary America, 1760–1781;* L. Einstein, *Divided Loyalties;* A. S. Flick, *Loyalism in New York*

During the American Revolution; P. H. Smith, *Loyalists and Redcoats;* C. H. Van Tyne, *Loyalists in the American Revolution.*

CHAPTER 5

1. *General*

J. R. Alden, *American Revolution, 1775–1783,* and *A History of the American Revolution;* T. S. Anderson, *The Command of the Howe Brothers during the American Revolution;* A. Bowman, *The Morale of the American Revolutionary Army;* H. S. Commager & R. B. Morris (eds.), *The Spirit of 'Seventy-six, the Story of the American Revolution as Told by Participants;* D. S. Freeman, *George Washington,* vols. iii-v; T. G. Frothingham, *Washington, Commander in Chief;* D. Higginbotham, *War of American Independence;* D. W. Knox, *The Naval Genius of Washington;* P. Mackesy, *War for America, 1775–1783;* J. T. Main, *The Sovereign States 1775–1783;* J. C. Miller, *Triumph of Freedom, 1775–1783;* R. B. Morris (ed.), *The Era of the American Revolution;* H. Peckham, *War for Independence;* E. Robson, *American Revolution in Its Political and Military Aspects, 1763–1783;* F. E. Schermerhorn, *American and French Flags of the Revolution;* P. Smith, *A New Age Now Begins;* W. M. Wallace, *Appeal to Arms;* C. Ward, *The War of the Revolution* (2 vols.); G. S. Wood, *The Creation of the American Republic, 1776–1787.*

2. *Supply and Finance*

A. Bezanson, *Prices and Inflation During the American Revolution;* C. J. Bullock, *Finances of the United States from 1775 to 1789;* R. A. East, *Business Enterprise in the American Revolutionary Era;* E. J. Ferguson, *Power of the Purse;* L. C. Hatch, *Administration of the American Revolutionary Army;* C. P. Nettels, *The Emergence of a National Economy, 1775–1815;* C. L. Ver Steeg, *Robert Morris.*

3. *Military Operations, through 1777*

J. R. Alden, *General Charles Lee, Traitor or Patriot?;* G. A. Billias, *General John Glover and His Marblehead Mariners;* G. S. Brown, *American Secretary: The Colonial Policy of Lord George Germain, 1775–1778;* L. Lundin, *Cockpit of the Revolution;* H. Nickerson, *The Turning Point of the Revolution;* J. M. Palmer, *General von Steuben;* H. Swiggett, *War Out of Niagara: Butler and the Tory Rangers;* W. B. Willcox, *Portrait of a General: Sir Henry Clinton in the War of Independence.*

4. *France and Diplomacy*

S. F. Bemis, *The Diplomacy of the American Revolution;* H. Butterfield, *George III, Lord North, and the People;* E. S. Corwin, *French Policy and the American Alliance of 1778;* V. W. Crane, *Benjamin Franklin and a Rising People;* G. H. Guttridge, *David Hartley;* F. Monaghan, *John Jay;* R. B. Morris, *The Peacemakers;* J. B. Perkins, *France in the American Revolution;* P. C. Phillips, *The West in the Diplomacy of the American Revolution;* R. W. Van Alstyne, *Empire and Independence;* C. Van Doren, *Benjamin Franklin,* and *Secret History of the Revolution;* G. M. Wrong, *Canada and the American Revolution.*

5. *Naval War and Military Operations, 1778–1782*

J. R. Alden, *The South in the Revolution;* G. W. Allen, *Naval History of the American Revolution* (2 vols.); W. B. Clark, *Lambert Wickes, Gallant John Barry,* and *Captain Dauntless;* W. M. James, *The British Navy in Adversity;* C. L. Lewis, *Admiral de Grasse and American Independence;* E. S. Maclay, *History of American Privateers;* Admiral A. T. Mahan, *The Influence of Sea-Power Upon History,* and *Major Operation of the Navies in the War of Independence;* S. E. Morison, *John Paul Jones, A Sailor's Biography;* T. Thayer, *Nathanael Greene.*

CHAPTER 6

1. *State Constitutions*

H. J. Eckenrode, *The Revolution in Virginia;* A. C. Flick, *History of the State of New York,* vol. iv; Z. Haraszti, *John Adams and the Prophets of Progress;* A. Nevins, *The American States during and after the Revolution;* J. P. Selsam, *The Pennsylvania Constitution of 1776.*

2. *Reform, Religion, and Slavery*

D. B. Davis, *The Problem of Slavery in the Age of the Revolution;* W. E. B. Du Bois, *Suppression of the African Slave-Trade;* H. J. Eckenrode, *Separation of Church and State in Virginia;* P. Guilday, *Life and Times of John Carroll* (2 vols.); J. F. Jameson, *The American Revolution Considered as a Social Movement;* W. D. Jordan, *White over Black;* G. A. Koch, *Republican Religion;* R. McCormick, *Experiment in Independence: New Jersey in the Critical Period, 1781–1789;* R. J. Purcell, *Connecticut in Transition;* M. Savelle, *Seeds of Liberty.*

3. *Arts, Letters, Education*

S. J. Buck, *The Planting of Civilization in Western Pennsylvania;* E. Ford, *David Rittenhouse;* N. Goodman, *Benjamin Rush;* S. E. Morison, *Three Centuries of Harvard,* ch. 7; E. C. Shoemaker, *Noah Webster, Pioneer of Learning;* R. E. Spiller, et al., *Literary History of the U.S.,* vol. i; D. J. Struik, *Yankee Science in the Making,* pt. 2.

4. *The West and Vermont*

G. H. Alden, *New Governments West of the Alleghenies before 1780;* C. A. Hanna, *The Wilderness Trail;* A. Henderson, *Star of Empire;* A. B. Hulbert, *Boone's Wilderness Road;* M. B. Jones, *Vermont in the Making;* L. P. Kellogg, *The British Regime in Wisconsin and the Northwest;* W. S. Lester, *The Transylvania Company;* J. Pell, *Ethan Allen;* F. J. Turner, 'Western State Making in the Revolutionary Era,' in his *Significance of Sections in American History;* S. C. Williams, *History of the Lost State of Franklin.*

5. *The Articles of Confederation*

L. B. Dunbar, *Study of 'Monarchial' Tendencies in the United States from 1776 to 1801;* M. Jensen, *The Articles of Confederation,* and *The New Nation;* A. C. McLaughlin, *Confederation and the Constitution;* R. B. Morris, *The American Revolution Reconsidered.*

6. *Land Policy and the Ordinances*

T. P. Abernethy, *Western Lands and the American Revolution;* C. W. Alvord, *The Illinois Country;* K. P. Bailey, *The Ohio Company of Virginia and the Westward Movement.*

7. *Foreign Affairs and Commerce*

S. F. Bemis, *Jay's Treaty;* F. Gilbert, *To the Farewell Address;* F. Monaghan, *John Jay;* S. E. Morison, *Maritime History of Massachusetts,* chs. 3–7; A. P. Whitaker, *The Spanish-American Frontier.*

8. *Debtors and Shays*

J. T. Adams, *New England in the Republic;* M. L. Starkey, *A Little Rebellion.*

CHAPTER 7

1. *General*

I. Brant, *James Madison,* vols. i-iii; R. Brown, *Charles Beard and the Constitution;* M. Farrand (ed.), *Records of the Federal Convention* (3 vols.); G. Hunt & J. B. Scott (eds.), *The Debates in the Federal Convention of 1787 . . . reported by James Madison;* F. McDonald, *E Pluribus Unum,* and *We the People;* A. C. McLaughlin, *Confederation and the Constitution;* J. T. Main, *The Antifederalists,* and *Political Parties Before the Constitution;* C. Rossiter, *Alexander Hamilton and the Constitution;* R. L. Schuyler, *The Constitution of the United States;* C. Page Smith, *James Wilson;* C. Warren, *The Making of the Constitution.*

2. *Ratification*

F. G. Bates, *Rhode Island and the Formation of the Union;* A. J. Beveridge, *Life of John Marshall,* vol. i; S. B. Harding, *Contest over Ratification of the Federal Constitution in the State of Massachusetts.*

CHAPTER 8

1. *General*

J. Flexner, *George Washington;* D. S. Freeman, *George Washington,* vol. vi; J. C. Miller, *The Federalist Era;* R. R. Palmer, *Age of Democratic Revolution;* N. Schachner, *The Founding Fathers.*

2. *Organization of the Federal Government*

E. C. Corwin, *The President, Office and Powers;* R. V. Harlow, *History of Legislative Methods in the Period before 1825;* C. Warren, *The Supreme Court in United States History* (2 vols.); L. D. White, *The Federalists.*

3. *Biographies*

I. Brant, *James Madison,* vol. iii; G. Chinard, *Honest John Adams,* and *Thomas Jefferson: The Apostle of Americanism;* D. Malone, *Jefferson and the Rights of Man;* J. C. Miller, *Alexander Hamilton;* R. B. Morris (ed.), *Alexander Hamilton and the Founding of the Nation,* and *John Jay, The Nation and the Court;* N. Schachner, *Alexander Hamilton.*

4. *The Birth of Parties*

W. N. Chambers, *Political Parties in a New Nation;* J. Charles, *Origins of the American Party System;* N. Cunningham, *The Jeffersonian Republicans;* D. Fischer, *Revolution of American Conservatism;* R. Hofstadter, *The Idea of a Party System.*

5. *French Revolution and Foreign Affairs*

S. F. Bemis, *Jay's Treaty,* and *Pinckney's Treaty;* A. L. Burt, *The United States, Great Britain, and British*

North America; A. De Conde, *Entangling Alliance;* F. Gilbert, *To the Farewell Address;* C. D. Hazen, *Contemporary American Opinion of the French Revolution;* H. M. Jones, *America and French Culture, 1750–1848;* E. P. Link, *Democratic-Republican Societies, 1790–1800;* C. M. Thomas, *American Neutrality in 1793;* A. P. Whitaker, *Spanish-American Frontier.*

6. *Whiskey Rebellion, Public Land, the West*

C. W. Alvord, *The Illinois Country;* L. D. Baldwin, *Whiskey Rebels;* T. Boyd, *Mad Anthony Wayne;* B. H. Hibbard, *History of Public Land Policies;* F. L. Paxson, *History of the American Frontier;* M. M. Quaife, *Chicago and the Old Northwest.*

7. *John Adams's Administration*

M. J. Dauer, *The Adams Federalists;* S. G. Kurtz, *The Presidency of John Adams;* C. Page Smith, *John Adams.*

8. *French Relations and Naval War*

G. W. Allen, *Our Naval War with France;* S. E. Morison, *Harrison Gray Otis,* vol. i; M. de Saint-Méry, *Voyage aux États-Unis, 1793–98;* M. Smelser, *Congress Founds the Navy;* A. P. Whitaker, *The Mississippi Question, 1795–1803.*

9. *Alien and Sedition Acts*

L. W. Levy, *Freedom of Speech and Press in Early American History,* and *Legacy of Suppression;* D. Malone, *The Public Life of Thomas Cooper;* J. M. Smith, *Freedom's Fetters;* V. Stauffer, *New England and the Bavarian Illuminati.*

CHAPTER 9

1. *General*

H. Adams, *History of the United States during the Administration of Jefferson* (4 vols., Commager ed. of 2 vols.); S. H. Aronson, *Status and Kinship in the Higher Civil Service;* A. J. Beveridge, *John Marshall;* D. J. Boorstin, *The Lost World of Thomas Jefferson;* N. E. Cunningham, Jr., *The Jeffersonian Republicans in Power;* W. E. Dodd, *Life of Nathaniel Macon;* R. E. Ellis, *The Jeffersonian Crisis;* T. Hamlin, *Benjamin H. Latrobe;* A. Koch, *Jefferson and Madison: The Great Collaboration;* A. T. Mahan, *The Influence of Sea Power upon the French Revolution* (2 vols.); D. Malone, *Jefferson the President;* M. D. Peterson, *The Jeffersonian Image in the American Mind,* and *Thomas Jefferson and the New Nation;* M. Smelser, *The Democratic Republic, 1801–1815;* L. D. White, *The Jeffersonians;* C. M. Wiltse, *The Jeffersonian Tradition in American Democracy.*

2. *Tripoli War, Louisiana, Lewis and Clark*

J. E. Bakeless, *Lewis and Clark;* E. S. Brown, *Constitutional History of the Louisiana Purchase;* I. J. Cox, *The West Florida Controversy;* G. Dangerfield, *Chancellor Robert R. Livingston of New York;* B. De Voto (ed.), *The Journals of Lewis and Clark;* J. A. Robertson, *Louisiana under the Rule of Spain, France, and the United States* (2 vols.); L. B. Wright & J. H. Macleod, *First Americans in North Africa.*

3. *Federalist and Burr Conspiracies*

T. P. Abernethy, *The Burr Conspiracy;* H. Adams (ed.), *Documents Relating to New England Federalism;* W. F. McCaleb, *The Aaron Burr Conspiracy;* S. E. Morison, *H. G. Otis;* N. Schachner, *Aaron Burr.*

4. *Embargo*

S. E. Morison, *Maritime History of Mass.,* chs. 12, 13; B. Perkins, *Prologue to War;* L. M. Sears, *Jefferson and the Embargo.*

CHAPTER 10

1. *General*

H. Adams, *History of the U. S. during the Administration of Madison* (5 vols.), and *The War of 1812* (reprint of the War chapters); F. F. Beirne, *The War of 1812;* I. Brant, *Madison,* vol. ii; R. H. Brown, *Republic in Peril: 1812;* A. L. Burt, *The United States, Great Britain and British North America;* A. H. Z. Carr, *The Coming of War;* J. P. Cranwell & W. B. Crane, *Men of Marque;* R. Horsman, *The Causes of the War of 1812,* and *The War of 1812;* R. Ketcham, *James Madison;* D. W. Knox, *History of the U.S. Navy;* C. P. Lucas, *The Canadian War of 1812;* A. T. Mahan, *Sea Power in Its Relations to the War of 1812* (2 vols.); B. Mayo; *Henry Clay;* B. Perkins, *Prologue to War;* J. W. Pratt, *Expansionists of 1812;* M. M. Quaife, *Chicago and the Old Northwest;* E. Rowland, *Andrew Jackson's Campaign;* C. M. Wiltse, *John C. Calhoun: Nationalist, 1782–1828.*

2. *Peace of Ghent and Hartford Convention*

J. Banner, *To the Hartford Convention;* S. F. Bemis, *J. Q. Adams and the Foundations of American Foreign Policy;* F. L. Engelman, *The Peace of Christmas Eve;* S. E. Morison, *H. G. Otis,* vol. ii, *Maritime History of Mass.,* chs. 12, 13, and *By Land and By Sea,* ch. 12; B. Perkins, *Castlereagh and Adams;* T. A. Updyke, *Diplomacy of the War of 1812.*

CHAPTER 11

1. *General*

H. Adams, *United States,* vol. ix; J. Q. Adams, *Diary* (selections from 12-vol. *Memoirs,* A. Nevins, ed.); S. F. Bemis, *J. Q. Adams and the Foundations of American Foreign Policy;* W. P. Cresson, *James Monroe;* G. Dangerfield, *The Era of Good Feelings,* and *The Awakening of American Nationalism;* S. Livermore, Jr., *The Twilight of Federalism;* C. Schurz, *Henry Clay,* vol. i; F. J. Turner, *Rise of the New West.*

2. *Marshall and the Judiciary*

A. J. Beveridge, *John Marshall,* vol. iv; E. S. Corwin, *John Marshall and the Constitution;* F. Frankfurter, *The Commerce Clause under Marshall, Taney, and Waite;* J. T. Horton, *James Kent;* R. Pound, *The Formative Era of American Law;* J. Story, *Commentaries on the Constitution of the United States* (2 vols.).

3. *Missouri Compromise*

G. Moore, *The Missouri Compromise;* D. L. Robinson, *Slavery in the Structure of American Politics, 1765–1820;* F. C. Shoemaker, *Missouri's Struggle for Statehood, 1804–1821;* C. S. Sydnor, *Development of Southern Sectionalism.*

4. *Monroe Doctrine*

A. Alvarez, *The Monroe Doctrine;* S. F. Bemis, *J. Q. Adams . . . Foreign Policy;* F. A. Golder, *Russian Expansion on the Pacific;* D. Perkins, *Hands Off: A History of the Monroe Doctrine;* A. P. Whitaker, *The U.S. and the Independence of Latin-America.*

5. *J. Q. Adams's Administration*

S. F. Bemis, *J. Q. Adams and the Union;* C. Eaton, *Henry Clay and the Art of American Politics;* H. E. Putnam, *Joel Roberts Poinsett.*

CHAPTER 12

1. *General*

T. P. Abernethy, *From Frontier to Plantation in Tennessee;* J. S. Bassett, *Andrew Jackson;* Lee Benson, *The Concept of Jacksonian Democracy;* W. N. Chambers, *Old Bullion Benton;* J. C. Curtis, *The Fox at Bay;* W. Hugins, *Jacksonian Democracy and the Working Class;* M. James, *Life of Andrew Jackson;* W. MacDonald, *Jacksonian Democracy;* M. Meyers, *The Jacksonian Persuasion;* E. Pessen, *Jacksonian America;* R. Remini, *Andrew Jackson;* A. M. Schlesinger, Jr., *The Age of Jackson;* J. A. Shackford, *David Crockett;* H. C. Syrett, *Andrew Jackson;* F. J. Turner, *Rise of the New West,* and *The United States, 1830–50;* G. G. Van Deusen, *The Jacksonian Era;* J. W. Ward, *Andrew Jackson, Symbol for an Age;* L. White, *The Jacksonians.*

2. *Political Conditions and Background*

E. M. Carroll, *Origins of the Whig Party;* C. R. Fish, *Civil Service and the Patronage;* D. R. Fox, *Decline of Aristocracy in the Politics of New York;* H. L. McBain, *De Witt Clinton and the Origin of the Spoils System in New York;* R. McCormick, *The Second American Party System;* H. Martineau, *Society in America,* and *Retrospect of Western Travel;* A. Nevins (ed.), *The Diary of Philip Hone;* R. Remini, *The Election of Andrew Jackson,* and *Martin Van Buren and the Making of the Democratic Party;* A. de Tocqueville, *Democracy in America;* F. Trollope, *Domestic Manners of the Americans* (Donald Smalley, ed.).

3. *Webster and the West*

R. N. Current, *Daniel Webster and the Rise of National Conservatism;* C. M. Fuess, *Daniel Webster* (2 vols.); R. G. Wellington, *Political and Sectional Influence of the Public Lands, 1828–42.*

4. *Calhoun and Nullification*

M. L. Coit, *John C. Calhoun: American Portrait;* W. Freehling, *Prelude to Civil War;* D. F. Houston, *Critical Study of Nullification in South Carolina;* D. Malone, *Public Life of Thomas Cooper;* A. G. Smith, *Economic Readjustment of an Old Cotton State;* G. G. Van Deusen, *Economic Bases of Disunion in South Carolina;* C. M. Wiltse, *John C. Calhoun, Nullifier.*

5. *Finance and the War on the Bank*

R. C. H. Catterall, *The Second Bank of the U.S.*; T. P. Govan, *Nicholas Biddle*; B. Hammond, *Banks and Politics in America from the Revolution to the Civil War*; A. B. Hepburn, *History of Currency in the U.S.*; J. M. McFaul, *The Politics of Jacksonian Finance*; R. C. McGrane, *Foreign Bondholders and American State Debts*; M. G. Madeleine, *Monetary and Banking Theories of Jacksonian Democracy*; W. B. Smith, *Economic Aspects of the Second Bank of the United States*; P. Temin, *The Jacksonian Economy*.

6. *Indian Removal*

A. Debo, *The Road to Disappearance*; G. Foreman, *Indian Removal, The Last Trek of the Indians*, and *The Five Civilized Tribes*; G. D. Harmon, *Sixty Years of Indian Affairs, 1789–1850*; W. Lumpkin, *Removal of the Cherokee Indians from Georgia*; F. P. Prucha, *American Indian Policy in the Formative Years*; R. N. Satz, *American Indian Policy in the Jacksonian Era*.

7. *Democrats and Whigs*

L. Benson, *The Concept of Jacksonian Democracy*; O. P. Chitwood, *John Tyler*; H. D. A. Donovan, *The Barnburners*; H. R. Fraser, *Democracy in the Making, the Jackson-Tyler Era*; D. B. Goebel, *William Henry Harrison*; R. G. Gunderson, *The Log-Cabin Campaign*; R. C. McGrane, *The Panic of 1837*; J. B. McMaster, *History of the People of the U.S.*, vol. vi; J. C. N. Paul, *Rift in Democracy*; C. Schurz, *Henry Clay*, vol. ii; R. Seager, *And Tyler Too!*; J. Silbey, *The Transformation of American Politics, 1840–1860*; T. C. Smith, *The Liberty and Free Soil Parties in the Northwest*.

8. *Taney and the Supreme Court*

F. Frankfurter, *Commerce Clause under Marshall, Taney and Waite*; C. B. Swisher, *The Oliver Wendell Holmes Devise History of the Supreme Court of the United States*, vol. v: *The Taney Period, 1836–64*, and *Roger B. Taney*; C. Warren, *Supreme Court*, vol. ii.

9. *Anglo-Canadian-American Relations*

J. B. Brebner, *North Atlantic Triangle*; H. S. Burrage, *Maine in the Northeastern Boundary Controversy*; W. Kilbourn, *The Firebrand: W. L. Mackenzie*; T. H. Raddell, *Path of Destiny, Canada 1763–1850*.

CHAPTER 13

1. *Cotton Kingdom*

K. Bruce, *Virginia Iron Manufacture in the Slave Era*; A. Conrad & J. Meyer, *The Economics of Slavery and Other Studies in Econometric History*; A. Craven, *Edmund Ruffin, Southerner*; W. E. Dodd, *The Cotton Kingdom*; J. W. DuBose, *Life and Times of William Lowndes Yancey*; C. Eaton, *A History of the Old South*; J. H. Franklin, *The Militant South*; F. P. Gaines, *The Southern Plantation*; E. D. Genovese, *The Political Economy of Slavery*; L. C. Gray, *History of Agriculture in the Southern States to 1860*; M. B. Hammond, *The Cotton Industry*; O. Handlin, *Race and Nationality in American Life*; F. A. Kemble, *Journal of Residence on a Georgian Plantation*; A. B. Longstreet, *Georgia Scenes*; F. L. Olmsted, *The Cotton Kingdom* (A. M. Schlesinger, ed.); U. B. Phillips, *Robert Toombs*; A. F. Scott, *The Southern Lady*; S. D. Smedes, *Memorials of a Southern Planter*; C. S. Sydnor, *Development of Southern Sectionalism, 1819–1848*; L. White, *Robert Barnwell Rhett*.

2. *The Negro*

H. Aptheker, *American Negro Slave Revolts*; F. Bancroft, *Slave-Trading in the Old South*; J. W. Blassingame, *The Slave Community*; H. A. Bullock, *A History of Negro Education in the South from 1619 to the Present*; H. T. Catterall, *Judicial Cases concerning American Slavery and the Negro*; D. Davis, *The Problem of Slavery in Western Culture*; C. N. Degler, *Neither Black Nor White*; S. M. Elkins, *Slavery*; R. Flanders, *Plantation Slavery in Georgia*; W. Fogel & S. Engerman, *Time on the Cross*; J. H. Franklin, *From Slavery to Freedom*; E. D. Genovese, *The Political Economy of Slavery*, and *The World the Slaveholders Made*; U. B. Phillips, *Life and Labor in the Old South*, and *American Negro Slavery*; K. M. Stampp, *The Peculiar Institution*; R. S. Starobin, *Industrial Slavery in the Old South*; C. S. Sydnor, *Slavery in Mississippi*; F. Tannenbaum, *Slave and Citizen*; R. C. Wade, *Slavery in the Cities*.

3. *Southern Culture*

C. H. Ambler, *Thomas Ritchie*; J. J. Audubon, *Birds of America* (William Vogt, ed.); P. A. Bruce, *History of the University of Virginia* (5 vols.); W. J. Cash, *The*

Mind of the South; V. Dabney, *Liberalism in the South;* C. Eaton, *Freedom of Thought in the Old South,* and *The Mind of the Old South;* S. W. Geiser, *Naturalists of the Frontier;* W. S. Jenkins, *Pro-Slavery Thought in the Old South;* T. C. Johnson, *Scientific Interests in the Old South;* E. W. Knight, *Public Education in the South;* V. L. Parrington, *Main Currents in American Thought,* vol. ii; L. Rhea, *Hugh S. Legaré;* C. G. Sellers, Jr., *The Southerner as American;* W. R. Taylor, *Cavalier and Yankee;* W. P. Trent, *William Gilmore Simms.*

4. *The North*

P. W. Bidwell & J. I. Falconer, *History of Agriculture in the Northern States;* P. W. Gates, *The Farmer's Age;* J. B. McMaster, *History of the People of the U.S.,* vols. v-vii; E. W. Martin, *The Standard of Living in 1860;* T. L. Nichols, *Forty Years of American Life, 1821–1861;* D. C. North, *The Economic Growth of the United States;* R. H. Shryock, *Medicine and Society in America, 1660–1860;* F. J. Turner, *The United States, 1830–50;* N. J. Ware, *The Industrial Worker, 1840–1860.*

5. *Transportation and Westward Movement*

C. H. Ambler, *History of Transportation in the Ohio Valley;* C. F. Carter, *When Railroads Were New;* A. D. Chandler, Jr., *Henry Varnum Poor;* A. S. Dunbar, *History of Travel in America* (4 vols.); R. W. Fogel, *Railroads and American Economic Growth;* C. Goodrich, *Government Promotion of American Canals and Railroads, 1800–1890;* C. Goodrich, et al., *Canals and American Economic Development;* A. B. Hulbert, *Paths of Inland Commerce;* E. Hungerford, *Story of the Baltimore & Ohio Railroad;* K. W. Porter, *John Jacob Astor;* J. Rubin, *Canal or Railroad?;* G. R. Taylor, *The Transportation Revolution;* R. L. Thompson, *Wiring a Continent;* D. B. Tyler, *Steam Conquers the Atlantic.*

6. *Immigration and Packet Ships*

E. Abbott, *Historical Aspects of the Immigration Problem;* W. F. Adams, *Ireland and Irish Emigration to the New World from 1815 to the Famine;* R. G. Albion, *Square-Riggers on Schedule,* and *The Rise of New York Port 1815–1860;* R. B. Anderson, *Norwegian Immigration to 1848;* R. T. Berthoff, *British Immigrants in Industrial America, 1825–1850;* R. A. Billington, *The Protestant Crusade, 1800–1860;* J. R. Commons, *Races and Immigrants in America;* R. Ernst, *Immigrant Life in New York City;* A. B. Faust, *The German Element in the United States;* F. E. Gibson, *The Attitudes of the New York Irish toward State and National Affairs, 1848–1892;* O. Handlin, *The Uprooted;* M. L. Hansen, *The Atlantic Migration,* and *The Immigrant in American History;* F. E. Janson, *Background of Swedish Immigration, 1840–1930;* M. A. Jones, *American Immigration.*

7. *Manufacturing and Cities*

S. Batchelder, *Introduction and Early Progress of the Cotton Manufacture in the United States;* D. H. Calhoun, *The American Civil Engineer;* V. S. Clark, *History of Manufactures in the United States;* A. H. Cole, *The American Wool Manufacture* (2 vols.); P. R. Knights, *The Plain People of Boston, 1830–1860;* K. W. Porter, *The Jacksons and the Lees: Two Generations of Massachusetts Merchants;* J. M. Swank, *History of the Manufacture of Iron;* R. M. Tryon, *Household Manufactures in the U.S.;* R. C. Wade, *The Urban Frontier.*

8. *Science and Technology*

G. Daniels, *American Science in the Age of Jackson;* A. H. Dupree, *Science in the Federal Government,* and *Asa Gray;* B. Jaffe, *Men of Science in America;* E. Lurie, *Louis Agassiz;* P. H. Oehser, *Sons of Science;* C. Resek, *Lewis Henry Morgan;* R. H. Shryock, *American Medical Research Past and Present;* M. Wilson, *American Science and Invention.*

9. *Education*

C. Bode, *The American Lyceum;* M. Curti, *Social Ideas of American Educators;* B. A. Hinsdale, *Horace Mann and the Common School Revival in the United States;* R. Hofstadter & W. Metzger, *The Development of Academic Freedom in the United States;* M. A. D. Howe, *Life and Letters of George Bancroft* (2 vols.), and *Classic Shades;* R. A. McCaughey, *Josiah Quincy;* S. E. Morison, *Three Centuries of Harvard;* F. L. Mott, *American Journalism,* and *History of American Magazines;* F. Rudolph, *The American College and University;* S. K. Schultz, *The Culture Factory;* R. Storr, *The Beginnings of Graduate Education in America;* D. G. Tewkesbury, *Founding of American Colleges and Universities before the Civil War;* C. F. Thwing, *The American and the German University;* C. G. Woodson, *Education of the Negro Prior to 1861.*

10. *Reformers and Utopias*

E. Abbott, *Women in Industry;* W. Bennett, *Whittier, Bard of Freedom;* G. Brooks, *Three Wise Virgins;* C. C. Cole, *Social Ideas of the Northern Evangelists, 1826–1860;* W. R. Cross, *The Burned-Over District;* M. Curti, *The American Peace Crusade, 1815–60,* and *The Learned Blacksmith;* W. A. Hinds, *American Communities and Co-operative Colonies;* S. M. Kingsbury (ed.), *Labor Laws and Their Enforcement;* J. A. Krout, *The Origins of Prohibition;* R. W. Leopold, *Robert Dale Owen;* L. Litwack, *The Negro in the Free States, 1790–1860;* G. B. Lockwood, *New Harmony Movement;* W. G. McLoughlin, *Modern Revivalism;* R. A. Mohl, *Poverty in New York, 1783–1825;* R. B. Nye, *Society and Culture in America, 1830–1860;* R. Riegel, *American Feminists;* D. J. Rothman, *The Discovery of the Asylum;* C. E. Sears, *Days of Delusion* (Millerites); T. L. Smith, *Revivalism and Social Reform in Mid-Nineteenth Century America;* L. Swift, *Brook Farm;* A. F. Tyler, *Freedom's Ferment;* N. Ware, *The Industrial Worker, 1840–60;* W. R. Waterman, *Frances Wright;* E. Webber, *Escape to Utopia.*

11. *Literature and Transcendentalism*

G. W. Allen, *The Solitary Singer* (Whitman); N. Arvin, *Longfellow,* and *Herman Melville;* V. W. Brooks, *The Flowering of New England, 1850–65,* and *The World of Washington Irving;* H. S. Canby, *Walt Whitman;* H. S. Commager, *Theodore Parker;* O. B. Frothingham, *Transcendentalism in New England;* W. R. Hutchison, *The Transcendentalist Ministers;* J. W. Krutch, *Thoreau;* F. O. Matthiessen, *American Renaissance;* P. Miller (ed.), *The Transcendentalists, an Anthology;* L. Mumford, *The Golden Day;* B. Perry, *The American Spirit in Literature,* and (ed.), *The Heart of Emerson's Journals;* R. L. Rusk, *Life of Ralph Waldo Emerson;* O. Shepard (ed.), *The Heart of Thoreau's Journals;* R. Stewart (ed.), *American Notebooks, by Nathaniel Hawthorne;* M. Wade, *Margaret Fuller;* R. Welter, *The Mind of America, 1820–1860;* S. Whicher, *Fate and Freedom* (Emerson).

12. *Anti-Slavery and Abolition*

G. H. Barnes, *The Antislavery Impulse, 1830–44;* W. Barney, *The Road to Secession;* M. Duberman (ed.), *The Antislavery Vanguard;* D. Dumond, *Anti-Slavery;* L. Filler, *The Crusade Against Slavery;* G. M. Fredrickson, *The Black Image in the White Mind;* L. Gara, *The Liberty Line;* A. S. Kraditor, *Means and Ends;* G. Lerner, *The Grimké Sisters from South Carolina;* R. B. Nye, *Fettered Freedom;* W. A. Owens, *Slave Mutiny;* B. Quarles, *Black Abolitionists;* G. Sorin, *Abolitionism;* B. P. Thomas, *Theodore Weld;* J. L. Thomas, *The Liberator;* C. Woodward, *American Counterpoint.*

CHAPTER 14

1. *General*

R. A. Billington, *The Far Western Frontier;* H. M. Chittenden, *The American Fur Trade of the Far West* (3 vols.); K. Coman, *Economic Beginnings of the Far West* (2 vols.); B. De Voto, *The Year of Decision, 1846,* and *Across the Wide Missouri;* N. A. Graebner, *Empire on the Pacific;* G. C. Lyman, *John Marsh;* F. Merk, *Manifest Destiny and Mission in American History;* H. N. Smith, *Virgin Land;* R. G. Thwaites, *Early Western Travels;* A. K. Weinberg, *Manifest Destiny.*

2. *Great Plains, Oregon, and Rockies*

H. C. Dale, *The Ashley-Smith Explorations and the Discovery of a Central Route to the Pacific, 1822–29;* D. O. Johansen & C. M. Gates, *Empire of the Columbia;* F. Parkman, *Oregon Trail,* and *Journals* (Mason Wade, ed.), and *Letters* (W. R. Jacobs, ed.); J. Schafer, *History of the Pacific Northwest;* W. P. Webb, *The Great Plains;* D. E. Wood, *The Old Santa Fé Trail from the Missouri River.*

3. *The Mormons*

F. M. Brodie, *No Man Knows My History: The Life of Joseph Smith;* C. A. Brough, *Irrigation in Utah;* B. De Voto, *Forays and Rebuttals;* W. A. Linn, *The Story of the Mormons;* W. Mulder & A. R. Mortensen, *Among the Mormons, Historic Accounts by Contemporary Observers;* T. F. O'Dea, *The Mormons;* G. Thomas, *The Development of Institutions under Irrigation;* M. R. Werner, *Brigham Young.*

4. *Polk and the Texas Question*

E. C. Barker, *Life of Stephen F. Austin;* E. I. McCormac, *James K. Polk;* F. Merk, *Slavery and the Annexation of Texas;* A. Nevins (ed.), *Diary of a President* (1-vol. abridgment of Polk's Diary); J. F. Rippy, *The United States and Mexico;* C. G. Sellers, *James K. Polk;* S. Siegel, *A Political History of the Texas Republic;* J. H. Smith, *The Annexation of Texas,* and *The War with Mexico* (2 vols.); N. W. Stephenson, *Texas and the Mexican War.*

5. *The Mexican War*

K. J. Bauer, *The Mexican War;* A. H. Bill, *Rehearsal for Conflict;* C. W. Elliott, *Winfield Scott;* H. Hamilton, *Zachary Taylor;* O. A. Singletary, *The Mexican War;* W. P. Webb, *The Texas Rangers.*

CHAPTER 15

1. *General*

A. C. Cole, *The Irrepressible Conflict, 1850–65;* A. Craven, *The Growth of Southern Nationalism;* E. Foner, *Free Soil, Free Labor, Free Men;* C. B. Going, *David Wilmot, Free-Soiler;* H. Hamilton, *Zachary Taylor,* vol. ii, and *Prologue to Conflict;* G. F. Milton, *The Eve of Conflict* (Douglas); A. Nevins, *Ordeal of the Union,* vol. i; R. F. Nichols, *Franklin Pierce;* J. F. Rhodes, *History of the United States from the Compromise of 1850,* vol. i; T. C. Smith, *Liberty and Free Soil Parties in the Northwest;* biographies of Calhoun, Clay, Rhett, Webster, and others already cited.

2. *California and the Gold Rush*

J. W. Caughey, *Gold Is the Cornerstone;* R. G. Cleland, *From Wilderness to Empire,* and *History of California;* C. Goodwin, *Establishment of a State Government in California, 1846–1850;* L. R. Hafen, *The Overland Mail, 1849–1869;* O. T. Howe, *Argonauts of '49;* A. Nevins, *Frémont;* R. W. Paul, *California Gold.*

3. *Opening of Japan*

A. B. Cole, *Yankee Surveyors in the Shogun's Seas;* T. Dennett, *Americans in Eastern Asia;* F. R. Dulles, *The Old China Trade;* W. E. Griffis, *Matthew C. Perry;* S. E. Morison, *Old Bruin* (Perry); I. Nitobe, *Intercourse between the U.S. and Japan;* P. J. Treat, *Diplomatic Relations between U.S. and Japan, 1853–95* (2 vols.); A. Walworth, *Black Ships off Japan.*

4. *Isthmian Diplomacy*

D. Perkins, *The Monroe Doctrine, 1826–1867;* B. Rauch, *American Interests in Cuba;* W. O. Scroggs, *Filibusters and Financiers;* I. D. Travis, *History of the Clayton-Bulwer Treaty;* M. W. Williams, *Anglo-American Isthmian Diplomacy.*

5. *Canadian Relations*

C. D. Allin, *Annexation, Preferential Trade and Reciprocity;* L. B. Shippee, *Canadian-American Relations, 1849–1874;* C. G. Tansill, *Canadian Reciprocity Treaty of 1854.*

6. *The Clipper Ship and Steam*

A. H. Clark, *The Clipper Ship Era;* C. C. Cutler, *Greyhounds of the Sea;* C. L. Lewis, *Matthew Fontaine Maury;* S. E. Morison, *Maritime History of Massachusetts,* ch. 22, and *By Land and By Sea,* ch. 2; E. L. Pond, *Junius Smith;* D. B. Tyler, *Steam Conquers the Atlantic.*

CHAPTER 16

1. *General*

A. Craven, *The Coming of the Civil War,* and *The Growth of Southern Nationalism;* D. E. Fehrenbacher, *Prelude to Greatness;* M. Holt, *Forging a Majority;* P. S. Klein, *President James Buchanan;* G. F. Milton, *The Eve of Conflict;* A. Nevins, *Ordeal of the Union,* vol. ii, and *Emergence of Lincoln;* R. F. Nichols, *The Democratic Machine, 1850–54, The Disruption of American Democracy,* and *Franklin Pierce;* J. A. Rawley, *Race and Politics;* K. M. Stampp (ed.), *The Causes of the Civil War.*

2. *Prairie Settlement, Kansas, and Nebraska*

F. W. Blakmar, *The Life of Charles Robinson;* C. A. Dawson & E. R. Younge, *Pioneering in the Prairie Provinces;* E. Dick, *Vanguards of the Frontier,* and *The Sod House Frontier;* D. Donald, *Charles Sumner and the Coming of the Civil War;* P. W. Gates, *The Illinois Central R. R. and Its Colonization Work,* and *Fifty Million Acres;* H. C. Hubbart, *The Older Middle West, 1840–1880;* W. T. Hutchinson, *Cyrus Hall McCormick* (2 vols.); S. A. Johnson, *The Battle Cry of Freedom;* J. C. Malin, *The Nebraska Question;* M. M. Quaife, *The Doctrine of Non-Intervention with Slavery in the Territories;* P. O. Ray, *Repeal of the Missouri Compromise;* R. Russel, *Improvement of Communication with the Pacific Coast as an Issue in American Politics.*

3. *Know-Nothings*

R. A. Billington, *The Protestant Crusade;* W. D. Overdyke, *The Know-Nothing Party in the South;* L. F. Schmeckebier, *The History of the Know-Nothing Party in Maryland.*

4. *Dred Scott*

R. M. Cover, *Justice Accused;* V. C. Hopkins, *Dred Scott's Case;* C. B. Swisher, *The Oliver Wendell Holmes Devise History of the Supreme Court of the United States,* vol. v: *The Taney Period, 1836–1864,* and *Roger B. Taney.*

5. *Lincoln-Douglas Debates*

P. M. Angle (ed.), *Created Equal?,* and E. E. Sparks (ed.), *Lincoln-Douglas Debates,* for the texts; H. V. Jaffa, *Crisis of the House Divided;* H. V. Jaffa & R. W. Johannsen (eds.), *In the Name of the People;* R. W. Johannsen, *Stephen A. Douglas;* C. Sandburg, *Abraham Lincoln, the Prairie Years;* P. Simon, *Lincoln's Preparation for Greatness.*

6. *Secession*

W. M. Caskey, *Secession and Restoration of Louisiana;* S. A. Channing, *Crisis of Fear;* A. M. B. Coleman, *The Life of John J. Crittenden;* E. M. Coulter (ed.), *The Course of the South to Secession;* O. Crenshaw, *The Slave States in the Presidential Election of 1860;* R. Current, *Lincoln and the First Shot;* C. P. Denman, *Secession Movement in Alabama;* D. L. Dumond, *The Secession Movement;* N. Graebner (ed.), *The Crisis of the Union;* W. J. Grayson, *James Louis Petigru;* R. Gunderson, *Old Gentlemen's Convention;* P. M. Hamer, *Secession Movement in South Carolina;* J. Hodgson, *The Cradle of the Confederacy;* G. H. Knoles (ed.), *The Crisis of the Union;* E. Merrill, *James J. Hammond;* G. F. Milton, *The Eve of Conflict;* D. M. Potter, *Lincoln and His Party in the Secession Crisis;* P. L. Rainwater, *Mississippi: Storm Center of Secession;* R. R. Russel, *Economic Aspects of Southern Sectionalism, 1840–1861;* H. T. Shanks, *The Secession Movement in Virginia;* E. C. Smith, *The Borderland in the Civil War;* K. Stampp, *And the War Came;* A. H. Stephens, *A Constitutional View of the Late War Between the States;* A. Whitridge, *No Compromise!;* R. A. Wooster, *The Secession Conventions of the South.*

CHAPTERS 17–18

1. *General*

D. Aaron, *The Unwritten War;* B. Catton (ed.), *American Heritage Picture History of the Civil War;* H. S. Commager, ed., *Official Atlas of the Civil War;* E. M. Coulter, *The Confederate States of America;* D. Donald, *Charles Sumner and the Coming of the Civil War;* C. Eaton, *History of the Southern Confederacy;* C. R. Fish, *The American Civil War: An Interpretation;* E. D. Fite, *The Presidential Campaign of 1860;* J. B. McMaster, *History of the People of the United States During Lincoln's Administration;* B. Mayo (ed.), *The American Tragedy;* A. Nevins, *The War for the Union* (4 vols.), and *The Emergence of Lincoln,* vol. ii, chs. 1–11; T. J. Pressly, *Americans Interpret Their Civil War;* J. G. Randall, *Civil War and Reconstruction;* J. F. Rhodes, *History of the United States,* vols. ii–v; C. P. Roland, *The Confederacy.*

2. *Abraham Lincoln*

C. R. Ballard, *The Military Genius of Abraham Lincoln;* R. Basler (ed.), *Collected Works of Abraham Lincoln* (8 vols.); R. Bruce, *Lincoln and the Tools of War;* R. N. Current, *The Lincoln Nobody Knows;* D. Donald, *Lincoln Reconsidered;* B. J. Hendrick, *Lincoln's War Cabinet;* W. B. Hesseltine, *Lincoln and the War Governors;* G. F. Milton, *Lincoln and the Fifth Column;* H. Mitgang (ed.), *Lincoln As They Saw Him;* J. G. Nicolay & J. Hay, *Abraham Lincoln* (10 vols.); J. G. Randall, *Constitutional Problems Under Lincoln,* and *Lincoln the President: Springfield to Gettysburg* (2 vols.); J. G. Randall & R. N. Current, *Last Full Measure;* C. Sandburg, *Abraham Lincoln: The War Years* (4 vols.); D. M. Silver, *Lincoln's Supreme Court;* H. Strode, *Jefferson Davis* (2 vols.); B. Thomas, *Abraham Lincoln;* T. H. Williams, *Lincoln and His Generals;* W. F. Zornow, *Lincoln and the Party Divided.*

3. *Biographies*

R. von Abele, *Alexander H. Stephens;* F. Brodie, *Thaddeus Stevens;* F. Cleaves, *The Rock of Chickamauga* (Gen. Thomas); B. Davis, *Jeb Stuart;* W. C. Davis, *Breckinridge;* D. Donald, *Charles Sumner and the Rights of Man;* G. E. Govan & J. W. Livingood, *A Different Valor* (Joseph E. Johnston); U. S. Grant, *Personal Memoirs* (2 vols.); G. F. R. Henderson, *Stonewall Jackson and the American Civil War* (2 vols.); B. J. Hendrick, *Statesmen of the Lost Cause;* T. Lyman, *Meade's Headquarters;* R. McElroy, *Jefferson Davis* (2 vols.); R. D. Meade, *Judah P. Benjamin;* J. Niven, *Gideon Welles;* J. Parks, *General Edmund Kirby Smith C.S.A.;* R. W. Patrick, *Jefferson Davis and His Cabinet;* W. T. Sherman, *Memoirs of General William T. Sherman* (2 vols.); R. Taylor, *Destruction and Reconstruction;* J. Thomason, *Jeb Stuart;* F. Vandiver, *Mighty Stonewall* (2 vols.); R. F. Weigley,

Quarter-Master General of the Union Army (Montgomery Meigs); K. P. Williams, *Lincoln Finds a General* (U.S. Grant) (5 vols.); J. Wyeth, *Life of General Nathan Bedford Forrest.*

4. *Military*

G. W. Adams, *Doctors in Blue;* R. Brownlee, *Gray Ghosts of the Confederacy: Guerrilla Warfare in the West;* B. Catton, *A Stillness at Appomattox, Glory Road, Grant Moves South, Mr. Lincoln's Army, Never Call Retreat, Terrible Swift Sword,* and *This Hallowed Ground;* D. T. Cornish, *The Sable Arm;* H. H. Cunningham, *Doctors in Gray;* D. S. Freeman, *Lee's Lieutenants,* and *R. E. Lee;* T. R. Hay, *Hood's Tennessee Campaign;* S. Horn, *The Army of the Tennessee;* R. U. Johnson & C. C. Buel (eds.), *Battles and Leaders of the Civil War* (4 vols.); F. Maurice, *Statesmen and Soldiers of the Civil War;* E. S. Miers, *The Web of Victory: Grant at Vicksburg;* J. Monaghan, *Civil War on the Western Border;* L. V. Naisawald, *Grape and Canister;* B. Quarles, *The Negro in the Civil War;* J. C. Ropes & W. R. Livermore, *The Story of the Civil War* (3 vols.); M. Schaff, *The Sunset of the Confederacy;* F. A. Shannon, *Organization and Administration of the Union Army* (2 vols.); A. Townsend, *Campaign of a Non-Combatant;* B. Wiley, *The Life of Billy Yank,* and *The Life of Johnny Reb.*

5. *Naval*

D. Ammen, *The Atlantic Coast;* J. P. Baxter, *Introduction of the Ironclad Warship;* F. Dorsey, *Road to the Sea: Story of James B. Eads and the Mississippi River;* H. A. Gosnell, *Guns on the Western Waters;* J. D. Hill, *Sea Dogs of the Sixties;* C. L. Lewis, *David Glasgow Farragut* (2 vols.); A. T. Mahan, *Admiral Farragut,* and *The Gulf and Inland Waters;* J. T. Scharf, *History of the Confederate States Navy;* G. Welles, *Diary* (3 vols.).

6. *Foreign Relations*

E. D. Adams, *Great Britain and the American Civil War* (2 vols.); H. Adams, *The Education of Henry Adams;* J. O. Bullock, *Secret Service of the Confederate States in Europe* (2 vols.); J. M. Callahan, *Diplomatic History of the Southern Confederacy;* M. Clapp, *Forgotten First Citizen: John Bigelow;* D. Jordan & E. J. Pratt, *Europe and the American Civil War;* J. Monaghan, *Diplomat in Carpet Slippers;* F. L. Owsley, *King Cotton Diplomacy.*

7. *Behind the Lines*

J. C. Andrew, *The North Reports the Civil War;* R. C. Black, *The Railroads of the Confederacy;* A. C. Cole, *The Irrepressible Conflict;* E. M. Coulter, *The Confederate States of America;* E. Crozier, *Yankee Reporters 1861–65;* E. D. Fite, *Social and Industrial Conditions in the North during the Civil War;* P. Gates, *Agriculture and the Civil War;* W. Gray, *The Hidden Civil War;* W. B. Hesseltine, *Civil War Prisons;* H. Hyman, *Era of the Oath;* E. C. Kirkland, *The Peacemakers of 1864;* F. L. Klement, *The Copperheads in the Middle West;* M. Leech, *Reveille in Washington;* E. Lonn, *Foreigners in the Confederacy,* and *Foreigners in the Union Army and Navy;* W. Q. Maxwell, *Lincoln's Fifth Wheel: The U.S. Sanitary Commission;* A. B. Moore, *Conscription and Conflict in the Confederacy;* F. L. Owsley, *States Rights in the Confederacy;* W. M. Robinson, *Justice in Grey: A History of the Judicial System of the Confederate States of America;* J. C. Schwab, *The Confederate States of America;* L. Starr, *The Bohemian Brigade;* R. C. Todd, *Confederate Finance;* T. Weber, *Northern Railroads in the Civil War;* C. Wesley, *The Collapse of the Confederacy;* B. Wiley, *Southern Negroes 1861–1865,* and *The Plain People of the Confederacy;* W. Yearns, *The Confederate Congress.*

Source Selections

P. M. Angle & E. S. Miers, *Tragic Years* (2 vols.); H. S. Commager, *The Blue and the Gray* (2 vols.), and (ed.), *Documents,* nos. 189–244; F. Moore (ed.), *The Rebellion Record* (12 vols.).

CHAPTER 19

1. *General*

P. H. Buck, *The Road to Reunion;* J. A. Carpenter, *Sword and Olive Branch: Oliver Otis Howard;* A. Conway, *The Reconstruction of Georgia;* E. M. Coulter, *The South During Reconstruction;* A. Craven, *Reconstruction;* C. Crowe (ed.), *The Age of Civil War and Reconstruction;* R. Cruden, *The Negro in Reconstruc-*

tion; R. O. Curry, *Radicalism, Racism, and Party Realignment;* D. Donald, *The Politics of Reconstruction, 1863–1867;* W. A. Dunning, *Reconstruction, Political and Economic;* R. F. Durden, *James Shepherd Pike;* J. H. Franklin, *Reconstruction;* H. M. Hyman (ed.), *New Frontiers of the American Reconstruction;* A. Nevins, *The Emergence of Modern America;* E. P. Oberholtzer, *History of the United States since the Civil War,* vol. i; O. H. Olsen, *Carpetbagger's Crusade: The Life of Albion Winegar Tourgee;* R. W. Patrick, *The Reconstruction of the Nation;* J. G. Randall & D. Donald, *The Civil War and Reconstruction;* J. F. Rhodes, *History of the United States,* vol. v; R. P. Sharkey, *Money, Class, and Party;* K. M. Stampp, *The Era of Reconstruction, 1865–1877;* A. W. Trelease, *White Terror;* I. Unger, *The Greenback Era;* F. G. Wood, *The Era of Reconstruction, 1863–1877.*

2. *The Negro as Freedman*

P. A. Bruce, *The Plantation Negro as Freedman;* G. W. Cable, *The Negro Question* (Arlin Turner, ed.); W. J. Cash, *The Mind of the South;* H. H. Donald, *The Negro Freedman;* W. E. B. Du Bois, *Black Reconstruction,* and *The Souls of Black Folk;* F. A. Logan, *The Negro in North Carolina, 1876–1894;* R. W. Logan, *The Negro in American Life and Thought, 1877–1901;* W. S. McFeely, *Yankee Stepfather;* J. M. McPherson, *The Struggle for Equality;* B. Mathews, *Booker T. Washington;* A. Meier, *Negro Thought in America, 1880–1915;* G. Myrdal, *An American Dilemma* (2 vols.); W. Peters, *The Southern Temper;* B. Quarles, *Lincoln and the Negro;* A. Raper, *Preface to Peasantry;* J. M. Richardson, *The Negro in the Reconstruction of Florida, 1865–1877;* O. Singletary, *Negro Militia and Reconstruction;* S. R. Spencer, Jr., *Booker T. Washington and the Negro's Place in American Life;* C. E. Synes, *Race Relations in Virginia, 1870–1902;* G. B. Tindall, *South Carolina Negroes, 1877–1900;* B. T. Washington, *Up from Slavery;* C. H. Wesley, *Negro Labor in the United States, 1850–1925;* V. Wharton, *The Negro in Mississippi;* J. Williamson, *After Slavery: The Negro in South Carolina During Reconstruction, 1861–1877;* C. G. Woodson, *A Century of Negro Migration.*

3. *Presidential Reconstruction*

H. Beale, *The Critical Year;* L. & J. H. Cox, *Politics, Principle, and Prejudice: 1865–1866;* J. Dorris, *Pardon and Amnesty under Lincoln and Johnson;* W. B. Hesseltine, *Lincoln's Plan of Reconstruction,* and *Lincoln and the War Governors;* C. McCarthy, *Lincoln's Plan of Reconstruction;* E. McKitrick, *Andrew Johnson and Reconstruction;* G. F. Milton, *The Age of Hate;* J. G. Randall, *Constitutional Problems under Lincoln;* W. L. Rose, *Rehearsal for Reconstruction: The Port Royal Experiment.*

4. *Congressional Reconstruction*

T. B. Alexander, *Political Reconstruction in Tennessee;* M. L. Benedict, *A Compromise of Principle;* G. Bentley, *A History of the Freedmen's Bureau;* W. R. Brock, *An American Crisis: Congress and Reconstruction;* W. M. Caskey, *Secession and Restoration in Louisiana;* W. L. Fleming, *Civil War and Reconstruction in Alabama;* J. W. Garner, *Reconstruction in Mississippi;* W. Gillette, *The Right To Vote: Politics and the Passage of the Fifteenth Amendment;* R. Shugg, *Origins of Class Struggle in Louisiana;* F. B. Simkins & R. H. Woody, *South Carolina during Reconstruction;* D. Y. Thomas, *Arkansas in War and Reconstruction;* C. M. Thompson, *Reconstruction in Georgia;* H. L. Trefousse, *Benjamin Franklin Wade.*

5. *Reconstruction and the Constitution*

H. Hyman, *A More Perfect Union,* and *The Era of the Oath;* J. B. James, *The Framing of the Fourteenth Amendment;* S. Kutler, *Judicial Power and Reconstruction Politics;* J. M. Mathews, *Legislative and Judicial History of the Fifteenth Amendment;* J. Ten Broek, *Antislavery Origins of the Fourteenth Amendment;* C. Warren, *The Supreme Court in United States History,* vol. ii.

6. *Radical Reconstruction*

M. L. Benedict, *The Impeachment and Trial of Andrew Johnson;* F. Brodie, *Thaddeus Stevens;* R. N. Current, *Old Thad Stevens;* D. Donald, *Charles Sumner and the Rights of Man;* W. R. Gillette, *The Right to Vote;* H. Hyman & B. P. Thomas, *The Life and Times of Lincoln's Secretary of War;* R. Korngold, *Thaddeus Stevens;* H. L. Trefousse, *Impeachment of a President,* and *The Radical Republicans;* H. White, *Life of Lyman Trumbull.*

7. *Grant and Domestic Politics*

H. Adams, *The Education of Henry Adams;* D. C. Barrett, *Greenbacks and the Resumption of Specie Payments;* W. A. Cate, *L. Q. C. Lamar;* M. Duberman, *Charles Francis Adams;* W. B. Hesseltine, *Ulysses S. Grant, Politician;* H. Larson, *Jay Cooke, Private Banker;* R. S. Mitchell, *Horatio Seymour of New York;* A. B. Paine, *Thomas Nast, His Period and His Pictures;* E. D. Ross, *The Liberal Republican Movement;* J. Schafer, *Carl Schurz, Militant Liberal.*

8. *Foreign Affairs*

S. F. Bemis (ed.), *The American Secretaries of State and Their Diplomacy,* vol. vii; J. M. Callahan, *The Alaska Purchase;* C. L. Jones, *Caribbean Interests of the United States;* A. Nevins, *Hamilton Fish;* C. C. Tansill, *The United States and Santo Domingo 1789–1873.*

9. *The Election of 1876*

H. Barnard, *Rutherford B. Hayes and His America;* H. J. Eckenrode, *Rutherford B. Hayes;* A. C. Flick, *Samuel Jones Tilden;* P. L. Haworth, *The Hayes-Tilden Disputed Election of 1876;* A. Nevins, *Abram S. Hewitt: With Some Account of Peter Cooper;* J. F. Rhodes, *History of the United States,* vol. vii; L. B. Richardson, *William E. Chandler, Republican;* C. R. Williams, *Life of Rutherford B. Hayes* (2 vols.); C. V. Woodward, *Reunion and Reaction.*

CHAPTER 20

1. *General*

R. Andreano (ed.), *New Views on American Economic Development;* A. D. Chandler, Jr., *Giant Enterprise* and *Strategy and Structure;* V. S. Clark, *History of Manufactures in the United States 1860–1914;* S. Coben & F. G. Hill (eds.), *American Economic History;* T. Cochran & W. Miller, *The Age of Enterprise;* R. Fels, *American Business Cycles, 1865–1897;* M. Friedman and A. J. Schwartz, *A Monetary History of the United States;* S. P. Hays, *The Response to Industrialism;* E. C. Kirkland, *A History of American Economic Life* and *Industry Comes of Age;* S. Kuznets, *National Income;* L. Mumford, *Technics and Civilization;* W. N. Parker (ed.), *Trends in the American Economy in the Nineteenth Century;* S. Ratner, *American Taxation as a Social Force;* R. Robertson, *History of the American Economy.*

2. *Special Industries and Industrial Leaders*

F. L. Allen, *The Great Pierpont Morgan;* S. Buder, *Pullman;* R. A. Clemen, *American Live Stock and Meat Industry;* A. H. Cole, *The American Wool Manufacture* (2 vols.); R. Current, *The Typewriter and the Men Who Made It;* P. de Kruif, *Seven Iron Men;* P. Giddens, *The Birth of the Oil Industry* and *The Standard Oil Company of Indiana;* R. and M. Hidy, *Pioneering in Big Business: The Standard Oil Company of New Jersey;* W. T. Hutchinson, *Cyrus McCormick* (2 vols.); M. Jacobstein, *The Tobacco Industry;* M. James, *Alfred I. DuPont;* H. Larson, *Jay Cooke;* S. E. Morison, *The Ropemakers of Plymouth;* A. Nevins, *John D. Rockefeller* (2 vols.) and *Abram Hewitt: With Some Account of Peter Cooper;* A. Nevins & F. E. Hill, *Henry Ford* (3 vols.); H. C. Passer, *The Electric Manufacturers;* C. C. Rister, *Oil;* P. Temin, *Iron and Steel in Nineteenth Century America;* H. F. Williamson & A. H. Daum, *The American Petroleum Industry;* F. P. Wirth, *Discovery and Exploitation of the Minnesota Iron Lands.*

3. *Trusts and Trust Regulation*

J. D. Clark, *Federal Trust Policy;* J. R. Commons, *Legal Foundations of Capitalism;* E. Jones, *The Trust Problem in the United States;* D. Keezer & S. May, *Public Control of Business;* O. W. Knauth, *The Policy of the United States Towards Industrial Monopoly;* H. W. Laidler, *Concentration of Control in American Industry;* G. W. Nutter, *Extent of Enterprise Monopoly;* W. Z. Ripley, *Trusts, Pools, and Corporations;* H. R. Seager & G. A. Gulick, *Trust and Corporation Problems;* H. B. Thorelli, *Federal Anti-Trust Policy;* A. Walker, *History of the Sherman Law.*

4. *Big Business and Its Philosophy*

C. Barker, *Henry George;* F. B. Copley, *Frederick Taylor;* S. Diamond, *The Reputation of the American Businessman;* J. Dorfman, *Economic Thought in American Civilization,* vol. 3; S. Fine, *Laissez Faire and the General-Welfare State;* R. Hofstadter, *Social Darwinism in the United States;* E. C. Kirkland, *Business in the Gilded Age;* R. G. McCloskey, *American Conservatism in the Age of Enterprise;* I. Wyllie, *The Self-Made Man in America.*

CHAPTER 21

1. *General*

D. Brody, *Butcher Workmen* and *Steelworkers in America;* R. Christie, *Empire in Wood;* J. R. Commons *et al., History of Labor in the United States* vols. 3 and 4; G. Grob, *Workers and Utopia;* A. L.

Harris, *The Black Worker;* H. Harris, *American Labor;* H. Pelling, *American Labor;* M. Perlman, *The Machinists;* S. Perlman, *History of Trade Unionism in the United States* and *A Theory of the Labor Movement;* P. Taft, *The A.F. of L. in the Time of Gompers;* L. Ulman, *The Rise of the National Trade Union;* N. J. Ware, *Labor Movement in the United States 1860–1895;* C. H. Wesley, *Negro Labor in the United States 1850–1925;* L. Wolman, *Growth of American Trade Unions 1880–1923.*

2. *Labor Leaders and Leadership*

C. Barker, *Henry George;* H. Barnard, *Eagle Forgotten* (Altgeld); C. R. Geiger, *The Philosophy of Henry George;* R. Ginger, *The Bending Cross* (Debs); E. Glück, *John Mitchell;* S. Gompers, *Seventy Years of Life and Labor* (2 vols.); J. Grossman, *William E. Sylvis;* R. E. Harvey, *Samuel Gompers;* B. Mandel, *Samuel Gompers;* A. E. Morgan, *Edward Bellamy;* T. Powderly, *The Path I Trod;* L. Reed, *Philosophy of Gompers.*

3. *Labor Conflicts and Industrial Violence*

L. Adamic, *Dynamite;* P. W. Brissenden, *The I.W.W.;* W. G. Broehl, Jr., *The Molly Maguires;* J. R. Brooks, *American Syndicalism;* R. Bruce, *1877: Year of Violence;* J. W. Coleman, *The Molly Maguire Riots;* J. R. Commons *et al., History of Labor in the United States,* vol. 4; H. David, *History of the Haymarket Affair;* M. Dubofsky, *We Shall Be All;* C. Goodrich, *The Miner's Freedom;* A. Lindsey, *The Pullman Strike;* B. S. Mitchell, *Textile Unionism in the South;* B. Rastall, *Labor History of the Cripple Creek District;* T. Tippett, *When Southern Labor Stirs.*

4. *Labor Legislation and the Courts*

E. Abbott, *Women in Industry;* E. Berman, *Labor and the Sherman Act;* J. R. Commons & J. B. Andrews, *Principles of Labor Legislation;* J. R. Commons *et al., History of Labor in the United States,* vol. 3; F. Frankfurter & N. V. Greene, *The Labor Injunction;* E. Freund, *The Police Power;* G. G. Groat, *Attitude of American Courts on Labor Cases;* C. E. Jacobs, *Law Writers and the Courts;* M. Karson, *American Labor Unions and Politics;* A. T. Mason, *Organized Labor and the Law;* E. E. Witte, *The Government in Labor Disputes;* I. Yellowitz, *Labor and the Progressive Movement in New York.*

5. *Immigration*

H. S. Commager (ed.), *Immigration and American History;* J. R. Commons, *Races and Immigrants in America;* O. Handlin, *Boston's Immigrants, The Uprooted,* and *Immigration as a Factor in American History;* M. Hansen, *The Atlantic Migration* and *The Immigrant in American History;* M. A. Jones, *American Immigration;* M. Rischin, *Promised City;* C. Wittke, *We Who Built America.*

6. *Special Groups*

K. C. Babcock, *Scandinavian Element in the United States;* G. Barth, *Bitter Strength;* R. Berthoff, *British Immigration to Industrial America 1790–1850;* K. O. Bjork, *West of the Great Divide: Norwegian Migration to the Pacific Coast;* T. C. Blegen, *Norwegian Migration to America* (2 vols.); T. Capek, *The Czechs in America;* J. Davis, *The Russian Immigrant;* A. De Conde, *Half Bitter, Half Sweet* (Italians); A. B. Faust, *German Element in the United States* (2 vols.); R. Foerster, *The Italian Emigration of Our Times;* M. Gamio, *Mexican Immigration to the United States;* E. F. Hirshler (ed.), *Jews from Germany in the United States;* F. E. Janson, *The Background of Swedish Immigration 1846–1930;* H. S. Lucas, *Netherlanders in America 1789–1950;* W. Mulder, *Homeward to Zion: Mormon Migration from Scandinavia;* H. Nelli, *Italians in Chicago, 1880–1930;* H. Pochmann, *German Culture in America;* C. C. Qualey, *Norwegian Settlement in the United States;* T. Saloutos, *The Greeks in the United States* and *They Remember America;* A. Schrier, *Ireland and the American Emigration 1850–1900;* B. Lee Sung, *Mountain of Gold: The Story of the Chinese in America;* W. I. Thomas & F. Znaniecki, *The Polish Peasant in Europe and America;* C. Wittke, *The Irish in America.*

7. *Immigration Restriction*

M. T. Bennett, *American Immigration Policies;* W. Bernard (ed.), *American Immigration Policy—A Reappraisal;* J. P. Clark, *Deportation of Aliens from the United States to Europe;* J. Higham, *Strangers in the Land;* R. Paul, *The Abrogation of the Gentlemen's Agreement;* B. Solomon, *Ancestors and Immigrants.*

CHAPTER 22

1. *General*

R. G. Athearn, *High Country Empire;* R. Billington, *Westward Expansion;* H. E. Briggs, *Frontiers of the*

Northwest; E. Dick, *The Sod House Frontier, 1854–1890;* G. W. Fite, *The Farmer's Frontier;* E. W. Hollon, *The Southwest;* P. Horgan, *Great River;* J. G. Malin, *The Grassland of North America;* E. Pomeroy, *The Pacific Slope;* R. E. Riegel & R. G. Athearn, *America Moves West;* F. A. Shannon, *The Farmer's Last Frontier;* W. P. Webb, *The Great Plains* and *The Great Frontier.*

2. *Railroads*

G. D. Bradley, *Story of the Santa Fe;* S. Daggett, *Chapters on the History of the Southern Pacific;* J. P. Davis, *The Union Pacific Railroad;* C. R. Fish, *Restoration of the Southern Railroads;* P. Gates, *The Illinois Central Railroad and Its Colonization Work;* J. Grodinsky, *Jay Gould* and *Transcontinental Railway Strategy;* E. Hungerford, *The Story of the Baltimore and Ohio Railroad* (2 vols.); G. Kennan, *Life of E. H. Harriman* (2 vols.); E. C. Kirkland, *Men, Cities and Transportation, 1820–1900* (2 vols.); W. Lane, *Commodore Vanderbilt;* O. Lewis, *The Big Four;* J. Moody, *The Railroad Builders;* E. H. Mott, *Between the Ocean and the Lakes;* J. G. Pyle, *James J. Hill* (2 vols.); E. L. Sabin, *Building the Pacific Railway;* E. Smalley, *History of the Northern Pacific Railroad;* J. F. Stover, *American Railroads;* G. R. Taylor & I. D. Neu, *The American Railroad Network;* N. Trottman, *History of the Union Pacific.*

3. *Railroads and the West*

T. Cochran, *Railroad Leaders, 1845–1890;* T. Donaldson, *The Public Domain;* R. W. Fogel, *Railroads and American Economic Growth* and *The Union Pacific Railroad;* L. H. Haney, *Congressional History of Railways, 1850–1887;* J. B. Hedges, *Henry Villard and the Railways of the Northwest;* R. C. Overton, *Burlington West;* J. R. Perkins, *Trails, Rails and War;* G. C. Quiett, *They Built the West;* R. E. Riegel, *The Story of the Western Railroads;* R. L. Thompson, *Wiring a Continent.*

4. *Indians*

American Heritage Book of Indians; E. D. Branch, *The Hunting of the Buffalo;* D. Brown, *Bury My Heart at Wounded Knee;* J. Collier, *Indians of the Americas;* C. A. Fee, *Chief Joseph;* G. Foreman, *The Five Civilized Tribes;* G. B. Grinnell, *The Story of the Indian* and *The Cheyenne Indians* (2 vols.); W. T. Hagan, *American Indians;* H. H. Jackson, *A Century of Dishonor;* J. P. Kinney, *A Continent Lost, a Civilization Won;* E. P. Priest, *Uncle Sam's Stepchildren 1865–1887;* P. Radin, *The Story of the American Indian;* R. N. Richardson, *The Comanche Barrier to the South Plains Settlement;* F. W. Seymour, *Indian Agents of the Old Frontier;* W. P. Webb, *The Texas Rangers.*

5. *The Mining Frontier*

H. H. Bancroft, *Popular Tribunals* (2 vols.); D. De Quille, *The Big Bonanza;* R. R. Elliott, *Nevada's Twentieth Century Mining Boom;* C. W. Glasscock, *Gold in Them Hills, The War of the Copper Kings,* and *The Big Bonanza;* W. T. Jackson, *Treasure Hill;* N. P. Langford, *Vigilante Days and Ways;* O. Lewis, *Silver Kings;* G. D. Lyman, *Saga of the Comstock Lode;* E. M. Mack, *Nevada, a History of the State;* W. P. Morrell, *The Gold Rushes;* R. Paul, *California Gold* and *Mining Frontiers of the Far West;* T. A. Rickard, *The History of American Mining;* C. H. Shinn, *Mining Camps;* C. C. Spence, *British Investments and the American Mining Frontier, 1860–1901;* W. J. Trimble, *The Mining Advance into the Inland Empire.*

6. *Cattle Kingdom*

A. Adams, *The Log of a Cowboy;* L. Atherton, *The Cattle Kings;* E. D. Branch, *The Cowboy and His Interpreters;* M. Burlingame, *The Montana Frontier;* R. Cleland, *Cattle on a Thousand Hills;* E. E. Dale, *Cow Country* and *The Cattle Range Industry;* J. F. Dobie, *A Vaquero of the Brush Country;* J. B. Frantz & J. Choate, *The American Cowboy;* G. R. Hebard & E. A. Brininstool, *The Bozeman Trail* (2 vols.); S. Henry, *Conquering Our Great American Plains;* E. Hough, *The Story of the Cowboy;* W. Kupper, *The Golden Hoof;* E. S. Osgood, *The Day of the Cattlemen;* O. B. Peake, *The Colorado Cattle Range Industry;* L. Pelzer, *The Cattleman's Frontier, 1850–1890;* S. P. Ridings, *The Chisholm Trail;* P. A. Rollins, *The Cowboy;* J. T. Schlebecker, *Cattle Raising on the Plains, 1900–61;* F. Shannon, *The Farmer's Last Frontier;* C. W. Towne & E. N. Wentworth, *Shepherd's Empire;* W. Webb, *The Great Plains;* P. I. Wellman, *The Trampling Herd;* E. Wentworth, *America's Sheep Trails.*

7. *Passing of the Frontier and Organization of the West*

L. J. Arrington, *Great Basin Kingdom;* R. G. Athearn, *William Tecumseh Sherman and the Settlement of the West;* M. Austin, *The Land of Little Rain;* H. E. Briggs, *Frontiers of the Northwest;* R. Cleland, *California* (2 vols.); E. Dick, *Vanguards of the Frontier;* P. W. Gates, *Frontier Landlords and Pioneer Tenants;* J. Ise, *Sod and Stubble;* M. James, *Cherokee Strip;* R. Lillard, *Desert Challenge;* J. C. Malin, *Winter*

Wheat in the Golden Belt of Kansas; J. C. Parish, *The Persistence of the Westward Movement;* R. N. Richardson, *Texas, the Lone Star State;* R. Robbins, *Our Landed Heritage;* F. J. Turner, *Significance of the Frontier in American History.*

CHAPTER 23

1. *General*

H. Agar, *The Price of Union;* J. Bryce, *The American Commonwealth* (2 vols.); J. Dorfman, *Economic Mind in American Civilization,* vol. 3; H. U. Faulkner, *Politics, Reform and Expansion 1890–1900;* S. Fine, *Laissez Faire and the General-Welfare State;* J. Garraty, *The New Commonwealth, 1877–1890;* E. Goldman, *Rendezvous with Destiny;* S. Hirshson, *Farewell to the Bloody Shirt;* J. R. Hollingsworth, *The Whirligig of Politics;* R. Jensen, *The Winning of the Midwest;* M. Josephson, *The Politicos;* P. Kleppner, *The Cross of Culture;* R. D. Marcus, *Grand Old Party;* H. Merrill, *Bourbon Democracy in the Middle West 1865–1896;* H. W. Morgan, *From Hayes to McKinley;* R. B. Nye, *Midwestern Progressive Politics 1870–1950;* D. Rothman, *Politics and Power;* L. D. White, *The Republican Era 1865–1900;* W. A. White, *Masks in a Pageant.*

2. *Reform*

G. Blodgett, *The Gentle Reformers;* C. R. Fish, *The Civil Service and the Patronage;* H. F. Gosnell, *Boss Platt and the New York Machine;* A. Hoogenboom, *Fighting the Spoilsmen.*

3. *Biographies*

H. Barnard, *Eagle Forgotten: Life of John P. Altgeld;* J. A. Barnes, *John G. Carlisle;* H. Bass, *'I Am a Democrat';* H. Croly, *Marcus Alonzo Hanna;* C. Fuess, *Carl Schurz;* M. A. Hirsch, *William C. Whitney;* G. Hoar, *Autobiography of Seventy Years;* G. F. Howe, *Chester A. Arthur;* M. Leech, *In the Days of McKinley;* A. Nevins, *Grover Cleveland;* W. A. Robinson, *Thomas B. Reed;* H. J. Sievers, *Benjamin Harrison;* T. C. Smith, *Life and Letters of James A. Garfield* (2 vols.); N. W. Stephenson, *Nelson Aldrich;* F. Summers, *William L. Wilson and Tariff Reform;* J. F. Wall, *Henry Watterson;* C. R. Williams, *Life of Rutherford B. Hayes* (2 vols.).

4. *Railroad Regulation*

C. F. Adams, *Railroads;* S. J. Buck, *The Granger Movement;* E. G. Campbell, *The Reorganization of the American Railroad System 1893–1900;* F. A. Cleveland & F. W. Powell, *Railway Promotion and Capitalization;* J. B. Crawford, *The Credit Mobilier of America;* F. Frankfurter, *The Commerce Clause under Marshall, Taney and Waite;* W. Larrabee, *The Railroad Question;* F. Merk, *Economic History of Wisconsin;* I. L. Sharfman, *The Interstate Commerce Commission* (5 vols.).

CHAPTER 24

1. *General*

L. H. Bailey, *Cyclopedia of American Agriculture* (4 vols.); O. E. Baker (ed.), *Atlas of American Agriculture;* M. Benedict, *Farm Policies of the United States 1790–1950;* E. L. Bogart, *Economic History of American Agriculture;* A. Bogue, *From Prairie to Corn Belt* and *Money at Interest;* B. H. Hibbard, *A History of Public Land Policies;* E. L. Peffer, *The Closing of the Public Domain;* W. Range, *A Century of Georgia Agriculture;* R. Robbins, *Our Landed Heritage;* A. Sakolski, *The Great American Land Bubble;* J. Schafer, *Social History of American Agriculture* and *History of Agriculture in Wisconsin;* F. A. Shannon, *The Farmer's Last Frontier;* C. C. Taylor, *The Farmers' Movement, 1620–1920;* U.S. Dept. of Agriculture, *Yearbook, 1940: American Agriculture, the First Three Hundred Years;* R. Vance, *Human Geography of the South;* W. P. Webb, *The Great Plains;* H. Wilson, *The Hill Country of Northern New England;* C. V. Woodward, *Origins of the New South.*

2. *Farm Problem and Agrarian Revolt*

A. M. Arnett, *Populist Movement in Georgia;* L. Benson, *Merchants, Farmers, and the Railroads;* R. P. Brooks, *The Agrarian Revolution in Georgia;* S. J. Buck, *The Granger Movement* and *The Agrarian Crusade;* J. B. Clark, *Populism in Alabama;* E. Dick, *The Sod House Frontier;* E. Ellis, *Henry Moore Teller;* N. Fine, *Labor and Farmer Parties in the U.S.;* P. R. Fossum, *The Agrarian Movement in North Dakota;* P. Gates, *Fifty Million Acres;* M. Harrington, *Populist Movement in Georgia;* F. E. Haynes, *James Baird Weaver* and *Third Party Movements Since the Civil War;* J. D. Hicks, *The Populist Revolt;* O. M. Kile, *Farm Bureau Movement;* S. Noblin, *L. L. Polk;* M.

Ridge, *Ignatius Donnelly;* T. Saloutos, *Farmer Movements in the South, 1865–1933;* T. Saloutos & J. D. Hicks, *Agricultural Discontent in the Middle West;* R. Shugg, *Origins of the Class Struggle in Louisiana;* C. V. Woodward, *Tom Watson.*

3. *The Money Question and the Panic of 1893*

J. A. Barnes, *John G. Carlisle;* D. R. Dewey, *Financial History of the United States;* M. Gresham, *Life of Walter Q. Gresham* (2 vols.); M. D. Hirsch, *William C. Whitney;* D. L. McMurray, *Coxey's Army;* S. Ratner, *American Taxation;* I. Unger, *The Greenback Era;* A. Weinstein, *Prelude to Populism;* M. S. Wildman, *Money Inflation in the United States.*

4. *The Populist Revolt*

A. M. Arnett, *The Populist Movement in Georgia;* H. Barnard, *Eagle Forgotten: John Peter Altgeld;* J. B. Clark, *Populism in Alabama;* J. D. Hicks, *The Populist Revolt;* A. D. Kirwan, *Revolt of the Rednecks;* W. T. K. Nugent, *The Tolerant Populists;* R. B. Nye, *Midwestern Progressive Politics;* N. Pollack, *The Populist Response to Industrial America;* F. A. Shannon, *The Farmer's Last Frontier;* W. D. Sheldon, *Populism in the Old Dominion;* F. Simkins, *The Tillman Movement in South Carolina.*

5. *Bryan and the Election of 1896*

W. J. Bryan, *Memoirs* and *The First Battle;* P. E. Coletta, *William Jennings Bryan,* vol. 1: *Political Evangelist 1860–1908;* H. Croly, *Marcus Alonzo Hanna;* R. F. Durden, *The Climax of Populism;* E. Ellis, *Henry Teller;* P. W. Glad, *The Trumpet Soundeth* and *McKinley, Bryan and the People;* P. Hibben, *W. J. Bryan;* S. Jones, *The Presidential Election of 1896;* H. W. Morgan, *McKinley and His America;* M. R. Werner, *Bryan;* W. Williams, *William Jennings Bryan.*

CHAPTER 25

1. *Philosophy and Religion*

A. I. Abell, *American Catholicism and Social Action* and *The Urban Impact on American Protestantism;* P. Carter, *The Spiritual Crisis of the Gilded Age;* H. S. Commager, *The American Mind;* M. Curti, *The Growth of American Thought;* J. T. Ellis, *American Catholicism;* C. H. Hopkins, *The Rise of the Social Gospel, 1865–1915;* H. F. May, *The End of Innocence* and *The Protestant Churches and Industrial America;* T. Maynard, *The Story of American Catholicism;* R. B. Perry, *The Thought and Character of William James* (2 vols.); S. Persons (ed.), *Evolutionary Thought in America* and *American Minds;* G. Santayana, *Character and Opinion in the United States* and *Winds of Doctrine;* H. Schneider, *A History of American Philosophy* and *Religion in Twentieth Century America;* A. P. Stokes, *Church and State in the United States* (3 vols.); H. Townsend, *Philosophical Ideas in the United States;* P. Weiner, *Evolution and the Founding of Pragmatism;* M. G. White, *Social Thought in America.*

2. *Social and Legal Thought*

S. Chuggerman, *Lester Ward;* J. R. Commons, *Legal Foundation of Capitalism;* B. Crick, *The American Science of Politics;* C. M. Destler, *American Radicalism 1865–1901;* J. Dorfman, *Thorstein Veblen and His America;* F. Frankfurter, *Mr. Justice Holmes and the Supreme Court;* R. Hofstadter, *Social Darwinism in America;* M. DeW. Howe, *Justice Oliver Wendell Holmes: The Proving Years;* W. Jordy, *Henry Adams: Scientific Historian;* M. Lerner (ed.), *The Mind and Faith of Justice Holmes;* H. Odum (ed.), *American Masters of Social Science;* E. Samuels, *Henry Adams: The Middle Years;* H. E. Starr, *William Graham Sumner;* B. Twiss, *Lawyers and the Constitution.*

3. *Literature*

H. Adams, *The Education of Henry Adams;* G. N. Bennett, *William Dean Howells;* V. W. Brooks, *New England: Indian Summer, Howells: His Life and World, The Ordeal of Mark Twain,* and *The Confident Years;* E. H. Cady, *William Dean Howells;* O. Cargill, *Intellectual America* and *The Novels of Henry James;* E. Carter, *Howells and the Age of Realism;* H. H. Clark (ed.), *Transitions in American Literary History;* M. Cowley, *After the Genteel Tradition;* B. DeVoto, *Mark Twain's America;* D. Dudley, *Forgotten Frontiers: Theodore Dreiser and the Land of the Free;* L. Edel, *Henry James;* M. Geismar, *Ancestors and Rebels;* A. Kazin, *On Native Grounds;* F. O. Matthiessen, *The James Family* and *Henry James: The Major Phase;* E. Neff, *Edwin A. Robinson;* V. L. Parrington, *Beginnings of Critical Realism in America;* R. E. Spiller *et al., Literary History of the United States,* vol. 2; W. Taylor, *The Economic Novel in America;* Y. Winters, *E. A. Robinson.*

4. *Journalism*

W. G. Bleyer, *Main Currents in the History of American Journalism;* G. Britt, *Forty Years, Forty Millions: A Biography of Frank Munsey;* O. Carlson, *Hearst: Lord of San Simeon;* H. S. Commager (ed.), *The St. Nicholas Anthology;* E. Davis, *The New York Times;* G. Johnson, *An Honorable Titan: Adolph Ochs;* J. M. Lee, *History of American Journalism;* F. L. Mott, *American Journalism* and *History of American Magazines,* vol. 3; D. Seitz, *Joseph Pulitzer;* W. A. Swanberg, *Citizen Hearst;* J. Tebbel, *George Horace Lorimer and the Saturday Evening Post;* B. A. Weisberger, *The American Newspaperman.*

5. *Education*

L. Cremin, *The Transformation of the School;* E. P. Cubberley, *Public Education in the United States;* M. Curti, *Social Ideas of American Educators;* C. W. Dabney, *Universal Education in the South* (2 vols.); H. Hawkins, *Pioneer: A History of the Johns Hopkins University;* R. Hofstadter & W. Metzger, *Academic Freedom in the United States;* H. James, *Charles W. Eliot* (2 vols.); E. Krug, *Charles W. Eliot and Popular Education;* T. LeDuc, *Piety and Intellect at Amherst College;* R. D. Leigh, *The Public Library in the United States;* P. Monroe (ed.), *Cyclopedia of Education* (5 vols.); S. E. Morison, *Development of Harvard University 1869–1929;* A. Nevins, *The Land Grant Colleges;* G. Pierson, *Yale;* E. D. Ross, *Democracy's College;* R. J. Storr, *Harper's University;* T. Veblen, *The Higher Learning in America;* L. Veysey, *The Emergence of the American University.*

6. *Art and Architecture*

W. Andrews, *Architecture in America* and *Architecture, Ambition, and Americans;* V. Barker, *American Painting;* C. Beaux, *Background with Figures;* J. Burchard & A. Bush-Brown, *The Architecture of America;* A. Burroughs, *Limners and Likenesses;* H. S. Commager, *The American Mind;* R. Cortissoz, *Augustus St. Gaudens* and *John La Farge;* W. H. Downes, *John Singer Sargent;* J. M. Fitch, *American Building;* S. Giedion, *Space, Time and Architecture;* I. Glackens, *William Glackens and the Ashcan Group;* L. Goodrich, *Albert Ryder, Winslow Homer,* and *Thomas Eakins;* T. Hamlin, *The American Spirit in Architecture;* J. Kouwenhoven, *Made in America;* O. Larkin, *Art and Life in America;* R. McKinney, *Thomas Eakins;* C. H. Moore, *Daniel H. Burnham;* L. Mumford, *Roots of Contemporary Architecture, The Brown Decades, Sticks and Stones,* and *The South in Architecture;* J. Myers, *Artist in New York;* E. P. Richardson, *Painting in America;* M. Ryerson (ed.), *The Art Spirit: Robert Henri;* M. Schuyler, *American Architecture* (2 vols.); F. Sherman, *Albert Pinkham Ryder;* L. Taft, *History of American Sculpture;* W. Walton, *Art and Architecture at the World's Columbian Exposition* (3 vols.); F. L. Wright, *Autobiography, Modern Architecture,* and *Writings and Buildings.*

CHAPTER 26

1. *General*

J. B. Brebner, *The North Atlantic Triangle;* F. R. Dulles, *The Imperial Years* and *America in the Pacific;* L. Gelber, *The Rise of Anglo-American Friendship 1898–1906;* A. W. Griswold, *The Far Eastern Policy of the United States;* G. F. Kennan, *American Diplomacy;* W. La Feber, *The New Empire;* H. W. Morgan, *William McKinley and His America* and *America's Road to Empire;* R. E. Osgood, *Ideals and Self-Interest in America's Foreign Policy;* D. Perkins, *Hands Off! A History of the Monroe Doctrine;* D. W. Pletcher, *The Awkward Years;* A. K. Weinberg, *Manifest Destiny;* A. Whitaker, *The Western Hemisphere Idea: Its Rise and Decline;* B. M. Williams, *Economic Foreign Policy of the United States;* W. A. Williams, *The Roots of the Modern American Empire* and *The Tragedy of American Diplomacy.*

2. *Rise of Imperialism and Manifest Destiny in the 'Nineties*

H. C. Allen, *Great Britain and the United States;* H. K. Beale, *Theodore Roosevelt and the Rise of America to World Power;* E. J. Carpenter, *America in Hawaii;* P. E. Corbett, *The Settlement of Canadian-American Disputes;* T. Dennett, *Americans in Eastern Asia;* W. Livezey, *Mahan on Sea Power;* F. Merk, *Manifest Destiny and Mission in American History;* A. Nevins, *Henry White;* G. O'Gara, *Theodore Roosevelt and the Rise of the Modern Navy;* E. S. Pomeroy, *Pacific Outpost: American Strategy in Guam;* W. D. Puleston, *Admiral Mahan;* G. H. Ryden, *The Foreign Policy of the United States in Relation to Samoa;* H. & M. Sprout, *The Rise of American Naval Power;* S. K. Stevens, *American Expansion in Hawaii 1842–1898;* R. West, *Admirals of American Empire.*

3. *The Spanish War*

F. R. Chadwick, *Relations of the United States and Spain: The War* (2 vols.); F. Freidel, *The Splendid Little*

War; W. Millis, *The Martial Spirit;* B. A. Reuter, *Anglo-American Relations During the Spanish American War;* J. Wisan, *The Cuban Crisis as Reflected in the New York Press.*

4. *Imperialism and Anti-Imperialism*

R. Beisner, *Twelve Against Empire;* R. Cortissoz, *Life of Whitelaw Reid* (2 vols.); M. Curti, *Bryan and World Peace;* T. Dennett, *John Hay;* E. Ellis, *Henry Teller;* M. Leech, *In the Days of McKinley;* E. R. May, *Imperial Democracy* and *American Imperialism;* A. S. Pier, *American Apostles to the Philippines;* J. Pratt, *Expansionists of 1898.*

5. *The Open Door*

M. J. Bau, *Open Door Doctrine in Relation to China;* J. M. Callahan, *American Relations in the Pacific and in the Far East;* C. Campbell, Jr., *Special Business Interests and the Open Door Policy;* H. Chung, *The Oriental Policy of the United States;* P. H. Clements, *The Boxer Rebellion;* T. Dennett, *Americans in Eastern Asia* and *John Hay;* A. L. P. Dennis, *Adventures in American Diplomacy;* J. W. Pratt, *America's Colonial Experiment;* P. A. Varg, *Open Door Diplomat—The Life of William W. Rockhill* and *Missionaries, Chinese, and Diplomats;* M. Young, *The Rhetoric of Empire.*

6. *Foreign Affairs in the Progressive Era*

T. A. Bailey, *Theodore Roosevelt and the Japanese-American Crisis;* H. K. Beale, *Theodore Roosevelt and the Rise of America to World Power;* C. S. Campbell, *Anglo-American Understanding 1898–1903;* T. Dennett, *John Hay, Roosevelt and the Russo-Japanese War,* and *Americans in Eastern Asia;* L. E. Ellis, *Reciprocity, 1911;* R. Esthus, *Theodore Roosevelt and Japan;* L. M. Gelber, *The Rise of Anglo-American Friendship;* A. W. Griswold, *The Far Eastern Policy of the United States;* D. Miner, *The Fight for the Panama Route;* C. Vevier, *The United States and China 1906–1913.*

CHAPTER 27

1. *General*

D. Aaron, *Men of Good Hope;* J. D. Buenker, *Urban Liberalism and Progressive Reform;* J. R. Chamberlain, *Farewell to Reform;* L. A. Cremin, *The Transformation of the School;* R. Daniels, *The Politics of Prejudice;* C. M. Destler, *American Radicalism 1865–1901;* J. Dorfman, *Economic Mind in American Civilization,* vol. 3, and *Thorstein Veblen and His America;* R. Ginger, *Age of Excess;* S. Haber, *Efficiency and Uplift;* S. Hays, *The Response to Industrialism 1885–1914;* R. Hofstadter, *The Age of Reform* and *The Progressive Historians;* G. Kolko, *The Triumph of Conservatism* and *Railroads and Regulation, 1877–1916;* C. Lasch, *The New Radicalism in America;* A. Mann, *Yankee Reformers in the Urban Age;* E. E. Morison, *Turmoil and Tradition* (Stimson); D. W. Noble, *The Paradox of Progressive Thought;* R. B. Nye, *Midwestern Progressive Politics;* R. Wiebe, *Businessmen and Reform;* R. Wilson, *In Quest of Community;* C. V. Woodward, *Origins of the New South, 1877–1913.*

2. *Political Reform and Era of the Muckrakers*

R. M. Abrams, *Conservatism in a Progressive Era;* C. Barker, *Henry George;* W. E. Bean, *Boss Reuf's San Francisco;* H. F. Bedford, *Socialism and the Workers in Massachusetts;* C. Bowers, *Beveridge and the Progressive Era;* J. Braeman, *Albert J. Beveridge;* D. M. Chalmers, *The Social and Political Ideas of the Muckrakers;* D. D. Egbert & S. Persons (eds.), *Socialism and American Life* (2 vols.); E. Ellis, *Mr. Dooley's America;* L. Filler, *Crusaders for American Liberalism;* E. A. Fitzpatrick, *McCarthy of Wisconsin;* D. Grantham, *Hoke Smith and the Politics of the New South;* F. E. Haynes, *Third Party Movements in the United States;* F. C. Howe, *Confessions of a Reformer;* I. Kipnis, *The American Socialist Movement 1897–1912;* A. D. Kirwan, *The Revolt of the Rednecks;* A. S. Kraditor, *The Ideas of the Woman Suffrage Movement, 1890–1920;* B. C. and F. La Follette, *Robert M. La Follette* (2 vols.); E. R. Lewinson, *John Purroy Mitchel;* P. Lyon, *Success Story* (McClure); R. S. Maxwell, *La Follette and the Rise of Progressives in Wisconsin;* G. E. Mowry, *The California Progressives* and *The Era of Theodore Roosevelt;* R. E. Noble, *New Jersey Progressivism before Wilson;* C. W. Patton, *The Fight for Municipal Reform;* H. Quint, *The Forging of American Socialism;* C. C. Regier, *The Era of the Muckrakers;* D. A. Shannon, *The Socialist Party of America;* L. Steffens, *Autobiography;* H. L. Warner, *Progressivism in Ohio;* A. & L. Weinberg (eds.), *The Muckrakers: An Anthology;* Brand Whitlock, *Forty Years of It.*

3. *Humanitarian Reform*

G. Adams, Jr., *Age of Industrial Violence;* J. Addams, *Forty Years at Hull House;* R. H. Bremner, *From the Depths;* A. F. Davis, *Spearheads for Reform;* J. C. Farrell, *Beloved Lady* (Jane Addams); G. P. Geiger, *Philosophy of Henry George;* J. R. Gusfield, *Symbolic Crusade;* R. M. Lubove, *The Progressives and the Slums* and *The Struggle for Social Security, 1900–1935;* A. E. Morgan, *Edward Bellamy;* W. L. O'Neill, *Divorce in the Progressive Era;* J. Riis, *The Battle with the Slum* and *How the Other Half Lives;* L. Wade, *Graham Taylor;* L. Wald, *The House on Henry Street* and *Windows on Henry Street;* S. B. Wood, *Constitutional Politics in the Progressive Era.*

4. *The Struggle for Negro Rights*

W. J. Cash, *The Mind of the South;* L. Dinnerstein, *The Leo Frank Case;* W. E. B. DuBois, *Dusk of Dawn, The Philadelphia Negro, Color and Democracy,* and *The Souls of Black Folk;* J. H. Franklin, *From Slavery to Freedom;* T. F. Gossett, *Race: The History of an Idea in America;* L. Harlan, *Booker T. Washington;* A. Locke, *The New Negro;* A. Meier, *Negro Thought in America;* A. Meier & E. M. Rudwick, *From Plantation to Ghetto;* S. Redding, *The Lonesome Road;* S. M. Scheiner, *Negro Mecca: A History of the Negro in New York City, 1865–1920;* A. H. Spear, *Black Chicago: The Making of a Negro Ghetto, 1890–1920;* C. V. Woodward, *Strange Career of Jim Crow.*

5. *The Progressive Era*

J. Blum, *The Republican Roosevelt;* C. Bowers, *Beveridge and the Progressive Movement;* H. U. Faulkner, *The Decline of Laissez Faire;* J. S. Garraty, *Henry Cabot Lodge* and *Right-Hand Man* (George W. Perkins); E. Goldman, *Rendezvous with Destiny;* W. H. Harbaugh, *Power and Responsibility* (Roosevelt); J. Holt, *Congressional Insurgents and the Party System, 1907–1916;* P. Jessup, *Elihu Root* (2 vols.); W. Johnson, *William Allen White's America;* R. M. Lowitt, *George Norris;* M. N. McGeary, *Gifford Pinchot;* G. E. Mowry, *The Era of Theodore Roosevelt* and *Theodore Roosevelt and the Progressive Movement;* H. F. Pringle, *Theodore Roosevelt* and *Life and Times of William Howard Taft* (2 vols.); N. W. Stephenson, *Nelson W. Aldrich.*

6. *The Extension of Government Regulation*

S. Fine, *Laissez Faire and the General-Welfare State;* S. P. Hays, *Conservation and the Gospel of Efficiency 1890–1920;* A. Martin, *Enterprise Denied;* A. T. Mason, *Bureaucracy Convicts Itself: The Ballinger-Pinchot Controversy;* J. Penick, Jr., *Progressive Politics and Conservation;* E. R. Richardson, *The Politics of Conservation;* H. B. Thorelli, *The Federal Anti-Trust Policy.*

7. *Woodrow Wilson*

R. S. Baker, *Woodrow Wilson: Life and Letters* (8 vols.); H. C. Bell, *Woodrow Wilson and the People;* J. M. Blum, *Woodrow Wilson and the Politics of Morality* and *Joe Tumulty and the Wilson Era;* W. Diamond, *Economic Thought of Woodrow Wilson;* C. Forcey, *The Crossroads of Liberalism;* J. A. Garraty, *Woodrow Wilson;* A. Link, *Woodrow Wilson* (5 vols.) and *Woodrow Wilson and the Progressive Era;* A. T. Mason, *Brandeis;* F. L. Paxson, *The Pre-War Years;* M. J. Pusey, *Charles Evans Hughes;* C. Seymour (ed.), *The Intimate Papers of Colonel House* (4 vols.); A. L. Todd, *Justice on Trial: The Case of Louis D. Brandeis;* M. I. Urofsky, *A Mind of One Piece* (Brandeis) and *Big Steel and the Wilson Administration;* O. G. Villard, *Fighting Years;* A. Walworth, *Woodrow Wilson* (2 vols.).

CHAPTER 28

1. *General*

A. Arnett, *Claude Kitchin and the Wilson War Policies;* R. S. Baker, *Woodrow Wilson: Life and Letters,* vols. 5 and 6; R. S. Baker & W. E. Dodd (eds.), *The Public Papers of Woodrow Wilson* (6 vols.); E. H. Buehrig, *Woodrow Wilson and the Balance of Power;* H. F. Cline, *The United States and Mexico;* J. Cooper, *The Vanity of Power;* C. H. Cramer, *Newton D. Baker;* R. W. Curry, *Woodrow Wilson's Far Eastern Policy;* M. Curti, *Bryan and World Peace;* B. J. Hendrick, *Life and Letters of Walter Hines Page* (3 vols.); T. Iyenage & K. Sato, *Japan and the California Problem;* A. S. Link, *Wilson the Diplomatist* and *Wilson* (5 vols.); V. S. Mamatey, *The United States and East Central Europe, 1914–1918;* E. R. May, *The World War and American Isolation, 1914–1917;* A. J. Mayer, *Political Origins of the New Diplomacy, 1917–1918;* A. Nevins (ed.), *The Letters and Journals of Brand Whitlock* (2 vols.); H. Notter, *Origins of the Foreign Policy of Woodrow Wilson;* R. E. Osgood, *Ideals and Self-Interest in America's Foreign Relations;* F. L. Paxson, *American Democracy and the World War,* vol. 1; R. Quirk, *An Affair of Honor;* C. Seymour, *American Neutrality, 1914–1917* and *American Diplomacy During the World War.*

2. *Struggle for Neutral Rights*

T. A. Bailey, *The Policy of the United States Towards Neutrals;* K. E. Birnbaum, *Peace Moves and U-Boat Warfare;* E. M. Borchard & W. P. Lage, *Neutrality for the United States;* D. M. Smith, *Robert Lansing and American Neutrality* and *The Great Departure;* C. Tansill, *America Goes to War;* B. Tuchman, *The Zimmermann Telegram.*

3. *Propaganda*

T. A. Bailey, *The Man in the Street: Impact of American Public Opinion on American Foreign Policy;* C. J. Child, *The German-American in Politics 1914–1917;* L. Gelber, *Rise of Anglo-American Friendship;* H. C. Peterson, *Propaganda for War;* A. Rappaport, *British Press and Wilsonian Neutrality;* C. E. Scheiber, *Transformation of American Sentiment Toward Germany 1898–1914.*

4. *Mobilization*

D. R. Beaver, *Newton D. Baker and the American War Effort;* G. B. Clarkson, *Industrial America at War;* B. Crowell & R. F. Wilson, *How America Went to War* (6 vols.); R. Cuff, *The War Industries Board;* S. W. Livermore, *Politics Is Adjourned;* F. L. Paxson, *American Democracy and the World War,* vols. 1 and 2; P. W. Slosson, *The Great Crusade and After;* H. Stein, *Government Price Policy During the World War;* G. S. Watkins, *Labor Problems and Labor Administration During World War* (2 vols.); W. F. Willoughby, *Government Organization in War Times and After.*

5. *Public Opinion and Civil Liberties*

Z. Chafee, *Free Speech in the United States;* D. Johnson, *The Challenge to American Freedoms;* J. R. Mock & C. Larson, *Words that Won the War;* H. C. Peterson & G. C. Fite, *Opponents of War, 1917–1918;* H. Scheiber, *The Wilson Administration and Civil Liberties.*

6. *Military and Naval History*

T. G. Frothingham, *Naval History of the World War* (3 vols.) and *American Re-enforcement in the World War;* L. Guichard, *The Naval Blockade 1914–1918;* E. Morison, *Admiral Sims and the Modern American Navy;* F. Palmer, *America in France* and *Bliss: Peacemaker;* D. Trask, *The United States in the Supreme War Council.*

7. *Intervention in Russia*

T. A. Bailey, *America Faces Russia;* W. S. Graves, *America's Siberian Adventure 1918–1920;* G. Kennan, *Russia Leaves the War* and *The Decision to Intervene;* C. Lasch, *The American Liberals and the Russian Revolution;* B. M. Unterberger, *America's Siberian Expedition 1918–1920;* W. A. Williams, *American-Russian Relations 1781–1947.*

8. *The Treaty, the League, and the Peace*

T. Bailey, *Woodrow Wilson and the Lost Peace* and *Woodrow Wilson and the Great Betrayal;* R. S. Baker, *Woodrow Wilson and World Settlement* (3 vols.) and *What Wilson Did at Paris;* P. Birdsall, *Versailles Twenty Years After;* A. Cranston, *The Killing of the Peace;* D. F. Fleming, *The United States and the League of Nations* and *The United States and the World Court;* J. Garraty, *Henry Cabot Lodge;* L. E. Gelfand, *The Inquiry;* W. S. Holt, *Treaties Defeated by the Senate;* J. M. Keynes, *Economic Consequences of the Peace;* N. Levin, *Woodrow Wilson and World Politics;* E. Mantoux, *The Carthaginian Peace;* D. H. Miller, *The Drafting of the Covenant* (2 vols.); H. Nicolson, *Peace Making, 1919;* K. F. Nowak, *Versailles;* H. R. Rudin, *Armistice, 1918;* G. Smith, *When the Cheering Stopped;* R. Stone, *The Irreconcilables;* H. W. V. Temperley *et al., History of the Peace Conference* (6 vols.); S. P. Tillman, *Anglo-American Relations at the Paris Peace Conference of 1919.*

CHAPTERS 29–30

1. *General*

F. L. Allen, *Only Yesterday;* J. Braeman *et al.* (eds.), *Change and Continuity in Twentieth-Century America: The 1920's;* P. Carter, *The Twenties in America;* R. Crunden, *From Self to Society, 1919–1941;* J. D. Hicks, *The Republican Ascendancy;* G. H. Knoles, *The Jazz Age Revisited;* I. Leighton (ed.), *The Aspirin Age;* W. E. Leuchtenburg, *The Perils of Prosperity, 1914 32;* G. Ostrander, *American Civilization in the First Machine Age: 1890–1940;* J. Prothro, *Dollar Decade;* G. Tindall, *The Emergence of the New South, 1913–1945.*

2. *Politics*

J. Allswang, *A House for All Peoples;* W. Bagby, *The Road to Normalcy;* J. L. Bates, *The Origins of Teapot Dome;* D. Burner, *The Politics of Provincialism;* C.

Chambers, *Seedtime of Reform;* P. Coletta, *William Jennings Bryan;* O. Handlin, *Al Smith and His America;* W. Harbaugh, *Lawyer's Lawyer;* J. J. Huthmacher, *Massachusetts People and Politics, 1919–1933;* I. Katznelson, *Black Men, White Cities;* M. Keller, *In Defense of Yesterday;* B. C. & F. La Follette, *Robert M. La Follette* (2 vols.); L. Levine, *Defender of the Faith* (Bryan); R. Lowitt, *George W. Norris;* K. MacKay, *The Progressive Movement;* D. R. McCoy, *Calvin Coolidge;* A. T. Mason, *William Howard Taft: Chief Justice, The Supreme Court from Taft to Warren,* and *Harlan Fiske Stone;* E. Moore, *A Catholic Runs for President;* R. Murphy, *The Constitution in Crisis Times, 1918–1969;* R. Murray, *The Harding Era* and *The Politics of Normalcy;* B. Noggle, *Teapot Dome;* H. Quint & R. Ferrell, *The Talkative President;* F. Russell, *The Shadow of Blooming Grove;* E. E. Schattschneider, *Politics, Pressures and the Tariff;* A. Sinclair, *The Available Man;* W. A. White, *Puritan in Babylon;* H. Zinn, *La Guardia in Congress.*

3. *Intolerance and Civil Liberties*

J. W. Caughey, *In Clear and Present Danger;* Z. Chafee, *Free Speech in the United States;* S. Coben, *A. Mitchell Palmer;* H. S. Commager, *Freedom, Loyalty, and Dissent;* R. Cushman, *Civil Liberties in the United States;* T. Draper, *The Roots of American Communism;* R. L. Friedheim, *The Seattle General Strike;* E. M. Morgan & G. L. Joughin, *The Legacy of Sacco and Vanzetti;* P. Murphy, *The Meaning of Freedom of Speech;* R. Murray, *Red Scare;* W. Preston, *Aliens and Dissenters;* E. M. Rudwick, *Race Riot at East St. Louis;* F. Russell, *Tragedy in Dedham;* D. Shannon, *The Socialist Party of America.*

4. *Political Fundamentalism*

C. C. Alexander, *The Ku Klux Klan in the Southwest;* D. M. Chalmers, *Hooded Americanism;* V. Dabney, *Dry Messiah;* N. Furniss, *The Fundamentalist Controversy, 1918–1931;* W. B. Gatewood, Jr., *Preachers, Pedagogues, & Politicians;* R. Ginger, *Six Days or Forever?;* K. T. Jackson, *The Ku Klux Klan in the City;* D. Kirschner, *City and Country;* J. M. Mecklin, *The Ku Klux Klan;* R. Miller, *American Protestantism and Social Issues, 1919–1939;* A. Sinclair, *Prohibition: The Era of Excess;* J. Timberlake, *Prohibition and the Progressive Movement, 1900–1920;* J. Weinstein, *The Decline of Socialism in America, 1912–1925.*

5. *Foreign Affairs*

S. F. Bemis, *The Latin American Policy of the United States;* D. Borg, *American Policy and the Chinese Revolution 1925–1928;* H. Cline, *The United States and Mexico;* R. Current, *Secretary Stimson;* A. De Conde, *Herbert Hoover's Latin American Policy;* L. Ellis, *Republican Foreign Policy, 1921–1933;* J. K. Fairbank, *The United States and China;* H. Feis, *Diplomacy of the Dollar 1919–1932;* R. H. Ferrell, *Peace in Their Time;* D. F. Fleming, *United States and World Organization 1920–1933;* B. Glad, *Charles Evans Hughes and the Illusions of Innocence;* A. W. Griswold, *The Far Eastern Policy of the United States;* H. Nicolson, *Dwight Morrow;* R. W. Paul, *The Abrogation of the Gentlemen's Agreement;* D. Perkins, *The United States and the Caribbean* and *Hands Off! A History of the Monroe Doctrine;* M. Pusey, *Charles Evans Hughes* (2 vols.); E. O. Reischauer, *The United States and Japan:* S. Smith, *The Manchurian Crisis 1931–32;* H. L. Stimson & M. Bundy, *On Active Service in Peace and War;* J. Tulchin, *The Aftermath of War;* J. C. Vinson, *The Parchment Peace;* B. H. Williams, *Economic Foreign Policies of the United States;* J. Wilson, *American Business and Foreign Policy, 1920–1933.*

6. *The Economy*

A. A. Berle & G. C. Means, *Modern Corporation and Private Property;* A. R. Burns, *The Decline of Competition;* C. Chapman, *Development of American Business and Banking Thought;* J. K. Galbraith, *American Capitalism* and *The Great Crash;* S. Giedion, *Mechanization Takes Command;* M. Heald, *The Social Responsibilities of Business;* H. Jerome, *Mechanization in Industry;* S. Kuznets, *The National Income and Its Composition 1919–1938;* H. W. Laidler, *Concentration of Control in American Industry;* W. W. Leontief, *The Structure of American Economy 1919–1929;* A. Nevins & F. E. Hill, *Ford: Expansion and Challenge 1915–1933;* G. W. Nutter, *Extent of Enterprise Monopoly 1899–1931;* O. Pease, *The Responsibilities of American Advertising;* The President's Committee, *Recent Economic Changes in the United States* (2 vols.); R. Sobel, *The Big Board* and *The Great Bull Market;* G. Soule, *Prosperity Decade;* E. R. Wicker, *Federal Reserve Monetary Policy, 1917–1933;* R. Wik, *Henry Ford and Grass-roots America;* T. Wilson, *Fluctuations in Income and Employment.*

7. *Labor and Agriculture*

H. Barger & H. Landsberg, *American Agriculture 1899–1939;* M. R. Benedict, *Farm Policies of the United States 1790–1950;* D. Brody, *Labor in Crisis: The Steel Strike of 1919;* J. R. Commons *et al., History of Labor,* vol. 4; J. D. Durand, *The Labor Force, 1890–*

1960; G. Fite, *George Peek and the Fight for Farm Parity;* T. Saloutos & J. D. Hicks, *Agricultural Discontent in the Middle West;* P. Taft, *The A.F. of L. in the Time of Gompers;* J. Weinstein, *The Decline of Socialism in America, 1912–1925.*

8. *Social Developments*

J. Burnham, *Psychoanalysis and American Medicine: 1894–1918;* W. Chafe, *The American Woman;* N. Hale, *Freud and the Americans;* D. Kennedy, *Birth Control in America;* J. Lemons, *The Woman Citizen;* R. and H. Lynd, *Middletown;* W. F. Ogburn (ed.), *Recent Social Changes in the United States;* W. O'Neill, *Everyone Was Brave;* G. Osofsky, *Harlem.*

9. *Literature*

C. Baker, *Hemingway;* V. W. Brooks, *The Confident Years;* H. M. Campbell & R. E. Foster, *William Faulkner;* O. Cargill, *Intellectual America;* R. Chase, *The American Novel and Its Tradition;* M. Cowley, *After the Genteel Tradition* and *Exile's Return;* B. Duffey, *Chicago Renaissance in American Letters;* C. A. Fenton, *The Apprenticeship of Ernest Hemingway;* L. Fiedler, *Life and Death in the American Novel;* M. Geismar, *Rebels and Ancestors, The Last of the Provincials,* and *Writers in Crisis;* R. Gilbert, *Shine, Perishing Republic: Robinson Jeffers;* D. Heiney, *Recent American Literature;* F. J. Hoffman, *Freudianism and the Literary Mind* and *The Twenties;* I. Howe, *William Faulkner;* N. Huggins, *Harlem Renaissance;* R. Jarrell, *Poetry and the Age;* M. Josephson, *Portrait of the Artist as an American;* A. Kazin, *On Native Grounds;* W. Manchester, *Disturber of the Peace: H. L. Mencken;* F. O. Matthiessen, *The Achievement of T. S. Eliot;* H. F. May, *The End of American Innocence;* A. Mizener, *The Far Side of Paradise* (Fitzgerald); H. J. Muller, *Thomas Wolfe;* E. Neff, *Edwin Arlington Robinson;* W. V. O'Connor, *The Tangled Fire of William Faulkner;* S. Persons, *American Minds;* L. C. Powell, *Robinson Jeffers;* M. Schorer, *Sinclair Lewis;* R. Sklar, *F. Scott Fitzgerald;* R. E. Spiller *et al., Literary History of the United States,* vol. 2; E. Wilson, *The Shores of Light.*

10. *Art, Painting, and Music*

J. Baur, *Revolution and Tradition in American Art;* M. Brown, *American Paintings from the Armory Show to the Depression;* E. Cary, *George Luks;* M. Cheney, *Modern Art in America;* I. Glackens, *William Glackens and the Ashcan Group;* S. Hunter, *Modern American Painting and Sculpture;* S. Janis, *Abstract and Surrealist Art in America;* S. Kootz, *Modern American Painters;* N. Leonard, *Jazz and the White Americans;* C. Rourke, *Charles Sheeler;* J. T. Soby, *Contemporary Painters.*

CHAPTER 31

1. *General*

I. Berstein, *The Lean Years;* J. Braeman *et al.* (eds.), *Change and Continuity in Twentieth-Century America* and *The New Deal;* P. Conkin, *The New Deal;* W. Droze *et al., Essays on the New Deal;* M. Einandi, *The Roosevelt Revolution;* M. J. Frish & M. Diamond (eds.), *The Thirties;* O. L. Graham, Jr., *An Encore for Reform;* C. Kindleberger, *World in Depression, 1929–1939;* W. E. Leuchtenburg, *The Perils of Prosperity, 1914–32* and *Franklin D. Roosevelt and the New Deal, 1932–1940;* B. Mitchell, *Depression Decade, 1929–1941;* R. Moley, *After Seven Years;* R. H. Pells, *Radical Visions and American Dreams;* A. M. Schlesinger, Jr., *The Age of Roosevelt,* vol. 1: *The Crisis of the Old Order,* vol. 2: *The Coming of the New Deal,* and vol. 3: *The Politics of Upheaval;* R. J. Simon (ed.), *As We Saw the Thirties;* G. Tindall, *The Emergence of the New South, 1913–1945;* D. Wecter, *The Age of the Great Depression, 1929–1941.*

2. *The Hoover Administration*

W. S. Myers & W. H. Newton, *The Hoover Administration;* A. U. Romasco, *The Poverty of Abundance;* J. Schwarz, *The Interregnum of Despair;* R. L. Wilbur & A. M. Hyde, *The Hoover Policies.*

3. *Roosevelt and His Circle*

B. Bellush, *Franklin D. Roosevelt as Governor of New York;* J. M. Blum, *From the Morgenthau Diaries: Years of Crisis, 1928–1938;* J. M. Burns, *Roosevelt: The Lion and the Fox;* F. Freidel, *Franklin D. Roosevelt* (4 vols.) and *F.D.R. and the South;* D. R. Fusfeld, *The Economic Thought of Franklin D. Roosevelt and the Origins of the New Deal;* T. Greer, *What Roosevelt Thought;* T. K. Hareven, *Eleanor Roosevelt;* H. Ickes, *The Secret Diary of Harold L. Ickes* (3 vols.); J. Lash, *Eleanor and Franklin;* F. Perkins, *The Roosevelt I Knew;* A. Rollins, Jr., *Roosevelt and Howe;* E. Roosevelt, *This Is My Story* and *This I Remember;* S. Rosenman, *Working with Roosevelt;* R. Sherwood, *Roosevelt and Hopkins;* R. Tugwell, *The Brains Trust* and *The Democratic Roosevelt.*

4. *Politics and Elections*

E. C. Blackorby, *Prairie Rebel* (Lemke); F. Broderick, *Right Reverend New Dealer: John A. Ryan*; R. Burke, *Olson's New Deal for California*; J. Farley, *Jim Farley's Story*; G. Q. Flynn, *American Catholics and the Roosevelt Presidency*; J. J. Huthmacher, *Senator Robert F. Wagner and the Rise of Urban Liberalism*; R. Ingalls, *Herbert H. Lehman and New York's Little New Deal*; F. Israel, *Nevada's Key Pittman*; D. B. Johnson, *The Republican Party and Wendell Willkie*; B. Karl, *Executive Reorganization & Reform in the New Deal*; D. R. McCoy, *Angry Voices* and *Landon of Kansas*; G. Mayer, *The Political Career of Floyd B. Olson*; Rev. A. Ogden, *The Dies Committee*; J. T. Patterson, *Congressional Conservatism and the New Deal* and *The New Deal and the States*; R. Polenberg, *Reorganizing Roosevelt's Government*; B. Stave, *The New Deal and the Last Hurrah*; C. J. Tull, *Father Coughlin and the New Deal*; F. A. Warren, *Liberals and Communism*; T. H. Williams, *Huey Long*; G. Wolfskill, *Revolt of the Conservatives*.

5. *Industry and Finance*

A. W. Crawford, *Monetary Management under the New Deal*; R. de Bedts, *The New Deal's SEC*; J. K. Galbraith & G. C. Johnson, *Economic Effects of Federal Works Expenditures, 1933–1938*; E. W. Hawley, *The New Deal and the Problem of Monopoly*; G. G. Johnson, *The Treasury and Monetary Policy 1933–1938*; H. Johnson, *The Blue Eagle, from Egg to Earth*; S. Kennedy, *The Banking Crisis of 1933*; D. Lynch, *The Concentration of Economic Power*; L. S. Lyon *et al.*, *The National Recovery Administration*; J. R. Reeve, *Monetary Reform Movements*; K. D. Roose, *Economics of Recession and Revival*.

6. *Agriculture*

M. R. Benedict, *Farm Policies of the United States*; G. Fite, *George N. Peek and the Fight for Farm Parity*; R. S. Kirkendall, *Social Scientists and Farm Politics in the Age of Roosevelt*; E. G. Nourse *et al.*, *Three Years of the AAA*; J. Shover, *Cornbelt Rebellion*.

7. *Relief, Social Security, and Labor*

A. J. Altmeyer, *The Formative Years of Social Security*; J. Auerbach, *Labor and Liberty*; I. Bernstein, *The New Deal Collective Bargaining Policy* and *Turbulent Years*; J. C. Brown, *Public Relief*; P. Conkin, *Tomorrow a New World*; D. E. Conrad, *The Forgotten Farmers*; M. Derber & E. Young (eds.), *Labor and the New Deal*; S. Fine, *The Automobile Under the Blue Eagle* and *Sit-Down*; W. Galenson, *The C.I.O. Challenge to the A.F. of L.*; H. Harris, *American Labor*; A. Holtzman, *The Townsend Movement*; D. S. Howard, *The WPA and Federal Relief Policy*; R. Lubove, *The Struggle for Social security*; R. & H. Lynd, *Middletown in Transition*; J. Mathews, *The Federal Theatre, 1935–1939*; J. A. Salmond, *The Civilian Conservation Corps*; E. E. Witte, *The Development of the Social Security Act*.

8. *The TVA and Conservation*

W. H. Droze, *High Dams and Slack Waters*; W. E. Leuchtenburg, *Flood Control Politics*; D. E. Lilienthal, *The TVA: Democracy on the March* and *Journals: The TVA Years*; T. McCraw, *TVA and the Power Fight, 1933–1939*; C. H. Pritchett, *The Tennessee Valley Authority*; P. Selznick, *TVA and the Grass Roots*.

9. *Supreme Court*

L. Baker, *Back to Back*; D. Carter, *Scottsboro*; H. S. Commager, *Majority Rule and Minority Rights*; R. Cortner, *The Wagner Act Cases*; E. S. Corwin, *The Twilight of the Supreme Court*, *Court Over Constitution*, *The Commerce Power vs. State Rights*, and *Constitutional Revolution, Ltd.*; J. P. Frank, *Mr. Justice Black*; E. C. Gerhart, *America's Advocate: Robert H. Jackson*; S. Hendel, *Charles Evans Hughes and the Supreme Court*; R. Jackson, *Struggle for Judicial Supremacy*; S. Konefsky, *The Legacy of Holmes and Brandeis*, *Justice Stone and the Supreme Court*, and *The Constitutional World of Mr. Justice Frankfurter*; A. T. Mason, *Harlan Fiske Stone*; A. T. Mason & W. M. Beaney, *The Supreme Court in a Free Society*; J. Paschal, *Mr. Justice Sutherland*; C. H. Pritchett, *The Roosevelt Court*; M. J. Pusey, *Charles Evans Hughes* (2 vols.); B. Schwartz, *The Supreme Court: Constitutional Revolution in Retrospect*.

10. *Documents*

D. Congdon (ed.), *The '30s*; L. Filler (ed.), *The Anxious Years*; M. Keller (ed.), *The New Deal*; W. E. Leuchtenburg (ed.), *The New Deal* and *Franklin D. Roosevelt*; E. Nixon (ed.), *Franklin D. Roosevelt and Conservation* (2 vols.); F. D. Roosevelt & S. Rosenman (eds.), *The Public Papers and Addresses of Franklin D. Roosevelt* (13 vols.); J. Salzman & B. Wallenstein (eds.), *Years of Protest*; D. Shannon (ed.), *The Great Depression*; B. Sternsher (ed.), *The New Deal*; H. Swados (ed.), *The American Writer and the Great Depression*.

CHAPTERS 32–33

1. *Roosevelt's Foreign Policy and the Coming of the War*

C. A. Beard, *American Foreign Policy in the Making, 1932–1940* and *President Roosevelt and the Coming of the War, 1941;* R. P. Browder, *The Origins of Soviet-American Diplomacy;* F. A. Cave *et al., Origins and Consequences of World War II;* M. Chadwin, *The Hawks of World War II;* W. S. Churchill, *The Second World War* (6 vols.); W. I. Cohen, *The American Revisionists;* W. S. Cole, *America First* and *Senator Gerald P. Nye and American Foreign Relations;* G. Craig & F. Gilbert (eds.), *The Diplomats, 1919–1939;* E. Cronon, *Josephus Daniels in Mexico;* R. N. Current, *Secretary Stimson;* R. Dallek, *Democrat & Diplomat;* R. A. Divine, *The Illusion of Neutrality;* D. Drummond, *The Passing of American Neutrality;* T. R. Fehrenbach, *F.D.R.'s Undeclared War;* H. Feis, *The Road to Pearl Harbor;* R. Ferrell, *The Diplomacy of the Great Depression;* L. Gardner, *Economic Aspects of New Deal Diplomacy;* E. D. Guerrant, *Roosevelt's Good Neighbor Policy;* W. H. Heinrichs, Jr., *American Ambassador* (Grew); C. Hull, *Memoirs* (2 vols.); M. Jonas, *Isolationism in America, 1935–1941;* T. Kase, *Journey to the Missouri;* W. L. Langer & S. E. Gleason, *The Challenge to Isolation 1937–1940* and *The Undeclared War 1940–1941;* E. E. Morison, *Turmoil and Tradition;* A. D. Morse, *While Six Million Died;* J. W. Pratt, *Cordell Hull* (2 vols.); B. Rauch, *Roosevelt from Munich to Pearl Harbor;* E. O. Reischauer, *The United States and Japan;* P. W. Schroeder, *The Axis Alliance and Japanese-American Relations;* C. C. Tansill, *Back Door To War;* F. J. Taylor, *The United States and the Spanish Civil War;* H. L. Trefousse, *Germany and American Neutrality;* M. S. Watson, *Chief-of-Staff: Prewar Plans and Preparations;* J. E. Wiltz, *In Search of Peace* and *From Isolation to War, 1931–1941;* R. Wohlstetter, *Pearl Harbor: Warning and Decision;* B. Wood, *The Making of the Good Neighbor Policy.*

2. *General*

J. P. Baxter, 3rd, *Scientists Against Time;* A. R. Buchanan, *The United States in World War II* (2 vols.); Bureau of the Budget, *The U.S. at War;* V. J. Esposito (ed.), *A Concise History of World War II;* J. F. C. Fuller, *The Second World War, 1939–45;* K. R. Greenfield, *World War II Strategy Reconsidered* and (ed.), *Command Decisions;* R. Hewlett & O. Anderson, *The New World;* J. A. Isely & P. A. Crowl, *The U.S. Marines and Amphibious War;* G. H. Johnston, *The Toughest Fighting in the World;* L. Lansing, *Day of Trinity;* W. Millis (ed.), *The War Reports of General George C. Marshall, General H. H. Arnold, and Admiral E. J. King;* S. E. Morison, *Strategy and Compromise* and *The Two Ocean War;* T. Roscoe, *U.S. Submarine Operations, World War II.*

3. *Biographies and Memoirs*

H. H. Arnold, *Global Mission;* General Omar Bradley, *A Soldier's Story;* A. Bryant, *The Turn of the Tide* and *Triumph in the West* (2 vols.); R. L. Eichelberger, *Our Jungle Road to Tokyo;* D. D. Eisenhower, *Crusade in Europe;* W. F. Halsey & J. Bryan, 3rd, *Admiral Halsey's Story;* E. J. King & W. Whitehill, *Fleet Admiral King;* S.L.A. Marshall, *Blitzkrieg, Bastogne, Island Victory,* and *Night Drop* (Normandy); Viscount Montgomery of Alamein, *The Memoirs;* R. Payne, *The Marshall Story;* F. Pogue, *George C. Marshall;* T. White (ed.), *The Stilwell Papers.*

4. *Comprehensive Multi-Volume Histories*

U.S. ARMY. K. R. Greenfield *et al.* (eds.), *The U.S. Army in World War II* and *The American Forces in Action;* W. F. Craven & J. L. Cate (eds.), *The Army Air Forces in World War II.* U.S. MARINE CORPS. *History of U.S. Marine Corps Operations in World War II; Marine Corps Monographs.* U.S. NAVY AND COAST GUARD. J. A. Furer, *Administration of the Navy Dept. in World War II;* S. E. Morison, *History of United States Naval Operations in World War II;* M. F. Willoughby, *The United States Coast Guard in World War II.*

5. *Wartime Diplomacy*

J. M. Blum (ed.), *From the Morgenthau Diaries: Years of War, 1941–1945;* R. Butow, *Japan's Decision To Surrender;* R. A. Divine, *The Reluctant Belligerent;* H. Feis, *The China Tangle, Churchill-Roosevelt-Stalin, The Potsdam Conference,* and *Japan Subdued;* T. Higgins, *Winston Churchill and the Second Front;* G. Kolko, *The Politics of War;* W. L. Langer, *Our Vichy Gamble;* R. Murphy, *Diplomat Among Warriors;* W. L. Neumann, *Making the Peace, 1941–1945;* C. F. Romanus & R. Sunderland, *Stilwell's Mission to China;* G. Smith, *American Diplomacy during the Second World War;* J. L. Snell, *Illusion and Necessity* and (ed.), *The Meaning of Yalta.*

6. *Mobilization and American Society in Wartime*

A. A. Blum, *Drafted or Deferred;* B. Catton, *War Lords of Washington;* L. V. Chandler, *Inflation in the United States, 1940–1948;* M. Clinard, *The Black Market;* R. H. Connery, *Navy and Industrial Mobilization in World War II;* E. S. Corwin, *Total War and the Constitution;* J. Dos Passos, *State of the Union;* H. Garfinkel, *When Negroes March;* J. Goodman (ed.), *While You Were Gone;* M. Grodzins, *Americans Betrayed;* H. D. Hall, *North American Supply;* W. Hassett, *Off the Record with FDR 1942–1945;* E. Janeway, *The Struggle for Survival;* U. Lee, *The Employment of Negro Troops;* F. Merrill (ed.), *Social Problems on the Home Front;* D. Novik *et al., War-time Production Control;* W. F. Ogburn (ed.), *American Society in Wartime;* D. H. Riddle, *The Truman Committee;* J. Seidman, *American Labor from Defense to Reconversion;* H. M. Somers, *Presidential Agency: OWMR;* J. ten Broek *et al., Salvage: Japanese American Evacuation and Resettlement;* G. Tindall, *The Emergence of the New South, 1913–1945;* War Production Board, *Industrial Mobilization for War,* vol. 1; R. Young, *Congressional Politics in the Second World War.*

CHAPTERS 34–35

1. *General*

Congressional Quarterly, *Congress and Nation;* C. Degler, *Affluence and Anxiety;* M. Gelfand, *A Nation of Cities;* E. Goldman, *The Crucial Decade;* A. Hamby, *Beyond the New Deal;* W. Johnson, *1600 Pennsylvania Avenue;* W. Leuchtenburg, *A Troubled Feast;* B. McKelvey, *The Emergence of Metropolitan America;* L. Wittner, *Cold War America;* H. Zinn, *Postwar America, 1945–1971.*

2. *Foreign Affairs: General*

J. F. Byrnes, *Speaking Frankly;* W. G. Carleton, *Revolution in American Foreign Policy;* J. Davids, *America and the World in Our Time;* L. J. Halle, *The Cold War as History;* G. F. Kennan, *The Realities of American Foreign Policy;* J. Lukacs, *A History of the Cold War;* H. Morgenthau, *Dilemmas of Politics* and *Politics Among the Nations;* R. Osgood, *Limited War;* W. Reitzel *et al., United States Foreign Policy, 1945–1955;* W. W. Rostow, *The United States in the World Arena;* J. W. Spanier, *American Foreign Policy Since World War II;* R. P. Stebbins, *The United States in World Affairs* (annual volumes); H. B. Westerfield, *Foreign Policy and Party Politics: Pearl Harbor to Korea.*

3. *Liquidating the War*

R. Benedict, *The Chrysanthemum and the Sword;* V. H. Bernstein, *Final Judgment: The Story of Nuremberg;* W. Friedman, *Allied Military Government of Germany;* S. Glueck, *Nuremberg Trial and Aggressive War;* G. Herring, *Aid to Russia;* R. Jackson, *The Case Against the Nazi War Criminals;* E. H. Litchfield (ed.), *Governing Postwar Germany;* A. F. Reel, *The Case of General Yamashita;* E. Reischauer, *The United States and Japan;* D. Ross, *Preparing for Ulysses;* R. Woetzel, *Nuremberg Trials in International Law;* H. Zink, *American Military Government in Germany.*

4. *Organization for Peace and the Control of Atomic Weapons*

G. Alperovitz, *Atomic Diplomacy;* R. Batchelder, *The Irreversible Decision 1939–1950;* P. M. Blackett, *Fear, War and the Bomb;* D. Bradley, *No Place to Hide;* B. Brodie, *The Absolute Weapon;* H. Brown, *The Challenge of Man's Future;* D. Clemens, *Yalta;* N. Cousins, *Modern Man Is Obsolete;* R. A. Dahl & R. S. Brown, *The Domestic Control of Atomic Energy;* P. Gallois, *The Balance of Terror;* G. Gamow, *Atomic Energy in Cosmic and Human Life;* J. M. Gavin, *War and Peace in the Space Age;* R. Gilpin, *American Scientists and Nuclear Weapons Policy;* R. G. Hewlett & O. E. Anderson, Jr., *The New World;* H. Kahn, *On Thermonuclear War;* G. Kennan, *Russia, the Atom and the West;* H. Kissinger, *Nuclear Weapons and Foreign Policy;* R. Lapp, *Atoms and Peace;* P. McGuire, *Experiment in World Order;* J. Muther, *History of the United Nations Charter.*

5. *Relief and Recovery*

D. A. Baldwin, *Economic Development and American Foreign Policy;* W. A. Brown, *American Foreign Assistance;* M. Curti & K. Birr, *Prelude to Point Four: American Missions Overseas;* S. Harris, *European Recovery Program* and *Foreign Economic Policy for the United States;* J. M. Jones, *The Fifteen Weeks;* G. Woodbridge (ed.), *UNRRA* (2 vols.).

6. *The Cold War*

D. Acheson, *Present at the Creation;* C. Bohlen, *Witness to History;* E. H. Carr, *Soviet Impact on the West-*

ern World; W. P. Davison, *The Berlin Blockade;* R. Drummond & G. Coblenz, *Duel at the Brink;* H. Feis, *Between War and Peace, Contest over Japan, From Trust to Terror,* and *Potsdam;* H. Finer, *Dulles Over Suez;* D. L. Fleming, *The Cold War* (2 vols.); J. Gaddis, *The United States and the Origins of the Cold War, 1941–1947;* L. Gardner, *Architects of Illusion;* N. Graebner, *The New Isolationism;* M. F. Herz, *Beginnings of the Cold War;* T. Hoopes, *The Devil and John Foster Dulles;* B. H. Ivanyi & A. Bell, *The Road to Potsdam;* G. Kolko, *The Roots of American Foreign Policy;* W. H. McNeill, *America, Britain, and Russia;* R. E. Osgood, *NATO: The Entangling Alliance;* H. L. Roberts, *Russia and America;* A. A. Rogow, *James Forrestal;* G. Smith, *Dean Acheson;* E. Stillman & W. Pfaff, *The New Politics;* L. Wittner, *Rebels Against War.*

7. *The Korean War*

C. Berger, *The Korea Knot;* R. Caridi, *The Korean War and American Politics;* M. Clark, *From the Danube to the Yalu;* H. Feis, *The China Tangle;* L. M. Goodrich, *Korea;* T. Higgins, *Korea and the Fall of MacArthur;* R. T. Oliver, *Why War Came to Korea;* D. Rees, *Korea: The Limited War;* R. Rovere & A. M. Schlesinger, Jr., *The General and the President;* J. Spanier, *The Truman-MacArthur Controversy;* A. Whiting, *China Crosses the Yalu;* C. Whitney, *MacArthur;* C. A. Willoughby & J. Chamberlain, *MacArthur, 1944–1951.*

8. *Latin America*

R. Alexander, *Communism in Latin America;* D. M. Dozer, *Are We Good Neighbors?;* R. Schneider, *Communism in Guatemala;* A. P. Whitaker, *Argentine Upheaval* and *The United States and Latin America: The Northern Republics.*

9. *Politics*

S. G. Brown, *Conscience in Politics: Adlai Stevenson;* A. Campbell *et al., The American Voter;* P. David *et al., Presidential Nominating Politics in 1952;* K. S. Davis, *A Prophet in His Own Country;* H. Eulau, *Class and Party in the Eisenhower Years;* R. Garson, *The Democratic Party and the Politics of Sectionalism, 1941–1948;* V. O. Key, Jr., *Southern Politics in State and Nation;* S. Lubell, *The Revolt of the Moderates;* N. Markowitz, *The Rise and Fall of the People's Century;* H. J. Muller, *Adlai Stevenson;* J. Patterson, *Mr. Republican;* C. A. H. Thomson & F. M. Shattuck, *The 1956 Presidential Campaign;* D. B. Truman, *The Congressional Party.*

10. *Truman and the Fair Deal*

S. K. Bailey, *Congress Makes a Law;* E. R. Bartley, *The Tidelands Oil Controversy;* B. Bernstein (ed.), *Politics and Policies of the Truman Administration;* P. A. Brinker, *The Taft-Hartley Act After Ten Years;* J. G. Burrow, *AMA;* J. Daniels, *The Man of Independence;* R. Davies, *Housing Reform During the Truman Administration;* R. S. Kirkendall (ed.), *The Truman Period as a Research Field* and *The Truman Period as a Research Field: A Reappraisal;* R. A. Lee, *Truman and Taft-Hartley;* A. J. Matusow, *Farm Policies and Politics in the Truman Years;* H. A. Millis & E. C. Brown, *From the Wagner Act to Taft-Hartley;* C. Phillips, *The Truman Presidency;* H. S. Truman, *Memoirs* (2 vols.).

11. *Civil Liberties*

J. Anderson & R. May, *McCarthy;* A. Barth, *The Loyalty of Free Men;* D. Bell (ed.), *The New American Right;* E. Bontecou, *The Federal Loyalty-Security Program;* R. Brown, *Loyalty and Security;* R. K. Carr, *Federal Protection of Civil Rights, The House Committee on Un-American Activities,* and *To Secure These Rights;* J. W. Caughey, *In Clear and Present Danger;* W. Chambers, *Witness;* H. W. Chase, *Security and Liberty;* H. S. Commager, *Freedom, Loyalty, Dissent;* A. Cooke, *A Generation on Trial;* C. Curtis, *The Oppenheimer Case;* T. Draper, *The Roots of American Communism;* O. D. Fraenkel, *Supreme Court and Civil Liberties;* R. Freeland, *The Truman Doctrine and the Origins of McCarthyism;* W. Gellhorn, *Security, Loyalty, and Science, The States and Subversion,* and *American Rights;* R. Griffith, *The Politics of Fear;* M. Grodzins, *The Loyal and the Disloyal;* L. Hand, *The Spirit of Liberty;* A. Harper, *The Politics of Loyalty;* A. Hiss, *In the Court of Public Opinion;* S. Hook, *Heresy, Yes—Conspiracy, No;* D. J. Kemper, *The Decade of Fear;* M. Konvitz, *The Constitution and Civil Rights;* E. Latham, *The Communist Controversy in Washington;* R. P. Longacker, *The Presidency and Civil Liberties;* D. McCoy & R. Ruetten, *Quiet and Response;* C. H. Pritchett, *Civil Liberties and the Vinson Court;* M. P. Rogin, *The Intellectuals and McCarthy;* R. Rovere, *Senator Joe McCarthy;* D. Shannon, *The Decline of American Communism;* E. A. Shils, *The Torment of Secrecy;* S. A. Stouffer, *Communism, Conformity and Civil Liberties;* A. Theoharis, *Seeds of Repression;* J. A. Wechsler, *The Age of Suspicion.*

12. *The Eisenhower Government*

S. Adams, *First-Hand Report;* M. Childs, *Eisenhower: Captive Hero;* E. L. Dale, *Conservatives in Power;* R. J.

Donovan, *Eisenhower: The Inside Story;* E. J. Hughes, *The Ordeal of Power;* A. McAdams, *Power and Politics in Labor Legislation;* M. Merson, *The Private Diary of a Public Servant;* R. M. Nixon, *Six Crises;* H. Parmet, *Eisenhower and the American Crusades;* M. J. Pusey, *Eisenhower the President;* G. Reichard, *The Reaffirmation of Republicanism;* R. Rovere, *The Eisenhower Years: Affairs of State;* J. L. Sundquist, *Politics and Policy;* A. Wildavsky, *Dixon-Yates.*

13. *Civil Rights*

N. Bartley, *The Rise of Massive Resistance;* M. Berger, *Equality by Statute;* R. Dalfiume, *Desegregation of the Armed Forces;* B. Daniel (ed.), *Black, White and Gray;* R. Harris, *The Quest for Equality;* A. Lewis *et al., Portrait of a Decade;* D. R. Matthews & J. W. Prothro, *Negroes and the New Southern Politics;* A. Meier and E. Rudwick, *CORE;* C. Mitau, *Decade of Decision;* W. F. Murphy, *Congress and the Court;* B. Muse, *Ten Years of Prelude;* A. M. Rose, *The Negro in Postwar America;* R. H. Sayler *et al.* (eds.), *The Warren Court;* D. Shoemaker (ed.), *With All Deliberate Speed: Segregation-Desegregation;* J. W. Silver, *Mississippi: The Closed Society;* F. E. Smith, *Congressman from Mississippi;* B. M. Ziegler, *Desegregation and the Supreme Court;* H. Zinn, *SNCC: The New Abolitionists.*

14. *The Warfare State*

M. Berkowitz & P. G. Bock, *American National Security;* D. Caraley, *The Politics of Military Unification;* P. Hammond, *Organizing for Defense;* S. Huntington, *The Common Defense* and *The Soldier and the State;* W. R. Kintner *et al., Forging a New Sword;* E. A. Kolodziej, *The Uncommon Defense and Congress, 1945–1963;* E. R. May (ed.), *The Ultimate Decision;* W. Millis, *Arms and the State;* C. Rossiter, *The Supreme Court and the Commander-in-Chief;* J. M. Swomley, *The Military Establishment.*

15. *Growth and the Economy*

W. Adams & H. M. Gray, *Monopoly in America;* F. M. Bator, *The Question of Government Spending;* S. Donaldson, *The Suburban Myth;* E. S. Flash, Jr., *Economic Advice and Presidential Leadership;* Editors of Fortune, *America in the Sixties;* J. K. Galbraith, *The Affluent Society* and *American Capitalism;* D. Hathaway, *Government and Agriculture;* A. E. Holmans, *United States Fiscal Policy, 1945–1959;* R. Lekachman, *Age of Keynes;* M. Lerner, *America as a Civilization;* D. E. Lilienthal, *Big Business;* A. Shonfield, *Modern Capitalism;* L. Soth, *Farm Trouble in an Age of Plenty;* C. E. Warne & K. W. Lumpkin *et al., Labor in Post War America;* R. Wood, *Suburbia.*

16. *Arts and Letters*

J. Aldridge, *After the Lost Generation;* I. H. Baur, *Revolution and Tradition in Modern American Art;* H. Harper, Jr., *Desperate Faith;* R. Jarrell, *Poetry and the Age;* J. Kramer, *Allen Ginsberg in America;* L. Lipton, *The Holy Barbarians;* A. C. Ritchie, *Abstract Painting and Sculpture in America;* B. Rosenberg & D. M. White (eds.), *Mass Culture;* S. Stepanchev, *American Poetry Since 1945.*

CHAPTER 36

1. *JFK AND LBJ*

R. Berman, *America in the Sixties;* D. Burner *et al., A Giant's Strength;* J. M. Burns, *John F. Kennedy;* M. Davie, *LBJ;* A. Donald (ed.), *John F. Kennedy and the New Frontier;* H. Fairlie, *The Kennedy Promise;* H. Golden, *Mr. Kennedy and the Negroes;* D. F. Hadwiger & R. B. Talbot, *Pressures and Protests;* L. Heren, *No Hail, No Farewell;* H. Miller, *Rich Man, Poor Man;* B. Muse, *The American Negro Revolution;* W. O'Neill, *Coming Apart;* P. Salinger, *With Kennedy;* A. M. Schlesinger, Jr., *A Thousand Days;* H. Sidey, *John F. Kennedy: President;* T. Sorenson, *Kennedy;* J. L. Sundquist, *Politics and Policy;* T. Wicker, *JFK and LBJ;* B. H. Wilkins & C. B. Friday, *The Economists of the New Frontier.*

2. *Politics*

L. Chester *et al., An American Melodrama;* B. Cosman & R. J. Huckshorn (eds.), *Republican Politics;* M. C. Cummings, Jr. (ed.), *The National Election of 1964;* G. F. Gilder & B. K. Chapman, *The Party That Lost Its Head;* H. Graham & T. Gurr, *Violence in America;* S. E. Harris, *Economics of the Kennedy Years;* R. D. Novak, *The Agony of the G.O.P. 1964;* R. H. Rovere, *The Goldwater Caper;* T. White, *The Making of the President, 1960, The Making of the President, 1964,* and *The Making of the President, 1968.*

3. *Foreign Affairs*

G. Allison, *Essence of Decision;* J. R. Boettiger (ed.), *Vietnam and American Foreign Policy;* C. Bowles, *Promises to Keep;* J. Buttinger, *Vietnam: A Dragon Embattled;* C. Cooper, *The Lost Crusade;* B. Fall, *The Two Vietnams* and *Viet-Nam Witness, 1953–66;* F. Fitzgerald, *Fire in the Lake;* J. W. Fulbright, *The Arrogance of Power;* J. Galbraith, *Ambassador's Journal;* P. L. Geyelin, *Lyndon B. Johnson and the World;* R. N. Goodwin, *Triumph or Tragedy;* D. Halberstam, *The Best and the Brightest;* R. Hilsman, *To Move a Nation;* K. Meyer & T. Szulc, *The Cuban Invasion;* M. G. Raskin & B. B. Fall (eds.), *The Viet-Nam Reader;* A. M. Schlesinger, Jr., *The Bitter Heritage;* R. Shaplen, *The Lost Revolution;* R. Stebbins, *The United States in World Affairs* (for appropriate years); R. Walton, *Cold War and Counter-Revolution.*

4. *From Nixon to Reagan*

C. Bernstein & R. Woodward, *All the President's Men;* H. Brandon, *The Retreat of American Power;* R. Evans & R. Novak, *Nixon in the White House;* R. Evans & R. Novak, *The Reagan Revolution;* H. Fairlie, *The Spoiled Child of the Western World;* S. Graubard, *Kissinger;* R. Harris, *Justice;* J. Hersey, *The President;* E. Kahn, Jr., *The American People;* D. Landau, *Kissinger;* F. Mankiewicz, *Perfectly Clear;* New York Times (ed.), *The End of a Presidency;* R. Reeves, *A Ford not a Lincoln;* R. Scammon & B. Wattenberg, *The Real Majority;* J. Schell, *The Time of Illusion;* M. Schram, *Running for President 1976;* L. Silk, *Nixonomics;* K. Stroud, *How Jimmy Won;* T. White, *Breach of Faith;* G. Wills, *Nixon Agonistes;* J. Witcover, *Marathon;* J. Wooten, *Dasher.*

Statistical Tables

ADMISSION OF STATES TO THE UNION

State	Entered Union	State	Entered Union	State	Entered Union	State	Entered Union
Alabama	1819	Indiana	1816	Nebraska	1867	South Carolina	1788
Alaska	1958	Iowa	1846	Nevada	1864	South Dakota	1889
Arizona	1912	Kansas	1861	New Hampshire	1788	Tennessee	1796
Arkansas	1836	Kentucky	1792	New Jersey	1787	Texas	1845
California	1850	Louisiana	1812	New Mexico	1912	Utah	1896
Colorado	1876	Maine	1820	New York	1788	Vermont	1791
Connecticut	1788	Maryland	1788	North Carolina	1789	Virginia	1788
Delaware	1787	Massachusetts	1788	North Dakota	1889	Washington	1889
Florida	1845	Michigan	1837	Ohio	1803	West Virginia	1863
Georgia	1788	Minnesota	1858	Oklahoma	1907	Wisconsin	1848
Hawaii	1959	Mississippi	1817	Oregon	1859	Wyoming	1890
Idaho	1890	Missouri	1821	Pennsylvania	1787		
Illinois	1818	Montana	1889	Rhode Island	1790		

President	Vice President	Secretary of State	Secretary of Treasury	Secretary of War	Secretary of Navy	Postmaster General	Attorney General
George Washington 1789	John Adams	T. Jefferson 1789 E. Randolph 1794 T. Pickering 1795	Alex. Hamilton 1789 Oliver Wolcott 1795	Henry Knox 1789 T. Pickering 1795 Jas. McHenry 1796		Samuel Osgood 1789 T. Pickering 1791 Jos. Habersham 1795	E. Randolph 1789 Wm. Bradford 1794 Charles Lee 1795
John Adams 1797	Thomas Jefferson	T. Pickering 1797 John Marshall 1800	Oliver Wolcott 1797 Samuel Dexter 1801	Jas. McHenry 1797 Samuel Dexter 1800	Benj. Stoddert 1798	Jos. Habersham 1797	Charles Lee 1797 Theo Parsons 1801
Thomas Jefferson 1801	Aaron Burr George Clinton 1805	James Madison 1801	Samuel Dexter 1801 Albert Gallatin 1801	H. Dearborn 1801	Benj. Stoddert 1801 Robert Smith 1801 J. Crowninshield 1805	Jos. Habersham 1801 Gideon Granger 1801	Levi Lincoln 1801 Robert Smith 1805 J. Breckinridge 1805 C. A. Rodney 1807
James Madison 1809	George Clinton Elbridge Gerry 1813	Robert Smith 1809 James Monroe 1811	Albert Gallatin 1809 G. W. Campbell 1814 A. J. Dallas 1814 W. H. Crawford 1816	Wm. Eustis 1809 John Armstrong 1813 James Monroe 1814 W.H. Crawford 1815	Paul Hamilton 1809 William Jones 1813 B. W. Crowninshield 1814	Gideon Granger 1809 R. J. Meigs, Jr. 1814	C. A. Rodney 1809 Wm. Pickney 1811 Richard Rush 1814
James Monroe 1817	D. D. Tompkins	J. Q. Adams 1817	W. H. Crawford 1817	Issac Shelby 1817 George Graham 1817 John C. Calhoun 1817	B. W. Crowninshield 1817 Smith Thompson 1818 S. L. Southard 1823	R. J. Meigs, Jr. 1817 John McLean 1823	Richard Rush 1817 William Wirt 1817
John Q. Adams 1825	John C. Calhoun	Henry Clay 1825	Richard Rush 1825	Jas. Barbour 1825 Peter B. Porter 1828	S. L. Southard 1825	John McLean 1825	William Wirt 1825
Andrew Jackson 1829	John C. Calhoun Martin Van Buren 1833	Martin Van Buren 1829 Edward Livingston 1831 Louis McLane 1833 John Forsyth 1834	Sam D. Ingham 1829 Louis McLane 1831 W. J. Duane 1833 Roger B. Taney 1833 Levi Woodbury 1834	John H. Eaton 1829 Lewis Cass 1831 B. F. Butler 1837	John Branch 1829 Levi Woodbury 1831 Mahlon Dickerson 1834	Wm. T. Barry 1829 Amos Kendall 1835	John M. Berrien 1829 Roger B. Taney 1831 B. F. Butler 1833
Martin Van Buren 1837	R. M. Johnson	John Forsyth 1837	Levi Woodbury 1837	Joel R. Poinsett 1837	Mahlon Dickerson 1837 Jas. K. Paulding 1838	Amos Kendall 1837 John M. Niles 1840	B. F. Butler 1837 Felix Grundy 1838 H. D. Gilpin 1840
William H. Harrison 1841	John Tyler	Daniel Webster 1841	Thos. Ewing 1841	John Bell 1841	George E. Badger 1841	Francis Granger 1841	John J. Crittenden 1841
John Tyler 1841		Daniel Webster 1841 Hugh S. Legaré 1843 Abel P. Upshur 1843 John C. Calhoun 1844	Thos. Ewing 1841 Walter Forward 1841 John C. Spencer 1843 George M. Bibb 1844	John Bell 1841 John C. Spencer 1841 Jas. M. Porter 1843 Wm. Wilkins 1844	George E. Badger 1841 Abel P. Upshur 1841 David Henshaw 1843 Thomas Gilmer 1844 John Y. Mason 1844	Francis Granger 1841 C. A. Wickliffe 1841	John J. Crittenden 1841 Hugh S. Legare 1841 John Nelson 1843

President	Vice President	Secretary of State	Secretary of Treasury	Secretary of War	Secretary of Navy	Postmaster General
James K. Polk 1845	George M. Dallas	James Buchanan 1845	Robt. J. Walker 1845	Wm. L. Marcy 1845	George Bancroft 1845 John Y. Mason 1846	Cave Johnson 1845
Zachary Taylor 1849	Millard Fillmore	John M. Clayton 1849	W. M. Meredith 1849	G. W. Crawford 1849	Wm. B. Preston 1849	Jacob Collamer 1849
Millard Fillmore 1850		Daniel Webster 1850 Edward Everett 1852	Thomas Corwin 1850	C. M. Conrad 1850	Wm. A. Graham 1850 John P. Kennedy 1852	Nathan K. Hall 1850 Sam D. Hubbard 1852
Franklin Pierce 1853	William R. King	Wm. L. Marcy 1853	James Guthrie 1853	Jefferson Davis 1853	James C. Dobbin 1853	James Campbell 1853
James Buchanan 1857	John C. Breckinridge	Lewis Cass 1857 J. S. Black 1860	Howell Cobb 1857 Philip F. Thomas 1860 John A. Dix 1861	John B. Floyd 1857 Joseph Holt 1861	Isaac Toucey 1857	Aaron V. Brown 1857 Joseph Holt 1859 Horatio King 1861
Abraham Lincoln 1861	Han'ib'l Hamlin Andrew Johnson 1865	William H. Seward 1861	Salmon P. Chase 1861 W. P. Fessenden 1864 Hugh McCulloch 1865	S. Cameron 1861 E. M. Stanton 1862	Gideon Welles 1861	Horatio King 1861 M'tgomery Blair 1861 Wm. Dennison 1864
Andrew Johnson 1865		William H. Seward 1865	Hugh McCulloch 1865	E. M. Stanton 1865 Ulysses S. Grant 1867 Lorenzo Thomas 1868 J. M. Schofield 1868	Gideon Welles 1865	Wm. Dennison 1865 Alexander Randall 1866
Ulysses S. Grant 1869	Schulyer Colfax Henry Wilson 1873	E. B. Washburne 1869 Hamilton Fish 1869	G. S. Boutwell 1869 W. A. Richardson 1873 B. H. Bristow 1874 Lot M. Morrill 1876	John A. Rawlins 1869 Wm. T. Sherman 1869 Wm. W. Belknap 1869 Alphonso Taft 1876 Jas. D. Cameron 1876	Adolph E. Borie 1869 George M. Robeson 1869	John A. J. Creswell 1869 James W. Marshall 1874 Marshall Jewell 1874 James N. Tyner 1876
Rutherford B. Hayes 1877	William A. Wheeler	William M. Evarts 1877	John Sherman 1877	George W. McCrary 1877 Alexander Ramsey 1879	R. W. Thompson 1877 Nathan Goff, Jr. 1881	David M. Key 1877 Horace Maynard 1880
James A. Garfield 1881	Chester A. Arthur	James G. Blaine 1881	William Windom 1881	Robert T. Lincoln 1881	William H. Hunt 1881	Thomas L. James 1881
Chester A. Arthur 1881		F. T. Frelinghuysen 1881	Charles J. Folger 1881 Walter Q. Gresham 1884 Hugh McCulloch 1884	Robert T. Lincoln 1881	William E. Chandler 1881	Thomas L. James 1881 Timothy O. Howe 1881 Walter Q. Gresham 1885 Frank Hatton 1884
Grover Cleveland 1885	Thos. A. Hendricks	Thomas F. Bayard 1885	Daniel Manning 1885 Charles S. Fairchild 1887	William C. Endicott 1885	William C. Whitney 1885	William F. Vilas 1885 Don M. Dickinson 1888

Attorney General	Secretary of Interior	Secretary of Agriculture
John Y. Mason 1845 Nathan Clifford 1846 Isaac Toucey 1848		
Reverdy Johnson 1849	Thomas Ewing 1849	
J. J. Crittenden 1850	Thomas McKennan 1850 A. H. Stuart 1850	
Caleb Cushing 1853	Robert McClelland 1853	
J. S. Black 1857 Edw. M. Stanton 1860	Jacob Thompson 1857	
Edward Bates 1861 Titian J. Coffey 1863 James Speed 1864	Caleb B. Smith 1861 John P. Usher 1863	
James Speed 1865 Henry Stanbery 1866 William M. Evarts 1868	John P. Usher 1865 James Harlan 1865 O. H. Browning 1866	
Ebenezer R. Hoar 1869 Amos T. Akerman 1870 G. H. Williams 1871 Edward Pierrepont 1875 Alphonso Taft 1876	Jacob D. Cox 1869 Columbus Delano 1870 Zachary Chandler 1875	
Charles Devens 1877	Carl Schurz 1877	
Wayne MacVeagh 1881	S. J. Kirkwood 1881	
B. H. Brewster 1881	Henry M. Teller 1881	
A. H. Garland 1885	L. Q. C. Lamar 1885 William F. Vilas 1888	Norman J. Colman 1889

President	Vice President	Secretary of State	Secretary of Treasury	Secretary of War	Secretary of Navy	Postmaster General
Benjamin Harrison 1889	Levi P. Morton	James G. Blaine 1889 John W. Foster 1892	William Windom 1889 Charles Foster 1891	Redfield Proctor 1889 Stephen B. Elkins 1891	Benjamin F. Tracy 1889	John Wanamaker 1889
Grover Cleveland 1893	Adlai E. Stevenson	Walter Q. Gresham 1893 Richard Olney 1895	John G. Carlisle 1893	Daniel S. Lamont 1893	Hilary A. Herbert 1893	Wilson S. Bissel 1893 William L. Wilson 1895
William McKinley 1897	Garret A. Hobart Theodore Roosevelt 1901	John Sherman 1897 William R. Day 1898 John Hay 1898	Lyman J. Gage 1897	Russell A. Alger 1897 Elihu Root 1899	John D. Long 1897	James A. Gary 1897 Charles E. Smith 1898
Theodore Roosevelt 1901	Chas. W. Fairbanks	John Hay 1901 Elihu Root 1905 Robert Bacon 1909	Lyman J. Gage 1901 Leslie M. Shaw 1902 George B. Cortelyou 1907	Elihu Root 1901 William H. Taft 1904 Luke E. Wright 1908	John D. Long 1901 William H. Moody 1902 Paul Morton 1904 Charles J. Bonaparte 1905 Victor H. Metcalf 1906 T. H. Newberry 1908	Charles E. Smith 1901 Henry C. Payne 1902 Robert J. Wynne 1904 George B. Cortelyou 1905 George von L. Meyer 1907
William H. Taft 1909	James S. Sherman	Philander C. Knox 1909	Franklin MacVeagh 1909	Jacob M. Dickinson 1909 Henry L. Stimson 1911	George von L. Meyer 1909	Frank H. Hitchcock 1909
Woodrow Wilson 1913	Thomas R. Marshall	William J. Bryan 1913 Robert Lansing 1915 Bainbridge Colby 1920	William G. McAdoo 1913 Carter Glass 1918 David F. Houston 1920	Lindley M. Garrison 1913 Newton D. Baker 1916	Josephus Daniels 1913	Albert S. Burleson 1913
Warren G. Harding 1921	Calvin Coolidge	Charles E. Hughes 1921	Andrew W. Mellon 1921	John W. Weeks 1921	Edwin Denby 1921	Will H. Hays 1921 Hubert Work 1922 Harry S. New 1923
Calvin Coolidge 1923	Charles G. Dawes	Charles E. Hughes 1923 Frank B. Kellogg 1925	Andrew W. Mellon 1923	John W. Weeks 1923 Dwight F. Davis 1925	Edwin Denby 1923 Curtis D. Wilbur 1924	Harry S. New 1923
Herbert C. Hoover 1929	Charles Curtis	Henry L. Stimson 1929	Andrew W. Mellon 1929 Ogden L. Mills 1932	James W. Good 1929 Patrick J. Hurley 1929	Charles F. Adams 1929	Walter F. Brown 1929
Franklin Delano Roosevelt 1933	John Nance Garner Henry A. Wallace 1941 Harry S. Truman 1945	Cordell Hull 1933 Edw. R. Stettinius, Jr. 1944	William H. Woodin 1933 Henry Morgenthau, Jr. 1935	George H. Dern 1933 Harry H. Woodring 1936 Henry L. Stimson 1940	Claude A. Swanson 1933 Charles Edison 1939 Frank Knox 1940 James V. Forrestal 1944	James A. Farley 1933 Frank C. Walker 1940

Attorney General	Secretary of Interior	Secretary of Agriculture	Secretary of Commerce and Labor	
Wm. H. H. Miller 1889	John W. Noble 1889	Jeremiah M. Rusk 1889		
Richard Olney 1893 Judson Harmon 1895	Hoke Smith 1893 David R. Francis 1896	J. Sterling Morton 1893		
Jos. McKenna 1897 John W. Griggs 1898 Philander C. Knox 1901	Cornelius N. Bliss 1897 E. A. Hitchcock 1898	James Wilson 1897		
Philander C. Knox 1901 Wm. H. Moody 1904 Chas. J. Bonaparte 1906	E.A. Hitchcock 1901 James R. Garfield 1907	James Wilson 1901	George B. Cortelyou 1903 Victor H. Metcalf 1904 Oscar S. Straus 1906	
G. W. Wickersham 1909	R. A. Ballinger 1909 Walter L. Fisher 1911	James Wilson 1909	Charles Nagel 1909	
			Secretary of Commerce	Secretary of Labor
J. C. McReynolds 1913 T. W. Gregory 1914 A. Mitchell Palmer 1919	Franklin K. Lane 1913 John B. Payne 1920	David F. Houston 1913 E. T. Meredith 1920	W. C. Redfield 1913 J. W. Alexander 1919	William B. Wilson 1913
H. M. Daugherty 1921	Albert B. Fall 1921 Hubert Work 1923	Henry C. Wallace 1921	Herbert C. Hoover 1921	James J. Davis 1921
H. M. Daugherty 1923 Harlan F. Stone 1924 John G. Sargent 1925	Hubert Work 1923 Roy O. West 1928	Henry C. Wallace 1923 Howard M. Gore 1924 W. M. Jardine 1925	Herbert C. Hoover 1923 William F. Whiting 1928	James J. Davis 1923
W. D. Mitchell 1929	Ray L. Wilbur 1929	Arthur M. Hyde 1929	Robert P. Lamont 1929 Roy D. Chapin 1932	James J. Davis 1929 William N. Doak 1930
H.S. Cummings 1933 Frank Murphy 1939 Robert Jackson 1940 Francis Biddle 1941	Harold L. Ickes 1933	Henry C. Wallace 1933 Claude R. Wickard 1940	Daniel C. Roper 1933 Harry L. Hopkins 1939 Jesse Jones 1940 Henry A. Wallace 1945	Frances Perkins 1933

President	Vice President	Secretary of State	Secretary of Treasury	Secretary of War	Secretary of Navy	Postmaster General
Harry S. Truman 1945	Alben W. Barkley	Edw. R. Stettinius, Jr. 1945 James F. Byrnes 1945 George C. Marshall 1947 Dean G. Achenson 1949	Henry Morgenthau, Jr. 1945 Fred M. Vinson 1945 John W. Snyder 1946	Robert P. Patterson 1945 Kenneth C. Royall 1947	James V. Forrestal 1945	Frank C. Walker 1945 R. E. Hannegan 1945 Jesse M. Donaldson 1947
				Secretary of Defense		
				James V. Forrestal 1947 Louis A. Johnson 1949 George C. Marshall 1950 Robert A. Lovett 1951		
Dwight D. Eisenhower 1953	Richard M. Nixon	John Foster Dulles 1953 Christian A. Herter 1959	George M. Humphrey 1953 Robert B. Anderson 1957	Charles E. Wilson 1953 Neil H. McElroy 1957 Thomas S. Gates 1959		A. E. Summerfield 1953
John F. Kennedy 1961	Lyndon B. Johnson	Dean Rusk 1961	C. Douglas Dillon 1961	Robert S. McNamara 1961		J. Edward Day 1961 John A. Gronouski 1963
Lyndon B. Johnson 1963	Hubert H. Humphrey	Dean Rusk 1963	C. Douglas Dillon 1963 Henry H. Fowler 1965 Joseph W. Barr 1968	Robert S. McNamara 1963 Clark M. Clifford 1968		John A. Gronouski 1963 Lawrence F. O'Brien 1965 W. Marvin Watson 1968
Richard M. Nixon 1969	Spiro T. Agnew Gerald R. Ford 1973	William P. Rogers 1969 Henry A. Kissinger 1973	David M. Kennedy 1969 John B. Connally 1971 George P. Shultz 1972 William E. Simon 1974	Melvin R. Laird 1969 Elliot L. Richardson 1973 Jas. R. Schlesinger 1973		Winton M. Blount 1969*
Gerald R. Ford 1974	Nelson A. Rockefeller	Henry A. Kissinger 1974	William E. Simon 1974	Jas. R. Schlesinger 1974 Donald H. Rumsfeld 1975		
James E. Carter 1977	Walter F. Mondale	Cyrus R. Vance 1977 Edmund S. Muskie 1980	W. Michael Blumenthal 1977 G. William Miller 1979	Harold Brown 1977		
Ronald Reagan 1981	George Bush	Alexander M. Haig, Jr. 1981 George Schulz 1982	Donald T. Regan 1981	Casper W. Weinberger 1981		

*On July 1, 1971 the Post Office became an independent agency. After that date, the Postmaster General was no longer a member of the Cabinet.

†The Department of Health, Education and Welfare, created by Congress April 11, 1953, was divided by Congress September 27, 1979, into separate departments of Education, and Health and Human Services. The Secretary of each is a cabinet member.

Attorney General	Secretary of Interior	Secretary of Agriculture	Secretary of Commerce	Secretary of Labor	Secretary of Health Education and Welfare	Secretary of Housing and Urban Development	Secretary of Transportation
Francis Biddle 1945 Tom C. Clark 1945 J. H. McGrath 1949 James P. McGranery 1952	Harold L. Ickes 1945 Julius A. Krug 1946 Oscar L. Chapman 1949	Claude R. Wickard 1945 C. P. Anderson 1945 C. F. Brannan 1948	Henry A. Wallace 1945 W. A. Harriman 1946 Charles Sawyer 1948	Frances Perkins 1945 L. B. Schwellenbach 1945 Maurice J. Tobin 1948			
H. Brownell, Jr. 1953 Wm. P. Rogers 1957	Douglas McKay 1953 Fred Seaton 1956	Ezra T. Benson 1953	Sinclair Weeks 1953 Lewis L. Strauss 1958 Frederick H. Mueller 1959	Martin P. Durkin 1953 James P. Mitchell 1953	Oveta Culp Hobby 1953 Marion B. Folsom 1955 Arthur S. Flemming 1958		
Robert F. Kennedy 1961	Stewart L. Udall 1961	Orville L. Freeman 1961	Luther H. Hodges 1961	Arthur J. Goldberg 1961 W. Willard Wirtz 1962	A. A. Ribicoff 1961 Anthony J. Celebrezze 1962		
Robert F. Kennedy 1963 N. deB. Katzenbach 1965 Ramsey Clark 1966	Stewart L. Udall 1963	Orville L. Freeman 1963	Luther H. Hodges 1963 John T. Connor 1965 Alexander B. Trowbridge 1967 C. R. Smith 1968	W. Willard Wirtz 1963	Anthony J. Celebrezze 1963 John W. Gardner 1965 Wilbur J. Cohen 1968	Robert C. Weaver 1966 Robert Wood 1968	Alan S. Boyd 1967
John N. Mitchell 1969 Richard G. Kleindienst 1972 Elliot L. Richardson 1973 William B. Saxbe 1974	Walter J. Hickel 1969 Rogers C. B. Morton 1971	Clifford M. Hardin 1969 Earl L. Butz 1971	Maurice H. Stans 1969 Peter G. Peterson 1972 Frederick B. Dent 1972	George P. Schultz 1969 James D. Hodgson 1970 Peter J. Brennan 1973	Robert H. Finch 1969 Elliot L. Richardson 1970 Caspar W. Weinberger 1973	George W. Romney 1969 James T. Lynn 1973	John A. Volpe 1969 Claude S. Brinegar 1973
William B. Saxbe 1974 Edward H. Levi 1975	Rogers C. B. Morton 1974 Stanley K. Hathaway 1975 Thomas D. Kleppe 1975	Earl L. Butz 1974 John A. Knebel 1976	Frederick B. Dent 1974 Rogers C. B. Morton 1975 Elliot L. Richardson 1976	Peter J. Brennan 1974 John T. Dunlop 1975 W. J. Usery 1976	Caspar W. Weinberger 1974 Forrest D. Mathews 1975	James T. Lynn 1974 Carla A. Hills 1975	Claude S. Brinegar 1974 W. T. Coleman, Jr. 1975
Griffin B. Bell 1977 Benjamin R. Civiletti 1979	Cecil D. Andrus 1977	Bob Bergland 1977	Juanita M. Kreps 1977	F. Ray Marshall 1977	Joseph A. Califano, Jr. 1977 Patricia Roberts Harris 1979	Patricia Roberts Harris 1977 Moon Landrieu 1979	Brock Adams 1977 Neil E. Goldschmic 1979
William French Smith 1981	James G. Watt 1981	John R. Block 1981	Malcolm Baldrige 1981	Raymond V. Donovan 1981		Samuel R. Pierce, Jr. 1981	Andrew L. Lewis, Jr. 1981

Sec. of Energy
James R. Schlesinger 1977
Robert W. Duncan, Jr. 1979
James B. Edwards 1981

This department was created by federal law August 4, 1977.

Secretary of Education	Secretary of Health and Human Services†
Shirley Hufstedler 1979	Patricia Roberts Harris 1979
Terrel Bell 1981	Richard S. Schweiker 1981

POPULATION OF THE UNITED STATES, 1770–1860

Estimates for 1770 taken from *A Century of Population Growth* (1909), others from the United States censuses

State	1770	1790	1800	1810	1820	1830	1840	1850	1860
New England									
Maine	34,000	96,540	151,719	228,705	298,335	399,455	501,793	583,169	628,279
New Hampshire	60,000	141,885	183,858	214,460	244,161	269,328	284,574	317,976	326,073
Vermont	25,000	85,425	154,465	217,895	235,981	280,652	291,948	314,120	315,098
Massachusetts	265,000	378,787	422,845	472,040	523,287	610,408	737,699	994,514	1,231,066
Rhode Island	55,000	68,825	69,122	76,931	83,059	97,199	108,830	147,545	174,620
Connecticut	175,000	237,946	251,002	261,942	275,248	297,675	309,978	370,792	460,147
Middle Atlantic									
New York	160,000	340,120	589,051	959,049	1,372,812	1,918,608	2,428,921	3,097,394	3,880,735
New Jersey	110,000	184,139	211,149	245,562	277,575	320,823	373,306	489,555	672,035
Pennsylvania	250,000	434,373	602,365	810,091	1,049,458	1,348,233	1,724,033	2,311,786	2,906,215
South Atlantic									
Delaware	25,000	59,096	64,273	72,674	72,749	76,748	78,085	91,532	112,216
Maryland	200,000	319,728	341,548	380,546	407,350	447,040	470,019	583,034	687,049
Dist. of Columbia			14,093	24,023	33,039	39,834	43,712	51,687	75,080
Virginia	450,000	747,610	880,200	974,600	1,065,366	1,211,405	1,239,797	1,421,661	1,596,318
West Virginia									
North Carolina	230,000	393,751	478,103	555,500	638,829	737,987	753,419	869,039	992,622
South Carolina	140,000	249,073	345,591	415,115	502,741	581,185	594,398	668,507	703,708
Georgia	26,000	82,548	162,686	252,433	340,989	516,823	691,392	906,185	1,057,286
Florida						34,730	54,477	87,445	140,424
South Central									
Kentucky		73,677	220,955	406,511	564,317	687,917	779,828	982,405	1,155,684
Tennessee		35,691	105,602	261,727	422,823	681,904	829,210	1,002,717	1,109,801
Alabama					127,901	309,527	590,756	771,623	964,201
Mississippi			8,850	40,352	75,448	136,621	375,651	606,526	791,305
Arkansas				1,062	14,273	30,388	97,574	209,897	435,450
Louisiana				76,556	153,407	215,739	352,411	517,762	708,002
Oklahoma									
Texas								212,592	604,215

North Central									
Ohio			45,365	230,760	581,434	937,903	1,519,467	1,980,329	2,339,511
Indiana			5,641	24,520	147,178	343,031	685,866	988,416	1,350,428
Illinois				12,282	55,211	157,445	476,183	851,470	1,711,951
Michigan				4,762	8,896	31,639	212,267	397,654	749,113
Wisconsin							30,945	305,391	775,881
Minnesota								6,077	172,023
Iowa							43,112	192,214	674,913
Missouri				19,783	66,586	140,455	383,702	682,044	1,182,012
North Dakota			}						4,837
South Dakota									
Nebraska									28,841
Kansas									107,206
Mountain									
Montana									
Idaho									
Wyoming									
Colorado									34,277
New Mexico								61,547	93,516
Arizona									
Utah								11,380	40,273
Nevada									6,857
Pacific									
Washington									11,594
Oregon								13,294	52,465
California								92,597	379,994
	2,205,000	3,929,214	5,308,483	7,239,881	9,638,453	12,866,020	17,069,453	23,191,876	31,443,321

POPULATION OF THE UNITED STATES, 1870–1980 (in Thousands)

State	1870	1880	1890	1900	1910	1920	1930	1940	1950	1960	1970	1980
New England												
Maine	627	649	661	694	742	768	797	847	914	969	992	1,125
New Hampshire	318	347	377	412	431	443	465	492	533	607	738	921
Vermont	331	332	332	344	356	352	360	359	378	390	444	511
Massachusetts	1,457	1,783	2,239	2,805	3,336	3,852	4,250	4,317	4,691	5,149	5,689	5,737
Rhode Island	217	277	346	429	543	604	688	713	792	859	947	947
Connecticut	537	623	746	908	1,115	1,381	1,607	1,709	2,007	2,535	3,032	3,108
Middle Atlantic												
New York	4,383	5,083	6,003	7,269	9,114	10,385	12,588	13,479	14,830	16,782	18,237	17,557
New Jersey	906	1,131	1,445	1,884	2,537	3,156	4,041	4,160	4,835	6,067	7,168	7,364
Pennsylvania	3,522	4,283	5,258	6,302	7,665	8,720	9,631	9,900	10,498	11,319	11,794	11,867
South Atlantic												
Delaware	125	147	168	185	202	223	238	267	318	446	548	595
Maryland	781	935	1,042	1,188	1,295	1,450	1,632	1,821	2,343	3,101	3,922	4,216
Dist. of Columbia	132	178	230	279	331	438	487	663	802	764	757	637
Virginia	1,225	1,513	1,656	1,854	2,062	2,309	2,422	2,678	3,319	3,967	4,648	5,346
West Virginia	442	618	763	959	1,221	1,464	1,729	1,902	2,006	1,860	1,744	1,949
North Carolina	1,071	1,340	1,618	1,894	2,206	2,559	3,170	3,572	4,062	4,556	5,082	5,874
South Carolina	706	996	1,151	1,340	1,515	1,684	1,739	1,900	2,117	2,383	2,591	3,119
Georgia	1,184	1,542	1,837	2,216	2,609	2,896	2,909	3,124	3,445	3,943	4,590	5,454
Florida	188	269	391	529	753	968	1,468	1,897	2,771	4,952	6,789	9,739
South Central												
Kentucky	1,321	1,649	1,859	2,147	2,290	2,417	2,615	2,846	2,945	3,038	3,219	3,661
Tennessee	1,259	1,542	1,768	2,021	2,185	2,338	2,617	2,916	3,292	3,567	3,924	4,590
Alabama	997	1,262	1,513	1,829	2,138	2,348	2,646	2,833	3,062	3,267	3,444	3,890
Mississippi	828	1,132	1,290	1,551	1,797	1,791	2,010	2,184	2,179	2,178	2,217	2,521
Arkansas	484	803	1,128	1,312	1,574	1,752	1,854	1,949	1,910	1,786	1,923	2,286
Louisiana	727	940	1,119	1,382	1,656	1,799	2,102	2,364	2,684	3,257	3,641	4,204
Oklahoma			259	790	1,657	2,028	2,396	2,226	2,233	2,328	2,559	3,025
Texas	819	1,592	2,236	3,049	3,897	4,663	5,825	6,415	7,711	9,580	11,197	14,228
North Central												
Ohio	2,665	3,198	3,672	4,158	4,767	5,759	6,647	6,908	7,947	9,706	10,652	10,797
Indiana	1,681	1,978	2,192	2,516	2,701	2,930	3,239	3,428	3,934	4,662	5,194	5,490
Illinois	2,540	3,078	3,826	4,822	5,639	6,485	7,631	7,897	8,712	10,081	11,114	11,418
Michigan	1,184	1,637	2,094	2,421	2,810	3,668	4,842	5,256	6,372	7,823	8,875	9,258
Wisconsin	1,055	1,315	1,693	2,069	2,334	2,632	2,939	3,138	3,435	3,951	4,418	4,705
Minnesota	4	781	1,310	1,751	2,076	2,387	2,564	2,792	2,982	3,414	3,805	4,077
Iowa	1,194	1,625	1,912	2,232	2,225	2,404	2,471	2,538	2,621	2,758	2,824	2,913
Missouri	1,721	2,168	2,679	3,107	3,293	3,404	3,629	3,785	3,955	4,320	4,677	4,917
North Dakota	14	135	191	319	577	647	681	642	620	632	618	652
South Dakota			349	402	584	637	693	643	653	681	666	690
Nebraska	123	452	1,063	1,066	1,192	1,296	1,378	1,316	1,326	1,411	1,483	1,570
Kansas	364	996	1,428	1,470	1,691	1,769	1,881	1,801	1,905	2,179	2,247	2,363

Mountain												
Montana	21	39	143	243	376	549	538	559	591	675	694	786
Idaho	15	33	89	162	326	432	445	525	589	668	713	944
Wyoming	9	21	63	93	146	194	226	251	291	330	332	471
Colorado	40	194	413	540	799	940	1,036	1,123	1,325	1,755	2,207	2,889
New Mexico	92	120	160	195	327	360	423	532	681	951	1,016	1,300
Arizona	10	40	88	123	204	334	436	499	750	1,302	1,771	2,718
Utah	87	144	211	277	373	449	508	550	689	891	1,059	1,461
Nevada	42	62	47	42	82	77	91	110	160	285	489	799
Pacific												
Washington	24	75	357	518	1,142	1,357	1,563	1,902	2,379	2,853	3,409	4,130
Oregon	91	175	318	414	673	783	954	1,090	1,521	1,769	2,091	2,633
California	560	865	1,213	1,485	2,378	3,427	5,677	6,907	10,586	15,717	19,953	23,668
Alaska					64	64	55	59	73	226	300	400
Hawaii					154	192	256	368	423	633	769	965
Puerto Rico						1,300	1,544	1,869	2,211	2,350	2,712	3,196
Total	38,558	50,156	62,948	75,995	92,228	107,322	124,747	132,154	151,319	179,311	203,212	223,111

Source: U.S. Bureau of the Census

URBAN AND RURAL POPULATION, 1870–1980

	Urban*		Rural	
Census Year	Number (In Thousands)	Per Cent of Total	Number (In Thousands)	Per Cent of Total
1870	9,902	25.7	28,656	74.3
1880	14,129	28.2	36,026	71.8
1890	22,106	35.1	40,841	64.9
1900	30,159	39.7	45,834	60.3
1910	41,998	45.7	49,973	54.3
1920	54,157	51.2	51,552	48.8
1930	68,954	56.2	53,820	43.8
1940	74,423	56.5	57,245	43.5
1950	96,847	59.0	54,479	41.0
1960	125,269	69.9	54,054	30.1
1970	149,235	73.5	53,887	26.5
1980	166,965	73.7	59,539	26.3

*Urban: Includes all persons living in places of 2,500 or more and in densely settled urban fringe areas.
Source: U.S. Census of Population, 1980

Year	Candidate	Party	Popular vote	Per cent	Electoral vote
1789	*Washington*	none	—	—	69
	J. Adams	none	—	—	34
	Jay	none	—	—	9
	Harrison	none	—	—	6
	Rutledge	none	—	—	6
	Hancock	none	—	—	4
	G. Clinton	none	—	—	3
	Huntington	none	—	—	2
	Milton	none	—	—	2
	Armstrong	none	—	—	1
	Lincoln	none	—	—	1
	Telfair	none	—	—	1
	Votes not cast	—	—	—	12
1792	*Washington*	Federalist	—	—	132
	J. Adams	Federalist	—	—	77
	G. Clinton	Democratic-Republican	—	—	50
	Jefferson	—	—	—	4
	Burr	—	—	—	1
1796	*J. Adams*	Federalist	—	—	71
	Jefferson	Democratic-Republican	—	—	68
	T. Pinckney	Federalist	—	—	59
	Burr	Anti-Federalist	—	—	30
	S. Adams	Democratic-Republican	—	—	15
	Ellsworth	Federalist	—	—	11
	G. Clinton	Democratic-Republican	—	—	7
	Jay	Independent-Federalist	—	—	5
	Iredell	Federalist	—	—	3
	Washington	Federalist	—	—	2
	Henry	Independent	—	—	2
	Johnston	Independent-Federalist	—	—	2
	C. C. Pinckney	Independent-Federalist	—	—	1
1800*	*Jefferson*	Democratic-Republican	—	—	73
	Burr	Democratic-Republican	—	—	73
	J. Adams	Federalist	—	—	65
	C. C. Pinckney	Federalist	—	—	64
	Jay	Federalist	—	—	1
1804	*Jefferson*	Democratic-Republican	—	—	162
	C. C. Pinckney	Federalist	—	—	14
1808	*Madison*	Democratic-Republican	—	—	122
	C. C. Pinckney	Federalist	—	—	47
	G. Clinton	Democratic-Republican	—	—	6
	Votes not cast	—	—	—	1
1812	*Madison*	Democratic-Republican	—	—	128
	D. Clinton	Fusion	—	—	89
	Votes not cast	—	—	—	1
1816	*Monroe*	Republican	—	—	183
	King	Federalist	—	—	34
	Votes not cast	—	—	—	4

Year	Candidate	Party	Popular vote	Per cent	Electoral vote
1820	*Monroe*	Democratic-Republican	———		231
	J. Q. Adams	Independent-Republican	———		1
	Votes not cast	———	———		3
1824**	Jackson	No Distinct	152,933	42.2	84
	J. Q. Adams	Party Designations	115,696	31.9	99
	Clay		47,136	13.0	37
	Crawford		46,979	12.9	41
1828	*Jackson*	Democratic	647,292	56.0	178
	J. Q. Adams	National-Republican	507,730	44.0	83
1832	*Jackson*	Democratic	688,242	54.5	219
	Clay	National-Republican	473,462	37.5	49
	Wirt	Anti-Masonic Nullifiers	101,051	8.0	7
	Floyd	Independent	———	———	11
	Votes not cast	———	———	———	2
1836	*Van Buren*	Democratic	764,198	50.9	170
	W.H.Harrison	Whig	549,508	36.6	73
	White	Whig	145,352	9.7	26
	Webster	Whig	41,287	2.7	14
	Mangum	Anti-Jackson	———	———	11
1840	*W.H.Harrison*	Whig	1,275,612	52.9	234
	Van Buren	Democratic	1,130,033	46.8	60
	Birney	Liberty	7,053	.3	—
1844	*Polk*	Democratic	1,339,368	49.6	170
	Clay	Whig	1,300,687	48.1	105
	Birney	Liberty	62,197	2.3	—
1848	*Taylor*	Whig	1,362,101	47.3	163
	Cass	Democratic	1,222,674	42.4	127
	Van Buren	Free-Soil	291,616	10.1	—
1852	*Pierce*	Democratic	1,609,038	50.8	254
	Scott	Whig	1,386,629	43.8	42
	Hale	Free-Soil	156,297	4.9	—
1856	*Buchanan*	Democratic	1,839,237	45.6	174
	Frémont	Republican	1,341,028	33.3	114
	Fillmore	American	849,872	21.1	8
1860	*Lincoln*	Republican	1,867,198	39.8	180
	Douglas	Democratic	1,379,434	29.4	12
	Breckinridge	National-Democratic	854,248	18.2	72
	Bell	Constitutional Union	591,658	12.6	34
1864	*Lincoln*	Republican	2,219,362	55.1	212
	McClellan	Democratic	1,805,063	44.9	21
	Votes not cast	———	———	———	1
1868	*Grant*	Republican	3,013,313	52.7	214
	Seymour	Democratic	2,703,933	47.3	80
	Votes not cast	———	———	———	23

PRESIDENTIAL VOTE, 1872–1980

Year	Candidate	Party	Popular Vote	Per Cent	Electoral Vote
1872	*Grant*	Republican	3,597,375	55.6	286
	Greeley	Democratic, Liberal Republican	2,833,711	43.8	—
	Hendricks	Democratic	———	——	42
	Brown	Democratic, Liberal Republican	———	——	18
	Other	———	———	——	3
	Votes not cast	———	———	——	17
1876	Tilden	Democratic	4,284,885	50.9	184
	Hayes	*Republican*	4,033,950	48.0	185
	Cooper	Greenback	81,740	1.0	
	Smith	Prohibition	9,522	.1	
	Walker	American	2,636	.0	
1880	*Garfield*	*Republican*	4,449,053	48.3	214
	Hancock	Democratic	4,442,035	48.2	155
	Weaver	Greenback	307,306	3.3	
	Dow	Prohibition	10,487	.1	
	Phelps	American	707	.0	
1884	*Cleveland*	*Democratic*	4,911,017	48.9	219
	Blaine	Republican	4,848,334	48.2	182
	St. John	Prohibition	151,809	1.5	
	Butler	Greenback	133,825	1.3	
1888	Cleveland	Democratic	5,540,050	48.7	168
	Harrison	*Republican*	5,444,337	47.8	233
	Fisk	Prohibition	250,125	2.2	
	Streeter	Union Labor	146,897	1.3	
	Cowdrey	United Labor	2,808	.0	
1892	*Cleveland*	*Democratic*	5,554,414	46.0	277
	Harrison	Republican	5,190,802	43.0	145
	Weaver	People's	1,027,329	8.5	22
	Bidwell	Prohibition	271,058	2.2	
	Wing	Socialist	21,164	.2	
1896	*McKinley*	*Republican*	7,035,638	50.9	271
	Bryan	Democratic	6,467,946	46.8	176
	Levering	Prohibition	141,676	1.0	
	Palmer	Nat. Democratic	131,529	1.0	
	Matchett	Socialist-Labor	36,454	.3	
	Bentley	National	13,969	.1	
1900	*McKinley*	*Republican*	7,219,530	51.7	292
	Bryan	Democratic	6,358,071	45.5	155
	Woolley	Prohibition	209,166	1.5	
	Debs	Socialist Democrat	94,768	.7	

Year	Candidate	Party	Popular Vote	Per Cent	Electoral Vote
1928	*Hoover*	*Republican*	21,392,190	58.2	444
	Smith	Democratic	15,016,443	40.8	87
	Thomas	Socialist	267,420		
	Foster	Workers'	48,770		
	Reynolds	Socialist-Labor	21,603	1.0	
	Varney	Prohibition	20,106		
	Webb	Farm-Labor	6,390		
1932	*Roosevelt*	*Democratic*	22,821,857	57.3	472
	Hoover	Republican	15,761,841	39.6	59
	Thomas	Socialist	884,781		
	Foster	Communist	102,991		
	Upshaw	Prohibition	81,869	3.1	
	Harvey	Liberty	53,425		
	Reynolds	Socialist-Labor	33,276		
	Coxey	Farm-Labor	7,309		
1936	*Roosevelt*	*Democratic*	27,751,612	60.7	523
	Landon	Republican	16,681,913	36.4	8
	Lemke	Union	891,858		
	Thomas	Socialist	187,342		
	Browder	Communist	80,181	2.9	
	Colvin	Prohibition	37,609		
	Aiken	Socialist-Labor	12,729		
1940	*Roosevelt*	*Democratic*	27,243,466	54.7	449
	Willkie	Republican	22,304,755	44.8	82
	Thomas	Socialist	99,557		
	Babson	Prohibition	57,812		
	Browder	Communist	46,251	.5	
	Aiken	Socialist-Labor	14,861		
1944	*Roosevelt*	*Democratic*	25,602,505	52.8	432
	Dewey	Republican	22,006,278	44.5	99
	Thomas	Socialist	80,518		
	Watson	Prohibition	74,758		
	Teichert	Socialist-Labor	45,336	2.7	
	Misc. Independent		216,289		
1948	*Truman*	*Democratic*	24,179,345	49.6	303
	Dewey	Republican	21,991,291	45.1	189
	Thurmond	States Rights	1,176,125		39
	Wallace	Progressive	1,157,326		
	Thomas	Socialist	139,572	5.3	
	Watson	Prohibition	103,900		
	Misc. Independent		46,267		
1952	*Eisenhower*	*Republican*	33,936,234	55.2	442

	Barker	People's	50,232	.4	
	Malloney	Socialist-Labor	32,751	.2	
	Ellis	Union Reform	5,098	.0	
	Leonard	United Christian	518	.0	
1904	*Roosevelt*	*Republican*	7,628,834	56.4	336
	Parker	Democratic	5,084,401	37.6	140
	Debs	Socialist	402,460	3.0	
	Swallow	Prohibition	259,257	1.2	
	Watson	People's	114,753	.9	
	Corregan	Socialist-Labor	33,724	.3	
	Holcomb	Continental	830	.0	
1908	*Taft*	*Republican*	7,679,006	51.6	321
	Bryan	Democratic	6,409,106	43.1	162
	Debs	Socialist	420,820	2.8	
	Chafin	Prohibition	252,683	1.7	
	Hisgen	Independence	83,562	.6	
	Watson	People's	28,131	.2	
	Gillhaus	Socialist-Labor	13,825	.1	
	Turney	United Christian	461	.0	
1912	*Wilson*	*Democratic*	6,286,214	41.8	435
	Roosevelt	Progressive	4,126,020	27.5	88
	Taft	Republican	3,483,922	23.2	8
	Debs	Socialist	897,011	6.0	
	Chafin	Prohibition	208,923	1.4	
	Reimer	Socialist-Labor	29,079	.2	
1916	*Wilson*	*Democratic*	9,129,606	49.3	277
	Hughes	Republican	8,538,221	46.1	254
	Benson	Socialist	585,113	3.2	
	Hanly	Prohibition	220,506	1.2	
	Reimer	Socialist-Labor	13,403	.0	
	Misc.		41,894	.2	
1920	*Harding*	*Republican*	16,152,200	61.0	404
	Cox	Democratic	9,147,353	34.6	127
	Debs	Socialist	919,799	3.5	
	Watkins	Prohibition	189,408	.7	
	Cox	Socialist-Labor	31,175	.1	
	Christensen	Farmer Labor	26,541	.1	
	Macauley	Single Tax	5,837	.0	
1924	*Coolidge*	*Republican*	15,725,016	54.1	382
	Davis	Democratic	8,385,586	28.8	136
	La Follette	Independent, Progressive, and Socialist	4,822,856	16.6	13
	Faris	Prohibition	57,551		
	Johns	Socialist-Labor	38,958		
	Foster	Workers'	33,361	.5	
	Nations	American	23,867		
	Wallace	Com. Land	2,778		

	Stevenson	Democratic	27,314,992	44.5	89
	Hallinan	Progressive	140,023		
	Hamblen	Prohibition	72,949		
	Haas	Socialist-Labor	30,267		
	Hoopes	Socialist	20,203	.3	
	MacArthur	Constitution	17,205		
	Dobbs	Socialist Workers	10,312		
1956	*Eisenhower*	*Republican*	35,590,472	57.4	457
	Stevenson	Democratic	26,022,752	42.0	73*
	Andrews	States Rights	111,178		
	Haas	Socialist-Labor	44,450		
	Holtwick	Prohibition	41,937	.6	
	Misc. Independent		216,119		
1960	*Kennedy*	*Democratic*	34,226,731	49.7	303
	Nixon	Republican	34,108,157	49.5	219
	Byrd				15†
	Faubus	National States Rights	44,977		
	Haas	Socialist-Labor	47,522		
	Decker	Prohibition	46,203	.8	
	Dobbs	Socialist Workers	40,165		
	Misc. Independent		324,464		
1964	*Johnson*	*Democratic*	43,129,484	61.1	486
	Goldwater	Republican	27,178,188	38.5	52
	Haas	Socialist-Labor	45,219		
	DeBerry	Socialist Workers	32,720		
	Munn	Prohibition	23,267	.4	
	Misc. Independent		235,632		
1968	*Nixon*	*Republican*	31,770,237	43.4	301
	Humphrey	Democratic	31,270,533	42.7	191
	Wallace	American Independent	9,906,141	13.5	46
	Blomen	Socialist-Labor	52,588		
	Gregory	New	47,097		
	Halstead	Socialist Workers	41,300		
	Cleaver	Peace & Freedom	36,385	.4	
	McCarthy	New	25,858		
	Misc. Independent		36,680		

*In 1956 in Alabama one Democratic elector refused to vote for Stevenson and cast his ballot for Walter B. Jones.

†Six unpledged electors from Alabama, eight from Mississippi, and one Oklahoma Republican who re to vote for Nixon.

PRESIDENTIAL VOTE, 1876–1980 (continued)

	Candidate	Party	Popular Vote	Per Cent	Electoral Vote
1972	*Nixon*	*Republican*	47,169,911	60.7	520
	McGovern	Democratic	29,170,383	37.5	17
	Schmitz	American	1,099,482		
	Spock	Peoples	78,756		
	Jenness	Socialist Workers	66,677		
	Fisher	Socialist-Labor	53,814	1.8	
	Hall	Communist	25,595		
	Munn	Prohibition	13,505		
	Hospers	Libertarian	3,673		1
	Misc. Independent		36,758		
1976	*Carter*	*Democratic*	40,830,763	50.0	297
	Ford	Republican	39,147,793	48.0	240
	McCarthy	Independent	756,691		
	MacBride	Libertarian	173,011		
	Maddox	American Independent	170,531		
	Anderson	American	160,773		
	Camejo	Socialist Workers	91,314		
	Hall	Communist	58,992		
	Wright	People's	49,024	2.0	
	LaRouche	United States Labor	40,043		
	Bubar	Prohibition	15,934		
	Levin	Socialist Labor	9,616		
	Zeidler	Socialist	6,038		
	Miller	Restoration	361		
	Taylor	United American	36		
	Misc. Independent		44,969		1
1980	*Reagan*	*Republican*	43,901,812	50.7	489
	Carter	Democratic	35,483,820	41.0	49
	Anderson	Independent	5,719,722	6.6	
	Clark	Libertarian	921,188	1.1	
	Commoner	Citizens	234,279	.3	
	Hall	Communist	44,954		
	Rarick	American Independent	41,268		
	DeBerry	Socialist Workers	40,145		
	McCormack	Right to Life	32,327		
	Smith	Peace and Freedom	18,116		
	Griswold	Workers World	13,300	.3	
	Bubar	National Statesman	7,212		
	McReynolds	Socialist	6,895		
	Greaves	American	6,647		
	Pulley	Socialist Workers	6,271		
	Misc. Independent		31,147		

Source: *America Votes, Statistical Abstract of the United States,* and the Elections Research Center, Washington, D.C.

Name and State Appointed from	Service		Name	Service	
Chief Justices in Italics	Term	Yrs.		Term	Yrs.
John Jay, N.Y.	1789–1795	6	George Shiras, Jr., Pa.	1892–1903	11
John Rutledge, S.C.	1789–1791	2	Howell E. Jackson, Tenn.	1893–1895	2
William Cushing, Mass.	1789–1810	21	Edward D. White, La.	1894–1910	16
James Wilson, Pa.	1789–1798	9	Rufus W. Peckham, N.Y.	1895–1910	14
John Blair, Va.	1789–1796	7	Joseph McKenna, Cal.	1898–1925	27
Robert H. Harrison, Md.	1789–1790	1	Oliver W. Holmes, Mass.	1902–1932	29
James Iredell, N.C.	1790–1799	9	William R. Day, Ohio	1903–1922	19
Thomas Johnson, Md.	1791–1793	2	William H. Moody, Mass.	1906–1910	4
William Paterson, N.J.	1793–1806	13	Horace H. Lurton, Tenn.	1910–1914	5
John Rutledge, S.C.	1795–1795		Charles E. Hughes, N.Y.	1910–1916	6
Samuel Chase, Md.	1796–1811	15	Willis Van Devanter, Wyo.	1910–1937	27
Oliver Ellsworth, Conn.	1796–1799	4	*Edward D. White*, La.	1910–1921	11
Bushrod Washington, Va.	1798–1829	31	Joseph R. Lamar, Ga.	1911–1916	6
Alfred Moore, N.C.	1799–1804	5	Mahlon Pitney, N.J.	1912–1922	10
John Marshall, Va.	1801–1835	34	Jas. C. McReynolds, Tenn.	1914–1941	27
William Johnson, S.C.	1804–1834	30	Louis D. Brandeis, Mass.	1916–1939	23
Brock. Livingston, N.Y.	1806–1823	17	John H. Clarke, Ohio	1916–1922	6
Thomas Todd, Ky.	1807–1826	19	*William H. Taft*, Conn.	1921–1930	9
Joseph Story, Mass.	1811–1845	34	George Sutherland, Utah	1922–1938	16
Gabriel Duval, Md.	1811–1836	25	Pierce Butler, Minn.	1922–1939	17
Smith Thompson, N.Y.	1823–1843	20	Edward T. Sanford, Tenn.	1923–1930	7
Robert Trimble, Ky.	1826–1828	2	Harlan F. Stone, N.Y.	1925–1941	16
John McLean, Ohio	1829–1861	32	*Charles E. Hughes*, N.Y.	1930–1941	11
Henry Baldwin, Pa.	1830–1844	14	Owen J. Roberts, Pa.	1930–1945	15
James M. Wayne, Ga.	1835–1867	32	Benjamin N. Cardozo, N.Y.	1932–1938	6
Roger B. Taney, Md.	1836–1864	28	Hugo L. Black, Ala.	1937–1971	34
Philip P. Barbour, Va.	1836–1841	5	Stanley F. Reed, Ky.	1938–1957	19
John Catron, Tenn.	1837–1865	28	Felix Frankfurter, Mass.	1939–1962	23
John McKinley, Ala.	1837–1852	15	William O. Douglas, Conn.	1939–1975	36
Peter V. Daniel, Va.	1841–1860	19	Frank Murphy, Mich.	1940–1949	9
Samuel Nelson, N.Y.	1845–1872	27	*Harlan F. Stone*, N.Y.	1941–1946	5
Levi Woodbury, N.H.	1845–1851	6	James F. Byrnes, S.C.	1941–1942	1
Robert C. Grier, Pa.	1846–1870	24	Robert H. Jackson, N.Y.	1941–1954	13
Benj. R. Curtis, Mass.	1851–1857	6	Wiley B. Rutledge, Iowa	1943–1949	6
John A. Campbell, Ala.	1853–1861	8	Harold H. Burton, Ohio	1945–1958	13
Nathan Clifford, Me.	1858–1881	23	*Fred M. Vinson*, Ky.	1946–1953	7
Noah H. Swayne, Ohio	1862–1881	20	Tom C. Clark, Tex.	1949–1967	18
Samuel F. Miller, Iowa	1862–1890	28	Sherman Minton, Ind.	1949–1956	7
David Davis, Ill.	1862–1877	15	*Earl Warren*, Cal.	1953–1969	16
Stephen J. Field, Cal.	1863–1897	34	John M. Harlan, N.Y.	1955–1971	16
Salmon P. Chase, Ohio	1864–1873	9	William J. Brennan, Jr., N.J.	1956–	
William Strong, Pa.	1870–1880	10	Charles E. Whittaker, Mo.	1957–1962	5
Joseph P. Bradley, N.J.	1870–1892	22	Potter Stewart, Ohio	1959–1981	23
Ward Hunt, N.Y.	1872–1882	10	Byron R. White, Colo.	1962–	
Morrison R. Waite, Ohio	1874–1888	14	Arthur J. Goldberg, Ill.	1962–1965	3
John M. Harlan, Ky.	1877–1911	34	Abe Fortas, Tenn.	1965–1969	4
William B. Woods, Ga.	1880–1887	7	Thurgood Marshall, N.Y.	1967–	
Stanley Matthews, Ohio	1881–1889	8	*Warren E. Burger*, Minn.	1969–	
Horace Gray, Mass.	1881–1902	21	Harry A. Blackmun, Minn.	1970–	
Samuel Blatchford, N.Y.	1882–1893	11	William H. Rehnquist, Ariz.	1972–	
Lucius Q. C. Lamar, Miss.	1888–1893	5	Lewis F. Powell, Jr., Va.	1972–	
Melville W. Fuller, Ill.	1888–1910	22	John Paul Stevens, Ill.	1975–	
David J. Brewer, Kan.	1889–1910	21	Sandra D. O'Connor, Ariz.	1981–	
Henry B. Brown, Mich.	1890–1906	16			

DISTRIBUTION OF INCOME, 1950–1980

	1950		1960		1970		1980	
	white	nonwhite	white	nonwhite	white	nonwhite	white	nonwhite
Population (in thousands)	—	—	41,123	4,333	46,535	5,413	52,710	7,599
Income:								
under $2,500	7.8	21.8	3.8	12.3	1.8	4.7	1.6	5.0
$2,500–$4,999	7.5	18.0	5.8	16.5	3.4	9.8	3.3	10.2
$5,000–$7,499	10.9	20.1	7.2	13.9	5.0	10.9	5.3	12.3
$7,500–$9,999	12.0	15.6	7.8	12.8	5.7	9.8	6.0	9.8
$10,000–$12,499			11.9	12.1	6.5	10.4	7.1	8.7
$12,500–$14,999			8.3	7.4	6.5	8.6	6.8	7.4
$15,000–$19,999			23.8	13.2	20.0	17.1	14.1	12.7
$20,000–$24,999	61.7	24.5	11.1	5.2	11.6	8.7	14.2	10.6
$25,000–$34,999					23.8	13.7	20.8	12.9
$35,000–$49,999			20.3	6.7	9.8	4.4	13.6	7.6
$50,000 and over					6.0	1.8	7.2	2.8
Median Income	$11,792	$6,398	$16,235	$8,987	$21,722	$13,828	$21,904	$13,843
Mean Income	$13,600	$7,233	$18,038	$10,776	$24,394	$16,467	$24,939	$17,280

Source: Dept. of Commerce, Bureau of the Census.

The Constitution of the United States

We the People of the United States, in order to form a more perfect union, establish Justice, insure domestic tranquility, provide for the common defence, promote the general Welfare, and secure the Blessings of Liberty to ourselves and our Posterity, do ordain and establish this Constitution for the United States of America.

ARTICLE I

Section 1. All legislative Powers herein granted shall be vested in a Congress of the United States, which shall consist of a Senate and a House of Representatives.

Section 2. The House of Representatives shall be composed of Members chosen every second Year by the People of the several States, and the Electors in each State shall have the Qualifications requisite for Electors of the most numerous Branch of the State Legislature.

No Person shall be a Representative who shall not have attained to the Age of twenty-five Years, and been seven Years a Citizen of the United States, and who shall not, when elected, be an Inhabitant of that State in which he shall be chosen.

Representatives and direct Taxes shall be apportioned among the several States which may be included within this Union, according to their respective Numbers, which shall be determined by adding to the whole Number of free Persons, including those bound to Service for a Term of Years, and excluding Indians not taxed, three fifths of all other Persons. The actual Enumeration shall be made within three Years after the first Meeting of the Congress of the United States, and within every subsequent Term of ten Years, in such Manner as they shall by Law direct. The Number of Representatives shall not exceed one for every thirty Thousand, but each State shall have at Least one Representative; and until such enumeration shall be made, the State of New Hampshire shall be entitled to chuse three, Massachusetts eight, Rhode-Island and Providence Plantations one, Connecticut five, New-York six, New Jersey four, Pennsylvania eight, Delaware one, Maryland six, Virginia ten, North Carolina five, South Carolina five, and Georgia three.

When vacancies happen in the Representation from any State, the Executive Authority thereof shall issue Writs of Election to fill such Vacancies.

The House of Representatives shall chuse their Speaker and other Officers; and shall have the sole Power of Impeachment.

Section 3. The Senate of the United States shall be composed of two Senators from each State, chosen by the Legislature thereof, for six Years; and each Senator shall have one Vote.

Immediately after they shall be assembled in Consequence of the first Election, they shall be divided as equally as may be into three Classes. The Seats of the Senators of the first Class shall be vacated at the Expiration of the second Year, of the second Class at the Expiration of the fourth Year, and of the third Class at the Expiration of the sixth Year, so that one-third may be chosen every second Year; and if Vacancies happen by Resignation, or otherwise, during the Recess of the Legislature of any State, the Executive thereof may make temporary Appointments until the next Meeting of the Legislature, which shall then fill such Vacancies.

No Person shall be a Senator who shall not have attained to the Age of thirty Years, and been nine Years a Citizen of the United States, and who shall not, when elected, be an Inhabitant of that State for which he shall be chosen.

The Vice President of the United States shall be President of the Senate, but shall have no Vote, unless they be equally divided.

The Senate shall chuse their other Officers, and also a President pro tempore, in the Absence of the Vice President, or when he shall exercise the Office of President of the United States.

The Senate shall have the sole Power to try all Impeachments. When sitting for that Purpose, they shall be on Oath or Affirmation. When the President of the United States is tried, the Chief Justice shall preside: And no Person shall be convicted without the Concurrence of two thirds of the Members present.

Judgment in Cases of Impeachment shall not extend further than to removal from Office, and disqualification to hold and enjoy any Office of honor, Trust or Profit under the United States: but the Party convicted shall nevertheless be liable and subject to Indictment, Trial, Judgment and Punishment, according to Law.

Section 4. The Times, Places and Manner of holding Elections for Senators and Representatives, shall be prescribed in each State by the Legislature thereof; but the Congress may at any time by Law make or alter such Regulations, except as to the Places of chusing Senators.

The Congress shall assemble at least once in every Year, and such Meeting shall be on the first Monday in December, unless they shall by Law appoint a different Day.

Section 5. Each House shall be the Judge of the Elections, Returns and Qualifications of its own Members, and a Majority of each shall constitute a Quorum to do Business; but a smaller Number may adjourn from day to day, and may be authorized to compel the Attendance of absent Members, in such Manner, and under such Penalties as each House may provide.

Each House may determine the Rules of its Proceedings, punish its Members for disorderly Behavior, and, with the Concurrence of two thirds, expel a Member.

Each House shall keep a Journal of its Proceedings, and from time to time publish the same, excepting such Parts as may in their Judgment require Secrecy; and the Yeas and Nays of the Members of either House on any question shall, at the Desire of one fifth of those present, be entered on the Journal.

Neither House, during the Session of Congress, shall, without the Consent of the other, adjourn for more than three days, nor to any other Place than that in which the two Houses shall be sitting.

Section 6. The Senators and Representatives shall receive a Compensation for their Services, to be ascertained by Law, and paid out of the Treasury of the United States. They shall in all Cases, except Treason, Felony and Breach of the Peace, be privileged from Arrest during their Attendance at the Session of their respective Houses, and in going to and returning from the same; and for any Speech or Debate in either House, they shall not be questioned in any other Place.

No Senator or Representative shall, during the Time for which he was elected, be appointed to any civil Office under the Authority of the United States, which shall have been created, or the Emoluments whereof shall have been encreased during such time; and no Person holding any Office under the United States, shall be a Member of either House during his Continuance in Office.

Section 7. All Bills for raising Revenue shall originate in the House of Representatives; but the Senate may propose or concur with Amendments as on other Bills.

Every Bill which shall have passed the House of Representatives and the Senate, shall, before it becomes a Law, be presented to the President of the United States; If he approves he shall sign it, but if not he shall return it, with his Objections to that House in which it shall have originated, who shall enter the Objections at large on their Journal, and proceed to reconsider it. If after such Reconsideration two thirds of that House shall agree to pass the Bill, it shall be sent, together with the Objections, to the other House, by which it shall likewise be reconsidered, and if approved by two thirds of that House, it shall become a Law. But in all such Cases the Votes of both Houses shall be determined by Yeas and Nays, and the Names of the Persons voting for and against the Bill shall be entered on the Journal of each House respectively. If any Bill shall not be returned by the President within ten Days (Sundays excepted) after it shall have been presented to him, the Same shall be a Law, in like Manner as if he had signed it, unless the Congress by their Adjournment prevent its Return, in which Case it shall not be a Law.

Every Order, Resolution, or Vote to which the Concurrence of the Senate and House of Representatives may be necessary (except on a question of Adjournment) shall be presented to the President of the United States; and before the Same shall take Effect, shall be approved by him, or being disapproved by him, shall be repassed by two thirds of the Senate and House of Representatives, according to the Rules and Limitations prescribed in the Case of a Bill.

Section 8. The Congress shall have Power To lay and collect Taxes, Duties, Imposts and Excises, to pay the Debts and provide for the common Defence and general Welfare of the United States; but all Duties, Imposts and Excises shall be uniform throughout the United States;

To borrow Money on the credit of the United States;

To regulate Commerce with foreign Nations, and among the several States, and with the Indian Tribes;

To establish an uniform Rule of Naturalization, and uniform Laws on the subject of Bankruptcies throughout the United States;

To coin Money, regulate the Value thereof, and of foreign Coin, and fix the Standard of Weights and Measures;

To provide for the Punishment of counterfeiting the Securities and current Coin of the United States;

To establish Post Offices and post Roads;

To promote the Progress of Science and useful Arts, by securing for limited Times to Authors and Inventors the exclusive Right to their respective Writings and Discoveries;

To constitute Tribunals inferior to the supreme Court;

To define and punish Piracies and Felonies committed on the high Seas, and Offences against the Law of Nations;

To declare War, grant Letters of Marque and Reprisal, and make Rules concerning Captures on Land and Water;

To raise and support Armies, but no Appropriation of Money to that Use shall be for a longer Term than two Years;

To provide and maintain a Navy;

To make Rules for the Government and Regulation of the land and naval Forces;

To provide for calling forth the Militia to execute the Laws of the Union, suppress Insurrections and repel Invasions;

To provide for organizing, arming, and disciplining the Militia, and for governing such Part of them as may be employed in the Service of the United States, reserving to the States respectively, the Appointment of the Officers, and the Authority of training the Militia according to the discipline prescribed by Congress;

To exercise exclusive Legislation in all Cases whatsoever, over such District (not exceeding ten Miles square) as may, by Cession of particular States, and the Acceptance of Congress, become the Seat of the Government of the United States, and to exercise like Authority over all Places purchased by the Consent of the Legislature of the State in which the Same shall be, for the Erection of Forts, Magazines, Arsenals, dock-Yards, and other needful Buildings;—And

To make all Laws which shall be necessary and proper for carrying into Execution the foregoing Powers, and all other Powers vested by this Constitution in the Government of the United States, or in any Department or Officer thereof.

Section 9. The Migration or Importation of such Persons as any of the States now existing shall think proper to admit, shall not be prohibited by the Congress prior to the Year one thousand eight hundred and eight, but a Tax or duty may be imposed on such Importation, not exceeding ten dollars for each Person.

The Privilege of the Writ of Habeas Corpus shall not be suspended, unless when in Cases of Rebellion or Invasion the public Safety may require it.

No Bill of Attainder or ex post facto Law shall be passed.

No Capitation, or other direct, tax shall be laid, unless in Proportion to the Census or Enumeration herein before directed to be taken.

No Tax or Duty shall be laid on Articles exported from any State.

No Preference shall be given by any Regulation of Commerce or Revenue to the Ports of one State over those of another: nor shall Vessels bound to, or from, one State, be obliged to enter, clear, or pay Duties in another.

No Money shall be drawn from the Treasury, but in Consequence of Appropriations made by Law; and a regular Statement and Account of the Receipts and

Expenditures of all public Money shall be published from time to time.

No Title of Nobility shall be granted by the United States: And no Person holding any Office of Profit or Trust under them, shall, without the Consent of the Congress, accept of any present, Emolument, Office, or Title, of any kind whatever, from any King, Prince, or foreign State.

Section 10. No State shall enter into any Treaty, Alliance, or Confederation; grant Letters of Marque and Reprisal; coin Money; emit Bills of Credit; make any Thing but gold and silver Coin a Tender in Payment of Debts; pass any Bill of Attainder, ex post facto Law, or Law impairing the Obligation of Contracts, or grant any Title of Nobility.

No State shall, without the Consent of the Congress, lay any Imposts or Duties on Imports or Exports, except what may be absolutely necessary for executing its inspection Laws: and the net Produce of all Duties and Imposts, laid by any State on Imports or Exports, shall be for the Use of the Treasury of the United States; and all such Laws shall be subject to the Revision and Controul of the Congress.

No State shall, without the Consent of Congress, lay any Duty of Tonnage, keep Troops, or Ships of War in time of Peace, enter into any Agreement or Compact with another State, or with a foreign Power, or engage in War, unless actually invaded, or in such imminent Danger as will not admit of delay.

ARTICLE II

Section 1. The Executive Power shall be vested in a President of the United States of America. He shall hold his Office during the Term of four Years, and, together with the Vice President, chosen for the same Term, be elected, as follows

Each State shall appoint, in such Manner as the legislature thereof may direct, a Number of Electors, equal to the whole Number of Senators and Representatives to which the State may be entitled in the Congress: but no Senator or Representative, or Person holding an Office of Trust or Profit under the United States, shall be appointed an Elector.

The electors shall meet in their respective States, and vote by ballot for two Persons, of whom one at least shall not be an Inhabitant of the same State with themselves. And they shall make a List of all the Persons voted for, and of the Number of Votes for each; which List they shall sign and certify, and transmit sealed to the Seat of the Government of the United States, directed to the President of the Senate. The President of the Senate shall, in the Presence of the Senate and House of Representatives, open all the Certificates, and the Votes shall then be counted. The Person having the greatest Number of Votes shall be the President, if such Number be a Majority of the whole Number of Electors appointed; and if there be more than one who have such Majority, and have an equal Number of Votes, then the House of Representatives shall immediately chuse by Ballot one of them for President; and if no Person have a Majority, then from the five highest on the List the said House shall in like Manner chuse the President. But in chusing the President, the Votes shall be taken by States, the Representation from each State having one Vote; A quorum for this Purpose shall consist of a Member or Members from two thirds of the States, and a Majority of all the States shall be necessary to a Choice. In every Case, after the Choice of the President, the Person having the greatest Number of Votes of the Electors shall be the Vice President. But if there should remain two or more who have equal Votes, the Senate shall chuse from them by Ballot the Vice President.

The Congress may determine the Time of chusing the Electors, and the Day on which they shall give their Votes; which Day shall be the same throughout the United States.

No Person except a natural born Citizen, or a Citizen of the United States, at the time of the Adoption of this Constitution, shall be eligible to the Office of President; neither shall any Person be eligible to that Office who shall not have attained to the Age of thirty five Years, and been fourteen Years a Resident within the United States.

In Case of the Removal of the President from Office, or of his Death, Resignation or Inability to discharge the Powers and Duties of the said Office, the same shall devolve on the Vice President, and the Congress may by Law provide for the Case of Removal, Death, Resignation or Inability, both of the President and Vice President, declaring what Officer shall then act as President, and such Officer shall act accordingly, until the Disability be removed, or a President shall be elected.

The President shall, at stated Times, receive for his Services, a Compensation, which shall neither be encreased nor diminished during the Period for which he shall have been elected, and he shall not receive within that Period any other Emolument from the United States, or any of them.

Before he enter on the Execution of his Office, he shall take the following Oath or Affirmation:—"I do solemnly swear (or affirm) that I will faithfully execute the Office of President of the United States, and will to the best of my Ability, preserve, protect and defend the Constitution of the United States."

Section 2. The President shall be Commander in Chief of the Army and Navy of the United States, and of the Militia of the several States, when called into the actual Service of the United States; he may require the Opinion, in writing, of the principal Officer in each of the executive Departments, upon any Subject relating to the Duties of their respective Offices, and he shall have Power to grant Reprieves and Pardons for Offences against the United States, except in Cases of Impeachment.

He shall have Power, by and with the Advice and Consent of the Senate to make Treaties, provided two thirds of the Senators present concur and he shall nominate, and by and with the Advice and Consent of the Senate, shall appoint Ambassadors, other public Ministers and Consuls, Judges of the supreme Court, and all other Officers of the United States, whose Appointments are not herein otherwise provided for, and which shall be established by Law: but the Congress may by Law vest the Appointment of such inferior Officers, as they think proper, in the President alone, in the Courts of Law, or in the Heads of Departments.

The President shall have Power to fill up all Vacancies that may happen during the Recess of the Senate, by granting Commissions which shall expire at the End of their next Session.

Section 3. He shall from time to time give to the Congress Information of the State of the Union, and recommend to their Consideration such Measures as he shall judge necessary and expedient; he may, on extraordinary Occasions, convene both Houses, or either of them, and, in Case of Disagreement between them, with Respect to the Time of Adjournment, he may adjourn them to such Time as he shall think proper; he shall receive Ambassadors and other public Ministers; he shall take Care that the Laws be faithfully executed, and shall Commission all the Officers of the United States.

Section 4. The President, Vice President and all civil Officers of the United States, shall be removed from Office on Impeachment for, and Conviction of, Treason, Bribery, or other high Crimes and Misdemeanors.

ARTICLE III

Section 1. The judicial Power of the United States, shall be vested in one supreme Court, and in such inferior Courts as the Congress may from time to time ordain and establish. The Judges, both of the supreme and inferior Courts, shall hold their Offices during good Behaviour, and shall, at stated Times, receive for their Services, a Compensation, which shall not be diminished during their Continuance in Office.

Section 2. The judicial Power shall extend to all Cases, in Law and Equity, arising under this Constitution, the Laws of the United States, and Treaties made, or which shall be made, under their Authority;—to all Cases affecting Ambassadors, other public Ministers and Consuls;—to all Cases of admiralty and maritime Jurisdiction;—to Controversies to which the United States shall be a Party;—to Controversies between two or more States;—between a State and Citizens of another State;—between Citizens of different States,—between Citizens of the same State claiming Lands under Grants of different States, and between a State, or the Citizens thereof, and foreign States, Citizens or Subjects.

In all Cases affecting Ambassadors, other public Ministers and Consuls, and those in which a State shall be Party, the supreme Court shall have original Jurisdiction. In all other Cases before mentioned, the supreme Court shall have appellate Jurisdiction, both as to Law and Fact, with such Exceptions, and under such Regulations as the Congress shall make.

The Trial of all Crimes, except in Cases of Impeachment, shall be by Jury; and such Trial shall be held in the State where the said Crimes shall have been committed; but when not committed within any State, the Trial shall be at such Place or Places as the Congress may by Law have directed.

Section 3. Treason against the United States, shall consist only in levying War against them, or in adhering to their Enemies, giving them Aid and Comfort. No Person shall be convicted of Treason unless on the Testimony of two Witnesses to the same overt Act, or on Confession in open Court.

The Congress shall have Power to declare the Punishment of Treason, but no Attainder of Treason shall work Corruption of Blood, or Forfeiture except during the Life of the Person attainted.

ARTICLE IV

Section 1. Full Faith and Credit shall be given in each State to the public Acts, Records, and judicial Proceedings of every other State. And the Congress may by general Laws prescribe the Manner in which such Acts, Records and Proceedings shall be proved, and the Effect thereof.

Section 2. The Citizens of each State shall be entitled to all Privileges and Immunities of Citizens in the several States.

A person charged in any State with Treason, Felony, or other Crime, who shall flee from Justice, and be found in another State, shall on Demand of the executive Authority of the State from which he fled, be delivered up, to be removed to the State having Jurisdiction of the Crime.

No Person held to Service or Labour in one State, under the Laws thereof, escaping into another, shall, in Consequence of any Law or Regulation therein, be discharged from such Service or Labour, but shall be delivered up on Claim of the Party to whom such Service or Labour may be due.

Section 3. New States may be admitted by the Congress into this Union; but no new State shall be formed or erected within the Jurisdiction of any other State; nor any State be formed by the Junction of two or more States, or Parts of States, without the Consent of the Legislatures of the States concerned as well as of the Congress.

The Congress shall have Power to dispose of and make all needful Rules and Regulations respecting the Territory or other Property belonging to the United States; and nothing in this Constitution shall be so construed as to Prejudice any Claims of the United States, or of any particular State.

Section 4. The United States shall guarantee to every State in this Union a Republican Form of Government, and shall protect each of them against Invasion; and on Application of the Legislature, or of the Executive (when the Legislature cannot be convened) against domestic Violence.

ARTICLE V

The Congress, whenever two thirds of both houses shall deem it necessary, shall propose Amendments to this Constitution, or, on the Application of the Legislatures of two thirds of the several States, shall call a Convention for proposing Amendments, which, in either Case, shall be valid to all Intents and Purposes, as Part of this Constitution, when ratified by the Legislatures of three fourths of the several States, or by Conventions in three fourths thereof, as the one or the other Mode of Ratification may be proposed by the Congress; Provided that no Amendment which may be made prior to the Year One thousand eight hundred and eight shall in any Manner affect the first and fourth Clauses in the Ninth Section of the first Article; and that no State, without its Consent, shall be deprived of its equal Suffrage in the Senate.

ARTICLE VI

All Debts contracted and Engagements entered into, before the Adoption of this Constitution, shall be as valid against the United States under this Constitution, as under the Confederation.

This Constitution, and the Laws of the United States which shall be made in Pursuance thereof; and all Treaties made, or which shall be made, under the Authority of the United States, shall be the supreme Law of the Land; and the Judges in every State shall be bound thereby, any Thing in the Constitution or Laws of any State to the Contrary notwithstanding.

The Senators and Representatives before mentioned, and the Members of the several State Legislatures, and all executive and judicial Officers, both of the United States and of the several States, shall be bound by Oath or Affirmation, to support this Constitution; but no religious Test shall ever be required as a Qualification to any Office or public Trust under the United States.

ARTICLE VII

The Ratification of the Conventions of nine States, shall be sufficient for the Establishment of this Constitution between the States so ratifying the Same.

DONE in Convention by the Unanimous Consent of the States present the Seventeenth Day of September in the Year of our Lord one thousand seven hundred and Eighty seven and of the Independence of the United States of America the Twelfth. IN WITNESS whereof We have hereunto subscribed our Names.

G^{o} Washington
Presid^{t} and deputy from Virginia

AMENDMENTS
ARTICLE I

[THE FIRST TEN ARTICLES PROPOSED 25 SEPTEMBER 1789; DECLARED IN FORCE 15 DECEMBER 1791]

Congress shall make no law respecting an establishment of religion, or prohibiting the free exercise thereof; or abridging the freedom of speech, or of the press; or the right of the people peaceably to assemble, and to petition the Government for a redress of grievances.

ARTICLE II

A well regulated Militia, being necessary to the security of a free State, the right of the people to keep and bear Arms, shall not be infringed.

ARTICLE III

No Soldier shall, in time of peace, be quartered in any house, without the consent of the Owner, nor in time of war, but in a manner to be prescribed by law.

ARTICLE IV

The right of the people to be secure in their persons, houses, papers, and effects, against unreasonable searches and seizures, shall not be violated, and no Warrants shall issue, but upon probable cause, supported by Oath or affirmation, and particularly describing the place to be searched, and the persons or things to be seized.

ARTICLE V

No person shall be held to answer for a capital, or otherwise infamous crime, unless on a presentment or indictment of a Grand Jury, except in cases arising in the land or naval forces, or in the Militia, when in actual service in time of War or public danger; nor shall any person be subject for the same offence to be twice put in jeopardy of life or limb; nor shall be compelled in any Criminal Case to be a witness against himself, nor be deprived of life, liberty, or property, without due process of law; nor shall private property be taken for public use, without just compensation.

ARTICLE VI

In all criminal prosecutions, the accused shall enjoy the right to a speedy and public trial, by an impartial jury of the State and district wherein the crime shall have been committed, which district shall have been previously ascertained by law, and to be informed of the nature and cause of the accusation; to be confronted with the witnesses against him; to have compulsory process for obtaining Witnesses in his favor, and to have the Assistance of Counsel for his defence.

ARTICLE VII

In suits at common law, where the value in controversy shall exceed twenty dollars, the right of trial by jury shall be preserved, and no fact tried by a jury shall be otherwise re-examined in any Court of the United States, than according to the rules of the common law.

ARTICLE VIII

Excessive bail shall not be required, nor excessive fines imposed, nor cruel and unusual punishments inflicted.

ARTICLE IX

The enumeration in the Constitution, of certain rights, shall not be construed to deny or disparage others retained by the people.

ARTICLE X

The powers not delegated to the United States by the Constitution, nor prohibited by it to the States, are reserved to the States respectively, or to the people.

ARTICLE XI

[PROPOSED 4 MARCH 1794; DECLARED RATIFIED 8 JANUARY 1798]

The Judicial power of the United States shall not be construed to extend to any suit in law or equity, commenced or prosecuted against one of the United States by Citizens of another State, or by Citizens or Subjects of any Foreign State.

ARTICLE XII

[PROPOSED 9 DECEMBER 1803; DECLARED RATIFIED 25 SEPTEMBER 1804]

The Electors shall meet in their respective states, and vote by ballot for President and Vice-President, one of whom, at least, shall not be an inhabitant of the same state with themselves; they shall name in their ballots the person voted for as President, and in distinct ballots the person voted for as Vice-President, and they shall make distinct lists of all persons voted for as President, and of all persons voted for as Vice-President, and of the number of votes for each, which lists they shall sign and certify, and transmit sealed to the seat of the Government of the United States, directed to the President of the Senate;—The President of the Senate shall, in the presence of the Senate and House of Representatives, open all the certificates and the votes shall then be counted;—The person having the greatest number of votes for President, shall be the President, if such number be a majority of the whole number of Electors appointed; and if no person have such majority, then from the persons having the highest numbers not exceeding three on the list of those voted for as President, the House of Representatives shall choose immediately, by ballot, the President. But in choosing the President, the votes shall be taken by states, the representation from each state having one vote; a quorum for this purpose shall consist of a member or members from two-thirds of the states, and a majority of all the states shall be necessary to a choice. And if the House of Representatives shall not choose a President whenever the right of choice shall devolve upon them, before the fourth day of March next following, then the Vice-President shall act as President, as in the case of the death or other constitutional disability of the President. The person having the greatest number of votes as Vice-President, shall be the Vice-President, if such number be a majority of the whole number of Electors appointed, and if no person have a majority, then from the two highest numbers on the list, the Senate shall choose the Vice-President; a quorum for the purpose shall consist of two-thirds of the whole number of Senators, and a majority of the whole number shall be necessary to a choice. But no person constitutionally ineligible to the office of President shall be eligible to that of Vice-President of the United States.

ARTICLE XIII

[PROPOSED 31 JANUARY 1865; DECLARED RATIFIED 18 DECEMBER 1865]

Section 1. Neither slavery nor involuntary servitude, except as a punishment for crime whereof the party shall have been duly convicted, shall exist within the United States, or any place subject to their jurisdiction.

Section 2. Congress shall have power to enforce this article by appropriate legislation.

ARTICLE XIV

[PROPOSED 13 JUNE 1866; DECLARED RATIFIED 28 JULY 1868]

Section 1. All persons born or naturalized in the United States, and subject to the jurisdiction thereof, are citizens of the United States and of the State wherein they reside. No State shall make or enforce any law which shall abridge the privileges or immunities of citizens of the United States; nor shall any State deprive any person of life, liberty, or property, without due process of law; nor deny to any person within its jurisdiction the equal protection of the laws.

Section 2. Representatives shall be apportioned among the several States according to their respective numbers, counting the whole number of persons in each State, excluding Indians not taxed. But when the right to vote at any election for the choice of electors for President and Vice President of the United States, Representatives in Congress, the Executive and Judicial officers of a State, or the members of the Legislature thereof, is denied to any of the male inhabitants of such State, being twenty-one years of age, and citizens of the United States, or in any way abridged, except for participation in rebellion, or other crime, the basis of representation therein shall be reduced in the proportion which the number of such male citizens shall bear to the whole number of male citizens twenty-one years of age in such State.

Section 3. No person shall be a Senator or Representative in Congress, or elector of President and Vice President, or hold any office, civil, or military, under the United States, or under any State, who, having previously taken an oath, as a member of Congress, or as an officer of the United States, or as a member of any State legislature, or as an executive or judicial officer of any State, to support the Constitution of the United States, shall have engaged in insurrection or rebellion against the same, or given aid or comfort to the enemies thereof. But Congress may by a vote of two-thirds of each House, remove such disability.

Section 4. The validity of the public debt of the United States, authorized by law, including debts incurred for payment of pensions and bounties for services in suppressing insurrection or rebellion, shall not be questioned. But neither the United States nor any State shall assume or pay any debt or obligation incurred in aid of insurrection or rebellion against the United States, or any claim for the loss or emancipation of any slave; but all such debts, obligations and claims shall be held illegal and void.

Section 5. The Congress shall have power to enforce, by appropriate legislation, the provisions of this article.

ARTICLE XV

[PROPOSED 26 FEBRUARY 1869; DECLARED RATIFIED 30 MARCH 1870]

Section 1. The right of citizens of the United States to vote shall not be denied or abridged by the United States or by any State on account of race, color, or previous condition of servitude.

Section 2. The Congress shall have power to enforce this article by appropriate legislation.

ARTICLE XVI

[PROPOSED 12 JULY 1909; DECLARED RATIFIED 25 FEBRUARY 1913]

The Congress shall have power to lay and collect taxes on incomes, from whatever source derived, without apportionment among the several States, and without regard to any census or enumeration.

ARTICLE XVII

[PROPOSED 13 MAY 1912; DECLARED RATIFIED 31 MAY 1913]

The Senate of the United States shall be composed of two senators from each State, elected by the people thereof, for six years; and each Senator shall have one vote. The electors in each State shall have the qualifications requisite for electors of the most numerous branch of the State legislature.

When vacancies happen in the representation of any State in the Senate, the executive authority of such State shall issue writs of election to fill such vacancies: PROVIDED, That the legislature of any State may empower the executive thereof to make temporary appointments until the people fill the vacancies by election as the legislature may direct.

This amendment shall not be so construed as to affect the election or term of any senator chosen before it becomes valid as part of the Constitution.

ARTICLE XVIII

[PROPOSED 18 DECEMBER 1917; DECLARED RATIFIED 29 JANUARY 1919]

After one year from the ratification of this article, the manufacture, sale, or transportation of intoxicating liquors within, the importation thereof into, or the exportation thereof from the United States and all territory subject to the jurisdiction thereof for beverage purposes is hereby prohibited.

The Congress and the several States shall have concurrent power to enforce this article by appropriate legislation.

This article shall be inoperative unless it shall have been ratified as an amendment to the Constitution by the legislatures of the several States, as provided in the Constitution, within seven years from the date of the submission hereof to the States by the Congress.

ARTICLE XIX

[PROPOSED 4 JUNE 1919; DECLARED RATIFIED 26 AUGUST 1920]

The right of citizens of the United States to vote shall not be denied or abridged by the United States or by any States on account of sex.

The Congress shall have power, by appropriate legislation, to enforce the provisions of this article.

ARTICLE XX

[PROPOSED 2 MARCH 1932; DECLARED RATIFIED 6 FEBRUARY 1933]

Section 1. The terms of the President and Vice-President shall end at noon on the twentieth day of

January, and the terms of Senators and Representatives at noon on the third day of January, of the years in which such terms would have ended if this article had not been ratified; and the terms of their successors shall then begin.

Section 2. The Congress shall assemble at least once in every year, and such meeting shall begin at noon on the third day of January, unless they shall by law appoint a different day.

Section 3. If, at the time fixed for the beginning of the term of the President, the President-elect shall have died, the Vice-President-elect shall become President. If a President shall not have been chosen before the time fixed for the beginning of his term, or if the President-elect shall have failed to qualify, then the Vice-President-elect shall act as President until a President shall have qualified; and the Congress may by law provide for the case wherein neither a President-elect nor a Vice-President-elect shall have qualified, declaring who shall then act as President, or the manner in which one who is to act shall be selected, and such person shall act accordingly until a President or Vice-President shall have qualified.

Section 4. The Congress may by law provide for the case of the death of any of the persons from whom the House of Representatives may choose a President whenever the right of choice shall have devolved upon them, and for the case of the death of any of the persons from whom the Senate may choose a Vice-President whenever the right of choice shall have devolved upon them.

Section 5. Sections 1 and 2 shall take effect on the 15th day of October following the ratification of this article.

Section 6. This article shall be inoperative unless it shall have been ratified as an amendment to the Constitution by the legislatures of three-fourths of the several States within seven years from the date of its submission.

ARTICLE XXI

[PROPOSED 20 FEBRUARY 1933; DECLARED RATIFIED 5 DECEMBER 1933]

Section 1. The eighteenth article of amendment to the Constitution of the United States is hereby repealed.

Section 2. The transportation or importation into any State, Territory or possession of the United States for delivery or use therein of intoxicating liquors, in violation of the laws thereof, is hereby prohibited.

Section 3. This article shall be inoperative unless it shall have been ratified as an amendment to the Constitution by convention in the several States, as provided in the Constitution, within seven years from the date of the submission hereof to the States by the Congress.

ARTICLE XXII

[PROPOSED 21 MARCH 1947; DECLARED RATIFIED 3 MARCH 1951]

Section 1. No person shall be elected to the office of the President more than twice, and no person who has held the office of President, or acted as President, for more than two years of a term to which some other person was elected President shall be elected to the office of the President more than once. But this Article shall not apply to any person holding the office of President when this Article was proposed by the Congress, and shall not prevent any person who may be holding the office of President, or acting as President, during the term within which this Article becomes operative from holding the office of President or acting as President during the remainder of such term.

ARTICLE XXIII

[PROPOSED 17 JUNE 1960; DECLARED RATIFIED 3 APRIL 1961]

Section 1. The District constituting the seat of Government of the United States shall appoint in such manner as the Congress may direct:

A number of electors of President and Vice President equal to the whole number of Senators and Representatives in Congress to which the District would be entitled if it were a State, but in no event more than the least populous State; they shall be in addition to those appointed by the States, but they shall be considered, for the purposes of the election of President and Vice President, to be electors appointed by a State; and they shall meet in the District and perform such duties as provided by the twelfth article of amendment.

Section 2. The Congress shall have power to enforce this article by appropriate legislation.

ARTICLE XXIV

[PROPOSED 27 AUGUST 1962; DECLARED RATIFIED 4 FEBRUARY 1964]

Section 1. The right of citizens of the United States to vote in any primary or other election for President or Vice President, for electors for President or Vice President, or for Senator or Representative in Congress, shall not be denied or abridged by the United States or any State by reason of failure to pay any poll tax or other tax.

Section 2. The Congress shall have power to enforce this article by appropriate legislation.

ARTICLE XXV

[PROPOSED 6 JULY 1965; DECLARED RATIFIED 23 FEBRUARY 1967]

Section 1. In case of the removal of the President from office or of his death or resignation, the Vice President shall become President.

Section 2. Whenever there is a vacancy in the office of the Vice President, the President shall nominate a Vice President who shall take office upon confirmation by a majority vote of both Houses of Congress.

Section 3. Whenever the President transmits to the President pro tempore of the Senate and the Speaker of the House of Representatives his written declaration that he is unable to discharge the powers and duties of his office, and until he transmits to them a written declaration to the contrary, such powers and duties shall be discharged by the Vice President as Acting President.

Section 4. Whenever the Vice President and a majority of either the principal officers of the executive department or of such other body as Congress may by law provide, transmit to the President pro tempore of the Senate and the Speaker of the House of Representatives their written declaration that the President is unable to discharge the powers and duties of his office; the Vice President shall immediately assume the powers and duties of the office as Acting President.

Thereafter, when the President transmits to the President pro tempore of the Senate and the Speaker of the House of Representatives his written declaration that no inability exists, he shall resume the powers and duties of his office unless the Vice President and a majority of either the principal officers of the executive department or of such other body as Congress may by law provide, transmit within four days to the President pro tempore of the Senate and the Speaker of the House of Representatives their written declaration that the President is unable to discharge the powers and duties of his office. Thereupon Congress shall decide the issue, assembling within forty-eight hours for that purpose if not in session. If the Congress, within twenty-one days after receipt of the latter written declaration, or, if Congress is not in session, within twenty-one days after Congress is required to assemble, determines by two-thirds vote of both Houses that the President is unable to discharge the powers and duties of his office, the Vice President shall continue to discharge the same as Acting President; otherwise, the President shall resume the powers and duties of his office.

ARTICLE XXVI

[PROPOSED 23 MARCH 1971; DECLARED RATIFIED 30 JUNE 1971]

Section 1. The right of citizens of the United States, who are 18 years of age or older, to vote shall not be denied or abridged by the United States or any state on account of age.

Secton 2. The Congress shall have the power to enforce this article by appropriate legislation.

Index